HARDPRESS.NET
HOME OF HARD-TO-FIND BOOKS

The Southern Spectator
by Richard Fletcher

Address:
HardPress
8345 NW 66TH ST #2561
MIAMI FL 33166-2626
USA
Email: info@hardpress.net

THE

SOUTHERN SPECTATOR;

A MAGAZINE

OF

Religious, Philanthropic, Social & General Literature.

FROM AUGUST, 1857, TO JUNE, 1858.

EDITED BY REV. R. FLETCHER,

ST. KILDA, MELBOURNE.

VOL. I.

MELBOURNE:

W. FAIRFAX & CO., PRINTERS AND PUBLISHERS.
SYDNEY: SHERRIFF & ARMSTRONG.
HOBART TOWN AND LAUNCESTON. WALCH & SONS.
ADELAIDE: E. S. WIGG.

1858.

The Southern Spectator.

No. 1.   AUGUST, 1857.   VOL. I.

EDITOR'S ADDRESS.

WHY start a new Magazine? Have not many attempts been made in these Colonies to establish periodicals; and have not all, with the exception of one or two now on their trial, languished and died? and can any other fate befal the present undertaking? The fact of so many attempts having been made, indicates a sense of want in the community for publications of this kind,—a craving which will certainly not rest satisfied till it meet with its appropriate food. *When* magazines shall permanently exist here, is clearly a question of time only. They are sure to come forth, and to secure a footing when the community is ripe for them. But how shall that period be ascertained? By successive experiments alone. The chief causes of failure heretofore, have been the limited number of contributors, the contracted circle of readers, the difficulty of distribution of the works and collection of money returns, and the extraordinary fluctuations in the condition of the community. The sudden rise in the labour market, and in the monetary value of all articles of consumption in particular, extinguished not a few. These causes are now daily diminishing; population receives perpetual additions, and becomes more consolidated and settled in its habits; more and better channels of intercourse are opened up continually; and it is believed that the disposition to appreciate publications of this kind, the means of purchasing them, and the desire to obtain them are sensibly on the increase. Whether they have reached the required point of development, so as to enable a periodical to secure for itself a lasting existence, can perhaps only be determined by putting the experiment to the test. The present attempt has this advantage over most, if not all its predecessors, that it is not local in its nature, the scheme of any one particular colony, and designed for it mainly. It is essentially an Australasian project, having its originators, contributors, subscribers, and general supporters, in all the Australias, including Tasmania. As the field of sympathy and support is thus widened, it is hoped that the aid rendered and the circulation secured, will be sufficient to keep the publication alive. In order to give time for a fair trial, sufficient funds have been subscribed to keep it in existence for one year at least.

B

The time has gone by to speak at any length in praise of periodical literature. Unrivalled as a channel for the quick conveyance of intelligence, as a medium of intercommunion of thought, as a means of collecting and using for the public good the musings and teachings of numerous able minds that never would have ventured on a volume, as a convenient depository for the discoveries of science as they come to light and the inventions of ingenuity as they are rapidly produced; and unrivalled too as an instrument of power for working upon the public mind in every possible way, it has won for itself a place in the estimation of the community, from which nothing can now dislodge it. Recent in its origin, and insignificant in its beginning, what a prodigious magnitude and wide-spread influence has it now attained! Probably, the larger portion of the authorship of the day—certainly of professional authorship—flows in this channel. Its operation is consequently felt and owned in all directions, on the opinions and conduct of every class, on the consultations of cabinets, the movements of armies, the tactics of party, the devices and labours of philanthropy. Religious, literary, scientific, mercantile, and political men, derive their most healthful impulses from the daily and weekly journals, or the monthly and quarterly serials, and are indebted to them for the chief means of carrying out their projects. Periodical literature has indeed become a necessary of mental, moral, social, and religious life in all civilised communities. One cannot but wonder how our forefathers did without it. In what manner the political rivalries and philosophical disputations of ancient Greece, the vast and complicated affairs of mighty Rome, the evangelizing efforts and the earnest controversies of the primitive Christians, were managed and sustained without the aid of a single periodical, seems to us inconceivable. One can hardly believe that so recently as the spirit-stirring times of Elizabeth and Cromwell, such a thing as a magazine or a newspaper was unknown. Now, however, that the value of this class of publications has been found out, they have become indispensable. And there can be little doubt that the peculiar character of the present age, marked and rapid progress, is to be mainly attributed to this class of works, as they are the most powerful of instruments in concentrating public attention upon any one object, and in calling forth the union of energy necessary to its accomplishment. Periodical literature, carries forward, on the one hand, the education and mental development of the community more than any other instrumentality, and on the other, provides rich, varied, entertaining, and useful reading for the appetite it creates.

We, emigrants from such a country as Britain, where reviews and magazines abound, naturally miss them when we arrive on these shores. Of course, endeavours are made to supply the lack by importation. But we receive our supplies irregularly. When they do come they come in heaps. Instead of being invited by a single number or two, we are appalled by the magnitude of a pile, the accumulation of months. They also taste somewhat stale from age, freshness being a chief charm in a magazine. And who is not conscious of a decaying interest in some at least of the periodicals we receive from home, as the changes every mail announces in the *Dramatis personæ* on the stage of Europe, remove so many familiar names, and introduce others of whom we know nothing? In proportion as the affairs of this southern region, which we have adopted as our home, acquire a stronger hold upon our thoughts and our affections, those of the northern hemisphere sensibly diminish and decay.

The periodical we propose to establish, will necessarily be more mixed and varied in its character than those of the fatherland. There, the wants of separate classes, the limited objects of particular sections of the community, the variety of taste, and even the whims and fancies of the eccentric, can be provided for by special magazines. There, every profession, every science, each department of art, every form of philanthropy, has its own periodical; high church and low church, high doctrine and low doctrine; the old theology and the new, orthodoxy and heterodoxy, have their appropriate organs. There are elaborate "Quarterlies" for the learned and studious, and simple "Pennies" and collections of scraps for the young and illiterate.

This country will doubtless one day possess all this array; but the time is not yet. Many years may have to pass over it, before it be ripe for such a variety. In the mean time we must begin with our literature as we begin with everything else. Our houses, our stores, our places of worship, are, in the first instance, extremely *colonial*. This term has a special significancy here, which our friends at home cannot well understand. We are compelled to put up with many inconveniences, and to shut our eyes to many inelegencies until our necessities are supplied. Our stores and shops contain many incongruous goods. In young townships, a tradesman must not be very particular as to the articles he sells. It would not pay for every separate business to have its own depot. Our periodical literature must, we presume, run a somewhat similar course. It will be varied at first, and more select afterwards. We are, therefore, only yielding to the necessity of our position, when we propose that our new publication shall be a *miscellany*, embracing literature and science, philosophy and political economy, education and philanthropy, morality and religion.

But still our main element will be *religion*. The project has originated with a religious body; its articles will be written, in all probability, chiefly by religious men; our principle dependence for readers will be among religious communities; and our leading object is a religious object. We shall not here lay down the articles of any creed, to which every statement in our pages must be rigidly conformed, nor give a detailed explanation of what we mean by religion. The work will, in the course of time, speak for itself on these points. But this much we must explicitly avow at the outset, that the religion we shall advocate is that usually denominated evangelical. This we firmly believe to be the truth, the most momentous of all truth—the element which it is of the utmost importance to infuse largely into any community, especially a young and rising one in the act of granulating and taking a form and feature to be transmitted to coming ages. To those, who like ourselves have abandoned the sweets of intercourse with relatives and friends, and the attractions of a native country, second to none on the face of the earth in all that can make a country delightful to live in, to cast in their lot among the founders of this new southern empire, we shall deem ourselves real benefactors, if we can be the means, in however small a degree, of instilling into their minds, along with other useful knowledge, the principles of a religion which, while it will teach them the secret of turning to the best account the advantages of the land of their adoption, will at the same time furnish them with topics of consolation under the troubles inseparable from humanity, and turn their thoughts to securing an inheritance in another and a better country.

This publication, as announced in the prospectus, originated in resolutions passed in two conferences of Congregationalists, held, the first, in Melbourne in January, 1855, and the second in Sydney, February, 1857 ; and it comes forth under the sanction, and aided by the liberality of several gentlemen who then met. From this circumstance, it is natural to suppose that a large part of its circulation will, in the first instance at least, be among the members of that body of Christians, and as a consequence it is not unlikely that a more frequent reference to their affairs, than to those of others may possibly concur, simply arising from better information respecting them ; and it is not improbable that some may fancy they can detect a certain tinge and hue here and there pervading some classes of subjects, arising from the standpoint from which the authors contemplate them. But the work is by no means meant to be sectarian and exclusive. It is honestly intended to be conducted on Christian and Catholic principles, and to take free and liberal views ; and as it will be open to the contributions of all Protestant evangelical denominations, so it is hoped it may be read by the universal brotherhood of Christians, without offending the prejudices of any but the bigoted and narrow-minded. It will be the aim of the Editor to breathe through its pages, a spirit of affection and good-will to all who love the one Saviour, and hold fast by the Common Salvation ; and he will deem it an ample reward for his labours, and a source of rich consolation to his own mind, if the work he superintends should in any marked degree promote among the various churches "the unity of the spirit in the bond of peace." We wish it, however, from the first to be clearly understood, that on the subjects of State Aid and Voluntaryism, we shall advocate the latter firmly and decidedly, but in a temperate and kindly spirit,—not because we think it will promote the interests of any one denomination, but the vitality and purity of the whole.

In concluding this address, we bespeak the candour and patience of our readers in our first attempts. Several able writers have promised contributions, but a regular staff of writers, whose abilities are approved and whose communications may be relied on, has, as a matter of necessity, in a great measure yet to be formed. It is believed that there exist in these colonies materials in abundance to constitute such a staff; and that many at present unknown will be forthcoming in due time, possessing the requisite ability, spirit, and diligence to furnish useful and acceptable articles, without the Editor being compelled to have recourse to extracts from works already published, or writers at a distance. Measures are indeed on foot for securing regular correspondence both with Europe and America; but it will be chiefly for the sake of obtaining religious and literary information; and some time must necessarily elapse before the fruit of these arrangements can be reaped. But our main reliance for material for our pages will be on the colonies themselves; and our aim will be to give the work the colonial stamp, and to impart to it a character of appropriateness and adaptation to the condition, the wants and the tastes of the people of this Austral Hemisphere.

SUNDAY READING.

[IT is our intention to furnish, in each number of this work, an article or two more particularly designed for Sunday Reading, for the use of such persons as may, from distance or other causes, be unable to enjoy the benefit of public worship; and it is hoped that some of these papers may not be unsuitable to read to small congregations, in the bush or elsewhere, where regular ministerial services cannot be obtained.—ED.]

The Sabbath.
No. I.

THE Sabbath question has awakened great interest of late in our Father-land. Powerful attempts have been made, and in influential quarters too, if not to secularise the Sabbath to purposes of business, at least to divert the current of observance into channels of recreation and amusement. Happily the good sense, the pious sentiment, and the conscientious convictions of the people, have been aroused in such strength against the contemplated innovations, as to check, if not utterly to discomfit the machinations of the "Sunday League." In this young country, where everything is in the course of formation, where usages are becoming established and habits gradually fixed, it is of the utmost importance that right views on this momentous subject should prevail from the beginning. It is a pleasing feature and hopeful

symptom of colonial life, that a very respectful attention is paid
to the external observance of the Sabbath, so far as a general
cessation from business, the shutting up of public houses, and
other matters of that kind are concerned. Yet it must be remembered that observances which derive their sanction solely
from custom, and are not founded on conviction and spring not
from principle, are very precarious in their tenure, and are in
danger of being at any time swept into oblivion. There is no
security for the permanent preservation and right observance of
the Sabbath Day, but the thorough conviction that it is a
Divine Institution and binding on the conscience.

The views of the community are divided upon the subject.
Some appear animated by a spirit of bitter hostility to the Sabbath. From their manner of speaking about it they might deem
it the greatest pest to society, and the strict observers of it as
the enemies of human happiness ; and their strenuous efforts
are bent, by engaging as much in business as decency will allow,
by encouraging travelling, pleasure, and trading on the Lord's
Day, and by taking every opportunity of holding up to ridicule
those who make a conscience of keeping it sacred, on obliterating
it altogether. A second party regard it as a good, useful, civil
institution, resting entirely upon human laws and customs, but
having no divine authority. They think that cessation from
wearisome toil about once in seven days is an excellent thing for
health, and a fine opportunity for recreation and social intercourse ; and perhaps they deem it no objection to a weekly
Sabbath, that it affords an outlet for the enthusiastic superabun-
dance of religious emotion and zeal with which some people are
unfortunately troubled. A third party hold the Sabbath to be
authoritative and obligatory, but only in an ecclesiastical sense.
Their idea is that the Scriptures have not enjoined it but the
Church has ; that the Church, from primitive times and in every
following age, has separated the first day of the week from
common uses to be enjoyed as a christian festival, and therefore
it should be kept. Another portion of the community regard
the Sabbath as the appointment of God himself, as instituted
when man was created, and as continuing in force through every
dispensation, and—though altered and modified in some respects
under the christian economy—as still the solemn command of
Heaven, addressed to all Christians faithfully to keep it holy.
The greater part of evangelical Christians hold this opinion.

Some may imagine that it is of little consequence which of
these opinions they embrace, if only they fall in with the usual
arrangements for keeping the day sacred. But this is a mistake,
for the manner in which it will be kept and the degree of zeal
for maintaining it inviolate, will be essentially affected by the
principle on which it is supposed to rest. Its honor and sacredness will be preserved with ardour and consistency without
giving way to motives of expediency, if it be believed to rest on

an authority which is Divine; but one infraction of it after another will be tolerated, until few traces of it remain, if the basis on which it rests be regarded as anything less than the command of God.

But how comes it to pass that such diversity of opinion upon this subject exists? If the Sabbath be so very important, a Divine Institution still binding on Christians, will it not be clear and unmistakeable from Scripture? Here we have to confront the most plausible of all the objections to the Divine Authority of the Sabbath, the alleged silence of the New Testament respecting it. It is maintained that Christians take their religion from the teaching of Christ and his Apostles; the code of laws for the regulation of the Church is to be found in the New Testament, not in the Old: and it is inconceivable that so little, and that so vague, should be said upon this momentous topic in this later portion of the Word of God, if the Sabbath were designed by the Head of the Church to be a law to Christians. The following hints are thrown out by way of reply:—

1. It is a very dangerous ground of objection to take to any doctrine or duty, not that there is nothing said about it in Scripture, but not much. Upon this principle, if there be little enjoined, however clear that little may be, it goes for nothing; it must be repeated many times before it becomes obligatory. Almost every essential doctrine of Christianity has been assailed on this plea; such as the Trinity, the Deity of Christ, the personality of the Holy Spirit, the depravity of human nature, the separate state of souls after death, the permanence of baptism and the pastoral office, and many others. Now who shall determine the number of texts requisite to establish any article of faith? Different minds will demand different amounts of evidence to satisfy them. We surely are insufficient judges of the quantity of proof it becomes God to furnish to us; our duty is to examine what he has given, be it little or much; and if one clear text or one sound argument be adduced from Scripture, that should be enough to satisfy a teachable mind that the truth therein taught is the truth of God and must be implicity received.

2. From the structure of the Scriptures, the frequency with which any subject is brought forward depends upon local and passing events, and this remark applies equally to the New Testament and to the Old. The Gospels contain a report of our Lord's discourses, but the greater part of them arose out of incidental circumstances, and these circumstances occasioned a special prominence to particular topics, and imparted a peculiar colour to the illustrations. It was the same with almost every Epistle we find in the Sacred Canon. Hence there were, at that time, some things elaborately argued and defended in which we, of the present day, see little difficulty, and others largely insisted on in which we take but slight interest; such as the controversy

about circumcision, the admission of the Gentiles to equal privileges with the Jews, and the eating of meat offered to idols; and others are but slightly alluded to, or are to be gathered only by induction and inference, which have become of great prominence and moment in subsequent times. The probability is that, with respect to the Sabbath, there was no dispute in primitive times, and that the oral instructions and uniform practice of the Apostles in relation to it meeting with no opposition, there was no special need to refer to it in their writings.

3. It is a mistake to affirm that the New Testament is our only rule and guide in matters of religion. "All Scripture is given by inspiration of God and is profitable for doctrine, for reproof, for correction, for instruction in righteousness, that the man of God may be perfect throughly furnished unto all good works." In this very text the Apostle refers to the ancient Scriptures. Throughout all the teachings of Christ and his Apostles, the Divine authority of the Old Testament is taken for granted, and it is often appealed to in support of New Testament doctrines. The harmony of the two, and their substantial oneness as a revelation from heaven, are throughout maintained. No doubt a great number of enactments, in force under the former economies, are abrogated under the present; and which of these are permanent and which temporary, which are still binding and which annulled, we must judge of by a careful perusal of the whole document. What is the law of Britain at this moment? We shall not find it in any one Act of Parliament or set of Statutes. Neither old acts nor new taken singly will give us the true state of the law. Modern Acts often supplement ancient ones without repealing them, and repeal parts leaving the rest in force; so that the whole body of law, common and statute, ancient and modern, must be studied and compared, to ascertain what is really at the present day the law of the land. This is a fair illustration of the Law of Holy Scripture: it is all from God; and to know what his will is, we must look at the entire book, diligently compare one part with another, and thus learn what is superseded and what yet remains in force. Upon this principle, if the Sabbath be of Divine appointment and *unrepealed* it is still obligatory.

4. As each portion of Scripture was designed, in the first instance, for the use of a particular class of persons living in a particular age, and was written in the vernacular dialect that all might understand it, so the knowledge then prevailing upon the subject was taken for granted; certain things were assumed as received and understood; and with respect to these no special additional revelation was deemed requisite. Baptism, Singing of Hymns, and Prayer are enjoined; certain well-known usages in relation to these ordinances existed at the time; no minute directions were therefore necessary; it was sufficient to give general commands which no one in that age

was in danger of misunderstanding, while we at this distance of time can only infer what the practice respecting them was by comparing passage with passage, and looking at the incidental circumstances which happen to be noticed. So it was with respect to the Sabbath. The institution was universally known to the Jews and universally observed by them. Its authority was not called in question. No new enactment was required, and all that the case demanded was the adaptation of the old established law, which none disputed, to the new constitution of things under the Gospel.

5. It has further been the method of the Divine Legislator to take up, incorporate, and give sanction to existing usages, and to continue old ones, in whole or in part, altered amended and adapted to the new state of things as the case may require. In passing from one economy to another *all* the old laws and customs were not violently abrogated and an entirely new set instituted; but much of the old was retained and used, with perhaps additions and modifications, or in a new and more significant sense. And in introducing a new law the old one was not always repealed in so many words and required to be disused all at once, but was rather gradually displaced by the new enactment. Thus it has been found by learned research that many of the Laws of Moses had a previous existence, and that God directed him to adopt and put under suitable regulation much that he found already in use. This was the case with circumcision, and sacrifice, and ceremonial ablutions, the laws relating to the avenger of blood, the Sabbath itself, and many others. So in the New Testament. The bread and the wine of the Lord's Supper were on the table as part of the feast of the Passover, and the blessing and breaking of the bread, and giving thanks for the cup, were already Jewish customs to which a new significancy was given by the Saviour. Baptism, as a rite of initiation, was found existing when John and Jesus began their ministry, and was adopted into the Christian economy. In like manner the system of Synagogues, which had sprung up and was everywhere in use, became in many respects the model of the Christian Churches that were planted. Even the whole Mosaic ceremonies, while strenuously resisted as binding on the Gentiles, were allowed to be still observed by the Hebrew Christians, it being clearly foreseen that time, and the new arrangements, would gradually lead to their disuse. Thus the Sabbath existed among the Jews at the time of the foundation of Christianity; it was never abrogated; its Divine authority was universally admitted and acted upon; and the observance of a new day, the first day of the week, was commenced under the auspices of the Apostles; this co-existed for a time with the seventh-day Sabbath, but ultimately superseded it altogether.

6. It was the way of Christ and his apostles to teach by example as well as by express precept. What they did in their official capacity had equal authority with what they said. Thus

they gave few direct injunctions about church government and worship, but they founded churches upon certain principles, and instituted a certain mode of worship in them; and their example, as far as it can be ascertained, is justly considered binding upon Christians in all ages. So with the Sabbath; if it should be found that the Apostles seldom refer to it, because local circumstances did not call upon them to do so, no difference of opinion respecting it then existing and no one disputing its authority; yet if they observed it themselves, and practically transferred it to the first day of the week, and changed its usages from those that were peculiarly Jewish to such as were in accordance with the gentleness, spirituality, and happiness of the Christian dispensation, we deem it quite as much an obligation resting upon us to follow their example, as it would have been to obey injunctions expressly and repeatedly commanded.

(To be continued.)

The One Foundation.—1 Cor. iii. 11.

"It is appointed unto all men once to die," and this our destiny is inexorably fulfilled. While a young generation is ever springing up, the old one is as constantly passing away. "Our Fathers, where are they? and the prophets, do they live for ever?" Where are the friends of our childhood, and youth, and the companions of our riper years? How few but feel that the world, though as replete with population as ever, wears an increasingly untenanted aspect, from the loss of those who were once the chief charm of social life. And whither do men go when they leave this world? Is death annihilation? Is the grave "the land of darkness and the shadow of death; a land of darkness as darkness itself," where no light shall ever penetrate? or, shall we live again, and live for ever?

The instinctive yearnings of our nature after immortality, and the conclusions of reason and philosophy, have been fully confirmed by revelation. "Life and immortality are brought to light by the Gospel." But will *all* men be happy hereafter? The same authority which assures us of the certainty of a future state, assures us likewise that it is a state of retribution. There are abodes of light and abodes of darkness in that world, mansions of felicity, and dungeons of woe.

It must strike every reasonable being that it is of the utmost importance to have, if it be possible to acquire it, some definite and well-grounded idea of the state we shall be in, when we pass into the regions of immortality: and especially, if a hope of happiness *be* indulged, that it should not be a vague and baseless one, but one built upon a solid and sure Foundation.

Our condition is obviously such as should awaken solicitude about the future. No thoughtful person will consider that the happiness of the human race in the world to come is so demonstrably certain that all anxiety about it is superfluous. Indeed, with the consciousness of guilt in every human heart, and the immortality of the soul conceded, indifference on this subject is manifestly inexcusable. Even if a doubt cloud our prospect, every practicable effort should be made to have that doubt removed.

There are many, however, who give themselves very little trouble about their prospects in reference to eternity. They put away the unwelcome subject altogether, and wilfully shut their eyes to the consequences. They stake every thing upon the merest chance, comforting themselves perhaps with the thought that they will be no worse off than the bulk of their neighbours. But is this determination, to leave all to hazard, wise? Is it the part of a reasonable, a reflecting, an accountable being? Would not such a course, in regard to worldly matters, brand a man with insanity? But when he carries his folly into religion no such stigma is attached! What, however, is the judgment of Scripture? "Yea also the heart of the sons of men is full of evil, and madness is in their heart while they live, and after that they go to the dead." "They are a nation void of counsel, neither is there any understanding in them. Oh that they were wise, that they understood this, that they would consider their latter end!"

Many excuse themselves on the plea that *no certainty* regarding a future state, and a right preparation for it, can be obtained. They allege the difficulty and perplexity of the subject, one which has baffled the profoundest thinkers and the best of men. The disputes among Christians powerfully confirm them in this opinion. If men zealously pious cannot agree among themselves as to what religion really is, and what a right preparation for another world consists in, the subject must be hopelessly involved; and without personal enquiry they hold themselves excused for refusing to meddle with it. Is not this a sad symptom of a wrong state of mind? Would men be content to act thus in relation to their temporal interests? Were health impaired, would they refrain from all efforts to restore it because of discrepancy of opinion among medical advisers? Were a fortune at stake, would the perplexity of the case and the conflicting views of lawyers be deemed a sufficient reason for indifference and inaction?

The assumption, however, is false that no certainty can be had on the subject of men securing "a good foundation against the time to come, that they may lay hold on eternal life." The inspired Scriptures were given by God for the express purpose of showing how this may be done; and it were a reflection on the wisdom and goodness of the Divine Being, if they should necessarily fail of their object. He that comes to them in a docile spirit, with a real desire to find out a sure resting-place for his hopes, shall not be, cannot be, disappointed. As to the disagreements among Christians, so industriously magnified, they are much less important upon essential points than some would represent. Among most denominations, saving truth may be found, and the way to heaven learnt. Let all frivolous excuses as to the perplexity of the problem, all lethargic indifference on a question of such surpassing interest, be thrown aside, and serious attention be given to the securing a good foundation of hope for the eternal world.

Not a few, who manifest a laudable concern in regard to a future state, fall into serious mistakes in attempting to gain their object; and in contravention of the apostle's declaration, " Other foundation can no man lay than that is laid which is Jesus Christ," go about to lay others; and, as may be expected, what they do lay, rests upon the loose and shifting sand, and what they build upon it, will totter and fall.

Some it is to be feared try to persuade themselves that *sin* is a comparatively *harmless thing*. The representations made of it by preachers they affect to regard as exaggerated. Men's vices they consider frailties rather than faults. The *only* view they take of the Divine Being is, that of an indulgent parent who will leniently pass over the infirmities of his children. God is merciful they say, and will not be very strict with us. It is impossible that one so good should visit our errors and weaknesses with so dire a punishment as perdition. If we throw ourselves on his mercy at last, all will be well. These are very flattering and pleasant thoughts to those who are not willing to part with their sins. But are they not delusions? Is not this an abuse of the glorious paternal character of God? What says God himself?—" Know, therefore, and see that it is an evil thing and bitter, that thou hast forsaken the Lord thy God, and that my fear is not in thee, saith the Lord God of Hosts." " The wages of sin is death."

The only foundation that others rest upon is the *consciousness of integrity*, virtue and honor. Fair in their dealings, scrupulous in speaking truth with their neighbours, never descending to a mean or dishonorable action, and giving occasionally of their surplus stores to help the needy, they flatter themselves that they have nothing to fear. And this is the whole basis of their hopes. They are " alive" and full of confidence, but is it not " without the Law"? Granting that they are as faultless as they imagine in their duty to their neighbour, how do they stand in relation to the first and greatest commandment of all? Where is that love to their Maker, that holiness of heart, that humility and devoutness of spirit, that spirituality of mind, which form the fundamental requirements of the Law the Creator has imposed upon his accountable creatures. Without these, all the rest are but " as sounding brass or a tinkling cymbal." Vain are all hopes built on human virtues ; for " by the deeds of the Law shall no flesh be justified."

But most feel the necessity of some *religion* being added to their morality. They cannot deny that something is due to God as well as to man. Even the Pagans and Mahommedans admit this. Witness the temples and ceremonies of the one class ; the mosques, prayers, and pilgrimages of the other. And not a few among ourselves, it is to be feared, in laying a foundation for their hopes, construct it of materials which, though religion is a chief ingredient, prove to be weak and deceitful. Dependance may be placed upon external relationship to a visible corporate society which is regarded as the true Church, just as the Jews of old deemed themselves safe from their being the true Israel. To this may be added something personal that is considered religious. A correct creed is deemed indispensable ; such a zeal, it may be, for certain Articles of Belief and Confessions of Faith as to make a man an offender for a word, if he do not utter the shibboleth of their party. More than this, careful and systematic attendance upon the public ordinances of religion, and the punctual recital of private prayers, may form a conspicuous ingredient of that piety on which dependance is placed. Still further, various feelings are experienced, tears flow, gratitude and joy arise, sacrifice and service for what is deemed the cause of God are displayed ; and these become the basis of hope, the ground and reason why the favour of God is claimed, and future happiness deemed secure.

Is this a safe and Scriptural Foundation ? Did religious observances, combined with a fair morality, avail the boasting Pharisee, who said, " God, I thank thee that I am not as other men, extortioners, unjust, adulterers, or even as this Publican : I fast twice in the week ; and I give tithes of all that I possess." Did they save Paul, who declared that if any man had reason to trust in such things he had : " circumcised the eighth day, of the stock of Israel, of the tribe of Benjamin, an Hebrew of the Hebrews ; as touching the law, a Pharisee ; concerning zeal, persecuting the church ; touching the righteousness which is in the law, blameless ?" Did he not declare that though he gloried in them once, in the days of his ignorance, he had, when better taught, learnt to discard them utterly as grounds of acceptance with God : " What things were gain to me those I counted loss for Christ?" The taint of imperfection and sin pervades the best of human endeavours and renders them unworthy, for their own sake, of the Divine acceptance. If any virtue, any creed, any religious ceremony, any pious service, any good works, or any of the pleas or excuses already noticed, be relied on as the basis of hope, the Foundation being of the wrong materials and therefore deceptive, the hope will inevitably perish : " I will even rend it with a stormy wind in my fury ; and there shall be an overflowing shower in mine anger, and great hailstones in my fury to consume it.   So will I break down the wall that ye have daubed with untempered mortar, and bring it down to the ground, so that the foundation thereof shall be discovered, and it shall fall, and ye shall be consumed in the midst thereof."—Ezek. xiii. 13, 14.

In contradistinction from every thing whatever of merely human construction, the Scriptures present us with a *Divine* foundation, the *only* one on which so precious a fabric as the hope of eternal life can safely rest, and this is emphatically pointed out in the words of the Apostle Paul :—" Other foundation can no man lay than that is laid which is Jesus Christ." The great personage who visited our earth 1,800 years ago, to whom the prophets and apostles bore witness, stands prominently forth in the world's history, as furnishing in himself the basis of human hope.   In a peculiar and emphatic sense, he is the Redeemer and Saviour of men ; in a sense totally different from that in which a Bacon, a Socrates, or a Luther have emancipated their fellow-men from the thraldom of error, of vice, or of superstition.   It is not his doctrine only, but his person ; not his words merely, but his doings; not even his example, taken by itself, but his sufferings and death and reign in a glorified state, to which we are directed to look as the basis of our confidence.   His words are precious, his example is faultless ; but it is *himself* in his personal qualities on whom our trust must repose.   The Scriptures profess to reveal the secret by which eternal life may be secured—and what is the sum of their information ?   Is it not comprised in what relates to the person, and the work of the Lord Jesus ?

In ancient prophecy it was predicted, that the Divine Being, out of love and pity to mankind, would provide them with a firm resting place for their · hopes of salvation.   "Thus saith the Lord, behold I lay in Zion for a foundation ; a stone, a tried stone, a precious corner stone, a sure foundation ; he that believeth shall not make haste."   The reference of this prediction is not left in doubt.   The New Testament writers apply it expressly to Christ :   He is the " Chief corner stone, elect, precious : " " Other foundation can no man lay than that is laid which is Jesus Christ."   The simple meaning of all which is, that we are to expect future happiness, not from any vague and chance exercise of the Divine comparison ; not from any virtuous dispositions we may attain ; nor from any religious ceremonials we may perform ; but solely from the virtue and the worth inherent in the work, and sufferings, and expiatory death of the Lord Jesus Christ.   The only safe thing sinful man can rely on, in cherishing a hope of felicity beyond the grave, is the obedience the Saviour has rendered, the sufferings he has endured, the death he has accomplished, and the mediation and advocacy he carries on within the veil in the sanctuary above.   " *This* is life eternal, to know thee the only true God, and Jesus Christ, whom thou hast sent." "Behold then the Lamb of God, who taketh away the sin of the world." Look unto Him and be saved." Let the superstructure of Hope rest upon the rock of ages, and no power in the universe shall ever involve in ruin.

PUBLIC QUESTIONS.
State Aid to Religion.

THE propriety of affording State Aid to religion, has been already keenly agitated in each of the Australian colonies, and in all but one of them is still one of the leading unsettled questions of the day. This is not to be wondered at; indeed, a little consideration will shew that it was inevitable. In the mother country two conflicting elements have long been in existence. On the one hand, there has been the National Church with its social and political supremacy; on the other, Dissent with its unceasing protest. In every British colony to which there is a large and indiscriminate emigration of the middle and working classes, members of both these ecclesiastical parties are sure to find a place, who will transfer to the new land the antagonism originated in the old. But a very short time suffices to shew, that by changing the field of conflict, the relative position of the combatants has been greatly altered, and that the battle must be waged for the future under very different auspices.

It is no breach of charity to say that the Church of England is not a theoretical institution, constructed after the fashion of a modern revolutionary constitution. It is not the result of an attempt to realise an ideal. It was the result of circumstances, and bears conspicuously all the marks of the age and country in which it was established, and of the men by whom its foundations were laid. How it came to be what it is, and how much of it is the result of a compromise between the forces in conflict at the time of its origin, the student may read in the brilliant pages of Macaulay. As an institution, it is essentially national. It is no copy of a similar model elsewhere. It is racy of the soil. It is an historical product—a living result of the activities of preceding ages. But for that very reason it is untransferable. Part and parcel as it is of the British constitution, twining in and out through the whole social and political framework of the State, it can never enter in a similar manner as a component part into any other constitution,—not even in a British colony, where British sympathies and the wish to imitate British antecedents are the strongest. The children of the English Church find themselves in the colonies somewhat at a loss. They have their ancient liturgy, and they can retain the main features of their ecclesiastical polity, but this is all. Except by tradition and descent they are no longer members of a National Church.

Facts and logic are often at variance. A thing gets established on grounds very different from those on which it is subsequently defended. Admirers and apologists of the Established Church in Britain have striven to demonstrate its justice and excellence, by arguments which never entered the heads of Henry the Eighth or Cranmer. But when an institution is assailed by vehement opponents, it is necessary to say something in its behalf; and where many interests are dependent upon it, there is sure to be no lack of ingenious and ardent advocates. There are treatises almost without end in support of the existence, and in vindication of the righteousness of the English Church, and out of these its members find no difficulty in selecting reasons which they readily accept as sufficient to fortify their allegiance.

Many of these reasons, however, cannot survive emigration. They lose all their vitality in a new land. Their virtue evaporates, and after a short effort to make use of them, they are abandoned as no longer serviceable. The exclusive endowment in these colonies of any single sect is impossible,—so much so that no one ventures to propose it. All the unendowed would remonstrate loudly, and even the members of the favored sect would be forced to admit the political injustice of such an arrangement. The smaller scale on which colonial governments are erected, and the greater simplicity of their construction, as compared with that of the parent State, admits of more complete insight into their form, and more searching criticism into their character. Their outlines are not concealed beneath " the rust and verdigris of antiquity." There is no haze and obscurity overhanging them, arising from vague claims of vested interests or undetermined rights. There is no involution of functions, which it is difficult to disentangle. All is recent and clearly defined. The first principles of law, of authority, of social order, of political philosophy, are seen in their simple and elementary application. State policy is intelligible here even to those who are confused by the complexity and vastness of that of the mother country. Thousands who have been puzzled in England by the contradictory arguments about the value and equity of national establishments, see at a glance that there can be no national church in the colony, and that there ought to be none. The great principle involved presents itself to the judgment in its naked simplicity, undisguised by those wrappings, which in an older and more complicated social polity, concealed its outlines. Decision upon its merits is, therefore, more quickly obtained, more sharply pronounced, and more generally comprehended.

This elementary, social, and political condition of the colonies rids us at once of two classes of defenders of a State Church. We hear nothing in these latitudes about the identity of the Church and the State. We are delivered from theorists who try to persuade us that the Church is as inseparable from good government as courts of justice are, and that a State is not a proper State which is not also a compact Church. Such theories could not gain a patient hearing where they are so obviously unrealisable. We are also free from those who support an ecclesiastical establishment as a buttress to aristocratical and monarchical institutions. We have no such institutions in the Colonies, and need no national hierarchy to keep them company. The well-used watchword of "the altar and the throne" has parted with its charm. While remaining loyal and integral parts of the British Empire, the Colonies are in their local institutions essentially democratic, and do not reproduce the social grades of the parent country.

The direct and old-fashioned alliance of Church and State, by the exclusive endowment of any particular sect, being instinctively abandoned on all hands as an impossible policy, (all the customary arguments in its favor and which still hold their ground in the old country, notwithstanding,) the Church question descends to an inferior footing. Its very nomenclature is changed. It appears now as the question of "State-aid to Religion." The obligation of the State to teach the *truth* being surrendered, something else is clung to which it is the duty of the State to patronise,—something more vague and general than truth,—viz., religion. And as religion is supposed to belong to all sects, which truth evidently cannot, it is thought that the main result is secured, and the political injustice avoided by endowing each sect in proportion to its numbers. This, it is said, is merely redistributing amongst the sects a part of the general taxation. The State levies the money through the Custom House, instead of leaving it to be collected at the church doors. By this means every man is made to pay for his own religion; and he does this, when he is smoking his pipe or drinking his toddy, without the exercise of much grudging. This plan is lauded, too, as having the advantage of levying the assessment with tolerable equality, and spreading it over the whole community, instead of devolving it on a few liberal persons, as is too much the case in the voluntary system. If it should be alleged that the greater part of the customs revenue is derived from tobacco and spirits, and that therefore the support of religion falls most heavily on those who consume those luxuries, it may be retorted, that those who smoke and drink most are those who most stand in need of religious instruction, and so a rude justice is still maintained.

This universal endowment plan chimes in so well with the indolent apathy of those who wish to see religious ordinances decently maintained, but who dislike the uncertainty, trouble, and annoyance of perpetual subscriptions, and is so agreeable to the views of those that look forward to the pulpit as offering a good social position, together with a guaranteed salary, that it might have been established with general consent, and have had

a long lease of life, till it had begotten abuses which made the
world weary of it, if all the denominations had been willing to
acquiesce in it.   But the time has gone by for giving it such a
trial as would really embrace all.   It was not propounded as a
piece of State policy till the doctrine of Christian voluntaryism
had struck deep root into society.   The defection of any denomination from the scheme spoils its symmetry; and when
several denominations collectively, forming a large part of the
community, stand aloof, it becomes glaringly inequitable.   This
is the case at present.   There are bodies of Christians who hold
firmly to the notion that the Church is to be sustained by free-
will offerings alone, and who cannot be bribed by any temptation
into accepting State-aid for their own relief.   They are regarded
by the supporters of State churches as possessed with a troublesome crotchet, as acting a kind of dog-in-the-manger policy, and
as preventing by their obstinate fanaticism the establishment of
a convenient system for the satisfactory support of religion.
But their doctrine, so stoutly held and so strongly denounced, is
steadily making its way, in a manner quite unaccountable to
those who see in it only the narrow views of perverse minds.   In
these, and indeed in almost all the British colonies, there are
only four sects who take the public money for their Church purposes.   These sects comprise, collectively, the greater portion of
the wealth, the population, the fashion and the influence of
colonial society.   Yet they are unable to make headway against
the voluntary heresy.   They receive the grant in aid yearly, with
a presentiment that they will soon receive it no more ; and foresee
that they will be compelled, however reluctantly, to rely on that
system of free-will offerings they so much dislike and mistrust.
   The gradual but irresistible advance of the belief in Christian
voluntaryism is a fact which may well challenge the attention
of the politician, and may perhaps force the conviction, that its
success can be owing only to its intrinsic truth.   At the first
planting of Christianity, the notion of its being supported by the
State was, for obvious reasons, never entertained.   It was enough
for the early Christians if they were not persecuted.   But when
an absolute emperor became a Christian, then the idea of
making the nation Christian found place.   It was a very natural
one under the circumstances—in fact, inevitable.   It seemed
part of the ordained development of Christian principles.   We
do not read that objections were taken to it, or that dangers
were anticipated.   It was welcomed as a good thing for religion.
It needed time to produce all the consequences.   At the Reformation, the relations of Church and State were not much discussed or understood.   The reformers protested against existing
corruptions, without seeing distinctly one great and constant
source of those corruptions.   The reform movement in no small
degree, trusted for aid to the civil power.   But freedom of
thought was secured by Luther's struggle, and one inevitable

consequence of that freedom was, that the doctrine of Christian Voluntaryism, as the proper basis of Church support, began slowly to rise above ground. Its adherents were few and despised; yet now it not only gains a patient audience amongst statesmen, but has been already adopted as a fundamental national policy in more than one instance. It is a distinctive feature of the great American republic, and important British colonies have also recognised it as the true ecclesiastical policy. In no case, where it has been adopted, has it as yet been, after trial, rejected; and where it is still opposed, there is felt to be an inevitable tendency towards its realisation. So steadily has this opinion made its way—dead against the opposition of rank and wealth and power!

It is this doctrine which is now contending in Australia against the universal endowment principle. The two opinions are brought face to face, and Christians and politicians are called on to choose between them. The basis of the opposition to voluntaryism lies in a distrust of its efficacy. There is not much desire to maintain the principle of state-churchism on its own account, nor is there any wide-spread feeling that to dispense with it would be sin. What there is of such opinion is mainly the remnant of imported ecclesiastical polity, and is not a naturalised colonial doctrine. On the contrary, it is admitted that there are inconveniencies attaching to the grant-in-aid; and most of those who still advocate it would be ready to dispense with it altogether, but for a fear that the interests of religion would thereby suffer. It is on the low ground of expediency that the rest of the battle has to be fought out. Will religion be adequately supported without the aid of the State? This is the real question now pressed on the voluntaries, and which they are now challenged to answer. They may indeed demand that the question should be narrowed still further, and that they should be only compelled to shew that religion would be *as well* supported without the grant as it is with it. For they may contend that the grant has practically failed to realise the national Christianity it pretends to achieve—that the money has been swallowed up with comparatively little to shew for it—and that, therefore, if actual and not theoretical voluntaryism is to be pointed at on the one side, actual and not theoretical state-religion should be pointed at also on the other. But, waiving this consideration, the question in its double aspect presents itself now to the colonial legislatures, and their constituencies: Will state support secure national religion? and could that result be accomplished on the voluntary system? If these two questions are answered, the first in the negative and the latter in the affirmative, the dispute will be set at rest; and it is to these points, therefore, that those who are anxious to clear up the truth should address themselves.

What is it that is really wanted?   National religion—that is to say, that the people at large should be animated by religious motives.   But how is this to be secured?   The will of man is not a mechanical product that can be acted upon by mechanical means.   How can we buy religious motives for the people? obviously the thing is unpurchaseable.   Vital religion cannot be obtained like police or turnpike roads at so much per head of the whole population.   What can be done, and this is all, is to provide church accommodation and support religious teachers, in the hope that this instrumentality may beget the desired result. Strictly speaking, "State-aid to Religion" is a misnomer.   It would more properly be called "State-aid to church ordinances." It is possible to have all the outward organization of Christianity, with little or no vital and animating religion.   Such a state of things has been, and to this day is still, in certain quarters.   It appears then, that the state cannot secure national religion by ever so much endowment.   It can secure church forms, but cannot obtain a guarantee that the much desired spiritual life should accompany them.   It is only a contingency, not a certainty, that is acquired.   Yet, if the vital religion should not be forthcoming, the organisation set up is a failure, and the money spent is wasted.   No Christian man will deny the value of Christian ordinances.   On the contrary, he will tax himself heavily to support them where they are, and to plant them where they are not.   But their influence for good is proportioned, not to their outward aspect of efficiency, but to the force and fervour of the inward animating spiritual life.   Voluntaryism itself is not a protection against the churches becoming powerless.   If the zeal that originated the organization dies out, then Ichabod is written on its walls.   The Church is the body, religion is the soul.   In the early days of Christianity there was much religion with very little of Church forms apparent to the world.   In subsequent days, the Church externals stood out before the world, vast, splendid, and imposing, but the celestial tenant had gone.   The Church stands in constant need of salt to preserve it from decay.   It is an invaluable blessing to a nation and to the world, when filled with heavenly fire; it is useless, and worse than useless, when it has only "a name to live, and is dead."   When is a church most likely to be vitalised—when it constantly depends on the zeal of Christians, or when it is comfortably and securely quartered on the public treasury? Let all answer who have studied human nature, who have read ecclesiastical history, who can observe the various aspects of the different parts of Christendom at this day, and who know by personal experience what the working of Christian principle in the heart is.   We want a god-fearing people.   Shall we say, as our experience of the past, "this kind cometh not forth but by"—State endowments?

The voluntary advocate is not content to rest his case on theory. He appeals to the history of Christendom. Have not national churches existed in Europe in great variety, among people of various races, and under such diversity of circumstances as to afford a very wide basis of experiment? Can any instance be pointed to which was successful, which realised the theory, and which did not degenerate in proportion as the Church ceased to be an embodiment of Christian life, and became an instrument of State policy? Is it or is it not a fact, that national churches, under all forms, have been national failures; and that they have not only come short of their pretensions, but have proved themselves the prolific parents of not a few evils and distractions? Because, if so, it suggests that there must be something wrong in the principle itself. A good tree would bear good fruits. A constant crop of rottenness shews that there is unsoundness at the roots.

Some will say,—" Well, if we give up this principle of State support to religion—which it must be admitted has never proved itself satisfactory—what are we to trust to? Men are selfish, and are unused to giving liberally. Religion will be starved out of the world." It never has been starved out yet,—even when it abode only amongst the poor and persecuted. The Church has encountered more danger from contact with wealth than from exposure to poverty; but no one will deny that in Australia there is plenty of money. Taken altogether, there is not a richer population in the world, man for man, than there is here. If, therefore, people do not contribute liberally, it is not because they cannot, but because they will not. This want of will is a sign of deficient Christian life, for to give freely is a Christian duty. Will State endowments cure this evil? Christian liberality requires to be called more into exercise, and the duty of it to be pressed more upon the consciences of the public. Will this end be in any measure attained by suspending the exercise of this liberality in one of its most important directions, and providing for Church ordinances by taxation? Vigor comes by healthy exercise, both to the body and the mind. If there is prevailing langour, the remedy must be sought not in indolent repose, but in the infusion of fresh life.

When awakened to its duty, and with that duty cast wholly on itself, the Church is equal to the task before it. Why should this be doubted? The triumphs of Christian liberality are to be seen on every hand. In every quarter of the globe it has made itself felt, and has penetrated all grades of society, from the palace to the prison; and this has been done under discouragement, and in spite of the wide-spread adhesion to the doctrine that the spiritual culture of humanity had been sufficiently taken in charge by governments. What may it not be expected to do when set free from all trammels? " Be not afraid, only believe."

[The following article on the Marriage Laws may be deemed by some too
elaborate and technical for the pages of a Miscellaneous Magazine; but
as it is from a competent hand, and is extremely reasonable at the
present moment, when the unsatisfactory state of these Laws, in Victoria in particular, demands and must receive the early attention of the
proper authorities, it is hoped its appearance will be considered a public
benefit.—Ed.]

HISTORICAL NOTICES OF THE LAWS RELATING TO MARRIAGE IN THE AUSTRALIAN COLONIES.

THIS paper is intended to record the development of the Anglo-
Australian laws relating to marriage; to relate the past practice
in these colonies, and recite the remarkable cases by which that
practice has been illustrated; to set forth the opinions of the judges
and the conflict of the Courts, and finally to show the progress of
a more enlightened legislation. The statements given are derived
from original authorities; and will not be encumbered with special
references.	In this retrospect we shall see that the British
and Colonial Governments neglected to provide laws for these
colonies adapted to their condition, that they suffered the laws to
remain in doubt long after their purport had been called in
question, and that they declared and amended them, yet so as to
leave their fundamental principles unsettled.	We shall have to
mark the recklessness of certain ministers of religion, who, on a
theory of abstract justice, or a private interpretation of the law,
habitually disregarded legal restrictions, that by this course they
cast over thousands of families the most serious doubts; and thus
hazarded the social position of those families, their peace of mind,
and their rights of inheritance.	It was not until 1855 that the
New South Wales Legislature adopted a law worthy of statesmen—
a law which, while legalizing all marriages liable to be questioned
for want of form, and while providing for persons who wish to
dispense with religious rites, conferred equal privileges on the
same terms upon all sects and all ecclesiastics. To the bold and
liberal views of SIR ALFRED STEPHEN, Chief Justice of New South
Wales, who drafted the Bill, and to the support it received from
Mr. Plunkett, the first law officer of the Crown, the colonists owe
a Marriage Act more simple, clear, and impartial than any found
in the statute book of England, and not inferior to any in her
colonial dependencies.

The colony of New South Wales, founded in 1788, was first
peopled by convicts and their superiors. The appointment of
their first clergyman was an after thought. No care was bestowed
to ascertain the laws which affected their social life.	The
Governor for the time being usurped the functions of a legislature, and issued edicts grounded on temporary circumstances,
and irrespective of past British legislation. Detachments from
the principal settlement were drafted to others beyond the seas,
where there were often no clergymen of any persuasion.	Magis-
trates sometimes in these circumstances officiated at marriages and

gave a civil sanction, probably under the impression that the common law made such contracts valid. They were, however, merely witnesses. Some families of colonial consideration trace to this form of marriage. The rites of religion were generally afterwards added when they became accessible. The Governor of New South Wales, which country was then in the diocese of Calcutta afterwards of Madras, issued licenses to the clergymen to solemnize matrimony. The utility of this practice, as tending to check clandestine marriages, was clear, and it was continued to 1836. The greater part of marriages so licensed were solemnized by Episcopal clergymen; some licenses were, however, issued to Dr. Lang, then a clergyman of the Church of Scotland. The authority of the Governors to execute the functions of Surrogate under the Bishop was never ascertained; it was, however, attributed rather to their representative headship of the Church, than to Episcopal delegation.

In 1826, an ordinance passed the Colonial legislature, which assumed that there were parishes in New South Wales, and that there were "established ministers" over them. All other clergymen, whether of the Anglican Church or not, were required to certify the marriages they solemnized to "the established minister," to be inserted in the parochial register. The clergy, both of the Churches of Scotland and Rome, declined to comply. Dr. Lang did so in a manner to challenge prosecution. Proceedings being taken, the existence of legal parishes, and of established ministers, was disputed with success, and the ordinance fell into desuetude. It is thus remarkable that while the Governor, as head of the Church, or " Ordinary," issued licenses to Presbyterian ministers, the Anglican clergy were appointed to record marriages void under their own ecclesiastical system. The *existence* of legal parishes soon became an important question in the Courts, and entered deeply into the inquiry, whether the English marriage acts were of force in the colonies of Australia.

The marriage law of India came under the examination of the Courts of Westminster. It was admitted that the English law of 26 George II. did not extend to India. The statute 58 George III. c. 84, was passed to quiet the apprehensions of the Scottish colonists in India. Reciting the doubt whether marriages solemnized by ministers of the Church of Scotland were legal, it declared them of the same effect as marriages celebrated by clergymen of the Church of England.*

A similar declaration and enactment was necessary for New South Wales. Accordingly in 1834 an ordinance was passed adopting the words of the British Parliament in the Indian Act with some modification. It included the Roman Catholic marriages, and required, in the case of Scottish clergy, that they should take a declaration from either of the parties, that one of

---

* Roper on the Law of Husband and Wife, vol. ii. p. 460.

them was in communion with "the *Presbyterian* Church of
Scotland;" thus leaving it open to doubt whether any but one,
and that the smaller portion of Scottish population then in the
colony, could be married by their own clergy.

It had, however, been already decided that a marriage
solemnized in India by a Roman Catholic priest in a private
room was valid. It was the practice of the Catholic clergy to
follow this precedent in New South Wales, neither license nor
bans being considered essential. Accordingly in 1829 a
marriage was solemnized between John Maloney and the widow
Haley. The usual forms were observed ; two witnesses were
present, and a record of the marriage was found among the
papers of the officiating clergyman after his decease. Maloney,
his wife being alive, intermarried with one Mary Carmody in the
Episcopal Church, Liverpool (New South Wales.) Being indicted
for bigamy, his counsel at his trial disputed the validity of the
first marriage. On his conviction, it was referred as a
Special Case to the Supreme Court, and a majority of the Judges
sustained the verdict. The question raised was whether the
statutory laws of England applied to the colonies. The *common*
law undoubtedly did, but what the common law relating to
marriage was, had not then been decided. The question as it
came before the Court was, whether the English Marriage
Act of 1823 were in force or not.

In an Act of Parliament passed in 1828, for the government of
New South Wales, it was enacted, " That all laws and statutes in
force within the realm of England at the time of the passing of
this Act shall be applied in the administration of justice in the
Supreme Court of New South Wales, *so far as the same can be
applied within the said colony*." There were two methods pointed
out by the Act itself, to ascertain the applicability of laws—a
judgment of the Supreme Court, or a declaration of the Legislature. Up to this period neither had been given. The English
Marriage Act of 1823 required that marriage by license should
take place only in the parochial church in the parish where one
of the parties resided : that in marriage by bans, the bans should
be published in the church in which the marriage was celebrated ; and of course, in both cases, they should be solemnized by
the clergy of the Church of England. In this colony all sects
had celebrated marriages in private houses, and many were so
solemnized by the Archdeacon of the territory. If this Act
applied, all such marriages would be null and void. The Parliament, however, had unquestionably given a *primâ facie* claim to
consider this law binding on the colonies, and the judges were
to declare whether it was valid.

It was an established maxim of the English constitution—
" that the English carry with them so much of the law as is
applicable to their own situation and the condition of an infant
colony, such, for instance, as the general rules of inheritance."
" But English Acts of Parliament made in England without

naming the foreign plantations, cannot bind them." "What laws are in force must, in cases of dispute, be decided in the first instance by their own provincial legislature." Acts of Parliament, made for the purpose, bind the colonies, and such parts of the common or statute law as have by *long usage* and *general acquiescence* been received and acted under. *These*, though without any particular law of the country for that purpose, are to be continued in force." Mr. Justice Burton maintained that the English Act applied. He affirmed that it was a necessary law, to prevent clandestine marriages; that although not entirely like the parishes of England, there were parishes; and that although no parochial churches or clergy in the full sense, there were such sufficient to afford machinery for the application of the Act. If, on the supposition that the law applied, inconvenience and dissatisfaction should follow, he thought the opposite conclusion would lead to more disastrous results. In this case, children of fourteen and twelve years could marry at any time, by a mere verbal agreement, and in defiance of parental authority. It would appear from this opinion that Judge Burton thought the *common law* of Europe, as it stood before the Council of Trent (which law made a contract of marriage binding without the intervention of a priest), was the law of England before the Marriage Act of George the Second, and that it was only set aside by that Act, and the Act of 1823.

The Chief Justice, Sir Francis Forbes, combatted the views of Mr. Justice Burton in a very learned judgment. He maintained the marriage law of England was not intended to be applied to the colonies. "It is apparent," he said, "that some of the most material requisites of the English Marriage Act are entirely defective in the colony; that it wants the machinery necessary to its operation; that in fact it cannot be enforced." In support of his view, Sir Francis Forbes referred to an opinion, given by the English law officers of the Crown in 1812, on a question put to them by the Secretary of State, "That the Marriage Act of George the Second does not apply to the British settlements abroad." Sir Francis Forbes, however, rested his judgment chiefly on the view, "that marriage is a contract by general law, antecedent to civil society. In civil society it becomes a civil contract, and subject to regulation adapted to the circumstances of the community in which the contract is made." He also held that, before the Act of George the Second, by the law of England "the consent of two persons able to contract, expressed in words of *present* mutual acceptance, technically known by the name of *Sponsalia per verba de præsenti*, constituted an actual and valid marriage;" and he believed the place, the religious solemnities, the bans, and licenses were all immaterial. In this opinion Mr. Justice Dowling concurred; and thus a major part of the judges declared that the English marriage laws of the Georges did not apply. To this view the legislature of the colony by its silence assented.

The Colonial Ordnance of 1834, which pronounced marriages by clergymen of either Scotland or Rome of equal efficacy with those performed by clergymen of the Church of England, had declared all marriages void thereafter solemnized, unless the officiating clergymen obtained a declaration in writing, and in duplicate, that one of the parties was " a member of or in the communion with the Church of Rome, or the Presbyterian Church of Scotland." The Church of England, however, was under no such restriction, and could marry any parties who presented themselves. The Presbyterian clergy considered this " declaration" a burden and a snare, and a badge of inferiority. The words used were also of doubtful import, since " the Presbyterian Church of Scotland" was not then the only or the most numerous section of the Scottish Colonial population. Dr. Lang and Dr. M'Garvie, both clergymen of the Church of Scotland, neglected to require the declaration; and thus nullified all the marriages they solemnized so far as they depended on the colonial law. This alarming fact was disclosed in 1850, in the case Regina v. Roberts, who was found guilty of bigamy. The first marriage in this instance had been solemnized by a clergyman of the Church of England—the second by Dr. M'Garvie, of the Church of Scotland. As the validity of the second marriage was not necessary to sustain the conviction, the question as to what was the law, with reference to the intervention of a person in holy orders, was not then determined.

The Chief Justice, Sir Alfred Stephen, in an elaborate judgment, decided that Dr. M'Garvie, by neglecting to require this declaration, had omitted one essential condition to the validity of a marriage; unless, indeed he were to solemnize it independently of any local enactment; and then, if this were the fact, any other person—a postman or blacksmith, could have done so. Sir A. Stephen dwelt on the mischief which must befal society from the uncertainty in which this great social question was involved, and the importance of legislative interference. He unfortunately deemed himself precluded from going into the question, whether, irrespective of colonial ordinances, a marriage were good without the intervention of a person in holy orders. Mr. Justice Therry and himself concurred that where the first marriage was binding the crime of bigamy was complete, whether the second were legal or not. The entire Court agreed, that a Presbyterian clergyman was invested by colonial law with the power to celebrate a marriage only after the declaration prescribed by the Act of 1834 had been duly made, and that being neglected, the marriage, so far as its validity depended on that law, was void. Mr. Justice Dickinson not only confirmed the conviction, but asserted the validity of the second marriage considered in itself. It had been maintained by the Attorney-General that New South Wales was not an English, but a British colony; and that the laws of England do not exclusively extend to it, but that what would be valid in Scotland would be valid there. Mr. Justice Dickinson, however, replied that the Imperial Parliament having established courts, after the model and with the powers of those of Westminster, implied that their decisions were to be governed, not by Scottish, but English laws.

In a judgment of great power, he nevertheless maintained the validity of the marriage, that is to say its validity in itself but for the first marriage, irrespective of the colonial ordinance and the ecclesiastical status of Dr. M'Garvie. It was contended by the learned judge, that by the common law of England—the law of nature, and of nations—the marriage was good. "The efficacy of marriages in this colony depended, not on any portion of the *instituted*, but on the *natural* law of England. According to that law, marriage is constituted by consent." He asserted that "the ceremony before Dr. M'Garvie was valid by the law of nature, as being *nuptiæ per verba de præsenti ;*" that is, the consent of two persons able to contract, expressed in words of present mutual acceptance.

It was admitted that, by the laws of England of a date antecedent to legal memory (the accession of Richard I.), a marriage was not valid unless solemnized by a person "in Holy Orders." This had been decided upon an appeal to the House of Lords. George Millis, a member of the Established Church in Ireland, was married to Hester Graham a Presbyterian, by a Presbyterian clergyman ; he afterwards married another, Hester being still living, in an English Parish Church. The conviction for bigamy was set aside. The laws of Ireland at first allowed Dissenters to solemnize marriages without being molested in the ecclesiastical courts ; and afterwards authorized these marriages, both parties being Dissenters. These were, however, exceptions from the operation of the English law, which exceptions did not extend to a member of the Established Church. It had been long held by eminent lawyers that prior to the Act of George II. marriages by "mutual present acceptance," were valid according to the common law. This was the canon law of Europe before the Council of Trent. The ecclesiastical courts compelled the parties to fulfil these contracts, and set aside marriages solemnized in the face of the church in favor of those pre-contracted. The Council of Trent had however no authority in England, and it was long supposed that by the common law the intervention of a priest was not required. The decision in the case of Millis cleared all doubts on the subject, and declared that, where the marriage laws of England prevailed, the only marriages valid were those celebrated by a priest in holy orders, unless under special enactments which must be strictly construed. The English Judges referred to the Institutes of Edmund, and the statutes of a council held in Winchester, at the time of Archbishop Lanfranc, 1075. The first of these declared that "In nuptials there shall be a mass priest, who shall with God's blessing, join the parties together in marriage." The second enacted "that a marriage without the benediction of a priest should not be a legitimate marriage." The decision of the House of Peers was pronounced, upon an equal division of six law lords, of whom four had been Chancellors and two Chief Justices of the Common Pleas. The decision, which involved the highest interests, followed a rule that where the votes are equal, judgment shall be given in favor of the party denying; *presumitur pro negante.* It was however the decision of the highest Court of law, and no question could remain that in England since, as well as before the Reformation, a clergyman of the Established Church could alone solemnize a legal marriage. The opinion of all the judges had been taken, and a large majority were in favour of that proposition.

Whether these early laws were the *common* law of England, or whether they were to be considered laws within the definition of " an enactment" had not been explicitly determined. They were beyond the era of " legal memory." But " statute laws have been defined as laws in writing." Mr. Justice Dickinson held these early institutes to be included in the *statutes,* and therefore not the *common law* of England. As it was now admitted that the English Marriage Acts did not apply to the colonies, it followed, in his view, that the statutes of Edmund were comprehended in the general principles of their exclusion. He maintained that it was " an abuse of terms to say, when a record of a law is in existence, that it is a *lex non scripta,* and a confusion of ideas to deem a piece of positive institution to be a portion of the common law." The argument of the learned judge may thus be summed up. According to the law of nature, and, before the Council of Trent, by the law of Europe, a marriage by *mutual present acceptance* is a valid marriage. In the time of Edmund, a law was made requiring the intervention of a priest. This was an innovation, and then first became the law of England. It was, however, a *written* law,—it belonged to the *statutory* laws of England. These confessedly have no force in Australia, unless they are applied by competent authority. The marriage laws of England have been declared not to apply : the common law therefore prevails ; and by that law mutual " present consent" constitutes a legal marriage, except where it is set aside by colonial ordinances. Sir Alfred Stephen and Mr. Justice Therry both appeared to dissent from this opinion, but no competent authority has pronounced against it. It is probably held by these eminent judges that the common law was merely declared by the Saxon institutes, quoted above, and that they cannot be considered as bringing in for the first time, " the intervention of a priest." Or that if, on the contrary, those institutes were *innovations,* they nevertheless belong to the received *Common law* of the realm,—a large portion of which, as is well known, consists of lost or forgotten written institutes. The discovery of such writings leaves the nature of the law (in legal contemplation) just where it was before such discovery.

Although the views of Mr. Justice Dickinson appear to be in harmony with justice, the prevailing sentiments of the Court created the utmost alarm. Dr. M'Garvie had solemnized marriages informally, never taking the declaration without which the Court had decided that his special authority, as a *minister*, did not come into operation. All these marriages were illegal, except upon the views of Mr. Justice Dickinson, and persons contracting other marriages could not be prosecuted with success. In India, the judgment of the Lords had been followed by lamentable abuses, and there is too much reason to believe that similar mischief has resulted in the Australias. The Government, however, lost no time in passing an Act, declaring the Presbyterian marriages valid, but without amending the law. The Governor, in giving his assent (1850), reflected strongly on the neglect of the requirements of the law, and stated that he should be sorry to lend his aid again to remedy a defect which might have been avoided by a due observance of its provisions. He, perhaps, was not aware that, however culpable a systematic neglect of the requirements of the law might be, it was partly due to the ambiguity with which they were expressed.

The marriage law of 1835, authorizing dissenting ministers to solemnize marriages, was expressly limited to England. This enlargement of the privileges of the nonconforming sects led, of course, to similar changes in the colonies. The more offensive parts of the English marriage law were impracticable; there were no poor-law boards, or work-houses, in the colonies.

The course in New South Wales has been to extend, by separate Acts, to the different denominations, the privileges at first granted to the Catholics and Presbyterians. They were, however, required to exact the declaration of membership, which was liable to the most arbitrary definitions. In Tasmania, the English Act was adopted more nearly. The places of worship were licensed; registrars acted as surrogates; or recorded notices, which were equivalent to bans. The officiating ministers were bound to use certain words implying *mutual present acceptance*, and to transmit the certificates of marriage to the Registrar-General. They were, however, allowed to marry any persons, without reference to their religion. While this was the law respecting the minor denominations, the Episcopal, Scottish, and Roman Catholic ministers preserved their own usages as they existed before the law of 1835. The colony of Victoria still lives under the late law of New South Wales*; and there is reason to fear that the confusion which the latter country only lately escaped is likely to reveal itself in the former. The invalidity of marriage, in which the " declaration of membership" has not been made, was affirmed by the unanimous judgment of the Supreme Court of New South Wales, and may be presumed

* Modified in some respects by the Registration Act passed since the Separation.—ED.

to affect all in a similar position. When the exposition of the law of England, in the judgment of the Supreme Court, reached the Synod of Edinburgh, a petition was presented from that body to the Lords by the Duke of Argyle, complaining of the state of the law, and demanding imperial legislation. Earl Grey, then Secretary of State, cast on the colonies themselves the responsibility, and stated that since the laws of England *did not* extend to the colonies, they should adapt their own to their social condition.

In New South Wales the new marriage law passed with almost universal assent (1855), and, with a few unimportant exceptions, has been found remarkably acceptable. The solemnization of marriage is confined to officiating ministers of all denominations, and to official registrars. These, both ministers and registrars, must be gazetted as such. They must certify the marriages they perform. They must exact a declaration from both parties to the marriage that they are of age, and that there is no lawful impediment to the union. Falsehood is dealt with as perjury, and irregularity is highly penal : but no marriage can be set aside for want of form. The ceremonies of religion, the use of bans and licenses, the time and the place of celebration, and all other questions, more or less ecclesiastical, are left to be determined by the sects themselves. Provision is made for those who wish to be married in the office of the Registrar, for the sake of pagans, or others who object to ministers of religion, but whose natural rights it is the duty of society to recognize and protect. Considering the long contest on this subject, and, recollecting the difficulties which seemed to beset the settlement of the marriage question, and the all but unanimous satisfaction which has attended its accomplishment, the authors of the New South Wales Marriage Act are entitled to general gratitude.

The future legislation in the Australias respecting marriages, opens a subject of great and painful interest. It is perhaps to be deplored, that the statesmen of Britain have relinquished to numerous dependencies the task of adjusting the marriage laws to their various and conflicting prejudices ; and it has been predicted by Lord Campbell, with great probability, that this confusion will hereafter confound the highest tribunals of the empire. Already, in one of the colonies (South Australia) the law has declared itself with reference to the marriage of the deceased wife's sister, and it is highly probable that a law for facilitating divorces will be adopted in another. Without reference to the expediency of such laws, or their agreement with the dictates of revelation, it must be of universal concern that they should be considered from a more elevated stand-point than a single colony is likely to afford. They seem to form one of a numerous class of public questions, which demand the united legislation of the Australian world.

MISCELLANIES.

Fern Tree House.

(A SERIES OF SKETCHES.)

No, I.

"Our tallest rose,
Peeped at the chamber window; we could hear
At silent noon, and eve, and early morn,
The sea's faint murmur. In the open air,
Our myrtles blossomed, and across the porch
Thick jasmines twined; the little landscape round
Was green and woody, and refreshed the eye."

COLERIDGE

People in England talk much about the roughness of Australian life, its inconveniences, its "shifts," its want of comfort. If, on the voyage, some one who had only obtained his notions of Australia from the common opinions of English society, were to meet with the passage from Coleridge which we have taken as the motto for this chapter, he would perhaps heave a sigh, and say to himself, "All that is left behind." Our friends in Europe might, however, be induced to change their opinions if they could be transported, some summer evening, to the palace-like mansions in the neighborhood of Sydney, with their gardens of a luxuriance unattainable in even the grounds of Kew or Chatsworth. Or even if they could suddenly behold the pleasant suburban villas and numerous picturesque cottages which lie outside "young and half-formed Melbourne," they might perhaps think they were still in England, if it were not that the sky is brighter, and the vegetation more tropical.

We propose to introduce our readers to one of these quiet suburban retreats, and hope that we may spend some pleasant hours in the company of our friends who live at "Fern Tree House," which lies on the shores of the beautiful Bay of Port Phillip. And as we listen to their conversations with their numerous friends and visitors, we may perhaps, from time to time, gain some little insight into what is passing, and what people are saying, in this our new world. We are none of us too wise to learn; we none of us are so perfected in our opinions that they will not do with a little correction or enlargement, or our interest in our own opinions may need deepening.

It was one evening in the month of May of this year, when Mr. Hamilton was sitting in the bay window of his house, with his newspaper by his side and a book in his hand, waiting the arrival of his friend Mr. Churchill, who had promised to spend the evening with him. The window was open on to the verandah which encircled the villa, and through the arches of passion flow___ ___ ___ ___ ___ ___ the pillars, shone the rich glory ___ ___ ___ ___ ___ ___ nearly upon the horizon, and the ___ ___ ___ ___ ___ in bold relief the mountains on th___ ___ ___ ___ ___ when lighted up with the glory of ___ ___ ___ ___ sunset scenes, as viewed from the ___ ___ ___ merry voices, coming from those ___ ___ ___ toils of the day on the beach, ___ ___ ___ garden; but the thick shrubbery ___ ___ ___ prevented anything from being see___ ___ ___ ing onwards, apparently to a brigl___ ___ ___ seemed almost unearthly in their temp___ ___ ___

The sound of footsteps in the verandah announced the arrival of visitors. Mr. Hamilton looking up saw his daughter Clara coming towards him, and with her his friend Mr. Churchill. Before, however, he could offer his salutations to his guest, Clara took upon herself the task of introducing him.

"Papa," she said, "here is Mr. Churchill at last. Do you know he is quite a unique and rare specimen of the genus lawyer."

"That's a new way of introducing me to your home," he said, turning to her, "I suppose you want to wither me with your sly sarcasms. If so, I must give in at once; but still, I should like to know why I have such a judgment pronounced upon me, if my fair judge will condescend to explain why she condemns me as so curious a specimen of the genus lawyer. I——"

"It won't take much explanation. Do you know, Papa, this Mr. Churchill, who professes to be at home in Blackstone's Commentaries and Rutherford's—I forget what his most pleasing book is called—but no matter; this dry lawyer went, or tried to go, into poetic ecstacies on the view from the garden gate. I endured it for a little time, but was soon obliged to stop him; for, only think, he had in his hand his red bag there, and he held it out at arm's length, pointing with it to the setting sun!"

Mr. H.   Our friend, I see, scarcely knows what to reply to such a terrible charge, and I must undertake his case for him, and my argument shall be one by analogy. Perhaps our friend here acts on the same principle as our quondam acquaintance, Mr. Maitland, the poet and novelist (it makes no matter for our argument whether his books sold or not). But he said, when he came to the conclusion of an exciting love scene, or a grand rhapsody, he used to take up De Morgan's Differential Calculus by way of diversion; and I may readily suppose that our friend acts on the same principle, though reversing the operation, making poems on his way home from the Melbourne law courts, with the red bag under his arm.

Mr. C.   Then I must beg the pardon of my fair censor for my grievous offence. I own the charge is correct, and plead guilty to having admired the beauties of this quiet retreat, and of having allowed the better part of my nature to express its response to the enchantments of this scene, the choosing of my young critic herself.

Miss C.   You make, however, a rare confession: I was waiting impatiently until you had finished your sentence to notice it—"the better part of our nature" indeed!—then you lawyers spend all the hours of court business, to say nothing of hours lost over law books, in cultivating the worse part of your nature—and just occasionally, as when the sunset happens to be particularly beautiful, does anything better come out? I have often heard it remarked before, but never yet confessed.

Mr. C.   Don't you think, Mr. Hamilton, I had better hand over my gown and wig to my unmerciful antagonist? She would make a first-rate hand at puzzling a witness. I have a difficult and doubtful case to-morrow, and I shall be happy to hand it over to one who, like Portia, has "so young a body with so old a head," and who will certainly win the cause for my client.

Miss C.   Let me answer that question myself. If I then am to be like Portia, I should not be the first lady who donned a learned robe, and won her cause; and, with all due respect to my learned friend, no lawyer ever equalled "the young and learned doctor," (and she too contrived to be a poet as well). Besides, according to one sentence of that dry book you gave me to read, I am sure we ladies would beat you at getting through a mass of evidence.

Mr. C. And pray what was that?

Miss C. I don't profess to remember all you give me to read, even if I do read it; but this one extraordinary sentiment I do remember: "The female mind is eager to attain to truth by direct intuition; the masculine intellect arrives at the same result by a process of reasoning." That is, both you and I want to get across a field, you go round it, I run straight through.

Mr. C. I must really give in. It is too bad, after a hard day at the courts, not to have a little peace in a place like this. Is it not, Mr. Hamilton?

Mr. H. May be after tea your faculties will have recovered their elasticity, and Miss Clara have forgotten her sarcasm; and so we had better move in and close the window, especially as the glory of the sunset, the innocent cause of all this, has now departed.

The company then went into the sitting room through the window, which opened at once upon the verandah, and were joined at the tea table by Mrs. Hamilton, and one or two of the younger members of the family. Mr. George Hamilton (to which specimen of colonial character we may at some future time introduce our readers) was not present.

"I was so much perplexed," said Mr. Churchill to his host when they were all seated, "with the shafts aimed so mercilessly at me just now by my young friend here, that I forgot to ask after you—I expected to see you to-day."

Miss C. Very lawyerlike to be sure, to forget! I wish I was a witness, and you were examining me.

Mr. H. Never mind the law courts now, Clara, for if you go on this way, I must get Mr. Churchill to supplant you in your duties as president of the tea table. You will be pouring water into the tea caddy, and milk into the sugar basin.

Miss C. With all my heart, I am ready to give way to my learned friend as soon as he likes.

Mr. C. Thank you, I'll tell you when presently; but, Mr. Hamilton, I was going to ask you, if I had not been interrupted, how it was you were never in my office to-day, as you promised. I met the young man; he came at 12 o'clock, and I was sorry you were not there to listen to his story. I was very much affected by it: it was impossible not to be.

Mr. H. And what did you do? Did you take him into your office?

Mr. C. No! I thought I would let you see him first—there is so much deception, and clever deception too, among these fallen scholars, that I thought there would be no harm in waiting a few days and watching him. His enemies give him a wretched character, still I expect to find it without foundation. I am generally pretty correct in my reading of character; and though sometimes my compassion has led astray my reason, I don't think it is so in this case. He is a clever, noble-hearted boy, but broken down by his misfortunes. I wish you had been there; but as you were not, I have asked him to call on me in a day or two, and I will bring him up here to tea.

Mr. H. I regret I was not with you, but I could not avoid it. I had an unusual amount of correspondence to despatch by the mail this evening, and among the rest an article for an English Review, on the Australian aspects of the great question of Church and State. Since the decision of the House of Assembly on the question, and the probable dooming of the 53rd clause, I have felt an increased interest in the matter. I cannot tell you how glad I felt, when after sitting in the gallery of the House for four or five hours, I saw that grand triumph. It was well fought, and I longed to be among the combatants. I have

D

some hope now for the Christian character of our young country ; and to make this land as Christian as can be, is my earnest endeavour.

Mr. C.   I am not going to discuss that question with you. You and I may agree to help a poor outcast scholar, but on this point we shall, I fear, ever be at variance. I cannot help looking on your present earnestness as mistaken Christian zeal on your part. As a *Christian*, it is that I greatly regret the decision of our Assembly ; and on the same ground, I cannot but hope the measure will fail to pass the Upper House. I cannot endure the idea of a government in a land which is peopled chiefly by Christians, having no kind of recognition of those great truths and principles on which every measure ought to be based. It is preposterous.

Mr. H.   I trust the Upper House will have more sense and prudence than to jeopardise their position by opposing the Assembly upon so vital a question. I too have faith in my religion, and I have a faith which you seem not to possess, in the powerful response which religion elicits from the hearts of those who receive it. Let it have its perfect freedom, its independence, its native energy from Christ himself, and it will be strong indeed apart from the help of the State.

Mr. C.   True enough ; but we must use means. My definition of practical religion is this—looking at, and working out, common natural things as if they were supernatural. We must use every means in our power; and I believe the aid of the State, and the grand conservatism which follows upon a religious establishment, are both of them among the chief means for us to use in evangelising the world.

Mr. H.   We are both pretty much agreed upon the main question ; what we differ about is the means of accomplishing our object. My idea is, that if Christianity is elaborated from the heart, and the bible interpreted by the heart, then men will love their religion more, and have more faith in its power; and your being an English Churchman is no reason why you should fetter your own system,—for let religion be freer, and then all parties and denominations, including your own, will have more life.

Mr. C.   As to that, you will allow me to have my own opinion, and I am not disposed to talk the matter over now. But however we decide this question, you will agree with me in reprobating the style of " enduring patronage," which our public men bestow on religion in its various forms.

Mr. H.   I don't see what you mean ; explain yourself.

Mr. C.   This is what I mean. The sentiment and conduct of many of our public men towards religion is just like that of an American slaveholder, with a somewhat disorganised property, who has a handsome and efficient steward-slave. The slave, unfortunately, has some idea of his having a mind of his own, and likewise a right to exercise it. But he looks well about the estate—he is very useful and clever; but is too strong and too designing to put up with harsh treatment. What then must the master do ? He makes him his steward and his valet, gives him a gold chain and kid gloves, talks to him, sometimes pats him on the back, and thinks to himself he has hit upon the right plan for managing him, without making him either a friend or an enemy. Now is not that just the way that many of our respectable citizens treat all religion ? I took the pains the other day to transfer to my pocket-book a sentence which appeared from the pen of one of them. Here it is : it runs thus—" Looked at from the general and social, and not from the individual point of view, we apprehend that all forms of religious belief, which acknowledge and enforce the rules of moral duty, are equally useful to society." Equally useful, indeed !

Miss C. If you will allow me a word in your most serious conversation, I think I can make an improvement in your illustration, Mr. Churchill, about the slaveholder. That sentence you have just read suggests it to me. The case is rather as if your useful and handsome slave had a numerous progeny, all of them of the same ornamentally useful character, and for fear of offending the ornamentally useful father, and the similarly ornamentally useful children, when they grow up; one is dressed as a page, and so is still highly ornamental and contented; one is made a lady's waiting-maid, which if not ornamental, is yet honorable in the household and useful ; one is trained as a secretary, and another is made into a cook, to prepare the sops for all the rest. Isn't it so?

Mr. C. An excellent addition to my speech, and it makes no matter, as to its applicability, that this equitable and imaginative distribution of the ' ornamentally useful' family, by my fair censor, shows that she has not yet trod the shores of America. But however, to return to what we were saying, Mr. Hamilton : I have an unbounded and inexpressible contempt for that latitudinarian way of looking at religion. ' Equally useful,' indeed ! How does that sound to a man whose heart is burning with love to mankind, and who believes that the great Founder of our common faith is now alive for evermore ?

Mr. H. Yes, there I can agree with you, though perhaps from different motives. I believe in the innate power of Christianity, and look with you upon its holy principles as rightfully masters in the State, and on all the institutions of the country as justly its subordinates, and useful to it ; and to place religion in that position is all my energy directed. I wish for it an omnipotent rule in all the thoughts and deeds of society. But how is it you speak of this tendency as latitudinarianism ? I often hear you boast of your freedom from prejudice, and apply that word to yourself.

Mr. C. So I do ; but I should think you keen enough as an observer to have seen that there are two things passing under the same name ; one of which I abhor both as a man and a Christian; the other I hail as a welcome sign of better days, both among us Episcopalians and you Independents and Presbyterians.

Mr. H. And what are they ?

Mr. C. Why, there is first that ' equally useful' theory, of which I have been speaking, which is patronised by the so-called ' large-minded statesmanlike' young men, who boast of having no prejudices, no knots tying them to their mothers' apron-strings. They pooh-pooh all philanthropic societies, and talk over their wine of the narrow-mindedness of evangelical Christianity ; and the practical result of their glowing benevolence is a single subscription to some fashionable hospital. ' Religion is all very well ; it is very good for preserving within proper bounds the public morality,' is what they are fond of saying.

Mr. H. You mean, in short, those who, had they lived in the days of Cicero, would have patronised the gods of pagan Rome, as very good for the ' commonalty,' the ' profanum vulgus.' They have an interior sanctum of proud self-sufficiency for themselves, and an outer court of superstition for the multitude. In one corner of this outer court they erect a statue of Jupiter ; in another, a Virgin and Child ; in another (though they don't like to say so), a Christ on the Cross.

Miss C. And allow me to suggest that the gateway leading to the outer court is an exact copy of the Strand entrance to Exeter Hall, only with the addition of a grotesque laughing face hidden among the foliage of the Corinthian capitals, looking down with ridicule on the deluded multitudes who throng to the ‘May meetings.’

Mr. C. A portrait of that arch-cynic Gibbon, I suppose you would like to have in that elevated place.

Miss C. He might do; but I should think the face in the foliage might be changed every now and then with advantage; and the most fitting for this age would be an individual of the ‘fast’ species, with a cigar in his mouth, and trying to learn human nature from a sentimental novel—a modern St. Simon Stylites, about as sanctimonious as that illustrious head of those who are fond of climbing to the tops of pillars, and looking down with similar indifference on the quarrels of men below, comparing them to his two terriers, ‘At-’em’ and ‘Catch-’em,’ fighting over a rat, when there are no bets made.

Mr. C. You say truly, they look on religion with the same feling with which they look upon a dog-fight, and I cannot endure this form of latitudinarianism, especially when it rules the public journals. Nevertheless, I rejoice to see a spirit beginning to pervade all religious bodies which gives birth to a truly *Christian* latitudinarianism. Every right-minded godly man, looking on the Church of Christ, and seeing the perpetual strife of parties, who have yet all some measure of *the* truth, must feel grieved, and long for some common Christian platform whence he may view the whole Church, and feel, as the different sections fight under different flags, they are yet one army. Churchman as I am, I can do that—I can laugh at the foibles of many Christians; I can ride over the prejudices of others; I can welcome all as fellow-soldiers, whether they have a red or a white cross on their shields, if only they have a cross of some sort. A latitudinarianism, which makes the existence of the *Christian heart* the grand test of brotherhood, and not any form of Church government; which, too, loves and serves a personal living, acting Christ, who now is, and who now helps his people—that, I confess, is what I strive after. How, think you, do those who are full of the glorious loving activity of heaven, look upon the ecclesiastical squabbles down on earth?

Mr. H. All very well if we were already in heaven; but does not your experience tell you that those who are indifferent to minor principles often carry that indifference into the very heart of religion?

Mr. C. It need not be so. It is true we never can altogether prevent pride or prejudice from entering the heart of man, but we shall have less of this spirit if we can succeed in reaching this altitude of true Christian Catholicity. I am in earnest in this matter; and my plan for introducing the Christian element into this young nation, is to preach to it this exclusive devotion to the living head of the Church, and in addition, to give the people *plenty to do* in works of benevolence; and I cannot but rejoice, as one of the signs of the times, in the increase of such effort, as it is shown in the present more active working of our various Church of England societies; and among your people, in the establishment in the different Colonies of Congregational Home Missions, and in other movements of a similar kind.

Miss C. There now, that will do well for a conclusion; you have surely reached a climax, and you have given us altogether a capital sermon, with two heads, and illustrations thrown in. I think it would not be amiss if you were to put on the white surplice on the Sunday, instead of the week-day black gown—only mind, no wig.

Mr. H. And, my fair adjuster of all wrongs, social and political, as well as in the domain of sentiment, would it be a *very* dreadful spectacle to behold a lawyer preaching the religion of Christ?

Miss C. O dear no! for, without joking, I am very much obliged to you for your sermon, and so is Papa, for he is not often so demure as he now is—but will you be so kind as to finish your tea, if it be not too cold, and then we will go to the other room.

The First Sabbath.

(A free Translation from the German.)

THE sixth day of Creation was drawing towards its close—the sun had completed his course — the gloom of evening began to spread itself over the youthful world— the first-born son of Creation was standing upon one of the hills of Eden, and by his side was Eloah, his guardian angel and companion.

Round the hill it grew darker and darker. The twilight gloom passed into night and spreading, like a fragrant veil over hills and dales, hid them from view. The songs of the birds were hushed, and the joyful voices of the whole animal creation were heard no longer—even the sportive breezes seemed to slumber.

"What means all this?" said Adam to his heavenly companion, "Is the young Creation now going to depart, to be lost again in its ancient nothing?"

Eloah smiled and said, "It is the world *at rest* that you see."

Then appeared in the sky the lights of heaven, the moon arose and the hosts of the stars came forth in cheerful splendour, and Adam looked upwards towards heaven with joy and wonderment, and on that upturned gaze of the Son of Earth the Angel of the Lord looked down with pleasure.

The night became stiller, the nightingale struck ever deeper and stronger notes. Then Eloah touched Adam with his staff, and lying down upon the hill he fell into a deep slumber, and there came down to him from above his first dream. Meanwhile Jehovah formed for him his earthly mate.

When, at last, the morning dawn began to break, Eloah again touched the slumberer. He awoke and felt himself transfused with power and new life; out of the dawn arose too, the the hills of the valley, the light in the east glowed brighter and brighter, and illumined the spray of the fountains of Eden: then the sun itself arose and brought with it the full light of day; Adam looked upon his new made companion—the mother of all living—and wonder and surprise filled his heart.

"See," said Eloah, "It is in *rest* that the truly godlike is born; ought not you then to give up this day of joy to rest, and to keep it holy."

Thoughts on seeing the Sunrise in Australia.

I.

I looked forth on the sea, one early morn,
The night still brooded o'er it, but the morning grey
Gave promise in the east of breaking day;
No sound was heard, the air was cold and calm,
The faint light of eastern clouds reflected lay
Upon the glassy surface.   All seemed to say
" The air, the sea, the clouds, and those dim mountains,
Are lost in rest."   But then a sunbeam's play
Upon the fringes of the cloud—a radiance gay
With hope,—told of those hidden fountains
Filled with light, which bursting forth, give life and form
To hills and trees, and write a rainbow charm
Amidst the dashing spray, tossed by the angry storm.

II.

Thus lay all before me—unmoved, yet strong
With hope of coming strength : then burst a view
Of vaster glory on me—how great, how new,
Will be the splendour of this land in the long
Years yet to come !   All now is strangely calm—
The forests' voice is silence—free from harm ,
The gay plumed birds now rule the scene.
All is at rest, save when the axe is heard among
The trees, and calling forth an answering throng
Of echoes to a strange prophetic song—
" E'er long," they say, " the iron roads will pass between
" Our hills and vales,—then full of life, and green
" With a new verdure.   Led by a heavenly hand
" Unto a destiny, so sure, so grand,
"How full of joy is this our young and freeborn land ! "

[*Short Biographies of such Ministers of Religion, and other public and useful men, as present anything instructive in their lives or deaths, and who have died in Australia, will be thankfully received by the Editor, as it is his wish to preserve a record of all such.*]

SKETCH OF THE REV. JAMES SAWLE, OF ANGASTON, SOUTH AUSTRALIA.

THE subject of the following brief record was born at Gerrans Portscatha, in Roseland, Cornwall, England, April, 1795.   In his eighteenth year he became associated by membership with one of the Wesleyan congregations, so numerous and large in that county.   In his twentieth year he began to exercise his gifts in preaching, in which he continued more or less engaged for the remaining forty years of his life.   This early step, so critical in the case of every young man, so questionable in the case of many, and so disastrous in that of some, was in this instance vindicated by his long continued acceptableness and usefulness. To a commanding person, a noble voice, and a free utterance, there were added strong sense, fine natural powers, great faithfulness in the pulpit, and a good reputation out of it.   After a while he removed to Truro, where he resided for many years.   There one of those questions arose which have since so extensively agitated the Wesleyan body.   The dispute ended in the secession of Mr. Sawle and his friends, nd their joining the New Connection Methodists.   This took place in 1834.   In this w relation Mr. Sawle was prominent and active up to the time of his leaving

England for Australia, where he arrived 1840. In Adelaide he aided in forming and sustaining by his counsels, efforts, and ministrations, a society of his own denomination, which for a time promised to take a respectable stand in the colony, but which has since dissolved and merged into other bodies. In 1843 Mr. Sawle went into the interior, and settled at the locality now known as Angaston, fifty miles from Adelaide, named after G. F. Angus, Esq., to whom the lands there and extensively around belonged. This township with its neighbourhood, from its beauty of scene and other agricultural and pastoral advantages, soon became attractive; and for moral and social condition is certainly one of the selectest spots. It owes much to the enlightened attentions of the public spirited and benevolent proprietor long before he left England, of which one proof remains in the erection at his own cost of the chapel, which was used by the congregation for about eleven years. Much good influence is also attributable to some valuable Christian families settled in the district. But we should lose sight of the most powerful element in the good condition secured, did we not remember the important fact that for eleven or twelve years Mr. Sawle constantly kept up public worship, and faithfully preached the gospel of Christ amongst these early settlers. It is not easy, without thinking well upon the matter, to form a full and proper estimate of what a neighbourhood really owes to the advantage of being taken thus in hand at the first, when the settlers are few and slowly receiving additions, and of being in this manner quietly formed to the habits of Sabbath observance, of public worship, of hearing sermons, of Sunday School duties, and of other occasional assemblings—religious, social, benevolent and semi-festive. The effects upon the adult portion of the people are valuable and happy; but their telling upon the children and youth will be better computed some twenty or thirty years hence, though even then but imperfectly. A considerable number of persons attending the ministry of Mr. Sawle were members of the church in Freeman-street, Adelaide. The pastor of that church was requested to come up and form them into a distinct church, which duty he cheerfully and thankfully performed, with the full concurrence and assistance of Mr. Sawle. The new society was placed, though not on a denominational, yet on a congregational basis. Of this newly constituted church Mr. Sawle took the pastoral oversight. He avowed that such changes had taken place in his ecclesiastical views as not only reconciled but decidedly inclined him to Congregational usage. He retained his doctrinal sentiments, but this occasioned little or no inconvenience. Though conscientious, he was discreet. He did not assail his theological opponents. He preached Christ; he preached grace; he preached justification by faith; he preached regeneration; he preached experimental godliness; he preached practical holiness: and the Calvanism that sat in the pews was of a kind that did not object to his preaching all this as pointedly, as invitingly, as freely, as pressingly, as his own peculiarities even could dictate. On the morning of November 1st, 1854, Mr. Sawle started from Angaston to attend the half-yearly meeting of the Congregational Union, at Gawler Town. On the way the horse took fright, and he was thrown from the vehicle with great violence, much injured, and for a time insensible. As he was alone, when consciousness returned, he remained for hours in the agony of his wounds, and under the burning heat of the sun. When found, he was taken home in a German waggon. On the way he did not expect to reach his house alive, and he said to the friend who was then with him, " Tell my dear wife and family that I die in peace; tell the church that I die in peace; tell the world that I die in peace." On Nov. 3rd the Rev. E. Aggett saw him; and, though in great pain, he was composed and tranquil. On the Sabbath morning, the 5th, Mr. A. again saw him, whose report of him is, " he was reposing calmly on the Christian's foundation—Christ crucified." He said to me " I am a poor worm, but my hope and strength are in him." With great emotion he said, " I dare not look within, nor can I look around for comfort now; but I can look up; yea, blessed be God, I can look up!" He was much interested respecting the new chapel, the foundation stone of which was laid during his short illness. He also enquired eagerly as to the services of the Sabbath, and expressed thankfulness when assured of the satisfactory arrangements that had been made. On the Monday morning he asked for " the blessed book," but could not read it. After a short sleep, on attempting to relate a pleasant dream, as he said, of a visit home, he gently expired. On the 9th the Rev. Mr. Philps conducted the funeral ceremonies, in the presence of a large assembly, mourning deeply for their friend and pastor. It so happened that the Rev. J. L. Poore, of Melbourne, visited Angaston on the Sabbath following, just in time to supply the vacant pulpit for the day, and to preach the funeral sermon.

MISSIONS.

CHINESE MISSION.

The important and perplexing question as to the amount of restriction that should be put upon the immigration of the Chinese into Australia, is now engaging the serious attention of the Colonial Governments. Without assuming to give an opinion upon this point, Christians have to do with a great and momentous fact, the actual presence in the colony of Victoria of nearly 40,000 of these heathen strangers. While they are in the midst of us, they have a claim upon our sympathies to do them all the good we can; and it may turn out that the Providence of God has permitted their coming hither, that they might learn the way of truth. The great barrier to intercourse with them, especially on the subject of religion, is their peculiar language. Possibly this may be more easily overcome in the course of time, as communications with them increase. In the meantime, little or nothing can be done for them by the personal efforts of British Christians. In June, 1856, the arrival in Melbourne of two Chinese young men, who were brought up in the Mission schools at Hong Kong, and who were members of the Christian Church there, seemed to furnish the agency adapted to work upon their countrymen in Australia. Much interest was manifested in them; several meetings were held, and a Chinese mission on a Catholic basis was formed. One of these young men has since become Chinese interpreter at the Ovens gold-fields; but two others have since arrived, so that there are at present three of these agents engaged in the work. Two are labouring in the neighbourhood of Castlemaine, and one at Ballaarat. The Rev. W. Young, thirty years a Missionary of the London Missionary Society, to the Chinese in China, Java, &c., happening to be in Sydney, where his wife's illness had compelled him to come for change of air, was induced to remove to Victoria, and superintend the labours of these native evangelists. The expenses are met by subscriptions and collections from all evangelical denominations. The funds have been obtained with difficulty, but the Society at present is not in debt. The friends at Castlemaine, at Geelong, and Ballaarat, contribute their share towards the maintenance of the Missionaries in their respective neighbourhoods. The Wesleyans make an annual grant from their Mission fund to this object. The Chinese are visited in their encampments, the Scriptures are read to them, addresses delivered to groups, conversations held with individuals, and worship is conducted in tents or rooms when a sufficient number can be collected. The migratory habits of these strangers greatly interfere with the success of the Missionaries and prevent the gathering into organized congregations those that are favourably impressed. Nevertheless, some visible fruit has been seen; a few have been baptized, and a place of worship expressly for the Chinese is about to be built at Forest Creek, towards which the Chinese themselves have subscribed about £60. It is strongly felt by the Committee, that an extension of the Mission is required; that Chinese agents should be placed at Bendigo and the Ovens; that while Mr. Young superintends the Mission at Castlemaine, another European Missionary is required for the Ballaarat District; and a third could be most usefully occupied among the Chinese in and about Melbourne. Will the Christian public furnish the needful funds? The American Christians have established a Mission to the Chinese in California. They have built a Mission house in San Francisco, at a cost of 20,000 dollars, and settled a Mission family there. The Rev. Mr. Speers is labouring there with great assiduity. Could not the same be done in Melbourne?

PACIFIC OCEAN.

The islands in the South Pacific Ocean open up a wide field for missionary operations. The Church of Christ has expended large sums of money on them, and many labourers have been employed. The results have been sufficient to encourage the labourers, and to stimulate the missionary zeal of the churches. As we look on the map of the South Pacific, and mark the numerous islands which appear on its surface, we are almost bewildered with their multitude.

Let us mark out the islands on which successful missionary operations have been carried on. There are the two islands of New Zealand. The work has been carried on there by missionaries belonging to the Episcopal and Wesleyan Churches. The Romish Church has a bishop and several priests on the island, but they have made few converts.

From New Zealand we pass on to Tahiti, the main island in the Society group, the scene of the early operations of the London Missionary Society. It is about a fortnight's sail from New Zealand. Missionaries reside in Eimeo, Huahine, and Raiatea; Tahaa and Borabora are visited by the missionaries, the work being carried on by native evangelists. There are several islands within one or two days' sail of Tahiti, which are regarded as out-stations.

The Marquesas Islands, to the north of Tahiti, are occupied by an agent of the American Board of Foreign Missions, with native teachers from the Sandwich Islands.

The Hervey group, which is about six days' sail from Tahiti, consists of Rarotonga, Aitutaki, Mangaia, and several small islands a short distance from the main islands of the group. The natives of this group have advanced in the use of mechanical arts, have adopted generally European clothing, and made considerable progress in civilization.

West of Samoa lie the Tonga and Fegee Islands. They are under the care of Wesleyan missionaries, who have reaped much fruit from these fields of labour. The Romish priests have attempted the establishment of missions on Tonga with little success. They are found also in the Fegees. There is an island not far from Tonga called Uea; the priests have this island almost entirely under their power. They have a training establishment for native assistants on a small island called Fotuna. The priests make use of the most intelligent of the natives, and take them to other islands to assist them in the work of proselytism.

A few days' sail from Tonga brings us to the New Hebrides Islands. Missionaries reside on Aneitum, and native teachers on Tana, Fotuna, Eromanga, and Nina. The Loyalty group, which is a day's sail from the New Hebrides, has two foreign missionaries residing on Maré, and native evangelists are stationed on Tolka and Sifu.

The Isle of Pines and New Caledonia are under the Romish priests. Their principal station is on the Isle of Pines. They have made little inroad upon the strongholds of heathenism.

The above islands are all south of the Line. North of the Line the American Board of Missions have long laboured on the Sandwich Islands. They have opened a new station on Strong's Island, a little north of the Line; they have not extended their operations beyond the Sandwich Islands until the last few years.

The islands enumerated embrace the field of missionary operations in the South Pacific. There is great need for more labourers to meet the pressing calls for help. The cry sounds in our ears from many an island just emerging from heathenism, "Come over and help us."

THE "JOHN WILLIAMS" MISSIONARY BARQUE.

The "John Williams," belonging to the London Missionary Society, on her fourth outward voyage to the islands, touched at the Cape of Good Hope, Hobart Town, Melbourne, and Sydney. Her visit excited great interest. The friends at Hobart Town, who have been warm supporters of the London Missionary Society, gave her a hearty reception. Upwards of a thousand children went on board, and were highly delighted with the treat.

The vessel anchored in Hobson's Bay, December 12th, 1856, and remained until the end of the month. Sermons were preached by the missionaries and ministers on behalf of the society, both in Melbourne and its suburbs: also at Geelong. A large public meeting was held in Dr. Cairn's church, Eastern Hill; collections were made, and a considerable sum raised. The most novel and interesting circumstance connected with this visit was the trip to the ship by the children of the various schools. About two thousand persons went to Sandrige Railway Pier, alongside of which the vessel was moored. The children, entering at the gangway, walked round the vessel, and then passed on to the pier; the stream was kept up for two or three hours. The children were addressed by the missionaries, and Isaiah a native of Rarotonga. A beautiful lithograph of the scene has been executed by a Melbourne artist, and many copies have been purchased as mementoes of a very pleasant day, which passed without the slightest accident having occurred to any of the children.

A public breakfast was held on the 31st December in the Mechanics' Institute, to take leave of the missionary brethren Howe, Barff, and Gordon.

The friends of missions in New South Wales gave the vessel a hearty welcome, and the scenes in Hobart Town and Melbourne were reproduced in Sydney.

Our last communication from the islands informed us of the safe arrival of the vessel at Tahiti, in March, 1857. She left the same month for the Hervey Group.

It cannot be forgotten that the Christians in Australia stand in such close proximity to the South Sea Islands, that the friends of missions in England are looking to them to take up the mission work in the South Pacific. The pressing nature of the claims of the population in Australia, and the little surplus wealth at the disposal of the church for foreign missions, may not be sufficiently considered perhaps by friends at home, yet the fact stands before us that the Wesleyans in Australia have taken upon themselves *the support of the South Sea missions in Tonga and the Fegee Islands*. They raise upwards of £6000 for foreign missions, and receive but a small sum from the Board of Missions in England. Their example ought to stimulate others to organise, and do something at once.

The Reformed Presbyterian Church in Scotland are preparing to send *two* missionaries to Western Polynesia. The Presbyterian Church of Nova Scotia has been so much cheered with the success of their mission, that they are ready to send out more men as soon as suitable persons offer. The friends of missions in Sydney support *two* missionaries, who are labouring on the island of Maré in the Loyalty Group. Why should not Melbourne or Tasmania send *two* missionaries to help in the great work of evangelizing the South Sea Islanders? " The harvest truly is great, but the labourers are few ; pray ye therefore the Lord of the harvest, that he would send forth labourers into his harvest "

TAHITI.

A letter has been received from the Rev. W. Howe, since his return to Tahiti, stating that the impediments put in the way of English pastors of the native churches in discharging their duties are so embarassing, that it is extremely desirable that *French Protestant Pastors* should be sent out, who would have a political status in the country, and be able, as subjects of the French Government, to claim the protection of French law in the exercise of their ministry. This suggestion is approved of by the London Missionary Society ; but Mr. Howe apprehends that the Society will be able to do nothing more than send out the men. From the urgency of the demand upon its funds for extending the work in China, Africa, and elsewhere, he does not expect they will have it in their power to maintain them after their arrival. The money for that purpose must come from some other quarter, and he naturally looks to the Christians in Australia to come forward in this emergency to do something to preserve and consolidate the Tahitian Mission.

RELIGIOUS INTELLIGENCE.
New South Wales.

GENERAL SOCIETIES.—BIBLE SOCIETY.—Meetings in connection with the above Society, have lately been held at Darlinghurst, St. Leonards, and Windsor, and addressed by the Secretaries,—the Revds. F. Ashwin and S. C. Kent, and other gentlemen.

YOUNG MEN's ASSOCIATION.—A valuable lecture was delivered to the Members of this Institution early in June, in their rooms, George-street, Sydney, by the Rev. R. Barker, on John Bunyan and his Times.

TEETOTALISM.—Extraordinary efforts have recently been made by the advocates of Total Abstinence, to revive and increase the Teetotal Societies of New South Wales. Large meetings have been held in Sydney in the School of Arts, the Lyceum, and the Prince of Wales Theatre. A monster soiree was held on Thursday, June 25th, at which upwards of three thousands persons were present. The Rev. R. Mansfield presided,—and addresses were delivered by the Revds. Archdeacon McEncroe, G. Mackie, and S. C. Kent.

WESLEYANS.—CHURCH BUILDING.—The Wesleyans have recently held a meeting in West Maitland to make arrangements for the erection of a more commodious chapel than the one at present occupied by them. They have determined to build a Gothic structure, capable of accommodating at least a thousand hearers, and have already raised such an amount as ensures the early accomplishment of their purpose.

At Macquarie Plains, in the Bathurst district, the foundation-stone of a plain and substantial Wesleyan Chapel was laid on June 1st, by Mr. W. M. Fulton.

MISSIONS.—At the York-street Chapel, Sydney, in the early part of the last month, the first Annual General Meeting of the Australian Wesleyan Missionary Society, as an independent association, was held under the presidency of George Allen, Esq., M.L.C. According to the report, the total expenditure of the past year was £10,839 5s. 8d. ; the net receipts from the colonies and mission districts, including native (Polynesian) contributions, in oil, were £9,082 14s. 9d. ; leaving a balance to be paid by the committee in London of £1,807 0s. 11d. The operations of the various missions in New Zealand, in the Friendly Islands, and in Fejee, were fully gone into in the report. The progress appeared upon the whole to have been very great, although further missionary aid was greatly needed, especially in Fejee, where the disposition to accept Christian teaching was extending far more rapidly than teachers could be supplied. A strong appeal was made for assistance. The following was given as a general summary of the society's missions:—

Number of chapels	...	...	302	Full & accredited church members				13,079
Other preaching places	...	...	296	On trial	...	...	...	2,181
Missionaries	...	...	31	Sabbath schools	...	...	...	188
Assistant Missionaries	...	...	13	Sabbath scholars	...	...	...	5,319
Catechists	...	...	164	Day schools	...	...	...	420
Day school teachers	...	...	1,223	Day scholars	...	...	...	17,779
Sabbath school teachers	...	..	462	Total number of hearers, including				
Local preachers	...	...	864	Church members and scholars				64,268
Class leaders	...	...	178	Printing presses		...	...	2

EPISCOPALIANS.—Trinity Church, Sydney, which promises to be one of the best ecclesiastical edifices in the city, although at present incomplete, was opened for public worship on May 31st. The Rev. Forster Ashwin, one of the Secretaries of the Bible Society, is its incumbent.

A meeting has been held in St. Paul's, Redfern, presided over by the Rev. A. H. Stephen, at which it was resolved to add a new wing to that building.

ARCHDEACON COWPER.—We have just seen a half-length portrait of our venerable friend, beautifully engraved from a painting of Claxton's by Mr. G. B. Shaw, and forming an appropriate companion print to the one lately published by him of the Bishop of Sydney. We hope the time is not far distant when we shall be able, following in the wake of our excellent contemporary *the Evangelical Magazine* of the fatherland, occasionally to present to our readers engravings of the more prominent of our ministers and friends.

CONGREGATIONALISTS.—PITT-STREET CHAPEL.—The Congregationalists are about enlarging the church in Pitt-street, Sydney, in consequence of the great increase of congregation under the ministrations of the Rev. W. Cuthbertson, B.A.

THE CONGREGATIONAL CHURCH BUILDING SOCIETY.—The annual meeting of this Society was held in the large school-room adjoining the Pitt-street Congregational Church, on Thursday evening, June 4th. The Hon. D. Jones, Esq., M.L.C., in the chair. The Chairman, having explained the object of the meeting, and the purposes for which the Society was originated, called upon the treasurer, Mr. Fairfax, to read the general and financial report. The Treasurer then read the following Report:—

" The Congregational Church Building Society of New South Wales was established in August, 1858. Its existence dates from a period of great colonial prosperity. Money was plentiful, and a few Christian men belonging to the Congregational Board were strongly impressed with the idea that the time had arrived when a combined and zealous effort should be made to erect new places of worship, and thus extend the means of spreading the gospel of Christ in this increasing and wide-spread colony. They believed in the power of principles altogether antagonistic to state-aid ; were anxious to manifest to other denominations of Christians that the religion of of Jesus Christ does not in these days, any more that eighteen hundred years ago, require that support ; and were especially desirous to take their share in enlightening the human mind and extending the blessings of salvation. Impressed with these feelings the Society was formed under the presidency of the Rev. Dr. Ross, and sums amounting to seven thousand pounds were promised in the following twelve months. Rules and regulations for the conduct of the Society were adopted, and its business at once commenced. In about a year after the period of the formation of the Society, the first annual meeting was held. One of the resolutions then passed was the following :—' That this meeting, convinced that the object of this Society is of such a magnitude that it cannot be realised by restricted, feeble, and parsimonious support, but only by the help of each and all, and that to their utmost ability, pledges itself, in imitation of the noble example set by its promoters, and deeply conscious that God requires, on this occasion, deeds of sacrifice at its hands, to a liberality worthy of the object and demanded by the emergency.' This was moved by Mr. James Dawson, seconded by Mr. George A. Lloyd, and supported by the Rev. Mr. Poore. Mr. Lloyd, with his usual earnestness and zeal, proposed that the sum for church building purposes should be raised to £20,000, the payments to be spread over a period of five years. This suggestion was warmly and enthusiastically taken up by Mr. Poore. It was arranged that a tea-meeting should be held on a subsequent evening, and at the latter meeting promises making up the sum to the £20,000 were made. Three years have elapsed since the last mentioned period, and the committee have now the pleasure of meeting the subscribers to give an account of their stewardship. Towards the £20,000 promised to be paid in five years, there has been collected in four years the sum of £15,799 1s. 1d. In the purchase of land, and grants and loans for church building, the Committee have expended £16,368 6s. 10d., leaving a balance owing to the Treasurer of £559 5s. 9d. The churches which have been either entirely or partially assisted by this Society are eight in number, viz., at Ipswich, Balmain, Petersham, Surry Hills, Maitland, Newcastle, Wollongong, and Newtown. The extent to which aid has been rendered will appear from the balance-sheet, which will presently be read. It will be seen that the bold and energetic effort made a few years ago has abundantly succeeded. A few of our friends predicted failure. The promises, it was suspected, were made under exciting circumstances. The result proves that the men who put their shoulders to the wheel, and whom God had blessed with the means, have not disappointed the expectations of your committee. The work has been done so far, and will go on. Give, however, the glory only to God, whose is the gold and the silver; believe in His promises, trust in His grace, and the work of Church extension shall go on; and we, whose lot is cast in this beautiful land of Australia—not by accident—but by the special appointment and guidance of our Heavenly Father, shall be instrumental in laying the foundation of an empire which shall be freed from the evil power and worldly trammels of state endowment. The time will come when the strange sight shall no longer be witnessed of the Priests of Rome, the Presbyters of the Reformed Church of England, the Ministers of Scotland's old Kirk, the followers of John Wesley, and the professors of the Jewish faith—going, month after month, to receive a miserable pittance from the hands of the Executive."

The report further exhibited the list of subscribers, and the amount which had been given or granted on loan to the different churches. For Ipswich, the land had been purchased at a cost from the Government of £191 1s., and granted to the people, and a loan towards building the church was made of £400. To the committee for building the church at Balmain a free grant of £1,000 was made, and a further loan of £2,000 without interest. The iron church in Bourke-street, Surry Hills, was built at the entire cost of the Society. The land, the church, and freight, the building of it on stone foundations, gas fittings, &c., entailed an expense of £4,594 5s. 9d. In West Maitland, the church is approaching completion. The land was sold at a nominal price, rendering it nearly a gift, by the Hon. D. Jones, to the local committee. The Society had given and loaned towards this edifice £2,331 7s. 2d. At Newcastle the Society had purchased land from the Australian Agricultural Company, and had assisted towards the building to the extent of £2,101 0s. 10d. To Wollongong, towards a church building on a most eligible piece of land in the centre of the township, the gift of Mr. Henry Gilbert Smith, a free grant of £300 had been made. The Newtown Congregational Church had been built on a central piece of land granted by two members of the committee. The entire cost of the erection was £2,577 16s.; towards this the Society had given nearly £1,000. There were, besides, grants for Petersham and Sydenham, £120. These items with sundry expenses, which were given in detail, made up the sum expended to £16,358 6s. 10d.

The report was received with the utmost satisfaction.

A series of resolutions, accompanied with appropriate speeches, from Revds. Joseph Beazley, W. Slatyer, E. Griffith, G. Charter, S. C. Kent, J. West, and Messrs. T. Hogg, and J. Morris were then adopted.

A committee was appointed, consisting of Mr. Robert Garrett, secretary; Mr. John Fairfax, treasurer; and Messrs A. Foss, A. Fairfax, D. Jones, George A. Lloyd, George Rees, R. Nott, John Morris, John Thompson, Samuel Thompson, N. H. Eager, and Edward Hunt.

CONGREGATIONAL CHURCH, REDFERN.—The completion of the seventh year of the Rev. Joseph Beazley's pastorate, was celebrated on Wednesday, May 13th. His friends assembled in large numbers to testify their respect and esteem, and were addressed by the Revds. Messrs. Cuthbertson, Slatyer, and Kent.

BAPTISTS.—On July 5th a new Baptist Chapel was opened at Hinton, near Maitland, on which occasion sermons were preached by the Rev. J. Voller, of Sydney, and the Rev. E. Griffith, of Maitland. On the following day nearly four hundred persons partook of tea together, and were suitably addressed by various ministers and friends. About £300 remain to be raised to cancel the debt incurred by the erection of the above place.

Victoria.

GENERAL SOCIETIES.—BIBLE SOCIETY.—This institution, greatly revived by the visit last year of the Rev. W. M. Becher, the deputation from the British and Foreign Bible Society, has engaged commodious premises in Swanston-street as its depôt, and has secured the important services of Mr. J. T. Hoskins as secretary and agent. A large stock of Bibles and Testaments ordered from London has recently arrived, and is in active demand for various parts of the colony. The report of the Rev. W. M. Becher presented to the parent Society, on his return from his mission, has arrived here, and is an able and interesting document, giving a comprehensive view of the state of these colonies in relation to the supply of the Scriptures, and the most likely means of securing a wider circulation of them.

A TRACT SOCIETY, upon the catholic basis of the Religious Tract Society of England, has recently been formed in Melbourne, and is proceeding satisfactorily. A good stock of tracts has been obtained from Sydney, and more are expected from England, and the demand for them is steadily on the increase. The depôt is in Swanston-street, in the same premises as that of the Bible Society.

EVANGELICAL ALLIANCE. — On Friday, May 29th, a numerous meeting of Christian ministers and members of various religious denominations was held in the Protestant Hall, Melbourne, to take into consideration the desirableness and practicability of establishing an Evangelical Alliance in Victoria. Henry Langlands, Esq., M.L.A., presided. The Bishop of Melbourne opened the proceedings with prayer. Addresses approving of the object were delivered by the Bishop, the Revds. Dr. Cairns, D. Seddon, J. Harding, Jas. Ballantyne, and others. Resolutions were then passed, formally constituting an Alliance on the basis of the Alliance in Britain, and the following officers were appointed :—President, Judge Pohlman ; Vice-Presidents, H. Langlands, Esq., M.L.A.; D. Ogilvy, Esq.; Treasurer, H. Jennings, Esq ; Secretaries, Rev. Jas. Ballantyne, Mr. J. T. Hoskins; Committee, Revds. Dr. Cairns, R. Fletcher, J. Harding, W. Jarrett, D. Seddon, J. Sunderland, J. Taylor, Messrs. T. T. a'Beckett, H. Budge, W. Little, J. S. Ogilvy, and J. Russell.

A second meeting was held, June 12th, in the same place, when additional Rules were agreed upon for the regulation of the Society.

The first Quarterly meeting was held in the same Hall, on the evening of July 7th. Owing to the inclement state of the weather, the attendance was not so numerous as it otherwise would have been. The chair was occupied by Mr. Justice Pohlman, the president. Prayer was offered by the Rev. Richard Fletcher ; the Bishop of Melbourne delivered an address upon Christian Union, which was most catholic in its spirit, and deeply interesting. Addresses were then delivered by the Revds. Dr. Cairns, R. Fletcher, T. Harding and others. The basis was read by Mr. J. T. Hoskins, secretary, and parties present were invited to become members. Full information may be obtained as to the rules, basis, and mode of admission, from Mr. Hoskins, at the Bible Society Rooms, Swanston-street, Melbourne, or any of the officers of the Alliance. The formation of this Union is a happy omen for the cause of christian charity in Victoria, and it is to be hoped that the example will be followed in the other colonies.

BETHEL UNION.—A Bethel Union has been formed for the purpose of supplying religious ordinances to seamen frequenting Port Phillip. It is composed of members of all Evangelical Denominations. A vessel, as a Floating Church, has been lent to the Society by Government for six months ; numerous gentlemen have subscribed to meet the expenses, and the Rev. Kerr Johnston, late of Hobarton, has been appointed Chaplain. The opening services were held on Wednesday, July 1st, on board the vessel in Hobson's Bay, when the Bishop of Melbourne read prayers, and preached the first sermon. Refreshments were provided, and a public meeting was held in the ship, when the Hon. C. Vaughan, M. L. C., presided, and the Bishop and Dean of Melbourne, the Revs. Messrs. Harding, Moss, W. R. Fletcher, and Johnston, and Messrs. H. Langlands, M. L. A., C. Ferguson, J.P., W. Fairfax, Mathews, A. Bonar, T. Dickson, and others, addressed the meeting. Excellent arrangements had been made to convey visitors by railway and steam-boat ; but the extreme inclemency of the weather detained great numbers who had promised to be present. As it was, the attendance was very encouraging. The Society is at present not in debt, but its future liabilities were stated to be likely to amount to £1,000 per annum.

PRESBYTERIANS.—PORTLAND.—INDUCTION SERVICE.—On Sabbath the 28th June, the Rev. Wm. Ridley, B.A., formerly in connexion with the Synod of New South Wales, was formally inducted into the pastoral charge of the church and congregation worshipping in the above place ; the Rev. A. M. Ramsay, as commissioner from the United Presbyterian Presbytery of Melbourne, officiating on the occasion. Three services were held in connexion with the settlement. In the forenoon, after sermon by Mr. Ramsay, the members of the church observed the communion of the Lord's Supper ; in the afternoon the ceremony of the induction took place ; and in the evening Mr. Ridley preached. The weather was very propitious, and the attendance at the different services large and encouraging. The various exercises were solemn and impressive. Much benefit to this community is anticipated from the settlement of a minister of Mr. Ridley's talents and high reputation as a scholar, and faithful minister of the Gospel. It may interest some of our readers to see the following queries, which were addressed to the minister and congregation in the course of the service. They constitute the Ordination Formula of the United Presbyterian Synod of Victoria; — 1. Do you believe the Scriptures of the Old and New Testaments to be the Word of God, and the only rule of faith and practice? 2. Do you acknowledge the Westminster Confession of Faith, and the Larger and Shorter Catechisms, as an exhibition of the sense in which you understand the Holy Scriptures; it being understood that you are not required to approve of anything in these documents which teaches, or is supposed to teach, compulsory or persecuting and intolerant principles in religion? 3. Are you persuaded that the Lord Jesus Christ, the only King and Head of the Church, has therein appointed a government distinct from, and not subordinate to, civil government? And do you acknowledge the Presbyterian form of government, as authorized and acted on in this church, to be founded on and agreeable to the Word of God? 4. Do you approve of the constitution of the United Presbyterian Church, as exhibited in the Basis of Union; and while cherishing a spirit of brotherhood towards all the faithful followers of Christ, do you engage to seek the purity, edification, peace, and extension of this church? 5. Are zeal for the glory of God, love to the Lord Jesus Christ, and a desire to save souls, and not worldly interests or expectations, so far as you know your own heart, your great motives and chief inducements to enter into the office of the Holy Ministry? 6. Have you used any undue methods, by yourself or others, to obtain the call of this church? Do you, the members of this church, testify your adherence to the call which you have given to Mr. William Ridley, B.A., to be your minister? and do you receive him with all gladness, and promise to provide for him suitable maintenance, and to give him all due respect, subjection, and encouragement in the Lord? 7. Do you adhere to your acceptance of the call to become minister of this church? 8. Do you engage, in the strength of the grace that is in Christ Jesus, to live a holy and circumspect life, to rule well your own house, and faithfully, diligently, and cheerfully to discharge all the parts of the ministerial work, to the edifying of the body of Christ? 9. Do you promise to give conscientious attendance on the Courts of the United Presbyterian Church, to be subject to them in the Lord, to take a due interest in their proceedings, and to study the things which make for peace? 10. And all things you profess and promise, through grace, as you shall be answerable at the coming of the Lord Jesus Christ with all his saints, and as you would be found in that happy company?

BEECHWORTH.—A new Presbyterian cause has been commenced here by the settlement of the Rev. John Grant, who has recently arrived in the colony. A temporary church on a government grant of land has been put up, and is occupied at present. The foundation of a permanent church was laid by the Rev. Jas. Nish, of Bendigo, on Monday, July 6th, and an overflowing tea meeting held the same evening. It is estimated that the new church, school, and manse will cost £3,500.

GEELONG.—UNITED PRESBYTERIAN CHURCH—This new and handsome church, situated in Ryrie-street, was opened on Sabbath, July 5th, on which occasion sermons were preached in the morning by the Rev. R. Fletcher of St. Kilda, in the afternoon by the Rev. J. Cooper the minister of the church, and in the evening by the Rev. John Ballantyne, of Emerald Hill, Melbourne. The attendance was overflowing, and the collections amounted to £110, which sum was augmented on the following evening to £141 17s. The soiree took place on Monday evening, July 6, in the capacious hall of the Mechanics' Institution. The demand for tickets was so great that they were with difficulty to be obtained. From seven to eight hundred persons are supposed to have sat down to tea. Rev. John Cooper, the pastor, occupied the chair. The platform contained a goodly array of ministers and other friends; a full report of the past proceedings of the church was read by the secretary; and the speakers were, besides the chairman, the Rev. J. Apperley, Rev. R. Fletcher, Rev. A. Love, Rev. M. Townend, Rev. A. Scales, Mr. Turner, &c. About six years ago the church was organized. No time was lost in building a suitable place of worship; but a storm laid it in ruins while in the course of erection, and a pecuniary loss was entailed amounting to £2,608 18s. 6d. This severe calamity checked the progress of the cause for a time. About three years ago the present pastor, the Rev. J. Cooper, settled there. Nothing daunted by their former loss, the congregation soon set about rearing the present structure. It is in a commanding and central situation. The style is Gothic, with a tower and spire at the entrance ninety feet high. It is felt by all to be an ornament to the city. The entire cost has been £4150, part of which remains as a mortgage on the property. The liberality, vitality, and growth of the congregation will appear from the following statement which was read at the soiree. The pecuniary history of the congregation, during the past six years, may be summed up as follows :—The total amount collected from all sources during the year 1851-52 was £905 11s. 8d.; ditto, 1852-3, £553 18s. 5d.; ditto, 1853-4, £1372; ditto, 1854-5, £716 17s. 7d.; ditto, 1855-6, £1,125 16s. 1d.; ditto, 1856-7, £1,207 17s. 10d; total, £5,082 2s. 7d.

BAPTISTS.—MELBOURNE.—An important movement has taken place in this body by the mission to Australia of the Rev. James Taylor, late of Birmingham, to promote the welfare of the denomination. An interesting breakfast meeting was held in the Mechanics Institution, shortly after his arrival, to welcome him to the colony, on which occasion a large number of ministers and friends of other denominations, besides the leading members of the Baptist body, were present. The Hon. C. Vaughan, M.L.C., presided; and the meeting was addressed by the Rev. Dr. Cairns, A. M. Ramsay, A Morison, J. Sunderland, D. J. Draper, T. Bradney, J. Taylor, &c. The most cordial spirit of brotherly love breathed through all the speeches. Mr. Taylor is settled at present as the minister of the Collins-street Baptist Chapel, Melbourne. It is understood that more ministers are to follow him from England.

BRIGHTON.—The recognition of Mr. Collins as pastor of the Baptist Church here took place on Thursday evening, July 9th, when the Rev. J. Taylor, of Melbourne, delivered an introductory discourse; and the Rev. R. Fletcher, of St. Kilda, delivered a charge to the pastor and church.

CONGREGATIONALISTS. — VICTORIA PARADE, MELBOURNE. — A temporary place of worship, at the corner of Victoria Parade and Fitzroy-street, for the use of the church and congregation under the pastoral care of the Rev. H. Thomas, B. A., was opened on Lord's day, May 10th. On the following Tuesday evening a public tea-meeting was held, which was largely attended and satisfactorily conducted. F. J. Sargood, Esq., M.L.A., presided, and the meeting was addressed by the Rev. Messrs. Morison, Odell, R. Fletcher, Sunderland, Clark, W. R. Fletcher, H. Thomas and T. Bradney. This congregation, recently worshipping in a store in Brunswick-street, have purchased this most eligible site, and intend erecting upon it a church worthy of the situation. A superior plan, selected out of several competing ones, has been adopted ; and the congregation is only allowing itself a little breathing time before commencing in earnest the arduous undertaking of giving embodiment to the masterly ideas of the architect.

FOREST CREEK.—The Independent congregation at Forest Creek has for some time worshipped in a tent; but the cause becoming sufficiently consolidated to warrant further proceedings, a plain, but good and substantial stone chapel has been erected. The opening services took place on Tuesday the 9th, and Sunday the 14th of June, when sermons were preached by the Rev. W. R. Fletcher, M. A., of St. Kilda, and the Rev. E. Day, of Castlemaine. The ordination of the Rev. J. F. Pitman, the pastor, was held on the evening of Wednesday the 10th, when the Rev. W. R. Fletcher read the scriptures and prayed, Rev. E. Day delivered the introductory discourse, the Rev. W. Young, missionary to the Chinese, offered the ordination prayer, and the Rev. R. Fletcher, of St. Kilda, delivered a joint charge to the pastor or and the people. Mr. Pitman gave a very interesting statement of his religious experience and doctrinal views. On the following evening (11th) a tea-meeting was held, when the attendance was so large that the tables had to be cleared for a second company, and then the room was scarcely sufficient. An animated meeting was held, and engagements were entered into by numerous persons present, to raise in the course of twelve months the £300 requisite to clear the place from debt.

NORTH COLLINGWOOD.—This church having been long without a pastor, the Rev. J. Mirams, for some years pastor of the Congregational Church, Chishill, Essex, having just arrived in the colony, was applied to to undertake the charge. He engaged to do so for a limited period on trial, commenced his labours a few weeks ago, and has since accepted a unanimous call to become its pastor.

BALLARAT.—The Rev. J. M. Strongman, of New Town, near Hobarton, having received an invitation from the Congregational Church at Ballarat, has removed thither, and entered upon his new sphere of labour on Sunday, July 12th.

ST. KILDA AND BRIGHTON.—The Congregational Churches of these two places have entered into an arrangement with the Rev. R. Fletcher, pastor of the St. Kilda church, and his son, the Rev. W. Roby Fletcher, M.A., recently arrived from England, to supply the two places alternately for a period of six months.

THE REV. J. L. POORE.—Letters have been received from Mr. Poore announcing his safe arrival in England, and his successful efforts in awakening the attention of the Congregational Churches at home to the claims of these colonies. Some ministers are now on their way hither, and more will follow in due time.

WESLEYANS.—BEECHWORTH.—The foundation-stone of a new and substantial church for the use of the Wesleyans in Beechworth and the neighbourhood, was laid on the first day of the present year, by the Superintendent of the Circuit, the Rev. J. C. Symons; and it was opened for worship on Sabbath day, April 12th, 1857. On this occasion the Rev. D. J. Draper, of Melbourne, Chairman of the Victoria District, preached morning and evening to overflowing congregations. On the following evening a tea-meeting was held in the adjoining school-room, which had been till then used also as the chapel. The attendance was very large. H. M'Lean, Esq., presided. The Rev. J. C. Symons presented the financial statement relating to the structure, and delivered an address. The meeting was also addressed by the Rev. D. J. Draper, Mr. Wilton, Mr. Witt, &c. The speeches were animating, and the meeting was much interested. It appears that the building which is plain and substantial, and in the Gothic style, cost altogether about £1,650; that to meet this expenditure a grant had been received from the Wesleyan Extension Fund of £500, a bazaar had raised £455 11s. 4d., and a balance of debt remained of £674. Towards this, about £180 was raised at the opening services.

Tasmania.

CANVASS FOR SABBATH SCHOLARS.—The important movement originated in Birmingham, and adopted in London, Manchester, and elsewhere in Britain, for making a general canvass for Sunday Scholars, has stirred up the friends of Sabbath school instruction in Hobart Town, to go and do likewise. The matter was taken up by the Tasmanian Sunday School Union, who invited the co-operation of ministers, superintendents, and teachers connected with all the Protestant Denominations, to combine in a general and simultaneous canvass of the city and its suburbs; to ascertain the number of children of age to attend school; the number connected with Sabbath schools, and the number unconnected; and to induce non-attendants to join themselves to some Sabbath school. All denominations (with the exception of the Episcopalian) seem to have responded to the invitation. The town was divided into thirty-one districts, two canvassers being appointed to each. The work was done very effectually. The sum of the results given in, is as follows:—Number of children between the ages of four and fifteen, 2,965; number attending Sunday schools, 1,813; number of promises of new scholars, 323. The canvassers not being armed with an authority to require answers, this notice can be considered only as an approximation to the truth, but it is sufficiently accurate for all practical purposes. The work was carried out in a most unsectarian manner, and the canvassers were generally received by the parents and others in a kind and cordial spirit. Though the number of young people who attend no Sabbath schools is large, 1,152, the Committee state that a greater number is in attendance than in any town of similar size in the United Kingdom. If the promises of attendance are fulfilled, the number of non-attendants will be reduced to 829. The report of these proceedings was given in at a public meeting held in the Wesleyan school-room, Melville-street, April 21st, when Henry Hopkins, Esq., J.P., presided.

The fourteenth Annual Meeting of the *Tasmanian Sunday School Union*, was held May 11th, in Collins-street Chapel, Hobarton. The Rev. G. Clarke presided. The Union embraces the Island, and reports were sent in from all quarters, some favourable, others unfavourable. Attention has been paid, with encouraging success, to Ragged schools in Hobarton. A depository is established for books suitable for Sunday schools, and books to the amount of £78 2s. 6d. had been sold during the year. The Committee suggested visits to the country districts by deputations, and, if possible, the employment of an agent after the American plan, to promote the establishment of Sabbath schools. On the whole the work of Sabbath school instruction seems to have secured in Tasmania a commendable amount of attention.

Printed at the Steam Press of W. FAIRFAX AND Co., Melbourne.

The Southern Spectator.

| No. 2. | OCTOBER, 1857. | Vol. I. |

TO OUR READERS.

EDITORS of Periodicals, in adopting the royal WE, have affected somewhat of royal state and reserve. From their invisible council chambers their decrees have gone forth without any kindly intercourse with those whom they treat as their subjects. The conductors of the present work would like to be upon better terms with their readers, and to hold a familiar *tête a tête* with them now and then. The subject of the first talk shall be the Magazine itself. Well, it has been launched at length ; and our readers would not believe us if we pretended to be indifferent as to its reception. The project has been too long in our thoughts, and taken up too purely from love, to make it possible for us to be otherwise than anxious for its success. How has it gone off? We have the pleasure of saying, Better than at one time we dared to hope. Upwards of three thousand copies were printed, and not many are left on hand. If those who have become purchasers will be so good as to go on as they have begun, make a little exertion to get a few more subscribers in their several circles, send advertisements for the covers, and be punctual in their remittances of payment, we shall have nothing to complain of so far as the business part of the work is concerned.

But how is it liked? Ah, that is a more delicate question. Perhaps it would hardly be prudent to divulge all that has come to our ears on this point. We may, however, say this much : that from those for whom it was more particularly designed, the members of Christian congregations, we have received much of commendation and encouragement. For this we are thankful, and also for the hints they have thrown out for future improvement. It always looks well when, instead of sulkily grumbling at what is amiss, some kindly efforts are made to mend it. And we can assure our readers that any practicable suggestions for making the work what is really wanted, shall have due consideration. But the general public, How has it gone down with them? We dare say that if the English public were shut up to the Evangelical Magazine, and the Christian Observer, they would think them "dry and heavy," just because they have little relish for the religion that is in them. But having plenty of choice, they let them alone for those that like them. Here, however, the choice is more limited, and works, religious in their tone, are in danger of receiving prompt condemnation, for not being, what they never pretended to be, of a light and amusing character.   A law book is dry to any but a lawyer ; a book on logarithms is dry to any but a mathematician, and so a book mainly religious will, we fear, ever be distasteful to those to whom religion itself is not a very pleasant subject.   It will be inferred from this that we have heard of these epithets, " dry and heavy," being applied to our first number.   So far as the religious element in it produces this impression, we cannot hold out much hope of change ; but it will ever be our endeavour to present religion to others, as it ever appears to ourselves, as a pleasant and cheerful theme.   Perhaps, however, we do the critics in question an injustice : it may not be the religion but the length and massiveness of the articles which act as repellents.   As to this we promise to aim at as much brevity and variety as we may find compatible with our object.   Still it will be our ambition to have a good thorough article on a useful topic when the occasion demands it, such as we believe the article on the Marriage Laws to be, one which may be referred to with advantage and satisfaction when lighter matter is forgotten.

One most cherished wish of ours is gained ; the Periodical is bonâ fide *inter-colonial ;* indeed, less Victorian than Australian.   The greater part of our subscribers, writers, and pecuniary supporters reside in New South Wales, Tasmania, and South Australia.   With the interest so extensively awakened in the work in parts so distant from the place of its issue, we have a fair prospect before us of opening up a channel of communication between colony and colony, and of binding closer the ties of sympathy and mutual interest among Christian brethren.   One inconvenience from this circumstance, however, we have already felt in part, and are likely to feel all along, with respect to which we beg the indulgence of our readers ; we mean the different state of feeling on particular questions in the different colonies.   A question may be utterly stale in one colony, because it has been argued out and long ago settled there ; in another, it may be just rising into notice, and every thing bearing upon it eagerly read. Particular laws may be all right in one portion of Australia, and all in confusion in another ; and any articles upon such subjects will consequently be regarded as matters, on the one hand, of mere curious enquiry, or, on the other, of vital importance, according to the nature of the case.   So with national education, prison discipline, and other public questions.   Now, we entreat our readers to bear this in mind, in passing judgment upon our productions ; that which does not suit them may be just the thing for others ; what is *passée* in one place may be full of freshness elsewhere.   Let our readers think of other people's wants as well as their own ; and let them accord to us a little credit for perceiving and attempting to supply a necessity in some part of our extensive field which may have escaped their own observation.   But this peculiarity of our position cuts both ways ; if it demand some indulgence from our readers, it may furnish also a hint to writers to restrain somewhat their ardour in desiring to bring into our pages matter which may have only a local and limited interest. The atmosphere of public opinion may have been violently agitated by some discussion in their own immediate vicinity; but not the slightest vibration may have been felt in the distant regions beyond. While they are anxious, therefore, to furnish something that may be useful to their neighbours, let them not altogether keep out of view how far it may be suitable and seasonable to the great bulk of our readers.

We have heard some enquiries as to what is to be done with the *profits*. Alas! for the simplicity of those who put such a question. With the low price charged, the style in which the work is got up, and the heavy costs and drawbacks of various kinds which are inevitable to such an undertaking, it is doubtful whether any amount of circulation would do more than just clear expenses. Should any profits arise, however, the character of the projectors is, we trust, a sufficient guarantee that they will not be applied to any private advantage. Again asking for the sympathy, co-operation, and hearty good-will of the Christian public, we leave these explanations and hints with them. And so ends our colloquy.

MISCELLANIES.

The May Meetings.

The recent mails have brought us full accounts of the Anniversary Meetings usually held in the month of May in the British metropolis. Side by side with the war of politics, the bustle of business, and the flutter of gaiety, when the London season is at its height, there is presented a spectacle of another order, which may well arrest attention and awaken admiration—the spectacle of benevolence in organized action. It may be seen day by day in the vast crowds who assemble in public rooms, and especially in Exeter Hall. It has become the fashion, with some writers, to sneer at what they call the " performances " in this celebrated place; to hold up its frequenters as narrow bigots, hot enthusiasts, or religious voluptuaries; to characterize its speaking as " braying," and its doings as folly. They tell us that fierce hatred is fulminated against the Papists, and eccentric fondness is lavished on the Jews; or, as it has been humourously expressed, brimstone is administered to the one and treacle to the other. Because an occasional meeting may have been characterized by zeal without discretion, all Exeter Hall gatherings are indiscriminately jumbled together to receive the stigma of a common opprobrium. The men who do this know not what they say, nor whereof they affirm. They must either be ignorant, or malicious, or bigotted in their own peculiar line. Taking the whole

E 2

range of meetings which occur in the month of May, we deem them an honor to the British nation, and to the age in which we live.

Societies may be formed, and meetings held, for innocent amusement, the promotion of art or science, the advancement of commercial or political objects ; and these may not only be lawful, but expedient and commendable. But they come far short of the "May meetings" in disinterestedness of motive, and dignity of aim. The leading character of the latter is *benevolence.* Their object is not so much to get good as to do good, and that in every possible way that ingenuity can devise. Indeed one is almost bewildered amidst the variety of the institutions whose object is the happiness of the race. The *bodily wants* and temporal comforts of the needy and distressed, are cared for by societies for the sick, the houseless, the orphan, the stranger, the ragged, the aged, and the enslaved. Others have in view the elevation of the *morals* of the community, by promoting temperance and peace, reclaiming criminals, and rescuing fallen females from their degradation. The educational wants of the community, in the absence of a comprehensive national scheme, are provided for by a vast and costly system of Schools and Educational Institutes, on the voluntary principle. But the feature most characteristic of the greater part of these meetings is their strictly *religious* object. They aim at the development and elevation of the divine part of man's nature. They seek to make man happy by making him good. They have respect to his future and eternal existence, as well as his present. By preparing him for the world to come, they seek to improve his condition and increase his felicity in this ; and in acting on this plan they copy the example of him who, when he descended to this world on an errand of "good-will to men," accomplished the redemption of the soul as that blessing which comprehends all others.

This grand object is carried out by organization. Instead of leaving zeal to expend itself in desultory and individual efforts, these Institutions combine the scattered resources of the community, arrange and systematize them. This may almost be regarded as a modern discovery ; at all events its application upon a large scale is of comparatively recent date. A hundred years ago there was scarcely one of these organizations in existence ; now they count by scores. Constructed in the first instance to give effect to Missionary zeal, they have now been applied to remove or ameliorate nearly all the varied wants of humanity. The advantage of these combinations is obvious. Previous to their existence what could the rich man have done, with thousands at his command, to evangelize the heathen, however deep his anxiety ? Now the pence of the poor are available for that object. The religious world seems to have taken a lesson from the Political Economists in the application of their favorite principle of division of labour. One Society provides Bibles, another Books and Tracts, and a third puts them in circulation. One class of Institutions provides for the education of children, another for the mental and moral wants of young men. The Missionary Societies undertake the Heathen as their care, and they divide the world among them,—one selecting

Western Africa and the East, another the Pacific South Africa and China, and a third the West Indies New Zealand and Western Polynesia. Some Societies give themselves to the evangelization of cities, others of rural districts; some to the European Continent and others to the Turkish Empire. Indeed to enumerate in detail all the departments taken up would be tedious. Now that the spirit of Christian benevolence is alive and active, it seems quick to discern any class of the community, or form of evil and distress, which existing organizations do not touch, and instantly to construct a new Society to meet the want. With all their variety and multiplicity, however, there are no signs of their being in each others' way. Like the celestial luminaries, each has an orbit of its own, and moves on without clashing with its neighbours. Indeed they form a harmonious system, acting and re-acting upon one another to their mutual benefit, and supplementing each others' operations.

These Societies betray no signs of exhaustion. The predictions of enemies, that the zeal which commenced them, being a temporary fit of enthusiasm, would would soon expend itself, have not been verified. The stream of Christian benevolence has gone on augmenting in volume year by year, with only occasional temporary checks, till now it has attained a magnitude perfectly astonishing. In 1856 the gross income of the British and Foreign Bible Society was £135,521, and this year it is £9,000 more. The aggregate of the receipts of all the Foreign Missionary Institutions, amounted last year to £517,337 ; and, so far as can be yet ascertained, this large amount will prove to have been exceeded by the receipts of the present year. This gradual growth of revenue, which has now continued for upwards of half a century, is a sure sign of the stability of these Institutions, and of the firm hold they have secured on the principles and affections of the Christian community.

Not only have the meetings been large and the state of the funds encouraging, but the speaking has been distinguished by a high order of christian eloquence. The platforms have been crowded by distinguished men of all professions, of the most exalted rank, and most influential stations ; several of these being the new Bishops and other dignitaries of the English Establishment. If the staple and quality of the oratory of the season be read and examined with a candid eye, it will be found little to deserve the sneers cast upon it by the ignorant or the prejudiced.

From the manner in which these meetings are sometimes referred to in the public prints, it might be supposed that the "May Meetings" were only one of the phases of London gaiety. As the fashionable world has its pleasures, so has the religious. These meetings are but the hobbies of the pious, from which they derive the agreeable excitement which their less fastidious neighbours derive from the race-course and the ball-room. But if there be a slight touch of truth in this representation in some instances, it is on the whole a gross calumny. The grand feature of these meetings is the amount of work they represent,—of earnest, persevering, patient, self-denying work. The vast sums reported come from thousands of collectors, and are furnished by tens of thousands of contributors. The organizations that supply them extend over all the Empire, and are at work all the year, and this description of labour is the result of solemn convictions of duty, and is carried on in quiet retirement where there is no excitement to stimulate. And then as to the operations of the Societies, what a world of patient and arduous toil do they embrace ! The reports of the great institutions are not rhetorical essays, but plain and condensed statements of multitudinous facts. No longer regarded as the " bore " of the meeting, the " Report " has become in many cases, the most interesting, as well as the most instructive part of the proceedings, from the value of the facts it details. What meetings of committees have been held, what journeys undertaken, what visits paid, sermons preached, translations made, books written printed and distributed, and instructions imparted to furnish materials for these reports ! The great meetings are only the visible indices of the vast and complicated interior workings of the Christian portion of the community throughout the world, and they testify that multitudes of our countrymen are occupied in "patient continuance in well-doing" all the year round. All success to these noble Institutions, the true glory of Britain ; and may this young country emulate its venerable parent in her sublime career of christian benevolence.

Christian Politics.

By the term Christian, as applied to an individual, we do not mean a member of any particular church, but every man who loves and serves the Lord Jesus Christ. By politics, we do not mean the principles or practices of any given party or country, but the science of human government for human well-being. There are men in the world who would have liked Christianity more if, as *a system* it had come as an expounder of natural phenomena, and an instructor in political ethics,—if, as *a power*, it had overturned all that is unjust, and established the reign of love and freedom,—if, as *a blessing*, it had conferred upon man a mastery over nature, and a long life of enjoyment,—without any reference whatever to his spiritual condition. There are others who regard Christianity as simply a revelation of spiritual truth,—a remedy for spiritual wants alone. Both err from defect. " The true development of Christianity is the practical application of its principles to man, in every aspect of his being." Christianity will do much that secularists deem desirable; it seeks the same noble ends by wiser means. Recognising all the evils that afflict man as springing from his depravity, it seeks to make the tree good that the fruit may be good also ; believing that " if the root be rottenness, the blossom will go up as the dust." Hence, true Christian reform is personal ; it begins with man in the higher aspects of his being, in his relations God-ward, and works downward to man's relation to his fellow-men,—brings him into just relations to the infinite and unseen, then embraces in the arms of its charity the finite and seen, with its duties and pleasures, its wants and woes. The citizen of heaven is the best one for earth. One God rules over both worlds, the same moral principles and duties are found in both, simply marked by specialities of adaptation. A divine religion is for man in every relation he sustains, the gift of One who " knoweth our frame." As there are duties toward God, so there are duties to our fellow - men ; not merely love justice honour to individuals, but " there is, and there ever will be, a Christian patriotism, a great system of duties, which man owes to the sum of human beings with whom he lives ;—to deny it is folly—to neglect it is crime."* Yet there are Christians who feel no interest in politics ; who plead their religion as an excuse, who urge that Christianity would be injured by attention to earthly duties ; that, forsooth, she cannot stoop to things of low degree, her sole object being to fit men for heaven—they should add—by a right discharge of their present duties. Are not politics and religion so often interwoven that to neglect one is to neglect the other ? Is slavery a mere " domestic institution," unsupported by any federal power? Did Britain abolish the monstrous iniquity before her Christians became politicians ? Does the cause of divine truth need human defenders ? or is it variable as sovereigns, or parliaments, or countries? Is the continuance of divine worship in the world dependent upon support from the national treasury ? or its seemly conduct regulated by the varying decisions of judicial tribunals? And can the errors be rectified apart from politics? It is a Christian as well as a Jewish duty to " seek the peace and welfare of the country" in which we live,—the reason holding good in both cases that, " in the peace thereof we shall find peace." The good and wise of past generations, and other countries, never attempted to put asunder what God had joined together,—their private interests and the public welfare, — their politics and their religion. Attending carefully to the duties of their day and generation, remembering who was above them, and what before them, they obtained for themselves, and for us, civil and religious rights which we must preserve and extend for future ages. We cannot expect civil and religious freedom and equity apart from endeavours to secure them. In addition to general reasons, as obvious to all men as they are common to all countries, are there not special reasons, in our colonial circumstances, for attention to public matters? We are entering upon a new career of effort and trial,—let us hope of success, and aim to make our hopes

---

* Sydney Smith.

self-fulfilling. Hitherto our free institutions have been, to a great extent, in their actual outworkings, the occasions for ignoble personal ambitions and party strifes. Our senators need to be taught wisdom; they have scandalised some by their folly, amused some by their puerilities. Others, belonging to the family of the " stand-stills," have drawn an inference unfavourable to representative government, or, at least, against the capability of the Australias for this purpose; whilst the satirist repeats that " collective wisdom often proves singular folly." We are not to commit the *Southern Spectator* to any school of economy or party politics, we simply urge attention to duties which all Christian politicians will confess to be binding, when we say—

1. Study the various public questions at issue, so as to form an individual opinion upon their merits and claims. The questions now pressing for solution are manifold and important. The disposal of the public lands seems one peculiarly fraught with difficulties to our statesmen, and perhaps on this question electors may have, in some of the colonies, to pronounce their views and wishes before it is definitely settled; rival schemes may form the battle-ground at the hustings and the polling-booth. Our tariff duties, poll taxes, our educational and ecclesiastical grants, are questions now being dealt with in some of the colonies, and soon to be dealt with in others. Law, civil and criminal, with its mystery and delay, confusion and expense, is susceptible of more harmony, condensation, and justice, and in some points must speedily be altered. The subject of the federal union of the Australias, for mutual counsel and helpfulness will yet receive more attention. For these and other public questions, a thousand-and-one replies and remedies will be constantly brought before the public,—each clamouring for partisans, vainly parading its little series of partial facts, and promising if accepted, all happy results. Now a Christian man may and ought to have opinions upon these points; not the opinions merely of the party with which he usually acts, but honest personal opinions, arrived at by the use of the powers and opportunities of gaining and sifting evidence and principles, with which God has favoured him. Opinions, we know, will vary, so long as men possess different degrees of reasoning power—different measures of information—and are swayed by local, personal, or party feelings; yet we have faith in honest thought as the cause of wise and united action.

2. Act according to your honest convictions when called upon by circumstances to do your part. See that your names are duly entered upon the electoral roll, and your qualifications fairly stated, and then vote when the polling-day calls upon every true citizen to record his views of the useful and the right. It is a cause of great regret that many, who have the power, neglect the duty of recording their votes. Very rare and

peculiar are the reasons which will justify such an entire dereliction of public duty. "Neutrality is a natural state for men of fair honesty, small wit, and much indolence, who cannot get strong impressions of what is true and right." But, surely, Christians are not usually men of this stamp—rather, may we hope they are active in duty, fervent in spirit, serving the Lord Jesus Christ by doing, for His sake, whatsoever things are true and just. If all were to be neutral, the reign of terror and darkness would soon return. It is no just defence that some Christians become entangled in political snares, and stumble in consequence. The same is true of all departments of human effort. We plead not for absorbing attention to politics, to the neglect of other duties, especially of religious ones; but when public duty is the duty of the hour, do it, and serve your day and generation according to the will of God.

3. Pray for the peace and welfare of the land in which you dwell. No Christian will deny that it is his bounden duty, " in everything, by prayer and supplication, with thanksgiving, to make known his requests unto God." Nor will he deny that Samuel, Ezra, Nehemiah, and many others of modern times and other countries, pleaded with God for the welfare, political and religious, of the land of their birth or adoption. Nor is it necessary that we should urge a man who has faith, and knowledge of the power of prayer, and a real desire for his country's welfare, to an earnest discharge of this duty. God's expressed or implied command is in itself a sufficient reason and hope. We venture to insist, however, that there is a right and a wrong way of praying. Our scripture readings lead us to believe that God hears the prayers of working and consistent men, that sometimes labor-worship is most acceptable in His sight; that we should not, in all cases, be satisfied with merely making our requests known, but should work to make our prayers self-answering. " Thy kingdom come," sometimes means, teach a class in a Sabbath-school. " Grant that our trade and commerce may flourish," means often, be wise in plans, energetic and persevering in action. " Send peace in our time, O Lord, we beseech thee,' signifies, have nothing to do with other people's business when they put down one reigning family to set up another: or it may mean again, "be content with such things as ye have," when other people have a previous and better claim to disputed possessions, and are indisposed to part with them. It is even so with many other prayers. God helps the workers. Let true Christians, then, labour and pray for the time when the kingdoms of this world, in spirit and practice, shall become the kingdoms of our Lord Jesus Christ, and the song begun in heaven be re-echoed back from earth,—" Hallelujah! for the Lord God Omnipotent reigneth." He is worthy to reign over man in his individual and collective aspects.

Don't Imitate.

FOR YOUNG MEN.

Good intentions are no security against mistakes. The noblest undertakings may be marred if ill-judged measures are adopted to promote them. In the great and arduous work of the formation of individual character, many young men are often sadly led astray by bad advice, and waste their time in well-meant but ill-directed efforts. Perhaps in nothing is this more visible, than in the futile endeavours that are made to imitate slavishly some imaginary model of excellence. The young orator twists and strains himself in the vain attempt to reproduce a Chatham or a Fox; the result being only, to use the felicitous phrase of Burke, "the contortions of the Sybil without the inspiration." So, too, many young aspirants to the pulpit acquire a fictitious habit, in the attempt to engraft upon their own natures, the most striking characteristics of celebrated preachers. "If I could only preach in the style of Melville, or Chalmers, or Binney," says the young student to himself, "I should win a share of their renown." So, too, young apprentices and pupils, in the various trades and professions, look at the steps by which their predecessors climbed to wealth or fame, and flatter themselves that, by following as closely as possible in the windings of their career, they will be likely to reach the same eminence. But it was not by imitation that those whose greatness is thus emulated achieved their success; nor will such a merely mechanical process confer distinction on those who seek to follow in their footsteps. It is not given to all men to be great, but the utmost possible degree of excellence that is attainable by every one, is to be gained by perfecting his own peculiar abilities, and making the best possible use of his own peculiar circumstances. Imitation usually degenerates into mimicry, and the model is parodied instead of being reproduced.

The legitimate influence of example is an admirable incentive te exertion. It stirs the blood and kindles the spirit of a young man to read how those who have gone before him have risen, step by step in the sight of all men, to positions of great honor and great usefulness. It awakens a noble emulation, and girds him up to start with fresh energy in the race of life. But it is the abuse of example, when its influence so degenerates as to inspire only a formal and slavish imitation. The *spirit* of a man's life is quite distinct from its outward details. If *that* can be appropriated in any way, a substantial benefit is indeed gained. If the emulous young aspirant can catch any of the animating genius of those who have worthily preceded him; if he can imbibe any of their self-reliance, their patient industry, or their unconquerable perseverance, he will do well. But any attempt simply to mimic their outward development, will only lead to a lamentable failure.

It is a frequent delusion with those who read biography, to

imagine that the circumstances of great men were particularly favorable to their advancement, and to flatter themselves with the thought, that if they, too, were as fortunately situated, they would be able to do far more than is possible for them in their existing position. Probably quite as many persons are deterred from attempting to emulate the success that others have achieved, by indolently persuading themselves that their unfavorable position renders the task hopeless, as have been led into the error of fruitless imitation. In both cases, too much importance is attached to circumstances. The non-possession of certain adventitious aids, is often of far less value than is supposed ; nor would the possession of them, to the fullest extent, be of service to those who, trusting in them, have not cultivated the faculty of using them wisely.

Young men should seek, not to reproduce exactly some model that they set before themselves, but to prosecute self-culture in the inspiring light of bright examples. The individualities which Providence creates are not evils which are to be eradicated. He that abandons himself in order to try and become somebody else, parts with his best and most personal possession, and gives up the substance to grasp at the shadow. Let every man build on his own foundation. Some people are too timid to be themselves. They are afraid of being singular. They speak not what they feel, but what they fancy they ought to feel. They do not act in accordance with their own promptings, but in order to harmonise with custom or fashion. This dread of differing too much from the established standard runs through society, and begets a stunted uniformity where there ought to be a free and various growth.

To those who are starting in the journey of life, and are animated with the desire of developing in themselves, with the aid of Divine assistance, those faculties that have been given them, we should say : " Don't imitate. In all things, be yourself. Superadd as much discipline and self-culture as you like, but let the substratum on which you operate, remain essentially yourself. Never destroy your own individuality. Depend upon it you will never gain anything by parting with your own characteristics—by cutting down your own growth to graft on something else. Take your own stand on your own nature. Say to the world—' I shall be myself, and nobody else.' Don't be too fearful of being thought peculiar. Respect the influence of your own emotions, and the genuine workings of your own mind. Let your aim be, not to denaturalise yourself, but to realise yourself. Develop your being : do not denude or overlay it. Blossom outwards from the vigor of your own internal sap ; but do not shake off your natural foliage in order to deck yourself with borrowed beauties which will never become you. Suck in strength and nourishment from all quarters, but let it fructify freely."

There is a very instructive moral to be drawn from the story which tells how David would not put on Saul's armour. The offer might have been well meant on Saul's part, but it was not judicious, and David did wisely not to ape a style of action for which he was not at the time fitted. It was far better for him just to be what he was, and to pretend to nothing else, whatever ridicule he might incur. If he had encumbered himself with harness he could not work in, he might have mimicked more successfully the gait of a warrior, but he would have paid with his life the penalty of his folly. He was but a shepherd boy—why should he affect the style of a veteran soldier? His prowess, humanly speaking, lay in his following the bent of his own training. By many a day's practice on the hill-side when watching his sheep, he had grown to be expert with the sling. The use of that simple weapon came natural to him. He could fight Goliah in that way but in no other.

The men that have most moved the world, and that still lead society, have been always profoundly original. They have drawn their inspiration from within, and not from foreign sources. They have given free play to their own impulses, and not waited to take their orders from custom or fashion. The first great charm of oratory, and indeed of all public action whatsoever, is sincerity. He who would sway others must impress them with an instinctive conviction that what they outwardly see and hear has been first inwardly thought and felt. Sincerity accredits itself. Heart responds at once to heart. "One touch of nature makes the whole world kin." Imitation may be clever; but it can never be a substitute for nature.

The Church's Duty to Colonists.

In this paper we shall give an outline of the history of Emigration, as preliminary to an enquiry into the duty of the Christian Church to those who have come and are still coming into these lands to make them their permanent abode.

In the Scriptures there is a striking passage indicative of God's goodness to mankind : " The heaven, even the heavens are the Lord's ; but the earth hath he given to the children of men." This gift was in a manner forfeited by the rebellion of the ante-diluvians, but restored when Noah left the ark. The value of the donation could be but imperfectly understood by the Patriarch. The arts and sciences were then of course almost unknown. The wonders of astronomy, as now understood, were not discovered. Geography had not brought to light the islands and continents, the lakes, rivers, and seas, with which we are now acquainted. Nor is it necessary to suppose, that Noah foresaw that teeming millions of human beings would, in due time, overspread the earth, and form themselves into permanent cities, states, and kingdoms. He could not conceive of the wide and wondrous circle of history which our race was destined to describe. To him the mighty future was a blank; the curtain of its solemn drama not yet lifted.

Admitting that Noah was aware of the intention of the Creator to let the earth, as the home of our race, continue through many thousands of years, his point of view, nevertheless, is not for a moment to be compared with ours. *He* could be aware only of the Divine purpose—*we* have seen that purpose to a large extent fulfilled. By the light of history, we see the world tenanted and enjoyed; its forests felled; its marshes drained; its plains and valleys cultivated; its lakes and seas and rivers made the high ways of trade and intercourse between distant communities. Nearly the whole globe has been made available for man—the home of a large and an ever-increasing family.

Few, indeed, were the persons who, as trustees for posterity, received from God the largess of a new world. From the primary seats of human life they at length found it necessary to spread themselves over the surrounding regions. We watch them as they migrate towards the East, and the West, and the South. At a very early period, numerous families are seen venturing forth into the unknown, unexplored portions of the earth. The descendants of Japhet push their way into Europe, and establish themselves in Greece, Italy, and the "isles of the sea." The posterity of Ham speedily diffuse themselves over the whole country lying between the Euphrates and the Mediterranean, and, at length reach and occupy the African Continent. Meanwhile the progeny of Shem take possession of Central Asia and India. Thus far our information is derived from the Inspired Word. (Gen. x. passim.)

The first colonies of which we have any intimation in profane history are the Phœnician. Occupying a strip of country bordering upon the eastern extremity of the Mediterranean, this people were happily situated for dispersion. Being intelligent and enterprising, they devoted themselves to commerce; and through them the precious products of the East were transmitted to the West. By means of their maritime trade they soon became acquainted with the shores of the Great Sea, from the Straits of Gibraltar to their own strand. They familiarised themselves with the countries and spots most eligible for the settlement of the growing numbers of their countrymen. In the first instance, probably, nothing more was attempted by them than the formation of emporiums, for the transaction an extension of the commerce of the mother country. They did not, therefore, contemplate the expulsion of the earlier inhabitants of the lands in which they established themselves. Subsequently, however, many of the Phœnicians were, by the tyranny of their rulers, ejected from their paternal dwelling-place, and compelled to seek a permanent home in a foreign land. From whatever causes, they are known to have had flourishing colonies in Africa, in Spain, in Cyprus, in Italy, and in Sicily. The Phœnicians are universally acknowledged to have been the earliest and the most successful colonizers of antiquity; and their location at different points must have had considerable influence in extending the conveniences and refinements of civilization in a rude age. In after times the Greeks followed in the footsteps of the Phœnicians. Their own narrow territories being insufficient to support a large population, offshoots were sent to the isles of the Ægean, to the shores of the Black Sea, of Asia Minor, of Southern Italy, and other places, and vast and elevating was the influence, and enduring the effects of this wide dispersion of the Grecian element in those regions. The scheme of colonization carried out by the Romans is well known. Their Empire, embracing, in the times of their greatest glory, the larger portion of the then known world, was studded over with colonies. "Wherever," says Seneca, "the Roman conquers, he inhabits." These Roman colonies, however, were as much of the nature of military posts for securing the allegiance of the surrounding countries, and centres of Roman influence for humanizing the inhabitants, as places of provision for the needy and adventurous. The settlers sought neither to exterminate nor expel the old inhabitants; on the contrary they were themselves at length amalgamated with the mass in the midst of which they dwelt.

We need not stop to trace the history of modern emigration as conducted by the Venetians, the Spaniards, the Portuguese, the Dutch, the French, and others; and by our own countrymen in the other hemisphere. From the most hasty glance at the world's history, it is clear that there has ever been a tendency in crowded populations to overflow into unoccupied and thinly peopled regions, partly by migrating in masses, and partly by emigrating and colonizing in detachments, thus accomplishing the Divine purpose of filling the earth with inhabitants: and the Immigrants who have come or are coming to the Australias, are, whether they mean it or not, acting in harmony with this beneficent intention.

Colonies have always, for longer or shorter periods, acknowledged a tie of sympathy and relationship between them and the parent state. Their political connexion has not been so uniform. Some have been independent from the first, as were for the most part those of Greece; others have, in the course of time, achieved their independence like the United States; while a few, like Cuba, retain a more permanent dependance on the country which gave them existence. In some cases, the aborigines have been extirpated,—in others, absorbed into the invading race, and in others again reduced to servile bondage. All colonists carry with them the habits, the laws, the faith of the mother country. The Romans transplanted their system entire. "Each of the Roman colonies," says Aulus Gellius, "was a Rome in miniature."

Britons do much the same now; not only is communication kept up with the old country, but the colonial Governor, the judges, and others, are chosen and appointed by the home Government. And hence, with slight modifications, the institutions of Britain have been planted in America, Africa, and Australasia.

We are of course chiefly concerned with the Australian colonies in which our lot is cast. These it becomes us to benefit by every means in our power, and the preceding paragraphs seemed necessary to prepare the way for an inquiry which every Christian must regard as of the highest importance, namely, " What is the duty of the Christian Church, in regard to the rising communities around it ?"

As Englishmen, we cannot look at our history in these lands without sorrow and humiliation. Captain Cook's visit was, as far as the aborigines are concerned, as disastrous as the visit of Columbus to the shores of the New World. With absorbing interest we read Robertson's narrative of the daring and successful voyage of the great discoverer, but we soon become sick at heart. We trace but too clearly the injustice, the cruelty, the avarice, which the Spaniards displayed towards the simple children of nature whom they found in South America.

With all our frequent boasting, we cannot affirm that we come far behind the bigoted and avaricious Spaniard of the fifteenth and sixteenth centuries. We found the aborigines of Australasia wandering over these vast and fertile lands, fishing in the rivers, and hunting the kangaroo in their native forests. They have since almost entirely disappeared. A few remain, the wretched remnants of tribes that have perished. That crime—the extinction of a race of God's creatures—remains, alas ! and must remain unexpiated and inexpiable. We now suffer little annoyance from aborigines. In Tasmania, and in the settled districts of all the other colonies, they create no apprehension ; not that they are now blended with the invaders,—not that they are won over and naturalised by the paternal kindness of those who have taken possession of their lands,—not that they have been rendered harmless, and useful, and happy by religious and civilising influences. The weapons, the vices, the selfishness of the Briton have swept them away as with the " besom of destruction." We have silenced them by slaying them. We, too, " have made a desert," and we " call it peace." Well might the mocking and bitter satirist exclaim,—" Perhaps you have been taught to anticipate this destruction as the inevitable result of your advent to these shores. Perhaps your mission was to destroy. Providence, indeed, gave the poor wretches the soil on which they lived. You arrived, invested with superior rights, with heaven's commission in your hands, to eject the old tenants from their ancient homes. You have faithfully fulfilled your assumed mission." We can but turn silently away from these reproaches.

Let us not dwell on the painful retrospect; let it pass from our view; and, not without a tear, let the poor ignorant races themselves pass to extinction and forgetfulness.

But, if we can do little or nothing for the aborigines, can we do nothing for our own countrymen? It must be evident to every thoughtful person, every student of morals and manners, every observer of the "signs of the times," that without powerful and persevering efforts on the part of the followers of Christ, these colonies, or some of them at least, may rush headlong to moral ruin. There is the convict element more or less mingled with the mass of free immigrants, —a marked peculiarity affecting these colonies, and one which, though transportation has now happily ceased, will be injuriously felt on the morals of the community for years to come. There are the strong bewildering excitements of the gold-fields, ever disappointing indeed yet ever attracting, ever stimulating, ever breaking up habits of application and quiet perseverance in the culture of the soil and in the prosecution of commerce. Yet these habits are all-important to the individual and to society. Facility in gaining money, and the hope of gaining it speedily, beget a recklessness in the expenditure, and often a general laxity of moral conduct and principle. The state of society and of life among us, is not that which we have witnessed in the fatherland. Colonial children differ widely from the children of British parents. The same may be said of the parents themselves,—of masters also and servants. The relations of life seem altered and deteriorated. The sanctities of Christian intercourse are less and less understood and recognised. There are in many cases indications of insubordination and conceit, which, unless a barrier firm and strong be raised up, may in due time produce disastrous consequences to the well-being of society. To none can we look to erect an effectual barrier, but to the disciples of Christ. Our reliance, under God, is upon the Christian church, in its various sections. Our eye is directed to the teacher of the young, to the preacher of the gospel, to the efforts and lives of all earnest servants of God. The spirit referred to must be checked. The population must be pervaded throughout all its extent with the leaven of truth and holiness. The community must be formed and moulded after the Christian type. To effect this, the Christian must exert his best energies, display his warmest zeal, continually present that fervent prayer which has power with God. Christians must aspire to be, what indeed they ought to be—the "salt of the earth," the "light of the world," the pervading and conserving power in the community,— and this view of our obligations as colonists is applicable to all Christian bodies alike.

Of the way in which we think this may be done, we shall reserve the discussion to a future opportunity.

QUARTUS.

SUNDAY READING.

The Two Shipwrecks.

Since the publication of our last number, two lamentable shipwrecks have happened on the coast of Australia, the tidings of which have sent a thrill of horror through the community. The ship *Dunbar* at midnight struck on the precipitous cliffs near the entrance to Port Jackson, and in less than an hour was reduced to atoms by the fury of the waves. The passengers and crew, to the number of one hundred and thirty, all perished, with the exception of one solitary sailor who was cast on shore at a spot where he was able to climb to a ledge of rock, on which he remained in safety till discovered and hauled up by a rope on the second morning after the disaster. The two steamers *Lady Bird* and *Champion*, on a quiet night came suddenly into collision off Cape Otway, the latter vessel being sunk and thirty-two persons suddenly launched into eternity.

These two calamities, both so unexpected, both so distressing, sent a shock through the heart of our Colonial Society. The most thoughtless and unfeeling yielded for a moment to the influence of the general sympathy, and for days the talk on every lip was the wreck of the *Dunbar*, or the collision of the steamers. The universality of death compels a fellow-feeling for those who have met the inevitable destiny under circumstances of peculiar terror and distress. It was midnight when the doomed voyagers were called to their account. They were mostly asleep, not dreaming of the fate that hung over them. Little time was allowed them for reflection. From the moment of their first awaking to the awful consciousness of their danger to the last sense of life, there was but the space of a few minutes.

To those who have no fear of death, a sudden decease is not absolutely more distressing than a lingering one. The general dread that exists of meeting death without timely notice has its root in a prevailing sense of an unfitness to die. It is "conscience that makes cowards of us all." Even amongst those who avow their faith in Him who has snatched the victory from the grave and plucked from death its sting, there are few who would not shrink from an unexpected and hurried summons to meet their Lord. There have been many who have ultimately met the last enemy with calmness and tranquillity, if not with triumph, who on first being brought to face their danger have trembled. And it has not been till they have reassured themselves by contemplating with eager ardour the great atoning work of the Redeemer, and have fastened their faith afresh upon the Cross, that they have been able to tread the dark valley with unfaltering step. There are thousands of timid disciples who live in constant apprehension that they will never be able to attain to this assurance in the dying hour, and who consequently, "through fear of death are all their lifetime subject to bondage." They are terrified at dissolution, even when they think of it as in the distance, and shrink from the fate of being forced suddenly and without warning to meet a struggle of which they have so many apprehensions. It sometimes surprises those who are not aware of the intrinsic power of Christian faith, and how it proves itself equal in emergencies to the demands made upon it, to see how the timid who are really disciples lose their fears in the crisis, when they most expected to find them, and enjoy a tranquillity as delightful to themselves, as astonishing to those who behold it. But the back is fitted to the burden. And the hand that fashioned the susceptibilities, knows how to apply the alleviating support. The " bitterness of death " is felt in its real extent only by those who, having been nurtured in Christian doctrine, and who, having never lost their faith in it even under the extremest outward appearance of carelessness or scepticism, have to meet, all of a sudden, a change for which they have made no preparation. To them the agonizing remorse of the last few moments of life—the sense of hopelessness, the bitter regrets, the self-accusation, the overwhelming dread, the despairing clutching at life, mingled with a flashing consciousness of the realities of the situation—all this, concentrated into a short interval, images to the mind a phase of human experience on which it cannot bear to dwell.

There is at first sight something so strange about the dispensations of Providence, that the mind not fortified by faith is apt to be bewildered. Frightful accidents in which whole masses of human beings are hurried at once into eternity, are so appalling that we are apt to feel a momentary rising against that Providential government which can admit of events so heart-rending, so reckless of human life. As the world's career advances, the great machine of destiny unrols its thread with such an apparent unconcern for human suffering or human interests as comes into collision with the warmer passions and even the best feelings of our nature. But sudden and frightful accidents only represent more sharply, and bring in a more concentrated form under our notice, what is going on constantly all over the world. Apart from the great fact of death itself, there is every conceivable form of sorrow, inequality, cruelty, and injustice ever to be found. Why all this should be allowed, is more than we can say. We cannot command the prospect which will enable us to take in all at once, and see the coherence of the various parts of the Providential scheme. But though it is beyond our reach to arrive at the explanation, we can find hints to show that there is an explanation possible, though at present out of sight, and with this our faith must rest content. We have sufficient assurance on other grounds to satisfy us that God cannot be otherwise than wise and good—an assurance strong enough to help us to bear in patience the " heavy and the weary weight of all this unintelligible world." "He that hath given us his own Son, how shall he not with him also freely give us all things?" Providence, which is God in events, cannot be at issue with grace.

The Sabbath: No. II.

Having in a previous paper laid down the principles of interpretation which should guide us in examining what is permanently enjoined in Scripture, we proceed to apply those principles to the question of the Sabbath.

The first mention of the Sabbath is in the account of the Creation in the book of Genesis. The mighty God, who in the beginning made the Heavens and the Earth, fitted up and furnished this globe for the residence of man, and formed man himself in his own glorious image; and this he did in a regular order and succession in the course of six days. On the completion of this great work the Divine Architect looked abroad upon the fair world he had constructed, with unmixed complacency and satisfaction, and "behold it was very good." "Then the morning stars sang together and all the sons of God shouted for joy." "Thus," adds the historian "the heavens and the earth were finished and all the host of them, and on the seventh day God ended his work which he had made; and he rested on the seventh day from all his work which he had made; and God blessed the seventh day and sanctified it, because that in it he had rested from all his work which God created and made."

This remarkable statement, occurring immediately on man's creation, is very important and clearly proves not only the extreme antiquity of the Sabbath, but its great dignity and, as we think, its universal obligation. The labour and rest spoken of had reference to *man* and not to *God*. The Divine Being had no need to occupy a succession of days even in the work of Creation; his fiat would have completed all in an instant. The consumption of time therefore in the work was designed to set his creatures an example of useful occupation; and for the same reason he rested on the seventh day, that they might periodically cease from *their* labours. *He* had no need either to work or to rest; it was done for the sake of man, and in condescension to the peculiarities of the nature with which man was endowed. The command is not simply enjoined because God did this, but God did it that it might be enjoined. And he must therefore have deemed an institution of this kind essential to the well-being of man as such.

Let it be remembered that the Sabbath was instituted before man fell, while he yet remained in a state of purity. Even *then*, as a being made both to worship his Creator and to work with his hands, he had need of the rest of the Sabbath. Though his labour in Eden could not have been excessive, yet his considerate Creator provided him a respite from that gentle exertion, and required him to repose one day in seven. Sinless, he was yet allied to earth as well as to heaven; he was composed of body as well as soul, and while the six days of labour were requisite for the support of the one, the seventh day's rest was requisite for the more full employment in religious duties of the other. How much more necessary for the toiling sons of fallen Adam is the rest of the holy Sabbath, both for the health of the body and the welfare of the soul!

The reason assigned for the sanctification of the Sabbath, viz., the repose of the Almighty from the work of Creation, is as cogent to men in every age, as it was to the men of the first age of the world. God is *our* creator as much as he was Adam's or the Jews': and it is as necessary for us, as it was for them, to remember our Creator, to praise, to love, to serve him, and to have sufficient time for that purpose. Hence if there was any thing reasonable and suitable in the Institution as originally established, there is equally as much at the present time.

The terms employed denote an absolute and permanent consecration of a seventh portion of time to the service of God; "God blessed the seventh day and hallowed it." This language clearly expresses a claim on the part of the Creator himself to this proportion of man's earthly existence, an appropriation of it to rest for the good of the body, and to holy services for the good of the soul and the glory of Him who made all things. And as this was done by the Creator at the beginning, as the first of all his enactments, taking precedence of every thing else,—such a law must be *perpetual* unless repealed by the same authority which enjoined it. The Sabbath is thus put upon the same footing as marriage. They were both enacted in the time of man's innocency, and were designed for the race wherever it should be scattered; and if one be an ordinance of Heaven and of a nature to be obligatory in every country and in every age, so is the other; and if a pure and unfallen nature required such enactments, much more does that nature in its present degenerate condition.

The silence of the historian of the lives of the Patriarchs has led some to assert that this institution was unknown to them. But mere silence in a case of this kind argues nothing. Something positive on the contrary side is necessary to annul a law, founded on such principles and for such reasons. The extremely brief and fragmentary character of the history, and the consequent omission of many other important matters, sufficiently account for the Sabbath not being named during that period. Nothing was noticed but what seemed to fall naturally in with the special object of the writer: and to enlarge further on the Sabbath, especially as it was not called in question, was doubtless deemed unnecessary. Nevertheless there are traces of the division of time into periods of seven days. Thus Noah sent forth the dove out of the ark at intervals of seven days; and Laban spoke to Jacob about fulfilling Rachel's week; indeed among all the ancient nations, vestiges may be discerned of the weekly division of time. The division into months is easily accounted for, arising as it does from the lunar motions: but the division into weeks is arbitrary, and its general prevalence must have sprung from a common and early source.

We now come to consider the evidence for the Divine obligation of the Sabbath in the laws of Moses. All admit that the Sabbath was a part of the Jewish Economy, and was binding upon the Israelitish nation while that economy lasted. But those who deny the perpetual obligation of the Sabbath, assert that it was peculiar to that system, and that when Judaism was abrogated, the Sabbath was abrogated along with it. To keep the Sabbath therefore, according to them, is to go back to the "beggarly elements" of an imperfect and preparatory dispensation. This notion seems founded for the most part upon the reason for keeping the Sabbath assigned in Deut. v. 15, by Moses when recapitulating the Law: Addressing the assembled nation he says: "Keep the Sabbath to sanctify it, as the Lord thy God hath commanded thee. Six days shalt thou labour and do all thy work; but the seventh is the Sabbath of the Lord thy God: in it thou shalt not do any work, thou, nor thy son, nor thy daughter, nor thy man servant, nor thy maid servant, nor thine ox, nor thy ass, nor any of thy cattle, nor thy stranger that is within thy gates; that thy man-servant and thy maid-servant may rest as well as thou: and remember that thou wast a servant in the land of Egypt, and that the Lord thy God brought thee out thence through a mighty hand and by a stretched out arm: *therefore* the Lord thy God commanded thee to keep the Sabbath day." It is alleged, that the reason here given for keeping the Sabbath is the national deliverance from Egypt, a reason therefore of force to that people but not to any other. It is doubtful whether this *is* the legislator's meaning, or whether he does not refer to the people's experience of the toils of servitude in Egypt, as a reason why their *servants* should enjoy the rest of the Sabbath as well as themselves. But waiving this point, and admitting that, at that time, part of the design of the Sabbath was to commemorate the deliverance from Egypt, it was certainly not the whole or the chief part. For in every *other* place, where the reason is given by Moses for keeping the Sabbath, especially in the version of the Sabbatical Law we have in the Decalogue, the reason is the *old one*, God's resting on the seventh day from the work of Creation. The deliverance from Egypt might be *added* to the original reason, without superseding it. That deliverance was a mighty work of God, and was well worthy of being commemorated by the Jews, along with the Creation, just as the Resurrection of Christ and our Redemption by him, are united with the Creation of the world, as deserving of commemoration in the Christian Sabbath.

From the manner in which the subject of the Sabbath is introduced by Moses, and always spoken of by him, we naturally infer that the Israelites were previously acquainted with it and in the habit of keeping it, and only required it to be impressed more deeply upon their memory, and enforced more powerfully upon their attention : "*Remember* the Sabbath day to keep it holy," is the formula employed. The first mention of it is in connexion with the fall of the manna. The people had gathered a double quantity of that miraculous food on the sixth day, that they might rest on the seventh. They did this in a natural way as if it arose out of an ordinary habit. As previous surplus collections of manna, above the day's allowance, had corrupted on the following day, the rulers of the Congregation seemed to apprehend a similar result to this extra quantity which had been laid up for the Sabbath, and they came to state their difficulty to Moses. He commended the people for what they had of their own accord done, and said to them ; " This is that which the Lord hath said : To-morrow is the rest of the holy Sabbath unto the Lord ; bake that which ye will bake to-day, and seethe that ye will seethe, and that which remaineth over lay up for you till the morning. Six days shall ye gather it, but on the seventh day which is the Sabbath, in it there shall be none."

The Ten Commandments were delivered after this event, and the law of the Sabbath occupies a central position among them. This is certainly a remarkable circumstance, from which the plain inference is that God designed the Sabbath to be of perpetual obligation. The peculiar significance of this circumstance will appear from the following remarks.

1. The Decalogue was separated and distinguished from the mass of ceremonial regulations, by being enacted by itself, and before any of the others.

2. It was further distinguished by being announced by the Divine Being himself, who, from the midst of thick darkness on the top of Sinai, with thunderings and lightnings and earthquakes, spake with his own voice in the ears of the affrighted people all the words of this law. No others of the laws of that economy had such an honor, and such an emphasis, impressed upon them ; for they were all delivered on the mount to Moses in a private manner, and by him communicated to the people.

3. The Ten Commandments and they alone had the further distinction of being twice written on tables of stone, not by human hands, but by the *finger of God*. They were ordered also to be put *inside* the ark, that precious type of Christ, while the general body of the Law was only placed near the ark on the outside.

4. The laws which constitute this code are *moral* in their character, founded on the nature and relations of man as such, and therefore immutable, binding upon all mankind at all times and in all places, irrespective of any peculiar or temporary dispensation of religion; and the law of the Sabbath is placed in the midst of

them. And why it should be so separated from the new moons, the Sabbatical year, the Jubilee, and other Jewish feasts, unless it partook of a moral nature and had an anterior and independent authority, it is impossible to explain. Its being placed among the precepts of the moral law is consistent, if we regard it as founded upon the constitution and nature of man in his present state of being, in force from the Creation, and remaining in force while man continues an inhabitant of earth : but if it be nothing more than a Jewish ceremonial, on the same level with sacrifices and circumcision, limited in its obligation as to time and place, its being exalted into the decalogue is wholly inexplicable.

5. While the *ceremonial* Law of Moses is in the New Testament regarded as a temporary institution designed to be abolished and superseded by the Gospel, the precepts of the *moral* Law are excepted. These—both Christ and his Apostles explained in their true sense, vindicated from false glosses, and re-enacted with the full weight of their authority. And unless the Sabbath were specially *excepted* we are bound to consider it as included among the rest.

As therefore we find the obligation to devote a seventh portion of our time to rest and devotion, to be a Law instituted at the beginning of the world, deriving its authority from God as the Creator, and placed, when the temporary laws of Moses were enacted, separate from them and exalted to a central place among the grand moral precepts which are universally and perpetually binding, what more can be requisite to prove, so far as the Pentateuch is concerned, that the Sabbath is a Divine and permanent Institution?

The testimony of the subsequent parts of the Old Testament is in full harmony with the teaching of the books of Moses on the subject of the Sabbath. It is not very frequently referred to, because circumstances and occasions seem not to have required it. But where it is mentioned, it is distinguished from the ordinary ceremonial laws, as specially important. Though all the laws God had enjoined were required to be observed, yet throughout the Psalms and the Prophets the moral is ever exalted above the ceremonial in point of intrinsic value, mercy above sacrifice, contrition of heart above sackcloth and ashes. And the Sabbath is in a similar manner signalized ; its violation is represented as peculiarly offensive to God, its faithful observance as peculiarly acceptable. Thus in the prophecies of Jeremiah (xvii. 21—27) special promises of good are delivered to the people if they would "hallow God's Sabbaths," and fearful denunciations of evil in the event of their profaning them. In the prophecies of Ezekiel too (xx. 12—21,) where the rebellions of the house of Israel are recounted as reasons for the fearful judgments which had already befallen the people, and were still further impending, marked prominence is given to their "polluting God's Sabbaths," as among the worst. And when Nehemiah built up the dilapidated ecclesiastical and civil system of his countrymen on their return from captivity, he makes emphatic mention of his deep solicitude to correct the lax notions and lax practices on the subject of the Sabbath, which the people had learnt in heathen countries, and of his zeal in restoring that institution to its ancient purity (Neh. xiii. 15—23.) It is not necessary to do more than refer to these passages; but one may be quoted in full from the prophecies of Isaiah (lviii. 13, 14,) as containing the essence and sum of the teachings of the Old Testament Scriptures on the subject in question: "If thou turn away thy foot from the Sabbath, from doing thy pleasure on my holy day, and call the Sabbath a delight, the holy of the Lord, honorable; and shalt honor him, not doing thine own ways, nor finding thine own pleasure, nor speaking thine own words; then shalt thou delight thyself in the Lord, and I will cause thee to ride upon the high places of the earth, and feed thee with the heritage of Jacob thy father; for the mouth of the Lord hath spoken it." The New Testament view of the question will be considered in a future paper.

Hymn to Beauty.

An Evening Melody.

I.

What fairy-like music comes over me now,
Blending its tones in this dreamy hour,
  Sounding in the river's flow,
  And from the forests murmuring low,
To the depths of my soul as a holy power?

II.

The charm of Beauty is softly falling,
  On hill, and meadow and tree:
And listen, listen, her voice is calling
  To the spirit that would be free.

III.

I hear it in the rustling bough,
  And in the nightbird's lay;
And in the winds that gently blow,
  From the dying light of day.

IV.

'Tis not the flowers and woods that speak,
  But Beauty dwelling there;
Whose spirits now in chorus seek—
  Re-answering feeling here.

V.

" Our leaves are pointed to the sky,
  " As to the realm of love;
" And all around the breezes sigh,
  " For beauty's home above.

VI.

" And every lovely thing on earth
  " Should lead to God on high ;
" Where purer beauty has its birth,
  " In joy that cannot die.

VII.

" Thence comes every ray that cheers,
  "(For there all beauty is light) ;
" And here where'er it shines, appears
  " A heaven of delight."

VIII.

Then this is the light which around me is spread
In these quivering moonbeam's glory :
And this, too, the light on the soul, which is shed
By love's old cherished story.

BIOGRAPHY.

[Short Biographies of such Ministers of Religion, and other public and useful men, as present anything instructive in their lives or deaths, and who have died in Australia, will be thankfully received by the Editor, as it is his wish to preserve a record of all such.]

MEMOIR OF THE LATE REV. J. M. LEWIS, OF GAWLER TOWN, SOUTH AUSTRALIA.

JOHN MELBOURNE LEWIS was descended from families in Wales, of sufficient distinction to preserve their lineage and records. John Bonner, an ancestor of his, was rector of Abergavenny, whose son became High Sheriff of Monmouthshire. One of the daughters of the latter was married to Mr. William Lewis, a country gentleman living in Hanover Court, near Abergavenny. Francis Lewis, the son of William, and grandfather of John Melbourne, became an earnest Christian, and was for thirty years a minister of a Baptist Church in Newberry. His son, John Lewis, became a bookseller in the same town, but dying suddenly in 1820, left the subject of this memoir, a little child, to the care of his widowed mother. Of his history for a few years no records are in the possession of the writer. It appears that at the age of seventeen or eighteen, he joined the Congregational Church in Newberry. He had early thoughts of the ministry, and enjoyed successively some educational advantages under Dr. Hewlett, the Rev. Spedding Curwen, and the Rev. H. March, and latterly with a view to the sacred office. Before he was twenty, he began to preach in the villages, but obstacles stood in his way of the entering regularly upon the Ministry. It did not seem practicable to leave his aunt, whom he assisted in the business. On her death a new difficulty presented itself,—for in 1844 he had married, and thus barred his entrance into college. His desire, however, of usefulness was not to be suppressed, nor entirely baffled. In 1845, leaving business, he offered himself to the London City Mission, and after examinations at Red Lion Square, and interviews with Dr. Morrison and the Hon. and Rev. Baptist W. Noel, he was accepted April 2nd. The event suggests the very pleasant reflection that such institutions are admirable, not only for the kind and amount of evangelical work they do, but for the opportunity they give for eliciting and developing valuable talents which otherwise would be hidden and lost, or remain cramped and dwarfed. Mr. Lewis soon justified the favourable decision of the Society. On the 14th of the same month he left Newberry, and settled in Clapton, the station to which he was appointed. The arrangement was a happy one. He became associated with the Rev. Algernon Wells, and acted in some sort under his direction and supervision. He felt himself happy in thus being thrown in the way of that noble, genial, and tender spirit, and Mr. Wells in his turn loved and valued his protegé, whose excellent sense, true piety, conciliatory manner, frankness and intelligence, combined with great activity, he could not but discern and appreciate. Here Mr. Lewis earned for himself the reputation of a good Missionary to the poor and wretched of his countrymen. But his health gave way, and on the ground of a medical certificate (now lying before the writer) he felt compelled to give up his connection with the City Mission, and seek health in distant lands. He arrived in South Australia September 27th, 1851,—a period of deep colonial depression, instantly followed by the perplexing exodus of the male population to the gold-fields, which in its turn was succeeded by the wild excitement caused by the return of the gold-laden diggers. Mr. Lewis after residing a few weeks in Adelaide, took his family to Lyndoch Valley, a deserted station of the Congregational Home Missionary Society. He hoped, however, to be useful, and commenced his work. But recent untoward circumstances and prospective difficulties, induced him to accept an urgent call from the Church at Gawler Town, where he began his labours April 13th, 1853. This step was a judicious one. A central and rising place, such as Gawler, was just the spot for him. His presence there was quickly felt. The hearers multiplied, the Church increased, the neighbourhood was favourably impressed, and there seemed to be the very fairest promise of extensive usefulness. Here his capabilities came into view. Thus one of his Gawler friends wrote of him after his decease :—" He was characterised by a force and activity of mind, a clearness of conception, and a power of discrimination rarely equalled. His judgment was sound, his imagination vivid, though always restrained by a taste highly refined, and severe almost to a fault. He had an intense love of the beautiful in nature. His knowledge of general literature, which was considerable, was remarkably accurate ; and his acquaintance with mental science profound. Whatever he had read he had mastered digested, and, made his own. Some of his pulpit discourses (none of which were fully written), were elaborate compositions abounding with original and striking thoughts." After making all due allowance for the ardour of Christian affection, and the sorrow then fresh and bleeding, we cannot read this extract and not form a high estimate of its subject, since the description itself shews its writer's competence to give an opinion. The writer of the present sketch has before him a packet of manuscripts left by the deceased. A beautiful pile—a convincing memorial of a " a workman that needed not to be ashamed." And these comely documents will bear close inspection. Whilst they shew great industry and, by their references, exhibit a large and judicious range of reading, and a habit of using and working in the best materials, they also manifest a fine mental vigour and freedom. Above all this, there runs through them "the form of sound words," in the presentation of which he evidently well knew how " to stir up pure minds by way of remembrance," and also not only to get within *speaking distance* of the consciences of sinners, which many fail to do, but to approach and grapple with them. Well might his people mourn so bitterly ! In the oratorical power of presenting this treasury of thought and sentiment, he was gifted in no mean degree. As he kept away from the " metropolis," he was not so well known as he ought to have been. He was only just beginning to be spoken of as a preacher and speaker, when he left us, " like a retiring bird whose form and plumage were no sooner observed, than it took its flight." The writer of this sketch had once an opportunity of witnessing at a public meeting at Lyndoch Valley, amidst the Borassa Hills, a display of spontaneous oratory, which for vividness of imagination, aptitude to the occasion, and complete effectiveness, he will never forget. Certainly, had Mr. Lewis's life been spared, he would have been in frequent demand for platform service in Adelaide. His ardour carried him beyond due bounds, and excessive labours prostrated his strength. On the 8th July, 1855, he swooned in the pulpit, and was taken to his home, where he lingered for a few months, struggling in the last stages of consumption. The same pen that pourtrayed him as a preacher, shall describe his sick chamber. " To the last he retained, with very brief interruptions, the use of his mental faculties. His case was a beautiful illustration of that passage of Scripture, ' Mark the perfect man and behold the upright, for the end of that man is peace.' I never witnessed an instance of more unaffected humility, and of more simple and confiding trust in the faithfulness of the Saviour, and the efficacy of his atonement, than that afforded in the case of the departed one. It was his to have the ' assurance of *understanding* '—the ' assurance of *faith* '—and the ' assurance of *hope*.' Throughout his illness he had almost uninterrupted ' peace.' On one occasion I said something to the effect, that the Saviour would be with him in the ' dark valley.' He looked up, smiled, and said : ' It is *not dark* yet ; and if it should become so, one can *cling in the dark* you know.' His mind was stayed on God. He knew ' in whom he had believed.' ' He rejoiced in hope.' He anticipated the ' eternal weight of glory.' On September 29th, 1855, he died, after a residence of two years and a half in Gawler, during which his labours, his Christian spirit, his blameless course, and his catholic bearing towards all Christian denominations, had concurred to make the day of his departure a season of deep and universal sorrow.

In the two cases—the present and that of Mr. Sawle, given in the number for August—there is something suggestive and instructive in relation to colonial evangelisation. Neither of them had been pastors in England. Neither of them had passed through a collegiate course. Neither of them had been sent by a public Society. Yet both occupied important positions as ministers of the Gospel in the colony. Both of them were adapted for their stations. And both did good service in their vocations. Shall we, then, in looking for ministers confine our views exclusively to the English Colleges, to English Pulpits, or to English Societies? Let Sawle and Lewis answer the question; and let Angaston and Gawler echo the response.

STATISTICS.

STATISTICS OF RELIGIOUS BODIES IN SOUTH AUSTRALIA.

LETTER FROM REV. T. Q. STOW.

Felixstow, South Australia, September 9th, 1857.

To the Editor of the Southern Spectator.

DEAR SIR,—Within the last year and a quarter, I have had many applications from the other colonies for information, relative to the effect upon the cause of religion—of the withdrawal of State-Aid in South Australia, six years ago. Had I been in health, I should have felt bound, for the sake of truth and usefulness, as well as courtesy, to pay due attention to all the enquiries alluded to. As the interrogatories have been recently renewed, and I am better able to give them attention, I crave through the *Spectator*, to give the enclosed "Statistics," which I beg my respected and enquiring correspondents to accept as an answer to their questions, whilst they may serve also for general information, and the correction of some misapprehension in the sister colonies; for *here* the subject is little talked of, so apparent are the results, and so acquiescent in the present system is the general mind of the people, including multitudes who were opposed to the change.

The tabular view I send you, I have collected with great care. I have drawn it from the friends, representatives, and printed documents of the various denominations,—for which obliging aid I tender my thanks; from the Government census; from the "Statistics of South Australia for 1856;" from the Almanac of 1851—the year in which the grant was abolished; and from my own knowledge and recollections, which I found of some service in collating the various other items of information. Every religious edifice has risen, and every minister in the colony landed or assumed office, since I arrived about twenty years since; and up to 1851 there were very few ministers whose names, stations, and even persons I did not know.

	1851.		1857.	
	Ministers.	Churches & Chapels.	Ministers.	Churches & Chapels.
Episcopalians	16 including the Bishop.	18	26 including the Bishop.	35
Wesleyans	6	19	12	47
Congregationalists	13	18	18	28
Roman Catholics	11 with Bishop	8	12 with Bishop	23
Presbyterians	3	6	8	11
Baptists	6	10	9	11
Bible Christians	2	2	10	35
Prim. Methodists	3	9	5	25
Free Wesleyans	—	—	1	2
Swedenborgians	—	1	1	1
Unitarians	—	—	1	1
Quakers	—	1	—	2
Jews	—	1	—	1
Lutherans	6	6	11	12
	65	99	114	281

The population on the 31st December, 1850, stood 63,700. In June, 1857, it stood, as nearly as I can get at it, 102,152 ; * which numbers show an increase for six years of 38,452. We have then during the six years since the cessation of the Grant, an increase of 60 per cent. in the population, but an increase of 76 per cent. in the regular ministers, and 136 per cent. in the churches and chapels. But this does not then shew the whole case. The different bodies have connected with them altogether 232 lay preachers and readers, of whom a large proportion are the accessions of the last six years, whilst the 15 or 16 lay readers of the Church of England are quite new, being only one of the signs of additional life and self-action consequent upon the change from State-Aid to self-reliance. Should it be thought that 99 ministers are insufficient for 234 churches and chapels, it should be remembered that the ecclesiastical systems of some of the denominations require that their ministers *circulate*, and in the smaller places especially, the occasional or periodic absence of the regular ministers is met by the lay agents. In denominations not thus organised, economical and temporary expedients suited especially to a young colony, are giving place to more permanent and more complete arrangements.

The above account does not bring into view some other large indications of religious and ecclesiastical activity and liberality; the rebuilding and enlarging in an improved style of many of our old places of worship; and the better appearance and greater size of erections altogether new.

I am, my dear Sir, with great esteem and cordiality, yours truly,
THOMAS QUINTON STOW.

TASMANIA.—Census.—The population of the island, according to a recent census, consists of 80,802 persons (exclusive of the military), and is distributed under the head of "Religion," as follows :—

Church of England	47,714
Church of Scotland	7,220
Wesleyan Methodists	4,721
Other Protestant Dissenters	3,820
Roman Catholics	16,852
Jews	429
Mahomedans and Pagans	46

VICTORIA.—We have received from the Census Office of Victoria the official returns of the population up to March in the present year :—

	Persons.	Males.	Females.
Enumerated population, [exclusive of Ships, &c.]	402,804	257,341	145,463
Population in Ships and Hulks	3,773	3,569	204
Total of enumerated population†	406,577	260,910	145,667
Estimated for un-enumerated population ...	4,189	3,424	765
Grand total	410,766	264,334	146,432

REVIEWS.

NOTICE TO OUR READERS.—Our Magazine is not large, and it only appears every second month : it cannot, therefore, be expected that we should give a complete survey of the literary world. So enormous has that world become, that not even the *Athenæum*, with its weekly issue and strictly literary purpose, can adequately daguerreotype for us the changing features of publishers' catalogues and booksellers' counters—what then can be expected of us? We will do our best to watch over and nurse the young literature of these

---

* In December, 1850, the population is stated to be 63,700. In December, 1856, the numbers stand at 104,708. To this must be added half 1857, which at the estimated rate of the increase of the previous year would raise the return to 108,571. But from this there are deductions to be made. 1st, For the increase of half 1851, as the grant was not abolished until the middle of that year—a reduction of 1,419. 2nd, As the "Analysis" published by the Government caused a reduction of the estimated numbers of 1851, 1852, 1853, 1854, and up to the end of March, 1855, to the extent of 10,436, it is believed that a similar analysis would have a similar effect upon the two years and a quarter following, that is, from March, 1855, to June, 1857.—say a reduction of 5,000. The two abatements would bring down the numbers to the 102,152 of the text.

† These numbers include 25,424 Chinese and 1,768 Aborigines.

colonies—some day it will be too big for us perhaps,—all the better if it is so:—but while it is little we will help it, encouraging and commending when we honestly can, but sometimes doing what may be rather more unpleasant.

English books of interest to us we shall notice, without professing to furnish an exhaustive catalogue, but we shall always consider that colonial publications have the preference. This has caused us to omit several notices which we had intended to insert, of various English books, which may perhaps find a place in our next.

RELIGIOUS CONTEMPORARY PERIODICALS.—A few colonial Magazines, having a similar object in view to ours, have reached us.

The Australian Messsenger; edited by the Rev. JAMES BALLANTYNE. Melbourne: Mason and Firth.

This is a monthly magazine of sixteen pages, and charged sixpence. It has reached the tenth number of the second volume. It is undenominational in its spirit. It consists of short original pieces, extracts, anecdotes, hints, religious intelligence, and other miscellaneous matter, all deeply imbued with the spirit of earnest piety. Its cheapness, its easy reading, its catholic spirit, its useful tendency, give it strong claims on the support of all classes of Christians. It is well adapted for gratuitous distribution as a tract by wealthy persons who can purchase a quantity.

The South Australian Union Magazine for Teachers. Adelaide: E. S. Wigg.

This is published quarterly, price sixpence, was commenced in January last, and has reached its third number. As its title impor's, it belongs to no sect. but to the whole Evangelical Church; and is designed chiefly to encourage and assist Sunday School teachers in their benevolent labors. It consists of addresses to teachers on their responsibilities and duties, specimen addresses to scholars, lives and obituaries, chiefly of such as have been connected with Sunday Schools, reviews of books adapted for young people's libraries and for affording assistance in teaching, Sunday School intelligence, and other matter bearing on the great work of the religious education of the young. It is a very respectable production, containing judicious and useful matter, well adapted to its object; and is got up in a manner creditable both to editor and publisher.

The Wesleyan Chronicle and Victorian Miscellany; a Monthly Periodical of Religious Literature and Intelligence. Melbourne: Shaw, Harnett and Co. Price 6d.

This magazine is meant chiefly for the Wesleyan body, to diffuse among its members intelligence of each other's proceedings, and to stir them up to increased zeal in the cause of God; and for these objects it is well adapted. Though strongly denominational, it contains much that all Christians may read with profit.

The Church of England Record for the Diocese of Melbourne. Published monthly, at 6d. Geelong: Heath and Cordell. Melbourne: J. J. Blundell and Co.

This, like the *Wesleyan Chronicle,* is an avowedly denominational magazine. and is largely occupied with the proceedings of the Episcopal Church of Victoria, and of that church exclusively. It is well adapted to its object. It contains, besides a number of short pieces, chiefly extracts of a religious and useful tendency.

G

Australia, Tasmania, and New Zealand.   By AN ENGLISHMAN.   Fifth
thousand.   London: Saunders and Otley.   Melbourne: G. Robertson, Collins-street.

It is one of the annoyances to which a free press, conflicting interests in
Britain and here, and a natural inquisitiveness and desire for eccentricity on
the part of observers, will subject us, in this young land of ours, to have all
sorts of tales told of us to the people in the old country.   One publisher
sends forth a book which paints us white; another, at the other end of
London, gets up a chaste-looking, well printed volume, which deals largely
in Indian ink and deep shades; and our friends on the other side of the
globe are expected to take it all in.   And so they do, judging from those
words, "fifth thousand," which appear on the title-page to this book.   It is,
however, all innocent child's play, for when they come here, they find us
neither black nor white (like the two disputants in the fable about the
colors of a certain chameleon), but a harmonious mixture of all the shades
which can form the promising picture of a young artist.   This book is
certainly a curiosity.   It comes to us with such an array of figures, of course
"well authenticated;" tables of imports, exports, duties, &c; speeches from
Governors; all most reliable and undisputed sources of information.   But
in spite of all this scaffolding, the building is made of rotten stone, and it is
only because the shower of rain, in the shape of a little better information,
has not yet fallen, that 5,000 of this book can have got abroad in England.
As an instance of our author's capability of putting broken spectacles on
when he wants to see a thing awry, observe what he says of the handsome
capital of Victoria   We collect a few out of many phrases:—" The site
of the town, had it been for a moment anticipated by the founders, at
the time of selection, that it would ultimately become the seat of government, and a great commercial city, is ill chosen.   It lies low, and without
any of the natural advantages possessed by places not far distant."   Our
author, of course, is ignorant of the fact of Williamstown, situated so
beautifully, according to theory and maps, at the mouth of the river, being
called after the king; whereas Melbourne, as a second-rate place (according to
bookwriters), was called after the prime minister; but circumstances have
outrun theory; Melbourne has eclipsed the King's town.   Here again—
"Most of the streets of Melbourne are narrow" (!!!)   Once more—
not only is it deplorably sunk in the swamps of the Yarra, with
narrow streets, but our "beautiful climate" (and here the censure extends
as far as Sydney and Adelaide) "is a fiction, and considered altogether,
having ourselves experienced the alternate seasons in each locality, we pronounce Australia, for reasons we shall assign, not only to be not the finest
climate in the world, but inferior to any other with which we are personally
acquainted."   To conclude, we would say to our readers in this part of the
world, they may enjoy looking at their portraits, as this "Englishman" has
drawn them, only they must remember it is a reversed photograph: they must,
in imagination, twist everything round.   And to our readers in England we
would hint that this Englishman seems to have come upon this splendid
young boy nation of ours and seen it, when it had the measles.   No doubt it
looked deplorable enough; but this shortsighted individual imagines,
evidently, that if a child has the measles one day, that therefore it must
have them all the days of its life.   Our friends in New Zealand (in spite of
the buzzing of the political "blue-bottles" of which our author complains),
may thank the writer of this work, for the book is evidently written in their
interest.

*" Durable Riches;" or, a Voice from the Golden Land; being Memorials
of the late* SARAH SUSANNAH PERRY, *of Melbourne, Australia:*
consisting of her Poems, Diary, and selections from her Correspondence, with a Biographical Notice.   Melbourne: Robertson and
Baker.

This work is a collection of memorials of the late Mrs. Sarah Susannah

Perry, of Melbourne, consisting of a short biography, and selections from her poems, diary and letters, which are all united under the title of "Durable Riches." We can well understand, on reading this book, the intense pleasure it must give to those who were personally acquainted with the subject of the memoir, and lived under the influence of her tender heart, to have these reliques of her, now that she is gone. And those who have only the means of knowing her through this book, may thank the warm attachment of her friends for having rescued these remains from oblivion. We cannot say the verses exhibit the highest style of poetry : they are deficient both in fancy and in imagination, in that high and extended meaning which Wordsworth has stamped upon the word ; but they have two of the elements of genuine poetry very prominent—music of versification and deep feeling. Some of the verses are exquisitely melodious : others, by a little more care, might have been made so ; but it is for their pure, unclouded brightness of feeling that we value the book,—the unrestrained emotion which seeks not the how and the wherefore of its existence, but, like a child, delights in the mere consciousness of being. This we especially value in the " Diary," as it saves us from a great deal which often disfigures religious biographies, a self-dissection which is both partial and incomplete. This is a stream from the heart, and therefore is genuine. The mind of the author seems to us like a fountain playing on a sunny day, when a gentle breeze is blowing : as the falling water waves in the wind, innumerable changing effects are produced, but they are all composed of fragments of rainbows floating in the spray. And on the earth here, we need such brilliant fountains to call off our thoughts to that world whence comes the light which causes this heavenly sparkling.

Memorials of WILLIAM JONES, *of the Religious Tract Society ;* compiled from his private papers and other authentic documents. By his ELDEST SON. Melbourne : G. Robertson.

This is a book of small pretension, but, we are happy to add, of considerable interest It is pleasant to obtain an insight into the character of any man whose influence over the world has been great. But, William Jones —does he deserve to be spoken of in this way ? Yes, if the Religious Tract Society can be said to have had any influence on the age we live in. He lived and worked for that Society : he travelled, wrote, spoke, preached on its behalf ; he was untiring in its service ; he made the Society what it is ; in fact, we may almost say he was the Society. With those who have no faith in the workings of religion in its purer and more active forms of benevolence, this volume will have nothing in common. But those who like to trace the underground operations of some of the great religious movements of this age will find considerable pleasure and profit in reading these pages. It is a simple unadorned narrative of Mr. Jones's labors, interspersed with several quaint anecdotes of his personal experience in dealing with the many phases of character he met with. The book is like the man,—unostentatious, yet earnest : humorous, yet Christian ; displaying no deep philosophisings, but the straightforwardness of an active, affectionate ingenuous mind.

Bible Stories for Young Australians. By JAMES BONWICK. Part I. Melbourne : J. J. Blundell and Co. 1857.

The Spirit of the True Teacher ; being a Lecture delivered before the Geelong Teachers' Association, on March 28, 1857, by JAMES BONWICK. Melbourne : J. J. Blundell and Co.

If all men who have the ability to write were possessed of Mr. Bonwick's impetuosity and earnestness, we should not long be left to complain of having no literature of our own. We should have it good and bad : whether it would pay or not : attract or repel readers. The cover of one of these pamphlets contains advertisements of no fewer than twelve works, of some size or other, by our author. Of the two, however, which stand at the head of this para-

graph, we have to say one word, and are happy to say that that word is
commendation. The first, the "Bible Stories," is intended to be a series of
forcible, vivid pictures of the scenes of Bible history, and are evidently told
by a mind which delights alike in the eternal freshness of these tales of
glorious heroism, and in making others love them too : but we cannot but
think that the end would have been answered better. if the same space had
been given to fewer subjects, and more care taken in the individual pictures :
for some of them bear the marks of too much hurry to be printed, whilst
others, in the strong Austral coloring given them, are excellent. The book
is fitted to be, and we think will be, a favorite with all Sunday School
teachers and scholars. In the second of the two books, we cannot but admire
the ardour and earnestness of the author in his great work. for great it is.
It is a word from an earnest Christian man, who wishes for the prosperity
of our nation, and sees that prosperity as mainly destined to arise from right-
minded education : and is addressed to those engaged in the same work with
himself. This earnestness it i which makes us not disposed to particularise
two or three hasty historical generalisations which occur as blemishes in it.
Mr. Bonwick is a downright Australian, and his work is full of healthy
Christian feeling. "Twenty years' experience in the school-room," he says,
"has not, I trust. cooled my ardor, though it may have checked some
sanguine expectations. I would picture no Utopia, for I believe in fallen
humanity. But only let the friends of education bestir themselves, and
provide such a body of earnest teachers as to purify our hearths and gladden
our homes, and the moral waste of Australia shall bloom with Eden-beauty."

The Month. Sydney : Cox and Co.

We have just received the third number of "The Month," a dashing-spirited
periodical, which we are happy to find is making its way, and taking a good
position. We have not space to analyse its contents. and such indeed,
judging from the first article, would be decidedly distasteful to our courageous
contemporary, who seems to have an especial dislike to small "pats on the
back" in the form of "faint praise." So we will say nothing, but just wish
our companion in the race for public favour, all success. We are almost of
equal ages. both equally ambitious, though in somewhat different lines ; and
may we both live till we expire by a voluntary death, in the belief that the
time shall then have come when some nobler offspring will arise out of
our ashes.

Two Years Ago. By the REV. CHAS. KINGSLEY, F.S.A., F.L.S. &c.,
Author of "Westward Ho!" &c. In 3 volumes. Cambridge :
Macmillan & Co. Melbourne : Robertson.

It is surprising how little in this country seems to be known of this
"Clergyman who writes Novels," as he has been defined. With a great and
increasing reputation in England, here he seems to be just known only as
an ordinary specimen of those whose business it is to supply the market
with the requisite quantity of romance for the demands of the public
appetite. But in England he has indeed a reputation. When first he came
forth before the public in the wild eccentricities of "*Alton Locke*," all stood
aghast at the daring genius of the young clergyman, who, in the strength of
his convictions, the fiery earnestness of his great soul, dared to ally himself
even with chartists and "sweating tailors." But the glow of a nature whose
genius was of no common stamp, whose earnestness was not of a day but of
a life-time, was manifest amidst all the brilliant mistakes of that his first
fiction ; and the world recognised even then a teacher, to catch whose spirit
was to learn much and who since then has taught us many things. It has
become now a sort of fashion to admire Kingsley, at least in England, and
when a new work of his is out, even drapers' apprentices may be seen carrying
it home from some circulating library, and eagerly devouring its contents
in the streets or on the roof of an omnibus. A fashion, say we, to read
Kingsley. Well, so much the better, for he must be a dull dotard indeed

who does not feel a better man after reading one of our author's glowing pictures of heroic virtue and Christian self-denial; and so much the better for us here if we too appreciate one whose spirit has so much in common with the life and energy of our country, and yet so Christian. We have not space to say much about this particular work of our author which stands at the head of this notice ; it is a story of English life two years ago, when the war-fever was at its height, and notwithstanding its lack for the most part of the pomp of circumstance in its scenes and incidents, it is yet one of the most fascinating of stories. The mere love of writing a fiction which shall be a work of art and nothing more, is far from being the motive which actuates Mr. Kingsley in this or any other of his works. He has an ideal *Christian* character or principle which he ever seeks to develope, and he chooses the form of fiction as that in which he thinks it to be most graphically and attractively exhibited. This Christian character is not in his mind a pattern to which all must be conformed so that all godly men become alike ; but it is a principle which must enter into and suffuse the most diverse dispositions—elevating, not supplanting, what is within. To shew this was one chief purpose in writing " *Westward Ho !*" and the same is seen in " *Two Years Ago;*" and, in our opinion, in this latter work he has succeeded in this better than in the other. To his exact idea of the Christian character we may perhaps take exception, but rather as a falling short of our estimate of what the man of God should be than as being in itself wrong.

The work is written with more than Mr. Kingley's usual power of description,—the pictures of scenery, which in many books are their most unbearable parts, give to all our Author's productions a brilliant charm,—no one who has read the vivid painting (for painting it is) of the American tropic forests, in " Wesward Ho," or the night ascent of Glyder Vawr, in Wales, in this work, can ever forget them. We do not say that this work is devoid of faults,—it has in our opinion many, especially viewed as an artistic *whole*.— The plot is awkwardly arranged. But for those who love nature, and feel any sympathy with those who are filled with the same love,—for those who admire the clever delineation of character, and the working of the noblest principles in the development of true manliness and heroism,—for those who desire to see fiction brought into the service of the well-wishers of humanity, there will be a rich satisfaction in this book. To those too who are troubled with any morbid notions about the world and providence, or whose actions consist more of sentiment than self-denying piety, this book will be a healthy medicine. To all we would say, if you read it, which do, do not forget to *think over it.*

Illustrated Journal of Australasia. Melbourne : G. SLATER.
We have received the monthly issues of this excellent Magazine, but must reserve a review till our next.

Australian Cricketer's Guide for 1856-7 ; edited by H. BIERS and W. FAIRFAX. Melbourne : Fairfax & Co.

This manual, the result manifestly of a vast amount of care and labour, must delight the heart of every true lover of the English game of Cricket. He has here every information he can possibly want on the subject of his favorite recreation. All young persons who take pleasure in this healthful exercise would do well to possess themselves of this Guide.

Reginald Mortimer ; or, Truth more Strange than Fiction. A Tale of a Soldier's Life and Adventure. Nos. I. to III. By H. BUTLER. STONEY, Captain 40th Regiment. Melbourne : W. Fairfax & Co.
We are ready to give a hearty welcome to any work that is Australian,— whatever it be, we must take what we can get, and put aside our tendency to be over fastidious, till our young country has got to an age when, having left school, it can appreciate books for learning sake. Otherwise, on receiving such a book as this for notice, we might enlarge upon its inflated style—the

alarming redundancy of its adjectives and adverbs, and especially its untruthfulness (for a fiction is often truer to all principles of character and scenery than a poorly sketched authentic narrative) This, however, we will not do, for in spite of all, the book is very interesting, and the heroism of character it displays in times of war, it would be well if we saw a little more of in men who imagine themselves heroes in this time of peace.

The Southern Phonographic Harmonia; edited by a Lady,—written in the Initiatory Corresponding and Reporting style. Melbourne: G. Slater.

This is a singular little periodical, which has now appeared every month since the beginning of the year, and has therefore reached its ninth number. It looks of course to the uninitiated as uninviting as a book of hieroglyphics. But it augurs well for the cause of Phonography, or rather Phonographic Shorthand, that any one should be found to take the trouble to prepare and publish a work of this kind in this hemisphere, and it unmistakeably indicates the extent to which the art must be diffused, when readers sufficient are found, as we presume there must be, to keep the publication alive. Though we have studied Pitman's system sufficiently to be convinced of its immeasurable superiority over all other systems of shorthand, yet having been long accustomed to another, we do not profess sufficient proficiency in the new system to pronounce a judgment upon the literary matter of the work ; but its object we heartily approve, and recommend all young people to acquire so valuable an art, especially when it is now set before them based upon principles not arbitrary, like all former attempts, but such as are soundly philosophical.

LIBRARY OF OLD AUTHORS.—The present age is distinguished for the re-production of old and almost forgotten authors, in every department of literature. The Library of Old Authors furnishes a list in poetry, the drama, history, and theology—re-edited and with notes, printed in the old style, both as to typography and paper, to which the high price alone forms an objection. THE CONFESSIO AMANTIS of GOWER pertains to this class, but it is reproduced in such a style of art as to place it beyond the reach of all but the curious in literature. Macaulay's frequent reference to LUTTERALL'S DIARY, in his 3rd and 4th vols. of the History of England, has led to the publication of the work complete, which is brought out in 6 vols. The discovery of some old edition of portions of Shakspeare's works, and of other authors of that period, by Professor Mommsen, in Switzerland, and other parts of the Continent, has resulted in the re-publishing of the tale, founded on the DRAMA OF PERICLES, Prince of Tyre, in fac-simile. It is hoped that the present discovery will induce a further search among the old libraries of the continent, especially in the Low Countries, which had a very close connexion with England in those times. Another of these antique books, is

THE LIFE OF DR. JOHN TAULER, and a selection of his sermons, for which we are indebted to Susannah Winkworth. This lady possesses a power of rendering the German into English so as to command the admiration of Germans themselves. Her perception of the finer shades of meaning that would elude an ordinary and even competent German scholar, enables her not merely to convey the suitable word, but the very spirit of the writer. Her translations of the " Theologia Germania, " and of " Bunsen's Signs of the Times," have elicited in our hearing, expressions of high admiration from a German minister of our acquaintance. She has been equally successful in the present instance. Dr Tauler belongs to the school of mystics. With him and his contemporaries, however, dates a new and profounder view of mysticism as a religious and philosophical system. Previous to the 14th century, the conception which was formed of divine influence was that of a transmission from God, as the centre of light and life divine, through widening circles of beings, from the Cherubim around His Throne, down to man as the remotest of the boundaries. The effect believed to be produced. was to raise and advance man from the outer to the inner circle, till he approximated the seraphic state. The views of Tauler and his fellow mystics differed from the former, in this respect, that they believed God was the object of immediate realization by the soul, and, was to be manifested from *within*, and not externally. This theory declares God to be everywhere present with all his power; heaven or hell to be realized in the present moment; denies that God is nearer on the other side the grave than this; equalizes all external states, breaks down all steps, all partitions between man and the Deity; will have him escape from all that is not God, and so know and find God everywhere. The effusions of Madame Guyon, as translated by our Cowper, embody such thoughts as these. The means of effecting these states or realizations differed according to the system. The first class considered themselves to become subject to possession by a divine AFFLATUS, and to be carried off their rational centre by inspirations of the Spirit, producing bodily commotions, extacy, trembling, and similar effects, like the Quakers of a former day and even of the present. The latter expect no such AFFLATUS, regard THE WORD as all of inspired truth' necessary, and by withdrawing the soul within itself, there in contemplation and prayer to realize God. The necessary effect of this doctrine is to withdraw the mind from the contemplation of the Cross of Christ, as presented in the evangelical point of view. The expiatory nature of the Atonement is not denied, but is not asserted. The example of our Lord is chiefly held up. There is abundance of divine communication supposed, but no medium through which it comes to the soul; an outflowing of grace, but no fountain visible or rightly acknowledged as existing. The soul is turned into itself to contemplate God there, and not directed to "behold the Lamb of God that taketh away the sin of the world."

As next in order with the above work, we may advert to THE LIFE OF HENRY CORNELIUS AGRIPPA VON NETTESHEIM, Doctor and Knight, commonly known as a Magician. By H. Morley. The work introduces us to a period nearly a century later than the times of Tauler, and to a man his superior in learning, if immeasurably behind him in piety. Agrippa was accounted a conjuror in his own age; and the object of this biography is to vindicate his character. It sets forth a life of storms and sorrows, of suffering and persecution. Born three years before Luther, Agrippa, at the age of 23, appears as a lecturer on Cabalistic philosophy, the rage of the day; and shortly after, as a perfect literary knight errant—in support of the superiority of the female sex. His next great work was in three books on magic; and at a later period, was produced the work on the vanity of the sciences, a savage attack on the learning of the age, and a vindication of the word of God. His life closed in clouds, as it had passed amidst storms. Mr. Morley lovingly combats the charge of charlatan and magician which the Monks attempted to affix as a stigma on him, and to hold him forth as a philosopher, who, like all such, are necessarily at issue with the age, because before it.

FALSE WORSHIP. By the Rev. S. R. Maitland.—This very curious work deserves notice in connexion with the preceding, as it has to do with Magic and Magicians The extraordinary phenomena of phreno-mesmerism, electro-biology, spirit-rapping, and table-turning, in all which manifestations Mr. Maitland reposes unquestioning faith, has led him into a new research on the origin of idolatry, and the rites connected with false worship. The book is full of suggestions, and leads to new regions of thought, as from the numerous facts adduced, it seems impossible to explain the phenomena, with anything like satisfaction, by a reference to known and established physical laws.

THE COMMUNION OF LABOUR. By Mrs. Jamieson.—The rights of woman is Mrs. Jamieson's object of advocacy; and in connexion with this, there is a list of works bearing on the general subject, which would separately deserve notice, such as EASTERN HOSPITALS AND ENGLISH NURSES, BY A LADY VOLUNTEER. REPORT OF THE PERSONAL LAWS COMMITTEE ON THE LAWS RELATING TO THE PROPERTY OF MARRIED WOMEN. The object of the works above referred to is to assert woman's right to property, and a training which will qualify her to understand, use and maintain such right ; that she also shall be so educated as to fit her for departments of labour and enterprise from which, by existing laws and social prejudices, she is debarred. The question is a grave one, and is not to be "poo-pooed" on the one hand, nor on the other to be hastily dealt with. There must be a reform in regard to existing usage: and such ladies as Mrs. Jamieson, and Miss Nightingale, with her sister heroines, are the persons to lead on to it.

AURORA LEIGH. By Mrs. Browning.—Aurora Leigh is a beautiful poem, whose text is the Rights of Woman. We had not read further than about the sixth line before we felt that it was poetry of the true stamp.   The work is an autobiography, but the principal social difficulties of the age are portrayed in the characters and incidents that mingle in Aurora's life.   The poem is full of life and characters, beyond the main line of the story ; episodes replete with beautiful and also bitter meaning ; female character approaching angelic beauty : and its opposite, aristocratic beauty, and grace concealing the hard and terrible selfishness of a nature incapable of a kindly feeling or generous sentiment.   We can heartily commend Aurora Leigh to the study of all who can appreciate poetry ;   read her again, and yet again.

PROFESSOR WILSON'S THIRD VOLUME OF ESSAYS.—Of this, more than one half is dedicated to the genius and character of Burns.   The Professor eulogizes his brother poet with intense and fervid eloquence.   We are to expect the strong feeling of nationality to be abundantly visible throughout his review of Burns, and that Scotland and the Scotch are duly (or rather unduly) glorified, but, this apart, Christopher's essay is a delightful and truthful tribute to the memory of Scotlands' greatest poet.

RELIGIOUS INTELLIGENCE.

New South Wales.

GENERAL OBJECTS.—YOUNG MEN'S CHRISTIAN ASSOCIATION.—The fourth annual meeting of the Young Men's Christian Association was held on Monday evening, August 31st, at the School of Arts. The chair was filled by John Fairfax, Esq., the President of the Association.   A report was read and adopted, showing the great amount of good which had been effected by this institution in its various operations— lectures, debates, classes, and above all, Christian instruction.   The meeting was addressed by many speakers, clerical and lay, and various resolutions were passed, declaratory of the advantages which the Association had secured to its members, and of the expediency of extending these advantages as widely as possible among the young men of the colony.

NEW CITY MISSION CHAPEL, SYDNEY.—Sermons in connection with the opening of this place of worship were preached on July 26th, and August 2nd, by the Revds. B. Quaife, W. Cuthbertson, J. Beasley, and S. C. Kent.   The chapel is situated at the south-western corner of Liverpool and Sussex streets, a neighbourhood where such a place was much needed. The building owes its origin to the friends of Mr. Pidgeon, the City Missionary, whose "Life and Experience" has lately been given to the public through the press.   This indefatigable man, as an out-door preacher, and a visitor from house to house amongst the lowest and most degraded of the population, has succeeded in doing an amount of good that is most encouraging to others who are disposed to work in a similar manner.   The chapel, which seats about 300 people, is built of wood, and is of a most inexpensive character.

BURWOOD CHRISTIAN INSTRUCTION SOCIETY.—On Tuesday evening, August 11th, a public Tea Meeting was held in a large tent, for the purpose of arranging for the erection of a place of worship, of an undenominational character, to be placed in trust for the use of all Evangelical Protestant Christians. Upwards of two hundred persons partook of tea together, after which the Rev. L. E. Threlkeld was voted into the chair, and addresses were delivered by Mr. Alderton, and the Revs. Messrs. Voller, Beazley, Boag, Cuthbertson, Kent, and Slayter. Mr. M. M. Cohen has kindly given a most eligible site for the building; upwards of £100 was raised previous to the meeting, and £40 16s. was collected after the effective appeals made by the speakers. Through the kindness of the railway directors, a special train was laid on for the accommodation of visitors from Sydney.

SABBATH OBSERVANCE.—On the same evening the first annual meeting of the New South Wales Society for Promoting the Observance of the Lord's Day, was held in the Castlereagh-street school-room, Sydney. The Bishop of Sydney, President of the Society, in the chair. The report was read and adopted. The meeting was addressed at considerable length by the President, and also by the Revds. R. L. King, W. M. Cowper, A. H. Stephen, J. Millard, and others; and various resolutions were adopted in furtherance of the objects of the society.

CONGREGATIONALISTS.—NEW CONGREGATIONAL CHURCH, WOLLONGONG. —On Thursday, August 6th, the above place was opened for public worship. In the morning the Rev. W. Cuthbertson, B.A., preached to a large and attentive congregation. The devotional services were conducted by the Rev. G. Charter (the resident minister), J. Beazley, and S. C. Kent. The collection amounted to £131 5s. In the afternoon a public tea was provided, after which a public meeting was held. A. Foss, Esq. presided. Mr. G. Waring read an interesting report, shewing the origin of this place of worship, and the steps which had been taken for its erection. The Hon. H. Gilbert Smith, Esq., M.L.C., had kindly presented the site; and the Sydney Building Committee had subscribed £300. The amount of money subscribed previous to the day of opening, was £1,028 14s. 8d. The entire cost was £1,459 17s. 10d., so that a sum of £431 3s. 2d. was required to liquidate the remainder. Addresses were delivered by the Revds. Messrs. Charter, Beazley, Cuthbertson, and Kent, after which an appeal was made, and the sum of £145 6s. 3d. was collected; besides which, several gentlemen entered into engagements to collect £189. The following is a brief description of the building:—The building is 54 feet by 30 feet, capable of seating 200 persons, and is fitted with cedar throughout. The roof is open, and the windows are Gothic. The seats are without doors, and the pulpit is very chaste and tasteful. The church is entered by an ornamental portico, approached by a flight of stone steps, and the ground on which it is erected is enclosed by a neat paling. The children connected with the Sabbath-school, to the number of ninety-two, assembled on the following day, to commemorate with their pastor, teachers, and friends, the opening of the new church. After their luncheon, they spent the afternoon most pleasantly in cricket and other games, and then partook of tea together, and were addressed by the Revds. S. C. Kent and G. Charter. On the following Sunday, two sermons were preached by the Rev. S. C. Kent, after which collections were made, and the small balance of the debt entirely cleared off. The architect, Mr. Waring, in addition to a handsome donation, gave his services and superintendence gratuitously.

PRESBYTERIAN.—PADDINGTON PRESBYTERIAN CHURCH.—A soiree was held on the evening of Setpember 3rd in the Scotch Church School-room, Paddington, in aid of the completion of the new Presbyterian Church, now in course of erection, and notwithstanding the threatening aspect of the weather the room was crowded to excess. After tea, the very Rev. James Mylne, Moderator of the Synod, took the chair, and after stating the object of the meeting moved the first resolution, namely, "That this meeting rejoices that a permanent church for the use of this district is being erected." Seconded by the Rev. James Coutts, of Parramatta, and carried unanimously. The Rev. R. Beag moved the second resolution, which was, "That this meeting use its utmost efforts to complete the building now begun." Seconded by the Rev. Dr. Fullerton, and carried unanimously. The Rev. Mr. Threlkeld urged the necessity of combined exertion to carry on the work of completing the church. A collection was made, and the Rev. Mr. Mylne having pronounced the benediction, the meeting separated.

AFFILIATED COLLEGES IN CONNECTION WITH THE UNIVERSITY.—The Synod of Eastern Australia has determined, after some discussion, to avail itself of the provision, of the Affiliated Colleges Act, by co-operating, on certain terms, with other Presbyterian bodies for the establishment of a Presbyterian College in connexion with the University of Sydney. The resolutions adopted for this purpose were carried by majority, and some grounds of dissent rem ain still to be recorded. A committee has however, been appointed to carry the decision of the majority into effect.

WESLEYANS.—WESLEYAN COLLEGE.—The amount promised towards this undertaking is now about £11,000.

EPISCOPAL CHURCH.—By the First Annual Report of the Diocese of Sydney, we learn that the licensed clergy of that Church numbered in 1855, 48 ; and at present they amounted to 70, increase 20. Besides the cathedral in Sydney, there are 38 projects for church building in various stages of advancement, involving a total expenditure of £40,000.

Tasmania.

EVANGELICAL UNION.—This Union was established in Hobart Town several years since, and holds a monthly prayer-meeting in such places of worship as may be available for the purpose. During the present year, meetings have been held, and addresses delivered by various ministers on appointed topics, as follows :—Wesleyan Chapel—"The Youth required by the present age," by the Rev. G. Clarke. Brisbane-street Chapel (Independent)—" The History and Present Prospects of the Protestant Churches in France," by the Rev. W. Day. St. John's Church (Presbyterian)—" True Peace in Death," by the Rev. F. Miller. Wesleyan Chapel—" The Christian's duty to to Unconverted Relatives," by the Rev. J. Downes. Brisbane-street Chapel—" The Profitable Hearing of the Word," by the Rev. B. McClean. St. John's Church—" A Holy Sabbath—a Happy Sabbath," by the Rev. H. Dowling. Baptist Chapel—" The Earnest and Progressive Church," by the Rev. S. Waterhouse. Congregational Chapel, Davey-street—" The Encouragements of the Discouraged," by the Rev. C. Simson.

CONGREGATIONALISTS.—HOBART TOWN.—The New Congregational Church in Davey-street, Hobart Town, was opened for public worship on Sunday the 16th of August, little more than twelve months after the foundation-stone was laid by Henry Hopkins, Esq. The Church has been erected by the congregation of Collins-street Chapel, under the pastoral charge of the Rev. George Clarke, at a cost, including the purchase of site, building, accessories, and architect's fees, of about £7,000. Of this large sum, there remained at the opening services only £600 to be provided for, towards which £350 were contributed in the course of the day. Further subscriptions have since been received, reducing the whole debt to a trifle over £200. The Rev. F. Miller, the pastor of Brisbane-street Chapel, and the oldest minister of the Independent body in the Australian colonies, preached in the morning from Psalm xlviii. 9, and availed himself of the opportunity to express his cordial sympathy with the minister of the new Church, whom he had known for many years, and whom he affectionately commended in his prayer to the grace of God. The Rev. W. Nicolson, of the Scottish Free Church, preached in the afternoon from Exod. xl. 33, 34. The reverend gentleman explained the spiritual use of a place of worship, and showed in a most impressive manner that the glory of God was manifested by active exertions in the cause of Christ, and by the holy lives of His disciples. The Rev. George Clarke conducted the evening service, and preached from Mark xvi. 15. The church was well filled at each of the services. The congregation have been about four years in making preparation for the work. They had previously occupied the chapel in Collins-street, which was built by Henry Hopkins, Esq., of Hobart Town, and generously given up to their use for many years. The limited accommodation, however, of the old chapel, and other considerations, rendered it advisable to build another and a larger place of worship. It may with propriety be remarked, that although members of other denominations have contributed most liberally to this enterprise, nearly nineteen-twentieths of the whole cost have been provided by the congregation itself. With his well-known liberality, Mr. Hopkins (on whose 70th birthday the church was opened) subscribed a large sum towards the building, and his example was promptly and cheerfully followed by the congregation. We understand that they contemplate building school-rooms behind the church, as soon as possible, and heartily wish them success in completing their noble enterprise.

As church building will occupy a good portion of the attention of the religious public for a long time, and as it is desirable to encourage the erection of tructures at once commodious and tasteful, we append an architectural description of this Church, which is deemed by good judges a model of its kind. The architectural design was furnished by Messrs. Tiffin and Davidson, and the contract for building was taken up by Mr. James Pretty. The church is in the early English style of the time of King John. It has a façade of a tower and Broach spire 96 feet high in the clear, with an entrance by one deeply recessed door way. This opens into a porch, whence springs a staircase turning right and left, which gives access to the galleries, while entrance to the body of the building is obtained by side doors also leading out of the porch. The church consists of a nave, two aisles, a chancel, and a vestry. Galleries run round three sides of the building. The roof is open timbered, consisting of hard native wood, boarded and slated, and supported by nave piers formed of eight alternated clustered and octagonal columns. The exterior is relieved by projecting buttresses. The chancel is lighted up by a three-light pointed window, bordered with stained glass. The side lights are plain pointed, with splayed jambs. The pulpit, of handsomely carved cedar, is placed at the junction of the nave and chancel; and instead of pews, open cedar benches lined down to the seats have been adopted. Altogether it is the purest and most beautiful specimen of ecclesiastical architecture in the colony, and an ornament to the city. Its interior construction is well suited to the voice. There is at present accommodation for more than 700 worshippers, and provision could easily be made for 800.

LAUNCESTON.—St. John's Square Congregational Church.—On Monday August 10th, a meeting was held in St. John's Square Chapel, to adopt measures for the enlargement of the building, so as to secure about 100 additional sittings. Above £220 were contributed on the spot, and the amount has since been increased to about £600; and a Committee was appointed to superintend the work. In this chapel, the Rev . J. West for some years exercised his ministry, but on his removal to his important post in Sydney, he was succeeded by the Rev. Wm. Law, formerly of the Samoan Mission.

A neat little chapel was recently opened at Prospect Village, in connection with the congregation of St. John's Square, Launceston. The cost of erection was chiefly defrayed by the friends for whose use it is designed. A Sabbath school has been opened with an encouraging attendance.

The Rev. Walter Mathieson, formerly of Westmoreland, recently of Market Drayton, county Salop, has arrived in Launceston, with the intention of occupying the Mersey and Don district, in connection with the northern branch of the Tasmanian Colonial Missionary Society.

Tamar Street Independent Chapel.—On Wednesday, September 3rd, a social Tea Meeting was held in the school-room of Tamar-street Chapel, Launceston, to commemorate the completion of a quarter of a century's ministerial labor in Australia by the Rev. Charles Price. On this occasion, the Church and congregation presented to him the complete works of the present Archbishop of Canterbury, and Owen on the Hebrews. The "old scholars" presented Poole's Annotations. Mr. Price duly acknowledged the kindness of his friends. Mr. Price's only son is now studying with a view to the Christian Ministry.

A vigorous agitation has commenced in Tasmania, to obtain the abolition of State Aid to ecclesiastical bodies. The subject is awakening considerable interest and attention.

Victoria.

GENERAL SOCIETIES.— Evangelical Alliance.—The first Quarterly Meeting of the Evangelical Alliance of Victoria, was held in the Protestant Hall, Melbourne, on the evening of Tuesday, the 7th July, at half-past 6 o'clock. The Hon. Judge Pohlman, the President of the Alliance, occupied the chair. The Bishop of Melbourne delivered an interesting and able address on Christian Union, and the mode of its manifestation and promotion. . The Rev. Dr. Cairns, and the Rev. R. Fletcher, followed in addresses upon the same subject. The devotional exercises of the evening were conducted by the Revds. Messrs. Fletcher and Harding, and the Hymns were read by J. T. Hoskins, Esq. The next quarterly meeting of the Alliance will take place on the first Tuesday of October, when an address will be delivered by Dr. Cairns on the subject of "the Sabbath." The Members of the Alliance meet once a month, for breakfast, and social and religious fellowship; when breakfast is over the engagements commence by the offering of prayer; a portion of scripture is then read, and a few observations are made upon it partaking of the nature of an exposition. This service, for the last two months, has been conducted by the Rev. R. Fletcher, and the Rev. D. J. Draper. After this introductory address, free remarks from any of the gentlemen present follow; and the whole concludes precisely at ten o'clock, to allow gentlemen to proceed to their several avocations. From twenty to twenty-five gentlemen of nearly all the Evangelical denominations, have thus met in harmonious brotherhood.

BIBLE SOCIETY, BENDIGO.—The first annual meeting of the Bendigo branch of the British and Foreign Bible Society, was held, August 4th, at the Wesleyan School-house, Sandhurst, and was numerously attended. The President, W. Bannerman, Esq. Manager of the Bank of New South Wales, occupied the chair, apparently to the great satisfaction of the meeting. The report was read by the Rev. J. Nish. It stated that a general depot for the Society had been established at Mr. Wheeler's, View-place, and branch depots at the White Hills, and other places. It appears that two colporteurs are about to be employed to carry the scriptures to every tent throughout the district. More progress would have been made had there been a larger stock of Bibles in hand. The Treasurer's report was read by Mr Valentine. The adoption of the report was moved by the Rev. Mr. Butler, and seconded by the Rev. W. Henderson, of Williamstown, and was supported by J. T. Hoskins, Esq., Secretary to the Victoria Bible Society, in an interesting, instructive, and happily delivered speech. The committee for the ensuing year was proposed by the Rev. J. D. Brennan, seconded by Mr Jones. After the usual votes of thanks the meeting concluded with a hymn.

RELIGIOUS TRACT SOCIETY.—The Annual Meeting of the Religious Tract Society of Victoria, was held in the Protestant Hall, Melbourne, on Thursday, the 30th August. The attendance was not so numerous as might have been anticipated. In the absence of the Bishop of Melbourne, Dr. Wilmot was called to the chair. The report was read by Rev. R. B. Dickenson. It showed that 20,000 tracts had been presented by Henry Cooke, Esq., for gratuitous distribution, and that £100 worth of tracts had been bought of the Sydney Tract Society, on liberal terms. Several considerable orders for tracts had been received, and applications were numerous. The Treasurer's Report was read by W. Fairfax, Esq., which shewed that the subscriptions for the year amounted to 216l. 2s.; the donations to 64l. 13s. 4d.; and the sales of books to 52l. 18s.; total 338l. 14s. 1d. The balance in treasurer's hands amounted to 60l. 11s. 6½d. Resolutions were moved and seconded by the Rev. J. Mirams, Rev. J. C. Searle, Rev. W. R. Fletcher, Mr. R. Smith, Rev. J. Ballantyne, and Mr. Fairfax. The meeting closed with singing a doxology.

CHINESE MISSION.—The Annual meeting of the Mission to the Chinese in Victoria, was held in the Protestant Hall, Melbourne, on Tuesday evening, the 4th August. The Hall was densely crowded. His Excellency Sir H. Barkly, K.C.B., the Governor, occupied the chair and delivered the following address, in introducing the business of the evening :—

Ladies and Gentlemen, we are met to-night in support of the Mission which has for two years past been quietly and unobtrusively endeavouring to diffuse the blessings of the Gospel light among the Chinese immigrants into Victoria. A good many meetings have recently been held in the colony in connection with this singular and ingenious race of people, not generally, I am afraid, in the same spirit of Christian charity, or with the same benevolent intention, as that by which we are actuated to-night. I am most unwilling at all times, and especially on an occasion like the present, to trench on debateable ground, but I certainly do feel, in the position I have to-night been asked to take, that a few words may be expected from me on the Chinese Question in general. I am quite aware that the great majority of those persons who have attended the meetings to which I have referred, whilst conscientiously opposed to the continued immigration of the Chinese into this Colony, repudiate as heartily and as entirely as I am sure we all do, the cruel, and I may say, the un-English acts recently perpetrated at one of the remoter gold fields. With regard to the continued influx of the Chinese, I must say that I fully share in the apprehensions on that subject. I think that there are very grave objections to the continued influx into the colony of an inferior race, not recognizing even the moral sanction of the Christian law, unaccompanied by their wives and families, and in almost every instance not intending to make the colony their permanent home. I shall be very glad, therefore, if with the aid of the neighbouring Governments, it should be found possible to make those restrictions (which have hitherto so very much failed) more effectual in preventing the introduction of these people. I shall be glad also if the Legislature, in its wisdom, can devise regulations under which the Chinese already at the gold-fields may be brought to live without any fear of collision with the European miners; and I consider it quite fair and proper, that such portion of special taxation as their foreign habits, and the difference in their type of civilization may require, in order to prevent expense and burden being inflicted on this country, should be levied on them. I am quite prepared to agree that such an amount of taxation should be levied on the Chinese, but I should be sorry for the sake of our boasted English civilization, and for the credit of the people of Victoria, that it should be proposed to go further; and I have no hesitation in saying thus publicly, that, in my own opinion, it would be neither right nor expedient that anything like an attempt should be made to expel the Chinese either from the gold-fields or the colony.   I do not think it would be expedient or politic; for, whatever their faults may be, there is a great deal in the sobriety and industry of the Chinese race that is well worthy of imitation;—and I feel convinced that anything like the sudden withdrawal of some 30,000 or 40,000 industrious laborers and great consumers, would, at any rate for a time, affect very much the general prosperity of the colony.   That it would not be right is equally clear to me. I do not think, however, that I need enlarge on a point like this.   I do not think, that in the gospel of our Lord Jesus Christ, which we are met to disseminate, there is any varying rule of conduct laid down for us with regard to different classes of our fellow-creatures; there are no rules that should regulate our conduct with regard to the Chinese differently from our conduct to the rest of our fellow-men.   We are bound to do them, as far as possible, all the good that lies in our power, and that is the motive which has caused us to assemble to-night.   It falls as a duty on all of us as Christian men to disseminate the truth of the Gospel; but on this head it is not necessary for me to enlarge, in the presence of others before whom I stand.   We ought to regret that it has been in our power to do so little, and rejoice at having so special an opportunity for our exertions as is given to us amongst the Chinese in the Colony.   Next to the enmities and dissensions existing amongst Christians themselves, I know of no greater stumbling-block to the reception of Gospel truth, in an unregenerated mind, or of no subject of greater scoffing to the unbeliever, than the little comparative progress made by Christianity during the 1,800 years which have elapsed since its divine founder ascended into heaven, and commanded his disciples to preach the Gospel unto all nations.   However firmly we may be convinced in our own minds that the words of Divine Revelation will sooner or later be fulfilled, and all the kingdoms of this world become the kingdom of our Lord and of his Christ, it cannot but be a painful reflection to the christian mind that, after all, the doctrine of Christ has made little more advance than that of the false prophet, Mahomet; and that at the present moment the majority of mankind are plunged in the greatest ignorance; nay it is to be doubted whether all the Christian sects in the world can equal in number the 400,000,000 of heathens in the Chinese Empire alone.   It may be said, admitting this,—what effect can we here produce on the general heathen population of the world?   And I answer—Much in every way;   and this the Report about to be read will show; but I will turn to the general question, and consider what effect a movement of this kind may have upon the Chinese Empire itself.   We all know that for many years past a rebellion has been raging in that country against the Tartar dynasty, and we remember that in the earlier stages of that movement, great hopes were entertained by the christian world that it might tend to the extension of the gospel through the Chinese Empire   The leaders of that movement seemed to have a certain acquaintance with the doctrines and precepts of Christianity, and it was hoped that this might eventually lead to the spread of those doctrines amongst the Chinese.   After a time it was found that these hopes were likely to be disappointed,—for these leaders were guilty of dreadful atrocities towards their fellow-men, and were inclined to make use of the small amount of religious faith they had acquired for their own personal advantage, and even went so far as blasphemously to pretend that they had communications with the Divine being himself.   But I am induced to believe, from a speech of the Bishop of Hong Kong—incongruously styled the "Bishop of Victoria,"—that we still should not despair, and that the balance of that revolutionary movement may be still turned in favor of Christianity.   Most of the leaders I have referred to have been slain, and those who survive seem more likely to be actuated by the doctrines of the gospel.   They have in common use amongst them already, the Lord's Prayer and the Ten Commandments, translated into the Chinese language, and there seems to be a strong disposition on their part to conform more fully to the Christian belief.   Now I would ask what may not be the effect of such a Mission as this on the general question, in turning the scale in favor of Christianity in the great Chinese Empire?   By a return recently laid before our Parliament, it seems that during the twelve months ending the 30th of June, 2954—or, in round numbers, 3000—Chinese returned from the ports of this Colony only, to China. What, I ask, might have been the result had it been possible to conduct the Mission on such a scale that all these Chinese should have been converted to Christianity ?—If it had been possible that every one of them should have been furnished with a copy of the New Testament in the Chinese language ? Or even if only ten per cent. of these people had been converted to Christianity, what an effect might be produced on the Chinese Empire at the present moment ?—We see therefore that the Mission is of importance, not only as regards the Chinese in this Colony, but that it may be a grand and wonderful auxiliary in support of the progress of civilization and the Christian religion throughout the world.

The Rev. B. Fletcher, one of the secretaries, read the report, which stated that the Rev. Mr. Young, for many years a missionary in China, and Lo-Sam-Yuen, Chu-A-Luk, and Leong-A-Toe, Chinese Christians, were at present labouring among the Chinese of Ballarat and Castlemaine. Steps have been taken with a view to erect a new and more substantial place of worship for the Chinese at Castlemaine, and a considerable proportion of the sum required for that object has already been subscribed by the Chinese themselves. The receipts of the Mission for the past year amounted to £556 16s. 7d., and the disbursements to within £40 of that sum. The meeting was addressed by Bishop Perry, the Revds. J. P. Sunderland, D. J. Draper, J. Taylor, S. L. Chase, B. Fletcher, and Messrs. W. Little and H. Jennings. A collection was made amounting to £30, including a donation of £10 from His Excellency. The Bishop having pronounced the benediction, the meeting closed.

EPISCOPALIANS.—The ASSEMBLY of the Episcopal church of Victoria is now in Session under the presidency of the Right Rev. Bishop Perry. It sits daily, from half-past one till six o'clock. Various important matters regarding the discipline and government of this branch of the Church,—the appointment of ministers,—the raising of funds, &c., are under consideration; from which the good order, purity, and vigorous action of the community are anticipated.

CHRIST CHURCH, ST. KILDA.—The opening of this new Church took place on Sunday, August 2. The Bishop of Melbourne preached in the morning: the Dean in the afternoon, and the Rev. D. Seddon, the incumbent, in the evening. On the following evening a Tea meeting was held in the adjoining school-room, in which worship has heretofore been conducted. The meeting was addressed by the Bishop, the Dean, Dr. Cairns, the Revs. D. Seddon, and C. T. Perks, and Messrs. Jennings and Winter. The collection on the sabbath and the contributions at the social meeting amounted to nearly £500. The total expenditure up to the present time has been about £11,000; towards this sum £6,000 has been subscribed and paid, £2,000 granted by Government, leaving a debt of £3,000, which is guaranteed by thirty gentlemen, in £100 each. The Church is well seen from the Bay, and from the Melbourne side, and when the spire is up will be a very conspicuous object. It is a much admired structure, built in the early English style of Gothic; in extreme length 111 feet, width 32 feet, with transept, chancel, vestry, porches, and high-pitched open-timbered roof, &c., and will accommodate 600 people. The architect was Charles Swyer, Esq.

STEIGLITZ.—A Public meeting of the members of the Episcopal Church was held on August 5. when a Committee was appointed to provide for a permanent place of worship, the school-room having proved insufficient to accommodate the Sunday evening congregations.

OPEN AIR PREACHING.—At a meeting of the Clergy of the Archdeaconry of Melbourne, held at the deanery, Tuesday, August 18, it was agreed to preach in the open air during the approaching summer, at such times and places as might be hereafter selected. The Rev. R. B. Dickinson was to commence on Sabbath, August 30, at Sandridge.

MISSION TO THE ABORIGINES.—On the evening of Wednesday, Aug. 19th, a numerously attended meeting in connexion with the Episcopalian Mission to the Aborigines, was held in St. Paul's Schools, Swanston-street, Melbourne. The report gave a favorable account of the proceedings of the mission.—The following resolutions were adopted:—1. That the openings for the preaching of the Gospel demand our utmost exertions, and our proceedings during the past few months call for the devout acknowledgment that God has graciously prospered our way, since we associated ourselves together for Missionary purposes. 2. That God having provided the means for the evangelization of the heathen, we ought continually to bear in mind, and to practice, the duty of intercession for their salvation. 3. That this meeting rests on the command to preach the Gospel to every creature, as the strong foundation for persevering in the endeavour to win the Aborigines to the Saviour, and rejoices in those first fruits which have already been gathered.

Essendon.—Immediate steps are to be taken with a view to the erection of an Episcopalian Church at Essendon. The church is designed in the early English style of architecture, and will consist of a nave 55 feet in length, by 38 feet 6 inches in breadth; and a chancel 20 feet 6 inches in length, by 15 feet in width. There will be a vestry and a bell-turret on the north-east angle of the nave. It is calculated to seat about 300 persons. The walls are to be built of blue-stone rubble with axed dressings. The Architects are Messrs. Knight and Kerr.

PRESBYTERIANS.—Prahran Free Presbyterian Church.—The report of this congregation, under the pastoral care of the Rev. G. Divorty, for the year ending 2nd July, 1857, is very encouraging. It shows that, in addition to the ordinary expenses, the sum of £739 2s. 7d. has been expended in the liquidation of the debt upon the church and manse, and the payment of interest. This sum has been raised by means of private subscriptions and monthly collections. The debt, which originally amounted to £5000, has been reduced to £1803 18s. It is expected that through the consideration and liberality of the people, a large portion of this may be liquidated during the current year. The sources of congregational revenue are chiefly three, viz., the ordinary collections at the church door, the seat-rents, and the sustentation fund. The Day-School is attended by upwards of 100 scholars, and were the accommodation larger, the numbers might be much increased. The Sabbath-school is attended by about 50 scholars. It is proposed to enlarge the school-room at a cost of about £400. A ladies' visiting society has been formed, from which much good is anticipated.

NEW SCOTCH CHURCH.—Essendon.—The foundation stone of this new Church was laid by His Excellency Sir Henry Barkly, on the 7th August, in the presence of a considerable body of spectators. The Rev. T. Craig gave out a hymn, and offered prayer. A silver trowel, bearing a suitable inscription, was presented to His Excellency by one of the trustees. A parchment scroll, containing the name of the architect and builder, the name of Sir Henry Barkly as its founder, and the date of the foundation, was deposited, and along with it the papers of the day, and the coins of the realm, and thereafter the stone was lowered into its proper place. His Excellency and the Rev. T. Craig addressed the spectators. The proceedings were closed with prayer. The new edifice is to be constructed of bluestone, and is intended to accommodate 500 persons. The estimated expense is £2,600, and the architect is Mr David Ross.

FREE CHURCH.—St. Kilda.—The misunderstanding in the synod of the Free Church has led to the opening of a second Presbyterian Church in St. Kilda, the Rev. A. Paul having commenced worship in a new temporary building, in the Alma Road. On the church recently occupied by him being vacated, it was re-opened by the Rev. Dr. Cairns, and it is at present supplied by the ministers in turn. It is understood that a minister has been sent for from Scotland to fill the vacant post.

UNITED PRESBYTERIAN CHURCH.—Melton.—During the last twelve months the Rev. Alexander M'Nicol, of Bacchus Marsh, has been accustomed to preach every alternate Sabbath in the rapidly rising township of Melton. As the population is steadily growing, it was felt desirable that a place of worship should be erected. Nearly £290 have been subscribed for the purpose of accomplishing this. A wooden structure has been raised in the Gothic style of architecture, which is capable of accommodating 100 persons. The new church was opened on Sabbath the 5th of July, by the Rev. Mr. M'Nicol, who preached two appropriate sermons on the occasion. The attendance was numerous and encouraging. A tea meeting was held on Monday evening, which was also well attended. A report was read by the secretary, which showed that the funds were in a very flourishing condition. An address was presented to Mr. M'Nicol, acknowledging his valuable services in connexion with the young cause, and expressive of the esteem and affection entertained for him as a minister of the gospel, which Mr. M'Nicol suitably responded to.

WESLEYANS.—Melbourne.—The eligible building site, on which stands Collins-street Wesleyan Chapel, has been sold for, it is understood, the large sum of £40,000. The proceeds are to be applied partly to the erection of a church of large capacity and superior architecture, in Lonsdale-street, with minister's house and schools, and partly to the building of other churches. A church extension fund of £10,000 additional, is also in the course of being raised, 4000l. being already subscribed. This money is to be lent without interest for limited periods to parties building new chapels, and when repaid, is to be used again in the same manner.

Pentridge.—The foundation-stone of the Wesleyan Methodist Chapel, Pentridge was laid on Wednesday, the 6th current, by the Hon. Nehemiah Guthridge, M.L.C.,

The Rev. D. J. Draper opened the proceedings with a hymn, and the Rev. H. Waddington read a portion of scripture, after which the Rev. T. Williams offered up a prayer. A sealed bottle containing the record usual on such occasions was placed in the stone cavity beneath the corner stone, together with a copy of the *Argus* and *Herald* of the day. Mr. Guthridge was presented with a silver trowel which displayed considerable artistic skill. The meeting was addressed by the Revs. W. L. Binks and D. J. Draper. The architect is T. J. Crouch, Esq.

PRIMITIVE METHODISTS.—A Missionary Tea-meeting was held in the Primitive Methodist Chapel, La Trobe-street, on the evening of Tuesday, 4th of August. The Rev. M. Clark, Pastor of the Church, occupied the chair. A number of interesting and encouraging statements in reference to the progress of the cause of Primitive Methodism were laid before the meeting. It was mentioned that an effort was being made to raise 100*l.*, to be sent home with the view of bringing out additional labourers to the Colonial field. Addresses were delivered by the Rev. H. Thomas, B.A., Rev. Mr. Foster, the Rev. James Ballantyne, and by Messrs Allan and Hotchin. The principle topic of the evening was the subject of Missionary effort for the more extensive diffusion of the Gospel.

CONGREGATIONALISTS.—NORTH COLLINGWOOD INDEPENDENT CHURCH.— A public meeting in connection with the settlement of the Rev. James Mirams as pastor of this church, was held on Thursday evening, August 6th. George Harker, Esq., M.L.A. presided. Amongst the ministers and friends present, were the Revds. A. Morison, W. Moss, James Ballantyne, T. Odell, J. P. Sunderland, W. R. Fletcher, M.A., H. Thomas, B.A., W. Jarrett, T. Williams, Bradney, W. B. Landells, Brien, R. Hamilton, and J. Taylor, most of whom took part in the proceedings of the evening. The place of worship was crowded,—the audience cordially responded to the expressions of fraternal regard with which the new pastor was welcomed. In the course of the evening, Mr. William Poole (who had supplied the pulpit for some months), was presented by Mr. Mirams, in the name of the Church, with a handsome silver tea service, " As a token of Christian esteem and grateful acknowledgment of his gratuitous pulpit ministrations, August, 1857." Mr. Mirams has entered upon his labours in this locality with every prospect of success. Already both the stated congregation and communicants have greatly increased.

THE REV. W. ROBINSON, late of Ampthill, Bedfordshire, the first of the ministers sent out by the Colonial Missionary Society, as the result of the visit to England of the Rev. J. L. Poore, has arrived in Melbourne, together with his lady and family, by the ship *Adelaide*, after a long passage. He was received by the Committee of the Victoria Congregational Home Mission in a full meeting, and cordially welcomed. By the time this number is printed, a Tea Meeting will have been held in Mr. Thomas's Chapel, Collingwood, to give him a public welcome. He has been engaged to preach for the present to the Independent Congregation at Williamstown, to make trial of the place.

THE REV. A. SCALES, minister of Mackillop-street Independent Chapel, Geelong, has recently resigned his charge, but is likely to continue his ministry in the same town in some other place of worship.

OPEN AIR PREACHING.—Since our last publication, a series of open air services have been carried on by the Revds. J. Mirams, of North Collingwood Independent Church, Bradney, and Brien who continue to preach every Lord's Day afternoon (weather permitting) in Victoria Parade, near the Water Tank. The congregations thus far have been good—sometimes there have been from 300 to 350 present, and on all occasions they have listened with the most respectful attention. Other ministers have promised their aid in this movement.

STATE AID TO RELIGION IN VICTORIA.—The third reading of the Bill for the Abrogation of the 53rd Clause of the New Constitution Act by which State Aid to Religion will be entirely done away with from the 31st December, 1860, passed the House of Assembly in the Victorian Parliament, on September 9th, by a majority of 17 ; viz. 33 for, and 16 against. As the New Constitution Bill requires that the alteration in question should receive the sanction not only of a majority of the members present, but of the whole House, and as the House consists of 60 members in all, the voters for the third reading being 33, the condition has been fulfilled. The Bill, however, has still to pass the ordeal of the Upper House.

The next number of this Magazine will be issued on 1st December. Communications for Editor care of W. FAIRFAX & Co., *Melbourne.*

Printed at the Steam Press of W. FAIRFAX AND Co., Melbourne.

The Southern Spectator.

| No. 3. | DECEMBER, 1857. | Vol. I. |

MISCELLANIES.

The Indian Mutiny.

THE year 1857, now drawing to a close, will henceforth be a memorable one to all future historians of India. That thousands of native soldiers receiving the Queen's pay and wearing her uniform as defenders of her royalty and possessions, should actually conspire together and levy open war against her throne and majesty, using her arms and ammunition, their acquired military skill and perfect knowledge of the country, to overturn her government : seizing towns and arsenals, and holding them for a period against all comers,—are events of no common importance, and will give rise to many alterations if not improvements. The news of the outbreak has awakened considerable surprise and anxiety. There may be observed a feverish desire to antedate our mail steamers, some fears as to its immediate results, and many speculations as to its remote consequences. The suddenness of the outbreak—its opposition to our ideas of the "faithful Sepoy" —its wide-spread character, and the fearful atrocities that have marked its progress, with the general unpreparedness to repress it, are all points of special interest. Scarcely have we closed our well-fought strife with the Russian autocrat, and made Alma Inkermann and Sebastopol words to stir the blood, before we find ourselves involved in a serious internecine war. The massacre of Hango pales, in atrocity, before that of Cawnpore, and in revenge ten thousand Sepoys are said to bite the dust for foul insults offered to British matrons and maids. That we owe this Indian mutiny to Russian intrigue we deem a popular delusion. Our Anti-Russian mania need not be perpetual. The autocrat need not be credited with all political evils any more than Satan with all moral ones. Other causes more tangible and real, and easier to deal with because of our own creation, lie upon the surface. Collating together the scattered items of intelligence provokingly scanty and disjointed—availing ourselves of previous facts for illustration and exposition, and looking upon the revolt

H

as a Christian spectator, we should regard some of the causes as unavoidable, some as highly criminal, and others as purely military. All our readers must be aware that this is a transition period in the history of India. A spirit of change is passing over the land, making all things new as to religion, social usages, and material circumstances. From an almost fabulous antiquity the modes of thought, social customs, and religious observances of our Indian fellow-subjects, have been stereotyped up to the close of the last century. At that period the coral strand of India was trodden by the feet of those whose work it was to preach a pure faith, men who went in the " irresistible might of weakness" to win a new empire for the Saviour. Science, too, built her schools and taught ascertained truths, thus aiding to unsettle the minds of the people,—their false religious views being intimately associated with false ideas of the physical world. New ideas were thus imparted, new impulses awakened. The people of India are now generally dissatisfied with their ancient faiths ; yet prejudice custom and sin, prevent them still from accepting Christ and His cross, in whom and in which are hid all the treasures of wisdom and knowledge. We accept as true the inuendos of the *Times* and other papers, that the zeal of mission-aries, the formation of churches, the establishment of schools, and the gradual undermining of the old superstitions have unsettled the minds of the people. We deem this to be unavoidable, except by withholding Christianity and science from them altogether. Christianity is not the guilty cause, but the innocent occasion of the disquiet. It turns the people from darkness to light, and from the power of Satan unto that of God, while parties who are interested in the continuance of former evils seek to oppose its onward career of light and blessing. In so far as Christianity has anything to do with the revolt, it is as an opponent ; mission-aries and native Christians are alike opposed to it. But the labours of the one and the increase of the other, occasion a new version of the uproar at Ephesus. The images once believed to have fallen from heaven, are found to be waning in popular estimation, and the gain of the Brahminical craftsmen is in danger. The offerings of the devotees are fewer in number and less in value, and Brahmins betake themselves to military life. In one Sepoy regiment, one thousand strong. there are six hun-dred Brahmins, in another four hundred. It is impossible to effect great moral and social changes without injuring the interests of men who have identified themselves with doomed evils. Hence transition periods are periods of chronic rebellions.

A grave crime must be charged upon the so-called Christian government of India, inasmuch as for a long period the *prestige* of British support was given to some of the worst mummeries of idolatry. The time can still be remembered when British officers were accustomed to bow in policy to heathen shrines, and officiate as grand masters at heathen ceremonies. The Christian

Government of India had a per centage upon the proceeds of the pagoda, and drew from its three Presidencies, after paying the salaries of the dancing girls, &c., about £30,000 per annum. When this grievous evil was represented to the Court of Directors, the reply was, that three lacs of rupees were too much to sacrifice to the orators of Exeter Hall. Under native rulers in the Mysore, the pagodas and idols were neglected and fast falling into disrepute. On the British assuming the sovereignty, a tax was laid upon every house in a certain village for the due support of the idol and his temple,—his devotees loudly complaining that they had never been so taxed under their native Rajah. * Even so late as 1836, a memorial was presented to the Government of the Madras Presidency signed by 150 civil and military officers, praying that they might not be compelled to superintend heathen temples and festivals of idolatry; to present arms and fire salutes to a senseless idol. This memorial was supported by Bishop Corrie, who for more than thirty years was an example of piety to all India. The Secretary of the Government replied, " that he was directed to inform the Bishop that the sentiments of the governor were not in accordance with those of the memorialists; and the governor was sorry the bishop did not attend to his own peculiar duties in moderating the zeal of over-heated minds, instead of agitating questions that were calculated to endanger the peace of the community." After much agitation of the question in India and England, the prayer of the memorialists was first granted, then again refused, and stringent resolutions passed to bind the officers more firmly to idol cars and festivals. On the promulgation of this law in 1839, Judge Nelson resigned his connection with the company. He sacrificed all his honors and emoluments, and a prospective pension of a £1000 a year, to which a little longer service would have entitled him. Sir Peregrine Maitland resigned his office as commander-in-chief for the same reason, and laid, as an offering upon the altar of Christian consistency, an income of £15,000 a year. The scenes which rendered famous the plains of Dura and immortalised the three Hebrew children, have been enacted again upon the plains of India.

Native Christians have received no more sympathy. Previous to leaving India, Lord William Bentick abolished flogging in the native army, making no distinction as to religion. A Christian native shortly after committed a grave military offence, and was sentenced to receive two hundred lashes. The commanding officer referred the matter to the judge advocate for his opinion, who replied,—" There is not room for a doubt upon the subject; the act of abolition was only intended for Hindoos and Mohammedans, and not for native Christians at all—the sentence should therefore be carried into execution immediately."† After a long agitation Exeter Hall has prevailed over the Court of Directors;

---

* Campbell's " British India," chap. xxv., &c.
† British India, p. 485.

infanticide and the immolation of widows are prohibited; toleration is granted to British officers and native Christians; the pilgrim tax is abolished; a new law has been recently issued, preserving to every native who makes a profession of Christianity his property and possessions, and a beginning has thus been made for dissolving government connection with idolatry. This has greatly exasperated both Brahmins and Mahommedans, Government, though reluctantly, having at last been impartial in its favors. Any act of simple equality is now regarded as an act of persecution or an insult; and thus the Government reaps a large harvest of disquiet from its former misdeeds. Had there been from the beginning equal tolerance to all religions and support to none; had Government confined itself to its own sphere, the present mutiny might not perhaps have been prevented, but would have certainly wanted one element of peculiar intensity. Expediency is often the root-principle of a large harvest of evil; and the Bengal mutiny, apart from the justice of a retributive Providence, is not a little owing to policy having in former times superseded truth and justice, in the Calcutta as well as in the other Presidencies.

The purely military causes have been much insisted upon by Calcutta correspondents, and deserve the gravest censure. In the Bengal army there has long been an utter want of sound military discipline. By far too much respect has been shewn to the caste prejudices of the Brahmins in the army. In the mutiny that occurred in 1849, the Brahmins were the chief instigators. Sir C. J. Napier in his work on Indian Misgovernment (pp. 28-29, second edition) thus refers to the matter:—" When the mutinous spirit arose with our Sepoys, the chief leaders were undoubtedly Brahmins, and Brahmins, having a religious as well as a military character, enjoy an immense influence. . . . . . Their religious principles interfere in many strange ways with their military duties. . . . . . Having two commanders to obey, caste and captain, if they are at variance, the last is disobeyed, or obeyed at the cost of conscience and duty." Such things are utterly subversive of sound military discipline. In the army regulations no attention should be paid to caste prejudices—the Sepoy should not be a Brahmin but a soldier. Better far, said C. J. Napier, to have a low caste man for a soldier, upon whom caste prejudices sit lightly, and who will snap his fingers at them when duty or convenience come in the way. In the Bengal army, the men have been allowed to dictate too much as to promotion, where the senile rule of seniority has not been adhered to. The general absence of the superior officers from their regiments is a great evil. Each regular regiment of Sepoys has on its muster roll the names of about twenty-four European officers, yet so numerous are civil and staff appointments that usually not more than twelve or thirteen young subordinate officers, and these to a great extent ignorant of the language, are in barracks with the men. The general body of European troops has not been increased in a proportionate ratio to those of the native troops, and the latter have in consequence assumed airs of importance. The minor causes referred to are the curtailment of certain petty privileges : the Sepoys cannot frank their letters as formerly ; once they paid no tolls on roads ; provisions were also cheaper, and their pay consequently of greater relative value.

Particular prominence should be given to the absence of the superior officers and the want of discipline. Sir C. J. Napier writing on the Bengal military system in 1844, observes :—" The great military evil of India which strikes me is this : all the old officers get snug places, and regiments are left to boys. The 8th Native Infantry were on parade for inspection last week, 800 strong, and there were only three officers, of whom two had not been dismissed drill ! This will not do : the men look to the native officer; and he, teaching the *saheb*, naturally looks upon him as his pupil not his master. Some day, evil will arise from this." An evil of scarcely less magnitude is the ignorance of the native language on the part of the officers thus left in charge of regiments. It is well known that the revolt in Lower Canada was extensively planned by the rebels, " without the knowledge of the Government, or doubt being entertained as to their loyalty and intentions," there being a want of proper officers among them versed in the language of the disaffected districts. The same result has been shown among the military in India as among the civilians in Canada. No man should hold a civil or military appointment in India, unless he can intelligently converse with the natives ; interpreters and hearsay evidence are bad data.

The present Governor-General of India is reported to have said that the danger and the revolt have been greatly overrated. We regard, however, the Calcutta petition to the Home Legislature as a more trustworthy informant, and by the petitioners the crisis is regarded as being of the gravest character. Of its speedy suppression we cannot entertain any reasonable doubt, should the mutiny be confined to the Bengal Presidency. Hitherto the Sepoys seem to have no clearly defined and common purpose. They are without an influential leader and at variance among themselves. The appointment of Sir Colin Campbell to the chief command of the faithful troops is cause for hope. His acquaintance with the mutiny of 1849, the first symptoms having appeared at his station of Ramil Kindee, where he acted with great prudence and firmness, along with his military skill and personal bravery, give promise of his yet greater usefulness.

We see but little reason at present to fear an Indian famine, as one of the immediate effects of the mutiny. Hitherto the revolt has been confined to the troops in large towns, and cannot to any serious extent have interfered with the usual processes of cultivation. There is more to be feared—an alienation of races. Hitherto there has been but little of this in India,—the relations subsisting have been those of fellow-subjects, the conquered and

conquerors living peaceably together. This mutiny with its
horrible atrocities and treachery, will awaken vindictive feelings
of a deplorable character. We hope no attempt will be made to
conciliate the heathen portion of the community by attempts to
neutralize missionary agency. Let both have a fair field and no
favour. Who ever knew truth put to the worse in a fair and open
encounter? One fact stands out broadly—there must be a
thorough re-organisation of the Bengal army. It will also
become a question whether at no distant day the Government of
India must not be assimilated to that of the British Colonies
generally; it is at present an anomaly, expensive too in its
character, and not at all adapted to the changing circumstances
of the people.

We cannot close without adverting to the fact how the revolt
illustrates and confirms the statement of Scripture : " The dark
places of the earth are full of the habitations of cruelty." Nor
can we fail to hope that these overturnings are preparing the way
for a Prince and a Saviour, who by the might of his love can still
" the tumult of the people."

A Glance at the Religious State of Britain.

Much as we are engrossed here with our own concerns, we cannot
be indifferent to what is passing among the multitudes of our
fellow-subjects in the other hemisphere. Our eagerness, indeed,
for the arrival of every mail, and the appetite with which we
devour its supply of news, show anything but indifference. Whatever charms may invest political, literary, and other secular
intelligence, to earnest Christian minds nothing will be felt of
equal importance to the state of religion ; and to do somewhat to
meet this desire we purpose to summarize what we have gathered
from recent arrivals, not so much in the form of distinct items as
of a glance at the more salient points in the several Churches.
In some respects we are in a more favorable position to take an
impartial view of affairs than the actors themselves, just as persons
on a height, surveying the surging movements of the hosts contending in battle on the plains below as they sway to and fro in
their struggle for the mastery, may have an exacter idea of the
plan of operations and the state of the field than those absorbed
in the turmoil.

What a contrast does the aspect of the religious community of
Britain present, at the present time, to the dull monotony and
self-satisfied apathy of the last century, when nothing was stirring
but the great Methodist movement ! The Established and Nonconformist Churches were alike lax in doctrine, cold in piety,
and utterly wanting in zeal. Now, everything betokens excitement
and action. Jealousy for the truth, sensitiveness to abuses,

measures of reform, schemes of extension at home and missionary enterprises abroad, characterise every branch of the Church of Christ. Clergy and laity, male and female, rich and poor, are taking their several shares in the work of instructing the young, reclaiming the vicious, and supporting measures for converting the heathen to the faith of Christ. Alas! for the old *beau ideal* of sound orthodox Churchism,—a comfortable living, a brief and cold sermon, no dissenters, no Sunday schools, no prayer meetings, no missionary fanaticism,—the Church and the world in jovial fellowship with each other. Such a state of things is now only to be found in some remote rural corner.

The Established Church of England manifests signs of renewed life and vigour. The Evangelical element, fostered at first by Romaine and Newton, Scott and Cecil, for a long time distinguished but a small minority of the clergy. Still it grew and spread, and at length its progress, alarming High-churchmen, led to the Tractarian reaction. Hailed as this was by many, as at least a symptom of earnestness, it soon developed its really superstitious and Romanist tendencies, and then naturally produced a second reaction. The inroads of Puseyism and the dread of Popery induced Lord John Russell to raise the pious Sumner to the Archiepiscopal see of Lambeth, and this step has been followed by a succession of Episcopal and other preferments, as grateful to the lovers of Evangelical truth as they are novel in the proceedings of statesmen. The effect of the elevation of so many devoted Christians and able preachers to these dignities seems quite electrical. Formalists of all sections are confounded; the friends of earnest religion are taking courage. The cause of missions and Bible circulation at home and abroad, has received a new impulse; every description of agency for diffusing religious influence is invigorated; unwonted measures, long deemed irregular, for reaching the masses, are now openly patronised by the hierarchy,—Bishops and other dignitaries are preaching to listening crowds of operatives in Exeter Hall and other unconsecrated places; and out-door preaching is being adopted by the parochial clergy in many parts of the country. A happy day, we trust, is dawning for England in the renewed activity of what is certainly the most extensive, and ought to be the most powerful, of all the ecclesiastical organizations existing in that country.

Another new feature of the religious state of England is the appearance of some remarkable young preachers among the Nonconformists. The fame of Whitfield and Wesley is almost paralleled by that of Spurgeon, while, as it regards the quality of some of the persons attracted, it is surpassed. It is a new thing, now-a-days, to hear of ten or twelve thousand people being congregated together to listen to one man; and, since the days of Irving's early popularity, there has been nothing like the present rush of the nobility to Spurgeon's ministry. His style, too, of preaching is a phenomenon. Like that of his great predecessors just named, the founders of Calvinistic and Wesleyan Methodism, it abjures all philosophy, all arguments about the evidences of Christianity or the truth of Evangelical doctrine, all refinement in thought or taste in composition, and is eminently doctrinal and experimental, plain, racy, and dogmatic. Mr. Spurgeon preaches "as one having authority, not as the scribes." Many good people have lamented a tendency, which they declare to have been increasingly shewing itself in preachers, to keep back the peculiar doctrines of Christianity and to substitute in their place a negative theology; and have been laboring hard, by argument and persuasion, controversy and rebuke, to correct the evil. Mr. Spurgeon cuts the knot at once, by shewing to the nation what he considers a more excellent way. He does not say what he thinks should be done, but does it, and certainly with marvellous effect. Nor does he stand alone in this new department. Other stars are rising above the horizon, whose quality of light is similar if their brilliancy is not quite equal. Among those spoken of are a brother or brothers of Mr. Spurgeon, and a Mr. Guinness, who are likewise producing a great sensation. Whether all this will prove only a nine days' wonder, or whether wide spread effects,— beneficial and permanent, like those which followed the labors of the itinerant preachers of a century ago,—will result, time alone can determine.

For some time the Congregational body has been sadly agitated by doctrinal controversy, or rather by a controversy not about the doctrines themselves, respecting which all profess to be agreed, but whether they are or are not preached with sufficient prominence. The storm, however, has been chiefly confined to debates at the Union meetings, and letters and articles in newspapers, and pamphlets, unaccompanied by organic disruption, the displacement of pastors, or other permanent effects. It seems now to have subsided. While it lasted, doubtless it tended to check the practical working of the ministry and the spread of vital religion; now that it is over, it is to be hoped that the combatants on both sides will betake themselves to their work of evangelising the people with renewed earnestness and zeal.

The serious check to the onward progress of the Wesleyan Methodists by the reform agitation has, after a vigorous struggle of a few years, at length been effectually removed. That Church is renewing its youth, and evinces elastic power of reaction. Its statistics show an increase in all departments,—in members, in ministers, and in finances. Its great Missionary Society has enjoyed a gradual augmentation of funds from its very beginning, and now realises the vast sum of £119,205 per annum.

The Evangelical Presbyterians in England, no longer a branch of a Scottish Church, but now an independent body known under the name of the English Presbyterian Synod, is making its way gradually. Its college, in London, is doing well, and we hear of new places of worship rising up, from time to time, in various parts of the country. Its mode of conducting worship, being the same as that which prevails in Scotland, has not altogether suited the taste of English people; and to that circumstance may perhaps be ascribed the fact that the congregations consist almost wholly of immigrants from the North. A feeling of this kind seems to have led to recent attempts to Anglicise the public services, by the introduction of organs and modern hymns; but these attempts, so far, have been unsuccessful.

The most noticeable thing in the religious affairs of Scotland we have recently met with, is a lay movement, under high sanction, to bring about an amalgamation of the Free and the United Presbyterian Churches. A series of eight admirable resolutions, recognising the actual agreement between the two bodies in doctrine, discipline, and worship, and pleading for forbearance on the few theoretic points wherein they differ, has been signed by the Marquis of Breadalbane, Lord Panmure, General Sir Thomas Brisbane, Mr. Knight, M.P. for Glasgow, and John Henderson, of Park, together with a large number of other eminent laymen of both churches.

The ecclesiastical affairs of Ireland seem to have been remarkably quiet for some time, if we may except the unclerical violence of some of the Romish clergy at the late elections, and the still increasing inroads making among the Catholics, chiefly of the west, by the persevering labours of the Irish Missions of the Established and other Churches. One other little but significant incident may be mentioned: Archbishop Whately was violently opposed to the Evangelical Alliance at its commencement, and forbad his clergy to join it, actually withdrawing his license from one who had dared to disobey him. Now, one may almost fancy he has changed his mind upon the subject, for his Grace has recently attended and taken part in a meeting convened in Dublin, in company with Presbyterian and other ministers, to assist the Presbyterian Vaudois Church.

One of the great signs of the times, however, and one affecting all bodies of Evangelical Christians alike, is the progress of the Evangelical Alliance, an institution which was looked upon with great suspicion and doubt at the first, and has had to fight its way through a host of difficulties. It has, nevertheless, steadily adhered to its principles and prosecuted its work; and, so far as its constitution would allow, has exerted its influence in behalf of such measures as unite the suffrages of all Evangelical Christians, doing, in particular, good service in throwing the shield of protection around not a few on the Continent who were suffering persecution for righteousness' sake. The proposal to hold its periodical Conference at Berlin, and the marked favor shewn to that step by the King of Prussia, have produced quite a commotion among the Protestant Churches of the Continent, and something like it also in England. The Archbishop of Canterbury has received at Lambeth the deputation which had waited upon the

King of Prussia at Berlin, to hear the report of their visit; and there, in that ecclesiastical palace, at his invitation, a goodly array of Bishops and other high dignitaries of the Established Church united with Dr. Steane a Baptist, W. M. Bunting a Wesleyan, and other nonconformists, as fellow members of the one universal Church, in an extemporaneous religious exercise, conducted by Mr. Bunting. This example of mutual and kindly Christian recognition, in such a quarter, will doubtless not be without its effect on many timid and wavering minds.

It was our intention to have extended our notice to the state of religion on the continent of Europe, but this we shall reserve to another occasion, perhaps till the news of the Alliance meeting at Berlin shall have arrived, when much additional information will doubtless be furnished.

Catholic Colportage.

In Australian politics reference is constantly made to the political institutions of America. The wisdom of carefully studying the history and present government of a great nation, presenting in the past the very national phases through which we are now passing; and even in the present, in much of her outlying territory, possessing a remarkable similarity to the condition of these colonies, must be apparent to every thoughtful person. If in the arena of politics such study be a necessity, in the equally important department of Christian agency a like examination must prove useful. 'Tis true that if the modes of Christian labour be already stereotyped, if fresh phenomena demand no new adaptation, our study is wasted; for as it was in England so must it be in Australia, however different the circumstances amid which we live. We have, however, read the signs of the times to no purpose, if an *a priori* objection to all new kinds of Church agency is entertained by a large portion of any of the sections of the Church of Christ in this land. We believe it to be the earnest desire of all denominations energetically to prosecute any mode of effort which presents a reasonable prospect of extending the kingdom of Christ among us.

The spirit of the Apostle, whose rule of action was " if by any means I may save some," is shared, we trust, by all. Our various ecclesiastical polities are undoubtedly cherished by each of us; yet in these matters we severally believe in the theory of development, and insist upon their applicability to whatever requirements colonial life may make upon us. The denomination which cannot, or will not, comply with this condition, must become limited in influence, and fail in its duty both to God and man. Fortunately for Australia, all the Evangelical sects have adopted this belief. Freed from the trammels of prejudice by emigration, compelled almost by the necessities of colonial life with its theory of religious equality, and very many elevated by the Spirit of God into loftier and purer desires, Christians in this land denounce alike the childish or selfish spirit which either refuses to labour for the advancement of religion through dislike to new methods of work, or forbids men casting out devils because "they follow not us." In this young land we fully endorse a sentiment uttered by the Archbishop of Canterbury in the House of Lords on the 28th of May last, extending its reference to all sections of the Christian Church:—"I cannot imagine that any greater reproach or disparagement could be cast upon the Church than to suppose it was incapable of accommodating itself to the changing necessities of the age." Our belief then is, that Christians in Australia are perfectly prepared for, nay more, that they are intensely desirous of incorporating with their present agencies any method of doing good which possesses adaptation to the spiritual necessities of the colonies. We have been led to make these remarks by a perusal of the Annual Report of the American Tract Society for the year ending May 7th, 1856, thinking that, in that report, we have pointed out to us a mode of evangelizing the Bush districts of our country, at least worthy of being attentively considered by every Christian in Australia. The necessity of having a preached Gospel throughout this land is not a question which requires much discussion. Happily all are agreed on that point. Nor, when the different denominations attempt practically to meet this necessity, do they find their chief difficulty in the cities or larger towns of the colonies. True, with regard even to such we have still stern work and sacrifice before us ; but we are doing something, and to an extent which will bear comparison with much older countries. Our difficulty is the Bush, and there it is twofold. Either the population is so sparse, or so separated by religious opinion, as to render the establishment of a settled Church and Congregation for the time an impossibility ; or the present number of dwellers within a limited area, combined with future probable increase, is sufficiently enticing to act upon Christian zeal, deepened perhaps by the love of denominational extension, so as to set the more powerful denominations to work to rear separate sanctuaries, and retain their respective recognised Ministers, with at best but little assistance from the people to be benefitted, and without any well grounded hope of obtaining anything like a Congregation.

No true follower of Christ will say the former of these difficulties is sufficient to exonerate the Churches from the responsibility of carrying the Gospel to the most thinly populated district ; and yet the means of overcoming this difficulty have still to be devised. We further think no reflective Christian can feel perfectly satisfied with what we have presumed to point out as a second obstacle. Supposing we waive the objection of the danger of Christian zeal in a limited community degenerating into sectarian rivalry, and admit that in proportion to the number of Ministers and Churches will be their beneficial influence upon the population, there remain, as serious considerations, the effect of a necessarily comparative want of success upon the minds of the Ministers themselves, the continual drain such weak causes make upon the not overflowing treasuries of the self-sustained Churches, and the consequent general injury to the denominations, when the mission stations increase in a ratio disproportionate to the strength of the several bodies as a whole. In a word, the progress made is not legitimate. It is the forcing of the hot-house, not the gradual ripening of nature. At first sight, our remarks may seem to militate against the sufficiency of the voluntary principle in a young colony. A little reflection will show the deduction to be false. No advocate of Voluntaryism asserts it must ever work in a stereotyped form. Its freedom to adapt itself to circumstances is its glory. The question is not whether, if limited to advancement by the power to build costly structures and to sustain ordained Ministers, Voluntaryism could supply at once the spiritual wants of a thinly populated but extensive country, that population moreover still in a nomadic state; but the question we are called upon to face is, can the friends of religion, unassisted by government treasuries, devise and carry out *any plans* by which the Gospel of Jesus Christ can be made known even to the isolated dwellers in the far bush. We think they can; and the report we have referred to, in our opinion, demonstrates our position.

As we have already hinted, our Christian brethren in America have to encounter some of the very difficulties in Evangelisation with which we are now struggling. In one of the speeches given in the report referred to they are thus enumerated :—

1st. Sparseness of population.

2nd. Heterogeneousness of population in language, manners, and religion.

3rd. The general deterioration of character ever to be observed in a new population. And finally, the restless and unsettled habits of such a population.

To a greater or less extent each of these obstacles to the diffusion of the Gospel exists in this country. How then, we eagerly ask, are they overcome in America? Is there any one particular agency capable of adoption by us which efficiently reaches the thinly peopled districts? The Committee of the American Tract Society declare they have found a mode of overcoming these serious hindrances, and to this they have given the name of "Catholic Colportage." The name of course implies what the Constitution of the Society would suggest, that all Evangelical denominations unite to support this method of Christian work, and that consequently it is entirely unsectarian.

Its Catholicity is its conquering power. In supporting, in every way possible, this agency of the Tract Society, each denomination feels it is responding to the claims which the spiritually waste places of the land have upon it, and that a narrow sectarianism would only obstruct the glorious work which Christian charity and union are alone powerful enough to perform. It is stated in the Report to which we have alluded, that at present there are nearly six hundred colporteurs actively at work. The *modus operandi* is as follows. The Agent selected, a large district is assigned to him, every family in which he must endeavour to visit at least once in the year. Necessarily he travels on horseback, and has with him for sale or gift as many religious tracts or books and Bibles, as he can carry. His work, however, is not that of the mere salesman. In the different households he visits, he remains as long as other claims will permit and the work he has to do demands. He is invariably received with hospitality and respect. He engages the family in household devotion, converses with single inmates on religious subjects, and when opportunity offers with the family together, reads to them the scriptures: and, if sufficiently gifted, preaches to as many as can be gathered together the glorious Gospel of the blessed God. Thus, week after week he presses forward, until he has gone through the entire district assigned to him. All this time the population is increasing; and such has frequently been the influence of his instructions, and of the books he left behind him, that before his third circuit has been accomplished a settled minister has been sent for, a church organised, a school opened, and a prosperous Mission Station established.

To give something like a full idea of the adaptation of this agency, the extent to which it has been carried in America, and the grandeur of its results, we subjoin the following table of statistics.

If our readers carefully ponder the figures they will see that the scheme of operations extends over the whole of the States embraced by the Union. They certainly exhibited the characteristic energy of the American people in carrying out vast plans of organized action. Can we learn nothing from them? Bearing in mind the spiritual wants of our country, its wide extent of surface, and its scanty population, and having this table before our eyes, we ask the following questions. Should we refuse to adopt and extensively to employ an agency which the trial of years has shown, in a country closely resembling our own, to be eminently adapted for Colonial evangelization? Is there anything in the relationship of the Evangelical sections of the Church of Christ in the Colonies which ought to prevent them uniting on the platform of our Tract Society, for the immediate establishment of the agency of " Catholic Colportage"?

SUMMARY VIEW OF COLPORTAGE IN THE SEVERAL STATES.

STATES.	Colporteurs.	Time of service.		Volumes sold.	Volumes granted	Public or prayer meetings.	Families destitute of all religious books.	Families destitute of the Bible.	Families Roman Catholics.	Families habitually neglecting evan. preaching	Families conversed or prayed with.	Whole number of families visited.
		M.	D.									
New England	18	74	24	33,778	6,652	232	1,431	58	390	4,359	6,390	12,690
Conn'cticut..	2	6	26	2,199	508	37	52	7	159	108	369	3,186
New York ..	62	509	7	63,429	16,563	1,909	8,593	6,846	20,095	23,490	71,830	128,379
New Jersey..	9	49	9	6,697	1,376	77	569	565	1,445	3,003	4,982	14,155
Pennsylvania.	61	402	10	70,803	22,124	1,025	4,519	4,004	8,965	17,240	50,916	91,748
Delaware	3	29	20	4,080	1,265	111	819	555	509	1,346	4,889	6,475
Maryland	7	46		2,729	690	93	1,091	877	1,406	2,610	4,482	13,061
Dis. Columbia	1	8		2,822	506	48	490	120	395	435	2,325	2,813
Virginia	54	332	18	42,011	19,337	1,672	1,801	1,267	720	2,886	16,333	37,780
N. Carolina..	41	225	26	30,476	11,706	1,417	2,816	1,135	225	1,452	14,571	26,541
S. Carolina ..	21	125	17	14,651	4,764	304	911	478	75	617	4,705	11,290
Georgia......	16	80	20	11,023	4,232	558	1,456	672	125	1,146	5,524	10,912
Alabama	13	31	20	3,942	1,108	100	126	95	5	7	1,127	3,249
Mississippi	11	23	12	2,815	669	157	74	42	3	67	924	1,792
Louisiana	11	62	11	5,474	1,795	83	1,195	1,455	4,749	1,604	4,433	19,863
Texas	9	54	5	7,090	2,278	220	1,179	172	27	1,546	2,435	5,065
Arkansas	1	2	14	585	257	72	61	36	8	71	126	257
Tennessee ..	20	77	16	9,878	2,791	503	1,017	433	77	1,043	3,189	8,194
Kentucky ..	14	84	21	8,910	2,365	227	855	1,136	1,273	1,170	5,104	11,077
Ohio	50	203	7	27,246	9,765	437	1,121	858	1,833	2,309	13,636	26,391
Michigan	10	57	5	4,662	1,737	133	559	509	642	1,766	5,169	8,983
Indiana......	21	126	17	16,889	6,342	531	3,063	1,674	1,714	4,555	9,227	21,889
Illinois	33	210	28	30,144	7,470	764	2,171	1,606	2,882	4,549	17,967	36,904
Missouri	15	109	19	12,523	3,807	298	1,645	902	1,909	1,990	5,202	19,850
Wisconsin ..	15	90	22	11,789	4,162	376	1,591	1,408	2,195	3,762	7,117	21,794
Iowa	10	60	1	12,676	2,021	189	885	350	760	3,059	4,466	11,355
Minnesota ...	1	5	8	707	235	133	3	11	21	181	401	811
Oregon	1	3		924	494	7	120	10	1		50	125
Canada	17	138	22	32,264	4,625	480	2,598	1,061	857	2,543	9,584	20,067
Total	547	3,232	15	473,306	141,634	12,198	42,316	28,426	53,750	88,914	277,482	586,131

SUMMARY OF COLPORTAGE BY STUDENTS FOR VACATIONS, 1855-56.

New York ..	21	41	..	9,129	2,256	165	1,150	558	990	1,824	4,401	12,406
New Jersey..	3	4	23	1,097	487	2	11	26	71	67	363	1,547
Pennsylvania.	31	60	12	14,442	2,668	133	1,345	453	870	1,433	4,594	15,027
Dis. Columbia	2	5	10	735	134	13	5	4	5	27	342	578
Virginia	6	9	29	1,561	368	37	43	46	31	47	814	1,498
S. Carolina ..	6	10	6	1,586	389	11	11	10	3	13	608	985
Tennessee ..	5	10	16	1,642	684	71	11	12	..	..	286	818
Kentucky ..	1	2	1	565	81	1	27	19	19	46	129	412
Ohio	10	18	27	4,126	991	31	279	107	60	545	898	4,944
Michigan	1		14	34	11	..	4	8	..	65	78	100
Indiana......	1	3	16	1,587	343	20	227	90	22	55	578	954
Illinois	11	28	18	6,283	1,166	64	356	369	871	933	1,570	5,973
Wisconsin ..	1	1	15	243	185	6	32	2	17	74	315	564
Minnesota ..	1	3	..	985	92	14	25	15	79	165	296	565
Canada	15	25	6	9,533	1,273	61	374	149	340	723	1,301	5,891
Total	115	225	10	53,548	11,029	629	3,900	1,861	3,431	6,017	16,561	52,207
Total by Colporteurs & Students..	662	3,457	25	526,854	152,663	12,827	46,216	30,287	57,181	94,931	294,043	638,338

National Education.

THE object of this paper is not to vindicate any special principle, to support any pet theory, or defend any particular system. A glance at the colonial aspect of the question—such as befits a *Southern Spectator*—is all that is intended. A review of all the systems that obtain in other countries and other colonies, pointing out their merits and defects, and how far they would be applicable, either in whole or in part, to Australia, is a task which, however worthy, is beyond our present scope.

By *national education* is to be understood a system supported by public funds, and embracing the whole people. If either of these two conditions is wanting, the thing falls short of its title. There might be a complete education of the people by voluntary effort, but this would not be considered a national system, any more than the voluntary support of religion would be regarded as a national church. Nor could a system be properly called national, which applied only to one sect, or to several specially favored sects. For the system to be truly national, all must be included, and at the cost of all.

Ought there to be any such national system? Is it necessary or expedient? This question would seem to lie at the threshold of all enquiry, but it is not much raised in these colonies. In England it has been very keenly discussed. Many of the advocates of voluntaryism carry their theory into the question of education, and maintain that State education is not only not necessary, but would be a political evil. There is much in the peculiar condition of England that gives countenance to this view of the case. The accumulated result of voluntary effort in supplying schools is so great that comparatively little is now left for the State to do, while the existence of the national Church awakens a justifiable jealousy on the part of the unendowed sects, lest a scheme of national education should be a fresh buttress to an institution they desire to see detached from State connection.

These reasons do not apply to the colonies, and proposals for national schemes of education do not meet with this kind of fundamental hostility. Voluntaryism in education is not a necessary corollary to voluntaryism in religion. There is, or need be, no violence done to conscience by a national system of education. In the United States, where no State-aid is given to religion, there is State-aid to education, and with universal approval. The same thing occurs, also, in the British colonies of Canada and South Australia. Voluntaries in these countries find no incongruity in acquiescing in a system of State education, if only ample provision is made for securing religious liberty. It is not so necessarily the duty of the State to educate the people that it should be under positive obligation to forbid its being done by private zeal, any more than it is necessarily the duty of the Church. Either organisation may undertake the duty if it is neglected, or either may resign it to the other. It must be regarded purely as a matter of expediency which shall be the prime agent, or how far they shall mutually co-operate. In England, the sects, stimulated largely by mutual competition, have exerted themselves to such an extent as almost to take the work out of the hands of the State. In these colonies, on the other hand, the services of the State, so far from being rejected, are sought, the only quarrel being whether it should undertake the work exclusively or share it with the denominations.

In New South Wales, (and Victoria inherited the same condition of things from its parent,) a portion of the denominations are at issue with the rest of the public, as to who should have charge of the education of the young. The former do not warn the State off the domain altogether, and offer, unassisted, to undertake the task. They demand pecuniary help from the State, but claim to be the chosen instrumentality for carrying out the work. The whole of the denominations are not united in opinion on this matter, nor all the members of any denomination. Leading men of all sects are seen to detach themselves from the bulk of their brethren, and give their support to the rival system. But, as a general rule, we shall not be far out in saying that a very considerable proportion of the most active members, and nearly all the clergy, in the four denominations,—the Episcopalian, the Catholic, the Presbyterian, and the Wesleyan,—are in favour of the denominational system.

The reasons for this preference it is not difficult to discover. Denominational schools are under direct ecclesiastical influence. The character of the religious teaching, therefore, can be determined more directly than is possible in a national school, where children of all sects meet as on neutral ground, and with equal rights. A very strong feeling exists in many minds as to the importance of the religious element in education,—a feeling which is strong in proportion as it is conscientious; and it is thought that the security for this religious instruction is minimised if the clergy are removed from direct control over the schools. The assertions made by the opponents of the denominational system, to the effect that the religious teaching in schools is nominal and perfunctory more than real and thorough, may be true to a great extent; but it is met by the counter-assertion that, whatever deficiencies exist in this respect are capable of removal,—that the denominational system contains unlimited capabilities for extending and improving the religious education offered, while the national system places an impassable limit to it. Many of those who dread the exclusion of religion from public schools feel, or imagine, that in order to prevent it, a complete divorce between the Church and the school-house must not be allowed, and that, therefore, the only way open to ensure clerical supervision is to educate the people through the agency of the denominational organisations.

A second cause which prompts the support of the denominational system is sectarian zeal. If all denominations were equal in numbers, or were so distributed that each could always include its own members in its own school, this cause would hardly exist. But the professed adherents to the different denominations, as well as those who are careless about religion altogether, are scattered indiscriminately all over the colonies. In the great cities each sect can have its own school, and can manage to fill it; but in the country townships and hamlets this is not the case. There, only one or at most two schools can exist. The denomination, therefore, that can first get a footing and establish itself, holds a vantage ground, so far as the chances of proselytising are concerned. There being, for some time, no scope for a second school, all the children in the neighbourhood must come to its school, or go without public education altogether. It, therefore, not only secures the bringing up of its own youth in all the articles of its creed and the peculiar forms of its worship, but it stands a fair chance of winning over others. It does not, of course, follow that children brought up in the school of a particular denomination will be attached to that denomination through life. But early impressions, especially if pleasing, are often permanent, and, where there is no counteracting influence may have a wonderful predominance over the character. The educational grant, therefore, is capable of being made a very powerful auxiliary for the promotion of denominational interests; and we accordingly observe that there is often a scramble amongst the different sects to secure the first possession of an unoccupied district. It is obvious that the most numerous and powerful sect has the best chance, since, in localities where its adherents are numerically fewer than all the other residents if put together, it may be the strongest, considered separately, and consequently able to take the lead and compel submission on the part of the rest. If there had happened to be any one denomination so very strong as to overshadow all others, there would probably have been a combination against it, to prevent its using State funds still further to aggrandise itself. But the four most numerous denominations are, on the whole, so evenly balanced, that each has an equal chance of benefiting by the educational grant; and therefore, though jealous of each other, they are all content to accept a system which gives them in common an advantage as against the rest of the public. The small and miscellaneous sects have no opportunity of training their own children in their own faith. To them the liberal offers of the system are little better than a mockery. Unable, except in a few places, to fill a school of their own, the assistance that is promised to them, if they could do so, is an assistance they can rarely secure, for they can seldom fulfil the required conditions. Their children must mostly attend schools conducted by persons of a different faith, and the loss of influence and *prestige*, to which their denominational position is thereby exposed, is compensated by no reactionary influence in their favour in other ways. So far, therefore, as the denomina-

I

tional system affects the relative prosperity of the different sects, it is obvious that it is to the advantage of the stronger sects to support the system, and, if possible, to make it the exclusive one; while, on the other hand, the weaker sects are interested in the establishment of a system on a broad, national, and undenominational basis.

It is considered by some that the denominational system has the advantage of enlisting in the cause of education the religious zeal of the country, thus securing, without cost to the State, the services of a very powerful and constantly operating force. All mere official departments of the government, they say, have a tendency to become inert. There is in them a want of self-acting stimulus, or competitive emulation, which keeps other agencies perpetually up to the mark. It is thought that a wide scheme of national education, unopposed by any rival system, would deaden all inventive industry by its uniformity, remove all stimulus to special exertion, and induce on the part of the whole official staff that minimum degree of exertion which is described in colonial parlance as " the government stroke." By setting sectarian jealousy to work, a force is undoubtedly called into play which would do much to prevent inertness in the cause of education, though, when the country is once schooled and mapped out amongst the different sects, there would be less scope for the effective exercise of this jealousy, only so much indeed as it afforded by the increase of population. But, though sectarian zeal is a powerful agency, it has its drawbacks. Apart from the spirit of philanthropy or conscientiousness which is generally more or less mixed up with it, it is of somewhat dubious worth on moral grounds, and certainly is not a spirit which the State as such is justified in encouraging.

The fact, too, that the educational grant, when distributed denominationally, is capable of being applied as a church grant in disguise, forms one of the chief difficulties in the way of a parliamentary settlement of the question in that direction. The *odium theologicum* is imported into the question none the less surely because it is done covertly. A zeal for education is professed when it is really a zeal for denominational extension that actuates. This has been the case in England. It is not less the case in these Colonies. Those who object on principle to the State aiding religion at all, feel therefore an objection to a denominational system of education similar in kind, if not equally strong in degree; and this, combined with the unseemly rivalries to which this scheme gives rise, its capricious distribution of schools throughout the country, and its defects as a system for imparting a really sound education, may account for the obvious tendency of enlightened statesmen of every denomination, to give the preference to a good national unsectarian plan as the only satisfactory solution of the question.

To this we may advert in a future paper.

Popular Proverbs.

Proverbs, containing as they do moral judgments, cannot but be, as far as they obtain currency, mightily operative for good or for evil. The proverb is the supposed portable wisdom which every man carries about with him; that which moves him to act or restrains him from acting; to which he appeals for warrant and sanction for what he is and what he does; it is the salt with which he seasons his good deed, the flattering sweet with which he sugars over the bad. "Let me have the making of a nations' ballads," said a shrewd observer of human nature, "and I care not who makes its laws;" and a proverb in point of influence is upon a par with the ballad. He who strikes off one and secures its circulation among his countrymen, acquires a moral ascendancy, and that through centuries, which legislators and statesmen might well envy. If the proverb be true to the nature and condition of humanity, it will pass on from lip to lip, from region to region, and from age to age, swelling as it rolls like the snowball of our childhood, and augmenting in power; but if it be untrue to fact and nature, though taking, it may be, from a felicitous collocation of words, it will, after a temporary run, in all probability melt and die away, as doubtless thousands have done. This, however, is not uniform, and the observation must be taken with due limitation and caution, for wisdom is not always the heritage of the masses; human nature has not yet attained the goal of perfection. We receive from the past its poisonous streams of error as well as its healthy flow of truth. A sound and intelligent mind will not, therefore, indolently take for granted as genuine all that obtains circulation in society, but will "prove all things, and hold fast that which is good." Let none pass as current coin but such as have stamped upon them the undoubted image and superscription of Truth.

Proverbs when analysed are found to be, some wholly true, some wholly false, and others partly true and partly false. Sometimes also they are true when looked at from one point of view and false from another. We have culled a couple for present observation, and gathered them from around our own door. "Honesty is the best policy." This is a well known adage, an old favourite, often inculcated upon us in our childhood by the sage and the thrifty as the very embodiment of sound advice, and the secret of success in life. "My boy," says the expectant father to his hopeful son, "whatever you do stick to business, and mind 'Honesty's the best policy.'" There is no doubt a measure of truth in this maxim, if it be understood as meaning that honour and honesty, when consistently and uniformly carried out, will in the main and in the majority of instances, be more successful than fraud and deceit. But as it is worded, and as it is sometimes inculcated, it is not wholly unobjectionable. It may seem a rather chivalrous piece of knight-errantry to attack so established a favorite: nevertheless truth requires the venture.

When this sentiment is brought forward as a *motive*, that policy demands honesty; that, on a prudent estimate, the shortest and surest way to make money is to be honest, does it not sanction a low, calculating, and simply utilitarian code of morality, a morality in connection with which the higher and nobler sentiments, the purer and more disinterested virtues of humanity are kept in the back-ground? When I am told that honesty is the best policy, with a view to inculcate upon me the principle that it is my policy to be honest, I feel as a truly honest man that the presentation of such a motive is an insult to my inherent and unbribed love of integrity. Whether it be the best policy or the worst I do not stay to enquire; but whether it be right in itself, and that which becomes me as an upright man, the thing from which I cannot depart without losing my self-respect and the approbation of my own conscience, this is all that concerns me. Policy is a questionable make-weight to honesty,—indeed honesty loses the quality of a genuine and pure virtue in the degree in which the alloy of policy is intermixed in its composition. Let us be honest from principle, not from policy. Let honest courses be pursued, whatever be the consequences: "Fiat justitia ruat cœlum."

But is this proverb true as a *fact?* Is honesty *always* the best policy? We have admitted that it is so often; but is it so uniformly and to a certainty? If the honest man pursue the "honesty policy" system as a policy, will he be always the gainer? Will he not frequently find himself outstripped in the race of policies by those who adopt a more cunning and knavish one? In this world of ours poor honesty is often beaten in the race, and successful fraud carries off the prize. While many an honest man is smarting for his scrupulous conscientiousness, many a swindler is revelling in the abundance of his ill-gotten gains. We cannot, therefore, believe that real honesty derives much advantage from this much-used proverb. "Sophron," says Coleridge, "is well informed that wealth and extensive patronage will be the consequence of his obtaining the love and esteem of Constantia; but if the foreknowledge of this consequence were, and were found out to be, Sophron's main and determining motive for seeking this love and esteem, and if Constantia were a woman that merited or was capable of feeling either the one or the other, would not Sophron find (and deservedly too) aversion and contempt in their stead?" Now honesty may be considered as occupying the position of Constantia. If we woo her for her dowry, the pure, serene, and unworldly eye of honesty turns away from her abject and mercenary votary, with haughty disdain and with merited contempt.

"A stitch in time saves nine." This homely proverb is the second on which we shall offer a remark or two. All honour to the man or woman who first invented the needle; and all honour to the fair who have acquired the skill to ply it well. The needle say we before the bayonet any day: Here is a subject to evoke the spirit of poesy, as Cowper and others could testify. Among its other virtues is the proverb it has furnished us with,—for the poetry, or even for the rhyme of which we cannot say much, but its practical prudence is of sterling value. The timely replacement of the lost button, the speedy reparation of the prophetic rent, are pregnant with ideas of economy, comfort, and orderly habits. But the great and comprehensive lesson taught is the value of promptitude in action.

The measure of success in life to be attained by any, we are disposed to think, depends very much upon the cultivation of this habit. We see two men, one is possessed of a tolerable share of ability and good intentions; he seems likewise always to be uncommonly busy; but somehow or other there is movement without progress—the action is *circular* rather than *onward*—and the whole life is one never-ceasing promise, yet one huge failure. Trace all this to its source, and in innumerable instances you will find that it proceeds from the want of "the stitch in time"—from the baneful spirit of ruinous procrastination. The trite Shakespearian authority may be given once more for the sake of the last two lines, which are not so often quoted—

> " There is a tide in the affairs of men
> Which taken at the flood leads on to fortune;
> *Omitted, all the voyage of their life*
> *Is bound in shallows and in miseries.*"

The other man never allows his deed needlessly to lag behind his purpose; he does not, so to speak, give credit to himself and book his intentions, to be paid for on some future favourable occasion, which he might flatter himself will surely come; his life is one of cash payment, of daily settlement and balancing of all calls and duties. By this promptitude in action, he just escapes about half the bewilderment and fruitless toil of the other, while he ensures double the profit, finding, in truth, that the hand of the so diligent maketh rich. Shun then the spirit of procrastination! Whatever your hand findeth to do, do it at once with all your might; for, as a military veteran once said in the House of Commons when referring to the small hope of promotion for the British soldier whatever his merit and daring might be, " We are beaten by time, your promotion comes when we are worn out by age, or comes when we are gone." Yes, the thought is stirring, time will verily beat us unless we are prompt and active, and old age, should we be spared to reach it, may find us with long procrastinating arrears, which eternity may not be long enough to settle.

What is it to be a Hero?

(FOR YOUNG MEN.)

WE have heard a great deal in late years about "heroes" and "hero worship," and it is curious to see how some try to make us believe that this age of steam-engines and railways is the most heroic the world has ever seen ; while others lament over it as far, far beneath the glorious centuries of the past. Be that as it may, there is plenty of scope in this age and in this country for heroic feeling and heroic enterprise, if our opportunities are only properly used. We are inclined, however, to believe that this era in which so much good has been done and so much more attempted, will, when distance has lent its enchantment to the view, be looked upon as one of the most favorable in the history both of the world and the christian church. But what is heroism ? what is true greatness ? is it attainable ?—many a young man has said to himself. Perhaps he has been reading some of the records of immortalised greatness, of the deeds of chivalry, of noble purposes producing noble results, of self-sacrifice, of fame acquired by despising it ; and he has longed to emulate these doings which humanity delights to honor. Or he has tried to go beyond reading and dreaming, and has actually attempted to mount the ladder of glory, as others have done, and then has been ready to say with quaint old Humphrey— "O that the wretched rolls and red herrings of the world should have power to drag down the spirit to earth when it is soaring amidst the clouds !" If so, what is the reason of this perpetual failure of the dreams of heroism which every young man more or less has cherished ? Some do not fail, it is true, but ninety-nine hundredths do. They try to flap their wings and rise heavenward, but come back again very speedily to live ordinary lives down below. How many imaginary "Paradise Losts" have loomed in the distance, flattering young poets ? How many prime ministers' careers have been sketched among the political youth of our age ? How many "Laws of Gravitation" have been conceived of as not yet found out, but which only awaited discovery to give fame to some scientific juvenile aspirant ! It is all very well for old and experienced heads to smile at this, but young people *will* hope, will build castles, will try to imagine themselves great. Not all the experience of all the ages the human family has lived on earth has changed this propensity of the rising generation to sacrifice common sense to bright and impossible prospects. It will not do then to ignore it, it must be directed. An encouraging hint, which is meant rather to guide than to repress this ambition, will not only often save a young man from wasting himself, but will enable him actually to grow up into true greatness. How ? *True heroism or true greatness is within the reach of all,* and no one with ordinary energy or determination of character need fail to reach it. This will plainly appear if we only think what it is that constitutes that quality in those men called heroes and which is admired by all. *It is not splendour or rank,* for it is a singular fact, which any one of common intelligence can substantiate, that but few out of the ranks of princes,—those born to thrones and dominions of course we mean—have entered the noble company of heroes. They may have been men who well filled their station, who were discreet, wise, able in the position in which they were placed by providence ; but all that did not make them heroes. Among the deceased sovereigns of Britain since the accession of the Stuarts, who is it that merits this high name ? Not one, except perhaps William III. ; yet there have been tolerably good governors among them. But, if a man, not born to such station, by his own energy reaches it, then we esteem him as high in the ranks of earth's greatest sons, as for instance Cromwell. Rank, station, opportunities do not make a hero ; but if a man has the spirit of a hero in him they are a lofty platform for him to start from. Again, *it is not talent*, nor *education*, nor *taste* ; for who calls that man a hero, who, with the finest faculties, trained and exercised throughout youth with the greatest care, and with the keenest perceptions of the beautiful cultivated within him, lives merely for the pleasure of exercising such gifts and acquirements? We do meet with such men occasionally whose business it is to make an elegant waste of life, which they do with such a display of dexterity and æsthetic ingenuity that their refined literary and artistic epicureanism appears at first very enviable. But are they *heroes*, clever and polished as they are ? Are they half as noble as many a man that may be found in these colonies who, once thrown in his struggle with destiny, determines to make his way yet in the world, and begins by felling trees, and making fences, and sleeping under a bush tent ? Heroes ? Are those deserving of the name who have had much given them and have done nothing with it ? It is not talent, nor education joined with talent, that makes a man great. What is it then ? It is *the conquest over circumstances*,—making hindrances into stepping stones, —resolutely taking hold of everything and making it the man's own for some good purpose. Is not that heroism ? If so cannot all become heroes ? Think over the countless roll of heroes from monarchs to peasants, and is it not that which all admire in them ? And the more noble the purpose the more noble the life—the more unselfish the end the more does it claim admiration. Some heroes have been selfish, that is, they have conquered circumstances for themselves, for their own benefit exclusively. The career of such may dazzle by their brilliancy but they never attract ; for true nobility of nature, we all feel, is kindly and genial. The lives of such men as Alexander and Napoleon are splendid pictures, but as we see them we are ready to say—" thank God there are not many such." The truer forms of the heroic character appear when there has been something for which this conquest has been effected, apart from the man's self-interest. These unselfish aims of heroic action are very numerous and different one from the other. They vary in the life of each. This characteristic appears in the heroism of Demosthenes in Greece ; Brutus in ancient, and Rienzi in mediæval Rome ;

our own Cromwell in England and Washington in America, in all of whom patriotic feeling went beyond personal considerations. And in the service of *science* we might enumerate many noble men who have proved self-sacrificing martyrs, in eliminating discoveries which have blessed the world. But is that the highest end for heroic action to achieve ? Is there not something nobler still, which has consecrated the labors of our great philanthropists, our missionaries, the modern martyrs to the cause of humanity ? Nor is this all, may we not go beyond the mere benefit of man in our aim, *and aspire to God ?* May we not conquer circumstances in order to serve and honor him more earnestly, more efficiently ? These are the truest heroes, and such all may be. *All* we say ; for some may conquer impediments that in the field of action their arm may be stronger ; and others by resignation may prove themselves indomitable in faith, and thus deserve the title "heroes in suffering." Some like Hugh Miller may rise from the condition of a simple stonemason to being a power for good in the nation, while others may become models of endurance by energetic devotion to the highest, that is Christian, ends. What more can we say, young men ? Is not a life of heroism within the reach of every one of you ? All that is wanted is *energy* and an *object*. Seek for that energy from God, and let that object be Christ and his cause, and your names will be enrolled among the lists of God's nobility.

SPEECH

Of Sir H. Barkly, K.C.B., Governor of Victoria, at a Public Déjeuner, given at the Exhibition Building, on Nov. 7, 1857, to Dr. Barker, Bishop of Sydney, on the occasion of his Visit to Melbourne.

(Taken from the Argus).

The BISHOP of SYDNEY proposed the Governor's health.

HIS EXCELLENCY, after the toast had been drank, rose and was received with loud and prolonged cheers. He said he felt the high compliment which the Bishop of Sydney had paid him by inference, by the comparison which he had drawn between himself and the Governor of New South Wales. He appeared before them that day less as Governor of Victoria than as a private individual. He begged to say that, while he yielded to no one in respect for the Church of England, he had deemed it wise and discreet to decline the honor which had been proffered him of filling the chair on that occasion. While he hoped, as an humble member of the Church, he should never shrink from the duties thereby incumbent upon him, as Governor of the colony he filled a somewhat peculiar position. As the Queen's representative—the Queen who was the head of the Church to which they belonged, wherever it existed—it might be supposed he was more closely connected with that Church than with any other. That, however, was an accident of his position. He could scarcely be considered as in any way concerned in the government of the Church, in a colony where there did not exist the the principle of connection between the two. He formed no part of the Ecclesiastical Constitution. Governor of a country in which there were no immediate relations between the State and the Church, it would have been wrong, he thought, to have allowed himself to have occupied an apparently official connection with the Church, and for that reason he had felt bound not to consent to act as chairman. Englishman as he was, and Churchman as he was, he still thought it desirable that the actual indep ndence of the Church and State here should be suff-red to appear. Some of them might think a State Church to be a State necessity ; but it was a remnant of a by-gone time, when the minority had to keep their opinions pretty much in their own bos ms. An institution it was that, no doubt, possessed many advantages, but it had also many disadvantages. The powers claimed by Parliament as to the Church had involved the whole question in many difficulties. Therefore it was that their Roman Catholic fellow-subjects had been so long excluded from a voice in the making of the common laws of their country. The Jews, by this feature, more than by anything beside, were still shut out from Parliament. He had always, when himself in Parliament, felt that question one of the most difficult of all to deal with. He spoke as a liberal and, at the same time, conscientious Church of England man. It was undoubtedly a false principle, on the one hand, to say that a born subject of England should not be allowed to assist in the making of the laws under which he lived ; but then, again, to let the Jews take part in the internal working of the Church to which they were opposed seemed to him an anomaly fraught with danger to the institutions of the Church itself. An able writer had said that religion could not possibly share in temporal power without partaking of the animosities which the disputes about that power were certain to call forth. This feature had, in his (the Governor's) opinion, impaired the Church's efficiency down to the present time ; and in this country the Church, by relinquishing some influence and visible power, had escaped many snares and difficulties to which otherwise it might have been exposed. He sincerely hoped her influence here would grow, and the benefits of her existence be felt on all sides around her. In England it might perhaps be said that the Church was too much a Church of the rich ; here, he trusted, such a reproach would never be brought upon her, for she existed under different auspices. An effort for political federation was now making in the Australian colonies. The Church already, to a certain extent, enjoyed analagous benefits, but how greatly would these be increased by the formation of an intercolonial Synod, composed of members from the various colonies. He trusted they would again be visited by their respected metropolitan, for from such visits great benefits to them all would unquestionably accrue. He hoped the ladies would accept his apologies for having obtruded upon them a dry, and perhaps distasteful, speech ; and he would conclude by thanking them all for the patience with which they had listened to him. (Loud cheers).

A SOFT PILLOW.

Whitfield and a pious companion were much annoyed one night at a public-house, by a set of gamblers in the room adjoining where they slept. Their noisy clamour and horrid blasphemy so excited Whitefield's abhorrence and pious sympathy that he could not rest. "I will go in to them, and reprove their wickedness," he said. His companion remonstrated in vain. He went. His words of reproof fell apparently powerless upon them. Returning, he lay down to sleep. His companion asked him rather abruptly, "What did you gain by it?" "A soft pillow," he said patiently, and soon fell asleep. Yes, " a soft pillow " is the reward of fidelity—the companion of a clear conscience. It is a sufficient remuneration for doing right, in the absence of all other reward.

SUNDAY READING.

The Church's Duty to Colonists.

The term Church is used without any reference to sectarian distinctions. The Church of God is not to be identified with a sect. It is composed of such as call Christ master, and are ready at his bidding to work for the destruction of ignorance and ungodliness, and for the establishment of the kingdom of righteousness, peace, and joy in the Holy Ghost. Such are ready to spend and to be spent; to employ head, heart, and purse for the honor of their master. These, including ministers, office-bearers, teachers, and private members form the instrumentality by which these colonies are to be taught, guided, and elevated. All hope of healthy progress is under God in the Church of Christ.

If, however, the church is ever to fulfil her mission, she must solemnly realize her position in reference to the world. The Redeemer prayed not that his followers might be " taken out of the world."——He taught that they are " the light of the world,"—the " city set on a hill." They are " put in trust" with his Gospel, which they are to preach to every creature. This is their appointed work, nor dare they decline it. It is to be feared that christian men often satisfy themselves with very inadequate views of the mission of Christianity. It is a remedial system. It answers the great question, " What shall I do to be saved?" Its design is to sanctify and guide the individual to peace and holiness. This is doubtless its immediate object. But is this all it aims at? Does it not regard men in their collective capacity? Does it not aim to control and guide cities and states? —to make itself felt in the mart of business, in the court of justice, and in the halls of legislature. Surely Christianity seeks to form the mind of a people, to mould their manners and their social habits, to impress its stamp upon their life. It aspires to be a national religion—not in the sense in which that expression is most commonly used; for Christianity cannot become efficient by force of human law, or as coerced into one form, or as an instrument of political power, but only as a spirit of freedom and health. It is a matter of high moment that good men should regard the Gospel as meeting the enquiry of the heavy laden sinner. But it is almost equally important that they should regard it as placed like the pillar of cloud at the head of communities, to lead them forward on their appointed journey.

Liberal views must be formed and carried out. Christ must be honored, the full breadth of his religion exhibited, although it should lead to some sacrifice of sectarianism, or even scatter its minor peculiarities to the winds.

The lessons of history are before us, and deserve to be deeply pondered. Christianity has ever been the great civiliser; but during the middle ages her influence was mixed with, and limited by, the covetousness and ambition of men who breathed little of her spirit. The church so called did not fairly expound the messages of God to the nations. Men, even when led in the right path, were led very much in darkness. Their obedience was the obedience of slaves, instead of that of children. Religion was a craven superstition, not a service of perfect freedom. Christianity, apart from ecclesiastical tyranny, could not work itself out into a broad national power. How difficult it is to appreciate the strength of Christianity as consisting in truth and love, separate from all other influences, may be seen in the case of the excellent puritans on their first settlement in America. They attempted to bind the spirit of religion to civil force. Driven out from their own land by persecution, these God-fearing men did not fully understand the doctrine that truth can fight her own battles and win her own victories.

At the distance of two centuries, colonies are rising on these remote shores. There are, blessed be God, not a few intelligent and devoted men among us—men who call Christ Lord, and who long for the highest welfare of these communities. It becomes them, amid the excitements of the time and the political privileges now conceded and freely exercised, to review their position and to consider their responsibility as the servants of Christ. They have it in their power, by the blessing of God, to do a glorious work for their master and for posterity.

1. Christian men should feel that the work of moulding the sentiments and character of the colonies, in a religious point of view, is committed to their hands by him to whose authority they bow. If this work be not done by them, it will remain undone. The Bible contains within itself the seeds of human well-being and progress. Its doctrines are friendly to all the interests of man. That book asserts man's responsibility and immortality. It affirms a moral government, and points to a day of reckoning. It exhibits God as the King and Father of his creatures. It makes little of outward circumstances. It regards the soul as of infinite worth. It rebukes injustice and protects the weak and oppressed. It claims for man a common origin, and explodes all notions of caste. It accords to men equal rights, equal freedom, equal laws. It concedes to woman her rights and responsibilities as the partner and equal of man. It proclaims the tender sympathies of God towards his chosen servants. It reveals a system of forgiveness, and bids the Christian ever remember that he is bought with a price. These truths lie at the foundation of human welfare, individual or collective. They are preeminently necessary in a growing community. Such a community may in the absence of these truths increase in numbers, and in commercial importance, but not in true greatness nor in moral worth. The salt of the earth, the power which at once stimulates and preserves, is the truth of God. But who are the parties that are to assert that

truth ?—to keep it before the public eye? that, loving the truth, see and feel the necessity of its being received and acted upon by all around ?   Obviously the servants of Christ.

2. It behoves the Church of Christ in these colonies—the church consisting of devoted men of all sects—to feel that she has been made a church, and placed in her present position, with a view to her holding forth the word of life and leavening with truth and goodness the whole community.   Christian men should feel that they are fully committed to this work ; that a "necessity" is laid upon them, nay that "woe is unto" them if they are unfaithful to their Great Master.   For what purpose has God given them his Holy Word?   Why has he filled that word with truths which not only guide the individual wanderer to peace, but which are so adapted, so essential to social advancement? Unless these truths are recognised, no State can attain to permanent greatness.   None qualified to judge will deny that the Bible is the basis of modern civilisation.   The Law of God is the foundation of all other law ; but the book of which these things are said, is the "book of the Church:" by the Church it is held dear, and, but for her, its voice would soon cease to be heard among men.   How urgent the motive then that should impel pious men to declare and expound the truth of God through the pulpit, the platform, the press, and by every available means.   And it is not too much to affirm that these colonies will be elevated or degraded as they are faithful or otherwise to their Lord.

3. Nor is it unimportant to remind the reader, that although these colonies have been in existence from twenty to sixty years, they may still be said to be in their infancy,—for that is but a small period in the life of a nation.   The question then is not impertinent : What is to be the moral character of their manhood? What is to be the predominant social power pervading them? Is Christianity to rule?   Are all questions to be referred to her decision?   In old countries certain abuses have incorporated themselves with religion, and they defy all attempts to remove them. Are similar abuses to re-appear on these shores ? Things are taking shape.   Institutions are rising and becoming powerful. It becomes our men of influence carefully to watch and guard against all errors and mistakes in the State and in the Church, in Societies and Committees, and thus preclude the evils which, once established, become invincible.   Every immigrant stepping on these shores should find that his highest interests are cared for ; that his rights as a man and a citizen are understood ; that there is among us a public opinion in favor of what is true and right, and intolerant of what is false and unjust.   This state of society depends, however, upon the Church of Christ,—not merely on her attempts at individual conversions, but on the power of the influence she exerts upon the complicated machinery of colonial social life.

QUARTUS.

Another Shipwreck.

WE have scarcely recovered from the shock produced by the fearful wreck of the " Dunbar," and the running down of the "Champion " steamer, when all the emotions awakened by those events have been quickened into fresh sensibility by another appalling catastrophe — the wreck at the Sydney Heads of the " Catherine Adamson," by which another multitude of our fellow-creatures, including the pilot who guided the vessel, and a minister of religion, who had come out to devote his energies to these colonies,* were suddenly consigned to a watery grave. The passengers and crew, like those of the Dunbar, just entering the desired haven, after the weariness of a long sea voyage, had, in a moment, their joy cut short, and met a melancholy death instead. Why this new calamity on the heels of the others? Do these things occur by chance? Is there not a cause and an object? And is there not a voice in these events? Perhaps the impressions produced by the former strokes were likely to have proved evanescent, and therefore the stroke is repeated. A Divine hand must be recognised. Every Christian mind will exclaim— "This is the finger of God."

There is, and always has been, a strong tendency to practical atheism in the world. Because events are brought about by the laws of nature, or through the agency of man, many persons rest satisfied with these proximate causes, and look no higher. Everything is attributed to the seen and natural, nothing to the unseen and spiritual. A gross materialism excludes the Deity from his own world. Any acknowledgment of divine interposition is stigmatised as enthusiasm or cant. A smile of incredulity and pity greets the least reference of public or private calamities to the hand of God, or the remotest hint that such events are designed to have a moral significancy.

" Shall there be evil in a city and the Lord hath not done it?"† asks a Hebrew prophet. Disasters had occurred among his people, and others were impending, but the infidels of the day deemed them mere accidents. They saw nothing of God, nothing of warning, in them. Their inward thought was—all things come alike to all. How sternly is their atheism here rebuked! and how forcibly are the people instructed to trace up their troubles to the Governor of all, and to read in them the lessons of wisdom and piety he was obviously teaching them.

There is no doctrine more deeply impressed upon the Old Testament Scriptures than that of a Divine providence in human affairs. This great truth is interwoven in the very texture of the book, and cannot be disengaged from it without destroying the fabric. The histories of individuals and of nations there recorded

---

* The Rev. Jacob Jones, late of Milksham, Wilts, sent out by the Colonial Missionary Society for New South Wales.

† Amos iii. 6.

were not designed to amuse, or even to give historic information, but to teach the world that the Creator has not abandoned the universe he has made, but is its actual and ever-vigilant Governor. The blight that has come upon man's moral nature shows itself in nothing more obviously than in the tendency to overlook this great fact, and a chief part of the mission of the prophets was to rouse attention to it, and to demand its constant recognition And did they not do this in every possible way,—by sublime descriptions of the Deity, by earnest and impassioned exhortations, by vivid reproductions of past events, and varied and striking predictions of those that were to come? "The Lord reigneth," said they; "He is a great King over all the earth;" "His eyes are upon the ways of man, and he seeth all his goings;" "God is judge; he putteth down one and setteth up another." They even introduce the Divine Being himself as saying, "I kill and I make alive, I wound and I heal;" "I form the light and create darkness, I make peace and create evil; I the Lord do all these things."

And let it be remembered that it is not miraculous events alone, or such remarkable ones as cannot be explained by natural causes, that are thus ascribed to Divine agency. Sunshine and shower, seed-time and harvest, summer and winter, food and raiment, health and friends—all the ordinary comforts and felicities of life—are the bountiful gifts of "our Father which is in heaven." And the sicknesses and pains, the anxieties and disappointments, —the various "ills that flesh is heir to"—are his paternal chastisements for his children's good. The passions and energies of men or the established laws of nature, may be the instruments of bringing about these results, but "the hand that moves them is Divine." The Egyptians, the Philistines, the Assyrians, the Romans, who harassed the Israelites of old, and the mighty conquerors of antiquity, who led them captive, are described, with all the force of Oriental imagery, as the sword, the staff, the hammer of the Almighty, by which he punished his rebellious people. Mildew and caterpillars, drought and barrenness, the raging of the sea, and the convulsions of air and land, the ravages of flood and pestilence, are alike the operations of the Supreme Being. "He maketh the winds his messengers, and the flaming lightnings his ministers." The writers of Scripture, in tracing all such events to the providence of God, seem innocently unconscious of any difficulty. They were not embarrassed by a speculative or materialistic philosophy. And in this they show both the correctness of their reasoning and the strength of their piety. For surely to exclude God from the government of the world he has made is as contradictory to sound logic as it is offensive to the religious susceptibilities of our nature.

Nor is the doctrine of providence peculiar to the Old Testament Scriptures—the production, some would have us believe, of a mythical, a superstitious, and an obsolete age. It is equally characteristic of the New. If the blessed Saviour himself assures us that not a hair of man's head, nor even a common sparrow, can fall to the ground without our Father, he surely teaches us to recognise the providence of God as extending through the universe at large. The doctrines, the precepts, the promises and prophecies of the New Testament, all assume, and some assert, the continued presence of the Deity among men, his agency in controlling every circumstance which affects their destiny, and his doing all this for purposes infinitely wise and good.

It might seem superfluous to affirm so strongly so plain a point as a Divine Providence in human affairs, extending to all events that concern us. But the tone of too many writers in the present day, the scorn with which any reference to God in public calamities is met, the obstinate reluctance to look no farther than to the causes nearest at hand for a solution of such occurrences, indicating a wide-spread scepticism upon the subject, or, at all events, a *wish* to disbelieve, must be our apology. There is clearly no alternative between an absolute infidelity, amounting to practical atheism, on the one hand, and the recognition of a watchful providence in all human concerns, on the other. If we are Christians at all, we must be believers in Providence.

The ordinary workings of providence are uniform, tranquil, and beneficent. Under their silent and serene influence myriads of sensient and conscious beings are sustained, protected, and made happy. Their "bread is given to them, their water is sure." They lie down in peace, sleep in safety, and arise refreshed, to renew their daily occupations. But this very quietud and regularity are perverted to the purposes of unbelief and indifference. When all things continue without material change God is overlooked. When the machine of Providence goes on with the precision of clock-work, the secret spring that moves it, the mighty power that keeps it in order, is forgotten. It requires something uncommon and unexpected to break this profound repose and arouse public attention. Hence it is, that in the order of providence startling events occur from time to time. The elements are let loose from their ordinary restraints, and spread havoc over sea and land. The human mind, in its skill and in its caution usually acting with such constancy that thousands confidingly trust their lives to these qualities in their fellow-men, suddenly and unaccountably fails, as if infatuated, and multitudes perish as the consequence. A district is reduced to poverty—a town is clad in mourning—grief and lamentation are heard on every hand.—Is there not a purpose in this? and must it not be a benevolent one? If the peaceful and faithful regularity of providence, for the most part, should nourish in the heart gratitude and love and trust towards the Being that does all this, are there not lessons equally valuable taught us by the storm, the shipwreck and the flood? When God thus loudly speaks shall not his creatures reverently hear?

Moral and religious truths may be more effectually impressed upon the mind by suffering than by didactic instruction. Not unfrequently it is, that through the sacrifices, sufferings, and bloodshed entailed by despotism, and continued age after age, the sweets of liberty are won. Through mistakes and grasping monopolies, and clashing interests and dear-bought experience, correct principles in legislation and commerce are wrought out. Through the protracted and bitter experience of error and superstition and national deterioration, a people are prepared to welcome and appreciate the true religion. So it may be that through startling calamities and accidents by sea and land, truths which are generally acknowledged, but little heeded, may come to be seen in a stronger light, and acquire a new importance. Not to insist upon the frailty of human life, and the necessity of constant preparation for another world—lessons which occur to us at once, as obviously suggested by such events — may not their purpose further be to lift us out of our selfishness, and place us where charity spontaneously rises in the heart, and help is readily extended by the hand—where the ties of our common brotherhood are more tenderly felt, and the deepest sympathies of our nature are stirred towards our fellow-creatures in distress? Above all, are not such events designed to force attention to the Divine government in human affairs—to evoke emotions of awe and reverence and humility before a Being who wields such tremendous agencies of destruction? " Is there evil in the city and the Lord hath not done it?" And the voice of Him that does it may be heard above the storm, addressing us and saying, " Stand in awe and sin not;" " Be still and know that I am God." Who does not see the wisdom, the duty, the benefit of submission to such a power, and of the cordial and willing acceptance of the overtures of reconciliation which are so graciously made to us by the same Being in the Gospel of peace?

The Cross : A FRAGMENT.

CHRIST on the Cross ! Strange union of thoughts and words ! Christ and a Cross ; the Son of God dying the death of a slave ! We feel no perplexity in meeting the Incarnate One on the Mount of Beatitudes, on " Tabor's glorious steep," at Lazarus' tomb, at Bethany, or even at the well of Sychar. But Christ on the Cross ! This startles and shocks. Yet there he is ; the nails are through his hands and feet, the thieves are on either side, the noisy thoughtless crowd around, the Pharisees intoxicated with malicious joy, the devout women watching in the distance. Yes, it is He—there can be no mistake as to his identity—He who wrought the wondrous miracles, who uttered the rich deep wisdom.

Christ on the Cross ! Yes, and he is there by the permission, the ordination of God; there by his own choice; there to the joy of the Church. The Christian gazes at the sufferer, drops a tear, yet says, " It is well !" The right Being " is in the right place." True, never was the Redeemer more in his place,—not when he said to the raging sea, " Peace, be still !"—not when he said, " Lazarus, come forth ! "—not when he took his seat on the mediatorial throne. But it is not enough to say God *permitted* the crucifixion ; he *rejoiced* in the spectacle. Never had such virtue, such self-denial, such consecration appeared before, either among angels or men. Jesus delighted to do his Father's will. He ran, he flew, to this goal of the Cross ; he eagerly leaped on to this hill of humiliation and suffering. The Christian delights to turn to that Cross. Moses smote the rock, and there gushed out a stream of water : Jehovah smote his Son, and there gushed forth a richer and more lasting stream,—a stream which to the end of time shall " make glad the city of God." Oh ! my soul ! hast thou dwelt amid the mysteries of the cross ? Glorious sufferer ! art thou indeed my Saviour ?

Before thou canst realise the magnetic power of Calvary thou must have an eye to see and a heart to feel. Suppose there had been present at the Cross a representative from every known country of the globe,—a philosopher from Athens, another from the Eternal City, another from Alexandria, a half-civilised man from distant Albion,—the spectacle to them would have been vapid and commonplace, or odious and disgusting. But let the " heavy laden " one come, whose conscience is up in arms, around whose head the thunders of Sinai are rolling and threatening destruction ; let the soul wounded by the barbed arrows of conviction, over whom a dread eternity has cast its silent and awful shadow,—the soul whose agitation is rapidly transferred to the whole material world, so that, affrighted, it feels as though the world were striking on a rock and threatening to break up into fragments. Let *him* look at the Cross, learn that the transaction of Calvary is God's sovereign method of grace for fallen man : let him learn that Christ is a Saviour, heaven a home, and God a friend. Then the burden drops from his shoulders,—then he feels the truth of this word, " And I, if I be lifted up from the earth, will draw all men unto me."

Christ on the Cross settles conclusively the question of man's immortality, for the life he procures is " eternal life," and the punishment from which he delivers is "everlasting punishment." I know little of the invisible world, but the God of Calvary reigns there ; and his eternal government of his Church shall be a luminous commentary on the cardinal event of time—the " lifting up " of his Son.

FEAR OF EVIL.

In the commission of evil, fear no man so much as thine own self. Another is but one witness against thee ; thou art a thousand. Another thou mayst avoid, but thyself thou canst not. Wickedness is its own punishment.

Memoir

OF THE LATE MRS. ISABELLA WHITNEY, HOBART TOWN.

Matured Christians uniformly renounce self-glorifying, especially as they approach eternity. The Rev. Thomas Scott avowed, in the final scene, that the prayer of the publican, from which he had preached his last sermon, was *his own*. Hannah More, when reminded of her good deeds, said, " Talk not so vainly : I utterly cast them from me, and fall low at the foot of the Cross." The Rev. Richard Watson, when addressed in a similar strain, exclaimed, " God forbid that I should boast ! Oh, no ; I am a poor vile sinner." The Rev. Charles Simeon deprecated " a dying scene," and said that he wished to be alone with God, and to lie before him as utterly unworthy. In like manner, the subject of this sketch, after long maintaining an honorable Christian walk, celebrated the Divine mercy as the source of all her hopes and joys.

Mrs. Whitney (whose maiden name was Crager) was born at Laytonstone, in Essex, but removed to London when a child. She had a pious mother, but during her life gave no heed to the best counsel. She was addicted to amusements, and was passionately fond of dancing. She was led, however, to accompany some friends to the chapel where the Rev. Andrew Reed (now Dr. Reed) then exercised his ministry : there she heard him preach from the passage—" Is anything too hard for the Lord ?" As he exhibited the manifold forms in which the Divine potency may be displayed, she listened in a captious spirit, and said in her heart, " Who does not know all this ?" But presently she was startled by the announcement that there was one thing which *was too* hard for the Lord. This statement excited her surprise, and even indignation ; but the preacher proceeded, saying, with deep solemnity, " There is one thing which the Lord cannot do—He cannot save a sinner *in* his sins." This was the awakening call which God's mercy supplied. She was led to Christ, and united with the Church under Dr. Reed's care, when she was about eighteen years of age. She continued in that fellowship nearly thirteen years, and then, partly on account of health, left England for Hobart Town. There, in March, 1833, she joined the Church under the charge of the Rev. F. Miller, and remained in that fellowship to the end of her days an enduring and consistent Christian. According to the testimony of one who resided with her upwards of twenty-three years, as well as that of her most intimate friends, she was distinguished for decision, veracity, integrity, and conscientiousness ; for spiritual-mindedness, for thankfulness, contentment, and uniform consistency of character, and for warm interest in the advancement of Christ's kingdom. She passed through varied scenes of care and sorrow, but her principles endured the test. On the bed of sickness, more than twenty-one years since, in the midst of sore distress, she said, with an emphasis which has never been forgotten by one who heard her, " Though he slay me, yet will I trust in him." During the closing months of her pilgrimage she was sustained by like precious faith. Continuous suffering was endured with so much patience and placidity that to this cause was ascribed the prolongation of life, contrary to medical expectations. Frequently she urged those around her to seek that religion which supplied to her solace and strength. Shortly before her departure she breathed out these significant words—" More than conquerors." Thus she realised an answer to the prayers of earlier years. Some records of her Christian course, which she kept as a diary or journal, she desired to be preserved from observation or publicity. Such a request should be respected and appreciated, for it may certainly be questioned whether a record of Christian experience can be kept with due fidelity, if there be even the latent impression that it will be seen by others. But reference has been permitted to another journal, which chiefly relates to her voyage to the colony, and which probably was intended to be seen by some of her friends. In that journal, in November, 1832, she thus wrote :—" May we be continually looking to Him who has promised to cover our head in the day of battle, and to make us *more than conquerors* through Him who hath loved us." Such was her earnest desire a quarter of a century since ; a desire which subsequently, without doubt, often found prayerful expression. What was the issue ? The utterance of her feeble voice in a dying hour indicated that her " heart's desire and prayer to God " *was answered*. She retained consciousness to the last. She died on her birthday, aged fifty-four years.

ENVY.

Other passions have objects to flatter them, and seemingly to content and satisfy for awhile ; there is power in ambition, and pleasure in luxury, and pelf in covetousness ; but envy can give nothing but vexation.—*Montaigne*.

The Power of Rest.

I.

A scarce-felt breeze is blowing, and the sea
Spangled with ripples, lies beneath the hill
Like to a smiling beauty in a dream,
While in the enchantment of the sunlight's gleam
The waves are hushed, no longer wildly free,
But telling us that Peace should all things fill ;
While in the centre of the bay, a sail
Though spread to find the breeze, yet rests asleep,
Her eager canvas for a time must fail
Of motion,—for the spirits of the gale,
Charmed with the beauty of a slumb'ring deep,
Will in *silence* for a while their vigils keep.

II.

But there may be an unseen strength in rest,
Though seldom known,—for I had turned away
My eyes from looking on that ship, and lay
Wrapt a while in thought, and in communion blest
With him whose mantle is the light of day,
And in my dream of joy was trembling lest
Ought should disturb me, when I looked, and lo !
That sail, with quiet speed, had crossed the bay,
Strong in that strength which gentlest breezes know.
Then spake to me a voice in that mild hour—
" Might is not only where wild tempests lower
" In seeming useless rest, may dwell a heavenly power."

LIFE.

Life bears us on like a stream of a mighty river. Our boat first glides down the mighty channel—through the playful murmuring of the little brook, and the winding of its grassy borders. The trees shed their blossoms over our young heads, the flowers on the brink seem to offer themselves to our young hands ; we are happy in hope, and we grasp eagerly at the beauties around us ; but the stream hurries on, and still our hands are empty. Our course in youth and manhood is along a wilder and deeper flood, amid objects more striking and magnificent. We are animated at the moving pictures of enjoyment and industry passing us : we are excited at some short-lived disappointment. The stream bears us on, and our joys and griefs are alike left behind us. We may be shipwrecked, we cannot be delayed ; whether rough or smooth, the river hastens to its home, till the roar of the ocean is in our ears, and the tossing of the waves is beneath our feet, and the land lessens from our eyes, and the floods are lifted up around us, and we take our leave of earth and its inhabitants, until of our further voyage there is no witness save the Infinite and Eternal !—*Bishop Heber.*

WHAT IS THE WORLD ?

A dream within a dream ; as we grow older, each step is an inward awakening. The youth awakes, as he thinks, from childhood – the full-grown man despises the pursuits of youth as visionary—the old man looks on manhood as a feverish dream. Is death the last sleep ? No ; it is the last awakening.—*Walter Scott.*

FOLLY.

A fool, says the Arab proverb, may be known by six things—anger without cause, speech without profit, change without motive, inquiry without object, putting trust in a stranger, and not knowing friends from foes.

K 2

STATISTICS.

TASMANIAN CENSUS.—We have received a letter from a correspondent guarding against the false impression the Government Statistics of the Colony, published in our last number, are likely to produce as to the relative numbers of the different denominations. The Episcopal Church is put down as 47,714, whereas our correspondent states that by a published return the actual attendants on worship were only 5,700, which number includes a large body of convicts who are compelled to attend. We presume that in the census returns that vast number of persons who are, unhappily, nothing at all in religion, are put down to the Church of England, and thus have the effect of swelling the amount of the public grant apportioned to that body.

NEW SOUTH WALES.
From the *Sydney Morning Herald*, 18th August, 1857.
OFFICIAL STATISTICS.
Education of the Churches in Sydney.

Proportion of those persons who are educable members of each Church, *who can read and write*:—

For each 1000 in Roman Catholic Church	570
„ Church of England	769
„ Presbyterian Churches	800
„ Independent and Wesleyan Churches &c.	801

Among 1000 educable children in the above bodies, there are who can read and write—

In Roman Catholic Church	386
„ Church of England	483
„ Presbyterian Churches	510
„ Independent and Wesleyan Churches, &c.	547

To the Editor of the Southern Spectator.

DEAR SIR,—In the October number of the *Spectator*, "Quartus," writing on the Church's duty, intimate that a tear for their sad extinction is all that can be rendered to the Aborigines of Australia.

It is natural for one who has seen Australia only in the neighbourhood of its cities and the larger seaport towns, to write thus. But it is important for the Church of Christ to have the fact clearly and fully presented that, in the distant interior, and along the coast to the northward of Moreton Bay and to the west of Adelaide, the aborigines are still numerous.

The Diocesan Board of Missions in N. S. Wales collected information, three or four years ago, as to the number of aborigines within that colony,—information which led to the conclusion that there were about eleven thousand within the occupied territory.

Those who travel outwards from the cities and towns of the colony, toward the unoccupied regions, find that as the number of colonists decreases, the aborigines begin to be more numerous. A traveller, at 200 miles distance from Sydney, meets two or three blacks at a station here and there; after two or three days' journey onwards, camps of half-a-dozen are seen; and, in a few more days he comes occasionally across parties of twenty, thirty, or a hundred; and, by the time he has reached the furthest cattle stations, he may be surrounded by much larger crowds of aborigines.

Have not the reports of the Missionaries at the Murray and at Port Lincoln proved, at least, that there are still many aborigines there?

In the year 1854, between the McIntyre and the Bundarra Rivers, I fell in with a large party of aborigines who were returning from a "bora," at which the three usually hostile tribes of the McIntyre, Bundarra, and Namoi Rivers had met in peace for the celebration of their national mysteries. From reports of the various parties who went in other directions, it was evident there could not have been less than 600 met at that time. These blacks live in a district which has been occupied by squatters for fifteen or twenty years. In that company I saw many a hoary head, and many an infant at the breast,—proofs that the extinction of the race (unless by the hand of violence) is not near. And if there be tens of thousands in the territories occupied by our colonists, there must be many more tens of thousands in the regions beyond.

If we had here two or three men of the spirit of Moffatt and Livingstone, our colonial Churches would soon be aroused to substitute for the desponding "tear" with which we "let the poor ignorant races pass to extinction and forgetfulness," the rallying cry, "Up! for the time is come to sound forth among the heathen who are perishing for lack of knowledge in Australia the glad tidings of redeeming love, and to gather in from this hitherto desolate field many precious souls to the harvest of eternal life."

I am, dear Sir, yours sincerely,

WILLIAM RIDLEY.

Portland, 22nd October, 1857.

REVIEWS.

Victoria and the Australian Gold Mines in 1857. By WILLIAM WEST-GARTH. London: Smith, Elder and Co. Melbourne: G. Robertson and J. J. Blundell.

Mr. Westgarth's fruitful pen has favored the world with another volume on Victoria, and a goodly one too of 460 pages. Like all his former works it is well written, and abounds in common sense views and kindly feeling. It is of course more designed for Britain than these colonies, aiming to give our friends at home a correct idea of what is passing here. Nor is this unnecessary, for we are not unfrequently amused and sometimes amazed at the gross ignorance that prevails on Australian affairs, even in circles that might be presumed to know better. Where New South Wales is, where Victoria, where South Australia, where Western Australia, are questions that would puzzle not a few who would not like to be thought bad geographers. We, therefore, rejoice in anything which helps to diffuse correct and reliable information among the people of Britain concerning us and our doings. Unlike the works of Howitt, "An Englishman," and others of the book-making stamp, the information in this volume may, as all who know Mr. Westgarth and are aware of his long residence in Victoria and his thorough acquaintance with it, be fully depended on. His volume is very comprehensive: it takes a glance at the physical and aboriginal aspects of the country; sketches its early colonisation, and its progress from its feeble beginning to its present magnitude. The commerce, the squatting, the agriculture, and the gold-fields come under review. Each of the principal gold-producing regions (except the Ovens) is described, and a sketch of a tour to them is given, which has the advantage of being written by Mr. Westgarth, while one of a Commission sent on purpose to examine the state of the mining population, and on the other hand the disadvantage of being nearly three years old. All the rest is fresh up to the time when Mr. Westgarth left the colony in February last. But the rapid changes that take place in colonial life are remarkably shewn in the somewhat stale and post-date character of many of his remarks on politics and other matters relating to progress. It is not needful to go into an examination of the volume, as there is little in it which Australians did not know, or might not have known, beforehand. The writer, however, throws out shrewd and valuable hints on all subjects as he passes along. and few can read the book without deriving more or less profit from it. One or two of his suggestions may be briefly noticed. Mr. Westgarth recommends a tax on all lands sold, cultivated or not. He suggests confining the aid given by the public funds to Immigration, to well-regulated *female* Immigration. He seems more favourable to private Railways guaranteed by the State, than to Railways directly undertaken by the Government. He throws out some suggestions for improving Prison Discipline, which are deserving of consideration. See page 363.

Notes of the Overland Route are appended, which constitute a new feature. They are very pleasant reading, and contain a correct representation of what the returning colonists see or may see as they pass homeward by way of Ceylon, the Red Sea and Egypt

Wild Adventures in Australia and New South Wales, beyond the Boundaries, with Sketches of Life at the Mining Districts. By FREDERICK DE BREBANT COOPER. London : James Blackwood. Melbourne : Robertson.

The more common novelists and second-rate tale writers have long been in want of a new scene for their plots. or some fresh style of decoration for their exciting incidents. What a boon India has been to such ! How many fortunes have been made there—How many rich uncles have died there, towards the end of the third volume ! What a convenient place to ship some character off to, which had became unmanageable by the author ! Then as India was getting stale, America got into the market, and we had scenes laid in ' dense primeval forests,' encounters with the red men, ' Hawk eyes,' ' Dear Skin,' ' Swift Foot,' &c. : fierce chases after herds of buffaloes on the burning prairies, and pictures of the backwoodman's retreat among the pines of Canadian forests. And now that American Indians have become *passés*, Australia has come up just at the right moment, and we are having the first few drops of a perfect storm (so we expect) of adventures, travels, descriptions, poems, and novels, founded on the experiences of squatter-life, and a bushman's half-civilised existence on the runs ; and perhaps a still more prolific progeny will spring from some poor unfortunate digger's luckless experiments at Bendigo or Ararat, or from the fortune-making storekeeper's on the gold-fields, who may call to mind, when he has made his money, that there was a time in his life when he was proud to see his name written with B.A. after it. How many of these yet unknown literary "sinkings" will be " shicers" to both writers and public ? Time will show.

In this book of Mr. Cooper's, we have a straightforward graphic description of the wildest bush life—life beyond the boundaries : and we must give our author the credit of having written a very interesting work. It is too much disfigured by the introduction perpetually of technical phrases, both nautical and Australian ; but putting that aside the book is for the most part well and vividly written. The scene of the bulk of the narrative is laid in the northern part of New South Wales, in the bush beyond the runs. where the land has to be won from the savages by hard fighting ; and many are the bloody battles Mr. Cooper himself has been engaged in. The scene of the latter part of the book is laid in the Victorian Gold-fields, and is much inferior in interest to what precedes it.

The Testimony of the Rocks ; or Geology in its bearings on the two Theologies, Natural and Revealed. By HUGH MILLER, author of "The Old Red Sandstone," "Footprints of the Creator," &c. Sixteenth thousand. Edinburgh : Constable. Melbourne : Robertson.

As we turn over the pages of this the most brilliant work of the late Hugh Miller, we feel that there is a melancholy interest connected with it, which would prevent our employing the language of censure even were we disposed or qualified to do so. Few men have lived their short earthly sojourn more nobly, or striven more sincerely to make their energies useful to the cause both of science and religion, than the great Scotch geologist. And as we meet with this the last effort of his genius, which has called forth more care, thought, foresight and eloquence than appear in any of his earlier works ; and then remember how this very work seemed to overcome the master who produced it, and led him to seek refuge from the world in voluntarily quitting it, we would rather let it tell its own story than examine into its details critically. We presume that few of our readers are unacquainted with the life of our author, and have not followed with interest his romantic career from his boyhood among the rocks and caves of Cromarty, when under the tutelage of nature alone, his genius began to develop itself, till the time came when he stood forth acknowledged by the world as at once the most eloquent, and one of the most original, expounders of geological science. The world has much to thank him for ; but still more are the acknowledgments of the Christian church due to him, for it was to the service of religion that his talents were made chiefly to contribute. He has contended earnestly for the faith, and has converted Geology from being an enemy to revealed religion into a faithful ally. When geological investigation was bringing to light, some few years ago, so many new and startling facts, infidels and the opponents of scriptural inspiration looked upon the new science as about certainly to overturn old narrow religious theories. Time has proved the contrary to have been the result of the severe scrutiny the Bible has undergone in consequence. Geology is now the handmaid of even revealed religion ; and that it is so, we in great measure owe to the labours and patience and christian devotedness of Hugh Miller. This last effort of his genius has more especial reference to the biblical questions involved in geological science than his other works. It consists of a series of lectures, some of which were delivered and some never intended to be, on a variety of subjects. Some of them are more scientific and technical, and not so suited to the general reader, but the others on the Creation and Deluge are at once the most interesting and the most eloquent of the series. It is not our purpose to speak of the arguments used in support of his theories, but simply to draw the attention of our readers to this book, especially those who feel interested in the questions which arise out of the Mosaic narratives of the formation of the Earth and its inhabitants. We cannot but think that the question is here placed before us in a more satisfactory light than it has ever been before, in a light at once more in accordance with the spirit of Holy Writ, and the undeniable facts of the advancing science of Geology. At all events the views of Hugh Miller claim the serious consideration of the divine and the christian.

VARIETIES.

SAVING.

The origin of wealth is in a moral feeling—self-denial. " Here is something I will not consume or throw away—I will take care of it, store it up for the future use of myself or others." The man who first said and acted thus laid the foundation of a virtue upon earth. The savings of each man are a diffusive blessing to all, and therefore, so far, frugality is a thing which all may and ought to applaud.

FACTS FOR THE CURIOUS.

If a tallow candle be put in a gun, and shot at a deal door, it will go through without sustaining any injury ; and if a musket-ball be fired into water, it will not only rebound, but be flattened as if fired against a solid substance. A musket-ball may be fired through a pain of glass, making the hole the size of the ball, without cracking the glass ; if the glass be suspended by a thread, it will make no difference, and the thread will not even vibrate. Cork, if sunk 200 feet in the ocean, will not rise, on account of the pressure of the water. In the Arctic regions, when the thermometer is below zero, persons can converse more than a mile distant. Dr. Jamieson asserts that he heard every word of a sermon at a distance of two miles.

FEELING AND JUDGMENT.

Feeling without judgment is a washy draft indeed; but judgment untempered by feeling is too bitter and husky a morsel for human deglutition.— *Charlotte Bronte.*

THE SWEETS OF REVENGE.

" Something of vengeance I had tasted for the first time. As aromatic wine, it seemed on swallowing, warm and racy ; its after-flavor, metalic and corroding, gave me a sensation as if I had been poisoned."—*Ibid.*

LIFE A TRUST.

Life brings with it requirements, and claims, and responsibilities. The burden must be carried, the want provided for, the suffering endured, the responsibility fulfilled.—*Ibid.*

INFLUENCE OF TEMPER ON HEALTH.

Excessive labour, exposure to wet and cold, deprivation of sufficient quantities of necessary and wholesome food, habitual bad lodging, sloth, and intemperance, are all deadly enemies to human life; but they are none of them so bad as violent and ungoverned passions. Men and women have survived all these, and at last reached an extreme old age; but it may be safely doubted whether many instances can be found of a man of violent and irascible temper, habitually subject to storms of ungovernable passion, who has arrived at a very advanced period of life. It is, therefore, a matter of the highest importance to every one desirous to preserve " a sound mind in a sound body," so that the brittle vessel of life may glide down the stream of time smoothly and securely, instead of being continually tossed about amidst rocks and shoals which endanger its existence, to have a special care, amidst all the vicissitudes and trials of life, to maintain a quiet possession of his own spirit.—*Bailey's Records of Longevity.*

MORAL COURAGE.

Sydney Smith, in his work on moral philosophy, speaks in this wise of what men lose through deficiency of moral courage, or independence of mind : " A great deal of talent is lost in the world for the want of a little courage. Every day sends to their graves a number of obscure men, who have only remained in obscurity because their timidity has prevented them from making a first effort; and who, if they could have been induced to begin, would, in all probability, have gone great lengths in the career of fame. The fact is, that to do anything in this world worth doing, we must not stand back, shivering, and thinking of the cold and the danger, but jump in, and scramble through as well as we can. It will not do to be perpetually calculating tasks, and adjusting nice chances; it did very well before the flood, where a man could consult his friends upon an intended publication for a hundred and fifty years, and then live to see its success afterwards; but at present, a man waits, and doubts, and consults his brother, and his uncle, and particular friends, till one fine day he finds that he is sixty years of age: that he has lost so much time in consulting his first cousin and particular friends, that he has no more time to follow their advice."

EXTEMPORE MICROSCOPE.

When a microscope cannot be obtained for some special purpose, a tolerably good extempore one may be made by filling with water, or any other limpid fluid, two small bottles or test tubes, crossing them at right angles, and looking at the object to be examined through the crossed parts.

RELIGIOUS INTELLIGENCE.

New South Wales.

GENERAL OBJECTS.—BRITISH AND FOREIGN BIBLE SOCIETY.—The annual meeting of the New Town Branch of this Society was held in the Congregational Church, New Town, on the evening of October 5th. The chair was occupied by T. C. Breillat, Esq. The Rev. Hulton King and S. C. Kent attended as a deputation from the New South Wales Auxiliary, and the meeting was addressed after the Rev. W. A. Quick had read an encouraging report by the deputation, the Hon. Thomas Holt, Esq., M.P., and Messrs. Toy, Mills, and Walker.

RELIGIOUS TRACT SOCIETY.—The adjourned annual meeting of the Australian Religious Tract and Book Society was held on Monday, Nov. 9th, in the hall of the School of Arts. The President of the Society, the Hon. G. Allen, Esq., M.L.C., occupied the chair. The report was read by the Rev. J. M'Dougall, and the following gentlemen took part in the meeting:—The Revs. Messrs. Farrer, Cuthbertson M'Gibbon, Whiteford, Kent, and Messrs. G. W. Allen, Caldwell, Hogg, Foss, an

M'Arthur. From the report we extract the following:—"In the twelve months which have elapsed since the last general meeting, there have been sold in the depot 44,434 books, and 101,699 tracts. Upon reference to past reports, it will be found that the amount of sales is nearly double that effected in any of the previous years. This is peculiarly gratifying, as giving evidence that, even in a strictly commercial point of view, the society is attracting an increased degree of attention, and promises speedily to become not only self-supporting, but to have a surplus for gratuitous distribution. The sums received from sales at the depot amount to £1525 10s. 4d.; from colporteurs, £399 4s. 8d.; in all, £1924 15s. The public contributions are considerably less than last year; but the increased amount then announced was owing to several special efforts made to relieve the society from its difficulties. The ordinary subscriptions of the year amounted to £169 2s. 8d. Besides the books and tracts distributed throughout the colony by sale, the society has also circulated, by way of grants, the very large number of 448 books and 42,080 tracts, being, in all, a greater amount than has been disseminated in this way in any year since the commencement of the society."

ALLIANCE FOR THE SUPPRESSION OF INTEMPERANCE.—A lecture was delivered before the members and friends of this association on the evening of October 22nd, at the hall of the School of Arts, by the Rev. W. Cuthbertson, B.A. The subject chosen was "John Gough." The lecture, which was an elegant and forcible exposition of Gough's history and powers, was extemporaneous, and occupied two hours in the delivery. The hall was thronged, and at the close a vote of thanks was rapturously carried.

PITT-STREET BAND OF HOPE.—The second anniversary of the Pitt-street Band of Hope was commemorated on Wednesday evening, November 11th, by a soiree, held in the School of Arts. Mr. H. Burnell was voted to the chair. Addresses were given by the Rev. J. Voller, Rev. Joseph Beazley, and several other gentlemen.

CONGREGATIONALISTS.—CONGREGATIONAL HOME MISSIONARY SOCIETY.—Sermons on behalf of the Society were preached in the several Congregational Churches of Sydney and its suburbs on Sunday, October 25th. On the following Tuesday the seventh annual meeting was held in the Congregational Church, Pitt-street. The Rev. Dr. Ross presided. The Rev. S. C. Kent read the report in which the objects, operations, and prospects of the Society were noticed at length, and from which we extract the following:—"Our indefatigable friend, the Rev. J. L. Poore, who is at present in England, in obedience to the resolutions with which we closed our last report, secured for us the services of the Rev. Jacob Jones, late of Melksham, Wilts, for whom a Valedictory Service was held in Percy Chapel, Bath, in which the Revs. J. Poore, Thomas James, R. Brindley, and others took part. It is stated in the advices which have reached us, that Mr. Jones addressed the meeting under great emotion, and briefly gave his reasons for the step he was about to take. From many sources we have heard of the excellence of his character and his adaptation for the work of our mission. We were all anxiously looking for his arrival, and every preparation was made to give him a most cordial welcome. But, alas! as you have all heard with deepest sorrow, the Catherine Adamson, in which he was a passenger, was wrecked at the entrance of our harbour on Saturday morning last, and he with twenty others found a watery grave. For him, we doubt not, "sudden death was sudden glory;" but for us this calamity is so inexpressibly painful that we cannot yet think or speak of it with calmness. "I was dumb, I opened not my mouth because thou didst it." "It is the Lord, let him do what seemeth him good." It is scarcely necessary that we should bespeak your prayers for his friends and relatives in the fatherland, that they may be prepared for the reception of these mournful tidings, and may be able to bow with resignation before Him who "is too wise to err, too good to be unkind;" and from the heart to say—"The Lord gave, and the Lord hath taken away; blessed be the name of the Lord." Had we but the necessary funds there are several openings in the colony we could advantageously fill, and of which we cannot think without deep regret and earnest prayer that we may speedily be furnished with agents for the work and means to support them, so that we may not continue unrepresented in many of our most important towns, and that those who dwell in the far off bush may no longer have occasion to say, No man careth for our souls. As an instance of the earnestness with which ministers are desired and the readiness with which they would be supported were they forthcoming, your committee inform you that in the early part of the present year they received a guarantee for the annual sum of £200 towards the support of a missionary in the Burnett and Leichhardt districts, a guarantee which they regret to add has since been withdrawn, in favour of another denomination, in consequence of their inability promptly to take it up." George Rees, Esq., the Treasurer, presented the financial statement, from which it appeared that the total income for the year had been £1,755 17s. 6d. The meeting was addressed by the Revs. Joseph Beazley, W. Cuthbertson, J. West, E. Griffith, G. Charter, J. Voller, and the Hon. Thomas Holt, and J. Fairfax, Esquires. On Wednesday a United Communion was held in the same church, when a larger number of communicants were present than on any previous occasion. Suitable addresses were delivered, and the service was felt to be most solemn and impressive.

INDIA.—A special public prayer meeting, on behalf of our countrymen in India, was held in the Congregational Church, Pitt-street, on the evening of October 28. Between five and six hundred persons were present. The Rev. W. Cuthbertson presided, and explained the object of the service, which occupied nearly two hours. The Rev. Messrs. West and Kent delivered suitable, instructive, and deeply affecting addresses on the past and present state of India, especially as to the condition in which our fellow countrymen and women are now situated. The devotional parts of the service were conducted in a solemn and appropriate manner by the Rev. Messrs. Griffith, Charter, and Cuthbertson.

WESLEYANS.—CHURCH EXTENSION.—On Monday evening, October 12, a public meeting was held in the Wesleyan Chapel, Surrey Hills, in aid of the Wesleyan Church Extension and Contingent Fund. Mr. T. W. Bowden presided. The amount raised last year was £582 19s. 5d. Ten circuits are in receipt of assistance from this source, but for which some of them could not exist. The Rev. J. Eggleston, W. T. Mayne, W. Schofield, and the Rev. W. Hessel, addressed the meeting in support of various resolutions. The collection amounted to £23 5s.

South Australia.

CONGREGATIONALISTS.—CONGREGATIONAL UNION.—The half-yearly meeting of the Congregational Union of South Australia was held recently, in the Congregational Chapel, Happy Valley. The proceedings of the day were introduced by a devotional service in the morning, conducted by the Revs. Messrs. Hodge, Newland, Nichols, and Cheetham. The business meeting was held in the afternoon, on which occasion about 30 ministers and delegates from various Congregational Churches were present, besides other friends from Adelaide and elsewhere. On the assembling of the ministers and delegates an introductory address was delivered by the Chairman, the Rev. C. W. Evan; after which a statement of the past half-year's proceedings was presented by the Rev. T. Q. Stow, one of the secretaries of the Union. The statement in question referred to the connection of the South Australian Congregational Union with corresponding unions in the other colonies; also, to the new periodical originated by the Congregational body—the Southern Spectator—to the education of ministers, and to the expected arrival, in this colony, of five or six Congregational ministers through the instrumentality of the Rev. J. L. Poore. After the delivery of the Secretary's statement, the meeting proceeded to discuss and to adopt a scheme of regulations under which the Committee of the newly-organised Chapel Building Society are to appropriate the funds now placed at their disposal. The objects of this Society are to aid, by loans or grants, in the erection or rebuilding of chapels belonging to the Congregational body, and also to assist in the liquidation of debts upon such chapels. It was stated that the sum of £500 was already available for chapel extension, and with a view to obtain the requisite public sanction to the movement, the Provisional Committee were instructed to take steps for calling a public meeting in Adelaide as speedily as possible. At a later stage of the proceedings the question of the amalgamation of the Union with the Home Missionary Society was introduced, but was withdrawn by the mover after considerable discussion. The forthcoming conference at Hobart Town was then brought under consideration, and resolutions were adopted, appointing the Rev. C. W. Evan to visit Tasmania, as the representative of South Australian Congregationalists on that occasion, and authorising the Executive Committee of the Union to select and appoint some lay gentleman to accompany Mr. Evan in the same capacity. Other business relating to the internal affairs of the denomination was afterwards considered and disposed of. In the evening an appropriate sermon was preached by the Rev. T. Q. Stow, the Rev. Mr. Harris conducting the introductory service. The meetings are stated to have been the most encouraging of the kind ever held in the colony. The numerous visitors on the occasion were most hospitably entertained by Mr. Young, M.P., Dr. Montgomery,

Rev. A. R. Philps, and others. The Rev John H. Barrow was elected by ballot as Chairman of the Union for the next 12 months.

MOUNT BARKER.—The foundation stone of a new Congregational Church was laid at this place on Tuesday, the 29th September, at three o'clock, by the Rev. T. Q. Stow. After the ceremony a Public Tea Meeting was held, at which Mr. Giles presided. The meeting was addressed by the Chairman, and the Rev. Messrs. Stow, Austin, Harris, Watts, &c. The Rev. J. B. Austin, who originated the effort, preaches at this place.

GAWLER.—Public religious services have just been held in the Congregational Chapel, Gawler, in connection with the Northern Association of Congregational Ministers, and in behalf of the South Australian Home Missionary Society, as follows :—On Tuesday evening, 20th October, the Rev. T. Q. Stow preached the Association sermon ; and on Wednesday evening, the 21st, a public meeting was held, Mr. W. Peacock, of Adelaide, in the chair, when the Revs. T. Q. Stow, J. D. Mudie, W. Oldham, J. P. Buttfield, J. Ayling. T. W. Charlesworth, and J. Leonard, and a deputation from the Home Missionary Society, Adelaide, consisting of the Rev C. D. Watt and Mr. T. Davis, severally addressed the meeting. Votes of thanks were then presented to the deputation, to the Rev. T. Q. Stow, and to the Chairman, for the kind and valuable services rendered by them severally. The collections, amounting to £7 7s., will be appropriated to the objects of the Home Missionary Society.

WESLEYANS.—WESLEYAN MISSIONARY SOCIETY.—On Monday evening the annual meeting in connection with the Australian Wesleyan Mission was held in the Pirie-street Chapel, which building, at an early hour, was densely filled by the friends and promoters of the objects of the meeting. His Excellency the Governor, after the proceedings had been opened by prayer and singing, was called to the chair, and commenced the business of the evening by expressing his great gratification at presiding on that occasion. He had owed much to the good-will and zeal of the Wesleyans in his former Governments at the West Indies and in West Africa, and he was pleased to see one minister of that church, whom he had seen engaged on more dangerous services, taking a part in the evening's proceedings. He had once had the pleasure, in one of the countries referred to, of appointing a Wesleyan minister as Colonial Chaplain—an appointment highly approved of by Earl Grey. But if that Church was influential there, it was also here, for he saw—and he was glad to see it—from published statistics, that the Wesleyans were two to one in their attendance on Divine Service, as compared with any other persuasion in the colony—even with that of the Church of England, to which he was afraid a great many persons were returned as members from the single fact of their being nothing at all. His Excellency, after the reading of the report (from which it appeared that the last year's expenditure of the mission was about £10,000, and their income about £9,000), was followed by the Rev. Mr. Gardiner, who, dwelling upon the arduous labour of the South Sea missionaries, took occasion most eloquently to reply to an article undervaluing the labours of those missionaries, which appeared in the August number of *Colburn's Monthly Magazine*. The Rev. Mr. Butters also brought forward proofs on that subject, and instanced the numerous cases of self-devotion and heroic courage on the part of the Feejee Island missionaries, which were known to himself ; whilst the Hon. Mr. Forster, after reading an extract from and commenting on the article referred to, argued that the presence among them that night of a native Feejeean converted to Christianity, and able to expound the Gospel, was a sufficient answer to such calumnies. The Rev. Mr. Waterhouse, a returned missionary, then introduced Solomon Ramisi, the convert referred to by the last speaker. Mr. Waterhouse gave a brief sketch of this man's life, and described the amusing impressions which were produced on his mind by the civilised scenes which he came in contact with at Sydney and Hobart Town. The snorting steam-engine was, according to Mr Ramisi, "a big canoe crawling along the ground ; " a snow-storm was a flock of " little birds ; " and altogether his idea of white men seemed to be something like that of the American Indians when they first caught sight of the plumed and glittering Spaniards.

MACLAREN VALE.—Recently a large number of friends assembled at Maclaren Vale to witness the interesting ceremony of the laying of the foundation stone of a Wesleyan chapel. The service was commenced by Rev. J. B. Waterhouse, of Willunga ; after which the Rev. W. Butters, of Adelaide, proceeded to lay the stone in due form, and delivered an appropriate address. The company then adjourned to an unfinished building kindly lent by a friend, where a thronged and delightful tea-meeting was held. From the statement presented to the meeting, it appears that the proposed chapel is to be in the Gothic style, and that the present engagements of the Trustees amount to £315. After an excellent speech from the Rev. W. Butters, the donations already promised were announced by the Rev. J. B. Waterhouse, who invited additional subscriptions. The appeal was liberally responded to. Including the proceeds of the tea, and the collection at the laying of the stone, the subscription list was found to have reached the goodly sum of £203 1s.

UNITED PRESBYTERIANS.—UNITED PRESBYTERIAN CHURCH, GOUGER STREET, ADELAIDE.—Three sermons were preached in this place in connection with the settlement of the Rev. James Lyall as Pastor, on Sabbath day, October 25th. In the morning by Mr. Lyall himself, in the afternoon by the Rev. Wm. Ingram, and in the evening by the Rev. James Binney. On Monday, 26th, a Public Soiree was held in White's Room, King William-street, when addresses on interesting subjects were delivered by the Revs. Messrs. Ingram, Ross, Evan, Binney, Lyall, &c.

Tasmania.

CONGREGATIONALISTS. — COMMEMORATION SERVICES AT TAMAR-STREET CHAPEL, LAUNCESTON.—On the completion of the twenty-fifth year of the ministry of the Rev. C. Price, a series of services was held. On Sunday, Aug. 30, Mr. Price preached a special sermon on the occasion. On the evening of the same day a devotional meeting was held to return thanks to God for his abundant mercies to pastor and people. On Wednesday, September 2nd, a social tea meeting of the Church, Congregation, and old Sabbath School scholars took place in the school-room. An address was presented to Mr. Price on behalf of the Church and Congregation, and also a testimonial consisting of Archbishop Summer's works, and Owen on the Hebrews. 15 volumes in all, as a token of esteem. Another address and another token of grateful respect, consisting of Poole's Annotations on the Bible, were next presented by an old Sunday School scholar on behalf of a number who had been formerly scholars in the school. Mr. Price made a reply full of feeling and thankfulness. He stated that when he came to Launceston in 1832 the colony was chiefly a penal establishment. He and the Rev. F. Miller, of Hobart Town, were then the only Independent Ministers in all Australia, now there were upwards of seventy. In Launceston he had neither church, people, nor provision. Many difficulties had been encountered, and great changes experienced. A Sabbath School was commenced from the first, which had continued to this day. Home Missions, the Bible Society, Christian Union, the Temperance Cause, the Mechanics Institute, and other Public Institutions had been all zealously assisted by the pastor and his people during this long period. Mr. Price's commemoration sermon was preached from the appropriate text,—"Ebenezer, hitherto hath the Lord helped us."

MEETING FOR ABOLITION OF STATE PAYMENT OF MINISTERS OF RELIGION.—A meeting was held on November 16th, at the Alliance Rooms, Hobarton, for the purpose of preparing a petition to the Legislature for the discontinuance of the State Aid to religion. Among those present were Messrs. Hopkins, Crouch, G. W. Walker, Mather, S. Westbrook, J. Facey, W. C. Smith, J. Dickenson, J. Hiddlestone, J. Andrews, G. Rolwegan, and the Revs. Messrs. Nicholson, Downes, Fry, and Clarke. Mr. Henry Hopkins having been called to the chair, and the Rev. Mr Clarke having been appointed Secretary, the draft of a petition was read and adopted, and arrangements were made for obtaining signatures. A letter was read from J. A. Dunn, Esq., M.H.A., stating his intention of doing everything in his power to promote the object of the meeting in the withdrawal of the State Aid from the various denominations, and that he should be ready to give his unqualified support in the House of Assembly to the petition for that purpose. A committee was appointed to carry out the objects of the meeting.

Victoria.

GENERAL OBJECTS.—BIBLE SOCIETY.—The first Annual Meeting of the St. Kilda Ladies' Bible Association was held on Thursday, October 8th, in the Rev. R. Fletcher's Congregational Church, Alma Road. His Honor Judge Pohlman occupied the chair, and in his address congratulated the meeting upon the establishment of a branch of the Victorian Bible Society, that the ladies of the neighbourhood had formed the Society, and more especially on the fact that individuals connected with various denominations were about to take part in their proceedings. The Rev. D. Seddon read the report, which showed that the ladies of St. Kilda had collected about £170 during the year, to be appropriated for the purchase of bibles from the Victorian Society. The Rev. R. Fletcher read the Treasurer's report, which was considered highly satisfactory; after which the Very Rev. the Dean of Melbourne proposed the adoption of the report. The Revs. J. P. Sunderland, C. Searle, T. Harding, W. R. Fletcher, M.A., and Messrs. J. T. Hoskins (deputation from the Melbourne Society) Frederick Haller, and H. Jennings, severally addressed the meeting.

EVANGELICAL ALLIANCE.—The Second Quarterly Meeting was held on the evening of Wednesday, the 7th October, in the Hall of the Mechanics' Institution. The attendance was very good. The Honorable Judge Pohlman occupied the chair. The Rev. Dr. Cairns delivered a masterly and eloquent defence of the Sabbath as a divine institution, which was listened to with profound attention. Bishop Perry, the Rev. William Jarrett, the Rev. Mr. Divorty, the Rev. J. T. Hoskins, and the Rev. James Ballantyne also took part in the proceedings of the evening. The next Quarterly Meeting is to be held in January, 1858.

TEMPERANCE.—The Temperance Hall, Russell-street, has recently undergone alterations, which have cost nearly £450. A soiree in connexion with the re-opening of it was held on the evening of Monday, the 28th September. Richard Heales, Esq., M.P., occupied the chair. After tea, the meeting was addressed by the Chairman, the Rev. James Ballantyne, the Rev. James Sunderland, the Rev. James Mirams, Henry Harmer, Esq., Secretary to the Temperance League of Victoria, and — Cooper, Esq. A bazaar on behalf of the Hall was held during the first week of October.

A SUNDAY SCHOOL UNION, embracing all evangelical denominations, was formed at PORTLAND, in the Wesleyan Chapel, on Oct. 20, the Rev. J. Knight in the chair. The speakers were Messrs. Hill, Hearne, Andrews, Jennings, and the Rev. W. Ridley. A series of five resolutions, containing some excellent regulations and suggestions for the effectual working of the Union were passed.

CONGREGATIONALISTS.—CONGREGATIONAL HOME MISSION FOR VICTORIA.—A meeting of this Society was held in Victoria Parade Chapel, Collingwood, Sept. 29, 1857, for the purpose of welcoming to the Colony the Rev. W. C. Robinson, lately sent out by the Colonial Missionary Society, and generally to promote the interests of the Victoria Mission. Tea was provided, after which G. Rolfe, Esq., was called to the chair. A hymn was given out, and prayer offered by the Rev. W. R. Fletcher, M.A. The chairman gave an introductory address, in which he strongly advocated the claims of the Society, and showed its necessity for the establishment of new congregations. He also adverted to the safe arrival of the Rev. W. C. Robinson, addressed him in a few words of congratulation, and, in the name of the assembly, gave him a cordial welcome to the Colony. Mr. Robinson then responded, related the steps by which he had been led to think of coming out to Victoria, the opening which had at once presented itself to him at Williamstown, and the favourable impression he had received of Victoria, from the general aspect of the place, and the kindness with which he had been received. Several other ministers then addressed the meeting.

REV. J. L. POORE.—Letters have been received from the Rev. J. L. Poore, giving encouraging accounts of the success of his mission in England. He has visited most of the towns in England and Scotland, lecturing on the colonies of Australia, and pleading the cause of colonial Missions. He has obtained a sufficient sum of money from the British public to supplement the £2,400 subscribed in Australia to bring out a supply of ministers. Twelve ministers have been already engaged, and six or eight had already sailed or were on the point of sailing at the date of last advices. One, alas! the Rev. Jacob Jones, as is notified in another place, is now no more. Mr. Poore is expected to return about April next.

OPENING OF INDEPENDENT CHAPEL, WILLIAMSTOWN.—On Tuesday evening, Nov. 3, the celebration of the commencement of the ministerial labors of the Rev. W. C. Robinson took place in the new iron chapel, situated in Stevedore-street, North Williamstown, and was attended not only by many of the families resident in the municipality, but by upwards of one hundred ladies and gentlemen from Melbourne and its suburbs. Amongst those present were Thomas Mason, Esq., J. P., Chairman of the Municipality; Captain Ferguson, R. N., Harbor Master; and several captains of the ships lying off the township; besides these, were Messrs. Langlands, M.L.A.; Sargood, M.L.A.; Embling, M.L.A.; Fulton, Rolfe, &c.; also, the Revs. W. C. Robinson, W. B. Landells, W. R. Fletcher, M.A., W. Moss, Thomas Odell, J. Mirams, K. Johnston, &c., who all took part in the meeting. Henry Langlands, Esq., M.L.A., presided. Messrs. Pickersgill and White gave a financial statement of the position of the cause, and detailed the circumstances by which Mr. Robinson had been invited to come amongst them. It appeared that the building and ground had been purchased for £300, and that other engagements were entered into to the amount of £70. The amount obtained at the meeting was upwards of £200. Williamstown is the first station furnished with a minister brought out by the Congregational Home Mission, and consequently the settlement of Mr. Robinson excited no little interest amongst the friends and supporters of the society.

NEW CONGREGATIONAL CHURCH, RICHMOND.—The foundation-stone of the new church in Lennox-street, Richmond, was laid by F. J. Sargood, Esq., M.L.A., on Monday, October 5th, 1857, at four o'clock in the afternoon. The Rev. J. Mirams opened the service by giving out a hymn; the Rev. B. Fletcher, of St. Kilda, offered the dedicatory prayer; the Pastor of the Church, the Rev. J. P. Sunderland, read a copy of the document deposited in the foundation-stone; the Rev. W. B. Landells, of Collingwood, delivered an address, and the Rev. H. Thomas, B.A., pronounced the Benediction. There was a good attendance of ministers and friends of the various Evangelical denominations. A public tea meeting was held at six o'clock in the evening. After tea, F. J. Sargood, Esq., the chairman, opened the business of the evening. The following ministers and friends spoke to the topics placed in their hands : Revs. T. Odell, Mirams, B. Fletcher, W. B. Fletcher, M.A., A. D. Kininmont, W. C. Robinson, late from England, H. Langlands, Esq , M.L.A., T. Fulton, Esq., J.P., and F. Haller, Esq. The church is to hold, with an end gallery, 900 persons. It is built of bluestone, in the Gothic style. Messrs. Robertson and Hale are the architects. It is to cost, without seats, about £2,590.

OXFORD-STREET INDEPENDENT CHAPEL SABBATH SCHOOLS, COLLINGWOOD.—The annual sermons of the above schools were preached on Sunday, September 27th : that in the morning by the Rev. James Ballantyne, that in the evening by the Rev. J. P. Sunderland. On the following Wednesday evening, September 30th, the anniversary tea and public meeting was held. The Rev. W. B. Landells presided. The report stated that 360 children were in attendance; that a fund had been commenced with a view to the erection of additional school accommodation ; and concluded with an earnest appeal for more teachers. The Rev. James Ballantyne moved the adoption of the report. Dr. Embling, M.L.A., seconded the report,—after which the Rev. W. B. Landells addressed the meeting, and in the name of the teachers and scholars presented a testimonial to the late superintendent, who had well sustained the office upwards of three years. It consisted of a quarto Bible, and contained the following inscription :—" Presented to Mr. James Giles Robinson, by the teachers and scholars of the Oxford-street Independent Chapel Sabbath-school, as a token of christian love, and expressive of the high value they attached to his services, whilst acting as their superintendent.—Collingwood, September 30th, 1857." Mr. Robinson acknowledged the testimonial, and gave a brief history of his connection with the school. The meeting was also addressed by the Rev. J. P. Sunderland, and Messrs. Wilkinson, Stillwell, Walker, and Hills.

PORTLAND.—We have to record a movement made by the Independent body towards the formation of a church and congregation in the rising sea-port of Portland. Some short time since the Government steam vessel conveyed certain of the members of Parliament to visit and report on the Western harbours, and while at Portland, one of the members, Mr. Sargood, an Independent, met with a few friends accustomed to worship in a small building, hired by them for that and school purposes. We understand that Mr. Sargood, after the morning service, took the opportunity of encouraging the people in their work of faith. On the following morning, several of the friends sought his advice as to the purchase of a piece of land for Church purposes, and we now learn that a most eligible site has been secured, and further, that a design has been agreed upon for a plain but commodious place of worship at a small cost. It is earnestly desired that when the claims of this Church are presented to the public they will be met with ready help.

BAPTISTS.—CHURCH EXTENSION MEETING.—A meeting was held October 20th in Collins-street Baptist Chapel for the purpose of taking steps for the enlargement of that place of worship. After tea the objects of the meeting were stated by Mr. Kerr, who fulfilled the duties of president. It appeared from his statement that it was the intention of the committee to extend the chapel in the rear forty feet by a width of fifty feet,—such extension being arranged so that it might be continued to the street front at some future period at an uniform width of fifty feet. The cost of the present proposed extension, it was calculated, would be £2,500, towards which £800 had already been raised by the members of the church and congregation. The Rev. J. Taylor narrated the various results which had attended his visits to Sydney and some of the gold-fields of this colony. His statements of the position of the Baptist denomination in the Australian colonies were of an encouraging character, but also shewed that there was great necessity for additional ministerial aid. Conversational addresses followed, and before the proceedings closed a collection was made, which yielded a very handsome sum, and subscription cards being issued, it is anticipated that the required amount will be speedily realised.

EPISCOPALIANS.—BISHOP OF SYDNEY'S VISIT TO MELBOURNE.—Dr. Barker has recently made an overland journey from Sydney to Melbourne. On the occasion of his visit to the latter city, a public *dejeuner* was given to him in the Exhibition Building, on Saturday, November 7th. About 120 persons assembled. The Hon. Sir James Palmer, President of the Legislative Council, occupied the chair. On his right was the Bishop of Sydney, and on his left His Excellency the Governor of Victoria. Several healths were given and speeches delivered. The guest of the day was most cordially received, and greeted with many compliments. The most remarkable feature in the speeches was the foreboding of an entire separation between Church and State being at hand. The Hon. Chairman made some remarks on the condition and prospects of the Episcopal Church in these colonies under the great experiment of the separation of Church and State, which he said "none could doubt was about to be attempted in Australia. Under its new destinies, the strength of the Church would lie pre-eminently in the union of its individual members. While he hoped to see the dominion of the Church of England enlarged, he felt how probable it was that the designs of Providence were compatible with a number of forms of faith, and hence how gratifying a feature of the times was the development of the principles of religious toleration and liberality. A great change in this respect had distinguished the course of the last two centuries, and he looked forward to the time when religious intolerance would be no longer known." The Bishop of Sydney in the course of his reply observed,—" Should it prove that the Church's independence of State aid was here a thing possible, and that the prosperity of the Church without endowments was also possible, then the hearts of many of her sons would revive, not only in England, but all over the world. If fourteen years after the placing of a bishop here, sixty clergymen, zealous and faithful, had been appointed, the Bishop of the Mauritius, and the Church throughout India, would take courage, and feel the necessity of making an effort which might be equally successful there." He also spoke in a very kindly spirit of the efforts of other denominations. He said, "the charity of the age, as the chairman had said, was advancing, and people were not now burnt for not agreeing with others in matters of religious belief. It was not in this manner they now sought to make willing those who were unwilling. For himself, he desired to feel the enlarged charity of the apostle towards all men. The efforts of all denominations of Protestants were most beneficial, and who was he, or who were they, that they should in any way hinder them?" But the speech of his Excellency Sir Henry Barkly, the Governor, is most noteworthy, and is given at length at page 120 of this Magazine. We commend it to a careful perusal.

THE VICTORIAN EPISCOPAL CHURCH ASSEMBLY.—This body commenced its adjourned session on September 1st, and closed on the 23rd. The Assembly was chiefly occupied with the consideration of measures for the appointment of ministers to congregations, the exercise of clerical discipline, and the raising of finances.

A CHURCH OF ENGLAND SUNDAY SCHOOL INSTITUTE was established at a meeting held in the Mechanics' Institution, Melbourne, September 9th. The object is to encourage the establishment of Sunday Schools, and to help to make them efficient. Its operations will be confined to the episcopalian body. The Bishop of Sydney was present on the occasion.

METHODISTS.—UNITED METHODIST FREE CHURCH.—The opening of a church of this denomination took place on Sunday, October 25th, in Lower Church-street, Richmond, when two sermons were preached by the Rev. M. W. Bradney, and the Rev. J. P. Sunderland. On Monday a public meeting was held, and Mr. W. H. Alsop was voted to the chair, who congratulated the members upon no less than three new chapels having been opened in the neighbourhood of Pentridge, Kew, and Richmond, within the last three months. The Rev. M. W. Bradney then read the report, which stated that the cost of the ground and building of the compact little place of worship amounted to £380; the proceeds of the subscriptions, collections, and tea, being £240; leaving a debt of about £140, towards the liquidation of which Mr. Bryant contributed the handsome sum of £120.

PRESBYTERIANS.—PRESBYTERIAN CHURCH, HAMILTON.—The foundation-stone of this building was laid on Wednesday, the 21st October, in the presence of large assembly of people, many of them having come a great distance to witness the ceremony. The Rev. Angus Macdonald, pastor of the congregation, conducted the devotional exercises, and delivered a suitable address. The stone was laid by William Skene, Esq., of Kanowalla. An address was also given by Alex. Learmonth, Esq. The building is to have a tower, with a spire sixty-five feet high, which is intended for a bell and clock, for the convenience of the inhabitants of this rapidly increasing township.

The Rev. Mr. Fraser and family sailed from Liverpool on the 8th August, per the *Morning Light,* for Melbourne. Mr. Fraser comes to enter on the pastorate of St. Andrew's Free Church, formerly under the ministry of the Rev. Dr. Mackay.

Messrs. Proudfoot and Wilson, preachers in connexion with the Free Church, have recently arrived in the colony.

UNITED PRESBYTERIAN CHURCH, EMERALD-HILL.—A Congregational Soiree was held on the evening of September 29th. The Rev. John Ballantyne, the pastor of the congregation, occupied the chair. The Rev. John Cooper, of Geelong, engaged in devotional exercises. After tea, addresses were delivered by the Rev. D. McDonald, of the Free Church, Emerald-hill; the Rev. Mr. Taylor, of the Baptist Church, Collins-street; the Rev. H. Thomas, of the Congregational Church, Victoria-parade; the Rev. James Ballantyne, of the United Presbyterian Church, Lonsdale-street; and Mr. Robert Black, United Presbyterian student.

The Rev. Mr. Moir and lady have arrived from Penang, per *European.* Mr. Moir is one of the missionaries of the Free Church.

WESLEYANS. — CHURCH EXTENSION. — GEELONG.—A numerously attended meeting was held in the Yarra-street chapel, on Monday evening, September 7th. The Mayor of Geelong took the chair. The first resolution was moved by the Rev. I. Harding, and seconded by Mr. Alderman Wright:—" That anticipating the speedy removal of the Government Grant for religious purposes, this meeting deems it desirable that active measures be at once taken for carrying on the work of God in this colony." After this and some other resolutions were carried, a subscription was opened, which soon reached the sum of £615 7s. 6d., and it is expected that the entire proceeds of the Geelong circuit will amount to £1,000, towards the £10,000 proposed to be raised in the colony.

WESLEY CHURCH, MELBOURNE.—Sixteen of the architects of Victoria put in drawings for the approval of the trustees, and after two days' close deliberation, the choice fell by an almost unanimous vote upon the design of Mr. Reed, who has already received instructions to call for tenders, and proceed, with as little delay as possible, to the erection. The buildings will comprise a most handsome church, a minister's residence, a school-house, master's residence, and book depot. The entire cost is to be £19,000.

AT CALIFORNIA GULLY, SANDHURST, a chapel has just been erected, of the Gothic style, at a cost of £430. A highly interesting meeting was held at the opening, when Mr. Padwick presided. The proceeds were £140.

WARRNAMBOOL.—The foundation-stone of a suitable Wesleyan Church was laid on the 15th instant, by R. W. Naphine, Esq., and the Rev. R. Hart, assisted by the Rev. Mr. Currey and others. The proceeds amounted to the sum of £100.

A NEW CHAPEL AT AMHERST was opened on September 6th, Messrs. Albiston and Kaw being the preachers. The chapel cost rather more than £400, towards which £300 has been collected.

ANOTHER NEW CHAPEL WAS OPENED AT CARISBROOK on September 27th, by the Rev. D. J. Draper. At the public meeting, on the following evening, it was stated that the building had cost £600, and the total contributions amounted to £270.

NEW WESLEYAN CHURCH, ST. KILDA.—On Tuesday afternoon, October 27, the ceremony of laying the foundation-stone of the new Wesleyan Methodist chapel, in Fitz Roy-street, St. Kilda, was performed, in the presence of a large number of spectators, by Alexander Fraser, Esq., J.P. The usual formalities were observed, and hymns sung, and prayers offered, appropriate to the occasion. The 84th Psalm having been read, the stone was laid. There was afterwards a tea meeting.

THE NEXT NUMBER OF THIS MAGAZINE WILL BE ISSUED ON 1ST FEBRUARY.

Communications for Editor care of W. FAIRFAX & Co., *Melbourne.*

The Southern Spectator.

| No. 4. | FEBRUARY, 1858. | VOL. I. |

MISCELLANIES.

Pulpit Efficiency.

A long and interesting correspondence has recently appeared in the Melbourne *Argus* on the alleged decline of the power of the Pulpit. A writer under the signature of "Luther" first mooted the question, and his letter has been followed by a long list of others. Luther's complaint referred more specifically to the Episcopal Church of Victoria, but others have extended the charge of declension and inefficiency more or less to all churches. The controversy in the main has been conducted in a tolerably fair spirit, and not a little may be learnt from it both by preachers and hearers.

The inferiority of the Colonial to the British Pulpit seems to be assumed ; but this assumption admits at least of question. Conceding that such specimens of surpassing oratory as may be found at home cannot be paralleled here, and that such men as would be considered among the more able and effective there though not exactly of the first class, may not be numerous in these regions ; yet, taking it as a whole, the pulpit of this country may we conceive stand a fair comparison with the pulpit of Britain. The number of regularly accredited ministers of all denominations in these colonies probably does not exceed 500, while those in Great Britain and Ireland amount to not less than 30,000. If any 500 ministers of all denominations in England were indiscriminately taken, including a due proportion of country ministers, we believe the existing ministers in these colonies would not materially suffer in comparison if at all with such a selected portion.

Should this however be denied, and should the preaching in the colonies be, on the average, inferior to that of Britain, it need not greatly excite surprise. The men of largest attainments, of greatest grasp of mind, of most popular talents, and the widest personal influence, have spheres of usefulness at home of far greater magnitude than they can possibly find here ; and they are, generally speaking, so fixed in their spheres that it would be difficult indeed to remove them, if it were right to attempt it. Then, the young men of most promise just coming out of college are not likely, in any great numbers, to think of these distant colonies, when so many influential posts

L

just at hand are waiting to receive them.   There is as great a cry for
superior men to occupy important vacancies in England as there is
here, and the inducement is not small to prefer what is near and certain and obviously influential, to what is remote, contingent, and for
the most part yet to be developed.   The danger therefore is great
of feeble men, who have failed at home, turning their attention to the
colonies as a field of labor where they may have a better chance of
success.   Those on the spot know indeed that this is a great mistake,
and that of all places in the world a young colony is the last where
feebleness can hope to succeed.   But this perhaps is not so well
understood at home.   Christian communities, however, cannot be too
much on their guard against this danger, discouraging all such from
attempting to come hither, and using every endeavour to obtain men
of education, of mental power, of good preaching abilities, and, above
all, of unspotted character.

For some time to come it is obvious we must look to the mother
country for ministers.   The colonies have done well to found Universities, and to furnish each of them with a staff of able professors ; but
it will be a long, long time before they are in full working order and
amply supplied with students.   The population now in the colonies,
and the immigrants coming in, are for the most part adults who are
past the university age, and are, besides, not from that class at home
devoted to literature, but from those whose taste is for commerce :
the families rising up here are too young as yet to furnish pupils, and
too few if they were grown up to furnish many : and the class of
persons of whom the colonists are composed are too entirely, it is to
be feared, of the money-getting order to furnish the universities with
a fair quota, according to their numbers, as compared with the old
countries of Europe.   Time alone can, and doubtless will, correct
these evils.   Families in good circumstances will be desirous of giving
their sons a superior education, the good working of an improved
system of national schools will appear in due time in increasing
numbers of the youth of the country desiring to go forward to the
university, and the usual proportion of persons evincing a taste for
literature, for learning, and for the professions, will doubtless be forthcoming.   It is the duty and interest of the community to foster the
development of this spirit, to make provision for it as it arises, and to
turn it to the best possible account.   The existence of well appointed
universities at the present stage of the history of Australia is, in this
view, a happy circumstance, for they both create a taste for learning
and supply the means of gratifying it.   All this applies to ministers
of the gospel as well as to general students ; indeed, since only a portion of the general body of students think of devoting themselves to
the church, it applies with greater force.   If under graduates be few,
candidates for the ministry will be fewer still.

If we are therefore to have well filled pulpits in the colonies we
must, for the present, look to home for the men.   Nor can we expect
many of the best class of men,—such as the complaints in question
imply are wanted, to come of their own accord.   Before they are ascer-

tained to *be* men of power they must be proved ; already, therefore, must they be in stations of influence and usefulness and attached to them doubtless by strong and tender ties, and they are not likely voluntarily to abandon those posts and come to the antipodes on what may appear to them a wild speculation,—going, they scarcely know whither or for what. A sort of suspicion, justly or unjustly, is apt to arise when a minister becomes a voluntary emigrant, as if he were of a roving turn, or conscious of failure, or had done something wrong. The best men for the most part—for there are bright exceptions—wait to be solicited. They must be *selected* and sent for ; respectable provision must be made for them beforehand, and all help given to them to forward their settlement when they arrive. Where this has been fairly done it has generally succeeded. It is the duty and interest of all denominations of Christians to act upon this principle, and certainly the claims of these growing, and, on the whole, intelligent communities urgently require the most strenuous efforts in this direction.

We have thought it right to present this common sense view of the actual state of the Colonial pulpit, and to call attention to these practical suggestions for its improvement. But in the correspondence we are now referring to, notions have been broached, incorrect in our opinion, as to what the pulpit really is, and vague and crude as to what it ought to be. Possibly much of what the writers long for is unattainable, and undesirable if it could be attained. The charges of inefficiency are not confined to preachers in the Colony wholly, but extend to preachers of the present day generally. It is a symptom of the age. The British pulpit it is said, has declined ; it is not what it once was ; it has ceased to be a power in the country. Is this true ? Where is the evidence to support the charge. We think that a dispassionate view of the case will lead to the opposite conclusion. *When* was the Pulpit a power in Britain ? At the Reformation ? That great event was brought about more by books than by sermons, and preaching was confined to a few places, such as St. Paul's Cross, and to a few gifted men, such as Latimer and his fellow laborers. Was it a power in the reign of Elizabeth ? Incumbents indeed were found to hold the livings and read the service, but men qualified to preach were so rare, that one or two had to suffice for a whole county. During the ascendancy of Puritanism, preaching was indeed a power, but it will be admitted by the complainants that its influence was confined to a class which, though energetic enough, was numerically a minority in the community. Between the Restoration and Revolution, preachers were never perhaps held in less esteem, nor were sermons ever at a greater discount. Throughout last century, moderatism in Scotland, Arianism among the English Nonconformists, and cold and careless formalism and heathen morality in the English Church, were the characteristic of the times ; and were ever the congregations thinner, or the pulpit less powerful ? That dreary period, dreary as it respects sacred eloquence, in all or nearly all churches, was only relieved by the appearance of the despised Methodists, the Whitfields and the Wesleys and men of their

school, who were mighty in word and deed, but not after a fashion
which many in modern times who demand improvement would wish
to see revived.   But during the present century and up to the present time in Britain, what a change, we might say what a contrast
presents itself!   Places of worship are multiplied far beyond the
ratio of increase of the population, congregations are larger, the
standard of ministerial qualification for the practical work of the
ministry is higher, and instances of real, effective eloquence are far
more numerous than perhaps at any previous period.   We speak not
of individual cases, but of the general condition of the British Pulpit
and its aggregate result upon the people ; and we may challenge
those, who mourn over the *decline* of its power, to produce a period
at all equal to it in influence, with the sole exception of the primitive
days of Christianity.

Some of the writers assert that the preaching of the day has no
hold upon the educated mind of the community.   This vague charge
is difficult to deal with.   *Where* is the educated mind to be found ?
Are not ministers of religion on the whole as well aducated, as well
read, and as intelligent, as lawyers, medical men and merchants ; are
not church and chapel goers on a par at least with the rest of the population in mental culture ?   We suspect that the complainers in question,
when they speak of intelligence, have a particular *sort* of intelligence
in view.   Are they not thinking of the popular authors and periodical
writers of the day, and of their readers and admirers ? or of men
who confine their attention to scientific pursuits ?   Possibly the pulpit may not have much hold upon these classes.   But if so ; is there
anything new in this ?   When was it otherwise ?   Were many of the
Dramatists, the Essayists, the Poets, the Novelists, the Pamphleteers,
the Writers for Periodicals of former times, much under the power of
the pulpit, and disposed to bow to its teachings, any more than those
of the present day ?   This may or may not be a matter of regret :
all we contend for is that there is nothing novel in the circumstance ;
it is no sign of a *decline* in sacred oratory.   And the matter is easily
explained.   The pulpit is specifically an institute for the promotion
of *religion*, and the writers of the class named do not, in their published works at least, trouble themselves much with that subject.

While deeply anxious to raise the standard of preaching to the
highest attainable elevation, and while therefore fully sympathising
with those who are earnestly desirous of its improvement, we suggest
the desirableness of moderating expectations within the bounds of
what is practicable.   Let it be remembered that the power of effective speaking is a rare possession among any class of men.   There
was but one Demosthenes among the Greeks, and one Cicero among
the Romans.   A Baxter and a Whitfield among preachers, an Erskine,
a Burke and a Brougham among lawyers, and a Pit, a Fox, and a
Canning among statesmen, are not of every day's occurrence.   A
company of educated gentlemen meet for festive compliments at the
Lord Mayor's dinner ; an assembly of savans at the anniversary of the
British Association for the Advancement of Science

deep learning or relate interesting scientific discoveries, but how few of either have tongues competent to give decent expression to their thoughts! There are 658 members of the British House of Commons, comprising is is said "the first gentlemen in Europe," but the vast majority never attempt a speech at all, and five-sixths of those who do, speak to empty benches or to noisy and impatient hearers. Hosts of gentlemen of the highest education are called to the bar; their profession is that of speakers; yet the great majority never open their lips; and when a really effective speaker does make his appearance, he monopolises the practise of the circuit and carries all before him. Here, with every advantage of education, with every inducement to excel, with the most splendid prizes glittering before the eyes of the competitors, only a small number succeed. Eloquence, the power of fixing the attention, delighting the fancy, and moving the passions of an audience,—seems, like poetry, to be a natural gift, though one capable doubtless of being improved by study. In any conceivable change for the better in the ministry, therefore, we fear that true eloquence will be confined to a favored few, and that the bulk will not rise above mediocrity. And in passing judgment upon the ministers of religion, all we ask for them is, that they should not come in for a greater share of censure than falls to the lot of other public speakers.

Day School Instruction.

This article was in type before Mr. Ireland's speech and the leaders in the *Argus* advocating many of the same views appeared in the papers.

PASSING over for the present the systems of State support to education in operation in Tasmania and South Australia, it is our intention in this paper to advert to public education in New South Wales and Victoria, with more particular reference to the latter, and to the measure now before the Legislature of that colony.

In New South Wales and Victoria it is well known that *two* systems are in contemporaneous operation, the Denominational and the National. Both are worked by boards of commissioners appointed by Government. The Denominational Board imparts education through the agency of the several religious bodies who are willing to work with it, and who are at liberty to teach their own peculiar tenets in the schools. The National system allows no sectarian teaching, but gives the power to the several religious bodies to make provision for instructing in their own peculiarities the children belonging to them, but apart from the other pupils. These two boards occupy the position of rivals rather than allies, each being anxious to get as much as possible of the education of the country into its hands. This keen competition is felt by all to be unseemly; and the desirableness of unity of action is so generally acknowledged, that the abrogation of the duplicate system is regarded only as a question of time. Which of the two plans shall be adopted by the country is the point to be settled.

The advantages and disadvantages of the Denominational system were impartially stated in a former number. It has the zealous support of the Roman Catholics, and from their extreme earnestness at the present moment in Victoria in its defence, it may be inferred that they suppose it answers their purpose, or hope it will, in promoting their denominational interests. The system also is understood, as was stated in the previous article, to be preferred by the greater part of the Episcopal, the Wesleyan, and the Presbyterian clergy, and a considerable number of their active laymen. The Congregationalists are not at one upon the subject of education; some upholding the Denominational system; a few deprecating *all* legislative interference; but the greater part inclining to the National scheme, or some modification of it. While we believe this to be a fair representation of the state of feeling and opinion among the more prominent and earnest men of the several religious bodies, it is pretty obvious that such of the *public* men and the community at large as are not included in the classes just named, are decidedly in favor of a broad unsectarian scheme. And even numbers who prefer the Denominational system show little disposition to struggle to preserve it, as appears from the approval given by the Episcopal Church Assembly of Victoria to Professor Hearn's scheme, upon which the bill now before the Victorian Legislature is largely based, and by the absence of all petitions, except from the Roman Catholics, against that measure.

There are no indications just now, that we are aware of, in South Australia and Tasmania, of agitation on the subject of education. In New South Wales the matter once and again has been before the Legislature and discussed in the public journals; but we hear little of it at the present time. Doubtless, however, the existing quiet is only a temporary lull. In Victoria, the case is different; the ill-working of the two rival schemes, and the unsatisfactory results to the country at large, having stirred up a general desire for a reconsideration of the whole subject. Mr. Michie, the Attorney-General, has brought in a bill to establish one general system, and this bill is now under legislative consideration, and is already so far approved, that the second reading has been carried in the Assembly by a majority of 33 to 11.

This bill, though constructed in its details specially for Victoria, is, in its main principles, if adapted to one of the Australian colonies, equally adapted to them all. Indeed, it is understood to be in substance derived from the Canadian scheme, and to resemble in many respects the Common School system so long established and so universally approved in America. It is not our intention to give a minute analysis of the bill, or to consider its several clauses. Its leading principles are what we are concerned with; if these be satisfactorily settled, details will not be difficult to adjust.

One of the main principles of this measure is its municipal, self-sustaining, self-governing character. It is proposed to school districts throughout the country, with defined boundaries necessity for them arises, and to alter their extent from time to time to suit convenience ; to give power to the inhabitants to elect boards of managers, to establish schools, appoint teachers, and to levy rates upon themselves to meet the expenses. Special care is taken that no denominational interests shall be served. There is still, however, proposed to be a central board, who will act as the main spring throughout the country in constituting school districts, assisting them to begin their schools, and co operating with them in carrying them on with efficiency; and the principal organ of this board is to be a salaried secretary or " chief commissioner," whom it is proposed to invest with powers which are very generally thought to be unconstitutionally large. The greater or less degree of power, however, of this officer or of the board itself is a subject for regulation, and, perhaps, for change from time to time. The great principle of the measure, its municipal element, is the thing we are chiefly concerned about.

We cannot help regarding this principle as of unspeakable value, and a vast improvement upon any organisation of pure centralised power, whether it be called a Ministry of Instruction, a Committee of Privy Council, or a National Board of Commissioners. All writers on the American Day School system represent the direct action of the people living in the school district upon their own seminaries as its very life and soul.

Pure centralisation is not popular with Englishmen accustomed to trust to themselves and lean but little upon government. They are jealous of the accumulation of authority in any single focus. Schemes of education of the Prussian stamp are lauded to the skies for their completeness and symmetry of form, their clock-like precision and uniformity of action, and the rigor and the certainty with which they penetrate and pervade with their influence the entire body of the nation; and their satisfactory statistical results are paraded by most writers and speakers on education. But all this is vitiated in the eyes of our countrymen by the whole being done *for* the people and nothing *by* them ; by the extensive patronage and dangerous influence over the mind of the community the system puts into the hands of a few men at head quarters ; by the nepotism and corruption to which it is sure to give rise ; and by the servile spirit apt to be gendered in a whole people who are from their infancy taught only what the Government is pleased to dictate. This is paying too dear for the whistle. An evil of such magnitude, then, is sought to be avoided, in the proposed measure by the constitution of *school district municipalities*, by which the inhabitants themselves will have, to a great extent, the matters relating to their own schools in their own hands and under their own direction.

Yet without some central authority the scheme, as a general one, would in all probability be a failure. Districts would not be organised in many parts of the country, and when organised, they might soon sink again into inaction or fall into gross blunders and mistakes, especially in remote and rural parts. From incapacity or indifference

the law might become a dead letter.   Hence, the appointment of a
board of commissioners to see it carried out, and to assist by their
experience and by their agents in its practical application and due
development ; while the evils incident to a central authority would
be brought to a minimum by the check imposed upon it by the
existence of self-taxing and self-governing municipalities, through
which alone it must operate.

Supposing the system to work as well as it may reasonably be
expected to do, the following advantages would result :—

1. The schools would be located where they are most wanted, as
the inhabitants would be best able to judge what would suit their
own convenience.

2. A needless multiplicity of schools would be avoided.   This is
the opprobrium of the Denominational system.   The churches often
being built near each other, the schools are also clustered all together,
where they rival and compete with one another as if they were private
speculations.

3. The education would be improved in quality as the schools
were increased in size from being diminished in number.   The *one*
teacher in a small school, who must teach everything, cannot be
expected to teach anything so well as the *many* teachers in a larger
school, who are selected for their proficiency in particular departments.*

4. The people at large may be expected to take a deep interest in
the common schools of the district.   What they pay for ; what they
elect officers to manage ; what is planted in the midst of them ; and
what is designed, not as a charity for others, but as an institution for
the use of their own children, can scarcely fail to awaken in them an
interest far beyond what is witnessed at present.

5. Undue and lavish expenditure, so likely to occur in all simply
Government outlay where the money is at the disposal of parties who
do not furnish it out of their own pockets, would be checked in the
present case by the people holding the purse-strings themselves.

6. Abuses, so sure to arise in all public institutions, would more
easily be detected, and the remedy with more facility applied, when
the victims were on the spot and had the the power of correction in
their own hands.

We now come to the most difficult part of this or any other scheme
of day school instruction,—the religious aspect of the question.
Whether religion shall be taught in the schools ; and, if it be, *what*
religion ; and *how* it shall be taught ; these are the *questiones vexatæ.*

All earnestly religious persons feel that not only should children be
instructed and trained religiously, but that religion should constitute
a fundamental and essential principle of their education ; but the
several denominations think, of course, that their own views of what
religion is are the only right views, and insist upon having them
taught ; hence, the difficulty of combined action.   A middle party

---

* This is shewn admirably in Professor Hearn's Pamphlet on Education.

steps in and suggests that what is common to all religions and must constitute the essence of them all,—morality and a general reverence for the Deity,—should be alone taught. But this is begging the question as to the nature of religion, and is looked upon as dangerous latudinarianism by not a few of the religious bodies.

This difficulty has led to the formation in England of a society to promote voluntary education, on the ground that all good education must be intermingled with religion, and that, as religion is beyond the proper province of the State, education also must be withdrawn from its province, and promoted wholly by voluntary effort. Those, on the other hand, who have no scruples in receiving State-aid to religion, can readily, of course, fall in with the denominational system, which permits them to teach their own religion in their own way ; but how can they coalesce with a scheme which is meant to embrace the whole community, consisting of every shade of religious sentiment ?

The Bill before the Victorian Legislature proposes to cut the knot after the manner of the Irish National Education scheme, by making specific provision for *secular instruction* only, which is to be communicated for a certain number of consecutive hours each school day ; and by giving liberty to the several denominations to make their own arrangements, at certain times allotted for that purpose, for supplementing the religious teaching to the children belonging to the various bodies respectively. If any should not avail themselves of this permission, specific religious instruction would not be imparted at all to their portion of the pupils. In the actual working of the system the probability is that some would, and some would not, use this permission. Where the population is considerable an arrangement might possibly be made among the several congregations to meet the case, but in thinly-peopled districts we apprehend it would, for the most part, be impracticable ; and the safest way to prevent disappointment is for the public to regard the scheme as one which will *not* provide religious instruction.

Shall the scheme, therefore, be ignored ? We think not ; and in making this avowal we do not withdraw what we have already said, that religion ought to be an essential part of education, and that parents and guardians do not discharge their duty to the young unless they give it a prominence second to no other element. But *education*, in its full sense, includes *all* the influences which are brought to bear upon the formation of character,—parental example, domestic instruction, social connections, family and public worship, private reading, Sunday school tuition ;—and day school teaching is only one among many such influences. The children are learning good or evil at all times and everywhere : at home among their relatives, in the playground, in the midst of their companions out of school hours, and on Sundays whether at church or in the fields seeking recreation. It is only a *part*, and that a small part, of the entire education that is, or possibly can be, given in ordinary day schools. If the question now before the public were the establishment of *boarding schools*, people concerned about religion would have no option but to require them to be thoroughly religious : but the actual case is widely different ; it concerns the institution of seminaries for imparting a few elements of secular learning ; and if it were thoroughly known and understood that nothing more than this were professed, no one would be deceived, and parents and churches might then make such arrangements to complete the education as they felt to be necessary or found to be practicable. The error all along has been in calling and regarding the teaching in day schools " education;" it is, at best, but " instruction," and that in certain things only.

And if such a system as the one proposed were universally adopted, would there be, after all, such a great change in the religious education of the young as many seem to apprehend ? Do the existing day schools, even the Denominational ones, actually teach much religion, or sensibly affect the religious characters of the children ? Little, we apprehend, is really done in this way, even where most is attempted. We scarcely ever met with a case either in this country or in England where deep religious impressions were made at a day school ; nor, generally speaking, is it reasonable to expect it. The chief things taught *must* be secular. For these the parents send their children ; for these the schools are established. The children's heads are full of arithmetic, geography, history ; their minds are anxious about their lessons and tasks ; the rule that is over them is one of authority, enforced, if necessary, by punishment ; and altogether the atmosphere which pervades the place is uncongenial to seriousness of thought and depth of emotion ; and if sacred feelings do happen to be temporarily excited, they are pretty sure to be dissipated as soon as the buoyant group are let loose in the playground. In the Sunday school it is totally different. There the attendance both of the teachers and scholars is voluntary, and the teaching is a service of love. The government is one of tenderness and affection, not of compulsion. The day is sacred ; the teaching is sacred ; the exercises, prayer and singing reading and exhorting, are all sacred. Religion is all in all ; and the consequence is that deep and holy impressions and permanent transformations of character are happily of common occurrence among the youth trained in well-conducted Sunday schools.

If, therefore, the religious communities could bring themselves to consider that they are striving after what is next to an impossibility in trying to make common day school instruction sensibly productive of religious training ; if they would accept it as simply furnishing a part, and that the inferior part, of education, instruction in certain necessary and useful things ; and if they would then address themselves with assiduity and earnestness to make up the important remainder by such arrangements as would secure a really religious training for the young people belonging to them ; if they would do this, we see no reason why they might not heartily concur with their fellow-citizens at large in a measure like the one now proposed, supposing all its minutiæ be made otherwise unexceptionable, in order to secure the best secular instruction for the youth of Australia which modern improvements in tuition have placed within their reach.

Christmas at the Antipodes.
WHAT IS ITS SIGNIFICANCY?

It is proverbial what a powerful influence is possessed by old association and long habit, in making us feel as both fitting and probable what has really very little, if any, foundation in fact. We know, too, how difficult it is to surrender that faith which we have placed in any favourite theory, even if it should be plain to our reason that all facts are against us. We often are disposed to say when inclination and prejudice are thus brought into collision with stubborn and unmistakable truths, " So much the worse for the facts." In some things this love for our old habits and customs is very much in the way of the progress of truth and enlightenment—as when an Ecclesiastical Court puts an astronomer in prison for telling the world that the old opinion of the sun's going round the earth is untrue—whilst in other things this poetic attachment to the antique is harmless, and even beautiful. This we all feel to be the case with respect to the observance of Christmas in the Old World. Not a shadow of an argument (not even from remote tradition) can be urged in favour of December as the month of our Saviour's nativity, yet who would wish to see Christmas kept in September or April, either of which months is more likely than December to be the true anniversary of that great event? We love the old associations connected with the warm and cheering festival of Christmas, as it comes to break the monotony of the dull and cold winter of Britain. The light of that joyous time breaks over the snows of Europe like the flashes of the Aurora over the ice-fields of the Polar regions, and we cherish long the memory of the recurring Christmas days of the past. What matter to us does it make, whether that day be the true day or not? Our dearest associations are clustered around it, and that is enough. It is like some fine old ruin covered with ivy, looking beautiful in its poetic adornments as it stands before us bathed in moonlight and hoary with age. If we were gazing upon such a venerable relic of the past, would it not sound sacrilegious to hear any one find fault with the architecture, and complain of its want of fitness and harmony, and talk of the discomforts the narrow chambers and cold stone floors must have inflicted upon those who were unfortunate enough to dwell there? What is that to us who only see, and desire to see, the beauty of a romantic ivy-covered castle as it looks mournfully down from its elevation on the degenerate civilization around it?

But here in Australia all is changed. There is no past to dwell upon, nothing to call up old associations ; and so completely are all things reversed here, that it is not possible with us, as it was with the Pilgrim Fathers, to transplant in its integrity the old festival of Christmas to these shores. The cold short days of an European winter give place to the long burning days of an almost tropical summer. Instead of a mantle of white covering all with desolation, we have the desolation of parched and sun-burnt fields and gardens. Instead of hearing on all sides of social gatherings around the Christmas hearth, every one deserts the streets and business places of the city for the shady nooks in the bush, or the cooler shores of the Bay. Pic-nics, and not dinner parties are the order of the day here. All seems reversed, and many are the sighs which are heaved over the necessary departure of the charm of this glorious old festival.

But with all due deference to this spirit of devotion to antiquity, we cannot but think that, if rightly considered, the gain is all upon our side. A man, whose feelings of veneration for Christmas are grounded solely upon the beauty of preserving and perpetuating a time-honored observance may indeed feel that its glory is departed, but *a Christian* man who wishes to trace some harmony between the original of this great feast and our modern mode of keeping it, will find, after a little reflection, that far from having thrown aside, when he came here, all that was suggestive of the birth of our Lord, he has only cast away what confused his ideas, in favour of a new series of associations, far more truthful and consequently far more beautiful. Let him think of the shepherds as they lay reclining on the hills of Judea, tending their flocks while they wandered over their pastures by night rather than by day; let him imagine their pastoral lay broken by a heavenly voice among the stars which shone in the clear sky of the warm east. Surely he will think that Christmas loses none of its suggestiveness because it happens at a season of the year when night is more lovely than day. Let him remember too, how, by " the decree of Cæsar Augustus," all were required to go to their own city to be taxed, and how many, to carry out this decree (among whom would be Mary and Joseph) would have to traverse almost the entire length of Palestine ; and let him pourtray to himself the scene which such an emigration must have presented—young and old, parents and children passing on in family and neighbourly groups from city to city until they arrive at their own, resting on the way in crowded inns, or because there is no room for them there, in the meaner accommodation of the stables—and surely such a picture must appear impossible when placed amidst the scenery of a cold snowy winter in Northern Europe. It is far more natural to think of this when the cessation of our winter rains permits to us free access to the interior, and makes the distant cities of our land seem near at hand. And so too with the visit of the Magi who, travelling by night and guided by " his star in the east," undertook a long journey to greet the heavenly visitant, as he lay in the manger of the stable of the inn outside Bethlehem. In the pictures which painters have drawn of the homage of these wise men, they have always been obliged to violate the common scenery of Christmas and have had to change winter into summer. Again, how impossible would seem the flight of Joseph and Mary and her new-born infant into the distant land of Egypt, if we picture to ourselves the hills of Palestine covered with snow, the trees leafless, and all the region barren and uninviting for such a protracted journey. In fine, putting all together and trying really to place before us the incidents of the biblical narrative of the advent of our Redeemer, we must come to the conclusion that they are far more in accordance with the new-found Christmas customs which are forced upon us here in Australia, than with the old associations of the merry Christmas time which we used to spend before we left Europe.

Milton, as we all know, in his grand poem the " Ode on the Morning of Christ's Nativity," has succeeded in tracing a sublime harmony between the desolation of winter and the great event of our Saviour's Advent ; and in truth he seems to be, as he says, " touched with hallowed fire" as he strikes his harp to such noble strains :

> " It was the winter wild,
> While the heaven born child
> All meanly wrapped in the rude manger lies ;
> Nature, in awe of him
> Had doffed her gaudy trim,
> With her great Master so to sympathise ;
> It was no season then for her
> To wanton with the sun, her lusty paramour."
> &c.

But it is far more the resistless power of the poet's genius and enthusiasm, than the sober basis of probability and fact which makes us admire that hymn.

And again, to a thoughtful mind, how suggestive of the ultimate truth of the Angel's prediction of " peace " and " goodwill " to all the earth, is this new empire rising up in the knowledge of Christianity. There have been but few nations of whom it could be said they were lights to the whole world, but if the various sections of the Church of the Redeemer do their duty here, we may fairly predict that this country will shine, in the moral progress of the family of mankind, with a more brilliant lustre than any other has yet been invested with. We are starting with more energy, more life, more knowledge, more of the means of material advancement, and more wealth, than have been afforded to any other germinant empire ; and at the same time fewer impediments are in our way. We have not the deep-rooted prejudices and vested interests of Britain to make our freedom of religion a thing to be attained only at some far off future day ; and we have not our moral and religious harmony disturbed by the unseemly disputes on the slavery question, which make the world point to many of the Christians of America as the best samples of bigoted, self-interested incon-sistency. No ! the recurrence of Christmas in this region of

converse seasons, is far from unmeaning; for as it comes round
year after year, it seems to bring nearer and nearer that time
when the whole earth will be able with truth and with sincerity
to take up and prolong upon our world the song, which hitherto
has been confined to the choirs of a better world, "Glory to God
in the highest."

Evangelical Preaching—is it a Power?

In the recent correspondence in the Melbourne *Argus* on the
supposed decay of pulpit power, various hints were thrown out
expressive of a dislike to the doctrinal and evangelical tone of the
preaching of the day as if it were an element of weakness, and of
a longing for something more simply moral.   It is thus assumed
that the evangelical strain of preaching makes it uninteresting
and feeble, and that a change in the contrary direction would give
it influence and strength.   In this paper we confine ourselves to
one single point: is the presence of evangelical doctrine and
exhortation an element of weakness or of power in the pulpit?
It is pretty well known that most of the preaching in Victoria
is characterised by the peculiarities of the evangelical school of
theology.   That of Presbyterians, Congregationalists (Baptist
and Pædobaptist), and Methodists of every section is here, as at
home, universally so.   And through the influence of Dr. Perry,
Bishop of Melbourne, who has presided over the Episcopal
church since Victoria was constituted a separate diocese, it is
understood that none but evangelical appointments have been
made in that church.   It is assigned as a ground of complaint
and a reason for the alleged decay of pulpit efficiency, that the
attention of congregations is taken up, not with the enforcement
of moral duties and practical truths, but with unprofitable
dogmas, disputed points of theology, and expositions of creeds
and confessions which gender sectarianism, bigotry and strife.
This is a favorite mode with some of speaking of those great verities of the gospel to which evangelical preachers give prominence.
The doctrines are regarded with dislike, and the inculcation of
them as a source of weakness.   It is maintained that the adoption
of an ethical strain of address, in which the holders of all sorts of
faith, or of no faith at all, might cordially join, would restore
power to the pulpit, and be a means of awakening interest and
producing impression.   At home there is a choice of preachers
and of styles, and hearers, in large towns at least, if they dislike
the evangelical flavor in one church, can generally find something
to their taste in another.   But in their position here they are
without option, and being compelled to put up with what is unpalatable, they give vent to their dissatisfaction in murmurs.   We
do not say that this feeling is quite so openly avowed as we have

expressed it, but we have ventured to put in plain words what we think we can detect in the correspondence as one main ground of dissatisfaction with the preaching of the day.

Now, without mooting the question as to the right or the wrong, the truth or the falsehood of evangelical peculiarities, we ask, whether the preaching in which these peculiarities are wanting is usually more powerful—whether it produces a deeper impression upon the mind of the community, educated or uneducated—than that in which they form the main staple of discourse? The evangelical element is eschewed by Roman Catholics and Tractarians, by the Rationalists of Germany, the Moderates of Scotland, and Unitarians everywhere, and by a large portion of the Church of England. Are these parties characterised by more attractive and more effective preaching—by greater power in the pulpit—than those who are known as evangelical? Is it not notorious that wherever the preaching is confined to hierarchical and sacramentarian doctrine on the one hand, or to elegant essays and moral disquisitions on the other, *there* the congregations are slender, the people uninterested, and the ministry wanting in energy and life? Exceptions will occur to this as to any other rule, and there may arise a Bourdaloue, a Massillon, and a Wiseman among Romanists; a Channing and a Martineau among Unitarians; a Newman and a Pusey among Tractarians, and a Hugh Blair among Church of Scotland Moderates; but these are *rara aves in terris*, and do not alter the general fact that extreme feebleness and utter inability to produce *any* sort of impression are characteristic of preachers of this order as a class. On the other hand, is it not in the evangelical churches that crowds are gathered, eloquence is displayed, and powerful impressions are produced?

The cause of this is obvious enough. The improvement of the understanding, the refinement of the taste, the gratification of the fancy, and even the inculcation of morals, are not objects sufficiently immediate and direct, or even sufficiently important in the estimation of most, whether speakers or hearers, to excite that earnestness which is the soul of eloquence. Where do we meet with true power in speaking in secular affairs? In the senate, where a measure is to be carried,—at the bar, where a jury is to be convinced,—on the hustings, where votes are to be won. Even the exciting themes of politics and law would cease to inspire orators or to attract hearers, were they removed from the arena of active life and practical ends, and treated as mere matters of dissertation and lecturing, especially if people were doomed to hear these disquisitions every week of their lives.

But the aim of evangelical preaching is direct and momentous. It is built upon the idea that preaching itself is not a human but divine institution, existing nowhere apart from Christianity; established by the authority of Christ himself for a specific purpose, and that purpose the salvation of the soul. Men are regarded as lost, and the object of the preacher is to save them. He calls them to repentance and conversion if they would secure their final safety; and even exhortations to morality and consistency of conduct, after men become real Christians, are founded in the belief that these are important, not only or chiefly on account of the honor and comfort they bring in this life, but because they are necessary to the working out of the soul's complete and final salvation. By evangelical preaching, characterised by power, we do not mean either strong hyper-Calvinistic statements, or violent diatribes against Roman Catholics, or a controversial style of treating subjects of divinity, or disquisitions strongly systematic and theological, but the exposition and enforcement of the leading truths of Christianity, as taught by Christ and his apostles, in an earnest, affectionate, and practical manner, with a view to an immediate effect upon the heart, and a permanent transformation of the character. These were manifestly the views and aims of the apostles themselves, when they went forth to execute the commission of their Master. It was not a mere change of creed—proselytism from Judaism to Christianity, from idolatry to the worship of Jehovah—nor the reformation of manners in that corrupt age which inflamed their zeal, gave them the tongue of fire and the self-denial and courage of heroes; it was the prospect of saving their fellow-creatures from the wrath to come, and presenting them to their Lord as trophies of their success. And if eloquence and power characterised the preaching of Luther and Knox among the reformers, Baxter and Howe among the Puritans, Whitfield and Wesley among the Methodists, and, in modern times, Chalmers and Gordon among the Presbyterians, Newton and Melville in the Episcopal Church, Spencer and Hall and Spurgeon among English Nonconformists, they owed that power to the strength and vividness of their convictions on the importance of the truths which distinguish the evangelical school. And if the evangelical pulpit, regarding it as a whole, be more effective and influential than any other, as it unquestionably is, the cause is to be found, not in the men happening to be better orators than others, but in the influence of their creed upon them and their hearers. Take away from them the evangelical element, as some in their simplicity would wish to do, and you deprive them of the lock of their strength.

Thus some of the hearers in Victoria complain of the effeteness and feebleness of the pulpit in the colony, and hint, as one remedy, at a change from an evangelical to a moral strain of preaching. Let them look at the Episcopal pulpits in New South Wales and Tasmania. The former bishop of the one, and the present bishop of the other set their faces against evangelical clergymen, and the pulpits, to a large extent, are supposed to be occupied by men of an opposite class. Are the churches there better attended? Are the preachers more attractive, the hearers better satisfied?—The colonial pulpit, none can deny, needs improvement. Let no pains or expense be spared to furnish it with the best men that can be got; let it be elevated to as high a standard as would satisfy the warmest wishes of intelligent Christians;—but let none delude themselves with the idea that they will accomplish this longed-for reformation by making it less evangelical than it is.

SUNDAY READING.

Be Consistent.

Consistency is a jewel which a Christian man should wear for his own sake, and that of the Lord Jesus Christ. The first point is to be a Christian; the second, to appear such. We should have a form of godliness, with a real power giving life to the form, prompting it, moulding it, using it as the outward visible sign of an inward spiritual grace—such a form, according to God's appointment, ever nourishing the life that animates it. There are two forms of Christianity in the world: the form of the New Testament—simple, beautiful, strong in its truth, and mighty in love—and that of the Christian Church generally. These forms are not often very much alike: copies of all kinds are said to be always inferior to the originals, yet the disparity between the divine original and the human copy need not, ought not, to be so great as is actually found to exist. The world usually accepts the two forms as one—regards the professed living epistle as a fair transcript of the written one—and, finding Christian men often to be very ordinary mortals, charges their failings upon the system they profess, and argues and acts accordingly. We see the folly and fallacy of this; the boasted wisdom of the world here fails to discern between things that differ; the logic is false, but the false life giving occasion to it is worse still. Christian professors and preachers write books and deliver lectures on the evidences to prove to the world that Christianity is true, and yet live so as to lead the world to disbelieve their books.

We wish the professors of Christianity to feel that they are as responsible to God for the general influence of their conduct, as for their time, talents, and opportunities of personal service. A man in joining a Christian Church professes to know more, in some respects to be and to do better, than the generality of men around him. If he be a real believer in Christ, his eyes have been opened; he has become a new creature; he is made a partaker of the Divine nature; he is zealous of good works; he lives, yet not he, but Christ liveth in him—that is, in every true believer the Saviour multiplies himself—as He was, so are we in this world; witnesses to God's character, to the purity

M

of his law, dwelling in love, and so in God.   Hence, the true
and ultimate idea of Christian profession is illustrating by holy
practice the character of God.   Let a man realize this : I have
to show my fellow-men the true character of God, the maker of
all.   As the sun shines, and the moon and the stars give light to
declare His eternal Godhead, so must I show in my little sphere
the moral attributes of God—justice to all, affectionate goodwill,
mercy and patience untiring.   All we ask is, that a Christian
man should be consistent with his profession—that he should
not merely seem, but be—not talk, but do—not have a name to
live, and yet be dead.

If Christians were to carry out the principles of their holy
faith, their lives would form the best of all pictorial illustrations of the bible, the most striking commentary, the most
eloquent sermon ;   the caviller would be silenced, the
opponent subdued, and the wide world would be speedily
brought to the obedience of the faith.   Whilst Satan, sin, and
ignorance continue together to keep from the Saviour his purchased and rightful dominion, how unspeakably important that
his professed friends should not join the unholy alliance, by
their moral influence being adverse to the speedy and universal
recognition of the Saviour's kingly claims.   One sinner de-
stroyeth much good ; and one inconsistent professor in a church
or neighborhood will blunt the edge of the Spirit's sword, and
confirm the wicked in their wickedness.

Example is better, because more powerful, than precept—"words
are but air, and tongues but clay"—but to do justice, love mercy,
and walk humbly with God, are tangible facts which possess too a
self-multiplying power.   Deeds are better than precepts, as they
more clearly manifest the duty.   The Saviour's example shows
me better what it is to love my fellow-man than any moral
precepts can ; there is no mistaking his meaning ;   he went about
doing good ;   he had compassion upon the ignorant, and taught
them ;   he removed the common wants and miseries of human
nature ; his pathway was strewed with blessings ; his train composed of the once blind, lame, deaf, leprous, dumb and diseased,
who had been healed by him of all their afflictions.   Howard,
Wilberforce, Clarkson, Fry, Nightingale, and Livingston, following in his footsteps, explain most clearly the nature of true
compassion, and the character of our holy faith.

Example is better than precept, inasmuch as it shows the duty
to be practicable.   You urge upon me self denial, zeal and liberality,
patience and perseverance, the diligent practice of life's duties and
courtesies to all men, and special love to the brotherhood of the
saints : prove to me that all these things are possible to him that
believeth.   While you point to brighter worlds, lead the way over
these intervening mountains of evil customs and habits, and
seeming interests.   You visit me in my low moral estate ; you
urge me to burst asunder by God's help my moral chains, and

leaving my prison and bondage, to become God's freeman, to ascend the lofty moral heights of consecration service and daily communion with God before His glorious throne, seen from which, earth's mountains are molehills and the world itself a very little thing. Gladly will I follow your leadership: whilst you cry "Excelsior," and scale the rugged mountain side of duty, I shall see that it is possible to be good. Show a man what a duty is, and that it is practicable, by your personal example, and you have done much; the feeling of emulation may then be awakened. "Bad as the world is, there is nothing that has so much influence over it as virtue." Individuals may be seen moulding a large circle by the force of their example; they do what is right; men admire, and not unfrequently imitate. "Herod feared John, knowing that he was a just man and holy, and observed him; and when he heard him, he did many things and heard him gladly." "William Wilberforce grew up, and the grace of God made him a Christian. In the Bible he found the model on which God would have him form his character. He studied it. He prayed over it. He watched himself, and struggled with his evil tendencies. God's spirit strengthened him, and gave him wonderful self-conquest. With his pen he expounded to the highest classes that system of vital piety, which Whitfield and Wesley had already preached to the populace: and carrying it to the dinner tables of Clapham, and the evening assemblies of Piccadilly, many who fancied religion too severe in the sermons of Bishop Porteous, or the strictures of Hannah Moore, confessed to its loveliness in the life of Mr. Wilberforce." The force of example is frequently seen in its most powerful form in the case of children; they can understand pictures before they can read the letter-press, and can imitate the actions of men before they know the reason of such actions. The influence of godly parents upon their children is often as gentle, silent, and powerful as the law which binds this world to its sun, and all worlds to the Father of Lights. The earnest exhortations of pious parents, their fervent prayers, the silent force of their holy example, often awaken many youthful feelings of reverence for the Bible, love to the Saviour the Sabbath and the sanctuary, which have finally developed into a bright example of the advantages of pious parents and early religion.

A Christian man should aim at strict consistency for his own sake. It will preserve him from many doubts and misgivings. Some never rise to the joy of an assured interest in Christ; they go mourning all their days, because they do not watch unto prayer, nor lay aside every weight and the sin that doth so easily beset them, nor walk worthy of the Lord unto all well pleasing. Christian assurance can never be attained save by the path of Christian obedience. "And hereby we do know that we know him, if we keep his commandments." "Whoso keepeth his word, in him verily is the love of God perfected : hereby know we that we are in him."

A Christian man is bound to glorify God by his body and spirit, which by creation preservation redemption and personal consecration belong to God.   He may do this by his praises, prayers, offerings, and personal services.   His whole life, in its varied manifestations, may be a song of praise.   Men will see his good works, and glorify his Father in Heaven—glorify God on his behalf.   No sight is more impressive, none more to be desired, than to see one of the royal priesthood offering his personal sacrifice, and causing others, as by the magnetic attraction of his moral influence, to follow in his train to the same altar, and worship the same glorious God.   " Let your light so shine before men that they may see your good works, and glorify your Father who is in heaven."

The Church's Duty.

It is clearly the duty of every Christian to labor for the spread of Christianity in his own sphere of life. This duty has, however, been transferred almost entirely to the office-bearers of the Church.   The great body of Christ's servants have not, in modern times, been considered as included in this responsibility. They have come to be looked upon as a passive, not an active, portion of the Christian community. They have been practically taught that except as to giving money, it is not " more blessed to give than to receive."   The "laity" have been baptized, taught the catechism, instructed from the pulpit in Christian doctrines. They have enjoyed ministerial visitation in their afflictions and trials ; after death, have been committed to the grave with the solemnities of Christian burial. Thus, through their whole earthly course, the view under which they appear is that of persons *for* whom much was to be done, and not that of persons *by* whom anything was to be done.   They were to be cared for, but were not expected to care for the spiritual welfare of others.

For the pernicious views which have led to such a state of things we have largely to thank the Roman Church.   That Church has done much to rob Christianity of its power as a means for the development of individual mind and character.   It has encouraged *giving* to an unlimited extent.   It has, after a fashion of its own, cultivated the element of devotion.   But it has wofully failed to bring out that manly form of piety which implies personal thinking and reading, and the communication of the fruits of this to others.   In the history of the dark ages there is not a more melancholy picture presented to the mind of the Protestant, than that of a so-called Christian congregation, say of some five hundred persons.   It is sad to observe the vast stores of unappropriated talent and zeal lying there The whole amount of *agency*—of actual working energy, would be found limited to not more, perhaps, than some four or five persons.

It is not in reference to doctrine alone that that community has showed itself so cruelly unfaithful to its trust, although the charges of history against her are, on that score, not light. But she sapped the zeal of the Church; she failed to enforce upon private Christians, we may say she ignored, the duty of personally *working* for the honor of their Lord. She thus inflicted serious injury on each of her members: for it may be laid down as a principle, that no Christian can secure the full advantages of Christianity, unless he labor for its extension. "If any man will not work, neither shall he eat," may be applied to the mind as well as the body. Luther demolished the deadly error of justification by works, and established the life-giving doctrine of justification by faith; and for his heroic struggles in this service his name will be held in reverence through all ages. But he is not equally entitled to gratitude for anything he did to awaken, to call into activity, the slumbering energies of the members of the Church. There is scarcely a church now existing, to which the finger can be pointed, as exemplifying the requirements of the New Testament on this head. The majority of modern churches come far short of their duty of making individual attempts to spread the truths of salvation. Thousands of the descendants of the Puritans are " in the same condemnation." They hear the gospel from youth to age. They have a full understanding of the " truth as it is in Jesus." They have ability and culture. They have high fitness for preaching the gospel, yet they continue dumb and inactive. Alas! what talents are laid up in napkins; what eloquent tongues are bound in guilty silence. What noble faculties lie unused!

Thousands of souls wait, blindly " feeling after God," but those who have the light of life decline to lead and guide them. The fields are, in all these colonies, " white unto the harvest," but the laborers refuse, except in very insufficient numbers, to be " thrust into the harvest."

"But," the reader will ask, " is it the duty of *every* Christian to exert himself to diffuse the great salvation?" Let the appeal be made to the word of God " What saith the Scripture?" "Freely ye have received, freely give," said the blessed Redeemer. " As every man hath received the gift, even so minister the same as good stewards of the manifold grace of God," is the exhortation of Peter. We are informed in the Acts that, upon the dispersion of the primitive church, its members " went everywhere preaching the word." When John Bunyan appeared before the magistrates of his day and was called upon to give an account of himself, as in their view an unauthorised preacher of the Word, he appealed at once to passages of the class now quoted.

And it is remarkable how the plain untutored sense of the Bedford tinker coincides with the conclusions of the most accomplished modern critics. These commentators dare not limit the command of Christ,—" preach the gospel to every creature,"—to any body of men less than the "universal Church." (See Alford, on Matthew xxviii. 19, 20). Moreover, earnest ministers of all bodies are becoming more and more convinced that they must enlist the services of the humblest members of their respective churches, if religion is indeed to leaven the entire community. And if these considerations have force in Christian England, how is that force increased when the subject is looked at from a colonial point of view?

But suppose the point contended for is admitted, and the individual Christian to long to perform his duty to his Lord, how can his wishes be realized?

1. Let each Christian householder in the colonies aim, by every judicious means in his power, to bring his children and servants to know and serve Christ. The duty of making this attempt will not be denied. Yet how few serious direct efforts are made in Christian families for the salvation of servants. Little instruction is given; few appeals are made to them on the subject of religion. In some instances, it is to be feared, they are allowed to come into a family, and go from it, without a single endeavour being made to " turn them from the power of Satan unto God." Yet how much might our churches be replenished from this important class.

2. The neighborhoods in which Christians live form spheres of action which should be diligently worked. It may be assumed as true, that not one half of the inhabitants of any given locality attend the house of God. Many of these non-attendants probably never hear of their danger or their refuge. Yet it may be affirmed that, were the Church " up and doing," were its private members to exert themselves as they ought, there need be scarcely an individual left untaught or unadmonished. It is not intended that Christians should disregard the usages of society by being offensively forward and officious. Certainly not. But without any approach to this, might not many of the ignorant and indifferent be reached by regular tract distribution? Might not others be favorably impressed by kindly visitation and sympathy in the hour of accident and affliction? Might not many, from time to time, be invited to the sanctuary? and might not the Christian people of a district, in these and other ways, convey to their neighbors their views of the infinite value of the soul, and of the redemption which is by Christ? Surely the Christian should feel himself responsible, as a witness for God, for conveying such an impression to all around him.

3. Passing by the Sabbath school as an institution universally approved, and, on the whole, worked with tolerable efficiency, let us make a more distinct reference to the exercise of preaching and

exhortation. It is manifestly impossible to supply all the agency that is needed in our colonies for conducting public worship and imparting religious instruction by means of the more regular ministry. Where there is one engaged in this work on the Lord's day, the church should furnish at least twenty. But no amount of funds would suffice to sustain so great a number. It does not seem possible that the case can at present be met, unless by enlisting the services of the gifted and experienced laymen belonging to the Church. They *must* go forth in the name of the Lord into the highways and hedges, and "compel" men by holy persuasion to come in. And if this be not done upon a much larger scale than at present, multitudes of souls will wander in ignorance and danger, as sheep having no shepherd. Let the honored men to whom these remarks apply, ponder their responsibility, and with prayer and earnestness address themselves to the work for which God has fitted them. Let them remember that the blood of souls will be found upon them if they remain silent and inactive. Unless this activity on the part of members of churches be displayed, it is idle to look for large success. The strong passions at work in these colonies, require to be met and checked by a most vigorous and aggressive zeal, or the aboundings of ungodliness will be fearful in the extreme.

The present colonial era calls for no ordinary effort. In the struggle between the Church and the world, a small detachment of the soldiers of the cross is insufficient; trivial skirmishes will not meet the urgency of the case; the whole army of God must move forward "to the help of the Lord against the mighty." On the other hand, it is easy to anticipate the results of combined and unanimous efforts in such a campaign. In the churches thus jointly laboring for the salvation of men, there would be prosperity. There would be happiness—for happiness always comes from the discharge of duty and the united pursuit of high aims. There would be harmony, for Christians seldom quarrel while they are heartily engaged in doing their Master's work. There would be multiplication of numbers; and there would be, as the crown of all, the rich presence of him at whose command Christians labor.

The true notion of a church we deem to be that of a hive of bees in full work; that of a community of Christ's disciples zealously laboring in the cause of their Master; saved themselves, striving to save others; each one asking, "Lord, what wilt thou have me to do?" and each cheerfully doing what he indicated. We would respectfully urge on ministers to have this subject thoroughly understood by every candidate for Church fellowship. The most vital point to be satisfied upon, in the first instance, is the *conversion* of the candidate to Christ. The second should be his readiness to *labor in the vineyard of the Lord.*

Would it not be well to suggest to every convert that there are several departments of work ready to receive him, and to let him select the kind for which he feels himself best fitted by nature, education, and grace? Should not the minister seek to indoctrinate his church with these views? Could he not often remind his people that as Christ exists, and fulfils his high office as the Mediator for the Church, for its present and final happiness, so should the Church live, exhibit her excellencies, employ her strength and zeal, and devote all her resources to arousing, enlightening, and saving the world? Surely such a course would, under the blessing of the Holy Spirit, tend to invigorate the Church, make her more and more mighty as a chosen instrument in the hand of God for filling the land with his glory. In her experience he would graciously fulfil his promise, " I will make them and the places round about my hill a blessing : there will I cause the shower to come down in his season ; there shall be showers of blessing." 　　　　　　　QUARTUS.

The Forerunner.
Matt. iii. 2.*

" BEHOLD, I send my messenger before thy face, who shall prepare thy way before thee," was the language of God in prophesy to the Messiah. Why was a Forerunner necessary to herald his advent ? Were not the Jews universally expecting his appearance, anxiously desiring it, and eager to give him a hearty welcome ? True, but the Omniscient God saw that they were not really prepared for him, and that they should be faithfully told beforehand what sort of kingdom he was about to set up. At length, a voice was heard in the wilderness, crying " Prepare ye the way of the Lord : make his paths straight." John the Baptist had nothing of the character of an ordinary royal herald ; no gaudy livery ; no prancing horses ; no flourish of trumpets ; no retinue of attendants. He made no processional entry into the streets and halls and palaces of crowded cities, but took his station in the barren and lonely desert.

He came as a humble field preacher ; and his pulpit was a grassy hillock, a broken rock, or the trunk of a tree. His robe of office was a rude garment of camels' hair secured by a leathern girdle about his loins. No dainty food was provided for his palate; " his meat was locusts and wild honey." Was all this eccentricity ? or was there a meaning in it ? It was indeed in keeping with his character as a Jewish prophet, it being the wont of those venerable men to adopt a simplicity of manners bordering on austerity. But, had it not a deeper significance ? Did it not harmonise with the purport of his mission, and the seriousness of his doctrine ? Was he not a living embodiment of the unpalatable truths he had to teach, and the hard work he had to perform ?

He was sent to " make the rough places plain, and the crooked places straight," and " to form in the desert a highway" for the

---

* It is suggested that this paper may be read as a sermon to country congregations where there is no officiating minister.

Prince of Peace. What *were* those rough and crooked places which required rectifying? What was the kind of preparation the case demanded? It is summed up in the preacher's first words —words which may be considered as the text of all his following discourses—" Repent, for the kingdom of heaven is at' hand."

Did the Jews need any repentance, in order rightly to appreciate God's Messiah? It is well known that their idea of the promised Deliverer was that of a temporal monarch, possessed of vast resources, of supernatural wisdom, and surrounded by a halo of external glory and magnificence, of which that of Solomon was but a faint and feeble type. The Roman yoke, which galled them so sorely, they expected him to break. He was to set the nation free, and to exalt it to a supremacy above all the kingdoms of the earth. They were now, as prophecy had foretold, in respect to military and political affairs, "the tail;" and they expected, under the leadership of the long-looked for Prince, to become the " head" and chief, when, the power being theirs, they would pay their oppressors back with interest all the suffering they had endured at their hands.

Had these expectations been correct, what sort of people would have been fit to constitute the subjects, the agents, the companions of such a Messiah? Plainly, men like the Romans themselves; proud, ambitious, warlike, tyrannical, with the super-added garnish of oriental gorgeousness and show. The secular, the covetous, the revengeful, even the vicious and ungodly, would not have been disqualified for membership in a kingdom of this description. Had the prevailing ideas respecting the Messiah been correct, there would have been no need of a harbinger to prepare the way. The way was prepared enough already; the people were ripe for such a leader. With a sprinkling among them of enlightened and pious men, it is no breach of charity to say that, as a whole, they were fallen into a state of deep moral degeneracy. Can it be otherwise, when He, whose knowledge of men's hearts was infallible, and whose love and gentleness and consideration for human infirmity were unequalled, pronounced the men amongst them, most in repute for their piety and goodness, to be hypocrites, deceivers of the people, devourers of widows' houses, serpents, a generation of vipers, whited sepulchres—fair outside but within full of dead men's bones and all uncleanness?

The Messiah, whom John came to introduce, required a totally different class of subjects to welcome and value him; and the kingdom he came to establish demanded materials of another order wherewith to construct it.

What were the external circumstances of him who, in the fulness of time, claimed to be the Messiah? No army owned him as commander; no throne waited his occupancy; no ministers of state surrounded his person; no grandees attended his levees. Instead of this, what do we see? The child of a decayed house;

a member of the operative class; the inhabitant of a remote town, the very name of which was a reproach; the associate of fishermen and peasants; so poor himself that he had not where to lay his head; an obscure itinerant preacher, wandering about from place to place, and taking upon himself to address such groups of people as gathered around him, on moral and religious subjects, —matters which the learned thought far beyond his province. And was *this* the Son of David, the anti-type of the sumptuous Solomon, the Mighty King so celebrated in prophetic song, whose glory was to eclipse that of all his predecessors and contemporaries?

And what was the character of this long-expected king, now in such humble guise? Was he indignant at his country's wrongs, burning with patriotic ardor to break the oppressor's yoke and set the people free? Was he ambitious, daring, warlike, eagerly aspiring to the supreme power, and only waiting a fit opportunity to set up the standard of revolution? What a perfect contrast to all this did Jesus of Nazareth present! Refusing to assume the functions of a judge, and declining, when asked, to exercise lordship; hiding himself from the people, when they would by force have made him a king; meek and lowly in heart; gentle and forgiving in temper; when reviled, reviling not again; "holy, harmless, undefiled, separate from sinners"; engaged in no scheme for self-aggrandizement, but going about unweariedly doing good; seeking for the sick that he might heal them; for the sorrowful, that he might comfort them; for the ignorant, that he might instruct them; for the vicious and the fallen, that he might cleanse and restore them.

And what was the *work* he set himself to do—the kingdom He began to found and organise? certainly, anything but what his countrymen expected. Declining to meddle with the earthly politics of his nation, he engaged in matters of a nobler kind. He spake as never man spake on the deep things of God. He threw a flood of light upon the whole subject of morals. Life and immortality, so obscure to the most far-seeing philosophers, he brought clearly to light. He sought out and saved a few lost and wandering souls, imbued them with his spirit, patiently instructed them in the purest knowledge, and formed them into the nucleus of his new kingdom. Above all, he became the Saviour of men, by offering himself a sacrifice and atonement for their sins, that he might bring them back to God; thus proving himself to be a Redeemer and a Deliverer of a higher order, and upon a greater scale, than if he had restored independence to his country by dethroning the Cæsars, and assuming the imperial purple. His aim was spiritual: to rescue the nobler part of man's nature from its peril, and cure it of its deep-seated moral maladies; to found a dominion, not of this world, but holy heavenly and divine, in the hearts and consciences of men.

If such were the character of the Messiah whom God sent,

and if such were his objects, a people in the state the Jews are described to have been, needed a Forerunner to summons them to repent, to alter their views, correct their expectations and reform their lives, before they could appreciate the heavenly stranger. Otherwise, when he came to his own, his own would not receive him; they would turn from him with scorn as not the deliverer they wanted, charge him as an impostor, and persecute and punish him as a criminal. Therefore it was that John the Forerunner cried, saying " Repent, for the kingdom of heaven is at hand." The Messiah is coming, prepare for his approach. He is on the point of setting up his long-promised kingdom: see that ye be fit to enter it. The Lamb of God is about to offer himself a sacrifice for the sins of the world ; behold him, believe in him, attach yourselves to him, imbibe his Spirit, and live! Alas, for the hardness and inveterate secularity of the human heart! The warning voice was lifted up in vain. A few, we know, listened, repented, and received him gladly; but the nation as a whole excluded themselves from the new reign, of righteousness, and became outcasts and wanderers in the earth. This believing few, however, saved the Forerunner's mission from being a failure. They proved the germ of the new dispensation ; the first subjects of an empire destined to become universal and perpetual.

Does the Forerunner's cry—"Repent, for the kindom of heaven is at hand"—apply at all to mankind in the present day? Is there any need *now* for a change of mind, and a special preparation, as there was among the Jews in the time of the Saviour's advent? Most certainly ; for the Apostles, in establishing their Master's kingdom, "commanded *all men everywhere* to repent." Whence arises this universal necessity for a change of mind and altered views, in order to become incorporated in the kingdom which the Son of God has established? From the same reasons as those which affected our Lord's countrymen and contemporaries. It arises from the nature of that dominion of which Christ is the head, and the moral condition and carnal likings of mankind at large.

"Art thou a king?" asked Pilate. "I am a king," replied Jesus; " to this end was I born, and for this cause came I into the world : but my kingdom is not of this world." "The kingdom of God is not meat and drink, but righteousness and peace, and joy in the Holy Ghost." Christ's dominion is over the heart ; he assumes the regal power to subjugate to himself the affections, the will, the imagination, the thoughts, the services of men ; and only those who yield him this inner, this loving, this holy, this undivided allegiance, belong to the spiritual kingdom over which he reigns. His kingdom is not fixed to a local territory, is not determined by creeds however sound, or rites and ceremonies however scriptural. " Circumcision availeth nothing nor uncircumcision, but a new creature." No visible community of Christians includes all Christ's subjects, nor is composed wholly of such. His is an eclectic society, made up of individuals of a certain character, and taken doubtless from many varied churches. All whom he acknowledges as his are justified through his atoning blood, partakers of his disposition; subordinating the secular to the spiritual, the temporal to the eternal; and living with the constant aim to please and serve their Maker, by obedience, love, and cheerful devotedness. This is the true Church, "the Church of the first-born which are written in heaven," that Church which Christ "loved", and for which he "gave himself" that he might "sanctify and cleanse it," and "present it to himself a glorious Church, not having spot or wrinkle, or any such thing; but that it should be holy and without blemish."

Now, are men, as we universally find them, fit to be members of a kingdom of this nature, without a change in their dispositions, any more than the men of Judea were fit, in the state of mind in which John found them, to become at once incorporated in the kingdom then about to be established?

To prove the necessity of this change it is not requisite to make out that there is in man no sense of God, no trace of virtue and goodness, no benevolence and kindness, no disinterestedness and magnanimity, nothing but unmixed corruption and vice. This—to make man a demon—were to ignore the most obvious facts, and to libel our race. But, taking the most lenient view of human nature, and giving it credit for all the excellence we find in it, is it not "far gone from original righteousness"; forgetful of God, averse to thinking of him, to loving him and serving him; tenaciously clinging to the present world and indifferent to the future; the prey of evil passions, only kept within bounds for the most part by the restraints of law, the dictates of self-interest, or the force of custom? Glancing at the Pagan, the Mahommedan, and even the nominally Christian portions of mankind, are the dispositions and characteristics which prevail in harmony with that holy kingdom of which Jesus is the founder and the head? Apart from the vicious and the vile, is it not obvious that the heart of humanity itself is morally diseased; that the taste and preferences of men jar with the purity, the spirituality, the heavenly character of the moral dominion of Jesus? To enter his kingdom, therefore, it must be necessary for all to undergo a renovation. The Saviour's words are universally applicable—— "Except ye be converted, and become as little children, ye shall not enter the kingdom of heaven." "Except a man be born again, he cannot see the kingdom of God." Let every one examine and search his heart to ascertain his condition; and not be satisfied without the testimony of his conscience, that his inward state and outward life are in harmony with the mind, the will, and the religion of Jesus.

Sacramental Hymn.

"Do this in remembrance of Me."

I.

If human kindness meets return
    And own the grateful tie;
If tender thoughts within us burn,
    To feel a friend is nigh.

II.

Oh! shall not warmer accents tell,
    The gratitude we owe,
To HIM, who died our fears to quell,
    Our more than orphan's woe.

III.

While yet his anguish'd soul survey'd
    Those pangs he could not flee,
What love his latest words display'd—
    "Meet and remember Me!"

IV.

Remember Thee! Thy death and shame,
    Our sinful hearts to share!
Oh! memory leave no other name
    But this recorded there.

Memoir

OF THE REV. GEORGE COWIE MORRISON, A.M.
Congregational minister, Kyneton, Victoria.

The subject of this memoir was a son of the Rev. Patrick Morrison, and was born in or about the year 1829, at Duncanston, Aberdeenshire, Scotland, where his father was for many years the pastor of the Independent Church. From his earliest to his last days his bodily constitution was weak, which made him an object of more than ordinary parental solicitude, and tended not a little to prepare him in youth for religious impressions, and raise him in his manhood to eminence in spirituality of mind. Blessed with parents of distinguished piety, the influence of religion was brought to bear upon him in his boyhood, restraining him from evils peculiar to this stage of life, inducing obedience and filial affection, and leading him to think on the importance of salvation, and to resolve from day to day to give himself up to Christ. Thus he continued until his 16th year, when delay began to weaken his impressions, to bring on indifference, and induce a tendency to hardness of heart. Several months passed on; then a crisis came. What was he to be here? and what was to be his condition hereafter? were questions which started up in his mind as he returned one day from school; and whilst he contemplated the past, the present, and the future, he became alarmed, fell upon his knees, and poured out his youthful heart in prayer. His anxiety increased. The Bible and James's Anxious Enquirer became his constant companions. He opened his mind to a schoolfellow, and found him in a similar state of mind. Sympathy bound them together. Unknown to friends they met every night for two months to read and pray with each other. After experiencing much agony of mind in seeking salvation, both found it at length—both believed, and realized peace and joy. Mr. Morrison shortly after made a public profession of religion, and joined the church under the pastoral care of his father.

About this time he entered King's College, Aberdeen, where he studied four years, and took the degree of Master of Arts. After leaving the university, he became a tutor in a private family for about a year. As soon as he gave his heart to Christ, he became desirous to devote the remainder of his life to the work of the ministry, and this desire he cherished until his path to it was made clear. On resigning the office of private tutor, he entered the Theological Academy at Glasgow, conducted by the late Dr. Wardlaw and Professor Thompson, where he continued two years. On finishing his academical course, he accepted an invitation to become the pastor of the Independent Church at Berwick-on-Tweed, where he labored for about two years. By his catholic spirit and gentlemanly bearing he won the affection and confidence of all parties in the town of Berwick. He was on intimate terms with the Episcopal minister, the rector of the parish, who, on Mr. Morrison's coming to Australia, gave him a commendatory letter of introduction to the Bishop of Adelaide, in case he should visit that colony.

In the year 1855 Mr. Morrison came to Victoria, under the auspices of the Colonial Missionary Society in England, having long had a desire to labor in the colonies. The pastoral office of the Independent Church at Kyneton being vacant on his arrival, he was requested to spend a few weeks on probation there, with a view to his ultimate settlement over that church. In due time he was elected to the office. During the fifteen months which elapsed between his settlement at Kyneton and his death he labored perseveringly and successfully in the promotion of literature, education, civil rights, social feeling, and especially of pure and undefiled religion. He was both a pastor and a teacher—a preacher of the gospel both in word and deed. Earnestness, sincerity, and faithfulness to Christ, marked his entire course. It was impossible to be with him and not feel that he was a man imbued with the spirit of his Master. As might reasonably be expected, he grew in the esteem of all denominations of Christians, and of all classes of society. The work of the Lord prospered in his hand; the church increased, the chapel filled—accommodation could not be provided for those desirous of sittings, and plans were in course of preparation for enlarging the building, or erecting a new and more commodious one, when he was suddenly called away to the upper sanctuary.

On Lord's Day morning, the 28th December, 1856, he preached from 1 Pet. iv. 7,—"The end of all things is at hand; be ye therefore sober, and watch unto prayer,"—which proved to be not only a suitable subject for the close of the year, but also, unconsciously to himself and his congregation, a farewell discourse to them, and a funeral sermon for himself. At the close of the day he was attacked by hæmorrhage of the lungs, to which he had been occasionally and slightly subjected, both in Britain and this colony. During the week following his attack he was forbidden by his medical attendant to speak more than was absolutely necessary, and directions were given to his friends to keep him as quiet as possible. Incessant watchings, assiduous ministrations, and frequent variations of improvement and relapse, are all that can be narrated of his sick chamber up to Monday, the 5th January, 1857, the ninth day of the attack. On the morning of that day it became evident to the medical attendant that Mr. Morrison's end was near. Intelligence of this was communicated to him. He received it as a man of God a true believer in Christ—prepared for the coming change, although he had not, up to that time, expected that his sickness would be unto death. Though the force of his attack—greater than on any previous occasion—led him once, at least, in the early stage of it, to the momentary supposition that in his case the end of all things was at hand, yet so strongly was he impressed with the idea that God had much more work for him to do upon the earth, that the prevailing conviction of his mind, up to the morning of the day of his decease, might have been expressed by him in the language of Paul :—" And having this confidence, I know that I shall abide and continue with you all, for your furtherance and joy of faith." But when the intelligence of his drawing near to the gates of the grave was given to him, he withdrew all anticipations of recovery ; he broke the silence which had been imposed upon him, he directed that every calling friend should be admitted to his dying bed, and he spent the day—the last day of his life, for he died at nine o'clock the same evening—in declarations of his faith in Christ, his love to God, and his assurance of heaven ; in earnest exhortations to those who waited on him, and in fervent prayers to the Most High for them all. To one of the deacons of the church he gave a description of a gloom which had gathered round his spirit on the preceding Saturday, and of the ecstasy which followed it, and for which it seemed a preparative. " I have passed," he said, " in effect through a state in which I seemed as though standing in the universe alone, where there was nothing to cheer the eye, and nothing to please the ear—it was a vast wilderness—but suddenly the Lord appeared to change the scene, and fulfil the prophecy sung by Isaiah (xxxv. 1, 2) :—

" ' The wilderness and the solitary place shall be glad for them ;
And the desert shall rejoice and blossom as the rose.
It shall blossom abundantly,
And rejoice, even with joy and singing.
The glory of Lebanon shall be given unto it,
The excellency of Carmel and Sharon ;
They shall see the glory of the Lord,
And the excellency of our God.' "

The friend to whom he spoke, thinking that his soul was panting for heaven, and wishing to hear his sentiments stated distinctly, asked him whether he desired to be with Christ, which was far better than remaining in the flesh ? The holy and dying man, remembering the marriage state into which he had entered only four months before, the church over which he had been placed as pastor fifteen months previously, and the congregation still needing his care, showed that he was in the strait experienced by Paul—having a desire to depart hence for his own personal happiness, and to stay here for the benefit of others—for he said, turning his eye as he spoke first to his sorrowing wife, and then to the rest around his bed, " I love natural affections ; I love to be engaged in the work of Christ ; I love to write the name of Jesus upon the human heart." His state throughout Monday, the day of his departure, was one of holy and seraphic rapture. The day glided away—the shades of evening gathered around him—the voice became more and more inarticulate —the last intelligible expression escaped his lips,—it was, "Victory!" Nine o'clock came, and he fell asleep in Jesus.

In Mr. Morrison's death a mournful vacancy was created in the newly-formed household of love, piety, and happiness, which has since been cheered by the birth of a son—a posthumous orphan child it is true—but still, an image of the departed ; in the pastorate which he filled with efficiency, success, and bright prospects ; and in the social circle which he adorned by his gentlemanly bearing, true friendship, a well cultivated mind, and a benevolent heart.

MR. J. S. WADDELL, OF LAUNCESTON, TASMANIA.

(Being portions of a sketch read at the close of his Funeral Sermon on Lord's Day evening, 20th December, 1857).

Our departed friend was born in the month of September, 1806, at Nayland, in Suffolk, where his father was minister of the Independent Church. His early years were marked by serious attention to religious duties, and very early in life the Spirit of the living God impressed his mind with the necessity of a Saviour. In entering upon the active duties of life, he passed through many changes, and while waiting for some further opening of God's providence, he complied with the invitations of his friends, and accompanied them to these shores. Having received the truth of the Gospel as the only hope of sinful man, previous to leaving England, he soon after his arrival in Launceston made a public profession of his faith by joining the church in Tamar St. Chapel. His first reception of the Gospel was marked by a cheerful confidence in the power and grace of the Saviour. At a subsequent period of his history he passed through severe mental and spiritual depression, from which he was mercifully delivered by returning health. His life-course was a very even one ; for many years previous to his death there was but little of outward change ; he kept on "the noiseless tenor of his way," walking in the path of Christian self-denial and labor to a better country, that is, a heavenly one. Soon after his return from Sydney, his friends became alarmed at his altered appearance and manifest signs of weakness, yet nothing serious was apprehended within a short period of his decease. Advice, however, was early sought and active measures employed, in the, alas! vain hope of averting the progress of the disease, which had long, undetected been undermining the vital powers of his frame. For the first few weeks he struggled manfully against his complaint, and yielded not till the disease had fairly mastered him. When he became conscious that his recovery was all but hopeless, he patiently sought to resign himself to the will of the Gracious Being all whose acts are mercy and love. On one occasion he lamented that he should feel such a clinging to life, mournfully adding, "Fond of our prison and our clay." During his illness, I saw him at intervals of two or three days, and was much pleased with his humble confiding trust in the Saviour. He frequently expressed his thankfulness for the simplicity of the Gospel—"All is done for us;" "Look, and live,"

The time drew near that he must die. The Saviour led him by a very gentle descent into the dark valley, keeping close to his side all the way through. A short time before his death I quoted the verse, "Jesus can make a dying bed, &c.," which he repeated with as marked fervor as his strength would permit. He also referred to the passage, "Though I walk through the valley, &c." Almost his last words related to the Lord Jesus as his hope. His humble hope was well founded : the angel of death came to his bed with a gentle step, and quietly led him to his glorious home.

Ended now were the night watchings and the hours of anxious grief; past now our hopes and fears as the disease went on in stealthy and painless progress to a dreaded termination. Ended, too, the burning thirst and restlessness of the patient sufferer. It was evening, and wearied with the labor, sorrow, and sickness of life's day, he fell asleep in Jesus.

In offering a few remarks upon his character, we wish to be as honest and impartial as the Egyptian judges of the dead, and would aim to realise the godly simplicity of the ancient sage who knew not how to give flattering titles unto man, lest his Maker should take him away. All who knew him will bear cheerful witness to his gentle deportment. He gave himself no airs of superiority; of assumption he was entirely guiltless. The pride that springs from self ignorance, from imagined mental power, from rank or riches, had no home in his bosom; he knew it to be offensive to man and to God. His humility was founded upon a clear knowledge of himself—was deepened by his devout acquaintance with God's requirements and his frequent communion with One, who, for man's sins humbled himself and became obedient unto death, even the death of the cross ; and was still more intensified by his knowledge of the unsullied holiness of Jehovah : wherefore he repented and abhorred himself as in dust and ashes.—He was characterised by the love of order and punctuality. He kept his word as to engagements, and kept time. He was seldom late either in business or sanctuary worship. These are important virtues, and busy men appreciate their worth — for time is money. Delay we would cheerfully leave to those who think it an honor to be waited for. We never devolved business upon him but we found it done to our complete satisfaction. His services as secretary to the Colonial Missionary Society were of great value. The records were carefully kept, and all details faithfully carried out ; while as superintendent of the Sabbath School he was a model of diligence. Orderly and punctual in every engagement, he sought to redeem his own time without wasting that of others.—He was marked by a spirit of Christian liberality ; money was a talent, himself a steward ; he was such a giver as the Lord loveth. His general consistency gave a completeness to his character which awakened respect. There may be many Christians who possess one or more graces in greater perfection than he did, yet few who combine so many excellencies and so much of general consistency. He gave of the firstlings of the flock, and did not withhold the living sacrifice. There was no attempt to compound for a sin hard to be forsaken, by the diligent practice of a cheap and easy virtue. The consecration was entire ; he accepted the ten commandments of the Old, and the new one of the New Testament as his moral code, and Christ as the embodied living expression. The former esteemed pastor of this church* thus testifies : —"I have known him intimately as an honorable, sincere, and humble

---

* Rev. J. West, now of Sydney.

Christian, and none of my acquaintance have left on my mind a fuller conviction of the reality and earnestness of piety." We do not say that he was perfect, in a world where there is not a just man that doeth good always and sinneth not. He is not held up as a model of saintly virtue worthy of being canonised by his holiness the Pope. He was a man of like passions with ourselves, and had, doubtless, to mourn over many failings and short-comings. But we do say that, admitting all that the most rigid censor could fairly urge, there still remains a large measure of positive Christian excellence, alike honorable to the man himself, to the common nature he wore, and still more to the grace of God, which made him what he was on earth, and has now presented him without fault before the throne of God in heaven.

The lessons of his life are important. Parents may learn much for their guidance and to encourage their hopes. During his illness he often referred with thankfulness to his early advantages. One who was much with him thus writes : — " Early associations were greatly endeared to him ; I have heard him revert with much feeling to the hallowed influence of the Sabbath as spent under his father's roof." On another occasion he said, " We cannot be too thankful for early religious instruction. I often derive great comfort from hymns and passages learned in youth. Watts's Divine Songs help me when I cannot think for myself." He instanced :—

" Lord, at thy feet ashamed I lie." &c.
" Remember all the dying pains," &c.

" Train up a child in the way he should go, and when he is old he will not depart from it."

There is a lesson for young men. He had been successful in business and had attained a comfortable competence. It was obtained by the slow gains of honest industry. It was a process of ant-hill accretion, little by little. He confined himself to daily toil and yearly gains. A few may become suddenly rich by fortunate speculations, but more fail. Make haste slowly ; —success usually crowns the painstaking and diligent. We would say to young men in business, as the moral of his history : Be courteous and diligent : content yourselves with the slow gains of safety ; consecrate a portion of your income to God's service ; and, with His blessing, you will find godliness to be profitable to all things, having promise of the life that now is and of that which is to come.

Finally, we would commend his example to Sabbath school teachers. If personal piety, a sincere desire to benefit the children, a spirit of faith, patience, prayer, and hope, be the essential attributes of a true teacher, he had these, with a large measure of scripture knowledge and a most untiring spirit of perseverance. " Be not slothful, but followers of them who through faith and patience now inherit the promises."   W.L.

THE EFFECT OF THE SAVIOUR'S PRESENCE ON EARTH.

" We know what the church was when it received the epistles fresh from the living apostle. We know its enduring faith, its holy hope, its sufferings which were triumphs, its earthly defeats which were heavenly victories. In that new-born church, human nature, as if recent from its contact with Deity in the person of the incarnate God, seemed once more to have issued in primitive beauty from the divine hand, and again to have caught the original impression of its Maker. Eternal purity had been on earth in the form of Jesus Christ, and, though he had passed away, the world where he walked was still fragrant with his presence. The sun himself had set, but the clouds yet burned with his glory, and twilight was still to the darkness to come."—*Archer Butler.*

BOOKS.

ENGLISH CORRESPONDENT'S LETTERS.

[We have been favored with the following letters from our Correspondent in England, who promised to supply us from time to time with some of the gossip current in literary circles. We have to apologise to our readers for having to present to them two letters in one number of our Magazine, but our excuse is (and every body will admit it as sufficient) the confusion of the mails, which has annoyed everyone the last three months.]

To the Editor of the " Southern Spectator."

Dear Sir, September, 1857.

It would seem not unreasonable that your correspondent, who purposes to furnish you from time to time with a little literary, scientific, or artistic gossip selected from the incessant babble of this old country's decaying days, should preface his intended communications with his own ideas on the nature and capacities of gossip in general ; but as I have not much time to spare if I am to catch this mail, I will forego, and proceed at once to what I have to say to you this month.

I don't know how it is with you people at the antipodes, but our cousin Jonathan is making such improvements in the English language, and, with his go-a-head enthusiasm, introducing such startling novelties, that, knowing you to be of strongly progressive tendencies, I am half afraid lest the costume of my thoughts should appear as antiquated as the dress of Rip Van Winkle after his long sleep. Of course wilful and headstrong young people will have their own way, but if you take my advice, you will be at some pains to preserve intact the purity of your mother tongue. If you are thus minded and have any anxiety on this point, I am glad to inform you that, if all goes well, you may expect one of these days a valuable aid in the shape of a real " *Lexicon totius Anglicitatis*," which has been projected by the Philological Society. It is intended to supersede both Johnson and Richardson, including, along with the results of their labours, a great number of true English words and phrases which are not noticed by them : these it is said are to be found mainly in the writings of Roger Ascham, Philemon, Holland, Henry Moore, &c., since Chaucer, Robert of Gloucester, and the early ballad writers, have been pretty accurately surveyed already. The carrying out of the enterprise is committed to R. Chevenix French, Dean of Westminster, F. J. Furnival Esq., and Herbert Coleridge, Esq., who are inviting the co-operation of all devotees disposed to bury themselves alive in musty old accounts of state trials, royal progresses, and quaint translations of the classics. Let us hope they may obtain plenty of assistance and that we may enter into the fruits of their labours.

Talking of good old English, there is a splendid edition of Bacon's Essays out, now some little time, with annotations by Whately, in which the notes are worth almost as much as the Essays. In my haste, however, I am not equal to the weight of Bacon, and must pass on to something lighter. I presume the last number of " Little Dorrit ' has reached you, and I wonder what you think of it. As for us, we are as unanimous as a hungry jury that scents dinner . we are calling it everything that is bad, and wondering what has become of " Boz," and the Editor of the " Pickwick Papers." Have you seen anything of him ? Has he gone over to you with so much of the vital power, the bone and muscle of this old land ? Certainly his old clothes are left behind, but the general impression is that they cover nothing but a convulsive scarecrow, jer ed about by a kind of galvanic sentimentalism, or blown hither and thither by every wind of whimsy. I suppose I need not give you any account of the somewhat angry warfare which has arisen between Mr. Dickens and the Edinburgh Review, which in its last number has taken upon itself to defend the Executive, or, as it is called in " Little Dorrit," the " Circumlocution Office ;" from the attack Mr. Dickens has made upon it. The article in question is entitled " The License of Modern Novelists." and joins with " ittle Dorrit." Mr. Reade's notorious book " It is never to late to mend ;" on both of which the writer fixes the charge of gaining melodramatic effects fro u perverting and colouring truth till it becomes falsehood. The article is bold, spirited, and interesting : perhaps, however, with your mighty ideas of a " nascent empire." you will think this a storm in a tea kettle, and so we will pass on.

What next ? well. I wish I had left myself more space to talk about the Life of that heroic woman, *Charlotte Brontë*. The worst of it is, the Life as written by Mrs. Gaskell, is more like a novel than a sober narrative of fact, and that unfortunately not always in a good sense But one redeeming feature in the book is the extent to which Mrs. Gaskell has allowed her heroine to tell her own story : and a wonderful story it is ! Talk of Pegasus in harness ! What could equal the indomitable perseverance in self-martyrdom. the almost unearthly power of self-compression displayed. in compliance with the irksome restraints of the lowliest earthly duties, by this extraordinary being. with a heart fiery enough and soul daring enough to conceive and paint the parting scene between Jane Eyre and Rochester ? This is what seems to me to come out most strongly, in her life. This is what must make it influential for good with all young. ardent, aspiring minds, for it shows us that even a woman that acquired such great and sudden fame found it necessary " *to do with all her m gue whatever her hand found to do.*" She is gone ; and the lives of the strongest and brightest seem, perhaps, short because we could desire them to live for ever.

November, 1857.

We can hardly think or speak of anything here but India ; and no wonder. I am not, however, about to enter on political questions. But it is natural, under present circumstances, that *maps of i dostan* and *books on the war* should take up more of our attention than anything else in the realm of literature. Indeed, I do not believe there is much else to invite notice at all ; for there is a general complaint about the dearth of good new books.

The most interesting announcement I have to make to you by this mail, is the appearance at length of *Dr. Livingsto e's* eagerly-expected *Account of his Trae s*, and observations in Central Africa. It forms a thick octavo volume, illustrated by excellent plates, and is published at the somewhat high price of a guinea. At this rate, its publisher, Mr. Murray, and it is to be hoped its author likewise, must be making a good thing of it ; for nearly fourteen thousand have already been sold, probably to-day more than that number, although it has only been out a week ; and another day or two will certainly see the first edition (20,000) exhausted. The unassuming, manly modesty of the great traveller and missionary is as evident in the pages of the book, as it has been in every assembly that Dr Livingstone has honored with his presence : and this always heightens the charm that attaches to the recital of great and heroic deeds. Almost equal in interest to the narrative of his own adventures is the information given concerning the resources of the unknown lands he has traversed, and their availableness for the purposes of commerce. It is wonderful to hear of the eager desire for an outlet for the productions of their country manifested by the savage chieftains of inland tribes. So strong was this, that one of them thought the discovery of a path to the coast an ample remuneration for the liberality with which he had fitted out an expedition for Dr. Livingstone, though, through the difficulties experienced on a first passage, it returned empty-handed. Perhaps the perusal of this narrative of what can be accomplished by high Christian principle, and unassuming but indomitable energy. may stimulate you, our antipodean friends, to see what you can do towards exploring the unfathomable abysses of your wilderness, and developing its resources, if there are any.

The next thing I have to tell you is that *Mr. Spurg on* has written a book. Perhaps in your distant seclusion you are unable to appreciate the import ance of this announcement ; but I assure you, we who revolve in the imme diate dazzling rays of this pulpit phenomenon of the nineteenth century

roused to almost as eager attention as though Tennyson's epic were proclaimed. The other evening (6th of Nov.) we were as usual burning our fingers and risking our eyesight in honor of the deliverance of our English Solomon from Guy Fawkes. By the way, I suppose the little boys of your rising continent will be too advanced and philosophical for this *sporting* custom. However, all I want with it at present is to obtain a figure expressive of Mr. Spurgeon's career hitherto. For it is wonderful what a flaming display is created, and sustained for an unexpected length of time, by an insignificant and apparently sober little Catherine-wheel. It looks like a bit of waste-paper, twisted up by the fingers of an idle child; but only let it be properly placed, let the spark be applied, and what a shower of glory suddenly bursts upon the sight! Stars and burning diamonds and jets of fire, flung abroad in dazzling profusion, startle the juvenile beholders, and keep their gaze entranced. But such a little unpretending thing cannot surely last long! "Ah! it is nearly done," they cry, after a few revolutions; but the wheel, as though insulted by the observation, blazes up defiantly, and brighter than ever. Again it is confidently expected to expire, and again does a fresh halo of glory falsify the prediction. So has it been with Mr. Spurgeon—an unknown, insignificant, illiterate young man; but, when placed in the pulpit of New Park-street Chapel, and touched with the fire of evangelic zeal, the greatest preacher of modern times. I say, the greatest preacher; for what right have you to take a pet parson of your own, whether beloved for the softness of his heart, or admired for the hardness of his head, and, either by your solitary vote, or that of a few who think like you, place your favorite on that eminence? "By their fruits ye shall know them." What a man does, is the best proof, at least to men, of what he is; and on this principle you ought to judge of preachers by the power with which they bring truth to bear on the greatest multitudes. Judged in this way, Mr. Spurgeon has no competitor in the present century,—perhaps not in any other century either, unless it be Peter the Hermit. I know that such men as Robert Hall have done much; but the tens of thousands, who in business-hours will fight and push and smash windows and break balustrades in frantic eagerness to catch a few deep mellow notes from that incomparable voice, have no parallel. Constant have been the predictions of his failure, but they have only seemed like oil to the flame of his glory. It was out of all reason that an uneducated youth, who despises the advantages of learning, should long continue in so extraordinary a position. But he is higher than ever now, and treads steadily on his giddy height. His power may be a puzzle, but it is a great fact for all that. As you can hardly expect to get his living voice over amongst you, your best plan is to order his book, viz.: "*The Saint and his Saviour*:" London: J. S. Virtue: a small 8vo volume of addresses, suitable to successive stages of Christian experience. I think you will acknowledge the power of the writing, and yet you will feel a difficulty in accounting for it. It seems to go right into you, and stir up the depths of your soul. It revives the work of God in you, and makes old truths look like new ones. I am greatly mistaken if that book is not the result of many a fervent prayer. You may dislike the doctrine, you may deprecate the grammar, you may disdain the display that is made of superficial reading, but you will feel, notwithstanding all, that there is a wondrous power of life therein.

To change the subject, I see that *Lord Macaulay's History* (you are aware of his new dignity) is to be issued in a new form. Volumes I. to IV. of the former editions are to be distributed into 7 vols. post octavo, which will come out at intervals of a month, the first in the beginning of December. The price will be 6s. a vol.—A library edition of *Dickens's Works* is also announced, complete in 22 vols, crown octavo, at 6s. a vol. The first will be issued in January.—A second edition of that whimsical individual, George Borrow's, whimsical book "*The Romany Rye*," is out; 2 vols. post octavo, London, John Murray. Perhaps few books contain more nonsense; and not many are more entertaining. Indeed, I think more than entertainment may be gained from it by a serious man who has patience to read it. Of course plenty of *books on India* are coming out. The two that seem most worth mentioning to you are, one by J. P. Ferrier, entitled "*Materials towards a History of Affghanistan;*" and another by the inexhaustible Miss Martineau, called "*British Rule in India.*"—The author of "The Eclipse of Faith" has just published a new book. entitled "*Selections from the Letters o" R E H. Greyson, Esq. Edited by the author of 'The Eclipse.' &c.*" Mr. Greyson is a fictitious person, and the epistolary form of the book is well adapted to its miscellaneous character. A variety of subjects are embraced, theological, metaphysical, and social; while at times the same subject is continued through several letters; but there is no unity in the book. It consists of two vols small octavo, published by Longmans and Co.—There is another book, intended mainly for boys, which has reached a third edition in a very short time. I mean "*Tom Brown's Schooldays. By an Old Boy.*" London : Longmans and Co. It is the narrative of a boy's experience at Rugby in the days of Dr. Arnold. It appears to be a capital book, healthful, bold, and thoroughly English in its tendency, not without a natural and unaffected spirit of godliness infused.

REVIEW.

The Philosophy of Education, or the Principles and Practice of Teaching. By T. TATE, F.R.A.S. Second Edition, revised and enlarged. London : Longmans. Melbourne : Robertson.

MR. TATE is too well-known to need any introduction now. He has already made numerous friends among those who are favorable to advancement in the science and art of education ; and among those who are wedded to the old-fashioned learn-and-repeat style of training, which spurns an explanation, but loves a rule, he has likewise made many enemies. In saying this, we give utterance to what may be taken as praise of our author,—for it is not every man who is able to make enemies out of the quiet jog-trot teachers of some of our educational establishments, and when we do find a man who can give a home thrust at that dead conservatism which was and is so paralysing to the prosperity of our schools, all hail to him. Be he right or wrong, we welcome him. He has done good service, even if he can go no further. Out of free and earnest inquiry it is, that we gain those truths either of theory or practice, which are of service in helping forward any right-minded work, and he who promotes such investigation deserves the thanks of all friends of progress. This Mr. Tate has done, both by the book now before us, and by his numerous educational works whose more immediate object is tuition. But we afford him more than this mere negative praise. Though not prepared to agree with every point in his theories, we yet think them in the main soundly philosophical, and based on a careful and accurate investigation into the capabilities and faculties of the mind in the double light of common sense and mental philosophy. Nor is it all theory : throughout the whole of this work our author never for a moment loses sight of the object before him : to show a teacher how in the best the most efficient way, he can train up those entrusted to his care. He wants to make schoolmasters not stiff, starched pedagogues, but educators; and to redeem their work from the degradation into which it has fallen, by showing it to be a work which requires as complete a development as possible of all the various faculties in the mind of the instructor—a careful and searching insight into the individual character of each child, and a knowledge of the principles on which the *science* of education is built, and by which it must become efficient as an *art*.

It is impossible to give in this short notice anything like an adequate epitome of the contents of Mr. Tate's *Philosophy of Education*. The work commences with a discussion of *method* as applied to education, i.s history, its various forms, its importance. Mr. Tate's method we may concisely state to be this. Having ascertained the nature of the being to be educated, it is the work of the instructor so to direct his energies and enforce his lessons, that there may be a harmonious progressive *self-development* in the mind of the child. In accordance with this idea there follows naturally a philosophical chapter on the powers of the human mind, and the means of cultivating them in the juvenile understanding. Then comes an examination into the various modes or methods of tuition adopted in schools, and the remainder of the work is occupied with a practical application of our author's own principles to all the subjects of elementary instruction, and to the organisation and discipline of schools.

In Britain, they have become heartily tired of the old school-system of appointing masters to their posts because they had broken a leg, and so could be no longer soldiers, or who were too paralysed to serve behind the counter of the village shops, or too old to act as the gardener of the parsonage. It was time there should be some change, and that change is happily fast taking place, and such characters as these are now only occasionally to be found. But also, in better schools there was sadly needed some reform. Education was *teaching to repeat* and nothing more. The first book of Euclid was best mastered when the propositions could be said forwards and backwards. He was the best grammarian who could say fastest his *verbum personale, &c.*; and when the student of arithmetic after being "driven mad" by practice, innocently passed on to what he hoped was more lucid, and asked for an explanation of division of fractions, he was told, " invert the divisor and proceed exactly as in multiplication." Sometimes this style of teaching arose out of ignorance on the part of the teacher, who dared not trust himself away from his book, and sometimes from prejudice and a conservative abiding by worn-out habits. Education was in nearly all schools and schoolbooks nothing but a thing of routine. The *rationale* of the growth of the immortal soul was never dreamt of, or if vaguely perceived to exist, was practically ignored. But the day of these things is gone by, and in this young country there is no need that they should ever be at all. Whether we love stir or repose in these colonies, we have no choice but to advance. It is so with education — we have few obstructions to clear away, — we may make this land as it developes as remarkable for its intelligence and literary spirit, as it is for wealth and enterprise, if we will only be guided in all our proceedings (as Mr. Tate is in his journeyings to and fro between theory and practice), by the light of a vigorous Christian common sense.

To all who love teaching in its highest sense we would recommend this book as a pleasant and profitable companion ; and likewise to those who, having influence in the establishment of schools or the appointment of schoolmasters, desire to know what are the best characteristics of a really good educator.

Young Men's Department.

CONGREGATIONAL BOOK CLUB, Pitt-street Chapel, SYDNEY.—A Society under this name has recently been formed in connection with the congregation of which the Rev. W. Cuthbertson is the pastor. Its *objects* are the promotion of social intercourse, a taste for Christian literature and mental improvement among the members, and the diffusion of Christian, Biblical, and congregational literature throughout the community generally. And its *methods* are monthly meetings to devise plans and to hold conversations and friendly discussions; the circulation of books and periodicals among the members themselves, and the adoption of such means as may, from time to time, seem advisable for acting upon a wider scale. Membership is obtained by ballot, and a subscription is required of 2s. 6d. per month. This endeavor to promote intelligence among the members of a congregation and especially its young men, and to cherish in them a relish for wholesome reading and self-culture has our hearty approval ; and it is hoped that the example so worthily set, may be followed by many congregations throughout Australia.

THE COLLINGWOOD YOUNG MEN'S CHRISTIAN ASSOCIATION in connection with the INDEPENDENT CHAPEL, OXFORD-STREET. — The first half-yearly soiree of the above association, was held in the school room, on Tuesday evening, January 12th. About 120 persons sat down to tea, after which Rev. W. B. Landells, the president, occupied the chair and opened the business by dwelling upon the importance of such associations and the benefits to be derived by young men meeting occasionally to consider calmly and discuss temperately subjects of importance.

The secretary read the half-yearly report. The association was instituted last July, and commenced with 12 members : during the session the members had increased to 30, with an average attendance of 20. The programme agreed upon had been carried out in a satisfactory manner, the subjects generally were interesting, and the discussions were carried on in a manner which reflects credit upon those concerned. The committee are desirous of getting a library for the use of the members as soon as the funds will admit.

The treasurer reports the receipts during the session to be £7 7s. 6d , the expenditure £3 11s., leaving a balance in hand of £3 16s. 6d.

The adoption of the report was moved by Dr. Embling, M.L.A., and seconded by Mr. Thorpe and carried.

The following subjects were spoken on, during the evening :—

The advantages of Young Men's Associations ; by Mr Curtis.

Religion and Literature ; by Mr. Wilkinson.

The claims of the times upon Young Men ; by Mr. Mason.

Young Men and Sunday Schools : by the Vice-president, Mr. Stillwell.

An almost-overlooked Christian Duty ; by Mr. Hills.

A vote of thanks was given to the ladies who had kindly prepared the tea, after which the meeting terminated with prayer.

YOUNG MEN'S CHRISTIAN ASSOCIATION. - A social meeting was held in the Hall of the School of Arts, Sydney, on Monday, November 30th. About 200 persons sat down to tea, after which, addresses on " Individual Effort," " United Effort," and " Success," were delivered by Messrs. Stock, Langley, and Halley. The special object of the meeting was to present Mr. S. H. Lewis, one of the secretaries of the association, with a valuable silver tea service, which was done on behalf of the subscribers by the president, John Fairfax, Esq.

South Sea Missions.

IN our August number we inserted a sketch of the Missions now carrying on in the islands of the South Pacific, and an account of a visit to Australia of the " John Williams" missionary ship, with a further account of her return to the islands. and of her safe arrival at Tahiti, where she landed the Rev. W. Howe * When Mr. Howe was in Melbourne, some steps were taken to promote a union of various denominations of Christians to raise funds for assisting the South Sea Mission. Several meetings were held, but no practical result has yet followed. Mr. Howe refers to this attempt in the following letter, just received. Two other letters are appended, previously received by the friends to whom they are addressed, which give interesting information of the progress of the missionary work.

    Rev. R. Fletcher.   Papeete, Tahiti, Nov. 9, 1857.

MY DEAR SIR,—I wrote to you in April last, giving to you an account of our safe arrival here, and of our reception, with a brief account of the state of things among the people ; and, as a vessel has unexpectedly put in here on her way to Melbourne, I avail myself of it to state a few more particulars.

The " John Williams" arrived here from visiting the out stations of this mission, namely, the Austral group of Islands, consisting of Rurutu, Tupuai, Raivavai, &c.

---

* News has just been received of the arrival of the " John Williams " in Sydney.

Rapa, on the 1st of October. Tupuai is the only one over which the French protection has been extended. In this group, a body of American Mormons located themselves some years ago; their success, however, was very small, and when the interference of the French compelled them to leave Tupuai (which was their chief place of residence), coupled with other circumstances, they left in a body, and none of them have again returned. The deputation appointed to visit this group were the Revs. Messrs. Barff, Senr. of Huahine, and Chisholm, of Raiatea. They brought a very pleasing account from them all, having found the churches, as well as the governments, in a far better state than they had reason to hope for, from the long period which had elapsed since the last visit of the vessel to those islands. No direct attempt has yet been made by the Catholic Bishop to extend the influence of his system to that group, and, unless he has a large reinforcement to his body of priests, he will not be able very soon to do so. In the meantime, it becomes us to be earnestly alive to the wants of that people, which still remain to be supplied, lest they be permitted to lose by our supineness that which they have already obtained. They are endeavouring to supply this lack for themselves, to the best of their ability, each of the islands having furnished one or two students for Mr. Barff's seminary, which is to be held at Tahaa, in the neighbourhood of Raiatea, and to the support of which some of our Melbourne friends, I believe, subscribed. This step is one of great importance for the future advancement of the people in knowledge and judicious superintendence, but it will by no means meet the case for some years to come; for, although a little knowledge is not always "a dangerous thing," we have too many painful proofs that it is too often so to the native mind.

What is wanted there, is an European missionary who would take the entire charge of this group, which, with a small schooner at his service, he might very efficiently do; and in a few years he might be able to leave them to their own supervision. The expense would not be more, I think, than £150 per annum, including the expense of the schooner; articles for barter, for paying those who have charge of the schooner and for other purposes, being furnished from the Melbourne or Sydney market.

Probably this would be one of the best and readiest modes of bringing into operation your auxiliary, according to the terms in which it was originally proposed. Should the brethren composing your committee be disposed to entertain the subject, we will then furnish you with more particulars as to size, distance from each other, population, number of villages and churches &c., of this interesting group.

It is a source of great gratitude to the God of all grace to be able to say that the Gospel influence is still progressing in Tahiti. There is much activity in all the churches, and very considerable numbers are being added to them; and, although some extravagances are growing up in their church government (such as looking for deacons in the upper ranks, and admitting members on exceedingly short trial, and some other things that may ultimately give trouble) it is gratifying to see so many willing to give up the pleasures of sin (which they are compelled to do) to enjoy church communion.

A census of the population of Tahiti, Eimeo, and of a small island in the neighborhood, was published in the *Messenger* of yesterday, a small government Sunday paper. The population is divided into four classes.

	Males.		Females.	BIRTHS FOR NINE MONTHS.	
Old people	367	...	316	Males	85
Adults	1289	...	982	Females	59
Mature	794	...	652		
Children	1295	...	1211	Total births	144
	3745		3161	Excess of males	26
Deduct females	3161			BIRTHS AND DEATHS.	
				Total births	144
Excess of males	584			Total deaths	111
Total of the population			6906	Excess of births over deaths	33

As compared with the census of 1848, there is a deficiency of nearly one-fourth. This deficiency is accounted for in three ways—first, the fearful ravages which the measles made among all ages of the people; secondly, the number who have gone during the period to the Leeward Islands; and thirdly, the present census is probably much more accurate than the preceding one, the authorities having been more exact in obtaining the correct account of the people in each locality, and in more fully excluding those who belong to other islands. The disparity of sex is the most singular part of this statement, as no greater mortality has taken place among the females than among the males; indeed, the list of births appears to give the true reason. The excess of births over those of deaths, for the last nine months, gives hope that the population is again rallying.

Yours very truly,

WM. HOWE.

Robert Smith, Esq., Melbourne.   Rarotonga, April 10th, 1857.

MY DEAR SIR,—   *   *   *   *   *   *

The valuable box we have now received will assist us much at this time, as we are about to visit some of the most destitute portions of our missionary field, where some of the things sent will be much prized, and some of them will be very useful to the native missionaries.

We have now five young men set apart to the work, who are about to embark in the missionary barque for distant and dark lands: each of these have been furnished with a good black coat from your box. Some of them, being of a large size, fitted them nicely, and made them look like gentlemen.

We had a most deeply interesting meeting with them last evening, when each of them spoke with much feeling and effect; they were addressed both by Mr. G. Gill and myself, and one of the senior Deacons gave them also a parting address. It was a delightful meeting: it was good to be there.   *   *   *

God has seen fit to lay his hand upon me; for six months I have been laid aside, and at times the affliction was so severe that I appeared just at the door, and expected soon to be before my Saviour, but God has partially restored me to health; I do not, however, expect to be able to resume labor in the tropics. We know not what is before us. It is our intention to visit the colonies on the return of the *John Williams*, and there wait the indications of the cloud. It is now more than thirty years since we embarked for the South Seas, and we are now spending our thirtieth year at Rarotonga.

Few are permitted to labor on heathen ground so long: and, what is best, God granted success to our labors. A goodly number are already surely landed on the heavenly shore, and many more are thither bound whom God has given us. To God be all the praise.

With kind remembrance to your old pastor, the Rev. A. Morison, and kind regards for Mrs. Smith, in which Mrs. Buzacott and daughter unite,

Yours affectionately,

A. BUZACOTT.

To the Rev. A. Morison.   Mangaia, South Pacific, May 21st, 1857.

MY DEAR SIR,—I had hoped to receive a few lines from you per *John Williams*: but I presume that press of business prevented you. You were all doubtless pleased by the recent visit of the missionary vessel to your "golden city." I trust that it has been the means of increasing the interest in the cause of missions

Long and anxiously did we await the arrival of the *John Williams*. At length, on March 31st, after an absence of upwards of two years, she came to her missionary station, in the solitary islands of this vast ocean—she is indeed a messenger of peace.

On this occasion, however, sorrow was mingled with joy, on account of the removal of our fellow-laborers, the Rev. and Mrs. George Gill. Our brother proceeded to Rarotonga, per *John Williams*, to succeed the Rev. A. Buzacott (who is laid aside by sickness) in the important duties of the Institution [for training Native Teachers]. We are now left alone in this rarely visited island, with the care of the three Mission Churches. This is indeed a heavy responsibility. May I entreat your prayers, that an increased portion of the Holy Spirit's influences may rest upon us. You need not be assured that nothing can be more cheering to the far distant missionary, than to know that he is not forgotten in the prayers of our fellow Christians at home.

A very interesting revival of religion has lately occurred at Ivirua, the smallest of the three villages on this island. At one time the village to which I refer was remarkable for the number of open transgressors. During the early part of the year 1857 there seemed nothing whatever to encourage,—not an enquirer presented himself. This led, I believe, to self-examination and prayers on the part of the native Pastors, and the Deacons. A place was set apart for prayer by the Deacon's wives. The wife of Kaluke, the native teacher, presided. The spot selected for this purpose is somewhat wild—a solitary crag of rock, overshadowed by two trees. There, prevailing prayer was offered to God. The little band increased in numbers; their earnestness and faith augmenting with success. In these sacred meetings for prayer they were in the habit of pleading for certain individuals mentioned by name; and following up by personal visits to their dwellings, and exhortations suited to their various characters. It was not long before there was a shaking among the dry bones. Numbers came forward expressing a concern for their spiritual welfare. At the close of the last year, my colleague had the pleasure of admitting twenty-seven individuals to church fellowship; all of whom had long been on probation. The single solitary gathering amid the rocks had by this time increased to four well-attended prayer meetings, held twice a week in the open air. in secluded spots Six young men were admitted to church fellowship by Mr. G. Gill on his departure for Rarotonga. Last month I admitted forty-four individuals to the Communion of Saints below, upon an intelligible confession of their ardent love for the Saviour, and their entire trust in his atoning blood for salvation. I should perhaps add that ALL these parties had long been on probation : thus, in considerably less than twelve months, seventy-eight persons have been admitted to the Church in that little village. out of a population of about six hundred souls. What hath God wrought! We have been constrained to regard it as a blessed outpouring of the Holy Spirit, in answer to the fervent prayer of his people. I have felt the more liberty in describing these events, as they did *not* occur in connection with my own direct and stated labors; but under the superintendence of our faithful and zealous native pastor, Katuke. Let, then, the friends of missions rejoice. and do what they can to sustain the labors of such worthy native Evangelists; and let them unite their supplications with ours, that these young converts may be kept from the evil influences of this world, and be preserved faithful even unto death.

May I solicit any contributions of clothing and useful articles for the benefit of our people? Mrs. Gill has a school of girls. who are very dependent upon us for clothing. Of course, I have a number of native lads under my own special care and instruction. Two years since we were much encouraged by the contributions of Melbourne friends. May I hope that we shall *again* receive similar encouragement?

I remain, my dear brother,

Yours, very truly, ·

WILLIAM WYATT GILL.

RELIGIOUS INTELLIGENCE.

STATE-AID TO RELIGION.—The measure for abolishing all State-aid to Religion in Victoria having passed the House of Assembly through all its stages, was rejected in the Legislative Council, on the second reading, by a majority of *one*. It is much to be regretted that the abolition thus sanctioned by the ministry, by a large majority of the people's house, and by the general sense of the country. and regarded even by those who are opposed to it as inevitable ere long, should not have been allowed quietly to pass. A vexed question would have been removed for ever out of the way. The delay only keeps open an irritating wound in the body politic, which nothing can heal but the removal of the exciting cause. The friends of Abolition. however, will not relax their efforts ; a new agitation has been determined on, and the occurrence of a suitable time for action is only waited to prosecute it vigorously. The same question is now occupying the attention of the public in Tasmania, where the associations previously stated to have been formed to bring about abolition of all State aid to religion, are proceeding prosperously. In New South Wales, the only form in which it is exciting public attention at present, is in relation to affiliated colleges for the several denominations towards which public grants are made. This subject will be adverted to in a future number.

REV. THOMAS BINNEY, LONDON.—Intelligence has been received of the intended sailing of this distinguished minister, accompanied by Mrs. Binney, in the " Royal Charter," which was expected to leave for Melbourne early in January. Mr. Binney's health has been impaired by over excitement, and a sea voyage is recommended to recruit it. His intention, we believe, is to visit the different colonies, and to preach as much as his strength will permit.

REV. J. L. POORE'S MISSION TO ENGLAND.—Mr. Poore, who went to England thirteen months ago to procure ministers for Australia, backed by a fund of £2400 raised in the Colonies, had, by last advices, nearly accomplished his object. He has preached, lectured, and attended public meetings incessantly, for a period of six months, in various parts of England and Scotland, and procured subscriptions amounting to more than £1000, to supplement the Australian contribution. About two-thirds of the ministers have arrived, or are on their way, and the rest will soon follow. Since our last issue, there have reached Melbourne the Rev. J. Sleigh, from Hockliffe, Beds; the Rev. W. R. Lewis, from Lutterworth; and the Rev. J. Summers, from Bridgford, Notts. These ministers have entered on missionary labors; the first at Portland, the second at Brighton, and the third at Sandhurst. Mr. Poore was intending to sail in the same ship ("Royal Charter") with Mr. Binney; and there will accompany him the Revs. Messrs. Bowman, late of Hull; Reed, of New College, London; and Jackson, of the Lancashire Independent College, all designed for Victoria.

New South Wales.

GENERAL OBJECTS.

SYDNEY BETHEL UNION.—The seventeenth anniversary of this Institution was held in the Exchange Hall, on Tuesday evening, January 5. His Excellency Sir W. Denison, Governor, in the chair. The Report was largely occupied with an account of the erection of the New Mariner's Church, upon which there has been expended about £4600, and to complete which about £1400 more will be required. It appears that upwards of 16,000 seamen visit the port of Sydney each year, and about 200 of this number become inmates of the Infirmary. Upwards of 5000 tracts, and several copies of the Scriptures, in British and Foreign languages, have been distributed among the seamen by the chaplain in the course of the year, and services have been regularly conducted in the present inconvenient chapel, and the hospital and refuge visited, and other means adopted to benefit the seamen. The receipts of the year amounted to £787 10s., and the expenditure to £1137 3s. 10d., leaving a balance against the institution of £349 11s. 10d. The meeting was addressed by the Revs. Dr. Mackay, Dr. Fullerton, J. Eggleston L. E. Threlkeld, J. Dougall, and by Captains Williams, Morison, Finlay, Eldred, &c.

BURWOOD CHRISTIAN INSTRUCTION SOCIETY.—A place of worship in connection with the above society was opened at Burwood, on Sunday, December 27. Sermons were preached by the Revs. J. Voller, W. Cuthbertson, and J. Dougall. On the Monday a social meeting was held, when suitable addresses were delivered, and a liberal effort made to liquidate the debt incurred.

CONGREGATIONALISTS.— NEWCASTLE CONGREGATIONAL CHURCH.— The annual meeting of this Church was held on December 21st, when the Hon. David Jones, M.L.C., of Sydney, presided. The report, read by the pastor, the Rev. J. Gibson, stated that the school-room beneath the church (the church is built on the slope of a hill) had been completed at a cost of £327, the whole of which had been paid by subscriptions, collections, a bazaar, and the proceeds of six months' teaching in the day school by Mr. and Mrs. Gibson. The room has a day school in it of one hundred and ten children, and a Sunday school of ninety. Besides being used for week evening services, it is allowed to be used gratuitously for lectures and reading, for the benefit of the working classes,—an arrangement which has been very successful. A piece of land adjoining the church having been granted by the A. A. Company for a parsonage, the next effort of the congregation will be directed towards its erection. The report, in other respects, speaks favorably of the progress of the cause. The chairman congratulated the congregation on their efforts and advancing condition, and exhorted them to persevere, as Newcastle was inadequately supplied with Christian ordinances. The meeting was also addressed by the Rev. Mr. Woolnough, Wesleyan, R. Nott, Esq., J.P., and others, and by the Rev. W. Cuthbertson, from Sydney, who delivered a powerful speech.

WEST MAITLAND CONGREGATIONAL CHURCH.—On December 22nd, the Rev. W. Cuthbertson preached at the opening of the above church, a spacious and elegant Gothic edifice, which has been erected at a cost of £4700. On the following day a public meeting was held, J. Fairfax, Esq., in the chair, which was addressed by the Revs. Messrs. Griffith, Gibson, Turner, and the Hon. D. Jones and R. Nott, Esqs. On Sunday, the 27th, the Rev. S. C. Kent, of Newtown, preached in the morning and evening, and the Rev. E. Griffith (the pastor) in the afternoon. It was announced that £4100 had been raised towards the erection of the church, and that a debt of only £600 remained.

NEW TOWN CONGREGATIONAL CHURCH.—Anniversary sermons, in commemoration of the opening of the above church, were preached on December 13th, by the Revs. Messrs. Cuthbertson and Beazley. On the following Wednesday a tea meeting was held, and afterwards a public meeting; J. Fairfax, Esq., presided. From the Report of the Rev. S. C. Kent, the pastor of the church, we gathered that the entire expenses of this, its first year, had been met by the free-will offerings of the people, that a church of eighty members had been formed, and that more that two hundred children were under instruction in the Sabbath school. It appears also that all the sittings in the church are let, and that it is proposed immediately to commence an enlargement. Resolutions were spoken to by the Revs. Messrs. Beazley, Slatyer, Sunderland and Voller, and by Messrs. Rowe and Robinson.

CONGREGATIONAL CHURCH, PITT STREET, SYDNEY.—This church, formerly occupied by the Rev. Dr. Ross, and now by the Rev. W. Cuthbertson, B.A., having needed en argement from the increase of the congregation, additional accommodation to the extent of two hundred and fifty sittings has been provided, at a cost of £1967 15s. The church will now seat one thousand two hundred and fifty persons. The old organ has been disposed of, and a large organ, imported by the late Bishop Davis, and recently in the Hall of the School of Arts, has been purchased, for which a new gallery has been erected behind the pulpit. Special services in connection with this effort were held on Sunday, January 17th, when two impressive sermons were preached by Mr. Cuthbertson, and large collections made. The whole congregation were appealed to beforehand to make an effort to liquidate the debt, partly by cash payments in the plate, and partly by promises at three and six months. The result of this appeal on the Sabbath day was, in money, £639 17s. 4d., and in promises. £867 7s. 4d. This includes a handsome donation of £25 each from Sir Daniel and Lady Cooper. The total amount raised was £1507 6s. 3d., leaving only about £450 unprovided for.

Victoria.

BIBLE SOCIETY.—The Annual Meeting of the Victoria Auxiliary Bible Society was held in the Mechanics' Institute, on the evening of Wednesday, the 23rd December. Though the evening was unusually hot, the attendance was numerous His Excellency Sir Henry Barkly presided, and delivered an admirable speech. A large number of ministers of the different denominations were present. Mr. Hoskins, the Secretary, read the Report, from which it appeared that there were sixteen branch societies, in addition to which several depositories had been formed, by whose means several thousand copies of the Scriptures had been circulated in Victoria. The Treasurer read the financial account, from which it appeared that the receipts of the year amounted to £1502 4s. 5d., being an excess of £179 2s. 11d. over the receipts of last year. The expenditure amounted to £1367 9s. 8d., showing a balance in hand of £134 14s. 4d. A large portion of the outlay has been for Bibles, of which a considerable stock is now on hand. Appropriate addresses were delivered by Bishop Perry, the Revs. Dr. Cairns, Harding, W. R. Lewis, Mr. Williams, and Solomon Grand-Merci, a native of one of the Fejeean Islands. A collection was made in aid of the funds, and after a vote of thanks to his Excellency the meeting separated.

CONGREGATIONALISTS.— F. J. SARGOOD, Esq.—This gentleman, who has taken a leading part for several years in the affairs of Independency in Victoria, both in parliament, where he persevering y advocated the abolition of State aid to Religion, and in Home Missionary and other efforts to multiply Congregational churches, being about to return to England with his family, a meeting, convened by the newly revived Congregational Union of Victoria, was held in Oxford street Chapel, Collingwood, January 7, 1858, to present an address to him on the occasion of his departure. A goodly number assembled for tea in the school; afterwards they adjourned into the chapel, when the Rev. W. B. Landells, Chairman of the Union, presided. There were present most of the Independent ministers of Melbourne and its vicinity, together with several of the principal laymen of the body. After prayer, and a speech from the Chairman, the Rev. R Fletcher read an ADDRESS to Mr. Sargood, which had been prepared at the request of the Union. It expressed regret at Mr. Sargood's departure, and good wishes for the safety and comfort of himself and family in their voyage and visit to England. It adverted to his success in life, to his parliamentary labors in promoting freedom of religion, and to his liberality and personal efforts to extend the operations of the Independent denomination in Victoria; it assured him of the confidence reposed in his consistency as a private Christian, in his integrity and uprightness as a merchant, and his honor and virtue as a public man; and the conviction that he had been a benefit and a blessing to the land which he had made his home for eight years. The address was adopted by the meeting, and was then followed by a feeling and suitable reply from Mr. Sargood. Various speakers followed; G. Harker, Esq., M.L.A, Dr. Embling, M.L.A., F. Haller, Esq., the Revs. Messrs. Sunderland, Thomas, Moss, Summers (just arrived from England). &c. The Revs. Messrs. Ramsay and Hamilton, of the United Presbyterian Church, were present. The address was subsequently engrossed on parchment, and given to Mr. Sargood. He and his family embarked in the *Anglesey*, January 13th, and the vessel sailed from the Heads on the 14th. It is expected that Mr. Sargood will return in, perhaps, a couple of years.

INDEPENDENT CHURCH, NORTH COLLINGWOOD.—This Chapel has been enlarged, and was opened for divine service on Sunday, the 13th ult. The Rev. James Taylor preached in the morning, and the Rev. James Mirams, the pastor, in the evening. The attendance was good on each occasion. On the Tuesday evening following a tea-meeting was held, which was numerously attended. George Harker, Esq. M.P. presided. The Chairman opened the proceedings with an appropriate address, in which he congratulated Mr. Mirams on the extension and improvement of the building, and the increase of the congregation. The following ministers and others took part in the proceedings of the evening:—Rev. Messrs. Sleigh, Lewis, Morison, Odell, Moss, Bradney, and the Pastor, and Henry Langlands Esq., M.P. and Robert Smith, Esq. The collection at the Sunday services amounted to £25. The chapel is now capable of accommodating 650 individuals.

BOROONDARA.—At this place, about six or seven miles east of Melbourne, a neat Gothic chapel has been standing unfinished for some time. Having been recently covered in and made capable of service being conducted in it, it was opened for public worship on Sunday. December the 20th, by the Rev. R. Fletcher, of St. Kilda, and a tea-meeting was held on Tuesday evening, the 22nd; Thomas Fulton, Esq., in the chair. Mr. Kemp, through whose exertions chiefly, the chapel had been made available for worship, stated that the additions had cost about £170, of which from £40 to £50 was still unpaid. Before the meeting closed the whole sum was raised. Several of the Independent ministers of Melbourne and the neighborhood were present and spoke. They have made an arrangement to preach in turns at the chapel on Sabbath afternoons, for the present.

NORTH MELBOURNE.—The Rev. H. Thomas, late of Victoria-parade chapel, has commenced a new cause on the north side of Melbourne, between the University and Carlton Gardens. A temporary weather-board chapel has been put up, and preaching commenced in it. The opening sermons were preached by the Rev. W. B. Landells and Rev. H. Thomas, on Sunday, January the 17th, and a public tea-meeting was held on the 21st, when most of the congregational and several other ministers were present. The district is an inviting one for a new cause, as there is only one Protestant place of worship, and that a Gaelic one, for a considerable and a growing population.

ARARAT.—Some Independents at this new gold-field, anxious to gather a congregation, have been communicating with friends at Geelong and Melbourne with a view to obtain ministerial help. The Rev. A. Scales has paid a preliminary visit, and it is probable he may go there for a longer period with a view to prepare the way for a settled minister.

BAPTISTS.—The Baptist Church at Ballarat is in want of a minister, but it would appear that our Baptist friends have the same difficulty to contend with which most other denominations feel more or less, and that is, the difficulty of inducing ministers of superior attainments to come to these colonies. At Sandhurst there is a church in course of organisation, under the pastorate of Mr. Henderson. A chapel is in course of erection, and the cause is a promising one.

The Rev. James Taylor, who is in Victoria as the delegate from the Baptist Missionary Society, is unremitting in his endeavours to obtain suitable ministers from England. He has been so far successful that the Rev. Isaac New, of Birmingham, is now on his way to Melbourne, with the intention of taking the oversight of the church at Albert-street. Mr. New is a gentleman of high standing in the denomination, and will be an able and influential fellow-worker with Mr. Taylor. Strong hopes are entertained that two other ministers will speedily follow Mr. New, the one for Geelong, and the other for North Melbourne, the necessary amount for their outfit having been remitted to the London committee some months ago.

WESLEYANS.—NEW CHURCH, LONSDALE-STREET, MELBOURNE.—This church is designed to take the place of the present one in Collins-street, and is to be built with a portion of the proceeds of the sale of the latter. The foundation-stone was laid by His Excellency Sir H. Barkly, the Governor, on Wednesday, December 2nd. The Rev. Messrs. Binks and Wells conducted the devotional service. His Excellency delivered a liberal and Christian address on the occasion. A handsome silver trowel was presented to him N. Guthridge, Esq., M.L.C., the Revs. W. L. Binks, Dr. Cairns, and D. J. Draper, took part in the engagements. The church will be in the Gothic style with a lofty spire; it is intended to accommodate 2000 persons, and will cost upwards of £15,000.

NEW CHAPEL, BALLARAT.—The foundation-stone of a Wesleyan chapel was also laid by Sir H. Barkly, the Governor, on the occasion of his first visit to the Ballarat gold-fields. The day was fine and the concourse of people large. A trowel, made of Ballarat gold ornamented with nuggets, was presented to His Excellency. He delivered an address worthy of his reputation for Catholicity and Christian feeling, and was loudly cheered. The Rev. Messrs. Bickford, Mackay, and Porter, took part in the proceedings.

UNITED METHODIST FREE CHURCH.—Two ministers, the Revs. Wm. Middleton and Jas. Sayer, have recently arrived in Melbourne, sent out by this Church from England. We understand this body are about to send twenty ministers to this colony, and £3,000 with them, to help on the work in which they are embarked. On Sunday, the 20th December, sermons were preached on behalf of the missions throughout the Melbourne Circuit. The pulpit in George-street chapel, Collingwood, was occupied by the ministers just named. On Monday, following, a public meeting was convened in George-street chapel, to give a cordial Christmas welcome to the newly arrived ministers, to celebrate the amalgamating of the Wesleyan Association and the Wesleyan Reformers, and to promote missionary operations.

PRESBYTERIANS.—PRESBYTERIAN CHURCH, HAMILTON.—The foundation-stone of this building was laid on the 21st October, in the presence of a large congregation. The Rev. Mr. M'Donald engaged in devotional services, and delivered an appropriate address. William S. Kerr, Esq., of Wanowalla, laid the stone. Alex. Learmonth, Esq., also delivered an address. The church is to be ornamented with a tower and spire, and will also have a clock and bell.

FREE CHURCH, KYNETON.—The foundation-stone of a Free Church at Kyneton was laid by the Rev. Dr. Cairns, on Thursday, the 3rd December, in the presence of a very large assemblage of people. Prayer was offered by the Rev. Donald M'Donald, of Emerald Hill. The manuscript scroll to be deposited in the cavity of the foundation-stone was read by the Rev. Dr. Cairns. The Rev. Dr. delivered an appropriate and eloquent address, and afterwards divine service was held in a tent, with a view to the people giving a call in favor of the Rev. E. MacDonald to become their pastor. This gentleman is brother to the Rev. Mr. MacDonald, of Emerald Hill, and has hitherto been located among the Presbyterians of Kyneton. Contracts for the new building have been entered into to the amount of nearly £1000, and it is intended to accommodate 300 persons.

UNITED PRESBYTERIAN CHURCH, COLLINS-STREET.—On Tuesday evening, Jan. 5th, a congregational soirée was held in this church The pastor, the Rev. A. M. Ramsay occupied the chair. The Hon. Charles Vaughan, J.P., John Dinwoodie, Esq., J.P., and other gentlemen, together with the Rev. Messrs. Taylor, Hamilton, Fletcher, Odell, Sunderland, M'Nicol, Mirams, and Young, were present. The church was well filled with a large and respectable audience. A collection was made to defray the expense of a new pulpit and platform, which is now in course of erection. During the evening, Mr. Ramage, who has till lately very kindly given his gratuitous services as precentor, was presented with a handsome mahogany writing-desk and a bible. A soirée for the children attending the sabbath-school was held on the following evening, at which about seventy or eighty children were present. A magic lantern, kindly lent for the occasion by Mr. Browning, tended greatly towards the pleasure of the evening.

UNITED PRESBYTERIAN CHURCH, LONSDALE-STREET, MELBOURNE.—The foundation-stone of a new church in Lonsdale-street, was laid in the afternoon of January 5th, by the Rev. James Ballantyne, the minister, assisted by Mr. Walter Bell, the chairman of the congregation. Addresses were delivered by the Rev. John Ballantyne, the Rev. W. Jarrett, and the Rev. James Ballantyne. The Rev. John Cooper, of Geelong, offered prayer. There were also present the Revs. Dr. Cairns, J. Hetherington, J. Sunderland, and J. Mirams. The new church is in front of the one in present use. It is to be in the Grecian style, with Doric columns and pediment, and will cost £5000.

PRESBYTERIANISM, NORTH MELBOURNE.—On Thursday evening, January 14th, a congregational meeting, in connection with the Scots' Church, was held in the Grammar School Hall, off Curzon-street. The members of the Presbytery of the connexion and other clergymen attended, the object being the induction of the Rev. George M'Cullagh Reed, as pastor, and the ordination of the Rev. Robert Hogg, recently arrived from England. The Rev. Peter Gunn, the Rev. Irving Hetherington, of the old kirk, the Rev. Dr. Cairns, and the Rev. William Fraser, of the Free, and the Rev. James Ballantyne, of the United Presbyterian Churches, took part in the ceremony of induction and ordination. Mr. Hogg was then appointed to the district of Horsham, on the banks of the Wimmera.

DEATH OF THE REV. MR. PARNETT, OF BELLARINE.—Mr. Barnett was on his way to one of his out-stations, when he had to cross a creek swollen with water. His horse went down the slope and the abrupt descent to the bottom, and must have plunged or fallen so as to throw the rider. The stream was strong, and it bore away the unfortunate gentleman to a considerable distance down the stream, where the body was found on the following day by two persons who themselves had been two days lost in the forest. His pocket bible was found in his side pocket, and his countenance was remarkably placid. The funeral took place at Camperdown, before the bereaved family near Geelong could be informed of the event. A large attendance of the principal persons of the district for many miles around, and very many of the people in the humbler walks, attended the funeral. Business was suspended, and the greatest seriousness and solemnity pervaded the people. At the grave the Rev. Mr. Hamilton delivered a very suitable and impressive address, and the deepest sympathy was manifested for the widow and fatherless children, for whom a subscription was at once opened and raised to the handsome sum of £320, which it is intended to increase to the total sum of £500. Mr. Barnett had only recently received his call to his new sphere, and had for some time previously been a faithful servant of the Lord Jesus, at Bellarine. In both places he was much esteemed by his people, and more especially by the poorer portion, with whom he was remarkably affable and sympathising.

Tasmania.

WESLEYANS.—The Annual Conference of the Wesleyan Methodist body, including all the Australias, is about to hold its sessions this year in Hobart Town. Statistics laid before some of the district meetings have been forwarded to us; but we refrain from publishing them till the set is completed at the Conference.

CONGREGATIONAL CONFERENCE, HOBART TOWN.—A Conference is to be held at Hobart Town, commencing February 9th, of ministers and delegates from the different Australian colonies. It was agreed upon by a resolution of the Conference held in February last, at Sydney, when the Rev. R. Fletcher, of St. Kilda, was elected by ballot, to be the Chairman. The Rev. T. C Evan, of Adelaide, has passed through Melbourne on his way to Tasmania, and delegates are expected from New South Wales and Victoria.

PRESBYTERIANS.—The foundation-stone of a new manse for the Rev. William Nicholson, of Chalmers' Free Church, Bathurst-street, Hobart Town, was laid by Mr. Nicholson, on Tuesday, the 24th November.

South Australia.

SOUTH AUSTRALIAN BIBLE SOCIETY.—The twelfth annual meeting of the South Australian Bible Society, was held in White's Assembly Rooms, Adelaide, October 28th last, His Excellency Sir R. G. Macdonnell, in the chair. The report was read by Archdeacon Woodcock, and the cash account by Mr. Whiting. The several resolutions were submitted to the meeting by the Rev. Messrs. Barrow, Lya'l, Evan, Ingram, Woodcock, Gardner, Rowe, Butters, and Farr, and by the Hon. T. Reynolds and C. Smedley, Esq., M.P. It appears from the report that the Society is in a prosperous state. Its receipts for bibles and testaments sold during the year amounted to £693 6s. 9d., and the free contributions received from all sources amounted £613 6s. 1d. There are thirteen branch societies in the colony, and these have connected with them upwards of thirty different depôts in various convenient parts, where bibles may be obtained. The issues of the scriptures have been considerably in excess of former years, the stock of bibles has been augmented, and rather over £400 has been remitted to London as a free contribution to the British and Foreign Bible Society, to assist it in its great work of supplying the world with the word of God.

N.B. We have not received our usual packet of intelligence from South Australia for the present number.

THE NEXT NUMBER OF THIS MAGAZINE WILL BE ISSUED ON 1st APRIL.

Communications for Editor care of W. FAIRFAX & Co., *Melbourne.*

The Southern Spectator.

| No. 6. | APRIL, 1858. | Vol I. |

MISCELLANIES.

The Evangelical Alliance.

The Conference of this body at Berlin, in September last, has turned out a most important and significant event. It was looked forward to with deep interest by multitudes, and has more than realised the most sanguine expectations. The Alliance commenced its career amidst much misgiving on the part of the friends of Evangelical religion, and amidst much scorn on the part of its enemies. Doubts were naturally entertained as to the practicability of parties holding opinions so diverse on numerous points, and long accustomed to regard each other with jealousy, suspicion, and in some cases even with hostility, being brought to act together with cordiality for any considerable time; and yet it was felt that the disciples of the same Master, believers in the same Saviour, *ought* to do so, as the points wherein they agreed were more numerous and important than those wherein they differed. A conjunction of circumstances favored the experiment. The growing dread of Puseyism, united opposition to Maynooth, the great disruption in Scotland, and the appearance of several tracts and books on christian union, contributed to prepare the way. The first invitation to meet came from Scotland; an invitation signed by a goodly number of the leading ministers and laymen of all denominations in that country. The first assembly was held in Liverpool in October, 1845. Its success was complete, so far as the meeting itself was concerned, and arrangements were immediately made to organise an Alliance. All Scotland was with the movement; the leaders of the Wesleyans were hearty in it; the majority of the Independents and Baptists gave in their ready adhesion, and a small section of the Evangelical portion of the Church of England were among its warmest friends. Still many stood aloof. The *Record* on the one hand, and the *Banner* on the other, poured forth fulminations; not a single Bishop or dignitary of the English Establishment gave it countenance, and some of the clergy, conspicuous for their support of the Bible and other general societies, published their reasons for not joining this new organisation. It took root notwithstanding;

o

meetings were held in Birmingham, Manchester, and London, to complete the organisation, and at length, after not a little struggle with difficulties, a great gathering of Evangelical Christians, from all parts of the world, was ventured on in the summer of 1846 formally to found a grand Alliance. The meetings were held in the Freemason's Tavern, London. The gathering was a noble one, all branches of the universal Church being well represented, and great numbers of distinguished foreigners being present. A basis of doctrine was agreed upon, and the Institution was fairly launched. The great fundamental principle was, a union of individual Christians, not of Churches. No recognition or sanction of any form of Church government was implied by membership. The foreign element in the Alliance has ever been one of its main elements of strength. Weak and scattered in their own countries, the foreign Christians were craving for sympathy and for some sensible communion with the universal brotherhood of believers. Some of them too were suffering persecution, and needed the shield of protection thrown over them. The Council in London took action in promoting Sabbath observance, resisting the attacks of Infidelity, checking the progress of Popery, and succouring those in Continental States who suffered for their religion. They interfered successfully on behalf of the Madiai in Italy, and the Baptists in the north of Europe, and in other cases ; they boldly sent influential deputations and made representations to foreign courts and cabinets on behalf of those whose rights of conscience were invaded. Thus the Alliance has been kept before the public by its activity in behalf of Evangelical Christians where most needed, and has won for itself a growing number of friends. Advantage was taken of the Great Exhibition in London in 1851, and the Exhibition in Paris in 1855, when strangers were gathered together from all parts of the world to hold conferences in those cities, and both those occasions added strength to the organisation.

The proposal to hold a conference in Berlin came from Berlin itself. There was a branch of the Alliance there containing in it some earnest friends ; among these was Krumacker, the Royal Chaplain, an eminently pious and Evangelical clergyman ; and, probably through his influence, the King of Prussia himself gave the measure his warm support. The invitation to the Council in London came with the royal sanction. Hints have been thrown out that reasons of State policy had their influence with his Majesty ; but there is the strongest evidence to believe that the King is a truly pious man, and has given his countenance to the Conference from a genuine interest in evangelical truth ; and, till the contrary is proved, charity requires that credit should be given to him for sincerity. This high sanction had a magic effect ; a deputation from England to Berlin was resolved upon to make preparations, an interview with the King was granted, and, on the return of the deputation, a report of this interview was laid before the venerable Archbishop of Canterbury, several Bishops and dignitaries of the Established

Church, and ministers of other communions at Lambeth Palace. This open sanction of the Alliance by the Primate has decided many waverers in its favor, and these circumstances, altogether, have greatly strengthened its position in Britain.

The Conference at Berlin has been pronounced by the most unprejudiced authorities a pre-eminent *success.* Its numbers were upon a large scale. According to the printed lists, which, however, do not contain nearly all the names of those who took part in the proceedings, Prussia contributed 876 members, other German States 103, England 166, France 12, Spain 1, Italy 2, Hungary and Bohemia 7, Switzerland 11, Holland 10, Belgium 4, Denmark and the German Duchies 11, Sweden 2, Russia 12, Turkey 2, and Greece 2. Thus, Europe altogether sent 1222, Asia 3, Africa 3, America 23, Australia 3. The total of these printed names amounts to 1254, of whom 689 belonged to the clerical profession. The only European States of any consequence that did not contribute any quota at all to the above number were, naturally enough, the Papal States, Austria (the Crown Lands), Portugal, Naples, and Tuscany. The above figures, 1254, have, however, no reference at all to the number of hearers present at the Conferences, of whom no account was kept, but their numbers can be guessed at, as the Garrison Kirche, which was used for the purpose, is capable of containing 4000 persons, and during the eight meetings that were held was on the average two-thirds full. The expenses, which were considerable, were borne entirely by the Berlin Committee, the King himself contributing liberally out of his private purse. At some of the sittings the King and Queen were present, and the members of the Conference were invited to the palace at Potsdam, and were honored with a royal audience.

During the successive days on which the Conference sat numerous devotional services were conducted, a great variety of papers read, and speeches delivered by the most eminent individuals in the various Protestant churches of Christendom, on subjects of interest to Christians generally. A vast fund of information was collected relating to the state of religion in all parts of the world, and more especially the continent. Free and cordial intercourse took place between Christians of different communions who had rarely before come into friendly contact with any besides members of their own bodies; and various standing committees were appointed to carry out measures of common interest to all Christians discussed in the Conference, the fruits of which will doubtless appear at a future day.

The advantages resulting from this Conference it is impossible to calculate. Prussia itself, will, of course, derive the greatest share, and, next to that country, the Protestant States of Germany generally. Meetings for free discussion, the reporters of the press being admitted without restriction and no police exercising surveilance, were a novelty in Berlin. Their harmlessness to the Government, their obvious utility to the public, may, we hope, lead to repetitions of such gatherings until they become as common in Prussia as in England. Bunsen, in his "Signs of the Times," had been advocating the broad principles of Religious Liberty after the English fashion, and the whole empire was agitated with the controversy; and it may be hoped that during the prevalence of this feeling, the presence in the capital of the representatives of so many different churches, and the equal recognition given to all alike, may help forward the cause of religious equality and full liberty of conscience.   As the Conference consisted of *Evangelical* Christians, all professing to hold the great doctrines of the Reformation, a check will probably be given to the philosophical scepticism on the one hand, and the ultra-hierarchism on the other, which have been the bane of Germany, and encouragement will be taken by the earnest friends of pure Christianity to abound in their endeavors to spread the truth once delivered to the saints.   The hands of persecutors all over the Continent will be weakened, and the down-trodden and oppressed for righteousness sake will be animated with fresh courage in giving their testimony for Christ and his cause.   The watchful eyes of the Alliance will be upon the religious movements of Europe, and deputations and remonstrances will be forthcoming where oppression may be exercised. Already has a deputation waited upon the Emperor of Russia on the subject of the restrictions imposed upon the circulation of the Scriptures in the vulgar tongue in his vast dominions, and a remonstrance addressed to the Danish Government on its illiberal treatment of the Lutheran inhabitants of Schleswig; and other measures of a like kind will follow where needed.   A bold front has also been presented before the eyes of Romanists of the substantial union of Protestant Churches founded on a common Basis of Faith. A correcter knowledge of each other, and, as a consequence, more mutual respect and charity are sure to result from the close intercourse which has taken place among members of communions hitherto strangers to one another; and thus all the great objects contemplated by the Alliance will approach nearer to realisation.   The whole movement is an augury of better days to come.   The process of amalgamation of Christians may be slow, but we cannot but think the tendency of the age is towards it.   It took centuries to rear the separating walls which divide the different folds of the Church from each other; we need not wonder if it takes years to level them.   For the sake of the Church's credit, and its influence in the conversion of the world, all Christians should pray for that period and strive to hasten it on, when the essential unity which really exists among them shall be more fully and harmoniously exhibited before the eyes of mankind.

We are indebted for a few of the facts above stated to a remarkable article on the Berlin Conference in the London *Times*, an article which is in itself a significant sign of the change of public opinion in favor of the Evangelical Alliance.

Day School Instruction.

A word of explanation seems necessary respecting the remarks made on the subject of day schools in our last number. The article was written and in print when Mr. Michie's bill was before the Victorian Parliament, and before Mr. Ireland's amendment was brought forward. It referred to the bill as originally proposed, not as subsequently altered. We spoke of the bill as being framed on the model of the Irish National System, so far as the difficult subject of religious teaching is concerned. Arrangements were proposed to be made for each denomination, which might choose to avail itself of them, to impart religious instruction to the pupils belonging to its own communion. We expressed a doubt whether this permission would be extensively used, or would have much effect in securing a really religious training, and suggested that those anxious on this point should chiefly rely on distinct and independent agencies ; still, others might think differently, and the permission was to be granted. The amendment, which was carried, wholly altered the bill in this respect, inasmuch as it positively *forbad* religious teaching at all, or the employment of the school premises in any way whatever for religious purposes. This change was sure to raise the hostility of those who, though they might prefer the denominational system of imparting secular and religious instruction simultaneously, would yet have fallen in with the proposed plan of separating them, rather than have no religion at all taught ; and such has proved to be the fact. The introduction of the amendment has sealed the doom of the bill.

While regretting this consequence of altering the measure, we further object to the amendment on principle. It is one thing to make provision for nothing but secular instruction, and another positively to forbid, by specific enactment, all religious training. While the State has no right to meddle with religion in the way of imparting it, it passes beyond its province when it undertakes to interdict it. If it may rightfully spend its money and apply its organization to supply the secular element, it may also, without violation of principle, put no hindrance in the way of any voluntary arrangements the parties interested are willing to make to secure what they think the spiritual element. If the regular school hours, during which the attendance of the scholars is required, be occupied wholly in continuous secular teaching, and no books but such as relate to that department are then used, there need be no hindrance to the employment of other hours, when attendance is optional, in such religious exercises as the parents, guardians, or ministers of the children may be willing to provide for and carry on. All that the State is bound to look to in such cases is that no compulsion or unfair influence be employed, and that no invasion of the fullest liberty of conscience be allowed.

We go further still further in limiting the power of the State to *interdict* religion so far as regards its treatment of the teachers employed in secular schools. It is taking a false view of the teachers' province to regard him as a mere machine. He is a living voluntary agent whose mode of communicating instruction, and whose whole character will be constantly acting for good or for evil upon his pupils. If he be an unworthy man no stringent enactments will prevent his want of principle from oozing out ; if he be a conscienciously religious man, it will be equally impossible to prevent his religion from becoming manifest. The temper he displays, the tone of voice he employs, the reasonings he uses, the disciplinary measures he adopts, will be all affected by his personal character and principles. The opponents of a merely secular scheme of day school instruction have attempted to reduce it to an absurdity by asking how a teacher is to inculcate truth and honesty if he be forbidden all reference to the Diety and religious sanctions. If he *be* so forbidden his liberty is infringed on, and the interdicting power is passing its due limits. He is employed to teach secular knowledge and moral virtues : leave it to his own judgment to fulfil the task he has undertaken, as well as he can. If he be fit for his post, confidence should be reposed in him. If in accomplishing his object he use methods which are complained of as interfering with the religion of the children or as tending to proselytism, let inquiry be made, and if the rights of conscience *have* been invaded, let him be censured or dismissed as the case may require. But let no general law be laid down forbidding him to discharge his duty to his employers in the way that best approves itself to his own conscience.

We would have the State, in employing teachers to train youth in secular learning, act in the same way as men of business do in engaging servants to perform their work. They specify the duties they wish to have discharged, but do not make it an *express stipulation* that no religion shall be allowed to appear. If the shopman be a profligate and his vicious habits interfere with his duty to his master, he is dismissed ; if he be a pious man his master will reap the benefit of his diligence and conscienciousness without any offensive manifestation of his peculiarities : should, however, he injudiciously obtrude his religion upon customers when he ought to be selling goods, he will probably be censured, and if incorrigible, parted with. But if the different tendencies of character are kept within bounds, so that the duties of the station are satisfactorily fulfilled, no interference takes place. Let it be so in secular schools. Let the Boards or Councils (or whatever the governing bodies may be called) see that the work for which they hire the teachers is thoroughly done, but let them not limit and hamper a free and responsible agent as to the manner in which he tries to do his duty. If any overt act be committed violating the spirit of his engagement, let it be dealt with as it deserves.

The promoters of secular instruction in England, who brought out their scheme first for Lancashire alone and afterwards for the whole kingdom, made a fatal and needless mistake in expressly and in words *forbidding* religious teaching. Numbers who approved of the schools being secular declined giving their support to the system because of the proposed positive interdict. They argued that restrictions would be put upon the teachers which were not imposed upon any other class of the community ; that no man of spirit and conscienciousness would consent to be thus shackled and restrained ; that they ought to be left to their own judgment and discretion as to how they should perform the duties they undertook, provided they *did* perform them ; and that the effect of this positive prohibition would be to repel the most valuable teachers, and to invite to the work men of lax principles. The promoters of that scheme would have found more favor with the public if they had simply provided for secular instruction in their proposed schools, and *said nothing about religion at all*, unless it might be, as in the case of the Irish system, to allow it to be taught in other than the regular school hours.

Dr. Libingstone.

"A man with heart, head, hand."—TENNYSON.

"GOD hath chosen the foolish things of the world to confound the wise, and God hath chosen the weak things of the world to confound the things which are mighty." So writes St. Paul, as he meditates on his own eventful career, passing from city to city, carrying with him the doctrine of the crucified Nazarene, and by its means giving truth to his enemies' assertion that he "turned the world upside down." And so it has ever been in the history of the world. Its greatest changes have been wrought, and its most marked progress achieved by the most unlikely instruments. Not only in the onward course of religion and the developments of Christianity, but in all that has to do with human advancement, it seems as if the all-wise Governor of the earth would rebuke the pride of mankind by showing that he can accomplish much from but small means. It is as if the creative energies of the Deity were perpetually manifested, and the wonders of the "six days in which God created the heavens and the earth " were to find their counterpart in every movement of providence. It makes no matter where we look, we find the same truth enforced upon us. In the history of the development of science, civilization, or particular nations, the great names, the leaders, have ever been, for the most part, such as would have been called "base," "despised," among "the things that are not." It is not the scaffolding that constitutes the building, and in our day some of our proudest structures have been erected without any other aid than that afforded by the part already formed. Storey upon storey has been piled up, with no other support for the builders than the work already accomplished. Scaffolding might be obtained, but such help is unneeded. And so in society there are appliances in abundance for making great and learned men ; but the advantages of a university education do not make the man ; and with all the favoring circumstances of wealth, opportunity, and talent, a man may fail, and does often fail, to become what society might justly expect him to be—an ornament to his generation ; while some of those who are honored by all for their great and noble doings, have risen to their present eminence by the power of their own energy conquering circumstances for them.

Such a one is Dr. Livingstone, who alone, even at this time of war excitement, can claim any great share of public attention. The bloody victories in India, and the peaceful conquest in Africa, stand side by side as the recipients of popular applause ; and this great conqueror, who has passed in such a grand and simple triumph through Britain, as a hero of the noblest stamp, is *one of the people.* In a village of some few thousand inhabitants on the banks of the beautiful Clyde, dwelt an honest, humble tea-dealer, whose principal support was in the custom given him by the numerous hands and adherents of the large cotton manufactory of Messrs. Monteith and Co., called Blantyre Works.   He was poor, and " too conscientious ever to become rich," yet by his " kindliness of manner and winning ways he made the heartstrings of his children twine around him as firmly as if he possessed, and could have bestowed upon them, every worldly advantage !"   But kindliness will not maintain a rising family ; so at the age of ten his son David was " put into the factory as a piecer, to aid by his earnings in lessening his mother's anxieties."   To those who know what a factory is, who have seen its busy, heartless toil, and the pale faces of those who flock there and breathe its atmosphere tainted with the smell of oil and filled with cotton dust, it would seem as if even an unknown Milton must, in spite of the fire of genius rebelling against fate, remain " mute " and " inglorious." And no doubt this frequenntly happens ; but when genius is joined with energy and perseverance, then no circumstances can quench its warmth, nor often prevent it manifesting itself. This young boy had both ambition and patience, and so we find him saying, " With a part of my first week's wages I purchased Ruddiman's ' Rudiments of Latin,' and pursued the study of that language for many years afterwards, with unabated ardor, at an evening school which met between the hours of eight and ten.   The dictionary part of my labors was followed up till twelve o'clock, or later, if my mother did not interfere by jumping up and snatching the books out of my hands.   I had to be back in the factory by six in the morning, and continue my work, with intervals for breakfast and dinner, till eight o'clock at night.   I read in this way many of the classical authors, and knew Virgil and Horace better at sixteen than I do now."   Study was a passion with him, everything " except novels " was eagerly devoured by this studious " mill hand."   Scientific works and books of travel were his especial delight, and absorbed his attention.   Not long afterwards he discovered the beauty of religion, and joined to his previous study the investigation of the word of God, rejoicing to find that religion and science were far from being hostile to each other. The truths of Christianity passed from without to within; he never had any difficulty in understanding them, but now he made them his own. "The perfect freeness," he says, "with which the pardon of all our guilt is offered in God's word drew forth feelings of affectionate love to him who bought us with his blood; and a sense of deep obligation to him for his mercy has influenced in some measure my conduct ever since!" The young Christian, in the ardor of his zeal, resolves to become a missionary. He undertakes fresh courses of study with that end, but is still too poor to leave the cotton-mill. Evening hours are not enough for his aspiring mind. He must study and work at cotton-spinning too. He has been promoted from "piecing" to having the charge of a "jenny," and in his new duties he is able to catch literally every alternate minute and make it his own. He thus "keeps up a pretty constant study undisturbed by the roar of the machinery," and by a perpetual interruption occurring five or six times every five minutes. He becomes a student, but still must support himself at the factory; and, promoted still further to having a loom to manage, the harder work was "excessively severe upon a slim, loose-jointed lad." To make it worse, study becomes impossible in this new employment, and so he works in the summer, and on the results of his six months' labor lives a life of still severer mental exertion for the winter. His exertions are so far crowned with success that this factory operative, and while he still is a factory operative, is admitted a "Licentiate of the Faculty of Physicians and Surgeons." He is anxious to go to China, as a medical missionary, and with a spirit of noble independence, desires to go without being under the wing of any society; but the opium war compels him to give up his purpose. God has other work for him to do. He is advised to offer himself to the London Missionary Society, and with "some pangs, as one accustomed to work his own way," he does so. He is then sent to Africa to second Mr. Moffatt, and to follow out the course begun by that noble pioneer, and in 1840 he embarks for the Cape. After a short residence there, he leaves the haunts of civilisation, and among the barbarous tribes of the interior he "spends the following sixteen years of his life, namely, from 1840 to 1856, in medical and missionary labors, without cost to the inhabitants."

It is not our intention to follow Dr. Livingstone through his extraordinary travels. It would require too much space, and to all our readers who are interested in the doings and sacrifices of one of the greatest of men, if Christian heroism can make a man worthy of that title, we would recommend his own work. It is at once so simple and yet so manifestly the work of a keen observant mind, so terse and vivid in expression, so abounding in incident and novelty, and so absorbing in the fascination produced by looking through it upon a new field for mankind's energies, that when once entered upon it cannot be thrown aside till finished. And even then its effects must still be felt, for he must be dull indeed who does not feel himself stirred up to nobler and better thoughts after its perusal. In our next number we may probably give, not an account of, but a paper upon the journeys of Dr. Livingstone. We would now merely speak of the man—the character which could prompt to such philanthropic and arduous labors, and as we do so we find him to be one who, notwithstanding the opposition of the circumstances, yet, alone, struggled for and attained the highest advancement. *He is an example for all,*—not some far off chimerical ideal, but a man from the ranks, whose only heritage was honesty and a good name,—a "man with heart, head, hand," one who better than any other we can at present recollect realises the description given by the great unknown Junius of a well-balanced mind ; "But neither should I think the most exalted faculties of the human mind a gift worthy of the Divinity, nor any assistance in the improvement of them, a subject of gratitude to my fellow creatures, if I were not satisfied that really to inform the understanding corrects and enlarges the heart."

Affiliated Colleges.

WITH a natural impatience to emulate the educational institutions of the mother country, the two wealthiest colonies of Australia have of late years both established universities. They have not progressed gradually towards this end, by beginning with grammar schools, rising to colleges, and then crowning all with a university. But suddenly, and by Act of Legislature, each university sprang up fully equipped. The apparatus for teaching and conferring degrees was erected, and the professors were left to hunt for students. These latter have hitherto come in rather slowly, a score or two being all that have been caught at present. The hasty and premature manner in which these universities have been constructed has naturally led to the contracting of a disproportionate expenditure. The total charges of the university divided among the *alumni* make the cost of each student somewhat serious. But this, after all, is but a trifling evil. Our colonial governments are so addicted to extravagance, that a little surplus outlay in the matter of education is comparatively a venial transgression. They waste so much needlessly, that the university expenditure is by no means the most vulnerable point in the estimates. The mere number of students at present attending lectures, moreover, must not be taken as the guage of the present effectiveness of the university. Its stimulating influence on the higher classes in the schools must be taken into account. The introduction into our colonial society, too, of half a dozen professors has been of no slight value. The effect of their presence has been beneficially felt in many directions. Amid the overwhelming pressure of mercantile affairs, and the too general pursuit of grossly material objects, the existence and activity amongst us of a class, however small, of men who make intellectual culture the main object of their labors, is a good not to be overlooked. They invite us to better things than the acquisition of wealth, and remind us of the higher possibilities of our nature. We are not at all disposed, therefore, to complain much of the cost of our universities. Would that all our public funds were laid out in a manner that gave as little cause for regret!

But we cannot help feeling that the constitution of our universities would have been more satisfactory, if they had not been so hurriedly constructed, if more time had been given to mature the plans, and more popular feeling had been directed to them. As it is, having been established in advance of the demand for them, and before there was any general interest felt in their existence, or any comprehension of the method of their working, the arrangements fell into the hands of little coteries of literary men, all or most of whom were naturally affected with prejudices in favor of the practices of particular universities to which they were attached. A quasi-imitation of the old country, rather than a happy adaptation to the new, was the natural result. Liberality and prejudice have been jumbled together.

Universities in their origin were regarded as seats of *learning*. The granting of degrees was an adjunct. They were places where the highest form of education, as well as the completest course, was to be obtained. In the course of time, however, the distinction between the *examining* functions and the *teaching* functions of the university has become more sharply defined, the former rising into a prominence they had not originally possessed. In many cases *colleges* have sprung up which have assumed the task of teaching, while to the central university authority, little has remained but general oversight and the responsibility of *testing* the education imparted. This separation of functions is, perhaps, most completely observable in the case of the University of London, which, though it commenced its existence as a college, has outgrown its original dimensions. The university proper—the only body recognised or assisted by Government—is not a teaching institution at all. Its functions are confined to general management and examination. The senate appoints no professors, regulates no classes or lectures. It simply appoints examiners, who report on the proficiency of the students that come up from the several affiliated colleges. These colleges perform the whole work of education. They are entirely uncontrolled by each other or by the central senate. They are scattered far and wide over the kingdom, some even being situated in the colonies. They have no connection whatever with the Government, and are subject to no common regulations.

It may seem to many that this is the model which it would be most desirable to imitate in these colonies, and undoubtedly it would present many advantages. But the limited number of literary men amongst us interposes a difficulty. It would not be easy to select competent examiners from the circle of educated men not engaged in tuition. To introduce gentlemen from England to be examiners only, would be a great waste of resources. Superior teachers is the first want, and in each colony there is not room at present for more than one good college. Of necessity, therefore, at first starting, our colonial universities followed the primitive type. Our universities are colleges, and our colleges universities; the professors are both teachers and examiners.

But a multiplication of colleges has been in one colony speedily introduced. Not because students multipled to that extent that the original professors could not attend to them all. Not because in all the great inland towns a passion for the higher forms of education was manifested, and local colleges were demanded. No, but because students of different creeds could not study together; or rather because their parents and priests resolved that they should not. Educational disunion was demanded, not as a national necessity, but in the name of religion. The most frightful consequences to the religion and the morality of the country were predicted unless the score of students were distributed amongst half a dozen separate colleges, each sufficiently charged with a sectarian bias. The Legislature yielded to the cry. Affiliated colleges have been established and endowed at an immense cost, and if each denomination had accepted the offers made, there would be altogether as many colleges and more professors than students. The temptation to each sect to chime in with this scheme is by no means inconsiderable, and it requires more than philosophy—it requires principle—to withstand the bait. A handsome site for a college, a grant of money in aid of its erection, and a perpetual endowment, are benefits of too solid a character to be rejected if they can be lawfully accepted.

Can they be lawfully accepted by Congregationalists? That is the question. The grant, disguised as it is under the name of education, is really a grant in aid of sectarianism. It is not even for the sake of religion generally that the money is voted—not for the sake of those common truths in the reception of which all Christians agree, but for the special preservation and inculcation of denominational dogmas. In this view, the Affiliated Colleges Act of New South Wales is open to all the objections which are urged against the grant in aid of religion. It is in fact an application of the denominational system to adult education. If separate sects like to have separate colleges of their own, they certainly ought not to be prevented; but there is as certainly no obligation resting on the State to encourage this subdivision prematurely.

The identity of the principle in the Colleges Act and the grant in aid of public worship, is sufficiently illustrated in the manner in which the different sects have acted. Those that conscientiously oppose State religion have declined to receive all for colleges the essential characteristic of which is religious education. Those that have no scruples on the subject have readily accepted the aid. The Free-Church Presbyterians waver between the two courses of action. Voluntaries in practice, but not in theory; ready to accept aid on their own terms, but not satisfied with the conditions on which it is offered, they are divided in opinion. In Sydney, the meetings of the Free-Church Synod have been marked by a great division of opinion on the subject, though the latest decision is against accepting the grant. With the spirit of that decision we fully sympathise. To us it seems the only decision which is consistent with the avowed doctrines and policy of the Free Church, and any other course would have fatally affected the future action of that church in any protest it may hereafter be called upon to make with respect to indiscriminate endowments.

The offer made by the State is, as we have said, so tempting, that it was hardly to be expected that it should be declined without a strenuous effort being made to prove that it was innocuous. We have before us a pamphlet by the Rev. Dr. Mackay, in which that gentleman pleads hard with his brethren not to throw away so good a chance. We have perused this pamphlet with all the respect due to the talent, the piety, and the long service of Dr. Mackay, but we must confess that we do not think he has made out a case. The most eloquent and persuasive portion of his address is that in which he enlarges on the benefits of the University, and the denominational prestige which would result from official connection with it—every word of which may be admitted. Yet if compliance would be wrong, Dr. Mackay's eloquence only gilds the fatal bait for his brethren. He makes the temptation almost irresistible. It is from no self-deprivation, from no want of natural ambition, from no inability to recognise the value of social distinctions, that the uncovenanted sects stand aloof from the Government scheme. They know what they are refusing, as well as those who accept the boon know what on their side they gain. It is not pleasant to forego advantages, or to be sent to the rear in any social classification, but there are some things more precious than fictitious promotion. Principle is dearer to the hearts of those that love it than prosperity. Were the offer ten times greater than it is, it should be peremptorily refused, if it cannot be touched with clean hands. It is a great thing, doubtless, to have all the *eclat* that belongs to a national institution, yet Dr. Mackay and his associates surrendered all the privileges attaching to a national church, parted not only with social rank but with their prospects of competency and ecclesiastical preferment, and came out on to the lower level of a voluntary sect, rather than compromise what they considered to be the truth. Surely men who have made this great sacrifice are capable of resisting a smaller temptation to the infringement of what is fundamentally the same principle.

The weakest part of Dr. Mackay's pamphlet is that in which he endeavors to prove the harmlessness of taking State-aid for a religious college.   He cannot in consistency surrender his hatred of indiscriminate endowments, and he believes the fundamental principle of the College Act to be wrong.   But he seems to think it sufficient to enter a protest against this.   In other words, he would take the money, but denounce the principle on which it is given.   But what moral worth has a protest given under such circumstances ?   He who protests and refuses vindicates his honesty in the sight of the world.   He may be a fanatic, or a fool, but at least he gives proof of sincerity.   But he who takes public money and protests against the principle on which alone the arrangement is founded by virtue of which he receives anything, exposes his sincerity to suspicion.   The common sense of mankind will not consent to believe in the heartiness of any man's opposition to a scheme by which he is a gainer.   If Dr. Mackay wishes his protest to be effective, he should make it as forcible as possible.   But that protest is emasculated the moment he touches the public money.   It is obvious that if Dr. Mackay could succeed in persuading the Legislature to abolish all indiscriminate endowment, he would secure the cessation of endowments altogether.   A Free Church grant could not survive the destruction of all other ecclesiastical grants.   Special favoritism is impossible.   The acceptance by any sect of a grant in aid is an encouragement to the State to go on with the existing system —an encouragement that far outweighs any verbal protest against it that may be made by those who do not refuse to participate in its advantages.

The affiliated colleges exist for the sake of secular as well as religious instruction.   But they would not have been established for the sake of the former alone.   It is specially to secure the latter object that they have been brought into existence, and it is therefore as religious establishments that they must be regarded when their connection with the State is considered.   They are not mainly secular and incidentally religious, but primarily religious, and secondarily secular.   This distinction is often confounded in discussions on the subject, and a grant in aid of religion is made to appear as a grant in aid of education.

The above remarks apply chiefly to New South Wales.   In Victoria grants of land and money have unfortunately been made to establish sectarian grammar schools, and some of these are being proceeded with, but nothing has been done to found affiliated colleges.   A noble university exists, which is well supplied with professors, and is slowly but surely developing its powers for good.   An ample space of land also surrounds it, which has been reserved, it is supposed, with the intention of being offered in due time to the differents sects for college sites. But no appropriation that we are aware of has yet taken place, and no votes of public money have been passed to assist in the erection of college buildings. It would be a pity that there ever should; for the clustering of a number of State-aided colleges around the central university would not help but hinder it. The colleges, unless they were failures, would practically absorb all the students, and render the public university, as a teaching institution, an expensive nonentity. But there is little danger of such a gross mistake being now committed. The state of public opinion on the application of public money to further denominational objects is too far advanced to allow of another movement in that direction being attempted.

Easter.

LEST the reader should feel the heading of this article to be repelling, it may be as well to state at once that what he fears will probably not be found in these remarks. It is not intended to give an explanation of the ancient festivity of Easter, as that may be readily found in any theological dictionary. Nor is it necessary to trace the controversy, relating to the day thought proper for this observance, through its alternations of storm and calm, of conflict and reconciliation, as ecclesiastical history will supply all this. And still less is it our intention to present gloomy selections of scenes and distractions and horrors from the long and bitter controversy, as these will be found with sufficient prominence, and more than sufficient zest, in other histories than those which are ecclesiastical. Nor is it any part of the present design to discuss the lawfulness or necessity or expediency of this annual church celebration, as all can consult the literary guides of their respective parties; or, if some are moved by the impulses of a more searching spirit and would wish to read both sides of the question, they can find the combatants duly arrayed, and examine for themselves their respective arguments.

Without entering upon any portion of this ground, the subject has some aspects and relations of another kind that are suggestive and interesting.

The difference of usage in the time of keeping Easter, prevalent in the ancient churches, furnishes a trustworthy and useful clue in ecclesiastical inquiries, the more valuable, as we find it conducting us to conclusions of deep interest in relation to the first propagation of Christianity in our own favored father-land. The ancient inhabitants of Britain with their kinsmen of Wales, and the Irish with their ecclesiastical children the Culdees of Scotland, all followed the Eastern Churches in their rule regarding Easter, whilst they avowed and pleaded tradition from these churches as their defence against the demands of the

Roman and Saxon bishops. We conclude, therefore, that it could not have been by an *Italian* route that Christianity first came to Britain, and that it must have come by some other path. As Rome had been so early, and so uniformly pertinacious on this point, and as the British held the opposite, as a tenet so strongly and as an usage so uniformly, no historical inference would seem to be clearer than that it could not have been from Rome or by Roman action and influence that Britain had her first instructor in the Christian religion. This reasoning might not apply to some other points of difference which existed, as, for instance, celibacy and auricular confession. For it could be alleged, that the agency, whether incidental or formal, which evangelised Britain, might have gone forth from Italy before these points sprang up; and all that could be proved therefore would be, that Britain drew her views of Christianity from some source purer than that of Rome in the sixth century, and that source might have been Rome herself, when her own views and usages were more free from innovations and additions. But the case is vastly different with regard to Easter. The practice of Rome and of the Western Churches in this matter was so early and so uniform, that it must have accompanied all out-going agency, whether in the occasional or systematic diffusion of Christianity. As the Roman Church had kept Easter all along, in that manner would her missionaries and members teach and practice everywhere. How came, then, churches in the far west to have the Eastern rule rather than the Roman one? The following would seem to be the fair solution. It is not difficult to understand how Christianity should pass over from Gaul to Britain; and the oldest authenticated Church in France, and, as it would seem, the most influential in the propagation of Christianity in that country, was that of Lyons; a Church holding also the Eastern and not the Roman view of Easter; a Church planted by Christians from the East; a Church of which Pothinus, a missionary from the East, was bishop. The zeal which carried missionaries from Asia to Lyons and from Lyons over Gaul, could also carry them across the Straits to Britain. On two accounts such a conclusion possesses interest:—First, Christianity must have come early to Britain; for in the latter part of the second century Trenæus, successor to Pothinus, as Bishop of Lyons, gave in his adhesion to the Roman See on this point of Easter. Britain therefore was evangelised before this, or there could not have been such uniformity in the British Churches, in the practice of the Eastern rule, on the disputed point. Secondly, The Church of Lyons appears to have been one of the most pure and vital of all Christendom. The account of the Martyrs of Lyons, and the Letters to Eastern Churches, in which it is given, constitute the most precious document of the ancient Church. The evangelical views, the spiritual feeling, the Christian temper, and the noble constancy of those suffering Christians, form one of the most edifying passages of all ecclesiastical history. It is delightful to think that British Christianity should have come from such a quarter. No wonder it formed so serious an obstacle to the imperious demands of the Romish Saxon Hierarchy at a later period.

The next thing noticeable in the celebrated controversy, is the unreasonable importance sometimes attached to subordinate matters. How very inconsiderable some things come to appear which once were absorbing! How disturbed was Christendom for ages upon the question whether one particular day of the week, or a different one, should be observable as an anniversary of Christ's resurrection! And it was not the corrupt advocates, or hopeless slaves of despotism only, but the wisest and holiest and kindest that were agitated. How do the holiest and wisest and kindest look upon that point now? There is a remarkable passage in the venerable Bede in relation to this very matter, well worth remembering. Speaking of the exemplary and devoted Aidan, one of the Iona missionaries and Bishop of Landisfarne during the reign of Oswald King of Northumbria: after enumerating his virtues, his peacefulness and charity, his disinterestedness, his lowliness and devotion, his faithfulness, his tenderness of spirit, he says:—"These things I much love and admire in the aforesaid bishop, because I do not doubt that they were pleasing to God, *but* I do not praise or approve *his not observing Easter at the proper time*, either through ignorance of the canonical time appointed, or if he knew it, being prevailed on by the authority of his nation not to follow the same; yet this I approve in him, that in the celebration of his Easter, the object which he had in view in all he said, did, or preached, was the same as ours; that is, the redemption of mankind through the passion, resurrection, and ascension into heaven of Jesus Christ, who is the Mediator betwixt God and man." We smile at his grave exception. But is it not probable that many things even now are said and written by great and good men upon some subordinate or minor matters which posterity some centuries hence will also smile at, just as we now do at the qualifying clauses of the good old historian? How will some things be reduced to their proper relative dimensions by the subsidence of traditional and party prejudices, the broader views, the higher spiritual altitude, the more uncramped yet correcter principle of interpretation, and the stronger intellectual development altogether, which shall form indications of the Church's progress and means of her efficiency!

One suggestion more shall close these reflections. It is most satisfying to have it demonstrated, that however time and development and advance may change and reduce the little things which ignorance has made great, yet no change, no disturbance, no reduction can happen to what is really great and precious. Whatever befals the opinions and usages of men regarding the commemorations and symbols of Christ's birth, death, and resurrection, the great facts themselves stand unmoved on their eternal basis of truth, and the great principles they involve unclouded in their light of evidence and glory. A truly Christian posterity, to whatever height elevated and to whatever degree enlightened, will never say that we have made too much of the Incarnation, or the Atonement, or the Resurrection of Christ Jesus our Lord. The purest and the brightest age which awaits the Church will never rebuke us for an excess of appreciation of these great things, or an extravagant earnestness in them, but probably will have some lamentations to utter over the narrowness of our views, the deficiency of our earnestness, and especially over the misapplication of that enthusiasm to secondary, or perhaps insignificant points, which should have been given to the weightier matters of our faith.

Free Conferences.

THE Evangelical Alliance Conference at Berlin, and the Congregational Conference at Hobart Town, both noticed in the present number, may be regarded as signs of the times.

They are not to be confounded with the Ecclesiastical Councils of former ages, which were mere gatherings of the Hierarchy for settling disputed points of doctrine, government, and discipline: nor with modern Wesleyan Conferences, Presbyterian Synods and Episcopal Church Assemblies, which are Ecclesiastical courts, armed with power for governing their respective communities. They are associations of men who may express opinions but cannot pass decrees. The question has been put respecting them, *cui bono!* what is their utility? They may afford opportunities for pleasant trips, healthful excursions and agreeable social intercourse; but is their public benefit worth the time and the money they cost? In these widely dispersed colonies it requires no doubt a considerable amount of both these precious articles to insure the gratification in question, and it is very difficult to estimate the value of mental and spiritual good in hard cash or in fleeting hours. But the growing tendency to such conventions seems to indicate a feeling and conviction that the benefit is worth the sacrifice.

We say that Free Conferences for comparing, discussing, and expressing opinions, are a sign of the times. If they are not strictly peculiar to the present age they are certainly one of its characteristics. The *Anti-slavery agitation*, if we mistake not, produced some of the earliest of modern conferences. They were found to be invaluable in collecting and diffusing information on the great evil sought to be removed, in devising and agreeing on organised modes of action, and in strengthening the hands of abolitionists when discouragements caused them to droop; and they contributed in no mean degree to the final emancipation of the slaves. The *Anti-Corn Law League* made great use of these conventions. Its leading friends were brought together at different times and in various places to discuss the great question of " Free Trade *versus* Monopoly," and to enlighten the public mind on the subject by their speeches and their resolutions. The Ministerial Anti-Corn Law Conference of 1841, when 650 ministers of religion gave utterance to their opinions on the sin of laws designed to raise artificially the price of the people's food for the benefit of a class, did untold service in securing at length their removal from the Statute book. The members of the *Peace Society* have held conferences in London, Paris, Berlin, and elsewhere, for the discussion and diffusion of their principles, and if they have not yet seen their cause triumph, it may be because they are advocating an impossible theory. But it cannot be questioned that their meetings have tended to abate the ardour for war too common to our nature, and to encourage amity and good understanding among the nations of Europe and America. The friends of *Temperance* have had frequent recourse to conferences on a scale varying from provincial gatherings to such as partook of a world-wide character. The miseries resulting to individuals, to families and to society from intemperate habits have thus been set before the whole world, and methods devised and discussed and put in operation which are visibly tending to promote the moral reformation of the human race. *Sunday School Instruction* owes much to meetings of this character. Besides the anniversary meetings of " Unions," which afford opportunities for speeches on the benefits of Sabbath schools, conferences of Superintendents and Teachers have been and still are periodically held in some parts of Britain, to discuss questions relating to order, instruction, classification, the management of elder scholars, and other points involving the efficiency of Sunday schools, with manifest advantage to all parties. What are the annual meetings of the " *British Association for the Advancement of Science*," but simply " Conferences " of learned and scientific men, who read papers, report discoveries, discuss difficulties, suggest investigations, and stimulate each other by mutual interchange of thought to the culture and diffusion of knowledge? Besides the general benefit they effect in this way, they doubtless exert a great local influence favorable to science in the places where the meetings are successively held.

But perhaps the most marked use of the " Conference " is in connexion with the *Evangelical Alliance.* It was strongly objected to that institution at its commencement that it *did* nothing, and proposed to do nothing but *talk*; its history and growing influence however seem to shew that its talking has been to some purpose. Its first experimental gathering held in Liverpool was a season never to be forgotten by those who had the privilege of being present. Eminent ministers and laymen, prominent members of all the evangelical denominations, who had only heard of each other by the hearing of the ear, met for the first time face to face, not in acrimonious conflict contending for their several peculiarities, but in sweet accord as fellow christians to converse with one another on the things wherein they were agreed, to pray together, and to confer on the methods best adapted to promote christian union. Some of them had taken opposite sides in great controversies, and had seasoned their productions with not a little of the *odium theologicum;* now they melted in tears together before the throne of grace, and were ashamed of their bitterness and uncharitableness of spirit. The hallowed influence arising from good men forgetting their minor differences, lamenting their infirmities of temper, and heartily embracing each other as brethren, was a fore-shadowing of the heavenly state where all shall see eye to eye and live in perfect love. Some of the subsequent meetings of that body were less pleasant and profitable for the simple reason that they ceased to be " conferences " in the sense which we are now attaching to that term, but were occupied in the dry and uninteresting work of framing regulations for a vast and unwieldy organization. But the grand Conference held in London in 1846 was a heart-stirring event. It was an œcumenical gathering; choice spirits from most parts of the world were there. And what was the object that drew these Christians to one spot from places so remote? Merely to *confer* and communicate with each other on the cultivation and diffusion of Truth and Love; and as might be expected, from the nature and composition of the assembly, the interest awakened and the hallowed effect produced could scarcely be surpassed.*

The *Congregationalists* of England have been much in the habit during the last quarter of a century of holding conferential meetings. Their ecclesiastical principles not allowing of any central organization for the purposes of government, the want was deeply felt among the scattered members of the body, of opportunities of intercourse and interchange of thought. The Congregational Union was formed to meet this want; and the annual and autumnal meetings of that body are nothing more than conferences: they have no appeals to hear, no laws to enact, no decrees to promulgate, no government to exercise. All they do, besides devotional services and exercises designed for edification, is to discuss such topics of the day as they consider of importance to the interests of religion; and to express, in the form of addresses and papers, speeches and resolutions, the opinions upon them of the parties then present; such opinions

---

* These meetings of the Alliance are referred to in page 195 of the present number.

having no further force than that which attaches to the reasons alleged in their support: and while some jarrings have occasionally marred the harmony of the proceedings, as might naturally have been expected where a large number of independent thinkers come together, the influence of the meetings on the whole has been eminently beneficial in encouraging manly thought, continued and vigorous action, and a general feeling of hopefulness and strength throughout the denomination at large.

The Congregationalists of Australia have early adopted the measure of holding conferences. The population of the separate colonies is too small to give to the meetings of their respective Congregational Unions the dignified character of "conferences," but the whole colonies united furnish materials sufficient to constitute meetings which may without presumption be called by that name. The isolation of many of the ministers and churches from their brethren, arising from the distance of the colonies from each other, their consequent ignorance of the feeling and sentiment on important questions pervading each other's minds, and the desirableness of concerting measures for the general good, are strong reasons for holding intercourse on matters common to all as often as may be found practicable. This want led to the convening of the first conference in Melbourne, in Feb., 1855. The pleasure and benefit arising from this meeting led to the summoning of a second in Sydney in the February of 1857; and that again to a third which met in Hobart Town last month. These have all been "times of refreshing," from the agreeable and profitable intercourse enjoyed, from the ventilation afforded to opinions on matters of difficulty, and from the mutual stimulous given and received to increased exertion and sacrifice in the cause of Truth. Another is proposed to be held in Adelaide at the latter end of next year; and we trust the practice will not then be suffered to fall into disuse, but will become a standing custom in the body to be handed down to posterity.

SUNDAY READING.

Religion and Labor.

By religion we mean, as a science, those facts and doctrines revealed in the scriptures of the Old and New Testament; as an experience, those heavenly influences brought to bear upon the human spirit by the Holy Ghost; as a result, those feelings and acts of penitence, faith, worship and obedience, which serve to distinguish the people of God. The author, then, of religion is the only wise God ; the record of it, the Bible ; the best example of it, the Lord Jesus Christ ; the experience of it, spiritual life ; and the final issue, glory and immortality. It is not knowledge merely, not feeling alone, not good works exclusively—but all these combined in due proportion and place. Very grievous is the misconception which some people have of religion, that it is a mere provision for their escape from perdition ; a blessing simply to ask for and enjoy ; a sublime gratification of their selfish views, in making them heirs of all things to the neglect if not the absolute exclusion of all others. The record says "Let not every man look on his own things—i.e., exclusively—but also on the things of others." "No man liveth unto himself, and no man dieth unto himself"—whilst the great example of all truth and goodness embodies and illustrates in his life these noble principles in a manner too plain to be misunderstood, and too gentle to be resisted. Hence, a true Christian, one who has the spirit of his master, is a benevolent, earnest, working man. His inspiring motive is not pay, but principle ; not the applause of men, but the "well done" of an observing and gracious God—his guiding example, that of one who in life went about doing good, and dying, gave his life a ransom for many. A man in becoming a child of God has duties to discharge as well as privileges to enjoy. A voice which he recognises as that of our Father in heaven speaks thus to him—"Son, go work to day in my vineyard." As Christians "we are all one man's sons," and have our own work assigned us. With many the day is far spent : with all, it is short, while the work is momentous and difficult. Hence, the importance of wise and earnest labor to the utmost tasking of our time and talents, for "the night cometh when no man can work."

We need not establish by any lengthened induction of scripture passages the general principle already assumed, that every Christian man as such is responsible to his Great Task-master for the diligent prosecution of some effort specially designed to promote Christianity in the world. We all confess that we are not our own, that Jesus died for us, and called us by his grace that we might be a peculiar people zealous of good works : we are to let our light shine before men, to hold forth the word of life ; to preach the gospel to every creature ; to have compassion upon the ignorant and upon those who are out of the way ; and by our likeness to Christ to lead the world to love and esteem our Master.

Neither need we vainly endeavour to indicate the path of personal duty. It varies with individuals and circumstances; from the manifest duty of some to enter heathen lands and so stand "in the forefront of the array in the aggressive onslaught," down through all the varied walks of Christian enterprise and duty, to giving a cup of cold water to a disciple in the name of a disciple. Where there is a willing mind, an honest heart ready hand, and a trustful dependence upon God's guiding providence, we shall not greatly stray from the path of personal duty. Begin with work near at hand, the little duties of more importance by their number and results than by their individual magnitude, and which are too frequently neglected because little, forgetful of the fact that all great works are a series of little things. Whether it be to build a Leviathan, explore a continent, or give the Bible to the Chinese, the mighty result is the aggregate of little endeavors.

When we are fully committed to our work we must be prepared to labor on with patience, nothing discouraged by the opposition of craftsmen, by the predictions of prudent men and soothsayers, or by the want of immediate success; with constancy when the love and zeal of many shall wax cold; and with assured faith that, in the ultimate issues of spiritual endeavors, according to God's unchangable decree, "he who goeth forth weeping bearing precious seed shall doubtless return again with rejoicing bringing his sheaves with him." As soldiers in the moral strife, we must enter the lists with high and holy endeavor, with the boldness of the war-horse when the battle can be smelt afar off, and with all

"The stern joy which warriors feel
In foemen worthy of their steel,"

ever keeping in view the Captain of our Salvation, and emulating his example, who has already brought many sons unto glory; in the hope of being able to sing "Thanks be unto God, who always causes us to triumph in Christ, and maketh manifest the savour of his knowledge by us in every place."

Manifold are the encouragements of the Christian laborer. He may rejoice in the thought that he is a fellow-laborer with God. The Mighty One has girded himself for the work: it is especially His. He has given his Son to die; he has promised his Spirit, armed with a sword, quick and powerful to convince and convert. He has pledged his life that the cause of goodness and truth shall triumph—"I have sworn by myself, the word is gone out of my mouth in righteousness and shall not return, that unto me every knee shall bow, every tongue shall swear" loyalty and obedience.

It is a work which will promote the highest interests of our race. The gospel is sent to supply our greatest want. It is the bread of life for the perishing, an ark for the ship-wrecked, a balm for the sick and the weary, a resting place for the pilgrim of earth in the eternal love and happy home of his Heavenly Father. Give a man the gospel, and you do more for his happiness than if you gave him the wealth of either India, or the collective riches of our new gold fields with old names. It is only by the gospel that man rises to the dignity of his nature. Well does Pascal observe that "out of Christ there is nothing but mystery darkness and despair, whether in the Divine nature or our own, whilst in Him we see safety, dignity and hope." The kindliest office to the race is to hasten forth with the knowledge of Christ crucified : it is the herald and pledge of all earthly and heavenly blessings.

It is labor which will eventuate in our own welfare. He that watereth others shall be watered himself. It is safety to work : "Whosoever heareth these sayings of mine, and doeth them, I will liken him unto a wise man who built his house upon a rock." It is future glory to persevere unto death—"Blessed are they that do his commandments, that they may have right to the tree of life, and may enter in through the gates into the city."

> Work on and win !
> Life without work is unenjoyed ;
> The happiest are the best employed ;
> Work moves and moulds the mightiest births,
> And grasps the destinies of earth ;
> Work on !

Christian Faith—what is it ?

THE belief of the gospel, or saving faith, involves first, *the assent of the judgment* to the great facts and fundamental doctrines of the gospel. The facts referred to are recorded in the first four books of the New Testament. These books are separate histories of the leading events connected with the birth, life, teaching, death, resurrection, and ascension of our Lord. As historical books they have the same claim on our attention and credence as other books of a similar character. Our belief of the facts recorded in them may rest on the same kind of evidence as that on which we receive statements in ordinary historical books. A circumstance recorded by one who professes to have been an eye witness of it, gains ready belief, unless the character of the narrator be open to suspicion, or the circumstance be in itself highly improbable. Three of the sacred historians before us were eye witnesses of most of the important events which they have recorded.

The evidence in favor of any supposed event is increased in proportion to the largeness of the number of those who bear testimony to it ; so that while the testimony of one historian of intelligence and probity is not likely to be set aside, that testimony, if confirmed by a second of like character, is universally regarded as being raised above reasonable doubt, unless met by some counter evidence. Now, in the case of the gospels, all the most important facts recorded in them are confirmed by the independent but harmonious testimony of four intelligent and, as all must admit, honest men.

Testimony in confirmation of any fact is considered more valuable and reliable when given by those who have no personal interest to serve by their statements. From this consideration, the evangelical narratives gain no little weight.   The men who wrote them had no expectation of gaining thereby wealth, honor, or influence.   The religion founded on the facts which they promulgated was " everywhere spoken against," its doctrines ridiculed, and its adherents persecuted, imprisoned, beaten, martyred.   The testimony of men who " suffered the loss of all things," and were ready to sacrifice their lives for what they affirmed to be true, is above all reasonable suspicion.

There is another consideration which tends greatly to confirm the truthfulness of the evangelical histories.   They were all written at a period so near to that during which the events recorded were said to have occurred, that if they had contained anything which was not at least substantially true, it is impossible to believe that they would have remained uncontradicted.

What, then, are the facts which we are required to believe, to which our judgment is called upon to assent ?

That there was, some 1860 years ago, such a person as Jesus, born at Bethlehem in Judea—that he was born of a virgin—that he lived some thirty years with his mother and supposed father—that he then began to preach, and to work miracles ; and continued to be thus employed about three years, more or less—that at the termination of that period he was unjustly condemned, and suffered death by crucifixion —that on the third day he arose again from the dead—that he gave abundant and satisfactory proof of his resurrection ; appearing at intervals, for forty days, to many different persons, speaking to them on various subjects about which he had, prior to his death, given them some intimations—and that, at the expiration of the forty days, and in view of eleven competent witnesses, he left the earth, ascending towards heaven in a cloud.

The *great doctrines* of the gospel, to which the judgment must assent, are the following :—

That every human being who has attained to such mental development as to know "right " from " wrong," has violated the divine law, and is therefore a sinner and liable to condemnation and eternal woe—that Jesus Christ led a life of absolute conformity to the Divine law—that in him the Divine nature was really though mysteriously united with the human—that his death was not a penal infliction for sin committed by himself, but a vicarious sin-offering, or sacrifice for the sins of others—that the benefits of this sacrifice are conferred on every human being who " believeth in Jesus "—and that the benefits thus conferred comprehend the pardon of sin, or exemption from the punishment due to the sinner ; the gift and indwelling of the Holy Spirit to renew and sanctify the nature ; the favor and eternal friendship of God ; and a right to endless bliss in heaven.

To all this— or at least to this in the main—and with but few and unimportant modifications—the judgment must cordially assent. We say not that saving faith consists in this assent of the judgment ; but that this assent of the judgment is included in " saving faith ;" that it is one of its elements and constituent parts.   There can be no evangelical faith without this assent of the judgment, though there may be the assent of the judgment without evangelical faith. A man may admit as true every fact and doctrine of the gospel, and yet be as far from the "the kingdom of God" as "an infidel."

Saving faith, then, includes next, *submission*, on the part of the *will*, to the terms on which pardon and eternal life are to be enjoyed. It is easy to conceive of an individual whose mind is well informed on religious truth, and whose views opinions and sentiments, are highly evangelical, but whose heart and will are averse to all that is good. He may be quite aware—that is, his *judgment may assent to the statement as a truth*—that, in order to salvation, it is necessary to *repent*, while there is *no willingness* on his part to repent. His love to his sin, his indolence, or his aversion to that mental suffering which is inseparable from repentance, may have a more constraining influence on his will, than has his conviction of the necessity for immediate and sincere repentance. Again: a man's judgment may assent to the truth, that the gospel requires constant watchfulness and self-denial; that it demands holiness of life and heart, and never encourages the hope of salvation without these things; and yet have no *will* to comply with these conditions. Once more: a man's judgment may be convinced, or, in common parlance, he may believe that the gospel plan of salvation involves trust in the righteousness and merits of Jesus; but there may be lacking the inclination to rely on the Saviour and his work for pardon and eternal life.

Now it is obvious that, in such cases, there is no evangelical faith. The mere assent of the understanding to all the grand truths, revelations, and doctrines of our holy religion, apart from the concurrence of the will with its requirements, only entitles a man to be considered as "believing lightly," as having "a faith" which is, by the Scriptures, emphatically declared to be "*dead*," a faith which is without that *vitality* which sanctifies the heart and life, and can, therefore, neither give present peace, nor secure future bliss.

Christian or "saving" faith involves, lastly, a cordial and grateful *reception* of the blessings of the gospel on God's own terms. Viewed in its commencement, and therefore as *an act* of the mind, it is a grateful acceptance of pardon, peace, and everlasting life, as those blessings are gratuitously offered in the gospel. It is thus in effect the whole mind—the judgment, the will, and the affections—putting itself *into harmony* with the Divine will, as expressed in the plan of redemption. Hence, evangelical faith is said to be "of the heart;" "man believeth with the heart unto righteousness."

Viewed in its after stage, that is, as *a state* of the mind, it is a loving belief of "the truth;" and such belief first "purifies the heart," and then induces that obedience to the Divine law in which consists outward holiness; and thus we see how those two scriptural statements, "without holiness no man shall see the Lord," and "whosoever believeth shall be saved," harmonise. From the first of these statements it appears that "holiness" is the condition on which heaven is to be attained, and from the other that "faith," or "believing," is that condition. This apparent contradiction disappears, and the two statements are seen to agree, when it is borne in mind that there is not, and that there cannot be, in human nature any real "holiness" without "Christian faith," and that this "faith" can no where dwell in any human heart without inducing "holiness."

Thus we find that saving faith includes in it an intellectual conviction of the truth, the submission of the will to its claims, and the accordance of the heart the temper and the life with its spirit. Reader, hast thou that faith? Happy is he who can sincerely say to the searcher of hearts "Lord, I believe!" and who yet, consciencious of the moral weakness of his nature, earnestly adds "help thou mine unbelief."

The truly Honorable in Character.

A SHORT HOMILY FOR YOUNG MEN.

"Jabez was more honorable than his brethren."—1 Chron. iv. 9.

In what respect was he more honorable? Perhaps in learning, for "the families of the scribes dwell at Jabez," which university town was probably named after him. Perhaps in patriotism, for he sought to "enlarge his coast" at a time when a Divine command required the expulsion of the Canaanites. Certainly in piety, for his pre-eminence in devotion is mentioned to his honor. He was a man given to prayer, and a summary of his devotions is recorded: "And Jabez called on the God of Israel, saying, Oh that thou wouldst bless me indeed, and enlarge my coast, and that thine hand might be with me, and that thou wouldst keep me from evil, that it may not grieve me! And God granted him that which he requested." A noble and comprehensive prayer! presented, doubtless, if not in the same words, yet in substance, in his daily closet devotions, at the family altar, and in the public assemblies of worshippers. Here was a man, in a remote age, who became honorable among his contemporaries, and an inspired authority points out those elements of character which won him esteem. Young men who are aspiring after honor may learn something from this example.

There is a conventional sense in which the term *honor* is applied to the code of maxims and usages by which men of education and position in society regulate their conduct. Gentlemen obey the "law of honor," their high ambition is to be men of honor. But other classes, as well as they, have their points of honor: the merchant has, the tradesman, the mechanic, and the servant; custom has sanctioned certain principles which are accepted by each class as its law of honor, the violation of which is visited with degradation and expulsion. Transgressors are looked upon as unworthy to be associated with, and are carefully shunned.

But how capricious, loose, and accommodating is this law ! Among *gentlemen* falsehood, meanness, insult, cowardice, repudiation of " debts of honor," are deemed disgraceful, and the offender is instantly banished from society.   But swearing, drunkenness, seduction, the non-payment of tradesmen's bills, irreligion and infidelity are liberally tolerated.   A gentlemen may be guilty of all these, and yet be an honorable man.   In the British Parliament it is now deemed disgraceful to take a bribe or pilfer the public funds, but it is no disgrace to procure a seat by grossly bribing and corrupting others.   One member unblushingly avowed before the House that it was well known that *all* paid for their seats in meal or malt ; yet he was unrebuked, and still held his position as a man of honor. It is deemed dishonorable among *soldiers* to take an insult meekly ; among *merchants* to swindle and cheat ; among *artisans* to work for less than the current wages.   The culprit is degraded and ignominiously driven from his class ; it would be a disgrace to speak to him. But if a man be only careful on such points as these, he is esteemed a man of honor, worthy of being associated with, though stained, perhaps, with the foulest vices of another kind, sunk in profanity and debauchery.

To be *truly* honorable is to rise far above this low and arbitrary standard to one loftier, nobler, more consistent, and more certain. Cull from the laws of honor, which regulate the behaviour of the various classes of society, whatever is really virtuous and excellent, and add to it that which is " honorable in the sight of God."   True honor is made up of a variety of elements.

Labor and *Industry* are honorable ; it is no disgrace to work ; the mind and body were both made for exertion ;   the Creator designed their various faculties to be dependent for their healthy condition upon activity.   The world is so constituted as to require labor in the great mass of mankind.   Thorns and thistles are the spontaneous outgrowth of the soil ;   useful products are the result of human toil. *All* men can never attain to a state of independence of work, or how could food be grown, or clothes made ?   No conceivable inventions in machinery or advance in society can produce such a revolution as will liberate the great majority of the human race from the necessity of toil.   Labor therefore is honorable ;   the worker is more useful, and hence more honorable than the idler.   Be never ashamed of honest work ; it cannot degrade, it may often exalt you.

Integrity is honorable.   There is no honor without honesty. All cheating, however secretly, skilfully, and successfully carried on, is disgraceful.   Every dishonest act makes a man sink in self-respect, and would sink him in public esteem if it were known.   Practices partaking of the nature of deceit and fraud are too common in the commercial world, and are thought, if not quite fair, yet indispensable to success ; but they are dishonorable, and should be scrupulously shunned.   Be faithful and just in little as well as great things ; let integrity and uprightness preserve you, and they will bring you to honor.

Truthfulness enters largely into the composition of honor. This might come under the category of dishonesty, for lying is a species of fraud. It is an attempt to rob your neighbour of the precious jewel of truth ; to pass off as genuine coin a base counterfeit. It is a violation of the golden rule, " All things whatsoever ye would that men should do unto you, do ye even so unto them." Falsehood, when detected, destroys confidence ; you can never thoroughly trust a man's word who has been found capable of deceiving you with a lie. It is mean, paltry, low ; nature revolts at it and despises it ; no man can be a man of honor who is not a man of his word. " Upon my honor," say men when they wish to be believed, their honor being vouched for their veracity. Avoid all approach to untruth, prevarication, exaggeration, misrepresentation, and the "white lies " so common in business. If you would be truly honorable, and thoroughly respected, be conscientious and ever punctilious in speaking truth in the smallest particulars.

Self-control belongs to respectability. You respect a man who can command himself ; who is not hurried away by paroxyisms of rage, or the cravings of appetite. The gluttonous, the drunken, the unchaste, the violent, debase their nature below the level of brutes, and deserve to be branded for the dishonor they do to it. They have no right to be classed among honorable men. Disdain to allow the appetites of the body to lord it over the noble faculties of the soul, or the passions of your nature to be stronger than its principles. Gird up the loins of your mind, be sober and self-possessed, and you will be respected, or deserve to be.

Generosity is an ingredient in true honor. Can you esteem a man who cares for none but himself ; whose thoughts are wholly engrossed with his own comfort, interest, or aggrandisement ; who has no heart to feel for, no hand to help, his fellow-creatures in distress ? Whether his selfishness take the form of indulgence, covetousness, or ambition, it is contemptible. It violates the second great Commandment, " Thou shalt love thy neighbour as thyself." If all were like him, a self-inclosed monopolist, what would become of the suffering, the needy, and the helpless ? Who are the most honored among men ? Are they not the generous, the self-sacrificing, the philanthropic, the benefactors of our race ; the Pauls, the Howards, the Wilberforces, who lived for the good of others ? To be truly honorable you must adopt and exemplify the Christian motto, " No man liveth to himself."

Learning is honorable. A man may certainly be worthy of esteem and honor who is not educated, but his ignorance in this case must have been his misfortune, not his fault. He is, however, an imperfect specimen of human nature, his nobler capabilities being undeveloped. The high mental faculties God has given us are meant to be cultivated, and cultivated by ourselves. No species of culture is more effective than self-culture. Those who have the opportunity of improving their minds and neglect it are guilty of a breach of trust. They have not made the most of the talents committed to them, and they do injustice to themselves; for "knowledge is power." Mental culture increases a man's sources of happiness and means of usefulness. It enhances the value and enlarges the sphere of every faculty he possesses. It makes his virtues shine more brightly and operate more influentially. He therefore pursues an "honorable" course who does his best to furnish himself with useful knowlege and to invigorate the powers of his mind by exercise and discipline.

There cannot be the best and highest kind of honor without true *Piety*. This, though last named, is first in importance. For the highest authority of all has said, "Seek ye *first* the kingdom of God and his righteousness." It was, pre-eminently, the marked piety of Jabez that made him "more honorable than his brethren." The religious faculty of the soul is the highest and noblest that belongs to it. It is that which assimilates us to angelic beings, the most exalted of created intelligences. It is that which brings us into union with God himself, and makes us "partakers of the divine nature." We fulfil the first and greatest functions of our being, the noblest end of our creation when we are sincerely and earnestly religious. Must not piety then be a main ingredient in the "truly honorable?" So thought Solomon, who, from his position, apart from his inspiration as a writer of Scripture, ought to be admitted as a competent judge: "Wisdom (religion) is the principal thing; therefore get wisdom, and with all thy getting get understanding. Exalt her and she shall promote thee; she shall bring thee to honor when thou shalt embrace her: she shall give to thine head an ornament of grace, a crown of glory shall she deliver to thee."

But what *is* the piety we recommend? No puly sentimentalism; no austere asceticism; no wild enthusiasm; no pharisaic formality; no rigid and narrow sectarianism. It must be something deeper, holier, more genial and genuine than any of these. The piety we urge is not that loose and easy sort which fashion accepts as sufficient, nor that narrow and artificial kind which may be imposed as the Shibboleth of a sect; but the piety of the Bible itself. In that sacred book we find it summed up in "repentance toward God and faith in the Lord Jesus Christ;" in a "new heart;" an unreserved surrender to God; in the enjoyment of pardon first, peace next, and obedience as flowing from these; in the love and practice of prayer, a life of practical obedience and self-denying usefulness; and a constant preparation for another world. In that blessed volume, also, we find it exemplified in instances like Joseph, Moses, and David of the olden period, and Paul, Timothy, and John of the new; "whose faith follow, considering the end of their conversation, Jesus Christ the same yesterday, to-day, and for ever."

To crown all there must be *Moral Courage* in the truly honorable character. What you are, dare to avow. Be not ashamed of your colors or your captain. If physical cowardice be a dishonor, moral cowardice is a deeper disgrace. Be faithful to Christ and fear not the face of man. Be bold enough to confess him before the world whatever be the consequences, and you will find your account in it good conscience, the blessing of God, and probably in the end the approval of men. But should you be misunderstood in the present life and your name be cast out as evil, He, on whose head are many crowns and who is the fountain of all that is truly honorable, will amply reward you at last. He will recognise you as belonging to the highest "Legion of Honor," and will invest you with badges of distinction more pure, more noble, more enduring, and more satisfactory, than all the medals, stars, garters, and orders of merit that ever were heaped on the world's favorite and fortunate heroes.

BIOGRAPHY.

SARAH TICE BEAZLEY.

Sarah Tice Beazley was born in Hertfordshire, England. She came of an honorable line. Among her father's ancestors there were several nonconformist ministers of considerable name and influence. Through her mother she could trace her connexion with the illustrious Admiral Blake, whose name was such a terror to the Spaniards at the period of the Protectorate. It seems, also, that in the same line there were some who suffered in the foolish and cruel persecutions of their day.* Mrs. Beazley always felt an honest pride in her godly ancestry, and often repeated the well-known words of Cowper :—

> " My boast is not that I deduce my birth,
> From loins enthroned, and rulers of the earth,
> But higher far my proud pretensions rise,
> A child of parents passed into the skies."

Very early in life she felt the supreme importance of religion, and often, in after days, referred to the impressions that were made on her youthful heart

---

* Family tradition to is that one, a Rev. Mr. Blake, was very near tasting the tender mercies of Judge Jefferies, of infamous memory. The house of Mr. Blake was often entered by those who, by Jefferies' authority, sought his life. It was singular, however, that they never found him at home. They did not understand that Mrs. Blake had a way of her own of managing the matter. She used, when her enemies were at hand, to hang out a table-cloth to signal to Mr. Blake his danger. Mr. Blake would watch, and read the signal sometimes from amidst the straw in the stable or the barn, and sometimes from a field of standing corn. When the men rushed rudely in the house, they found Mrs. Blake plying her domestic duties with great vigor and calmness, when she would politely inform them that Mr. Blake was not in just then.

On one occasion Blake was drawn from his house by the minions of Jefferies, whom he had empowered to take the life of the servant of the Lord. The persecuted family hurried from their house across hedges and fields, and at last reached an inn. Here they thought they were safe for the night. While they were preparing for rest the servants of Jefferies came in; one whispered to another, " That is Blake ; " he replied, " Let him go to bed, we will have his head off before morning." The landlady heard this colloquy, and in the dead of the night crept to the bedroom door of Mr. Blake, and told him of the purpose of his enemies. The family instantly arose, and were let out at the back door of the house. The landlady drove them in a cart across a ploughed field, and set them on the public road at some distance from the house, and thus they escaped.

by books, sermons, and by the Christian conduct of her parents. She was accustomed, however, to name the death of a beloved sister as the event which, by the blessing of God, led her to decision. She was at a distance from home when this event occurred, but was speedily sent for to mingle her tears with those of her bereaved parents and brothers and sisters. And it was while alone in the death chamber, and while gazing on the remains of her beloved, and, as she was fully persuaded, glorified sister, that she consecrated herself to Christ in a covenant that was never afterwards broken. Her early experience had something of terror in it. She was slow to believe that "God is love." Hence she had many doubts of her acceptance with God, even after she had surrendered her heart to the Redeemer. At length, however, she attained clearer views. She saw God in Christ reconciling the world unto himself, and henceforth rejoiced in his love. During the many years of her life that followed, she did not, for any length of time together, doubt of her personal interest in Christ. She walked in the calm and steady light of the Divine countenance.

She resided in the colonies of Tasmania and New South Wales since 1832, and her career as a consistent Christian, through the whole of that period, is known to many. In 1838 she married, and has since resided at Green Ponds, Tasmania, and Redfern, Sydney. The first ten years of her married life she spent in Tasmania. This was a period of great usefulness. She spent much time in visiting the poor and others, and in establishing a Sunday school, which, under her management, became very prosperous, numbering 75 children. While there she became the happy mother of four children, two of whom have since died, and two yet remain to mourn over the death of their excellent mother, and, it is hoped, to tread in her steps.

In 1846, her health gave way, and she visited Sydney with a view to its restoration. Afterwards she was advised by her medical attendant to reside permanently in New South Wales. Accordingly, and as Providence graciously opened the way, she and her husband and family settled in April, 1847, at Redfern.* There can be no doubt that this movement was most providential, and that the change of climate was the means, in God's hands, of adding several years to her valuable life. She still remained an invalid, but was able, from time to time, to visit the sick, and in various ways to promote the cause of the Master she loved.

During the last year it became evident that her complaint was gaining strength, and but for the great skill and attention of her medical attendant, must have proved fatal at a much earlier date. About six weeks before her death she became much worse, and her friends saw that her end was approaching. This was her own opinion. It was touching to see the evidences of increasing weakness. She withdrew with trembling steps from the public services of the sanctuary—then from the limited circle of her immediate friends—then she retreated from the family table—then was confined to one floor of her house, and ultimately to the room in which she died; and at last gave up the long but vain struggle, and sank under the

---

* It may not be amiss to notice how Providence opened the way for the removal of the family from Green Ponds to New South Wales. While Mrs. Beazley was trying the effects of the Sydney climate, her husband was preaching to the church and congregation of the Rev. Dr. Ross. His ministry proved not unacceptable. This led to an inquiry whether, as the climate seemed to suit Mrs. Beazley, a permanent opening might not be made for Mr. Beazley to exercise his office as a minister of Christ. At length, and with the concurrence of the Rev. Dr. Ross, the Redfern Congregational Church was erected, which Mr. Beazley has occupied for nearly eleven years.

power of the enemy. It would answer no good purpose to tell of the sufferings which were crowded into the last few weeks of her life. Suffice it to say that she had the sympathy and help of Him who wept at Lazarus' grave, and who graciously placed around her those who anticipated her wants, watched over the turns of her disease, calmed her agitation, and smoothed her passage to the tomb.

At 8 o'clock on Saturday morning, January 30th, she received the sentence of death. Her friends were summoned. The doctor was soon at her side, and materially mitigated her extreme distress. She then became calm, and free from pain, and, as usual in persons suffering from the same disease — consumption—spoke with great confidence of returning health, told her attendants that she should soon dismiss them, and herself attend to the duties of the family. At 10 o'clock the same day there was another alarming attack, which seemed to threaten immediate death. From this attack she did not rally. She felt the mortal hour was at hand, and said, " I begin to think this is death." There remained to her now but six or seven hours of life. Her friends watched and sought every word that fell from her lips, not that they needed any assurance as to her safety, for her life had been that of a disciple of Christ, an extended preparation for the other and better world. Still they were anxious to see how far the gospel would go in sustaining the heart amidst the struggles of expiring nature ; how far the soul could triumph amidst the decay of the body. They waited for a practical comment on those blessed words of the Apostle. " Though our outward man perish, yet the inward man is renewed day by day ; " and they give devout thanks to the Lord for what they saw and heard. When distinct utterance had failed, she looked tenderly at those who stood around, and with much difficulty exclaimed, " Far better." At intervals she said, " Come, Lord Jesus, come quickly ; " " Pity, pity, pity me, oh ! my God ; " " The weary one shall rest." And then, as though she had displayed impatience, she added, " Not my will, but thine be done." Thus did she speak in extreme suffering, when the fires of death were consuming her; thus did she display in a manner at once touching and sublime, her fellowship with the sufferings of her Lord, and her conformity to his death. She now seemed to lose consciousness, and in a few seconds the " weary one " fell asleep, and became, in the twinkling of an eye, a subject of the unsuffering kingdom of God.

On Monday morning, February 1st, her body was committed to the grave, amidst the tears and sympathies of many who had known her worth. She rests side by side with her beloved child Henry, who had been laid in the same spot three years before. Happy child! happy mother! they assuredly await the resurrection of the just.

A few words may be added on the character of Mrs. Beazley, for, as those who knew her will bear testimony, she had a character. She was not led and influenced in her acts and opinions solely by the judgment of others. She thought, and decided, and acted, and lived, as a responsible being, as one who feels that she has to give an account of herself to God. It was quite necessary for her to have grounds of action before she acted, and reason for an opinion before she adopted it

Perhaps the most remarkable feature of her mind, and it was one of singular prominence, was sincerity—Christian honesty. From this resulted an extraordinary detestation of whatever is of a contrary character. She could not sway with pretence or duplicity in any of their forms. She never

Q

sought her object by subterfuge or management, or in an indirect manner: it was perfectly natural for her to seek it directly and openly, and if the thing sought could not be effected in that manner, she resigned the attempt. The writer of this knew her intimately for twenty years, and does not recollect a single instance of conduct inconsistent with the simplicity that is in Christ.

She was very zealous in the work of the Lord. Before disease had subdued her strength, she labored incessantly, and much beyond her power. She was convinced of this herself, and said but a few weeks before her death that, had she her time again, she should consider it her duty to be more careful than she had been of the strength which God had given her.

Her mind was one of more than average quickness and power; she had read much, especially of poetry, biography, and history. She sometimes wrote verses on domestic and other occasions, and some of these display considerable force both of language and thought. We may give a specimen or two extracted from a poem addressed to her husband on the occasion of the death of Henry, one of their three sons :—

" Our harps are on the willow
    That bends o'er sorrow's sea,
And many a stormy billow
    Has broke o'er you and me.
Our triple cord is broken,
    Our Henry is no more ;
With anguish deep, unspoken,
    Our last one we deplore ;
Our youngest cherished darling
    Dwells in our home no more."

"Thy wit, thy merry laughter,
    In life's sweet day-spring wild,
Leave echoes long, long after
    Our sad farewell, my child."

" Death could but touch the mortal,
    Beyond he had no power ;
We felt heaven's open portal
    Waited the parting hour.
On came the last sad mystery,
    Watching the expiring breath
That closed dear Henry's history,
    The brothers first saw death."

" This cloud has silver lining,
    Which faith and hope shall see,
And soon God's sun, clear shining,
    Shall bid the darkness flee."

Her imperfections were such as might have been expected from the character of her mind. Her scorn of meanness was, perhaps, sometimes carried to excess. She did not always make sufficient allowance for minds less firm than her own. But her faults were few, and some of them were the results of a nervous anxiety to serve and honor her Saviour. Reviewing her character as a whole, we may safely affirm that it is worthy of the remembrance, the admiration, and the imitation of all who watched her course. They may be pointed to her, and addressed in the words of the apostle, " Imitate her faith, considering the end of her conversation, Jesus Christ, the same yesterday, to day, and for ever."

RELIGIOUS INTELLIGENCE.

Congregational Conference.

The third Conference of Delegates from the Congregational Churches of New South Wales, South Australia, Victoria, and Tasmania, has recently been held in Hobart Town.

On Monday evening, February 15th, an introductory devotional meeting was held in Brisbane-street Chapel, presided over by the Rev. C. W. Evan, of Adelaide, who delivered an impressive address on the occasion; the devotional exercises were conducted by the Revs. C. Price, and S. C. Kent.

The Conference commenced its sittings on Tuesday morning, February 16th, under the presidency of the Rev. R. Fletcher, St. Kilda, Victoria. After introductory devotional exercises conducted by the chairman, the Rev. F. Miller, provisional Secretary, reported the proceedings which had been taken in preparation for the Conference, and presented the following list of delegates :—

NEW SOUTH WALES.—Sydney: Rev. S. C. Kent, Mr. John Fairfax, and Mr. Samuel Thompson.

SOUTH AUSTRALIA.—Adelaide: Rev. C. W. Evan, B. A., Mr. G. M. Waterhouse.

VICTORIA.—Melbourne: Rev. R. Fletcher, Mr. Thomas Fulton.

TASMANIA. - Hobart Town, Brisbane-street Church: Rev. F. Miller, Rev. W. Day, Messrs. Wooley, Lumsden, George Salier, Perkins, Rolwegan, Dear, W. Giblin.

Davey-street Church: Rev. G. Clarke, Messrs. Hopkins, Basil Rout, Joseph Facy.

New Town: Rev. J. Nisbet, Mr. Le Vicount.

Launceston, Tamar-street Church: Rev. C. Price, Messrs. Pescodd, Aikenhead, and Room.

St. John's Square Church: Rev. W. Law, Messrs. Button and Powell.

Green Ponds: Rev. W. Waterfield, Messrs. Speak, and T. Gorringe.

Cambridge: Mr. Blackwood.

Franklin, Huon: Mr. Giles.

It was moved by the Hon. Mr. Button, seconded by Mr. Basil Rout—

That the Revs. F. Miller and C. Price be Secretaries to the Conference.

Moved by the Rev. F. Miller, seconded by Rev. G. Clarke—

That the Rev. S. C. Kent, Messrs. Hopkins and Fairfax, constitute an Executive Committee to arrange the order of proceedings.

The Chairman then delivered the following address :—

CHAIRMAN'S ADDRESS.

BELOVED BRETHREN,—Permit me in the first place to give utterance to the high gratification I experience in assembling, in our united and representative capacity, in Hobart Town the very spring and source of Australian Congregationalism. The gentleman who first sent home to England for an Independent Minister to come over and settle in these distant and then almost unknown regions; and the first minister who had the courage to respond to the call to adventure on a voyage to the antipodes, at that time no slight affair, and to accept, as his lot in life, of a voluntary banishment to a penal colony, are still living, and both are with us this day. It must be a high gratification to these gentlemen to see whereunto their first and feeble effort has grown. Little, I ween, did they expect to behold the day when there should be gathered, in their own city of Hobart, a body of ministers and laymen who virtually represent some sixty or seventy churches. We share with them in their grateful emotions and rejoice in their joy. The progress, from the day of small things to the present period of comparative strength, was well traced by the hand best able to do it—my respected predecessor in this office—the beloved minister just referred to*, in his address at Sydney last year, and I shall not therefore here enlarge upon it; but I could not deny myself the pleasure of this passing reference, in which I am sure I have the hearty sympathy of all present.

With respect to the progress since our last meeting at Sydney, of the cause with which we are identified, the time has been too brief to furnish much material for comment. The most noticeable circumstance is, the accession to our ministry resulting from the visit of Mr. Poore to Britain. The labors of my friend there have been upon the most gigantic scale. He has astonished the home authorities by his indomitable energy and perseverance. The towns and villages he has visited, and at which he has conducted services, in England and Scotland, amount to little short of a hundred. His efforts have been directed to *three* objects: diffusing information respecting these colonies, looking out for ministers to send out hither, and collecting £1,000 to supplement the £2,400 subscribed by these colonies to defray the expenses of bringing the ministers out. This he has done, by popular lectures, by speeches at public meetings, and by sermons. The money has been raised, though not without considerable difficulty, arising in part from the commercial crisis. It was, however, if possible, a harder task to procure the *men*; not that there was lack of applications: these were numerous enough; but few were of the kind that could be entertained. Mr. Poore preferred looking out for himself, and to make application to such brethren as he thought suitable. But he met with many and grievous disappointments; the effective men being difficult to dislodge from their present positions. He has, at length, obtained the full number he undertook to send out. *Five* have arrived in Victoria, who have all found spheres providentially opened for them. *Two* more are daily expected, and for them also unoccupied posts are ready. We believe that these brethren will prove a real accession of strength to the cause of Evangelical Religion and Congregational Church Polity. You are all aware of the melancholy loss of one of our esteemed brethren, who perished as he entered the Heads at Sydney, in the wreck of the *Catharine Adamson*—a mysterious exception to the otherwise successful carrying out of all these measures. We are now in the daily expectation of the arrival once more among us of Mr. Poore himself, accompanied by my old friend and companion in youth, Mr. Binney, whose visit I trust may not only prove beneficial to his shattered health, but also useful to our churches and the cause of religion generally.

Perhaps a sweeping tour like this of Mr. Poore's can only be made at very distant intervals. It would be more difficult to get a second £1,000

---

* Rev. F. Miller

than the first, and, perhaps, still more difficult to obtain sixteen more ministers all at once. But I trust permanent arrangements will be made to secure a continued supply of faithful men of God, at the rate, at least, of six or eight per annum, and also to provide for them suitable spheres when they arrive.

If I desire the spread of Independency, it is not, I trust, from party spirit, or love of sectional peculiarities for their own sake, but from a conviction of the Scriptural basis of our principles, their adaptation as a vehicle for the conservation and diffusion of vital religion, and from their wholesome action upon other bodies of Christians. With respect to our prospects of growth and extension in these colonies, my hopes are sanguine, not grounded wholly upon the reasons just adverted to, but largely upon practical considerations. Good arguments upon church government are something, but it is no easy matter to induce people to give heed to them. Very few, in point of fact, unite themselves with any body of Christians, because they have carefully examined into its principles and become convinced of their truth. Other circumstances sway them; and on the whole that system takes best with the community which works best, not that which boasts the most goodly theory, and shews the most imposing array of proof. Hence, we find different systems have prevailed in different countries and different districts, simply because they were most suited to the tastes and habits and, may-be, prejudices of the people.

Now let us look at the present and prospective state of these colonies religiously considered. The country is sown with mixed seed. The immigrants are not all Episcopalians, or Presbyterians, or Romanists, or Wesleyans, or Baptists, or Independents. Every ship contains an assortment of nearly all these. Every city, every township, every rural district is peopled by these varieties variously proportioned. No established church, no dominant sect, no rigid uniformity can exist. Whether all this is an advantage or a misfortune is not now the question. It is a simple fact and cannot possibly be helped; and it is a fact which cannot but exert a powerful influence upon the future. New comers bring with them, no doubt, their old predilections and prejudices, and these may cling to them to the last; but on the whole they cling less closely here than they do at home. Colonists, detached from their old habitudes and freelymingling with people who differ from them, are more open to be acted on by other bodies of Christians than they were in the fatherland, where they were surrounded by their old associations. Their children will be still more unshackled. It will be impossible to convey to *them* the same strength of Churchism, whether English, or Scotch, or Romish, or any other, as their parents imbibed in their own early education. As time rolls on, a collision and friction of opinion and usage must ensue. The different denominations of Christians will necessarily rub down and modify each others peculiarities, and the minds of all will be more accessible to influence and action from quarters against which they were once firmly closed. A process of disintegration will go on, and then, doubtless, new formations will take place.

If these statements be correct, a condition of society is preparing which will try all denominations of Christians, and in which any one, whose principles and usages are characterised by common sense simplicity and easy adaptation to the wants and tastes of a community comparatively unprejudiced, will have a fair chance of success. And such we have the vanity to

RELIGIOUS INTELLIGENCE.

think *ours* in no mean degree is. It appears to me we have as little about us that is artificial and peculiar or merely traditional, as most other bodies, and less than many ; and supposing any parties desirous of change, they will meet, probably, with as few things among us likely to strike them unfavorably as elsewhere. Our system is not only based on Scripture but common sense. We do in religion as we should be naturally led to do had we no Scripture principles or warrants, and no prescriptive usages to guide us. If we take care to have goodly places of worship occupied by able and right-hearted ministers, we are little in danger of being confined for Congregations to such only as were ranked as Independents in England. I mention this not in the way of self-gratulation ; but as an indication in providence of a great work being assigned to us in these rising colonies ; and as a motive to use every endeavor to multiply churches in suitable localities, to cherish and exhibit the goodly spectacle of union and concord among ourselves, and to do our utmost to create and diffuse throughout the body a healthy sound public sentiment.

An objector might be disposed to say, " All this is fine talking, but what have you *done ?* What is your present state ? Are you not far behind many other denominations ?" We admit it ; and think we can account for it without impugning what has been already advanced. Congregationalism had great disadvantage in the start. Other denominations entered on the race before us. This arose from the nature of the case. The colonies being at first penal establishments, thoroughly Governmental and almost military in their structure, were anything but inviting to free emigrants. The criminals sent over were under the charge of the State as it regards religious provision, as well as in other respects. All Englishmen were regarded as of the Church of England, all Scotchmen as of the Church of Scotland, all Irishmen as Roman Catholics, and Government State-paid chaplains were provided for these varieties. Thus these three bodies were in at the very beginning, and long had sole possession of the field. There was no room, no opening for Independents. In the course of time the Wesleyans made their appearance, and their being here, at so comparatively early a period, is easily accounted for from 'the fact that their great Missionary Society is not confined in its fields of labor to strictly Heathen lands, but embraces any country beyond the limits of England where an opening offers. Operations in Ireland, in France, and in English-speaking colonies were strictly within its province. Hence this organisation enabled them to commence missionary labors here as soon as an opening presented itself. But it was not so with us. The Missionary Society we support (the London) was confined by its constitution strictly to the *Heathen*, and could not send ministers here to preach to the English, and there was no other institution in existence that could ; and the formation of a society specially for the *colonies* was not likely to take place till some pressing necessity called it into being. Such necessity did not arise till Independents had begun to emigrate, and, finding no ministrations to their mind, to write home to their friends to persuade ministers to come out. One or two came in this manner ; and at last rose the Colonial Missionary Society in 1836. By this time the other bodies had got firmly rooted, and had spread their ramifications far and wide, and much lee-way had necessarily to be made up before a parallel course could be run by Congregationalists. In *South Australia* the case was different ; there, the system of colonisation was free from the first, and the Colonial Society, coming into existence about the time, was at hand to send out ministers to supply the colony as it increased ; and the result is what might be expected. We hold a more important position there in relation to the community at large, considering the extent of the population, than in any of the other colonies.

Most of the systems in operation previously to our own received. and some of them mainly relied upon, *State-aid.* It is of the nature of such assistance to stimulate a premature development which is generally followed by a corresponding reaction of languor and debility. Ministers are placed where congregations can scarcely be gathered ; and, where the people are sufficiently numerous, the paralysing influence of the unnatural help afforded is found in the long run to impair their energies. In addition to this. some of the forms of Christianity with which we are familiar are distinguished by compact organisation and a structure of government somewhat resembling a monarchy or an oligarchy. Such bodies, with a strong central executive, can act more energetically and promptly at first, not having to wait for the tardy growth of public opinion ; but freely constituted communities, if their condition be healthy, though slower in their first movements, are more powerful in the end. Their weakness is in their infancy. When they pass the stage of childhood and dependance they acquire strength with their years. Our churches are like free republics, dependent on the good opinion and voice of the people. The chief difficulty is in the commencement ; when this is overcome they contain the elements of development and of easy, rapid, self-multiplication. Such has been the history of Independency in England during the present century, as I have had, for the latter half of that period, large opportunities of witnessing. Such, it appears to me, is likely to be its career in Australia. In 1838, for instance, there was but one small church of our order in New South Wales, and that without a minister : not a single congregational pastor was there in all that vast colony. That church has now grown to great magnitude and power : a few years ago it was able to raise £20,000 for church extension; now it sees a numerous progeny springing up around it : and though *they* are at present in their infancy, and some of them partly dependent on their parent, yet time will strengthen them : and they will by and bye become centres of influence in their several localities, and contributors to the general fund for further missionary operations. In Victoria we have some ten or twelve churches which have surmounted their earliest difficulties and are now in the second stage, building goodly chapels and paying off debts, and about as many more just commencing their career : in a few years, by the blessing of God, these will constitute a body strong and powerful for further extension : and so, I presume, it is in the other colonies. For these reasons, I am full of hope that the cause of religion, as connected with our principles and polity, will advance in future years with a self-multiplying progression. Its progress, we hope and believe, will be marked by an ever-increasing momentum.

It is well, however, to be reminded that these anticipated results will not take place as a matter of course, by a species of happy fatality independently of care and fidelity and of the blessing of Almighty God. The principles may be good, but they must be brought prominently and vigorously into action. The body may be fair and well-proportioned, but it must be animated by the principle of life and the vigor of health, to accomplish the end of its existence. In particular let me say, that whatever zeal we may display for the sacred right of private judgment. for freedom of opinion. for the liberties of the Christian people, and the independence of the churches of all foreign control, all will be in vain to secure either usefulness or extension, unless we are *sound in the faith* once delivered to the saints, holding fast by the cardinal doctrines of the glorious Gospel of the Blessed God. Nor will this be sufficient, if it be nothing more than zeal for a dead and sapless orthodoxy, a cold and rigid and logically arranged system of Theology. The *life* and *power* of religion must be amongst us. Personal piety in Church members is a vital principle of Independency. We believe that churches should be composed not of baptised persons only, nor of the outwardly moral, nor of regular attendants, nor of money subscribers, nor even of inquirers after salvation, but of *Christians*; of persons professing to be penitents, believers, new creatures in Christ Jesus, and sustaining their profession by sufficient evidence. We dare not lower the standard beneath this scriptural level. This principle is our glory and strength. By adhering to it we may make less show in statistics than some others, but we retain the elements of real energy. If we have vital churches we shall have a vital ministry; and with a vital ministry and a vital church we may reasonably calculate on the presence and power of the Spirit among us. It was from laxity in this respect that so many of the Nonconformist Churches in old England and the Congregational Churches in New England declined during last century into Unitarianism apathy and death. Let us therefore be jealous on this point; and, while excluding none of Christ's little ones because they are not full-grown in knowledge and experience, and, while careful not to put needless barriers to admission in the way of the timid. still let genuine piety be a condition of membership. Let us be content, if this *must* be the alternative, to be rather few and strong, than many and weak.

It would be superfluous to press fidelity to the principle of refusing all STATE AID TO RELIGION. We were the first, or among the first, to take a stand upon this point; and we are not likely to abandon it now, when others are coming over to our views, and the Legislatures themselves are wavering. Pure Congregationalism is incompatible with State support in any form whatever. Religion is an affair of the heart, between God and the human soul. Its essence consists in its willinghood. An act professedly religious, or in favor of religion, loses the very nature of religion, if it be not voluntary. The *State* is the nation acting by law, that is, by *force;* and aid from the State is aid wrung from compulsory taxation. To give or to receive such assistance has no religion in it at all. This we have perceived, and this we have acted upon. Others have accepted the bait, and *we* appear to have suffered for a time: but we believe we shall gain in the end. And it cannot but be matter of rejoicing to see that the public sentiment is setting in strongly in the direction of our views. Men of all denominations in the various Legislatures, struck with the common-sense reasonableness of our principles, are advocating them now in high places. They are denying not only the policy but the right of the State to interfere in things sacred. Hence we see how opinions long peculiar to ourselves and a few others, and for a long time thought to be mere denominational crotchets, are gradually leavening the community at large: and this may encourage us to hope that others of our principles, equally simple and reasonable, will work their way into other systems and will modify and improve them. The abolition of

State-aid, as a political question, has, you are aware, made rapid progress. South Australia furnished the example of settling the question boldly and at once. In Victoria it was passed by triumphant majorities in the Assembly and only lost in the Council by one vote. The agitation of the question is progressing favorably in Tasmania, and New South Wales we hope will not long lag behind.

The question of Education, or Day School Instruction, is exciting attention in some of the colonies, and probably will in all ere long. And it is desirable we should form some definite views upon it, and, if possible, agree upon some uniform line of action. Perhaps, however, the time is not yet come for this : for I am aware there is a difference of opinion among ourselves on this momentous subject. I have put forth my own opinions without reserve in the present month's "Southern Spectator." The state of things in Victoria, seeming to warrant, almost to necessitate, my doing so. It is far, however, from my wish to dictate. The question has many sides, and may well admit diversity of opinion. I can only say the views I have expressed are not hastily taken up; I have long held them, and they are the result of large opportunities of observation in England. Many of our congregations there strained themselves to sustain day schools, with but little profit. They diverted the current of their strength from its appropriate channel to their own ultimate loss. The mission of the Church, as such, is exclusively religious. The Church is the salt, the leaven, the light of the world. That which it has to diffuse is the blessed Gospel; that which it is to aim at is the *salvation* of the *soul*. This is its one exclusive object. For this it has been instituted and organised. To this Christ and his apostles and the early Churches confined themselves. It was no part of their mission to teach literature, science, and mathematics. As a matter of charity, when opportunity offers, Christians must feed the hungry, clothe the naked, heal the sick, or they may help the secular instruction of neglected children; but no one of these things is their special and direct vocation. If any one of them were, more than another, it would be healing the sick, judging from the examples set by Christ and his apostles. Even these charitable labors, however, were done with the ulterior view of benefitting the soul. And there may be cases, as so generally happens to missionaries among uncivilized tribes, where help in secular matters is the shortest way to induce the people to attend to the Gospel. But let us remember that the real business of Churches, as such, is the spiritual, and not the secular. The Church is not the academy, nor the minister the schoolmaster. Nor is a schoolmaster, for secular learning, among the officers provided by Christ for the working of his own peculiar institution ; that Church of which he is the head.

I shall refrain at present from saying anything upon the "Southern Spectator" and Denominational Literature, as that matter will come up by-and-bye for separate and serious consideration. Nor shall I attempt to anticipate my brethren in the views they may have to express on the subjects assigned to them in the programme, which I doubt not will all receive the attention they respectively deserve.

May a spirit of love, of power, and of a sound mind, of wisdom and of utterance be poured out upon our Conference, that all that shall be said and done may contribute to the refreshment of our own spirits, and through us to the revival of religion in our Churches, and the diffusion of the Gospel throughout the Australias, the Islands of the Great Pacific, and the world at large.

On the motion of the Rev. G. Clarke, seconded by Mr. G. M. Waterhouse, it was resolved, "That the warmest thanks of the Conference be and are hereby presented to the Rev. R. Fletcher for his appropriate and valuable address, and that he be solicited to place it in the hands of the Congregational Union of Tasmania, with a view to its publication." The Chairman intimated his willingness to comply with the request of the Conference.

Mr. Fairfax introduced the subject of an "Educational Institution for the children of Ministers and Missionaries;" and, after considerable discussion, it was agreed, on the motion of Mr. Hopkins, seconded by Mr. Thompson :—

That a committee be formed, consisting of the Rev. Messrs. West, Cuthbertson, and Kent, and Messrs. Fairfax, Thompson, and Mills, to raise and provide a fund to assist in the education of the children of those missionaries of the London Missionary Society in the South Seas who may be disposed to avail themselves of such aid; that such committee apply the funds as occasion may require, and report their proceedings at the next Conference.

The Rev. W. Law introduced the subject of a "Provident Fund," which was freely discussed; and, on the motion of Mr. G. M. Waterhouse, seconded by Rev. W. Law, it was agreed :—

That this Conference strongly recommends to the Congregational Union of each colony the necessity of providing a fund for the relief of superannuated ministers, and of the families of deceased ministers; and that for that purpose an annual collection should be made in each congregation, or such other steps adopted as may seem desirable to each Union.

The Conference resumed its sitting on Wednesday morning.

After devotional exercises, the Rev. G. Clarke brought under the consideration of the Conference, "The paucity of candidates for ministerial and missionary service." Nearly all the members of the Conference having expressed their views on the subject, it was moved by the Rev. G. Clarke, and seconded by the Rev. S. C. Kent :—

That this Conference is of opinion that the resolution originally adopted at the Conference in Melbourne, is worthy of confirmation—that the Rev. R. Fletcher be solicited to receive young men under his care for Theological training—that the advantages offered by the Melbourne University be embraced, as far as may be deemed desirable—and that such churches and unions, in the several colonies, as may wish to place their young men under his care, be recommend d to make their own arrangements with him.

The subject of "South Sea Missions," was then introduced by the Rev. S. C. Kent. After a full and careful discussion of the condition and claims of these Missions, in which nearly all the brethren expressed their opinions, it was ultimately agreed, on the motion of Mr. Fairfax, seconded by Mr. Fulton :—

That this Conference earnestly recommends to the churches in the colonies, enlarged contributions to the funds of the London Missionary Society, with the hope that the directors will increase the support to, and number of their agents in the South Sea Missions.

The Conference resumed on the following morning.

Mr. George Waterhouse read a paper on "The law of Marriage and Divorce."

After which it was moved by Mr. Fairfax, seconded by Mr. Basil Rout—

That Mr. Waterhouse be requested to hand over the paper now read to the Executive Committee, to be dealt with as the Conference may direct.

It was moved by Mr. George Waterhouse, seconded by Rev. S. C. Kent—

That, in the opini n of this Conference, ministers of all denominations should be placed on one and the same footing, as regards the power of celebrating marriages.

It was then moved by Rev. Mr. Law, seconded by the Rev. G. Clarke—

; hat this conference would call the attention of the various Congregational Unions to the state of the marriage laws as existing in their respective colonies, with a view to effecting such alterations where necessary, as shall place all religious bodies on a perfect equality, as soon as practicable.

It was then moved by the Rev. C. W. Evan, seconded by Mr. Fulton, and carried—with three dissentients :—

That this Conference views, with satisfaction, the progress of enlightened opinion on the subject of marriage with a deceased wife's sister, and would express the hope that all legal hindrances to such marriages, (where such hindrances exist), will at an early period be removed.

The Rev. R. Fletcher gave a full account of the *Southern Spectator*, and read several letters expressing opinions respecting the future management of this publication. The subject was discussed at length, when the Rev. Messrs. Clarke, Evan, Kent, and Fletcher were appointed a committee to prepare a plan for the future management of the magazine.

On the following morning the report of the committee in reference to the *Southern Spectator*, was presented by the Rev. S. C. Kent.

The following resolutions were then adopted by the Conference :—

1. That the best thanks of this Conference are due, and are hereby presented to the Rev. R. Fletcher for his able and gratuitous services as Editor of the *Southern Spectator*.

2. That the *Southern Spectator* consist of 32 pages; that it be published monthly, and sold at one shilling per copy, or ten shillings to subscribers for the year, payment in advance.

3. That the title in future be the *Southern Spectator*—a Magazine of Religious and General Literature, connected with the Congregational Churches of Australasia.

4. That the Delegates representing the different Congregational Unions in this Conference be requested to form themselves into local committees, with power to add to their number, for the purpose of promoting the circulation of the *Spectator*, and that each committee be earnestly desired to obtain, if possible, the sum of £50 to secure the continued publication of the Magazine, and to communicate the result to the editor before the 15th May next.

5. That pastors of different churches be requested to introduce to the notice of their deacons, at their monthly meetings, and to urge upon their churches, the importance of subscribing for, and promoting the circulation of the Magazine.

6. That the thanks of this Conference be tendered to those friends who have contributed papers to the *Southern Spectator*; and that the pastors of the various churches keep constantly in view as a duty the supply of suitable articles for the magazine, from themselves or others they may be able to influence.

A letter was read from Mr. J. Salier, in reference to a " Hymn book and tune book."

After some discussion it was moved by the Rev. S. C. Kent, seconded by the Rev. W. Law—

That this Conference is obliged to Mr. Salier for his letter on the subject of a hymn book for the Congregational Churches of the colonies, and deems it desirable that no change be made until such time as the hymn book now in course of publication by the Congregational Union of England and Wales shall have reached the colonies.

The Rev. F. Miller introduced " Congregationalism in New Zealand," and read several letters from that colony on the subject.

It was then moved by Rev. F. Miller, seconded by Mr. Hopkins—

That this Conference, while regretting the inability of the Congregational ministers and churches in New Zealand to send a delegate to its meeting, regards with much interest the communications which have been received from them in relation to Congregationalism in that colony; and trusts that by the instrumentality of the Colonial Missionary Society, an earnest and sucessful minister may speedily be established in Wellington. That the chairman of the Conference be respectfully requested to transmit to the Colonial Missionary Society in London the appeal from the friends in Wellington, and to call special attention to it.

The Rev. J. Nisbet introduced the subject of " Statistical Returns."

After some discussion, a tabular form was presented and approved by the meeting, and it was resolved to transmit it to the several Unions with a recommendation that it be used in future statistical returns.

The subject of " Divorce " was introduced by Mr. G. M. Waterhouse, after which it was moved by Mr. G. M. Waterhouse, and seconded by Rev. F. Miller—

That considering the moral and social evils resulting from some of the bearings of the present law of marriage, this Conference would refer with satisfaction to a measure recently passed by the British Parliament to afford facilities for divorce and legalised separation, and expresses the hope that some similar measure may be early adopted in the Australian colonies.

The Rev. C. W. Evan in the name of the Congregational Union of South Australia requested that the next Conference should be held in that colony.

It was then moved by the Rev. G. Clarke, seconded by Mr. Fairfax—

That in accordance with this invitation this Conference recommends that the next meeting of Delegates from the different colonies, be held in Adelaide, if practicable in October 1859, and not later than October 1860 ; and that the Rev. Joseph Beazley, of Sydney, be the Chairman of such Conference, and the Rev. C. W. Evan, be Secretary to arrange for its meeting.

It was moved by the Rev. S. C. Kent, seconded by Rev. J. Nisbet :—

That the Rev. R. Fletcher, as Chairman of the Conference, be solicited to call the attention of ministers in England, in the way which shall seem to him most desirable, to the importance of giving suitable testimonials to all members of their churches emigrating to these colonies.

It was moved by Rev. S. C. Kent, seconded by Rev. C. W. Evan, supported by Mr. Fulton—

That the Delegates attending this Conference desire to express their sense of obligation to their friends in Hobart Town for the kind and generous hospitality with which they have been received and entertained by them during their sojourn in this city.

It was moved by Mr. B. Rout, seconded by the Rev. J. Nesbitt—

That the cordial thanks of the conference be given to the Rev. R. Fletcher for his able Presidency, and to the Secretaries the Revs. F. Miller and Charles Price and the members of the Executive Committee, for their efficient services during its sittings.

The Chairman responded to this vote as did also the other gentlemen whose services were acknowledged. The preceding resolutions, with one exception, as recorded above, were passed unanimously.

On the evenings of the days on which the Conference sat, the following public meetings were held. On Tuesday evening the Annual Meeting of the Colonial Missionary Society was held in the Congregational Church, Davey-street. The Chair was taken by John Fairfax, Esq., of Sydney; an interesting report was read by Mr. Dear: various resolutions were passed, and addresses were delivered by the Rev. R. Fletcher, S. C. Kent, C. W. Evan, C. Price, W. Law, and Messrs. Fulton, Thomson, and Aikenhead. On Wednesday evening a Social Meeting was held in Brisbane-street School-Room, Thos. Fulton, Esq., presided, and the assembly was addressed by Messrs. Thomson, Fletcher, Fairfax, Law, and Miller. The meeting was largely attended. The speakers were chiefly occupied in detailing the progress of the Congregational Churches in the various colonies. On Thursday evening another Public Meeting was held in Davey-street Church for the " Enunciation of Congregational Principles." Mr. James Aikenhead, presided. Resolutions affirmatory of these principles were submitted to the meeting and formed the basis of speeches by the Rev. S. C. Kent, R. Fletcher, G. Clarke, W. Law, and John Fairfax, Esq. The meeting seemed deeply interested in the statements and arguments produced. These various proceedings were brought to a close by the celebration of the Lord's Supper at Brisbane-street Chapel, on Friday evening. The attendance of members of other besides Congregational Churches, was invited, and several responded to the call. The Rev. S. C. Kent presided, and the Revs. C. Price, R. Fletcher, W. Law, and G. Clarke, took part in the service.

Victoria.

SEAMEN'S CHURCH AND SAILORS' HOME, MELBOURNE.

(Abridged from the Argus, March 20th, 1858.)

The amelioration of the social condition of seamen is a matter for the exercise of a true practical philanthropy. The sailor's lot at best is not a very enviable one, and he is in an especial degree a most fitting subject to engage the attention of the benevolent who seek to humanize the neglected and ignorant among their fellow-creatures. It is well-known that if the sailor is but too often the victim of degraded habits, it is because his better nature has been obliterated by ill-treatment, and that kindness and attention to his legitimate wants, produce almost invariably the most satisfactory results on his manners, and general life.

To sow the seeds of improvement during the sailors stay in the Port of Melbourne, a society of gentlemen, countenanced and aided by the support of Sir Henry Barkly, have, under the name of the Bethel Union, from which all sectarian differences are banished, succeeded in establishing a Sailors' Mission, with a floating church in Hobson's Bay, of which the Rev. Kerr Johnston is the chaplain. The Bethel ship was opened for Divine service on the first of July last year, and the first public meeting to advocate the claims of the society took place on Thursday evening, February 25th, 1858, in the Hall of the Mechanics' Institute, Collins-street. His Excellency Sir Henry Barkly, K.C.B., Governor of Victoria, the Patron of the institution, occupied the chair. The attendance was large, and the meeting most enthusiastic. On the platform were Lieutenant Bancroft, A.D.C.; the Hon. J. Hodgson, M.L.C.; the Hon. C. Vaughan, M.L.C.; Captain Perry, M.L.A.; Captain Charles Ferguson, Chief Harbor Master; Captain B. R. Mathews, Lloyd's Agent; Captain Norman, of H.M.C.S.S. *Victoria*; Captain D. M'Callum; the Rev. S. L. Chase; the Rev. James Ballantyne; the Rev. D. J. Draper; the Rev. J. Mirams; the Rev. J. P. Sunderland; and H. Langlands, M.L.A., T. Dickson, F. Haller, A. Bonar and J. Ballingall, Esqrs.

The Rev. J. P. Sunderland offered prayer, after which

His Excellency the Governor said—Ladies and Gentlemen,—As patron of the Victoria Bethel Union, it becomes my pleasing duty to preside at the first public meeting held on its behalf in Melbourne. It is possible some of you may not be aware of the object of the institution, because its title, though well known at home, is not suggestive of its design, which is to support a floating church for seamen arriving in Hobson's Bay. When I mention that about 30,000 seamen annually visit this port, and that on no day are there fewer than 1,400 in the Bay, it will be clearly seen that a great necessity exists for an institution of this kind here; for sailors, it must be remembered, are only birds of passage—they are here to-day, and away to-morrow, and therefore it cannot be expected that they could join themselves to any of the churches ashore; and even if they did belong to any church ashore, it would be difficult for them to leave their ships and come on land to divine worship, especially looking to the fear of captains that their crews, or some of them, would take advantage of going to church to desert. Therefore, it will be seen that a necessity does exist for an institution of this kind. Of the obligations under which the rest of the community are placed, as regards the sailors of this colony, I think I need hardly enlarge; at least it would be unnecessary to occupy much of your time in doing so, for in the report to be read the claims of seamen are warmly and eloquently advocated. Moreover, in a colony like this their claims press with peculiar force, for there are few among those who now listen to me who have not made a long voyage in coming to this country, and probably acquired some experience in the hardships and perils to which sailors are exposed; and I think we all must have seen in our voyage here, that though Jack was a little coarse in his exterior, and sometimes in his language, he is, on the whole, rather a devout fellow. We must all remember there is no class of the community that seems to live with a more constant sense of a superintending Providence than the sailor; and we cannot but think it is natural he should do so, when we remember the expressive words of Dr. Johnson, that the sailor passes his days with only a two-inch plank between him and eternity. I think it will be found from the report of the chaplain of the mission there is this degree of susceptibility of impression to be found among the maritime population who frequent this port; and it will be proved to your satisfaction that a wide and extensive field for Christian exertion is to be found among the seamen who frequent Hobson's Bay, and it depends on the Christian liberality of those who are present to-day that this field be properly cultivated. There is another subject on which I would like to touch, though briefly, and that is, the necessity that exists for the establishment in this city of something of the nature of a sailor's home. When I state to you that more than 10,000 seamen are every year discharged at this port and enter into fresh engagements under the shipping master, it will be seen that it is necessary that respectable and cheap lodgings should be provided in some suitable and convenient locality in this city, for seamen. Sailor's Homes are to be found in most seaports in Britain and the United States, and the rising importance of this emporium of the south demands that we should not be behind in establishing a home for the sailors frequenting this port. But I would not wish to withdraw your attention from the fact that the object of our meeting to-night is to aid the Bethel Union which we have established here. Before I sit down, I have to state that letters of apology have been received for the non-attendance of the Lord Bishop of Melbourne, the Very Rev. the Dean, the Rev. Dr. Cairns, the Rev. Isaac New, and other gentlemen, who would have been happy to attend had it been consistent with their other engagements to do so.

Mr. W. Fairfax, Honorary Secretary then read his report, and Captain B. R. Mathews, the Treasurer read the financial statement from which it appeared that £732 15s. 3d. had been received and £719 13s. expended. It will require about £1000 a year to work the institution efficiently and nearly £800 of this has been already obtained for the year just closed. The several resolutions were spoken to by most of the gentlemen already named.

The Society has a further project in view, to complete the good work begun in the Bethel ship, the founding of a Sailors' Home, where provident habits, and feelings of self-restraint and self-respect, may be encouraged and practically inculcated.

Sailors' Homes were first established in London in the year 1835, and the advantages which they are ascertained to have conferred during the twenty years they have been since in operation, are of the most extensive and practical character. The last report of the Directors of the Sailors' Home, Wall-street, London Docks, states that " the great aim of the founders of the Institution was to improve the religious and moral character of the seamen of all countries, by pious instruction, and by keeping them out of the clutches of the harpies, crimps, and prostitutes who are always on the look out to rob them of their hard-earned wages. Since the opening of the Sailors' Home in May, 1835, the sum of *five hundred and sixty-nine thousand pounds* (£569,000) has been deposited by sailors in the Institution, of which *one hundred and ninety-three thousand six hundred and seventy-two pounds* (£193,782) have been remitted to ' Jacks' relatives and friends. Mr. Green, the eminent shipowner, who opened an excellent ' Sailors' Home' in the East India-road, Poplar, for the crews of his own vessels, has liberally extended the admission to all seamen of good character. Sailors' Homes are now established in Aberdeen, Belfast, Bristol, Cardiff, Chatham, Cork, Devonport, Dover, Dublin, Falmouth, Folkestone, Greenwich, London, Liverpool, Plymouth, Portsmouth, Stornaway, and Sunderland."

With such an example before them there can be little doubt that the Society of the Sailors' Friends in Melbourne will be stimulated to bring about equally beneficial results for the seamen frequenting Hobson's Bay. The same evil influences which so demoralised seamen in Great Britian, are equally active in Melbourne, and here sailors are cheated, robbed, and ill-treated by harpies, who look upon them as their special prey, pretty much as they were formerly in London, Liverpool, and New York; and the field for plunder at the mercy of these miscreants is not less fruitful; for we find from a letter addressed to the Secretary of the Society by Mr. M'Culloch, the late Commissioner of Trade and Customs, that "from 1st of March, 1856, to the

31st of December, 1857, a period of 22 months, there were 19,017 sailors engaged and discharged before the Shipping Master at the Port of Melbourne, and that the amount of money advanced to them during this period was £88,000." How much of this large amount has Jack been able to put in the savings bank, we should like to know.

It is considered that £8,000 would be sufficient to establish a Home in Melbourne or Williamstown capable of accommodating 200 sailors, and supplying the advantages of a school, reading-room, hospital, shipping office, and savings bank; and as these Homes are always self-supporting establishments, little doubt can be entertained that the Society will early succeed in their desire to provide the seafaring community visiting our shores with this great *desideratum*. A deputation has been appointed to confer with the Chamber of Commerce on the subject, and to unite the co-operation of that body in effecting the object in view; and under such good auspices there is every reason to expect a successful termination of the labors of the Sailors' friends in this matter.

SUNDAY TRAFFIC.—A Conference of ministers and laymen was held in the Mechanics Institute, on Friday, February 19th, for the purpose of adopting measures for resisting the attempt making in the Victorian Parliament to open public-houses on part of the Lord's day. Richard Heales Esq., M.L.A. presided, and various resolutions were submitted to the meeting by the Revs. Messrs. Ballantyne, Morison, Binks, Hetherington, Mirams, Messrs. Fawkner, Little, &c. Petitions to the Legislature were agreed to be presented, and a Committee was appointed to convene a public meeting.

BALLAARAT CHINESE MISSION.—On Sunday and Monday, January 24 and 25, some interesting services were held in connection with the opening of the first place of worship built and paid for exclusively by the Chinese. The building, of wood, erected on an eminence, is 40 x 25 feet, and surmounted by a belfry. It is nicely fitted up with benches, pulpit, &c., and will bear comparison with any English place of worship. The opening services on the Sabbath afternoon were conducted in English by the Rev. J. M. Strongman, and in Chinese by the Rev. W. Young and Lo Sam Yuen. About 150 Chinese were present, and paid the most marked attention, while the English friends felt it to be a hallowed and delightful service. On Monday a public tea-meeting was held, which was well attended by the Chinese and Europeans. The place being too small and the night moonlight, the meeting was held in the open air. Members of all our Churches attended and were addressed by the Revds. Messrs. Gates, Niquet, Potter, Lane, Searle, McLauchlan, and Strongman, Messrs. Oddie, Dixon, and Booth. The Chinese listened with great attention to the speeches of the Rev. W. Young, Lo Sam Yuen, Alpheny and Ahsam, in their own language. It is gratifying to know the chapel is filled every Sunday afternoon with a Chinese audience, for whom also a school has been opened.

BALLAARAT SUNDAY SCHOOL UNION.—A Union of Teachers connected with all the Protestant Sunday schools on Ballaarat, except the Episcopalian, has been recently formed, with a view to improve existing schools and open new ones in destitute places.—It already comprises nearly one hundred members. On Tuesday, March 10th, the first of a series of lectures to Sunday School Teachers, was delivered by the Rev. J. M. Strongman, in the Wesleyan school room. Subject:—"The objects of Sabbath School Instruction."

PRESBYTERIANS.—FREE PRESBYTERIAN CHURCH, INKERMAN ROAD, ST. KILDA.—The Induction of the Rev. C. Moir (recently a missionary at Penang), to the pastoral charge of this Church took place on Friday evening, March 19th. The Rev. Dr. Cairns conducted the service, preaching an impressive Sermon, and proposing the questions which are usual on such occasions, to which assent was given by Mr. Moir On Sabbath the 31st the Rev. D. McDonald of Emerald Hill preached, in continuation of these services, and on Monday Evening the 22nd a public Soireé was held. The Meeting which was crowdedly attended was presided over by the new pastor and was addressed by the Revs. R. Fletcher, Dr. Cairns, D. McDonald, J. Harding, W. Roby Fletcher Jas. and John Ballantyne, and J. Clarke, lately arrived from Scotland. The whole series of these interesting services was concluded by the Children of the Schools assembling for Tea on Tuesday evening.

BAPTISTS.—Melbourne. On Tuesday evening, February 9th, the Victoria Auxiliary to the Baptist Missionary Society was held in Collins-street Chapel. The Hon. C. Vaughan, M.L.C., presided. Mr. Mouritz read the Report, from which it appeared that upwards of £700 had been remitted to the parent society during the year. The meeting was addressed by Messrs. Collins, Poole, Sprigg, Jackson, Mouritz, and Kerr. The Rev. J. Taylor propounded a scheme for organizing a Baptists' Union to embrace all the Australias and New Zealand, in order to raise a fund to bring out ministers, and another to build places of worship; and also to establish a Denominational Magazine. Collins-street Chapel, where the Rev. J. Taylor officiates, is undergoing an extensive enlargement in order to accommodate the increasing attendance; and while the alterations are proceeding, Mr. Taylor's congregation and that of the Rev. A. Ramsay worship together in Mr. Ramsay's commodious Church. The alterations and additions are expected to cost upwards of £3000.

The Rev. Isaac New, late of Birmingham, has recently arrived in Melbourne to take the pastoral charge of the Baptist Church, Albert-street, Collingwood, and has entered on his labors with every prospect of raising and extending that cause.

WESLEYANS.—An extensive Bazaar, for which preparations have long been making and towards which contributions has been coming in from England as well as the colonies, was held in the Exhibition Building for five or six days in succession, beginning with the 16th March. The object is to raise funds to build a Wesleyan Grammar School on a site granted by Government. The proceeds amounted, it is understood, to over £2000.

CONGREGATIONALISTS.—THE REV. THOMAS BINNEY.—Several paragraphs have been copied from English journals into colonial newspapers, respecting this distinguished Nonconformist clergyman. As some inaccuracies have occurred, we may take the opportunity of mentioning the facts of the case, and we are able to do so from personal correspondence with the reverend gentleman himself. It is known to many of his friends in the colony that he has discharged the responsible duties of pastor of the Weighhouse Chapel for nearly 30 years; in addition to which he has been actively connected with and engaged in many of the noble and philanthropic institutions of the city of London, as well as the various societies of his own religious denomination. A London minister's life, especially if he hold a popular position, is one of wear-and-tear, mentally and physically. The consequence of this, in Mr. Binney's case, has been a prostration of power, rendering him unequal to study and public ministration. Twelve months' entire cessation from all official duty was recommended by his medical attendants. The Colonial Missionary Society, established in London about 20 years ago, was first suggested by Mr. Binney; and throughout its subsequent operations he has been its warm friend and continued advocate. Directly and indirectly, this society has been instrumental in sending forth to the colonies of Australia, East and West Canada, New Brunswick, Newfoundland, Nova Scotia, &c., upwards of 150 ministers. Seeing, therefore, the deep obligation under which these (Australian) colonies especially were laid to the reverend gentlemen, it was the suggestion of a colonist (Mr. John Fairfax) when in London about 5 years ago, on taking leave of him to return to Sydney, that he should obtain leave of absence from his large church and congregation, and spend 12 months in visiting the Australian group. This suggestion was repeated by several colonists in England, when Mr. Binney's health failed, and all arrangements being satisfactorily made, on the 25th December, with Mrs. Binney, he sailed, in company with the Rev. J. L. Poore and the Rev. Mr. Reed, from Liverpool in the *Sultana* a ship of 1300 tons, and by this time should be in Melbourne. It is earnestly hoped that his strength and energies, by the long sea voyage and change of climate, will have returned to their wonted power; and that his numerous friends on this side of the Globe may again listen to his masterly discourses. But we quote his own words: "I come as an invalid, and may not be able to open my mouth in public." We have thought it best to state these facts, so that his friends on his arrival might be prepared for disappointment. It will be a happy circumstance if the sojourn here should prove beneficial. After spending a fortnight at Melbourne Mr. Binney will come on to Sydney.—*Sydney Morning Herald.*

INDEPENDENT CHAPEL, RICHMOND.—The new Chapel built on a site adjoining the old one, for the accommodation of the increasing congregation to which the Rev. J. Sunderland ministers, was opened for religious worship on Sabbath, March 7th. The Rev. W. B. Landells preached in the morning, the Rev. I. Taylor in the afternoon, and the Rev. Isaac New in the evening. The attendance was large and the prospects of the cause are highly encouraging. It is intended to hold a public meeting in connexion with this movement on the arrival of the Rev. Messrs. Binney, Bowman and Poore, who are expected daily.

OXFORD STREET INDEPENDENT CHAPEL, EAST COLLINGWOOD.—The fifth anniversary of this place was celebrated on the 16th February. About 300 persons sat down to tea. The Rev. W. B. Landells the pastor presided. Addresses were delivered by the Revs. Messrs. Lewis, Mirams, Sunderland, Robinson, Odell and Thomas; and Dr. Embling, M.L.A., J. P. Fawkner, M.L.C., and others. The balance sheet, read by Mr. Rogers, treasurer, showed the receipts for the year to have been £1100 and the expenditure £1140. It was announced that £250 had been promised towards liquidating the debt of £1000 still remaining. The Report of the proceedings of the Church and Congregation was read by Mr. Goodhugh. The increase in Church Members had been 22; the number of Sunday scholars is about 350, and teachers 24. A day school commenced in July last, and now under the National Board, numbers 250 children. A Ladies' Tract Distribution Society, and a

Young Men's Christian Association, have been originated, and are accomplishing much good. Several Members of the Church devote themselves to village preaching. The Report altogether showed the cause to be prospering greatly and enjoying many tokens of the Divine blessing.

Tasmania.

ST. JOHN SQUARE CONGREGATIONAL CHURCH, LAUNCESTON.—This church, after being much enlarged and improved, was re-opened for Divine worship on Lord's Day, February 28th, on which occasion two excellent sermons were preached by the Rev. R. Fletcher, of St. Kilda, Melbourne. The congregations were good, and much interest was excited. On the following Monday, March 1st, a social tea-meeting was held in the new school room, when nearly 300 persons were present; Thomas Fulton, Esq., of Melbourne, in the chair. From the financial report read by the pastor, the Rev. W. Law, it appeared that the entire expense of enlarging the chapel, and building a new school room and vestry, amounted to £1,200. Toward this sum, there had been raised about £750. The meeting was addressed by the Rev. R. Fletcher, Rev. M. Dowling. Rev. Jas. Lindsay, Hon. W. S. Button, M.L.C., his Worship the Mayor of Launceston, Messrs. J. G. Jennings, Aikenhead, T. Button, and Law. This cause, founded and consolidated by the valued labors, for many years, of the Rev. J. West, of Sydney, is progressing favorably under his successor. The additional accommodation provided is already nearly all occupied; the Sunday school is in a satisfactory state, and pleasing accessions are being made to the communion of the Church.

South Australia.

GAWLER.—CONGREGATIONAL CHAPEL.—Public religious services in commemoration of the sixth anniversary of this place of worship were held in November last, as follows, viz.—on Sunday, the 29th, when the Rev. C. W. Evan, B.A., of Adelaide, preached morning and evening, and on the following evening, when there was a tea-meeting in St George's school-room and a public meeting in the chapel afterwards. The services on the Sunday were attended by large and attentive audiences, and were deeply impressive. The tea was patronised by a full attendance, despite the excessive heat and dust of the day. The public meeting was likewise so largely attended that numbers were obliged to remain outside. It was presided over by Mr. Walter Duffield, M.P., and effectively addressed by the Revs. J. Ayling, J. Hannay, J. D. Mudie, T. Lloyd, S. Keen, T. W. Charlesworth, and J. Leonard; and by Messrs. W. Barker, W. Filsell, and J. Jones. Thanks were passed to the ministers present, and to the Revs. Messrs. Evan and Moir, for their services and sympathy; also to the ladies, for their liberality and exertions in providing the tea; to Mr. L. S. Burton, for the use of the school-room; and to the chairman, for so ably presiding. The proceeds of the services, which are being devoted to the construction of a fence round the chapel, and of a shed for the convenience of horses on Sundays, were over £40. It is due to Mr. Duffield to add that that gentleman has just made a handsome present of two pairs of iron gates, value £20, to be placed in the fence at the front of the chapel.

Western Australia.

EPISCOPALIAN —A portion of the diocese of Adelaide has been cut off, and constituted a separate bishopric, by the Church of England authorities at home. The first Bishop of Perth (such is the new title) is Dr. Hale, archdeacon of Adelaide, who was duly consecrated and set apart to his office at Lambeth in July last.

CONGREGATIONAL.—FREEMANTLE.—The Congregationalists of this town, finding their place of worship too small for the numbers desiring accommodation, held a public tea-meeting in October last, for the purpose of commencing an effort towards its enlargement and improvement. The meeting was held in the boys' school, which was lent for the occasion, and the provisions were gratuitously furnished by the several ladies who presided at the tea tables. About 300 persons were present, and the assembly was addressed by the Revs. Z. Barry (Episcopalian), S. Hardy (Wesleyan), and J. Johnston, the pastor. Sacred music diversified the evening's proceedings, which were of a gratifying and encouraging character. The proceeds amounted to about £20.

THE NEXT NUMBER OF THIS MAGAZINE WILL BE ISSUED ON 1ST JUNE.

Communications for Editor care of W. FAIRFAX & Co., *Melbourne.*

The Southern Spectator.

No. 6. | JUNE, 1858. | Vol. I.

MISCELLANIES.

Livingstone's "Geographical Feat."

This phrase is Livingstone's own; the sentence of which it forms part, " the end of the geographical feat is the beginning of the missionary enterprise," having almost become a proverb. In our last number we gave a few particulars of the Doctor's personal characteristics and history; in this, we purpose presenting a bird's eye and comprehensive view of what he has accomplished. Many of our readers have doubtless read the original volume, but many have not, and those that have may acquire a clearer idea of the great work done by glancing at an epitome of the whole. We shall not attempt any detail of the incidents of the journey; they are too numerous to extract and too interesting to abridge, and the work itself should be read through by all who can procure it.

Mr. Moffat, Dr. Livingstone's father-in-law, had long occupied the most advanced post to the northward in the South African Missionary field, the Kuruman Station, about 800 miles from Cape Town. Dr. Livingstone selected for his position, Kolobeng, 200 miles more to the north, and distant therefore from the Cape 1000 miles. Beyond this Europeans had not penetrated, but during his many years residence there he received various verbal descriptions, from intelligent natives, of portions of the interior regions, and made occasional excursions of more or less extent.

His first journey for the direct purpose of exploration was undertaken in company with two fellow-countrymen, Mr. Oswell and Mr. Murray, June 1849, when, after crossing with immense difficulty the Kalahari Desert, he discovered the large river Zouga, 300 miles to the northward, and the great Lake Ngami, 300 further still in a north-west direction. Here he saw rivers, and heard of others, flowing from the north and north-west into the Lake, and found a well-watered region. This was an important discovery as throwing a new light on the Geography of Central Africa. He returned to Kolobeng, having travelled over 600 miles of new country.

B

In 1850 he visited the Lake again, taking with him this time Mrs. Livingstone and their children, with the intention of occupying some advanced post as a Missionary station, if a suitable one could be found, and from thence carrying his explorations still further into the interior as opportunity might offer ; but sickness and other misfortunes compelled their return with little more result than an increased knowledge of the nature of the country, the temper of the inhabitants, and the requisites for successful travel.

Still bent upon his purpose, and aided by the experience of former journeys, Dr. Livingstone set out in the spring of 1851, in company once more with his old friend Mr. Oswell, to prosecute his researches. He followed his former track till he struck the Zouga again, when, instead of descending that stream westward to the Lake, he crossed it and pursued a northward and north-westward course. He at length was rewarded by the discovery of a large river called the Chobe, which he found flowing to the eastward, being about 300 miles further in the interior than he had previously penetrated. Down this noble river he sailed till he reached Linyanti, a native town and a sort of capital of a large region, where he was enthusiastically received by the chief and people. From this point he descended the Chobe still further till he reached its junction with the Great Zambesi, the grand artery of this part of Africa. Here a new world opened to his view, a flood of light was thrown upon the nature of the country, and a multitude of fresh questions pressed upon him for solution. He had not yet found a salubrious spot fit for a missionary station, the districts he had passed through being infected with malaria. Partly excited by missionary zeal to supply this desideratum, and partly inflamed with the spirit of discovery which his very success had enkindled, he resolved to trace the course of this grand river, to see whence it came and whither it went, to ascertain the nature of the country through which it made its way, and the character of the people dwelling on its banks. But a journey of such magnitude would require some two or three years to accomplish, and necessitate vast and careful preparation. He determined therefore to return to Kolobeng, and thence to take Mrs. Livingstone and family to the Cape and ship them off to England, that they might be safe among their friends while he addressed himself to his arduous enterprise. All this he promptly carried into execution.

It was on the 8th of June, 1852, that Dr. Livingstone left the Cape on this his memorable and chief exploratory journey. On reaching Kolobeng he found his station had been plundered and reduced to ruins by the Dutch Boers, who were hostile to all his measures for elevating the native races. Nothing daunted by this cruel disaster, he proceeded with the oxen he had procured at the Cape, and such equipments as experience had taught him to be neceesary, in company with a chosen band of natives, but

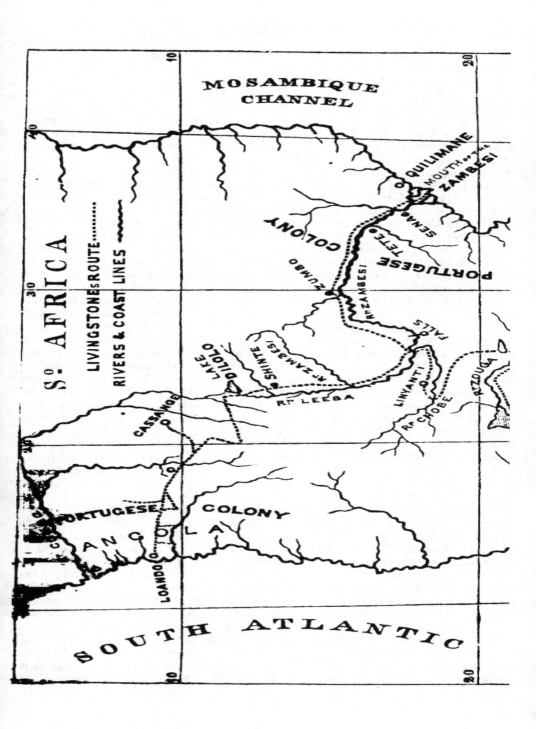

without a single European companion. His first point was Linyanti, where as we have seen he had twice been before, the seat of Sekeletu, the powerful chief who had manifested great interest in his proceedings. He varied his route to avoid the fly tzetze) so fatal to domestic cattle, and met with obstructions rom the flooded state of the country enough to have appalled any heart but his. The friendly chief entered warmly into his plans, and rendered him most valuable assistance in carrying them out, especially by furnishing him with a trusty band of men to accompany him all the way (Dr. Livingstone's own men returning to Kolobeng), and by giving him favorable commendations to the tribes beyond.

It was not till the end of July, 1853, that all things were ready for the final start into countries never before traversed by Europeans, and known but for a very short distance to his African companions themselves. His general object in this journey was to reach Loanda, in the Portuguese settlement of Angola on the west coast. He embarked on board a canoe with thirty able rowers, in the sight of the king and a vast concourse of his people. For a short distance they had the stream in their favor till the Chobe entered the Zambesi, and then, reversing their course, they had to make their way up that powerful river. They proceeded in this way as long as the navigation would permit, but at length rapids and shallow water compelled them to take to their bullocks and the river banks. They found the Zambesi a right noble stream, often a mile broad, and abounding with marine animals and aquatic birds, and the country bordering it covered with a profuse vegetation and occupied with incredible quantities of game, including elephants, lions, camel leopards, zebras, and antelopes. The influence of Sekeletu extending far up the river, the travellers met with every assistance in the supply of food and other helps from the petty chiefs on their way. About lat. 14, long. 23, finding the Zambesi coming from the east north-east, which lay out of their course, they left it and ascended a large tributary, the Leeba, in the direction of Angola. About a 100 miles up this river they abandoned it and prosecuted their journey by land, the route being shorter and easier, for another 150 miles, till they reached a lake called Dilolo, which proved to be the water-shed of this central river system. On the eastern side of this lake they met the waters coming down to feed the river they had ascended, on the western side they found them flowing out in the opposite direction and supplying the rivers running to the west coast. They were now, in fact, upon one of the feeders of the Casai river, which is itself in all probability one of the tributaries of the Congo or Zaire, well known on the western coast of Africa. In proceeding north-west to Cassenge they crossed numerous rivers, and then came to the great Congo itself, flowing through a grand valley, 100 miles wide, and bounded by mountain ranges of considerable elevation. They had long passed beyond the limit of Sekeletu's influence, and had had considerable trouble from the covetousness and suspicion of the strange tribes through whose territories their route lay, especially those bordering upon the Portuguese colony of Angola. Here the slave-trade carried on by the Portuguese had debased and corrupted the people. Their rapacity and selfishness were such that Dr. Livingstone had to part with everything he possessed to procure the barest means of subsistence, and he and his party were more than once in great peril of their lives. As soon as he entered the Portuguese colony his troubles of this kind were over; he met with the kindest possible reception from the Portuguese, and had his wants generously supplied. After being refreshed he pursued his way westward for 300 miles farther, until at last he reached the city of Loanda on the coast, on the 31st May, 1854, having been ten months in performing the journey from the time he parted from Sekeletu near Linyanti. It is scarcely possible to exaggerate the difficulties of this celebrated journey. Dr. Livingstone had travelled through flooded and swampy grounds a great part of the way, not being dry for weeks together night or day, constantly exposed to pestilential malaria, suffering at times from dysentery so severely that he could not retain his seat on his ox for more than ten minutes together, and having to endure upwards of thirty attacks of intermitent fever. He had been compelled to subsist for a considerable time on the most miserable diet, short in quantity and innutricious in quality. How he lived through all this seems a miracle. When he arrived at Loanda he was nearly dead, and owed, under God, the preservation of his life and his restoration to health to the devoted attention and careful nursing of Mr. Gabriel, the only Englishman in the city. The kindness of this gentleman was unbounded, and left an indelible impression on the grateful heart of Dr. Livingstone.

Here the traveller had the satisfaction of receiving letters from his friends both at the Cape and in England, and had a tempting opportunity of finishing his labors and visiting his native country, where his family were residing. But he was restrained from yielding to this inducement, first, by a point of Christian honor; he had promised to convey the faithful companions of his journey back to their own country, and he could not break his word; and, secondly, by the consideration that he had not in this journey yet found the great object of his search, a healthy eligible spot for a missionary station. He therefore resolved to retrace his steps to Linyanti, and thence to proceed eastward, so as to complete his investigations across the entire continent. His companions were amazingly impressed and delighted with what they saw and heard of the wonders of civilization in the city of Loanda, and were sent away laden with presents.

After a stay of about three months at Loanda, our traveller set out on September 20th, 1854, on his return journey. He lingered awhile in the colony of Angola, visiting various spots to take astronomical observations and fix uncertain positions; and then entered upon his old track, varying it occasionally when he had some special purpose to answer. The rainy season was now over; the country was not so pestiferous; he was better furnished with provisions and necessaries, and consequently enjoyed better health and more comfort. He had also an opportunity of correcting his former observations, and increasing the extent and accuracy of his knowledge of the country. He nevertheless had to encounter various hazards and adventures. After a journey of eleven months, at the end of August, 1855, he safely reached Linyanti. Great was the joy of Sekeletu and his people on the return, without a single death, of the travellers whom they had long ago given up for lost, and deep was the veneration they felt for the missionary who had performed so marvellous an exploit. It may readily be supposed that the Makololo men had wonderful tales to tell to their countrymen of all the strange things they had seen and heard, especially in the white man's country. Among other things, they stated that (having reached the sea) they had been to the end of the world.

Dr. Livingstone had now explored the continent of Africa from his station at Kolobeng to the western coast. But, as he had not discovered a salubrious locality whereon to settle as a missionary, so neither had he found what he ardently desired— a practical outlet for the teeming productions of this most fertile region. His project therefore of proceeding to the eastward in search of these two desiderata he determined at once to carry into effect. His plan was a simple one, to follow the Zambesi down to its discharge into the ocean, leaving the river occasionally, when by so doing the way might be shortened or made easier. There was no lack of volunteers to accompany him. The travels of his former companions had too much distinguished them among their countrymen not to have inflamed the ambition of multitudes to emulate their example.

After a rest of two months at Linyanti, two hundred natives being selected as companions and all preparations completed, Dr. Livingstone commenced his journey eastward, Nov. 3, 1855. He followed the course of the Zambesi till he arrived at some extraordinary Falls, of which he had heard a great deal, and which he named the Victoria Falls, a natural phenomenon nearly as wonderful as, and in some respects more remarkable than, the Falls of Niagara. Finding the passage down the river suddenly broken off, he cut across the country in a direction nearly parallel to its supposed course, for three hundred miles, till he struck the river Lafue; and then, following it, soon came to the Zambesi again. He took the northern shore, proceeding by the margin of the noble river. He found it flowing between two ranges of high hills, and not bounded by swampy flooded land as in the west. The whole aspect of the country was different.

Extensive tracts of arable and pasture land of the best description, on the slopes of the hills and in the vales, were discovered. Here were a good soil, plenty of rain, no floods, no malaria, the very region he had been in search of. Cheered with this discovery, he pushed on to Tete, the most inland of the Portuguese settlements on the east coast of Africa, which place he reached March 2, 1856. Though he had enjoyed much better health in passing through this salubrious district than in his western travels, yet he suffered greatly both from fatigue and from privation, arising, as on the other side of the continent, from the extortion of those natives who had become selfish and corrupted by contact with European slave-traders. At Tete he met with great kindness from Major Sicard, the Portuguese Governor; and after recruiting himself there, and waiting till the healthy season for descending the Zambesi through its swampy delta arrived, he at length reached Quilimane, on the coast of Mozambique, on the 26th May, 1856, thus successfully completing his grand exploratory journey across the whole continent of Africa. Here he found Her Majesty's ship of war the *Frolic* waiting his arrival to convey him to the Mauritius ; and thence he travelled by steamer up the Red Sea and across Egypt to England, which he safely reached, December 12th, 1856, to the joy not only of his friends but of the nation at large.

Dr. Livingstone thus traversed the western half of the continent twice, and the eastern portion once, crossing from sea to sea, travelling over some 4,000 miles of new country, and not less than 10,000 miles altogether, partly by canoes, partly on foot, but chiefly on ox-back. His volume must be read to become acquainted with all the interesting incidents he met with in so long a journey, all the perils he encountered, the privations he endured, the patience he manifested, the resolution, courage, perseverance, and intuitive tact with which he met every emergency, and above all, the admirable Christian spirit (so becoming a missionary of the Cross) which he ever breathed. Not that these qualities are paraded by him, for he says nothing in his own praise, but the circumstances force them on the reader's notice in spite of the writer's modesty. The book must be read too to become acquainted with the vast mass of information the traveller collected on subjects relating to the zoology, botany, geology, and ethnology of the country. His watchful eye never slumbered ; nothing seemed to escape his keen observation, which is the more wonderful as his frequent prostration from fever might have been held a sufficient excuse for ceasing to notice or record. It is perfectly marvellous how he managed in such circumstances to take his 2,812 astronomical observations, which the Astronomer Royal of Cape Town has lauded for their reliable accuracy and extreme value in fixing the chief points in the whole of his route.

And what are the practical results? They are not unimportant to Science. The discoveries of Dr. Livingstone have solved a great geographical problem, as to the formation of the continent of South Africa. The space between the Tropic of Capricorn and the Line, 23½ degrees of latitude, has been till now a blank upon our maps, or has only here and there been occupied with an imaginary line or name. Some conjectures made this *terra incognita* a vast barren desert like the Zahara of North Africa; others, a mass of lofty snow-clad mountains like the centres of Asia and America. Both are proved to have been wrong; for it is found to be a vast valley abounding in lakes and rivers. The primitive granite elevations, instead of being in the heart of the country, as they are in Britain, South America, Asia, and elsewhere, with rivers flowing down either side to the ocean, are, as in the case of Ireland, near the coasts forming a kind of frame work, inclosing a central portion of country comparatively depressed. The section of the country furnished by Dr. Livingstone (partly conjectural) shows the cropping out of primitive rocks similar in kind near the two opposite coasts, and the intervening space filled up with later formations on a lower level. The water-shed where the rivers diverge to the west and the east, is not a mountain ridge, as in the Alps, but a lake, the lake Dilolo (s. lat. 12½°, w. long. 22½°), which presents the singular phenomenon of discharging its waters in two opposite directions, and being the fountain head of the eastern and western river systems. Sir Roderick Murchison, president of the Royal Geographical Society, had, from the data furnished him, in a great measure by Livingstone himself, conjectured this to be the character of the continent, and had published his opinion to the world three years before the Doctor knew of it; but it remained for the traveller not only to form a similar independent theory of the country, but also to verify it by actual discovery and observation. This is not the solution of a mere curious point in physical geography, but one fertile in useful results; for the enormous valley, stretching between the two border ridges, is fed with copious rains, abounds in noble rivers and rich alluvial soils, is covered with a profuse vegetation, and teems with animal life; and being placed under a tropical sun, its capabilities of produce are beyond calculation. Its river system gives it a ready means of communication between place and place throughout its entire extent, and, on its eastern side in particular, there is easy access to it from the ocean. This region is everywhere occupied by inhabitants. Their number per square mile is of course very much smaller than in civilised countries; but the aggregate is immense. They are mostly of the negro stamp, though with great varieties as to the depth of their hue and the contour of their countenances.

The bearing of these discoveries upon commerce and the slave trade is deemed by Dr. Livingstone to be very important, and this conviction has powerfully stimulated him to persevere in making them. In this region, cotton, indigo, coffee, sugar, and rice may be grown to any required extent. Slavery and the slave-trade are little known in the interior, but they are a fearful curse in the countries on the sea-board, where Europeans have located themselves, and have stimulated the native tribes to steal and sell each other for the sake of the European goods they receive in exchange. According to Dr. Livingstone's observation, the people have no particular liking to this work of kidnapping, but would much rather engage in lawful commerce to supply their wants and gratify their tastes. It is on this favorable tendency of their character that he builds his hopes of supplanting the internal slave traffic by legitimate trade. If the natives can be furnished with a market for the produce of their rich country, and can get a fair return for it, he believes they would willingly give up selling their fellow creatures; and probably the example, when once set, would be followed by the tribes to the northward, and along the western coast towards Guinea. This would be applying the axe to the root of the tree, and accomplishing the very object contemplated by the splendid but abortive "Niger Expedition."

But higher and nobler aims even than these inflamed the zeal and stimulated the perseverance of Dr. Livingstone. He went forth as a Christian missionary. Dissatisfied with his position at Kololeng, partly from its extreme aridity and consequent uncertain productiveness, and partly from its proximity to the hostile Boers, he sought a more suitable spot where he might carry on his operations for the benefit of the native tribes undisturbed; and when he found the centre of the country filled in all directions with inhabitants, and (like the vale of Sodom before its overthrow) as the garden of the Lord, well watered everywhere, he properly considered this a new and inviting field for missionary enterprise. But rain and heat and profuse vegetation breed pestilential fevers, as poor Dr. Livingstone found to his cost, and it would be the height of imprudence to fix a missionary station in the midst of conditions so sure to be fatal to European life, if a healthy place could be found. His first journey to the west was, as we have seen, unsuccessful in discovering what he so much wanted, but his journey eastward has accomplished all he desired. In the extensive elevated lands through which the Zambesi flows on to the coast, lying between the 29th and 33rd meridians, lie localities perfectly and in every respect adapted to his purpose. And the man of God deems this the most valuable of all his discoveries. Somewhere in this region it is contemplated to found a Mission Station, which may prove a centre and a source of Christian, philanthropic, and civilizing influences to all the region round about.

Dr. Livingstone has sailed again for his field of research. A government subsidy and a government appointment, together with a staff of well-qualified coadjutors, will aid him in more minute and accurate investigations. Nor will the London Missionary Society be behindhand in taking advantage of these magnificent openings to prosecute its benevolent objects. The liberality of the public has placed at its disposal a considerable sum of money, with which it will be enabled to fulfil Dr. Livingstone's wish to establish Mission Stations in such localities as he may select.

It is gratifying to see the high appreciation of Dr. Livingstone's labors and successes manifested by the public. All party and sectarian feeling has been laid aside in his ovations. In Cape Town, the governor, the chief members of the legislature, the Astronomer Royal, a Church of England bishop, and men of all sects and parties, in public meeting assembled, did honor to his genius and perseverance. In Britain, he has been *fêted* almost to satiety. The Royal Geographical Society, with its large-hearted and noble president, Sir R. Murchison, has heaped such honors and attentions upon him as it never did on any other individual. Even Oxford and Cambridge forgot that he was a dissenter, receiving him with acclamations and rewarding him with university degrees. His native Scotland has conferred upon him the freedom of its most important cities. And all this has been borne with a meekness, modesty, and humility, which have won all hearts, and which appear, in the circumstances, as wonderful as his sagacity, attainments, self-sacrifice, and indomitable perseverance.

The Congregational Year Book and Chapel Architecture.

Before us lies the Congregational Year Book for 1858. To say one word in praise of its cheapness, completeness, and value, is needless; no gentleman's library in the Australias, who is connected with the Congregational body, can be deemed complete without it. We give a right hearty welcome to the Year Book, affording, as it does, the year's history of the Congregational body, and bridging over the distance between our present abode and many a well-remembered spot in the land that is now far away. The list of ministerial changes and settlements is fraught with lessons of instruction as to the movements of One who is ever concerned in the " perfecting of the saints, the work of the ministry, and the edifying of the body of Christ." The ministerial Obituary shows that many whose names were once familiar as household words have gone the way of all flesh. Being dead, they yet speak by their blessed memories, their pious examples, and their eloquent books. Varied were their talents, different their dispositions, unequal their attainments, diverse their labors and achievements, yet all were serving the same Master, inspired by the same motives, and contributing with varied success to the same grand and glorious result. Such records remind us of the fleeting character of our own life, and enforce afresh the ever solemn and abiding admonition—" Whatsoever thy hand findeth to do, do it with thy might." The usual literary register contains some names as yet unknown to fame ; of some of them we shall hear again, however, at a future day. The engravings of new chapels are striking and suggestive ; a fresh feature is observable in the introduction of three Australian chapels, which we hope will not be the last nor long the best. One can imagine, but not adequately describe, the surprise of a stern old puritan of the nonconformist era, on revisiting the land of his children and observing the change in the construction of the meeting houses. Would he be grieved at the degeneracy of his religious descendants in these later days, " shrinking from the simplicity of the puritanic sanctuary, and trying to rival the architectural extravagance of a system which derives its funds from the national wealth ?" Undoubtedly all extravagance and foolish rivalry would be condemned by those men of stern materials and simple make, but not the improvement of our sanctuaries in a ratio consistent with the improved taste and circumstances of the present generation. Their occasionally expressed dislike of some of the architectural glories of England, was owing to the association of those edifices with a dominant and persecuting hierarchy—the preachers in them had strenuously upheld the " divine right of kings to govern wrong," and denounced all freedom of thought as an insult to God and the king. Clerical intolerance and adverse political views, not vandalism or envy, were the moving causes of their contempt for the places where such views and actions were proclaimed and defended. The proverbial plainness of their own places of worship is easily accounted for when their poverty and persecutions are remembered, and the jealousies which imposing structures would have awakened. With the times and the men the necessity for mean structures passed away ; a gradual improvement has since taken place, especially within the last few years ; and some of the specimens given in the Year Book are all that the most fastidious in church architecture could possibly desire. We are aware that a rapidly diminishing class protest against the great cost of such structures ; but where they are opened free from debt, who shall deny the subscribers the pleasant propriety of having a temple for worship corresponding to their improved habitations and circumstances ? If it be said that the money expended upon one such chapel would suffice to build a dozen respectable sanctuaries in destitute districts, our reply is that the statement itself is probably true, while the principle in its entirety would forbid Christian people to enlarge and beautify their habitations, or add to their elegancies and comforts while there is a child of want within the reach of their benevolence ; and who shall draw for us the line of distinction between necessaries and luxuries ? or say how far a resulting, and to a great extent indiscriminate charity would prove a blessing?   Besides, the fact must not be overlooked, to gainsay it we deem impossible, that in some of the larger towns and cities to collect new congregations or increase old ones in antiquated chapels, offensive in their " brick and mortar ugliness," is a difficult and, humanly speaking, an impossible task.   A graceful and well-built chapel will attract an audience, when a building seemingly at studious variance with good taste and acoustics will deter or repel.   We know no just reason why the science of chapel building should lag behind all modern improvements ; and while beauty is combined with utility even in factories and steamships, we should still be doomed to servile copies of worn-out buildings, with their gable ends and pigeon cotes where one could keep watch over the narrow entry, and their straight highbacked pews, in which without observation our forefathers could sleep during the sermon measured by the triple hour-glass.   As well plead against organs on the ground that in former days men were accustomed in religious worship " to play with a loud noise, more or less skilfully, upon the flute, the serpent, and the bassoon."

Surely there is a limit to mere utilitarianism, and the just one is to combine it with beauty, as God has done in all the works of his hands.   It will not do to condemn æsthetical beauty in a world like this, with its landscapes and flowers, and with the glorious stars above us, and with natures so constituted that " we rarely rise to the beauty that thrills the spirit, except through the beauty that strikes the sense."   The love of the beautiful is one of our purest instincts, and for which God has provided abundant and ever-varying gratification.   Nina's logic about the roses and flowers we deem much better than the corrections of her sober aunt : " We might have been so formed as to fulfil all the material functions of our present existence unheeded and unsoothed by the faintest glimpse of visible beauty and grace.   We might have all been like the utilitarian, who could see in Niagara, or Terni, but so much water power for the turning of a factory."   It is no valid objection to adduce instances of perversion or abuse— of false taste—straining after effect.   Such things we confess and deplore.   But let us not forget that, with beauty as with the world, there is use as distinguished from abuse ; and why can we not use aright this beautiful world, with all there is in it of grace and goodness, so as to link our destiny with that of " the new heavens and the new earth, wherein dwelleth righteousness?"

So far as we can judge, the testimony of scripture is altogether in favor of the general principle of offering to God our best endeavours, and of special intimations of the application of this principle to places built for Divine inhabitation and worship.   The tabernacle, even in the wilderness, was built of the most costly materials, by workmen of great skill, qualified and instructed by God himself.   The temple built by Solomon was in part composed of wood and stones of a rare and costly character ; silver and gold were lavished in the choicest forms of ornamentation; cunning workmen were obtained from foreign lands, and all the skill of Israel was employed in the construction of this glorious temple. Concerning future events, the prophet predicts "the glory of Lebanon shall come unto thee, the fir tree, the pine tree, and the box together, to beautify the place of my sanctuary; and I will make the place of my feet glorious." Now if it can be shown that moral beauty is the essence of the prediction, it would still be manifest that moral beauty is associated with and often shadowed forth by material splendour. We disavow all sympathy with the spirit of what will simply do, when wealth and prosperity give an opportunity of showing what can be done; when love and gratitude prompt, and when God is to have the glory. With all humility, we venture to utter our emphatic protest against the divorcement of religion and beauty—what God hath joined together let not man put asunder. We shall venture to hope and ask that our Australian chapel builders will emulate the noble example set by many at home; and, as soon as possible, dispense with their weather-board structures, keeping at the same time out of the company of the man with one idea about chapel building.

We observe that most of the new buildings are designated congregational *churches*. We were once averse to this change but subsequent reflection has led us to regard it as an improvement upon the old nomenclature. *Chapel* is pre-eminently a papistic and middle-age term, signifying "a building adjoining to a church, as a parcel of the same;" or separate, "a chapel of ease," a mere diminutive either way. Its third and more modern sense is, "the staff of men employed in their associate capacity in a printing office," a meaning acquired from well-known historical facts. Moreover, the term has come to signify, in the ears of many unreasoning and ignorant people, "a place where persons meet for worship after a fashion of their own—neither pious nor wise." By the mere association of such ideas with the word much harm is done both to themselves and the attendants at such places. The term church is well understood in ordinary speech to designate a building where Christians meet for worship. It is, we confess, an accommodation of the term; but one so obvious, so general, and so strikingly analogous to other cases, that no danger can arise of its setting aside the just and original application of the word. Indeed, our readings in the ancient ecclesiastical history of Britain and Ireland, lead us to the belief that the term from its first application to Christianity in colloquial usage was ever employed in this twofold sense. Long before the British and Irish churches acknowledged the authority of Rome, it is so applied. The pages of our earliest church historians supply many examples. Of course no one needs to be told that the English term "church" is not the New Testament word to designate "a congregation of faithful men;" it is itself an accommodation.* The term "kirk" is doubtless the same word as "church" in a varied orthography, both coming from κυριακός, itself a derivative from κύριος (lord) one of the titles of the Lord Jesus. The twofold use of the word "kirk" in Scotland, to denote the congregation or church, and the place of assembly, is well known, and prevails as generally as the word "church" in the southern portion of Britain in the same senses. To designate then our religious edifices as "churches" we deem far more ancient, honorable, and protestant, than "chapels,"—it points directly to the glorious owner, and denotes them as the Lord's property. At the same time we have no serious objection to the use of "chapel" by those who love it from long use and pious associations; only let us be charitable and not deem the use of the more ancient and fitting term "church" to be a deviation from congregational principles. These, in the estimation of their advocates, are too true and holy to be put in jeopardy by a building with a steeple and stained glass windows, called a congregational church.

We have simply to say in conclusion, that the Year Book gives all attainable information respecting Congregationalism in the British Empire; and in looking over the lists of Congregational ministers in the different Australian colonies, the pride of place must be given to South Australia, for the number of its ministers as compared with the population.

Fault Finding.

There are none of us perfect. We all have our faults, and have plenty of room to mend. If any should try to improve us, which would be the best way to succeed? To do nothing but pick out our faults and always blame us, or, sometimes, to glance kindly at our little excellencies and endeavors to do our duty, and speak a word of commendation and encouragement?

A gentleman received a letter from a friend in England, requesting him to visit a youth who had taken to the sea, when his ship should come into port. The lad duly sent a note to announce his arrival. The gentleman went on board, saw the youth, and found he was doing well; he liked his ship, was satis-

* The New Testament term for church is Ἐκκλησία. If we had to begin de novo we might adopt that term. This is the plan adopted in many modern versions of the Bible, while the phrase to designate the building, is in those languages, "the house of God," "the sacred house," or "the house of assembly." We however employ the word ecclesia not to designate the church but its outworks; hence the phrases "ecclesiastical arrangements," "ecclesiastical purposes," &c.

fied with the officers, and did not repent his choice of a seafaring life. The captain was ashore, but the visitor seeing the mate at hand, inquired how the youth was going on. "Oh!" said he, "he is a very fair lad; he is doing very well, and gives entire satisfaction." "I am truly glad to hear it" rejoined the inquirer, "it will be a comfort to his good father to know that, and I shall take care to write him word." The youth being near, the gentleman went up to him and told him for his encouragement, what a good character his superior had given him, "Don't tell him that," cried out the mate, who overheard the remark, "it will make him conceited; I never praise the apprentices." "I suppose you tell him his faults though?" "Oh, yes" said the mate, "I take good care of that whenever I see any, which isn't often." "That's not fair," said the gentleman, "find fault with him when he does ill, but commend and encourage him when he does well."

This mate is not the only one who acts upon this fault-finding principle. He is the type of a class. Are there not some families where the reins of authority are drawn tight, and the regime is uniformly austere? where the keen eye sees every little defect, and the sharp tongue severely blames it, but where scarce a word of commendation is ever let fall? Displeasure is quickly shown, but satisfaction is studiously concealed. The young folks who may be trying hard to please their seniors, never have the comfort of knowing, from word or look, whether their endeavors are successful or not.

Does not the reign of terror prevail in many a school? Is not the master a stern despot, who rigorously punishes every infraction of his laws, but who never rewards their faithful observance, not even by an approving look? His face is so used to pucker itself up into a frown of displeasure, that it knows not how to relax into a smile of satisfaction. The consequence is, the school is dreaded, not loved; the bold are hardened and the timid discouraged; and those that would aim at improvement, seeing their effort is not observed or appreciated, give it up in despair.

Are men in business apt to speak a word of encouragement to the youths in their establishments, their apprentices, clerks, and salesmen? Some no doubt do, but is not this the exception to the rule? Is not the omission, the mistake, the failure quickly noticed and sharply reprimanded; but where is the sign of pleasure and satisfaction at the punctuality, the diligence, the integrity, the skill, the success, the endeavor to please, which a candid eye might easily discern in the young man's general deportment? Perhaps a kindly word is never spoken, an approving glance is never given by the head of the establishment; and the anxious youth can never tell what value is put upon his services, and is never stimulated to further improvement by any thing in the shape of encouragement.

Nor is this fault-finding confined to the domain of secular and social life. Do not some ministers of religion pride themselves in what they call their "faithfulness," a sort of reformer-like sternness in denouncing errors and follies, and pointing out faults, always dealing out censures and rebukes, and acquiring for themselves the reputation of being first-rate scolds? Is such a minister likely to attract or repel, to produce pleasure and edification, or resentment and disgust? Are there not private Christians who feel themselves called upon to be Catos among their brethren, as if they were specially invested with the office of censor; who make it their main business to pick out defects and administer rebukes, and who discharge their function in a tone and manner which shows how they relish their work? It is impossible to say how much these worthy men exasperate the evils they profess to be anxious to remove. Nay, do not some congregations treat their ministers in a similar spirit? There may be good abilities, blameless character, sound doctrine, edifying preaching, entire devotedness to the work—in short, the main requisites of an effective ministry; but if all the minute details of personal attention, according to the standard of expectation that may happen to be set up, be not paid, all the rest goes for nothing; the good is forgotten, the defects alone are seen; and the pastor's anxious heart is seldom cheered by a word of encouragement, but often depressed by murmurs of complaint.

Now, that the administration of rebuke is a duty, no one will deny. Faults should be observed, and reproof faithfully given by the proper persons, at the proper time, and in the proper manner. But it requires no small measure of prudence, and skill, and meekness, to meet these conditions. The object of the reprover should be, not the gratification of a censorious disposition, but the cure of the evil; and the question is, whether the perpetual dwelling upon the faulty side of a man's character, does not tend to make matters worse, by producing sourness of spirit and an indisposition to profit by hints so officiously given?

As human nature is constituted, a little commendation is found to be a more powerful stimulus to excellence than everlasting fault-finding. We are cheered on by approval more effectually than urged on by censure. A kindly notice of a little that is good and hopeful is likely to make it grow; a sullen rebuke for a failing is not sure to uproot it. The genial warmth of commendation, where the character in the main is worthy of it, will act as the sun upon the flowers, stimulate their growth and exhale their fragrance; the selecting of a single defect from a number of virtues and dwelling on it alone in frowning rebuke, will be felt as a chilling frost of discouragement on all attempts at self-improvement. It is said that the late Rev. R. Knill, who was so extensively useful in England, in promoting the revival of religion, always looked out for what was hopeful in every person, every minister, and every congregation he came in contact with as a monitor, and generally found something of the kind, and then dwelt upon and encouraged this germ of good; and that in this very much lay the mighty power of his great success.   Let us go and do likewise.

Thoughts for Thinkers.

"Wise men lay up knowledge."* Such is the description of wise men by one of themselves. A miser is a man who adds house to house, and land to land ; who believes competence to be three hundred pounds a year more than he ever possesses. So wise men lay up knowledge, little by little ; a process of ant-hill accretion. The acquisitions of to-day will be pressed into the service of to-morrow, to lengthen the ladder or the sounding line.

1. Consider the conduct which characterises wise men, " they lay up knowledge." Such men are called wise in a relative and comparative sense, as compared with their former childish period of ignorance ; as compared with other men. By the term knowledge we understand wisdom, in its widest and most comprehensive sense. A distinction has been drawn between wisdom and knowledge. Philosophers, such as Bacon and Whately, define wisdom as " the employment of the best means to accomplish the best ends ;" or again, as " the ready perception of analogies." They include in it virtue ; while knowledge consists merely in a comprehensive acquaintance with events and causes. Divines distinguish between them ; knowledge is with them a clear conception of scripture facts and doctrines, wisdom their proper and judicious application. Poets do the same ; one sings :—

> " Knowledge and wisdom, far from being one,
> Have oft times no connection ;
> Knowledge dwells in heads replete with thoughts of other men,
> Wisdom in minds attentive to their own."

In scripture, however, as in popular speech, the terms are generally used in a synonymous sense ; " the beginning of wisdom is the fear of the Lord, and the knowledge of the Holy is understanding." Men who are thus wise, seek to lay up knowledge.

The knowledge that cometh from above ; such knowledge as God has been pleased to give of himself. In the Bible God reveals himself ; Jesus Christ is his accredited representative. Knowledge concerning ourselves, our nature, duties, dangers, responsibilities, way of our redemption, final destiny. Wise men become acquainted with these things by reading, hearing, meditation, faith and prayer ; and lay them up as true, important, practical and consoling.

There is the knowledge which relates to our fellow-men, and wise men

---

* Proverbs x. 14.

B

lay it up. Men are a very instructive series of picture books, deserving careful study. Those around us may be studied in their variety, their individual excellencies and weaknesses; that they never settle controverted points by disputing about them. Not only the living but the dead. History unfolds her ample page, and her lessons are manifold. The sum of human happiness is very much the same in all ages and countries, by the sure operation of self-acting laws. All forms of government, unless carefully worked and watched, have a tendency to become despotic. Great hazards of various kinds attend all Revolutions. Religious intolerance is the evil genius of most churches. All men are sinful. Wise men thus seek to eliminate the philosophy of history, and lay up knowledge.

Wise men seek to lay up knowledge of the world around them. "Through desire a man having separated himself, seeketh and intermeddleth with all wisdom." Solomon was such a man, he spoke of the cedar of Lebanon, and of the hyssop that groweth out of the wall. The works of the Lord are great, and are still sought out of all them that have pleasure therein. There is Geology, with its books of rocks, written long ago; Chemistry with its quantities and qualities striking insights into nature's mighty forces; Botany with its lessons of beauty and love; Zoology with its types, gradations, and wonderful mechanical appliances; Astronomy with its glories and foreshadows, its connections and contrasts. Wise men seek to acquire knowledge of these things, and lay it up to teach them obedience and adoration.

2. The manner in which the duty is discharged. Wise men do not act without rules; they employ wise methods to obtain the best ends. They seek knowledge and lay it up,—*With diligence.* Wisdom must be wooed and won. We are to search for her, as for hid treasure. Just as the miner when he has reason to believe that there is gold beneath the surface digs patiently, so must the wise man. Treasures of knowledge, can only be had by seeking. There is no royal road to knowledge. Much study is a weariness to the flesh—weary eyes, aching head, throbbing brain, and the want of that sweet restorer which the labouring man enjoys, whether he eat little or much. Yet even then knowledge is cheaply bought.—*With caution.* There are many counterfeits; we must prove all things, and hold fast that which is good. There is tinsel, there is gold, chaff and wheat, the true and false, fancies and facts. Every falsehood is either inconsistent with itself or something else, sometimes both. The falsehood about Christ's resurrection is inconsistent with itself. If the watch really slept, they could not know that the disciples stole him away. Further, it is inconsistent with the fact of Christ's living appearance. The implied falsehood was that he was stolen away *dead*, yet he was seen of many and gave them infallible proofs of his living personality.

"Believe not every spirit," is a command wise men obey, knowing that many false spirits of plausible speech and appearance are gone abroad into the world.—*With earnest prayer.* " If any man lack wisdom let him ask of God, who giveth to all men liberally and upbraideth not." God is the teacher who can teach to profit. His knowledge is infinite, embracing the past, present, and future, incapable of addition or decrease; hence he is the Only Wise God. Happy those who are wise enough to feel their own ignorance, and the feebleness of their powers, and who seek to have their knowledge increased, purified, and perpetuated by fellowship with God.

3. The great uses to which wise men apply their knowledge. However extensive a wise man's knowledge, he always regards it as a means to an end. It has its own pleasures and uses, in seeking and possessing, but it is material for the will and conscience to apply and shape it into earnest action.

Wise men use their knowledge to acquaint themselves with God. A man may know God as the eternal One, the Creator of all, and the God whose tender providential mercies are over all his works. But he must make further acquaintance with God, as delighting in pardoning mercy, before he can be at peace with him. " This is life eternal to know thee the only true God, and Jesus Christ whom thou hast sent." Fearful is the condition of those who perish for lack of knowledge; still worse the doom of those who say to God, " depart from us, for we desire not the knowledge of thy ways;" and worst of all the fate of those who knowing not the day of their merciful visitation, find the throne of mercy eventually to be hidden from their eyes.—*To purify their characters.* Knowledge and goodness should ever advance with equal steps; we must grow in grace and in the knowledge of our Lord Jesus Christ. It is a fearful thing to gaze upon a born idiot, whose body has ever been a living grave for his spirit. Worse still, is the sight of a man of once noble intellect like Southey, with the mind's powers enfeebled; yet sadder still is the sight of a man whose powers of mind are clear and vigorous, yet with a heart destitute of piety. Such a man is a mystery and a grief. To have all knowledge without love, prompting to cheerful, universal, constant obedience, is but an aggravation of our guilt. —*To benefit others.* We are to have compassion upon the ignorant, and upon those out of the way of wisdom and peace. A wise man is only a steward, and as he hath received the gift so he must minister. Freely he hath received from God, freely he must give to his fellow men. It is the way to confirm and increase his own knowledge. He that watereth others shall be watered himself. He shall also, if wise to win souls to righteousness, have a still better reward. He shall shine as the stars for brightness, in the kingdom which is for ever and ever. We must not excuse ourselves on the ground of humble gifts or slender attainments. The servant with one talent is not to hide his Lord's money, not to bury it in indolence, or destroy its power, by a false humility. The rule is, as he hath received so let him minister.

Let us then seek to lay up knowledge. Search for real wisdom with the true fervor of a student spirit ; obey all her precepts with childlike docility ; love her as the young man his bride, and die for her if need be with a martyr's zeal and firmness. Hail to the glorious future, when the knowledge of the Lord shall cover the earth ; when we shall not have to teach every man his neighbor, but when all shall know the truth, from the least even to the greatest. Happy the men who shall live in that golden period of the world's future. Still happier however we deem those who are permitted to usher it in by faith, prayer and personal service.

SUNDAY READING.

Christ as a Teacher.

Jesus Christ came to be a teacher ; true, but this was clearly not the whole of his work, for if it were we should even be compelled to confess that he did it incompletely—not indeed as to the manner, but as to the matter—not as to quality, but as to quantity. He did not teach in all its fulness the whole of Christianity, and his abstinence in this matter seems to have been designed : he taught what was necessary to explain his own appearance and mission, and said enough to put his claim and pretensions beyond doubt. He laid down the great essentials of Christianity, that they might stand on no secondary authority ; but he left much that was of importance to be afterwards taught and developed by his disciples, under circumstances when the Church would be better fitted to receive the entire truth. The Apostles were the real expounders of Christianity : they taught the world what it was, and how it stood related to Judaism and heathen philosophy. Is not this a strong as well as a fair argument against the doctrine of those who hold that Christ was merely a profound thinker and a good man ? Because viewed in that capacity alone, some of the Apostles certainly surpassed him in the fulness of their teaching.

Jesus uttered the short saying " I came not to destroy the law, but to fulfil it." What a sermon on this text was produced by the author of the Epistle to the Hebrews ! How he amplified and illustrated the truth ! What a multitude of new thoughts, some doctrinal, some practical, he grouped together round this one idea ! Again, Christ said "ye cannot serve God and Mammon." What an elaboration of this thought is to be found in the epistle to the Romans.   How the history of heathenism and the experience of every man's conscience are laid bare to shew in a strong light the nature of that inward struggle over self which Christianity proclaims to be indispensable for all who would be saved.   Christ laid down the moral law, " Thou shalt love the Lord thy God with all thy heart, and all thy mind, and all thy soul, and all thy strength, and thy neighbor as thyself."   What a commentary on this was furnished by the beloved apostle ! How he unfolded the workings of human affection, and shewed in what way alone they could be sanctified !

It may be said, perhaps, that his superiority to them would still be manifest, inasmuch as it is the characteristic of the highest order of minds to discover truth and utter it oracularly, while it is the function of the second order of minds to comprehend these discoveries and explain them to the popular understanding. But in reply to this it may be urged, in the first place, that if this were the true view of the case, it would make the difference between the Apostles and Jesus Christ one of degree only, and not of kind ; and, secondly, that it is not the fact, for the Apostles did not confine themselves to mere exposition, but introduced many new and important truths.   How much is there of what we regard as revealed Christianity which is not even hinted at in Christ's discourses ?   The epistles are the great storehouses for doctrinal theology.   Let any one take up a system of divinity by any author, and examine to what part of Scripture references are made in support of the doctrines laid down, and he will find that for one reference to Christ's words, there will be at least two to the writings of his followers.   It may be said that Christ taught his disciples, and that what they announced to the world, they had previously learned from him in their private conversations.   This certainly could not have been the case with Paul, who was not converted till Christ had ascended, and who declares he received his gospel not from man, but by direct revelation.   Nor was it the case with the rest of the Apostles, for at the time of his ascension they were ignorant of much which they afterwards clearly preached.   They received the promised gift of the Spirit, and that led them into the way of all truth.   It is clear, therefore, from the manner in which Christianity has been expounded to the world, that Christ was not the exclusive teacher of it, nor yet even the principal teacher ; and that, therefore, though revelations and instructions were part of his work, they were not considered by himself to be the whole, or even its chief portion.   Christ came to do and to suffer—to live a perfect life, and die an expiatory death.   He thus on a basis of momentous facts founded Christianity, but he devolved on his followers the task of fully explaining it.   He avowed himself the promised Messiah, but he left it to his disciples, after he had risen from the dead, to prove from the Scriptures what the Messiah truly must have been. His work was rather practical than didactic, and his teaching, except so far as it asserted the divinity of his person and of his mission and the spiritual character of the dispensation he came to introduce, must be regarded, to some extent, as incidental.

His satisfaction at the close of life consisted in " having finished the work that was given him to do ;" and the Apostles after his departure for heaven, when they went forth to preach his gospel to the world, seldom referred to what he said, but often and much to what he did——perpetually dwelling upon the great facts of his history, his obedience, his sufferings, his death, his resurrection, as constituting his work, the accomplishment of which was the real occasion of his visit to our world.

The Present.

" Trust no future, however pleasant,
    Let the dead past bury its dead ;
Act, act, in the living present,
    Heart within and God o'erhead."   LONGFELLOW.

Some love to live in the Past. To cross the gulf of twenty centuries, and to mingle with those that were acting their part then on earth's busy stage, but who are so silent now, is felt to be delightful. To let imagination take her flight and to enter into the plans and projects, the hopes and fears, the joys and sorrows of that dim antiquity ; to watch the building of the ark, the piling up of the pyramids, the adorning and the opening of Solomon's temple, seems in a manner to identify us with the men and their doings of a by-gone age. We can enter into the tents and the battle-fields of Alexander, Hannibal and Cæsar ; we can sit among the audience, and listen to the soul-stirring strains of Demosthenes and Cicero, and fancy we catch the spirit, and share the greatness, of those heroes of the olden time. We fondly linger among the scenes where Abraham, Moses, and Paul performed their parts, for we are conscious of a soul governed by the same laws, obedient to the same motives, and subject to the same influences as theirs. The tie of a common brotherhood unites us, for "as face answereth to face, so doth the heart of man to man." Above all, how lovingly does the Christian mind go back to the days of the Incarnate One, the Redeemer of the World : dwell upon the incidents of his eventful career, and mark and appreciate the perfections of his glorious character. The fascination of the Past is exquisite, and if used aright may be truly ennobling.

Some love to live in the *Future*. They delight themselves in anticipations of what is to come. They gild the horizon that is before them with hues from their own fancy. They revel in visions of human progress, the development of the race in knowledge, in art, in material abundance, in virtue and happiness. The humble disciple of Him who brought life and immortality to light, who walks by faith not by sight, feels it glorious, above all others, to anticipate the future and to expatiate in a life to come. His treasure being in heaven, his heart is there too. He strains his faculties to form conceptions of the " house not made with hands," of the final union of unfallen angels and redeemed saints, of the endless progress of the Church in heaven ; of the radiancy of the " many crowns " that will encircle the brow of the King of Kings and Lord of Lords in his consummated glory. It is felt to be elevating, consoling and stimulating, amid the sorrows and humiliations of time, to look forward to and to ante- date the purity and the joys of eternity.

But with all deference to those who look so wistfully to the past and to the future and who love to live in those fairy regions, and with not a little sympathy in their musings, there is something nobler, more glorious still ; and that is, to *live in the Present.* This life may be as sacred, as pathetic, as grand to us as to the heroes and servants of God in ancient days. We live on the same wondrous globe as did Abraham and Moses, David and Paul. The same sky bends over us in serene and awful beauty. We gaze on the same sun by day, the same moon by night, and the configuration of the constellations of heaven is unchanged. To us the earth brings forth similar fruits and flowers. Day brings like toils and night like sweet repose. Our duties, our temptations, our sorrows, our joys, our sources of strength and encouragement are the same, for to us there is the same God and Father, who is above all and through all and in us all.

The *Past !* all consciousness and life have died out of it. It is dead, except as we breathe over it the breath of sympathy and shed upon it the glow of warmth and fancy. The *Future !* as yet it is not. It exists but in imagination and faith. But the *Present !* how real, how vital is the present. In it we emphatically *live.* Here it is that our joys and sorrows have a substantial, veritable existence. The present is the moment for action, for resistance, for conflict. To live energetically and well in the present is more glorious than to live a dreamy existence in the past, or to while away time in feasting the soul with hopes of what the future may yield. What so noble as to witness the Christian relying on his Saviour, enduring life's trials and temptations with courage, meeting his spiritual foes without flinching, discharging his daily duties with fidelity, denying himself for the benefit of others, and doing battle for truth in the name of the Lord of Hosts?

What have we to do with the past which is gone for ever, or the future which is not yet, except to derive motives and incite- ments to present and immediate action ? The passing time with its teeming opportunities of useful exertion, with its demands for principle and for strength, this, this is our appointed heritage. The spot on which we now stand is the stage on which we must act our part ; the present moment is the period in which feeble man must courageously, in the strength of God's Spirit, fight the dread battle of life, " a spectacle to the world, and to angels, and to men."

Christian, thou must daily discharge thy duty; daily please thy Saviour and honour his name ; and then thou wilt find thy life honorable and happy, like the lives of the godly that have gone before thee, and an example to those who shall come after thee. Accustom thyself to see a value in fragments of time, however brief; a dignity in daily duties, however mean : " whatever thou doest, do it heartily, as unto the Lord," and thus advancing step by step, each day will bring thee nearer in spirit as it will in point of time to the heavenly world. There is one glory of the past and another glory of the future, but the highest glory possible to thee as an accountable being, is to be achieved and won as the present hour passes silently over thee.

Restlessness on the Day of Rest.

SEARCHING QUESTIONS.—The prophet Amos supplies a significant illustration of this spirit. Worldly-minded persons in his time, could but ill brook the interruption of their ordinary business which was occasioned by the observance of sacred seasons: expressing the impatience of their minds, and their anxious desire again to engage in their secular pursuits, they said—" When will the new moon be gone, that we may sell corn ? and the Sabbath, that we may set forth wheat ?" Two questions are thus suggested for the consideration of our readers.

I.—IS THIS STATE OF MIND CHERISHED BY ANY OF YOU ? In order to determine this point, let the following tests be faithfully applied.

What are the feelings with which you regard the Day of Rest, and the sacred exercises which it involves ? Do you call the Sabbath a delight, the holy of the Lord, honorable ? Or do you feel it to be a dull and cheerless day ? Do you enter into the business of the week with zest and promptitude, and allow no unfavorable weather, or slight sickness to detain you from it ? Do you, on the other hand, regard the engagements of the Sabbath with comparative indifference and readily permit the passing shower or the trifling ailment, to keep you from sacred services ? You then attend to them, as custom or conscience may constrain you, but your heart is not in them.

What are the thoughts which usually occupy your mind, while en-

gaged *in the exercises of the Sabbath and the sanctuary?* The righteous man whose delight is in the law of the Lord, and who meditates therein by day and by night, will be prepared to attend upon the Lord with holy musings, and with deep sympathy with his truth and worship. True it is that those who thus seek their happiness in God experience an inward conflict, and frequently suffer from mental confusion and distraction. But the " vain thoughts" which mar their worship they abhor and resist. Where, however, the prevailing bias of the mind necessitates no such contest; where the schemes of earth readily engage attention, and exclude the higher themes which the Sabbath and the sanctuary suggest, the cry of these carnal worshippers is virtually re-echoed. To *cherish* thoughts of the world and its concerns, while professedly engaged in sacred services, implies that the Sabbath is a weariness and its hallowed rest an irksome restraint.

What are your habits during that portion of the Sabbath which is not devoted to public worship? What is the ordinary character of your *conversation?* Does it harmonise with the design of the day? Or does it indicate, by its current strain, the restless mind, long-ing to be occupied in the engagements which await you in the world? It may be asked further—how are the hours employed that intervene between the services of the sanctuary? Do you devote them to sacred studies, to prayer and meditation, or to active efforts in doing good? Or do you spend them in idleness and sloth? Instead of searching the Scriptures, do you take the newspaper or the novel; or, it may be, attend to your worldly affairs, such as writing letters or examining your accounts? In either case, it is manifest, that the heart is restless on the day of rest, and that the abridgement or suspension of the Sabbath would afford sad and guilty relief.

II.—Is NOT THIS STATE OF MIND PECULIARLY CRIMINAL?

It involves a direct violation of the first and great commandment. Supreme affection is claimed by God, and is due to him as the best and most glorious of beings—as the fountain of all good, and the Father of all our mercies. But this law is manifestly violated by those whose thoughts and affections are centred in the world : their own consciousness must attest that they cherish no love to God, and that they take no delight in contemplating the glories of his character, or in celebrating the riches of his grace. " They mind earthly things." This state of mind *indicates a prefe-rence which is as grovelling as it is sinful.* Those who might be invest-ed with everlasting righteousness, and be prepared for regal honors at the coming and kingdom of our Lord Jesus Christ, refuse to be ennobled for eternity, and choose rather the acquisitions or dignities of this fleeting scene, which they must speedily exchange for the woes of a self-wrought perdition. But even in the present life they suffer mournful loss. Their earthly prefer-ences *are hostile to peace and tranquillity of mind.* " The Sabbath was made for man;" it affords an opportunity to him who is burdened with the cares of this life to come to the Bible and the mercy-seat, and find refreshment there. Its sacred exercises are designed to soothe and to elevate the troubled spirit, to strengthen the mind for enduring difficulties, and to cheer it by the prospect of the rest that remaineth for the people of God. But the man whose heart clings to the world, and who devotes the Sabbath, in spirit or in conduct, to the secularities which absorb him, cannot realise this pause in the world's turmoil—this moral refreshment which his chafed and heated spirit so much needs. See the contrast between the Christian observing the Sabbath and enjoying the blessing, and the man of the world, neglecting the day of rest, and reaping the curse. It is said of Mr. Wilberforce—" On each returning Sabbath his feelings seemed to rise, in proportion to the sanctity of the day, to a higher degree of spirituality and holy joy, which diffused a sacred cheerfulness to all around him. He often remarked that he never could have sustained the labor and stretch of mind required in his early political life, if it had not been for the rest of the Sabbath : and, that he could name several of his contemporaries in the vortex of political cares, whose minds had actually given way under the stress of intellectual labor, so as to bring on a premature death, or the still more dreadful catastrophe of insanity and suicide, who, humanly speaking, might have been preserved in health, if they would but have conscientiously observed the Sabbath."

Such is the wreck of mental peace and physical vigor which this restlessness on the day of rest induces : but it entails yet more grievous evils—*it is utterly incompatible with preparation for heaven*. If there be no relish here for spiritual engagements— if the Sabbath, unless it be profaned, be a wearisome day, and the Bible an insipid book—if the gospel be heard without interest, and celestial treasures be practically regarded as unreal, no moral aptitude exists for the felicity of the heavenly state. The soul that deems worship a form or a burden, and thirsts not after God but after gold, cannot sympathise with the pleasures which are at God's right hand for evermore. Unless this vitiated taste be corrected, exclusion from heaven must be a moral necessity.

Religion in the Bush.
(A NARRATIVE.)

On Sunday afternoon, 3rd April, 1858, being Easter Sunday, a public service was held at the village of Dulcot, midway between Cambridge and Richmond, in Tasmania, for the purpose of dedicating to the service of God a humble stone bush hut, recently erected in that village by a laboring man, who, at the late government land sale, had purchased, from his savings, the land upon which this house was erected. The individual had lived for several years as a servant on the farms of various settlers, and being an exceedingly good and useful hand, was valued wherever he was employed. While residing in the Cambridge district, he attended the ministry of the Rev. Mr. Blackwood, who supplies the Congregational chapels at Richmond and Cambridge, and resides at the latter place. The means of grace were blessed to him ; the heart of the worthy man was effectually reached, and he became a decided and earnest Christian. He in consequence, became very active in his endeavours to carry into the lonely bush huts of the working people in that district, the knowledge of the truth as it is in Jesus ; and it is believed that his labors have not been in vain.

Suddenly he was missed from the chapel he attended, and from the district where he resided, and it was not known whither he had gone ; when, quite unexpectedly, as his minister was returning on a Sunday afternoon from the public service at Richmond, he was hailed by his former hearer, who most cordially welcomed him, and invited him to turn off the road a little way to see his house, then in course of erection. The poor man then explained to Mr. Blackwood, that he had, out of his long continued small savings, purchased the land on which the house was being built, and that when it was finished, he intended to dedicate it to the service of God ;—that it should be (as he expressed it) " the house of prayer for all neighbors ; " and he then urged the minister to hold a public service there, on the afternoon of Easter Sunday, to open his house as a place of public worship ; to which a joyful assent was given.

Mr. Blackwood having named this purpose to a friend in Hobart Town, he at once promised, with the aid of a few other friends, to present to this infant cause a bible and a hymn book for the minister's use, and six copies of the Hymn Book for the use of the congregation. To these were added, a small volume of " Sermons preached to the working classes," to be used occasionally when no minister or lay-preacher could be found to conduct the public services at this humble temple.

Accordingly, on Easter Sunday morning, April 3rd, 1858, Mr. R. E. Dear, the agent of the Colonial Missionary Society, with the writer of this account, the Rev. Mr. Blackwood, and a few others, went to Dulcot, where they found several of the neighbors awaiting their arrival. About 32 persons assembled, of ages varying from five to more than fifty years, some of whom had never before attended any place of worship. After introductory services, conducted by Mr. Dear, the Rev. Mr. Blackwood addressed the people from Isaiah lvi. 7, " For mine house shall be called an house of prayer for all people ; " thus carrying out the earnestly expressed wish of the builder and owner of the house, that that passage should form the subject matter of his address. He then presented to the congregation the books brought by the friends and pronounced the benediction, and the little band dispersed to their homes ; some of them, it is to be hoped, to offer thanks to the great Head of the Church, for putting it into the heart of one their own class to provide for them a sanctuary in the wilderness.

Thus, then, has there been opened in a hamlet, containing some 200 or more inhabitants—living at a distance of five miles on either side from any place of public worship—a " house of prayer " to which all neighbors are invited to come and worship God, and to hear the glad tidings of salvation ; and at which, on each Sabbath, service will be conducted, either by ministers or friends from town, or by the owner of the house himself, who is not destitute of education. Meetings for prayer on some of the evenings in the week, and a daily and sabbath school will also be held. From this nucleus it is hoped greater things will grow. This earnest, good man hopes, with the assistance of some neighbors, to erect, in the course of a few months, a more commodious weather-boarded building on his own land, to serve as the place for the meeting of a larger congregation than his small stone hut will accommodate. May the great Head of the Church bless him abundantly, and may the " house of prayer " thus opened prove the birth-place of many a soul, to the joy of the builder of the house and the glory of our God.

It is earnestly hoped that the perusal of the foregoing account of the zeal of this laboring man, may induce many in the bush throughout Tasmania and Australia, to go and do likewise. Were there more of this spirit of earnest endeavor to spread the gospel put forth by residents in the less frequented portions of these colonies; were they to say to their neighbors " come with us, for we will do you good, for the Lord hath spoken good concerning Israel, " how many who now live in entire neglect of religious ordinances, might have the gospel brought to their doors, and how many poor wanderers might thus be brought into the way of peace !

Hobart Town, April 10, 1858.

Obituaries.

THE YOUNG CHRISTIAN.

It is painful and pleasing to look back upon the short life of one who was peculiarly blessed of God from her earliest days. The little child was good tempered, and delighted to please companions and parents. She was early charmed with flowers, birds, and pleasant scenery ; which caused her to speak of the wonders they displayed, and the great God who made them all. Sweetness reigned in her temper, and love dictated her actions. " You should not hurt anything ; you should always help the weak and poor," were her characteristic expressions. The influence of Bible truth manifested itself, in her yielding her own wish to please others. Self-denial was thus beautifully illustrated in the childish circle, by her saying, " if it will please you, I will try to be pleased." From the lispings of infancy she most conscientiously observed the times of prayer. Sweet, simple, affectionate prayer for herself and others often affected more minds than her own. In the deepest weakness, the tender lamb clung to the Good Shepherd. The name of Jesus was sweet to her ear. The Bible and other books which told of Him were her constant companions. From Christ, her affections extended to his beloved people, and soon she learnt how it was they could suffer for Him they loved. With painful interest she read " Fox's Book of Martyrs," and took delight in inquiring about the worthies whose sufferings are there unfolded, shewing an insight into character, and a sympathy with God's people, much beyond her years. Her regard for the Sabbath led her to sanctify it in thought, word, and deed. It was delightful to see how she sought to please God on the holy day, by trying to bring neglected children to the Sabbath school. We shall never forget the pleasure which beamed in her intelligent countenance, when by perseverance she had overcome the unwillingness of parents, and induced them to let her take their little ones to the Sabbath school. She felt this to be a triumph of love, in which her happy mind received a present reward.

Thus, looking to Jesus, and putting forth the first efforts of a young disciple's love to Him, she sank into a lingering affliction in her twelfth year. Days and nights of pain and weakness were appointed her, but no murmuring escaped her lips. Her strength declined, but her patient, tender, loving spirit, made her more dear to all around. In the deep waters she prayed and looked to Jesus. As the spring returned she was restored to apparent health. But this only afforded a little space to develop sustaining mercy and maturing love to her dear Saviour. The winter came, and the disease returned with more virulence; when the young Christian yielded to the stroke with a peaceful mind, and amidst acute, continued pain, sank to rest. On the verge of eternity, at the moment of departure, she intimated that she loved Jesus. Nature sinks when one so lovely is called away, but faith follows to the skies, and exalts the soul to adoration and praise, as it sees the youthful disciple amidst the bright scenes, where pains and sorrows are unknown, with Jesus, who possessed the earliest affections of her heart.

CATHERINE ANN PRICE

Died February 22, 1851; aged 12 years and 11 months.
Launceston, Tasmania.

THE EXPERIENCED CHRISTIAN.*

Mrs. Mary Ann Pitt's death has produced some impression among her neighbors, and many perhaps have said, "O that I might die such a death as hers!" But such a death will not come as a matter of course. It will not come by *wishing* for it. It must be anticipated. Preparation must be made for it. The character and life of the righteous must be attained.

She was not converted upon her death-bed. Hers was no sudden transport, unconnected with her previous life, but what naturally arose out of it. She became a Christian when she was a young woman. She was converted to God under that eminent servant of God, the Rev. James Sherman, of Surrey Chapel, London. She was then not more than seventeen years of age. Powerful convictions of sin seized her. She saw the danger her soul was in : she became alarmed, and was anxious to be saved. These impressions did not wear off, as they too often do; but led her to Christ. While she felt she could not save herself, she saw that Christ could save her. She flew to him, cast herself upon his mercy, believed, and was happy. She gave her whole heart to the Saviour, and resolved to be his for ever.

This was no youthful fervor, which time and reflection cooled. It became a principle of life, an element of character. Old things passed away, all

---

* Extract from an address delivered in a cottage near South Yarra, Melbourne, shortly after Mrs. Pitt's decease, for the benefit of the neighbors, who knew her well.

things became new, and remained so. The ministry of her pastor she enjoyed exceedingly : under it she throve and grew in grace, and in the knowledge of our Lord and Saviour Jesus Christ. But this growth did not take place without diligence. She sedulously attended the public ministry, and was a careful hearer of the word. She kept a record of all the sermons she heard, and examined herself by them, to mark her progress in knowledge and piety. These are some of her self-questionings : " Am I more prepared to die ? Have I had sweeter communion with God than last year? Have I delighted to hear meekly his word ? Have I sung his praises with my heart, or only with my lips? Have I invited others to hear the word ? Have I prayed fervently for a blessing ? "

Nor did she live selfishly, but laid herself out for usefulness, embracing such opportunities as she had of doing good to the souls of others, and by watering others she herself was watered and refreshed. Nor did her profession of religion cost her nothing. She met with opposition in quarters where encouragement would have been more natural ; but this she meekly bore, rejoicing to be counted worthy to suffer for Christ's name.

Providence directed her steps to this country in the year 1848. She did not lose her religion on the voyage, but landed with it. She did not lose it after she landed, as so many have done, but carried it with her wherever she went. The want of a place of worship at hand was not a sufficient excuse for neglecting her soul : she sought out the means, and took trouble to go to them ; and when she could not enjoy them, she walked with God in secret.

She was first employed in a family as an instructress of children ; but her health was all along delicate, and she was not long in this colony when she became ill of the complaint of which at last she died. It was while she was thus suffering that her husband, then a scripture reader, first met with her. He was struck with her deep piety, and found in her a congenial spirit. They never had cause to regret their marriage, for like Zachariah and Elizabeth, they endeavored to walk in all the ordinances and commandments of the Lord blameless ; and the Lord blessed them, and made them happy in each other and in their children.

She had several attacks of illness during her married life, and other afflictions, especially the loss of a dear child ; and in them all she was sustained by the presence and promises of her God and Saviour.

Her last illness was not of long duration, and it had a threatening look from the first. Though she suffered much, her mind and speech were left unimpaired ; so that she could think clearly and speak without difficulty, and throughout she was calm and serene. She had no preparation to make, being already safe in Christ ; her lamp had oil in it, and was already lit ; it only required trimming to go forth and meet her Lord. The fear of death was taken away, for its sting was extracted.

She enjoyed conversation and prayer with her friends, and many delightful sayings she uttered on her dying bed. On being asked by her husband if she found the Saviour precious to her in her sufferings, she replied, " He is my rock ; the chief among ten thousand, and altogether lovely." In a time of great pain she said, " Our light affliction, which is but for a moment, worketh for us a far more exceeding and eternal weight of glory." Feeling herself a sinner in the sight of God, she quoted with delight the passages, " Who his own self bare our sins in his own body on the tree;" " The blood of

Jesus Christ his Son cleanseth us from all sin." She had often, in health, been harassed by temptations and depressing thoughts, but on her death-bed these all fled, and she was calm and peaceful, exclaiming, " Though I walk through the valley of the shadow of death, I will fear no evil, for thou art with me ; thy rod and thy staff, they comfort me ;" " Lord, let thy servant depart in peace, for mine eyes have seen thy salvation." When reminded by a friend of the unwavering love of the Saviour, she replied :—

> " His love in times past forbids me to think ‧
> He'll leave me at last, in trouble to sink."

On beholding the rising sun, she exclaimed, " The Sun of Righteousness is rising, with healing in his wings ;" and when an attendant, in endeavoring to alleviate her thirst, repeated the words, " Let him that is athirst come, and whosoever will, let him take the water of life freely," she replied, " Lord, I come, I come." When the last struggle came on, she seemed to suffer much. On being a little relieved, she desired to be raised up in bed, and, making an effort, she uttered the words, "Hallelujah! hallelujah! hallelujah!" and shortly afterwards resigned her spirit into the hands of her Redeemer.

Many who have been witnesses of these scenes have been struck with this happy death. Let it not be forgotten that the simple secret of it consisted in early consecration to God, a consistent profession, and humble trust in the Saviour of sinners for acceptance and eternal life; and the same means of living and dying happily are open to all.

REVIEWS.

Be Men. A Sermon by the REV. THOMAS BINNEY. W. Fairfax & Co. Melbourne.

The arrival of the Rev. Thomas Binney of London in these colonies, was looked forward to with great interest by a large portion of the public as soon as his intention to come out was known ; and when it was conjectured that he would preach multitudes flocked to hear him. The sermon, with the above brief but emphatic title, was preached in the Congregational Church, at St. Kilda, and was the first he delivered in the colony. Its publication was immediately demanded ; and though we understand that, as Mr. Binney was in infirm health and not adequate to a long service, he selected this particular sermon chiefly on account of its brevity, and was averse to its publication, yet as reporters were present and it would probably have appeared at any rate, he consented to furnish a correct copy and to revise the sheets.

Though a passing production of this kind, delivered and published in the manner stated, ought not to be regarded as a "crack sermon," a special specimen of Mr. Binney's powers, it is nevertheless, short as it is, a noble production, bearing on it the unmistakable signature and stamp of Mr. Binney's mind. It has all that lucid order, logical demonstration, vigorous tone of thought, and idiomatic racy nervous English, which are characteristic of all his productions. It furnishes a clear exposition of an important text and throws not a little fresh light upon it, and enforces a high and noble duty on those who bear the Christian name and are favoured with Christian

privileges. Did but Christians generally imbibe the spirit of this sermon
and carry its recommendations out in practice, what a different spectacle
would the Church present! How much more of unity, dignity, and impressiveness in its character, vigor in its movements and efforts, and success
in all its plans for the good of the world!

The visit of Mr. Binney to these colonies is hailed with delight by the
public generally, and strong hopes are entertained that his health may be
sufficiently restored to enable him to do good service to the cause of his
Master ere his return home. As he is a faithful minister of the Cross, and
preaches the " glorious Gospel of the blessed God" not excluding its evangelical peculiarities, as well as sound moral truths, it will not be a matter of
surprise if his doctrine should not suit every palate. We must not expect
that the unbelieving, Pantheistic, Unitarian, or even the merely secular and
literary portion of the public should relish the doctrine of the Crucified One ;
for the "offence of the Cross" still remains. But the author may console
himself with the assurance of the highest appreciation of his labors, whether
from the pulpit or the press, by all Christians of every section of the Church
of Christ

George Mogridge: his Life, Character, and Writings. By the REV.
CHARLES WILLIAMS. London : Ward and Locke.

FEW perhaps of our readers have ever heard of George Mogridge, but even
in this country we should imagine there are few who do not know " *Old
Humphrey.*" For many succeeding years did that kind, hearty, unknown
friend of mankind send forth his thoughts to the world. His pen seemed
ever ready to give expression to an inexhaustible store of keen observation,
quaint sarcasm, and genial feelings treasured up by him from all sources ;
yet nothing was ever known to escape from him which betrayed a heart
otherwise than full of benevolence, and overflowing with Christian joy.
The world began speedily to do more than admire their unknown friend ;
it began to cherish an affection for the garrulous old censor, who united
the chattiness of age with the sprightliness of youth, and whose love for
religion made his love for life all the stronger. But who was he ? and why
has he been silent of late ? have been questions often asked. He has gone
to his rest ; and we have got as a memento of our old friend, this " Life of
George Mogridge." And as we look behind the scenes, penetrate the
incognita, and see the man himself in common life, in his study,
amidst his family, or walking up and down the picturesque scenes of both
town and country, we find him to be just what we expected ; the same
character, as years came upon him, that he has given us in " Old Humphrey." But this biography has further value than merely as satisfying our
curiosity as to what " Old Humphrey " really was in every-day life. It is
a record of a most heroic struggle with difficulties. A struggle more manfully
conducted, with a more honest endeavour, combined with a firmer trust in
providence, we scarcely remember to have read. At first, engaged in business, life was easy to him ; but he was no business man, and in the course of
time he failed, and his life, after that was one long hard hand-to-mouth
encounter with starvation, which lasted almost till his death. But he never
loses heart, never desponds, always looks upwards to God, and within, to
see what energy is left there, and in consequence is very rarely unhappy and
never wretched, and his life is one continued victory.

The biographer has executed his task tolerably well. The great excellency
of the book is the large quantity of Mr. Mogridge's own writings, his letters
poems &c., which is introduced. We only wish there had been less of the
biographer's own adornments. We especially complain of the descriptions
of scenery which are needless, and, compared with those given by Mr. Mogridge himself, are pointless and tedious. One fact connected with the
literary success of Mr. Mogridge's career we give, as it may interest our
readers, and with that we close this brief notice : " More than *eighty products*
of his pen were issued by different publishers. And for the Tract Society,

in addition to miscellaneous papers in its periodicals, too numerous to be readily counted, he prepared no fewer than *a hundred and forty-six distinct publications*. The question is an interesting one, how many of these have been put in circulation? But it is not possible to obtain a correct answer. Of the currency they secured through the publishers mentioned we have no information, but in 1851 the Tract Society stated that of "Honest Jack the Sailor," they had distributed 494,450 copies; and that these with the aggregate of only six other of his works, including "Old Humphrey's Addresses" and "Observations," amounted to 739,564. As to the remaining 139 productions we have no intelligence; but if they have been circulated to the extent of the rest, the total issues more than five years ago, were fifteen millions and a quarter." The diffusion of Mr. Mogridge's works in America has been equally or still more extraordinary.

A Sketch of Boroondara. By JAMES BONWICK. Melbourne: Blundell.

Mr Bonwick's pen seems as if it could not rest. It has already produced a library; and, judging from present appearances, will ere long produce another. One thing we notice in all his works—they are Australian. We should imagine that he would greatly disapprove of the common mode o speaking in this country of England—calling it "home," and the voyag across the ocean as "going home." Everything Australian is tinted with the colors of paradise by the brush of this patriotic painter; and, though the effects may be rather too glowing, we do all honor to the feeling of the artist. Mr. Bonwick in this new pamphlet, undertakes so to describe the garden of Eden on the hither bank of the Yarra, that no one can resist its charms; and we advise all land speculators in the neighboring districts to use every means for the suppression of this little work, for Boroondara is such a charming region that everybody who reads the book will be sure to go and settle there. Sydney Harbor is tame compared with it, and the slopes of Mount Wellington not to be mentioned in the same breath: it is even a place where the business man returning in the evening can dig gold in his garden. Mr. Bonwick, in addition to his brilliant description, has given us a plain common-sense and well-executed map of his favorite El Dorado.

The British Workman and Friend of the Sons of Toil.

This is one of the most attractive little publications of the day, and admirably adapted to its purpose. It is a large single folio sheet, covered all over with scraps and pictures, and the Editor has apparently determined to make his motto " variety is charming," for it is always impossible from having seen one number, to say what the next will be like, yet they are all equally pleasing. We must especially commend the style of the wood engravings which are of the very first class, and by the best artists in that till lately, so despised a mode of illustration. It is a great mistake to think that working-men can be pleased with anything. They soon learn to know and appreciate what is good, be it a speech, a sermon, a book, a magazine in a picture; clap-trap and shams will not for long maintain their influence. But here we have a light, clever, and highly moral broadsheet which we feel convinced will be always popular wherever it is introduced. Its circulation of England is about 100,000 copies, and we are rejoiced to hear that there are 4,000 copies now on the way here. No one could be doing a greater service to the diggers than by letting them become acquainted with this cheap periodical. In England its price is only a penny, and in our rich colony perhaps our laboring men can more readily afford twice that sum, if such a price be necessary, than in the old country the bulk of people can spare a penny.

T

POETRY.

Light out of Darkness.

The morning broke in gloom and haze,
  No golden tints adorned the sky,
No smile was seen on Nature's face,
  The winds and waves played angrily.

The clouds when rent but closed again,
  No brighter light was seen behind,
The gusts roared over sea and plain,
  Their breath was cold, their touch unkind.

Their voice was harsh, " Sweet Peace is fled
  " For ever from the human heart,
" War reigns o'er all, and Hope is dead,
  " Heaven and earth are far apart."

All was so wild,—but yet I knew
  There had been days when all was glad,
When spoke a voice more strong, more true,
  "In heaven is peace though earth be sad."

I waited till the day was passed,—
  The winds were almost hushed, yet bore
Great piles of cloud against the west,
  To close by force light's only door.

Then rent the veil ; and shewed the gleams
  Of brighter light confined behind,
It caught the clouds, the captive beams
  With far off rolling mists entwined.

Above, below, to south, to north,
  The radiant arrows clove their way,
The dark sky glowed, the light poured forth,
  The gloom was powerless,—could not stay.

I looked what power this change had wrought.
  By whom the proud storm's head was bowed :
But lo ! the lines of light all sought
  A centre hid behind a cloud.

The source was hid, but faith was strong,
  For splendor flashed around the screen ;
I knew such light could but belong
  To some life-giving Sun unseen.

So earth has gloom, its heart is sad,
  And storms of sorrow roam abroad,
But light is here—light true and glad,
  Shed from that city built by God.

The Spirits of the Departed.

They are all gone into the world of light,
  And I alone sit lingering here ;
Their very memory is fair and bright,
  And my sad thoughts doth clear.

It glows and glitters on my cloudy breast
  Like stars upon some gloomy grove,
Or those faint beams with which the hill is drest
  After the sun's remove.

I see them walking in an air of glory,
  Whose light doth trample on my days;
My days, which are at best but dull and hoary,
  Mere glimmering and decays.

O holy hope! O high humility!
  High as the heavens above!
These are your works, and you have shewed them me
  To kindle my cold love.

Dear beauteous death, thou jewel of the just!
  Shining nowhere but in the dark:
What mysteries do lie beyond that dust,
  Could man outlook that mark!

And yet, as angels in some brighter dreams
  Call to the soul when man doth sleep,
So some strange thoughts transcend our wonted themes,
  And into glory peep.

If a star were confined into a tomb,
  Her captive flame must needs burn there;
But, when the hand that shuts her up gives room,
  She'll shine through all the sphere.

O Father of Eternal light, and all
  Created glories under thee!
Resume my spirit from this world of thrall
  Into true liberty!

Either dispense these mists, which blot and fill
  My perspective still as they pass:
Or else remove me hence unto that hill
  Where I shall need no glass.

        HENRY VAUGHAN, 1651.

MISSIONS.

SYDNEY.—VALEDICTORY MISSIONARY SERVICE.—About 200 of the members and friends of the Congregationalist body assembled, on Wednesday, 24th March, in the Pitt-street Church, for the purpose of bidding farewell to the three missionaries who are about to leave for their scenes of labor, and also to hear from the Rev. S. C. Kent an account of the proceedings of the late conference at Hobart Town, and to give a welcome to the Rev. G. Wight, who had lately arrived from Edinburgh. The chair was taken by the Rev. W. Cuthbertson, B.A., who opened the proceedings with singing, and the Rev. James Voller engaged in prayer. The chairman having delivered a few introductory remarks, the Rev. W. Slatyer, being called upon, proceeded to address himself to those missionaries who were about to take their departure. The qualities of mind to be expected from them in the discharge of the work they had engaged in need not be the highest, but above all things they required a quality of heart which would meet the demands of their mission. In view of all the features of that mission, it was not too much to say that trials and sacrifices were involved which were not to be experienced anywhere else.

The rev. speaker proceeded to counsel his brethren in a fervent valedictory strain. In bidding them "good bye," they (the Church) said "the Lord be with you." They could not say more; they dare not say less. In expressing the sentiments he had done for their well-being and prosperity, he had said what every friend desired.—The Rev. Mr. Murray next addressed the meeting. He begged to express, on behalf of himself and his brethren, his and their heartfelt thanks for the sentiments expressed and the kindness which had been bestowed on them. It was not that the missionary was shut up to betake himself to the fountain-head, from being cut off from the ordinary privileges of Christian life. But still he said for himself, and for his brethren, "not unto us but to thy name be the glory." It was on account of the interest manifested in the blessed work to which they were devoted, that he felt thanks particularly due. It was manifest that God was working with the missionaries, and this was a fact which should command sympathy. Yet the cause of missions was not supported as it ought to be. There were few effective missionaries in the Tahitian Group, and in the Harvey, comprising the Raratonga and others, there were only three. The Navigators had more, but were scantily supplied, and because these missions were so deficient in help, the laborers in them were sinking. There was only one source to which they could look for assistance, and that was the Australian Group; and he really believed the hand of Providence pointed to them for the deliverance so much needed. The Rev. Mr. Creagh next addressed the meeting. The thought of a departure from friends, and of the arduous duties they were to be delivered over to was trying, and though it was a blessed thought that they did not rely on the help of man, yet it was a happy thing to know that they had the continued sympathy of friends. He believed if the Church were fully alive to the importance of the work, it would be more effectually carried out. A short time ago he tried to get the means of obtaining a printing press to take down to the Island of Mara, but he had hitherto been unsuccessful. What they wanted was a printing press, and the necessary materials for printing the Scriptures and profitable books.—The Rev. Mr. Cuthbertson offered an apology for the absence of the Rev. Mr. Mathieson, a missionary lately out from England, who was to have addressed the meeting. He would call upon the Rev. Mr. Buzacott, who had labored arduously in the missionary cause for many years, to next address the meeting.—The Rev. Mr. Buzacott said his feelings were of a peculiar nature upon the departure of the John Williams. He had labored through 30 years —the work was endeared to him, yet to return to live in a tropical climate he felt, and was assured by his medical adviser, would be fatal to him. He was thankful, however, that it had pleased God to send his dear daughter back, to assist in carrying on the glorious work.—The Rev. S. C. Kent being called upon, proceeded to give an account of the Congregational Conference, lately held at Hobart Town. There were several matters brought before the Conference, which was presided over by the Rev. Richard Fletcher, of St. Kilda, Victoria. The particulars would be published in the *Southern Spectator* of the ensuing month, and he (Mr. Kent) hoped all the persons present would avail themselves of the forthcoming number.—Mr. Cuthbertson next introduced the Rev. G. Wight, late of Edinburgh, who had just arrived as a Congregational minister in New South Wales. From all he had heard of Mr. Wight, and from all he had seen of him, he could say nothing but what was in his praise. He stated the determination made last year, to cause two additional ministers to be sent out here, and in choosing Mr. Wight, Mr. Poore had chosen an accredited minister, who came to them as a Christian minister, and as one who had held a position of honor amongst those who loved him, and whom he loved; but alas! the second who was sent out, Mr. Jones, was no more. The ministers and the members of committee had united in giving a most cordial welcome to Mr. Wight. He trusted many more such men would follow, and that the principles he expounded would greatly extend. He called upon Mr. Wight to address the meeting.—The Rev. Mr. Wight said that since he resolved to come out to Australia—and the difficulties in his way were considerable—he had in no way felt regret. The rev. gentleman recalled the pangs incident to a departure from fatherland, and claimed for many present a participation in the feelings he had experienced in the act of severance from loved associations and connections. He indicated with lively anticipation a great and glorious future for this the land of his and their adoption, and concluded by returning his sincere thanks for the Christian reception and kind feeling which had been shown towards him since his arrival.—The Chairman then introduced to the meeting a Christian Chinaman, H. Laou Appa, a resident in Melbourne, who gave a very interesting narrative of his efforts in connection with the spread of the Gospel.—The Rev. S. C. Kent stated for the information of the meeting that this Christian gentleman had called upon him, and procured a number of testaments which he had engaged in actively distributing. The services were brought to a close at 10 o'clock, by singing and a benediction.

AUSTRALASIAN WESLEYAN MISSIONARY SOCIETY.—The annual general meeting of the Australasian Wesleyan Missionary Society, was held in the York-street Chapel, May 3. There was a large attendance, and the various speeches were listened to with great attention. The chair was taken by Mr. G. Allen, M.L.C. The business of the meeting having been commenced by singing and prayer, the chairman stated very briefly the object of the meeting, and called on the secretary to read the report. The Rev. John Eggleston then read the report—a very lengthy document—from which it appeared that, although the contributions were still increasing, the late period to which many of the anniversaries had been gradually postponed, had involved the Society in considerable difficulty and expense; that the total expenditure of the past year was £12,963 6s. 3d., and the net receipts from the colonies (including £1,594 18s. derived from native contributions of oil) £9,350, leaving a balance to be paid by the committee in London of £3,603 6s. 3d. The report then alluded to the engagement of new missionaries, and proceeded to give a description of the religious state of the various missions. The number of chapels was 397—other preaching places, 388; missionary and catechists missionaries, including supernumeraries, 55; catechists, 215; day-school teachers, 1,564; Sunday school teachers, 428; local preachers, 176; full and accredited Church members, 15,136; on trial for membership, 3,222; Sabbath schools, 198; Sabbath scholars, 10,410; day schools, 572; day scholars, 28,369. Total number of scholars under instruction being 31,791; and the total number of attendants at public worship, 8,635.

RELIGIOUS INTELLIGENCE.

New South Wales.

PUBLIC INSTRUCTION.

The Board of National Education in New South Wales have recently introduced a modification of their original plan, which promises to be very acceptable to a great body of the colonists. They have intimated their intention of supporting a class of schools, similar to those known under the Irish National Board as "non-vested." In these schools due security will be taken that instruction of the same efficient and unsectarian character as that required in schools purely National shall be given, during an adequate number of hours in each day, and that any special religious instruction shall be confined to stated periods, either before or after the ordinary school business, and to those children whose parents approve of their receiving it. One of the rules published by the Commissioners runs thus:—"During the hours appropriated in the time table to the ordinary instruction of the pupils, the usual routine of a National School must be observed in 'non-vested' schools; but the Commissioners will not exercise any control over the use of the school at any other time." In an explanatory note, it is added;—"Any religious exercise or instruction peculiar to the private character of the school, must, therefore, occupy some time before or after the hours fixed for the ordinary duties, so as to admit of the convenient absence of any children whose parents object to their attendance." It thus appears, that while all the children will study the Scripture lessons, which form part of the regular exercise of a National School, and will thereby have an opportunity of learning the essential and leading parts of the Christian religion, the master, or any others commissioned by the promoters of the school, may cause the children to read the Bible, or to learn catechisms, or engage in any religious exercise that they may deem advisable, provided only that parents approve, and that those things are not done in the hours fixed for the ordinary duties of the school. To balance this concession to denominational leanings, the board will give no aid towards the building or maintenance of "non-vested" school-houses, their contributions being limited to salary and books.

An ordination service was held on Monday evening, April 26th., in the Centenary Chapel, York-street. After singing and prayer, the Rev. John Eggleston, secretary of the Australasian Wesleyan Missionary Society, introduced to the Rev. Stephen Rabone, chairman of the New South Wales district, and to the congregation, the candidates for ordination—Frederick Langham and William G. R. Stevenson, who, having passed the usual introductory course, and having been by their respective quarterly and district meetings recommended to the office and work of the ministry, by the last Conference were admitted as ministers into the Wesleyan connexion. The candidates were then called upon to declare the grounds upon which they founded their belief that they were called to preach the Gospel : after which the authority was given them by the imposition of hands (the Revs. S. Rabone, J. Eggleston, S. Iron-side, and W. Hessel officiating) to exercise the office of a minister in accordance with the rules and principles of the Wesleyan Methodist Church. The sacrament of the Lord's Supper having been administered, the chairman addressed to the young ministers a few pertinent and affectionate warnings and counsels founded upon the apostolic injunction, "Take heed to yourselves," and the service closed with prayer by the Rev. W. Hessel. The Rev. W. Langham proceeds by the John Wesley to Vewa, Feejee, and the Rev. W. G. R. Stevenson to Habai, Tonga.

TEMPERANCE ANNIVERSARY.—This entertainment took place on the evening of the 14th of April, in the Hall of the School of Arts, on the occasion of the celebration, by a *soirée*, of the first anniversary of the New South Wales Alliance for the Suppression of Intemperance. About 500 persons assembled. The Rev. R. Mansfield, as chairman, stated in a general manner the purpose for which they were met, and the aims they had in view, and he took a retrospect of progress made by the society during the past twelve months. The Secretary then read the first annual report which, among other important matters, stated that seventeen temperance meetings had been held, and two *soirées*, one of which numbered 3000 persons. Several very important lectures had been delivered in behalf of the society, and these raised the number of their meetings to thirty-eight. About 700 pledges had been taken since the society started. The erection of a Temperance Hall had engaged the attention of the committee, and £500 had been paid on account of the purchase-money, which was £3000. About £30 was now in the Treasurer's hands, and the rent of the grounds (which were situate in Pitt street, nearly opposite the Congregationalists' Church) was more than sufficient to pay the interest on the balance of purchase money. It was intended to relieve the society of its expenses in hiring the School of Arts Hall amounting to about £200 a-year, by erecting a temporary building of their own, and they anticipated the aid of friends in carrying out that desirable project. It was also stated that the Band of Hope, numbering 990 young people, had been formally incorporated with the Alliance. Something, moreover, had been done in the shape of publications, not the least important of which was the *Band of Hope Journal*, conducted by Mr. Lee. On the motion of Mr. Robinson, seconded in a humorous speech by Mr. Griffiths, the report was adopted. Several charming pieces were sung by Mr. Chizlett's accomplished class, with organ accompaniment by Mr. Packer. The Rev. S. C. Kent spoke with excellent effect, and the meeting was also addressed by the Rev. Mr. Sharpe. At 10 o'clock the meeting closed.

CONGREGATIONALISTS.—The Rev. Thomas Binney has arrived in this colony, and his health is so far restored, that he is able to preach and speak with comfort to himself and to the great delight of the large assemblies which gather wherever he is announced to appear. On Sunday, May 9th, he preached in the evening at Pitt street Congregational Church, on behalf of the Congregational Home Missionary Society. The congregation was immense and the discourse instructive and eloquent, 1. Cor. 8. iii., "Are ye not carnal and walk as men." The Rev. W. Cuthbertson, B.A., preached in the morning. The collections amounted to £108 9s. 8d. On Sunday, May 16, Mr. Binney again preached to a large congregation in the Congregational Church, Surrey Hills. We understand our reverend friend intends visiting the Hunter River District and Moreton Bay before leaving this colony, and that he has consented to lecture to the "Young Men's Christian Association."

UNITED PRESBYTERIANS.—A new church is erecting in Sydney for the use of the congregation of the Rev. Hugh Darling, at present worshipping in the Supreme Court. The walls are now up and the building is covered in, and when completed it will be a very neat and indeed superior structure.

MORETON BAY—IPSWICH.—OPENING OF NEW CONGREGATIONAL CHURCH AND SCHOOL-HOUSE, BREMER BANK SAW MILLS (MR. FLEMING'S).—On Good Friday last, and the following Sunday, services in connection with the opening of this new building were held. In the morning (Friday) many friends started from Ipswich per *Breadalbane*, to return in the evening by the *Brisbane*. In the early part of the afternoon the children of the day-school were examined in the presence of the minister and friends, by their teacher, Mr. Davenport. Although at present they have been under his tuition but for a very short time, yet very satisfactory evidence was furnished of their steady application, as well as of the efficiency of their teacher's labors. At five o'clock tea was served in a large tent adjoining the church, to which the company afterwards adjourned. The chair having been taken by the Rev. J. T. Waraker, a short financial statement was presented by Mr. Reeve, from which it appeared that the cost of the building was about £150, of which £120 had been paid or promised, leaving about £30 still to be subscribed. The building, 25 feet by 25, is a neat and commodious one, of painted chamfer board, and will accommodate about 100 persons. The ground on which it stands (half an acre) has been kindly presented to the Congregational Church Mission by Joseph Fleming, Esq. In addition to the day-school a Sabbath-school is held every Sunday at two o'clock, and public-worship commences every Sunday afternoon at a quarter to four. As this mission station is distant from Ipswich about five miles, it is hoped that not only the immediate residents, but many in the surrounding district may avail themselves of the means of public-worship and instruction thus provided. On the following Sabbath the opening services were continued by the Rev. T. Deacon preaching in the morning and the Rev. J. T. Waraker in the afternoon. The circumstances and attendance of these services were of an interesting and auspicious character, and kindled sanguine hopes in many of the best results from the establishment of this Mission.

PRESBYTERIANS.—PRESBYTERIAN CHURCH OF EASTERN AUSTRALIA.—(Free Church).—The Synod of this Church met within Macquarie-street Church, Sydney, on Wednesday, the 5th of May, and was constituted by the Rev. Hugh M'Kail, Moderator, with praise, reading the scriptures, and prayer. The parties present were, the Moderator, Rev. Alexander Salmon, of Sydney; William Grant, of Shoalhaven; William Lumsdaine, of Sydney; James Cameron, of Penrith, Richmond, and Castlereagh; and S. F. Mackenzie, of Bowenfels, ministers; and Messrs. John Moon, William Thorburn, Henry L. Black, Archibald Colville, George Bowman, David L. Waugh, and John M'Lennan, elders, members of the Presbytery of Sydney; and Revs. William M'Intyre, of Maitland; Allan M'Intyre, of the Manning river; James M'Culloch, of Singleton; and A. M. Sherriff, of Clarence Town and Dungog, Synod clerk, ministers; and Mr. James Hamilton and Mr. Hugh Mackay, elders, members of the Presbytery of Maitland.

With respect to any plan for union with other bodies of Presbyterians, the following resolution was passed:—" Rev. Mr. Salmon, convener, gave in the report of the committee on Union, which was approved of, and the committee re-appointed, with instructions—

" To take special care that it do not agree to any basis of union that does not contain a full and explicit enunciation of the distinctive principles of this church, and provide for the maintenance of them, not only in the administration of the internal affairs of the United Church, but also in its intercourse with other churches."

With regard to the College question, this Synod, while recognising the vast importance of college education, were of opinion that the time was not come for entering on any immediate course of action. This will appear from the following resolution:—

" Taking all the circumstances of our present position into consideration, your Committee conceives that, in the meantime, the proper course for this Church would be to make an effort to procure subscriptions towards the erection of college buildings, and the endowment of professorships; abstaining, however, for the present, until such an institution is actually needed, and until it is seen whether there is a prospect of union on a satisfactory basis with the other Presbyterian bodies in the colony, or any of them, from applying the funds subscribed. And, until it should be considered that the time for applying them had arrived, it would, of course, be unnecessary to raise them. In the event of a satisfactory union, they should be applied by the united body, and by this Church, failing such a union. Even after it became advisable to institute classes, it might still for some time be unnecessary to erect buildings. Accommodation for such classes might be provided otherwise."

As this Church has not compromised its noble principles, as a branch of the great protesting Free Church of Scotland, by taking any portion of the state aid, offered by Government to all churches indiscriminately, it is consequently thrown upon its own voluntary resources. There are thirteen congregations, and they have raised in the course of the year, in the aggregate, for the support of the ministry and the different schemes, £3,733 2s. 3d., which gives an average of £287 for each. The congregational fund, raised in each congregation for its own minister, amounts, altogether, to £2,923 16s. 6d. This, of course, being determined by the numbers, wealth, and liberality of the several congregations, is very unequal. But this is supplemented by the Sustentation Fund, which amounts to £1,444 7s. 5d., yielding an average to each of the thirteen ministers of £111 2s. 10d. These sums appear to be irrespective of moneys raised for church building and enlargement, of which no report is given. The Rev. Dr. Mackay has been deputed to visit Scotland with the view of bringing out an additional supply of ministers.

Tasmania.

EVANGELICAL UNION.—The monthly meetings of this Union have been held in Hobart Town during the present year, as follows:—*January*—Wesleyan Chapel, address by the Rev. J. Buller of New Zealand. *February*—St Andrew's Church, address by the Rev. C. Price. *March*—Congregational Chapel, Davey Street, address by the Rev. J. Downes, on "The Vaudois Churches." *April*—Wesleyan Chapel, address by the Rev. F. Miller, on "Chesterfield, Voltaire, and Paul."

BIBLE SOCIETY.—The annual meeting of the Tasmanian Auxiliary Bible Society was held on April 27, in the Mechanics' Institute, Hobart Town. His Excellency Sir Henry Young, the President, being absent at Launceston, the chair was taken by one of the Vice-Presidents, Mr. G. W. Walker, of the Society of Friends. The report supplied an encouraging account of the labors of the Colporteur, Mr. Livermore, who during 8 months, had visited upwards of forty places, made 2,981 calls, and sold 3,103 volumes of the Sacred Writings. An urgent appeal was made for enlarged pecuniary aid, and the services of the ladies were solicited to canvass Hobart Town for contributions towards a "Special Bible Fund for India;" Mr. Hopkins generously offering to *double the amount* that should be so raised, within a month from that time.

TEMPERANCE.—The Tasmanian Temperance Alliance is prosecuting its labors, and securing the co-operation of Christian ministers. Sermons in connexion with its anniversary were to be delivered in the month of May, at Brisbane-street Chapel, the Bethel, and Knox's Church, by the Rev. Messrs. McClean, Downes and Miller.

SUNDAY SCHOOL UNION.—The fifteenth annual meeting of the Tasmanian Sunday School Union was held on May 18th, in Brisbane Street school rooms, the Rev. F. Miller in the chair. After the teachers and friends assembled had taken tea together, the report was read by Mr. Lodge, embracing notices of various schools connected with the Union, and of plans and agencies calculated to advance its objects. The resolutions proposed were advocated by the Rev. Messrs. Nicolson, Clarke, Waterfield and Downes; Messrs. Barrett, Hopkins, Dear, Blackwood, John Salier and Piesse. The attendance was encouraging, and many valuable suggestions were offered in furtherance of the Sunday School cause.

CONGREGATIONALISTS.—Davey Street Church, Hobarton. The sum of £250 has been raised by a bazaar, towards the cost of erecting school rooms in connexion with this place of worship.

Victoria.

GENERAL.—THREE MILE CREEK, NEAR BEECHWORTH.—On Monday evening, May 10, a Public Room was opened at this place by a Tea Meeting. Its object, as its name imports, is to afford accommodation for public purposes, unconnected with any denomination, such as a school, public meetings, preaching, &c. The cost has been £65 10s., which has been all defrayed. Rev. T. Jackson, Independent Minister of Beechworth, presided, and a considerable number of local friends addressed the meeting with pleasing effect.

PRESBYTERIANS.—UNITED PRESBYTERIAN CHURCH, EMERALD HILL, MELBOURNE.—The third anniversary of this Church was held on Wednesday, March 11th; the Rev. John Ballantyne, the Pastor, presided. After tea addresses were delivered by the chairman, the Revs. W. Jarrett, J. M. Reid, D. McDonald, W. B. Landells, J. Cooper, Jas. Ballantyne, and by Messrs. Watson and Black. During the three years of the existence of this cause, it has been favored with continued and growing prosperity.

UNITED PRESBYTERIANS, LONSDALE STREET, MELBOURNE.—Erskine Church. This new Church was opened for public worship on Sabbath. the 18th of April; the Rev. Dr. Cairns preached in the morning, the Rev. James Taylor preached in the afternoon, and the Rev. James Ballantyne, the pastor, preached in the evening. The attendances on the various services were large; a deep interest seemed to be taken in them, and the collection amounted to £135. A tea-meeting was held in the new church on the evening of the Tuesday following, commemorative of the occasion. Upwards of 700 were present. The Rev. J. P. Sunderland of the Congregational Church, Richmond, implored the Divine blessing. The Rev. James Ballantyne, after a few introductory remarks relative to the position of the church, called upon the following ministers in succession to address the meeting: Revs. D. J. Draper, and Mr. Williams of the Wesleyan Church, Rev. Dr. Cairns of the Free Church, Revs. W. B. Landells, H. Thomas, James Mirams, William Roby Fletcher, of the Independent Church: and Revs. William Jarrett, John Cooper, of Geelong, and John Ballantyne, of the United Presbyterian Church, the Rev. Mr. Craig of the Scotch Church, Essendon, Rev. Wm. Moss of Prahran, and Rev. Mr. Wells, were also present. This new church is the largest in the United Presbyterian Denomination in the colony. In its internal arrangements it is neat and comfortable. The ornamental front, which is yet to be erected, according to the design is to be of freestone with Doric columns and pediment. The church is henceforth to be known as Erskine Church, in memory of the distinguished men of that name who founded the oldest branch of the U. P. denomination.

REV. A. M. RAMSAY.—On Wednesday evening a valedictory *soirée* was held, in the United Presbyterian Church, Collins-street, on the occasion of the departure of the Rev. A. M. Ramsay, per *Victoria*, on a visit to Scotland. Amongst the gentlemen present were the Rev. Dr. Cairns, H. Langlands, M.L.A., Robt. Kerr, J.P.; and the Rev. Messrs. Taylor, New, Fletcher (sen.), Mirams, Young, Sunderland, Poore, Odell, Williams, Hamilton, M'Nicol, Goethe, Johnston, Fletcher (junr.), and Morison; and Mr. Meek, a newly-arrived missionary from Scotland. The Rev. James Taylor was voted into the chair, and during the course of the evening, a valedictory address was presented to Mr. Ramsay, by John Macgregor, Esq., solicitor, signed by the elders and deacons on behalf of the congregation.

BALLAARAT.—The German Lutheran Church at Ballaarat was opened for Divine service on Sabbath, the 28th of March. The Rev. Mr. Goethe, of Melbourne, preached an impressive discourse, in the German language, on the subject of Christ stilling the tempest. There were upwards of 300 persons present on the occasion. The structure is a wooden one, and is capable of accommodating about 400 individuals. The collection, on behalf of the building fund, amounted to £23.

FREE CHURCH.—CHALMERS' CHURCH (REV. DR. CAIRNS').—A social meeting of the congregation was held in the church on the evening of Tuesday, the 27th of April. The area of the spacious building was filled, and there were about 800 present on the occasion. The Rev. Dr. Cairns occupied the chair; around him on the platform were the Rev. D. J. Draper, Rev. James Ballantyne, Rev. D. McDonald, Rev. Mr. Divorty, Rev. Mr. Williams, Rev. J. P. Sunderland, Rev. James Taylor, Rev. G. M. Reed; and David Ogilvy, Esq. The Divine blessing was implored by the Rev. Mr. Draper. After tea the meeting was addressed by the Chairman, and the Rev. Messrs. Divorty, Ballantyne, Sunderland, Williams, McDonald, and Taylor. The best spirit prevailed in the meeting, and the numerous audience appeared to be much delighted.

FREE CHURCH, PRAHRAN (REV. MR. DIVORTY's).—This congregation has recently made an effort to clear off the debt which rested upon it. In February last a meeting was held for the purpose of considering what could be done. The Managers of the congregation initiated a scheme by subscribing among themselves the large sum of £1100. The greater portion being thus removed, the remainder, it is expected, will speedily follow. The example set by this congregation is well fitted to stir up others to follow in their train. While a load of debt remains upon a congregation, it cannot be in a position to do much for the evangelisation of the bush districts of this colony.

FREE CHURCH, BEECHWORTH.—This church, of the laying of the foundation stone of which a notice was inserted in a previous number of this magazine, was opened for public worship on Sabbath, Feb. 21st. The Rev. Mr. Grant, the pastor, preached in the morning, and the Rev. D. H. Ballantyne, of Albury, in the evening; the attendance on both occasions was encouraging, and the two collections amounted to £60. On the Thursday evening following, a social meeting was held in the new church, when about 170 persons sat down to tea. The Pastor presided, and among the speakers were the Rev. Messrs. Symons, Wesleyan; Jackson, Independent; Ballantyne, Presbyterian; Smith, of Sydney, Baptist; and Mr. J. A. Thompson, Evangelist and schoolmaster. The meeting went off with great spirit. The church is a plain, neat structure in the Gothic style, with a tower and wooden spire, and is considered an ornament to the town. The entire cost, including fencing, painting, &c., will be about £3000, and of this £2100 has been obtained.

METHODISTS.—UNITED METHODIST FREE CHURCHES.—Under this designation the Wesleyan Methodist Association and the Wesleyan Reformers in England have amalgamated and become one united body. The churches in Australia hitherto known as the Wesleyan Methodist Association have adopted the new designation, and they commenced the sittings of their annual assembly on the 4th January last, in Kildare Chapel, Geelong. The Rev. M. W. Bradney was elected president, Mr. W. H. Allsop

connexional secretary, and Mr. J. M. Bryant connexional treasurer. The reported statistics of the connexion show—4 itinerant ministers 20 local preachers, 19 leaders, 259 members, 11 chapels, 4 preaching places ; 3 day-schools, having 4 teachers, and 150 scholars; 12 Sunday-schools, with 66 teachers and 669 scholars. The increase of members during the past year, irrespective of 16 removals and 3 deaths, is 71. Five fresh localities have been occupied during the year for the formation of churches. Several openings for further extension were urged upon the Assembly, and applications for ministerial aid laid before it. The application on behalf of Ballarat was the only one responded to. The Rev. M. W. Bradney was, with his consent, appointed to open the mission. Two ministers recently arrived from England were received and recognised as accredited itinerant ministers in connexion with the Australian Assembly. A book committee was constituted for supplying the connexion, and amongst the public movements of the day the cause of Total Abstinence and State Aid to Religion were specially noticed, and the following resolutions recorded :—
" The Assembly take cognisance of the proceedings in connexion with the great cause of total abstinence, and hail as an augury for good the recent recognition of this grand movement by ministers of various denominations. They pray this example may speedily be followed by all the heralds of salvation. "—" That the connexional committee be requested to watch closely the question of State Aid to religion, and, if necessary, take action as may be deemed advisable in opposition to its increase, and with a view to assist in procuring the withdrawal of such aid. "

CONGREGATIONALISTS.—REV. THOS. BINNEY.—This distinguished minister, whose expected visit to Australia was announced in our last number, safely reached Hobson's Bay in the *Sultana* on April 1st, in company with the Rev. Messrs. Poore and Reed. His health was considerably improved by the voyage, but he was not in a condition to undergo much excitement or undertake any considerable amount of service. He, however, preached in the Congregational Church, St. Kilda, on Sunday, April 11, a sermon, the publication of which was immediately demanded ; and a second time on the 18th, at the new Congregational Church, Richmond. Previous to these engagements, Mr. Binney had not been in a pulpit for nine months. He preached apparently with all his former energy and effectiveness. On the 13th, a number of ministers and laymen of the Congregational body entertained him at breakfast, and enjoyed some very pleasant and profitable social intercourse with him. He and Mrs. Binney have proceeded to Sydney to spend some time beneath the hospitable roof of John Fairfax, Esq. His health having still further improved, he conducted the services which are reported under the head of Sydney intelligence. His purpose is to visit the Hunter River, Moreton Bay, and Tasmania, before his return to Melbourne ; and strong hopes are entertained that he will now be able, wherever he may go, to do good service to the cause to which he has devoted his life, by preaching, lecturing to young men, and other means.

THE REV. J. L. POORE arrived, as reported above, on the 1st of April, with Mr. Binney. Mr. Poore went to England, commissioned to look out for sixteen ministers, for the four colonies of New South Wales, Victoria, South Australia, and Tasmania, taking with him upwards of £2000 to defray in part the expense of sending them out, and engaging to raise in Britain, if possible, whatever additional sum might be necessary. In performing this latter duty he travelled by rail nearly 10,000 miles ; lectured four and five times a week (in all, in more than 100 towns) ; preached twice or thrice every Sabbath day, and attended numerous public meetings besides. His Sabbaths were devoted wholly to English religious objects, and his week-day exertions to raising his Australian Fund. For the latter, he obtained some £1300. Several shipowners generously granted free passages to the ministers. All the money taken out from Australia and obtained in England was paid into the hands of the Treasurer of the Colonial Missionary Society in England, and all disbursements have been made by him. The greater part of the ministers engaged to be sent out have arrived ; but a few are yet on their way, or will shortly set sail. Mr. Poore had scarcely landed in Victoria before he found, by various letters received and from other sources, that the supply of ministers was still inadequate ; various openings presenting themselves where faithful laborers were much needed. As his knowledge of those ministers at all likely to come out was, by his recent visit, extensive correspondence, and personal intercourse with them, more full and accurate than that of any other person, it was thought the best, the shortest, and in the end the most economical way for him to return to England immediately, before becoming entangled in colonial engagements, and personally select and send hither an additional number of ministers. He accordingly went by the April overland mail, taking a return ticket. It may be proper to state that the whole of Mr. Poore's travelling expenses in England did not exceed £60, and this was all that was deducted from the money he collected there; and that the whole of his voyaging expenses, out and in, have been defrayed by himself out of his ordinary salary, with the exception of a small grant made by the Melbourne Committee towards his present voyage.

LOCATION OF THE MINISTERS SENT OUT BY MR. POORE.—The *Rev. W. B. Robinson* has settled at Williamstown with good prospects. A commodious temporary place of worship has been purchased, a considerable sum of money raised, and an excellent congregation gathered. An animated tea-meeting was being held at the moment the *Sultana*, bringing Mr. Poore, arrived in the Bay; and he landed in time to show himself before the meeting broke up, and met with an enthusiastic reception. —The *Rev. J. Sleigh* has settled at Portland, in very encouraging circumstances. Another paragraph (below) more fully details his proceedings.—The *Rev. R. P. Lewis* has undertaken an engagement at Brighton, near Melbourne, where an eligible piece of land has been purchased for a new place of worship, and a contract entered into for a new building to cost £800, to answer the purpose of a chapel for a time, but ultimately to be used as a school-room.—The *Rev. J. Summers* has proceeded to Daylesford, about twenty miles from Castlemaine, and between that town and Ballarat, a place which, with some adjoining localities, contains a population of nearly five thousand people, very slenderly provided with religious ordinances. The prospect here is encouraging.—The *Rev. J. H. Jackson* is located at Beechworth. He has gathered a good congregation, and is about to re-organise the church; and measures are expected to be taken shortly to erect a place of worship on land which is already purchased and paid for. Mr. J. also conducts services amongst the miners at various diggings around Beechworth. Everything promises success.—*Rev. R. Bowman*, late of Fish-street Chapel, Hull, has accepted the call of the Church at Victoria-parade, Melbourne, and is laboring with every prospect of collecting and consolidating a good congregation.—*Rev. J. G. Reed, B.A.*, was designed for Geelong, and the Church at M'Illop-street Chapel desire to secure his services, but his delicate state of health throws a doubt upon his settlement. He took one service a-day for four Sabbaths in succession, and is now resting for a while to recruit his strength. The people are willing to wait some time in the hope that God may spare his valuable life for service in this church.—Some of these brethren are already wholly supported by the people among whom they labor, and all are expected to be so ere long. In the mean time temporary and limited assistance is granted from the Victoria Congregational Home Mission where needed. We have not precise information respecting the ministers who have arrived in other colonies, or of their several settlements.

VICTORIA CONGREGATIONAL HOME MISSION.—The first annual meeting of this Mission was held in the Mechanics' Institution on the evening of Monday, the 12th April. The attendance was numerous, and much interest was manifested in the proceedings. The platform was occupied by the Rev. Messrs. Landells, Bowman, Moss, Robinson, Mirams, Poore, Lewis, R. Fletcher, W. R. Fletcher, M.A., and J. P. Sunderland; the Hon. George Harker, and Messrs. Fulton, Russell, Rolfe, Templeton, &c. The chair was taken by the Rev. Richard Fletcher, of St. Kilda. The chairman stated that the main object of the society was to provide ministers for the colony, secure for them a proper location, and aid in sustaining them until they became settled pastors. He was happy to say that the society had received many tokens of the Divine favor, since it had come into existence. The report was read by Mr. Goodhugh, the secretary, and the financial statement was submitted by Mr. Rolfe, the treasurer. The gross income of the society for 15 months had amounted to £1,231 14s. 6d., of which £782 12s. had been remitted to England for ministers £244 expended in the colony, while £205 2s. 6d. remained in the hands of the treasurer. There were however some liabilities to be met. The Rev. W. B. Landells moved the adoption of the report and financial statement. He congratulated the association on its success thus far, which was greater than had been anticipated, and which augured good in times to come. The Rev. J. P. Sunderland seconded the resolution. He spoke of the numerous districts which applied from time to time for aid, the inadequacy as yet of the churches to meet these claims, and the great and solemn urgency of the work which the Mission had undertaken. The chairman then called upon the Rev. J. L. Poore. He had gone home 15 months ago with £2000 for the purpose of bringing out ministers. He had lectured in many of the leading towns of England and Scotland, on Australia, having addressed some 40,000 or 50,000 people on the subject. By his labors £1300 had been raised in England, and £500 of passages for ministers had been given by shipowners. He believed that in 20 years Victoria would contain a population of 2,000,000 of souls. It belonged to the churches to see that its spiritual wants, which would rapidly increase, were efficiently provided for. The next speaker that was introduced was the Rev. Mr. Bowman, late of Hull. He said it might be supposed that he felt strange in the position which he that night occupied. He could not explain his feelings. Since he came in sight of land new visions had been continually breaking upon him. He could hardly bring himself to believe that he had left England. It seemed as if a large part of London, or of some other great city, had been dropped down here, and himself with it, where 30 years ago there was nothing but the trail of the savage. He perceived there was a very inadequate idea in England of the condition of this colony. Since he landed, on Thursday last, he had been trying to find wherein the descriptions in books failed. When a man comes into the Bay he sees what cannot be described. The bustle and activity in Melbourne quite astonished him, and he was surprised to see the substantial character and architectural pretentions of so many of the buildings. The colony seemed to be a thousand times further advanced than it was thought to be in England. He had left a large and loving congregation in Hull. The pain of parting was intensified by the thought that he was going among comparative strangers. He was much relieved, however, and gratified with the hearty welcome he had received. He had already learned that he had not left English feeling, English kindness and English religion behind him. Mr. Bowman remarked on the probable religious future of this great colony, and the great responsibility which lies on the present generation. He moved a vote of thanks to Mr. Poore for his great exertions on behalf of the society. The Hon. George Harker briefly seconded the resolution. T. Fulton, Esq., and the Revs. William Moss and James Mirams also addressed the meeting, and a committee was elected for the ensuing year.

NEW CONGREGATIONAL CHURCH, RICHMOND.—A public tea meeting was held on April 6th, 1858, to celebrate the opening of the above place of worship. After tea, which was taken in the adjoining school-room, the friends assembled in the new church. There was a large attendance. T. Fulton, Esq., J.P., occupied the chair. The meeting was opened by singing, and the Rev. W. C. Robinson, of Williamstown, offered prayer. Addresses were delivered by Rev. R. Fletcher, of St. Kilda; Rev. I. New, of Albert street; Rev. H. Thomas, B.A., of North Melbourne; Rev. J. P. Sunderland, the pastor of the church; Rev. J. L. Poore, agent of the Colonial Missionary Society; Rev. J. Lewis, of Brighton; and F. Haller, Esq. Ministers of various denominations were present. The church cost £2800. A collection was made for the building fund, and a considerable sum was realised.

PORTLAND.—The foundation of a Congregational place of worship was laid by the Rev. J. Sleigh, January 18th, 1858. The Rev. S. Knight, Wesleyan minister, assisted. The building will seat upwards of 150 persons. It was opened March 21st, when sermons were preached by the Revs. J. Sleigh, pastor, W. Ridley, United Presbyterian, and S. Knight. The attendances and collections were encouraging. Next day a tea meeting was held in the new building, when Mr. J. Andrew presided and spoke. The above ministers and other friends followed, having interesting topics assigned to them, and delivering impressive speeches. These services realised £33 5s. 10d. Liabilities, including a site for a larger erection when needed, will exceed £500. Towards this £228 16s. 5¼d. (including £57 8s. 0d. for surplus bricks) has been raised chiefly on the spot. It is hoped this people will receive the public sympathy, which they both need and well deserve. The Rev. J. Sleigh is unanimously requested to remain as minister, and is graciously favored with many tokens of the presence and power of God.

RECOGNITION OF THE REV. R. BOWMAN.—The Rev. R. Bowman, late of Hull, was publicly recognised as Pastor of the Congregational Church, Victoria Parade, on Tuesday evening, May 25th. The Rev. R. Fletcher presided. After prayer by the Rev. J. Mirams, Mr. Fletcher made some introductory remarks on the history of the Church, and the import of a recognition service. Mr. Barlow, deacon, read the call addressed to Mr. Bowman, and Mr. Bowman's acceptance. Solemn prayer was then offered by the presiding minister for a blessing on the Pastor and Church. Mr. Bowman next delivered an address expressive of his feelings in assuming this important charge, and his purposes and hopes for the future. This was followed by a short address to Mr. Bowman by Mr. Fletcher. Rev. T. Odell next spoke upon the subject of an "Earnest Ministry" and the Rev. W. B. Landells upon an "Earnest Church," both which addresses were appropriate and impressive. The Rev. Messrs. Lewis, Robinson, Taylor, Sleigh and others were present on the occasion. The Church was well filled with an attentive and deeply interested auditory.

VICTORIA PARADE CONGREGATIONAL CHURCH.—On Thursday evening, May 27th, a tea meeting was held to welcome the Rev. R. Bowman, who has accepted the pastorate. The Church was densely filled. The chair was taken by the pastor. Mr. Russell and the choir of the Richmond Church attended and sung several anthems. The speakers consisted of the Hon. J. P. Fawkner, Messrs. Rolfe, Fulton, Langton (treasurer of the Church), and Rev. Messrs. James Taylor, Isaac New, T. Williams, James Mirams, J. P. Sunderland and E. Bowman. From the treasurer's statement it appears that during the past year there had been raised for general expenses £570 and for the building fund £420. There was a floating debt of £203 which the church was anxious to get rid of and proposed to do so that night. The friends present at once subscribed £188 and with a little further effort the debt will be removed. The meeting was most interesting and cheerful, and all present seemed determined to let the new pastor see that he had come amongst friends.

South Australia.

CONGREGATIONAL HOME MISSIONARY SOCIETY.—The annual meeting of this society was held on Wednesday, April 28th, in Freeman-street Chapel, Adelaide. After tea in the school room the friends adjourned to the Chapel, when the chair was taken by G. M. Waterhouse, Esq., (late M. P.). On the platform were Mr. J. H. Barrow, M. P., Mr. A. Hay, M. P., Mr. Smedley, late member for Light, Alderman Glandfield, and several Congregational clergymen. After the chairman had delivered a suitable address, Mr. Shawyer read the report, which stated that the receipts of the year amounted to £544 12s. 4d., the expenditure to £492 17s. 11d. The stations which had been more or less aided by the society during the year, were, Hindmarsh, Alberton, Salisbury, Lyndoch Valley, Houghton, Shipley, Glen Osmond, Glenelg, Maclaren Vale and White's Gully, and the district including Middleton, Goolwa, Castlerange, and Hindmarsh Island. Hindmarsh has been happily settled with a pastor, the Rev. Mr. Wilson, one of the ministers lately arrived, who is laboring with great acceptance, and with every prospect of soon being independent of the funds of the society. At Alberton the Rev. C. D. Watt has accepted an invitation to settle; the people are exerting themselves to raise the requisite means, and are manifesting increased zeal and earnestness. Salisbury being vacated by Mr. Mudie, is now without a pastor, and without the immediate prospect of one. At Lyndoch Valley matters are reported as being stationery. Houghton has been supplied by several agents of the society, the attendance has been encouraging, and the sabbath school is flourishing. The friends at Houghton and Tea Tree Gully are making efforts to secure the services of the Rev. Mr. Howie, lately arrived from Scotland. Shipley is supplied by agents, and presents signs of progress. The same may be said of Glen Osmond and Glenelg. At Maclaren Vale and White's Gully not much progress appears to be making. At Middleton, Castlerange, and Hindmarsh Island, discouragements are complained of; but at Goolwa the cause is looking up, a church has been formed by the Rev. J. Roberts, and arrangements are in progress for erecting a plain but commodious place of worship. During the year the church at Port Elliott, under the pastoral care of the Rev. John Hotham, and the church at Gawler, under that of the Rev. James Leonard, B.A., have ceased to receive pecuniary aid from the society. The settlement of the Rev. C. D. Watt, at Alberton, leaves the society without a ministerial and travelling agent; but the arrival of several ministers from England, renders such an officer less necessary. Mr. Watt has given the committee great satisfaction from the earnestness and ability with which he has discharged his duties. During the year a number of special meetings, of a devotional and public character, have been held at the different stations, with the happiest results. The society appears to be in a vigorous state, and various resolutions were passed pledging the friends to continued and increased exertions. These resolutions were spoken to by Mr. Brown, M.P., the Revs. Messrs. Wilson, Evan, Dixon, Cox, Hotham, Ayling, and others.

CONGREGATIONAL UNION.—On April 29th, the day after the above anniversary of the South Australian Home Mission, the Congregational Union held its meetings. In the morning a devotional service was held at Ebenezer Chapel, presided over by the Rev. F. W. Cox. In the afternoon the meeting for business was held at the same place. The chief points which engaged the attention of the Union were the resolutions passed at the conference held in Hobart Town in February last, which were discussed and concurred in. The Union specially resolved zealously to co-operate in the support of the friends to the *Southern Spectator*. The meetings were greatly enlivened by the presence of the four new ministers from England, and by the statements of Mr. Waterhouse, and Mr. Evan, the Deputies to the Hobart Town Conference. In the evening a sermon appropriate to the occasion was preached at Freeman street Chapel by the Rev. F. W. Cox, recently arrived.

Western Australia.

CONGREGATIONALISTS.—Extract of a letter from Freemantle, dated March 11, 1858:—

" I thought it might not be uninteresting to you to forward you a little statistical information respecting Congregationalism in Western Australia. You are aware that this colony falls far behind the other Australian colonies in point of population and progress. The superior attractions of Victoria, ever since the discovery of gold, have drawn away great numbers of the young and enterprising, and I suppose we shall continue to suffer from the same cause for some years to come. Still there is a gradual improvement made in population, commerce and agriculture, and the future prospects of the colony are hopeful. The present number of inhabitants in Western Australia is about 14,000. Perth, the capital, contains a population of 2600; Freemantle, the port where I reside, 1600; and the small towns of Bunbury, Guildford and York about 700 each. At present, only four denominations exist here : of these the Church of England is most influential, as it is the most favored by the government, and receives the lion's share of the ecclesiastical grant. There are a bishop and about twelve clergymen, who all receive aid either from the colonial or home governments. The next in point of numbers is the Roman Catholic Church. Connected with this body are two bishops, several ecclesiastics, lay brothers and sisters of mercy, nearly all of whom are either Spaniards or French. The Wesleyans have two ministers here, both excellent men, and their chapel in Perth is large and well-attended. Both they and the Roman Catholics receive some aid from the government. The Congregational Denomination is perhaps numerically the smallest. The father of Independency here is Mr. Trigg of Perth, who for many years was Clerk of the Public Works. Some years ago, in order to supply the spiritual destitution of the place, he commenced preaching in his own house in Perth. He then erected a small chapel, which was subsequently enlarged, of which for several years he was the minister. He gathered a congregation, and formed a church on Congregational principles. In consequence of his advancing years, the Colonial Missionary Society sent out a minister, Mr. Leonard, about six years ago, to whom Mr. Trigg resigned the pastorship. Mr. Leonard remained about four years, and then removed to Gawler Town, South Australia. He was succeeded by Mr. Charlesworth, who was formerly a clergyman of the Church of England. He continued about a year, and then removed to South Australia. In the meantime Mr. Trigg continued to preach at out-stations, and now regularly supplies four different places; and is usefully and honorably employed in his Master's work in his old age. The chapel at Perth was closed after Mr. Charlesworth's departure; but we are hoping to have another minister from England before long. Mr. Trigg was instrumental in procuring the erection of a neat chapel at Guildford, where Mr. A. Jones preaches with acceptance, and is sustained partly by his own exertions and partly by his congregation. At a place called Australind, a farmer named Allnutt has built a small chapel, where he preaches every Sabbath day, and has formed a small Congregational Church. He also preaches once a fortnight at Bunbury. The cause in Freemantle was originated by Mr. Trigg, who some years ago induced a few persons to commence the erection of a chapel, and send home for a minister. In answer to their appeal, the Colonial Missionary Society in 1853 sent the Rev. Joseph Johnson, who had labored for eleven years as a missionary in Tahiti. He found only an unfinished building, and but three persons who held Congregational principles. God, however, has blessed his labors : he has been successful in gathering a good congregation, who supply a part of his income, the Society still granting some aid. Just now the people are enlarging the chapel, at a cost of £300; as soon as this is paid off, it is expected that the congregation will be in a condition to support their minister wholly themselves. Owing to the fluctuating character of the population, a church has not yet been regularly organised; but Mr. Johnson administers the Lord's Supper to about twenty pious people, who will probably form the nucleus of a church."

THE FIRST NUMBER OF THE NEW SERIES WILL BE ISSUED ON 1ST AUGUST.

Communications for Editor care of W. FAIRFAX & Co., *Melbourne.*

EDITOR'S ANNOUNCEMENT.

THIS number of "Southern Spectator" completes the twelve months' issue at the promised rate of a number every alternate month. The projectors of the work have thus kept faith with the public, and with those subscribers who paid for the six numbers beforehand, in fulfilling their promise to continue the publication through one year at least ; and the Editor has endeavored to keep faith in other respects, by conducting the work according to the prospectus, so far as the means at his disposal would allow.

He stated that the work was designed to be colonial in its spirit, and colonial in its production ; and, in this respect, the original intention has been honestly carried out. The whole of the articles have been original, and nothing introduced in the way of extracts but a few scraps ; and the writers have been, in every instance, resident in one or other of the colonies, with the exception of a letter or two on books from an English correspondent. Nor have the productions of one colony preponderated much over those of any other ; they have been furnished in pretty equal proportions from all the four :—New South Wales, Victoria, South Australia, and Tasmania. The circulation has also held about the same proportion in each colony, according to the population. The fulfilment, therefore, has corresponded with the pledge that the periodical should not be Victorian, but Australasian.

It was announced that the work would not be Denominational, but Catholic, with the view of promoting the interests of the whole Church of the Redeemer, and not of any particular branch. And, to

T

this announced purpose, the Editor has the testimony of his conscience in having faithfully adhered. Judging by the event, however, little credit has been given to this declaration, for not the slightest countenance has been shewn to the undertaking, or interest taken in it, by any other denomination than the Editor's own. He has been favored with no articles, or communications of any sort, from Presbyterians, Baptists, Wesleyans, or Episcopalians, with one or two rare exceptions. This attempt at Catholicity may, therefore, be regarded as a practical failure. The Editor deeply regrets this, for it would have been a high gratification to him, and a great means, he believes, of usefulness, if the publication had been taken up by the general body of Evangelical Christians as their own, and made an organ for interchanging thought and sentiment, and mutually stimulating each other to love and good works.

It would seem, however, that the time is hardly yet come for this, in a population so comparatively small and scattered as inhabit these colonies. The number of persons sufficiently emancipated from the denominational spirit, and sufficiently detached from denominational interests, is scarcely large enough to support a periodical. A " Christian Times," or an " Evangelical Christendom," may find a constituency of writers and readers in England, but not in Australia. For a little time longer, therefore, we must, it is to be feared, fall back upon our sectional connections, and be content to have " Church of England Records," " Wesleyan Chronicles," " Baptist Magazines," and " Congregational Spectators," and, if the Presbyterians were only sufficiently united among themselves, "Presbyterian Witnesses."

Experience has taught the conductors of the work the lesson that the price at which it is sold is not sufficient to cover the expenses ; nor is the circulation in fault, for that has been large enough to have been remunerative, had the charge not been too low for the quantity of letter press produced. But the cost of printing, publishing, advertising, carriage, etc., is such as to entail a loss, for which the Editor will have to avail himself of the original guarantee fund.

These various matters came under the careful consideration of the Conference of Congregationalists, held in Hobart Town in February last. The Magazine originated at a previous session of that body, and it was proper that its future should be determined by the same authority. A committee was appointed to examine into the facts of the case and report to the Conference. The committee considered, from the information laid before it, that the Magazine in the main was a success and ought if possible to be continued ; that, as the circulation for the most part was confined to the Congregationalists it should in the event of its continuance be more ostensibly connected with that body ; that, as a work of this kind could not be expected to live permanently unless it cleared its own expenses, it should be reduced from three to two sheets, to bring down the expenses, while by increasing the size of the page the amount of matter would be but slightly lessened ; that, to meet the general wish and to keep up and increase the interest in the Magazine, it should appear once a month instead of bi-monthly ; that, as advertisements from which a revenue was expected, though their number had been considerable, appeared really to have entailed a loss, none should hereafter be printed, except on the cover, unless at the publishers' risk ; and, finally, that, a fund should be raised in equal proportions in the four colonies to form a capital for conducting the undertaking with advantage. A report, embodying these views, was laid before the Conference. Among the resolutions agreed upon (the whole of which appeared in our last number), it is necessary to insert here only the two following :—

"That the ' Southern Spectator ' consist of thirty-two pages, and that it be published monthly, and sold at one shilling per copy, or ten shillings to subscribers for the year, payment in advance."

"That the title in future be, ' The Southern Spectator, a Magazine of Religious and General Literature, connected with the Congregational Churches of Australasia.' "

The Editor, therefore, has to announce that it is intended to issue the "Southern Spectator," henceforth, on the first of every month ; that the first number, however, of the new series will not appear till August 1st., so that there will be only five numbers issued during the remainder of this year ; and that this portion of the work will be entitled Vol. I., part 2, so as to bind up in one volume with what has already been published. The way will then be clear for a fair start with Volume II., on January 1st, 1859.

In making these announcements, the Editor begs to state that though he will not, henceforth, be restricted from inserting articles avowing Congregational principles, the general spirit of the work will be as Catholic as ever.   He will study brevity and variety in the articles admitted, and endeavor to secure such as are adapted to the class of persons among whom it is expected the Magazine will chiefly circulate.   His great object will be to cultivate the intelligence of the people and to promote their piety.   He asks the cordial support of his brethren in the ministry, and of intelligent laymen, in furnishing him with articles and essays, biographical sketches, histories of colonial churches, interesting incidents and anecdotes, and other miscellaneous matter.   And, with respect to the circulation, he would ask the present subscribers who approve of the work and think it likely to be useful, not only to continue to take it in, but to exert themselves to procure additional subscribers among the friends ; and would suggest to ministers and deacons of churches the appointment of some *one active individual*, in each congregation, to manage the Magazine department, by canvassing for subscribers, delivering the numbers as they come to hand, receiving payments and remitting the moneys promptly as they come in.   To prevent loss to the parties ordering the Magazine, and secure a steady circulation, the plan of *pre-payment*, for the next five numbers up to Christmas, should if possible be universally adopted.

INDEX.

W. FAIRFAX AND CO., STEAM PRINTERS, COLLINS-STREET EAST, MELBOURNE.

THE

SOUTHERN SPECTATOR

A MAGAZINE

OF

𝕽𝖊𝖑𝖎𝖌𝖎𝖔𝖚𝖘, 𝕻𝖍𝖎𝖑𝖆𝖓𝖙𝖍𝖗𝖔𝖕𝖎𝖈, 𝕾𝖔𝖈𝖎𝖆𝖑 & 𝕲𝖊𝖓𝖊𝖗𝖆𝖑 𝕷𝖎𝖙𝖊𝖗𝖆𝖙𝖚𝖗𝖊.

From July, 1858, to June, 1859.

EDITED BY REV. R. FLETCHER,

ST. KILDA, MELBOURNE.

VOL II.

MELBOURNE:

W. FAIRFAX AND CO., PRINTERS AND PUBLISHERS,
78, COLLINS STREET, EAST.

1859.

The Southern Spectator.

| No. I. | AUGUST, 1858. | VOL. II. |

OUR NEW SERIES.

It may seem soon, after the commencement of this periodical, to announce a new series; but our first year was altogether experimental and our future course was to be determined by its results. Those results, as stated in the editorial announcement appended to our last number, are such as to encourage us to go on; but not exactly in the same way. To prevent a perpetual drain upon private funds, we are compelled to diminish the number of our sheets, without, however, materially lessening the quantity of letterpress. At the size and in the style now presented to the reader, the *Southern Spectator* will pay its own way, if it meet with a support equal to that which it has already received; and if it be favored with some additional support, it will be a complete success. It has been found expedient, as previously announced, to connect it more closely with the denomination with which it originated. As it was almost wholly sustained by the adherents of that body when it stood on common ground, it is natural to suppose that it will receive warmer and more extended support from them now that a greater prominence is allowable to Congregational principles and Congregational proceedings. We, therefore, earnestly call upon the members of our several churches, the worshippers in assemblies, the teachers in our Sunday schools, the young persons in our Bible classes and classes for mutual improvement, to exert themselves to increase the circulation. If each would do a little, the aggregate would be considerable, and the periodical be put beyond the risk of failure. And not so, but means would be put into the hands of the Editor by which the only quality and usefulness of the work might be further improved.

One of our greatest difficulties has arisen from delays in transmitting the successive numbers of the magazine to their destination, when that happened to be distant. Steamers have been irregular or have been occasionally missed; parcels have been detained in warehouses, or left unopened in vestries, and subscribers have complained that the magazines have reached them long after date. Perhaps this was inevitable in the first working of such an undertaking. But a road once open can be trodden more easily a second time. When it is ascertained where obstructions lie there is a better chance of avoiding them afterwards. Every attention shall be given to the prompt and punctual despatch of parcels, and we are full of hope that the complaints in question will soon greatly diminish, if not entirely cease; but the subscribers will have it in their own power to abolish these obstructions and delays altogether. The *Southern Spectator* is now *registered for transmission by post;** it may, therefore, be sent to

---

* The copies must be posted within seven days of publication, in a cover open at the ends, with 1d. stamp affixed. The name and address of the person to whom sent is the only writing allowed.

any part of these colonies, or of the United Kingdom, at the small cost of *one penny* per number. If those who desire the magazine, therefore, will only subscribe each five shillings (see slip inserted) for the first five numbers, which will embrace the issues up to the end of the present year, and remit the money beforehand, the numbers shall be sent to them with the regularity and the speed of letters, without any additional charge for postage. Some individual in a church or district might collect the moneys together and remit them in one sum to the Publishers, together with the addresses of the subscribers ; and in the case of other colonies than Victoria, some arrangements will be made to send the sums from the outlying districts through an agency in the chief cities. Whether these suggestions approve themselves or not, we would earnestly press the adoption everywhere, and in all cases, of the system of *prepayment*. It would enable the conductors of the work, with money in hand, to combine economy with efficiency in its preparation ; it would prevent, to the individuals who may interest themselves in canvassing for subscribers and supplying the magazine, losses through bad debts and the accumulation of odd numbers from subscribers leaving off without notice. The system is easily and satisfactorily managed when resolutely set about and persevered in.

When the magazine was first projected, the Editor stated his belief that a periodical of a medium style and price, and of a character somewhat mixed as to its contents, would be best adapted to the present state of these colonies. During the working of the experiment various opinions and suggestions have reached us, some recommending a journal of a higher class, and others something smaller and cheaper. On carefully considering all these suggestions, our opinion remains unchanged (and it was the same with the Conference Committee at Hobart Town), that the kind of publication most suited to existing circumstances, taking all things into account, is such an one as has already been furnished. That it is susceptible of improvement in details, none is more ready to admit than the Editor, and no pains will be spared to make it as useful and generally acceptable as possible ; but it will still aim at meeting the wants of more classes than one. The members constituting the several classes of which Christian congregations are composed, and who might wish for a periodical suited to their particular ideas and taste, are still too small to sustain one for themselves. Some readers may find something in our pages which does not interest them, but we trust most will find something which does ; and let all remember that the portions they do not care for, are the very portions others may want most to see. Let the readers of our magazine exercise the same indulgence and the same allowance they do in the use of newspapers, select those portions which best suit them, and leave the rest to others. And we, for our part, will make an endeavor to turn every practicable hint to good account, and to provide as great a variety as the case may seem to require, and of as good a quality as we can command.

It is our earnest wish, our fervent prayer, and our strong hope, that the *Southern Spectator*, about to make its appearance more frequently, with additional monetary and literary strength, and with the advantage of some experience, and in a fair way, we trust, to reach every church in connexion with the Congregational body in all the Australias, and most of the individual members, may become under God an efficient help to the minister in his anxious labors for the good of his flock, to the Sunday school teacher in his class-instruction, to the tract distributor in his visitations, to the young man in his aspirations after knowledge and excellence, to the missionary and Bible collector, and to the Christian in his private reading ; and if in any appreciable degree this hope should be realised, we shall not deem the labor and the time bestowed upon it as expended in vain. We again throw ourselves upon the sympathy of our friends, and particularly of our brethren in the ministry, and ask their co-operation in extending the sale of the work, and in enriching its pages with such materials, original or collected, as they may have at their command and think may be useful.

THE NEWSPAPER PRESS AND RELIGION.

Some movements have been recently made in Melbourne towards the establishment of a religious newspaper. The chief reason assigned for this attempt is an alleged neglect on the part of the Press in reporting religious proceedings. Not that these proceedings are entirely omitted, but that they are only occasionally noticed ; and then, generally speaking, in a very abridged and imperfect form. The religious interest in the colony, it is stated, does not receive that amount of attention to which its importance entitles it as compared with other interests. We presume there must be some ground for these complaints or they would not be so oft and so loudly repeated.

One of the defences set up is the sectarianism of the religious bodies, or rather of their clergymen. They are represented as cooped up within the narrow limits of their own sect, bent on denominational objects, and indifferent to those of a general nature. Much of this charge really resolves itself into a compliment to their diligence in their proper duties. For where should a minister devote his chief energies but upon his own flock and district ? Of course he has his anniversaries and social meetings to promote the welfare of the special charge committed to him, and he attends, also, larger gatherings for objects connected generally with his own body. But need he therefore be sectarian ? Is it not a very common thing to see these very ministers showing sympathy and rendering aid to brother ministers of other denominations at their public meetings ? Surely the men that do this, and do it so frequently, cannot be so very bigotted and exclusive. But are all religious meetings narrow and sectional? The Bible and Tract Societies, the City and Chinese Missions, Sunday School Missions, Bethel Unions, and Evangelical Alliances, do not contemplate and do not promote the increase of a congregation or the aggrandisement of a sect. Yet in the committees and on the platforms of such institutions these narrow sectarians are wont to meet and cordially to co-operate.

We are given to understand that the editors dislike, what they would probably call, the sermonising strain of speeches at religious meetings, and consider them unsuitable for the columns of a newspaper. But is it expected that they should themselves approve of everything they put in their papers ? Do they not record and publish the sayings and doings of others, leaving these for the most part to speak for themselves ? The complaint against them is not that they do not compose homilies for leaders and admit sermons for ordinary letters. It is not that they refuse to advocate some specific religious opinions and press religious duties, but, that religious proceedings of a public nature are not reported with sufficient care and fulness. We suspect they consider that such matter would not be palatable to their readers. But have they not readers of various tastes, and can they consult the taste of each in every article or paragraph they insert ? The community is divided into classes of different pursuits and different predi-

lections.   In a good newspaper each reader finds something to his mind.
But who reads everything?   Some see nothing but advertisements, others
never deign to cast an eye upon them.   Some fly at once to the births,
marriages, and deaths ; there are others that hardly know there is such a
corner in the paper.   The respective departments of shipping and markets,
law and police, science and literature, music and recreation, crime and accidents, agriculture and mining, politics legislation and general news, have
their several admirers and devotees, who, in not a few instances, confine
their worship to their own idols.   He must be a rare reader who is omni-
vorous and reads all before him.   There is often much that is not only
not attractive but positively offensive to many of the general approvers of
the paper.   But their distaste is not heeded, because there are others who
have a relish for these things.   Every class is catered for, though that class
may constitute but a fractionable portion of the community.   Now, is the
religious portion so very contemptible in number and influence that it alone
should be overlooked ?   Are not those who compose it nearly all newspaper
readers, taking the papers in for general purposes, but feeling also a special
interest in their own proceedings, just as the man of science or frequenter
of the theatre does in his ?   As a part of the general public, we contend,
they are entitled to have their public proceedings, those which they themselves deem important, as fairly and as fully reported as any other class.
No claim is put in for preference to be shewn to any particular denomination or set of opinions.   Let equal justice be done to all, whether orthodox
or heterodox, Protestant or Catholic, Jew or Christian.   Thus all will have
an opportunity of knowing what the rest are doing.   Some, perhaps most,
of the conductors of the Press, engage to insert reports of religious proceedings if sent in to them ready prepared by the parties themselves, and not
too long.   This is all very well in certain cases, especially such as are only
of a semi-public character.   But as a general rule we deem it but fair to
the religious bodies, and what would be conducive in the end to the interest
of the newspaper proprietors themselves, if they not only gave a proportionate amount of space to the proceedings in question, but took the responsibility also of providing the material as they do for other interests.
    To one thing more we must allude.   Space may be desirable, but
quality is still more important.   As things are, one or two reporters are
generally seen at advertised meetings, and *something* appears in the papers
next morning.   While it may be mortifying to see the account reduced to
a meagre skeleton, it is still more so to find the main points missed through
ignorance or inattention.   Reports, generally, must be greatly condensed ;
and it requires persons who know what they are about to condense properly,
to leave out the unimportant matter, and to seize the substance.   Men
are chosen to furnish commercial, political, legal, and theatrical intelligence
from their familiarity and sympathy with those departments ; why should
not a like course be adopted in reference to the important department of
religion ?   How could an infidel, or a man unfamiliar with religious ideas
and modes of speech, enter into the spirit of a religious meeting and satisfactorily report its doings and sayings, unless, indeed, he took down the
speeches *verbatim*, and printed them *in extenso* ?   As religion *is* a matter
of greatest moment to a large portion of the community, and as adequate
reports of public proceedings in relation to it *are* deemed of great consequence by vast numbers of newspaper readers, why should not the conductors
of a large daily paper, both as a matter of duty to their supporters and of
policy as regards their own interests, take care that they should have one,

at least, on their staff of reporters who, while answering the purpose of his employers in other respects, understands the subject of religion, has sympathy with it, and can give a trustworthy representation of measures publicly taken to promote it ?

We hope these remarks will be taken in good part, as they are meant. We would wish to see the regular newspapers in their ordinary course of business deal fairly with the religious portion of the public, whatever religious papers may be specially established to supply the want that is so much felt ; and the public mind may perhaps be ripe for one. Such papers are necessary for specific purposes, and when the population is larger, and its different interests are more fully developed, they will doubtless appear in greater numbers, but they can never supersede the functions of that great power in the community, the Daily Press.

SMALL BEGINNINGS.

HOW TO GAIN A CORRECT AND IMPRESSIVE ESTIMATE OF SMALL BEGINNINGS IN CHRISTIAN ENTERPRISES.

Is it then peculiar to Christianity alone, that large results should flow from seemingly inconsiderable commencements ? Assuredly not. The operations and productions of nature, the industrial trials of man, the advancement of intelligence, the progress of society, political organizations and changes, all admonish us, as clearly as our religion does, not to despise the day of small things. Half a dozen grains of rare corn planted in a garden by a careful hand, may, in a few years, cover vast regions with waving crops. The quiet studies of a single mind may revolutionize a science by startling discoveries, or supplant time-honored arts by brilliant inventions. A conversation between three intelligent men may convulse empires or rend in twain old hierarchies. Still, even in those things, it is not always seen how inconsiderable and how unimposing was the commencement ; it is not always remembered how small and unpretending was the first movement. And if in things material or involving material interests, attention has sometimes to be awakened to the small origin of vast affairs—to the seeds of events—how much more may this be expected when the objects do not appeal to the senses, or obtrude themselves upon the observation, when development came more stealthily and noiselessly into view, and when the spaces lying between the first agencies and the observable results are often so lengthened as to conceal the connexion between them. "But," say Christian philantropists, "we believe :—we believe that the worm Jacob shall thrash the mountains ; we believe that the handful of corn thrown upon the top of the mountain shall shake like Lebanon ; we believe in the grain of mustard seed ; we believe in the leaven hid in three measures of meal ; and we just act upon our faith, we fulfil our commission, do our allotted work, and leave the results with him whose it is to prosper and to bless." True ; but does not faith take cognizance of what God does in the world, as well as of what he says in his word ? If we know that Jacob does thrash the mountains and make them small as dust ; if we see the golden harvest waving on the mountain top ; if we find the lump leavened from the small deposit ; if we walk in the shade of the spreading tree sprung from the minute grain, is not our faith in the power that does it, all the stronger, our hope all the livelier, and our zeal all the warmer?

INSTANCES of usefulness, great, wide and lasting, from limited beginnings, will rebuke our incredulity, prevent discouragement, and eminently prompt to persevering effort. Great ultimate effects of incipient evangelical labors will neither be despaired of nor unattempted. It must not be supposed that the first wide spread of Christianity is a case inapplicable to our point. Notwithstanding the miraculous element it contained, it is still an analogy and a model. Miracle was to prove Christianity and to awaken attention. Christianity has that proof still as strongly as historical testimony can convey it to us; and each age has its appropriate means of exciting attention. We are thus brought upon the same footing with that despised company that met in an upper room for prayer, and which, issuing from that room took with them over the known world as the only means of the wonders they wrought, that same Gospel which we hold, and which we also use to produce the same effects. Nor should the immediately succeeding evangelists, who spread themselves throughout the Roman empire, and beyond it, be neglected in this inquiry on account of some fancied mystic power by virtue of proximity to apostles and miracles. How instructive would be the details of such labors could we have them! But the very want of them significantly bears on our present object. Their first efforts in various countries were too little observable to leave deep vestiges. Subsequent monuments do not shew, though they prove, their earliest conquests.

Into what importance would some of our present missions rise, could we compare their seemingly small, slow and discouraging condition with the same stages and aspects in those ancient missions which laid the foundations of all Christendom! In Britain, the records of such labors, if they existed, perished with the Britons themselves, whilst heathenism again covered the land. But we get some glimpses of the kind of work by which a second conquest over idolatry was gained. We do not look for it, however, in the proceedings of that marshalled company which under Austin, with much pomp and circumstance, left Rome for Canterbury, in order to convert the Saxons. Far more satisfactory was the influence of the simple monks of Iona. What a picture has Bede, himself a Romanist, given of Aidan! And after him, were individuals, who though yielding at length to the claims of the men of Canterbury, carried with them to several of the northern, the central, and even the eastern parts of the heptarchy, much of the simplicity, piety, and evangelism of the school of the Culdees. Such were the brothers, Cedd and Chad. England again became in name and profession Christian, and the earliest traces of her becoming in any degree vitally so, are found in connexion with the unostentatious missionaries of the western isle; whilst North Britain remains a conquest—glorious conquest—to this hour, of their lowly toils and teachings. Nor should we exclude from the catalogue of examples illustrative of our topic those few marvellous instances in which men, without miracle, or thought of miracle, produced impressions so extensive and so deep that we do not see how any considerable part of the world will escape the influence, nor how the traces can be trodden out to the end of time. Such are our legitimate witnesses; for it was simply the

Gospel that they spread, and their first essays were humble and limited. Wickliffe, Luther, Calvin, Knox, Whitfield, the Wesleys, all give their testimony to the value of a *first* attempt, however obscure, diminutive, or neglected.

To be continued.

————◆————

FRUIT IN OLD AGE.
To the Editor of the Southern Spectator.

My dear Sir,—When recently on a visit to a friend at Parramatta, a letter was shewn to me written by his mother, an old lady nearly ninety years of age, with which I was so much pleased that I requested to be favored with a copy of it. The aged saint has been taken to her rest, but to her children and children's children "though dead, she yet speaketh;" her holy life and pious counsels will long be remembered by them, and will ever be felt to be instructive and admonitory. I have permission to make any use of the letter referred to that I might think desirable; I send it for insertion in your work, as I am persuaded it will both interest and benefit many of your readers. The "old disciple" will thus speak to a larger audience than she ever thought of addressing, and in a way she never dreamt of; I am much mistaken, however, if her simple, but wise and weighty words do not find their way to the heart with far more facility and effect than those of many an ingenious or elaborate discourse.—Yours, &c.,

T. BINNEY.

July, 1858.

January 1st, 1854.

My very dear and only son,—I sit down to address to you probably the last letter you will have from me. I suffered much on account of your and my ever to be beloved Sarah's heavy trials on your beginning the world a second time; but my faith is immovable in all these things working out for you both, and for myself "a far more exceeding and eternal weight of glory." I am now near ninety years old, but I consider myself one of the happiest beings in existence, for most of my trials are gone through, and under the apprehension of those to come, I am happy to tell you that my feet are on the Rock. I have a husband, three children, and two grandchildren beyond the boundary line of sin and sorrow. God was manifestly glorified in the deaths of those who came to maturity, and the rest are quite as safe. My health is just as good as ever it was,—only the infirmities incident to old age, and fewer of these than perhaps any other creature of my age. My memory is good; I seldom forget anything I hear; I can read a little, and hear middling well; I have food to eat, and raiment to put on; and, when sick, tender hands to aid my infirmities. I feel as if a volume would not be too much for me to fill, if I told you all I think of you both, and the dear, dear children. When overwhelmed with the thoughts of you all, I can only ease my full heart by crying to heaven in the language of the apostle, "that the God and Father of Our Lord Jesus Christ would bless you all, with all spiritual blessings, in heavenly places, in Christ Jesus." I know and often say that our prayers are reciprocal, for I feel you are asking for me; and the blessed access I feel, tells me that I am heard for you. But one thing above all things I would enforce,—the necessity of teaching the dear children that this religion I am recommending is a thing not to be found in books, sermons, or knowledge, but at a throne of grace; it is a casting off the works of darkness and putting on the armour of light; it is putting off the old man, and a putting on the new; a crucifying the flesh, with its affections and lusts ; it is set about by a knowledge of themselves, a repentance towards God, a faith in Christ, a passing through the strait gate, a new birth, Christ formed and brought forth in the soul, enabling the new creature to walk in Christ, with a knowledge of salvation by the remission of sins ; a self-denying life.   I tell my dear grandchildren that these are my views of religion, after sixty-four years' experience, for so long has my Saviour kept me ; and now I know that " neither life nor death," nor any of the dangers in the catalogue, " shall be able to separate me from the love of God which is in Christ Jesus my Lord."   I shall ever, while life remains, remember you all in my prayers night and day, and I trust you will do the same for me, for I am still in the field, and the wolf of the evening is still going about ; but after sixty-four years' conflict, the sword of the Spirit is still bright, and oh ! to have the promised land in view ! this is what John Bunyan called " the Land of Beulah," or the prophet Isaiah " the land that is afar off, where the King is seen in his beauty."   I was reading of this to-day, the first of the year, and I trust, ere another year rolls round, that faith will be lost in sight.   But before I let the pen be dropped, again I would say, tell the dear children that in searching for religion, Jacob " wrestled," David " wept, and watered his couch with tears," Paul " prayed," the publican " smote upon his breast," the jailor cried " what shall I do ?" and, above all, Jesus, when asking *for* us, " rose a great while before day, and went into a solitary place, and there prayed ;"——everything, for life or death, is to be got at a throne of grace ; but the soul must be on the stretch for all we want.   And now, my dear children, I have told you what I longed to say before I leave this vale of tears.   Meet me above, that I may say, " Here am I, and the children that thou hast given me."   May the good Lord keep you all till we meet in " a house not made with hands," is the prayer of, my dear son,

Your affectionate mother,

*** ***

THE HONORS OF FORGIVENESS OF INJURIES.

   " The discretion of a man deferreth his anger ; and it is his glory to pass over a transgression."*   One cannot fail to be impressed with the great dignity thus ascribed to a virtue, of which men make but small account, by a Being who knows the relative and actual worth of the actions of all intelligent creatures.   His thoughts are not as our thoughts ; man's general estimate of glory is of a widely different character.   Wise men glory in their wisdom, in the results of patient thought and experiment, in the treasures of the past which they have made their own, in the secrets they have wrested from Nature's keeping ; and they receive glory from men as the priests and expounders of hidden things.   Rich men glory in the riches they have obtained by inheritance, in virtue of musty parchments, ancestral rolls and accidents of birth, or received as a gift, or won in the race of commerce by personal skill and effort.   Mighty men glory in their strength ; it is a great thing with them to stand in the imminent deadly breach, in the fierce and fiery aggressive onslaught, with unquailing heart and unfailing arm, acting a soldier's part, ever pressing on through opposing hosts till the city is won and victory crowns the banners so proudly borne.   It is not our object in this brief paper to limit and define the nature and amount of

* Proverbs, xix. 11.

human glory which a man may justly covet, nor to show how soon it must be left ; we point to a nobler glory. Show us a man in whom all earthly honors and glories centre—an admirable Crichton, a merchant prince of largest wealth, a hero brave as Tell, or the men who sealed the doom of the Cashmere Gate at Delhi. A yet nobler glory, we aver, belongs to the man who passes over a transgression, saying, like Stephen, "Lord, lay not this sin to their charge ;" or a greater than Stephen, "Father, forgive them ; for they know not what they do." This celebration of forgiveness as the crowning glory of man is pre-eminently a Scripture doctrine. You may read books, converse with men in many climes, but nowhere do you find this truth set forth as an intuitive principle, or as a generalised result from human experience. We owe it unquestionably to the source of all that is gentle, beautiful, and holy. The world had to be taught it, Christ to illustrate it, the Bible to record it, Apostles to explain and enforce it. Long as men may need and exercise forgiveness, it shall now ever remain a great truth, full of love and noble beauty, that it is the glory of a man to pass over a transgression.

Because it illustrates his humility. A man imbued with the true spirit of the Bible, on receiving a deliberate and wilful insult or injury, will not be anxious and hasty to devise means of immediate vengeance. His discretion will defer his anger until he has observed all the related circumstances. Humility prompts the question, " Is there not a cause ? Have I injured him, so that he is measuring back my injustice ? Have I acted unwisely, so as to lead him with a fair show of reason to suspect me ? If so, I shall not do well to be angry, but must extend forgiveness even unasked." More, such a man will humbly remember how often in the course of his life he has injured others by indiscretion, folly, ignorance, selfishness, and sin ; and if all such transgressions had been punished, his life would have been a constant penance for guilt. Nor will such a man fail to remember how numerous and aggravated by many circumstances are his own transgressions in the sight of God ; if he hopes to obtain forgiveness of these great transgressions, it can only be in the exercise of a spirit of forgiveness ; "For if ye forgive not men their trespasses, neither will your heavenly Father forgive your trespasses." Not that the spirit and act of forgiveness to a fellow-man ensures our forgiveness by God, and is the sole ground of it,—God forgives sin for Christ's sake only ; yet a forgiving spirit on our part is an essential preliminary to the receiving of divine forgiveness, just as penitence is. " Forgive us our trespasses, as we forgive them that trespass against us," is a divinely constructed petition for man in the only liturgy we care to recognise. A lowly heart, conscious of its own imperfections, charitable in its construction of other men's words and actions, humbly relying upon God's mercy, is an object upon which God looks with complacency and deems it glorious.

Because it illustrates his intelligence. A man cannot do a wiser thing for his own peace than to pass over a transgression. A rankling sense of evil received, with a burning desire for revenge, is the enemy of all enjoyment. Haman had a bright catalogue of honors and a full cup of joy, but so long as Mordecai failed to give him the reverence he thought his due, all this availed him nothing ; he had put his happiness in another man's keeping,—into the hands of his supposed foe. Better far for a man to construe an action charitably, or, if manifestly evil, to forgive and forget, especially as schemes and agencies of vengeance frequently recoil back upon himself in proportion to the energy expended upon them, as Haman found to his cost.   Moreover, a man cannot take a more likely course to secure a sincere friend than to forgive an enemy ; nothing melts like mercy, or moves to penitence like manifested love : it is the Redeemer's own plan to secure friends.   If Henry Martyn had penned no other truth than the following :—"This also I found, that the power of gentleness is irresistible," the world would have been greatly his debtor.

Nor will an intelligent man fail to perceive that his foes can do him no lasting harm if faithful to his duty ; his character, in the long run, is in his own keeping, and all little aspersions, as Boerhaave wisely said, are but sparks, which, if we do not fan them, will go out of themselves.   Let, then, a wise man cherish a forgiving spirit, and do it in order to be wise.

Because it shows his imitation of a high and holy example.   God delighteth in mercy ; we are required and permitted in some respects to be merciful, even as our Father in heaven is merciful.   As we have been made partakers of the divine nature, so must we perform divine acts ; if it is manly to resent an insult or an injury that we know,—we believe that it is God-like to forgive.   The Scripture argument to enforce the duty and glory of forgiveness, as drawn from divine procedure, is twofold.   There is first the argument drawn from the bounties of a common Providence.   God causeth his sun to shine upon the evil and the good, and sendeth rain upon the just and the unjust.   Next we are required to "forgive one another, even as God, for Christ's sake, hath forgiven us."   Solemn, touching truths here meet us face to face,—our own sinfulness, the incarnation, death, and intercession of the Saviour, the moment when we received for his sake a free, a full, a lasting forgiveness, with its newborn joys and heavenly aspirations.   Can a man remember these things and fail to extend forgiveness to an erring fellow-man ?   Will he be like God ? or like the servant in the parable, whose master forgave him a large debt, but unmindful of that, went out and found a fellow-servant who owed him a hundred pence, and most cruelly treated him, because he could not at once make restitution ?   The closing portion of the parable is of an eminently warning character.   Let us still forgive, even as God does, until seventy times seven ; a definite number for an indefinite one.

We are aware that the duty we have enforced is a difficult one, and the resulting glory rarely attained ; but this is no excuse for its neglect, it rather furnishes a reason for its diligent cultivation.   The Christian value of our good qualities, as is well known, depends upon there being a victory over some depraved and opposite active quality.   If a man's natural disposition be irritable, if his daily circumstances have a tendency to develop and foster the evil, all the more important is it that he should watch and pray,—all the more honor to him if he overcomes.   There is a great difference in virtues ; some, as the love of parents, country, friends, are easy ; but it is more noble as it is more difficult to love our enemies. If we win this glory, we may hope to dwell in a land and in a society where it will only exist as a reward.   It is a virtue the exercise of which is not known in heaven ; it belongs to earth.   Hail to the world of the future, where dwell the spirits of the just made perfect !

————

SUBSTANCE OF A SERMON
ON THE OCCASION OF THE DEATH OF THE REV. J. G. REED, B.A.,
RECENTLY COME OUT FROM ENGLAND.

1 Kings viii. 17—19. And it was in the heart of David my father to build an house for the name of the Lord God of Israel. And the Lord said unto David my father, Whereas it was in thine heart to build an house unto my name, thou didst well that it was in thine heart; nevertheless *thou* shalt not build the house, but thy son who shall come forth out of thy loins, he shall build the house unto my name.

In this young country, where old people are few, and the population is still small, funeral sermons, especially for ministers, are comparatively rare. When, therefore, deaths of sufficient public importance as to call for special notice do occur, it is the more desirable to turn them to good practical account. Such an event has just taken place among ourselves. A young minister, whose heart was burning with desire to be employed in his Master's service, and who has several times joined us here in worship, has been called to his rest. We recently sent home to England for an additional supply of ministers to assist in evangelizing this country; it pleased God to dispose the hearts of many to respond to the call. Sixteen in all left the shores of Britain for service in these different colonies as the result of Mr. Poore's visit, and of this number two have been snatched away by death, one, Mr. Jacob Jones, being lost by shipwreck at the entrance of Sydney harbour; the other, Mr. Reed, designed for an important station at Geelong, has fallen a victim to a wasting disease. Two out of sixteen is a large proportion of loss, for which, perhaps, we had not sufficiently prepared ourselves. But God is teaching us by these events both to use our best endeavours for his cause, in the belief that our labor shall not be in vain, and at the same time not to calculate too confidently on everything turning out exactly as we had planned. At one time we see the beautiful connection between the means and the end; and at another that connection seems suddenly broken off, and we hear a voice saying, "Be still and know that I am God." The young minister whose loss we now deplore was earnestly intent upon his Master's service. His eagerness for his work, like that of a young officer with the prospect of a great war before him, amounted to a passion. But a severe cold, caught in England by exposure to the night air of the winter season, fixing, perhaps, upon a constitution exhausted by excessive study, planted in him the seeds of that malady whose fruit is death. He clung to life and the hope of life, not for its own sake, but from his desire to do something for God before he died; and the greatest trial his faith and submission were put to, was, to be willing to be called off from the war without being allowed to share in its toils, and dangers, and successes. Though declining in health when he arrived, it was impressed upon his mind that God had a work for him to do in this colony, and it required all the grace which was ultimately given him to say, "The will of the Lord be done," when he learnt that that work was to be done not by his life, but by his death.

It was this feature in our friend's character and experience which has led me to select the subject I have announced for a brief consideration.

I. Look at David's case as here stated by Solomon, his son: "It was in the heart of David, my father, to build an house for the name of the Lord God of Israel." David had many things to engage his attention and inflame his ambition if he had been covetous of human glory; he was a great poet, a great musician, a great warrior, a great king. In all these respects he was, perhaps, the first man of his age, certainly of his country.   But these things seemed not to fill his soul ; to excel in these departments was not his leading object in life, they were only a sort of bye-play, occupations and pursuits subordinate to a higher and nobler aim.   The main feature in his character was his religion, and to glorify God the chief purpose of his life.   To this everything was made to bend. His music was sacred music ; his poems were psalms and hymns ; his wars were the wars of the Lord, undertaken by divine command against the oppressors of the chosen people ; and all the wealth, and power, and influence he acquired he laid upon God's altar and devoted to his cause.

In particular he was a lover of public worship, a constant attendant upon the Tabernacle services.   He did not make the cares of state an excuse for absence.   He had no wish to be absent, and therefore he arranged to be present, and made other things give place ; and when public duty did take him away from Jerusalem his chief trouble was that he was not within reach of the house of God.   " My soul longeth, yea even fainteth for the courts of the Lord."   " When shall I come and appear before God ? "   " A day in thy courts is better than a thousand.   I had rather be a door-keeper in the house of my God, than to dwell in the tents of wickedness."

A man of this holy turn of mind was naturally desirous of improving the public worship of God ; and, in harmony with the spirit of the period, when the visible was the symbol of the invisible, the outwardly magnificent was typical of spiritual glory, and the present was prophetic of the future, he sought the realization of his ideas of what it became him to do, in the rearing of a temple worthy of the God he worshipped.   He saw around him in Assyria and Egypt, vast temples of gorgeous grandeur, built to the honor of false gods ; while the ark, the symbol of the presence of Jehovah, the King of kings, Lord of lords, God of gods, dwelt in a humble tent, screened off from vulgar gaze by curtains.   This was well enough in the days of Israel's wanderings, poverty, and weakness ; but now that the nation had swollen into a great and wealthy empire, it seemed to the pious David unsuitable to these altered circumstances, and he conceived the purpose of erecting a temple which should excel all others in magnificence.

God approved of the purpose : he said to him, " Thou didst well that it was in thine heart."   He that searches the human spirit saw that the motive was pure ; not ambition, but piety ; not even his nation's glory, but the glory of the God of the nation.   The monarch was sincerely desirous of turning to the account of religion the influential position he had gained, and the vast wealth he had amassed, and God accepted of his purpose. Not only the motive but the plan itself was approved by heaven.   The temple with all its sumptuousness, the worship with all its imposing ceremonials, as parts of a carnal and typical dispensation foreshadowing better things to come, and as the Divine wisdom had determined, that, to that youthful age of the world, a visible glory should be the emblem of the spiritual glory that excelleth, it was meet and proper that the temple which was to be the embodiment of all this, should be as gorgeous as human hands and royal wealth could make it.   It was therefore well that this thought entered David's heart, and that the purpose was pursued through David's life ; all this was right, noble, and in the highest sense religious, and acceptable to God.   Indeed, the idea came from heaven itself ; it was the inspiration of the Almighty which led the monarch to conceive the design and to keep its execution steadily in view.

Yet with all this divine commendation of the project, strange to say, David was not permitted the honour and the pleasure of carrying his desire into effect ; the heavenly oracle thus addresses him : " It was well that it was in thine heart ; but thou shalt not build the house ; but thy son he shall build the house unto my name." What a disappointment ! not to see realized the fondly cherished dream of his life ; to have it approved and yet postponed, and postponed till the period of his removal to another world ! And why was this ? why was not the man after God's own heart indulged in this his favorite desire ? He had been, by the necessity of his position, a man of war ; this was to be a house of peace. He had been compelled to subdue with a rod of iron hostile nations ; here was to be held forth the sceptre of grace. His reign had been the exemplification of subjugation by force ; the house was to be the house of prayer for all nations, the grand symbol on earth of atonement for sin, and of mercy and reconciliation from God. Besides, David had done much, but he was not to do everything. It was enough for one man to be the instrument of fulfilling the promises and predictions of the glory and dominion of Israel made to the Fathers ; to his successor must be left the further development of this grand the-ocrasy. " One soweth and another reapeth ; other men labor and we enter into their labor."

David submits without a murmur. He utters no complaint, as if hard measure had been dealt out to him. How touchingly, but without a tinge of repining, does he relate the circumstance to his people in public assembly, and to his youthful successor : " Hear me my brethren and my people : as for me I had in mine heart to build an house of rest for the ark of the covenant of the Lord, and for the footstool of our God, and had made ready for the building, but God said unto me, Thou shalt not build an house for my name, because thou hast been a man of war and hast shed blood. Howbeit the Lord God of Israel chose me before all the house of my father to be king over Israel for ever, and he said to me, Solomon thy son, he shall build my house and my courts, for I have chosen him to be my son, and I will be his Father." And then with a noble disinterestedness, and sacrifice of all petty jealousy, he handed over the plans and patterns he had devised for the structure, or rather which had been communicated to him by inspiration, with all the abundant and costly materials he had been collecting for years, to his son and successor, whose name and not his own he knew would be affixed to the grand undertaking ;—it was to be Solomon's Temple not David's—and said to him—" Be strong and of good courage and do it ; fear not nor be dismayed, for the Lord God even my God shall be with thee ; he will not fail thee nor forsake thee, until thou hast finished all the work for the service of the House of the Lord." And then pouring out a noble thanksgiving to God for giving him and his people the ability and the heart to consecrate their property to such an object, and for raising up one of his own blood to do the work, the doing of which had been denied to himself, he concluded by saying to all the congregation : " Now bless the Lord your God ; and all the congregation blessed the Lord God of their fathers, and bowed down their heads and worshipped the Lord," and were so struck with admiration of the aged monarch's magnanimous bearing, that they paid to him a special act of homage. The will of God, not his own fancy and wish, thus became his law. The Judge of all the earth must do right. If the work were only done he would cheerfully surrender the honour of being the doer of it. And though it would have been an untold satisfaction to him to have feasted his eyes with a sight of the structure all complete in its adornments, he was content to "die without the sight," with the assurance that it would rise in all its glory when he was sleeping in the dust.

II. The lessons taught us by this incident may be briefly summed up.

1. To cherish desires for great usefulness in connection with the diffusion of Christ's religion, and to form plans for carrying them into effect, is a thing right and good in itself and commendable in the sight of God. The heart of man is a busy workshop, where devices and schemes of all kinds are for ever being fabricated. For the most part, however, they are limited in their objects to the present world, and in their period to the present life. Some of them take the higher aim of philanthrophy and the public good; but the great majority are essentially selfish, springing from self-love, and terminating in self-indulgence and self-interest, such as the promotion of ease, the gratification of passion, the accumulation of wealth, the acquisition of fame. Hence, all these devices are cut short by death, and are buried in the grave with their framers.

But the Christian lives a nobler life. He is linked to a higher and a better world, to which the present is only subordinate and introductory. He has the promise of the life that now is, and of that which is to come. He sows to the Spirit, that of the Spirit he may reap life eternal. For him, to live is Christ, and to die is gain. But, while he remains upon earth, there is important work for him to do. The master says to him, "Go work in my vineyard, work while it is day; the night cometh when no man can work." The Christian is constituted a steward, with the instruction from his Lord, "Occupy till I come;" and when his Lord comes, he will say "Give an account of thy stewardship." It is, therefore, not only permitted, but obligatory to work for God, and to do the work well. It is commendable in itself and pleasing to our master, that our hearts should be set upon his service, busy in devising methods to promote it, and in making attempts to execute them. Besides the ordinary works of usefulness which lie near our door, circumstances may warrant, as in David's case, the conception of schemes upon a large scale. One may purpose to found a school, and another a church. One may endeavor to reform the haunts of vice in the city; another to spread the gospel through a neglected country district. A man may feel his spirit stirred within him to write a book that may speak for him when he is dead. Schemes of vaster scope for the diffusion of Christ's religion may be entertained: a germinant thought may enter the mind, adapted to be prolific of good to distant regions and to future times, as when Raikes formed the idea of the first Sunday school, Nasmyth of the first city mission, Hughes of a Bible society for the world, and Fuller, Carey, Bogue and others of organised missions to the heathen. Not a few Christians, when converted to God in their youth, feel a strong desire to devote themselves to the work of the ministry. Perceiving that the wants of the world are urgent —that the harvest is great, but the laborers few—feeling as they imagine a conscious ability to do something for God, and seeing that all life lies before them—they, hearing a voice from the sacred word asking, "Whom shall I send, and who will go for us?" in the ardour of their youthful zeal exclaim, "Here are we; send us."

As the object in such cases is good, in harmony with the spirit and purposes of the gospel and with the Christian vocation, if the motive also be good, he that knows the heart says, "It is well that it is in thine heart." God commends the thought, the desire, the purpose. The intention is received in heaven as " an odour of a sweet smell, a sacrifice acceptable, well pleasing to God."

But possible disappointment must be taken into account. The inward thought and wish, in the simplicity and integrity of the heart, is one thing ; its actual realization among the events of time is another. God may approve of the motive, but not the plan. He may approve of the plan, but not the time for carrying it out ; other things may have to be done, before the proper season shall have arrived for this particular one to take effect ; or, the plan and time may be in accordance with the divine will, but the all-wise Head of the church may not approve of the deviser being the performer. Fitter instruments may be in store ; or, a mere commencement of the work may be permitted ; the foundation only must be laid, and the rest be reserved for other and future hands. As in Wycliffe's case, who was honored to be the " morning star of the reformation," but not its full-orbed sun. The Divine Ruler over all thus allows his people in their love and in their zeal, to wish, and purpose, and devise ; but he ever exercises a sovereign control over the work itself, as to who shall do it, and how much each shall do.

When the high prerogative is exercised in a way that seems to us mysterious and inexplicable, what is the duty of creatures so dependent and fallible as we are ? Is it not uncomplaining submission ? Shall a murmuring word escape our lips, or even a repining thought enter our hearts ? Does it become us to be pettish and discontented, because we cannot have our own way ? Surely full confidence may be placed in the unerring wisdom of the Captain of Salvation, in selecting, from the crowds of candidates for service, such as he pleases for the posts where men are wanted. Acquiescence in the Master's decisions is our duty, and should be our delight. David's noble example is worthy of imitation. Like him, we should be willing to do, or not to do, as God determines for us ; or, to do a part of the work on which we have entered, however small or however humble, and to leave it to others to finish it when we are gone ; to sow in hope, content that our successors should reap the harvest.

Whether enlarged purposes of services, reaching to future days and distant places, be accepted or rejected, it is incumbent upon all Christians to do the work which lies near at hand, and is within reach ; to seize existing opportunities of serving God and benefitting their generation ; to do the work of the spot on the spot, and the work of the day in the day ; and calmly and resignedly to leave all the rest to the wise Disposer of their lot.

MEMOIR OF THE REV. J. G. REED, B.A.

John Gibbon Reed was born at Stoke, near Coventry. His education was principally carried on at a grammar school in Coventry, where he was always remarkable for his persevering industry and fondness for books. Being intended for business, his attention was ultimately directed to one of the staple trades of the town. Having a good taste for drawing, he became a ribbon-pattern designer. For three or four years he followed this pursuit, and followed it with success ; but, intent upon self-improvement, he read and studied unceasingly in all his spare time. While quite young, he gave several lectures, and spoke frequently at public meetings, being a warm advocate of the temperance cause, and of other philanthropic objects.

His parents and friends were members of the Established Church, but amongst his companions were some who were teachers in a suburban Sabbath school connected with West Orchard Independent Chapel, Coventry. He attended for some time the services held in this schoolroom, became a teacher in the school, and afterwards worshipped regularly at the chapel to which it belonged.

In the year 1850 he left Coventry, through a desire to extend his knowledge and his business. He lived first in the neighborhood of Huddersfield, then near Halifax, and lastly in Manchester. In the two former places he thoroughly enjoyed the beauties of the surrounding country, where he could indulge to the full that strong relish for nature which always distinguished him. It was during his residence in Manchester, however, that he arrived at the great turning point in his life. Soon after his settlement there, he became a constant attendant upon the ministry of the Rev. James Griffin, who, by his open-heartedness and sincerity, completely won the affections of the young man, and prepared his mind for the full reception of that gospel which makes " wise unto salvation." He had made many friends, also, by this time, among young men of religious character, and with literary tastes like his own, whose influence was favorable at once to spiritual and intellectual progress. Some of these were students at the Lancashire College ; and his thoughts and desires, even then, often turned to a student's life. He thus expresses himself in a private paper written at this time :—" It seems to me that the six or eight hours per diem which I devote to my business is so much time thrown away, as it neither contributes to my own mental and moral growth nor to the benefit of anybody else. And this thought is always attended by a wish that I could find some work which would give employment to all my faculties, and leave some permanent result behind it, besides enabling me to live."

From early years his mind and heart had been seeking religious light and rest. He had thought much and deeply on God, and on the things connected with our spiritual nature ; he had prayed often and earnestly ; his progress was very gradual, but it brought him at last to the happy conviction that Christ's perfect righteousness and obedience unto death were the only grounds upon which he could plead with God, and be accepted of him. We again quote his own words :—" I was summoned home on the 31st of March [1853], to my father's death-bed, and did not arrive in time to see him die. My poor father had been waiting and wishing for me to pray with him, and had declined the services of the curate, hoping I should reach home before he died. I, for my part, had been examining myself with such questions as these : What can I direct him to ? How much of Christianity can I urge upon him from an experience of its efficacy ? Can I direct him to the atonement as a means of reconciliation with God ?—and, after all this, to find I was too late to be useful to him at all, was a bitter sorrow to me. My poor mother was so cast down with grief that I had to hide my own emotions as much as possible, to comfort her. My father's body was laid in the grave, but my internal questionings with myself still continued, and, after some anxious and troubled thought, resulted in a more complete conviction that Christ is the Divinely-appointed Saviour of sinners, as well as their Teacher, and that my hope was bound up in him. All my difficulties being removed, I resolved to devote myself henceforth to the preaching of Christ. I wrote to the Rev. Thomas Delf about it, and he approved ; I communicated with Mr. Griffin, who approved also. I also consulted with Mr. Johnson, of Darwen. All these reverend gentlemen concurred, and concurred further in recommending London as a place of study. Guided by their advice, I at length resolved on applying for admission to New College."

His business had been tolerably lucrative ; it enabled him to amass a large number of books—the wealth he most delighted in ; but it was immediately given up, and he retired to Coventry to prepare himself for entering college. After residing there for a time for this purpose, he proceeded as a student to New College, towards the close of 1853. On his removal to London, he was transferred by his friend and pastor, Mr. Delf, from the church at Coventry to that under the pastoral care of the Rev. Thomas Binney. He pursued his studies with diligence and success ; and, in due time, graduated at the London University, taking his degree of B.A. He had worked hard, and obtained the confidence and respect of his professors. He enjoyed college life much ; but before his course was finished he was impatient for the end, earnestly longing to be in the world and at work. His Sabbath days were his pleasantest, because he was then doing something more directly for the cause he had at heart. For a long time before he left college, he never had a vacant, idle Sunday, and never wished to have one, although it often entailed severe mental and bodily fatigue.

After a week's hard study, he would frequently have to prepare, on the Saturday, for one, and sometimes for two services on the coming day. He became acceptable as a preacher, and his services were often specially requested. During one session he preached every alternate Sabbath for a church in London which was without a pastor, and was offered by it a more permanent engagement. During the college recesses he ministered to churches at Leeds, Reading, and Mortlake, in the absence or illness of their respective pastors ; and in all those places he is lovingly remembered and respected.

At the beginning of the year 1857 he preached several times in the large chapel at Portsea with great success, and to crowded congregations. As the church was then seeking a co-pastor, many wished to invite Mr. Reed. But a severe cold caught about the same time disabled him for some time from duty. Later in the spring, another severe cold renewed his cough. His own account of the beginning of this fatal ailment was, that in preparing a discourse as a college exercise, he went out in the evening to meditate and collect his thoughts. While doing so, he became so absorbed in the subject that he forgot himself, and stayed out too long, when he felt the cold night air strike upon his chest, infixing some painful sensations there which he never afterwards lost. In May, Professor Godwin advised him to go home for rest and change of air. He went home, but did not relax from preaching. During the summer, he supplied six weeks at Plymouth, and at the end of that period received a unanimous call from the church.

At this time, the anxiety of his friends increased ; and, through their earnest solicitation, he went up to London to consult the highest medical authority for diseases of the chest. Dr. Walshe ordered him to leave off preaching, and go to the south of France for the winter. This was a severe blow to him, as it laid him aside from active service for some months. On the eve of his departure for France, he received letters from the Rev. Thos. James and Professor Godwin, proposing that he should try Australia. On learning from the doctor that a sea voyage and residence in this country would, in all probability, re-establish his health, and allow him to pursue his great object, and on hearing from Mr. Poore of the wide field open for exertion in these new colonies, he gave up his plans and prospects in England,

and set his mind and heart to prepare for work in Australia. He and Mrs. Reed, in company with Mr. and Mrs. Binney and Mr. and Mrs. Poore, embarked in the *Sultana*, at Liverpool, in December last. The first part of the voyage seemed to agree with him and do him good, but the tropical weather and the cold immediately succeeding tried him much, and he became considerably weaker. He landed here on the 31st of March, 1858, and was met by a deputation from the church assembling in M'Killop street chapel, Geelong, to request his services there for a month, as probationer for the pastorship. After a week's rest at St. Kilda, he went down to Geelong. A public meeting was held in the chapel to introduce him to the people, and welcome him among them. Though very weak, he spoke feelingly, sweetly, and effectively, and awakened an interest in him which grew from day to day. An arrangement was made that he should preach once each Sabbath for a month, and then rest for a couple of months, to give him opportunity to recruit. He had strength given him to fulfil the engagement, preaching five times in all during the month. The result of his stay at Geelong was to create a strong desire among the people for his permanent residence there. He then visited Queenscliffe, with the hope that sea air might be beneficial, but not finding it agree with him, he returned to St. Kilda, where by the kindness of Mr. Rolfe and Mr. Fulton, he had every possible attention paid to him during his last illness, and where at length he ended his days in peace. Moreton Bay was thought of for him by these and other kind friends, but doctors forbade his removal. The disease and weakness gained upon him so gradually that he hardly perceived it himself, and until the last week of his life he believed that as God had brought him here there was something for him to accomplish. In a conversation Mr. Fletcher had with him upon the guidance God vouchsafes to his people when they seek to know and do his will, he remarked, " In no step I ever took in life had I a firmer conviction of being in the path of duty than in coming out here, and I have a strong conviction that God has a work for me to do in this country." It was remarked to him, " It is well that it is in your heart to serve your Saviour ; but God may say, ' *Thou* shalt not build the house ;' the service may have to be done by death, and not by life ;"—to which he meekly assented. He dictated a letter to the church at Geelong, full of affection, the purport of which was to release them from their engagement to him, from his growing weakness ; but it contained strong intimations of a hope that he might, in the course of time, be restored, and enabled to resume his beloved labor once more. When he heard Mr. W. Roby Fletcher give an account of his plans for active service, he said emphatically and with a sigh, " I wish I could join you." Notwithstanding his rapidly declining health, he occupied himself constantly in thinking of and preparing for his work in the future, and exactly a week before his death he dictated a sermon on the words, " Behold the Lamb of God, which taketh away the sin of the world."

When he was told by the physician that there was no hope of his life, and that the end of it was near, his bodily frame received a severe shock, from his having so cherished the impression and hope just referred to. At first he seemed unable to give himself up to God's will, but after a night of wrestling with himself, and of earnest prayer (his last Gethsemane), he was enabled to " take the cup," was reconciled to it, and at peace. From that time he did not express a wish to live, but said he should like to do some little good in the short time he yet had before him in this world, and especially in the family (Mr. Fulton's) which had shown him so much kindness. He appeared to be full of love—love to God and to his fellow-creatures. He often used such expressions as these: "How much has Jesus done for me! O that I had loved and served him better!" One night, on asking for a text, "Come unto me, all ye that labor and are heavy laden," &c. was repeated, when he said, "I think I see Jesus weary and toilworn, footsore and stained with blood—and he suffered all this for us!" He often prayed aloud—for himself, that he might have strength, patience, and submission; for the church at Geelong, and for dear friends here and at home.

His experience generally was more calm and hopeful than ecstatic and exulting; but one morning he told Mr. Fletcher that he had enjoyed in the night watches, such a special season of communion with God, and of impression of the glory and blessedness of heavenly things, that, filled with delight, he roused his beloved partner from a slumber, and called upon her to rejoice with him, and to unite with him in praying and giving thanks to God.

He was much concerned for his mother, and asked the Rev. R. Fletcher to break the news to her. He also expressed a wish to see the Rev. T. Binney once more.*

Day by day, his powers of body and mind grew weaker; but when he spoke sensibly it was generally a text of Scripture, or a word of advice and love to those about him. On Sunday morning, July 4th, he asked for the 23rd Psalm, and himself quoted another. But by this time he spoke with great difficulty. Later in the day he said "Christ is glorious," three times over. It may be truly said that he fell asleep in Jesus, for his departure was like a sleep. No suffering disturbed his last moments—no sigh or groan escaped him; and no change was perceptible when he gently ceased to breathe, and the spirit had passed away whither we could neither see nor follow, at twenty minutes after the end of the day of rest, on Monday morning, July 5th.

His remains were deposited in the St. Kilda cemetery, on Wednesday the 7th, when ten brother ministers, and several friends from Geelong, and others, paid their last tribute of affection at his grave. The funeral services were conducted by Messrs. Sunderland, Fletcher, and Landells.

May his great desire, that Christ should be glorified by him, be still fulfilled, though not in his life, yet in his death!

---

* This feeling and desire on the part of Mr. Reed and his former pastor was reciprocal. Mr Binney, on hearing of his increased illness, formed, while at Sydney, and communicated to the Editor, a plan for getting him to Moreton Bay for the remainder of the winter. This, however, was rendered nugatory by the unfavorable opinion of the physicians. On hearing of this, Mr. Binney immediately determined on leaving New South Wales and coming to Melbourne, in hope of seeing him before he died. In this he was disappointed, as, just on the eve of his leaving Sydney, he received intelligence of his death. We have been favored by Mr. B. with the following extract from a journal kept by him on board the *Sultana*, in which he and Mr. Reed came together to Australia. The passage, though brief, is pregnant and suggestive, and, from the circumstances under which it was written, is invested with an interest more touching, perhaps, than could now be imparted to anything expressly written for publication:—"Saturday, Feb. 6.—Mr. Poore continues very unwell; neither he nor Mr. Reed can do anything to-morrow. Mr. R.'s case appears at times very serious. I hope and trust he will be spared for work. He is highly qualified for it; well educated, very intelligent, deeply devotional, and earnestly and beautifully good. His prayers, in our private morning service, are exquisite for sentiment, expression, copiousness, and depth; his voice is very musical, and, in some of its tones, exceedingly touching. His poor young wife, who, by the way, is a superior and admirable woman, is, I think, often a good deal depressed about him." It need hardly be added, that Mr. B.'s testimony to the piety and excellence of our deceased friend is always expressed in the most earnest and decided terms.

c 2

ONE ASPECT OF THE CHRISTIAN RELIGION.

THE GOSPEL GLORIOUS.—1 Tim. i. 2.

ONE grand object had in view by the Divine Being in all his works—in creation, providence, and grace,—has been and is the *manifestation of himself*—of his natural attributes and moral qualities.

In the first creation of the matter of which the physical universe is formed, and in the wonderful and mighty revolutions of those vast heavenly bodies which astronomy treats of, we see glorious displays of *almighty power.*

In the relative magnitudes of the several planets composing the solar system, and in their relative positions, taken in connexion with their relative velocity of motion ; in the adaptation of the entire vegetable world to the soil in which it grows, and to the atmospheric influences to which it is exposed, and to the measure and nature of the solar light and heat in which it luxuriates ; and in ten thousand other adaptations visible on every hand around us, we see striking exhibitions of *divine wisdom.*

In the creation of innumerable distinct species of things having *life ;* and in the creation of countless myriads of individuals belonging to each species ; in their being endowed with various senses, the exercise of each of which affords direct and immediate gratification ; in their being placed in positions adapted to their instincts and natures, and where a multitude of things around them continually minister to their comfort and happiness : and, again, in the varied forms, observable on every hand, of elegance and beauty, both in the vegetable and animal kingdom, of greatness and grandeur in the lofty mountains and the rolling sea, and in the varied and beautiful coloring of earth and sky,—filling the human mind sometimes with calm and sometimes with intense delight ;—in all these things we have indisputable manifestations of *divine goodness.*

So we have a further exemplification of him, in the way in which God has met and dealt with moral evil.

A multitude of intelligent beings—whether an entire race, or a part only of the race to which they belong we know not—known in the Scriptures as " the devil and his angels," dare to disregard and set at nought the principles by which their conduct and character were to have been regulated. It is the first time the authority of heaven has been doubted. It is the first violation of law. It is the first instance in which the creature has set himself in opposition to the Creator. It is a grand and fearful experiment. Where will it end ? What will be its result ? The universe looks on with breathless and intense anxiety. Will the Almighty allow the reins of government to fall from his hands ? Will he retire and fail to vindicate the honor of his great name ? Will he allow that there henceforth should be a ground for suspicion that with him there is a want of power, or holiness, or truth ? Will the creature be justified in the future in entertaining a *want of confidence* in the Creator? No ! There shall be, not a bare vindication of his character, but a further and more glorious manifestation of it. A fiat goes forth from the Eternal throne ; it is the expression of unbending *justice*, of unsullied *truth*, of infinite *holiness ;* and " the angels which kept not their first estate are reserved in everlasting chains, under darkness, unto the judgment of the great day !"

Another revolt occurs. The arm of rebellion is raised in a new quarter. Earth sets itself in opposition to heaven. But John sufficiency shall again be displayed. Again the " High and Lofty One" will " bring good out of evil." Other attributes of the Deity shall be discovered. There shall be a further and more illustrious revelation of himself still !

The guilty culprit stands trembling in the expectation of his doom. Forebodings of unutterable anguish affright his guilty soul. Every passing breeze seems to his disturbed and agitated mind to utter a curse. The words ring in his ears : " In the day thou eatest thereof thou shalt surely die." He expects "wrath to come upon him unto the uttermost." But how shall retributive justice smite ? Shall the curse come secretly and without warning, and destroy "suddenly and without remedy ;" or shall " the throne be set," and a formal trial instituted, and divine justice display its terrors and its honors in the sight of an assembled universe ? The terrors and honors of justice have already been fearfully and illustriously displayed. But " the truth of God must stand." Something out of the ordinary course of nature and providence must be done ; and something fitting the august occasion. The time arrives. " The voice of the Lord God is heard walking in the garden." It is a moment big with the destinies of a world. Contrary to all expectation, it is the voice of *Mercy* that speaks ; and ten thousand times ten thousand bright, intelligent forms fall prostrate at the manifestation of an attribute so lovely in its aspect and benign in its influence, but which was unknown and unimagined till now. The "Most High uttereth his voice ;" "The seed of the woman shall bruise the serpent's head. One shall be given in your own nature—bone of your bone, and flesh of your flesh—who shall destroy the power, influence, and dominion of the evil one by whom you have been seduced, and are now enslaved." Thus the Lord pities the souls which he has made.

This expression of grace melts the culprit. Emotions, unfelt before, of exquisite tenderness, swell his grateful heart ; and hope and joy beam in his uplifted and tearful eye.

Time rolls on ; and there is a gradual development of the plan by which God may be " a just God," and yet " a Saviour ;" and when "the fulness of time is come, God sends forth *his Son*, made of a woman, made under the law, to redeem them that were under the law, that we might receive the *adoption of sons*." His name is "Immanuel "—"*God with us*." The Creator takes upon himself the form of the creature, and dwells and associates with the works of his own hands. Here is condescension !—condescension that is measureless. It is the wonder of all worlds. Angels desire and delight to look into it : but fail fully to explore the riches of the grace manifested in it. Yet it is but the first step in the wondrous plan of redemption ; each succeeding one being replete with its own wonders. Sublime truths and glorious characteristics are evolved in every after-step. Time fails us even to enumerate them. Go, therefore, in imagination, to the land that bears the mystic marks of the frequentations of angels, and the footsteps of the blessed Saviour. Let your mind, for a moment, dwell in solemn si'ence on Bethlehem, and on each of the various scenes of his arduous labors ; let it tarry a little at Gethsemane, and then go to Calvary. Thus pursue the history of the " man of sorrows," from the " manger " and his early and hasty " flight into Egypt," to the " judgment hall," and the " cross." And as you reflect that all was endured by the Lord of life and glory on behalf of the guilty and wretched, but impenitent, " for while we were yet sinners, Christ died for us," say whether there ever was, or can be, such another exemplification of pity, and mercy, and grace, and love ; or whether any other plan could have reached the offender's heart and kindled his affections like this ! It is the sight—the full, clear, realising apprehension of this peculiar " manner of love," that subdues our rebellious nature ; that overcomes our pride ; that induces the repentance that needeth not to be repented of ; and makes us delight to prostrate ourselves before God : " for we love God because he hath first loved us." It is this which shall bind us, both in this world and in that which is to come, to the throne of God, with a chain stronger than iron, and more enduring than adamant.

It will always, through eternity, remain a fact that *we have been sinners.* And the remembrance, or rather perpetual consciousness of this, will induce and preserve in us a profound humility : not that low, mean, cringing spirit, which sometimes falsely bears the name on earth ; but that softened, subdued, chastened state of mind, which well comports with bliss. And whatever unwelcome thoughts and unpleasant feelings might otherwise be excited by the remembrance of our low origin and past degradation, they will be for ever excluded by the living visible fact, which, in the person of Jesus Christ, will be patent to the universe, that *the Diety has identified himself with the race ;* and thus, instead of its being a mark of degradation or inferiority, it will be, among all the various " hosts of heaven," a *glory to be a man !*

And while the " glorious gospel " thus puts peculiar honour on human nature, it will secure for redeemed humanity, *more* than *seraphic bliss.* Through eternity, the unmerited and boundless pity, grace, and love of our God, as manifested in the gift of his Son, will be a theme to warm, and kindle, and fire to ecstacy our enraptured souls ! The joy of the redeemed, shall be a peculiar joy : more melting and refined than can be experienced by the unfallen sons of God. These will love God as the infinitely holy and good, but not as their redeemer. Angels shall never sing the " song of Moses and the Lamb." None can " learn that song but the redeemed from the earth !" It need not, however, be supposed that the happiness which will result from redemption will be confined to man. He, indeed, is the immediate, and so far as we know, the *only* recipient of its *saving power,* but all " the host of heaven " will be interested in the contemplation of those moral attributes of the Deity which are manifested in the incarnation, life, and death of the Son of God ; and instead of envying man his high felicity, and the nearness to which he is brought to the Eternal, and the honor and dignity put upon his nature by the Son himself partaking of it, they will draw from the contemplation of all that is involved in the great scheme of which we speak, their richest measure of immortal bliss. Still, the tenderest emotions, and the finest feelings, and the highest and most soul-absorbing joy known *among the whole range of created mind,* shall be that which will be experienced by the " great multitude, which no man can number, out of all nations, and kindreds, and people, and tongues," as they stand before that throne round about which is " a rainbow like unto an emerald "—

" The green memorial of earth ;"

and " before the Lamb, clothed with white robes, and having palms in their hands, and cry with a loud voice, saying : This *salvation* be ascribed to our God which sitteth upon the throne, and unto the Lamb !"

Here, then, in the method of salvation, and in these anticipated results, we see the propriety of the epithet used by St. Paul, " glorious ;" " the glorious gospel of the blessed God."

PASTORAL REMINISCENCES.

Many years since, an elderly man, occupied in active avocations, applied for church fellowship. After due inquiry and conversation, he was received. For some time he continued to attend upon public worship and to exhibit a deportment which, so far as appeared, was free from serious spot. I felt, however, as his pastor, sorry to find that he was disinclined to assist in useful service, in furtherance of Christ's cause. I wished him to become a tract distributor, but he pleaded, as an excuse for declining the work, his physical infirmities, although he was quite ready to undertake long and toilsome walks in prosecuting his secular pursuits. He resembled another person who, in urging to me the heat of the climate as an excuse for Christian inaction, seemed to overlook the fact that no such barrier was presented to the gainful activities in which he and others were engaged. It may be feared, in many such cases, that the difficulty arises, not from physical but moral infirmity; not from the hot climate, but the cold heart.

The course of the old man was, at length, marked by a melancholy change. One of the deacons heard that his wife (who was not a member of the Church) had died suddenly in . fit. Although it was late in the evening, he hurried to his house, and there he found the bereaved husband lying on the bed, *drunk, by the side of his wife's corpse.* This startling discovery, in connection with subsequent events, led to the conclusion that both S—— T—— and his wife had been addicted to *secret tippling:* During the day, they appeared sober and industrious; but it was probably their custom at night, when no visitors were expected, to indulge in the fatal habit. On the following day I visited the unhappy man, who, stung by shame, had continued to take intoxicating liquor. He ordered me to leave the house, but I refused to go, until the counsel and warning which the case required were supplied. Eventually he professed penitence; but there was no permanent amendment. Having been detected in his evil courses, he seemed to become reckless, and exclusion from the Church was inevitable. He pursued the downward path with accelerated speed. Business was neglected, property sacrificed, and health destroyed. As a diseased pauper, he was removed to the hospital; there, when the end was at hand, I reminded him of that Saviour whose name he had once professed, and of the grace and mercy which might yet be realised by *him.* With a look, and in a tone which betokened calm despair, he replied:—" *The harvest is past, sir ; the harvest is past, sir ;—you know what I mean.*"

It is a sad and startling fact that the very deacon who discovered this old man's sin afterwards *fell into a similar snare.* Ultimately he was reclaimed, and became a total abstainer; but his intemperance had occasioned or aggravated disease, which issued in a death awfully sudden. He fell down and expired in the street.

These painful reminiscences will account for the statement that the pastor, who has so sorrowfully witnessed the ensnaring influence of strong drink *in the Church* as well as in the world, has long felt it important to recommend and practise total abstinence from all intoxicating liquor as a beverage. F.M.

ENGLISH CORRESPONDENCE.

April 8th, 1858.

In a late communication, I spoke of Spurgeon, the pulpit phenomenon of the age. But he is by no means alone in his glory, as is testified by two volumes of popular lectures lately issued, the one set delivered in Liverpool by the Rev. Hugh Stowell Brown, and the other in the Free Trade Hall, Manchester, by the Rev. Arthur Mursell. They are published respectively by Gabriel Thomson in Liverpool, and by Bremner in Manchester. Both these courses have been delivered on Sunday afternoons, and have been attended by dense crowds, mainly from the upper ranks of the working classes, who have fought hard for an entrance an hour or an hour and a half before the time of commencement. Perhaps this is enough to show that there is *something* remarkable in the lectures, or in the manner or circumstances of their delivery. They both boast extravagancies in the way of title, such as "The devil's meal is all bran," "Punch," "What ails thee, my son, Robin?" &c. But here the similarity ends; and they afford a curious illustration of the futility of any general rules as to the taste of mobs. A well known Quarterly, in its comments on Spurgeon, some time ago, attributed all the sensation. "to the charms of simple gospel" clearly and uncompromisingly enunciated. This, and nothing but this, plainly would delight the ears of the common people. I wonder what the editor of said Review would pronounce to be the attraction of " Punch," or the "Devil's meal," or the greater number of these two series, which are simply moral essays, enlivened by ridicule, peppered by sarcasm, and fired off with a pungent explosive power of language, or blazing with holocausts of superlative adjectives and adverbs, sacrificed at the shrine of a many-headed and firework-loving divinity?   To do justice to the Manchester series, however, the gospel is certainly " brought in" generally before the end ; and a lecture on " Who's dat knocking at de door," is made to wind up with an enforcement of a very solemn demand on the part of Christ for entrance into the heart of man ; but it would require some hardihood in support of a theory to say that the "simple gospel" is the attraction in either volume.   Not only however, are they diverse from Spurgeon, but almost more so from each other.   The discourses of Mr. Brown are a clear, straightforward, upright, downright, hammer and anvil sort of production, forming in most respects admirable models of popular eloquence.   There is no flowery display, no elaborate sentimentality here.   Half his power consists in calling a spade a spade, and pronouncing the word very clearly.   Indeed, I am glad to mark a growing opinion, testified by the press, that this man is not only the strongest but the truest of all our popular phenomena ; an intellectual blacksmith, doing rough and grimy work, with a heart as honest as his hand is firm.   I am not aware that he ever made a royal progress through the multitude, hat in hand, as is the case with our London prodigy ; and, what is more, I cannot fancy him at it.

Mr. Mursell's lectures, on the other hand, are flowery, high flown, elaborately pathetic or denunciatory discourses, with an undue proportion of adjectives and adverbs, together with a number of phrases introduced evidently for their sound and nothing more.   But he is much younger than Mr. Brown, and these are juvenile defects.   Let us hope he will grow out of them.   Never was mortal shot up into the heavens of fame with such rocket-like speed. Before these Free Trade Hall exploits he was utterly unknown, and now he is everywhere coupled with Spurgeon, which is saying a great deal.

All this is worthy of earnest thought, as indicative of considerable movement in the hitherto stagnant minds of the masses.   From the Irwell to the Cephissus—travelling is cheap in these days, and we are obliged to accustom our minds to a corresponding activity. " Andromeda, and other poems, by Rev. Chas. Kingsley.   London, J. W. Parker. 1858," has just come out.   Andromeda is another attempt at classical hexameters in English, and perhaps an improvement on any former ones.   But it is very like galvanising a beautiful corpse to introduce the Greek style of feeling and imagery into our living language.   Just fancy Homer arrayed in a swallow tail and an all-rounder.   There are some pretty ballads in the book ; but it is *ephemeral* poetry at best.

Have any of you a notion of making a pilgrimage to Rome from your Thule, for the health of your souls ? If so, I would advise you to read H.E. Cardinal Wiseman's "Recollections of the last four Popes," Hurst and Blackett, London, 1858 ; for here everything in the Eternal City is so represented *Couleur de Rose*, that any wavering in your purpose will be effectually banished.   Of course, it is a clever, an attractive, a powerful book, since it is by Cardinal Wiseman.   I think you would enjoy reading it ; though the conviction would press itself on you, that the author was rather too free with the trowel.   But, anticipating complaints of this, he candidly informs us that he has not thought it necessary to notice faults, since there are so many ready to do that.   The book contains some glowing descriptions of Romish ceremonies, and much interesting information about learned and literary people.

There is a dreamy, discursive book, which I mention, although it is getting old, because it has just attracted my attention, and interested me greatly.   I mean "Thorndale, or the Conflict of Opinions," by William Smith, author of Athelwold, a drama.   Blackwood and Sons, 1857.   The subject—hardly to be called the hero—of the work is a consumptive patient, who, while slowly dying at Naples, pens down his flitting thoughts on freedom, progress, and immortality, together with conversations held with different friends representative of various schools of thought.   There are many beautiful gleams in it ; but there is too much also of this morbid self analysis, so characteristic of thoughtful literature at the present day.

Havelock's life, by Brock, published by Nisbet, has had a tolerable run already, from the intense military, religious, and personal interest attaching to the subject, which certainly presented such an opportunity as is seldom given for an exercise of biographical power. Unfortunately, however, the prevailing impression seems to be that the book is a failure, and another book is eagerly looked for from another source.   Brock's book is introduction of supererogatory preachments, which is certainly a very false step in connection with so telling a life. Few more majestic characters have ever trod the earth than Havelock; mighty in the Scriptures and dauntless in war; at once ambassador of heaven and champion of outraged innocents, prophet and warrior, soldier and saint. It is not every one who knows how to treat such a subject.

Talking of India, if you want to read an account of the siege of Lucknow, don't get that by E. L. Runt Rees, unless it is a matter of interest to you to see by what process human dulness can succeed in making a thrilling narrative more intolerably tedious than the drone of a pair of bagpipes. The narrative of a staff officer is preferable, but is nothing very great.

An eighth edition of A. P. Stanley's "Life of Arnold" is just issued. I am not aware that it contains any important addition. Fronde's third and fourth vols. of the "History of England" are out; but, as I have not had an opportunity of reading them yet, I am not able to say how the hitherto impossible process of washing the blackamoor white is succeeding.

DOMESTIC MISSIONS.

SOUTH AUSTRALIAN BUSH MISSION.

A Bush Mission has been in operation about a year and a half in South Australia, which appears to give a practical answer to the question, "How are the pastoral portions of Australia to be supplied with religious instruction? From the nature of the case, the ordinances of religion cannot be brought, in a permanent and settled form, within the reach of the thinly scattered inhabitants. Such a scheme as that whose operations are here detailed, at all events does something towards supplying the want which all deplore. Whether more may not be done experience alone can determine.

On the 27th of January, 1857, shortly after the formation of the Institution, the mission agent, Mr. Luther B. Martin, was sent over to Yorke's Peninsula, a district with which he was tolerably acquainted, and where he felt very anxious to make his first essay in the work. During the six months following, he was there actively employed; visiting almost every station in the district, holding religious services on every available opportunity — sometimes a prayer meeting, sometimes a simple address from some passage of Scripture.

In August last it was considered advisable to afford Mr. Martin some help; and a young man (Mr. J. J. Smith), well disposed to the work, and earnestly desirous to be useful to his fellow-bushmen, was engaged. A horse and cart and various travelling accoutrements were purchased, and on the 6th of August the two agents started on their travels, chiefly in the north and north-east, between the Burra Mine and the Reedy Creek — in this locality they are at present engaged. An additional horse was after a while found to be necessary in their constant journeyings from station to station. This want has been met by the loan of one, in the meantime, from a warm friend of the mission.

Journals of their daily movements and work have been regularly kept and forwarded to the committee punctually month by month. There is in them much, very much, to interest and encourage; and any friend will be amply repaid by a perusal of a large portion of them. At times the agents have been much tried and cast down by the crosses inseparable from such an undertaking and the obstacles thrown in their way by some opposed to the light; but far oftener have they been greatly encouraged by the kindness and courtesy shown, and the urgent wish expressed at many stations that their visitations might be often repeated; and here and there some wonder that until now no movement of this sort had been made by the zealous activities of the Christian community in South Australia.

During a period of twelve months from the commencement of this Mission, there have been visited 88 head stations, 129 sheep stations, and 9 shearing sheds, and nearly 400 services held of the nature indicated above. At the same time the agents have acted as colporteurs having distributed, in the course of their travels 47 Bibles and Testaments, and 1,620 religious tracts and books. There have likewise been very many opportunities where the agents have sought to speak a word in season to those with whom they have been brought in contact. Thus has the work been commenced. The field is large, and with more extended help from the Christian public, many other districts might be occupied. The committee respectfully ask this pecuniary help, with all confidence in Him whose work it is, and who alone can dispose the hearts of all to give acceptably.

The Mission does not belong to any one denomination, but is established upon a catholic basis. The expenses of the year have amounted to £300, which has been covered by subscriptions and collections; but more funds are required to extend the operations.

MELBOURNE AND SUBURBAN CITY MISSION.

The first annual meeting of this Institution, in its new and revived state, was held on Monday evening, July 19th, in the Mechanics' Institution. His Honor Judge Pohlman occupied the chair. From the report which was read by the Rev. H. H. P. Handfield, we learn that the original City Mission had died out for want of funds, and that the Institution in its new form owed its existence and success to the zeal and devotedness of some Christian ladies. Four missionaries are employed, one in the heart of Melbourne, one in North Melbourne, one in Collingwood, and the fourth in Prahran and Richmond Flat. The expenditure is about £800 per annum; the sum collected amounts to £812 12s. 8d. The monthly expenditure, nearly £70, has been met and paid off as each month came round, though, sometimes, with difficulty The missionaries employed are spoken of as laborious and faithful men, and the results of their labors as encouraging. The loss, by death, of Mr. Buchanan, one of the missionaries, and of Mr. Oliver, an earnest friend of the mission, and of Mrs. Bonar, one of the Ladies' Committee, is much lamented. The wants of the districts embraced by the mission are so great that there is ample scope for a much larger number of missionaries. Laborers might be obtained if the funds were forthcoming. Mr. Wm. Fairfax read the financial statement, and the meeting was addressed by the Revds. Dr Cairns, A. Morison, H. H. P. Handfield, T. Odell, Dr. Embling, M.L.A., and Mr. Hoskins. We append the substance of Dr. Cairns' remarks He moved a resolution for the adoption of the report and financial statement, and expressive of the gratitude of the society to Almighty God for its progress, and of hopefulness for the future. He commented upon the great necessity which existed that the pastors of regular congregations should be largely supplemented by a staff of lay readers, or pastors, whom he might call "Evangelists." The peculiar duty of such persons was to investigate the spiritual wants of the various districts of the city, and to minister to them with tact, and not in the spirit of a controversialist. The history of the mission was interesting; inasmuch as it had been commenced some few years ago in a spirit too sanguine, and on a scale too large for the means at its disposal; like a large balloon, it collapsed. It had been, however, revived by the energetic efforts of a few Christian ladies, and now prospered to the extent indicated in the report. The society was largely indebted to the zeal and piety of its missionaries, whose labors had been crowned with many instances of success. Their journals exhibited much care, tact, and diligence, and their visits seemed to have been appreciated. Dr. Cairns proceeded to comment upon several of the cases recorded in the journals, and noticed, with peculiar approbation, the relief and sympathy often afforded by the missionaries in instances of physical affliction. This he thought one of the most interesting features in the mission. Another useful effort was made in the correction of habits of intemperance and debauchery in husbands and fathers of families—efforts often resulting in the reclamation of the children in Sunday-schools. Dr. Cairns concluded with a reference to the labors of the *colporteurs* of the continent of Europe, and recommended that an effort should be made to convert the missionaries as far as possible into *colporteurs* by furnishing them with useful books.

MISSION TO THE CHINESE IN VICTORIA.

The annual meeting of this Mission was held on Tuesday evening, July 20, in the Protestant Hall, Melbourne, and was numerously attended.

HIS EXCELLENCY THE GOVERNOR arrived shortly after 7 o'clock, and took the chair His Excellency was attended by his Aide-de-Camp, Captain Bancroft. The proceedings commenced with the singing of a hymn, and prayer.

HIS EXCELLENCY said they must all feel they were met together under more favorable circumstances than last year. The general objections to a Chinese immigration remained, perhaps, undiminished; but still there was less prejudice against the Chinese among the people, and especially on the gold-fields. The policy pursued by New South Wales had some effect in perpetuating the immigration, and the latter was now looked upon with more indifference, and almost as a necessary evil, and to this was superadded a forgetfulness of the duty of spreading among the immigrants the knowledge of Christianity. To this only could be attributed the inability which the society had experienced in extending its efforts over the country at large on the scale which had been contemplated last year. This deficiency in progress had arisen from that universal cause—want of means. The number of missionaries had to be reduced in consequence. And another difficulty had been the non-arrival of the type necessary for printing Chinese works. He hoped the meeting of that night would tend to a revival of this important Mission in this wealthy community The spreading of the blessings of Christianity among the Chinese was leading to the evangelization of the whole of the human race. He had written to his friend, Sir John Bowring, to send some Chinese interpreters to Victoria; but Sir John had not been able to comply with the request from the scarcity of Chinamen who understand the English language. It was very important that as far as it was possible should be made of the presence of those Chinese who remained in Victoria, not only for their own sakes but because they might hereafter become missionaries in their own country. He would now call upon the Secretary to read the report

The Report stated that the arrangement which located the Rev. Mr. Young, the European missionary, at Castlemaine, visiting Ballarat and Melbourne at intervals, was found to be inconvenient; and that in October last the head-quarters had been transferred to Melbourne This being the centre to and from which the Chinese are constantly coming and going, the fixed residence of a considerable number of storekeepers and others, and the port of embarkation to their own country, it afforded the best opportunities for acting upon them generally. Two rooms have been hired in Little Bourke Street, where the Chinese chiefly dwell, for Mr. Young's use through the day, for depositing and issuing Chinese tracts and Testaments, and for holding interviews with any who desire to see him privately. Here, placed in the midst of them, he goes in and out amongst them continually, and visiting and conversing with them in their shops and houses; he has easy access to them, can readily gain their ear, and has obtained considerable influence over them, being often referred to in cases of difficulty. Religious services are held in the house on Sabbath days and week evenings. The attendance varies from five or six to thirty persons. In conducting the services, the Rev. Mr. Young is assisted at times by different Chinese Christians. Besides these services, constant opportunities are presented in the city of conversing with, and reading the Scriptures and tracts, to the permanent residents, and also to those Chinese who pass through it from time to time. Opportunities, as far as possible, are also taken advantage of for visiting the hospital, the penal establishments, the Joss-house at Emerald Hill, where there are always some Chinese residing, and the emigrant ships returning to China. It is hoped the labors of the past have not been barren of results, and that salutary impressions have been made in the minds of not a few. The lot of the Chinese missionary, however, is that of one who must wait for the precious fruit of the earth and have long patience for it. One of the chief impediments is the instability of the Chinese immigrants. There were, a few months ago, three or four Christian Chinese who assisted Mr. Young in his meetings; but, at present, they are all dispersed.

It was proposed in the course of the year to secure a site for mission premises in the locality of Little Bourke street, and to erect thereon a place for Christian worship for the Chinese. A sum of money was raised amongst the Chinese themselves, which they promised would be available for this purpose; but subsequent experience has afforded too painful proof of the duplicity of the heathen character: a division which took place amongst those of the Su-i-ap clan—the most numerous in Melbourne and on the diggings—has furnished them with a pretext for repudiating their engagement, and of retaining the money. It is hoped, however, that where pagan infidelity has abounded, the liberality and zeal of Christians will much more abound, to furnish the necessary means for carrying out this object; and so of establishing a centre of action, which could not fail to prove a most important advantage to the mission.

The Committee became impressed with the importance of obtaining a fount of Chinese types, as a most useful means of communicating religious truth to the Chinese, and of diffusing useful knowledge amongst them. A meeting was held for the purpose of originating a special subscription for this object, and it was resolved that so soon as the amount necessary (which was ascertained to be about £300) could be raised, to send for the types without further delay. Up to the present time, however, the matter rests in abeyance from want of the necessary funds.

At Castlemaine, two native agents, Chu-A-Luk and Leong-A-Toe, were associated in the work up to January last. The Committee were unable to retain the services of more than one agent there from want of funds. Chu-A-Luk, having served the Mission faithfully returned to China in March.

Leong-A-Toe now labors alone, occasionally assisted by Fan-A-Wye, a native convert, who has lately gone to reside at Forest Creek. Visits, for the purpose of reading and expounding the Scriptures, have been paid to the Chinese in their tents, and numerous discussions on subjects connected with the Christian religion have been held with them—some of these of a most interesting nature. The Chinese also, in turn, visit the agent, and follow up the same animated and interesting discussions at his house, in a manner which shows the pleasing spirit of inquiry to be found amongst some of them.

The sick in the hospital have also been regularly visited, some of whom express their determination to renounce the worship of their idols. Two religious services, and sometimes three, are held for the spiritual benefit of the Chinese every Sabbath-day, the attendance at which varies from 20 to 50 or 60 persons. Besides these, two evening services are held during the week at the chapel, the attendance at which is encouraging. Tracts and copies of the New Testament are also given away as opportunities are presented.

At Ballaarat, the mission—superintended and maintained by the Geelong Chinese Evangelisation Society—is prosecuted on the same plan as at Castlemaine. Lo Sam Yuen, the agent laboring there, has been successful in raising the sum of £2 0 amongst his countrymen, with which a neat weatherboard chapel for Christian worship has been erected. It was opened in the month of January last. Two or three services are conducted here by the agent every Sabbath. The attendance at these services is larger than at Castlemaine. From 100 to 150 Chinese generally attend. Five or six Chinese married to European women have expressed a desire to be baptised, but it has been considered necessary to defer this till they shall have been sufficiently instructed in the knowledge of Christian truth, and shall have undergone a satisfactory probation.

The cash account was read by H. Jennings, Esq, the treasurer. It showed a balance against the society of £157, and that, notwithstanding the reduction in the number of agents.

The meeting was then addressed by the Very Rev. the Dean of Melbourne, Mr. Langlands, M.L.A., the Revds. Messrs. Wells and Odell, Leong-A-Toe, Chinese agent at Castlemaine, the Archdeacon of Geelong, the Rev. Messrs. Sunderland and Chase, the Bishop of Melbourne, and the Rev. R. Fletcher. The Rev. W. Young, the missionary, read two papers written in Chinese, being applications for baptism by two Chinamen. Translations of these autobiographies were read by him, and are here subjoined, slightly abridged. A collection was made at the close of the meeting, which amounted to £16 15s.

ACCOUNT OF LEONG-PONG-SUEN, BY HIMSELF.

From my boyhood I have been attached to books, and learned diligently the doctrines of Confucius and Mencius. At the age of seven I was sent to school, and was taught to pay regard to the five invariable laws of conduct, viz., benevolence, righteousness, politeness, wisdom, and truthfulness. At a still more advanced age, I was put under a superior master, and associated with men of learning. Out of five and twenty years, nineteen were spent in companionship with the learned, and studying what they studied. After a time, the rebels caused an insurrection, which extended to my native village, and all the wealth that I had accumulated in past times was now plundered. Such being my misfortune, I was resolved not to reside there any longer.

Hearing favorable accounts from the gold-fields, that the rulers were wise and good, and looked upon the people just as they looked upon their own children, and made no distinction between Chinese and foreigners; that the inhabitants were peaceably disposed, and regarded all living within the four seas as brethren; and, moreover, hearing that gold was to be obtained there, I engaged a passage to come to this very productive country. If in the course of two or three years I should be so fortunate as to get a large quantity of gold, it was my intention to return to my country to repair the damages done to my patrimonial estate. This intention, however, sprung only from the love of worldly gain; it had no reference to the honor of God. For what do our Chinese classics contain? Only disquisitions concerning matters pertaining to this life; they make no reference to the future, nor to the retribution that is to come. These things men rarely think about. How can they know the good news of the kingdom of God?

At Simpson's first, and Forest Creek next, I pitched my tent. It was there I heard Leong-a-toe preach the Gospel. He accidentally passed the place where I was digging, and spoke to me about the mercy of God, our maker and preserver, Christ dying to atone for the sins of men, and also of his having power to save the soul. He spoke, moreover, of heaven and hell, of the impropriety of worshipping idols and deceased ancestors, and the duty of worshipping the only one and true God, in order to obtain the happiness that has no end. On these topics he conversed with me several times. When I first heard them, I thought they were strange and empty doctrines, not worthy of men's belief. In consequence of this, we had constant discussions and arguments. I thought that after having deeply investigated the teachings of Confucius and Mencius, there was no more truth further to seek. I had spent years in studying their great productions, and had found nothing to equal them. But at that time I had never seriously reflected that the teachings of these sages were excellent only for regulating families and administering affairs of state, and that the study of them could not bring any to obtain salvation. But the doctrines of God were, indeed, important, inasmuch as they had respect to the soul;—if one studies these, he may cherish the hope of attaining the glory beyond the grave. When I first heard these doctrines, I was strangely perplexed, and did not feel capable of determining between the true and the false. When I had time, I used to go to A-toe's house, to be instructed by him in the deep doctrines of the gospel, and sometimes he used to come to my house and elucidate the divine book. By degrees its doctrines removed my ignorance. At this time I went to Ballaarat, on a speculation, which proved a failure, and then went back to Castlemaine in quest of my friend, A-toe. We conversed together about different matters. I received much consideration as well as comfort from him, and he advised me not to let external matters burden my mind, and again instructed me in the true doctrines of God. He told me that we should make the care of our souls our highest concern. A-toe then gave me a copy of a tract entitled "Gospel Teachings," "The Pilgrim's Progress," a Catechism, and a copy of the Old and New Testaments. I have seriously considered these. With the teaching of God's Spirit, added to the clear instructions received from A-toe, my mind has become illumined, and I feel inward joy. I am like one aroused from a dream, and for the first time feel that my former life has been all wrong,—that my resistance of the truth has been one of my greatest sins. Day and night, and at all times, I think of God as the Great Father, and offer him my highest adoration, and constantly address the Redeemer as the Lord of Mercy. But I mourn that I cannot get quit of sin, and that even now I do that which is wrong. If my countrymen, who see what I am now about to do, shall reproach me for giving up the system of the learned of my country to embrace one that is foreign, and for throwing away the talents I have acquired by more than a score of years' study of Confucius and Mencius; if, in derision, they shall raise their eyebrows and hiss with their tongues; or if with their mouths they shall justify, while in their hearts they condemn me,—say one thing of me in my presence, and another thing behind my back; this will cause me no grief, and will produce no fear. What my heart fears and grieves about is the dreadfulness of divine punishment. As to the slanders of men, they are not worth grieving or fearing about.

I desire now to be baptised. As in wisdom and experience I am young and raw, I beg to be taught. And further, I trust God and our Lord Jesus will add to me wisdom and strength, help me to keep the Commandments, and make me steadfast to the end, so that I may enjoy the inheritance that is incorruptible. This is the desire of my heart.

I entreat all the different ministers of the gospel to give me their instructions; they may then fill my life with pleasure and my soul with hope.

ACCOUNT GIVEN BY WONG-A-KI OF HIMSELF.

I was born of poor parents, and by profession am an agriculturist. I have studied very little, indeed, the books of Confucius and Mencius, and have no learning whatever. I am not extensively acquainted with the customs of China: of her literature how much more ignorant am I? I had two brothers, who came before me to this honorable country to dig for gold; they both returned to China with their profits, with ecstasy and delight. When I saw this, I also made arrangements to come hither, and considered the distance of thousands of miles as nothing, so I could but get riches. Contrary to my expectations, after mining for several years, my means gradually diminished; in addition to this, I was attacked with a swelling in my legs, so that I could not move a single inch. My means having been all expended, and all the Chinese doctors having failed in curing me, I looked to the gods for recovery. One day, Chu-a-luk and Leong-a-toe, whilst publishing the gospel, came to my tent. They sat down, and expressed their sympathy with my diseased and distressed condition; they told me not to be over grieved, and imparted to me the truth of the Gospel. They told me also not to pray to spirits, nor to supplicate the help of Buddha;—that what I had done during my past life was only calculated to bring down misery upon me. They taught me about the great Lord, who made all things, and about the miracles performed by the Saviour of the world; how he made the blind see, the deaf hear, the lepers clean, and the lame walk. After they spoke to me for two hours, I said to them—"I never heard before what country's God this Saviour is, who is able to do such wonderful things, and I desire to seek his help; nor do I know the place of his residence." The teachers told me that the Saviour was the all-powerful Lord, and that he was present everywhere; that he was Jesus, the Son of God, who assumed human nature and came into the world; that he could not only heal the diseases of the body, but had also power to cure the maladies of the soul. The two teachers came several times after this to teach me. On one occasion, Leong-a-toe mentioned that the English had erected a hospital for taking in patients, both English and Chinese. He asked me whether I should like to be received into that institution, and that if I did I need not pay anything. I begged Chu-a-luk to take me there. A skilful doctor attended me, and gave me medicines which proved effectual; and moreover, during the time I was in hospital, the two teachers often came to see me, and to tell me about salvation. I became convinced of my former errors, and that the dumb idols, Buddhas, and deceased ancestors that I formerly worshipped, had no power whatever to help, and were nought but stupid things. I now desire, morning and evening, to worship God, to put my trust in Christ, and to receive the transforming influences of the Holy Spirit. After being six months in the hospital, I was completely cured. I will ever regard the true God as my great Father, Jesus as my Redeemer, and henceforth will believe in him without wavering. I earnestly request the teachers to continue instructing me in the true doctrines of the holy book, otherwise my body will not survive, and my soul will have nothing on which to lean.

I present this to all the different ministers of the gospel, that they may consider my application; and may the triune God bless them with happiness that is unending. Amen.

CHINESE ON THE VICTORIAN GOLD-FIELDS.
Obtained from the Government returns, Melbourne.

BALLAARAT Mining District.—Sub-divisions: Ballaarat, 4,670; Creswick, 2,530; Smyth's Creek, 800; total, 8,000.

CASTLEMAINE Mining District.—Sub-divisions: Castlemaine, 4,450; Fryer's Creek 2,117; Maldon, 760; Mount Franklin, 800; total, 8,127.

AVOCA Mining District.—Sub-divisions: Avoca, 1,850; Amherst, 1,730; Dunolly, 1,200, Maryborough, 1,740; total, 6,520.

ARARAT Mining District.—Sub-divisions: Ararat, 2,505; Raglan, 450; Pleasant Creek; 70; total, 3,025.

SANDHURST Mining District.—Sub-divisions: Sandhurst, 2,430; McIvor, 500; total, 2,930.

BEECHWORTH Mining District.—Sub-divisions: Beechworth, 931; Snake Valley, 445; Three-Mile Creek, 889; Buckland, 228; Woolshed, 387; Yackandandah, 96; Omeo, 13; total, 2,489.

Grand total, 31,091.

CHINESE SERVICE.—SYDNEY.—On Sunday afternoon, July 4th, a religious service in the Chinese language was celebrated in the large school-room adjoining the Congregational Church, Pitt-street. The service was conducted by a Chinese Christian, named H. Lean Apps, who is engaged in mercantile pursuits in the colony; and who, in a true spirit of philanthropy, volunteered to officiate on the occasion. The ceremony gone through consisted of reading, prayer, and sermon, but no singing. H. Lean Apps expounded, apparently with great earnestness, the 5th chapter of the Gospel of St. Matthew, dwelling on the 12th and 18th verses. The service commenced at 4, and terminated shortly after 5 o'clock, and was listened to evidently with much attention by the congregation, which consisted of about 200 Chinamen, most of them recent arrivals in the country. The general deportment of the assemblage was throughout extremely creditable.

EXTRACTS.

THE WEAKNESS OF PHILOSOPHY.

" As to *moral education*, if that were indeed *all* that was required, have we not our men of fancy and our men of thought ? If a corps of ordained philosophers would suit the wants of an unhappy world, the numbers ambitious of distinction in the pursuits of mind would always be sufficient to supply the demand. But the world, in all its corruption, nevertheless feels and knows that such guides would leave its wants ungratified. They may expound the malady, but they can poorly tell the cure. They can ally themselves with every folly, as well as with every virtue ; and whatever influence they may have over our hours of calm, they are lost in the tempest of the passions; unheard or despised when " deep calleth unto deep," when the flood-gates are burst and the winds are up."

NARROW THEORIES IN RELIGION.

" You can conceive that if a naturalist had but a single leaf or flower to study, or limited *himself*, by some perversity, to it alone, he would endeavour to discover a *world* in his specimen, and exhaust all the powers of the microscope to detect wonders within wonders, without limit How this tendency to find all things in all, is increased by the urgencies of controversy, it is needless to remark. If the botanist had to overthrow a rival theory of fructification, or to establish one of his own, you know how preternaturally augmented would become his powers of microscopic vision. Every visionary notion of religion boasts its text or two, and can boast no more ; but its supporters hold the text or two so near their eyes that they hide the rest of the Bible."

FAITH DIVORCED FROM WORKS.

" So subtle is the dexterity of the human heart in evil, that even from the most salutary truth it can extract a poison. That principle of religious dependence, which in the Scriptures is called faith,—that principle which, restoring the communication between fallen man and his Maker, must obviously be the highest and purest state of mind on this side the grave,— that principle which in its essential quality is formed to be the master-spring of the whole system of life's duties,—the principle which, in a word, puts our human souls in the full sun-light at once of the divine favour and divine holiness, has been perverted into a barren act of speculative conviction, an audacious assumption of divine favour, and a secret internal justification of indolence, covetousness, and unspirituality. This subject has been so beset by the thorns of controversy, that I suppose it may be necessary to say, that in making these melancholy assertions, I allude to no professed sect, party, or denomination whatever. No, Christians and brethren ! the only sect I allude to, is that terrible and wide-spread sect which began at the fall, and will, I fear, continue till the judgment ; that sect whose birth is in the unchanged evil of the human heart,—of which the Devil is arch-heretic and founder,—that sect, without a name, which in one form or another, has, in every age, compromised between heaven and h ll, by giving its *beliefs* to the *one*, and its *conduct and heart* to the spirit which governs the *other*."

THE MUTUAL RE-ACTION OF LOVE AND KNOWLEDGE.

" If Christianity, which gives new objects and purposes to all our faculties, be formed to correspond to our desires, it must not anticipate but excite them—excite in order to gratify. This supposes the Divine objects of such holy desires to be constantly increasing in brilliancy and loveliness, in order that the desires of the purified heart may never expire in gratification, or fade into satiety. Now, what *is* holiness but this brightening presence of God, worshipped by affections which grow as they gaze ? The very property of spiritual enlightenment is to *see* excellence more vividly the more we *love* it. But must not the better sight of perfection quicken in its turn the very love that gave that better vision ? And thus the object more prominent and the love more animated will perpetually call each other into new and brighter existence ; every perception of God will set the heart on fire, and every burning emotion of love will in return bring God nearer to the soul. His presence will answer the demand of the adorer, and the adorer will rise, as his demand is granted, in prayers for a closer and yet closer presence ; and where—where—shall this progress to infinite perfection end ? Never in this world; never, perhaps, in the next. Our perfection for eternity may be our progress for eternity. Such at this hour may be the perfection of angels. And the whole universe of pure-born and regenerate beings may be conceived as scattered at different points along one vast highway, leading to the light inaccessible, where God dwells alone in the secret sanctuary of his own infinite attributes; all tending incessantly towards the light, which grows brighter and brighter upon them as they advance; for the progress is their happiness. *We*, alas for fallen human nature, are far behind in the course ; but still it is a *common* course to all, and the good and growth of all are our fellow-travellers to God.

GOD IS LIGHT.

1 John i. 5.

Eternal Light! Eternal Light!
    How pure the soul must be,
When, placed within thy searching sight,
It shrinks not, but, with calm delight,
    Can live, and look on Thee.

The Spirits that surround Thy throne
    May bear the burning bliss,
But that is surely their's alone,
Since they have never, never known
    A fallen world like this.

Oh! how shall I, whose native sphere
    Is dark, whose mind is dim,
Before the Ineffable appear,
And on my naked spirit bear
    The uncreated beam?

There is a way for man to rise
    To that sublime abode,
An offering and a sacrifice,
A Holy Spirit's energies,
    An Advocate with God.

These prepare us for the sight
    Of Majesty above;
The sons of ignorance and night
Can dwell in the Eternal Light,
    Through the Eternal Love!

                REV. THOS. BINNEY.

RELIGIOUS INTELLIGENCE.

EVANGELICAL ALLIANCE.—The quarterly meeting of the Evangelical Alliance was held in the Mechanics' Institute, on the evening of Monday, the 21st June. The attendance was numerous. His honor Judge Pohlman presided. On the platform were the Revds. Dr. Cairns, Richard Fletcher, Seddon, Young. Jarrett, Divorty, M'Donald, Ballantyne, Moss, J. Mirams, R. Bowman, and J. P. Sunderland, Messrs. Ogilvy, Russell, Perry, Haller, Jennings, A'Beckett, Hoskins, &c. The Rev. Mr. M'Donald read a portion of the Scriptures, and the Rev. Mr. Seddon engaged in prayer. The chairman introduced to the meeting the Rev. R. Bowman, who delivered an eloquent address "On the claims of young men on the church of Christ." A few remarks were thereafter offered by Dr. Cairns, Mr. Fletcher, and others. Mr. Seddon apologised for the absence of the Bishop, on the ground of indisposition. A vote of thanks to the Rev. Mr. Bowman for his able address was carried unanimously.

FORREST CREEK INDEPENDENT CHAPEL.—This place of worship, after having been newly roofed and otherwise repaired, in consequence of its imperfect structure in the first instance, was recently re-opened by sermons on the Sabbath, and a week-evening tea meeting. At the social meeting, the Rev. E. Day, of Castlemaine, presided. Mr. Nicholls read the report, and the meeting was effectively addressed by the Revds. Messrs. Pitman (the Pastor), Storie, and Hall, and by Messrs. Blythe, Burns, Waite, and Collins. Great efforts had been made to meet the expenses of the re-building and improvements, but a debt still remained of £210. The re-edified structure was much commended by the speakers for its commodiousness, substantiality, and elegance. The speeches were very effective, and the prospects of the cause here, with Mr. Pitman's improved health, are very encouraging.

PRAHRAN INDEPENDENT SABBATH SCHOOLS.—The eighth anniversary services in connection with the Prahran Independent Sabbath Schools, were held on the 20th June, when two sermons were preached, in the morning by the Rev. R. Lewis, of Brighton; that in the evening by the Rev. James Ballantyne, Melbourne. On the following Tuesday a public tea-meeting took place, at which about 300 friends connected with the congregation were assembled. A report of the schools for the past year was submitted to the meeting, from which it appeared that 260 children are connected with the schools, and the average attendance during the year had been nearly 150. Addresses appropriate to the occasion were delivered by the Rev. R. Fletcher, Rev. G. Divorty, Rev. R. Lewis, Rev. B. Lemmon, and Rev. —Firth. The Revs. James Ballantyne and R. Bowman, who had been invited, were unavoidably absent.

HINDMARSH CONGREGATIONAL CHAPEL, SOUTH AUSTRALIA—REV. WILLIAM WILSON. —On Monday evening a public meeting was held in the Congregational Church, at Hindmarsh, to welcome the Rev William Wilson, late of Falkirk, to the pastorate. The building has been much improved in appearance, and was decorated for the occasion. After tea, the Rev. T. Q. Stow presided over a large meeting, and in his opening address referred to the past state of things at Hindmarsh, when nearly twenty years ago, they thought a sanctuary of ' good honest mud' a positive improvement over the first tenement, and Hindmarsh formed the first country congregation in the colony. He first called on the Rev. Mr. Hodge, who delivered an earnest address to the young on the necessity of decision of character. The Rev. James Howie, late of Nairn, N.B., said he felt an interest in Hindmarsh, from its being his resting-place on the way to Adelaide, when he found a temporary home in the manse. Referring, also, to the grief of Mr. Wilson's father on parting with his son, and the solace which the present scene would be to the good man's soul, he then addressed the meeting on individual responsibility. The Rev. William Wilson, minister of the place, then rose, and, with much emotion, spoke of the tender chord his friend had made to vibrate in his heart. He begged to propose a vote of thanks to the Home Missionary Society, whose lay-preachers had maintained so long the worship of God in that house, and to couple with that vote the names of Messrs. Giles and Barclay as those who had ministered longest in the place. Mr. Barclay responded, congratulating the friends there on the inproved state of things. The chairman remarked that they were threatened with an invasion of the Picts and Scots, but as they come with only spiritual weapons, they would gladly welcome them, and therefore he would call on the Rev. Mr. Lyall, United Presbyterian minister. who told the meeting that their pastor and he were not strangers when they met in Adelaide. They had studied together at Glasgow University ten years ago, and he knew him as a hard and successful student. The Rev F. W. Cox said he had to speak to a topic not so interesting as some. Church finance was a difficulty even in the Apostles' days, and the national budget was so to the Chancellor of the Exchequer. There was dissatisfaction at home with the usual machinery of seat-rents, &c., and he thought a twofold application of the scriptural principle would meet all difficulty—first, the actual setting apart a certain proportion of income for sacred uses; and, second, the working well of the principle of the first-day offering in God's house by everyone, rich and poor, according to the measure in which God had prospered him. Messrs Mytton having proposed and seconded a vote of thanks to the young people who had labored so well in the cause lately, and coupling also the names of the gentlemen who had assisted that evening, the meeting was closed with the benediction.

COLLINGWOOD YOUNG MEN'S MUTUAL IMPROVEMENT ASSOCIATION —This association held its first half-yearly meeting on Thursday, 24th June, in the North Collingwood Independent Church; the occasion was celebrated by a Soiree, at which about 150 persons were present. The chair was occupied by Mr. Templeton, the president, who opened the proceedings with a few introductory remarks. The Secretary, Mr. S. H. Mirams, read the report, which was followed by a financial statement from the Treasurer, Mr. Walker. Mr. Jackson gave a descriptive account of a painting he had prepared, representing the rise and progress of locomotion. The meeting was further addressed by Mr Vale, as the representative of the Richmond, and Mr. Taylor of the Melbourne Associations. Speeches were also delivered by the Rev. J. Mirams, Messrs Oxley, and B. H. Rogers. The evening was enlivened by a recitation by Mr. Hendy, and selections of music on the concertina by Mr, J. Oaten.

BAPTIST CHAPEL, COLLINS-STREET, MELBOURNE.—This chapel, which with its large additions will seat 700 persons, was re-opened for worship on Sunday, June 13th. Sermons were preached by the Revds. Messrs. Bowman, Broad (on a visit from England), and New. A social meeting was held on Tuesday evening, the 22nd, on the platform of which nearly all the Protestant denominations were represented. R. Kerr, Esq., presided, and the Revds. Dr. Cairns, J. Ballantyne, A. Morison, W. S. Binks, and I. New, addressed the meeting on topics assigned to them. The alterations and additions had cost £8,600, of which £1,200 had been subscribed. Towards the remaining debt of £2,400, money was collected and promised at the meeting amounting to £700. About 600 persons were present, and the meeting went off with great spirit.

REV. THOMAS BINNEY.— After the services in Sydney recorded in our last number, Mr. Binney preached in various other places of worship. He also delivered a lecture on the Apostle Paul to an audience convened by the Young Men's Christian Association, in Pitt-street Congregational church. 1,500 tickets were sold, and the place was densely crowded. Sir W. Dennison, Governor-General, presided. The lecture is described to have been most instructive and impressive, and the impression produced on the vast audience such as will not soon be forgotten. The rev. gentleman subsequently visited Ipswich and Brisbane, where he also lectured and preached. He called at the Hunter River on his return, and preached in the Independent Chapel. He arrived in Melbourne on 14th July, much recruited in health. He preached at St. Kilda on the evening of the 18th, and on the 25th twice at McKillop-street, Geelong, on all the occasions to crowded congregations. He leaves by first steamer for Adelaide, where he purposes remaining several weeks.—July 27th.

W. FAIRFAX AND CO., STEAM PRINTERS, COLLINS-STREET EAST, MELBOURNE.

The Southern Spectator.

No. II.   SEPTEMBER, 1858.   VOL. II.

RELIGION AND THE WORKING CLASSES.

Deep and long have been the lamentations over the great estrangement of the operatives in England from sympathy with religion and its promoters. A portion of them is found in nearly all communities ; and in country places the congregations are made up very largely of the poorer classes, while all over the country the Sunday-schools are freely supplied with scholars from their families. But the vast masses of workmen in towns and manufacturing districts have kept aloof from active religionists, whether ministers or laymen, and have manifestly regarded them with suspicion, as if devoid of sympathy with their condition, and perhaps as in league with the interests of the masters, in distinction from those of the men. Many benevolent hearts have yearned over them, prayed for them, and longed to secure their confidence, in order to do them good ; but access for the most part was debarred. At length, we see a remarkable religious movement, if not *among* them, at least *towards* them, on the part of more than one denomination of Christians.

The *popularis aura* is proverbially uncertain. The masses have ever been fickle in their humors and changeable in their tendencies. The last hundred and fifty years have witnessed not a few of these fluctuations. When Whitfield and Wesley, with their coadjutors, went forth on their evangelistic campaigns, the rude populace met them not only with gibes and hootings, but with the more formidable artillery of rotten eggs and brick-bats. Not a few, however, were eventually brought under the influence of religious truth, as in the case of the colliers of Kingswood and the north of England, the miners of Cornwall, and nearly the whole population of Wales. And the good effects remain to this day. Forty years later, in the time of Lord George Gordon, we find the populace of London and Edinburgh excited even to riot by a dread of Popish innovations, and loyal to excess to the House of Brunswick and the Protestant interest. Another twenty years witnessed the working men of Birmingham collecting in mobs, shouting lustily for Church and king, and against the French revolution, and putting down Dr. Priestley and the Unitarians by conflagration and breakage. These were the unreflecting impulses of ignorance and rudeness. Little was done during all this time, scarcely anything even attempted, for the educational improvement or the religious instruction of the great body of the people. The only dawn of better days was to be seen in the unostentatious movement in Gloucester, the establishment in weakness of a humble Sunday-school, which has proved the fruitful parent of a mighty offspring.

But an important change passed over the working men of England during the first thirty years of the present century. The extraordinary development of the manufacturing system rapidly aggregated huge masses of population in various localities. The revolutionary principles of France, driven from their own country, found an asylum in Britain, and to no small extent leavened the popular mind. And when the great war with Napoleon was brought to a close, and the reaction of a state of peace threw multitudes out of work, the masses were ripe for radicalism. Hunt and Cobbett could collect and control their thousands and tens of thousands ; and the fashion of the day was to lay all the blame of scarce employment and bad harvests upon the Government and the constitution of Parliament. This manifestation of wild discontent gradually took the form of organized Chartism, and for a time Feargus O'Connor became the king of the people.

But all this while education was silently extending, and intellect awakening. The labors of Bell and Lancaster, the establishment of British and Foreign, Jubilee, and National Schools, the exertions of Brougham and other friends of popular enlightenment, were gradually producing an effect. But that effect seems at first to have been distrust of the upper classes, as if for their own interest they had hoodwinked and deceived their inferiors ; and, by way of reprisals, all the received opinions of these classes, and religion among the rest, came into popular disfavour. The people in this mood of mind became the easy dupes of infidels and Socialists. Taylor first, and Owen next, became the gods of the populace ; lectures were delivered to crowded audiences ; Halls of science and Rotundas sprung up in every direction, co-operative shops were opened, model farms with community of goods projected, and the inauguration of a " New Moral World " was confidently believed to have taken place. The mania had its day ; but, when it closed, the tendency to infidelity had not quite died out. Holyoak and the Secularists next appeared upon the stage ; and they attracted, to hear their blasphemies, assemblages of working men more numerous and enthusiastic than could be collected around the most popular preachers of the day. These impulses seem, at length, to have expended themselves : at all events, they are much diminished in force ; and now we hear of vast multitudes of people being gathered together by religious teachers.

It has been the lamentation of all denominations of Christians that their ministrations scarcely touched the great body of the working classes. The population was nearly unapproachable, and would respond to scarcely any calls addressed to them to give heed to religion, from whatever quarter they might come. The Sabbath was all but universally disregarded, except for recreation : the house of God was forsaken, and the people seemed to live without the fear of God before their eyes.

Notwithstanding these unfavorable symptoms, a silent change we believe had been extensively going on ; at all events, indefatigable and wide spread efforts were in progress to bring about a change. If the ear of the people could not be secured in large crowds, access might be had to them in a more quiet and unostentatious way. For half a century, the Bible and Tract Societies had been increasing their issues, year by year, till they reached an almost fabulous amount. The regular religious press was not idle, the number of newspapers, magazines, and small books, whose main element was religion, was something prodigious. The population could not be deluged with these publications without being more or less affected by them. City missions had come into vogue. The houses of the operatives had been systematically visited ; the sick comforted and prayed with, cases of distress relieved, kindness and sympathy manifested ; and, though these labors produced no sudden revolution, they doubtless had a softening tendency, abating prejudice and disposing the popular mind to a more candid construction of the motives and aims of those who were seeking their welfare.　Above all, there had been time for Sunday-schools to prepare a new generation.　It has ever been a striking and a hopeful fact that, while so many of the adult operatives would attend neither church or chapel, they never showed any reluctance to allow their children to go to Sabbath-schools.　This has been the case all over England and Wales.　The per centage of the present race of working men and their wives, who have never attended a Sabbath-school, must be very small indeed.　Where no specific religious impression was made when at school, a kindly feeling towards the teachers and patrons of those institutions must have been kindled, and doubtless still lingers in the breast.　Sunday-schools have often been mourned over as comparative failures ; but we cannot help thinking that the aggregate result must be a state of mind, to say the least, considerably less prejudiced against religion and religious men, than the fathers of the present generation displayed.　To all these ameliorating causes must be added the political concessions which have been made to popular demands, the failure of the hopes that had been raised by the promises and plans of not a few of the popular leaders, and the generally improved condition of the people.　Whether these explanations are sufficient to account for a change in large numbers of the working classes in regard to religious teachers or not, the fact of such a change cannot be denied.

For some time the mails from England have brought tidings of unwonted efforts to arouse the attention of the operatives to the all-important claims of religion.　Many apprehended this would prove a mere fit of spasmodic zeal on the one side, and curiosity on the other, which would soon exhaust itself.　So far, however, the result is otherwise.　The movement goes on, increasing in breadth and momentum from day to day, and promising to produce the happiest effects upon our countrymen.　Last winter special services for the working classes were held in Exeter Hall by dignitaries of the Established Church, to the great scandal of Puseyitic churchmen, but to the great delight of the people, who met the call by attending in crowds.　These services being interdicted by the parochial authorities, have been taken up and successfully carried on in the same place by leading Nonconformists.　The Episcopalians, however, foiled in one direction have taken action in another.　The Bishop of London not long ago announced special services to be conducted by himself, in a large church situated in the midst of the Spitalfield weavers, and the place was too strait for those who came.　The warmth of zeal has even reached those regions of cold decorum, the cathedrals of England.　These glorious structures, the marvellous monuments of a bygone zeal, and long regarded as now useless, except to enshrine formality and sacerdotal dignity and to delight architects and antiquarians, are being at length applied to a really practical purpose.　The grand nave of Westminster Abbey, heretofore used only as a receptacle for monuments, is now fitted up with benches to accommodate the working classes, who are invited to come and listen to the Dean and Prebends ; and what is more, the people accept the invitation and fill the ample space Sunday after Sunday.　The example has been followed at St. Paul's, and multitudes now congregate there for other purposes than to pace the polished floor and gaze upon the lofty dome.　The movement has extended to the country, the authorities of Gloucester and other cathedrals treading in the steps of their metropolitan brethren; and it is to be hoped that the salutary impulse will not be arrested till it has embraced within its influence every one of those venerable establishments.

Were this hope realized, however, the provision for meeting the wants the working classes would still be very inadequate. With few exceptions the cathedrals are not placed where the population is densest ; nor, for the most part, are the occupants of prebendal stalls celebrated for those popular talents necessary permanently to interest large assemblies of plain men. Other and more appropriate agency must be brought to bear upon the masses ; and such agency Providence is bringing forth. It is well known that Spurgeon has now for some time been attracting unparalleled crowds at the Surrey Music Hall. A junior brother of that gentleman, Mr. Guiness, and other young orators among Nonconformist ministers, are successfully laboring in the same line. In Manchester, Mr. Mursell, a youthful Baptist minister, has engaged the noble Free-trade Hall for Sunday afternoon lectures to the working classes, and every week preaches there to five thousand of them. Mr. Stowell Brown, of Liverpool, is adopting a similar course with similar success. Birmingham is appropriating her noble Town-hall to the same purpose, and these signs of the times are shewing themselves in various parts of the country.

We trust that these delightful symptoms of zeal on the part of able men in various branches of the Church, and of improved feelings on the part of the operatives of Britain, will not prove to be transient. It will be a happy thing for the latter, conducive to their welfare in this world as well as that which is to come, and an augury for good to our fatherland, if they discover at length that the middle classes and the ministers of religion are their best friends and would prove their most judicious advisers. They would thus be kept from wasting their resources and their energies upon wild and impracticable schemes, and be led to devote them to such as would tend to increase their material comforts, improve their homes, raise their status in society, and prepare them for a tranquil deathbed and a blessed immortality.

It may be long before we see an equally promising movement in these colonies, from the unsettled habits of so large a portion of the working men and the sparce distribution of the remainder, and from the small amount of social organization and social sympathy pervading the community. But let not Christians and christian ministers despair : let them aim at great things, and expect great things. Above all, let them persevere in well-doing in the face of discouragements and difficulties, remembering that great moral and religious changes are not brought about in a day, but that in due time they *shall* be brought about if the laborers faint not in their work of faith and labour of love.

RELIGIOUS AWAKENINGS IN AMERICA.

Amercia is a strange contradiction ; the land of revivals and the land of slavery. Side by side we see the blackest national crime and the brightest display of the power and grace of God. It is no new thing, however, in Providence, to see moral contraries in juxta position. Cowper sung of London as a city in which is found "All that's good and all that's ill," each in its intensest degree. Perhaps they act upon each other by way of repellancy and concentration. Without attempting to settle this point, or to solve the mystery it involves, **the fact** of these revivals cannot be questioned, and it is one deserving the serious attention of the whole Christian Church. Some may scoff at these manifestations as the getting-up of hypocrites, or the outbreaks of a wild and senseless fanaticism. But none who are acquainted with the religious history of America will regard them in either of these lights. They are no new thing in that land. The era of Jonathan Edwards (1731) was signalised by extraordinary awakenings which, taking their rise in Portland and its vicinity, spread over the New England churches in a wonderful manner, producing the most happy and permanent results. A full and minute account of these, by Edwards himself, has been handed down to us, combining the cool analysis of the philosopher with the approving sympathy of the divine. A chronic susceptibility of such awakenings seems to have been induced, which was powerfully and successfully worked upon by Whitfield in his repeated visits to that continent. And after his day, they still continued more or less, during the remainder of the century, to characterise the religious history of the country; and the same peculiarity attaches to it up to the present time. Scarcely a memoir of any American minister comes out, which does not contain notices of such seasons having occurred in his ministerial experience. Of the celebrated Mr. Dwight, it is related that one impressive sermon of his, delivered on four several occasions, resulted each time in a great awakening. Revivals have now become a normal feature of the religious condition of America. They are sometimes confined to particular congregations; sometimes they embrace those within a town or district; and at others spread over an entire State, or a great part of the Union itself. Every pastor expects them in the course of his ministry. Churches look forward to them to cure the evils which reaction and time are found to produce. Individuals, who are evading the present claims of religion, soothe their consciences with the hope that they shall be brought to decision in some future revival.

How comes it to pass that America possesses this peculiar susceptibility?—that her people, in their successive generations, show a tendency periodically to awaken up to the claims of the momentous verities of religion; that they are liable to a contagious excitement on the subject, diffusing itself over wide districts of country, and embracing indiscriminately all denominations of Christians? And this, too, while neither Protestant Britain, the parent country whence her people emigrated, nor any of her other dependencies, present phenomena of the same kind. This question is not one of mere curiosity; it involves much that might prove eminently instructive. Something is probably due to the general excitability of the American character. In all their proceedings they are liable, in popular language, to "go-a-head." In politics, in commercial matters, in schemes for the improvement of the country, they are notorious for their impulsiveness and vehement onwardness of motion. And the same tendency, doubtless, is transferred to their religious doings, and stamps them with the national characteristic. But this does not exhaust the explanation nor, properly speaking, does it touch the main difficulty; for why should a people so intensely earnest in the pursuit of secular things show a tendency to throw all their energies into the pursuit of religion at all? Individuals, or other communities, of an impulsive nature may take up one secular thing after another and pursue it with characteristic eagerness, but serious vital religion is the last thing thought of.

All real believers in the divine authority of the Bible will attribute the work ultimately to the good pleasure and sovereignty of God; yet as God works by appropriate means, through the instrumentality of natural and pre-disposing causes, some solution of the problem may be found in the traditions, the training, the habits of the men of America. The Americans, those of them at least who lead public opinion, are mostly descended from the Puritans; and the Puritans were a remarkable order of men. Eminently religious themselves, they took care that all their institutions should be pervaded with the element of religion. They gave special heed to found in abundance educational establishments, in order to transmit their principles to their descendants. Among other usages they had seasons of extraordinary religious observances. The sacramental occasions were solemn and impressive. The periodical gatherings of their ministers were turned to account to deepen the sentiment of religion in the public mind. And above all, it was a customary thing with them to have days of fasting and special prayer frequently set apart by public authority; and these were observed by the people, not as holiday recreations, but really as intended, as times of solemn and earnest devotion. It thus became in a manner a national peculiarity to have at intervals seasons of a special kind, for penitential exercises and extraordinary prayer.

The features of the Puritan fathers are still stamped upon their children,—Puritan theology, Puritan worship, Puritan notions, Puritan sympathies are hereditary in the country,—the people were made familiar with them in their childhood, and they cannot shake them off in their adult years. This is not the case merely with a small denomination or two, as in England, or with a single class of the people, but with the nation as a whole. Not only the common people, but the men of trade and men of cience, the physicians and the lawyers, heads of colleges and editors of newspapers, judges, legislators and governors have been, as a general rule, brought up in this school, with Puritan ideas in their heads, whether they have or have not retained Puritan habits in their lives. And with respect to Revivals, in particular, they have been familiar from childhood with their history, most of them have witnessed something of the kind, they are accustomed to regard them as realities, and as events to which public opinion awards a high estimation; and their promoters, being probably among their personal friends, and of the class they have ever been accustomed to regard with respect and veneration, they cannot rank among hair-brained fanatics. When the rumour of a revival reaches them it does not therefore provoke the stare of ignorance or the sneer of contempt, as it probably would do in the corresponding classes in England, who have lived totally beyond the range of such excitements, or have only heard of them to despise them. The Americans, on the other hand, from these predisposing causes, treat them with respect, and if they happen to be near the scenes where they occur, a solemnity of mind is likely to come over them which may be the precursor of a deeper influence. All this may in some measure tend to account for what appears to the English public so inexplicable, namely, that a religious awakening once begun, the merchants, lawyers, and public men of New York and other great cities should be drawn into its vortex.

Attempts have not unfrequently been made to " get up " revivals, and ministers have appeared, after the stamp of Mr. Finney, whose profession and business it was to create them; and methods not always unexceptionable were had recourse to, to produce the necessary excitement. It is generally understood that the effects of revivals of this description were to a large extent spurious and evanescent; but where no such artificial expedients were adopted, remarkable men have appeared in America, whose ministry was almost uniformly attended with awakening effects. Such a man was Nettleton, who, without any *outré* measures, with nothing that the most fastidious could object to, either in his style of preaching or manner of proceeding, scarcely ever visited a church without producing an extensive awakening. And while many of the apparent conversions, which were the result more or less of artificial means, proved transitory, *his* converts nearly all stood, many of them becoming missionaries, ministers, office-bearers, and leading members of the churches of New England. Not less than thirty thousand persons are known to have been brought to religious decision through his labors. No one can read his memoirs, with a spark of candour, without being convinced of the genuineness and intrinsic value of the awakening which resulted from his wonderful ministry. Wherein lay the secret of this extraordinary power? It is difficult to answer. When his reputation was once established it is easy to conceive that expectation would be excited when he was known to be be about to visit any particular church or neighborhood, and a state of mind induced extremely sensitive and favorable to deep impression. But this would not account for the uniform success of his early ministrations when he was comparatively unknown.

And now it appears that the American churches are visited with another shower of sacred influences upon a larger scale, extending over a wider area, and producing more extraordinary effects than, perhaps, any other manifestation of the kind upon record. The commercial public had long been under a delirious excitement through various speculative manias; and the eager grasp after wealth was only equalled by the extravagant profusion with which it was expended. The fearful reaction came, bringing with it universal panic, and wide-spread bankruptcy. Perhaps this was a preparative in providence for an excitement of another and more salutary kind. Religion was admitted on all hands to be at a low ebb. The winter before last, complaints were manifold and loud over the lamentable state into which the churches were declining—places of worship were thinly attended, conversions were few, the colleges were scantily supplied with students for the ministry, missionaries to the heathen were not forthcoming in the usual numbers; everything was flat, retrograde, and discouraging. But it appears to have been the midnight hour to be followed by the dawn of a bright and glorious day. The chill of a morbid state has been succeeded by the glow of health; paralysis by vigour and activity. Testimonies to the genuineness and extent of this work will be given elsewhere in this number.

THE CHURCH'S STRENGTH.*

"Be strong," say the Scriptures to every individual Christian; "Put on thy strength, O Zion," to the Church at large. Why? Because the Church has a great work to do, and strength is needed to do it. Her work everywhere and at all times is great; in these colonies and at this time it is pre-eminently so. Looking at her position generally she has a new empire to leaven with her salutary principles; regarding it specifically she has incongruous materials to assort and organize, deep vices to uproot, broken habits to repair; she has even for the most part, her own institutions to found, her ordinances to establish, and her agents to bring from

---

* Isaiah lii. 1.

afar. Like the handful of brave Britons in India contending with multitudinous foes, she has to do battle against vast odds, with her forces scattered and her munitions of war scanty. She has need therefore to consider well where her strength lies, to husband it with care and to use it with skill. Now, wherein does the strength of the Church consist?

There is strength in numbers. A small body is weak, a large body is strong. The majority of the community naturally prevail over the minority, the many over the few. Hence a numerous church has, all other things being equal, more power to influence the world around it than a small church. There is more strength in it.

There is strength in riches. Wealth is another term for those physical means which are necessary, in the present life, for human subsistence and comfort. To possess riches is to possess the power to command a large portion of food, clothing and conveniences. Now, upon a great scale, to diffuse intelligence and promote religion, it is necessary that agents should be employed, and consequently sustained; that buildings be erected and paid for, and various other matters done which entail expense. With these means the needful agency can be supported, without them it cannot. Hence a church possessing surplus wealth, after defraying its own expenses, possesses a powerful element of strength for producing an impression on surrounding minds.

There is strength in rank, station, position in society. We may argue against this as unreasonable, and contend for the absolute equality of all men; but the fact is, and ever has been, that men in a higher position in civil life have an influence over a wider circle than those in a lower; and a Christian community, in which such persons form a considerable element, possesses, provided it is equal in other respects, a greater power to affect public opinion and to impress society, than one in which no such element forms a part.

There is strength in genius and learning. It is natural to pay deference to superior mental endowments. The thoughts and opinions of master spirits impress and mould the age in which they live. Knowledge too is power. An educated community is more mighty in affecting other minds than one sunk in ignorance. This is seen in the superior influence of civilised over savage races when they are brought into contact. A church of Christians, therefore, whose vocation it is to sway the intellect and heart of man, if it consist largely of persons of superior abilities and good education, is necessarily stronger than one composed of men inferior in these respects.

There is strength in these things; but they do not constitute the peculiar strength of the Church. They may, under proper influence, prove powerful auxiliaries; but regarded in themselves, they would contribute nothing towards the Church's objects. More than this, the Church may possess all the elements of real strength and go on from conquering to conquer without these. Was it not so with the Primitive Churches? All will admit that they were clothed with power: yet at first, and at the period when they were strongest, their numbers were scanty; their wealth was small; they were composed for the most part of unlearned and ignorant men in humble stations of life: not many wise men after the flesh, not many mighty, not many noble were called in those days; yet the mightiest things of this world gave way before them; they possessed a strength which nothing could resist. Where lay the secret of their strength?

The Church's strength consists in that, whatever it is, which will favourably affect other minds, will produce conviction, and bring mankind over to her side. It consists in *truth*. There is strengh in truth, there is weakness in error. Truth is possessed of inherent energy. It lives in the light ; courts inquiry and has nothing to fear. It girds the loins, nerves the arm, and fortifies the heart with confidence. But error is suspicious and evasive. It induces misgivings, failing of heart, distraction and feebleness. A few earnest men holding a great truth are more mighty than a host of erring opponents clothed with every other attribute of power. We have seen, in our own day, great political and economical truths advocated by very slender minorities against the united phalanx of authority, rank, wealth, learning and vested interests, and yet come off signally victorious. It is so with religious truth. The "Truth once delivered to the saints," the "Glorious Gospel of the blessed God" was the weapon with which the apostles and first preachers did their execution. The doctrine of Christ crucified is a power, the power of God to salvation. It is a sword of ethereal temper and certain effect when rightly wielded ; and, when brought fairly into collision with the false systems of the world, it is more than a match for them, whether they be the superstitions of the vulgar, or the speculations of the learned. The early Christians were aggressive and invulnerable while faithful to the truth ; they only ceased to conquer when they debased the quality of their weapon by the alloy of gross errors.

This truth is unpalatable to the corrupt taste of man ; and the temptation is not slight to hold back part of it, to dilute it, to soften it down, to mix a little flattering error with it, in short to make a compromise in order to render it more agreeable and popular. In the degree in which this temptation is yielded to, the end in view is defeated. Instead of bringing over the world to the Church, the Church herself is the conquered party. God's truth, with which she is entrusted, is strong because it *is* truth, and that special kind of truth which is adapted to man's necessities ; and the moment she parts with it she parts with the lock of her strength.

In *piety*. There can be no piety without some portion of saving truth, but truth may be held in theory without piety. In such cases the truth itself becomes weak. The sword of the Spirit requires a fitting arm to wield it, and that arm must be moved by piety. If a church be soundly orthodox but spiritually dead, it is paralysed and unfit for action. The truth itself falls powerless to the ground if presented by those who do not deeply feel it and earnestly enforce it. The Great Teacher not only uttered truth, but made disciples. He collected a few choice spirits, constituted them a normal school, imbued them with his own principles, and then said to them, " Ye are the salt of the earth," assuring them that if they lost the savour of their piety, they would be "good for nothing." The strength of a body of soldiers consists in the spirit of the men, as well as the quality of their armour. The millions of Persia were weaker than the few thousands of Greece. Gideon's army was stronger when reduced to three hundred stout-hearted warriors, than when it consisted of thirty-two thousand cowards. In like manner the strength of the handful of apostolic men who undertook to bring back a rebellious world to the allegiance it owed to its Maker, consisted in the sincerity and ardour of their personal religion in union with the heavenly truth committed to their trust.

So long as the primitive Christians retained their first love, they retained their strength. They went on from conquering to conquer : " mightily grew the word of God and prevailed." While they were " good men, full of the Holy Ghost and of faith," " much people was added to the Lord." But when in the course of time the spirit of the world invaded them, when formalism took the place of experimental piety, and unconverted men became ministers and leaders, then they were shorn of their strength and ceased to spread. But piety to be effective should be earnest as well as real. There should be not only light, but brilliancy; not life only, but health. As the sick are unfit for the active duties of life, so sometimes Christians, though possessed of the vital principle of religion, have so feeble a spiritual constitution that they are powerless for good. They breathe, but can neither walk nor work. They are "saved," yet "so as by fire," and contribute but little towards saving others. The power lies with the earnest men, who are strong in faith, ardent in love, filled with compassion for souls, zealous for God, mighty in prayer. These do the work of extension.

The Church's strength consists in practical *holiness*. Orthodoxy, fired by enthusiasm, would without virtue still be weak. Human nature, bad as it is, revolts at such glaring inconsistency. Deeds are more eloquent than words, and good deeds the most eloquent of all. Worldly men cannot understand the Christian's private feelings nor appreciate his experience, but they can see a good life; they understand it, they feel it. More than this, they expect it; and from the high professions Christians make they have a right to expect it; and when they do fall in with it, it arrests their attention, and wins their admiration. The primitive Christians (to recur to them again) were strong because they were truthful, just, sober, pure, disinterested, benevolent, meek and forgiving. Their entire example was a new moral spectacle, a phenomenon the world had never beheld before; mankind were awed by such an array of virtues; it overpowered and subdued them. And oh! if Christians now were only equal in this respect to their professions, how mighty would they be for good!

What is the opprobrium of Christianity but the want of consistency in the conduct of its professors? What weakens the minister's appeal but the scarcity of living specimens of the religion he recommends? What so effectually fortifies the sinner's heart against the claims of the Gospel as the conspicuous blots on the character of many who are well known as its zealous advocates? How much harm has been done to the minds of children and domestics, of customers and fellow-tradesmen, of workmen and employers, by the bad tempers, the questionable integrity, the deficient truthfulness, the grasping covetousness, the selfish indulgences of professing Christians? The Church will never be strong till she is holy: by "well-doing," she must "put to silence the ignorance of foolish men;" and when, armed with truth, and fired with piety, her professions and conduct correspond, she will meet with little that may not be overcome.

MEMOIR OF THE REV. J. R. DALRYMPLE.
WARRNAMBOOL.*

The Rev. JAMES RICHIE DALRYMPLE was born in Ayr, West of Scotland. Nothing is known here of his parents, or of his early training, but from the number of his near relatives who are ministers of the United Presbyterian Church of Scotland, it may be inferred that the fear of God

---

* Abridged from an excellent Funeral Sermon, preached at Warrnambool to the bereaved congregation, by the Rev. Robert Hamilton, of Collingwood, and since published by William Goodhugh and Co., Melbourne.

was, in an eminent degree, found among his kindred, and that he enjoyed all the advantages of christian example, and godly upbringing in his youth. It appears that, when a boy attending the Ayr academy, he displayed great aptitude for learning, stood among the highest in his classes, and endeared himself to his teachers by his amiable disposition, and correct behaviour. The seed of divine truth, which had been early cast into the virgin soil of his heart, gradually developed into a life of entire devotedness to the service of his Lord and Master, Jesus Christ.

With a view to the holy ministry he commenced his studies in the University of Edinburgh in the year 1825. He passed through the entire curriculum of study, in the classics, philosophy and science, required by the United Presbyterian Church. During five years attendance at the University, he distinguished himself in different departments of learning, and proved himself capable of taking a first place either in languages, metaphysics or science. Both in these and in moral and religious questions, he won the high commendation and esteem of the College Professors. Having finished the course of preparation required for students for the ministry, he was duly licensed in 1836, by the Presbytery of Edinburgh, to preach the Gospel, and his name entered on the list of probationers. Mr. Dalrymple was not many months engaged as a preacher, when the church of Thornliebank, in connection with the Glasgow Presbytery, called him to take the oversight of them in the Lord, and he was duly set apart, in April, 1837, by prayer and "the laying on of hands" to the office and work of an ordained pastor. Here he labored during eight years, with great ability and zeal, beloved by his people, and highly esteemed by his ministerial brethren in the neighbourhood.

During the course of his labors in this place, his mind became deeply impressed with the duty of devoting himself to the work of preaching the gospel in a foreign field. Accordingly, towards the end of the year 1845, he resigned his charge, much to the regret of his people, who were extremely reluctant to lose the services of so talented and excellent a minister, and resolved to devote himself to the work of God in the flourishing colony of Canada. His brethren in the ministry, after eight years intercourse, bore the highest testimony to his worth as a man, a scholar, and a minister of Christ.

Having arrived in Canada, he officiated at first in vacant churches and preaching stations. No fewer than three localities competed for his settled ministrations. The object of his choice was Hamilton, Canada West. Here he was inducted in November, 1847. In this place he labored with acceptance for about three years, till the state of his health constrained him to seek again release from his pastoral connection, with a view to his returning to the parent country.

He remained at home about two years, recruiting his health from the severe effects of the Canadian climate. Returning vigour brought renewed desire to be employed in ministerial work, in foreign service. Australia, from its mild and healthful climate and its rising importance as a gold country, presented itself to his view as the most eligible field, on the cultivation of which he might expend his energies for his Master's glory. On the eve of his departure for this country, he received from the Mission Secretary of the United Presbyterian Church the following testimony :—
"I have personally known Mr. Dalrymple for several years, and I have a high and favorable opinion of his talents, attainments and unblemished character, and I believe that, wherever it is his lot to labor in the service

of his Divine Master, he will prove a devoted, acceptable, and useful minister of the Gospel of Christ. ·

Mr. Dalrymple arrived in the *Strathfieldsaye*, in April, 1853. He soon commended himself to the confidence and esteem of the brethren already on the spot, by his unassuming manners, his intelligence, attainments, and Christian deportment, and was received into connection with the Melbourne Presbytery of the United Presbyterian Church. He seemed well qualified, in many respects, for a charge in the city of Melbourne, but no opening presenting itself there, he had to look for a door of usefulness in another quarter.

The Rev. Lachlan McGillivray of Warrnambool, was at that time leaving the colony and returning to Scotland, and Mr. Dalrymple was invited to visit the place on trial. The result was his permanent settlement. For several years he occupied three stations, a few miles apart from each other, Warrnambool, Woodford and Towerhill. Among the three localities he divided his labors, by a judicious arrangement, so as to accomplish the greatest amount of good compatible with his strength. It was while on the way to conduct his usual ministrations, riding from Towerhill, that he received, about two years ago, a sun-stroke which contributed to lay the foundation of those affections under which he at length fell prostrate. From that period, he more or less complained of general weakness, and surrendered the station at Towerhill altogether. During the last twelve months, particularly, he was observed to give decided symptoms of declining health. His usual elasticity of mind, and energy of body, both afforded marked indications of decay. Of this he was perfectly sensible himself, and he frequently spoke of the likelihood of his being obliged to retire from his pastoral labors, and again visit the land of his birth. It was a subject of great lamentation to him that he was not able, as formerly, to visit the members of his congregation residing at a distance from the town.

There seems little room to doubt that he fell a martyr to his studiousness and zeal in his Master's cause, and his devotedness to his people's interests. Private study and public labor absorbed his time. His labors were abundant, and were all bestowed without grudging. In the spirit of the Gospel, he sought to distribute freely what the grace of God had bestowed upon himself. During the greater part of his life, he was a devoted student, endeavoring to store his mind with those treasures whereby he might enrich the people of his charge. To a mind eminently active, united to a physical frame of delicate construction, the labors of study, prolonged for many years, at length induced such susceptibility, that he fell at once under the first stroke of disease. From his ardent zeal in the discharge of duty, he refused to yield to the kind admonitions of friends to desist, at least for a time, from further toil. The season for celebrating the Lord's Supper was at hand : though unfit for so exciting a service he mustered all his energies to go through it ; he was enabled to finish the sermon, to call upon his people for the last time in his Master's name, to " Examine themselves, and so to eat of that bread and drink of that cup," when his mental powers failed. He was observed to be incapable of proceeding with the service. The desire of his heart to eat of the Christian Passover once more before he died was denied him, but he lost his last feeling of consciousness in the act of preparing himself and others to do it. It was an affecting scene to witness, in the midst of so solemn a ceremonial, the derangement of the intellectual powers through physical exhaustion. Symptoms of mental aberration manifested themselves ; this was an indica-

tion of the entire breaking up of the system ; soon the vital springs lost
their tension, and every energy became paralysed. Medical skill on the
spot was employed, but in vain. It was thought desirable to remove the
invalid to Melbourne to secure the best assistance obtainable for such cases ;
but his glass was run. The kind offices and care of his friends was of no
avail. Within a week and a half of his last public service he breathed
his last in quietness and peace, but without returning consciousness.
The medical attendant stated the cause of death to be "chronic inflammation
of the brain, with softening of its substance." He died on the evening of
July 1st, 1858, and the funeral took place on Monday the 5th. The
friends met in the United Presbyterian Church, Collins-street, Rev. A. M.
Ramsay's, and service was conducted by the Rev. D. McDonald, of Emerald
Hill. His remains were followed, by a number of friends belonging to
different churches in town, to their final resting-place in the public
cemetery in Melbourne, where they wait " the resurrection of the just from
among the dead." " Blessed are the dead who die in the Lord, from
henceforth. Yea, saith the Spirit, that they may rest from their labors, and
their works do follow them."

Mr. Dalrymple was one who was respected by all, esteemed by his
acquaintance, and beloved by those who stood related to him by the ties
of ecclesiastical connection and of christian fellowship. He was one of
the few who enjoyed golden opinions among all classes, while he is never
known to have made himself an enemy ; nor was this from any spirit of
tame subserviency, but from pure christian courtesy.

He sometimes felt himself called upon either to state and defend his own
opinions or to oppose others, but this was always done in a christian spirit.
So candid was his expression of sentiment, so faithful his attachment to
principle, so thoroughly free from the bigotry of sect, and so full of
charitable respect to the conscientious convictions of others, it was impossible for any reasonable adversary, while differing from his views, not to
respect his opinions and his moral consistency.

Although conscientiously attached to the Presbyterian form of Church
Government, he had too much of the mind of Christ to suppose that his
principles and character would suffer by lending a helping hand to the
members of other denominations. He was a United Presbyterian in
preference to other Presbyterian sections, and a Presbyterian in principle in
preference to Episcopacy, Wesleyanism, and Independency ; yet the Christian
was always beheld in his spirit and life, rather than the sectary. Catholicity
in spirit was not with him mere theory, but a practical manifestation ; not
a piece of platform ostentation, but a living reality.

Mr. Dalrymple was not only opposed to State-aid to all sects indiscriminately, but to the principle altogether ; he deemed it alike the privilege and the duty of Christians to maintain the ordinances of the Gospel by
their own free-will offerings, according as God has prospered them ; and
believed it hurtful to the purity and efficiency of the Church to receive a
support exacted by compulsion and administered by the secular powers.
At the same time he never allowed his views on this important matter to
interfere with his enjoying cordial fellowship with those who differed from
him on that point. He was a zealous advocate of a general union of the
different sections of Presbyterians into one body. Although he was not prepared himself to surrender, or to approve of others surrendering, any
principle conscientiously held, in order to effect this object, it was yet a

matter of surprise and grief to him that so many difficulties should continually arise to postpone its consummation.

As a preacher Mr Dalrymple shunned the ornament of mere literary embellishment, as well as oratorical display; and endeavored by a comparatively quiet, yet impressive and effective delivery, to win his way to the understandings and hearts of his hearers, mainly by the force of truth, by the power of argument, and above all, by the energy of the Holy Spirit. His expositions of divine truth clearly proved him to be well skilled in the holy oracles, apt in unfolding the rich resources of the mind of God as revealed in the scriptures. His preparations for pulpit work were faithful and laborious. He did not serve God with what cost him nought, nor present " the halt, the maimed, the lame, and the blind," for sacrifice. Animated by a becoming sense of the responsibilities of his office, he sought to be well qualified for his Master's service.

In his visitations of the sick, Christianity shone forth with mild yet impressive lustre. The earnestness of his prayers on these occasions, the tenderness of his sympathy, and the rich communications of gospel truth which flowed from his mind, evinced the extent of his communion with God, of his christian experience, and the attainments he had reached in the divine life.

In the private circles of friendship he was peculiarly beloved. Distinguished for studious habits, he was yet peculiarly social in disposition. He was in his proper element among his people in their homes. He manifested his genial disposition, with select companions of christian friends, displaying great affability and kindness. His manners were equally opposed to gloomy austerity and to boisterous mirth. His Christianity was cheerful without frivolity, and grave without moroseness. His deportment was of the most unassuming character. Humility, among all the graces of his life stood forth conspicuous. He was not lifted up with pride, nor was he ambitious of display. He did not court notoriety. Instead of indulging in ostentation, he was disposed rather to take the lowest room. At the same time, when occasion called, he could stand up, without any air of obtrusiveness, and assume the leadership which his qualifications might have entitled him to claim.

This estimable servant of God though dead, yet speaketh in the remembrance of his instructions, the impressiveness of his example, and the solemn circumstances of death. He was conveyed to the tomb within two days of the time of the interment of the lamented young minister, the Rev. J. G. Reed, a memoir of whom appeared in our last number; and Melbourne thus witnessed, in one week, the funeral processions of two pious, devoted, and able ministers of the New Testament, neither of whom were worn out by age, and both of whom were prepared to have spent a longer time in the service of Christ on earth, had such been the will of their Master. While strenuous efforts are put forth and large sacrifices are made to obtain additional supplies of pastors and evangelists for these needy colonies, is not the Church, in all its branches, significantly taught, by these mysterious events, the uncertainty and precariousness of its best arrangements, and its absolute dependance for success upon the will and blessing of the great Head and Governor of all ? " Pray ye the Lord of the harvest that he may send forth more laborers into his harvest."

CORRESPONDENCE.

Dear Sir,—From the announcement given in the last number of the "Southern Spectator," that its pages would be open to subjects immediately identified with the progress of the Redeemer's kingdom, especially in these colonies, I have ventured to pen the following thoughts, which if you think worthy of a column in that magazine, will I trust in some measure, tend to awaken an interest in the minds of Church Members, in reference to the subject of which it treats.

The question, sir, is often asked; How is it, that with so many faithful and devoted ministers as now occupy the various pulpits of the Christian Church, so little apparent good is the result of their labors? It is not that they do not faithfully proclaim the "glad tidings of salvation." It is not that they are not found "constant in season and out of season." But I am much inclined to think, that there is a more intimate relation between an "earnest ministry" and a devoted and praying people, as it regards the success of that ministry, and the spiritual prosperity of the people, than has yet been felt. Ministers may preach, and labor ever so faithfully, yet if there is a lack of genuine heartfelt piety, of an earnest desire that God's kingdom on earth may prosper; if there is coldness and indifference manifested by those who are professed members of our churches, if there is a restraining of prayer before God, and if the seasons appointed for church and prayer meetings are neglected or forgotten, or only attended by a comparatively scanty number, what wonder is it that there are so few conversions to God, so few gathered from the world, to add to the strength of the Church, and to participate in the blessings of redemption? Yet is it not a mournful fact, that such is the case? We have only to observe the very meagre attendance at the usual week evening meeting for prayer to establish this, and the question involuntarily presses itself on every reflecting mind—Where is the genuine piety, the heartfelt religion of Jesus, the humble dependencies, the experimental knowledge of the truth, the wrestling in prayer, which is the privilege of the Christian, and which ought to characterise every disciple of the Saviour? Alas, where? This state of things ought not to be, and I cannot but think, that before any special blessing will attend the labors of our ministers, the Church must be awakened to a sense of her responsibility, as well as her privileges. I know that many are prepared to make excuses for non-attendance at these meetings, but none that I have met with (unavoidable circumstances alone excepted) appear to me to harmonize with a right state of mind; especially in a colony like this, when the duties of the day in most cases are over at an early hour. Surely if the disciples of Jesus were alive to their best interest, if they felt, that public as well as private prayer was necessary, not only to their spiritual growth in grace,—as a privilege unspeakable, amid the "turmoil and bustle of life," to find composure calmness and peace in waiting upon God, and with one accord in casting every burden upon him "who careth for them,"—but as a means by the exercise of which they can alone expect that God will bless both the pastor and the people, and prosper their united efforts to promote his glory, I cannot but think that our week evening services would present a very different aspect. And what might we not expect, if all our Church members were actuated by such feelings? I all assembled at the "hour of prayer," and if the united and earnest supplications of the Israel of God, were to ascend with fervent desires to the throne of grace, might we not expect that God, who has been so often arrested by the voice of prayer, would give such manifestations to his people now, as would convince them that He is still a "God hearing and answering prayer;" would he not accompany a preached Gospel with the outpouring of his Spirit, and thus not only strengthen the faith and piety of his own people, but send conviction also to the hearts of unbelievers, leading multitudes to the Cross, as the only refuge of a guilty world? I have met with a beautiful extract from the pen of that eminent and venerable minister of Christ, the Rev. J. A. James, so appropriate to the point, and so well adapted to repay a frequent perusal, that I venture to give it, trusting that the importance of the subject will be an apology for its length. He says, "I love to see the people of God come cheerfully, gravely, devoutly and earnestly, wending their way through the busy and thoughtless crowd, to the house of prayer, saying in effect to the multitude around them, 'Come with us and we will do you good, for the Lord hath spoken good concerning Israel.' I love to see the portals of the sanctuary open of a week evening, which, while the doors of the theatre, the ball-room and the tavern are drawing in the lovers of pleasure, shall send forth the voice of wisdom, saying, 'How long ye simple ones, will ye love simplicity?' 'Wherefore do ye spend money for that which is not bread,' &c. Where is the disciple of Jesus who will not say, 'I love to hear the lecture bell on a week-day evening, and to see my brother with me at the week-day service.' Let ministers be affectionately urgent with their people on this subject and they will be gratified by their success. They need line upon line, invitation after invitation. If the invitation is felt to be the fruit of love, if it is kindly and lovingly given, it will be taken by many, who, without such invitation, would never think of attending. Try, brethren to attend the week-day service, do all in your power to be there. It will be a good thing for yourselves, and will be very encouraging to your ministers. Let us have crowded 'Lectures' and 'Prayer meetings' over the entire country; let not your business form an hindrance, let it be a matter of conscience, not of taste merely to attend the week-day services; you need them,' and they will help and bless you. Be regular in your attendance; do not let it be a mere occasional thing to be there, when an admonition has been delivered on the sabbath, calling upon you for the performance of this duty, or when something extraordinary is to be heard. This is the case with too many. We see them sometimes, but oftener miss them. Be it with you an ordinance fixed as the sabbath, keep the evening free from all occupation, make no other engagement. When invited to something else, say 'No, that evening is given to God,' 'The diligent soul shall be made fat.' This is diligence, may it be yours."

I am, dear sir, yours faithfully,   J. V.

A GOLD-FIELD DISTRICT.
To the Editor of the Southern Spectator.

Sir,—It is impossible to conceive of a locality inhabited by Britons, more unlike anything to be found in Britain, than one of our large digging towns. There is the old familiar English tongue indeed, with its well-known Irish and Scotch varieties; the same bustle and business in every turn of the streets that we remember at home, and yet all looks different. The business ideas are different; the ideas of every-day life are different; old associations are cut off; healthful conservatism has degenerated into spurious activity, and the *individual* life, intensified to a greater degree, absorbs all social life; and everything proceeds in one violent agitated whirling of single units. This of course was more the case in the first origination of these mushroom townships than now, when they boast some five or six years of existence. Humanity is naturally social, gregarious as moralists say, and "nature having been cast out at the windows is coming in at the door." Society is working its own cure, slowly, but surely. At first, nothing but the individual man was thought of; places of worship were all but unknown, and the only thing which could draw people together was either the selfish lust for strong drink, or the discussion of some of the selfish rights of the individual miner. Now we have gradually developing a taste for more united life, and this is especially manifested in the gathering together of Christian congregations and the "society" which must arise from such a state of progress. But we are far, far behind what ought to be. The single man is still the common idol, and the most influential inhabitants are generally those who cater for the amusements of the many, who stimulate the appetite while they supply with food the craving for strong drink. Where selfish publicans are the acknowledged aristocrats, no one can expect much true morality, or heroism, or society, or Christianity.

This is to a large extent the case in Sandhurst; but a change is taking place and a better order of things is, we see, in store for the rising community. We regard the improvement as mainly the result of christian energy, and look forward to all future development to the same agency. There is no knowing how much future generations may owe to one or two genuine Christians who have wrought here from the commencement, and have been, indeed, as "leaven, leavening the whole lump." Christianity is becoming felt to be one of the powers at work in the community, and before long we shall hear no more of "respectable" citizens and men of influence boasting that they have "never been inside the walls of a church since they left the old country."

We have here a large population scattered over a wide space of ground. The *Bendigo District*, of which Sandhurst is the capital, covers an area in round numbers, 10 miles long by 10 miles broad, and of course the scattered nature of the population makes it all the more difficult to cope with the evils which are at work, and to supply all the people with the means of worship and christian instruction. The system of our friends the *Wesleyans* seems the most adapted for this work of pioneering. They possess the light skirmishing artillery, which can be brought to play in a short time, and on any point. The breaches they effect are often built up again immediately by the enemy, but still they do a useful work, and God honors them. I have before me now the Wesleyan plan of operations for this district. It is an extraordinary statement of what mere energy and faith can do. I count no fewer than twenty preachers, who are marshalled and commanded by the ministers of the district, Messrs Dare and Dubourg. Then there is a long list of places of worship,—some of them mere tents 'tis true, but still, in the neighbourhood where they are placed, deserving, by comparison with other tents, the name of "chapels" or "school-houses." The list numbers fifteen of these erections for religious worship, with services once, twice, or thrice, on the Sabbath, and occasionally in the week day. These are the germs of enlarged operations; if the locality should be permanent, and if the population should again rush off, the house of God goes with it. Now when we think of fifteen *churches* it seems a great deal; but all in all, we cannot take more than 100 or 120 as the average accommodation of these several buildings. If even, therefore, these were all filled, they would be but a very poor provision for the wants of the people. Unfortunately they are not all filled, and besides, out of so many as twenty digging artillery-men you cannot expect all to be expert gunners. The *Church of England* has two or three school-houses in different gullies, but owing to the want of ministers some of these have to be shut up on the Sabbath. These and the *Catholic* schools are the only means of worship for the great masses of the digging population, if we except two Primitive Methodist chapels in Long and Eaglehawk Gullies. So you see, Mr. Editor, that there is yet wide scope for the most energetic christian action that the Church can put forth. Some of these outlying gullies are several miles away from Sandhurst, have their own townships, and will be permanent centres of population ere long, but they are as yet destitute of true religious instruction.

I am rejoiced to see that in Sandhurst itself, the different congregations are becoming settled and strong. Christians should be "wise as serpents," and it is accordant with wisdom to try to gain as much strength as possible at head-quarters in the first instance, that there may be a rallying point for future operations to work round. The *Presbyterians* have the largest congregation, and work well and harmoniously under their excellent minister, Mr. Nish. They have been worshipping in the school-room till they are crowded out, and have been compelled to commence building a new church. The foundation stone was laid the week before last, and the walls are already rising into view from the market-square. On the other side of the town is the "Holy Hill" of Sandhurst, "where the people most do congregate." There is the reserve for the Wesleyans, and the English church. The Wesleyans have a handsome schoolroom, the church is yet to be. The *Episcopalians* have obtained a complete establishment; school, church, and residences for the clergyman and his schoolmaster. The church will be a noble building, overlooking all the district,—I say, 'will be,' for like so many colonial structures, it wants its spire. The Congregationalists met in a store in the Market-place, where originally were piled bags of chaff, &c. It was made into a very respectable temporary church, and served its purpose as a place of rendezvous in which the scattered remnants of the body might gather together. Our congregation is only a few months old, and judging from the measure of success God has granted to our efforts hitherto, we may augur well for the future. Not long since, we had very heavy rain, which, getting into the foundation of the "walls of our Zion," made them sink and almost fall. We were compelled to look out for other quarters. We did not know what to do, but were soon relieved from our great difficulty by the trustees of the English Church kindly granting us the use of their school-room till such time as our own building might be ready. Such a fact speaks more for the union of evangelical sentiment in this country, than a dozen platform speeches We are taking active steps to have a building of our own this spring, if possible. We have decided upon purchasing a fine and valuable site for a church and school, and are only waiting now for the lawyers to have their part of the work finished, in order to commence at once with a modest building. We build first a school-room, which will for a few years serve all purposes, and then, at some future day we hope to see, rising over the town, a handsome church and perhaps a spire.

I hope, Mr. Editor, I shall not weary your readers with this long letter, but in future days when all has changed, and great towns and noble buildings adorn this beautiful country

E

and when we have a people of our own, institutions and societies of our own originating, and
are grown to manhood, then, perhaps, such a boy's sketch of this country's schooldays may
not be without its interest.

Your's sincerely,

Sandhurst, Aug., 1858.   FIDES.

AMERICAN REVIVAL.

We have, in a previous page, presented some general views on the subject
of American revivals, and shall now furnish our readers with a short account
of the remarkable one at present in progress. Our difficulty is with the abundance and variety of the materials which have come to hand. We shall chiefly
make use of a series of letters which appeared in the "Christian Times," written
by a Church of England Clergyman, the Rev. J. L. Bird, Rector of Wyton,
Huntingdonshire. That gentleman visited America, and was an eye and ear-
witness of what he describes, and we deem his testimony altogether unexceptionable.

ORIGIN OF THE WORK.—For some weeks before the end of January last,
accounts were received from various localities, stating that a great religious
interest had arisen among the congregations of several churches; but early in
February, what may be termed a revival commenced simultaneously over a great
part of the land. Boston, New York and Philadelphia, were the great centres of
the awakening; but equally gladdening accounts were received from Cincinnati,
Detroit and the great cities of the West. The great religious movement was
neither preceded nor accompanied by any extraordinary measures. A general
spirit of prayer had pervaded the churches, and early in February the expected
blessing came down, and overshadowed whole communities in a way by no
means looked for. The origin of the work cannot be located. It commenced
far and near at the same time. Unconverted men crowded the churches, and
petitioned to be instructed in the way of salvation. Presently the ordinary
Divine services were found insufficient for the thousands of awakened souls, of
whom the astonished ministers were led to ask, "Who are these that fly as a
cloud, and as the doves to their windows?" Special services naturally sprang
out of this necessity, and many of the churches were opened at half-past eight
in the morning and half-past seven in the evening. But this was not enough.
Men in business felt the oppressive influence of the world's whirl of care, and
"business men's" noonday prayer-meetings were organised, the superintendence
of which was gladly left to the *Christian laity*, by the overworked and exhausted ministers. One hundred daily prayer-meetings are now conducted in
this manner in New York, and a proportionate number in all the great cities of
the West and North. They are held in places convenient to the chief haunts
of business, and are indicated by a placard, inviting persons to enter, in these
words, "Step in for five minutes or longer, as your time permits." But so
universal is the religious interest, that notices of the hours of prayer are posted
up in the hotels, the exchanges, the merchants' offices, and even in the steam-
boats. Notices are hung on the walls inside, to the effect that prayers and
exhortations should be brief, and forbidding the introduction of any controverted
topics. The frequenters of these meetings are from all classes in society—the
adherents of all sects or of none.

EXTENT.—New York is the chief centre of the movement, but it reaches to
nearly every part of the Union. The great cities are everywhere powerfully
affected, including Philadelphia, Boston, Baltimore, Cincinnati, Washington,
and others, and smaller towns and villages and country churches in great
numbers. It has extended to the central and distant Western States, including
Ohio, Illinois, Michigan, Wisconsin, Iowa, as well as New England. The work
is confined to no one denomination. All the Evangelical bodies are partaking
the benefit of the refreshing shower. It seems strictly and truly a national
movement.

EFFECTS.—As the awakening still continues, and to which

continue, it would be premature to estimate its fruits. Already, however, they are remarkable. The wave of mercy is rolling over the continent, changing and reforming society, and the effects of the revival are very apparent. Figures can give no definite idea of the number of conversions which have occurred, but from the statements tremblingly yet hopefully made by the ministers, we learn that during these five months *three hundred and forty-five thousand persons have* forsaken their worldliness or open sinful courses, and have expressed a wish to be received into communion with the churches, when the months of probation have passed by. We learn that the fruits of the "passing from death unto life" are becoming manifest—that drinking has decreased—that the observance of the Sabbath, which previously put our country to shame, has become yet more remarkable—that the great principles of truth and right have begun to enter into political affairs—that the publishers and writers of infidel and immoral publications, the dealers in ardent spirits, and the proprietors of drinking, gambling and dancing saloons have forsaken their several trades in large numbers, and have destroyed the implements of their professions ; and that, in *several thousands of known instances*, restitution has been made to those who had been defrauded, while a spirit of largely-increased liberality to religious and philanthropic objects has been evoked everywhere.

CHARACTERISTICS.—The chief features of the present awakening differ in many respects from most that have preceded it. The extravagancies which have so often characterized these religious movements, and which have raised in so many minds a strong prejudice against them, have as yet had no place in the present one. The following characteristics are noticed by Mr. Bird and others :—

1. *Spontaneity.*—The awakening has sprung up without any attempt to produce it. No revival measures have been had recourse to, no machinery set in motion to work upon the feelings of the people. No Wesley, Whitfield, Edwards, Finney, or Nettleton has gone about from place to place to awaken the public mind, the effect being limited to the places where they officiated. Everywhere—in the cultivated cities of the East, and in the uncultivated districts of the West, in the North and in the South, in the halls of learning and in prisons, in polite and in debased circles, in the Church and in the family, in the common school and in the Sabbath-school, in the haunts of business and of pleasure, yes, even of vice—this wonderful influence has been felt. This mighty movement has sprung up wherever the Gospel has been preached in its simplicity, and even where there has been no preacher at all, and where the only agency at work has been the *united prayer* of private Christians ; and the meetings held have rather resulted from the awakened demand than produced it.

2. *Prayer*, rather than *Preaching.*—The pulpit has been wholly subordinate. No instance is mentioned of the work being commenced in any congregation or town by extraordinary preaching. But prayer has been universal. Prayer meetings are the great feature. The one hundred held daily in New York, mentioned above, are attended by 12,000 people.

3. *Lay Influence.*—This has not been a clerical movement. The meetings have been almost uniformly, at least in the large cities, conducted by laymen, and the names of clergymen seldom appear in any of the accounts. The ministers have rather followed than led their people. This has deprived the enemies of these revivals of one of their standing objections, that they are got up by professional men for their own interests.

4. *Absence of extravagant Excitement.*—Feeling and deep interest there must be in anything which deserves to be called an awakening or revival ; but the feeling in the present instance is that of deep seriousness. The early local revivals in America were marked by a degree of unnatural excitement, and boisterous gatherings, well known under the name of "camp meetings," during which seasons of ill-regulated enthusiasm persons used to experience shocks of the nervous system, while others in the midst of wild disorder were urged, moaning and howling, to the "anxious seats," when, after some noisy exhortations, they declared they were filled with the joy of pardon. The

awakening of this year is free from such demonstrations. The silent weeping of those who are contrite for sin, the solemn stillness in crowded churches and prayer-meetings, the hushed seriousness of the thousands who throng the streets of the cities on their return from the Sabbath and week-day services— these are the prominent external features of the "awakening" of 1858. Those who comprehend the nature of true religion know that noisy demonstrations are not its natural development. They may work upon the grossly ignorant, and throw the mind into a tumult beyond its control or comprehension; but among the enlightened and educated American people such has not been the mode of action. The work is earnest, quiet, solid, unattended by exhausting enthusiasm; and from this circumstance the happy result of permanent good, on a larger scale perhaps than the world has ever seen, may reasonably be hoped

5. *Catholicity.*—This has already been alluded to. No sectarian interests are sought to be promoted by it; and no disputes about doctrine or church government have marred its harmony or checked its onward progress. No sect is tempted to be jealous of another since the blessing has come impartially upon all. The prayer meetings are chiefly upon the Evangelical Alliance principle; ministers and laymen of various denominations blending their common supplications at the throne of grace.

6. *Universality.*—It not only embraces all evangelical denominations, but extends more or less throughout the greater part of the States, over an area of country equal to more than half of Europe.

7. *Simultaneousness.*—The outbreak of religious concern has been so nearly simultaneous that it is difficult to say where it first began, though New York is generally considered to have been first affected. But the fire, if it did emanate from that quarter, spread so instantaneously that the train must have been laid beforehand by the providence of God. Besides, several vessels arriving from their voyages were found to have awakenings on board without having had any contact with the land.

All these characteristics are unexceptionable, and when united together, so remarkable, that the hand of God cannot but be recognised in the movement. And though some abatement must, in the nature of things, be expected, it is to be hoped that not only the professed converts may prove genuine and constant, but that the tone of piety and standard of moral feeling may be permanently elevated.

We proceed to furnish a few instances of the operation of this awakening, both upon individuals and towns.

INSTANCES—*Individuals.*—One of the many remarkable features of the awakening is that its influences have been exercised more on men, and young men, than upon the more excitable and susceptible sex. Among the thousands converted, the young men predominate. They are to be found in the house of God, in the Sunday-school, in the prayer-meeting, in the active work of attempting to do good. The change of heart, conduct, and purpose of large numbers of young men will make a very sensible difference in the religious and temporal affairs of life.

The promise, "While they are yet speaking I will hear," was remarkably fulfilled in the case of three young men. These persons were totally destitute of religious feeling, and two of them were slightly sceptical in their sentiments, but they were the sons of a praying mother, and during the time of the revival she requested the prayers of the members of her Church on their behalf. They came from a distant western city to transact business at New York, and on their arrival they asked the usual question, "What's the news?" The reply was, "Why all the world's converted, and they are praying in Burton's Theatre." To see so great a novelty as prayer in a theatre induced the young men to attend the place, and the service was blessed to the conversion of the three, who, in the very theatre itself, were deeply convinced of sin, and have since become disciples of Jesus. A great many similar instances came under the knowledge of Mr. Bird of persons who went into these prayer-meetings out of curiosity and received a blessing. But if it be delightful to see the young consecrating the dawn of life to God, it is scarcely less, and yet more wonderful, when those on whose heads the snows of many winters have rested, and whose steps are tottering towards the tomb, bow the pride of their unbelief, and become as little children at the foot of the Cross. Mr. Bird was at a private prayer-meeting at New York at which a gentleman called upon his friends to join with him in thanking God for the conversion of his parents. His father was eighty and his mother seventy-five years old. They were both infidels; his father had shaken the faith of many, and had acquainted himself with the Bible in the search for arguments wherewith to combat its authenticity and authority. At the commencement of the revival the son visited his parents, whom he found strong in their infidelity, and deriding the work of conversion of which they heard, and he returned home mourning and disheartened. But shortly afterwards the cloud of Divine mercy settled upon the very town in which the aged, hardened couple resided. They attended no services, sought no mercy seat, but in the quiet of their house, into which no minister had ever been permitted to enter, a greater than a minister knocked at the door of their hearts. The Spirit entered, convincing both of sin; and after a period of deep sorrow, in which the hope of pardon scarcely mingled with the tear of penitence, they found peace and forgiveness in Jesus. The son paid them yet another visit, and had the joy of finding a family altar raised in his father's house, and the voice so often and so long heard in the language of the scorner, uttered in faltering tones the prayer of the contrite at the mercy-seat. It is on this deep conviction of sin, which generally prevails—this repentance, which implies not penitence only, but reformation, that we rest our steadfast hope of permanent good when the season of awakening has passed by.

Villages and Towns.—There was a village in the northern part of New York which was notorious for its Sabbath-breaking and infidelity. Out of a population of 1,650, only twenty-six persons were under any evangelical influence. But within the last three months, in answer, doubtless, to the earnest prayers of the Lord's believing people in the place, there has been a great and wonderful change. All ages and classes of men have been brought under the influence of the awakening. The cloud of Divine mercy has settled upon the whole town, and for many weeks religion has been the absorbing topic of conversation in nearly every house, and in the places of public resort, so that prayer-meetings have been held in the bar-rooms of taverns. The drunkard has given up his intemperate habits, the infidel his infidelity, the swearer his profanity, and the Sabbath-breaker joins in the services of the sanctuary. Men and women from thirteen to sixty years of age, husbands and wives, parents and children, share in the blessing. There has been very much opposition to the plain preaching of the Gospel, and much effort expended to draw people from the meetings. Card parties, drinking parties, and pleasure parties of several kinds, were tried to divert people from the house of prayer, but in vain. Sabbath solemnity rested upon the community during the busy days of the week; business gave way for once, and men devoted themselves with one consent to the great concerns of the soul. Preaching and prayer were kept up within the churches every evening for five weeks, and the ministers devoted four hours of each day to giving private instruction. As the result, a very large number of persons have forsaken their wicked courses, and have turned in contrition of heart to God. *More than two-thirds* of the families in this village are now praying families; the standard of piety is high, the aspect of business has been changed, and eighteen out of nineteen persons who sold spirituous liquors have given up the pernicious trade.

Mr. Bird gives the following account of what he saw in New York:—" After having seen a great deal of the revival work in other places, I arrived in New York on March 15th, and was astonished to see the side walks in the business-streets of the city completely darkened with the thousands of business men, who were returning from the several churches and rooms in which the mid-day prayer-unions were held. During the three subsequent days I had opportunities of seeing how really changed the tone of society was, and how religion formed the principle topic of conversation in circles which, on former visits, I had known as supremely worldly. On the 17th March, the Committee of the Young Men's Christian Association leased Burton's Theatre for a noon-day prayer-meeting, which I was privileged to attend on the 19th. This theatre is situated near Broadway, in one of the most crowded parts of the city. I found the stairways and entrance blocked up, and a crowd extending across the pavement, while hundreds were going away unable to get in. All classes were represented in this throng. There were clergymen, merchants, clerks, brokers, carmen, whose carts were standing at the door, ladies who had turned aside an hour from their shopping, students, and strangers from distant parts, attracted by the fame of these marvellously strange meetings, though it was obvious that the merely curious formed but a very small portion of those present. I was surprised to observe that in this closely-packed throng there was complete silence; none of that talking and jesting so usual in an American crowd, but a serious, earnest look, as though the people had come there on important business. In about ten minutes time I obtained a seat in the front row of the highest gallery, from which I had a good view of the singular spectacle.

I think I never attended such an impressive service, or one in which the presence of Him "who dwelleth not in temples made with hands" was more manifest. The contrast between the theatrical appearance of the edifice and the purpose to which, for this brief period, it was appropriated was very striking. For that hour a theatre became a house of prayer, instead of a haunt of profanity—a spot for the real tears of repentance, and not the scene of fictitious grief over fictitious sorrows. The building, though lighted by gas, was partially darkened with the crowds of people, who were clustered wherever standing or clinging room could be found, while numbers were standing with bowed heads and reverent aspect in the lobby, where they could only hear. The pit and both galleries were full, and about five-sevenths of the audience of 1,800 were men. On the stage were four gentlemen, one of whom presided, and at twelve o'clock opened the service by reading the verse "Now, therefore, are we all present before God;" after which he offered up prayer. The hymn was sung—

> "Not all the blood of beasts,
> On Jewish altars slain,"

to the old tune, Shirland. It was a magnificent and thrilling sound, as nearly 2,000 voices joined the many-toned harmony, which was caught up on the stairs, in the lobbies, and in the streets, with fervour and enthusiasm. Prayers, singing, and direct instruction, and faithful exhortations followed, and alternated, all of them being of a deeply solemn character. One gentleman rose in the pit and spoke from the words, "The blood of Jesus Christ, his Son, cleanseth us from all sin," and when he reached the end of the allotted time, he was requested to go on both from the pit and stage. He spoke of sin—the rebel heart, and life contrary to God—of the heart-searching Judge, and the great white throne, before which all that assemblage must shortly appear. He said that he, a "blasphemer and injurious," had found mercy, and to that congregation of sinners, hushed in solemn stillness, met in such an unwonted place and time, he spoke gloriously of the fulness of mercy in Christ. There was no "excitement," but there was deep though suppressed emotion, such emotion as those must feel who are aroused to a view of the pit to which sin is hastening them. As he spoke of Him who came not to condemn but to save the world, there was a suppressed sound of weeping. The big tears were coursing down the wrinkled cheeks of the world-worn business men, while many, with faces buried in their handkerchiefs, were doubtless presenting that petition for pardon which has never yet been offered in vain. It was a solemn moment as the speaker sat down and the assembly rose to unite in a fervent prayer for those for whom requests had been presented, and for themselves. The meeting concluded with the verses of the grand old hymn—

> "Blow ye the trumpet; blow
> The gladly solemn sound,
> Let all the nations know,
> The universe around,
> The year of jubilee is come,
> Return ye ransomed sinners home."

And after the blessing, the crowd silently dispersed, hundreds of them, we trust, to carry into the counting house and the store, and the busy walks of life, the hallowed influence of having been with Jesus. Few things could be calculated to produce a stronger impression than the spectacle of nearly 2,000 human beings met in the busiest hour of business for the simple purpose of prayer, with a quiet seriousness, a propriety, and absence of demonstration and excitement, which would have satisfied the most fastidious stickler for decorum of worship. Surely the Divine presence dwelleth not in temples made with hands—surely there was joy in heaven among the angels of God over sinners that repented. Never, probably, in earth's stateliest cathedrals, had the Holy Spirit performed such a mighty work as within the unconsecrated walls of that theatre. In illustration of the blessed results which may follow merely from hearing prayer, I may mention an instance which occurred at a prayer meeting which I attended in another hall. There was a very wicked man, the proprietor and keeper of an infamous, but pecuniarily a very successful, dancing saloon, near a large railroad station. Seeing crowds pouring into the hall, he went in out of curiosity, and the opening prayer sent conviction to his heart. He went home and closed his saloon; he put himself under the instruction of a Christian minister, in whose hands he has placed a not inconsiderable fortune—the gains of iniquity—to build a mission church on the former site of the saloon. He, a humble sinner, has found peace in Jesus, and is but one, among multiplied instances of which I heard, of those who went from curiosity, or " to scoff," and "remained to pray."

And this in New York city! "Lord now lettest thou thy servant depart in peace," exclaimed a white-haired Christian to a friend at the door of Burton's Theatre; and to his exclamation of thankfulness let us join a glad response. We mourn the coldness of our churches, the infrequency of conversions, the wickedness of the surrounding world; but are we not too well content with mourning only? Where is the spirit of united prayer, which brought the blessing down in still increasing floods? The voice of God's Spirit is "Come to the help of the Lord, to the help of the Lord against the mighty." Let us "*arise and pray.*" The promise still remains: "Prove me now herewith, saith the Lord of hosts, if I will not open you the windows of heaven, and pour you out a blessing, that there shall not be room enough to receive it." "Effectual fervent prayer availeth much" to bring down blessings, which shall make our "wilderness and solitary places to be glad, and our deserts to rejoice and blossom as the rose." I. L. B.

Wyton Rectory, Huntingdon, April 23.

HIGHEST FORM OF RELIGIOUS REVIVAL.
By Mrs. Stowe, Authoress of " Uncle Tom's Cabin."

There is perhaps a well-founded prejudice in our minds against sudden changes. Sudden resolutions, sudden impulses, are universally regarded with suspicion. Many minds extend this to the sphere of religion, and regard with scepticism all accounts of *sudden conversions.*

Without much examination they class them under the head of fanatical delusion; and consider those periods in which these become a frequent incident, as periods of a kind of epidemic enthusiasm utterly opposed to the normal and regular growth of a rational piety.

It is to be remarked, however, that religious crises, both in individuals and in communities, are not so sudden as they appear to the looker-on;—in this respect they, like certain apparently sudden changes in the natural world, have their invisible, silent, preparatory causes.

The ground around us is now sheeted with snow, and the buds of the apple orchard look as brown and still and sealed as if they were not within a few weeks of a glorious resurrection of green leaves and rose-tipped blossoms. But it does not follow that nothing is doing because we hear and see nothing. In every one of these long warm days the sun's power is gradually and silently awakening the torpid and dormant forces of the tree, whispering at the root, and thrilling through the branches; and by-and-bye, before we think of it, what a bursting forth, what a new creation!—as if angels descending in the night had wreathed the trees with the roses of heaven, and left them standing altars of perfume and beauty.

So also in what are called sudden conversions, there has often been a silent preceding mental history, a working of providential discipline, of which the beautiful spiritual dawn called conversion is the perfected flower.

Afflictions, months and years gone by—no longer spoken of but germinating with still-life forces in every silent, reflecting hour—losses, disappointments, mortifications, sicknesses, pains alternating with mercies, hopes, newly awakened loves—all these under the guiding hand of an infinite Power, have been working on in the soul, until at last some slight outward pressure, a little more determining force from the good Spirit of God, and the man comes out firm and decided in a marked spiritual change. Those who see only the *change* and know nothing of the preceding history, call it a *sudden* conversion.

So it is in communities. A "revival of religion" awakens some worldly man with a start—and he cries out, What sudden rush is this?—nothing but prayer-meetings and religious talk! enthusiasm! delusion! But the pastor who has been watching his flock with silent assiduity year in and out, who has been guiding the life-forces, the Sabbath-school, the Bible-class, the preaching of Sunday, the pastoral visitation of the week, the prayer-meeting and lecture,—he has watched the gathering of the precious cloud,—he has been as one who lays his ear to the ground in early spring when a hundred tender forces work and stir all day long beneath the ground, and he does not wonder at the spiritual buds and blossoms.

The great religious revival now in our country is a crisis in our national spiritual history—the result of many years' providential training.

The religious impulse which founded the great system of religious charities—the Foreign Mission enterprise—the Bible and Tract Societies—the Sunday-school and Home Missionary, was in its time a true and heavenly one. It was fragrant with the incense of self-denial and self-consecration; it raised for a while the mind of the American church to a pitch of Christian heroism, under which she advanced rapidly and gathered converts by the power of her real Christian example. But then came an era in which, like a plant that ceases to grow, she first stood still, and then her leaves began to turn yellow. People began to give to all these sacred causes, as they did to their other business, at the rate of such and such a per cent.; religious establishments came to be conducted much like other business establishments; and religious enthusiasm began to be calculated on coolly as the stream to turn the wheels of the sacred machinery. Anniversary meetings began to have a little clap-trap, and less prayer than speech-making, and people gave not with tears in their eyes, but with pens behind their ears—"they didn't need any more talking; they had set down *that* cause at so much a year, so there was the end of it." Then came in jesuitry, worldly expediency, suppression of unpleasant truths, concessions to popular sins;—all because here were great institutions to be preserved, and it was not possible for the world to be converted without them. And so the money changers' seats were made fast in the temple, and they that sold doves had it all their own way;—it was a pious trade—for how could there be sacrifices without them?

Meanwhile another cause came up—a cry, not of foreign heathen, but of heathen at our own door—a cry of oppression, not in Siam or Burmah, but in Christian America—a cry that children were torn from mothers; that husband and wife were separated; that Christian maidens were sold for abominable purposes—there was a cry that every oppression and cruelty that ever disgraced any despotism, was being enacted in the very Church of Christ; and what was done about it?

The American Church, as such, shut her ears and did nothing. She said her hands were full; that she had the heathen to take care of, and tracts to print, and Bibles to circulate everywhere, except to the American slave, and, therefore, that she could neither remonstrate nor condemn.

From this grew up scepticism. *There has been no scepticism in America except what has grown out of the Church's shrinking from the place which Christ ordained her to fill,* and actually leaving in the hands of those whom she called unconverted men the great work of the Gospel, "to set at liberty them that are bound." Had the Church taken the stand for the American slave which she did for the Hindoo and Caffre, multitudes of those men whom to-day she denounces as infidels, and who in turn denounce her as Antichrist, would have been ministering at her altars, and leading on her sacramental hosts. In 1850 and 1851 what a sight did we behold in our country! what a period of disgrace and humiliation to our churches! Everywhere the forlorn fugitive flying—cold, hungry, desolate; churches of poor industrious brethren scattered like trembling sheep, while ministers of Christ were expounding to their people the new doctrine, that there was no law higher than the law of the land. Webster scoffed at the idea of a law of God higher than the Constitution of the United States, and many in the churches did not tremble to re-echo the scoff! Prayers for the hunted slave were refused in some of the leading churches in our great cities; and for a while it seemed as if the majority of the religious community silently acquiesced in the iniquity of the fugitive slave law.

But this crop, sown to the wind, in time brought forth its fruitful harvest of the whirlwind. They who acquiesced in the fugitive slave law soon found the same oppressions turned on their own sons and daughters, who had gone to seek their inheritance in new territories; and every month, with deeper and deeper mortification, have they seen the circle of their own rights and liberties narrowing. The principle of no higher law brought forth also its fruitful crop of dragon's teeth;—God, defied and insulted, gave them up to the legitimate consequences which always attend the loosening of the great bonds of responsibility to him;—frauds, swindling, monstrous corruption crept into every department of business, secular and ecclesiastical, till finally came the hour of disclosure; and in a moment, crash went the whole system of national trust, burying under its ruins the wealth to save which men had denied their responsibility to God!

It was in this crisis—after so long a time, when God had broken every idol as by a lightning stroke—when old political parties lay headless and handless as Dagon, and the golden calf was stamped to pieces and scattered on the waters of bitterness—it was in an hour of national dismay and humiliation, that meetings were appointed for prayer in New York city. They were appointed in the business quarter, by business men—by men who felt themselves wrecked and broken, and who bethought themselves, in their extremity, of God. But it was not only there that the voice of prayer began to ascend. The stroke had spread desolation through our land, and thousands of households whose earthly all had been swept away, were looking to God in their extremity. This great affliction came like John the Baptist in the wilderness, saying, "Repent, for the kingdom of heaven is at hand!"

And now what we see is a work unprecedented in any former times. It is not to be ascribed to the career of any preacher,—it seems, in fact, not to have come primarily from the ministry at all, but to have *welled up from the heart of the people* toward the pulpit, rather than rolled down from the pulpit to the people. Instead of mass-meetings to hear preachers, we have mass-meetings of brethren moved with one accord to pray and to open their hearts to one another.

It is remarkable that no modern language can more fitly describe the existing state of things than that of the prophet Zechariah, uttered twenty-three centuries ago: "Thus saith the Lord of Hosts, It shall come to pass that there shall come people, inhabitants of many cities, and the inhabitants of one city shall go to another, saying, Let us go speedily and pray before the Lord, to seek the Lord of hosts."

No form of religious revival is more wholly unobjectionable than a universal spirit of prayer. Prayer is the natural and normal relation of child to parent. The little child, playing on the carpet, prays to its father and mother all day long, and thus in the nursery goes on an unceasing parable, explaining to us the relation in which our souls ought to stand to our heavenly Father:—our prayer to him ought to be as child-like, as uninterrupted, as constant.

Nor do we murmur, but rather rejoice at the notice in the prayer-meetings which some of our well-meaning friends seem to disapprove, viz., "No discussion of controverted subjects." There is a time for all things. Sailors do not alter the ship's course while they are taking their observation of the heavenly bodies; then their business is simply to look upwards, gazing on the unchanging, truthful, heavenly lights: afterwards come the reckonings, based on these observations, and the alterations of the ship's course, thence found to be needful. Prayer is a short vacation of the soul when she goes upward to breathe a purer air, and recruit her spiritual health; and when she comes down, seeing with new and healthier sight, she will perceive much to reform. If God should permit us now and then to spend a day in heaven, though we might not even think of one of our earthly relations while there, doubtless we should see wondrous changes needed when we came back. Oh, how different would all things look to eyes baptized with that celestial vision! We would be willing to risk the experiment, if for a season all religious denominations should agree to suspend intellectual controversy,—if all reformers should agree to postpone their projects,—and all together, in hearty, brotherly frankness, should unite daily on the knee in earnest prayer to their common Father. We have been, perhaps all of us, more sincere and well-meaning than the world knows. We must all be conscious that in many respects we are more faulty, infinitely more so, than the world ever said. We have each had our fragments of truth, dear and precious in our own eyes, which we have fought for, sometimes with more zeal than love; and there have been upbraidings, and criminations, and recriminations, and we are now much like a nursery of children, which the mother finds with flushed faces and tearful eyes, each one sure that he is right and all the others wrong.

LONDON MAY MEETINGS.

The last mail has brought intelligence of the proceedings at the anniversaries of the great Religious Societies of England. The accounts are in the highest degree cheering. The funds of nearly all are in a prosperous condition, augmenting from year to year, the commercial crisis of the past year not having affected them in the way of diminishing their incomes; but only, perhaps, in making the increase somewhat less than it would otherwise have been. And with respect to the success of these institutions, in accomplishing the objects they have in view, the reports generally abound with proofs of manifest tokens of the Divine blessing. Our space will allow us to give only a condensed summary.

COLONIAL MISSIONARY SOCIETY.

The twenty-second anniversary meeting of this society was held in the Poultry Chapel, on Monday evening, May 17th, the Earl of Shaftesbury in the chair. A hymn having been sung, the Rev. Dr. Spence offered up prayer. The Rev. T. James read the report, which gave a sketch of the Society's operations at Toronto, Nova Scotia, Newfoundland, New Brunswick, Cape of Good Hope, Cape Town, Natal, Victoria, Tasmania, Sydney, Adelaide, &c., &c. The receipts for the year were stated to have exceeded last years' by £294 17s. 5d., as those were considerably beyond any previous year. The total amount received, including last year's balance of £70 3s. 1d., was £6,513 16s. 7d.; the expenditure was £5,634 18s. 6d.; balance in hand, £878 18s. 1d.; of this, however, £721 6s. 2d. is due to the fund raised in Australia, by Mr. Poore, for the sending out of ministers thither. Of that fund there had been received £1,391 4s., and from friends in this country towards the same object, obtained by Mr. Poore's exertions, £1,291 19s. 10d.; separating this fund from the general resources of the Society, the balance in hand was only £157 11s. 11d., while bills under acceptance amounted to £334 2s. 8d. Whilst thankfulness was due for the past, anxiety was felt for the future; for besides an exhausted exchequer, there were numerous stations in Canada, Nova Scotia, New Zealand, and the Australias, to which ministers ought immediately to be sent.

The report, in adverting to Canada, states that there are between 50 and 60 congregational ministers now located in that province, and about ten or twelve churches vacant. At Toronto, Dr. Lillie and Rev. A. Wickson conduct a Theological Institution, through which thirty-eight students have passed, most of whom are now laboring as pastors. In New

Brunswick and the other Atlantic colonies, there are eight ministers settled and four churches vacant. Since last report the Rev. E. Solomon has undertaken the charge at Bedford, Cape of Good Hope, and the Rev. G. Y. Jeffreys, that at D'Urban, Natal. The claims of the Australian colonies, and the Rev. J. L. Poore's visit to England, occupied a large share of the report : his journeyings in the colonies, the sum of money he had brought over, the money he collected in England and Scotland by indefatigable exertions, the ministers he had sought and obtained were all noticed at length. Sixteen ministers had already left the shores of Britain for the Australian colonies, and one, the Rev. Thomas Arnold, of Smethwick, was on the point of embarking.

The meeting was largely attended, and the noble chairman gave great satisfaction by the liberality and heartiness of his address. The resolutions were spoken to by R. Baxter, Esq., M.P.; F. J. Sargood, Esq., of Melbourne; Revs. Sam. McAll, Newman Hall, T. Arnold, F. Tomkins, and Dr. Archer. The speeches were impressive, and the meeting altogether satisfactory.

CONGREGATIONAL UNION.

The twenty-eighth annual session of the Congregational Union of England and Wales commenced on Tuesday morning, May 11th, at the Poultry Chapel, when there was a very large attendance of pastors and delegates, with numerous visitors, who occupied the galleries. After the usual devotional exercises, the Rev. Dr. Alliott, of Cheshunt College, who is the chairman for the year, delivered the introductory address, which was in the main a very lucid and masterly defence of the orthodox doctrine of the Atonement.

The address was received with the most profound attention, and at its close, on the motion of the Rev. A. Jack, seconded by the Rev. J. Hill, the cordial thanks of the assembly were presented to Dr. Alliott for the address he had delivered, with the request that it might be published with the other documents of the Union.

The Rev. G. Smith then read the report of the committee, which announced the completion of the separation of the affiliated societies, and of the new trust for the management of the magazines connected with the Union; and said that a copy of the new hymn-book would be placed in the hands of the chairman before the sittings of the Union closed. The report was unanimously adopted, on the motion of the Rev. J. Sherman, seconded by E. Baines, Esq.

The Rev. J. Stoughton gave an interesting account of his visit, as a delegate of the assembly to the Scotch Congregational Union. He stated that he met with a most cordial reception from the friends at Edinburgh. He advocated the claims of British Missions, and especially of the Colonial Society. The day upon which he preached was the fast day, when all business was suspended. His discourse was on the "Sacrifice of Christ;" and at the urgent request of the Scotch friends, he had consented to its publication. He congratulated the meeting upon the spirit of love and peace that prevailed in their midst that day—a spirit which augured well for the interests of the Union.

The Rev. Henry Wight was then introduced to the assembly, as a delegate from Scotland, and received a hearty greeting. He gave a striking account of three lay gentlemen who had recently gone through the length and breadth of the land from which he came, preaching the Gospel to the poor with the most remarkable success.

F. J. Sargood, Esq., who was suffering from indisposition, was introduced as a delegate from Victoria, Australia, by the Rev. T. James.

Two interesting papers were read,—the one on "Ireland," by the Rev. A. M. Henderson; and the other on "Chapel Building," by the Rev. J. C. Gallaway.

The following took part in the proceedings of the day, the Revs. Dr. Burder, Dr. Halley, Dr. Legge, T. Mann, T. G. Horton, J. Parsons, J. Alexander, G. Rose, H. Allan, and C. Gilbert, and T. E. Plint, and A. Morley, Esqrs.

On *Friday*, the brethren met again, at half-past nine, in a much larger number than we remember to have witnessed before on the second day, owing, no doubt, in a considerable measure to the fact that it had been arranged for the whole of the morning to be devoted to the subject of a "Revival of Religion." Mr. Charles Reed read a very admirable paper on the American revivals, setting forth their origin and progress, which was received with marked attention. After prayer by the Rev. James Griffin, a deeply important and heart-stirring paper was read by the Rev. J. A. James, on the general question of religious revivals. A hymn was then sung, and fervent prayer offered by the Rev. S. Martin. The Revs. J. C. Harrison, S. McAll, J. Alexander, Dr. Brown, Newman Hall, Andrew Reed, B.A., Edward Ball, M P., and many others, took part in the conference which followed, and which was in perfect keeping with the spirit of the papers read.

It is impossible for us, in the brief space at our disposal, to give anything like an adequate idea of the valuable addresses delivered, the amount of business transacted, or the delight experienced at the entire absence from the proceedings of those matters which, on former occasions, so seriously disturbed the harmony of the Union. The great importance attached to the papers presented may be gathered from the fact that the assembly passed an unanimous vote in favor of their immediate publication, for distribution among the churches; and that the brethren were earnestly recommended to set apart the first Lord's-day in June, for preaching upon the importance of a revival of religion, and to hold meetings for special prayer on the following Monday, June 7th, to entreat the outpouring of the Holy Spirit on our schools and colleges, on our pastors and churches, and on the land. All were ready to exclaim "Behold how good and how pleasant it is for brethren to dwell together in unity;" and the one prayer of all hearts was, "O Lord, wilt thou not revive us again, that thy people may rejoice in Thee."

LONDON MISSIONARY SOCIETY.

The Directors preface their report of the proceedings of the 64th Anniversary with the following statement:—On the recurrence of another Anniversary of our time-honored Society, we have especial cause to thank God and take courage, on the review of the manifold mercies which have been mingled with the trying experiences of the past year. During the crisis of the revolt in India, nothing short of the destruction of some of our most flourishing Missions could be anticipated; but our fears have been rebuked, and a gracious Providence has so ordered events that this great catastrophe has been rendered instrumental in stimulating the zeal and efforts of British Christians for the wider spread of the Gospel in that country. And further, through the discoveries of Dr. Livingstone, in Central South Africa, a way has been opened for the messengers of mercy into regions hitherto inaccessible to the light of truth. In other parts, also, of the Mission field, witnesses have risen up to testify to the grace of God, in converting sinners from the error of their way, and in building up believers in their most holy faith. Moreover, the various Services connected with the Anniversary have been characterised by an earnest tone of piety, and by a concentration of aim and purpose which, under the Divine blessing, form the best guarantee for the success of our plans and efforts in furtherance of the Gospel, while the numerous attendance on the Public Meeting at Exeter Hall, and the sustained interest with which the statements of the various speakers were listened to, serve to attest that the cause of Missions retains a strong hold upon the judgment and affections of the friends and constituents of the Society.

On Monday morning, May 10th, an early prayer-meeting was held in New Broad Street Chapel, and in the evening, the sermon to the juvenile friends of the Society was preached in the Weigh House Chapel, by the Rev. R. W. Dale, A.M., of Birmingham. On the 11th, a sermon in the Welsh language was preached in Fetter Lane Welsh Chapel by the Rev. T. J Jones, of Moriston, Glamorganshire. On Wednesday, the 12th, the Annual Sermons were preached in the forenoon at Surrey Chapel by the Rev. E. Mellor, A.M., of Halifax, and in the evening at the Tabernacle, Moorfields, by the Rev. W. M. Punshon, of Leeds.

The Annual Meeting was held on Thursday, May 13, in Exeter Hall, which was densely crowded. Frank Crossley, Esq., M.P., presided. Among the gentlemen on the platform, in addition to those who took part in the proceedings, were Edward Ball, Esq., M.P.; George Hadfield, Esq., M.P.; J. Cheetham, Esq., M.P.; J. Kershaw, Esq., M.P.; Sir C. E. Eardley, Bart.; Rev. Drs. Halley, Archer, Morton, Brown; Revs. G. Osborne, one of the Secretaries of the Wesleyan Missionary Society; F. Trestrail, one of the Secretaries of the Baptist Missionary Society; P. Latrobe, Secretary of the Moravian Missionary Society; J. Stratten, J. Stoughton, J. C. Harrison, G. Smith, J. Sherman, J. Hall, J. Watson, J. T. Rowland, J. R. Campbell, P. Thomson, A. Thomson, R. W. Dale, E. Mellor, A. Jack, J. Parsons, J. Woodward, H. Batchelor; Messrs. G. H. Davies, one of the Secretaries of the Tract Society; E. Baines, T. Barnes, S. Job, J. Perry, E. Jupe, W. D. Wills, Eusebius Smith, H. Rutt, John Morley, Joseph East, &c., &c. After prayer had been offered by the Rev. P. Thomson of Manchester, and an impressive address delivered by the Chairman, the Rev. Newman Hall read the Report, of which the following are the leading points:—

The answer already given to the appeal for the twenty missionaries for India is sufficient to convince the Directors that, in this proposal, they have the hearty sympathy of their friends throughout the country. Within three months nearly £11,000 have been promised towards the object, and a confident hope may be cherished that, by the close of the year, additional funds will be realised adequate to its full accomplishment. The general contributions from Great Britain and Ireland, including subscriptions, donations, collections, and dividends, amount to £44,943 7s. 8d., being £1,779 4s. 3d. more than the year preceding. The generous bequests of departed friends reach £8,401 4s. 1d., being £1,702 15s. 8d. in excess of the legacies of last year. The sacramental offerings to the Widows' and Orphans' Fund, with the yearly dividends, present an aggregate of £2,321 17s. 9d., being £119 17s. 8d. more than those of 1857, and in addition, the fund has received an increase of £899 6s. 5d., 3 per cents., reduced, being a legacy of the late Mr. Flanders. The contributions from missionary stations have yielded £16,611 9s. 10d., being £2,191 13s. 2d. more than those of the year preceding. The total annual income from these ordinary sources is £72,143 11s. 3d. being an increase of £6,659 2s. 8d. The amount received from the Australian and foreign auxiliaries is £819 5s., being less than the preceding year by £1,048 1s. 6d. The expenditure of the Society, for ordinary purposes, has been £64,059 13s. 9d., being a decrease on that of the former year of £2,799 15s. 1d., without involving any diminution of the Society's operations. The preceding statement is exclusive of the fund for the establishment of New Missions in South Africa, amounting to £7,078 6s. 2d., and that promised for the extension of Indian Missions, approaching the sum of £11,000.

The number of the Society's ordained missionaries last reported was 152; and it is an unusual demand for gratitude, that, in the interval, death has not been permitted to diminish that number in a single instance; while two additional brethren, Messrs. Blake and Jones, have been sent forth to strengthen the missionary band in India.

SOUTH SEAS.—In Tahiti, the Rev. Wm. Howe, amidst many obstructions, continues in charge of the Bible depository and the press, and renders also most valuable services in the defence of the truth. and in animating and sustaining the minds both of the native pastors and their flocks. Though forbidden to commend the Gospel to the native Christians, he regularly preaches to the British and other foreigners located at Papeetee. In the Society Islands, the political strife that in former years occasioned so much pain and sorrow to our missionaries has happily ceased, and the condition and prospects of their several churches are truly encouraging. The mission churches of Harvey Islands continue to present the same aspect of vitality and beauty by which they have been distinguished in former years. The Rev. Aaron Buzacott has been compelled, by severe and long-continued suffering, to retire from his beloved work in Raratonga. In the Samoan, or Navigators' Islands, the restoration of peace has happily been preserved, and our missionaries have been able to prosecute, without interruption, their various efforts for the social and religious improvement of the people ; and, notwithstanding occasions of sorrow and discouragement, arising from the former degradation and the peculiar habits of the natives, they are cheered by the evident progress of their churches in knowledge, enjoyment and usefulness.

WEST INDIES.—The missions of the Society, both in British Guiana and Jamaica, have throughout the year afforded to their faithful ministers occasion for devout thankfulness. Few, very few instances have occurred, in any of the churches, demanding christian discipline, while in several instances the accessions have been unusually numerous. The progress of the congregations, and more especially of the junior classes, in general intelligence and Scripture knowledge, has been evident, and the prosperous state of the numerous schools affords sure ground for encouragement and hope. The aggregate contributions of the West Indian churches toward their own support amount to £7,540, and although £500 belongs properly to the year preceding, the actual increase for 1857 exceeds £1,600.

SOUTH AFRICA.—Although the Cape Colony suffered disorder and injury during the last year from the influx of many thousand starving Kaffirs, and although this had been preceded by the disease which destroyed the greater part of the cattle, yet the social condition of the people has continued to improve. The reports from the mission stations, both within and beyond the colony, are cheering; the churches, almost without exception, have received numerous additions, and vigorous exertions have been made to extend the blessings of the Gospel to the Fingoes and other strangers from the interior. The stations on the frontier, including Peelton, Knapp's Hope, and King William's Town, consisting of enlightened and converted Kaffirs, are examples of a people transformed from wild marauders, ferocious in their spirit and disgusting in their habits, into peaceful and industrious christian villagers. At the last annual meeting the Directors had the pleasure of reporting that the translation of the entire Scriptures into Sichuana, by the Rev. Robert Moffatt, was then nearly completed ; and later intelligence informed them that the work was finished. It is scarcely possible to overrate the importance of this great achievement. The Sichuana, under certain modifications, is the language of the interior of South Africa. After repeated conference with Dr. Livingstone, the Directors lost no time in making known their intended efforts in Central Africa to their faithful friend and veteran missionary, the Rev. Robert Moffatt, requesting his counsels and co-operation in the enterprise. Their letter reached him just at the time he had completed the translation of the Old Testament, and with all the ardour of youth he started forthwith on a journey of nearly 600 miles, that he might secure the countenance and support of Moselekatse, the Chief of the Matabele, for the establishment of a mission among his numerous people.

CHINA.—Hongkong, from its proximity to the scene of war, has been often in a state of excitement and alarm ; but, notwithstanding these hindrances, the Rev. Dr. Legge and the Rev. John Chalmers have continued their unwearied labours in the respective branches of the mission ; while Chin-seen, the pastor of the Chinese Church, has faithfully preached the Gospel, in season and out of season, to his countrymen. At Amoy, Messrs. A. and J. Stronach, Hirschberg, and Lea, have again been favored with manifold proofs of God's presence and grace. During the year, twenty-two converts have been added to the Church, making 193 since the establishment of the mission ten years since. The Church of the American Mission in this city includes 172 members, and that of the English Presbyterian Mission 53 ; making a total of upwards of 400 Christian Chinese. The converts consist of various classes, and among them are several individuals of high literary attainments.

INDIA.—At Benares and Mirzapore, Messrs. Buyers, Kennedy, and Sherring were exposed to imminent danger from the mutinous Sepoys, but God was their present help in time of trouble, and suffered not a hair of their head to perish. The Directors regret, however, to record that Mrs. Buyers, whose devotion to her husband and to the interests of the mission constrained her to remain at her post when others retired from the scene of danger, shortly after fell a victim to disease superinduced by labor and anxiety ; but her end was peace, and her character is embalmed in the memories and hearts of all who knew her. The defection of the Bengal army must be attributed to various causes, bothsocial and political, but in no degree to the influence of missions, inasmuch as the Sepoy, whether Hindoo or Mohammedan, was of all men the farthest removed from the approaches of the Christian teacher. On the other hand, the native Christians remained faithful to our Government, and in its support, exposed themselves to the intense hatred of their heathen countrymen, to whose vengeance many of their number fell victims. The mutineers went forth to battle trusting in the gods of their country for strength and victory—and shame, defeat, and death overwhelm them.

Already, as our missionaries tell us, the haughty looks of the heathen are brought low, and they are more disposed to hear of that kingdom to which none can enter who does not seek admission as a little child.

The meeting was then addressed successively by the Rev. Samuel Martin, of Westminster, Rev. C. G. Goodhart, incumbent of Park Chapel, Chelsea, Dr. Lockhart, medical Chinese missionary, the Hon. and Rev. B. W. Noel, Rev. J. M. Mitchell, Free Church missionary from Bombay, Rev. Jos. Mullens, missionary from Calcutta, Rev. P. Thompson, of Manchester, E. Ball, Esq., M.P., Rev. J. Edkins, missionary from China, Rev. Dr. Halley, E. Baines, Esq., and Eusebius Smith, Esq.

An evening meeting was held in Finsbury Chapel, when the Rev. James Parsons presided, and impressive addresses were delivered by the Rev. E. Storrow, missionary from India, Rev. E. R. W. Krause, from the South Seas, Rev. H. Ingham, from Berbice, and the Revs. C. H. Bateman and J. Curwen.

The whole of the solemn and interesting services closed with the usual sacramental services, on Friday evening, in various chapels in different parts of London.

BRITISH AND FOREIGN BIBLE SOCIETY.

The Annual Meeting of this great Institution was held in Exeter Hall, on Wednesday, May 5. There was an overflowing attendance, and the chair was occupied by the Earl of Shaftesbury. The business of the day was, for the first time, commenced with prayer, which afforded much satisfaction to all the best friends of the Society.

After a psalm had been read, the chairman addressed the meeting, alluding particularly to the fact that, when holding their anniversary last year, there appeared not the slightest cause to arouse suspicion or alarm; yet within one week from that time, there broke out that most fearful revolt in India,—the most awful exhibition of human cruelty and wickedness which had, perhaps, ever defaced any portion of the habitable globe, awaking the utmost consternation on every hand. He referred to the significant circumstance that, in the favoured Brahminical Presidency of ;Bengal, where the Scriptures had never been allowed to approach the Sepoy cantonment, and the missionary was positively interdicted, and where the chaplain was prohibited from giving instruction in the *Word of God*, there it was that the rebellion raged most fiercely.

The Report—which was read by the Rev. S. P. Bergne, secretary, and was an elaborate and able document—announced that the entire receipts for the year amounted to £162,574 3s. 6d.; being £11,551 12s. 2d. more than in any former year. The total expenditure of the year has reached the sum of £153,177 4s. 8d., being £4,136 10s. 11d. in excess of any previous year. The issues of Bibles and Testaments from the various depôts amount to 1,602,187 copies, being an increase of 84,329 copies. The total issues, since the Society began, now reach the enormous amount of 33,983,946 copies.

The various resolutions were very effectively spoken to by the Bishops of London and Ripon, the Rev. W. Brock, Baptist minister, Rev. Dr. Cumming, of the Scotch Church, Rev. Canon Stowell and Rev. W. Cadman, of the English Church, Rev. J. H. Wilson, Congregationalist, minister of the Ragged Kirk, Aberdeen, the Rev. C. Osborne, Wesleyan, and Dr. Lockhart, medical Chinese missionary.

A special resolution was adopted, expressive of the Society's obligations to the Earl of Shaftesbury; after which the vast assembly retired, more than ever convinced, by terrible recent events, of the desirableness, the duty, and the blessedness, of circulating throughout the whole earth the Word of God.

RELIGIOUS TRACT SOCIETY.

The annual meeting of this Society was held in Exeter Hall, on Friday evening, May 7th, presided over by John C Marshman, Esq.

The Secretary read the annual report, from which it appeared that during the past year the Society had issued 14,000,000 tracts, and that the circulation of the Society's periodicals was 11,000,000. The grants made by the Society to various libraries at home and abroad amounted to £3,578 4s. 3d. Numerous tracts and books had been distributed among the soldiers proceeding to India, and also among the natives of that country in the vernacular tongue, and instances were not uncommon in which the tracts were found to produce a highly beneficial influence on the native mind. The receipts of the year were:—for sales, £75,856; the benevolent fund, £12,874; total £88,730; being a larger amount than any previous year, and exceeding the receipts of last year by £6,854. The total circulation of books and tracts by the Society during the fifty-nine years of its existence was no less than 782,000,000. The report contained a variety of interesting particulars connected with the christian press in various parts of the world, and concluded with an appeal for increased support on the ground of the great work in which the Society was engaged and the openings presented in the Divine Providence for the diffusion of christian truth.

The assembly was addressed by the Rev. Canon Champneys, Dr. Lockhart of China, Rev. J. Smith, missionary from Agra, Rev. J. Murray Mitchell, from Bombay, Robt. Baxter, Esq. of Aberdeen, and the Rev. J. H. Wilson, of the same place. The latter gentleman among other things made the following statements:—On looking into the history of the Society, he found that in 1832 the total amount of its issues was 27,000,000, while in the same year the total circulation of the anti-Christian publications of the United Kingdom was no less than 29,000,000. In 1857, the total circulation of publications of an infidel and sceptical character had, as he was informed on the best authority, fallen to 20,000,000; and during the same year the circulation of the publications of the Religious Tract Society was, as they had learnt from the report just presented, 34,000,000. Nor was this all. While that society had been thus progressing, other societies having the same object had come to its aid. In Scotland, for example, they had a tract agency by which one man, Mr. Peter Drummond, had been enabled within the last few years to distribute twenty millions of tracts; in addition to which he had obtained for his *British Messenger* a circulation of 200,000 per annum. They had also in Scotland a society called the Scottish Tract Society, which was issuing publications to the amount of about 3,000,000 a year. Colporteurs were likewise employed in the same work, and their labors extended over the whole of Scotland. If to these several agencies were added some smaller ones which existed in various places, he had no doubt it would be found, on examination, that altogether there had been issued in Scotland thirty millions of tracts and other religious publications within the last seven years.

SUNDAY SCHOOL UNION.

The Annual Meeting of this Union was held on Thursday evening, May 6th, in Exeter Hall, which was, as usual, densely crowded. A hymn having been sung, prayer was offered by the Rev. W. Brock. The Hon. A. Kinnaird, M.P., who presided, expressed his regret that his Parliamentary duties obliged him to leave shortly, and introduced to the Assembly the Hon. George Fife Angas, of South Australia, who had taken so deep an interest in Australian Sunday-schools, and who would conduct the business in his absence.

Mr. Watson read the report, which set forth the grants of school materials and books which had been made during the year. 250 lending libraries had been voted, at a cost of £1,519 14s. 4d. A debt of £1,440 12s. 4d. still remained on the Jubilee Memorial Building, which had been transferred to the Benevolent Fund. The sales at the Depository had amounted to £12,556 19s. 6d. A legacy of £200 had been left by Mrs. W. Flanders, who had long been a warm friend to Sunday-schools. The report concluded by stating the painful fact that there are still more than 300,000 young persons in London alone, between five and fifteen years of age, who are not found in the Sunday-school, so that for every child inside there are two outside the walls. Mr. G. H. Davis, the Rev. Paxton Hood, the Rev. Dr. Archer, the Rev. J. P. Cook (of Paris), the Rev. Newman Hall, and Mr. Charles Swallow addressed the meeting.

The *Morning* conference was held at the Jubilee Building at seven o'clock, when the Committee, together with the officers of the London Auxiliaries and Branches, spent two hours in prayer, and in discussing important subjects connected with Sunday-school instruction.

THE BAPTIST MISSIONARY SOCIETY.

On Thursday, April 29th, the annual meeting of the Baptist Missionary Society was held in Exeter Hall, under the presidency of Sir S. M. Peto. The hall was tolerably full, and the platform crowded. Among those present were the Rev. Dr. Cumming, the Rev. Dr. Campbell, the Rev. Dr. Hoby, the Rev. Dr. Spence, the Hon. and Rev. Baptist Noel, Rev. C. H. Spurgeon, the Rev. J. H. Hinton, the Rev. J. P. Chown, of Bradford, and the Rev. W. Brock. After devotional exercises and an address from the chairman, the secretary, Mr. Trestrail, then read the sixty-sixth annual report, which, before adverting to the topics which the recent calamitous events in India naturally suggest, called attention to the society's finances. The total receipts for 1857 were 21,467l. 4s. 6d.; for the present year, 22,946l. 16s. 10d.; being an increase of 1,479l. 11s. 4d. The total expenditure for 1858 has been 23,593l. 13s. 8d., which, including the debt of 286l. 0s. 11d., balance due to the treasurer last year, left a balance against the society of 932l. 18s. 9d.

The society's operations being confined to India, the report was chiefly occupied with details of the disastrous calamities of the past year. The Sepoy rebellion had raged in that part of India where the Society's missionaries labor, and there had been an almost total suspension of missionary work throughout the year. Many of the missionaries had been placed in imminent jeopardy of their lives; some had had most marvellous and providential escapes, and one, the Rev. Mr. Mackay, of Delhi, had fallen a victim to the thirst for English blood. Great hopes were expressed that, on the country being quieted, a new starting point would be afforded for increased exertions, with better prospects of success than ever.

The meeting was then effectively addressed by the Rev. F. Tucker, Rev. Dr. Cumming, Rev. J. Smith, from India, Rev. Dr. Angas, Rev. Dr. Spence, and Rev. Dr. Evans, of Scarborough.

WESLEYAN MISSIONARY SOCIETY.

The annual meeting of the Wesleyan Methodist Missionary Society was held on Monday, May 3rd, in Exeter Hall, which was crowded in every part. The Right Hon. Lord Panmure K.T., G.C.B., &c., occupied the chair.

The noble Chairman having opened the business in an excellent address,

The Rev. Dr. Hoole then read the financial and general summary, of which the following are the results:—

Total home receipts	...	...	..	...	... £91,050 17 2
Total foreign receipts	...	...	...	...	... 32,012 1 9

£123,062 18 11

There has been a noble increase in the receipts at the Mission House and in the home districts, amounting to more than six thousand pounds, and an increase of more than six hundred pounds in the Juvenile Christmas and New Year's Offerings. There is also an increase of nearly four thousand pounds in the receipts from the Foreign Auxiliary Societies. The total net increase is £3,857 10s. 9d.

The following much lamented missionaries have been removed by death:—

Dr. Cook, at Lausanne; Mr. Barnabas Shaw, at the Cape of Good Hope; Mr. Ritchie, from the West Indies; Mr. Albert Des Brissay, in New Brunswick; Mr. Bennett, in Nova Scotia; Mr. Slight, in Canada. To this affecting record must be added that of Mr. Müller, of Winnenden, in Germany, and of three excellent females, the wives of missionaries, who have also exchanged mortality for life.

The following general summary presents a view of the Society's labors and agency:—

Central or principal stations called circuits	403
Chapels and other preaching places	3,903
Ministers and assistant-missionaries, including twenty-three supernumeraries	693
Other paid agents, as catechists, interpreters, day-school teachers, &c.	985
Unpaid agents, as Sabbath-school teachers, &c.	11,703
Full and accredited church members	121,479
On trial for church membership	8,234
Scholars, deducting for those who attend both the day and Sabbath-schools	113,601
Printing establishments	8

The meeting was addressed by the Revs. Dr. Hannah, Dr. Dixon, F. A. West, S. D. Waddy, J. Smith of Agra, S. Coley, B. Field, R. Wallace, and J. Heald, Esq. The meeting was deeply interesting, and a truly missionary spirit pervaded the proceedings, which will not soon be forgotten.

CHURCH MISSIONARY SOCIETY.

The annual general meeting of the members and friends of this Society took place on Tuesday, May 4th, at Exeter Hall, which was densely crowded. The Earl of Chichester presided.

The Rev. H. Venn, Prebendary of St. Paul's, the Secretary, read the report. It stated that during the past year the total ordinary income of the Society had been £130,766 18s. 4d. while the special fund for India up to March 31, 1858, was £24,717 16s. 11d., making the total received in the United Kingdom, £155,484 15s. 3d. The balance in hand, after providing for all payments, was £1,444 18s. 11d. The local funds raised in the missions, and expended there upon the operations of the Society, but independently of the general fund, were not included in the above statement. They were estimated at £3,915 18s. 11d. The total number of clergymen employed by the Society was 225. The total number of European laymen, schoolmasters, female teachers, catechists, &c., was 2,077. Adverting to Sierra Leone, the report mentioned the death of Dr. Weeks, who had been for some time bishop of that diocese, and congratulated the Church upon the appointment of the Rev. Dr. Bowen as his successor, the new bishop having travelled much in the East, and become well acquainted with the language and habits of the inhabitants of the various districts. The report proceeded to trace the operations of the Society in India, China, Africa, the Mauritius, New Zealand, North America, and the various places at which the missionaries are stationed. Towards its close it expressed a hope that the Government of India would openly proclaim its Christianity, and that it would admit the Bible into its public schools.

The Bishop of London, the Bishop Designate of Calcutta, Viscount Middleton, Revs. Dr. Marsh, G. Knox, Dr. M'Neile, J. Scott, Hugh Stowell, and other gentlemen, advocated the claims of this important and flourishing institution.

We understand that the friends of the German Church, Eastern Hill, Melbourne, under the pastoral care of the Rev. M. Goethe, are intending to hold a bazaar in the present month (September), to aid in the obtaining of funds for the permanent enlargement of their place of worship. It is hoped they will meet with the kindly co-operation of such ladies as may be able to afford them help.

We have to apologise to our readers for the non-appearance this month of the usual department of Colonial Religious Intelligence, and of several minor articles and varieties. This has arisen from our desire to furnish, as early as possible, information of the religious proceedings in England in the month of May, and of the extraordinary religious awakening in America. Next month the deficiency will be supplied.

W. FAIRFAX AND CO., STEAM PRINTERS, COLLINS-STREET, EAST, MELBOURNE.

The Southern Spectator.

No. III.	OCTOBER, 1858.	VOL. II.

REVIVAL OF RELIGION.

ADDRESS OF THE REV. J. A. JAMES, TO THE CONGREGATIONAL UNION, LONDON, FRIDAY, MAY 14, 1858.

Are these things so? Is it a fact that great masses of men, in the most intensely commercial, energetic and politically sensitive nation upon earth, have been simultaneously moved with a concern regarding their relations to God, and their eternal interests?—That an awakening up to the claims of religion has been, and still is, operating over the United States of America, unparalleled even in the history of that land of revivals?—That it has penetrated, not only into the ordinary spheres of religion, but has made the voice of God to be heard in the busy scenes of trade, the colleges of learning, the resorts of fashion, the ships, the schools, the hotels?—That it has drawn hundreds of thousands, men of all parties in politics, all denominations in religion, including Infidels, Unitarians, Roman Catholics, and even Jews, into a deep solicitude about salvation? If so, with what profound and serious attention should the report of this fact be heard—with what anxious and cautious research—with what freedom from prejudice and partiality, should it be investigated by us?

No constant and intelligent observer of the processes of nature will allow any remarkable phenomenon to escape his notice; nor will he stand by with idle wonder or uninquisitive scepticism, but will instantly examine its nature, causes and effects. Shall Christians, and especially shall Christian ministers, be less ready, or less eager, to notice and examine any great and unusual occurrence in the spiritual world? Shall the majestic displays of God's power arrest and fix the attention of the philosopher, and the manifestations of his grace be unobserved by the believer in revelation? Let us with reverence and awe turn aside and behold this great sight. If what has just been read to us be only a meteoric blaze of enthusiasm, it is really so splendid as to demand regard. Make what we will of it, come to what conclusion we may, inquiry is our obvious and imperative duty, and however I may regret that it had not fallen to some other hand than mine to direct attention to it, I do rejoice that the Committee of the Union have determined to set apart this morning to the consideration of the subject.

For my own part, I regard this work as intimately connected with the future of that wondrous people, and their destined influence over the world's coming history. With territory that would support half the world's existing inhabitants, and a population doubling in less time than twenty-five years; possessing all the progressive energy of the Anglo-Saxon race, and all the resources of the Anglo-Saxon language and literature; let any one imagine what that nation must be, and must do in another century; when, if its population go on increasing at the present ratio, it must number more than four hundred millions of the world's citizens. Can we not, then, see a reason why God should step out of his usual course with such a people, to prepare them for that great work in bringing on the world's population and evangelization?

I believe, then, most entirely that the present movement is a mighty work of God, a rich and glorious display of his new creating power; a loud call to the land in which it takes place, and to all others, to learn what he can do, and what they should do; a kind of type of that glorious event, when, amidst millennial power and glory, a nation shall be born in a day.

That it must, indeed, be a genuine revival is, I think, satisfactorily proved, not only by its origination, extent, and results, but by its character. Produced by no exciting means, no forcing hot-bed growth, no fervid appeals to passion or imagination; attended by no wild outcries, no physical convulsions, no bodily disorders, no frenzied emotions,—all, with few and small exceptions, is deep solemnity, and in strictest harmony with the profoundest devotion. It is not the crackling blaze of thorns beneath the pot, obstreperous and transient, but almost noiseless as the tongues of fire which sat upon the brows of apostles upon the day of Pentecost; it is not the ripple of the shallow stream, but deep and silent as the course of that river, which giveth life wherever it flows. One of the most convincing proofs of its divine source and causation is the spirit of catholicity which characterises the movement. Sectarianism, which is the wisdom that cometh from beneath, is, to a great extent, swallowed up by that wisdom which cometh from above; and if we may credit the accounts which come to us, it is introducing a finer morality into the pursuits of trade, and the habits of social life.

The great question for us to take up is, what practical influence this event should have upon ourselves? Now, there appear to me to be two extremes to be avoided. On the one hand, the *scepticism* which doubts whether it is a work of God at all,—the disposition to resolve into a mere American peculiarity, a matter to be wondered at, but not in any way to be considered a special work of God to be followed by us; and, on the other hand, the credulity which would regard it as a type, which should be exactly copied and immediately expected. We must, however, avoid the credulity which supposes that there is no admixture of a human element with God's work; that it is a movement which will extend over the entire surface of the United States, which will end in the entire moral revolution of that great nation; and a revolution which may be expected, in every particular, to have its counterpart in this land. God's method of dealing, both with individuals and with communities, is so various, and so adapted, usually, to the circumstances in which they are found, that it would be highly injudicious to look for the same order of Divine procedure, and the same extent of Divine operation, in all cases. But something more, abundantly more, than we have ever yet received, may be expected in our case. This event ought to have a powerful influence upon our British Churches, and there should be, there must be, and, I hope, will be, a pressing and universal solicitude that it might. Many of the coolest, wisest, and most philosophic minds in the country where it exists, and they are the best judges, tell us they believe it is a wondrous work of God, and shall *we* doubt it? Let us take heed how we mistake, misjudge, or despise the work of God's Spirit. It is too serious a matter for burlesque, too great for ridicule, too holy for levity. Oh ! let there be nothing remotely approaching to the mockery and contempt which, on the day of Pentecost, declared the work of the Spirit to be the incoherent ravings of " men full of new wine." Shall we refuse to learn a lesson from it ? Is it doing honor to the Spirit of God to take no notice of his most extraordinary operations ? Is it doing justice to ourselves not to endeavor to kindle to an intenser heat our own flame by our neighbour's fire ?

The next thing it should lead us to do is, to re-study our Bibles, and learn what real, personal Christianity is,—how holy, how heavenly, how spiritual, how loving, how morally and socially excellent a matter, pure and undefiled religion is ; what separation from the world, what devoutness, what intense earnestness, what conscientiousness, what enlarged benevolence, what unselfishness, what zealous activity, what unearthliness, what germs of celestial virtue, our profession of godliness implies ; and then, having examined this, and obtained an impressive idea of it, to survey the state of the Christian Church and our own state, and ask if we do not need, and ought not to seek, more of the prevalence of such a religion as this, which, in fact, is primitive Christianity. Is the spiritual condition of our churches what it ought to be, what it might be, what it must be before they can fulfil their high commission as the salt of the earth, and the light of the world ? A Christian church, acting up, in some tolerable measure, to its profession, walking in the holiness of the Gospel, is the strongest and most emphatic testimony for God to our dark, revolted world, next to that of Christ himself. But, tell me, brethren,—oh ! tell me, do not the lamps of the golden candlesticks burn dimly, and throw out only a pale, disastrous light ? If they are not sunk to the condition of Laodicea,—which I do not think they are,—do they not too nearly resemble that of Sardis ? In their liberality and activity they have some noble, Christ-like, God-like features, beyond any age since that of the Apostles. I rejoice in it, and pray for its increase ; it is the Church's glory, and the hope of the world. But I am sometimes afraid the flame of our zeal is not altogether fed by the oil of piety. Our churches, notwithstanding this public activity, are infected deeply with the spirit of the world, as is proved by their eager haste to be rich, and their unscrupulous means to become so ; by their taste for worldly amusements, by their increasing love of ease and luxury, by their declining spirit of prayer and serious attendance upon the means of grace, by their higher appreciation of talent than of truth, and by their lamentable neglect of family religion. I appeal to you, brethren, whether these things are not so ; and, if so, do we not need to be revived ? What I earnestly want to see is, our churches roused to a consideration of their state, and brought to a conviction that they need a quickening from God,—a new baptism of fire, a fresh consecration by the Holy Spirit.

The first impulse of Christians in a time of awakening is, to begin to talk with every one right and left on their souls' salvation. And this is right and proper. Individual effort of no ordinary kind has been carried on in America during the present revival, and must be carried on by us for the conversion of sinners. The whole Church must be instinct with life ; all the Lord's people must be prophets. The heads of families in their households, men of business in their establishments and connexions, Sunday school teachers in their classes, must all with renewed energy be up and doing. But is this all ? Is it even the *first* thing ? Should there not be first, a deep heart-scrutiny by the churches, a looking through one's whole life to see how it harmonises with the spirit of Jesus? "He who finds his heart cold, his views low, his feelings earthly, must not hope to talk himself out of this state by preaching to the impenitent, nor to pray himself out of it in public meetings." No. A deeper work than this must be done. Alone with God his Saviour, he must take his daily life and course, item by item, and see if it has been conformed to Christ. Has he no wedge of gold, no Babyloniah vest, no hidden idols, no pledges and gages of the devil laid away in his house, where he scarce dares to look at them? All these must be brought out and burned, and his whole life intelligently consecrated to Christ. Do we not need such "a spirit of burning" as this?

And, as regards the conversion of souls among us, I ask with deep and solemn emphasis, and with mournful feelings, do we not need a revival? My brethren in the ministry, does there not seem a suspension of the Divine power upon the ministry of the Word? Do we see the dry bones in the valley stir, and hear the noise of their resurrection, as we have in former times done? We prophesy; but where, oh! where is the breath of Heaven? I hear from nearly all quarters, both in the Church of England and out of it, deep complaints and lamentations of the ministers of the Gospel of a want of success in the way of conversion. Taking the statistics of the whole of our denomination into account, I believe that the clear increase of members, after deducting losses by death, emigration, resignation and expulsion, would not be more than two or three for each church. How many churches are there who go for years without the increase of a unit!—how many which are gradually declining! Is not this a melancholy fact? Ought it not to excite lamentation and inquiry? What slow inroads are we making on the domain of Satan! How, at this rate, is our country to be evangelised and the world converted? Can we be satisfied to go on at this rate? How shall we account for this state of things? Are we deficient in the matter and manner of our preaching? Are we losing from our sermons the converting element of truth, and from our hearts the converting power to handle it? Or is conversion not believed and not sought by us? Are we aiming to please, instead of seeking to profit? Are we endeavoring to gratify the few by an elaborate intellectualism, or to save the many by a direct appeal to the heart and conscience? Is there not, then, really a suspension, an alarming suspension, of Divine influence, which imperatively, urgently, immediately calls for a renewed spirit of prayer? I believe there is. Then, brethren, we need a revival.

Ought we not to *desire*, intensely to *desire*, and long for, a revival? What sort of ministers, what sort of deacons, what sort of professors, must we be if we do not? Recollect, do not set up this American type, or any other type, of revival, and say we ought to desire this method of Divine procedure. I drop all organizations, all concerted measures, all externalism, all imitations, to seize and hold up the abstract principle, —the very core and essence of a true revival,—a holier Church and a more useful ministry. What we should intensely long for is, a better world; a better Church, to *make* a better world;—and a better ministry, to make a better Church. *This* is a revival,—to have the Church brought to really consider its mission as a witnessing Church to the world,—and more than this,—the Church making itself energetically, continually, and extensively aggressive upon the domain of sin and Satan.

We must be *willing* to be revived. And are we *not* willing, then?

many will reply. No, we are not, or we should be revived. We want to be revived as the unbeliever wants to be saved—without giving up the sins that stand in the way of his salvation, and without performing the duties necessary to his obtaining it. If there come a revival to our ministry, we who belong to it must adopt a more earnest, direct, heart-searching, and converting style of public ministration. We must surrender much of our easy, semi-indolent, and occasionally sauntering way of life, —we must sacrifice some of the time devoted to the amenities and luxuries of literature for objects more intimately connected with our ministry,—we must lay ourselves out more for the conversion of souls,—we must take some of the hours we spend in the parlour, and even in the study, and give them to the anxious inquirers after salvation. Are we willing to do this ?

And then, as regards the Church, a willingness to be revived means their disposition to throw off their indifference, their lukewarmness, their worldliness, their inconsistencies, their unscrupulousness in trade, their unchristian tempers, their neglect of prayer and means of grace, their selfishness, their love of ease and show ; and, in addition to all this, it means their being willing, desirous, anxious to become more devout, self-denying, liberal, humble, and loving. Are our churches prepared for such a state of things as this, desiring it and longing for it ? Do they want to be really less conformed to the world, and are they willing to receive this spirit of self-crucifixion ?

Am I asked what means should be used, beyond a spirit of fervent, believing prayer ? I shall prescribe very little. I want God's work, not man's. There is one means, however, open to us all, on which too much stress cannot be laid. I refer to *prayer*. The mighty work on the other side of the Atlantic is, as we have said, the triumph and trophy of prayer. It is a new proof and display of the mighty force of this great motive power in God's moral government of our world. And God is lifting up a voice on this subject, which grows louder and louder continually, as if He meant that it should be heard at last. Notwithstanding the general spirit of propagation and organization by which this age is distinguished, evidence is but too demonstrative that all hope for the conversion of the world must perish if there be not some fresh outpourings of the Spirit, and some fresh power of prayer to obtain them.

Let the real era of prayer now appear to have come. Hitherto, it has not come. I may be wrong ; my hopes may be too low, and my fears too high ; but I give it as my deliberate judgment, founded upon what I have seen in my own congregation and town, and on what I hear from other quarters, that the spirit of prayer has rarely, if ever, been so low in our churches in modern times as it has been till lately. Christians seem to be more ready for everything than for prayer, and can do everything better than pray. No reason is apparent why a revival in this particular should not henceforth commence. Let the past be characterised as it may by coldness and neglect ; neither the present nor the future ought or needs to be. The end of the neglect of prayer is, I trust, at hand. A time will come, doubtless, when the place of meeting for prayer shall have more attractions than the eloquence of any mortal, or any angel's tongue. And why should not the present be the date of that period ? Let us all, brethren, this day, in this place, make a covenant with God and each other, to give ourselves to prayer. Let us call to mind how Abraham and Moses, and Elias, and Daniel, and Paul,—above all, how the blessed Jesus, labored in prayer, and resolve in God's strength to pray in like manner. Oh! what an influence upon the world's eternal destinies would the hearts and the closets of God's people have if they were stirred up thus to pray! What wonders of grace would be wrought in our churches, what accessions would be made to the ministry, what an impulse would be given to missions, and what brightness would then be thrown on the dark places of the earth and the Church's future prospects! The Church straitened in herself has no just views of the immensity of her Lord's resources; she seems afraid of indulging in excess in her petitions, when, in fact, she has comparatively asked nothing.

People are surprised, and ask, with a sceptical tone and look, is it a real work in America, and may we expect anything like it? Why should they be surprised? Are we not under the dispensation of the Spirit, and not under the arid economy of the law? We know this, and yet we do not give that special place and prominence to the fact which it holds in the Word of God. Ought we not to expect,—are we not authorised to expect, —some richer effusions, some more wonderful manifestations, some more convincing demonstrations of the Spirit's power than we have been accustomed to witness or receive? Is this Divine agent confined, and ought our expectations to be confined, to routine, formality, and fixed order and measure? Should we not look for times of refreshing, days of power, intimations of the coming millennial glory? Are not these awakenings the very things we have prayed for, longed for, waited for? Are they not the subject of inspired prophecy? Are they not given to support our faith in Divine prediction, and animate our languid hopes of the coming glory of the millennial age, when a nation shall be born in a day? And are there no hopeful signs of such an awakening amongst us? Do we not see a cloud, though no bigger than a man's hand, rising out of the sea, the auspicious portent of a coming rain? What means this universal stir about the working classes, this breaking down of the barriers of ecclesiastical formalities, this starting up of lay evangelists in the north, and of clerical irregularities in the south, this opening of our abbey churches and cathedrals for the preaching of the Word of God to the masses, this entrance of the Gospel into places of trade and amusement, this gradual removal of the distinction between things sacred and secular,—when the sacred are not becoming secular, but the secular sacred,—and especially this miniature representation of the American revivals in some parts of our own country? I could speak of what has occurred in a town in my own neighbourhood, as remarkable for its extent as anything that has taken place across the Atlantic. I have in my possession, at this moment, the account of a surprising work which has been carried on in his congregation by a devoted young minister of our own denomination, which, if there were time to read it, would instruct, surprise, and delight us. Let us not be desponding, then, but hopeful. The voice of this revival in America comes to every country and to every Christian, as the midnight cry of old, "Behold, the bridegroom cometh!" A new era is struggling in the birth: Christ is moving to reorganise the world. Is it a vision of my imagination? is it only a spectral form which I see? or is it,—oh! is it the Saviour Himself walking on the waters of the Atlantic, and moving with his face towards Britain? Is it an allusion, or a reality, which leads me to think I hear His voice saying to this country, "Behold I come quickly, and My reward is with Me?" Oh! brethren, shall we fear Him, neglect Him, repel Him? Shall we, like the mercenary Gadarenes, entreat Him to leave our coasts, or shall we not rather implore His presence, and say, "Come, Lord Jesus, come quickly, and land upon our shores ?"

> "Enter with all Thy glorious train,
> Thy Spirit and Thy Word;"

> "Thy churches wait with longing eyes,
> Here to behold and bless."

Before I conclude, may I, my beloved and honored brethren in the ministry, as one who has attained to patriarchal standing, though, I am duly aware, to few of its honors or its claims, beseech you with affectionate earnestness to give this momentous subject your calm, deliberate, solemn and prayerful attention ? Our responsibility is tremendous, and should make us fear and tremble, and in an agony of spirit to exclaim, "Lord, who is sufficient for these things ?" On us does it in some measure depend whether the heavens shall open, and the blessing in its fulness come down, —whether the life-giving power shall ooze and trickle in drops or flow in streams. How is it we can be so easy in such circumstances, and with such interests dependent upon us ? How is it we can sleep so soundly upon our beds, or sit so comfortably around our table and our fire ? Are we, indeed, watching for souls, or trifling with them ? Are we so stiffened into formality, so drilled into routine, so enchained by custom, that when anything new or startling comes across our orbit, or enters into our sphere of observation, we will not notice it, or ask what it means ? Shall we who are stationed on the walls of Jerusalem be unprepared with an answer to the question,—"Watchman, what of the night? watchman, what of the night ?" Shall we who are expected to form public opinion, to influence public sentiment, to direct and control public movement, stand by in this case with cold and careless gaze, or sneering contempt, or actual opposition ? Even supposing we take no new steps, shall we not quicken those we already take in our own course ? If we adopt no new measures, shall we not be stirred up to carry forward our old ones with more vigor ? Let us, oh ! let us recollect, that we are the servants of Him who maketh His ministers a flame of fire. Dearly beloved brethren, let this be such a meeting as we have never held ; let a new baptism of fire come upon us all to-day. Let this be a time of humiliation for the past, of consecration for the present, and of determination for the future. Let us enter to-day into covenant with each other, and with God, to be more diligent and devoted servants of Christ, and then, depend upon it, we shall be more successful ones. You cannot know, as I do, the solemnity of the feeling that is produced by the conviction that life is almost gone,—the awe that comes over the mind of him who knows that he is upon the border-country of eternity, and must soon lay down his ministry, and give in his account. Let him, then, in conclusion, conjure you and himself by the solemn vows of our ordination ; by the worth and danger of immortal spirits ; by the agony and bloody sweat, the cross and passion of Our Lord Jesus Christ ; by the felicities of heaven, the torments of hell, and the ages of eternity ; by the great white throne, and the presence of Him that sits upon it, before which we must soon appear,—let me, I say, conjure you to inquire what use we shall make of the extraordinary events which have called for this paper, and in what way we shall turn it to our own account in watching for souls, reviving the spirit of piety in our churches, and bringing back this revolted world to the dominion of Christ.

CHRISTIAN FRATERNIZATION.

Love to the brethren is one of the laws of Christianity, and therefore it must be an organic principle in the Christian character. The Divine Author exemplified it in perfection, and his disciples, after imbibing his spirit, imitated his example. Indeed, wherever the Apostles recognised the spirit of their Master,—wherever, and by whose instrumentality soever, a group of minds sprung up, doing all Divine honors in a spiritual manner to Jesus Christ, there they hailed a brother or a fraternity. The Pentecostal effusion multiplied Christ's exponents of his truth, and Providence speedily found them full employ, not only throughout all the realms of David's ancient kingdom, but amidst the vales and mountains of Asia Minor, the classic ruins of Greece, the mixed races of Macedonia, and the stern imperialists of Rome. The law of Christ was recognised over all this vast region by those who yielded to his authority ; and churches began to employ messengers to convey salutations, cordiality, and sympathy to the brethren in distant communities. It may be impossible to cite from ecclesiastical history proofs that this practice became a universal feature of primitive piety ; but it prevailed to a considerable extent. Brethren communed with brethren, bearing each other's burdens in the fierce battle of life. Fraternization could not at that time be carried out by personal interviews, nor in many cases was it safe to attempt to do it by epistolary correspondence. It was more conveniently and effectually done by employing a member for the special work, delegating all his instructions, and limiting him to a definite and spiritual mission. This mode of fraternization was dictated, not more by the necessary weakness incident to the infancy of the Church, than by the probable dangers that might result from isolation.

Here then, is a subject which commends itself to Congregational Christians, and, indeed, to all others throughout the Australian colonies. Here is a law which remains yet to be fully obeyed, a principle yet to be more extensively exemplified ; and possessing, as we do, so many facilities for intercourse between man and man, and church with church, widely separated from each other, we ought to lose no time in availing ourselves of such privileges as we possess. Here is our own periodical appealing to the sympathy of all our churches, and waiting the co-operation of every devout mind among us. This organ is obviously the best mode of giving expression to our Christian character to the brethren with whom we can hold no literal converse. It is already *our* denominational journal, and it waits to be invested with the mission of a messenger to go forth and elicit the fraternization of all our churches.

The question then occurs, how can the periodical be made to elicit and express a larger measure of fraternity between the different provincial churches in this hemisphere ? This question appeals to every minister and every Christian among us throughout the colonies for a reply. There are few of us who believe that we are so closely indentified, denominationally, with each other as we ought to be, or as we might be ; and nobody can doubt that the amount of information which the different colonial churches possess respecting each other is exceedingly limited indeed, and yet it is information of some kind or other that we must possess, respecting each other's existence and position, before we can love each other as brethren. Until the establishment of the *Spectator*, the different colonial churches knew almost nothing of each other. The churches in the senior provinces might have been strong or weak, wealthy or poor in social position, intelligence, piety and organization, but who knew all this beside themselves, or, perhaps, here and there a minister or a merchant? How many persons in South Australia possessed knowledge enough of their brethren over the border to awaken in their minds the tender and expressive emotions belonging to Christian love? And how much knowledge do we possess even now? And what is its nature? Whatever this may be is owing chiefly to the *Spectator*; but if this magazine commanded the sympathy of the churches to the extent of its merits, and especially according to the law of our Master, it would speedily become a more extensive vehicle of information, and a more cheering messenger of fraternity between all the churches throughout the Australias. Situated as we are, in a new country, where all our imported associations are liable to fade gradually from the mind, and our strongest and best convictions meet either with rude or stealthy hostility almost every day of our life, we cannot possess too much of each other's sympathy. We cannot render mutually to each other too much help, nor reciprocate valuable information with too much frequency. nor to too great an extent.

South Australia. FRATER.

THE CHURCH'S STRENGTH.

(*Concluded from page* 42.)

The strength of the Church consists further in *Union*. The phrase "Union is strength" has become a proverb. Separate efforts may do much, but combinations do more, and individual efforts accomplish the greater part of their results by setting masses in motion. The strength of each individual man is augmented by union with others, for such union imparts to him greater zeal and greater confidence. The momentum of an organised corps is greater than that of the same number of men acting separately, because the power being concentrated becomes more effective. This is the secret of the wonderful strength of armies, whose achievements depend less upon their numbers than the perfection of their discipline, and their consequent unity of action. These principles apply to religious as well as secular movements. Vast revivals have, indeed, been accomplished by individual energy and zeal, as in the case of Luther, Wesley, Whitfield; but the success in such case may be estimated by the combinations to which it leads. The external apparatus of means and ordinances scarcely can be supplied upon a large scale except by Christians uniting together. What single men and desultory fits of zeal, in translating and circulating the Scriptures, could not effect in eighteen centuries, the Bible Society has effected in half a century. The same may be said of the institution of Christian schools, the erection of places of worship, the supply of ministers and catechists for instructing and converting the heathen.

The Church, then, to be strong, must be united. To put on strength is to "keep the unity of the spirit in the bond of peace." If Christians cannot have one eye and see alike, they should have one heart and feel alike. No strength should be wasted in internecine warfare, but all husbanded and concentrated upon the foe without. For the sake of quickly and effectually executing the commission with which the Saviour has entrusted his people, every motive of policy and prudence urges them to attend to the Apostolic exhortation; "whereto we have already attained, let us walk by the same rule, let us mind the same thing." But ought not higher motives than policy to lead to Christian union ?　What is the Church but the assembly of genuine Christians ; and are not all Christians indebted to the same grace, bought with the same blood, renewed by the same Spirit, instructed by the same Scriptures, destined to the same home ?　If *they* cannot love each other and act in concert, who can ?　But alas ! what has been the fact ?　The quarrels and divisions of Christians have been the scandal and the weakness of Christianity.　As long as the followers of Jesus remained loving and united, they were the admiration of the world and bid fair to become its conquerors.　When they began to quarrel among themselves, the enemy first lost their respect for them, then took heart, rallied, and became the aggressors in turn.　Christians should remember that they are not independent atoms, but parts of a whole ; members of one body, whose vigour and comfort and health depend upon the vital connexion and harmonious action of its several limbs and organs. Let them expel all morbid humors, lay aside selfish aims, party spirit, bitterness, anger, clamor and evil speaking, and whatever else tends to alienate and divide.　Let them live in love and mutual charity, and they will be strong either for attack or defence.　Paganism, infidelity, vice and self-interest, all combined, could not resist a united church.

The strength of the Church consists in *activity*.　This may seem a truism, but it is more.　Do not stagnant waters corrupt, running waters retain and increase their purity ?　Does not inaction in the body induce languor and weakness ?　Exercise and training develop and invigorate the muscles ?　Are not the mental faculties, memory, reason, imagination, improved by use ?　Even so with the virtues and graces of the Christian character.　Faith and hope, love and zeal, grow sickly and feeble when not brought into frequent exercise.　The less they are exerted, the less capable will they be of exertion ; the more vigorously they are put forth, the more their strength will grow apace.　The Church at large, or any particular church, but faintly employing its capacities of service, will by degrees forget how to use them at all ; indolence will bring on paralysis, and that, if not checked, will eventuate in spiritual death.　But those that are zealous in the work of the Lord will be " blessed in their deed ; " being " faithful in a few things " they shall become " rulers over many things ; " for having worked hard they shall be rewarded by more and greater work being assigned them, as being now possessed, after such a training, of increased capacities of service.　Hence the prophet's exhortation to Zion : " Awake, awake ! put on thy strength, O Zion ! Shake thyself from the dust ! arise " from thy prostrate condition !　Throw off thy slumbers ; yield not to lethargy and languor : bestir thyself ; rouse and use all thy energies ! What slumbering faculties are there in the Church of God !　What mines of unwrought wealth ; what unused stores ; what time misspent ; what thought and influence utterly misdirected !　Bring them forth ! use your talents and they will multiply ; freely break the bread of life and it will grow in your hands ; liberally scatter and you shall increase ; abundantly water others and you shall be watered also yourselves.

The strength of the Church consists in *Faith* in God.　The work assigned to the Church is peculiar ; the resistance is special, and can only be overcome by a power that is Divine.　Did not Moses feel this when he exclaimed, " If thy presence go not with us, carry us not up hence " ?　And was it not faith in the promise, " My presence shall go with thee," that rendered the Israelites invulnerable ?　What was the secret of that strength by which the worthies of the olden time " subdued kingdoms, wrought righteousness, obtained promises, stopped the mouths of lions, quenched the violence of fire, escaped the edge of the sword, out of weakness were made strong, turned to flight the armies of the aliens ? " Was it not the " Power of Faith ?" May the Church now expect the presence and the power of God ? Yes, for the Captain of Salvation says to the soldiers of the Cross, as they go forth on their campaign, " Lo ! I am with you alway, even to the end of the world." And does he not say to each separate Christian, engaged in any work of difficulty, " My grace is sufficient for thee ; my strength is made perfect in weakness" ? But these promises become effective only by dependence and faith. God will be honored by the confidence and trust of his people ere he puts forth his strength on their behalf. Was it not faith in his Master that fortified the heart and nerved the arm of Paul, when he exclaimed, " I can do all things through Christ which strengtheneth me" ? What but this could have sustained him when he entered Philippi, Corinth, Rome, almost alone and single-handed, to overturn the heathenism which time and genius and national predilections had consolidated into an impregnable fortress ? Such confidence in God as the Apostles entertained was the sure presage of victory. If the soldiers of Cæsar, of Napoleon, and Wellington, were inspired with an energy which won them battles, from confidence in the genius and good fortune of their commanders, how much more mighty should the power of faith in the Lord of Hosts be to invigorate and energise those who are fighting the " good fight " against all ungodliness of sin ?

Finally, there is strength in *Prayer*. "This kind " of power, the divine power on which Christians lean, "goeth not forth but by prayer and fasting." The established order of heaven is, to regulate its gifts by the fervency of the Church's petitions. The blessing must be valued, and the degree of appreciation must be shown by the importunity of prayer. The command is, " Ask and ye shall receive ; seek and ye shall find." The Saviour's promise is, " Whatsoever ye shall ask the Father in my name he will give it you." The Christian warrior, though provided with a panoply complete, can do no execution with it without prayer. To use his armour with skill and effect he must " pray always, with all prayer and supplication in the spirit, watching thereunto with all perseverance." The voice of prayer from below must bring down the Divine power from above. Where death and barrenness prevail, prayer is restrained : " Ye have not because ye ask not ; ye ask and have not because ye ask amiss." In such a state of things the complaint may always with justice be made, "There is none that calleth upon thy name, that stirreth up himself to take hold of thee." A prayerless church is a weak church, a strong church one in which prayer abounds. The present American revivals are distinguished above all things by a spirit of earnest, wrestling, and prevailing prayer. As he, who is the " Strength of Israel," says to every believer, in every church, " Let him take hold of my strength that he may make peace with me ; and he shall make peace with me ;" so let each one avail himself of this blessed permission to clothe himself with power from on high, by approaching the throne of grace and with holy importunity saying, " I will not let thee go except thou bless me." Soon will he be rewarded with the response, " Be it unto thee even as thou wilt."

The strength of the Church then consists in truth, piety, holiness unity, activity and faith ; and all these energised and made effective by fervent prayer. The signs of the times and the position of religion in these colonies demand a strong church. Mind is awake ; evil is active.

Much of the mental energy of the age goes in the direction of infidelity, secularism and vice. How are these to be checked but by counter-activity ? Where is the antidote to come from, but from a wakeful, zealous, devoted church, clothed with all the attributes of zeal and effective strength ? "Awake ! Awake ! put on thy strength, O Zion," and thy Lord will go forth with thee " conquering and to conquer."

TO YOUNG MEN.
EXCELSIOR. [*]

THE subject upon which we have to speak to-night is Excelsior. The word means, as used by us, higher—still higher. It assumes that you have gained by patient effort a certain elevation ; it expresses your own resolve to reach yet loftier heights ; it is a word of sympathy and approval from those who behold you ; it is the voice of the High and Holy One calling you upward and onward. We trust that your future life-course will supply a fitting exposition and a true response. To three points we will call your attention, we assume—

I. That you have acquired some knowledge, and are seeking more. You have been created by God with powers for acquiring and retaining knowledge—the faculties of observation, of analysis, of classification, of judgment, of fancy, of memory, are all yours ; the common heritage of all sane men. The possession of such powers constitutes at once the glory and responsibility of your manhood. We do not deny the existence of instinct, nor of a feeble kind of reason in the lower orders of creation ; unquestionably they possess, more or less marked, the faculties of observation, memory, and what seems like judgment, or the power of discerning between things that differ though nearly related ; nay, even moral feelings, as gratitude, faithfulness, and lasting affection. Still, between an elephant, however sagacious, and a man, there is a broad and impassable gulph. The mystic power of imagination, the solemn elements of conscience and responsibility, the noble faculty of veneration and worship, the tremendous attribute of spiritual immortality, the fearful alternative of endless progression in love and bliss, or sinking lower and lower in the scale of being, belong to man alone, and serve to invest our powers of mind, our privileges and period of probation with the deepest importance. The mental powers, then, which you possess, we strenuously urge you to cultivate to the utmost tasking of your time and talents. Wide and varied are the fields where knowledge may be wooed and wisdom won. There is your own nature, in itself an epitome of the world, the tabernacle in which you live, its glory and vanity ; the soul, with its nature, destinies, aspirations and sins ; the harmony between both ; the facts and philosophy of the reciprocal action and influence of mind and body. There is the wide domain of nature, with the sciences, classifying plants and animals and unfolding the relations of one to another, and of this world to man. There is the past, as it lives in the page of history, in the works and monuments it has left behind ; the condition, employments and governments of past generations, with the bearing of these upon the great questions of our modern sociology. Chief of all, the great truths and doctrines of religion will receive your most constant and prayerful attention ; as they are supreme in

[*] Being the substance of an Address delivered to the Launceston Young Men's Christian Association, at the first Soirée, 17th August, 1858.

interest, so will they be in your thoughts and researches ; the Bible will be the man of your counsel and the guide of your youth. The church of the living God, with its history, its present position and duties, with its future triumphs and glories, offers a most fruitful and instructive theme. Upon all these points you are already in possession of a greater or less amount of knowledge ; you have left the low ground of ignorance where mists and vapours hide the heavens from your view ; you are climbing with slow but sure steps the hill of knowledge, you find the air grow clearer as you ascend, the prospect widens and discloses fresh charms, the acquisitions of to-day are the stepping-stones for to-morrows ascent ; cheered with your past triumphs you are meditating fresh efforts. We simply place ourselves abreast of you to-night, and say with a brother's voice—Excelsior ! Your discussions, essays, addresses and conversations are all designed to create a noble unity and fellowship in your efforts of mutual improvement. We would venture a caution : Do not think yourselves to be wiser than facts actually warrant ; keep from the young man's folly, a spirit of presumption. Extensive knowledge leads to humility and charity. Beware also of expecting that your meetings will supply the place of quiet, thoughtful reading at home. Cultivate home joys and affections,—there is a tendency to religious dissipation of an insinuating and dangerous character.

II. We assume that you are Christians already and are seeking to become better. We take it for granted, without question, that as you are members of a Christian association, you are Christians in deed and truth. You are then partakers of the divine nature, have dedicated your body soul and spirit to God, are striving to perfect holiness in the fear of the Lord, and are giving all diligence to cultivate those Christian, personal, and social graces which adorn the followers of a Saviour who knew no sin. We give God thanks for this, and pray that He may have you in His holy keeping. As Jesus loved the young man for all that was lovely in his character, so we admire and love all that is holy, noble, and truthful in your characters and doings. We come to you now as you are ascending the hill Difficulty, climbing its heights and wrestling with its impediments, and we say—Excelsior ! We point you to those lofty regions of self-consecration and fervent faith, where holy men live, and yet not they, but Christ liveth in them, and we urge you to mount upward to the throne of light and purity. Aim at holiness of character as well as correctness of creed, at self-subjection as well as self-cultivation, at the development of your spiritual instincts as well as your mental powers. Grow in grace and in knowledge. For this end study the example of Christ, of his apostles, of eminent Christians of all ages countries and denominations. Abound in prayer, Christian watchfulness, and self-examination, and " if ye do these things, ye shall never fall." Let me warn you against the idea so generally prevalent that your secular engagements present insuperable obstacles to the attainment of eminent personal holiness ; far from this, they furnish you with noble opportunities of self-improvement. Are you servants ? Be diligent, not with eye-service as men-pleasers, but as doing God's work. Are you in positions of trust ? Be faithful. Are you masters ? Be courteous ; avoid everything like insolence, remembering one is your master, even Christ, and all ye are brethren.

III. We assume that you are engaged in works of usefulness and urge upon you more zeal and devotion. No man in God's plan becomes a Christian for his own sake merely. No man liveth unto himself, and no man dieth unto himself. When God revealed his Son to the apostle it was with the ulterior purpose that he might preach Him among the heathen—each saved man is to seek to save and bless others—this honor have all the saints who are faithful to their duty.   We must recognise the necessity and glory of individual efforts, as well as our adhesion to societies and associations.   Some of you are already identified with our Bible Society, our Town Mission ; others labor as Tract distributors, more as Sunday-school teachers. We rejoice in this ; we cry—Excelsior ! Work on, redouble your efforts, watch for opportunities, keep near to Christ, love the men around you, for God's sake if for no other, and give them such help and counsel as you may be able.   The wants of men are pressing, the claims of the Saviour great, your own time short, the reward of faithful labor great and sure.

Now to conclude.   We know there are difficulties in your way,   There is no royal road to knowledge. You lack time, poverty may be an obstacle, the pressure of manifold duties wastes your zeal and energies ; so found one whose hard fate and early death give mournful interest to his touching lines :—

> " For me the day
> Hath duties which require the vigorous hand
> Of steadfast application, but which leave
> No deep improving trace upon the mind.
> But be the day another's—let it pass,
> The night's my own—they cannot steal my night,
> When evening lights her folding stars on high
> I live and breathe, and in the sacred hours
> Of quiet and repose my spirit flies,
> Free as the morning, o'er the realms of space,
> And mounts the skies, and spreads her wings for heaven."

Husband wisely and well your spare moments, especially your nights and you may acquire a portion of knowledge far beyond your present attainments and of great usefulness to yourselves and others.   There is a difficulty in the way of self-subjection ; the evil that is within you will not die—alas ! all feel this ; so felt one of the holiest and wisest spirits of modern times, " I see a terrible energy in human appetites and passions ; but I do not fear ; truth is mightier than error, virtue than vice, God than the evil man."   There are difficulties in the way of your usefulness ; the want of experience, of co-operation from those whose age and standing in society would aid you much, the lack of success and earnest appreciation. Heed not these things ; we all have to overcome them.   God's approval is sufficient—Excelsior !

The shades of night were falling fast, covering the earth with darkness, as a youth was seen hastening through an Alpine village, holding aloft with a firm hand a noble banner, on which the strange device was seen, " Excelsior."   He saw high in the heavens the glorious turrets of the city and tower where dwell the faithful and good ; with high and holy endeavour he resolved to reach the city of God. An old man beheld him and said, " Try not the pass, there is danger there ; the reward is great, but the labor is long and difficult ; the ascent is steep and many have failed ; stay on this plain ; take counsel of age and prudence ; why die before thy time ?" The youth replied, " Excelsior !" and pursued the upward path. A maiden saw him and stood in his way ; roses and lilies were on her cheeks ; the sunlight of love flashed in her eyes ; music was on her lips, and grace in every motion. " Try not the pass," the maiden said ; "stay with me ; here are youth and pleasure, riches and wine ; my name is Worldly Joy, my house is of ivory, and all precious things I can command : the pathway to the mountain top is beset with terrible dangers, come then with me." His heart fluttered for a moment, a tear came into his eye, a sigh was upon his lips, but his better feelings triumphed, and with a steady voice and quicker step he cried, "Excelsior !" Other temptations awaited him, but he kept his upward path. He grew stronger and stronger. And when he was seen no more among men, a voice, soft as that which said "Follow me," proclaimed that he had gone up higher. He now treads the fields of everlasting spring, he walks with angels and the spirits of the just, his song is, Gloria in Excelsis ! And as he rises higher in wisdom, love and devotion, his cry still is, "Excelsior !" I give you now a friendly greeting, and hope by God's grace to give you a greeting as part of the general assembly and church of the first-born in heaven itself.

W. L.

OBITUARY.

MR. DAVID ROUT.

Died in Melbourne, September 12th, 1858, of fever, aged twenty-four, Mr. David Rout. son of Basil Rout, Esq., Deacon of the Congregational Church, Davey-street, Hobart Town, of which the Rev. G. Clarke is pastor. Mr. Rout removed to Melbourne ten weeks ago, with a view to improve his acquaintance with the drapery business. Two of the young men who were lodgers with him in the same house having been taken ill of fever, he attended upon them with assiduous care. On their recovery, he himself was seized with the same complaint, but in a more violent form. All efforts to save him were unavailing ; and in less than a fortnight he breathed his last. He died as he had lived, in the true faith and hope of a Christian.

Brought up in the fear of God by pious parents, he gave signs of early seriousness. Not that decided religion marked his character in the first instance, for he himself mentions, in a few manuscript memoranda left behind him, that at school he had contracted some objectionable habits. "Though brought up," he says, " under the roof of pious parents, at school I learnt to swear, and continued the habit until it pleased God to renew my heart." The important change here referred to took place when he was about fifteen years of age. He specifies one night in particular, when he suffered deep distress of conscience on account of his sins ; and having struggled hard with anxiety and fear, he betook himself to the throne of grace, cried earnestly for mercy, pleaded the blood of atonement for pardon, and before another day had passed, not only had obtained a sense of forgiveness, but enjoyed some delightful manifestations of the Divine love. This was the turning point in his history. From that time he became a youth of decided and earnest piety, and lived in the high and pure enjoyments which true religion affords. In his nineteenth year he joined the Congregational Church above-named, at that time assembling in Collins-st. Chapel. When that event was impending, he made the following record :—" I am now eighteen years and six months old, and this night I have been proposed as a member of the Collins-street Independent Chapel. I have thus openly confessed before the world my love to the Saviour, and my resolution to live the life of a Christian. May I be enabled through God's aid to follow out this course of life faithfully, if it please God that I should live to the full age of man ; but, if it be his will to call me away within a short space of time, may I die in the sure hope of that blessed world which is prepared for those that love God." On his first communion Sabbath, he writes—" To-day, for the first time, I sat down at the sacrament of the Lord's supper, and partook of the emblems of the body and blood of him who died on the cross to save sinners.'

" Religion is the chief concern
Of mortals here below—
May I its great importance learn,
Its sovereign virtues know."

From this time he *did* make religion his chief concern, and both experienced and exemplified its gracious influence. He enjoyed and profited by the ministry of his valued pastor, and walked consistently with the profession he made.

Shortly after this, his health not being good, a voyage to Port Phillip was recommended as likely to improve it. He was absent nearly three months. On reviewing this journey, he makes special mention of the new and stirring scenes he had witnessed, and the pleasures, the gaieties, and temptations to which he had been exposed, and speaks gratefully of God's having preserved him from moral contagion, as well as brought him back in safety. The death, during his absence, of a venerated grandmother deeply affected him, though he felt assured that the change was a happy one for her. He records her last words—

> " A few more rolling suns at most
> Will land me on fair Canaan's coast,"

and concludes his notice in these words, expressive of his gratitude for God's goodness to his aged relative :—" Thus, Lord, thou hast permitted her to live to the age of eighty-six years, and see all her children members of thy Church." On the first day and first Sabbath of the year 1854, a joint communion of the Independent Churches in Hobart Town was held, a service which appears to have been preeminently solemn and impressive. Mr. Rout was present on the occasion, and he refers to it with deep emotions of gratitude for the hallowed privilege he then had of enjoying fellowship with Christian brethren upon a larger scale than was possible in ordinary circumstances.

As soon as he became a decided Christian, he laid himself out for a life of usefulness. He entered heartily into the scheme for building a new and larger place of worship for the congregation with which he was connected, and made it a matter of fervent prayer, as appears from his papers; and he had the satisfaction at length of beholding a structure reared and completed, which is an ornament to the city and a source of strength to the cause.

Objects of practical usefulness in which a young man might take a share, both of a strictly religious and also of a generally benevolent kind, soon attracted his attention and secured his services. Among these may be mentioned Sunday Schools, City Missions, Ragged Schools, Young Mens' Christian Associations, and Mutual Improvement Societies. The Sunday School found in him a zealous and devoted teacher, who entered into the work not by constraint, as a mere matter of duty, but willingly as an engagement congenial to his taste and productive of real delight to his heart. The kindness of his disposition found ample scope for exercise in the Hobart Town City Mission. He was in constant communication with one of the agents who brought before his attention cases of extreme poverty and deep depravity, and he was ever up and doing to impart relief, as far as lay in his power, both to their spiritual and temporal wants. To meet the case of the comfortless and neglected poor, in respect to domestic accommodation, he organized, with the co-operation of two other young men, a Model Lodging House, in one of the most depraved localities in the city. The kindred scheme of Ragged Schools also engaged his attention. The city of Hobart has, perhaps, a disproportionate number of poor and neglected children, " street Arabs," the remnant, doubtless, of the old penal population. For these outcasts a ragged school was commenced, to which Mr. Rout gave his warm support, and he became the superintendent of the Sunday school branch of that institution. Often would he, in a spirit of generous self-denial, debar himself of the public ministrations of his beloved pastor on a Sabbath morning, that he might address words of counsel to his youthful charge, consisting of children of the lowest class, sunk in the deepest ignorance, and already adepts at vicious practices. Instead of becoming, as time went on, weary in well-doing, his labors of love seemed to strengthen the benevolent principle and to enlarge his desires of usefulness. For some time he had a strong wish to separate himself entirely from secular engagements and to devote himself to a missionary life among the heathen, and with this view he commenced, experimentally, a course of study with his beloved pastor, being partially relieved from business for the purpose. During this period his nights were devoted to mental application, and, perhaps, his health suffered in consequence. Various circumstances, however, induced his friends to advise the abandonment of the project.

Mr. Rout was of an obliging and cheerful disposition, and the writer of this notice has a pleasant recollection of his liveliness and readiness to serve all about him, when he acted as conductor to a party of thirty or forty friends, who ascended Mount Wellington in February last. He seemed to think of every body's comfort but his own.

His constitution appears not to have been very vigorous. It was for the sake of his health that he paid his first visit to Victoria ; on his return he was still unwell, and was laid up for a time with a bad knee. In February, 1855, he makes the following record :—" The Lord has again been pleased to lay me on a bed of sickness, I have now for a week past suffered severely from a pain in my chest, for which the doctor has been called in, who advises me for the present to keep my bed. This is the first Sabbath I have been absent from the house of God since May last, at which time I was also ill." Nevertheless, he recovered from this attack, and there seems to have been of late years nothing to awaken apprehension in the minds of his friends on his account ; and when he last left home for Melbourne he was in good health and spirits.

During his last illness his mind was so affected with delirium, that there were but few opportunities of sensibly conversing with him. Had he not been previously ready for death, there would have been no time for preparation then. In his lucid intervals his great delight was to hear portions of holy Scripture read, and favorite hymns repeated, especially the one—" There is a land of pure delight," &c. But even in his wanderings the bent of his mind was clearly seen. On one occasion he seemed to fancy himself in the Sunday school, leading its devotions, and he offered a beautiful and connected prayer expressing his thanks for the mercy of good health for himself and those present, and earnestly invoking the blessing of God upon the labors of the teachers, in order that young souls might be saved. At another time he imagined a Sunday school class stood before him, and questioned and spoke to one and another of his supposed scholars, as if he were really and intelligently engaged in teaching them; to one he said—" Do you know who God is? He is a kind God." He was surrounded by affectionate, sympathising friends, young men like himself, whom he had known for years. These did all in their power to minister both bodily relief and spiritual consolation. The Rev. A. Morison visited him twice, and succeeded in awakening him to only temporary consciousness. When the last hour came he was not in a state to recognise those about him, or to give utterance to any expressions of feeling. As soon as danger was apprehended, word was sent to his father, in Hobart Town, but it is matter of regret that such was the violence of the disease, that death had occurred before it was possible for any of the family to arrive. On Tuesday, September 14, his remains were borne to the Melbourne Cemetery, followed in mourning coaches by a large number of Hobart Town young men, his former companions and acquaintances, and now residents in Victoria, and by the Revs. A. Morison, J. Sunderland, and R. Fletcher. Mr. Sunderland read the Scriptures and gave a brief and solemn address, and Mr. Fletcher offered prayer. On the following Sabbath the Rev. R. Bowman, of Victoria Parade chapel, on whose ministry Mr. Rout chiefly attended while in Melbourne, improved the event to a full congregation, from the words, " Be ye also ready, for in such an hour as ye think not the Son of Man cometh."

This event speaks loudly to all young persons, and especially to young men. Here is one of their own class, born and brought up in a good position in society, with excellent worldly prospects before him, cheerfully giving his heart and his services to God, to religion, and to benevolence, seeking his happiness in being and doing good. Is not this the most rational, the most useful, the most happy way of spending even the time of youth, and is it not the only satisfactory way of preparing for death? Youthful reader, go thou and do likewise.

VARIETIES.

INTELLECT AND FAITH.

The host of Israel stood awaiting the return of the spies whom they had sent into the promised land. Their messengers at last came back. "It is in truth a good land," they said, and the people believed them. "It is a land of war and difficulty and opposition," they added, and the chicken-hearted people trembled and could not enter in because of unbelief, but wandered about the wilderness till they perished.

Is it not in this way many a piously educated man deals with the convictions of his childhood? He stands on the threshold of religion; the spies of his mind, his intellectual apprehensions, go forth; they return and say, "The Bible is true and beautiful, but hard is the struggle with sin for those who enter in;" he hesitates, well for him if his prayer ascends for faith. Warfare may be his lot, but God gives him the victory at last. If his faith fails, God condemns him to wander for a long, long time in the wilderness of doubt, and may be he falls in the desert; or only in far off old age, a saddened, a wiser, a penitent man, he crosses the boundary into God's domain.

Would not the author of "The Purgatory of Suicides" say now, that this was true, and tell us how years of the misery of scepticism may result from trifling with religious convictions in the days when intellect, strong in its fancied wisdom, will go forth as a spy, and return boasting itself wiser than faith?

FAITH.

Faith is often called a telescope; the simile seems more and more appropiate the more the power of that wonderful instrument is developed. Worlds invisible to the naked eye are clearly seen, and the dull white light of the nebulæ is resolved into far off systems of suns and stars. So Reason, beautiful and proud, looks at the mysteries of creation and life, and either fails to perceive much that we know is there, or else is strangely contradictory in her interpretations: whereas, Faith, humble yet hopeful, points upward and tells us of the unseen and the eternal. "Add to your knowledge, faith," is the dictate of the bold spirit of intellectual youth. "Add to your faith, knowledge," is the advice of Peter, when old age had given him wisdom. If we search for an example, here is one—The keen fearless eye of Shelley looks on *death*, and he writes—

> "Death is here, and death is there,
> Death is busy everywhere—
> All around, within, beneath,
> Above is death, and we are death.
>
> First our pleasures die, and then
> Our hopes, and then our fears, and when
> These are dead, the debt is due
> Dust claims dust, and we die too."

St. Paul directs toward this impenetrable mystery, the telescope of his faith, and he writes, "O death where is thy sting! O grave where is thy victory! The sting of death is sin, and the strength of sin is the law; but thanks be to God, who giveth us the victory through our Lord Jesus Christ."

THE MOTTO ON THE BRIDAL RING.

A young gentleman of fine intellect, and of a noble heart, was suddenly snatched by the hand of death from all the endearments of life. Surrounded by everything that could make existence pleasant and happy, a wife that idolized him, children that loved him only as they can love, and friends devoted to him, the summons came and he lay upon the bed of death. But a few short years ago, she to whom he was wedded placed a bridal ring upon his finger, upon the inside of which he had a few words privately engraven. The husband would never permit the giver to read them, telling her the day would come when her wish should be gratified, and she should know the secret. Seven years glided away, and, being taken ill and conscious that he must soon leave his wife for ever, he called her to his bedside, and with his dying accents told her that the hour had at last come when she should see the words upon the ring she had given him. The young mother took it from his cold finger, and though heart-stricken with grief, eagerly read the words—"*I have loved thee on earth, I will meet thee in heaven.*"

JOHN LOCKE AND THE SCRIPTURES.

Locke spent the last fourteen years of his life in the study of the Bible; and he wrote "The Common Place Book of the Scriptures," which is an invaluable fruit of his Scripture studies. These facts of themselves give the strongest proof of the high estimation in which this profound thinker and acute metaphysician held the Christian writings. He admired the wisdom and goodness of God in the method of salvation they reveal; and, it is said, that when he thought upon it, he could not forbear crying out, "O the depth of the riches both of the goodness and the knowledge of God!"

He was persuaded that men would be convinced of this by reading the Scriptures without prejudice; and he frequently exhorted those with whom he conversed, to a serious study of these sacred writings. A relative inquired of him what was the shortest and surest way for a young gentleman to attain a true knowledge of the Christian religion "Let him study," said the philosopher, "the Holy Scriptures, especially in the New Testament. Therein are contained the words of eternal life. It has God for its author, Salvation for its end, and Truth without any mixture of error for its matter."

HOWE'S TURN.

During the days of the Commonwealth, the Rev. John Howe, one of Cromwell's Chaplains, was frequently applied to by men of all parties for protection, nor did he refuse his influence to any on account of difference in religious opinions. One day the Protector said to him; "Mr. Howe, you have asked favors for everybody besides yourself, pray when does *your* turn come?" He replied, "My turn, my Lord Protector, is always come, when I can serve another."

POETRY.

There was once, says an old German legend, a hero named Wolker, who had given to him a wonderful sword, with which in the midst of the battle he struck music out of the helmets of his enemies.

All day we strove, our foes were strong,
  Our swords flashed sunset's fiery light,
And wearied coursers bore along
  Our warriors eager still for fight.

With every knightly blade that fell
  On knightly crest, strange sounds arose,
And oft that crash rang out the knell
  Of heroes doomed to death's repose.

The wildest discord reigned o'er all,—
  Glad trumpet notes pealed up the sky,
Mocking the cries of those, whose fall
  Called forth the shouts of victory.

*   *   *

Our army's leader stood apart,
  He watched his friends hard pressed below;
Calm was his look, but his great heart
  Bursting to save us from our foe.

His hand grasped firm that wondrous sword,
  Tempered in heaven's own armoury;
At once his servant, and his lord,
  A certain guide to victory.

The blade flashed fire—that well-known sign—
  He raised his eyes to Him on high,
Then gladly rode into the line
  Whence loudest came defeat's wild cry.

We saw him come, our hearts beat fast,
  We nerved our arms for stronger blows;—
When suddenly all tumult ceased,
  And every champion paused in haste,
    For strains of heavenly music rose,
    From out that din of fighting foes,
    Like that which from God's presence flows,
    Music that never a discord knows,
Ne'er heard before on earth's sad waste.

It comes, it goes, peals loud, then dies,
  Its birth-place is our battle field;
Thence to God's heaven it seems to rise—
  Strange offering for a strife to yield.

Our captain 'twas, whose wondrous sword
  Rang harmony from every stroke,
No death-groans more, no cries were heard,
  War's tumult into music broke.

Thus closed our fight, and Victory came,
  And twined her wreaths around his crest;
And foes joined friends in one acclaim,
  To him with bloodless conquest blest.

Such are God's champions in the strife,
  Such *all*, for him who strike the blow;
E'en from the battle-field of life,
  Can *men of faith* make music flow.

Sept. 1858.   FIDES.

MISSIONS.

The following account of the Island of CEYLON was delivered as a Missionary Lecture, at Collins-street Chapel, Melbourne, by the Rev. A. Morison, on Friday evening, August. 27, 1858.

The Island of Ceylon is one of the most beautiful countries of the world. Situated between 5 deg. 54 min. and 9 deg. 50. min. north latitude, and between 79 deg. 50 min. and 82 deg. 10 min. east longitude, it lies to the south-east of peninsular India, but is almost connected with the main land by a long promontory projecting from the Carnatic shore, two small islands on either coast, and a succession of sand banks between them, which are called Adam's Bridge; its northern portion narrowing, it assumes an egg, or rather a ham-like shape. Towards the central and southern parts, the land rises in terraces of hills and mountains, which attain an elevation of between 6,000 and 8,000 feet above the level of the sea; the general level of the plateau, however, ranges between 2,000 and 3,000 feet. These mountains are covered by magnificent forests, and intersected with ravines, cataracts, and rivers. The climate, owing to the elevation of the lands, and the prevalence of sea breezes, is much cooler than that of continental India. A singular result arises from the configuration of the island, and the prevalence of the north-east and south-west monsoons, at different periods of the year, on the eastern and western slopes of the mountains. When the westerly winds blow, it rains on the western side of the island, then the inhabitants till their ground, while, at the same time it is harvest season on the eastern side. On the contrary, when the eastern wind blows, the eastern people till their land, while the western folks gather their harvest, so that all the year round there is, in one or other part, a harvest ingathering of the fruits of the earth.

The country produces every kind of fruit that is known in India. There is one kind called jombo, not seen elsewhere, in taste like an apple, juicy and pleasant, but unwholesome, white in color, delicately tinted with red. The cinnamon is almost peculiar to this island, or at least here chiefly is the place where it is produced.

Among the curious vegetable productions is also the tallipot tree. This is described as being big and tall as a ship's mast, and very straight, bearing only leaves, which are of great benefit to the people, a single leaf being so broad and large as to cover some fifteen or twenty men, and keep them dry when it rains. The leaf being dried is very strong and limber, folds like a lady's fan, and is not bulkier than a man's arm. Being very light, the people carry pieces of a triangular shape in their hands, or on their heads, as a shade from the sun. The soldiers also make tents of them on march. The cocoanut tree is one of the great treasures of the country. Its yield of flower and fruit, of sap, which may be made into spirit, vinegar, and sugar, of material for thatching houses, for brooms, and torches—of nuts with milky juice, and the kernel yielding oil, and husks as food for pigs and poultry; besides various other purposes to which the shells and stem of this tree are applied, make it indeed a treasure.

The palmyra tree flourishes in great perfection, is equally profitable as the cocoanut, and is celebrated in a native poem as having an hundred and eight different uses to which it may be applied.

The kettule tree yields a liquor, which is exceedingly pleasant and wholesome, not stronger than water. Its juice is obtained twice and even thrice a day, in amount three or four gallons; and, when boiled, produces a sugar called jaggory.

There is also a sacred tree called Bogauhah or the God tree—large and spreading, and the foliage sensitive, like the aspen. As Buddha was accustomed to rest under these trees, they have been consecrated to his worship. The Cingalese pave around them, set up their images, with table for sacrifices, and lamps beneath the shade; they plant them everywhere, in towns and highways, as it is considered meritorious to do so,—but only the oldest men plant them, as, they say, he that does so shall die in a short time and go to heaven.

The riches of the vegetable kingdom, in tree, shrub, and flowering herb, are so great that the delicious scent is experienced by those approaching the shores, and justifies the beautiful lines of Bishop Heber—

> " What, though the spicy breezes
> Blow soft on Ceylon's isle;
> Though every prospect pleases,
> And only man is vile."

And from the combination of such varied beauty of scenery, amazing fertility in production of fruits, gorgeousness and fragrance of flowers, all that is charming to sight and sense, we cannot wonder that native historians have claimed this as the traditional site of the Garden of Eden; nor be surprised that their highest mountain is named Adam's peak, on whose top and adown whose side the footsteps of the expelled progenitors of the human family may be traced; and that the sand banks connecting the island with the main land, should be named Adam's Bridge, along which the unhappy fugitives passed, when

> " Some natural tears they dropt, but wip'd them soon;
> The world was all before them, where to choose
> Their place of rest, and Providence their guide;
> They hand in hand, with wandering steps, and slow
> Through Eden took their solitary way."

The pearl fishery deserves a notice as among other things which render this island a place of interest. At the appointed period for the fishery the boats assemble, each having several divers, who go into the water by turns, plunging three, four, or five fathoms deep. They are tied to a rope fastened at the stern of the boat, a stone is tied to the feet, and a bag to the waist of the diver to collect the oysters, which he gathers quickly into the bag, or collects in a heap, and returns to take breath, and dives again, or a companion takes a spell. The oysters collected are left a few days to open, and then the pearls are washed through different kinds of sieves. The fishery, however, is, through the confluence of the people, and the stench of the corrupting oysters, a source of desolating disease. Mrs. Heman's poem, " The Diver," borrows all its pathos and beauty from this fishery.

> " Thou hast been, where the rocks of coral grew,
>   Thou hast fought with eddying waves ;
>   Thy cheek is pale, and thy heart beats low,
>   Thou searcher of ocean's caves.
>
> " Thou hast looked on the gleaming wealth of old,
>   And wrecks where the brave have striven ;
>   The deep is a strong and fearful hold,
>   But thou its bar hast riven.
>
> " A wild and weary life is thine—
>   A wasting task and lone,
>   Though treasure-grots for thee may shine
>   To all besides unknown.
>
> " A weary life ! but a swift decay
>   Soon, soon shall set thee free,
>   Thou'rt passing fast from thy toils away,
>   Thou wrestler with the sea.
>
> " In thy dim eye, on thy hollow cheek,
>   Well are the death-signs read :
>   Go ! for the pearl in its cavern seek,
>   Ere hope and power be fled !"

*   *   *   *   *   *   *

Among animals, Ceylon is famous for its breed of elephants. King of beasts the lion is said to be, but any one who has seen a wild elephant will own his right to this title. Lord of all beasts in sagacity and power, he roams his native forests, browses on the lofty branches, upturns young trees from sheer malice, and from plain to forest stalks majestically, monarch of all he surveys. "There are," says one, "no animals more misunderstood than elephants ; they are naturally savage, wary, and revengeful, displaying as great courage when in their wild state as any animal known. It is recorded that in the time of the Native Rule of the Island, these animals were trained to execute criminals, and were taught to prolong the agony of the wretched sufferers by crushing the limbs, avoiding the vital parts. In 1850 one such was put through the pantomime of this work. The Chief gave the word of command, ' Slay the wretch.' The elephant raised his trunk and twined it, as if around a human being, he then made motions, as if he was depositing the man on the earth before him, then slowly raised his forefoot, placing it alternately on the spots where the man's limbs would have been, then, as if satisfied that all these bones were crushed, he raised his trunk high above his head. The Chief then commanded him to ' complete his work,' when he placed one foot as if on the abdomen, and the other on the head, with all his strength, as if to terminate the misery of the criminal."

The chief cities are Trincomalee on the eastern coast, Colombo on the western, and Candy, the native metropolis of the country, situated towards the central part of the island. Colombo is at present the capital. A night scene at this place beautifully describes another part of the natural phenomena. " When night throws her sable mantle over the earth, myriads of fire-flies hover over the lake, clouds of them flitting about in the air, then alighting on the waving leaves of the palms, causing the foliage to appear illuminated. Some few will settle on the floating leaves of the lotus, two or three will creep into the flower, sparkling like brilliants, then more of these luminous insects will alight on other aquatic plants, and the waters will glisten with a million minute specks of light. Many will settle, possibly, on a tall banana, the outline of the gigantic graceful leaves being distinctly defined by the dazzling specks of fire upon them. Nothing can be imagined more exquisitely lovely than this varied natural panorama ; and, although in the mountainous parts of the island, the face of nature may assume a sublimer aspect, never does she wear a more pleasing and truly oriental one than in the vicinity of Colombo."

The Cingalese are described as an intelligent people, but crafty and deceitful ; courteous in discourse, but full of flatteries; temperate, but not chaste; extremely slothful and apathetic; and, like the Cretans of old, "liars all." The men wear a cloth about their loins, a coat buttoning at the waist and gathered round the throat like a shirt. The female's habit is a waistcoat of white calico, and a skirt ornamented with blue or red fringes, jewels in their ears, and ornaments about their necks, arms, and waists.

Another class are the *supposed* descendants of the ancient or aboriginal inhabitants of the country who had been subjected and enslaved by the Cingalese. These are called Veddahs. Mr. Walker, an elephant hunter, gives the following account of the Veddahs :—" I have frequently read absurd descriptions of their manners and customs, which must have been gathered from hearsay and not from a knowledge of the people. It is a commonly believed report that the Veddahs live in the trees, and a stranger immediately confuses them with rooks and monkeys. Whoever first saw Veddahs' huts in the trees, would have discovered on inquiry that they were temporary watch-houses, from which they guard a little plot of koorakan from the attacks of elephants and other wild beasts. Far from *living* in trees—they live nowhere, wander over the face of their beautiful country, and emigrate to different parts at diff+rent seasons, with the game which they are always pursuing. The seasons in Ceylon vary in an extraordinary manner considering the small size of the island. The wet season in one district is the dry one in another, and *vice versa*. Wherever the dry weather prevails the pasturage is dried up, the brooks and pools are mere sand gullies and pits. The Veddah watches at some solitary hole which still contains a little water, and to this the deer and every species of game resort. Here his broadheaded arrow finds a supply. He dries the meat in long strips in the sun, and cleaning out some hollow tree, he packs away his savoury mess of sun-cooked flesh, and fills up the reservoir with wild honey, he then stops up the aperture with clay. The last drop of water evaporates, the deer leaves the country and migrates into other parts where the mountains attract the rain, and other pasturage is abundant. The Veddah burns the parched grass wherever he passes, and the country is soon a blackened surface, not a blade of pasture remains, but this secures a sweet supply when the rains commence, to which the game and the Veddahs will return. Meantime he follows to other districts, living in caves, where they happen to abound, or making a temporary hut with grass and sticks. Every deer-path, rock, pool, and peculiar feature of the country is known to those hunting Veddahs.

" The Veddah is in person extremely ugly, short, but sinewy, his long uncombed locks fall to his waist, looking more like a horse's tail than human hair. He despises money, but is thankful for a hatchet, or gaudy colored cloth, or brass pot for cooking. The females are horribly ugly, and are almost entirely naked. They have no matrimonial regulations, and the children are squalid and miserable. Speaking a language of their own, with habits akin to those of wild animals, they keep entirely apart from the Cingalese. They barter deer's horns and bees' wax with the travelling moor-men pedlars in exchange for their trifling requirements. If they have food they eat it, if they have none they go without. They chew the bark of trees and search for berries, while they wend their way for many miles to some remembered store of deer's flesh and honey, laid by in a hollow tree."

(To be Continued)

MORAVIAN MISSION TO THE ABORIGINES.

166, Collins-street, East, Melbourne.

Our Mission Board being much grieved at the breaking up of the Mission at Lake Boga, resolved to resume their labors in that portion of the Lord's vineyard, if again a door of entrance should be opened for them, and did therefore only consider the Mission as temporarily suspended. This opportunity was given to them, when, after negotiating with the Government here, permission was given to them to renew their labors, in consequence of which they appointed me and Mr. F. A. Hagenauer to be sent for the purpose of renewing the Mission. We left London on the 15th February last, and after a favorable voyage, arrived here on the 14th May. We have been kindly received by His Excellency and several other friends, which was, indeed, a cause of thankfulness to us. On the 15th of June, we undertook, with the permission of the Government, an exploratory journey in the Wimmera District, to look out for an eligible spot for a mission station (for the Government considered it better not to go back to the old place), and we found such a one near the station of Mr. Ellerman, called Antwerp, on the banks of the Wimmera River, about twelve miles this side of Lake Hindmarsh; and we have, since our return from that journey on the 13th of July, sent an application to the Government requesting permission to occupy that place, with a view to preach the Gospel to the aborigines. We are now waiting for a reply. I beg to add that we earnestly desire the prayers of the Lord's people.

F. W. SPIESCKE,
Moravian Missionary.

Rev. Mr. Fletcher.

CORRESPONDENCE.

REVIVALS.

To the Editor of the Southern Spectator.

DEAR SIR,—After reading the very interesting accounts given in your last number of the Revivals going on in America, every reflective mind must, I think, be struck with several facts there related, which are well worthy the serious consideration of every Christian.

The writer there alluded to appears to have given a candid and unbiassed opinion, and one, too, that must convince the most sceptical that the present movement has not arisen from any undue excitement, or from any external effort made to produce it. But the rise, the progress, the result appear to be solely attributable to the ever wonder-working power of God, by his Spirit, upon the hearts of men. And I could not but think that some as yet hidden and to us unknown cause, has been the originator of this wonderful manifestation of God's power.

And yet, sir, why should it appear so wonderful when we remember the many promises given in reference to earnest, persevering, believing prayer? Could we trace its origin (which will one day be revealed to the sight of an assembled world), who can tell but that our steps would be guided, not to the marble halls, not to the scenes of gaiety and pleasure of that far-famed city;—no, not even to the sacred edifice itself,—but to some humble abode, to an upper room, away from the turmoil of the crowded streets, where a few disciples have been in the habit of meeting for earnest prayer, on behalf of the church, their fellow-men, and their country at large.

Alarm at the profanity exhibited, the headlong rashness to get rich at the sacrifice of every feeling of honor and justice, and the manifest disregard to the law of God—yes, and the supineness of the church too—has awakened, doubtless, in the breasts of a few disciples (it may be humble and unknown) a love for souls, and an earnest desire that God would interpose to save his people, and to save their country. This has led them to their closet and their knees, and with bitterness of spirit, and earnestness of purpose, and confiding trust, they have again and again besought their Father in Heaven to "Arise, and have mercy upon Zion," and manifest his power in the conversion of souls. Or it may be that some Sabbath school teachers, or tract distributors, in some secluded spots, have united for the same purpose, and the fervent believing prayer of these few righteous ones has availed much—God has heard, and is now making bare his arm, in reply. The church first takes the alarm, and begins in earnest to pray. The little leaven is beginning to leaven the whole lump, and bye and bye crowds are attracted within her walls; the sacred influence spreads—the Spirit is at work—the prodigal is reclaimed—the hardened sinner melted to penitence—the blasphemer led to pray—and all with one accord hasten to the foot of the Cross to be washed and made clean. Surely this is the Lord's doing, and it is marvellous in our eyes.

Such, I take it, has been the source, "prayer;" and now the blessing has come, how hard it is to believe it genuine. By some it is regarded as fanaticism; by others, yes, by professing Christians too, it is regarded with suspicion and doubt. But, what better evidence have we than its results? This, we are told, is the silent weeping of the contrite, the solemnity that prevails in the sanctuary, the deep the suppressed emotion of those convinced of sin, the silent but earnest petition for pardon presented to the throne of grace, and the turning unto God of so many who previously had been living without God and hope in the world. Well may we exclaim, "What hath God wrought!" Now, sir, if such blessings as these are the result of prayer, ought we not "go and do likewise?" Why should not we have such manifestations of the power of God? Surely we need it; and we know full well that the God of America is the God of Australia too: "That hand is not shortened that it cannot save; neither is that ear heavy that it cannot hear." Would that the Christians of Victoria were of one mind in reference to this; and, laying aside all peculiarities of views and opinions, with one consent would unite for this special purpose, that God would prosper his work here, and make this land, interesting as it is on account of its resources and productions, as a "land which the Lord hath blessed," and where righteousness shall be the characteristic of its people. Let ministers ponder the subject well—let private Christians be aroused to their duty—and let one and all who feel their responsibility, and who have professed their allegiance to the Saviour, unite in earnest supplications for this blessing; and then why should we not expect that "the windows of heaven would be opened," and such blessings descend as would fill all hearts with gratitude and praise? "Ask, and ye shall receive; seek and ye shall find."

J. V.

FAMILY WORSHIP.

To the Editor of the Southern Spectator.

SIR,—May I beg the favor of the admission of these few remarks in you valuable publication, on a subject which I think all serious and right-minded persons will admit to be of great importance, I mean that of family worship. I have been induced to address you on this subject, in consequence of my acquaintance with many families who regularly attend the house of God, and are zealous members of the Church of Christ, but who, notwithstanding, omit this most important duty altogether. Others attend to it occasionally, as when a minister of religion is staying at their house; then the bible is brought out, and the evening sacrifice is offered. I ask, is it necessary that the head of a family should have a minister to perform for him a duty which devolves upon himself as the minister of his own house? Others attend to it when everything is smooth and convenient, but take no trouble to make things so. Is it not solemn mockery to act thus? is it not our duty to acknowledge God's goodness and providence, and to seek his blessing every day of our lives? and should not every professing Christian who is head of a family feel that domestic worship is daily incumbent upon him, and that nothing should be permitted to stand in the way of its performance, for the sake of the salvation both of himself and of those near and dear to him, who are entrusted to his care?

One head of a family, a professing Christian, lives in the neglect of family worship, and when asked the reason, replies that his friends W. and T. are in the habit of stepping in to supper occasionally, and as the one belongs to a different sect, and the other to no sect at all, it would be disagreeable to them and inconvenient, and therefore he omits it. It is deeply to be regretted that this class of timid Christians, who fear the face of man, are ashamed of their religion and hide their light from view, are so numerous. If they would have a good conscience, and give in their account to their Lord with joy, let them take warning in time, and not put off till it is too late to please God rather than their fellow-creatures, and to let their light shine before men to glorify their Father who is in heaven.

Another pleads inability to conduct worship before others, even his own family. He views it as an arduous and difficult task. The difficulty is magnified: a little use would convert the exercise into a pleasurable and profitable duty: a little moral courage, a beginning once fairly made, perseverance, and trust in God, would overcome all impediments. The service should consist of the whole or a portion of a suitable chapter of holy scripture, and the offering of a concise, fervent prayer, acknowledging God's mercies, and praying for a continuance of the same. By doing this, a deeper sense of dependence on God, and more gratitude for his mercies would be felt, devout feelings and holy principles would be cherished, a good example to the younger branches of the family would be set, and the blessing of God might be reasonably expected. That these few remarks may be useful in producing some of these benefits is the humble wish of yours very truly,

T.

North Melbourne, September 12, 1858.

SOCIAL STATE OF THE GOLD FIELDS.
To the Editor of the Southern Spectator.

SIR,—I wish to lay before you a few thoughts on the general state of society here. Society I say, but the common complaint is that there is no society; that we are all a chaotic mass of thinking and working human atoms, pursuing our individual course in a neck-and-neck race of selfish ambition. "Nobody knows who anybody is" is a common saying here, and many are the regrets uttered over the loss of the happy friendships of the old country. We are assuredly in a strange state, but by no means so bad as many suppose. Society has yet to be evolved out of the confusion; but an observant man can see that the work of its formation has commenced already; and from what he knows of the laws of human civilization, he can calmly calculate the result of present circumstances, and find much interest in awaiting its arrival and watching its progress.

Just now, population is in a transition stage. The worst features of the social state are seen no more, but still there is much that opposes the progress of brotherly feeling. The people are not mere units, who live an isolated life through ignorance of each other, but are actually entertaining lurking suspicions of their neighbours. All, in coming hither, have disconnected themselves from old ties of friendship; but there are some who are endeavoring to regain a position which they have deservedly lost where known. This ignorance of one another, with the natural fear of an unknown acquaintance turning out an unworthy companion, breaks up the vast mass of human beings in Sandhurst into circles almost as numerous as are the houses and tents they dwell in. The good suffer along with the bad. Those who might be friends are not so, just because they do not know each other. It is not necessary that people should have "mixed in good society" to make them speak of England as the land of social feeling. Every tent can tell its tale of severed friendships, and the happy circle of old acquaintances. In a community like that of Britain every man seems in his position; here all are in the condition of the players at the nursery game of "turn the trencher," that is, rushing frantically and uncertainly in search of a place that will suit them; but, as in that interesting sport the laugh and the rush are generally succeeded by order and quiet, so in our large game, the eye of the prophet sees that a day of harmony will yet come.

Some of your readers may perhaps here find the philosophy of the Australian fondness for *tea-meetings.* They are a substitute for something lost, an opportunity for partially satisfying the the cravings of sociality, without being too intimate with those they don't care for. The eagerness with which "tea-parties" and "soirées" are attended is quite a singular feature in these rough gullies. They are always full, and generally inconveniently so; and though not very brilliant oratory may always be the order of the evening, yet happy looking faces indicate an enjoyment of some sort experienced, and one which will make all present seek it again the next time a placard announces a similar gathering.

The tendency of all religious and philanthrophic movements is in the same direction. They bring forth more or less of brotherly feeling; they unite men in the healthiest of all unions, the co-working to do good. Hospital committees, ladies' working parties, temperance societies, church building committees, all assist in breaking away the crust of individualism. The turbulent life of our populous gold field is not unlike the agitation of the atoms of some chemical mixture, which no amount of stirring can cause to coalesce; it requires the galvanic spark of true religious and moral feeling to strike through the mass, and then all is changed. Rough and imperfect mechanical admixture gives place to chemical union; and new compounds, clear of all turbulency, and of varied and beautiful color, are the happy result.

It will take many, many years before there is in these Australian settlements a really local feeling. The present generation will have to pass away, and perhaps their successors too, before the slowly opening flower of social life shall have attained its full bloom. The staple of the population must be those who have spent all their days on the spot, and then the presence of strangers and new arrivals will not interfere with its natural development.

Now, the whole adult population is an aggregate of foreigners, who dwell fondly on other scenes, and are but as sojourners and pilgrims while here. What, however, this land will become—what its people, what influence its national opinion will have in the world—who can tell?

Somewhat in this strain, Mr. Editor, my thoughts were running when, going out into the streets, and ascending the hill where the English church stands, I stood upon the foundations of the tower that is to be, and looked round upon the scene. The world presents some strange pictures, and one might think that the variety of its effects was pretty well exhausted before now, but certainly the view of an Australian gold-field is something new. It is not a camp; it is too irregular for that; and the sounds that break the stillness are the monotonous hammerings of crushing machines, not the sounds of war. It is not a manufacturing town; for smoke is unseen in the translucent atmosphere. It is far from presenting the pretty picture of an European village, embowered in orchards and corn fields; for, far as the eye can reach are straggling tents set in a sandy wilderness; of fields, there are none, and cultivation is almost unknown. I stood looking on all as it lay bathed in the pale beams of a crescent moon. Hundreds of lights were sprinkled below, and the hum of the busy valley hovered over the scene;—I thought of the many isolated stories that could be told of the dwellers in those tents, how little they would have in common—how, if we knew all about what they had done, nearly the whole world would be laid bare. How different this from an English hamlet! There, the history of one would be the history of all, and if we were acquainted with the secrets of all, our knowledge would not take us beyond their ramparts of orchards and fruit gardens. How charming is the presence of memory in moments like these. She came as a companion, speaking peace in the wild tumult of Australian life, and, as if evoked by her spells, at that moment there came floating up the hill the sound of a chorus of voices singing "Home

sweet home." It rose and fell with the wind. which was blowing gently, and sounded to me rather like the consolation of that kind enchantress, Hope, than the regrets of memory over the past. It came as the irresistible appeal from some unseen but present spirit to be up and doing, that so our land may in time to come be worthy of those much loved homes we have left in Britain.   FIDES.

Sandhurst, September, 1858.

CONGREGATIONALISTS OR INDEPENDENTS.

(From slips of *Fairfax and Co's Handbook to Australasia*, now in the Press.)

THESE two designations are indifferently applied to the same body of Christians. The former term refers to the congregation or church of the faithful, who voluntarily organise themselves into a religious society, and the latter to the independence of authority and control from without, which every such society claims. The Congregationalists recognise no power to govern or dictate in Diocesan Bishop, Presbytery, or Conference. Though regarding the Scriptures as the only rule of faith, and subscribing no confessions or creeds, the doctrines held and preached by them accord generally with those found in the standards of the Established Churches of England and Scotland. The Independents and Baptists are identical in every respect in their sentiments and usages, except on the point of baptism, the former practising pædo-baptism, the latter confining themselves to the baptism of adults. The Congregationalists sprung out of the Puritan movement of the 16th and 17th centuries. were nearly stationary throughout the 18th, but have made rapid progress during the present century, having, probably, quadrupled their numbers since 1790.

The commencement of Congregationalism in Victoria dates as far back as 1837, and was owing to the zeal of Henry Hopkins, Esq., of Hobart Town, who, on visiting Port Phillip, and seeing the opening a young colony presented for useful labor, wrote to the Congregational Colonial Missionary Society in England to send out a minister for the new settlement of Melbourne. The Rev. W. Waterfield accordingly came in the year 1838. Worship was for a time carried on in a temporary place, but on September 8, 1838, the foundation stone of the first permanent building in Victoria for ecclesiastical purposes, was laid on the Eastern Hill, Collins-street, then untouched bush; and the church was opened for public use on January 1st, 1841. The Hon. J. P. Fawkner, M.L.C., one of the founders of the colony, took an active part in these proceedings. In March, 1848, Mr. Waterfield removed to Van Diemen's Land, where he still labors at Green Ponds, and was succeeded in the course of the same year by the Rev. Alexander Morison, who was sent over by the Home Missionary Society of that colony, and who still continues to be the pastor of this parent church.

The want of a second church in the west end of the city having in the course of time been felt, some preliminary steps were taken, and in 1850, when the Rev T. Odell arrived, a church was formed, of which he became the pastor. Ultimately, the excellent Gothic chapel in Lonsdale-street, in which he now officiates, was erected. The arrival, in 1853, of the Rev. W. B. Landells, who left England on account of his health, led to the formation of a third church, at Collingwood, and the building of a handsome Grecian chapel in Oxford-street. As openings presented themselves, and as ministers arrived, initial steps were taken to organize congregations in various localities, and by 1853 churches were formed and ministers settled at Prahran, Richmond, Brighton, St. Kilda, Geelong, and Kyneton. Most of these were small at first, using temporary places of worship. The Colonial Missionary Society in England deeming it desirable, from the great influx of population arising from the gold discovery, to furnish an additional supply of ministers for Victoria, sent out the Revds. R. Fletcher, J. L. Poore, and E. Day, who arrived in March, 1854, and in the course of a year or two after, there arrived, under the auspices of the same society, the Revds. H. Thomas, B.A., G. Morrison, M.A., and W. R. Fletcher, M.A. The Revds. W. B. Curzens, J. Apperley, and A. Scales, of Geelong, and the Rev. J. P. Sunderland, of Richmond, and others, had also come to the colony, and settled over churches. Immediately on the arrival of Messrs. Fletcher and Poore, a Home Missionary Society was formed to further the work of evangelization, and a large sum of money was subscribed,—but the commercial crisis which followed soon after brought it to a close in about two years. A second society was established in January, 1857, and is now in active operation. A fund was raised for bringing out additional ministers for this and the neighbouring colonies, which amounted to near £2,400, of which £1,200 was furnished by Victoria, and Mr. Poore was sent to England to endeavour to augment this fund by subscriptions, and to look out for and send men suitable for the work. The result of this effort has been the arrival in Australia of sixteen ministers, eight of whom were destined for Victoria, and more are shortly expected. Two of the sixteen have been cut off by death.

The statistics of the body, as nearly as can be ascertained, are at present as follow:—About 27 congregations worshipping every Sabbath; 21 churches regularly formed, the remaining six being recently gathered and not yet fully organized. Of the 27 places of worship, about 13 are permanent structures, i.e. built of brick or stone, and 14 are temporary, built of wood or iron. There are about 23 ministers settled over congregations, whose names will be seen in *Bradshaw's Monthly Guide to Victoria*, and 5 or 6 without pastoral charges. In several cases a manse is provided for the minister's use. The number of persons who appear in the census as Independents is comparatively small; but this arises from their having no territorial distribution in England, and from the fact that few persons give in their names as Independents who are not actually attendants at some of their places of worship; whereas great numbers of Englishmen, Scotchmen, and Irishmen record themselves as Episcopalians, Presbyterians, and Roman Catholics, though living in habitual neglect of all religious ordinances.

The Congregationalists decline receiving State grants in aid of religion. The only exception is the acceptance, in the early times of the colony, of two sites of land for churches, one in Melbourne and the other in Geelong.

Though the fundamental principle of Congregationalism does not admit the authoritative control of any synod over the several churches, yet it allows and encourages unions for consultation. A Congregational Union for Victoria was formed, the last meeting of which was held in May, 1856. This has been succeeded by another, which was established in October, 1857, and of which the Rev. W. B. Landells is chairman for the present year.

Free Conferences of ministers and laymen, delegated from the unions of the four colonies of Australia, have been held; the first in Melbourne, in February, 1855; the second in Sydney, in February, 1857; and the last in Hobart Town, in February, 1858, when various resolutions were passed affecting the interests of the denomination at large. Under the auspices of these conferences a monthly periodical for the use of the four colonies has been established, the *Southern Spectator*, edited by the Rev. R. Fletcher, of St. Kilda. An organization was formed for providing education for ministerial candidates, but only one or two students have as yet presented themselves.

A Victorian Congregational Home Missionary Society is established. Its funds are raised by collections and subscriptions, and are applied to the bringing out of ministers, and to their partial support till their congregations are enabled wholly to sustain them. Nearly all the ministers now in the colony are sustained by their people without such aid. The assistance of the Colonial Missionary Society in England is chiefly confined to measures for furnishing a continued supply of ministers to the colony.

The Denomination cannot show imposing figures in relation to day-school education. They have but few schools in connexion with the Denominational Board as they have not generally supported that system, but for the most part have thrown in their influence to support the National Schools. A Sunday School is attached to nearly every chapel.

RELIGIOUS INTELLIGENCE.

SOUTH AUSTRALIA.—THE REV. THOS. BINNEY—This gentleman is still in South Australia. By letters just received we learn that he has visited most of the settled parts of the country, and has preached at all, or nearly all, the places he has visited. He has preached several times for the different Independent ministers in Adelaide, the Port, and the suburbs, at Hindmarsh, Salisbury, Gawler Town, Angaston, Kapunda, Higher-combe, &c. On Thursday, September 16th, Mr. Binney preached a sermon on behalf of the Bible Society in the large Metho ist Chapel in Adelaide, on which occasion there was an immense crowd of people. The Governor, his lady, the Dean, and other leading persons were present. Mr. Binney was engaged to lecture on Friday, 24th September, in the large public room, for some general object, on a literary topic; and after that to pay a visit to Encounter Bay, and preach there. On his return to Adelaide, he would again officiate there; and on Monday evening, October 4th, he would deliver another public lecture, the Governor having engaged to take the chair. He has excited great attention and drawn large audiences wherever he has gone. He is expected to return to Melbourne about the middle or latter end of the present month.

TASMANIA.—LAUNCESTON.—*Prospect Village.*—The first anniversary of the chapel in the above village was held on April 2nd last. Nearly 200 persons were present. After luncheon, which was provided by the friends, a public meeting was held in the open air. The Hon. W. S. Button, M.L.C., presided on the occasion. Addresses were delivered by the Rev. W. Law, Messrs. Powell, Connor and Sinclair. The proceeds were devoted to the chapel and school funds.

HOBART TOWN.—*Ragged School Association.*—The foundation-stone of the new school building off lower Collins-street, was laid by H. Hopkins, Esq , J.P., on Monday, August 23rd, in the presence of a numerous assemblage of all classes. There were present : Revs. Messrs. Clark, Nicholson, Downes, Gellibrand, Bennett and McLean; Messrs. Gray and Coggin, City Missionaries; His Worship the Mayor; Mr. Alderman Rheuben, Major Cotton, (the Inspector of Schools); Mr. Hone, Captain Chamberlain, Messrs. Hutton, G. W. Walker, W. Rout, Crouch, &c., &c., The children of the Watchorn-street, and lower Collins-street Ragged Schools were marched up to the site, under the guidance of Mr. Gray the Superintendent, Mr. James Salier Secretary, Mrs. James Salier Secretary to the Ladies Committee, and the teachers. The proceedings were commenced by the singing of the hymn,

"Here we suffer grief and pain, &c."

The Rev. W. Nicholson then offered prayer. Mr. Hopkins next proceeded to lay the stone with the usual ceremonies. Various articles were deposited in the stone with a parchment containing the following inscription:—"This edifice is reared for the education of poor children, whose parents or guardians may be unable to secure for them the advantages of regular instruction. The cost of the building will in part be defrayed by a grant from the Colonial Treasury, and in part by the voluntary contributions of the citizens of Hobart Town." Mr. Hopkins then mounted the stone and spoke as follows:—My friends, this stone is laid of a building to be devoted to the instruction of the rising generation who are destitute, whose parents have left their children to the public, and in the desire that the children should be trained up in the fear of God, to be useful members of society. It is to be lamented that there are children left to wander about in idleness in their early days, instead of being brought up to be industrious members of society, rather than injurious members of society. I see a number of young faces around me, who have been long under instruction, who have learnt their lessons in Scripture and their beautiful hymns. I hope they will have the love of God in their hearts, and that they will pray to God to be the guide of their youth, and that he may guide them in all their ways. Mr. Hopkins spoke of the cause of education in the colony for the last thirty years, and the efforts made in bygone days by visiting from house to house to induce persons to attend the preaching of the gospel. One case in particular was worthy of notice, that of a person who had had a family of twelve children, nine of whom, sons living, had been trained in the fear of God, and had become useful members of society; had it not been for the instructions they had received in their early days, they would not have been what they were now.   He would venture to look forward thirty years, and he hoped in that time every child would be taught the fear of God; and he doubted not that near where this foundation was, they would have a church, and that many would be found attending divine service.   Mr Hopkins addressing the working men present, told them that if they wished to be happy they must come to the house of God, for there was no peace or happiness without the fear of God.   He (Mr. Hopkins) was seventy-one years old, and he had found that " The ways of religion are ways of pleasantness, and all her paths are peace."   God had blessed him and he acknowledged his gifts, and he assured them all if they wished to be truly happy, they must live in the fear of God, and they would have happiness in this world, and happiness in the world to come.   They must all die; but they could not expect to die happily unless they repented of sin and turned to God; and they must not look to a death-bed for repentance; there were only two places to which they could go, heaven or hell; and he wanted them all to love God while they had health and strength.   That was the only way to be truly happy—to live in the fear of God; but it was to be lamented that so few attended the house of God.   Mr. Hopkins, in conclusion, addressed the children, telling them the same truth, that real happiness consisted only in the fear of God.   He exhorted them to remember their Creator in the days of their youth; to go to the Lord Jesus Christ, who said, " Suffer little children to come unto me, and forbid them not, for of such is the Kingdom of Heaven."   Let them come to Jesus Christ, who would save them from their sins.   He wished the blessing of God to attend them all (cheers).   The children then sang "God save the Queen," in which some of the adults joined.   The children then cheered right and left, giving three cheers for the Governor, three for Mr. Hopkins, also for the Ladies' Committee, Mrs Wooley, Mrs. Salier, the builders, the school itself, &c.   They were afterwards regaled with milk, buns, and fruit.   A public tea meeting was held at the same place in the evening, the chair being taken by the Hon. W. Henty, Colonial Secretary, and after tea able addresses were delivered on the following subjects:—Rev. G. Clarke—The necessity for Ragged Schools.   Rev. J. Cope—Efficiency of Ragged Schools.   Rev. W. Nicholson—Claims of Ragged Schools to the sympathy and support of the community.   Mr. E. E. Dear—Ragged Schools in relation to crime.   Mr. R. G. Gray—Some account of the Hobart Town Ragged Schools.   Several other gentlemen also addressed the meeting.

The following is an abstract of the address of the Rev. G. Clarke :—He said that he could imagine if they were to go to England, and mention their intention to promote Ragged Schools in Hobart Town, they would be very much startled; they would say. " Why we can understand the necessity for Ragged Schools in our own country, but Ragged Schools in a new country! a country only fifty years old, where honest and diligent industry is sure to meet with its reward!   That is indeed startling!"   And speaking of the necessity for Ragged Schools in a new colony demands therefore some explanation he would say, in reply, that there were two things which must be borne in mind; not only should they think of its being a new country, but how the country had been formed; they should think of the elements which, from the system of transportation, had gone to make up a portion of the population.   Truly, though a large per centage had recovered as far as possible their original status, a large per centage still remained of men from whom they could expect nothing but iniquity.   It was a true principle that as we sow we shall reap; if we sow vice, we must reap the fruits of vice.   There was one element to be taken into consideration, and it went far to meet the objection.   But there was another point; whatever their different views as to the question of temperance, that is, whether the use of that which taken immoderately intoxicates, ought altogether to be laid aside, or whether it might properly be taken in moderation; no honest man could look around him in this city, and observe the vast disproportion of public houses, without coming to the conclusion that such a state of things is an evil.   Sir W. Denison, at Sydney, had stated that at least ninety per cent. of the crime in the colonies was to be traced directly or indirectly to the prevalence of drinking habits (hear, hear), similar assertions also were made by judges and magistrates here and in England; and when such extra-ordinary facilities were given for the consumption of intoxicating liquors, by the number of licensed public houses, how could they be surprised at the state of things now existing? If they walked down the main streets, strangers would remark that good order was kept; but they would observe every here and there gateways, entrances into scores of lanes and yards, where there were people cold, wretched and perishing.   Children were frequently left destitute in consequence of their parents' crime, and these considerations would suffice to show that such an institution as the Ragged School was necessary in the midst of this community.

VICTORIA.—SANDHURST.—A movement, which promises to be successful, has been made at this capital of the Bendigo gold-fields towards the erection of a Congregational Church.   Worship was conducted for a few months in the German church on Sabbath afternoons while the Rev. J. Summers was there; but on his removal to Daylesford it was discontinued.   In the month of April, the Rev. W. R. Fletcher, M.A. went out up by the Congregational Home Missionary Society of Victoria, to endeavour to establish a congregation and establish a cause. He was generously received by the Free Church, Presbyterian, and Wesleyan ministers, who invited him to preach in their pulpits, and permitted him to announce a meeting of such Independents as were willing to take part in the proposed undertaking. A meeting accordingly took place, a committee was formed, an old store was hired and temporarily fitted up, and worship was commenced. This place was occupied till it became unusable, when the Episcopal school-room was generously lent without charge. Here encouraging congregations assemble from Sabbath to Sabbath. An eligible piece of land for a new place has been purchased, on which there is a house which is at present let at a rent, and will ultimately answer for a parsonage, and ample space for the erection of a school and a church. A commencement has been made in building a neat structure, which in the first instance will serve for both preaching and Sunday-school purposes, it being intended to erect a larger church when required. The money for carrying on these measures has been raised partly by loans and partly by subscriptions, the friends in Sandhurst and also in Melbourne having contributed liberally. The current expenses are already met by the people themselves, without being dependent on the Home Missionary Society. The new place is expected to be ready in a short time.

BRIGHTON.—The new Independent Church at Brighton, which has been in the course of erection for the last few months, is now nearly completed, and will be opened for divine service in a week or two. It is placed in a favorable position, and will be a neat and commodious structure.

CAULFIELD, NEAR ST. KILDA.—Worship on Sunday afternoons has been held for a considerable time in a hired room in this township. An eligible piece of land, where population shows a tendency to gather, has been purchased for the erection of a chapel. As the individuals taking an interest in this movement are partly Independents and partly Baptists, it has been agreed by mutual consent to construct the trust deed on union principles.

SCHNAPPER POINT.—This township, lying on Port Phillip Bay, between Melbourne and the Heads, has already a population of 1500 people. Two gentlemen have offered suitable pieces of land for a chapel, for the joint use of Independents and Baptists. A meeting of friends connected with both these bodies has been held, and a resolution come to to accept one of these offers, and to proceed without delay to build a place suitable for the locality.

PORTLAND.— PORTLAND YOUNG MEN'S CHRISTIAN ASSOCIATION. — On Monday evening, August 30th, a preliminary meeting was held in the Presbyterian Church, Tyers-street, for adopting the best means for the establishment of a society, to be called "The Young Men's Christian Association." The Rev. James Sleigh was called to preside. After prayer by the Rev. W. Ridley, and remarks by the chairman, Mr. Cuthbertson explained the nature and objects of the proposed association. A discussion ensued, in which the Revs. G. B. Richards and W. Ridley, and Messrs. Mott, Hearn, and Cuthbertson engaged. It was resolved that a provisional committee, consisting of the following gentlemen, be appointed to make preparation for a public meeting to inaugurate the proposed society.— Messrs. Mott, Cuthbertson, Andrew, Sindall, Lowe, and Stevenson.

PORTLAND.—LECTURE BY THE REV. J. SLEIGH.— On Monday evening, July 26th, a lecture on "Old Countries and New Colonies" was delivered in the hall of the Mechanics' Institute by the Rev. J. Sleigh. He stated that the Divine will is that the human race be spread throughout the habitable globe. Their dispersion at Babel was adduced in proof. The allotted destinations of the sons of Noah, as recorded in Scripture, as transmitted by tradition, and as elucidated by modern research, were exhibited. The exodus and its important bearings were alluded to. Definitions of colony and colonists were given, and the various causes by which God promotes colonisation were enumerated. A luminous historical view of Phœnician and Greek colonies was presented. The country and circumstances of each people were described. Facts were given illustrating the several causes of those colonies, their relations to each other and their mother countries, and their most striking effects. Remarks on the mythology, philosophy, government, poetry, illustrious legislators and generals of the Grecians, and on the effects of their diffusion concluded the lecture, by which in little more than an hour much suggestive and ennobling instruction had been imparted. Mr. Sleigh hopes to pursue and complete his work in a future lecture. Three members were added. The Rev. Wm. Ridley, who presided, added a few valuable observations, and a vote of thanks was given to the lecturer.

BAPTIST CHAPEL, PRAHRAN.—On Monday the 16th ult., a tea-meeting was held in connexion with this chapel. Nearly two hundred persons were present on the occasion. After tea the company united in singing a hymn. The Rev. B. Lemonn, the pastor, then addressed the meeting on the necessity existing for the erection of a larger church. He urged the facilities in the way of obtaining a site, and dwelt on the present as a favorable time for pushing forward the scheme with all the energy in their power. Addresses were afterwards delivered by the Revs. A. Morison, W. R. Lewis, R. Fletcher, I. New, and W. Moss. The meeting was closed with prayer and singing. Promises were received at the meeting to the extent of nearly £300.

PRESBYTERIANS.—FREE CHURCH. SANDHURST.—The foundation stone of a new church, for the use of the Free Church, at Sandhurst, was laid, July 28th, by the Rev. J.

Nish, the pastor, who delivered a suitable address upon the occasion. A social meeting was held in the evening, when the attendance was large and the impression produced good. Among the speakers were the Rev. Messrs. M'Donald, of Kyneton; Grant, of Beechworth; Storie, of Castlemaine; and W. R. Fletcher, of Sandhurst. The cost of the structure will be about £3000, towards which upwards of £1500 have been subscribed.

UNITED PRESBYTERIAN CHURCH, M'KENZIE STREET (REV. MR. KININMONT'S).—This congregation, which has hitherto worshipped in the Protestant Hall, has erected a new place of worship in M'Kenzie-street. The building is a wooden one, and will accommodate about two hundred individuals. It is intended to erect a more permanent church so soon as the congregation are able to undertake the work. The new place was opened on Sabbath, the 15th ult. The Rev. David Chapman, United Presbyterian, preached in the morning; the Rev. M. Goethe, of the Lutheran Church, in the afternoon; and the Rev. H. Thomas, B.A., of the Independent Church, in the evening. A tea-meeting was held in the church on the Tuesday evening following; the attendance on the occasion was good. H. Langlands, Esq., presided. Addresses were delivered by the Chairman, the Revs. Isaac New and James Taylor, of the Baptist Church; the Revs. H. Thomas, B.A., and A. Morison, of the Independent Church; the Rev. M. Goethe, of the Lutheran Church; The Rev. D. Chapman, of the United Presbyterian Church; and the pastor of the congregation. The meeting was a pleasant and instructive one.

WESLEYANS.—WESLEY CHURCH, MELBOURNE.—This new place of worship was opened on Thursday the 26th August, by the Rev. Messrs. Draper and Butters. The Rev. Mr. Draper conducted the preliminary and devotional services, and the Rev. W. Butters. of Adelaide, preached from Zechariah iv. 6, 7. The audience was large. The Rev. Dr. Cairns preached an eloquent discourse in the evening, from Matt. xxviii. 18, the church being filled. On the following Sunday the Rev. W. Butters preached in the morning, the Rev. L New in the afternoon, and the Rev. Mr. Dare in the evening, to large congregations. On the Monday evening a soirée was held in the adjoining schoolroom, and after tea the assemblage adjourned to the spacious church, where a platform was erected. Walter Powell, Esq., presided, and various ministers and lay gentlemen delivered addresses. From a statement which was read from the pulpit, it appears that the contract for the erection of the church amounted to £14,600 and that the extras amounted to £3,000, making in all £17,600. The amount placed at the disposal of the Trustees by the sale of the Collins-street property was £15,000, leaving a deficiency of £2,500, and as they were anxious to carry out the design in its entirety, a further sum of £2,500 would be required. The structure is in the decorated English style of architecture, and in its extent. the symmetry of its proportions, and its imposing grandeur as a whole, far surpasses any ecclesiastical building in these colonies. It is, we understand, capable of holding 2000 individuals. The spire, when finished, will be 175 feet high.

BALLAARAT.—His Excellency Sir Henry Barkly, K.C.B., Governor of Victoria, on the 19th of January, 1858, in the presence of fifteen thousand persons, laid the foundation stone of a new Wesleyan church, in the western municipality of Ballaarat. From that period the erection of the building steadily progressed; and, on the 18th July, it was solemnly dedicated to the service of the Most High. The Rev. D. J. Draper, of Melbourne, preached in the morning and evening to crowded congregations; and, in the afternoon, the Rev. James Bickford addressed the teachers and scholars connected with the township. Gravel Pits, Mount Pleasant, and Canadian Sabbath schools. On Tuesday, the 20th, a tea meeting was held in the school room, after which a public meeting was held in the church under the presidency of the circuit steward, James Oddie Esq., J.P. The speakers on the occasion were the Revs. Messrs. Draper, Henderson, Searle, Bickford, Taylor, Crisp, and James; also James Bonwick and John Crombie, Esqrs. On Sunday, the 25th, the Rev. Joseph Dare, of Sandhurst, occupied the pulpit; and the body of the church was again filled. On Monday evening the Rev. Mr Dare delivered an address to a select company in the school-room on the Constitution and Adaptation of Wesleyan Methodism to the peculiar circumstances of the Australian colonists. The Rev. T. Taylor occupied the chair. The amount collected at the services, and in aid of the erection of the building, was £400.

NEW SOUTH WALES.—THE LATE REV. JACOB JONES.—A very solemn and impressive sermon was delivered at the Independent Chapel, Melksham, Wilts, by the Rev. T. E. Fuller, to an overflowing and sorrowful congregation, improving the melancholy death of their late pastor, the Rev Jacob Jones, who was drowned in the wreck of the Catherine Adamson off Sydney, last October. Mr. Jones had been pastor of this church for six years, during which time he was sincerely beloved by his flock, and universally respected by all denominations. He left Melksham, deeply regretted, last July, to settle in Sydney, where a church had been provided for him under the Colonial Missionary Society. He was a man of superior talent and learning, and was educated at Glasgow and Spring Hill College, Birmingham. His death has caused a sensation not easily to be forgotten. His age was about thirty. It is in contemplation to erect a monument to his memory in the chapel.—Christian Witness, March, 1858.

The Southern Spectator.

No. IV. NOVEMBER, 1858. Vol. II.

THE COMET: ITS TEACHINGS.

All eyes are now star-gazing. Numbers who rarely look at the sun, the moon, the planets, or the constellations with any curiosity, stare night after night at the strange wanderer now passing over our sky. And what do they see? A comet, a body so called from the Latin word coma, hair, its appearance being somewhat like a bunch of streaming hair. Meteors of this class have come within the range of human vision, at intervals, since the world began, and history records many such appearances. They have always excited great attention, and in former times great alarm. Mystery hung about them, and superstition invested them with terror No one, not even the philosopher, could tell whence they came, what they were doing here, or whither they were going. It was therefore at once inferred that they were messengers of the avenging gods, a species of astral furies, commissioned to sweep through the heavens, and inflict dire calamities upon the conscience-stricken race of man. Famine, pestilence, wars, commotions, were sure to follow, and if anything disastrous *did* happen to occur about the time of a comet's visitation, all the blame was sure to be laid upon the unoffending stranger. Science has dispelled these illusions and assures us comets are very harmless. People may now gaze at them without trembling. They are said to be very numerous, many presenting themselves to the telescope of the astronomer which are never seen by the naked eye. Some authorities speak of them as amounting to millions, wandering about in all the interstellar spaces. Though they often come so unexpectedly, and seem to move so capriciously, they are found to have regular orbits, and to be subject to law as rigidly as our own familiar planets themselves. The orbits of several have been ascertained, their periods calculated, and their return to the sun accurately predicted. Their habits, however, are singular. They all resemble each other in having orbits, long, narrow, and extremely elliptical, very unlike the nearly round ones of the planets. But while they agree to move in this eccentric way, they agree in scarcely any thing else. The planes of their orbits instead of being nearly parallel, and confined within the limits of the zodiac, are inclined to it at all possible angles, some being almost perpendicular. Their orbits are not concentric, inclosing without crossing one another, like those of the planets; but they intersect and are intersected in all manner of ways. Nor do they all move in one direction, like all the other bodies of the solar system; some having retrograde motions. They obey no such law as Bode's, keeping at proportional distances from the sun, but vary so much, that some never travel farther than Jupiter, while others go away into the profound depths of space, far, far beyond the orbit of the most remote planet. A few are known to visit the sun within every three, five, or six

years ; but to some are assigned, by calculation, a period of thousands upon
thousands of years before they can return, while, probably, others of them
have no re-entering orbits at all, but wander off to distant suns and systems.
The nature of their substance is a moot point with astronomers : that they
are matter, and not an imponderable luminosity, like the aurora borealis or
zodiacal light, is obvious from their being subject to the law of gravitation.
They are, however, manifestly extremely light and vapoury, their particles
having very little mutual cohesion, for while they are so easily attracted,
they exert scarcely any sensible attraction upon other bodies, and stars
may be seen through their thickest parts.   The phenomenon of the tail,
too, is still an unexplained enigma.   The nucleus is always nearest the sun
and the tail in the opposite direction, whether in approaching to or receding from it, so that the comet retires backwards from that luminary.
This appendage is somewhat evanescent, as it occasionally disappears altogether.   Comets always contract in bulk as they draw near the sun, and
expand again the farther they go away into space.   Philosophers have
not yet settled whether they are self-luminous, like the stars, or owe their
light to reflection, like the moon and planets.

With regard to this particular comet, now in the heavens,—is anything
known about *it* ?   It is thought to be one that was expected near this
time, which is supposed to have a period of 300 years or thereabouts,
having been seen in the middle of the seventh, tenth, thirteenth, and sixteenth centuries, and being therefore due in the middle of the nineteenth.
This conjecture is remarkably confirmed by the recent discovery of manuscripts containing Joachim Heller's elaborate observations on the comet of
1556.   On the basis of these elements, the most recent calculations of
astronomers bring out the extraordinaay coincidence, that the comet would
make its nearest approach to the sun in August of the present year.   The
last mail brought the intelligence that a comet, supposed to be the one in
question, was discovered by an Italian astronomer in the month of June,
and would be visible to the naked eye, in Europe, in August ; and here
we are, probably looking at the same object in October, after it has passed
its perihelion, and is on its return to the remote regions of space.
We wait with interest the result of further scientific observations, to prove
or disprove these conjectures as to the comet's identity.

And can this strange object teach us anything ?   Its very *strangeness* is
instructive.   In the government and proceedings of the Supreme Being
there are two principles discernible, the ordinary and the extraordinary,
sameness and variety, the rule and the exception.   The ordinary and usual
is designed to inspire confidence in the uniformity and constancy of nature's
laws, and to stimulate action from the conviction that results may be
depended on.   But the common, however beneficent and perfect, is apt to
lose its impressiveness.   What can equal the beauty, the glory, the grandeur
of the spectacle over our heads, either when the sun in his strength is
pouring down his glorious beams, or the stars of heaven are irradiating the
crystal firmament with their mild lustre in a calm and cloudless night ?   But
how few do more than cast now and then a careless uninquiring glance at
this spectacle !   They can see it at any time, and they hardly ever give it
a thought at all.   But when a strange luminary of foreign and eccentric
aspect comes athwart our skies and mingles among our stars, all eyes are
turned to it ; the whole world wonders what it is ; everybody at once
turns astronomer.   Perhaps this, to us at least, is its special use.   It may
be sent to turn us away from looking always at this sordid earth, to lift

our eyes heavenward, to urge us to contemplate not the comet alone, but the whole of this celestial department of the Creator's work, and to notice in it the strongly marked traces of the Divine hand that framed it. And if it do this to a world of intelligent and accountable beings, its visit will not have been in vain.

But is it not a *mysterious* object, strange, incomprehensible ? Granted : but is there no *use* in mystery ? Man is proud, especially of his knowledge ; he needs a check, to be reminded that he knows, after all, but in part, and sees through a glass darkly. It does him good to teach him his ignorance, and, while he is straining his utmost to add to his acquisitions, it is still salutary for him humbly to submit to the limits imposed upon his knowledge in the present state. Let him be lowly minded in the presence of that mighty and omniscient Being, only a small part of whose ways he can search out ; and let him adore where he cannot comprehend.

These visitors from remote spaces help us to a conception of the *vastness and grandeur* of our own solar system, and even of the universe at large. We were astounded a few years ago at the discovery of the planet Neptune, lying in the cold and dimly lighted regions, so far beyond what were deemed the outside limits of our system. But this is nothing to the orbits of some of the greater comets. One is computed to have a period of 7000 years, another even of 100,000 ! *Where* must *they* go to, and yet be attached to the solar system ? What must the universe be, of which that system is but a leaf in the forest ? " Who by searching can find out God ; who can find out the Almighty unto perfection ? " If our conceptions of the greatness and glory of the Deity are thus aided by such celestial visitors, our impressions of his condescension and grace must be correspondingly deepened. Of God it is said, " He healeth the broken in heart and bindeth up their wounds ; he telleth the number of the stars ; he calleth them all by their names. Great is our Lord and of great power ; his understanding is infinite." His condescension is enhanced in proportion to his greatness. What food have we here to nourish our reverence, our confidence, and our love !

ADDRESS OF THE REV. DR. ALLIOTT,

CHAIRMAN OF THE CONGREGATIONAL UNION OF ENGLAND AND WALES, DELIVERED AT THE ANNUAL MEETING, HELD AT THE POULTRY CHAPEL, LONDON, MAY 11TH.

MY DEAR BRETHREN,—Allow me to thank you for the honor you have done me by electing me your chairman. I should rejoice if I had been more worthy of the position, and more competent for the discharge of its duties. I trust, however, that our prayers for the out-pouring of the Holy Ghost on our assembly will be so fully answered, and that such a spirit of love and fraternal confidence will prevail, as to render it a matter of subordinate importance who the individual may be, that is called to preside over your deliberations. I do not intend, in my introductory address, to take any review of our denominational history during the past year. Several valued brethren have entered into their rest ; some have changed their sphere of labor ; and many, full of youth and promise have gone forth from our different colleges, either to take the place of older brethren, or to collect new congregations. Our different religious and benevolent institutions have been pursuing their labors of love amidst more or less of difficulty and discouragement, whilst they have not unfre-

quently been cheered by indications of evident usefulness.   Many periodical and other religious and literary publications, which are circulated
amongst us, prove that the men of power and thought, combined with a
spirit of love and devotion, are not diminished in number.   May the Lord
our God still be with us as he has been with our fathers! let him not leave
us nor forsake us !

Instead of addressing myself to these or any other points of mere
denominational interest, I propose to take as the subject of the present
brief discourse a matter which has reference to the whole Church of Christ,
and to us simply as a particular section of it.   Some of you will perhaps
think that what is called the "new theology," is a theme which has stirred
up so much bitterness of feeling and asperity of language, that it had
better, at least for a time, be laid on the shelf.   I would wish that
bitterness of feeling and asperity of language were for ever laid on the
shelf.   God forbid that I should say one word which shall tend to foster
any such feeling or give occasion to any such language.   Whilst I contend
for what I believe to be truth, I will try rather to allay than to increase
irritation, to promote rather than to offend the charity that believeth all
things and hopeth all things.

Leaving, then, our own denomination out of special notice, and looking
upon the Protestant Church as a whole, it is a fact which no one will hesitate
to admit, that there has, of late years, sprung up a theology to which
different distinctive names have been assigned ; some have called it " the
new theology," others "the negative theology," others, "Germanism,"
others, "spiritualism," and others, "the intuitional theology."   I have
thought that it would be interesting and profitable to ask what this
theology distinctly is ; what in the old theology, or in the state of the
church, has given rise to it ; what measure of truth and what of error there
is in it ; and what lessons the fact of its existence should inculcate ? When
we ask what the new theology distinctly is, the question arises, where are we
to go for an answer ?   The men who are regarded as the leaders of the new
school, are, for the most part, characterised by independence of thought,
and hence have their individual peculiarities.   Still there are some general
principles by which they are all more or less influenced, and which may be
considered as constituting their distinctness as a school.   The grand foundation of the controversy between the old and the new theology respects the
proper place of the *objective* and the *subjective* in religion ; and hence
such questions as these have arisen : Is it of any consequence what a man's
intellectual faith is ? or, is the only matter of consequence what is his
feeling, his state of heart, his spiritual life ?

Again, granting that there is objective truth to be believed, is its Divine
origin to be ascertained by objective or subjective evidence? in other words,
are we, or are we not, to receive merely those truths of an objective revelation which commend themselves to a supposed inward light which God,
it is believed, has given to every man with more or less fulness ?

Further, passing by other truths objectively revealed, and granting that
there is sufficient evidence that Christ offered himself a sacrifice for us, are
we to judge of the nature and object of his sacrifice by the teaching of the
written word, or chiefly by the inward light referred to above ?   And
supposing it to be allowed that the teaching of the written word is to be
principally regarded, does that teaching authorise the belief that an objective end was to be answered by the sufferings and death of Christ, or does
it justify the conclusion that the end was simply subjective ?   On all these

questions some writers of the new school go much further than others. Time will not permit me to enter into all the different shades of opinion ; and hence I will simply observe, that my statements are not intended to apply to any individual whatever ; they will not be throughout fully applicable to any one individual, though, with more or less of modification, applicable, I believe, to the school as a whole.

The first question I have named is—Is it of any consequence what a man's intellectual faith is ? or, is it the only matter of consequence what is his feeling, his state of heart, his spiritual life ? The introduction of this question is perhaps primarily to be traced to the undue disregard of the state of the heart by some of the profoundly orthodox. There have been those who have taught that the faith required by the Gospel is a mere matter of intellect, and there have been, moreover, numbers who professed full assent to gospel truth, and yet have practically manifested that their heart, their affections, had little to do with their faith. There thus has existed in some a cold, lifeless, valueless orthodoxy ; nay, perhaps, there has been manifested, in the great bulk of professing Christians, a deficiency of the full influence which truths so weighty as those avowedly received might have been expected to exert over the whole nature and character.

Some thinking men, looking on this state of spiritual deadness, saw that there was radical defect somewhere, and hastily concluded that, as the evil existed in connexion with a full profession of orthodoxy, orthodoxy, if not itself radically wrong, must be of little importance ; they thus reached the conviction that it is of minor consequence what a man believes, and that the only thing of consequence is the state of his heart. I do not blame them for laying stress on the subjective, nor for regarding a mere intellectual assent to certain truths as of itself inoperative in producing the subjective effect so essential to true religion ; but I believe them to have rushed into the opposite error, and unduly to have disregarded the objective. Man is naturally prone to extremes ; hence, when he finds one extreme a failure, he does not stop to inquire whether there is any middle place between that and its opposite, but takes for granted that the other extreme must be right. So, it seems to me, it has been with the parties of whom I am speaking.

In thus disregarding the objective, there are two reasons why I think them wrong ; one is, that it is only by the objective that we can ascertain the real value of any supposed subjective. There is a false subjective as well as a true one, for it is not all supposed religious experience that is true, valuable or desirable. How, then, is a man to know whether his own experience is the true subjective or the false ? Has he any subjective test by which he can try it ? We shall, perhaps, be told that he has within him "a religious consciousness" which will pronounce judgment on his religious experience, and decide for him its true character. But is this so-called "religious consciousness" to be depended upon as a judge ? If it were worthy of the confidence some place in it, surely it would be uniform in its decisions ; whereas, if we look even simply to our own individual experience, we shall find its decision different at different times, accordingly as our frame of mind differs. Thus at one time our so-called religious consciousness will pronounce a particular experience right, and at another time enthusiasm. Nor is this the only evidence of its fallibility ; for if we look out of ourselves we shall find its decisions in different individuals still more varied, and especially when one of the individuals is educated and another uneducated, or when one is civilized and another uncivilized, or when one has acquired religious habits and another has been trained to irreligion and vice. A "religious consciousness" so inconstant in its decisions, cannot be infallible, and hence its judgment as to the rightness or otherwise of a particular experience cannot be trusted. But possibly it may be thought that if its direct estimation of a religious experience is unworthy of confidence, it may be better qualified to judge of the fruits of such an experience ; and hence that its indirect judgment may, any way, be rested upon. So far, however, from this, it will be found that its decisions are just as varied as to the fruits of a religious experience, as they are as to the experience itself. Acts proceeding from one species of religious experience are approved by a man who has been taught to regard such acts as religious, and disapproved by another who has been differently taught. Thus, penances and even human sacrifices are thought right by some, and pronounced wrong by others. Accordingly, when an individual embraces the notion that the objective is of no value in religion, he is left without any standard for the subjective but what is variable and fallible ; and hence, may imagine himself to have eminent religious experience, a high degree of religious life, when his religious experience is really false and spurious, and his religious life really self-deceiving and worthless. Whether any objective truth which can better serve as a standard can be ascertained by us, except such as is ultimately founded on the subjective. I shall just now inquire.

In the meantime, let me remark that there is a second reason why those who disregard the objective are in error ; not only are they left without any adequate standard whereby to test the subjective, they are left without any adequate means for producing the true subjective. I admit that a mere intellectual assent to objective truth will not produce it ; but the case is very different with a cordial, hearty, loving reception of truth, a reception accompanied with self-application, and including trust and confidence. This believing is not simply with the understanding, but "with the heart :" it is the believing which, according to Holy Writ, God requires of us, and by which "He purifies the heart." If the Scriptures are the word of God, such a believing is the divinely appointed means whereby spiritual life is to be obtained ; and hence, wherever it is wanting there is, and there must be, spiritual death. But I need not say, that where there is no intellectual assent to the truth, there cannot possibly be that believing with the heart which includes it ; accordingly, where the objective truth is disregarded, the appropriate means for gaining true spiritual life must be neglected. Whilst, then, there may be a dead orthodoxy, which is vitally wrong because it disregards the subjective love of the truth, the error is equally vital, if, in order to escape from a dead orthodoxy, we neglect objective truth as unimportant. The true way to escape spiritual deadness is not by a rejection or a neglect of truth, but by a warm, hearty, living reception of it.

We proceed now to the next question. Granting that objective truth is not to be disregarded as unessential to religion, how is this objective truth to be ascertained ? Let it be admitted that if there is truth without us, which it is important for us to receive and believe, such truth must come to us with Divine authority, and the question evidently arises, How are we to know what has that authority ? No one will affirm that the subjective has nothing whatever to do with giving us, or at least enabling us to gain this knowledge. Even those who look to external evidence alone, will allow that external evidence would be unavailing, except there were some within to appreciate and receive it.   Thus far the subjective lies unquestionably at the foundation of all our knowledge.   The evidence, however, which thus appeals to the subjective may be either wholly objective, wholly subjective, or partially objective and partially subjective.   If we ask for the evidence of miracles or of prophecy, we may either simply refer to miracles objective to ourselves, or may also include moral and spiritual miracles wrought on our own hearts : in the former case the evidence is wholly objective ; in the latter, it is partially objective and partially subjective. Again, if we ask for internal evidence, we may either simply refer to the evidence arising from the harmony of the truth professing to be from God with the revelation which he has made of himself in his works generally, and in the institution of our minds in particular ; or we may refer to the harmony of the truth with our own religious instinct or religious consciousness, looking upon such instinct or consciousness as the voice of God within us. The evidence in the former case is partly objective and partly subjective ; in the latter it is wholly subjective.

Now some parties, professedly of the old school of theology, have occasionally laid too exclusive a stress on external evidence, and particularly on the evidence of miracles and prophecy ; and, in addition to this, instead of thoroughly meeting the difficulties which many thinking men found in this species of evidence, they to a great extent ignored them.   Time will not now permit me to enter into these difficulties, nor indeed does my present object require I should do so.   I believe that they all may be satisfactorily met.   At the same time, let me remark that they never will be satisfactorily met except by thorough and impartial investigation ; and even when they are met, the evidence ought not to be neglected that arises from the adaptation of a professed revelation to the necessities of mankind, and from the effects produced by it on the subjective experience ; nor ought the evidence to be considered unimportant which arises from the harmony of a professed revelation both with itself and with the revelation made in nature. It is the concurrence of all those different species of evidence that gives weight to the whole.   The effect, however, of laying an undue and almost exclusive stress on one species of evidence—that of miracles, or of miracles and prophecy—and especially in connexion with a disregard of the objections and difficulties which many felt in reference to it, produced a natural reaction, and, as the result, a class of men arose, who, instead of trying to remedy the deficiency, gave up external evidence as affording but little satisfaction ; these first made the subjective within to a great extent independent of the objective, and next set it up as an infallible judge of the objective ; hence, they regarded that objective truth alone as demonstrably divine, which the subjective instinct, or consciousness, or whatever else it was called, pronounced worthy of reception.

I have already shown that this subjective instinct, called by some "religious consciousness," is unworthy of confidence as a judge of the spiritual life ; but if it may err there, is it not, at least, equally likely to err in judging of objective truth ?   Its decisions must necessarily be in harmony with the inward life which it approves ; and hence, if it may approve a a false, a spurious inward life, it may disapprove an objective truth, which could not, if it were truth, harmonise with such a life. Moreover, that it is unworthy of confidence as a judge of the objective is proved in the same way in which we showed it to be unworthy of confidence as a judge of the subjective, by the different decisions which it gives in different cases. Here, for example, is one man before whom the orthodox view of the atonement is placed, and he tells us that he sees a moral beauty and glory in it ; but here is another man who tells us that it is so revolting to his religious consciousness that he cannot possibly believe it to be of God.

We, perhaps, shall be told in reply that the religious consciousness is more fully developed in one man than in another ; moreover, that it may, after full development, become warped and blinded by education, authority, and other accidental circumstances. If so, who is to tell whether his own religious consciousness is sufficiently developed to lead him right ; and whether, if developed, it has not been injured by any of the accidents referred to ? It surely behoves us to ask what this religious consciousness is, and how far it is trustworthy, before we submit ourselves to be blindly led by it. Is it a separate, distinct faculty of the mind ? or is it simply a state of religious and moral feeling, resulting in part from the original constitution of the mind, and in part from the influence of the joint operation of all the faculties and of all the external agencies that have acted upon them ? If the former, it may possibly be regarded as the voice of God ; but if the latter, it cannot be infallible, except the mind was originally constituted infallible, which we know it was not, and except the faculties of the mind and the external agencies that have acted upon them are infallible, which we know they are not. If, however, it was a separate distinct power—a power independent of all the other powers of the mind, and especially if as such it has to be regarded as a Divine voice, it would be the same in the enlightened and in the unenlightened, in the civilized and in the savage, in the strong-minded and in the weak-minded. Besides, if it was a separate, distinct power, we should naturally expect that since the Creator does nothing in vain, its operations could not possibly be accounted for by the mere supposition of the existence of the other mental faculties ; and yet had I time, I think I could show you that its operations can all be thus accounted for. We conclude, then, that the religious consciousness is not the infallible voice of God, and is not to be trusted as an infallible guide.

But I shall be asked whether the argument I have adduced against the trustworthiness of the religious consciousness is not equally available against the trustworthiness of our power to judge of evidence at all ; and hence against our reception of any evidence by which objective truth can be established. The two cases, however, are not parallel : a man who implicitly follows the guidance of his religious consciousness as the voice of God cannot question any of its decisions ; if he did, he would practically admit that his intellectual powers are a superior authority, or at least a co-ordinate authority, and hence that his religious consciousness is not an infallible or even his only leader. But a man who does not implicitly trust his religious consciousness, but believes it possible for his religious feeling to lead him astray, is led to exert all his mental powers to discover truth, instead of indolently following wherever his feeling leads him—is led to view truth in all its possible aspects, and to examine every kind of evidence by which it is supported. Moreover, after he has arrived at conclusions, he is led to seek for additional light wherever it can be gained, in order that he may be confirmed in those which are really sound, and corrected in those in which he has been mistaken. Such a man, surely, is less likely to go astray ; if he does go astray, there is every probability that it will not be in utter and irretrievable darkness. I admit that the influence of the Spirit of God are essential to lead us right ; but we have no authority for regarding these influences as guiding us by a blind instinct, but rather as helping us to exercise our faculties aright, and guarding us against any erroneous conclusions which would be fatally injurious to our spiritual interests. Accordingly, if some professedly orthodox theologians are in error when they confine their attention simply to the objective evidence of revealed truth, those of the new school are not less radically wrong when they confine their attention to its subjective evidence, and especially when they make their so-called religious consciousness an infallible test of truth and error.

A third question remains. Grant that objective truth is not unessential, and that it is to be ascertained in other ways than by a simple appeal to the religious consciousness, what is objective truth? And here, as time limits me, I will confine your attention to one particular truth—that which has excited the most controversy : the truth in reference to the nature of the sacrifice of Christ. As to the design of his sacrifice, the old school teaches that it is to provide for the pardon of the sinner in consistency with the honor of the law and of the moral government of God, or to provide for his pardon in such a way as that, in the words of Scripture, "God may be just and the justifier of him which believeth in Jesus." No doubt, if this is its immediate design, it is so with reference to a subjective effect to be thereby produced on the heart of the sinner. If God gave up his Son to suffer and to die as the substitute of the guilty, that he might thus be both a just God and a Saviour, it was that by this manifestation of his love he might win the heart to himself, and by the manifestation of his hatred of sin might lead the sinner to regard sin as exceedingly sinful. This ultimate subjective end of the atonement has been by some too lightly regarded. They have dwelt too exclusively on the immediate, as though that were the only end. The consequence has been a re-action ; it was perceived that the Scriptures laid stress on the ultimate end, and hence those who saw the error I have pointed out were led to look exclusively to the end which had been neglected, and they regarded it as the immediate instead of the remote end. Accordingly, they passed over the objective end altogether as a mistake, and considered that the first and only direct object of the atonement of Christ was to manifest Divine love, and thus to draw the sinner back to God. Nor is reaction the only cause to which this view of the atonement is to be ascribed. Difficulties were felt to attend the theory of substitution, and it was thought that they were not fairly and fully met, that it was impossible to meet them satisfactorily, and, therefore, that that theory must be given up as untenable. This new view, it was supposed, escaped all these difficulties, and made the atonement less of a judicial transaction, and more completely paternal and loving in its manifestations of God.

From what I have already said, it will be perceived I do not dispute that what some parties of the new school consider the only end of the atonement is an important end—is an end intended to be ultimately gained. I believe that God gave his Son to manifest to men his love, that he might thus win them to love him. It is a mistake to ignore or even to pass over as unimportant the subjective effect which God intended to produce by means of the atonement ; but I think it an equal mistake to regard this as its immediate end. And there are two reasons why I think so ; one, that it is the objective end of the atonement which adapts it to produce this subjective effect ; and the other, that this subjective effect is not the only ultimate end, the ultimate end being an effect produced not simply on the sinners who are drawn back to God, but also on the universe of intelligent creation—an effect which could not be produced except by means of the objective end.

(To be concluded in our next.)

THE MINISTER AND THE NAVVY.

One fine Australian summer morning, early in 1858, the Rev. —— was walking near S—— along the tramway in course of formation. He was pleased to observe the vigour, industry, and cheerfulness of the workmen. On coming up to one who was preparing to remove a huge root of a tree from the centre of the tramway, the minister halted. After mutual salutations the navvy commenced the following dialogue with the theologian. N. "Can you tell me, sir, how this root is to be got up?" M. "I do not profess to understand that business so well as those practically engaged in it." N. "I wonder a learned gentleman like you don't know what means must be used to stub up a root." M. "In giving an opinion I should recommend that the stump be undermined all around, and then forced up by the lever power of a pickaxe or a crowbar." N. "Yes, there must be much strength applied to the work." M. "I should go about removing this obstacle somewhat as I would deal with a man living in wrong practices, and whom I might desire to set right. I would undermine his false principles, impart correct views, and urge him with powerful motives." Beloved reader, whether navvy, butkeeper, shepherd, stock-driver, farmer, or artisan, let us have a word or two together on "roads" and "roots," the way of truth, duty, and happiness, and the difficulties which beset that way.

The natural inclination of fallen man to wander from God and holiness, and his actual and universal deviations from what is right, are impressively taught in the sacred scriptures. "God hath made man upright, but they have sought out many inventions."—Eccles. vii. 29. "The wicked are estranged from the womb, they go astray as soon as they be born, speaking lies."—Psalm lviii. 3. "All have sinned."—Romans v. 12. "All we, like sheep, have gone astray; we have turned every one to his own way."—Isaiah liii. 6. Daily observation confirms these and similar words of inspiration. Various sins and their consequent miseries abound. Minds very simple and unlearned feel convinced that the character and conduct of mankind are not as when the holy God made man and pronounced him "very good"; and minds, the most acute and intelligent, can furnish no satisfactory explanation of human depravity and voluntary waywardness, apart from the authoritative teaching of the Bible.

That blessed book which declares our guilt and ruin, also announces the glad tidings of salvation. The same great bible-map that shews the common "broad way" and numerous winding paths of unhappy man's departure from God, exhibits also a way of return. To the convinced and anxious soul, far more cheering are the traces of that way than the yellow spots, which indicate the gold-fields to the eye of one eager after worldly gain. We do not condemn, but commend, industrious habits. Still temporal good must be sought in a right spirit, and earthly desire must be confined within proper limits, or the soul is debased and ruined. In these enterprising colonies the lust of gain, the love of pleasure, and the allurements of vice, are drawing into perdition many thousands. The broad road which conducts to darkness and death is trodden by many, while few are treading the path of light and life.

> "Broad is the road that leads to death,
> And thousands walk together there;
> But wisdom shows a narrower path,
> With here and there a traveller."

How can we account for this painful yet obvious fact? What obstacles deter so many from walking in the way to glory? In reply, we refer not at present to those who have never heard the Gospel, and we can but briefly notice two or three of the hinderances of some who hear the voice of God yet refuse to turn to him.

Many stumble for *want of light.* They need clearer and more comprehensive views. Their mental twilight and fogs make grand and beautiful truths appear like terrible monsters. For instance, some persons imagine that God must be harsh and forbidding if the sufferings and death of Christ were necessary to the forgiveness of our sins. A sensible working man, on an English railway, was found by a friend to be in this difficulty. "Well," he replied, "I do see that it is a different case from what I thought before; but now look here. I am a poor fellow, don't pretend nor profess; yet I have a quarrel with a mate, feel to hate him, will drub him well next time we light on one another. I think better of it, offer him half my bread and cheese when we chance of meeting, and we are friends. Now why can't God do a generous action like that, and forgive us outright?" We reply,—Kings and magistrates may not act from mere pity. God is a great king and will be our final judge. As such it is right and necessary that he forgive and bless transgressors only in a way that will uphold and honor his royal authority, that is by Christ's sacrifice for sin, his atoning death, "the just for the unjust," the ransom price of his precious blood. For this work God, in his infinite pity, gave up his divine and well-beloved son, and he as freely undertook the office of Mediator and Saviour. The Scriptures abundantly teach these truths. They exhibit the Cross as revealing God's holiness, justice, love, and mercy, all in sweetest harmony. We must get rid of hard, unjust, gloomy, partial views of God. We must see that " God is love," and loves us, or we shall not love him. A spiritual view of the love of God in Christ, will soften and melt the hard heart. Under the outpoured spirit we shall trust and pray. We shall " look upon him whom we have pierced, and shall mourn for him," on whom the Lord hath laid the iniquity of us all, with whose stripes we are healed, and unto him we, who " were as sheep going astray," shall return as " unto the shepherd and bishop of our souls." Take a simple illustration of the subduing effect of a sense of abused love.

A devoted Christian lady who had directed time and effort to the welfare of the sons of toil, learnt and relates the following incident.—" A young navvy, after receiving the best advice, disappoints hopes of his reformation by giving way to the temptation of drink. True, he was hocussed by false friends; but still he had gone into the hated ' public' of his own will, and had been served right. He is penitent, and wishes to see his friend, the woman who had been so kind to him. His ' mate' thinks he is afraid of a scolding, and says to him, ' she won't scold you, Henry, 'taint her way with us.' Mark the reply of the repentant Samson. ' No, I'm not afraid of that; *but it's them two tears I can't abear.*' If such is the power of human Christian kindness, how mighty the loving, pitying eye of Jesus, which caused Peter to go out and weep bitterly!

> " Turn and look upon me, Lord,
> And break my heart of stone."

Our self-righteousness and pride of heart blind our eyes to the glory of the way of salvation by freegrace, and also induce unwillingness to be saved by pure mercy, until we feel we are guilty, lost, and undone.

The *love of sin,* so deeply rooted in the heart, causes hatred of that only way to heaven which is a way of holiness. Those pardoned for the sake of Jesus are regenerated and sanctified by the operation of the Holy Spirit. Saving faith. " works by love," and love induces holy obedience. This " holiness without which no man shall see the Lord," makes the path of true religion so unpleasant to the carnal mind. This disrelish of things divine and heavenly, originates most of the objections raised against religion and its professors. The incapability of many to form an idea of happiness superior to low sensual enjoyments, is much to be lamented. Here is a navvy pitman's blind notion of heavenly pleasure:—" My mate and I were working in a pit, and says he, I wonder, Bill, whether it is true what they say of heaven being so happy, whether, now, it can be happier than sitting in the public over a good jug of ale with a fiddle going? I don't know a pleasure as comes up to that."

May the readers of this paper seriously enquire after Jesus, who is the way, and the truth, and the life: ascertain the snares, temptations, and errors which hinder their progress heavenward, and pray for the pardoning mercy and renewing grace of God. Then will angels rejoice that these repentant sinners read thoughts suggested by the "Minister and the navvy."

REVIVAL OF RELIGION.

The following account of a Rivival of Religion in the Highlands of Scotland in the years 1797-1799, was written by Alexander Stewart, minister of Moulin, in a letter to the Rev. David Black, minister of Lady Yester's church, Edinburgh, and was published at the time. It has been re-printed in the *Christian Witness*, from which it is abridged :—

DEAR SIR,—I was by no means surprised to find, by your late letters, that the communications which I had made to you, from time to time, concerning the state of religion in this part of the country, had been highly gratifying to our friends in Edinburgh. As you have signified to me the opinion of Dr. Erskine, Dr. Hunter, and other respected friends, that the happy revival of religion amongst us ought to be made more generally known, and that it might be useful to publish an account of it, I shall now endeavor to give a more circumstantial detail of its commencement and progress. I am able to do this with tolerable correctness, as my memory is assisted by written notes. I have no doubt that the concern about religion, which has been lately awakened in this place, is already the ground of much rejoicing among the angels before the throne. Pity it should not also engage, as extensively as may be, the praises of our christian brethren on earth.

In narrating the means by which the people were brought to pay a more serious attention to their eternal interests, it is necessary to say something of my own case. I was settled minister of this parish in 1786, at the age of twenty-two. Although I was not a "despiser" of what was sacred, yet I felt nothing of the power of religion on my soul. I had no relish for its exercises, nor any enjoyment in the duties of my office, public or private. A regard to character, and the desire of being acceptable to my people, if not the only motives, were certainly the principal motives that prompted me to any measure of diligence or exertion. I was quite well pleased when a diet of catechizing was ill attended, because my work was the sooner over; and I was always satisfied with the reflection, that if people were not able or did not choose to attend on these occasions, that was no fault of mine. I well remember that I often hurried over that exercise with a good deal of impatience, that I might get home in time to join a dancing party, or to read a sentimental novel. My public addresses and prayers were, for the most part, cold and formal. They were little regarded by the hearers at the time, and as little recollected afterwards. I preached against particular vices, and inculcated particular virtues. But I had no notion of the necessity of a radical change of principle; for I had not learned to know the import of those assertions of Scripture, that "the carnal mind is enmity against God;" that, "if any man be in Christ he is a new creature;" and that "except a man be born of water and of the Spirit, he cannot enter into the kingdom of God." I spoke of making the fruit good; but I was not aware that the tree was corrupt, and must first be itself made good, before it could bear good fruit. The people, however, were satisfied with what they heard, and neither they nor I looked farther. Almost the only remark made by any one on the discourse, after leaving church, was, "What a good sermon we got to-day!" to which another would coldly assent, adding, "Many good advices do we get, if we did but follow them." Such a heartless compliment was all the improvement made of the discourse, and I believe all the fruit of my preaching. The hearers hardly gave me credit for a desire to do my duty, and they as readily took credit to themselves for a willingness to be taught their duty. But whether any improvement was actually going forward, whether there was any increase of the fruits of righteousness, was a point which gave neither minister nor people much concern.

If there were any persons in the parish at that time who lived a life of faith, under the influence of pure evangelical principles, I did not know them, nor was I qualified to discern and understand what spirit they were of. I have since had reason to believe that there were a very few spiritually-minded persons, but their life was hid, and they had left this world, all but one or two, before they could acknowledge me as a brother. I was, in a great measure, ignorant of the peculiar doctrines of Christianity, the corruption of the human will, the fulness and freeness of the redemption which is in Christ, justification by faith, and the necessity of the Holy Spirit's agency on the human soul ; and what I knew not myself, I could not declare to others. I never thought of praying for divine direction in my search after divine truth. I believe I had read the confession of faith of our church before I declared my belief in its contents, but I had taken little pains to compare it with the Scriptures. I certainly did not distinctly understand, nor was I at all persuaded of the truth of many propositions contained in it. Yet I do not remember that I had any scruples about subscribing it as the confession of my faith, or about declaring my assent to it solemnly, in the presence of that congregation whereof I was about to take the pastoral charge.

While I was yet ignorant of the truth, and unacquainted with christain experience, two persons under conviction of sin, and terrors of conscience, applied to me for advice. They supposed that one in the office of the ministry must, of course, be a man of God, and skilled in administering remedies for the diseases of the soul. They were widely mistaken in their judgment of me, for I had learned less of the practice than of the theory of pastoral duty. I said something to them in way of advice, but it afforded them no relief. They were, however, under the care of the good Physician. He applied his own balm to their wounded spirits, and " healed, and bade them live." Being progressively and effectually taught of God, they are both now established, judicious Christians. These are the first that appear to have been converted since my incumbency, but they cannot be reckoned the fruits of my ministry.

The Lord was now preparing to gather to himself a fuller harvest in this place. He might have removed me as a useless encumbrance, or rather an intervening obstacle, out of the way, and subjected me to the doom of the unprofitable servant ; but he was graciously pleased to spare me, and visit me in mercy, and even to employ me as one of his instruments in carrying on his own work. Glory to his name, who commanded light to shine out of darkness! The writings of pious men, which were put in my hands by one and another Christian friend, were made the means of bringing me acquainted with the truths of the Gospel. Among these I may mention the works of the Revs. John Newton and Thomas Scott, as eminently useful to me. I was slow in receiving and embracing the doctrines maintained by these writers. By degrees, however, I was pursuadad that they were agreeable to Scripture, and that no doubt they must be admitted as true. I therefore durst not preach anything which I conceived to be directly contrary to these doctrines ; but I brought them forward rarely, incorrectly and with awkward hesitation. The trumpet was sounded, but it gave an " uncertain sound." My preaching now consisted of a mixed kind of doctrine. I taught that human nature is corrupt, and needs to be purified ; that righteousness cannot come by the law ; that we cannot be justified in the sight of God by our own works ; that we can be justified only by the righteousness of Christ, imputed to us, and received by faith. But, in explaining the nature of saving faith, I stumbled on that stumbling-stone of *sincere obedience*, in substance at least, if not in so many words ; imagining, like many in whose writings I have since met with that opinion, that the great favor procured to men by Christ's sufferings and mediation was a relaxation of the Divine law ; and that sincere, not perfect obedience, was all that was now required.   This was "another gospel," which could never be owned by God as the Gospel of his Son, nor accompanied by the sanctifying power which belongs exclusively to the truth.   If it set any of my people on thinking, it only bewildered and misled them.   They remained as before, unenlightened and unchanged.

The biographical sketches in the *Evangelical Magazine* were the principal means of impressing my heart, of opening my eyes to perceive the truth, of exciting a love to godliness, and a desire after usefulness.   The power of Divine grace appeared illustrious in the composure, the joy, the triumph, with which many pious Christians left the world.   I saw their triumphant hope supported, not by a complacent reflection on a well-spent life, but by a confidence in the unmerited love of Christ, and in his power and willingness to save even the chief of sinners.   I was particularly struck with the account of ministers who had labored with much diligence and success, and had died at an early period of life, full of good fruits ; while I, who had already lived longer, and been longer in the ministry than they, could not say that I had taken any pains with my people, nor that I had been the means of reclaiming one sinner from the error of his ways, or of saving one soul alive.   The conversation and example of some persons of a truly spiritual mind, to whose acquaintance I was admitted, and who exhibited to my view what I found only described in written memoirs, conduced much to impress on my mind the truths with which I was gradually becoming more acquainted.   I cannot omit mentioning, in this connexion, the blessing I enjoyed in the preaching, the prayers, and the conversation, of that much favored servant of Christ, the Rev. Charles Simeon, of King's College, Cambridge.   He was a man sent from God to me ; was my guest for two days in June, 1796, preached in my church, and left a savour of the things of God, which has remained with us ever since.

From that time I began to teach and to preach Jesus Christ, with some degree of knowledge and confidence.   From August, 1797, to January, 1798, I preached a course of sermons on the fundamental doctrines of Christianity.   I was now enabled to show, from Scripture, that all men are by nature enemies to God, disobedient to his law, and on that account exposed to his just indignation and curse.   I therefore addressed them, not as persons who were already, from education, birth-right, or local situation, possessed of saving faith and other christian graces, but as sinners under sentence of death, and who had not as yet obtained mercy.   I did not, as before, merely reprove them for particular faults or vices, and urge them to the practice of particular virtues ; but told them that the whole of their affections and inclinations needed to be pointed in a new direction, and even their virtues to be new-modelled.

The novelty of the matter, and some change in my manner of preaching, excited attention.   People began to think more, and sometimes to talk together, of religious subjects, and of the sermons they heard.   But I did not yet know of any deep or lasting impressions having been made.   The two persons before mentioned, as earliest converted, had by this time got clearer views of the Gospel, were enabled to derive comfort from the word of salvation, and began to bear their testimony to the grace of God their Saviour. They were in the habit of visiting occasionally a poor infirm woman, who had long walked with God, and who now lived alone in a mean cottage in the neighboring village.   It was proposed that they should come together to her house at a time appointed, and that I and some of my family should join them, and spend an evening hour or two in reading, conversation, and prayer.   In process of time, different persons, who were inquiring after the one thing needful, hearing how we were employed, and believing God was with us, were, at their own request, admitted of our party.   In this poor woman's little smoky hovel, we continued to hold our weekly meetings, to August, 1799, when she was called away to join the general assembly of the firstborn above.   Her growth in grace had been very conspicuous, and her death was triumphant.

The number of those who were brought under concern about their eternal interests was increasing.   This concern showed itself chiefly among the younger people under twenty-five or thirty.   Their knowledge was yet imperfect.   A natural shyness often hindered them long from discovering to others what they thought or felt. They had as yet no friend or intimate whom they judged able, from experience, to understand their situation, or to give them counsel. Some of them began to visit one of the two earlier converts formerly mentioned, from whose reading and conversation they derived considerable benefit. By means of this common friend they were brought more acquainted with each other. One might now observe at church, after Divine service, two or three small groups forming themselves round our few more advanced believers, and withdrawing from the crowd into the adjacent fields, to exchange christian salutations and hold christian converse together; while a little cousin, or other young relative, followed as a silent attendant on the party, and listened earnestly to their religious discourse.

In February, 1799, it pleased God to call home my dear wife, after we had been married little more than five years. She, too, had been growing in grace during the last two years of her life. She labored for some months under a gradual decline, which impaired her strength, and occasioned sometimes a langour of spirits; but her faith and trust in her Redeemer were on the whole uniform and steady. Her dismission from the body was gentle, without pain or struggle. Her meek and humble behaviour, her growing love to her Saviour, and the joy she expressed at the prospect of being soon with him, were blessed to the edification of our pious neighbours, who often called to visit her.

The following month, March, 1799, I began a course of practical sermons on regeneration, which I continued to the beginning of July following. These were attended with a more general awakening than had yet appeared among us. Seldom a week passed in which we did not see or hear of one, two, or three persons brought under deep concern about their souls, accompanied with strong convictions of sin, and earnest inquiry after a Saviour. It was a great advantage to these, that there were others on the road before them; for they were seldom at a loss now to find an acquaintance to whom they could freely communicate their anxious thoughts. The house of one of our most established Christians became the chief resort of all who wished to spend an hour in reading or conversing about spiritual subjects. Some who had but newly begun to entertain serious thoughts about religion, and who had not yet come so far as to speak out their mind, would contrive an errand to this person's house, and listen to her talk. She was visited, at other times, by those who were drawn only by curiosity or a disputatious spirit, who wanted to cavil at her words or draw her into controversy. Such visitors she did not avoid, and at last they ceased to trouble her.

Other experienced Christians among us have been extremely useful to their younger brethren or sisters. Their conversation and example have been the principal means of turning the attention of the young to religion, and of edifying those who have been already awakened. Such persons I find most serviceable auxiliaries. If they be neither *prophets*, nor *apostles*, nor *teachers*, yet their usefulness in the church entitles them to the appellation of *helps*, 1 Cor. xii. 28. Nor do I think an apostle would have hesitated to acknowledge them, both men and women, in the relation of *fellow-laborers*, Phil. iv. 3. Nor has success in this Divine work been confined to instruments raised up among ourselves. The same happy effects have, in a certain measure, attended the preaching, the prayers, or conversation of pious brethren, who have assisted at the celebration of the Lord's supper, or made us other occasional visits.

Having lately made an enumeration of those of our congregation whom, to the best of my judgment, I trust I can reckon truly enlightened with the saving knowledge of Christ, I find their number about seventy. The greater part of these are under thirty years of age. Several are above forty, six or seven above fifty, one sixty-six, and one above seventy. Of children under twelve or fourteen there are a good many who seem to have a liking to religion; but we find it difficult to form a decided opinion of their case. Of persons who have died within these twelve months, three, we are persuaded, and we hope two or three others, have slept in Jesus.

It is evident that the Scriptures represent all mankind as divided into two classes. These are distinguished from each other in the most explicit manner; and the distinction is marked by the strongest language, and most significant compari-ons. They are called the children of God, and the children of the devil, 1 John iii. 10; the children of the kingdom, and the children of the wicked one, Matt. xiii. 38; the just and the wicked, Matt. xiii. 49; they who are dead in trespasses and sins, and they who are quickened together with Christ, Eph. ii. 1—6. They are compared to wheat and tares, Matt. xiii. 25; to good and bad fishes, Matt. xiii. 47, 48; to sheep and goats, Matt. xxv. 32. In the general tenor of my preaching, especially in discussing the important doctrine of regeneration, I have endeavoured to keep in view this distinction, and to exhibit it clearly to the notice of my hearers. Many have been not a little offended at such a discrimination; have found fault with the preacher; have complained of uncharitable judgment; pleading that it was God's prerogative to judge the heart; that they hoped theirs was good, though they did not make such a parading profession of religion, &c. The truth has prevailed, however; and some have confessed to me, that their first serious thoughts about the state of their souls arose from the surprise and resentment they felt, on being classed under the character of unbelievers, along with murderers and idolaters, Rev. xxi. 8. But in giving such offensive, though necessary warnings, I had much need of the Spirit of Christ, to repress all asperity of language and manner, to awaken tender compassion for those whom I addressed, and to enable me to speak the truth in love.

I observe among our young converts a considerable variety of frames, but a striking uniformity of character. They are dejected or elevated, according as their regard is more fixed on their own deficiencies and corruptions, or on the glorious sufficiency of Christ. But all of them are characterised by lowliness of mind, by a warm attachment to each other, and to all who love the Lord Jesus, and by the affections set on things above. I know no instances among them of persons trusting for comfort or direction to dreams and visions, impulses or impressions; and hardly an instance of seeking comfort from external signs or tokens, arbitrarily assumed by the inquirer, after the example of Abraham's servant, Gen. xxiv. 14, and of Gideon, Judg. vi. 36—40.

We have not yet to lament any great falling of in those who appeared to have once undergone a saving change. There may be persons who were for a time inquiring, with some apparent earnestness, and afterwards fell back to their former unconcern. I have reason to suspect that there may be several in this situation, though I have not access to know the exact state of their minds. May the Lord discover it to themselves in time! But all, so far as I know, who seemed to have been once truely humbled for their sins, and made to feel in their hearts the grace of God in the Gospel, continue thus far to maintain a humble, spiritual, conscientious walk. They have a constant appetite for the sincere milk of the word, and for christian fellowship one with another. The younger sort have lost their former levity of speech and behaviour, and are become devout and sober-minded; those more advanced in life have laid aside their selfishness and worldly-mindedness, and are grown humble, contented, and thankful.

The external effects of a general concern about religion have appeared in the behaviour even of those who do not seem to have experienced a change of heart. While the younger people attended a Sabbath-school, those who were grown-up used to spend the evening of that day in sauntering about the fields and woods in gossiping parties, or visiting their acquaintance at a distance, without improving their time by any profitable exercise. Now there is hardly a lounger to be seen; nor any person walking abroad, except going to some house of meeting where he may hear the Scriptures read. Swearing, profane talking, foolish and indecent jesting, have, in a great measure, ceased. At *late wakes*, where people assembled to watch over the body of a deceased neighbour, the whole night used to be spent in childish, noisy sports and pastimes. Even the apartment where the corpse lay was the scene of their revelry. This unnatural custom, which is still pretty general over a great part of the Highlands, is almost wholly discontinued in this part of the country. They still assemble on such occasions, but they pass the time in reading the Bible or some religious book, and in sober conversation.

In reply to your request of relating a few of the more remarkable cases of conversion which have occurred among this people, I must say that I have little uncommon to communicate. I have mentioned already, that almost all our converts have been brought to serious concern and inquiry in a quiet, gradual manner. To an intelligent observer, the change in the conversation, temper, deportment, and the very countenance of individuals, is striking: the change, too, in the general aspect of the manners of the people, is conspicuous. The effect is thus, on the whole, obvious; yet there are few particulars in the case of each person, which, taken singly, will appear uncommon, or worthy of being detailed in a separate narrative. We have no instances of persons remarkable for profligacy of manners or profaneness of speech, who have been reclaimed from such enormities; because there was none of that description to be found in our society. The change has been from ignorance and indifference, and disrelish of divine things, to knowledge, and concern, and spiritual enjoyment. Neither are there among us examples of persons suddenly struck and impressed by some alarming event, or singular interposition of Providence. The word of truth proclaimed in public, or spoken in private, has been almost the only outward means of producing conviction of sin, and confidence in the Saviour. In every single case the power of God is visible in the effect produced; but there is little "diversity of operation." Instead of endeavoring to paint the beauties of holiness in the scene around me, I rather wish to prevail with you and other friends, who know how to enjoy such a spectacle, to "come and see."

I have thus, my dear sir, endeavored to give a concise view of the prosperous state of religion in this congregation, for the last two or three years. We still have the happiness to find, from week to week, that the same concern and awakening is spreading around, and extending to some neighboring congregations. Within these few weeks, persons from six or seven miles distant have called here on a Sabbath morning, under evident concern about their souls. On a succeeding Sabbath, the same persons have called again, introducing a relation or fellow-servant, under similar concern. All these, so far as can be judged from present appearances, are in a hopeful way. Such is the manifold grace and lovingkindness with which it has pleased the Lord to visit this corner of his vineyard. I trust that all our Christian brethren, who may receive the joyful intelligence, will join us in praying, that God may continue to water, with showers of blessings, "this vine which his own right hand hath planted;" and that no boar from the wood may be allowed to waste it, nor worm at the root to smite it that it wither.

INCIDENTS.

A BACKSLIDER RESTORED.

At the door of the inn where William lodged, stood the landlord's niece. She entered heartily into the wish to see him reclaimed; and led me into a quiet sitting-room, whither she sent for Mrs. W. The poor wife told me, that the day after Mr. Chalmers had left Beckenham, some old friend of William's had come to see him, near the palace grounds, and had reproached him for being too religious now to "treat" them, and had called him "near" (the fatal word which drives so many of these poor fellows back into sin). He was stung to the quick, and then sold his clothes, in order to feast his friends with the money thus made. Mrs. W. seemed much distressed, and joined fervently with me in prayer for her husband, and for grace and wisdom for herself, to enable her to win him gently back again. Then she went to see if she could persuade him to come and see me, but she said "he had almost vowed that he never would again." "Where was the good," he argued, "of being pulled up to be better for a day or two, only to go down the lower afterwards?"

"Tell him," I said, "that I shall stay here until he comes." A long time passed. It was close upon the hour of the cottage-reading. At length a slow unwilling step was on the stairs. It was William's. The door was opened by his wife; and closing it upon him, she slipped away. He sat down with a sullen, desponding countenance, and made no answer to anything I remarked or inquired, until at last he said, in a low but determined voice, "It is no use at all! I have sold my soul to the devil."

"But he shall not have it, William; it is not yours to sell! Jesus Christ has bought it with His own blood. Oh, William, I must, I will have it for Jesus Christ."

I could say no more, for my voice failed; but his whole countenance altered, like the face of a man from whom an evil spirit had gone out. The strong man bowed his head and wept. "What shall I do? What can I do?

"You can pray. Let us pray now?" He laid his head on the table as he knelt, and cried like a child. He had become "a little child" again in the sense of our Saviour's words, "Except ye be converted, and become as little children, ye shall not enter into the kingdom of heaven."

As he rose up, I asked, "Did you pray too?" "A little," he replied, with characteristic truthfulness.

He and his wife were at the cottage-reading almost immediately afterwards. When we sang the hymn, beginning :—

"Come, thou fount of every blessing,"

he was much affected; and he could only "make melody in his heart to the Lord" with lips that trembled too much to sing, as we came to the last verses:

"Jesus sought me when a stranger,
    Wandering from the fold of God,
He, to save my soul from danger,
    Interposed his precious blood.

"Oh, to grace how great a debtor
    Daily I'm constrained to be:
May that grace, Lord, like a fetter,
    Bind my wandering heart to thee.

"Prone to wander, Lord, I feel it,
    Prone to leave the God I love;
Here's my heart—Lord, take and seal it,
    Seal it from Thy courts above."

William became a permanently reformed and Christian character.—*English Hearts and English Hands. pp.* 171— 173.

NOBLE CONFIDENCE OF WORKING MEN.

Previously to this interview, I had offered to take charge of any portion of their large wages, which they chose to empower me to receive for them during their engagement in the Crimea, to deposit them in the savings' bank, in the form of a Friendly Club, and to keep a private account for each man. A large number of men gladly accepted this proposition. Many of them requested us to forward to needy relatives a portion of the money thus saved, which varied, from ten to twenty shillings weekly. Not only wives and children were thus provided for, but amongst the majority, who had no such ties, an aged mother, an infirm father, a widowed sister, a sickly brother, or orphan nieces, were remembered, with a generous care for their comfort, in this "time of their wealth," by those who toiled for it night and day in the service of their country, and in many cases paid for it by laying down their strong, young lives on that unhealthy shore.

Strangers, as the majority of those who daily arrived to swell the ranks necessarily were to us, and the rest only friends of a few weeks' standing, I thought it but right to give a stamped receipt to each man for the money-order which had been drawn out in my name, and carried these receipts to the crystal palace grounds on the afternoon of the 18th. It must have been a noble trustfulness in those manly natures which made them *fling back* those receipts into the carriage, by common consent, with something like a shout of disdain at the supposition that they could possibly require such a pledge of honesty from a friend and a lady.—*English Hearts and English Hands, pp.* 174, 175.

REVIEWS.

English Hearts and English Hands, or the Railway and the Trenchers. By the Author of "Captain Hedley Vicars." London: Nisbet, 1858.

Miss Marsh, daughter of the venerable Episcopalian clergyman of that name, who for so many years was leader of the Evangelical churchmen of Birmingham and the Midland Counties, has achieved a success in the book line which even popular novelists might envy. Her "Memorials of Captain Hedley Vicars" had reached its 80th thousand some time ago, and her "English Hearts and English Hands," a more recent publication, is following hard in the race, having, at the beginning of this year, been eagerly purchased to the extent of twenty-six thousand, and, probably, by this time to more than double that amount. Fiction is attractive to the multitude of readers, especially if it bear the impress of true genius, or be made piquant by a free use of satire, humor, or careless generous vice. But these latter qualities appear to be not necessary to popularity. Of this Mrs. Stow's "Uncle Tom's Cabin" is a remarkable proof, as well as the works now under notice. Even the subject of religion, so repulsive to many, will not check the general demand for the work, if there only be found in it other qualities which appeal to the heart of our common humanity. The piety of Captain Vicars, strongly evangelical, decided and uncompromising as it is, is forgiven for the sake of his sincerity, his earnestness, his disinterestedness, his self-sacrificing toils to benefit those beneath him in social position, his moral courage as a Christian, his heroism as a soldier, and his untimely death in his country's service. In like manner "English Hearts and English Hands" is popular, in spite of its being religious, spiritual, and thoroughly evangelical. How is this? There are many qualities in it that cannot fail to make it a favorite with all whose better feelings are not quite dead. It is genuine, simple, unaffected. It makes no pretensions in regard to composition beyond unadorned truthfulness. It is replete with common sense and shrewdness; with the noblest acts of generosity combined with consummate wisdom and tact. Above all, it reveals the secret of doing good by confidence rather than suspicion, by cherishing the latent seeds of good in human nature rather than by violent antagonism to the evil which obtrudes itself on the surface. It would appear that the power of kindness and of perseverance in well-doing, even on the roughest natures, is all but irresistible. Navvies are not less distinguished for their physical strength and manual skill in the construction of great works, than they are notorious for their rough exterior, their fondness for the beer shop, their volleys of oaths, their delight in fights, and their thoughtless generosity of nature. Miss Marsh residing at the Rectory at Beckenham, near the Crystal Palace, Sydenham, when that structure was in course of erection, brougt herself incontact with the navvies engaged on the works. She seized the opportunity to endeavour to do them good. And this book contains the history of her benevolent attempts, and a most extraordinary history it is. The promotion of religion among them was the object she avowedly aimed at; religion was the instrument she openly worked by; she visited the men, collected them in cottage meetings, talked with them, expounded the Scriptures to them, prayed with them, wrote letters to them, and encouraged them to write others in return; she endeavoured to induce them to save their money and became their banker, to refrain from the public house, to send for their forsaken wives, to remember and assist their old and needy parents. And all this, and more, she effected to a wonderful extent. And how was all this received by those rough and untutored natures? The men idolised their benefactress, placed unbounded confidence in her, treated her with undeviating respect and politeness, never suffered her to hear an oath, and never abused the trust she reposed in them. Many were reclaimed from drunkenness, not a few became Christians indeed, eminent for the genuineness and consistency of their piety and the circumstances of a large number of them were greatly improved by the thrift they were induced to adopt. Nor were these effects transient, confined to the period when her personal influence could act as a restraint. Numbers of the men were drafted into the army working-corps for service in the Crimea, and while far away, toiling at the railway and roads between Balaklava and Sebastopol, amidst all the sufferings from cold and exposure, and the perils from shot and shell, and exposed to the strong temptation to drown their sorrows in strong drink, those noble fellows felt and owned the mighty influence of the gentle christian lady in distant England who took so deep an interest in their welfare. That influence, like the electric wire, seemed to be unaffected by distance, it still strengthened their resolutions to live a godly and virtuous life, and powerfully stimulated them to do their duty to

themselves, their families, their country, and their God.   It is a delicious refreshment to read such a book, and all may learn from it, who are willing to be taught,
valuable lessons in the art of doing good.   The selection of cases can give but a
slight idea of the book as a whole.   But we insert an extract at page 113.

The Christian Times and Australian Weekly News.   Edited by the Rev.
JAS. TAYLOR.

We hail with welcome the appearance of a religious newspaper in Melbourne.
The ordinary press of the country, daily and weekly, occupied as it is entirely with
secular affairs, and giving, as many think, an insufficient attention to religious
proceedings merely as matters of public interest, can never render unnecessary
journals professedly religious.   The religious newspaper is simply a supplement, to
supply a felt deficiency, and not a rival.   The prospectus announces that the
present undertaking belongs to no sect, but is based upon the principles of the
Evangelical Alliance.   Prominent notices of religious proceedings will be given,
and a vehicle will be furnished for the utterance of religious sentiments, while all
public questions, which do not involve party politics or denominational differences,
will be discussed and contemplated from a christian point of view.   A guarantee
fund has been subscribed to secure the experiment a fair trial.   The editorship is
undertaken, for the present, by the Rev. Jas. Taylor, who has generously offered to
serve gratuitously.   At the time we write three numbers of the paper have appeared.
It is well got up and ably conducted.   All it wants is to be heartily adopted by the
Christian public of Victoria as their journal; to be well furnished with suitable
matter for its pages by ministers and other competent persons, and to be largely
circulated throughout the various congregations; and then it may be expected to
prove an effective auxiliary to all movements tending to the increase of religion
in the community.

MISSIONS.

The Rev. James Russell, Missionary in connexion with the London Missionary Society, at Nagercoil, South Travancore, India, having visited Melbourne and Sydney not long ago for the recovery of his health, and having
returned to his sphere of labor with Mrs. Russell (daughter of Ambrose Foss.
Esq., Sydney), some communications lately received from them may not be
uninteresting to many of our readers.   The first letter relates to the Sepoy
Mutiny, and gives an account of a remarkable meeting of the " British Indian
Association," composed of native gentlemen of the highest standing in society,
still, however, retaining their connexion with the old religion of the country.
The speakers at this meeting (all natives) freely and intelligently criticised
Lord Ellenborough's speech in the House of Lords, in which he attributed the
rebellion very materially to missionary operations.   This, these native heathen
gentlemen utterly repudiate, and attribute it to totally different causes.   Their
speeches are given but are too long to extract.

The second communication relates to the missionary operations of Mr.
Russell and his fellow laborer, Mr. Dennis.   There are two stations in connexion with the South Travancore Mission—Nagercoil and Jamestown. In these
unitedly there are congregations, 49 ; adherents, 4,836; church members, 359 ;
native agents, 105; scholars, 2,416.   Mr. Russell's letter mentions the baptism
of *fifty-nine* converts on one day ; there was a considerable diversity in their ages,
circumstances, history and manner of conversion.   The account contains
biographical sketches of a considerable number of them.

A third letter contains the following account of an interesting conference of
missionaries of various denominations laboring in the South of India.   " A Conference was held in April last at the Neiligaries Hills.   It originated with the
missionaries in Bangalore ; all missionaries, with the exception of the Leipsic
Lutherans, connected with the Protestant Evangelical Societies laboring in
Southern India and North Ceylon, were invited to join in the proceedings.
Thirty-two European and American Missionaries connected with the following
societies attended: Church Missionary Society, 5 ; London Missionary, 10 ;
American Board of Foreign Missions, 6 ; German Evangelical, 6 ; Wesleyan, 2 ;

Free Church of Scotland, 1; Reformed Protestant Dutch Church of America, 1; Society for the Propagation of the Gospel, 1; there were also several friends present as visitors. The Conference sat from five to six hours daily for fourteen days. On all important subjects much unanimity of judgment was found to exist, while the spirit of christian love and union which prevailed throughout the whole of the proceedings demands special acknowledgment. A most gratifying practical exhibition of that real christian union which exists among all truly Evangelical Protestant Missionaries was placed before the Church and the world--this we cannot but regard as one of the most delightful features of the Conference. Besides the three devotional services blended with the business of the Conference, one day was entirely devoted to that purpose. On the last day, May 5th, the members of the Conference, with the families of a few at present on the Hills for the restoration of their health, and a considerable number of christian friends breakfasted together ; the breakfast having been provided by two Christian Officers at present on the Hills. In the evening of the same day, a Public Meeting was held, when five of the Missionaries gave addresses on topics connected with the Conference and missionary work. At this meeting the Bishop of Madras was expected to take the chair ; he was, however, prevented arriving in time by the inclemency of the weather ; in his lordship's unavoidable absence, J. M. Cherry, Esq., Acting Collector of Coimbatore, kindly consented to preside. Considering the very unfavorable state of the weather the attendance was excellent, and all seemed much interested. The subjects brought forward amounted to twenty in number. The Rev. Mr. Cox, from Trevandrum, and the Rev. Mr. Baylis, from Negoor, went as our representatives."

The following account of the Island of CEYLON was delivered as a Missionary Lecture, at Collins-street Chapel, Melbourne, by the Rev. A. Morison, on Friday evening, August, 27, 1858. *(Concluded from page 87.)*

It cannot be wondered that the introduction of the Gospel to such a people is, and must be, a task of more than ordinary difficulty.

Besides these there are moor-men, a race of Arabs, who profess the Mahommedan religion ; the Portuguese, the first European conquerors of this country; the Dutch settlers, who succeeded them in power ; and the British, who in 1796 took possession of the coasts, and in whose power the island still continues. The Malabars, or Tamuls, a Hindoo race, occupy the northern and eastern parts of the island, who are devoted to the Hindoo superstition and worship.

Three principal forms of superstition prevail in Ceylon—Hindooism, Buddhism, and Devil-worship, which we require to know something about, before we can understand the difficulties that missionaries have to contend with in endeavoring to Christianise the inhabitants. Hindoos suppose that EVIL has come into the world in consequence of the union of SPIRIT with MATTER, and is to be done away by suffering, or acts of charity or religious observances· The soul which is supposed at death to pass from the body of one animal to another, is thereby prepared for a reunion with the divine spirit of which it is a part, as a drop of water with the ocean. After obtaining a human birth the soul may be doomed to be born a brute, or exist as a tree or plant. Good and evil may be entailed from one birth to another, and the fate of each is written in his head when he is born. They speak of heaven and hell in a different sense from Christians. Each god has his own heaven, where he receives his worshippers and grants them sensual indulgences according to their merits, after which they become subject to the vicissitudes of mortal birth. Even the gods are subject to this change. Such persons as die without merit are sent to the god of death to be tormented as in purgatory, until their sins are expiated : and they are allowed another birth. Others who rise to the highest merits are absorbed in the divine essence. This system destroys by its fatalism the sense of accountability and fear of the consequence of sin ; and the people's apathy is increased by the ease with which sin is done away. The putting a light in a temple, bathing in any holy water, marking the forehead and breast with holy ashes, and such things, will effectually atone for sin, and secure happiness after death. The following stories will explain some of these notions. A RAT was one night in a temple where the lamp had burned down before the idol. Being very hungry the rat went to the lamp for oil, and, in attempting to get it, pulled up the wick so as to make it burn brightly. The god was so pleased as to cause the rat to be born a king, to whom he gave the dominion of the three worlds—the sky, the earth, and the lower region—for a thousand years. A very wicked man, who had murdered his father and elder brother to obtain their wives, and had in consequence become mad, was standing by the Cavary, a holy river, when a woman washing a cloth sprinkled a little of the water on him. His senses were restored, when plunging into the river he bathed and went to heaven. A man driving a hog by the same river was pushed by the animal into the water. Both fell in and went to heaven. The body of a very vile man who died in the midst of his sins, was lying in an outhouse where a dog was asleep on a heap of ashes. The servants of Yuma, the god of death, came to take his soul, but as they approached the dog awoke, and as he ran out stepped on the forehead and breast of the man so as to leave the marks of the ashes. The servants of Yuma seeing the marks said, "he is a holy man, he has the marks of Siva," and left him. The servants of Siva immediately came and took his soul to heaven. With such notions as these it is all but impossible to alarm their fears or to awaken their consciences.

The religion of Buddha is in many points like the Hindoo system. Its adherents entertain the doctrine of the passing of the soul from the body of one animal to another, accordingly as a man has acted virtuously or otherwise, and the ultimate attainment of happiness to be absorption into the Deity; but there are various heavens of glory and hells of misery to which souls are consigned. Buddha was a reformer, who lived some centuries before the Christian era, who taught these doctrines, and along with them inculcated a moral code that is second only to Christianity. But the mass of the population of Ceylon are profoundly ignorant of the tenets of their creed. In their daily intercourse and acts, morality and virtue are rarely seen. Neither hopes nor fears restrain them from habitually violating all those precepts of charity and honesty, purity, and truth, which form the very essence of their doctrine. Thus, insufficient for time, and rejecting eternity, a Buddhist lives without fear and dies without hope.

Before the introduction of Buddhism, in early ages, to Ceylon, the people were devoted devil-worshippers, and this worship is still common among them. On every domestic occurrence and calamity, the services of the devil-priests are sought, and their ceremonies performed in a most barbarous and revolting manner. Especially in cases of sickness and danger the assistance of the devil-dancer is implicitly relied on. An altar, decorated with garlands, is erected within sight of the patient, and on this an animal, frequently a cock, is sacrificed for his recovery. Mr. Baker says of them—"The Cingalese have a thorough belief in demoniacal possessions; one sect are actually devil worshippers. There is no character to work upon in the natives—they are faithless, cunning, treacherous, and abject cowards, superstitious in the extreme, and yet unbelieving in any one god. A Buddhist will address his prayer to the Christian's God if he thinks he can obtain any temporal benefit by so doing; but, if not, he would be just as likely to pray to the devil." He then narrates a case of possession—"On our return to the post-holder's hut, we dined and prepared for sleep. It was a calm night, and not a sound disturbed the stillness of the air. The tired coolies and servants were fast asleep, the lamp burned dimly, and we were about to lie down to rest, when a frightful scream made us spring to our feet. There was something so unearthly in the yell that we could hardly believe it human. The next moment a figure bounded into the room. It was black, and stark naked. His tongue half bitten through protruded from his mouth, his blood-shot eyes with a ghastly stare were straining from their sockets, as he stood gazing at us with his arms extended wide apart. Another horrible scream burst from him, and he fell flat upon his back. The post-holder and the coolies then assembled, and they all at once declared that the man had a devil. His convulsions were terrible. Without moving a limb he flapped here and there like a salmon when just landed. I had nothing with me that could relieve him, and I therefore left him in the hands of the post-holder, who prided himself on his skill in exorcising devils. All his incantations produced no effect, and the unfortunate patient suddenly sprung to his feet, and rushed madly into the thorny jungle. In this we heard him crushing through like a wild beast, and I do not know whether he was ever heard of afterwards."

Knox, an Englishman, who was, some centuries ago, a captive in this island for many years, says—" This for certain I can affirm that oftentimes the devil doth cry with audible voice in the night; 'tis very shrill, and almost like the barking of a dog; this I have often heard myself, but never heard that he did anybody harm. Only this observation the inhabitants of the land have made of this voice, and I have made it also, that either just before or very suddenly after this voice, always the king cuts off the people. To believe that this is the voice of the devil, these reasons urge—because there is no creature known to the inhabitants that cries like it, and because that it will on a sudden depart from one place and make a noise in another quicker than any fowl could fly, and because the very dogs will tremble and shake when they hear it, and it is so accounted by all the people." Such is the testimony of an intelligent, observing and pious man, and it will serve to show how difficult it must prove to emancipate the duller natures of the superstitious natives from their addictedness to devil-worship, that slavery of soul by which they directly offer to the enemy of God and man, an homage of sacrifice and service to propitiate his clemency.

The Portuguese being the first Europeans who established, early in the sixteenth century, a regular intercourse with Ceylon, were the first to introduce any form of Christianity to that people; and Francis Xavier, the so-called Apostle to the Indies, lived and labored chiefly in this island. The Roman Catholic religion therefore spread among the people, and in 1848 there were stated to be 115,000 professors of this creed, a bishop, vicar apostolic, twenty-eight missionaries and 324 churches. They have few schools, and these poorly supported, their main object being to create members of their church, who, for the most part, are "baptized heathens." Lord Torrington, in a report, states that multitudes call themselves Christians, and attend to all the outward observances of the church, but in secret they are still more attached to the doctrines of Buddha and the Hindoo mythology; and, at the approach of death turn doubtingly from the sacraments of their nominal church to repose their last confidence in the ceremonies of devil-worship, and in the priests of Brahma and Buddha. The following fact will give some idea of this state of things:— " I once saw a sample of heathen conversion in Ceylon (says Mr. Baker, writing in 1854), that was enough to dishearten a missionary. A Roman Catholic chapel had been erected in a wild part of the country by some zealous missionary, who prided himself on the number of his converts. He left his chapel for a few weeks absence in some other district, during which time his converts paid their devotions at the Christian altar. They had made a few little additions to the ornaments of the altars, that must have astonished the priest on his return. There was an image of our Saviour and the Virgin—this was all according to custom—but there were also three images of Buddha, a colored plaster-of-Paris image of the Queen and Prince Albert, upon the altar, and a very questionable penny print in vivid colors hanging over the altar, entitled ' the stolen kiss.' So much for the conversion of the heathen in Ceylon." We may add that real conversion is impossible under a system of Christianity in which veneration of images cannot be distinguished by the heathen from their own primitive idolatry, but the argument cannot go any farther than this.

At the commencement of the 17th century, the Dutch, having wrested the island from the Crown of Portugal, attempted to convert the natives to the

Protestant faith.   Unfortunately this was by absurdly ordaining that no native should be admitted to any employment under government unless he subscribed the Helvetic Confession, and consented to become a member of the reformed church.   Hypocrites in abundance were found willing, as nothing was required from the candidates for baptism but a repetition of the Lord's prayer, the ten commandments, a short morning and evening prayer, and grace before and after meat.   Under this system, in the northern district, alone 62,558 men and women, and 2,587 slaves, professed Christianity, and within a few years 12,387 children were baptized.

Nearly a century later, that is in 1740, two Moravian missionaries endeavored to preach the Gospel to these baptized heathens, but their work was speedily stopped by the Dutch governor, and the missionaries were removed from the island.

In the year 1812 the Baptist Missionary Society made a commencement at Ceylon, by establishing a missionary station at Colombo.   In the course of years stations in the Cingalese district have been multiplied, and faithful laborers have gathered fruit in real conversions.   The great effort on the part of Protestant missionaries being to obtain as early as possible a translation of the Scriptures into the vernacular of the country, so that the natives in their own tongue may read and hear the wonderful works of God, the earliest labors therefore are the formation of grammars, and translations of the Bible, in which work the Baptist missionaries have been greatly distinguished.

In 1814 a Wesleyan mission to the island was originated under affecting circumstances.   The brethren who entered on this mission were warmly welcomed by the English Governor, and under his advice commenced at four different points, at Jaffna and Batticaloa, for the Tamuls; and at Galle and Matura, for the Cingalese.   These missions since that period have been greatly extended.   In 1848 there were 2,963 boys and 675 girls in their schools; and their congregations were estimated at 10,000.   Wherever a Wesleyan chapel or school is maintained, there is a marked improvement in the public morals of the locality.

The American Board of Missions were the next in the field.   In 1815 a company of their agents landed, and selected Jaffna and its vicinity as the scene of their future labors, and its Tamul population as the object of their care.   Of this first company one returned in 1848 to America.   There were then twelve, including a physician, who were associated as teachers, preachers, and printers, and the constitution of this society is so free from sectarianism, that it includes clergy of different denominations, living under the same roof, using the same pulpit, and engaged in the same pursuits, and all as a body have shown the greatest anxiety to co-operate with the missionaries of the Church of England, and the Wesleyans, in the promotion of the same object, the diffusion of intellectual and religious instruction and expounding the great principles of simple Christianity.   The object of the mission, as stated in one of their reports, is not to disseminate the tenets of any one party; their missionaries are chosen from Congregational and Presbyterian Churches, and are sent out to preach repentance of sin and justification by faith in Christ as the only way of salvation.   Up to that time, 1848, twenty-three natives were trained as missionaries: 93,000 children, male and female, have been trained in their schools, 25,000 have received a competent education.   There had been £100,000 of voluntary subscription in the United States spent on this work; they have established extensive boarding schools, where the children are trained under the care of the missionaries and their wives.   The effect of this system on the people generally, and, above all, the influence and example of the females who have received their education in these establishments, are now producing highly beneficial results in the aspects of the community generally, and are working by degrees a decided change for the better in the domestic habits of the people.   A Tamul college has been established at Batticaloa, and from 1823 to 1848, 570 students were admitted, from whom the majority of the native officers employed by the Government have been supplied.   The printing establishment of the mission gives employment to 82 workmen.

50.000 volumes a year are issued. In consequence of this eminent success attending the labors of this mission, and the fraternal Christian spirit of its agents, the Legislative Council of the island have confided their educational grants to the management of a committee or joint Board of American, Wesleyan, and Episcopalian missionaries, an arrangement that has been highly satisfactory in its working and results.

In 1816 the island was made a part of the Bishopric of Calcutta, and an archdeacon appointed to administer its affairs. The Church Missionary Society in 1818 sent four missionaries, who commenced their labors, one at Candy, one at Calpentym, one at Galle, and one at Jaffna. These were increased in the progress of years. The happy influence of these laborers over the minds of the natives is seen in the fact that most of the mission churches and chapels are proposed by the natives themselves, and are raised chiefly by their voluntary contributions of materials, labor, or money. In 1845 the island was erected into a bishopric. Much has been done towards the extension of education by the Church of England without the aid of Government. The Diocesan School Society, in which their bishop is zealously interested, had been most successful in its exertions. In 1848 about 1,000 children were instructed under it in 30 schools, either supported or assisted in different parts of the colony, and grants had been made by the Christian Knowledge Society to print 2,000 copies of the Gospels, and 3,000 of the Parable Discourses, and Miracles of the Saviour in Cingalese.

Last in the field is the Scots' Church Mission, which at Colombo commenced a number of female schools, in which 280 native girls are educated on Christian principles. The best results might be expected from the improved training of the native female mind under the supervision of ladies, which has been found difficult to carry out in the Government schools. The Scottish Ladies' Society for Female Education in India has contributed largely to the formation of these schools, and have established a boarding school for girls after the model of that of the American missionaries at Jaffna, which is so deservedly admired, and has been so beneficial in its results.

With so much of Christian zeal, guided by heavenly wisdom, and such extensive and enlarging means of Christian education, we may hope well for the future of Ceylon, and pray that in a land of such beauty and richness, where every prospect pleases, man, alone the blot in its fair scenery, will cease to be vile.

SOUTH SEAS.

The London Missionary Society. The *John Williams*, missionary barque, having visited Tahiti and the various mission stations in the Society Islands and the Hervey Groupe arrived at Samoa in the month of June last She was to leave the Navigators Islands the first week in July to make her westward voyage. The Rev. G. Gill, of Rarotonga, and the Rev. G. Stallworthy, of the Samoan missions, were appointed the deputation to visit the out-stations of the London Missionary Society, and to locate native teachers on the Western Islands. The Rev. S. Creagh and family were on board, and proceed in the *John Williams* to their station on the island of Mari, New Caledonian group; and the Rev. Mr. Matheson and Mrs Matheson, from the Presbyterian Church, Nova Scotia, were also on their way to join the mission in the New Hebrides, under the charge of the Revs. J. Geddie and J. Inglis. Two missionaries from Scotland arrived in Hobson's Bay about a month ago, in the *Clutho*—the Revds. W. Paton and Copeland, for the South Sea Missions. They were fortunate in getting a passage in the *Harlem Page* direct to Auciteum, and after a short residence with the missionaries there, they hope to occupy a station on the island of Tana. The Rev. Mr. Gordon, of the Nova Scotia Presbyterian Church, is labouring on the island of Eromanga. The missionary and the native teachers have been suffering much from a scarcity of food, "almost starving" and a few friends in Sydney, on receipt of the intelligence, purchased a quantity of rice, &c., but the rush to the Fitzroy gold-fields has caused the vessels trading to the islands to be laid on for Port Curtis, and the supplies cannot be sent for the present. It is to be feared the mission families will have to endure great privations, if no vessel calls at Eromanga in the meantime, to furnish them with an opportunity of purchasing supplies. In a letter dated April 10th, 1858, from the wife of the Rev. J. Jones, of the Mari Mission, she states " that about two months ago the 8i Medu tribe killed two Church members, who went to preach Jesus to them. The women, when the teachers had been struck down, gathered round to drink the blood of the poor men as it flowed from their wounds, and while they were yet alive. Nor did they scruple respecting their bodies, but devoured them like greedy wolves." Surely "the dark places of the earth are full of the habitations of cruelty."

AMERICAN REVIVALS.

ANOTHER LARGE ACCESSION TO PLYMOUTH CHURCH, BROOKLYN, NEW YORK.

Recently, another large accession, numbering one hundred and sixty-one persons, was made to Plymouth Congregational Church, Brooklyn. This gratifying increase occurs only four weeks after a similar accession of one hundred and ninety. The revival in this church, of which these are some of the fruits, has continually increased in power and extent from the beginning, and at present is rather advancing than declining. The work throughout has been of a most delightful character, marked with no unusual, and even with less than usual excitement. The only extra meetings have been those held every morning for prayer, which, as they have been continued without interruption for more than a year, are regarded, not as extra, but as regular and indispensable. The average attendance every morning is about four hundred, though upon some occasions the lecture-room, with its aisles and vestibule crowded, has been too small for the numbers that have attended. Many of the Wednesday evening lectures have been given in the body of the church, which has been filled.

Unusual interest is manifest also in the Sunday-school, and about sixty conversions have already occurred among the scholars. For a few weeks past, after the afternoon session of the school, a prayer-meeting for the boys and another for the girls have been held for an hour, at which some very remarkable manifestations of the Divine Spirit have been witnessed. Many of the children have risen, and with tears in their eyes and deep emotion in their hearts, confessed their sins, and solemnly vowed in the presence of their companions, to begin a Christian life; and many others who have already begun it, have also risen in tears, though in tears of joy, to express their gratitude to God that he had touched them by his Spirit, and brought them to the Lord Jesus! Some of the requests for prayer made by the children have been very affecting; as, when a little boy, not ten years old, asked his companions in the meeting last Sunday afternoon to pray for the conversion of his grandfather, and others asked for the conversion of their parents and many older relatives and friends. On Tuesday evening a prayer-meeting of almost unparalleled interest was held by the boys, at which before it concluded, ten conversions occurred! The spirit of these meetings is almost Pentecostal. The only adult persons present were one or two officers of the Sunday school, with whom the children are familiar, and whose presence does not produce restraint or intimidation. The interest in the Sabbath-school almost, if possible, exceeds that in the large congregation.

Among the large companies who have been received into the church at the last two communions, the instances of persons who have come in alone, without some of their own friends or their own family, have been comparatively few; while in some cases whole families unbroken, have come in together—father, mother, and children, side by side! In other children who came in at the May communion brought in their parents last Sunday; while very many of the children of parents who have been long members of the Church, have been gathered into the flock in answer to prayers that have gone up from the altars of many households. The entire body of the church was filled, including the aisles, while many persons remained in the galleries, as silent spectators of the solemn yet joyful scene. It is a happy day in the history of any church when more of the congregation remain at communion than go away from it! On this occasion not far from two thousand persons mingled in that festival whose partaken emblems are to "show forth the Lord's death till he come."—*New York Paper.*

TESTIMONY OF DR. MONOD.

As to the reality of the Revival most valuable testimony has been borne by the Rev. Dr Monod of Paris, who has returned to France, after a very extended tour over the United States. Recently, while at Havre, he bore the following public testimony, which is the more valuable, as he has been suspicious and sceptical of "American Revivals," so called, and was therefore ready to detect imposture or fanaticism. "He had attended many of their meetings —taken part in their services—his eyes and ears were open and attentive to all that was going on around him—he had stood in the midst of three or four thousand people, all assembled for prayer and praise—had heard short and touching narratives of individual conversions, that melted thousands into tears; short and tender addresses, earnest and pathetic appeals to Christians for their united prayers in behalf of special cases; yet, with all this, there was a stillness and a solemnity pervading the entire assembly, such as he had never witnessed before. Nor had he, in all the meetings he had ever attended, once seen anything that had the slightest approach to fanaticism, nor anything that he could take the least exception to. And to use the language of one of the American ministers, it was without controversy " a revival," not got up by men. but brought down from above! As for myself I have not the shadow of a doubt but that it is the genuine work of the Holy Spirit."

At a prayer meeting held at his brother's house, Dr. Monod related some thrilling facts, when without preconcert, in the spontaneous outburst of a new born soul, his own son—who had accompanied him in all his travels—gave a simple and touching account of what the Lord had done for his own soul, and of the faith which he now had in the prayers of God's people. It suffused all eyes with tears and melted all hearts.—*British Evangelist.*

DR. SCHAUFFLER ON THE AMERICAN REVIVAL.

A meeting was held at Willis's Rooms, London, to receive the statements of Rev. Dr. Schauffler, the eminent American missionary in Turkey—now in England *en route* from the United States to Constantinople—with regard to the religious awakening in America. The Earl of Shaftesbury presided. Sir Fenwick Williams, of Kars, and several clergymen and gentlemen connected with the Turkish Missions-Aid Society, supported his lordship on the platform. The proceedings having been commenced with prayer, the noble chairman made a few introductory remarks. The Rev. Dr. SCHAUFFLER then came forward, and, after some personal explanations, proceeded to state that one of his reasons for undertaking the duty then before him was, that the beginning of the American revival was but little understood in England. When he reached America from Turkey a year ago, there was no more than the common interest in religion—it was, indeed, rather at a low ebb, and he remembered that apprehension had been expressed with regard to the effect of the unexampled prosperity which then prevailed in that country. Ere long came the great monetary panic, the operation of which he graphically described. There was universal dismay and distress; and many of those who suffered, bowed with silent submission, being constrained to acknowledge that God had a controversy with the land. He bore testimony to the faithfulness with which the moral and religious lessons of this commercial calamity had been handled in the pulpit. He next described the preparatory process of house-to-house visitation in New York, organised by the American Sunday-school Union, primarily with a view to gathering into the Sunday-schools of that city some 50,000 neglected children. A day of fasting and prayer was observed in connection with this movement, and it was determined to divide the whole city into districts in order to the proposed canvass, in which all the orthodox churches were to take part. The plan was arranged, but there seemed a doubt whether it would be carried into effect, until several females came forward, and offered their services as visitors—among them was an old lady eighty years of age. This was decisive. The scheme was carried out, the visitation embracing every house, rich and poor alike. Where there were no children to enlist for the schools, a word in season was addressed to adults. The reception accorded to the visitors by all classes—from merchant princes down to the lowest—was very encouraging, and the entire result of this movement must have been most beneficial. This, however, was only preparatory. The revival itself began with three pious merchants who were led to commence a prayer-meeting in John-street. Dr. Schauffler described the rapid increase of this meeting, and the extraordinary manner in which it led to the multiplication of similar meetings, to which large and constant auditories were drawn, not to hear addresses from powerful speakers but simply for prayer. These meetings now appeared to be covering the whole land. They were carried on and conducted chiefly by laymen. Six minutes was the limit allowed for a prayer or an address, and the greatest particularity was observed in the times of commencing and closing the services. He dwelt on the absence of excitement; yet sometimes in an assembly of 3000 souls, the sight of hundreds of uplifted hands, giving token of a desire on the part of the unconverted for an interest in the prayers of the Lord's people, was so affecting as to cause tears; at others the feeling of being blessed by the Divine presence was so overpowering that the prayer-meeting became involuntarily a meeting of thanksgiving, all present seeming to feel that their cup was running over. On results he would touch but lightly, but they must be considered as great and good. As an example it was stated that in 125 Congregational churches in Massachusetts alone, there were received on the first Sunday in May, 11,000 new members. It was estimated that the weekly harvest of conversions in the entire States was as much as 50,000. The colleges had largely shared the blessing, as he showed, especially with regard to the remarkable work of grace among the 400 students in

Yale College, Newhaven. Although, as already stated, the laity took a prominent part in the revival movement, the ministry and the pulpit had risen to a degree of respect, not only among the pious but even among the worldly, such as they never before enjoyed. Another result had been the promotion of real Christian Union. The way in which the secular, and even some of the most unprincipled newspapers spoke of the revival, was a remarkable evidence of its power. This altered tone might lead some to think that the editors had been converted, but the fact was rather that the movement exercised an influence which carried them with it, whether they would or not. The revival had extended to the State Legislatures ; and he had heard that at Washington a place was being sought for prayer-meetings among members of the Senate—a thing greatly needed.

CORRESPONDENCE.

To the Editor of the Southern Spectator.

SIR,—In your last number your correspondent T. writes on Family Worship in consequence of " his acquaintance with many families who are zealous members of the Church of Christ, but who, notwithstanding, omit this duty altogether."

Can this be true? And if true, is it consistent with the discipline of any scriptural church to allow the heads of such families to remain members?

Also your correspondent says, " The service should consist of the whole or a portion of a suitable chapter of holy scripture, and the offering of a concise, fervent prayer, acknowledging God's mercies, and praying for a continuation of the same." Is this a proper directory for family worship? I am not sure that the direction for prayer goes far enough even for a beginner, at any rate I would rather recommend the Lord's Prayer. But can the worship be complete without praise? Are none of the commands to praise God and to *sing his praises* with which the Scriptures abound, imperative upon his worshippers in the family? It is evident the puritan fathers practised singing in their family worship, from their being reproached as psalm singers. I believe the christian converts from heathenism in the present day generally practise it. And does not the neglect of this "comely " part of domestic worship, by some who observe it as recommended by your correspondent, proceed from the same causes which, he alleges, prevent a class of timid Christians from observing it in any form, namely, that they fear man, are ashamed of their religion, and hide their light from view?

Of course there may be families that cannot sing, as there are that cannot read; but I think, in either case, no time should be lost before beginning to learn ; and now that singing is regularly taught in the schools supported by Government, most children can sing, and many of them can lead singing, consequently the cases in which a psalm or hymn cannot be sung in a family are few : and certainly, supposing it to be a duty, there can be no excuse for the habitual neglect of it where there is a musical instrument and some one who can play in the family.

I could give instances that have come under my observation of good effected through singing being a regular part of the family worship, but fear to intrude further on your space.

I am, A DELIGHTED READER OF YOUR MAGAZINE.

HARMONIOUS WORKING OF DIFFERENT CHURCHES.
To the Editor of the Southern Spectator.

SIR,—Nothing very remarkable has happened since last I attempted to give you a picture of the religious condition of our community. Although our town is the capital of one of the Australian gold-fields, which have a world-wide fame for commotion and progress, one day or one week is very like the week or the day that is past. Nevertheless there are changes, and if we could contrast our social state with that of one of our quiet English villages, we should see a wonderful difference in the rate of progression. To be stationary or be going back would be death to one of our mining capitals. The general complaint is that the various religious bodies are too active ; the call for contributions is incessant ; no sooner is one claim satisfied than another comes, and when all are satisfied the round begins again. At this present time there are, or have been, three distinct canvassings of Sandhurst for money. Our Scotch friends, who commenced their handsome new church not many months ago, have found that, although £1000 in the bank may be a good balance in hand to start with, it will not complete their work, and they are calling on all for help. The Church of England here is burdened with a very heavy debt, and they are likewise making an effort to lessen their liability. And we of the Congregational section of the Church, have likewise made our appeal to the public, and are thankful to say not without a substantial response. We are none of us going to sleep, but all wishful for the means and the opportunities of doing more. Beyond these direct solicitations for aid, our whole town is at present made aware of the existence of a Wesleyan Bazaar, by the multitude of flags and Chinese lanthorns which adorn one of the entrances to what is commonly a carriage repository. Under the superintendence of their energetic minister, Mr. Dare, they have succeeded in furnishing a very splendid bazaar, by which they hope to realise about £600 or £700. We are doing our best here to solve the problem as to whether it is possible for all sections of the Church to be active and not to clash, and so far it has proved quite practicable. We work together and all help one another. Ministers who are in earnest in their work cannot, without a great loss of the vital power of their own godliness, look with a jaundiced eye on the doings of their brother ministers. On the ocean of true Christian feeling these cockboats of prejudice and denominationalism get swamped. I have a great dread of our religious differences being a laughing stock in the eyes of the community. In England they seem to be the source of life in many of the sections of Christianity—as a high church clergyman once inferred, when he said dissent was a blister on the side of the Church, to correct its evils, and when the evils were gone the blister would be removed; but here I think it may be possible to be active from the mere love of the truth and energetic from the prospect of the work yet to be done, and all the while not to abate one principle that we esteem right. I wish we could carry out our union more into action. It has answered in exceptional cases, but it is difficult owing to the strict ritual of some of our Evangelical communions.

I have received and welcomed the first number of the *Christian Times*; if it can only live till it is appreciated and known, its permanent establishment will then be a settled question. It is greatly needed; more, however, as a corrective for the opposite tendencies of the majority of our newspapers, than as itself a substitute for them; yet it may take its place as a supplement. Religion is too great a power in the State now, to be neglected any longer by the public press, and the spirit of religion is too free to brook any longer its subserviency to men who care little for it, when it needs to speak with the world. At the same time I would express my fears as to this new journal obtaining a wide circulation at once on the gold-fields. People here are not in circumstances to feel the want of such a paper to the extent that those do who live within the influence of the metropolis. The want has to be created first, and it may take some years before our up-country society is sufficiently christianised to appreciate as it ought such a journal.   FIDES.

Sandhurst, Oct. 18., 1858.

———◆———

RELIGIOUS INTELLIGENCE.

NEW SOUTH WALES.—Wollongong.—The anniversary services in connection wi the Congregational Church of this place, have been held, according to previous advertisement. On Sabbath morning, October 10, the Rev. Joseph Beasley, from Sydney, preached from Rom. viii. 16. In the evening the same gentleman preached from Phil. 1st chapter, 1st and 27th verses. On Tuesday morning, at 11, Mr. Beasley preached from the 3rd of Phil., 8th verse. He referred to the disappointment all present must feel in not seeing Mr. Cuthbertson, but some circumstance had prevented his arrival, and none felt it more than himself. In the afternoon, at two, between 70 and 80 friends took tea in the verandah of Mr. G. Hewlett's house, the rain having rendered it impossible to assemble in the booth. At seven in the evening, a public meeting was held in the church, when speeches were delivered by various gentlemen; the speech of the evening being that of Mr. Beasley. Considering the inclemency of the weather, the attendance at the services was as well as could be expected. The collections amounted to about £15.

SOUTH AUSTRALIA.—Port Adelaide Bible Society.—Extracts from the Report for 1858:—"The Committee have to report that they have divided the district into eleven divisions,or sub-districts,for the purpose of collecting subscriptions,and they have no small satisfaction in announcing that for each district they have obtained regular collectors The number of the collectors is at present seventeen. They report that the districts are generally well supplied with Bibles. While on this subject the Committee would be both ungallant, as well as ungrateful, if they did not express their best thanks to those ladies who have so kindly undertaken, and so faithfully fulfilled, the office of collectors. To their labors and exertions, humanly speaking, the Committee owe all their success. The subscriptions of this year amount to £108 13s. 5d., to which may be added £9 3s. 5d. collected at the last annual meeting. This makes in all £117 16s. 10d. collected in this district since the publication of the last balance-sheet. This, bearing in mind the difference of the time during which collections were made (eleven months being embraced in this report and eighteen in the previous one) contrasts favourably with the £150 of the last report, the more so as two districts have at present made no return for the last quarter. The issue of bibles and testiments has also kept up. Against 174 bibles and 33 testaments, mentioned in the last report, there have been issued during the last eleven months, 113 bibles and 46 testaments. In free subscribers the past year shows an improvement, though many are reported to have fallen off. What, however, we have lost in one quarter we have gained in another, for there are now 95 free subscribers against sixty in the last report. While in all the main points the labors of the Society have been thus successful the Committee can record with less regret than they otherwise could have done the loss sustained by them during the terrible fire which broke out in the Port, on the 9th of November last, when the whole stock of books to the value of £30 was destroyed. The depôt, however, has since been replenished, and the sum of £79 10s. 6d. has been remitted to the Parent Society for books since the last annual meeting. The result of this loss has been that the Committee have not been able to give this year more than £30 as a free contribution to the Parent Society. In concluding this report, the Committee would simply remind the friends and subscribers of the object of the British and Foreign Bible Society, in which this branch is supposed to take a share—namely, of supplying the whole world with the Word of God. In mentioning this, it is hardly necessary to add how, though much has been done in the way of translating and circulating the Scriptures, still more remains to be done. The work is only yet in its infancy. Successful, then, as this Branch has been, it is not for us to relax our efforts; we cannot yet rest, as if our work was done either at home or abroad. Our donation is but a particle of a drop in the ocean. The Committee would, therefore, urge every Christian about them to take care that the donation from this Branch Society shall never be less; and, while praying for God's blessing on so good a cause, to be sure to bear his share of the burden—if it can be called a burden—of joining to bring about the time when 'knowledge (the true knowledge of God) shall be increased, and when they shall all know me, from the least of them unto the greatest of them, saith the Lord.'"

CHURCH AND CHAPEL EXTENSION.—The work of Church and Chapel building is progressing with every symptom of healthy action on the part of the different denominations, but we have no general reports to make. The same healthy tone also characterises our scholastic movements, but there have been neither examinations, statements, nor reports since our last summary.—*South Australian Advertiser, Summary for October*, 1858.

BIBLE CHRISTIAN MISSIONARY SOCIETY.—A numerously attended meeting of this Society was held on the 21st Sept., in the Bible Christian Chapel, Bowden, Mr. Pickering in the chair. The meeting was addressed by Messrs. J. Rowe, T. E. Keen, J. Ashton, and Crabb. The good already done by this and kindred societies, and the large amount of work still remaining to do, were dwelt upon; while the former afforded much encouragement, the latter called for redoubled exertion. The condition of the aborigines of this colony was referred to. Mr. Keen considered the Christian Churches of South Australia guilty of neglect of the aborigines, and spoke highly of the speeches made at the meeting held recently in Adelaide, on their behalf; but he thought one thing had been overlooked, viz., the manner in which attempts were made to evangelize the natives. Why not deal with the natives of this country as with those of Africa and other places? Why bring them into institutions and subject them to a regimen and style of living altogether uncongenial to their natural dispositions? Why not carry the Gospel to them in the bush and to their wurleys? In this matter let the missionary copy the example of the indefatigable Mr. Moffat. In order to civilize the natives let them first evangelize them. Three sermons preparatory to this meeting were preached on the preceding Sunday, to large audiences, by Mr. J Counter and the Rev. Mr. Wilson, Congregational Minister. An excellent tea was provided on the afternoon of the 21st, which was well attended and decidedly enjoyed. The proceeds of the above services were, in cash, £27 7s. 10¼d., in promises, £4; total, £31 7s. 10¼d.

SOUTH AUSTRALIAN BUSH MISSIONARY SOCIETY.—A meeting of about 40 or 50 of the friends of this Society was recently held in White's Committee Room. Amongst those present were the Hon. Captain Bagot, in the chair; Hon. Captain Scott, Revs. Schoales, Evan, Wilson, Cox, Howie, Dixon, Cheetham and Scott; and Messrs. Tomkinson, J.P., Moulden, Peacock, S. Bakewell, H. Gill, J. Smith, C. Bowen and C. Sabine. The Chairman briefly stated the objects of the meeting, which were the spreading of the Gospel in those distant and thinly populated portions of the colony where places of worship could not be erected, nor a settled ministry maintained. The Secretary read the report, from which it appeared that the receipts of the Society from January, 1857, up to date were £442 11s. 9d., and the expenses £441 18s., leaving a balance of 13s. 9d. The agents were in the habit of visiting the sheepstations, woolsheds and shepherds' huts, not confining their attention to those places only where considerable numbers of people could be got together, but ministering to the spiritual wants of small knots of men—generally met with in the evening. It was also stated that the agents generally met with a hearty welcome, and that in no case had a room been refused them by the overseers. Some instances were mentioned of the usefulness of the agents. The Secretary, in answer to an observation from a gentleman present, made a statement, which he believed was approximately correct, showing the number of persons visited by the agents (about 25 daily), the number of miles travelled, and the number of times the same individuals were met with. The last was the least satisfactory part of the statement It appeared that the agents of the Society did not come into contact with the same individuals oftener than about once in six weeks. A resolution was passed, commending the Society to the sympathy and support of the Christian community. A question arose as to the best means of collecting the £300 which it was said would be necessary for the ensuing year. No plan was finally decided on, but the following gentlemen were added to the already existing committee, and it is to be hoped they may be able to make all necessary arrangements as to funds:—Messrs. Abbott, Bakewell, Josh. Gurr, A. Macgeorge, Monk, D.A.C.G., Murray, Prince, Smedley, Bowen, Faulding, M. Good, Harvey, Morcom, Peacock, and J. Smith. Votes of thanks were then passed to the original Committee and the chair, and the meeting separated.

THE REV. THOMAS BINNEY. — The great event in the religious world of South Australia during the last few weeks has been the arrival of the Rev. Thomas Binney, of London. The reverend gentleman has been followed from place to place by admiring crowds, from the Governor downwards, wherever he has announced his intention of preaching or lecturing. The following notice refers to his lecture on St. Paul, delivered in Adelaide on the evening of October 7:—This far-famed preacher delivered on Thursday evening a lecture at White's rooms, on the "Character and Ministrations of St. Paul." With regard to his lecture we shall merely say that it was a masterpiece of oral biography. Mr. Binney has deeply drank into the spirit of "the chiefest of the Apostles." Whether in analysing the apostolic character, in elucidating the apostolic writings, in tracing the apostolic journeys, or in weighing the apostolic labors, Mr. Binney is equally at ease. He speaks of Paul as of a master from whose lips he has learned wisdom, as a friend at whose side he has stood, and with the lights and shades of whose innermost soul he has by long acquaintance grown familiar. He speaks of Paul reverently, as of one to whom he looks up, and affectionately, as of one with whom he has communed. Mr. Binney's views of Paul are not rash speculations, not superficial enconiums, but deep, true, manly conceptions. Nothing can be finer than the manner in which the lecturer exhibits to his hearers, first the human, next the divine, and thirdly the combination of both in the character of the great Apostle. Mr. Binney's forte is not rhetoric. He wins his way into the hearts of his hearers. It is not eccentricity; it is not pathos; although there is something of each. The flashes of humor with which Mr. Binney sparingly lights up his addresses, though they relieve the more massive portions, do not explain the secret of his mastery over his audience. That mastery is nothing more than the combination of the faith and simplicity of the speaker. Believing what he says, he scorns adventitious aids. He knows it is true, and he utters it, leaving the truth to do its own work Of course something is attributable to Mr. Binney's cultivated mind, to his stores of knowledge, to his emphatic manner, even to his noble personal demeanour and bearing. But he conquers by faith and simplicity. Where the mere rhetorician, doubting of his theme, overloads it with ornament, Mr. Binney, "full of faith," yields himself to the genuine impulses of his own heart, and pours forth simple words of vital truth. And those words are words of power. The lecture was a complete success, although we have heard Mr. Binney under more favorable circumstances and in happier moods. Early in the morning of the day the tickets sold at 1s. 6d. each, were exhausted; they then speedily rose to a premium; 10s. was offered, and we are told that, at evening, as much as £1 1s. was tendered for a card of admission to the room. But after all precaution, numbers rushed in without tickets. It will be readily conceived that it was needful to place a limit to the admission of the public. The safety of life and limb required it. As it was, the room was densely crowded; a thousand or twelve hundred persons at the very lowest estimate being present, notwithstanding the oppressive heat of the weather. Multitudes went away disappointed; whilst during the evening groups of persons lingered about the entrance of the building, which they would gladly have entered had it been possible. Mr Binney has reaped a harvest of golden opinions from the South Australian public, and from that portion of the public to whom the eloquence of a Chalmers, a Hall, a M'Neill, a Melville, a Raffles, and a Newton was known. We trust that Mr. Binney will yet afford to the people of South Australia other opportunities of hearing his voice; and that when he returns to his native land he may be long spared to prosecute the great and glorious career on which he is embarked.—*South Australian Advertiser*, Oct. 9th.

TASMANIA.— SPECIAL SERVICES OF THE EVANGELICAL UNION, HOBART TOWN —A series of special and united Meetings for Prayer and brief Addresses, with a view to the advancement of Religion, were held on successive Tuesday Evenings, during the month of September, 1858, in the following order:—September 7 — Congregational Chapel, Davey-street. Address: Subject—"Self Examination," by Rev. W. Lelean. Sept. 14.—St. John's Church, (Presbyterian) Macquarie-street. Address:—"Walking in the comfort of the Holy Ghost," by Rev. W. Law. Sept. 21.—Brisbane street Chapel. Address:—"The Christian Motive to glorify God," by Rev. R. McClean. Sept. 27 — St. Andrew's Church (Presbyterian) —Ordinary Meeting of the Union. Address:—"The Quickening Spirit," by Rev. J. G. Macintosh. Sept. 28.—Melville-street Chapel. Address:—"The Indwelling Spirit," by Rev. G. Clarke.

VICTORIA.—BALLAARAT.—The Rev. Wm. Alexander Lind, formerly of Tahiti and the Austral Islands, South Pacific, having received, and accepted, a unanimous call to the pastorate of the Congregational Church in this town, commenced his regular labors there on Lord's Day, October 10. On the following Tuesday evening, a members' tea-meeting was held in the chapel, for the purpose of welcoming the new pastor, when an interesting and profitable season was enjoyed by all present.

BRIGHTON.—The new Independent Church at Brighton, mentioned in our last as being nearly completed, was opened for divine worship on Sabbath, October 17th.   The Rev. R. Bowman preached in the morning, and the Rev. I. New in the evening, to full congregations. On Tuesday the 19th a social meeting was held in the church, when the attendance was so large that it was necessary to have a second course of tea for the overflow.   George Rolfe, Esq., presided, and the Rev. W. Moss offered prayer.   An interesting report of the proceedings in connection with the building, including a brief history of the cause from the beginning, was read by W. Wisewold, Esq.   The commencement was made in 1853 by the Rev. H. Kidgell, when a piece of land was given by Mr. Were, and a small temporary chapel erected.   In 1854 a christian church was organised, the Rev. R. Fletcher presiding.   Mr. Kidgell labored here till the early part of 1857, when he removed to Flemington.   The chapel was then closed for a time, except when an occasional supply could be obtained.   In July, the Rev. R. Fletcher and his son the Rev. W. R. Fletcher undertook to conduct between them the forenoon service for six months.   During this time another piece   of land, in a more central and eligible situation, was purchased, with a view to the erection of a more commodious chapel.   In January of the present year an opportunity was presented of securing the services of a resident pastor, by the arrival of the ministers sent out by Mr. Poore.   The Rev. W. R. Lewis was accordingly requested to make trial of the place, with aid from the Home Mission of Victoria, for six months.   His labors have been successful, and the erection of the present commodious chapel upon the piece of land previously purchased is the result.   The church is built of wood, but is much superior to most structures of that kind, being in the Gothic style, furnished with buttresses outside, and plastered within, and having an elegant open timbered roof of grained oak.   It will accommodate about 300 persons.   The cost of the land was £375, and of the building £800, total £1,175.   Prior to the opening, subscriptions amounting to £375 had been received and a mortgage obtained of £500, leaving a floating debt of £300. The meeting was addressed by the chairman, by the Revs. W. B. Landells, T. Odell, W. R. Lewis (the pastor), Thomas Fulton, Esq. Revs. R. Bowman, R. Fletcher, H. Kidgell (former pastor), and E. King (Wesleyan).   In the course of the evening a collection was made, and cards containing promises for the next six months were given in.   In this way, including the Sunday collections, the whole of the sum immediately required (£300) was raised.

COLLINGWOOD.—The foundation stone of the new Wesleyan Church, Fitzroy-street, was laid on Tuesday, August 31st, by the Rev. William Butters, President of Australasian Wesleyan Conference, assisted by the Rev. D. J. Draper, Chairman of the District, and the Rev. T. Williams, Superintendent of the Circuit.   The proceedings were commenced by devotional services, and the stone was laid with the usual formalities; and then the assembly was addressed by the President and Mr. Draper.   After the benediction was pronounced, a tea meeting was held in the old chapel, Rose-street; Trays being gratuitously provided by the ladies presiding.   In the evening, the Rev. J. Dare, of Sandhurst, preached a sermon in the Brunswick-street Chapel to a large and attentive congregation.   The church is to be built of bluestone : length, 45 feet ; width, 30 feet ; height, 18 feet ; estimated cost, including land £630.

REV. A. M. RAMSAY.—It will be gratifying to the friends of this clergyman to learn that, by the Emeu, R. M. steamer, news was received here of his safe arrival in Britain.   He arrived at Southampton, per Cambria, on the 20th June, in company with the Rev. Mr. Poore.   On the day following (Monday), they started for London, where they arrived at 11 A.M.   Mr. Ramsay's stay in London extended over about a week, and he was received with great kindness by Mr. Westgarth (late of this city), and numerous other friends in the great metropolis.   On visiting Scotland, he also received a most cordial and Christian welcome from many friends in the ministry and others, and has since been actively engaged in preaching and endeavoring to excite a deeper interest in the Australian mission than at present exists. In the town of Hawick, in the south of Scotland (where he labored for a period of thirteen years, prior to leaving for this country about twelve years ago), he met with a hearty welcome, and preached three times in some of the different churches to large audiences.   A soirée was arranged to be held on the last day of August, in commemoration of his visit, which in other respects is likely to be greatly blessed.

REV. J. L. POORE having arrived in England from Australia, on his return mission for additional ministers, the committee of the Colonial Missionary Society passed the following resolution in reference to his demand :—"That this committee, after hearing the statement of Mr. Poore, are both surprised and delighted to hear that in so short a time new openings for ministers should present themselves in the Australian colonies ; and finding that those who were sent last year have all been auspiciously settled, cordially welcome their friend on his return to this country, at the request of the committee in Melbourne, for an additional number ; and hereby appoint a special sub-committee to confer with him on the best method for carrying out the object which brought him to England."

W. FAIRFAX AND CO., STEAM PRINTERS, COLLINS-STREET, EAST, MELBOURNE.

The Southern Spectator.

No. V.   DECEMBER, 1858.   VOL. II.

ADDRESS OF THE REV. DR. ALLIOTT,

CHAIRMAN OF THE CONGREGATIONAL UNION OF ENGLAND AND WALES, DELIVERED AT THE ANNUAL MEETING, HELD AT THE POULTRY CHAPEL, LONDON, MAY 11TH.
(Concluded from page 99.)

I will not, however, confine myself to this generic view of the sentiment entertained by the new school on the doctrine of the atonement. Those who make its immediate end simply subjective, may be divided into three principal classes, each of which I will for a moment notice. The generic view I have just given is perhaps most applicable to one of these classes. The class I refer to describe the humiliation, sufferings, and death of Christ as a manifestation of the love of God to us with the view of drawing our hearts to God. This, if the objective end is not excluded, is, I repeat, an undoubted truth. If God gives us Christ for the sake of delivering us from a terrible penalty, from which he could not otherwise justly deliver us, we see a manifestation of love which is without parallel, and which constrains us to adopt the language of John : "Herein is love, not that we loved God, but that he loved us, and sent his Son to be the propitiation for our sins." But let us deny the objective end of the death of Christ, and suppose that God gives his Son to suffer and to die for no other reason but to prove to us that he loves us, that he may thereby attract us to love him ; and we ask, What is the proof? Are we told that the very fact of his doing anything to attract our hearts to himself is a proof of his love ? Grant this ; still, except it be supposed that we delight in suffering for its own sake, the bounties of Divine Providence which directly contribute to our comfort would surely be a stronger proof of love than giving up Christ to unnecessary sorrow—to sorrow which, so far as any direct benefit to us is concerned, is utterly useless. The doing us good is a proof of love ; the making a sacrifice to do us good is a proof of yet stronger love ; but the making a sacrifice which does not directly benefit us at all, and which has no other object than to manifest love, does not manifest love till we are told what its object is. Hence, it seems to me in itself no proof of love ; it requires an accompanying explanation to make it even a sign of love ; and accordingly has little more real force than a simple profession would have had without it.

I proceed to another class—one which represents the Christ not as an individual, but as the ideal man, the representative of the perfection of humanity. They speak of this Christ as perfectly exhibited in the man Jesus of Nazareth, who has thus become the model of the whole human race, and say that his sacrifice was a complete self-sacrifice—a sacrifice of self to God and to man—to God as being an act of obedience to God, to man as being to him a type and pattern of the self-sacrifice which should characterise every man.   No doubt, the sacrifice of Jesus was a self-sacrifice and no doubt it is, as to its spirit, a type and pattern of the self-sacrifice which should characterise every man ; but this is not the whole truth in reference to the sacrifice of the Saviour.   It cannot, I imagine, be supposed that a self-sacrifice in itself, and independently of any end to be answered by it, is the thing set before us as a pattern ; for, if so, fasting and other austerities would be good for their own sake and irrespective of any end to be answered by them; and, in like manner, everything like enjoyment or pleasure would be evil in its own nature.   It must, then, be supposed that the self-sacrifice of Jesus was good, and an example to us, either because others were to be benefited by it, or because it was an act of direct obedience to God.   Suppose the former ; and, if the objective end of the atonement is left out of view, it will follow that the excellency of the self-sacrifice of Jesus arises from its subjective influence on others.   This subjective influence, however, cannot be the influencing others to make a sacrifice of self ; because the influence must, by the supposition, refer to the nature of the example set to them, and therefore must be prior to any effect produced by example.   Accordingly, the influence can only arise from the manifestation of love ; and this would make the theory similar to the one we have already discussed, and therefore need not discuss again.

The only view, then, requiring notice, is, that the self-sacrifice of our Lord was good and an example to us, considered as an act of obedience to God.   If it is so considered, I allow that it was good, and that it is an example to us.   Still, God does not call for anything that involves humiliation and suffering, except some end is to be answered by it.   He does not delight in the suffering of his creatures, and hence does not enjoin what involves suffering except good is thereby to be accomplished either to the party himself or to others.   Accordingly, if the self-sacrifice of the Saviour was good, considered simply as an act of obedience to God, it must be admitted that God had a sufficient reason for calling for his self-sacrifice, and that this reason can only be some adequate good to be thereby accomplished.   In the objective end of the death of Jesus we see such a reason, and find that the end was worthy of the sacrifice made.   Leaving it out of view, we have truth, but yet only a one sided view of truth. Supposing God to have no other end than to make the self-sacrifice an example to us, is to suppose it good in itself—a proposition which involves the absurdity that misery is for itself desirable, and that happiness is for itself to be deprecated.

There is, however, a further error in the theory which I cannot entirely pass over ; though this error is not to be attributed to all who represent the sacrifice of the Saviour as simply a pattern to us of self-sacrifice.   The error to which I refer is that of representing Christ as an impersonality—something generic—which appeared, indeed, perfectly in Jesus, but which appears more or less in every man.   Christ is thus regarded as merely the ideal perfection of humanity.   I believe him to be, on the contrary, a true and proper person—an individual.   The Christ is not merely in Jesus—Jesus is himself the Christ.   Scripture so represents him.   I admit that he dwells by his Spirit in the hearts of his people, and that thus there is an intimate union between them and himself ; but this is a very different thing from the supposition that there is a generic Christ. In the former case we come into union with a personal Saviour ; but in the latter we simply possess some of the general characteristics which the man Jesus fully possessed.

There is still another view of the atonement of Christ. Some think that his sufferings were chiefly sympathetic, arising from his perfect sympathy with fallen humanity. This class represent him to be, as he undoubtedly is, a Being of perfect holiness and of infinite love ; and they say, that, whilst his perfect holiness led him to see the full evil of sin, his infinite love led him to feel the intensest sympathy with those who were subjected to this evil. Hence they tell us that, as we, in proportion to our love and sympathy, whenever we see a fellow-creature enduring grievous suffering and laid low by a terrible disease, so Christ, because he saw that sin was a worse, an infinitely worse evil than the direst disease and the most excruciating pain, and because he felt love and sympathy far beyond the greatest sympathy ever experienced by any mere human being, experienced the deepest grief and anguish at the sight of sin. This, they affirm, was the chief, the heaviest part of his sorrows. His thus showing how deeply he felt the evil of sin, they regard as a manifestation of the Divine estimation of sin : and his showing how deeply he sympathised with the sinner, as a manifestation of Divine love to man. As they thus regard his sorrows both as a manifestation of the Divine estimate of sin and as a manifestation of the Divine love for man, they say that man is in this way melted to return to God and to hate and forsake sin.

On this view of the atonement, let me remark, that it does not include the whole truth either as to the sufferings of Christ or as to the nature and object of the atonement. It is true that Christ was a perfectly holy Being, and that, as such, sin would be more grievous in his eyes than it is in the eyes of such imperfect beings as we are. It is true that he was also a Being of boundless compassion and love, and hence felt deeper sympathy with and regard to the fallen than any other being ever felt. But let it be remembered that he manifested his sympathy and love not simply by living amongst us, and subjecting himself to the pain and anguish to which contact with sinful beings would expose him, but by subjecting himself to other sufferings which could be more fitly regarded as the penal consequences of their guilt—certainly not simply sympathetic sufferings. By so doing he manifested that perfect holiness which approves of such consequences as the just desert of guilt, as well as that perfect love which was willing to endure them in the stead of the guilty. If his sufferings, as to their nature, had chiefly arisen from sympathy with the fallen, how is it that the weight of his sufferings was confined to his residence on earth ? Did he know as fully before he came down to this world what human guilt and human misery were, as when he lived amongst men, and did he not sympathise as deeply before he left heaven as he did whilst here below ? How, then, was it that his sufferings and anguish were not in heaven what they were on earth ? It is answered that, as God, he could not suffer, and that therefore he became man ? let me then ask whether he has not retained his manhood now that he has left earth, and, if so, how it is that his sympathy now does not occasion the same intense anguish which he bore in the garden and endured on the cross ? It is true that he sympathised, but it is not true that the chief part of his anguish is to be attributed as to its nature, to his holy sympathy. Moreover, his death is represented as an essential part of his atoning sacrifice, and his death was undoubtedly something more than a mere sympathetic suffering. He suffered and he died, not simply as indicative of the sympathy he felt, though that led him to submit himself to the stroke, but, if Scripture be truth, because the Lord laid on him the iniquity of us all. It pleased the Lord to bruise him, to put him to grief, to make his soul an offering for sin ; and it was because the Lord appointed and accepted the offering that his blood now cleanseth from all sin.

Before I finish, I will just allude to an objection often made to the orthodox view of the atonement. It is supposed that justice and love are inconsistent attributes, and therefore that, as God is confessedly a God of love, he cannot be also a God of justice. We admit that if a sinner is regarded simply in himself, the two attributes may possibly come into collision ; that justice may require the infliction of a punishment on a guilty party, which, as far as mere regard to the party is concerned, love would forbid. But, as it has been often remarked, the love of God is a love to his creatures as a whole ; and whilst it is also a love to the individual, it is so only as far as love to the whole will permit. God is a father, but he regards the interests of his whole family, and will not spare one child deserving punishment if his doing so will introduce disorder and evil into the whole family. If, however, because this is the case, God, as a God of love to the universe, is so essentially just that he cannot spare the sinner at the expense of that attribute, so far from there being cruelty and vindictiveness, there is infinite love and mercy, if, by giving up his Son to humiliation, suffering, and death, God has so vindicated justice as to be able to pardon and save the guilty consistently with the welfare of his intelligent creatures at large.

Whilst I have thus entered, as far as the limits of such an address at the present allowed, into the question of the old and the new theology, I wish to repeat what I intimated at the beginning, that I have not professed to give the sentiments of any one individual, and hence that, so far as details are concerned, there is perhaps no one whose opinions I have throughout described. The school, whilst it may be considered as agreeing in some general principles, receives these principles with various modifications, and its disciples differ as much between themselves as thinking men might à priori be expected to do.

I cannot conclude, brethren, without remarking that, whilst the foundation-truths of the old theology are, I believe, the truth of God and the truth on which subjective Christianity rests, there are two classes who are in danger of being unjustly accused of indifference to, if not of renunciation of them. One of these believe that the subjective aspect of Christianity has been too much disregarded, and hence they have not made its objective aspect as prominent in their discourses and published works as they would, under ordinary circumstances, have done. They firmly believe, however, in the objective aspect ; they regard faith in it as of the first importance, and hence are the furthest remove from indifference to it. If, then, we were to charge them with indifference merely because of the prominence which, under particular circumstances, they think they ought to give to a neglected aspect of truth, we should treat them with great injustice. I myself believe that they would better accomplish their end by giving full prominence to each aspect of truth, the objective and subjective ; but here the difference between us is not about truth, but merely as to the best mode of presenting it. The other class to which I refer, in like manner thoroughly believe the old doctrines, but they hold that stereotyped forms of expression often lose their intelligence and power, and hence prefer setting forth old truths in a new dress. Here the grand question is, whether the new dress diminishes from the intelligibleness of the expression, whether it renders it more ambiguous or less clear.

does either, the expression is faulty ; but even if this is the case, the difference is not about the truth, but simply about the mode of teaching it. Neither of these classes is heterodox, and from both of them lessons of practical wisdom may be learnt—from the one, never to lose sight of the subjective aspect of Christianity ; from the other, not to imagine terms and phrases for the expression of thought as intelligible merely because they are old, nor to object to new terms and phrases, when they are intelligible, merely because they are new.

Those of us who are ministers of Christ have a great work committed to us—the work of saving souls. Let us ever remember that this is our work, and that if we would successfully accomplish it we must preach Christ crucified ; that it is by this preaching that God is pleased to save those that believe. Some may call it foolishness, some may call it weakness ; but if it is foolishness, it is the foolishness of God ; and if it is weakness, it is the weakness of God ; and " the foolishness of God is wiser than men, and the weakness of God is stronger than men." May we all so preach, and so live, that we may be amongst the number of those who turn many to righteousness, and who will shine as stars in the firmament for ever and ever !

BACONIAN PHILOSOPHY.

ON THE OPERATION OF THE BACONIAN PHILOSOPHY UPON MODERN SCIENCE, RELIGION AND POLITICS.

It is now about 250 years since the great author of modern science sent forth as from a new fountain of light the then novel principle, that all enquiries after positive truths must rest upon a basis of FACTS—facts accurately observed, correctly stated, and closely subjected for their verification to the inductive reasonings of all thinking men in the newly created commonwealth of true learning.

The immortal Bacon left his name and fame " to foreign nations, and to England after a lapse of time ;" and well have the nations of Europe—heartily has England—accepted and executed the legacy. The astrologers of those days have become our accurate astronomers ; modern navigators, as the practical men of art thence resulting, sail and ever will sail on all earth's oceans under their banner. The alchymists of ancient times have become our chemists, to whose subtle enquiries creation has freely unfolded her secret affinities and antipathies, for the use of man. Nor is more than a fractional part contained in these two branches of modern science, of all the fruit ever springing from and germinating upon the quickening seed then cast upon the earth. A labyrinth of ten thousand threads was speedily formed for exploring the mechanism of the heavens and the earth ; for investigating the powers and forces, physical, electrical, chemical, physiological, vital, intellectual—beforetime seminally latent indeed in nature, though hidden from the deductive reasonings of human vanity and error, but which now begun to be compelled, under a better method of philosophy, to yield their secrets to the materialistic knowledge of the world in which man lives.

Nor has the course of the Baconian philosophy been confined, after the ancient model, to schools of science and learning. The very form and character of our social institutions, and society itself, participate in and are in a measure modelled upon the new principle, both materially and intellectually. Not a manufactory or work-yard, scarcely a shop or school, a bank or mercantile office exists, wherein the leading spirits and superintendent are not deeply imbued with the Baconian doctrine—of materialistic facts being the basis equally of all theories of truth, and all practical operations.   Political science is becoming scarcely less operated upon by the new method of employing man's intellectual faculties, as we see plainly in the statistical reports exacted from civilised governments. Religion alone, and Christianity in particular, seems to have been but little affected by the new philosophy.   Our German divines preach Luther's sermons ; our Calvanistic Protestants of many names, all preach Puritan discourses. This apparent want of effect upon religion is, however, in seeming chiefly.   Her day of trial is fast approaching ; neither can any earthly power prevent the application of the Baconian method of inquiry into the truth, value and efficiency of our church organizations ; and, in fact, it requires but the single element of popularity to enable a materialistic atheism to burst over our religious institutions, with all the darkness and destruction of a Noachian deluge.

Whenever any great advance is suddenly made in knowledge it always happens, and must be expected, that the original author is followed by men who give to his discoveries a power and universality of application of which he saw but the feeblest glimmer of an outline.   Kepler was followed by Newton ; he by the practical navigators.   Franklin by a host of electricians ; and, in our day, Bacon is followed by the positive philosophers of Europe, at the head of whom stands out as the chief originator, though excelled in eloquence and popularity by many disciples, M. Auguste Compte, the influence of whose writings upon the learning and arts of the nineteenth century is expected to exceed by far that of Bacon upon the seventeenth and eighteenth centuries.

M. Compte's essays on *"Philosophie Positive"* occupy about 4800 pages octavo, in a type somewhat smaller than newspaper type, published in six volumes.   This is the original fountain from which tens of thousands of the most powerful and popular European writers, in many languages, have for about twenty years past drawn their daily inspirations.   The truer title of this work would have been the one we have given to this article, with the additional clause, "and negative philosophy," to indicate how much more M. Compte has expounded the philosopher's right of negation in reasoning, than did our immortal Bacon.   In fact, the so-called "positive philosophy" is far more negative and critical than positive and organic ; rejecting a thousand moral and intellectual truths of antiquity to each new materialistic one that it demonstrates, or even accurately generalises, by the positive method.

M. C. assumes that whatever cannot be proved by the positive method must in our days be rejected as false, or placed at least completely out of our human sphere of inquiry.   Our world (according to the prevalent philosophy) is an assemblage of phenomena, governed by invariable laws : all real phenomena can be discerned by our organs of sense, or they exist not to us, as living only by organisation ; and processes can be reduced to the operation of the invariable and exclusively materialistic laws, or they are vain imaginings of a disordered brain.   All is materialistic and sensual or sensational.   Our astronomy, under this philosophy, is " the mechanism of the heavens," limited mainly to the solar system, by our senses explorable ; our physical electrical sciences—optics and such like—are operations of matter, themselves not perhaps ponderable, but purely material, as phenomenon or law.   And chemistry, in like manner, is an accumulation of facts respecting equivalents and non-equivalents of substances in contact. Physiological laws are of a similar nature ; and life itself, or *vital phenomena*, is discernible and explorable only as organisation with its manifestations.

In our world, therefore, under this philosophy, all idea of final cause, intention, purpose or design in nature, as if the world were a creation having reference to an intellectual being endowed with volition and exercising a will, is to be totally rejected ; and the idea of God, with every dependent inferential truth, is to be viewed as purely notional and unreal.

One great application of the positive method remained to be made, viz., to all religious, moral, social, and political questions, for the final conducting of the affairs of this world under a new spiritual hierarchy ; and this, Mons. Compte undertook to accomplish by negating, as childish and futile, all actual religions, and inaugurating, to comprehend the other three branches of modern learning, a new science which he terms SOCIOLOGY ;—a "first philosophy," essential to the coming state of society, when humanity must succeed Christianity, and every human interest and question become amenable to a positive solution of the highest capacities, as in times past to the infallible authority of the Vatican. More recently, however, he published a catechism of positive religion, with a view to retain in the new order of things, "without God in the world," whatever men will not relinquish of religion, though regarded as purely imaginary. The child would thus be taught, for the first seven years of its life, to pray to its mother ; afterwards, I infer (for I have not yet seen the work), it would pray to the apotheosized great men of the world ; then, to the primordial truths ; and finally it would be emancipated from all this childish bondage into the full freedom of positivism, under which man alone is God ; yet even then retaining fictitious prayers, both family and public, for society in its residue of fetichism.

The principle by which the positive philosophers thus undertake to conciliate truth and falsehood, reality and fiction, lies mainly in their fundamental doctrine—that all truth is *relative* rather than *positive*—and, in fact, is truth to us chiefly as relative. Thus the doll, which the child calls its baby, is not the same thing to the child as to you of adult intellect, nor even as it will become to the child when her mind attains to greater maturity. It is something real to her which it cannot be to you—demands therefore a recognition, not merely of courtesy, but of positive truth. Thus Positivism can have its fictitious prayers and vain ritualisms, like ancient Popery or modern Mormonism. And herein lies one basis of that shallow but deadly negation of many vital truths, found in unexpected alliance with a vivid recognition of many pernicious falsehoods, which constitutes the true character of modern philosophy: a philosophy which would directly transform much of our knowledge into ignorance, our ignorance into knowledge, in this world, as in a valley of dry bones, among which under its inspiration we may hear, or fancy we hear, a rattling ; but no sinews form, no flesh covers, no breath of life enters into them. We shall live when this new age dawns upon us under the deadly upas tree—a real tree, indeed, and perhaps nutritious to some of the serpent kind ;—but to a redeemed world of men deadly and poisonous beyond all the heretofore ripened growths of past ages.

I will not indeed affirm that every positive philosopher, much less scholar of such, goes this length in his negations. I speak of TENDENCIES. I do however affirm that the influence of such views, held consciously or unconsciously, is widely diffused, and in an extending sphere. The world in its positive science largely occupies the throne of Christ in men's minds. We may meet, everywhere, with multitudes of our thinking contemporaries, leaders of the industry of the age, and even working artizans and labourers, whose consciences, stupified by the medium of positivism in which they live, yet not entirely paralyzed, often utter to their ministerial guides, in effect, the cry of anguish that Schiller puts into the lips of his female convert to the new doctrine : "Where is my soul ?. Oh, give me back my soul !   I was happy when I held it in my peaceful bosom of innocent ignorance, and now I am miserable !" Hardly does the minister, even the wise and good, know how to reply to such a cry of wretchedness. He has been taught to expect a different kind of enemy ; he is ill furnished with weapons for this new warfare. Or, perhaps, the language of the living conscience is like that which the same author puts into the lips of another of his heroes : "Oh, that I could return into my mother's bosom ! and be again the innocent infant I once was ;" to whom indeed a better author in the modern school (M. Cousin) would reply, "Innocence and virtue are only attainable, to the mature mind, by the *convictive* preference of child-like innocence to giant-like guilt—of feeble virtue to strong crime." But the modern minister of the Gospel is perplexed, because he has no adequate method of grappling with the case at all commensurate to the method of modern philosophy to which it owes its existence and force. He feels that he cannot deal with such matters successfully as he would have done before the time of Lord Bacon ; and the inductive reasoning in science has not yet taught him a better method in religion than the one ancient and effete.

For ourselves—the Independent Churches—our forefathers were ever in the van of human and christian progress ; yet we (I will frankly confess my fears) are in danger of falling into the rear. They opposed the mitred and governmental corruptions of Christianity in their day, with the life and energy of a better and a freer Gospel ; and we, yet more strengthened under their arms of voluntaryism, defensive and offensive, have conquered ; and in some of the Australian colonies, at least, may rest upon our arms. But there are victories more disastrous than defeat ; there are generals and armies that know not how to follow up a conquest. If we imagine that we must for ever fight against shadows of the past, and can safely overlook our actual opponents of the present, we shall commit the error that Wellington would have fallen into, had he, after the victory of Waterloo, led his army perpetually to renew the conflict with the ghosts of dead Frenchmen on the field of past conflict. If, in short, as some seem to imagine, we Independents fancy that the *Apollyon* and *Doubting Castle* of the present day lie in bishops' mitres and government patronage, we shall not hold the position that our forefathers assigned to us in the forefront of modern conflict.

In fact, M. Compte suggests in his great work of 1846-7, for the realization of his views, the establishment of a modern "spiritual power," or new hierarchy of a priesthood of positivism, on the model, and having more than the intellectual (i. e. spiritual) power over all Europe, of the papal hierarchy in the middle ages. Innumerable social, moral, and political questions, he pleads, absolutely demand an intellectual solution, which cannot be found in our religious and literary interpretations ; and which, in the meantime, our ruling governors are, from the constant demand of practical works upon their energies, incompetent to furnish.

These questions must be referred to a confederated union of the positive philosophers of the five leading nations of Europe, as the modern world's natural leaders, France, Germany, Italy, England, and Spain : the new spiritual power, or congress of nations, to be independent of, and dictatorial to, the governments, although dependent upon them for pecuniary support ; and every question to be reduced to the mathematical form of a problem or theorem. He has subsequently proposed twenty thousand as an adequate number for the new European priesthood for a commence, nent ; and certain it is that associations do exist in continental Europe- helped by apostate Christians, for carrying out their Atheistical or Pan- theistical views. For England, Miss Harriet Martineau has translated M. Compte's work, condensed into two volumes ; and parties sympathising with the new views, as well as individuals converted to the theory, exist in considerable strength.

While conscious of the immense obstacles that exist in the way of attaining such a project, and the comparatively feeble means for its accom- plishment which visibly appear, we may clearly discern that the project itself is no less than to revive an " Image of the Beast," whose wound seemed mortal ; to bring into the world THE Antichrist so long expected ; and to open a wide way for that general apostacy of the latter times which many of us believe has yet to be verified, and only requires the element of popularity for its realization. Surely we must expect, if not blind to the signs of the times, a conflict for life or death, wherein we cannot but take our place in the van or the rear. Where shall it be ? With what weapons, beside those of our fathers, shall we fight ? Not assuredly with the weapons of a Christian rationalism, ever more destructive and negative than constructive and positive. Not with those of a vain Christian mysticism whose days of victory are centuries past ; nor yet with the weapons of Scotch metaphysics, which put on ever a new substance as well as form, under the pen of each new pro- fessor. We may, I know well, oppose the godless tendency of modern philosophy, on its own principles, by opposing to its negations, the nega- tive form of the divine decalogue—" *Thou shalt not* "—to him who would rest in a deadly materialism. We may oppose a better interpretation of the negative principle in the words of a better teacher—because ye are ignorant " WATCH *for ye know not.*" We may deny and question the fundamental generalization of the positive philosophy ; and we may expect new truths to arise out of the, at present, latent resources of God in crea- tion, to testify amply to his existence, attributes and word. But on these matters I cannot now enter. In the mean time we have the hearts of our people to deal with, and their heavenly hopes ; how must we extricate them from the grasp of the modern Giant Despair ?

In this mere fragmentary programme of a great subject, I put the question for stronger minds to discuss, and remain, Mr. Editor, &c., &c.

E. R. B.

CONCERNING THINGS INDIFFERENT.

The application of this phrase to the Christian life is plain enough to all diligent readers of the Bible. There are things that are, in themselves, indifferent. The act of doing them, or the neglect of them, does not, in itself considered, constitute an evil ; and by doing or not doing them no one is thereby brought under moral blame.   "One man esteemeth one day above another ; another esteemeth every day alike."   "One believeth that he may eat all things ; another, who is weak, eateth herbs."   Now, the setting apart one day for a specific purpose, and thus, as it were, lifting it above other days ; the choice that one may make—the caprice that one may manifest—in eating "flesh," or in eating "herbs," to the exclusion of "other meats,"—neither the one thing nor the other constitutes a sin. Viewing the matter abstractly, and as it bears upon one's self, it may be of no possible importance what we observe or neglect, what we eat or what we abstain from eating.   These may be to us things purely indifferent. They may have in them no moral element, and, consequently, they are destitute of all moral bearings, that is, so far as we ourselves are concerned.

But there is an aspect in which even such matters assume a degree of importance, which no Christian man is at liberty to overlook or undervalue. Christians constitute a brotherhood ; and every member of this holy frater. nity is bound to consider what may be the effect of his or her course of conduct, even in matters indifferent, on the faith and the feelings of the community ; and should it appear that by indulgence in things lawful, and safe to a spirit of strong faith and firm purpose, weaker brethren are scandalised, it is, on the apostolic principle, expedient that self-denial should be exercised.   "All things, indeed, are pure ; but it is evil for that man that eateth with offence.   It is good neither to eat flesh nor to drink wine, nor anything whereby thy brother stumbleth, or is offended, or is made weak."   The will and its sanctions are too often forgotten in our day. Many who would shrink with unfeigned horror from the crime of the first murderer, say, by very many of their doings in accents distinctly heard by all ears save their own (may even they not sometimes hear?), "Am I my brother's keeper?"

While, however, those Christians who may be considered stronger and more advanced than others, are, in such circumstances, to deny themselves what may be lawful, weaker brethren must have a care not to exact, or even to expect too much.   There are good grounds for this caution, as every one who has watched the working of Christian societies is aware. Who has not observed that in good and well-intentioned persons prejudices sometimes usurp the place of principles, and the crotchets of the passing hour bulk more largely in their estimation than the eternal verities of the word of God?   There are boundaries to the field over which Christian forbearance exerts her benign influence ; and while the strong are not to act regardless of the feelings, and it may be in some instances, of the prejudices of the weak, the weak are not, on the other hand, to set themselves up as, in all matters of faith and practice, a measure for the strong.   Mutual forbearance is the rule in all matters of practice ; mutual concession in all matters of opinion.   But the strong may surely feel a double sympathy for the weak.   "Let not, then, your good be evil spoken of, for the kingdom of heaven is not meat and drink, but righteousness, and peace, and joy in the Holy Ghost."   W.

INDIVIDUAL EFFORT.

A powerful writer on missions has said, "There is wanting a sense of *individual* obligation"—an observation of great truth.   Many causes have conspired to produce this.   Among these causes is the existence of societies and institutions of various kinds. By these, the work to be done by the Church of Christ is done by many, and done in a systematic manner; and done, too, to a greater extent than it could be done by means of separate and individual effort. We do not wish to see our useful and popular associations dissolved and destroyed. Far from it. Who can estimate the amount of good that has been effected by the Bible and Missionary Societies? This will not be known till the "day of the Lord." We have said thus much to show that, while we advocate individual effort, we are not insensible to the value of effort of other kinds.

We are disposed, however, and justly, to lay great stress on individual exertion. No man can read with attention the New Testament without perceiving the very great importance Christianity attaches to the individual. It does not deal with men as masses or groups, but as individuals. As individuals we are called to mourn for sin—to repent—to believe in Christ. As individuals we are to cultivate all the excellencies that can adorn the character. Our joy, faith, hope, love, must be individual; our intelligence and growth; our fitness for the heavenly state must likewise be individual: life, death, immortality have the same aspect. Yea, we must appear at the judgment seat of Christ, that "*every one* may receive according to the things done in *his* body."

Now, it is quite consistent with this general view of the matter to look at Christian effort as an individual thing. "Lord, what wilt thou have *me* to do?" "As every man has received a gift, even so let him minister the same as a good steward of the manifold grace of God." It is very desirable that every Christian should be impressed with a sense of his personal responsibility. It is perfectly right and important that each one should feel that he has talents given him by his Lord, for the adequate use of which an account must be rendered. Oh, that that were deeply felt—felt by all the disciples of Jesus! This would be the infallible forerunner of a great revival of the Church.

The extent to which individual effort has been blessed is most encouraging. Every reader of the history of the Church is aware that the glorious Reformation to which we owe so much light and liberty, originated, and was for a time largely carried on by one—the celebrated Luther. It is equally clear that the most useful institutions among us may be traced to some one mind. God inspired the thought of a Bible Society into one mind; that mind spoke the heaven born thought to others, and thus the thing took shape. The great thought became a "great fact." The cloud, small as a man's hand, spread until it covered the heavens, and shed copious showers on whole countries. Nor can the humblest servant of God know but that his instruction or his effort may be fruitful to an unlimited extent—nay, that the thought he imparts to a child may not produce fruit for centuries to come.

There is an admirable book published by the American Tract Society, called the "Life of Harlan Page." In that book we have an example of a working Christian. The excellent man was in no way extraordinary. He was not rich or learned, did not occupy an important position in society. He could not be named with such men as Wesley, Whitfield, Chalmers, and others with whose names we are familiar. He was a plain man—was possessed of great good sense—his mind was educated by Providence and the Bible. By trade he was a carpenter. When he became a Christian, he saw it to be his duty to work for his Master; and he did work, judiciously and patiently. He wrote, he visited, he prayed. He spoke to young people, to old people.   He watched for opportunities of usefulness, and he found them in great abundance.   God made him very useful; indeed, it is thought that that plain, unobtrusive mechanic was instrumental in bringing not fewer than one hundred souls to Jesus.   "Here comes Mr. Page, bringing another lamb to the fold," his pastor said of him once and again, as he saw him bringing an inquirer to the pastor's house. This case merits attention from every member of the Church, but more especially from those in the same rank of life.   If we were asked what were the exact steps Mr. Page took, we should not care to name them.   It is not the exact method he took we need to know.   It is the spirit of unquenchable zeal he displayed that we need.   The circumstances of the Colonies differ from those of America.   We cannot reason from one to the other.   But, where the love of Christ exists in constraining power, there will be scope found for its exercise.

In speaking of individual efforts in the cause of Christ, we have suggested to our memory the part of John Bunyan's life in which he speaks of the manner in which he dealt with unconverted persons, and mentions that he was led to desire the salvation of *particular* persons. For them he made frequent and special prayer—he visited them, spoke to them, considered them as a charge committed to him by God;—and no wonder that he was in many instances made the means of salvation to those who engaged his pious solicitude.   Dear reader! there is no reason why you should not go and do likewise.   We cannot expect to see some persons engage in such a work.   They do not feel sufficiently the worth of the salvation of Christ.   Many join our churches without a sufficiently deep conviction of sin, consequently they never regard Christ as a transcendantly glorious Deliverer, and consequently they never feel or realise the danger of the unrenewed soul.   If any one reads these lines, who has seen something of the honor of saving souls, but is panting after efficiency of a higher degree, we may say a few suitable words.   1.   Let there be much meditation on the state of man as a sinner—as exposed to eternal death—on the fitness of the Gospel to meet his case—on the power of God's spirit—on the efficacy of Christ's blood.   Meditate until the soul is pervaded by the spirit of the Gospel, until you feel as the Saviour felt, who "must be about his Father's business."   2.   To this meditation, frequently renewed, let their be added prayer to God, the fountain of all grace.   Remember, he is the "hearer of prayer."   Remember the intercession of Abraham and of Moses.   Remember that there is reason to believe that God looks with peculiar complacency on those prayers of his people that have respect to the welfare of others.   3.   Live much in fellowship with Christ.   Accompany him from place to place in his tours through Galilee.   Listen to his sweet, solemn, faithful words.   Visit the cross.   Ask why he died.   What must be the nature of that calamity which he died to avert?   4.   Seek his Spirit, to keep up in your minds right views of sin and of holiness.   "Live in the spirit," and you will possess some of the most important qualifications for Christian labor.   And seldom indeed, has a person who used such means of becoming an instrument "sanctified and meet for the Master's use" been suffered to labor in vain, or to spend his strength for nought.   Does the reader desire to have suggested to him motives for active zeal in the cause of his Master? Such are scattered very profusely in the word of God.   "He that converteth a sinner from the error of his way shall save a soul from death"—of amazing power, surely!   One glance at the Apostle Paul is set the soul on fire. See him travelling from city to city! behold his tears! "He warns night and day with tears." He alludes to the enemies of the cross "weeping." He addresses the Corinthians with "many tears." He is "ready to die"; he encounters any danger rather than not "finish his course with joy." He did "one thing" and would reckon his hours wasted had they not been appropriated to the securing of that one thing. With still greater power does the example of Christ occur to the mind. How deep his love to souls. How assiduous was he in doing good. How readily did he embrace every opportunity of teaching the children of men. He had a "baptism to be baptized with," and how did he labor till it was accomplished! He "stedfastly set his face to go to Jerusalem." The apostles followed him "amazed and fearful" at the super-human purpose he showed in facing his awful work. Christians, ponder these things, and by God's blessing the fire of zeal will begin to burn. You will turn with fresh concern to your children, to your neighbors, to all that God may place in your way. If this should be the case with any number of Christians ourchurches would assume a new aspect, would blossom as the rose. PASTOR.

SELF-RELIANCE.

Perhaps there is no organ so strongly developed in man (and which allies him so intimately with the animal creation) as, Imitativeness. We all want to imitate; from the young child to the full-grown man may be seen this constant working of the soul, to *imitate.*

Perhaps in no period of the age of the world has this tendency been in such active operation as the present. Wherever we turn, in whatever book we look, still is seen this, "*To Seem,*" and not, "*To Be.*" Society is entirely governed by it. It has now become a mighty wave sweeping on with accumulative force and with resistless power all that comes within the influence of its rushing and never ceasing current.

The desire in itself is noble and great, when springing from the spirit's (interior) consciousness of its own inferiority, in comparison with others, those others being characters of inestimable worth, who have unfolded their beautiful lives through adversity, sickness and trial. To obtain a clear conception of the different turning points that have made these spirits great, and to use them to advantage, in the formation of our own characters, is most assuredly praiseworthy in any human being who aims at the highest moral excellence. This is the noblest order of imitation, which does not descend to lose itself *in* another, but to make itself *through* another, ever retaining the sweet consciousness of possessing as the under current of all, that great and high-born individuality of character, without which, man is not man, but the shadow of a man. It is this individuality displaying itself in so many multiple forms, which gives such graceful variety to the human family, and were this utterly destroyed, there would be no longer that full-toned harmony which adds zest to the ever freshness of life, by the varied yet blended shades of individual existence.

It is the blending of the many that makes the whole. Each is perfect in its own way. Surrounding circumstances should only be taken hold of, moulded to the will of the spirit, and assimilated to its own nature.

This is self-reliance. There is in the soul an individuality, a divine element, which requires for its perfection that its idiosyncrasy should be retained. All possess it, and either crush it or elevate it. To develope and elevate it should be one great end and aim of our existence. We must be *ourselves* in whatever we feel. think, or do, and never stoop to the degradation of attempting to imitate what can never become our own, however closely the copy may re-semble the original. H. W.

Richmond, Victoria.

INCIDENTS.

THE SON AND HIS AGED MOTHER.

Young George Willis was one who had especially interested me in the summer. He was always ready to open the carriage, to pull off his neckcloth as quick as lightning to dust a book or parasol, if it fell to the ground, or to render any other of those delicate little attentions by which these strong men shew their sense of a lady's friendly interest in them. One day I had noticed the earnestness of his fine countenance, as he listened; so I said to him afterwards; "George, you have a good mother, I am pretty sure?" "Safe enough! Now, who could have told it to ye?" "And I think you are a good son." "Well! you are out there! But I should *like* to be, uncommon." "How do you mean to begin?" "Why, by leaving my money order with you, to allow mother something handsome out of it; and if I don't live to come back, you'll please give it all to her."

The excellent rector of the parish where George's widowed mother lived, wrote in the course of the autumn, to express the poor woman's joy in the dutiful consideration of her son, and the hope it raised within her that it might result from a real change of heart and principle, as he had, previously, been somewhat wild in conduct and neglectful of her wishes.

A sorrowful task was it, indeed, to have to say, in answer to that letter, that her son was dead, "the only son of his mother, and she was a widow." Little as there was to tell her of what had passed between us, there was enough for hope. I could not even write his name, without remembering that those young eyes used to fill with tears and light at every description of a Saviour's dying love. I besought her to reckon on seeing those tears exchanged for smiles of joy in paradise; for surely no single spark of love to Jesus ever went down to be quenched in everlasting darkness.

On our return home at the close of the autumn, amidst a large heap of letters there, we found one from George, written whilst he was in the full vigor of health, some weeks before his death. God only knows the depth of thankful joy with which it was sent to that widowed mother, with the words written upon it, without one haunting doubt, "This your son was dead, and is ALIVE AGAIN; he was lost, and is FOUND."

"From George Willis, Army Works Corps, gone to the Crimea."

"Dear Madam—i received your kind letter and was happy to hear from you. Will you be so kind as to keep my order and to let my Mother Mary Willis have 5s. a week until i do return, if it do please God that i may. if i never do return again, it will be for mother Mary Willis, at Queen's Camel. Madam you can let my Mother have it as you please, and i thank you kindly for your Prayer and Hymn-book and your blessing as well Which i am sure if i do put my trust in him, and i hope i shall for evermore. i hope to keep your Litel prayer constantly with me for your sake, and our Saviour's that shed His Blood for us!

"& I do remain your obedient servt.

"George Willis."

—*English Hearts and English Hands*, pp. 234—236.

ENEMIES MADE FRIENDS.

Two navvies had a desperate quarrel and fought with knives. The authoress of "English Hearts and English Hands" came and separated them, appealed to their better feelings and to Christian motives to induce reconciliation, and the following passage describes the result:

On the evening of the 18th of June, I walked through the village for the cottage-reading. William W— and his wife were waiting for me on the slope near the church; she was looking hopeful and happy, and he, full of earnest feeling.

At the cottage we read the fifth chapter of the Second Epistle to the Corinthians, and illustrated the words, "We must all appear before the judgment-seat of Christ," by the wonderful parable of Matthew xxv. I humbly believe that the Holy Spirit's life-giving presence was the words which the Lord Jesus Himself had spoken, "spirit and life" to our souls. We felt it to be our little Waterloo—and called it so. Battles were fought and won; souls were trampling down their old enemies, sin and Satan, by the mighty help of the great Captain of their Salvation.

Richard J— and William W—, two of the men who had lately fought with knives, were sitting near each other, with overflowing eyes, and with brotherly love in their countenances. The hands that wrung mine at parting had been lifted up in prayer to the King eternal, as they pledged themselves, by His grace, to be His faithful soldiers and servants to their lives' end.—*English Hearts and English Hands*, p. 176.

POETRY.

TO THE SUPREME BEING.

The prayers I make will then be sweet indeed,
If thou the spirit give by which I pray :
My unassisted heart is barren clay,
That of its native self can nothing feed :
Of good and pious works thou art the seed,
That quickens only where thou say'st it may :
Unless thou shew to us thine own true way
No man can find it : Father ! Thou must lead.
Do Thou, then, breathe these thoughts into my mind,
By which such virtue may in me be bred,
That in thy holy footsteps I may tread ;
The fetters of my tongue do Thou unbind,
That I may have the power to sing of thee,
And sound thy praises everlastingly.

WORDSWORTH.

CORRESPONDENCE.

TO THE CHRISTIAN FEMALES OF VICTORIA.

DEAR CHRISTIAN SISTERS,—On reading the Report of the Chinese Mission, I was very much impressed with the thought that the funds of that noble Institution might be greatly increased if we were to put our "shoulders to the wheel," and do what we could to help forward the good work. Is it not lamentable that there should be so few to instruct such a vast multitude, who are ignorant of the true God and the only means by which a sinner can be saved ? Oh! what would our forefathers have given could they but have had such free access to those poor deluded creatures ? They would have thought no sacrifice too great; nay, they would willingly have gone forth "with their lives in their hands" to proclaim to those perishing millions the unsearchable riches of Christ. Ought not we then as professing Christians to make some sacrifice ? But shall we call it a sacrifice in the eternal world, when we behold a Chinese brother there through our instrumentality, casting his crown at our adorable Saviour's feet, and uniting with us in ascriptions of praise to the Lamb for ever ? Shall we not rather greatly rejoice that we deprived ourselves of some gratification and devoted the money to a far nobler purpose? It is a special "talent" committed to our trust, and woe be to us if we prove unfaithful. I am persuaded if a vigorous effort were made, and we were to follow the example of two devoted females in Melbourne, the funds would very soon be greatly increased. There are very few gentlemen who would refuse to give a lady a subscription, if it be solicited in a respectful manner. Let us then go forward by two and two in the strength of the Lord, and in humble dependance upon his blessing, and then I believe great success will be the result. S. S.

October, 1858.

THE REV. T. BINNEY'S VISIT TO SOUTH AUSTRALIA AND CHURCH UNION.

Anxious to preserve the following important correspondence and documents on the subject of Church Union, which have arisen out of the Rev. Thos. Binney's visit to South Australia, we have postponed several articles, and the whole department of religious intelligence till our next number, and extended our space, in the belief that our readers will be gratified and benefited by reading in a collected and permanent form what they may have seen detached portions of in the passing columns of newspapers.

Correspondence between the Bishop of Adelaide, Sir R. G. MacDonnell, the Governor of South Australia, and the Rev. T. Binney, on the Union of Protestant Evangelical Churches.

No. I.

To the Editor of the Advertiser.

SIR,—You will oblige me, and many others, I believe, if you can find room in an early number of your paper for the insertion of the following letters. They will explain themselves. I would only beg leave to say, that it is with anything but comfortable feelings that I suffer to stand and go before the public certain expressions, in the letters to me, complimentary to myself. It is thought best, however, that the documents should be given without any alteration or omission, and in the reasons assigned for this I feel compelled to acquiesce.

I am, &c.,

Felixstow, October 22, 1858.　　　　　　　　　　　　　　　　　T. BINNEY.

No. II.

The Right Reverend the Bishop of Adelaide to the Rev. T. Binney, "on the Union of Protestant Evangelical Churches."

Bishop's Court, October 4, 1858.

DEAR SIR,—I send you some thoughts which have occurred to me on a subject which has often occupied my mind, but more especially since I had the pleasure of forming your acquaintance. Such as they are, and expressed in the words pretty nearly that first came to hand, I lay them before you in the hope that they will not widen, if they do not bridge, the gap that separates us ecclesiastically, though I trust not spiritually, nor for ever.

I remain, Reverend Sir, yours faithfully,

Rev. T. Binney.　　　　　　　　　　　　　　　　　　　AUGUSTUS ADELAIDE.

P.S.—I leave Adelaide to-morrow morning on a five weeks' tour, and I fear I shall not have an opportunity of bidding you farewell.

Bishop's Court, September 23, 1858.

1. REV. SIR,—During our social intercourse yesterday, at the house of a common friend, you were pleased to take notice of a remark which fell from me to this effect—that we in this colony had the advantage of occupying "an historic stand point," so to speak, from which we might look back upon our past social, political, and Church life in England, and, removed from the smoke and noise of the great mother-city, might discern through all its greatness somewhat of folly and meanness, of defect and vice, in its habits and institutions. The survey would not be unprofitable if it should lead us to perceive how we had been blinded by its attractions, so as to become unconscious of its faults; and so hurried away by its feelings and associations as to be insensible of the conventional bondage in which we then lived and moved.

2. It must, I think, be admitted that the clerical mind is peculiarly swayed by party principles and sectarian prejudices. Withdrawn very much from practical into contemplative life, and valuing abstract truth as the basis of moral obligation and excellence, clergymen are too apt to exaggerate the importance of certain truths which they conscientiously hold, and to treat as essential principles of the doctrines of Christ matters of inferential or traditional authority. I do not suppose that Nonconformist ministers are exempt from this failing, though it may be fostered in the Establishment at home by the alliance of Church and State.

3. Be this, however, as it may, both clergymen and ministers may look back with some degree of regret that a mid-wall of partition should so have separated kindred souls; pledged to the same cause, rejoicing in the same hope, and devoted to the same duty of preaching Christ and him crucified to a dark and fallen world. By the very discomfort, however, of thus "standing apart" we are thrust rudely back upon the principles in which we have been brought up, and are constrained to put the question to our consciences, "Are you so sure of your ground as true to your convictions? Are your views so authoritatively scriptural as to put you exclusively in the right?" And if, after careful review and earnest enquiry, you feel unable to quit the "old paths," yet does not this very inquiry dispose us to put a liberal construction on the conduct of others, and to respect their equally sincere and their conscientious convictions? A candid mind will not fail to see that such inquiry

on the other side of the question; and if with our present lights we had lived in the time of our fathers, we should not perhaps have been disposed to break up the fellowship of the Reformed Evangelical Catholic Church for non-essential points, or narrow its communion on matters of Christian expediency rather than Christian obligation.

4. I have thrown these remarks together by way of preface, in order to shew the course of thought into which an Episcopate of ten years in this colony has gradually led me. You yourself have given a fresh impetus to such reflections. Your fame as a preacher had preceded you. I knew that you would be welcomed by all who in your own immediate section of the Evangelical Church take an interest in religion, and by all in our own who are admirers of genius and piety, even though the echo s of your King's Weighhouse sermon had not quite died away. Hundreds I knew would ask themselves, "Why should I not go and listen to the powerful preaching of Mr. Binney?" And when they had heard you reason of righteousness, temperance, and judgment to come; of Christ, who he was and what he did, how he died for our sins and rose again for our justification, I felt assured that they would ask again, "Why is he not invited to preach to us in our churches?" What is the barrier that prevents him and other ministers from joining with our clergy at the Lord's table, and interchanging the ministry of the word in their respective pulpits? Was it any real difference with respect to the person, office, and work of the Redeemer, the power of the Spirit of God, or the lost condition of man without Christ and the Comforter?"

5. I am truly glad that so considerable a person as yourself should by your presence in this colony have forced me to consider again the question, "Why I could not invite you to preach to our congregations;" to review my position, principles, beliefs, and prepossessions; more especially as the absence of sectarian prejudice on your part, and the presence of all that in social life can conciliate esteem and admiration, reduced the question to its simple ecclesiastical dementions.

6. Again and again the thought recurred to me, *Talis cum sis utinam noster eses!* Still I felt that neither the power of your intellect, nor vigor of your reasoning, nor mighty eloquence, nor purity of life, nor suavity of manners, nor soundness in the faith, would justify me in departing from the rule of the Church of England; a tradition of eighteen centuries which declares your orders irregular, your mission the offspring of division, and your Church system—I will not say schism—but *dichostasy.**

7. But while adhering to this conclusion, I am free to confess that my feelings kick against my judgment; and I am compelled to ask myself, is this "standing apart" to continue for ever? Is division to pass from functional disease into the structural type of church organization? Are the Lutheran and Reformed, the Presbyterian and Congregationalist, the Baptist and Wesleyan bodies, to continue separate from the Episcopal communion so long as the world endureth; Is there no possibility of accommodation, no hope of sympathy, no yearning for union? Will no one even ask the question? none make the first move? Must we be content with that poor substitute for apostolic fellowship in the Gospel, "Let us agree to differ;" or an evangelical alliance which, transient and incomplete, betrays a sense of want without satisfying the craving? Or are we reduced to the sad conclusion that as there can be no peace with Rome so long as she obscures the truth in Jesus and lords it over God's heritage, so there are no common terms on which the Evangelical Protestant Churches can agree after eliminating errors and evils against which each has felt itself constrained to protest? Are not Churchmen, for example, at this day, just as ready as you, Reverend Sir, can be, to condemn the treatment of Baxter, Bunyan, and Defoe, by a high Church Government? And do not Independents and Presbyterians readily allow that a Leighton or Ken relieves Episcopacy from the odium brought upon it by the severities of a Laud or Sharp?

8. It appears to me in this colony we are placed in a peculiarly favorable position for considering our Church relations, because one great rock of offence has been taken out of the way—I mean the connection between Church and State. We can approach the matter in dispute simply as questions of evangelical truth and Christian expediency. Neither social nor civil, nor ecclesiastical distinctions interfere to distract our view or irritate our feelings. There is no Church-rate conflict here! I have accordingly seized the opportunity of laying before you a few thoughts on the possibility of an outward fellowship as well as inward union of the Evangelical Churches, with the hope that they may suggest inquiry if they lead to no immediate practical results.

9. The questions I would propose for consideration are—

First. Whether an outward union, supposing no essential truth of the Gospel be compromised, is desirable amongst the Protestant Evangelical Churches?

Secondly. What are the principles and conditions on which such union should be effected?

I submit my ideas to you with great diffidence, but from the desire to show that there is no unwillingness on my part to consider how we might possibly serve at one and the same altar, walk by the same rule, and preach from the same pulpits the words of this salvation.

10. With regard to the first point, I conceive outward union to be desirable, because it appears to me to be scriptural and apostolic. That all the congregations of the Universal Church were subject under Christ to the twelve Apostles, and that the decree directed by the Holy Ghost, but framed by James and Simon Peter, Paul and Barnabas, and assented to by

---

* Gal. v. 20, "seditious," literally "standing apart."

the elders and brethern, was delivered to the Churches to keep, is recorded in the Acts of the Apostles. That the whole Church was viewed as one visible body by St. Paul is evident when he bids the Corinthians give offence to neither Jews nor Gentiles, nor the Church of God : and whatever be the figure under which the Holy Spirit characterises the body of true believers in Christ, unity or organized life is the substratum of the idea; be it vine or olive-tree, family or household, city or kingdom. the body or spouse of Christ, the thought is still the same. What, then, should we think of a family, whose several members inhabiting the same house kept each to his own chamber, and though continually jostling on the common stairs rarely exchanged a friendly salute and never a visit. Is this family life? And is it true Church life to say I am of Peter, and I of Paul, and I of Luther, and I of Knox, and I of Wesley, and I of Whitfield, and I of the Fathers? Are we not carnal, and speak as men? In the apostolic age there must have been outward union of the Churches, so far at least as the general order of a common worship, the celebration of a common sacrament, the profession of a common creed. and preaching in common the Word of Life! The spirit of Diotrephes we may hope was rare.

11. If the *odium theologicum* be indeed the worst type of that disease, it might be expected that a real union of the Churches and their publicly acknowledged fellowship in the Gospel might arrest the progress of that malady. It is the effect of party feeling, jealousy, and suspicion, fostered by rivalry and contention. Thus christian sympathy, which is meant for mankind, is too often restricted to a system or a sect. On the other hand :

12. In what an attitude of strength would such union place the Gospel of Christ before Jew and Gentile; before Brahmin and Mahommedan? No subtle Pundit would then point to the differences of Christian teachers as indicating error at least in some, and uncertainty in all. No Bossuet could enumerate, and perhaps exaggerate, the variations of Protestants, and, unmindful of the like in his own communion, claim for the Church of Rome the symbol of Unity as the mark of its being the True Church. But now instead of fighting the Lord's battle as one great army, our resistance to the Powers of Evil is like the death-struggle of Inkermann; a series of hand-to-hand combats, broken regiments fighting in detached parties, never receding indeed, but incapable of combined effort or mutual support.

13. It may, however, be urged on the other side, that the divisions of the Christian Church are helps to its vitality, even as the troubled sea which cannot rest is thereby preserved from stagnancy and corruption; that rivalry promotes exertion, and exertion results in expansion. Yet has not the Bible Society attained its present strength by acting on the opposite principle? Is it not because all Protestants can unite in furthering its object, truly catholic, and because catholic, triumphant?

14. The union I contemplate is not a yoke of subjection—an iron rule suppressive of individual or sectional thought, aspiration, energy, and action; far otherwise. If the great Apostle of the Gentiles would provoke his brethren after the flesh to jealousy in order to save some—if he stirred up the Churches of Macedonia by the forwardness of Achaia, and reciprocally urged the Achaian Churches to be ready with their contributions lest he should be ashamed of his boasting concerning them—certainly a loving zeal striving for the mastery is not to be cast out as unmeet for the Christian commonwealth. Unity is compatible with variety, and variety is pregnant of competition. God has created but one vertebrate type of animal organisms; but how infinitely diversified are the specific forms! I know no reason why, in our reformed branch of the Catholic Church, there might not be particular congregations of the Wesleyan rule, or some other method of internal discipline, or usage, or form of worship, even as the Society of Ignatius Loyola, or Dominic or Francis exists in the bosom of the Roman obedience. The seamless coat of the Redeemer was woven from the top throughout. The Roman soldiers said " Let us not rend it !" Why should chronic disunion be the symbol of Evangelical Christianity? I cannot call alliance union : nay, it is founded on stereotyped separations. I pass to the second question :—

Secondly. What are the principles and conditions on which a union of the Protestant Evangelical Churches should be effected?

15. It must be evident, I should suppose, after an experience of 300 years, that neither the Episcopalian, nor Presbyterian, nor Congregationalist can reasonably hope to force upon the Christian world his own particular system. Is either one or the other entitled by the Word of God to exclude from salvation those believers who do not follow the same rule of Church government? If, however, submission may not be demanded on the ground of its necessity to salvation, then any negotiation for outward union may and must proceed on grounds of what is best and wisest, most likely to unite, as being most in accordance with Scripture and apostolic tradition. We must lay aside hard words—schism, Church authority, sectarianism. In the comity of nations, *de facto* Governments are recognised and treated with; the question whether they are *de jure* is left in abeyance. So must it be with respect to any union of the Churches. They must meet together like brethren who have been long estranged, yet retaining the strong affection of early youth; resolve to forget the subject of their dispute, and walk together in the house of God as friends. It will be unnecessary to ask " Which man did sin—this man or his parents ?" or to say, " Thou wast altogether born in sin, and dost thou teach us ?" or, " We forbade him, because he followed not us." No; we must meet in the spirit of godly fear, of mutual respect, with the earnest desire by all right succession to promote God's truth, and advance Christ's kingdom. We must please one another, but not to doubtful disputations.

16. A second principle is, " Whereto we have attained," or shall

must be publicly acknowledged, in that rule we must walk and by it stedfastly abide. I firmly believe with Mr. Maurice, in his "Kingdom of Christ," that the Church of the apostolic age embraced every principle for which in later times each section of the Christian world has felt it necessary to contend, even to separation from the main body of the brethren. But the Church of the apostolic age, the true visible model church, does more. It harmonises them all; giving to each its due place, its real proportion. Each portion of the truth, obscured, distorted, or denied in the mediæval Church, each detail of the outward building of God, has been jealously rescued from corruption or decay by sects or individuals. It remains, perhaps, for this or the coming generation to restore the original fabric, and take away whatever is inappropriate, unsightly, or inconvenient. But is the spirit as yet willing? Alas, I know not. It is certain that the flesh is weak.

17. Let me endeavor to state, as accurately as I can, what seems to be the leading idea, the characteristic principle, of each section of the Christian Church:—

The Church of Rome, then, contends for external unity, founded on one objective creed, in subjection to one visible head of the Church on earth.

The Lutheran for justification by faith, antecedent to and irrespective of works.

The Reformed Calvinistic Church upholds the free and sovereign grace of God.

The Anglican witnesses for a scriptural creed, apostolic orders, and a settled liturgy.

The Presbyterian asserts the authority of the Presbytery, as derived immediately from the Holy Ghost.

The Congregationalist claims unlimited right of private judgment, and the independent authority of each congregation as a perfect Church, over its own members.

The Wesleyan preaches spiritual awakening, sensible conversion and social religious exercises.

The Baptist contends for personal religious experience previous to admission to the Church.

Every one of these principles is substantially, though not exclusively, true. When their mutual relations are forgotten, each becomes exaggerated; the beauty of proportion is lost, and a faulty extreme is made the Shibboleth of schism. Is there no analytical process possible, no law of affinity, by which the spiritual mind could precipitate the error, and leave pure and limpid the Gospel stream? or remove from the much fine gold of the Temple the dross with which it is alloyed? Would there not still remain a scriptural truth, a godly discipline, a settled order, a common altar, a united ministry, a visible union as well as fellowship in the Spirit? Might there not still be variety in unity, partial diversity of usage, and a regulated latitude of divine worship? The Episcopalian, the Presbyterian, and the Congregationalist might consent to harmonize what they cannot exclusively enforce; they might surely "in understanding be men," and exercise the great privilege of spiritual men—that is, combine freedom with submission to law, and general order with specific distinctions.

18. But it is time to draw these general remarks to a close, and define with somewhat more of precision that Church of the future which is to conciliate all affections and unite all diversities. I scarcely know which to admire most, the pleasantness of the dream, or the fond imagination of the dreamer. Still, let me speak, though it be "as a fool." My object is not to dictate proceedings, but to suggest consideration; to provoke inquiry, but not force conclusions. And since concession in matters not absolutely essential to salvation or positively enjoined must be the basis of the system adopted by the various Evangelical Churches, it may be fairly put to me in the language of the proverb—"Physician heal thyself." I will begin, then, with the Church of England, and will state what appears to me can be given up for the sake of union. 1. A State nominated Episcopate. 2. Compulsory uniformity of divine worship. Already the former has given place in Canada and New Zealand to an Episcopate freely elected by the Church itself. The latter, it appears, even in England, is only required from the clergy in parish churches, but not when preaching in the fields, or streets and lanes of the city. In addition, then, to the separation of Church and State in this colony, and the absence of the legal machinery connected with that union, greater freedom and diversity in the modes of worship seem attainable; and an Episcopate, moderate in its pretensions as well as constitutional in its proceedings, associated with and not lording it over the Presbyters; above all, chosen by the free suffrages of the united clergy and laity.

I believe the doctrinal articles of the Church of England and many others among the Thirty-Nine are allowed on all sides to be scriptural. I conceive, then, that a settled form of sound words, a deposit of objective faith, would not be deemed a yoke of bondage, but a guide to truth. I conceive, also, in order that all might worship with the understanding as well as the spirit, that certain liturgical offices, such for instance as the Litany, might form part of the stated services, but not to the exclusion of extempore prayer in connection with the sermon at the discretion of the preacher. So also in the administration of the Sacraments and conferring Holy Orders, a portion of the office might be fixed and invariable, and a portion left to ministering pastors.

19. These points being settled, the trial, nomination, institution, or designation of pastors, the dissolution of their connection with their flock or removal, their mode of payment, the internal discipline of the congregation over their members and officers, are details which may well be left for after regulation; if indeed there is really much or any injurious difference at present existing in these matters. A spirit of mutual forbearance and real affection must be largely shed abroad before such a system as here spoken of can possibly be

maugurated. Even if thought feasible for the future, how can it be made to take retrospective effect? How can we, who are *de facto* ministers, and think ourselves to be *de jure* so, besides being pledged to our respective systems, throw ourselves out of the one to enter upon the other?

Let us search the Scriptures for guidance. The beloved disciple was instructed to write by the Holy Spirit to the seven angels of the seven Churches of Asia, and Titus was left by St. Paul in Crete to ordain elders in every city as he had appointed him. But besides these later exertions of apostolic authority, we find Barnabas and Saul separated by the Holy Ghost to a special mission through the laying on of hands and prayers of the prophets and teachers of the Church at Antioch, Simeon Niger, Lucius Cyrene, and Manaen. Assuming the existing ministers of the several denominations to be recognised as *de jure* by their congregations, and *de facto* as such by the Anglican Church, might not the Bishops of the latter, supposing the before-mentioned terms of union were agreed upon to take effect prospectively, give the right hand of fellowship to them, that they should go to their own flocks, and mission also as preachers to the Anglican congregations, when invited by the pastors of the several churches? If the license of the Bishop can authorize even lay readers and preachers, how much more men like yourself, separated to the work of God, eloquent and mighty in the Scriptures! Indeed, I do not feel sure that I should have violated any ecclesiastical law in force in this diocese or province, by inviting you to give a word of exhortation to each of our congregations.* In this way, then, of mission without compromise, but on declared assent to certain fixed principles and truths, existing Ministers might co-operate with us in the preaching of the Gospel, and under the benign influence of this brotherly love, a Reformed Catholic Church might grow up, and, like the rod of Aaron, swallow up our sectarian differences.

20. I have said nothing about hypothetical ordination, which has been suggested (like conditional baptism where irregularity in the administration may be suspected), because it savours of evasion or collusion, neither of which is agreeable to Christian simplicity and due reverence for God's ordinances. Neither have I suggested the consecration as Bishops of existing Wesleyan Superintendents and Presbyterian Moderators, or those who, like yourself, seem sealed alike by nature and the Spirit to be special overseers in the Church of God. Missions, as preachers to our congregations, without imposing the obligations incident to the incumbents and curates of Churches, but not until full evidence had been given before license of soundness in the faith, would seem to meet the exigencies of the case so far as regards the present generation of ministers who have received Presbyterian orders.

Having attained to this step, perhaps God would reveal to us a more excellent way. Old systems have, in fact, been found wanting. Which of the Churches now existing is so perfect, so scriptural, so apostolic, as to insure instant acquiescence from the enquirer to the exclusion and condemnation of all others? If there be none, will all the learning, and eloquence, and traditional authority devoted to the support of each, persuade the present or future generations to substitute another for that in which they have been brought up? A few may, perhaps, be convinced or converted, but the masses never. A fresh combination must therefore be sought; traditional prejudices must be set aside; cherished associations laid upon the altar of love, to rise, like angel messengers, in the flame of sacrifice, to purer and loftier spirituality! Oh, for that millenial reign of peace when a Chalmers or a Cumming, a Binney or a Watson, might serve at one altar and plead from one pulpit with the Bishops and Clergy of the Church of England! It is the cause of God and Christ, of truth and holiness, of righteousness and peace, of faith and duty, of grace and salvation, of man delivered and Satan bound, of God alone exalted on that day, and reigning on Mount Sion gloriously. Then might the fulness of the Gentiles come in, then Israel be restored, then Babylon overthrown, and that regenerated state of this fallen world be made manifest for which Jehovah reserved the last great display of his providential love—the union in the God-Man of the Manhood with himself.

I remain, dear Sir, respectfully yours,
AUGUSTUS ADELAIDE.

Bishop's Court, September 23, 1858.

No. III.

SIR R. G. MACDONNELL TO THE REV. T. BINNEY.

" Glenelg, October 16, 1858.

MY DEAR SIR,—I herewith return the Bishop's letter of the 22nd ult., on 'the union of the Protestant Evangelical Churches.' I have long felt deep interest in this subject, and as a more than usually healthy feeling in connection therewith seems to prevail here at present, I am well pleased that it has been thus prominently brought forward by the Bishop. Moreover, whilst the moment for this step seems well chosen, the truly catholic spirit in which the subject is treated by His Lordship is, in my judgment, matter of congratulation to us all.

2. As, however, you have asked what I think of the suggestions in His Lordship's

---

* Canon 54 of the Province of Canterbury, A.D. 1603-4, requires "conformity as a *sine qua non* to preaching in the parish churches of England." I do not know that it is binding in colonial dioceses. It shows that persons were licensed to preach who were not disposed to take upon themselves all the obligations of the parish priest under the Establishment.

letter, I shall give you my opinion, but only in such imperfect manner as the little time at my disposal permits.

3. I have no doubt we both admire the eloquent and forcible manner in which His Lordship dwells on the numerous fundamental principles of agreement in doctrine between the various Protestant Evangelical sections of the Church of Christ. We must both also deplore with His Lordship the great injury sustained by that Church in the inherent and inevitable weakness engendered therein by the absence of any systematised and united action available for the expansion of its limits, and the diffusion of the really vital principles of faith and doctrine common to all its sections.

4. Nevertheless, I do not find that the Bishop, when he treats of 'the principles and conditions on which a union of the Protestant Evangelical Churches should be effected'—either professes to devise a remedy *in presenti* for that deficiency, or speaks hopefully of accomplishing such union hereafter. His suggestions seem to me aimed too high in pointing to a 'Church for the future, which is to conciliate all affections and unite all diversities.' Nevertheless, the willingness of the Bishop—as representing the Anglican Church here—to recognise, for certain mission purposes, the *de facto* ministers of evangelical congregations—to give up a State Episcopacy—to modify the compulsory uniformity of divine worship, and to omit portions of the offices for the administration of sacraments and conferring of holy orders—evinces the tolerance of an enlightened Christian and breathes a spirit, in which, if we were all to meet one another, there would soon be but one section of the reformed Church of Christ.

5. Looking, however, to the practical expediency of his suggestions, and having regard to human nature as it is, I do not see—even here, where the ground is comparatively cleared for the erection of such a structure by the abolition of all State aid—that there is much immediate prospect of establishing a general Protestant Church holding by one set of articles, however few, or by any fixed form of liturgy, however curtailed—especially if its bishops be not elected by all denominations, placed for that purpose on terms of equality.

6. I admit that such a Church, with its affairs administered by bishops or overseers elected by the general body of the Church (which, however, does not appear to be altogether his Lordship's meaning,) and with its bishops, aided by representatives of the whole Church assembled in Synod, would be a Church well adapted to the spiritual wants of mankind, and eminently Apostolical in its constitution. Yet, although, as the Bishop truly says, we 'might thus exercise the great privilege of spiritual men—that is, combine freedom with submission to law, and general order with specific distinctions'—the main difficulty would still exist, and the real question would only be begged, not solved; for there would still be a law—a rule, in which, as the Bishop says—'we should walk, and by it steadfastly abide.' Now, whatever be the rule, it would be difficult to induce the various Protestant sections of Christ's Church simultaneously to adopt it, or *afterwards abide by it.* Men had, in the first century, the teaching of Christ himself; they had the Apostles for their ministers and bishops; they had the recent evidence of Christ's miracles, and yet schism even then arose. It would do so again, even if a United Protestant Church were for a space to gather within its fold all the evangelical denominations of the Reformed Church in this province, and in Great Britain also.

7. We may be, however—indeed it is our belief and hope—that such a consummation will yet be witnessed in the fulness of time; but meanwhile I sincerely hope that what the Bishop himself calls 'the pleasantness of this dream' will not divert us from more immediate and practicable exertions, which, without disturbing the existing internal organisation of the various sections of the Reformed Church, may yet eliminate, if they do not find ready to our hand, some, if not all, the elements for united action when pursuing the main objects of all Christian Protestant action, viz., the diffusion and application of the broad vital doctrines of the Protestant faith

8. And herein I do not see why we might not at least prepare for such united action, without waiting to break and fuse all varieties of Protestant worship and organisation for the purpose of recasting them in a uniform shape from one mould. For my part, though I much prefer the forms of my own Church, I do not object to the organization or practice of the Baptists, the Independents, the Wesleyans, or many other denominations of Protestant Christians. It might perhaps be better if they were all to form one denomination; but I have doubts on that point; whilst it would come nearly to the same thing, if we could but fully regard one another truly as brethren; and if we felt bound to aid one another in all that might develope the pure principles of our common faith, whilst we illustrated them in our practice by works of mutual charity and help.

9. I would, therefore, suggest that we should test the sincerity of our mutual advances either towards union or alliance, by *at once* commencing a more intimate and brotherly intercourse with one another in our schools, our pulpits, and our missions; and that we should thus prepare the way for such a further mutual understanding as may, with God's blessing, fit us hereafter to discuss the question of fusing into one denomination all the various evangelical sections of Christ's Reformed Church.

10. I would ask, are we to have for ever merely a community of faith and not a community of labour in all good works; a brotherhood of doctrine, but not of action? If the Bible be the foundation of our faith, why should any intelligent, pure-minded, and approved Protestant expounder of that Bible be excluded by an ecclesiastical rule or tradition from preaching the doctrines of any Church in one of its places of worship, if invited to do so by the special

minister of the building ? Is such a union of Christians impossible in carrying on Christian duties ? Whenever such interchange of pulpits is permitted, under no restrictions but those which are desirable to ensure fitness of education and character, as well as soundness of doctrine (and I trust a high standard in all those respects will ever be maintained), it will be time enough to meditate on a still more general fusion, in approved ecclesiastical form, of the Protestantism of this and other lands.

11. I do not, however, perceive that the Bishop suggests any immediate step in this direction, although His Lordship thinks he might have invited you to exhort the Church of England congregations here ‘ without violating any ecclesiastical law in force in this diocese or province.’ I am only surprised that he did not use this power, when he gives so many reasons why it might have been wisely and usefully exerted in your favor. Those reasons, however, are so well stated by the Bishop, that he cannot long resist the conclusion to which they point. Indeed, I consider it fortunate on the whole that you did not arrive here till men’s minds, having become reconciled to the abolition of State aid to religion, had begun to feel the necessity and probable advantage of a very different aid, viz., that which might be derived from greater unity of action amongst themselves. It is no small sign of progress that the Bishop should have stated the case so forcibly, even though he has not yet availed himself of his own argument.

12. I also think it fortunate that neither in public opinion, nor perhaps in his own, is any Clergyman of the Anglican Church in this province regarded as more powerful or truthful in expounding the faith held by that Church than yourself. It makes the fact all the more remarkable that a large portion of this community, as belonging to the Anglican Church, should agree in your doctrines and be anxious to benefit by your teaching, and yet be deprived of the opportunity of hearing you in any pulpit of their Church, simply because you hold no licence from their Bishop, and are not officially, therefore, regarded in this diocese as a *de jure* Minister of the Gospel, the preaching and illustration of which form, nevertheless, at once the labor and glory of your life.

13. I rejoice, therefore, that your visit has made people ponder on such a pernicious—I would almost say unchristian—distinction of man’s device without a spiritual difference. I sincerely hope the application of such a rule to yourself may produce results useful to us all and end in throwing open God’s work to all who may be worthy of the labor.

14. It is, I hope, unnecessary that I should here guard against the possibility of being supposed to imply that the occasional interchange of pulpits which I advocate should be allowed to prejudice the usages or internal discipline of any denomination. Thus, if a Wesleyan Minister were to exchange services for a day with our Dean, he could not expect to conduct the service at Trinity Church as he would at Pirie-street Chapel ; nor could the Dean conduct the service at Pirie-street Chapel otherwise than according to the usage of the congregation there. Therefore I do not contemplate any such interchange of pulpits as possible, except where there might be a previously existing common belief in the great and vital truths of the Protestant faith, and a comparative indifference to the details of ritual-service and discipline in use amongst the various congregations of that faith.

15. I would add that, whilst this first step seems to disturb no Church organization now existing, my own feelings convince me that an advance in this direction must be far more agreeable to many thousand others, than an attempt to form a common Church by the sacrifice of services and customs to which I and they are personally attached. More especially would I protest against a sacrifice of the greater portion of the Liturgy, as suggested by the Bishop. I have reverently listened in my childhood to those prayers and words of solemn beauty. They have often been the consolation of my manhood. They are fraught to me with a thousand hallowed memories and aspirations ; and I would fain hope they will be amongst the latest sounds which may soothe my ear. With such feelings I not merely protest against such a concession to the prejudice of others ; but my own reluctance to accede to this teaches me to deal gently with all who may refuse similar concessions to my prejudices.

16. I therefore own that I am not much troubled at present to give a theoretical uniformity of outward structure to the Reformed Church. I would rather look to the foundation before roofing the Temple The details of discipline and practice— if there be no wilful or marked violation of any Scriptural command or leading truth necessary to our spiritual welfare—may be left safely to the various congregations who are most affected by them. Such things need not, and ought not, to be any bar to the most unreserved spiritual intercourse and community of labor amongst Christians of Christ’s Church.

17. My life has been hitherto so much more one of action than of theorising, that, hoping to be more useful by practically doing something to effect what I recommend than by writing about it, immediately on reading the Bishop’s letter, which I did not peruse till this day, I took the first step towards realizing my suggestion. As a communicant of the Anglican Church I have signed a memorial to the Bishop requesting His Lordship to invite you to preach at one of our churches. It is clear that some one must take this first step, and that the objections thereto are no more forcible now than they would be if I were to defer that step for years. The right hand of fellowship, moreover, ought, in my opinion, to be offered first by the Anglican Church, as that which has hitherto been the most exclusive and exacting in such matters. I have, however, taken care that the memorial should express the conviction of those signing it that they are thereby assisting to develope His Lordship’s own views—a point which it is difficult to doubt after perusing his very interesting and eloquent letter.

18. I know not how far these views, which are entirely my own, and as yet communicated to none but yourself, may coincide with your own opinions. I am, however, certain that if you think you can usefully exert yourself in removing prejudices which narrow the sphere of usefulness of Christ's ministers you will not fail to do so.

19. To assist in establishing a greater unity of action amongst the ministers and congregations of the various sections of the Reformed Church would be indeed a noble vocation. I earnestly desire that your exertions in that respect here, where the field is more open than elsewhere, may yet produce results to which you will gladly recur hereafter as amongst the happiest mementoes of your trip to Australia.

Believe me to be, my dear Sir,
Most sincerely yours,
RICHARD GRAVES MACDONNELL.

This Correspondence was followed by the following Memorial :—

No. IV.

MEMORIAL

Signed by Episcopalians in *favor* of Mr. Binney being invited to preach in one of the Metropolitan Episcopal Churches.

" To the Lord Bishop of Adelaide.

" We the undersigned members of the United Church of England and Ireland, attached to the ritual and Church Government, yet desiring to promote union and Christian fellowship between the Churches agreeing in our common Protestant faith; believing also that your Lordship is most desirous of adopting all measures calculated to extend and establish the common Catholic principles of faith held by the Protestant Church of Christ into whatever sections that Church may be divided, and earnestly desiring to assist your Lordship's efforts in that behalf, seize the opportunity now afforded by the presence in Adelaide of a distinguished member and Minister of the Church of Christ, to offer a sign of good will towards our brethren of the Evangelical Churches, by requesting your Lordship to invite the Rev. Thomas Binney, previous to his departure from Adelaide, to fill one of our pulpits in this city; in the belief that Christian union and Christian love will be thereby promoted and diffused in the hearts of those who, holding like faith in the great saving doctrines of our common religion, have been hitherto kept asunder by differences in matters of form and discipline."

Adelaide, October 16, 1858.

The following is a list of the signatures that were appended to the memorial :—

His Excellency Sir R. G. MacDonnell	J. W. Allison
The Hon. Wm. Younghusband	J. W. Bull
The Hon. F. S. Dutton	Joseph Perry
* The Hon. Arthur Blyth	Alex. J. Wright
The Hon. Capt. Bagot	G. T. Light
Capt. O'Halloran	Thos. B. Murphy
Capt. Watts	Thomas Murphy
John Woodforde, J.P.	Chas. S. Poole
Wm. Gosse, J.P.	Henry Stodart
Samuel Tomkinson, J.P.	William Walters
Charles S. Hare, J.P.	Joseph Walter
* R. B. Colley, J.P.	* Edw. W. Wickes
L. W. Thrupp	Samuel Pearce
H. Edward Smith	T. B. Bernard
* O. K. Richardson	Joseph Murch
* Samuel Stocks	William Main
* Pitt Cobbett	* Henry P. Denton
* Fred. G. Morgan	W. H. Formby
* Wm. A. Hughes	Alfred Bonnin
Fred. S. Monk	John Hancock
Wm. Ross	Wm. Johnson
H. S. Needham	R. G. Symonds
Edward Andrews	Charles Fenn
N. S Quick	* Henry Jickling
John Taylor	Matthew Smith
Samuel Goode	John Richardson
James P. Boucaut	Robert Todd
Wm. M. Sandford	Robert Cottrell
Henry Martin	Thomas Coutts
John Bailey	Alfred Watts, J.P.
G. W. Haines	

Those marked (*) are members of Synod.

The following explanatory letter and official reply have been received :—

"Adelaide, October 19, 1858.

"GENTLEMEN.—I submitted the memorial which you did me the honor to present to me yesterday to a special meeting of the Chapter held here this day, and I herewith transmit to you the conclusion at which they arrived.

"We have not deemed it necessary to trouble you by stating the reasons upon which we have come to the resolution alluded to, but we trust you will give us credit for sincere respect for the opinions and wishes of the gentlemen making the request. I have the honor to be, &c..

"JAMES FARRELL.

"To His Excellency Sir Richard Graves MacDonnell, Messrs. W. L. O'Halloran, Tomkinson, and other members of the United Church of England and Ireland, who signed an address to the Lord Bishop of Adelaide."

"Chapter House, Adelaide, October 19, 1858.

"The Dean, in the absence of the Bishop, having submitted to the Chapter a memorial addressed to His Lordship, and signed by certain lay members of the Church of England, requesting that the Reverend Thomas Binney should be invited to preach in one of the city churches—

"It was resolved unanimously, that it is not within the province of the Dean and Chapter to comply with the above request.

"JAMES FARRELL, Chairman."

No. V.

The Reverend T. Binney to the Right Reverend the Bishop of Adelaide.

Felixstow, October 21, 1858.

MY LORD BISHOP,—The letter which your lordship addressed to me "on the Union of Protestant Evangelical Churches," with its accompanying note of the 4th instant, reached me on the evening of the 5th, the day on which you were to leave Adelaide "on a five weeks' tour." I felt myself in a difficulty to know what to do, either in the way of simply acknowledging the receipt of the document, or of addressing to your lordship such remarks in reply as the study of it might suggest. I was at the time, and have been ever since, quite unable to give it that attention which its importance demanded—at least so far as writing for your lordship's eye or with a view to publication, what might occur to me on carefully weighing its principles and suggestions. I mention publication, because it appeared to me that there was internal evidence in your lordship's letter that this was contemplated by yourself, and because I thought this was the only mode by which any practical result would be likely to issue from the discussion which you had initiated. Your lordship's absence, the prospect of my soon having to leave the colony, and the circumstances in which I was placed by the pressure of engagements, all concurred in leading me to think that the most respectful course I could pursue would be to wait till I had leisure fully to enter into the subject of your letter; to send you my thoughts, and then to ask you to concur in a joint publication which might bring the whole matter before those whom it more immediately concerned. I have been induced, however, to anticipate your lordship's consent to such a course by a series of circumstances, which I beg to be permitted to detail somewhat minutely, not doubting that you will become a willing "accessory after the fact" to what I am about to do.

On the evening of the 7th inst., the Venerable Archdeacon Woodcock, in seconding a vote of thanks after a lecture which I had delivered on the Life of St. Paul, alluded, before a crowded audience, much to my surprise, to a matter which he knew of, which he was not at liberty particularly to mention, but which was interesting in itself, and might have important results—or something to that effect. I was aware to what he referred, and thought he meant that your letter was about to be published. On inquiring of him, however, if that were the case, I found that this was not his meaning, though I was not mistaken in concluding that he was acquainted with what your Lordship had written. So public an allusion to the subject, coupled with the fact that I had mentioned (and very naturally) to some of my friends that I had received from your Lordship a long letter on Christian Union, excited attention, stimulated curiosity, and led to conjectures and inquiries which found expression in the journals of the day. Your letter was directed to me at Government House, as I was then on a visit of a few days to Sir Richard and Lady MacDonnell. Sir Richard expressed a wish to be favored with a sight of it—a wish with which I felt your Lordship would yourself have readily complied. In sending it to him, which I did last week, I requested him to oblige me by jotting down anything that might occur to him on its perusal, "for," I said, "we ecclesiastics, all of us, no matter to what denomination we may belong, are in the habit of looking at certain subjects from a narrow stand-point, and in lights dimmed and darkened by our traditions. I should really like, therefore, if only as a matter of curiosity, to see how the questions raised by his Lordship shape themselves to the mind of a liberal and intelligent layman." On Monday morning last I was greatly surprised to find in the newspapers a public intimation that a memorial to your Lordship, headed by His Excellency the Governor-in-Chief, soliciting the opening of your pulpits, in my person, to ministers of other bodies, was in your absence, to be presented to the Dean and Chapter. Calling upon Sir Richard that day, as I had arranged to do, to receive back your manuscript, I found that he had had an interview, previously to his seeing me, with the Dean and the Archdeacon, and had read to them a letter to myself which he had penned on the perusal of your Lordship's. He then said that the two gentleman referred to, Dean Farrell and Archdeacon Woodcock, were alike of opinion that the publication of both documents would be productive of good, and that they recommended such publication. I was so much engaged during the remainder of the day that I could not call as I wished to do on either the Dean or the Archdeacon, but the next morning I wrote and dispatched the following letter :—

"Beaumont, October 19, 1858.

"Reverend and dear Sir,—When I saw His Excellency the Governor-in-Chief yesterday, he intimated to me, as I understood him, that the Dean and yourself had expressed a wish for the publication of the Bishop's letter to me and his own. Unfortunately, his Lordship's absence prevents my applying to himself on the subject, as it has hitherto prevented my writing to him at all. From your having alluded, however, publicly, to the existence of his letter, I think it likely that your are in possession of the Bishop's mind in relation to it. Both the letters are exceedingly interesting, and their publication, I cannot doubt, would do much good; but I could not publish what to me is as yet a private document. May I inquire whether you have authority to sanction the publication? The letter seems to have been meant for publication; have you power to give me liberty to print it?

"I am, dear Sir,
"Yours, very respectfully,
"T. Binney.

"To the Venerable Archdeacon Woodcock."

To this note I received the following reply :—

"Parsonage, Christchurch, October 19.

"Rev. and dear Sir,—In answer to the inquiry contained in your letter of this morning's date, I beg to say that I have no authority to sanction the publication of the Bishop's letter. I am, however, aware that his Lordship is quite prepared for its being made public, although I have reason to believe that he did not originally contemplate such event.

"Both the Dean and myself are still of opinion that its publication, together with that of the Governor's, would do good.

"I am, rev. and dear Sir,
"Yours respectfully,
"W. J. Woodcock.

"The Rev. Thomas Binney."

Yesterday morning (Wednesday) at the public breakfast which then took place, I passed the Archdeacon's note to Sir Richard MacDonnell, with the question, "Could I act on this?" to which he wrote, in reply, "I should think so, and would recommend it."

Such, my Lord, were the circumstances which, up to yesterday morning, transpired, relative to the publication of your letter. The thought did not originate with me, though when it was suggested by some friends. I endeavored to ascertain how far I should be justified in acting upon it. I do not think, however, I should have ventured to act upon it, even though fortified by the opinions and recommendations of such high authorities as those referred to, but for the consideration which I shall now state. At the public meeting yesterday morning, the proceedings of which have been very fully reported, such frequent allusions were made to your lordship's sentiments, especially as contained in your letter to myself, that I think it becomes due to your lordship that what you have really said should be seen. It may be supposed that you have gone further than you have, or meant to do, or than your words imply; and the shortest way of ascertaining whether this be the case, and the most equitable towards your lordship, is for those who are interested in the subject to have the means of judging for themselves. I am sure your lordship will appreciate this motive, and would probably have been satisfied had I stated nothing else; but so anxious am I to do what might not seem improper, that I have thought it right, and due to myself, to set forth, with something I fear of tedious minuteness, the various circumstances which have been operating for some days past. I regret that I cannot append to your letter the thoughts which it has suggested to my own mind, and the remarks which some points in it seem to demand. I propose to give to it my best attention, and to embody my reflections and views on the two letters in a small pamphlet, as soon as I can command the requisite leisure. In the meantime the public mind of South Australia is so interested in the subject, and so excited by recent occurrences, that I think it best not longer to withhold from it what so many are anxious to see; the publication of which, like the writing of it—to use your lordship's own words—" will not, I hope, widen if it does not tend to bridge the gap that separates Christians ecclesiastically, though not, it is to be hoped, spiritually, nor for ever "

It may not be improper to say one or two things before I conclude, to avoid misconception with respect to myself. A very few words must suffice for the present. I beg, then, to assure your lordship that while I highly admire the kind and Christian feeling that prompted your communication, and cordially sympathise in the desires and aspirations after more visible union to which you have given utterance, I greatly fear that the "idea" you entertain and would seek to realise includes too much; and not only too much, but that it has that in its elements which must be softened or lost sight of before it can find acceptance with others. It sometimes has the appearance of the old attempts at "comprehension" by which the early nonconformist used to be solicited back to the Episcopal Church; at others, it looks like a wish to form a "church of the future" out of a fusion of the different bodies at present existing, all altering something, the result being a new order of things, in which, however, your ecclesiastical peculiarities shall predominate. Now, without entering into the question as to the likelihood of this being the case (which, however, I think likely), supposing amalgamation and fusion to occur, I content myself with saying that it is premature to indulge in visions of the ultimate before we have taken such steps as are possible to us—the only steps, perhaps, that may be possible for years to come. What we need *first*—before anything else can be thought of or hoped—is, *not* the absorption by one church of others—not the conformity of others to *it*, or the toleration by it of the peculiarities of others;—nor yet an attempt to constitute a platform of discipline or service in which all may give up a little (or *much*, perhaps, in some cases) and unite. No; it is not this. First and foremost and *alone* must come the honest and hearty recognition of each other, as churches and ministers (*de facto* only, if you like), by the different Protestant Evangelical denominations,—their members and clergy. Let such recognition be shown by the occasional interchange of pulpits; and let *this* again be understood to involve nothing and imply nothing but their substantial oneness in faith, as holding in common the essential truths of the common salvation. The *liberty* thus to invite service would compel no one to invite it, or any to open their pulpits to persons—good men in their way—whom, for many reasons, it might be inexpedient to receive. Then again, the *rendering* of service, so far as simply preaching is concerned, should be held to imply nothing, on either side, beyond the oneness of faith just referred to. Had your lordship, for instance, invited me to preach in the pulpits of your Church, you ought to have been considered as committing yourself to nothing but to the recognition in me of a preacher of that Gospel which we hold in common, and of a Minister of Christ according to the constitution of that portion of the Church to which I belong. It is obvious, also, that I could not have been required to receive any *licence* from your Lordship; you would not have become my bishop, though you are one in your own communion, and I respect you as such. Those who would have needed your licence would have been your own clergy, *they* might have wanted your permission to act. In the same way, neither you nor they would have been so far compromised as justly to be regarded as giving your sanction to notions or customs among the Congregationalists of which you may disapprove, any more than I, by consenting to preach the Gospel to your flocks should have been justly supposed by that to profess *anything else*—to accept, for instance, that interpretation of your "*offices*" (I distinguish them from the Liturgy), which involves sentiments which I do not hold: which sentiments, if required to be held and professed, are, in my view, an adequate ground of nonconformity. No Church, either, whatever, should suppose that it confers a favor on the minister of another, by receiving him to its pulpits, but rather that it does what is proper and seemly for itself. When something of this sort is understood, and the first step taken in harmony with it, other things will follow. All other things and theories however, must, I fear, be postponed until this be done. I believe it might be done by very many of the Protestant Churches in relation to each other—done without compromise and without dishonor; and that great and blessed results would soon follow from it. That your Lordship may have the happiness of helping on so desirable a consummation, and may thus realise that after which your spiritual nature seems to yearn and pant, is the sincere prayer of, my Lord,

Your friend and servant in our common faith,

T. BINNEY.

Further letters on Church Union arising out of the above correspondence:—

CHURCH UNION.

No. I.

To the Editor of the Advertiser.

SIR,—I shall be glad if you can find room for the two letters and the appended paper which I herewith forward. I think, also, that after reading the letter of Messrs. Hawkes and Oldham, if you saw your way to insert their memorial, it will gratify and oblige them. So far as the memorial casts light on their letter to me, its insertion will also confer a favor on myself.

Yours, &c.,

Highercombe, October 30, 1858.   T. BINNEY.

No. II.

MESSRS. HAWKES AND OLDHAM TO THE REV. T. BINNEY.

Adelaide, October 1858.

SIR,—Observing from an advertisment in the daily papers that you are about to edit a correspondence between His Excellency the Governor, the Lord Bishop of Adelaide, yourself, and other gentlemen on the subject of a prosposed Church Union in this province; that it is your intention to append to such correspondence a memorial from certain members of the Church of England—suggestive of the subject—and that, as a first step towards such a movement, an invitation should be given to you to preach from some of the pulpits of that Church, and above all that such publication is to be introduced by a preface from your own pen—we, who take a different view of the subject as members of the Church of England, are desirous that our counter-memorial should not be omitted from your pamphlet.

Thoroughly convinced of your desire only to represent faithfully the opinions of the members of the Church of England in this province, we forward to you a copy of a memorial now in course of signature, and which already has the subscription of the President of the Legislative Council, and various other highly influential gentlemen, and request that you will do us the honor to include it in your publication. Had you not however notified your intention to publish the documents specified in your advertisement, we, nevertheless, as a mark of courtesy and respect, should have sent you a copy of our memorial.

Although we are unable to entertain the hope that any practicable plan of union can be matured, you will observe that we are no less anxious than yourself that all difference should be swallowed up in the dominion of the Church universal.

But whilst we are at the present time unable to agree in the mode the best calculated to that great end, we cannot suffer any difference of opinion, however marked, to blind us to the talents and gifts with which you are endowed.

It is moreover our sincere wish that your voyage to the southern world may be the means of the renovation of your health and strength, which it was designed to promote.

We are, Sir, your faithful servants,

G. W. HAWKES,
NATHANIEL OLDHAM,

Acting for the memorialists who have signed the counter-memorial.

Rev. Thos. Binney, Adelaide.

No. III.
MEMORIAL

Signed by Episcopalians *against* Mr. Binney's being invited to preach in their pulpits.

To the Right Reverend the Lord Bishop of Adelaide.

MY LORD,—We the undersigned, members of the United Church of England and Ireland, feel that we should be wanting in respect to your Lordship's high office, and in faithfulness to the Church of which it is our privilege to be members, were we to withhold the expression of our deep regret, that a memorial urging the invitation of an unordained minister, and of a denomination in separation from our Church, to teach from her pulpits, should have been addressed to your Lordship, by certain of her members, professing at the same time attachment to her ritual and government, and to be animated with a desire to promote Christian union on catholic grounds, and of aiding your Lordship's personal exertions in that great object.

Relying on the forecast and wisdom of your Lordship to maintain our Church in its integrity in this our adopted land, and to preserve her alike from all unauthorized measures within, as well as every intrusion from without, which may tend to obliterate even the least of her time-honored and distinctive characteristics, we await with every confidence your Lordship's determination.

Well aware that the fallacies of the positions assumed in the introduction of that memorial will not escape your Lordship's notice, it would be out of place were we longer to dwell upon them to add, that while we earnestly desire and await the reduction of every profession of Christianity into the bosom of one communion, we are not at liberty, as reasoning and reflecting men, to forget, that the name of Christianity affords no security whatever for substantial unity: and that Christianity in any form without the proof of its being a revelation, is but a human opinion—reasons which lead to the inevitable conclusion that any such anticipated union as that which the memorialists so indefinitely and vaguely describe must be considered as purely ideal.

We are prepared with abundant reasons why it is not possible for us to consent, on the present or any occasion, that our Church should unite or ally herself, or make any conditions of mutual assistance with any man, or body of men, involving the slightest compromise of principle, but aware that your Lordship will anticipate us in all these respects, it seems only to remain for us to express the unfeigned satisfaction with which we have received the decision of the Dean and Chapter in your Lordship's absence.

We remain, Your Lordship's faithful servants,

J. H. Fisher, President of the Legislative Council.	Edward A. Hamilton.
A. H. Freeling, Capt. R. E., M.L.C.	E. Cestres Gwynne, M.L.C.
T. O'Halloran, M.L.C.	James H. Parr.
J. B. Hughes, J.P.	Charles Lowe
Henry Gawler.	Edward T. Wildman.
Thomas Gilbert, J.P.	J. G. A. Branthwaite.
Nathaniel Oldham, J.P.	Thomas O'Halloran, jun.
G. W. Hawkes.	Nathaniel A. Knox.
Joseph Stilling.	Alfred Heath.
Henry Holyrod.	C. A. Wilson.

No. IV.

THE REV. T. BINNEY TO G. W. HAWKES AND NATHANIEL OLDHAM, ESQRS.

Highercombe, October 30, 1858.

To G. W. Hawkes, Esq., and Nathl. Oldham, Esq.

GENTLEMEN,—I beg to acknowledge the receipt of your letter of the 28th instant, which reached me here last night. I was exceeding surprised by the mistake which ran through it from beginning to end;—a mistake which so fully possessed you as almost forcibly to obtrude itself in every sentence. I was totally ignorant of the existence of anything that could have so misled you. I was not aware of my being employed in editing any pamphlet, or of being about to publish one, or that any advertisement had appeared that could convey such an idea. I had not seen such an advertisement, and I certainly had not authorised the appearance of anything of the sort. On carefully examining the papers, however, this morning, I found one, which, on a hasty or cursory reading, might convey the impression under which you labored. It announces that a pamphlet is intended to be put forth, containing such and such articles, and it closes with the statement that it will be " with an introductory paragraph, by the Rev. T. Binney." Now, instead of limiting the connection of my name to *the four words* which immediately preceded it, a person might extend it to the whole advertisement. This you seem to have done ; and hence, instead of meaning *what it says*, that an "introductory paragraph" is to be furnished by me, the advertisement came to mean, in your apprehension, that the entire pamphlet was to be mine. I admit, then, that *on a cursory reading*, you might get this impression, but I beg most distinctly to say that a *careful* reading would instantly have corrected the mistake ;—such a reading as, you will excuse my saying, gentlemen ought to have given before writing such a letter as yours. The pointing,—there being no full stop after the word "paragraph ;"—"by" having only a small b, not a capital letter, and the obvious grammatical meaning of the sentence,—ought to have prevented the misconception which you have so elaborately built in two-thirds of your communication.

Allow me to explain to you how the thing originated and how it stood ; and permit me also to say, that, seeing that it is possible for persons like yourselves of education and ability to mistake the meaning of the advertisement, I am glad that your letter affords me the opportunity of a public explanation before it be too late.—On Monday last, just as I found that I could not get off that day by the Havilah ; and had succeeded in transferring the places I had taken to her next trip, a gentleman said to me, "I think of putting into a pamphlet the letters which have appeared on Christian union, with the speeches at the public breakfast on the same subject, and the comments of the press ;—would you favor me with a short preface ?" —I hesitated for a time. I did not feel sure that I ought. At length, knowing that the thing could be done, for there is no copy-right, I believe, in what is written in newspapers. the thought struck me that it might be well to take advantage of the request to say one or two things which I was anxious the public should keep in mind, or be made aware of. I also thought that I might, without offence, indulge in an explanatory, illustrative, or other remark that would not, perhaps, be without its use. On these grounds I consented to furnish a preface to the proposed collection of papers ; but so far from my writing the work— or its being mine—or my having any control over it—I assure you, gentlemen, that my knowledge of it is limited to the fact that it is to consist of a selection of such articles from the newspapers as have recently appeared on a certain subject. I have never seen a sheet of proof ; I don't know which or how many of the articles referred to the pamphlet is to consist of ; I have nothing to do with compilation, or arrangement, or anything else ; all that I am concerned with is, that the book is to refer to a subject and to proceedings in which I am personally interested ;—that the opportunity was offered to me to say something to the public in connection with it ;—and that I thought of glancing at one or two things which I wished the public should not overlook.

I am convinced, however, by your letter, that my promise to the editor has placed me in a false position. It was well intended on my part, but I see that my fulfilling it, and having my name on the title-page of the projected publication, will expose me to much misconception. I have determined, therefore, to withdraw from it. I have explained to the gentleman who asked from me the favor of a very small service, how I feel myself to be circumstanced. I have requested him to release me from my promise, and to allow me to retire from all connection with his work. He has complied with my request, so that my name will no longer be put forth along with it. Henceforth, I shall stand, as I have hitherto done. without being voluntarily mixed up with what others may write or do. My sole concern will be to take an opportunity of communicating directly with His Lordship the Bishop of Adelaide on the contents of the letters which he kindly addressed to me. I still feel, however, that I should like to put or keep myself right with the public, by having an opportunity of saying what I was intending to say in the promised preface, or "introductory paragraph." I had completed the piece before your letter came—every word of it. I say this on my honor as a gentleman. It is all the same to me, whether it goes before the public through the medium of the advertised publication, or in connection with this correspondence. I shall append it therefore to this letter, and send it with it to the newspapers. I act promptly, not losing a day, because I feel it important that the mistake under which you write should be at once publicly met. If gentlemen of your standing could fall into it, the probability is, that it is very general ; and I certainly think that, if it were to continue, it would be to me very serious.

I have no power, as you will perceive, to direct your memorial to be inserted in the forth-coming pamphlet. Its appearance in the newspapers, however, will place it among that class of things out of which the pamphlet is to be constructed. Whether the editor will use it, or find it suitable to his object, I cannot tell ; but to put it within his reach is all that I can do for you. I think that you are quite right in wishing it to go before the public. I will send it, therefore, to the papers with this correspondence, and request its insertion. It is almost necessary, indeed, to do this to make the correspondence fully intelligible, yet I should not have felt warranted to do so, but that your request to myself shows that I shall thus only be carrying out your own expressed desire.

I thank you, gentlemen, for the courteous terms in which you speak of me personally; I reciprocate your good wishes; and I earnestly pray that nothing that has occurred in connection with my visit to your city may have any result, but what we may all look back upon, whatever our difference of opinion, if not with affection or gratitude, at least without rancour or regret.

I am, gentlemen, Yours faithfully,
T. BINNEY.

P.S.—I give the paper that follows exactly as it was written before your letters came. Though not now intended to be a preface to anything, I suffer its language, as such, to stand, because I think it best not to change a single sentence in consequence of the receipt of your letters;—nor have I added one.

T. B.

No. V.

THE INTENDED PREFACE.

Having been solicited by the editor of this book to furnish him with two or three preparatory paragraphs, I shall beg leave to avail myself of the opportunity of saying one or two things which, all things considered, it may be as well for me to say.

Of course it will be understood, without my insisting upon it, that I am not responsible for anything which this pamphlet may contain beyond what was spoken or written by myself. Of what may be inserted besides, I can only have a general impression. I shall not become acquainted with the whole of its contents till the book is published. There will be articles and papers, letters and paragraphs, I dare say, which, from their constant allusions to myself, it will not be particularly pleasant to peruse. This, however, is incidental to the singular position which, by no will or purpose of my own, I have come to occupy. As such I must bear it as magnanimously as I can, in the hope that the general good—good to the cause of truth and charity—may spring out of it. Their are more modes of martyrdom, or of vicarious suffering, than those of the gaol, the pillory, or the stake.

The proceedings at the public breakfast took a direction a little different from what was projected—that is to say, one topic, or one class of topics, was kept principally in view, to the exclusion of others and of other speakers that were to have been brought forward. This naturally arose out of the extraordinary movements, which had just been initiated, with which His Excellency, who spoke first, was so much concerned. Every one knows how a first speech, especially when telling and eloquent, and in harmony with the sympathies of an audience, gives a tone and character to the subsequent proceedings of a public meeting. For myself, I accept the report of what I said as being, I have no doubt, substantially correct. But I spoke under great disadvantages from the painful indisposition of the preceding day and night. Some things were omitted which should have been thought of (and had been thought of), and others said not exactly in the way I could wish to have said them.

Passing, however, from these personal topics, I will offer a word or two on more general matters. Let it, then, be well and thoroughly understood that the question which has been brought before the public mind of this colony, and which gives to the following pages all their interest, is not in any respect a personal one. It has nothing to do with individual ministers, whoever they may be, it should be looked at quite irrespective of all such. That my name is mixed up with it may be said to be an accident, and in some respects (though not in all) it is one not without its penalties. The whole thing took me by surprise. I was surprised by the receipt of the Bishop's letter, not having the slightest ground for expecting such a communication. I was still more surprised by reading in the newspapers the very morning after I had publicly taken leave of what to me is the representative Church of my own denomination, an account of the movement that was on foot in relation to myself among leading members of the Episcopal body, and which had found expression in their memorial to the Bishop. My surprise was certainly not lessened by finding, when I called at Government House, that the Dean and the Archdeacon had just been with His Excellency, that he had read to them a letter which he had addressed to me on reading His Lordship's, and that they recommended the publication of both documents. Altogether, the whole thing, in its successive steps, was very singular, and singularly unexpected. But I had nothing consciously or actively to do with it. I was a mere spectator, though so much interested—the involuntary subject of others' proceedings.

When action was suggested, in the form of giving to the public a letter addressed to me by one who was absent, I had to consider and decide. I felt it to be a very serious thing to send a paper to the press without first obtaining the writer's consent. Although I have not now, and had not at the time, the slightest doubt that the Bishop, could he have been applied to, would have given that consent, I do not think I should have done what I did in the way of publication, but for the consideration, personal to His Lordship, which I mention in my letter of the 21st instant, to the statements of which I beg the reader's particular attention. Subsequent events have justified the judgment I then formed, and on which I acted, and they will justify my acting upon it, I have no doubt, in the opinion of the Bishop himself.

It would not be consistent with the feelings of respect which I cherish towards His Lordship, nor would it, in my view, be becoming treatment of such a letter as his, to enter into the discussion of the subject he has propounded to me, and on his views and suggestions respecting it, in a publication like this. I must content myself, for the present, with what

I have said in my letter of acknowledgment and explanation (October 21st)—the first of the series published on Monday last, and now re-published in this book. Anything more, indeed, just at present, is hardly required. For all practical purposes, it is sufficient to have expressed the conviction that His Lordship's "idea" of "the Church of the future" is one which cannot possibly be realised as an immediate result, and to have hinted, as courteously as I could to be intelligible, that what at present, or might be, must be sought for on more equal terms, than from His Lordship's position and antecedents, it is at all likely he can be prepared either to propose or to accept. His Lordship's letter is to me exceedingly interesting, touching, as it does, on many matters which have necessarily occupied much of my attention, and illustrating how a genuine Christian soul, freed in some measure from the inherited prejudices of the old land, by coming into contact with and breathing the air of the new state of things inaugurated here, yearns and struggles, as from an irrepressible instinct, after something more of union with others than aforetime, probably, he could have thought it possible he should ever have desired. I shall soon, I hope, be able to write to the Bishop in reply to his communication, and to explain to him how the matters on which he touches have long shaped themselves to my mind. This, however, will be an engagement partaking more of speculative interests than of practical utility—at least as bearing on immediate action. So far as that is concerned, it is of no use (except to prevent it) to enter into a discussion about the character and authority of the Council at Jerusalem, or the "separation" of Barnabas and Saul at Antioch, or the position of Apollos, whose instructors in the faith were two private Christians, who rose into and retained a position in the Church which Apollos himself recognized and respected, but who never seems to have received ordination at all from either Bishop or Presbyter. It is of no use, I repeat, going into a public discussion of these matters, or trying to investigate the nature of schism, or the shade of difference between schism and "dichostasy," or the official rank and special duties of Timothy and Titus, or as to who and what were the "angels" of the Apocalypse, or the probable authority with one body of Christians of the old and venerated traditions of another. On all these points I have my opinions, and some of those opinions happen to approach much nearer to the views of His Lordship than do those of some of my co-religionists; but for all that, it is my settled conviction that not much gain on the side of charity is likely to be the result of such discussions. I by no means think that the points referred to are trifling or unimportant, or that even the Bishop's Church of the future may not one day come; but I do think that anything like general agreement about the one and anything like the faintest dawn of the other, is most likely to succeed to our acting together as far as we can without first engaging in "doubtful disputations." The probability is, that any new order of things will spring from something altogether different. The inward life of the Church itself, the spiritual longings of the flock of Christ, may become so strong, active, and irresistible that, without breaking down the form of the folds peculiar to particular portions of the whole, they shall yet one day so overpass them as to reach and realize through an accomplished fact what never would have been secured by ecclesiastical negotiations. As women, by a quick reasoning instinct, often arrive at the best and wisest practical decisions, while men are thinking and hesitating on the subject, and getting more and more hopelessly perplexed, so a religious, zealous, and active laity will often be found ready for an advance, and will be prepared to settle some knotty question by positive acts, before the clerical mind can see its way. We divines, especially in relation to ecclesiastical matters, are apt to forge strong iron bolts with which to bar our doors against each other; the laity have not skill to draw these bolts, and we dare not or will not; but every now and then a time comes when the force of the confined and crowded mass presses against the limits which enclose it—the doors suddenly open—the bolts are broken or fly off, being found, after all, to have no better fastening than tin-tacks. Thus will it be, most likely, with practical measures of Christian co-operation between different Churches. Instead of everything being settled and arranged, first, by our all agreeing in certain specified ecclesiastical traditions, something will be done—somebody will act—arguments will afterwards be found to justify it; and then out of this may emerge at length "the Church of the future."

I have only to add that I presume the pages that follow are intended simply to be a record of what has been taking place during the last week or two in this colony, as of something interesting in itself, indicative of progress, and "an outward and visible sign" of the working of "inward spiritual grace." The book is not controversial, as the movement it refers to is not, though it is not impossible that it may prove the occasion of something of the sort. I trust, however, that it will not, or that, if it does, the writers or speakers will "remember that they are brethren," and that it is quite possible for such to differ in opinion and to engage in discussion with mutual respect and loving words. No angry or unhallowed feelings will, I trust, be suffered to interfere with what has hitherto been undisturbed by such elements. I should be exceedingly sorry if my visit to South Australia should become the innocent cause of religious strife. I shall hope it will be otherwise. Though the time has not come to attempt to realize the idea of the Bishop—though it may not be possible at present to carry out the more restricted practical suggestion of the Governor—I yet feel that much has been gained by the utterance of the views and aspirations of two such "representative men," and I deem myself happy in having been the cause or occasion of that utterance. I visited Australia with little hope of engaging in any public service whatever. I came to this colony with no intention of doing more than seeing and visiting my own friends as quietly as possible. If, by consenting to do more, I have done something to lessen the distance between Christian men of different denominations, to increase their fraternal estimation of each other, and to strengthen their desires for a more visible manifestation of that; looking at this, and at what may, in God's good time, flow from it, I can almost fancy I see a reason, but certainly a recompense, for my having had to undertake, in sickness and sorrow, an involuntary voyage round the world.

Highercombe, October 28, 1858.   T. B.

The result of all this correspondence and these memorials is, that Mr. Binney was *not* asked to preach in a church which had been consecrated by an Anglican Bishop. He is *unordained*, and therefore unqualified. We thus see that the venerable "tradition of 1800 years" that no man is a proper and authorised minister of the Gospel whose ordination is not derived immediately from a Bishop supposed to be in the direct line of descent from the Apostles, is the *real barrier* to an effective and thoroughly cordial union of Christians and churches of different denominations. Many individual Christians in the Anglican Church feel no hesitation in admitting the true ministerial status of Christian Pastors ordained according to the usages of their own communities; but it seems the *Church itself* flatly denies such eminence of gifts, graces and usefulness; the visible stamp and seal of Divine approval, and the full recognition of the whole Christian world besides, are not sufficient to qualify for admission to the humblest pulpit of the Anglican Church a Calvin or Melancthon, a Knox or Melville, a Howe or Baxter, a Watts or Doddridge, a Tholuck or D'Aubigne, a Chalmers, a James, or a Binney. To fit such as these for admission, they must ignore their previous "orders," acknowledge the invalidity of all their past ministerial acts, and begin *de novo*, by receiving from a duly consecrated Bishop, Deacon's orders, the lowest in the clerical scale, and rising to higher grades in due time. And yet Roman Catholic priests, if *they* turn Protestants, are not so treated: the anomalous "Canons" of the Anglican Church allow the validity of *their* orders, and admit *them* to its ministry without re-ordination. The compliment, however, is not returned by the Romanists; *they* treat the Anglicans as the Anglicans treat their fellow Protestants; and Mr. Newman and others, on entering the Romish Priesthood, had to enter as Acolytes, and submit to be ordained afresh; and if the Archbishop of Canterbury were to turn Catholic, all his orders would go for nothing; he would be regarded simply as an unordained layman. So that others besides the Church of England can play at this game. Whilst, however, the Anglican Church is so exclusive and sectarian as to consider all Wesleyan, Presbyterian, Congregational, and Baptist ministers—however eminent and honored of God—as unordained, its rule is so comprehensive and latitudinarian in another respect as to embrace every shade of doctrine, and almost every variety of character, and to afford no guarantee for ministerial fitness, or soundness in the faith. A Hervey and a Sterne, a Hawker and a Tomline, a Sumner and a Jowett, a Pusey and a McNeill; Puritans and free-livers, hyper-Calvinists and Pelegians, devout Evangelicals and German Rationalists, Papists in thin disguise and ultra Orangemen are all acknowledged as true ministers of Christ, if only they have passed through the mystic right of episcopal ordination. All this is in keeping with the *Romanist* community, which systematically makes the *opus operatum* everything, and the real element of true religion, apart from it, nothing at all; but for a Church which is professedly Protestant, based upon the right and the exercise of private judgment and the sufficiency of Holy Scripture, to take up such an entrenched position of assumption and exclusiveness, does certainly strike all other Protestant communities as singularly anomalous and inconsistent. Nay, more, they regard it as a melancholy and unfortunate peculiarity; the great barrier to that free, cordial, and compact union of Protestants which alone can make head against a Papistical and infidel world; and they cannot but believe it must be a grievous lamentation to many excellent laymen, clergymen, and even bishops, of the Anglican Church, who long to give the right hand of fellowship upon equal terms to Evangelical ministers of other communities, but dare not or cannot, by reason of the ecclesiastical fetters that bind them. May the yearnings of their hearts after a closer union be speedily gratified by the bursting asunder of those galling fetters!

A FUNERAL ON THE GOLD-FIELDS.

To the Editor of the Southern Spectator.

It was a long, low, narrow canvas tent; so long and narrow that it seemed a good step from one end to the other, so low that a person of but middling stature could walk erect only along the middle of the place. Resting on two blocks of wood, one at each end, the most imposing object on the spot was a long dark coffin, made of pieces of deal, hastily fastened together, covered all over with a dark cloth and bearing on the lid a metal plate on which were inscribed in large letters the initials and years of him who thirty-six hours before had departed this life for another. At the remote end of the tent, stretching right across from side to side, and raised only a few inches above the surface of the bare earth, could be seen a rude wooden structure, commonly called a colonial bed, which is evidently intended to serve the same purpose on the gold-fields as the easy and elegant Tudor bed at home; but it is quite another piece of workmanship, and looks quite another thing. It was evidently while lying on that rude piece of upholstery that the deceased had passed his last illness; there the last moments of probation had been spent, thence the immortal spirit, prepared or not prepared, had taken its flight out of the earthly tabernacle into the presence of the Father and the Judge of the spirits of all flesh, and thence all that remained here had been removed and placed in the sable tenement in which now the body was enclosed ready to be carried to the long home appointed for all living. That wooden structure, rough and unattractive in its exterior, I could not help surrounding with these and such-like thoughts. The widow and sons and daughters of the deceased collected about the coffin, as near as a very limited space would allow. Prayers were offered to that God in whose hands our breath is and whose are all our ways. Portions of sacred Scripture suitable to the occasion were read and some counsels and admonitions were given. And now we were ready to move towards the cemetery as it is called. A common horse and cart, which had carried many rich loads of quartz to the wheels or stampers of the crushing machine and which two days ago formed part of the personal property of him now dead, were waiting to receive and carry their recent owner to his last resting place. The coffin was lifted up and placed diagonally across the vehicle from one corner to the other. Without any perceptible order the attendants, all immediate relations of the departed, followed on close behind the cart. The women appeared in their ordinary Sunday attire, light dresses and blue veils being the order of the day, without any token of sorrow or mourning. The men put on their best, and the only thing expressive of sorrow was a narrow piece of black crape fastened round that kind of covering for the head well known here as the wide-awake. Off we started for the grave, over a portion of the diggings, itself a land of open graves and enough to remind men of their latter end and their final earthly destiny, into the bush, instinct just now with many forms of insect life and glowing with the most abundant and exquisite variety of wild flower I have ever seen, suggesting as they did some solemn contrasts to the still, inanimate remains we were accompanying to the grave. Bye and bye we enter a deep ravine having two lofty hills, one on each hand, with multitudes of granite rocks projecting from their huge sides in all sizes and running from the base right up to the summit, sometimes in groups orderly and picturesque. Through this natural scenery, among the grandest and most imposing I have ever seen, we had to thread our circuitous way for some quarter of a mile, when after that the two ridges of hills began to lower and diverge away to the right and left, and presented to our view, not far off, a level open space in the midst, interspersed plentifully with gum trees and some rugged boulders of granite rising up from the ground. That open plot of ground is the necropolis of *M*. It is situated about one mile and a half distant from the township. There are about 80 graves of immense size in which Europeans and Chinese, not far apart from each other, sleep till the morning of the resurrection, and at the end of each respectively may be seen stuck in the earth the crucifix of the Christian and the red tapers of the Celestials. On this spot and in the midst of these fellow-sleepers of different nations and religions we deposited the remains of the brother departed. Suitable religious service was performed, the grave was filled up, and we came away impressed, no doubt very differently with the solemn spectacle we had witnessed in common. A deep shade made up of pity, sorrow, and melancholy came over my whole spirit, and in spite of some efforts to throw it off, remained all the day after. I was conscious that it had been a perpetual struggle all the time for me to get those present to look thoughtfully at the relative value of those things which are temporal and those which are eternal. I feared that neither what God had done in taking away the life of one so nearly related, nor the religious services performed in connexion with the burial would be the means of producing any salutary impression or doing any good. I had never contemplated death and the grave, the most solemn and momentous of subjects, in the midst of such incongruous circumstances. To one accustomed at such solemn times to see the dark imposing funeral pall, or the dark hearse and coaches with horses and trappings all in keeping, the solemn, thoughtful procession all moving slowly and seriously on, as duly impressed with the solemnity of the occasion, to some consecrated burial ground, the circumstances before described did seem frightfully incongruous with the reality and solemnity of the occasion which brought us together. Of course they are but accidents, circumstances in some cases necessary on the gold-fields. It is simply as such that I look at them, yet while in the body, whatever some sublime transcendentalists may say to the contrary, we cannot help being affected, sometimes deeply, with outward material circumstances and the fitness of things. Is the immortal spirit right, good, safe, happy? That is the important thing. If so, it matters but little, comparatively, under what forms and circumstances the mortal body is committed to the ground, or whether there be any forms at all. " Ah ! " said the surviving widow respecting the departed husband, " when at home he used to go to a place of worship on Sundays, but he has not been since we came out here." Of how many colonists out here, especially on the gold-fields, is this remark true. How many there are who at home went regularly to the house of prayer, seemed to find pleasure in the means of grace, and promised fair for the kingdom ; but who, out here, never come to worship God with the great congregation and only sometimes think of those things which make for their eternal peace. How many there are whose pastors, parents, brothers, sisters, and relations would deeply grieve if they but knew at home into what indifference and deadness the objects of their solicitude and prayer have fallen, out here. Of how many shall it be said by their surviving friends, when they are about to be consigned to their last resting place, and when the day of grace is hid for ever from their eyes, as the weeping widow said the other day, not quite sure about her husband's safety, " When at home he used to go to a place of worship on Sundays, but he has not been since we came out here." Let those whom it concerns ponder this and begin a corresponding reasonable conduct. Those who will not worship God on earth shall not worship him in heaven.

M., October, 1858.   VERAX.

REVIEW.
American Congregational Year Books. 1855-57.

A short time ago we submitted a few thoughts suggested by the English Year Book to the readers of the Southern Spectator. Through the kindness of the Rev. F. Miller, we have been favored with the books specified at the head of this article, with a view to supplement the former article. The United States of America furnish matter for serious reflection to the politician, philanthropist, and Christian. In contemplating their origin, rapid increase, vast extent, commercial enterprise, scientific culture, glaring inconsistencies, and characteristic vanity, one is startled and fascinated—and still the wonder grows! The population, already equal to that of the United Kingdom, speedily doubles itself—an advance of fifteen miles per annum is said to be made upon the forest in the Western States—whilst the eagle, to quote an Americanism, already touches the Atlantic with one wing, and the Pacific with another. Unquestionably the United States have a part to play of no small importance in the drama of the future. If we saw no other reason for distrusting fashionable expositions of prophecy, the utter neglect of the United States, and all nations but European ones, would be sufficient. Expositors usually limit their favors to Russia, France, and the 'Beast,' using a wise reservation about England, and ignoring all other nations,

M

great or growing. No thoughtful man can look at the intermingling of nationalities on the American continent, without at times speculating upon its physical, social and religious aspect, and wondering whereunto it will grow. One thing is clear, analogy helps us but little, the phenomena are altogether unique; and, when fully resolved, will add a new chapter to the annals of nations of deepest significance. It is a shallow view to suppose that the United States have simply to solve the practicability of a republican form of government with a clear exposition of its advantages and defects—that has long been done—history teaches us that such a form of Government, as Milton well observes, requires a larger measure of private and public virtue than any other—it is simply a question of national worthiness. Deeper problems wait for solution, and we watch with no small interest for the full unfolding of those truths of which time alone will be our teacher. Meanwhile it is refreshing to see the efforts made to speed the Gospel of Christ in connection with distinctive principles of church polity, which we would hold with no feeble grasp. The books before us contain a record of some of the deeds and purposes of a denomination, historically connected with the early founders of the New England States. Very noble is the well known apostrophe of Carlyle to those founders and their little ship. " Hail to thee! poor little ship, Mayflower, of Delft Haven, poor common looking ship, hired by common charter party, for coined dollars—caulked with mere oakum and tar, provisioned with vulgarest biscuit and bacon ; yet what ship Argo, or miraculous epic ship, built by the sea-gods, was other than a foolish bumbarge in comparison ! Golden fleeces, or the like, these sailed far with or with out effect. Thou little Mayflower hadst in thee a veritable Promethean spark, the life-spark of the greatest nation on our earth ; so we may already name the Trans-atlantic Saxon nation. They went seeking leave to hear sermons in their own method, these *Mayflower* Puritans, a most indispensable search ; and yet, like Saul, the son of Kish, seeking a small thing, they found this unexpected great thing. Honor to the brave and true ! they really, we say, carry fire from heaven, and have a power that themselves dream not of. Let all men honor Puritanism, since God has honored it ! " Worthy successors of the men who thus sought ' a faith's pure shrine ' and liberty of prophesying, have ever graced the annals of the American Church, aud not least among the tribes of its spiritual search stands the congregational body.

The statistics which are given in the Year Books, aid us to see, though imperfectly, the geographical distribution of the Congregational churches. Denominationalism, the world over, seems to have local affinities. Wesleyan Methodism makes little headway in Scotland, though mighty in England. Essex is a stronghold of English Congregationalism from ancient times, whilst in other agricultural counties it is comparatively feeble. So in America,—Massachusetts, and Connecticut, are learned in Congregationalism while the Southern States art chiefly in other hands. Interesting and valuable information is supplied by stating the number of members in connection with the individual churches. Some difficulty, however, seems to exist in obtaining the necessary returns: surely there is no undercurrent of the old English prejudice about numbering the people ; there are ministers who deem ignorance on this point both bliss and safety, if not a duty ! The general increase of church members is deemed upon the whole highly satisfactory.

We notice a praiseworthy fact in connection with the Plymouth Congregational Church, Brooklyn, under the pastoral care of the Rev. H. W. Beecher. As part of their new and magnificent church accommodations there are two social circle parlors, each 24 by 32 feet, in which social meetings of the members of the church and congregation are held for the purpose of facilitating and extending their mutual acquaintance. "And to these social gatherings is to be attributed much of the harmony and of the marked cheerfulness and friendship which exist in the church and congregation." Pastoral visitation, except in cases of sickness, of such a congregation as crowds the Plymouth Church, is out of the question, but by these meetings the pastor is enabled to keep up a general acquaintance with the members. Many are aware that few complaints are more general, or more sincere, or better founded, than the one made by members of our churches, fresh from England as to the difficulty of forming Christian acquaintances and friendships. Is it not possible in many instances to adopt the above plan of bringing our people together ? There does seem something incongruous in the fact of our members knowing but little more of each other than the Polynesian converts. We do not advocate a meeting with set speeches, but tea and a *conversazione*. We think that the New Testament, church history and experience, give ample warranty for such meetings. The general increase of this particular church is set forth in a series of striking figures, and the writer adds, " It is believed, that the spiritual prosperity of the church and society has been in no small degree dependant upon its promptness in discharging its pecuniary obligations. The annual pew rents of the church amount to about 12,000 dollars, of which not more than one pew rent has ever been lost." During the six years of its existence the congregation has raised for its Church Building Fund, its current expenses and for various benevolent purposes, sums amounting in the aggregate to about 144,000 dollars.

The Revival Record is a singular feature of American religious life, and plainly shows that previous to the present great awakening many churches had been blessed with cheering manifestations of God's grace and saving power. A revival may consist of an increase of the piety, joy and activity of existing church members, or in large additions to Christian fellowship from those who were aliens and strangers, or, as is usually the case, in both united. The record gives many instances where a revival was singularly blessed to church members. "Many seem to have entered upon a new life not by the ephemeral influence of sympathy, but by the most rigid review and heart-searching before God." Under the influence of God's Spirit old sins were forsaken, neglected duties resumed, alienations removed and injuries confessed with many tears. It is truly said, "It is in this state alone that Christians are really fit to do anything for sinners either by labor or prayer." Most blessed results have followed in numerous conversions, one small church receiving an immediate addition of 'twenty-three members, mostly young persons.' Wilt thou not revive us, O Lord, that thy people may rejoice in thee?

The memoirs of departed ministers are, in many instances, beautifully written, and well adapted to awaken purposes which, if embodied in worthy deeds, would make us better men and preachers. Among them is the name of Dr. Woods, a divine of world-wide reputation as an accomplished expositor of many intricate problems in morals and theology. To him belongs the honor of having trained the earliest of the American foreign missionaries, men to be held in everlasting remembrance. Dr. Murdoch's memoir is a fitting tribute to his manly worth. Students of church history know him as the gifted and learned translator of Mosheim's great work. He was " a man learned after the old fashion," a thorough scholar, widely read, a patient painstaking man, a sturdy Congregationalist, and as a Christian, "without attaining to a full assurance, he never relinquished his hope of salvation through divine grace." Many incidents of toil and travel, of dangers encountered and victories won, of sacrifices made and blessed results following, grace these ministerial biographies. "One who had large and generous plans for future labors " in the midst of present triumphs met death with calm resignation. "Bury me where I fall," was his strict injunction, and devout men who carried him to the grave sang the beautiful hymn of Mackay's—

"Asleep in Jesus! far from thee
My kindred and their graves may be:
But thine is still a blessed sleep,
From which none ever wakes to weep."

The venerable age of many of the ministers is remarkable. In one annual list of 40 deceased ministers, there are five who were 80 years of age and upwards, eight who were between 70 and 80, nine between 60 and 70. In another annual list (1856) of thirty deceased ministers, there are five who were 80 and upwards, nine between 70 and 80, eight between 60 and 70. Clergymen, the world over, are on an average proverbially long livers, and should our Australian clergy equal their brethren in this particular, the Australian Mutual Provident Society will have a fair margin of profit after their considerate allowance of five per cent. discount, which from their advertisements we perceive they allow to ministers effecting assurances on their own lives.

The College Records are honorable to the American churches. They have ever been blessed with a ministry second to none for sound professional learning. In no country is greater attention paid to sound biblical exegesis. The old Puritan ministers of America were men of mark and power even in the English Universities where they had studied. Colleges were early founded by these noble confessors, which have since been taught by men of great philosophical insight, accurate learning and high-toned devotion. The present professorial roll includes many well-known names, as Stowe, Parks, Shedd, Finney, Woods, Robinson, and others of great mark and likelihood. The curriculum as appended is eminently complete and satisfactory.

A pleasing account is furnished of a fund for aiding in the erection of churches in the Western States. The report occupies eight pages and is worthy of careful perusal, as showing the power and adaptation of the voluntary principle to provide church accommodation for districts ever increasing in extent and population. As a minimum every church in some States is urged to contribute ten dollars per annum to the fund, on the ground "that the erection of meeting houses to be controlled by congregational churches hereafter to be formed, would often secure the speedy existence of such churches in communities where they do not exist and would not otherwise be gathered for many years to come." Many of the buildings already finished are highly commended " as ornaments to the towns and rural districts where they have been erected." In connection with the fund a book of church plans has been published, and every encouragement seems to be given to a superior style of church architecture. Thus religious houses are provided for pilgrim bands, and they have their holy place. Surely some such plan will soon be imitated in these colonies.

Many points of interest might be further noted, but our paper is already long enough for the " Spectator." The general results upon our own mind is, that there is a large amount of healthful manly piety in the congregational churches of America, with a clear and firm apprehension of their distinctive principles of church polity. Other religious bodies have been greatly influenced by them, they have a noble history, their present position is one of hope and promise, a bright future awaits them, and in its blessings and triumphs we hope our Australian churches may largely share.   W. L.

Launceston.

REV. THOMAS BINNEY.—Mr. Binney has closed his career in South Australia and arrived in Victoria. His reception in the former colony must have been highly gratifying to himself as it is honorable to the South Australians. Everywhere he was heard with pleasure and received with every mark of respect and consideration. From the Governor-in-Chief to the masses of the people, all have united in giving him a cordial welcome. This is partly owing to his eminence as a preacher and author, to his catholicity as a Christian, and partly to the fact of his having been closely connected with the founding of the colony and personally known to not a few of its leading men. After preaching to the delight of multitudes in various parts of the colony, lecturing (as previously announced in this magazine) on subjects both sacred and secular, the termination of his visit was signalised by a magnificent public breakfast, at which were present nearly all the notables of the colony. Deeply interesting speeches were delivered by the Attorney-General who presided, by His Excellency the Governor, the Rev. T. Q. Stow and others, and Mr. Binney himself in his farewell address kept the audience entranced for fully two hours. We deeply regret not being able to give a report of these speeches, but the large space we have given to the correspondence on Church Union renders this impossible.

WESLEYAN CHURCH, ST. KILDA.—This place of worship was opened on Sunday September 19, by the Rev. W. Hill, of Geelong, preaching in the morning, Rev. James Ballantyne in the afternoon, and the Rev. I. New in the evening. when the congregations were excellent. On the following evening, 20th, a soirée was held in the school-room adjoining, the party adjourning after tea to the new church. Peter Davis Esq., presided, and the meeting was addressed by the Revs. D. J. Draper, R. Fletcher, J. Ballantyne, Walter Powell Esq., and others. The collection and promises amounted to about £350. The building is an oblong Gothic structure, with narrow lancet windows, side buttresses, a square tower, &c. It is built of blue-stone with white-stone facings, and has a neat appearance. It will accommodate 500 adults besides Sunday school children. The cost will be between £4,000 and £5,000, towards which £1,500 has been granted by the trustees of Collins-street Melbourne, out of the sale of the chapel there.

THE JEWS.—POPULATION OF JERUSALEM.—Many of our readers will, we doubt not, read with interest the following statement of the number of persons who resided in the 'holy city' in the year 1854, giving, as it does, the proportion to each religion the population profess to follow. We give it upon the authority of Dr. Barclay, who says, 'all previous estimates of the population of Jerusalem are so very discrepant—not only as to details, but the general aggregate also (ranging from 10,000 to 35,000)—that I have taken none of them, even as a basis ; but have instituted inquiries entirely independent ; and, after much inquiry, observation, and investigation, I am persuaded that the permanent population may be fairly set down at 22,000—discounting one or two per cent. from the detailed estimates of the Jewish and Christian population for the sake of round numbers—composed as follows : Jews, 11,000; Mussulmans, 6,000 ; Christians, 4,500. This estimate, of course, is exclusive of pilgrims, the number of whom averages about 7,000 per annum, principally Christians. 'The Jews are composed of two principal classes—the Sephardim and Askenazim. Of the Sephardim, the Spanish Jews number about 9000, and the Mograbim only about 50. Of the Askenazim class, the Perushim (or Pharisees) number about 1,200 ; the Khassidim (Pious), about 800; the Khabaad (or Hebronites), 100 ; and the Kairaites (distinguished for discarding the Talmud), only 40. The remaining subdivision of the Askenazim—the German Jews—number about 100. About 246 Rabbis (so called) preside over these various classes of Jews, as lords temporal as well as spiritual ; and a more grinding despotism is not perhaps exercised upon the whole face of the earth.'

The Southern Spectator.

JANUARY, 1859.

EDITOR'S ADDRESS.

At the commencement of a new year and a new volume, the Editor begs a word with his readers.

In reviewing his experience in connexion with this attempt to establish a religious magazine for the Australias, the Editor has had much both to dishearten and encourage him. The discouragements have largely arisen from the apathy of many ministers and others, in regard to the success of the work, who have made few or no efforts to extend its circulation ; from those to whom orders have been sent allowing unsold copies to accumulate ; and from the slowness and difficulty with which money-returns come in. The other side is balanced by encouragements, from the hearty co-operation of several able contributors ; from the zeal of some thoroughly sympathizing friends who have exerted themselves zealously in their respective localities to procure subscribers ; and from not a few cheering opinions which have been given expressive of the value of the work itself, as supplying a want long felt and deplored. To these gentlemen the Editor tenders his heart-felt thanks.

His own conviction, after the experience he has gained, is, that such a work is very much needed; that it is, in many quarters, very highly prized ; and that it *might become* a means of very extensive usefulness in our churches, if it were duly patronized and encouraged. With this conviction he is resolved to persevere, so long as the pecuniary means at his disposal hold out. To make the work entirely successful, he respectfully but urgently offers the following suggestions :—

1. It is necessary that the work should be made *self supporting.* This might easily be done by an increase of circulation, and by *prompt payments.* The pre-payment system is the only safe one to prevent losses. It works with admirable effect where earnestly tried, as it has been in several cases. The pre-payments may be for three months, for six months, or the whole year, according to the circumstances and convenience of the subscribers. If the money be remitted at once to the publishers, with the addresses of the subscribers, each number will be sent direct by post.

2. To *increase* the *circulation,* the Editor is convinced that *ministers* must take a little trouble and make some exertion. Wherever this has been done, the result has been satisfactory ; where it has *not* been done, few copies for the most part have been taken in. The duty of sustaining this denominational organ should be urged from the *pulpit,* and *personal canvass* among the members of the congregation should follow.

3. A *right idea* of the *nature* and character of the work should be given to correct erroneous expectations and to prevent disappointment and dissatisfaction. The magazine ought not to be put in competition with

English periodicals either in respect to price or contents. The value of labor in these colonies makes it impossible to publish works at anything like the English prices, and if we are to have colonial works at all we must make up our minds to pay more for them. With regard to the contents, while we cannot compete with British literature in its variety and adaptation to the community at large, neither can it compete with ours in furnishing what we most want, something which bears the colonial stamp and is specially suited to the varying circumstances which affect our condition in this hemisphere. English newspapers, much as we value them, do not supersede local ones ; no more would English magazines supersede Colonial magazines, if the proper function of that kind of publication were duly considered. Subscribers must also be reminded, that a periodical such as this cannot fairly be expected to suit exclusively any one particular class. Society consists of different sections which have different wants. Some wish for elaborate dissertations ; others short papers, incidents and anecdotes. Argument and eloquence would suit one class, religious experience and devotional sentiment another. Till our social condition is more mature, and our population is larger, when each division of the community will have its own periodical, we must be content with a compromise. The editor would therefore urge upon his readers a little self-denial and consideration of others, for the sake of the general good. It is hoped that all may find something suited to their taste and condition, while what is not so, may be the very thing most adapted to the requirements of other persons.

4. As the *Southern Spectator* has now become avowedly connected with the Congregational body, it is the editor's earnest wish to make it both a bond of *union* and a channel of *intercourse* and fellowship between our widely scattered churches. In this point of view it may be eminently useful if heartily sustained. But in order to this, contributions of material must come from a larger number and a greater variety of writers. The editor has no reason to complain of want of articles ; he has never been put to straits on this account, and his writers are in *all* the colonies, the fewest being in Victoria itself, where the work is printed. But he would wish every pastor to be a correspondent, furnishing him with suggestions, incidents coming under his own notice, intelligence, and short articles. In this way the thoughts of one might become the property of all, and the whole denomination be benefited.

5. The editor would once more remind his readers that the *Southern Spectator* is very *nearly a success*, and a little effort, generally made, would firmly establish it. No small expense has been incurred in carrying the experiment to the present point, and this will all be lost if it be not carried a little further. Should the present opportunity of establishing the magazine be lost, an enterprise of this sort would be thrown back for years, and it might be long before another attempt could be made.

As three Conferences composed of delegates from all the colonies have, after careful consideration of the whole subject, expressed a decided opinion in favor of the establishment of a periodical in connexion with the Congregational body, and have each time requested the editor to undertake the work, he feels he has a strong claim upon the earnest co-operation, the warm sympathy, and the fervent prayers of his brethren in the ministry, and of the deacons and members of the churches at large.

THE PULPIT AND THE PEOPLE.

The complaint is often made by a certain class of critics that the modern pulpit possesses less power over the people than the pulpit of former times. This criticism is sufficiently grave to invite and to justify investigation ; for if true, it involves a series of consequences which imply degeneracy and guilt in the churches and ministers of the age ; and if false, the criticism implicates its authors in malignant slanders and wickedness. In either case the evils are appalling, and effort should be made by every Christian mind to ascertain the truth or falsity of the sentiment.

We therefore offer a few reflections to aid the readers of the *Southern Spectator* in conducting this investigation so as to arrive at an accurate conclusion.

We ought to know, as a preliminary guide, what period in the history of the pulpit is taken as the standard ? or in what age, and among what people did the pulpit possess more attractions and command more influence over the community, than it does at this day ?

There must be some idea of a standard in the mind of the critic, to give his sentiment the pretext of honesty, and that standard must belong to some past age ; but can antiquity supply any rule whatever which can be fairly applied to the present age ? From the most remote period until the last century and a half, or a little more, the pulpit was the almost exclusive source to the people of any knowledge, whether secular or religious. The influence which it possessed, during those long ages, was not always or even frequently of the kind the pulpit was intended to wield. Some of the Christian fathers collected vast crowds of people and kept them spell-bound by their oratory. Some early missionaries and, in a subsequent age, certain preachers of the Crusades moved, subdued, and controlled whole nations of men. Luther convulsed the papal world; Knox regenerated Scotland, and many other pulpit orators have made themselves felt and feared and loved by the whole of society ; but must it be forgotten that in all these instances the pulpit had to do work which was not properly its own ? It was then the people's only friend and instructor, and to the pulpit orator alone they looked for the redress of wrongs, the cure of social disease, the suppression of tyranny, and the improvement of their general condition. The sphere of the pulpit was not restricted as it now is, to the simple work of expounding and enforcing religious ideas, but it embraced everything secular as well as religious, and the secular more than the religious.

These facts are hinted at just to prepare the way for modifying the critical stricture under notice, and to repudiate any comparison between modern and ancient pulpit influence.

We cannot conduct this investigation, with fairness to the pulpit, without remembering the fact that many powerful auxiliaries have entered the same sphere. The *press* of modern times has become a mighty and almost universal instrument in disseminating thought, morality, and religion, and at this moment its teachings is often of the same kind, and even more accessible to many minds than that of the pulpit. This coadjutor publishes and diffuses throughout society, literature and ethics, and even the same teachings as the pulpit itself. We have books of every conceivable size and on every subject in religion ; reviews, magazines, biographies, histories, serials in endless variety ; expounding the Scripture, asserting its claims, defending its authority, illustrating its facts and diffusing its influence ; all this is done by the press with irreproachable accuracy and the most praiseworthy zeal. A mighty host of minds has entered the lists doing battle with ignorance, depravity, and crime. The avocation of these minds has invested them with an estate, in power, in authority and in importance, equal to the pulpit. No estimate of the pulpit can be accurate which assumes that it ought to supplant all the advantages and facilities and attractions of a written literature. No estimate can be correct which ignores the special adaptation of religious books to meet the secular requirements of modern society, and to relieve the pulpit of some of that miscellaneous labour which the ignorance of society for many ages imposed upon it as a main part of its mission.   To inflict censure upon the pulpit, with any show of justice, we must ascertain what actual and effective power it possesses over society, notwithstanding the mighty attractions of all the literature which everywhere abounds, and notwithstanding the restrictions which have been placed upon its range of subject, its style of illustration, its manner and point. It should be remembered that the pulpit never had to do its proper work amidst such antagonism as modern society furnishes ; it never had to surmount such obstacles, such prejudices, or such depravity as abound in this age.   Society everywhere, and particularly where the power of the pulpit is known and felt at all, is more intelligent, but withal more critical, more fastidious, more sentimental, and more incredulous than in any past age.   Let all these facts be remembered and duly weighed, and then let us ask whether the pulpit has lost its former power over the people, or whether the censure referred to contains valid truth.   We wish the reader of these lines to study the subject carefully.   It concerns every Christian to become familiar with the true nature of pulpit functions and the true standard of efficiency.   The Scriptures show very plainly what those functions are and ,what the efficiency should be.   Perhaps if we pursue our reflections a little further upon this subject, we shall discover more causes still to modify the stricture of the critic ; indeed it may possibly be true that the pulpit possesses greater power in the present than in any past age of the world, and that the criticism must be resolved either into gross mistake, or slander and wickedness.

Let us then inquire, in the spirit of candour, what is the standard of pulpit efficiency ?

It is a well known fact that very many persons, who frequent our religious houses, have received their principal educational training on every subject from the popular press.   They possess a large amount of general knowledge, of miscellaneous opinions, of literary sympathies and powerful prejudices ; and it often happens that all this intellectual training simply and necessarily unfits them for the exercise of criticism upon pulpit efficiency.   They form opinions and inflict censures upon religion and religious subjects, while they are destitute of religious sympathies.   They have religious ideas, but no religious feeling.   Yet they assume the right to say, in reference to the pulpit, " We want men in the pulpit of great power, of commanding intellect, of mental energy, of literary refinement, men of suavity, logic, elegance."   Now we cannot say one word depreciatory of such talents when we find them dedicated to the service of the pulpit, though we may venture to deprecate the spirit of that criticism upon pulpit efficiency. But pause, gentle reader, and inquire whether the above qualifications constitute the thing demanded, and whether they were the attributes of the pulpit in all former times, and especially when the humble and illiterate fishermen of Gallilee were elected to discharge its functions ? It is natural to suppose that whatever talents may be required to make the pulpit do its appointed work, were to be found in the ministry of those men who received their commission and training and supervision in their work, from the Head of the Church. The first preachers might not have been perfect models of what ministers should be in an age and among mind, every way superior to the ancient world ; but Christ himself was a perfect model in everything relating to the erudition, culture, dignity, instructiveness, familiarity, directness and pathos, which all minds require from the pulpit. His first ministers, so far as we are able to conjecture from the New Testament, were men with talents about as diversified as subsequent ministers have been. The current history of the Church presents the ministers of every age in precisely the same general relation to the people as modern ministers are seen to be. There have been a *few* men remarkable for learning and general and powerful talent, standing out prominently from all the rest of their age ; but must it be overlooked that these few did not sustain the Gospel universally ? Nor were they the only or even the principal instruments in dispelling the spiritual darkness and purifying the corruption which abounded in the world. It may be doubted whether the most popular pulpit ability has been always the most useful. The great orators and logicians have done vast service, but the diffusion and maintenance of spiritual life in the souls of men have been the work of the moderate talent of the pulpit. This is proved beyond doubt by the history of the Catholic Church in all its denominations. The really efficient men in the pulpit, among every sect, have been those of moderate ability, of deep piety, of earnestness and faith in God. These have made less noise in the world, attracted fewer minds around them, and their names have been sooner forgotten. But the day of God will discover them to have been the most powerful agents after all in executing the functions of the pulpit. All who employ themselves faithfully, prayerfully, and earnestly; holding forth, not the words of man and wisdom, but the word of life, and who try to bring the truth to bear upon the conscience and heart of mankind, will be found the true ambassadors of Christ.

If piety, then, be the foundation of pulpit efficieney, is it right—must it not be egregiously wrong—to prefer the orator to the theologian, or the gentleman to the Christian ? And yet nothing is much more prevalent among some professing Christians, than a style of criticism which proves utter want of sympathy with anything in the pulpit, except that style of thought which is continuous, elaborate and finished. Happily this is not the judgment and the wish of the devout part of the Christian community ; of those who value the pulpit according to its aim and competency to reach the heart through the understanding, to inspire the mind with anxiety, penitence, prayer, hope and faith, and to renew the spirit in the moral image of Christ. Let Christians, then, be careful not to give countenance to that estimate of pulpit efficiency which ignores the first principles in a minister of divine truth. Let them be vigilant in guarding the pulpit from the occupation and usurpation of those aspirants to the ministry whose chief recommendations appeal to the head rather than to the heart of mankind. Finally, let Christians seek to rule the current opinions of men in religious affairs, and supply those from among themselves who shall feed, not man's self-complacency, but his desire for immortality.   N.

IMPEDIMENTS AND INDUCEMENTS TO CHURCH-FELLOWSHIP.

When Christianity was first promulgated, those who were converted to the faith united at once in holy fellowship, and constituted that society of faithful men, designated the Church. It is too obvious that the course which was pursued in primitive times is not always adopted now. In many instances, the christian convert long hesitates to join a church, because he is restrained by peculiar difficulties, or because he is not duly influenced by the incentives to full consecration.

What then are the impediments to Church-fellowship? The difficulties which are encountered may be expressed in language which is often employed: "I am not yet fit to join a church, and especially to partake of the Lord's Supper." It may be, this is the language of one who is perplexed with doctrinal or practical difficulties; who fails to realise that peace and satisfaction of mind, and that victory over sin, at which he aims; and who thinks that till these attainments are his, he is not fit to join a church. The Scriptures, however, teach us that those who are weak in the faith should be received into fellowship, that they may be aided in their course. If their prevailing concern be, to look to Christ as their Saviour, and to live to him as their Lord, they should not permit the moral deficiencies, and fluctuations of which they are conscious, to deter them from the full avowal of their decision for Christ. Moreover, may not spiritual loss be involved in their neglect? May not darkness or doubt beset them, because they are not following the Lord fully?

But the difficulty may assume another form; it may be said—"I fear to partake of the Lord's Supper, lest I eat and drink damnation to myself." This difficulty arises from a misapprehension of the Apostle's language, in referring to the abuses which prevailed among the Corinthians. They perverted the Lord's Supper to the purposes of feasting and faction, and thus exhibited a demeanor which was "unworthy," unmeet, unsuitable. Thus too they brought upon themselves judgment, or chastisement, which God mercifully appointed, that they might "not be condemned with the world." Certainly, we should fear to offend by unworthiness or unsuitableness of demeanor in this or in any other sacred service. But none need dread to observe the Lord's Supper who sincerely desire to remember and honor Christ. He says to the weakest among his followers—"This do in remembrance of me."

Another difficulty is this—"I fear to profess religion, lest I afterwards bring a disgrace upon it." This objection, if it be valid at one time, must be valid at another; so that, on this principle, the convert may postpone his profession of religion till his dying day. But is the objection valid? It is well to fear lest we fall, but it is not well to question the ability of Christ to keep us from falling. It is well to dread dishonoring God at any future period, by bringing disgrace on the religion we have professed; but it is not well to dishonor God now, by manifest disobedience to His revealed will. We should "make haste and delay not to keep his commandments," looking to the Saviour to preserve us faithful even unto death.

Another difficulty is—"I dread the examination and inquiries to which I must submit, before I can be received into church-fellowship." This is the natural expression of a timid retiring mind, which shrinks from unfolding its anxieties or hopes, especially to strangers. But may not this obstacle be magnified in imagination? Ought it to be difficult to converse with a minister, and with one or two christian friends whom he may select for that purpose? It should always be arranged, where practicable, that candidates for communion may be visited by those with whom they have had some previous acquaintance. In this and other ways, the feelings of the mind will be consulted, and every needless barrier be removed out of the way. To facilitate such arrangements, the deacons and other members of churches should look out for those who may appear to be interested in divine truth; that, in friendly and unrestrained intercourse, they may encourage them to decide for Christ. Such persons will usually be the best parties that can be selected to visit, in behalf of the church, those whom they have thus wisely and kindly taken by the hand.

What are the inducements to church-fellowship? To the convert, it may be justly said—"Your duty to your God and Saviour demands it." If you turn from the world to God, from sin to the Saviour, should you not distinctly indicate your preference? Is not this avowal due to the God of salvation, who has delivered you from guilt and death? Is it not due to that gracious Saviour, who has redeemed you unto God by his blood? Should you not "confess him before men" in his own appointed way?

And then the Church claims you for its fellowship. Christians banded together in their Master's name are, after all, but few and feeble. They have to maintain their principles in the midst of adverse influences which are mighty and manifold. Hence, they need encouragement; and this they receive as the Lord adds to the Church "the saved." Ministers are thus encouraged. They see that they are not labouring without tokens of the divine presence and blessing. And other Christians engaged in efforts to do good, and anxious for the prosperity and extension of the Church, are thus encouraged. Their prayers are answered, their hands are strengthened, and they are excited to be "steadfast, unmoveable, always abounding in the work of the Lord, forasmuch as they know that their labour is not in vain in the Lord."

The world too supplies an incentive to church-fellowship. The true convert must remember, with shame and sorrow, the influence for evil which he exercised when he belonged to the world. If then, he would do good, if he would supply an antidote, as far as practicable, to his former conduct, he must be decided. For the sake of the world, he should unite with the Church, that he may bear his testimony, in word and in deed, against "the lying vanities" which he once loved, and by which multitudes around him are still enslaved.

It may be urged further upon the Christian convert—"It is due to yourself to secure church-fellowship." This is the way to realize spiritual enjoyment. You complain of your deadness and coldness, and assign this as a reason for standing aloof from the Church; whereas it is rather a reason why you should join, that in waiting on the Lord, in all his appointed ordinances, you may realise refreshment and invigoration of soul. This too is the way to experience moral preservation. You dread lest you should relapse into sin and folly; but church-fellowship is appointed that you may be preserved from such a course; and many have found the benefit of being thus restrained. It is true that God only can keep you from falling, but then He works by means, and among them is union with a church, which supplies incentives to devotedness and circumspection, and which usually places the convert in a position to be observed and admonished if he wander from the right way. Thus also may you realize extended usefulness in the Church. You may hope to receive and reciprocate the sympathy, prayers, counsels and co-operation of christian brethren;

and to feel, in your efforts to do good, that "two are better than one." Christians unite in church-fellowship, that they may observe sacred ordinances, promote mutual edification, and advance Christ's cause in the world. Recognise these lofty aims. Be fully devoted to the best Master, and to the highest interests of mankind; cultivate hallowed sympathies; and remember that your God and Saviour, the Church, the world, and your own well-being, all bid you to identify yourself, without delay, with the society of the Saved, and the service of the Sanctified.

THE BIBLE A GUIDE.

Some time ago I received an invitation from a friend to spend a few days at his country seat. The invitation was accepted; but, as I was to travel alone, and as the road after I should leave the railway was one of the ordinary bush roads of the colony, and as the distance to be travelled was several miles, I became somewhat apprehensive that I should lose my way. My friend foresaw my difficulties, and he provided for my surmounting them. Just before I started, the post brought me a letter, in which he not only described in language the various turnings of the road, but added a sketch in pen and ink, showing the line which I should follow. One strict injunction was appended to the whole, and marked with emphasis, "*Be sure and keep to the right all the way.*"

With this guide in my pocket, I set out on my journey. I soon found its value. At every turning that I came to, I took out my letter and followed its instructions. I felt its value was greatly enhanced as there were but few houses where inquiry could be made. Cross-roads and devious paths were constantly presenting themselves; but following its directions, I went through fences and opened gates, which seemed to be the entrances to private properties, *still keeping to the right*. At one place I doubted; I looked at my map, but I misunderstood its meaning, and I soon found that I was off the road. I consulted my guide again, and more attentively, and I saw where I had erred;—*its* directions were accurate and plain, the mistake was *mine*.

After several hours' ride, I saw before me, through the gums and iron bark which lined the road, spread out on an eminence, the house of my friend. As the desired object caught my eye, my first reflection was, "how kind and thoughtful was my friend to furnish me with such a guide, correct and simple, which has brought me to his house, in such a sequestered spot, without any trouble." I pushed on, giving the reins to my horse. As I drew near, I was enchanted with the view. The house stood upon a hill, which rose up with a steep ascent from the plain. Nearest the road there was an extensive lawn covered with rich grass, in the centre of which was an artificial lake, whose edges were studded with bending willows, and cattle were grazing around. Beyond, there were enclosed fields of ripening wheat, waving in the breeze. Then on the sides of the hill, which was fringed with a border of various species of rose-bush in full flower filling the air with fragrance, the vine, the orange, the fig, the lemon, the pear, the apple, and the pine tree displayed their attractions in most ample profusion. A clump of original gums on the summit of the hill, and as it were *behind* the house, and half encircling it, formed a beautiful background; so that the house appeared to look out from a bower, and to have been dropped amid the riches of nature. It was a lovely spot. As you emerged from the barren bush, it appeared a paradise.—I received, when I arrived, the expected welcome, and I made my stay.

A train of reflection now commenced. Thoughts sprang up of a Friend—an invitation—a journey—a paradise—a guide. There was no effort at spiritualizing. It was impossible to help turning to the moral and religious. The beauties of nature spread out before me in all their attractions; the blue sky, the wide horizon, the waving corn, the brilliant flower, the fragrant rose, and the forming fruit involuntarily led me to the contemplation of Nature's God. I thought of him as a *friend*—as *the* friend. How could I think otherwise when I was surrounded with manifold proofs of his goodness and mercy.

could not doubt his kindness to men, amid the profusion of his gifts which were scattered before me. Every opening bud, every swelling ear, every spreading leaf, every song of the bird, spoke of the kindness and care of God. Yet I looked at those gifts as the mere types of others, far better, which have come down from heaven. I thought of how God has magnified his word above all his name—of his unspeakable gift—of his grace which hath appeared bringing salvation—of "peace on earth and good will to men"—of the Gospel, that "God is in Christ Jesus reconciling the world unto himself, not imputing men's trespasses unto them;" and, as I thought of these things, the truth came upon my mind with irresistible power, *that God is indeed the friend of man.*

Nor could I avoid reflecting that, as our truest friend, God sends us *invitations* to enjoy his friendship. In nature, in providence, in grace, God invites to him the children of men. The testimony of the blushing flowers and waving fields was, "The hand that made us is divine." All things were vocal of God, inviting to acquaintance and communion with him. But such invitations are but the echoes of others, which are addressed to us in the pages of holy scripture : " Turn ye, turn ye, for why will ye die" ; " Come unto me all ye that are weary and heavy laden, and I will give you rest"; " Ho every one that thirsteth, and he that hath no money, come ye to the waters ; come ye, buy wine and milk, without money and without price."

The invitations of God are all *bonâ fide.* Once and again, and again, he addresses them to us with all the accompanying proofs of sincerity and love. He willeth not the death of him who dieth. He has no pleasure in the death of the wicked ; he would rather that he should turn unto him and live. He urges us by both gladdening and afflictive providences, by the motions of the Spirit, by the appeals of a preached Gospel, to accept his invitations. His servants are sent to say to us, " Come, for all things are now ready." Others are sent " to compel us to come in." Overtures of mercy are addressed to us daily. No earthly friend was ever so patient, and persevering , and loving as God ; for in spite of ignorance and ingratitude and contempt, in spite of repeated repulses, he still utters the language and performs the actions of a friend. " Behold, I stand at the door and knock ; if any man hear my voice and open the door, I will come in to him and sup with him and he with me ! " Oh, if ever a doubt crosses your mind as to the earnestness and goodness of God in his invitations to sinners, look back to Calvary, and see what was transacted there. The cross proclaims a world-wide invitation ; "Jesus was lifted up that he might draw *all* men unto him."

" Ah ! never, never canst thou know, What then for thee the Saviour bore, The pangs of that mysterious woe, That wrung his frame at every pore, The weight that press'd upon his brow, The fever of his bosom's core."	" Yes, man for man perchance may brave The horrors of the yawning grave; And friend for friend, or child for sire, Undaunted and unmoved expire From love, or piety, or pride; But who can die as Jesus died? "

I thought too of a *journey.* Life is a journey. We are travelling *somewhere.* The important question is whither? There is no tarrying on the road. Time hurries us along. Sometimes the road is rough, sometimes level, sometimes strewed with fruits and flowers ; but where does it lead to? It has a termination ; we are ever nearing it ; though we may imagine that we are standing still we are moving on. There is the " broadway," upon which, alas, many are travelling, " which leadeth unto death;" and there is the " narrow path, which leadeth unto life," and few there be who find it. On one of these we are making progress—let us examine which ! None of us knows how soon his journey shall end. How uncertain is the day of death ! How attenuated and brittle is the thread of life ! The aged may think that they are within sight of the resting place, and the young may be encouraging dreams of many years to come ; while it may be that the young shall reach the end first, and that years shall be added to the aged and frail. No one has a lease of his life for a specified term. No one can guarantee life to another. Who can tell what a day or an hour shall bring forth? Appearances are deceitful ! Let the aged consider—let the young and healthful beware—let all be concerned and diligent.

There is a *paradise*—a true paradise. The world, in all its collected choicest beauties, is but a faint representation of the paradise of God. From the elevation on which I stood, I saw for miles around all that could please the eye and excite the imagination—the glossy lake, the fertile meadow, and the golden grain; but what are such glories as these compared with those on which the eye shall gaze with wonder and delight from the summit of the hills of the New Jerusalem? The riches of language are exhausted to pourtray the splendours of the heavenly state. The unknown is shadowed to us by the finest and grandest of things that are known. "It is a house not made with hands, eternal in the heavens;" "a house of many mansions;" "the palace of the Great King." "It is a city that hath foundations whose builder and maker is God;" "the Holy City;" "the Great City;" "the city of the living God;" "a city whose foundations are precious stones, whose gates are pearls, whose streets are gold, pure as transparent glass; and which hath no need of the sun, neither of the moon, to shine in it; for the glory of God does lighten it, and the Lamb is the light thereof." There, death and sorrow and sighing are for ever unknown; there, are glory and immortality; there, are pleasures for evermore; there, the redeemed of the Lord walk in the light of his countenance; there, is the river of the water of life; "there, are never withering flowers;" And, there grows the tree of life, which yields twelve manner of fruits, and yields her fruit every month, the very leaves of which are "for the healing of the nations!"

Lastly, there is *a guide*. Our great friend in heaven has not left us to grope our way—has not addressed to us invitations to come to his palace and enjoy his friendship, leaving us to reach such safety and bliss *the best way we can.* No, like a true friend he has anticipated our wants. He knows our difficulties and infirmities, and he has provided for our surmounting them. *He has sent us a letter, and has sketched for us the way which will bring us to heaven.* He has given us an infallible guide. As far therefore as the road is concerned no difficulty need be experienced. Every devious path is marked, and the straight and right way is clearly delineated. Jesus Christ has trodden the way before us, and he has left his footprints on the road; these footprints neither wind, nor rain, nor enemy can obliterate—they are indelibly impressed, and the impression shall remain until the end of time. The *Bible* is our guide. It is God's letter, containing all directions and instructions necessary for our successful journeying from earth to heaven. It was sent us to be our pocket-book and manual. It is a light to our feet and a lamp to our path. It is a sure word of prophesy, unto which if we take heed we shall do well. By the light of this word, and following those footprints, we shall never go astray. If we doubt, if we misunderstand, let us read again and more attentively. The great precept of the Bible is, "*keep to the right;*" and the great effort of our life should be to keep to the right. To deviate is to err—to turn aside is to go into perplexity and danger. *Keeping to the right* may sometimes appear a folly, since by striking to the left many annoyances and trials may for the present be avoided; but there is no safety unless in following the guide. The way which the guide indicates may appear the longest, the roughest, the dreariest, but assuredly it is *the only safe,* the best way. And what though it be long and rough and dreary, if it bring you at length to the house of your Friend, the paradise of God, where by his welcome and joys your fatigues and self-denials shall be far more than compensated, where in the delights of his companionship you shall enjoy for ever peace and rest?

> "The law of the Lord is perfect, converting the soul;
> The testimony of the Lord is sure, making wise the simple.
> The statutes of the Lord are right, rejoicing the heart;
> The commandment of the Lord is pure, enlightening the eyes.
> The fear of the Lord is clean, enduring for ever;
> The judgments of the Lord are true and righteous altogether.
> More to be desired are they than gold, yea, than much fine gold;
> Sweeter also than honey and the honey-comb.
> Moreover, by them is thy servant warned;
> And in keeping of them there is great reward."

Portland, Dec. 16, 1858.

To the Editor of the Southern Spectator.

Dear Sir,—I have just received the enclosed tidings of the departure to glory of the Rev. J. J. Davies, Luton Beds, England. You may think its insertion calculated to edify. It has been my happiness to enjoy several social and public interviews with the deceased—I highly esteemed him as an able and faithful minister; and as a Christian his character was unusually symmetrical and beautiful.

Nor do I less venerate and love the minister whose funeral address is subjoined. His last fraternal and christian act towards me was that of presiding at my farewell meeting, ere I left for Australia. Seeing our time is short, let us diligently work " while it is called to day ;" and as earth's dearest ties are being sundered, and its attractions weakened, may our souls be more powerfully drawn towards heaven. whither our Saviour is gathering around his glorious throne all the matured fruits of his eternal love, from even the bleakest spots of his garden below.   I am, Sir,

Yours truly,   JAMES SLEIGH.

OBITUARY OF THE LATE REV. J. J. DAVIES, OF LUTON, BEDFORDSHIRE.

Died on Sunday, October 3rd, 1858, the Rev. John Jordan Davies, formerly a minister of the Old Baptist Meeting, Luton, aged 52 years.

Mr. Davies was interred on Friday, Oct. 8. in the old meeting where for so many years he had preached the Gospel. The Rev. T. Hand, J. Makepeace, and D. Gould, of Dunstable, conducted the service. Mr. Gould delivered the funeral address.

We cannot permit the demise of one so widely known and deservedly held in such high esteem as the Rev. J. J. Davies, to pass with a mere record in our ordinary obituary column. The event has cast a mantle of gloom over the entire town, and the intelligence of it will fall like tidings of disaster in the different circles in which he was known. It is due, therefore, alike to his memory and worth, as well as to his sorrowing family and friends that we present our readers and the public with some sketch of his life and character. He was a native of Cardigan—the son of highly respectable parents—was intended by them for the ministry of the Episcopal Church—but was led to adopt Nonconformist views and associate himself with the Baptist body. He pursued his studies in Bristol College preparatory to the pastoral work, and is still remembered there by the president and many of the committee as a delicate, urbane, devout, and highly promising man. Those who were fellow-students with him cherish his memory as one whose clearness and power of thought were in exquisite harmony with the transparency of his character and the seraphic order of his piety.

His first engagement with a Christian Church located him in Bath whence he removed to Tottenham, where he spent seventeen years of great usefulness not unchequered by much sorrow. His trials, combined with his heavy labors, and painful solicitude for the spiritual good of those for whom he toiled, greatly prostrated his energies and necessitated his removal to Bootle where he recruited his vigor, and nursed to considerable power a new Congregation based on thoroughly catholic principles. Finding himself equal to the responsibilities of a larger sphere he removed to Luton in 1849, and spent amongst us upwards of eight years of great devotedness and success. Failing health again compelled him to relinquish his favorite work and winter in Jersey. This time, however, disease had made such rapid inroads upon his constitution— never a robust one —that it speedily succumbed. He came home to die. And never in the memory of those now living has any death caused such a sensation among us. This is occasioned not by anything remarkable in the circumstances attending his demise; for he gradually sank into " Life's long sleep." The impression produced by his death is an approving response to his life. Its blameless integrity and exalted excellence—its self-sacrificing charity and " lovingkindness," won for him a place in all true hearts; and now that he has gone to his rest every one feels that he has lost a Friend. His name will rank with that of the sainted Daniel as one who has left the impress of his character on many behind him. The qualities which combined to form that character, and render his name a power, were great clearness and breadth of thought,—extensive and thorough research, leading to a calm and many-sided view of Truth—a firm grasp and bold maintenance of grand principles—an utter abhorrence of all claptrap and crotchets,—the exhibition of a large-hearted catholicity combined with steadfast adherence to his own personal religious convictions. All who thoroughly knew him and were honored with his friendship would unhesitatingly quote him as an example, and a fine one, of the harmonious interblending of marked decision of purpose, great intellectual power, childlike simplicity of nature, and Christlike meekness and kindness of spirit. With the docility of a child he sat at the feet of his master and heard his word,—and from that imperishable record he gathered and gave to his people and to the world, "thoughts that breathe" a glorious Life. His "Sketches from the Cross"— "Felix"—and "Abijah," may be regarded as an average specimen of his style of thinking and powers of analysis and synthesis. But the peculiarly emphatic manner of his address,—the benign smile that played about all the features of his manly countenance, like sunshine on the waters, and all that went to make up the individualities of his Pulpit efforts, can be chronicled only by those who "heard him gladly." In reviewing his chequered course and calmly estimating his intellectual dignity and untiring toil,—his perfect freedom from all narrowness of thought and creed—his sympathy and disinterestedness of spirit, unobtrusiveness of manner, and true moral greatness of soul and life,—one feels that anything like injustice or unkindness must have deeply wounded a heart so tender and lovingly kind. From all that afflicted and oppressed his noble nature he is now free; and whilst his ashes rest beneath the grateful shade of the spreading tree, his exalted spirit, mingling with the glorious throng, rejoices in presence of the Eternal Throne with "joy unspeakable and full of glory." "He was a good man and full of the Holy Ghost and feared God above many."

The following is part of the funeral address of the Rev. D. Gould:—

What an enemy is death apart from the provisions of the Gospel! At his touch the human frame is changed, so that even an Abraham is compelled to desire to bury the beloved Sarah out of his sight. How violently it rends ties which penetrate to the very depths of the soul—anguish is awakened, which time can but slowly and partially allay. Those who are of the greatest worth and excellence are not on that account spared. They are as ruthlessly cut down by the scythe of Death as if they were noxious weeds poisoning and encumbering the ground. Sometimes it seems as if Death coveted rich spoils; as if the grave sought to banquet on what is most excellent. We are apt to think that the most excellent go first. Truly to a certain extent it is so. Self-sparing indolence and apathy is never worn or exhausted on behalf of others. In many instances it is life itself that love spends and exhausts for the interests of others. Death has yet more formidable terrors. "The sting of death is sin;" to the unpacified conscience the very name of death brings insupportable dismay. Ah! is he not fitly named the "King of Terrors?" But we are not left at the mercy of this relentless enemy. We may composedly reckon up the whole catalogue of evils which he inflicts or menaces in the full assurance that we possess in the Gospel, a remedy and consolation for them all. No great or permanent evil can befall the innocent or the pardoned. We are not innocent, but if believers in Jesus, we are pardoned. A future state after death, which the most laborious reasonings of philosophy can only show to be probable, the Lord Jesus places beyond question. Christ assures his people that they shall "appear with him in glory." Death is even made to advance the interests of Christians. It is mentioned by St. Paul, 1 Cor. iii. 22, 23, among the "all things" which are theirs, because they are "Christ's and Christ is God's." Death releases believers from temptations, from "flesh and blood," which "cannot inherit the kingdom of God." Thus it may become to us an object of desire. The Gospel affords reasons for desiring and welcoming death.

How strong a consolation then may be felt on the death of a servant and minister of Jesus Christ. The more deeply we feel the loss on account of his

TASMANIAN HOME MISSIONS.   13

excellencies and virtues, the more may the sorrowing survivors feel that there is ground not for sorrow, but rather for triumph. Even the grief we feel over the Christian dead may be the means of death being subdued by leading us to think more seriously of their excellencies, of their instructions and their example, and to desire to be reunited to them. The thought of our dearest friends being with Christ will serve to make that heavenly state the object of more frequent thought and more earnest desire.

With what grateful joy then should we celebrate his mercy, who "through death hath destroyed him that had the power of death, and delivered them who through fear of death were all their lifetime subject to bondage." May all who bewail the loss of Christian friends be enabled to realize the power of the consolations of the Gospel of Christ, so that they "sorrow not as others who have no hope." Especially may the bereaved, with whom we now sympathize —the beloved partner and children of the much honoured, much loved, much lamented servant of Christ, whose body we now consign to the tomb, be enabled to realize all the sweet and sanctifying supports of the glorious Gospel. —*The Luton Times.*

TASMANIAN HOME MISSIONS.

DISTRICT OF THE HUON.

Hobart Town, December 13, 1858.

Dear Sir,—The following brief account of a visit made to the district of the Huon, by a deputation from our Colonial Missionary Society, consisting of the Rev. G. Clarke, Messrs. Hopkins and Dear, may prove not uninteresting to many of your readers.

The deputation left Hobart by the Monarch steamer on Monday, and on the evening of that day Mr. Dear delivered a lecture at the Mechanics' Institute, in which, after giving a brief outline of the rise, history and objects of such institutes, he proceeded with a description of the growth and physiology of plants, and to show the simple but beautiful developments of the "giants of the forest." The lecture was well received throughout, a vote of thanks was carried by cheers, loud, stong and hearty, such as, perhaps, few but the hardy sons of the Huon could give utterance to.

The day following, Tuesday, was spent in looking about the Franklin and seeing the friends of the Society ; and in the evening a meeting of the church and congregation was held in the Independent Chapel, the special object of which was to raise a stated sum for the support of the Missionary labouring in the district. Notwithstanding the low state of the timber market, one of the main branches of commerce upon the Huon, a very ready response was given to the appeal, and arrangements were made for periodical contributions in aid of the Mission.

On Wednesday, though the rain fell as it sometimes does fall at the Huon, the party proceeded up the river to Victoria, five or six miles beyond the Franklin, a district, we believe, first opened up some few years since by Mr. Walton, and now a thriving settlement, with its chapel and school, its sawmills and farms, its orchards and its quarries. Taking advantage of a temporary cessation of the rain, the deputation visited the chapel, and thence proceeded to meet a gathering of the good friends convened in Mr. Page's barn, which had been tastefully festooned and amply provisioned for a tea meeting, the object of which was to raise a fund to clear and fence the grave-yard. Mr. Hopkins was called to the chair, and after alluding to the more immediate design of the meeting, he was followed by Messrs. Giles, Skinner and Wild, Rev. G. Clarke and Mr. Dear. The two latter gentlemen after alluding to the more immediate purpose for which they had assembled, urged upon the friends present the importance of their endeavouring to sustain their own minister, and a special appeal was made to all to embrace the means offered for attendance on public worship. During the meeting a collection was made and a sum quite sufficient for the purposes of the grave-yard was paid down by the parties then assembled. Meanwhile, however, it was evident if the appeal to attend the sanctuary was responded to by all then present, the house would be, in fact at present was, too small for the district; a meeting, therefore, of some of the leading friends of the district was convened on the following morning (Thursday), to confer with the deputation on this matter. Mr. Hopkins spoke like himself; said he never willingly helped a lazy man or a lazy body of men, but hoped he should always be glad to help those who strove to help themselves; further, he reminded them that every pound they gave towards building a sanctuary for Jehovah was an investment for their children; and by way of reducing his remarks to practice he promised that if, before the end of the year, £150 could be raised towards the erection of a new chapel, he would give £25. The offer was promptly accepted and a response, amounting to £130, was made at the meeting, four of the gentlemen present undertaking at the same time to canvass the district for further supplies.

Thus cheered, the Deputation returned to the Franklin, where they had engaged to meet some of the friends in that locality, to advise with them as to the best means for enlarging their chapel; but when a report was given of what had been done at Victoria—when, moreover, it was evident that no satisfactory enlargement could be made; and when, further, Mr. Hopkins by his practical liberality shewed them his sentiments, and as at Victoria headed the list, they also determined that they would strain every nerve and have *their* new sanctuary erected for the worship of their Lord. On Friday the deputation proceeded to Geeves Town. There is a history connected with this place we may at some future day refer to, but now we will simply remark that the deputation were most cordially welcomed by Mr. Geeves and by the members of his family living around him. Here, then, is a place of worship recently fitted up and sufficiently commodious for the present requirements of the district. In the evening, service was held and a sermon preached by the Rev. G. Clarke, after which there was a public meeting, when addresses were delivered by the members of the deputation, by Mr. Giles, Mr. Hay, jun., and by other friends, when it was stated that a piece of land had that afternoon been measured and staked out, to be put in trust to the Colonial Missionary Society, for the inhabitants of the district, for the erection of a place of worship and for a graveyard.

Saturday the deputation returned to steamer for Hobart Town; on the pier a letter was placed in Mr. Hopkins' hand, from the friends at Victoria, stating that the result of the canvass was a subscription list of upwards of £190, and that they proposed at once to build, expressing at the same time their grateful acknowledgments to Mr. Hopkins, to whose timely visit, liberal contribution and friendly counsel, as the letter expressed it, they were mainly indebted for the prospect of a new and commodious place of worship.

But I must not enlarge, I fear I have already occupied too much of your space. You have the facts, let them speak for themselves. I am,

Δ.

VARIETIES.

EFFORT IN RELIGION.

You who think that the world can be deserted without a sigh, and heaven won without a struggle, turn your contemplation to the world that surrounds you. If to secure mere physical comforts, to gain a common livelihood (and remember one God is the God of all, his laws govern this world no less than the world to come) such a weight of toil is required, such patience, such endurance, such incessant demands upon the spirit and the intellect; shall we say that an eternity of happiness is to be won by no trouble at all? that for a good, uncertain in acquisition and perishable if acquired, the Providence of God has decreed the necessity of careful previous exertion? and that for a good, certain in acquisition and eternal in duration, he requires no cost or preparation of any kind, no discipline, laborious or protracted, no sacrifice beyond what fashion or convenience may please to dictate?—*Butler.*

PROGRESS.

Be always displeased at what thou art, if thou desirest to attain to what thou art not, for when thou hast pleased thyself, there thou abidest; but if thou sayest I have enough, thou perishest: always add, always walk, always proceed; neither stand still, nor go back, nor deviate. He that standeth still proceedeth not; he goeth back that continueth not; he deviateth that revolteth; he goeth better that creepeth in his way, than he that runneth out of his way.—*Quarle's Emblems.*

COVETOUSNESS.

Covetousness pretends to heap much together for fear of want; and yet, after all his pains and purchase, he suffers that really which at first he feared vainly; and, by not using what he gets, he makes that suffering to be actual, present, and necessary, which in his lowest condition was but future, contingent and posssible. It stirs up the desire, and takes away the pleasure of being satisfied. It increases the appetite and will not content it. It swells the principal to no purpose, and lessens the use to all purpose; disturbing the order of nature and the designs of God; making money not to be the instrument of exchange or charity, nor corn to feed himself or the poor, nor wool to clothe himself or his brother, nor wine to refresh the sadness of the afflicted, nor his oil to make his own countenance cheerful; but all these to look upon, and to tell over, and to take accounts by, and make himself considerable and wondered at by fools, that while he lives he may be called rich, and when he dies may be accounted miserable, and, like the dish-makers of China, may leave a greater heap of dirt for his nephews, while he himself hath a new lot fallen to him in the portion of Dives. But thus the ass carried wood and sweet herbs to the baths, but was never washed or perfumed himself; he heaped up sweets for others, while himself was filthy with smoke and ashes.—*Jeremy Taylor.*

ATTENTION TO DRESS.

Appearances should not be wholly beneath the consideration of any man or woman. Nature does not distain them. Nothing is omitted that can enhance its beauty. Everything is grouped and arranged with the most consummate skill, and with the direct and manifest object of pleasing the exterior vision. Those persons, therefore, who play the philosopher on the strength of neglecting their attire, who hope that the world will rate the superiority of their intellect in direct ratio with the inferiority of their dress, are not philosophers at all, because the truly wise man thinks of nature through himself.

LADIES' INFLUENCE ON ELDER LADS.

There is one thing in school-work which I wish to press on you; and that is, that you should not confine your work to the girls; but bestow it as freely on those who need it more, and who (paradoxical as it may seem) will respond to it more deeply and freely—*the boys.* I am not going to enter into the reason* *why.* I only entreat you to believe me, that by helping to educate the boys, or even (when old enough), by taking a class (as I have seen done with admirable effect) of grown up lads, you may influence for ever not only the happiness of your pupils, but of the girls whom they will hereafter marry. It will be a boon to your own sex as well as to ours to teach them courtesy, self-restraint, reverence for physical weakness, admiration of tenderness and gentleness; and it is one which only a lady can bestow. Only by being accustomed in youth to converse with ladies, will the boy learn to treat hereafter his sweetheart or his wife like a gentleman. There is a latent chivalry, doubt it not, in the heart of every untutored clod; if it dies out in him (as it too often does), it were better for him, I often think, if he had never been born: but the only talisman which will keep it alive, much more develop it into its fulness, is friendly and revering intercourse with women of higher rank than himself.—*Rev. Charles Kingsley.*

POETRY.

A New Year's Morning Hymn by Dr. Raffles, Liverpool.

NO NIGHT IN HEAVEN.

"And there shall be no Night there."—Rev. xxii. 5.

No night shall be in heaven—no gathering gloom
Shall o'er that glorious landscape ever come.
No tears shall fall in sadness o'er those flowers
That breathe their fragrance through celestial bowers.

No night shall be in heaven—no dreadful hour
Of mental darkness, or the tempter's power.
Across those skies no envious cloud shall roll,
To dim the sunlight of the enraptured soul.

No night shall be in heaven. Forbid to sleep,
These eyes no more their mournful vigils keep :
Their fountains dried—their tears, all wiped away ;
They gaze undazzled on eternal day.

No night shall be in heaven—no sorrow's reign—
No secret anguish—no corporeal pain—
No shivering limbs—no burning fever there—
No soul's eclipse—no winter of despair.

No night shall be in heaven—but endless noon :
No fast declining sun, nor waning moon :
But there the LAMB shall yield perpetual light,
'Mid pastures green, and waters ever bright.

No night shall be in heaven—no darkened room,
No bed of death, nor silence of the tomb ;
But breezes ever fresh, with love and truth,
Shall brace the frame with an immortal youth.

No night shall be in heaven ! But night *is here*—
The night of sorrow—and the night of fear.
I mourn the ills that now my steps attend,
And shrink from others that may yet impend.

No night shall be in heaven ! O had I faith
To rest in what the faithful Witness saith—
That Faith should make these hideous phantoms flee,
And leave no night, henceforth, on earth to me.

CHURCH UNION.

THE REV. T. BINNEY'S VISIT TO SOUTH AUSTRALIA AND CHURCH UNION.

Under this head we introduced to our readers last month a long and interesting correspondence, including letters from the Bishop of Adelaide, Sir R. G. MacDonnell, the Rev. T. Binney and others. The correspondence having been continued, we continue the insertion of it, that it may be better preserved than in the pages of a newspaper. Another letter, it will be seen, may yet be expected from Mr. Binney, which we shall hope to give next month. The following belong to, and are properly the continuance of the *first series of letters given* by us last month ; they are therefore numbered accordingly.

No. VI.

The Right Reverend the Bishop of Adelaide to the Reverend T. Binney.

DEAR AND REVEREND SIR—On my arrival yesterday at this place, I received your note accompanied by a printed copy of our correspondence. I was fully prepared to see it in print; but I forbore to suggest that course, being satisfied that you would choose the proper time and place for so doing. It was, however, rendered necessary by public allusion having been made to my letter, and a correspondent on no better grounds than his own surmise, having thought fit falsely to disparage an eminent lady, with whom I was not personally acquainted until after I had been consecrated Bishop of Adelaide. I should have preferred to have received from you at your leisure the matured conclusions of your judgment on the interesting topic to which I have drawn attention. The discussion, however, has been precipitated, I would fain hope, without prejudice, to the cause.

I must now beg to say a few words explanatory of my impressions on the proceedings which have taken place during my absence.

1. I think it "untoward" that His Excellency the Governor should have been mixed up with the correspondence between you and myself. Church and State have been separated in this colony, and I know not why an official character should have been given to a memorial concerning the administration of this diocese, by the signature of the Governor-in-Chief and Ministers of State.

2. If I have doubts how far the letter of this ecclesiastical statute law of the Established Church of England is applicable to this or other colonial dioceses, I have none as respects its spirit, nor of the inspired authority of the apostolic "tradition of eighteen centuries" on which that law is founded. The evidence even of Jerome, and the argument of Chillingworth, are to my mind conclusive on that head. I could not therefore, nor can I feel justified in departing from that traditionary rule, even in your case. Had I felt sure that no Statute Law would have been violated, I should not have transgressed the "custom" of our Church without first consulting the Metropolitan and other Bishops of the province of Australasia, as well as the Archbishop of Canterbury. Consequently I think that I ought not to have been invited by those high in authority in this colony to take a step on my own responsibility, which though possibly not an actual, would have been at least a virtual transgression of the law of our Church. You, sir, well enforced the duty of obedience to existing laws in your farewell speech.

3. Having stated why I was unable to invite you to preach to our congregations, I took occasion from thence to urge a consideration of the terms on which at some future time possibly that inability might be removed. The indispensable conditions appeared to me to be three.

A. The acceptance in common by the Evangelical Churches of the orthodox creed.

B. The use in common of a settled liturgy though not to the exclusion of free prayer, as provided for in the Directory of the assembly of divines at Westminster.

C. An Episcopate freely elected by the United Evangelical Churches, not (as I have been misapprehended) exclusively by our own.

No notice, however, of these preliminary conditions was taken in the memorial addressed to me. Without them there would be no security against the intrusion even of heretical preachers into our pulpits.

I have now done. The object of my letter to you has been answered. I have drawn attention to the possible future union of Evangelical Churches; but I have found, like another before me, that there are those who "when I speak unto them of peace, make themselves ready to battle."

Charles V., after his abdication, amused himself with trying to make some watches keep time together. Finding his hopes disappointed, he wondered at the folly of his own lifelong endeavours to make men "to be of the same judgment and walk by the same rule."

My letter certainly has not bridged the Ecclesiastical gap which separates us. On the other hand, I do not think it has widened the breach. I am content to bide the time, and allow the leaven to ferment. If the counsel be of God, it cannot be overthrown. Meanwhile, as the Evangelical watches, though all professing to be set by the sun, do not seem at present inclined professedly to go together, I must continue to set mine by the "old church clock," which after all is probably the surest going time-piece in the world, and as near perhaps as any other to the true time of the Sun of Righteousness. I remain, &c.,

Anama, November 5th, 1858.   AUGUSTUS ADELAIDE.

No. VII.

Sir Richard Graves MacDonnell, C.B., to the Right Rev. the Lord Bishop of Adelaide.

Glenelg, 15th November, 1858.

MY LORD.—1. My attention has been called to a paragraph in a letter, signed by your Lordship, and addressed to the Rev. Thomas Binney, which appeared in the *Advertiser* of the 11th instant.

You therein express yourself thus:—"I think it 'untoward' that His Excellency the Governor should have been mixed up in the correspondence between you and myself. Church and State have been separated in this colony; and I know not why an official character

B

should have been given to a memorial concerning the administration of the diocese by the signatures of the Governor-in-Chief and Ministers of State."

3. The obvious meaning of that paragraph is, that I and some members of my ministry by signing a memorial to the Bishop of the Diocese on a matter affecting the discipline of our Church, gave an official character to the transaction; and by so doing had somehow overstepped the bounds of propriety and duty. Hence I presume the "untoward" appearance which the transaction wears in your eyes.

4. As your lordship's letter is dated so long back as the 5th instant, from Anama, in the north, I at first imagined that as your mistake arose from not examining the memorial to which you refer, your letter had found its way to the papers without your having enjoyed an opportunity of correcting it. I have, however, ascertained that your letter has been published since your return to town and by your own desire. Therefore as in reality I never did sign the memorial otherwise than as stated therein, viz., as "a member of the United Church of Great Britain and Ireland," your lordship must have *published* the above comment without previously asking for, or at least referring to the document itself. If so I am sure you will admit that, however excusable such a mistake might be in a private letter, it is equally inexcusable in a public document, into which your letter was immediately transformed, when it was printed, with your sanction, for public information.

5. I may here further observe, that even if I had signed as Governor, the inference that an officer of the State could thereby give an official character to the memorial in a colony where, as you correctly remark, Church and State are separated; or, in other words, that I could extend an official character to matters beyond my office, is an inference entirely of your lordship's own reasoning.

6. My sincere respect for your lordship personally, and for your office, joined to your prominent allusions to my personal efforts to win for our church here a privilege (the utility of which would, however, depend mainly on its judicious application) induce me further to explain briefly what I really did do in this matter. Even then my conduct may seem to you "untoward;" but it is better your judgment should be based on what I did do than on what I did not do.

7. On the morning of the 16th ultimo, I was waited on by a mutual friend with a draft memorial to your lordship, suggesting that, "as a sign of goodwill towards our brethren of the Evangelical churches," your lordship should invite Mr. Binney to fill one of our pulpits. I was asked what I thought of such a memorial, and replied, that personally I was most anxious to recognise either in that or some other way the various Protestant denominations of the Reformed church, which I regarded as sections of one army, though each might retain its separate discipline and captain. I said, however, that as your lordship had written a long letter to Mr. Binney, which, I believed, touched on topics akin to the subject of the memorial, and as that letter had been sent to me with a request that I should state my views thereon, I felt bound to read it before giving a final answer, as I would not sign the memorial if I thought your lordship opposed to it.

8. I had not previously perused your lordship's letter, but I then did so, along with the friend to whom I have alluded. To our great surprise and pleasure, we found therein your lordship actually asking yourself the very question on which the memorial hinged—viz., "Why is not Mr. Binney invited to preach in our churches?" We found you looking back with regret to the "mid wall of partition" which so long "had separated kindred souls, pledged to the same cause, rejoicing in the same hope, and devoted to the same duty, etc., etc., etc." We found you stating, "that if with our present light we had lived in the time of our fathers, we should not perhaps have been disposed to break up the fellowship of the reformed church for non-essential points." We found you expressing yourself "as truly glad" that Mr. Binney's arrival "had forced you to consider again the question why you could not invite him to preach to our congregations?" We found you asserting that "in this colony we are placed in a peculiarly favorable position for considering our Christian relations with our Protestant brethren," in consequence of the separation of Church from State, and expressly saying that here "neither social, nor civil, nor ecclesiastical distinctions interfered to distract our view or irritate our feelings." We found you admitting that nothing constrained you from acting in the liberal impulse of such a Christian feeling, but a "tradition" of "the Church which declared Mr. Binney's orders irregular, and his mission the the offspring of division," etc., etc., etc.

9. So completely, however, was I at first resolved to give up my own judgment to your lordship, that I would even then have refused to sign the memorial on the ground that your lordship had really no freedom of action in the matter, notwithstanding the strong inclination which you professed before the memorial was thought of to do what the memorial asked. We found, however, on further examination of your letter, that your lordship observed, in reference to that tradition "that your feelings kicked against your judgment," and that you "were compelled to ask yourself whether this 'standing apart' was to continue for ever;" whilst you admitted that in any scheme for greater Christian union we should treat the various denominations of the Protestant Church as *de facto* governments, and justly so, because in your own words "unity is compatible with variety."

10. Finally we observed with pleasure that, in reference to the particular request contained in the memorial, viz., the inviting a Protestant clergyman, not a member of our church, to fill one of our pulpits, you actually stated that "you did not feel sure you would have violated any ecclesiastical law in force in the diocese or province by in[...]

son to give a word of exhortation to each of our congregations." We attached great force to this remark, especially when we found you had strengthened it by a note, which pointed out that " Canon 54, of the Province of Canterbury, A. D., 1603-4, requires conformity as a *sine qua non*, to preaching in the parish churches of England, but that you did not know that it was binding in a colonial diocese, and that it showed that persons were licensed to preach who were not disposed to take upon themselves all the obligations of the parish priest under the establishment."

11. Now, to what conclusion could I come on perusing a letter, the whole spirit of which was quite consistent with the above extracts ? I felt that I could come to none other, if I understood the English language, and was so fully assured, as I was, of the writer's sincerity than that your lordship was most desirous to hold out the right hand of fellowship to the *de facto* existing Protestant denominations of Christ's Church, and that you were only prevented doing so in the manner pointed out by the memorial, because you were in some degree hampered by a tradition against which " your feelings kicked," whilst you actually doubted the existence of any law prohibiting your giving way to those feelings.

12. Under these circumstances had your lordship been in town, I would at once have sought your advice, and made myself more fully acquainted with your wishes. You were, however, absent, and not expected to return until after the departure of Mr. Binney. Now, as I was contending for a general principle in attempting to strike off a fetter, which hampered alike the Bishop and the Church. I thought it wiser that the memorial should be published before the departure of the gentleman, whose presence here had evoked from your lordship such strong and eloquent testimony—" To his reasoning, eloquence, purity of life, suavity of manners, and soundness of faith." I felt that although it was comparatively immaterial whether the principle was first asserted in his case or not, yet that the absurdity of the "mid-wall of partition," was in his case placed with more than usual completeness and distinctness before the public, and was thus all the more likely to cause people to reflect thereon. How in fact, could I doubt this, when I found your lordship entirely attributing to his arrival amongst us your own reconsideration of the very question at issue, namely, why " you could not invite him to preach to our congregations ? "

13. I therefore said I felt free to sign the memorial but only on one condition, namely, that it should contain a clause, which I myself drew up, and which stated that those signing it " believed your lordship was most desirous of adopting all measures calculated to extend and establish the common Catholic principles of faith held by the Protestant Church of Christ, into whatever sections that Church might be divided, and earnestly desired to assist your lordship's efforts in that behalf." That clause was inserted, and I then signed the memorial, as explained therein, in my character of a " member of the United Church of England and Ireland, and not as Governor, as your lordship implies—clearly gathering your information from some other source than the document itself. May I not, therefore, fairly say that, if there be anything "untoward" in these transactions, it is that your lordship did not examine the memorial before publishing—as your first notice of it—a rebuke, unsupported by the language of the original document ? I may add that, till I saw it in print afterwards, I had no idea what parties signed the memorial subsequently to myself.

14. Your lordship may not be prepared to learn, that I never expected the prayer of the memorial could be complied with in your Lordship's absence, and that when I heard it was laid before the Dean and Chapter, I actually told the Dean it would not be courteous for any one to act in your lordship's name in so important a matter during your absence. The great object which I and most others had in signing it was to place your lordship *en rapport* with the members of your own church, in discussing a point which you had so freely discussed with one outside the pale of that church. We only asked you to do something which we inferred from your own letter you would gladly do if you could ; and we expected that you would have given us a well-considered and friendly exposition of any difficulties intervening between us and our common object. We also expected the aid of your advice and assistance in removing those difficulties. Surely that was a natural motive ; and, whilst it was respectful in every way to our immediate ecclesiastical head it was consistent with the loftiest and purest aspirations for Christian alliance with the brethren of our common faith and doctrine.

15. It may be that the results, though hereafter destined to be important, have hitherto fallen short—lamentably short—of our hopes. Greater difficulties than were at first anticipated may arise from the clerical mind " being peculiarly swayed by party principles and sectarian prejudices," as your lordship expresses it. It may be that we laymen are apt to go too straightforward to our point, and, waiving etiquette, to offer our hands, in all honesty of purpose and hearty good-will to those who have not been presented to us by the proper authorities. Still a word of admonition and advice addressed to us directly might not have been inappropriate, and might have corrected our too eager zeal to accept the aid of persons willing to help us in extending the vital principles and doctrines of our common faith.

16. It is certainly unfortunate that in your lordship's long letter of the 23rd September to Mr. Binney—a letter which it now appears was from the first written to be published—and therefore intended to affect the minds of members of our church here—it is, I say, unfortunate that when speaking therein so much of the propriety of occasionally admitting sound preachers of certain Protestant denominations to our pulpits, your lordship did not state more plainly, what you now inform us was all the time your real meaning and intention, viz., that even if there was no statute law to the contrary, you would not have transgressed a " custom of our church without first consulting the Metropolitan and other Bishops of Australia, as well as the Archbishop of Canterbury."

17. I am hereby reminded of a young officer, who was quartered many years ago in my neighbourhood, and who was so particular in his civilities to a young lady as to justify her friends in inquiring his intentions. It was a troublesome, though a simple question; for he was of age, apparently without relatives, his own master and had a small independence. To the surprise of every one he replied that he could take no steps in the matter "without consulting his cousin in India," which was the more unfortunate as it was feared no reply could be received before the departure of his regiment to a distant colony. This was not more discouraging to the inquirers in that case than it is now to us laymen to find that, even if no law had opposed, and if your lordship had been free legally to do a thing not merely right in your own judgment, but the expediency of which you had also so eloquently advocated, yet that, when the banns for the new Christian Alliance were all but proclaimed, your lordship, even if freed by law, would have forbidden them till you had consulted all the Bishops of Australasia in the first place, and afterwards the Archbishop of Canterbury. Even if His Grace were satisfied, might there not remain still some cousin in India to be consulted? I therefore would seriously ask, is it surprising if some of us, on "inquiring your lordship's intentions," begin to fear that the "Union," so far as you are concerned, is "adjourned sine die!"

18. Truly, life is short, and labour long, but there are those here who would wish to finish the task they have begun, and who, though most unwilling to abandon the services and customs of their church—even though their Bishop commended the sacrifice—in the vain hope of thereby purchasing the conformity of others, whose existing ecclesiastical organisations are already well enough adapted to their special feelings and requirements,—there are, I say, those here, who, whilst they will not make a sacrifice which they believe to be needless, and which is certainly repugnant to their feelings, cannot afford time to await the realisation of such a gorgeous dream as that of a general conformity and a future common church. They believe such schemes to be impracticable for the next century, though alliance might be possible in a few years. They are therefore resolved to lose no opportunity of freeing the church of their best and holiest sympathies from all fetters that impede its free religious action in alliance with other ministers and brethren of the pure evangelical protestant faith. In that freedom—of which an occasional interchange of pulpits would have been a symbol—they see the fairest prospect of the Anglican Church, proving by her future progress that although unaided by the State, she can keep pace with the efforts and extension of kindred protestant churches.

19. Amongst those who feel thus, but distinguished from many of them by still cherishing the hope of acting with your lordship in so good a cause, is the humble individual who now has the honour to subscribe himself your lordship's most obedient humble servant,

                                        RICHARD GRAVES MACDONNELL.

The above letter of Sir R. G. MacDonnell, was preceded, when published in the Adelaide newspapers, by the following letters, which we here insert:—

Messrs. O'Halloran and Tomkinson to Sir Richard Graves MacDonnell.

SIR,—Your Excellency having been so good as to favor us with a perusal of your reply to certain comments in the Lord Bishop's letter to the Rev. Mr. Binney, dated 5th November, from Anama, which letter appeared in a newspaper of the 11th, we cannot refrain from respectfully asking your Excellency if you have any objection to the publication of your remarks—as we feel assured that the publicity given to the Bishop's strictures demands an early explanation from the movers in the first memorial addressed to his lordship, and are, moreover, convinced that all the sentiments and views so ably expressed by your Excellency will be heartily shared by those who signed that address, and by the great majority of the Church in this diocese.

We are likewise of opinion that the light thrown by your Excellency on the question as it now stands will lead to a right apprehension of the matter at issue, and terminate the minor controversy that has arisen.   We have the honor to subscribe ourselves,
                                        Very faithfully, &c.,
                                             WM. L. O'HALLORAN,
Adelaide, November 17, 1858.   S. TOMKINSON.

Sir Richard Graves MacDonnell, C.B., to Messrs. O'Halloran & Tomkinson.

                                        Adelaide, November 18, 1858.
GENTLEMEN.—1. In reply to yours just received, of the 17th instant, I beg to say that under ordinary circumstances I should feel a great and natural reluctance in complying with a request for publication of a non-official letter written by me. After some hesitation, however, I am inclined to think you have a right to claim publication of my letter of the 15th instant to the Bishop, as being not merely from its nature more or less a public document, but also as having been written to explain the conduct and motives of yourselves and others as well as of myself in connection with our recent memorial to his lordship.

2. We have acted together from the first, as well in getting up the memorial as in the transmission of my explanatory statement to the Bishop. I do not, therefore, see how I can well separate myself from you now, or refuse to sanction your making as free a use of my letter defending you, as his lordship did of his letter reflecting on you.

3. I shall therefore desire a copy of my letter to be given you, together with copy of the reply thereto by the Bishop, explaining how he was so far misled as to attach an official character to a non-official publication. As, however, his lordship's remarks are only an explanation of a premature public reference to a document, which, being addressed to himself, he was expected to examine before referring to it, and as his remarks do not in any way correct the impression which his reflections on the general propriety of the memorial may make, I think there still exists a necessity for giving to the public some such full explanation as that in my letter to the Bishop of our motives in originating a movement which I trust will yet produce useful results.

4. I still hope that the members of our Church generally will ere long be more alive to the absolute and ever increasing necessity of giving the Church a greater freedom of action and alliance; a greater and wider choice of means to reach the hearts and sympathies of her Protestant Evangelical brethren beyond her pale—between whom and herself there is no wider distinction now existing than that created by the different degrees of freedom of action enjoyed by each.

5. I also trust that the discussion will no longer be hampered and obscured by comparatively petty misunderstandings and trivial explanations, but that the important question we have raised will not be lost sight of, viz., how best to manifest affection for our Church by giving her that freedom of action, even though purchased by the sacrifice of a fetter imposed by a venerable tradition. I have, &c.,

RICHARD GRAVES MACDONNELL.

No. VIII.

The Lord Bishop of Adelaide to Sir Richard Graves MacDonnell, C.B.

Bishop's Court, 15th November, 1858.

MY DEAR SIR,—I beg to acknowledge the receipt of your letter on the subject of my reply to Mr. Binney, containing a paragraph arguing on the supposition that you had signed a memorial to me in your official character. I think it due to your Excellency at once to state that I was misled by the signatures as printed in the *Register*.

I have been informed (for I have not yet received the memorial), that the signatures in the original were without any official designation. When or how, or by whose instrumentality this untoward addition was made, I cannot say, nor is it my business to inquire. I can only say I regret that it compelled me to write the paragraph in question.

I remain, yours very faithfully,
AUGUSTUS ADELAIDE.

No. IX.

The Rev. T. Binney to the Rt. Rev. the Lord Bishop of Adelaide.

Sandhurst, Bendigo, November 29, 1858.

MY LORD,—Your last letter, although dated Nov. 5th, only reached me (as your lordship is aware) on the evening of the 10th. It appeared in the newspapers the next morning—the day on which I left Adelaide for Melbourne. I had hoped to have written in reply on the passage, but that I found to be impossible. Duties awaiting me in Melbourne next interfered with my purpose; I am now moving about in this region, and engaging in various public services; but I will endeavor, as opportunity offers, to put down a few thoughts suggested by our late correspondence, beginning, however, with your last letter.

I beg, first of all, to express my satisfaction at your lordship's acknowledgement that the publication of your first letter had become "necessary." My conviction, indeed, that its publication had become "due to your lordship," was, as I said, what ultimately decided my course. I felt that I had done right when I saw the rude and most offensive letter to which your lordship refers. No one could be sorry that the writer received an immediate rebuke, for what could not but be regarded as a gross insult to the primary pastor of his church.

I would next remark, before passing to more important topics—first, that I believe it is now understood that no "official character" was given to the memorial by the gentlemen who signed it; they simply attached their names as members of the Episcopal Church. Secondly: that I a little regret that what looks like a reply to the memorialists should have been addressed to me. I was not a party to the memorial—I never heard of it till I saw a statement about it in the newspapers; it was painful to me that the question raised was accidentally so mixed up with personal references to myself. I quite admit that it was not unnatural that your lordship should refer to the matter in your letter to me; at the same time I regret the reference, and cannot but wish that your views and feelings had been directly communicated to those concerned in reply to their own document.

As, however, your lordship has referred to the Memorial and the Memorialists, I may be permitted, perhaps, to make a remark in passing on a statement in your letter bearing upon both. After the sentences marked A. B. C., your lordship says, "No notice, however, of these preliminary conditions was taken in the Memorial addressed to me." I believe it will be found, on inquiry, that the simple fact was, that the Memorial was at first in no way connected with your lordship's letter, or had any reference to it. It originated with parties who had never seen it and knew nothing about it. It was only when it was taken to Sir Richard

MacDonnell, as I understood, that, in consequence of his having just been reading your letter to me, an expression was added alluding to what was supposed to be your lordship's wishes. Not knowing the "preliminary conditions," the originators of the Memorial could not refer to them in first drawing it up; and, if they did not introduce a reference to them afterwards, when it may be supposed they might have become acquainted with them, I presume the reason must be found in this—that the "preliminary conditions" embody your lordship's idea of the "Church of the Future," an idea which the Memorialists would probably think was not likely to be realized as an immediate result, a first attainment, preparatory to something else; but rather to be looked for as an ultimate growth from previous preparatory processes. As practical men, therefore, they thought it best, I suppose, to confine themselves to their original suggestion of a practical measure—one, too, which they supposed to be practicable, and which they perhaps also imagined might be the first step towards something more.

Dismissing, however, these preliminary topics, I will now beg permission to submit to your lordship some thoughts which your last letter has suggested. I look at it, of course, in connexion with your previous communication; but I begin with it for a reason which will afterwards be explained. I think it not unlikely that some of my observations may surprise you; none, I hope, will offend. It is impossible, I should suppose, that your lordship can be so acquainted with the modes of thought and feeling prevalent in the non-Episcopal Denominations, or with the way in which they look at certain ecclesiastical subjects, as those are who belong to them. However, therefore, you may be surprised by some of our idiosyncracies, or may lament them, it may yet be interesting to you if I explain to your lordship—which I shall do in the most friendly spirit—how some of the statements and expressions of your letter would, as I think, appear or shape themselves to the minds of ministers of other churches.

Beginning with the section marked 3, I beg respectfully to submit to your lordship whether there may not appear to some to be more implied or assumed, in the first paragraph, than perhaps your words were meant to convey. "*Having stated that I was unable to invite you to preach to our congregations, I took occasion from thence to urge a consideration of the terms on which at some future time possibly that inability might be removed. The indispensable conditions appeared to me to be three.*" Such are your Lordship's words. At present you are "unable" to do a certain thing; but you suggest certain "terms," "indispensable conditions," on which "possibly" "at some future time" that "inability" of yours "might be removed." Now, my lord, although *I* understand you to mean that your own church would have to be one of the parties to these terms, in common with all the rest, I greatly fear that to others the language will seem to be pervaded by assumptions, which they not only cannot admit, but which, according to the temperaments of individuals, would be smiled at as harmless or resented as offensive. It looks like one party to a friendly arrangement beginning the conference, I will not say by *dictating* but by *offering* terms to all the rest,—terms on which alone *it* can be brought to consent to any thing. Of these terms some would regard the first as unnecessary, seeing that "Evangelical Churches" must, as such, have already accepted, and be known to hold, the orthodox creed; others would think the second inexpedient to be insisted upon as a first step, and without preparation, with the present fixed habits of different parties; while the third (to say nothing of its requiring in some the abandonment of what they hold *as principles*) would appear to many to demand what it would require the interposition of a miracle to secure. But the point that would be most felt, I think, would be this:—that all is asked for, apparently, on the ground that it is required in order to relieve one party only from a certain "inability,"—an inability, the removal of which might be something to *it*, but which would be nothing to the rest worth the price they would have to pay for it,—for there are those who think that what your lordship could grant if you had the ability to do so, is not a favor to be received, much less bought, but a fraternal courtesy which they have it already in their power to exercise if others were only able to accept it. How the matter thus put will appear to your lordship I feel quite at a loss to determine. I do not know whether, on the one hand, you will be shocked by the thought that your words should be imagined to imply so much more than you meant; or, on the other, whether you will be surprised that any one should hesitate to accept language which, with all that it implies, and *because* it implies it, may seem to you the most natural and proper imaginable. Persons like you and me, my lord, trained in different schools, accustomed to look at things from opposite points, to see them under lights and aspects altogether different, and to speak of them in language based on conclusions, assumptions, habits of association, accepted traditions, unquestioned assertions widely apart,—of which, as existing in the other, each may have little knowledge, and can have no sympathy, —why, we, at times, must of necessity use words and convey implications without the consciousness on our part that there is anything in them to surprise other people,—anything to be objected to in what is said, or questionable or offensive in the opinions or feelings of him that says it.

The different light in which the same thing appears to different persons, from being looked at from opposite stand-points, and under the influence of different church-systems and religious associations, may be illustrated by what your lordship says of the practical efficiency of your proposed scheme. The "terms" on which the "inability" at present felt by your lordship, might "possibly" "at some future time be removed," are described as "indispensable conditions," and, on that account, are thus spoken of:—"*Without them there could be no security against the intrusion of even heretical preachers into our pulpits.*"

Now to us who stand on the outside of the Episcopal Church, and who are accustomed to look not so much to mechanism as to life—not so much to what men subscribe as to what they believe—not to the letter and articles only of an orthodox creed, but to what living men actually teach and to what they are—to us the language of your lordship comes with but little force, especially in its bearing on the subject in relation to which it is used, namely, the security of the pulpit against the teachers of error. The stringent and solemn subscriptions of your Church are no security against doctrinal differences in the clergy of the most serious description. "Heretical preachers," is a phrase that may mislead. A Church may have the thing without the name. "There are many Anti-Christs," we are told by St. John; and there are many heresies, or forms of error, alike deadly though not marked by the same brand. In the Anglican Church, you have, on the one side, men who are Romanists in every thing but the name—who preach the Church, the priesthood, sacramental efficacy, any thing but Christ, in the New Testament import of the term; on the other side, you have men far more than tinctured with Rationalism—men who deny, or explain away, all the essential verities of the Gospel—every thing distinctive of Christianity as a redemptive system. You have no security against these "heretical preachers" in your "orthodox creed." Some of them when purposely tested by being required to re-sign your articles, sign without hesitation, and then just go on teaching as before. The mere fact of being a clergyman of the Church of England is no security to us that the man would bring with him into ours, if we received him, "the doctrine of Christ;" it is not therefore of itself a passport to any of our pulpits. Your lordship will permit me to observe that I am not objecting in the abstract to Church standards; I am not denying the propriety and importance of professed adherence in ministers to an orthodox creed; I am not one, either, who has no sympathy with the toleration in the clergy of great diversity of opinion; nor am I questioning, on the other hand, the necessity of "terms" and "conditions" as the basis of such an amalgamation of Churches as your lordship proposes. All that I wish to insist upon is, that the terms and conditions mentioned not only ask too much to secure a small result (the removal of a certain inability), but that of themselves they would not necessarily secure the purity of the pulpit in the exercise of the liberty sought.

Setting aside, for the present, the idea of such a union of churches as would combine all in one great confederacy on certain specified terms and conditions, and which would thus secure a community of labor in pulpit services among the ministers of the different united bodies,—suffer me to offer a word or two on the interchange of pulpits, as distinct from everything else, churches and denominations continuing as they are. This is a subject which may be looked at from a ground different from that taken by your lordship. It ought to be contemplated, too, in connexion with the principles and convictions of all parties concerned. Instead of looking to new ecclesiastical arrangements, either for liberty to act or security in acting, I believe that an interchange of pulpit services between ministers of different churches is a thing that should rather spring from and be regulated by their mutual knowledge of and confidence in each other. If, indeed, the ministers of any church are under an interdict, unable to act, their inability will need to be removed by some ecclesiastical change in their own body; but this being done, liberty to act secured to them, then, I submit, the exercise of that liberty might safely be left to the men themselves. There is no difficulty in knowing what bodies of Christians, as such, agree together substantially in the essential principles of the evangelical faith; within these, again, individuals or classes have affinities and attractions which, without law, draw them towards each other, and which are far more to be depended on than any that law could originate or prescribe. Presbyterians, Wesleyans, Baptists, Independents, thus, as bodies, know each other, and their ministers, as such, have the ability to interchange pulpits, if they please, and when they please, without their previously adopting, with a view to that, a common formula of belief. Now, for the sake of illustration, let us suppose that in each of these bodies there are schools and sections of "heretical preachers," Romanists and Rationalists in everything but the name,—the sound and orthodox portions in any one of them have already far more security against the introduction into its pulpits of the unsound ministers of the others than could be conferred by their all agreeing to your lordship's conditions. They have it in spiritual sympathy; in instincts and feelings belonging to a common inward life, in addition to their adherence to a common faith, for there is this amongst them though they have not signed a common formula. By these it is that interchanges are regulated,—public acts which involve fraternal recognition and indicate substantial doctrinal agreement, without leading to any misapprehension in observers without, or any clashing of the heterogeneous elements which (by supposition) there may be within.

In this way, and only in this way, does it appear to me that the liberty enjoyed by some denominations, might be extended to and participated in by others. The principle hinted at in your lordship's first letter, that ministers of different churches, waving all de jure discussions, might agree to recognise and regard each other as de facto ministers of Christ—this being understood, admitted, and acted upon on both sides, all might have the liberty of giving and receiving ministerial service, so far as to preach for one another; and then this being secured, everything else might be left, with perfect safety, to the operation of laws far more potent and certain than any verbal agreement in terms and conditions. They only would use the liberty who felt they could, and only with those with whom they could. But this, it might be objected, would have the appearance of the action of churches within churches; to which it would be sufficient to reply, "you have that now;—everywhere in a degree, but nowhere to such an extent, among professedly protestant bodies, as in that church, which, in the person of your lordship, insists on laying down certain 'indispensable conditions' as a security against it !"

The last paragraph but two of your lordship's letter is this :—" I have now done. The object of my letter to you has been answered. I have drawn attention to the possible future union of Evangelical Churches ; but I have found, like another before me, that there are those who when I speak unto them of peace, make themselves ready to battle." In the last paragraph of all. are these words :—" I am content to bide the time, and allow the leaven to ferment." On these statements permit me to say, that I hope your lordship is mistaken in supposing that any, because you have spoken to them of peace, have deliberately " made themselves ready to battle." With the exception of the offensive letter already referred to, I hardly remember to have seen anything written in an improper spirit. Your words obviously refer to the members of your own Church. But it should be considered that neither your lordship's novel and somewhat startling idea of " the Church of the Future." nor the memorialists' more limited suggestion in respect to the present, could possibly have been put forth without occasioning difference of opinion and being met by opposition somewhere ; especially among the members of a church so comprehensive, and, therefore, in its communion so mixed, as yours. " The object of your letter," it appears, was " to draw attention to the possible future union of Evangelical Churches." But this " union," in your lordship's scheme becomes (or, at first sight, at least it seems) to be fusion, amalgamation,—not a fraternization only of existing churches, but a new church of the future altogether, involving organic changes in some, and the giving up and altering of much by all ; and it is not surprising that the unexpected launching of such an idea should produce something like a ripple in the quiet tide of South Australian life. I really do not think, however, that there was anything like a " making ready to battle." Your lordship feels that your scheme is not likely to be realised at once ; that you must " bide your time," and that progress in the public mind with respect to it will not take place without some " fermentation." The fact is, that what your lordship contemplates as an ultimate result,—what you require in order to secure it,—what you cannot do to meet the wish of the memorialists,—the ground on which you rest this "inability,"—and a variety of other matters involved in the questions started by your lordship in the suggestions of your first letter, or implied in the language of the second, all these things are at once so grave and so exciting, coming as they do into close contact, if not into collision, with the habits, principles, prejudices, traditions, of all Churches, your own and ours alike, that it is not wonderful if the first effect should be somewhat startling. In respect to your lordship's scheme, your own mind has probably become so familiar with it from long and frequent thought, that you cannot realise the impression it produces on those who have it submitted to them for the first time ; and in the same way, the principles which underlie your lordship's words in referring to the request of the memorialists, are so essentially a part of yourself, have no doubt always appeared to you as so settled and certain, have been so unquestioned in fact, and have seemed so perfectly unquestionable in theory, that it is not possible for your lordship to understand how they appear to those who listen to and look at them from an opposite stand-point. I will not enter into controversy, and I beg that your lordship will do me the justice to believe that, in the remarks which I am about to make, I am neither engaging in battle, nor " getting ready " for it. Your lordship does me the honor to submit to me certain views on the union of Evangelical Churches, and to ask my judgment. To realise these views, or to take the very first step towards them, will involve modifications of opinion and habit on all sides. But it comes out, that your lordship is entrenched in a position, which, so long as it is maintained, will frown upon and forbid the slightest approach to united action between yourself and other Evangelical Churches. Now it is not my intention to attack that position ; I will not, as I have said, have any " battle " about it ; but I desire to explain to your lordship how it looks to us on the outside, and how completely it interposes a preliminary obstacle to approach, conference, union, confraternity, and every thing of the sort.

" My letter," says your lordship, has certainly not bridged the ecclesiastical gap that separates us ; on the other hand I do not think it has widened the breach." So far as the "gap" may be said to be personal, something interposed between you and me as Christian men, I can truly say that I care little about it ; I don't look at it, or won't see it ; it does not affect my feelings of affection or my sentiments of respect. But, ecclesiastically speaking, regarded as a barrier, a sunk fence, between different " Evangelical Churches" as such, that is another matter. In this respect I do not think your lordship has widened the " gap," but I think you have thrown light upon it—you have brought it fully into view—you have reminded us of its width and depth—you have shown it to be of such a nature that it never can be " bridged" by any human skill or contrivance. Disguise the matter as we may—lose sight of it as we often do—amid the courtesies of private life, from personal regard. in social intercourse, or on the platform of religious or philanthropic societies—hide it from ourselves, keep silent about it, do what we like to cover or conceal it, the fact is, and it is better at once honestly to look at it, that the Episcopalian clergyman cannot recognise the " orders" of the ministers of other Evangelical Churches—he cannot regard the men as ministers of Christ, in the full and proper meaning of the words—he cannot admit their official standing or recognise their official acts. He may respect them as men. love them as Christian men, admire and esteem them as earnest and eloquent advocates of the truth ; but to him they are not ministers—they have not been Episcopally ordained, and are therefore not ordained at all ; their sacramental acts are invalid ; their preaching is without authority,—properly speaking indeed, they cannot "preach," though they may give a word of exhortation ;" whatever they may be thought by themselves or others, the ministers of Non-Episcopal Churches are, in the view of the Anglican clergy, laymen and nothing else. All this necessarily follows from the "tradition of eighteen centuries," when, as in the case of your lordship, a man has no doubt of its being an "*apostolic*" tradition, and of "*inspired authority*." The gist of the whole thing lies here. This principle touches and colors all thought—it interposes a bar to all action. Every scheme, plan, proposal for union or co-operation will be wrecked upon this rock, shattered to atoms by the breakers which play around the position your lordship occupies, and from which you look out with such a calm consciousness of perfect security. Or, to take your lordship's own figure, *you* -tand on one side of the "gap" or gulf, and all Non-Episcopal Churches and ministers on the other; and that gulf, guarded, watched over, kept open by the divine powers that reside in the words "apostolic," "inspired," and such like, how in the world is it ever to be "bridged" by mortal man? It never can be; nor will it ever close to admit the separated parties to come together, till there shall be thrown into it, sent down to the bottom and buried there, a goodly number of the "customs" and "traditions" of past ages. Though I speak thus, I am by no means insensible to the good that there may be in traditions and customs; I am not ignorant, either, how far some churches may surpass others as to the degree in which they approach the customs and order of apostolic times; I am not indifferent to the questions and consequences involved in or flowing from this: but sure I am, that, with the mere hints and germs of things, which we have in the New Testament; with the uncertainty which belongs to the first age, the evidence of Jerome and the arguments of Chillingworth notwithstanding; with the fact facing us that your orders are as invalid as mine in the view of that Church which, in one sense, is the Mother of us all; on these and other grounds that might be mentioned—I feel that it is not wise for any Protestant Church whatever, either to assert that it is modelled exactly after an apostolic pattern, or to assume for itself, in relation to its ordinations and orders, such an exclusive validity as, in effect, to unminister all other Protestant ministers. But to this, my lord, your tradition leads,—a tradition, with you, "apostolic" as to its age, and of "inspired authority" as to its character and source. Consistently with this, it is impossible for you to recognise the ministerial acts, standing, or office of the clergy of the non-episcopal "Evangelical Churches;" and so long as that is the case, you can never co-operate with them, or they with you, on equal terms. I had intended to notice how this principle runs through the whole of your lordship's first letter, tinging its thoughts, modifying its phraseology, hiding from you what lurks in many of its suggestions and proposals, and so reducing the entire fabric to a piece of idealism. But I must defer this to a future opportunity. I had not thought of writing so much in acknowledgment of your second letter; but having done so it precludes my making any reference to the first. I shall still feel it due to your Lordship to give that letter my best consideration, but I do not regret that I have been accidentally led to give precedence to the second, since in it the principle on which the other must be interpreted is more distinctly advanced and more explicitly avowed.

Your lordship's concluding allusion to the "watches" and the "clock" reminds me of an illustration of Dr. M'Neil's which I once heard him use with admirable effect. "God," he said, "had, in the Scriptures, set up a sun-dial, by which, as by a Divine standard, the universal church was to note and measure the time. In front of this, over, and round about it, Popery had gradually erected a mass of masonry which completely concealed the dial from the public view, and at the same time had set up its own central clock, commanding all men to go by it. The Reformers, however, detected and denounced the change; they rose up against it; they pulled down the stone structure that covered the dial, brought it forth to the sun-light, set it up in the sight of all men, made it again, what it was intended from the first to be, the inheritance of the people, and thus put it in the power of the church, as a whole, to test the Pope's clock by the true time." Of course every public clock, whether belonging to a parish or a private company, needs to be tested in the same way. The "old church clock," to which your lordship refers, is no exception to this rule. It is very necessary, indeed, to see that it is submitted to it, for it is well known that former Rectors, with the Mayor and the Town Council for the time being, often tampered with it, altering the works and putting the hands backwards and forwards, and back again, as they thought best, a very small change occasionally involving an immense difference.* I do not deny that a clock may tell us the true time, and that it may be very expedient to set our watches by it. While, however, we may use things that are "expedient," we are not to be "brought under their power." "Blessed is the man that condemneth not himself in the thing that he alloweth." Your lordship, I am persuaded, acts conscientiously in going by "the old church clock"; you will, I am sure, accord to me like credit in treating all clocks as pieces of man's workmanship,—using them where I think they may be used with safety; but as none of them are of any worth except as they are in harmony with the shadow on the dial, preferring, rather, to go by *that*; testing and trying by it, as far as I can, whatever sounds from either Church or Conventicle. May we all do this honestly and earnestly, with humility and prayer, and be guided in doing it, that "in *God's* light we may see light!" I remain, &c.,

T. BINNEY.

---

* Once, for example, the hand of the clock pointed to this:—"Children, having been baptized, if they die, are undoubtedly saved, *else not.*" The pointer was put back two seconds, and "else not" disappearing, ceased to rule. But what a mighty difference was made by that little change! Instead of being obliged to hold the positive destruction of all unbaptized infants, the clergy and members of the English Church are allowed to believe in their *possible* salvation. This is all, indeed, for the Church simply affirms nothing, it does not decide, or rule, either way; but even that is a great relief,—the *possibility* of the one thing against the *certainty* of the other!

In addition to the above correspondence, our readers will be interested in the following extracts, which we have selected from Adelaide papers, not received till the foregoing was in type. In our last number, we gave the two memorials which had been presented to the Bishop, one *requesting*, the other *deprecating* the admission of Mr. Binney to the Episcopal pulpit. We are now able to give the Bishop's formal reply to each. The second memorial had, it seems, after its first publication, received many additional names.

I.

The Bishop's reply to the first memorial.

Bishop's Court, November 19, 1858.

MY DEAR SIR,—To you, in your private capacity as a member of the United Church of England and Ireland, whose name stands at the head of a memorial (forwarded to and received by me soon after 2 p. m., on Wednesday, November 17), requesting me " to take steps to invite the Rev. T. Binney to occupy one of our pulpits in this city," I beg to transmit the enclosed reply, and remain,

Yours very faithfully,
AUGUSTUS ADELAIDE.

To His Excellency Sir R. G. MacDonnell.

May it please your Excellency and Gentlemen,
The immediate object of your memorial, requesting me "to take steps to invite the Rev. T. Binney previous to his departure from Adelaide, to fill one of the pulpits of this city," being impracticable, permit me to remark that the spirit out of which that request proceeded appears to me worthy of all respect; but the obstacles in the way of giving effect to the principle involved in such an invitation are in my opinion little likely, under the present circumstances and views entertained " in the various sections of the Protestant Church," to be overcome.

I have the honor to remain,
Your faithful servant,
AUGUSTUS ADELAIDE.

To Sir Richard Graves MacDonnell, and the Gentlemen who signed the memorial.
Bishop's Court, November 19, 1858.

To the Right Revd. the Lord Bishop of Adelaide.

Government House, November 19, 1858.

My Lord—I have the honor to acknowledge receipt, this day, of your lordship's reply to the memorial (16th October) and of your note accompanying it.
I shall at present merely observe thereon that the discussion of the principle at issue seems really commencing only now, though your reply mentions the existence but does not explain the nature of certain "obstacles in the way of giving effect to that principle "—a statement which I presume is intended to discourage further prosecution of the subject.
If, however, it be a wise and Christian principle, I and others are prepared to accept the difficulties, and to leave the discouragements to those who are less earnest in its support.
I have the honor to be, my Lord,
Your Lordship's obedient servant
RICHARD GRAVES MACDONNELL.

II.

The Bishop's reply to the second or counter Memorial.

Bishop's Court, November 15th, 1858.

DEAR BRETHREN,—I should be "presumptious and self-willed" if I did not give due weight to a memorial signed by no less than 164 members of our Church, who address me on a subject of grave importance, from the conviction that not to do so would "show a want of respect to the high office" which I hold, and unfaithfulness to that Church of which they feel it a privilege to be members, as well as in "confident reliance upon my forecast to maintain the Church in its integrity," to preserve it from unauthorised innovations from within, and " intrusion from without, which might obliterate even the least of her time-honored and distinctive characteristics."
The memorial refers specifically to the admission of persons to the office of preaching in our pulpits who have not been ordained by the laying on of hands of the Bishop with the Presbytery.
For my views on this subject I have only to *repeat* that portion of my letter to the Rev. T. Binney in which I said " neither the power of your intellect, *nor* vigour of your reasoning, *nor* mighty eloquence, *nor* purity of life. *nor* suavity of manners, *nor* soundness in the faith, *would justify me in departing* from the rule of the Church of England, a tradition of eighteen centuries, which declares your orders irregular, your mission the offspring of division, and your Church system, I will not say schism, but 'dichostasy—that is standing apart.'"
It is true I added " that my feelings kicked against my judgment," but still I set my face to its overthrow.

It is true that "*I did not feel sure* how far" I was restrained by force of law from breaking through that tradition, but I never supposed it would be imagined that I *could on my own authority* settle that intricate and extensive question.

Grieving, however, at what I cannot but believe to be unscriptual "divisions" of the Orthodox Protestant Denominations and Churches, I cast about to see in what way union might be restored, and the work of God carried on in common by the co-operation of all evangelical ministers and people "who love the Lord Jesus Christ out of a pure heart fervently." I did not, however, flatter myself with the delusive expectation that my suggestions would be adopted. It was enough if they should be *considered ;* and I was not unwilling to show that the intolerant spirit which once silenced Baxter, and failed to employ Wesley, no longer animated our Church.

By recurring to the scriptural principles and usages of primitive Christianity, the midwall of partition which now separates men of God in preaching the Gospel I thought might be removed.

I, for example, have ever understood that the Orthodox Dissenters of England did not object to what are called the doctrinal articles of our Church.

I knew that a "stated form of prayer" (to say nothing of the hymnology of Watts or Wesley) was used by many Wesleyan and by some Independent congregations. I remembered that Richard Baxter had composed a liturgy for our Church.

I had read that both Luther and Calvin esteemed Episcopacy lawful, and would have retained it, had circumstances permitted, in their respective Churches.

I knew that the old Independents, while they denied "the divine right" of Presbyterianism, did not claim it for their own system.

I imagined that the founders of the Free Kirk would hardly insist upon it as a dogma of the faith.

It seemed therefore to me *possible*, that with the growth of brotherly love among the various portions of the Reformed Orthodox Church, a longing for closer union on the basis of the Primitive Church might arise, to which, in the language of Bishop Jewel, the Church of England had acceded when she seceded from Rome. If this is a dream, it is at least as harmless as it is pleasant ; but if it be the counsel of God, it will yet be accomplished. Be that as it may, it cannot be brought about by rudely breaking in upon cherished associations, deep-rooted convictions, or even reverend prejudices.

From the relations of colonial dioceses to each other and the Mother Church, it is plainly the duty as it is the wisdom of each Bishop, after he has ascertained the general feeling on any given question of the clergy and laity of his own diocese, to communicate their views to their brother Churchmen in the metropolitan province through the Metropolitan and their respective Bishops, so that in all matters affecting discipline and worship we may act in common, neither disregarding the supremacy of the Crown, nor the legitimate authority of the Mother Church at home.

It is a pleasing thought that the same rule and order of worship which link us with the earliest ages of the Gospel—those generations of martyrs and confessors which by patient suffering overcame the rulers of the darkness of this world—also associate us with multitudes of fellow Churchmen in more than thirty colonial dioceses, as well as in the vast territories of the United States.

I heartily wish that the wise and good and able of all Evangelical denominations may find it possible hereafter, by the adoption of common principles, to join the great confederacy in the Gospel. I desire no prominence for myself; I claim no dominion for my Church ; but if by the manifestation of kindly feelings and a just estimate of a really great man I can in the slightest degree further that object, I do not think I shall have done amiss in writing to Mr. Binney, nor yet have given just ground for imagining that I am willing or able to compromise one single principle or time-honored characteristic of our Reformed Branch of the Catholic and Apostolic Church.

> I remain, dear Brethren,
> Your faithful servant in the Lord,
> **AUGUSTUS ADELAIDE.**

To the Hon. J. H. Fisher, President of the
Legislative Council, and the other Memorialists.

Although our space will hardly admit of any further extracts we feel that the following letter is so worthy of preservation that we must make room for it.

III.

A. H. Davis, Esq., to the Right Reverend the Bishop of Adelaide.

MY LORD,—I address your lordship as one of the *dichostasy*, to whom the discussion on Christian Union appears to be now assuming proportions which justify every reflecting mind in giving earnest thought to its possibility as a fact, and to its practicability as a devout realization. It would be unjust to doubt your lordship's thorough sincerity in the expression of warm feeling and ardent desire for a more cordial demonstration of that Christian fellowship, which you felt that you could consciencously manifest towards the Rev. Mr. Binney, but which ecclesiastical fetters, and the conventionalism of a clerical life, forbade you to indulge. No Christian man candidly perusing your letter of the 23rd September last, to our late visitor, can resist the conclusion that some circumstances had aroused your mind to inquire how it was that the body with which you stand so highly connected was placed in the anomalous position of refusing to recognise, as a fellow-worker in Christ's Catholic Church, one of whose talents you avowed your admiration, with whose manners you were delighted, whose eloquence charmed you, whose purity of character you admitted, and whose soundness in the faith was undoubted. I read that epistle on its first appearance with mingled impressions. Believing all that I have just conceded, there remained a conviction that after all it was an ebullition of transient emotion, that the better feelings which kicked against the judgment would be powerless in effecting any happy result, and that the faint cries for liberation from the thraldom of Canons and Acts of Uniformity would be drowned by the hoarse roar of those who, while the universe is in magnificent progress around them, resolve to occupy the same stand-point which served their narrow-minded fathers in by-gone centuries, when the human intellect and religious life, paralysed by long ages of degradation, were only newly awakened to perception.

Rendering all justice to your lordship's yearnings for more definite forms of Christian fellowship, it appeared to me that the basis on which your hope of effecting any change in the exclusive system of your ecclesiastical polity was destitute of one grand element of success. It wanted that thorough recognition of other Churches on their own simple foundation of the views entertained by their members, being, in the exercise of an enlightened judgment, as accordant with the requirements of Scripture There lurked throughout an innate superiority and an affectation of concession, which seemed to me of ill augury to the reception of any scheme likely to emanate from your lordship's views. I thought there was an indefinite and vague impression that a plan of comprehension was practicable, in which the Nonconformist alone was to yield his prejudices, and forego any non-essential points of discipline or form of worship ; and I knew that, however disposed to sacrifice much for a real expression of cordial unity among Christians, there must be a corresponding readiness on the part of your Church to relinquish some assumptions and accept some practices which the rigidity and cherished traditions of Episcopalianism scarcely left possible. Dr. Arnold characterizes uniformity as " that phantom which has been our curse ever since the Reformation." Let not your lordship suppose that such a state of things is either attainable or desirable. Other and more definite bases may be laid on which to build a superstructure of Christian union, in which there shall be " Christianity without sectarianism and comprehension without compromise." But if we are to be beguiled by a " tradition of 18 centuries," which presumes to invalidate the very groundwork of all our churches, your lordship inevitably drives us back upon the proof you are able to afford us for such lofty pretensions. We can smile at them when alluded to as a reason for your own justification, but other feelings would be excited if they were presented to us as logical inferences for our guidance or authorities for our obedience. Does not your lordship substitute the Church—your Church *par excellence*—for the Church of Christ, when speaking of a hallowed tradition of so ancient a date? Arnold says :—" Episcopacy was never commanded, the reason being that all forms of government and ritual are in the Christian Church indifferent, and to be decided by the Church itself ' *pro temporum et locorum ratione*,' the Church not being the clergy, but the congregation of Christians." I accept the testimony of so good a Christian Churchman. I have no antipathy to Episcopacy : and although preferring Congregationalism, I am not blind to its many defects. It has, however, this advantage, that it is unbound and capable of moving freely with that onward march of social progress characteristic of our times.

The happy separation of the Churches from State dependence in this province having enforced some other method for conducting the support of your time-honored institution, and the case having been so freely and fully met by a local Synod, in which the laity are privileged to sit, I was prepared to hope for a fuller recognition of other Christian communities at some future day. The action taken by the laics of your communion on your lordship's letter seems to me fully justified ; you had, in fact, left it almost to be inferred by those who only judged by your feelings that you would be happy favorably to respond even to an irregular appeal, and with the fact that your Church here is divested of its supremacy, and left with more freedom to act for itself, it appeared clear that, in the absence of distinct law negativing your wishes, you would be disposed to acquiesce in the request of your people. Let me freely admit that there are difficulties in the way of the suggestion of surrendering a pulpit in an Episcopal Church even to such a man as Mr. Binney. But what great or good thing was ever accomplished without breaking through the restrictions which long usage and ill, not to say bigoted, feeling had constructed to thwart Christian union ? In his case, however, there was nothing to apprehend on the score either of direct or inferential attack upon the rites, offices, discipline, or government of the Church—none on her doctrines. Even in ordinary cases of such an interchange of pulpit services as is common among various sects, no one ever violates the courtesy of Christian wisdom and prudence by preaching either doctrine or practice offensive to the people whose sanctuary is occupied. There is really, as a general rule, less probability of hearing what may be deemed serious error in the churches of Nonconformists than in your own exclusive temples. I have heard or known to be preached the ethics of Epictetus and the mysticism of Swedenborg, with the innumerable shades between, from the pulpits of the Establishment. It is matter of notoriety that High Church, Low Church, Evangelical, &c., form large sections in her pale ; they have nothing in common but submission to her formularies and subscription to her Articles, which admit, it is avowed, of conscientious differences of interpretation. There is more real union of sentiment between half the "*dichostasy*" and yourself than between one-half of your own Church and the other. Visions, however, of licensing authorised ministers of other denominations to preach in your churches are indeed illusions; this would destroy all idea of Christian union. Nor is any such step desirable; it would only affect a uniformity which is unattainable. The tendencies of all attempts to produce uniformity, if acquiesced in and pursued, can only be to generate a stolidity and sameness, which first wearies and then deadens the sources of all religious action.

Before the dream of your lordship as to the Church of the Future can hope for realization, the Church herself must take lessons from the State. It is the glory of the British Constitution that it adapts itself freely to all the emergencies which arise from the progressive social and political habits of the people. We have had within the last fifty years the State admitting even organic changes in its structure, without diminishing the love for the Constitution, and decidedly augmenting the loyalty of the people. The repeal of obnoxious statutes —the reform of the representation—the abolition of the navigation laws—the great victory of free trade—have all signalised our epoch. What has the Church done? Her noble voluntary efforts do her infinite honor. But what has she effected in relation to her position with other bodies of Christians? Unhappily, her rulers have generally been found opposed to all the great changes to which I have adverted; little, therefore, could be hoped for in relation to herself. "As it was in the beginning, is now, and ever shall be," is apparently the creed and the practice. The same persistent policy has influenced those memorialists who urge you to retrogression in the course you had advocated; they resolve to hold fast every time-worn usage, and to preserve all those faded trappings of the older days, even should their tenacity endanger the safety of the venerable fabric itself. I do not care to meddle with a document which I cannot respect for its object, which is laboriously dull and fatuitously inconclusive. Your reply seems to have justly measured the claims it had on your consideration.

Your lordship's present position reminds me of that pleasant fiction in the Arabian Nights of the fisherman whose net brought up a jar, which, instead of rewarding his hopes by the discovery of a great treasure, upon breaking the seal and removing the cover, gave forth only a cloud of vapour, which gradually assumed the form of one of those powerful genii, who are such active agents in Eastern romance. Gladly would the fisherman have rejarred the liberated spirit, but that was hopeless. Your lordship has set free the captive, and it will be wiser to welcome and promote the grand moral principle you have evolved than to attempt its reconfinement in the antique vessel in which it has so long been enshrined.

I have the honor to be, my Lord, yours very truly,

Moore Farm, November 22, 1858.   A. H. DAVIS.

INTELLIGENCE.

Rev. Thomas Binney.—This gentleman reached Victoria about the middle of November much recruited in health by his visit to South Australia. He has been engaged in preaching every Sabbath since his arrival. On November 21, in the morning, he preached in the Congregational Church, Richmond (Rev. J. Sunderland's), when a collection was made towards liquidating the debt on the church; and in the evening of the same day, for the Rev. W. B. Landells, Collingwood, on behalf of the Congregational Home Mission. On Monday, the 22nd, the foundation stone of a new Congregational Church at Prahran having been laid by His Excellency the Governor, Mr. Binney delivered an address. On Tuesday evening he attended and spoke at a Social Meeting at the Richmond Congregational Church; and on Wednesday evening he presided at the Annual Meeting of the St. Kilda Church, and addressed the Sabbath School Children on the Thursday evening at the Anniversary *Soirée*. On Friday, Mr. Binney went to visit the gold fields. On Sunday, November 28, he preached two sermons at the opening of the new Congregational Church at Sandhurst, built for the use of the Rev. W. R. Fletcher, and attended a Social meeting, in connexion with the same occasion, the Tuesday evening following. On Thursday evening, December 2, he preached for the Rev. J. Pitman, Forest Creek, and on Sunday, the 5th, for the Rev. E Day, Castlemaine, morning and evening. He delivered an address at the Annual Social Meeting of Mr. Day's Congregation on the Monday evening. On Tuesday the 7th, Mr Binney paid a visit to Mr. Parker's, at Mount Franklin, and held a service in the house in the evening. On Wednesday, the 8th, he proceeded to Ballaarat, where he was met by a deputation, consisting of representatives of various evangelical denominations, inviting him to a public Tea meeting on the Friday evening, which they purposed to convene to give him welcome. This meeting was held accordingly. On the morning of Sabbath the 12th, he preached in the Congregational Chapel, the Rev. W. Lind's; and in the evening, to a crowded audience, in the large church recently built by the Wesleyans, on both which occasions collections were made on behalf of the funds of the Congregational cause at Ballaarat On Monday, the 13th, Mr. Binney returned to St. Kilda; and on Lord's Day, the 19th, he preached in Dr. Cairn's large Church, on behalf of the Bible Society; and in the evening, in the Victoria Parade Congregational Church, Mr. Bowman, the minister, being laid aside from illness—notwithstanding the deluge of rain that fell, the attendances were large. These exertions have been somewhat too continuous and severe for the present state of Mr. Binney's health.

Testimonial to the Rev. J. L. Poore, at Salford, Manchester.—A meeting of the congregation at Hope Chapel, Salford, was held on Friday evening, October 8, to take leave of the Rev. J. L. Poore, formerly its pastor, on his departure for the third time to

Australia, as the Agent of the Colonial Missionary Society. A numerous company sat down to tea ; after which the chair was taken by the Rev. G. B. Bubier, the present pastor of the congregation. The chairman reminded the assembly of the welcome given by them last year to their old minister on his first return from Australia, and said, that they were again met, animated by the same respect and affection for their friend, to do him honor, to assure him of continued remembrance, and to express their entire sympathy with the great work in which he is now engaged. George Wood, Esq., the senior deacon, then addressed Mr. Poore in an appropriate and interesting speech, and presented him with a purse of 100 sovereigns, and a time piece bearing the following inscription :— " Presented to the Rev. J. L. Poore, with a purse, on his third departure to Australia, by his attached friends worshipping at Hope Chapel, as a memento of their appreciation of his zealous and devoted labours during a pastorate of fourteen years, from 1839 to 1853." Mr. Poore suitably acknowledged the gift; and, after briefly reviewing his Salford ministry, expressed his gratification at this proof of the continuing regard and esteem of his former flock. Several sentiments were spoken to by members of the congregation ; and, on thanks being given to the chairman, Mr. Poore made some warm and pleasant remarks on the cordial relations existing between himself and the chairman, as successive pastors, and the only pastors, of the Hope Chapel congregation.—In the course of the evening, it was stated that not only was Mr. Poore successful, on his first visit to England, in obtaining the fifteen ministers he came to seek ; but that, on his second mission, also (undertaken within two or three weeks of landing in Victoria on his return from the first), he has accomplished the objects he had in view,—having engaged twelve more ministers, for congregations in different parts of the three colonies of Australia,—and having further made arrangements by which, it is hoped, the future supply of pastors to new churches may be conveniently and effectively secured. All the circumstances of the meeting with his Salford friends, and the spirit of the whole proceedings, must have come to Mr. Poore's feelings as an emphatic " God speed."—*Nonconformist.*

SOUTH AUSTRALIA.—CONGREGATIONAL UNION.—The half-yearly meetings of the Congregational Union of South Australia were held at Kapunda, on Monday and Tuesday, the 15th and 16th November, in the following order :—On Monday evening the Rev. M. Hodge, of the Port, preached from Jude 3, " Contend for the faith which was once delivered to the saints." A devotional meeting was held on Tuesday morning, when the divine blessing was implored on the general interests of religion in the colony, as well as the particular interests of the denomination. The business meeting, presided over by the Rev. T. Q. Stow, consisted of the following ministers and delegates :—Freeman-street Chapel, Messrs. Bowen, Smedley, Dowie, A. Hay, Davis; Ebenezer Chapel, Rev. F. W. Cox (Sec.), W. Peacock; Hindmarsh, Rev. W. Wilson, Mr. Pickering; Glenelg, Rev. J. Kelsey; Port, Rev. M. Hodge; Lyndoch Valley, Rev. J. Ayling; Gawler, Rev. J. Leonard, B.A.; Kapunda, Rev. W. Oldham, Messrs. Lewis and Darwen; Salisbury, Rev. R. Mudie; Alberton, Rev. C. D. Watt; Home Mission, Rev. J. Howie. The following business was brought forward at the meeting :—The question of a provident fund for aged ministers and widows was referred to a Sub-committee to report upon at the next meeting. On the *Southern Spectator* magazine, Mr. Bowen and Mr. Cox reported what had been done ; that a guarantee fund of £50 had been raised and paid in, and that some effort had been made to extend the circulation, but the results of which were not quite clear. The Chairman for the ensuing year was balloted for, and the Rev. F. W. Cox declared duly elected. The question of the new hymn-book was brought forward and referred to the Executive Committee for further inquiry as to whether or not a supply of the revised edition should be at once ordered from England. In discussing the pecuniary clause of rule 2 of the Constitution of the Union, the Chairman explained that it was needful the churches should remit their collections to the Union before the end of the year, as there was a debt of £35 on account of the deputation to Tasmania. It was resolved that every Congregational minister not already in the Union be constituted a member thereof, by resolution of a general meeting, being proposed by the Rev. Mr. Leonard, seconded by Mr. Davis, and carried unanimously. The Executive Committee was requested to consider the subject of the best mode of providing for the visitation of the country churches periodically, so as to strengthen the hands of brethren who labor in the less populous districts. Messrs. Evan, Cox, Howie, Waterhouse, and Smedley, were requested to prepare a plan for the best mode of providing for the Conference of 1859, to be held in Adelaide, and to lay such plan before the next annual meeting. Notices of motion for the annual meeting were given by Messrs. Oldham and Cox :—First that the question of the enlargement of the constituency of the Union be considered; second that the constitution of the Union be revised in reference to rules 2, 5, and 7, and that such revised constitution be issued after the annual meeting, with a list of the members and churches in connection with the Union. In the afternoon, notwithstanding dust and wind, a large company met in a spacious marquee adjoining the chapel, and partook of tea; then adjourning to the chapel, cleared off the debt of the beautiful new building to within £100 (total cost being £720). After which the Hon. Captain Bagot took the chair, and the crowded meeting was addressed by Rev. Messrs. Cox, Hodge, Stow, Howie, Leonard, Watt, Wilson, and Mr. Smedley.

VICTORIA.—PRAHRAN INDEPENDENT CHURCH.—The foundation stone of the new Independent Church, Commercial-road, Prahran, was laid by his Excellency Sir Henry Barkly, on Monday, the 22nd of November. There were present on the occasion the following ministers of various denominations : Revs. H. Hetherington, G. Divorty, A.

Ballantyne, W. Hopkins, B. Lemmon, T. Binney (of London), T. Odell, R. Fletcher, W. B. Landells, H. Thomas, B.A., J. P. Sunderland, W. R. Lewis, A. Scales, and others. The entrance to the site of the proposed building was decorated with an arch of evergreens, and near the stone a tent was erected, in which to receive His Excellency. Notwithstanding the extreme heat of the weather, a large and highly respectable concourse of people assembled to witness the ceremony. On the arrival of His Excellency he was received by the various ministers and the trustees of the church, who conducted him to the tent, where the designs of the new church were explained to him by Mr. Crouch, the architect. Immediately after, the proceedings commenced by the Revs. R. W. Lewis and H. Thomas, B.A., and the Rev. R. Fletcher conducting the devotional exercises; after which the Rev. Wm. Moss read an address to His Excellency, and presented him with a silver trowel. The Rev. gentleman stated that the jar deposited in the cavity contained a scroll with the following inscription:—"The foundation stone of this building, for the use of the Prahran Independent Church and congregation, was laid by His Excellency Sir Henry Barkly, K.C.B., Governor in-Chief of Victoria, on the 22nd November, 1858, the Rev. T. Binney, of London, taking part in the proceedings. Pastor of the Church, Rev. Wm. Moss. Deacons: Messrs. J. Craven, J. Dunn G. S. Searle, and R. J. Blackwell. Trustees: Messrs. F. J. Sargood, Thomas Fulton, Robert, Smith, J. Craven, J. Dunn, B. Hick, J. Stokes, T. G. James, J. S. Mortimer, and R. J. Blackwell. Architects: Messrs. Crouch and Wilson. Builder: Mr. John Young." The jar also contained a copy of the Herald, Age, Argus, St. Kilda Chronicle, Prahran Advertiser, Bradshaw's Guide, and the Christian Times; also, the Church of England Record, Wesleyan Chronicle, Australian Messenger, Australian Baptist Magazine, Southern Spectator, and various current coins.

His Excellency replied as follows: "I accept this memento of the ceremony of to-day, in the spirit in which it is offered to me in the address that has just been read. In compliance with your invitation to take part in that ceremony, I do so with much pleasure for two reasons, first, because I am always glad to witness the foundation of another Christian place of worship. Secondly, with the view of testifying my respect for a very distinguished minister of the religious denomination by whom this chapel is to be erected—the Rev. Mr. Binney, who is this day present amongst us. It seems somewhat strange that in a country where the State is entirely disconnected with any church—the Governor should be often called to perform a duty of this kind by almost every religious body. I would fain infer from the circumstance that whilst the separation of Church and State is held to be expedient to obviate the evils which, through human frailty, have in some instances arisen from their connexion, there is yet no disposition to undervalue the obligation which lies upon every individual citizen—from the highest to the lowest—in religious matters. For my own part, I can with sincerity say, I am always happy to assist on such occasions. For though I, of course, believe the doctrine and the ritual of my own Church to be the best, I regard, in accordance with one of her articles, the visible Church of Christ as comprising every congregation of faithful men possessing the acknowledged attributes of Christianity. In times past, no doubt a universal church, one in doctrine and in discipline, was looked for on the strength of Scripture promises. Some still cherish such an expectation, though, judging from the tendency of the age, to further separation and subdivision, through the operation of the right of private judgment, it would seem most probable that we ought to build our hopes of a visible Catholic Church, not on anticipations of the outward conformity of men generally to any particular standard of doctrine or of ceremonial observances, but on a gradual assimilation of the inner spirit of the various Christian bodies in the world—a closer imitation, in fact, of their divine Master. It is a remarkable confirmation of this view that the men most distinguished for Christian attainments in all ages, have ceased to be regarded so much as members of particular sects, their lives and reputations being cherished as the property of Christians generally. Who, for instance, cares to what branch of the Church belonged Sir Thomas More or Fenelon, Cranmer or Latimer, Wesley or Whitfield, Watts or Doddridge? And thus it is in the present day, when such men as Dr. Binney come amongst us, they are at once hailed as brethren in the Gospel by all liberal Protestants, of whatever denomination. Let me conclude by assuring you that no one more thoroughly reciprocates than myself the hope expressed in your address, that such feelings of mutual affection and of sympathy may, through God's grace, continue and extend throughout all classes of Christians in this colony." The jar having been deposited in the opening left for it, the mortar was then laid, and the stone lowered. His Excellency then tapped the stone three times, and pronounced it well and truly laid.

The Rev. Mr. Binney next addressed the assembly in an able speech, of which we regret that no good report has appeared. The service concluded with the Benediction. A large company assembled shortly after in a marquee erected on the ground, and partook of tea, after which the public meeting was opened with prayer, by the Rev. J. P. Sunderland. Thomas Fulton, Esq., J P., occupied the chair, and alluded with much gratification to the progress and success of Prahran, and more especially of the Independent cause. The Rev. Messrs. Sunderland, Scales, Fletcher, Lewis and others, addressed the meeting. Apologies for absence were made for Rev. Messrs. Odell, Taylor, and T. Binney. Mr. Binney, from extreme exhaustion, was unable to wait till the close of the proceedings. The financial report read by Mr. Craven, was considered very encouraging. The cost of the church, when complete, will be about £3000, of which there remains to be collected £1800; £600 of which is required in three months, and for the remainder a mortgage is to be effected. £500 of the sum already collected was raised by the ladies belonging to the church, in two months.   After a vote of thanks to the ladies for the admirable manner in which they made their arrangements for tea, to the ministers for their addresses, and the chairman, the meeting closed.

MISSIONS.

TASMANIA.—HOBART TOWN.—Aid to South Sea Missions.—During several years contributions have been supplied by the Sabbath Schools connected with the Congregational Churches in this city, and by other friends, towards the support of native teachers in the South Seas.   More recently, a portion of these contributions has been specially applied to aid in sustaining those who are under training for this work.   An institution has been established by the Rev. John Barff in Tahaa (one of the Society Islands), respecting which he writes:—" We commenced in November last, with six students.   We have now nine, and are expecting a tenth.   Almost the whole have been chosen by the respective Churches of which they were members."   He then supplies particulars with reference to three students, named respectively Peter Facy, Henry Hopkins and F. Miller.   The first name is owing to the members of a family engaging to sustain a student, in memory of a revered father.   May not other families " go and do likewise ?"—A missionary seminary has for some years existed at Malua, Upolu, Samoa (or Navigator's Islands), which is highly prosperous.   A box of useful articles (value £30) having been transmitted from the Sabbath Schools connected with the Brisbane-street Chapel, the receipt of it has lately been acknowledged by the missionary resident at Malua (the Rev. G. Turner), who anticipates similar and extended aid in time to come.   He writes to the Rev. F. Miller—" I will take you and the teachers in connection with Brisbane-street at their word, and rely upon you for an annual supply of goods for the seminary, say, not to exceed £50.   This sum, with the aid perhaps of occasional boxes which we have from various quarters, will meet our expenditure, and prevent our drawing further upon the Society.   The institution at present contains sixty-four young men under training for the work of the ministry, who together with their wives and children, and a select class of youths, form a population on the premises of about 260 individuals.   The agricultural habits of the natives are kept up, and the institution thereby made as far as practicable self-supporting.   There is still, however, an annual expenditure for clothing, tools, and stationery of some £60, and that sum the children in the schools referred to are determined to meet."   Mr. Turner then urges the following appeal :—" But we must not stop with the children : what about the grown-up Christians and Church members?   Here is a question of simple proportion for you.   If the children of the Sunday Schools connected with Brisbane-street support the teachers under training in the seminary in Samoa, what could the united Churches of Brisbane-street and Collins-street do. ?   It seems to me that they could, with perfect ease, support the two tutors of the institution.   I have seen the minutes of your last conference, and observe that the support of the London Missionary Society's Missions in these seas was again talked about   We want you to begin and do something which will be definite, telling and effective. With but a little organization and superintendence, you could easily in Hobart Town carry out my suggestion, and support two of the missionaries of the Society; Launceston and other parts of Tasmania could at least support another.   Let the other Colonial Churches only do the same, and the support of every missionary in connexion with the London Missionary Society, from Tahiti to Nangoni, might be at once accomplished. We might still, for a time at least, let the children of England keep up the ship ; and look to Bloomfield-street for a supply of missionaries, as they may be required.   May the Lord bless what I have said to stimulate the friends of Christ to do something at once which will be worth reporting at the next Conference, and which may be the means of drawing out the missionary energies of the Churches to a greater extent than ever."

Handbook to Australasia. Edited by WILLIAM FAIRFAX.   Melbourne: W. Fairfax and Co.

This is a work of immense labor and incalculable utility.   It furnishes information in a condensed and perspicuous form upon every conceivable thing relating to all the colonies of Australia, including Tasmania and New Zealand.   The arrangement of the multifarious materials is simple and of easy reference.   The information too has been obtained from the most authentic sources, has been condensed with care, and may be relied upon as accurate.   The work is one which every politician, merchant, professional man, clergyman, schoolmaster, and indeed every individual who desires to be correctly informed of all matters in which he feels interested in the land of his adoption, should have constantly at hand.

ERRATA.

Page 156, line 19, *after* "built in " *insert* " to."
Page 158, line 6, *for* " what at present," *read* " what is possible at present."
Page 158, line 21, *for* " which Apollos," *read* " which the Apostle."
Page 159, line 16, *for* " denies such eminence," *read* " denies such status : eminence, &c."

W. FAIRFAX AND CO., STEAM PRINTERS, COLLINS STREET, EAST, MELBOURNE.

The Southern Spectator.

FEBRUARY, 1859.

CHRISTIAN FRATERNIZATION.

The subject of this paper is just beginning in one form or other to command increased attention from Christian men in Europe, America, and Australia. A fact like this, so wide and so simultaneous in its development, demands our best consideration and prayer. It is connected with various new forms of religious susceptibility and serious thought, sometimes exhibiting very strong symptoms merely of desire, and then of determination, on the part of large multitudes of minds, to throw off the bondage of every tradition and formula in religion which derives its chief authority from man, and to value for no more than they are worth the assumptions, creeds and ceremonies which have been handed down from a bygone age, and which are now therefore effete and cumbersome, if not pernicious and destructive. There is much in this excitement—this deep and powerful, although quiet, development of modern piety—which every Christian must hail with gratitude and wonder. The leading minds and the superior piety of Christendom could not simultaneously, and without designed combination, become dissatisfied with sentimentality and disgusted with the dogmas of man's ecclesiasticism, if they were not moved thereto by the Great Head of the Church. The promulgation of opinions and doctrines resting on authority or tradition—the recognition of parties whose chief object seems to be to indoctrinate mind with creeds and to educate it in arts of imitation, of dissimulation, and moral servitude to man—these are soon to command our sincerest and strongest resistance so far as they lead to human substitutes for vital and practical religion.

And is the Church of Christ, that is, all who love God as he has revealed himself in the person of Christ, and who attest that love by "walking in his commandments"—is this Church, which is so promiscuously diffused among the modern sects of Christendom, about to put on one of her beautiful garments and to conduct herself meekly, fraternally, and Christ-like towards herself, and to offer a word of compassion towards a lost world ! Verily the current history of our times seems to establish this hope, for Christians are beginning, as they ought always and everywhere to have done, to estimate personal religion, that is, moral affinity to the word and nature of Christ, by the old golden rule of love to each other and to their race. They are becoming conscious of their divisions, their exclusiveness, and their assumptions, and feel that these are not merely pernicious in their influence upon themselves, but huge stumbling-blocks before all those persons who derive their knowledge of Christianity from its professors. Some Christians do not appear to comprehend the New Testament idea of Christian unity, for they would, if their power enabled them, demolish every sectarian prejudice and conviction but their own, and drag every conscientious, but in their view erratic brother to worship God in their building and to pray in their stereotyped form. Such unity as this, while it is unattainable in the very nature of things, is neither compatible with conscience and Scripture, nor is it adapted to the special work of Christ's Church in this present evil world.

But it is the one idea of Christian *fraternization* that we wish just now to command our reflection. Good men everywhere seem to be tending, both in sentiment and individual effort, towards a much closer and dearer, and holier communion with each other; and we may ask the question, what must some of the outlines of such communion and fraternization embrace? It seems exceedingly desirable to avoid all misconception on the subject, and therefore, and for the sake of distinctness, we remark that it cannot mean that every separate Church or individual Christian, in this or any other country, should maintain some visible mechanical fellowship with every other church or Christian; but that each should conscientiously and habitually cultivate a spiritual interest in every other church or Christian with whom acquaintance may, by any providential means whatever, be formed and maintained. It is a fraternization characterized less by human legislation and organization than by individual, spontaneous, divinely prompted sympathy. The Church knows too much of the inefficacy of human organizations to strengthen her internal unity, and to consolidate her power before sinful men; and the world knows, too, that the real fraternity of spiritual minds will never evince so much godliness, or humanity, or antagonism to evil, while led on by theories built on compromise. No, the visible unity of the Church, and the particular manner and extent of her fraternization, must obey the bidding of Christ. The measure of our fraternization will be according to the measure of our love, and our love to each other will be influenced very much by the rule of our recognition of each other's godliness.

Our principles then, as Christians, require us to learn all we can about the spiritual condition of our brotherhood; and is it not possible for us, who live in Australia although provincially separate, to learn much about each other, and take a profounder interest in each other's welfare? Churches and individuals, possessing the spiritual sympathies of Christians, whether they ever see each other in the flesh or not, may certainly commingle their best affections and energies in the common enterprise of love, of caring for each other, of bearing each other's burdens, and of so fulfilling the law of Christ. Our churches generally can become more solicitous about each other's welfare, more anxious to know each other's state, each other's advantages, labours, temptations, trials, and general experience.

Let us look at this question, as perhaps it may elicit the opinions of various minds upon the subject, and lead to something which has not yet characterized the spiritual life of our brotherhood—*By what mode can churches fraternize with each other?* It has been remarked that they cannot migrate from their several localities to one centre for the purpose of actual interview. Such a derangement of society would destroy the professional character and utility of every Christian and church in such a gathering. Yet a mode may perhaps be more within our reach as churches than is generally supposed, and be neither utopian nor impracticable. If the main object of fraternization among the followers of Christ be the cultivation of mutual acquaintance, sympathy, and co-operation, this can be attained by various means. We have a press, we have a railroad, we have a telegraph in almost every province in this hemisphere, and these are rapidly increasing. Secular men are using these agencies mighty scale and with amazing energy, in working out for themselves a unity of thought, of information, of enterprise, and of co-operation. Politicians, merchants, tradesmen, literary men of every rank, of every secular profession, and with all sorts of objects bearing upon their present life, vigorously employ every modern facility for bringing themselves virtually within the range of one community, and of sharing with each other in one general prosperity. Is not the same agency waiting to render the same and a greater service to the churches of Christ, in facilitating their recognition and knowledge of each other, and the unity, co-operation, and power of their spiritual influence? Look at the railroad and the electric wire. Who claims their servitude? who reaps the fruits of their energies? who rejoices most in their wondrous achievements? We cannot aver that Christians do not use them; but do they use them *enough* in the service of religion, in communicating and interchanging thought, sympathy and help? It appears very doubtful whether Christians generally have paid that attention to this view of the subject which it merits. Christians, as such, have more powerful motives to avail themselves of the energies of scientific achievement, because they have greater benefits to bestow upon mankind than any mere secular society. The genius of Christianity, too, and the capacity of mind universally for imbibing its pure spirit and exemplifying it in society, have usually anticipated the service of science. Science only developes powers, principles, laws belonging to the Christian's God and Saviour—powers which he doubtless created for the ultimate advantage of his cause in the world, and for the special use of his spiritual children—and which *they* only will ever employ gratefully, admiringly and lovingly in promoting the purest social and spiritual benefit of mankind.

If there is truth in these remarks, should not Christians make the appliances of science subservient to fraternization? Here is the *press*, and our character, our growth, and our power, as men fearing God, can be immensely improved by making more use of it. Here is the press in our actual employ. Alas, it is appreciated, worked and encouraged by a number immensely disproportionate to our duties, our wants, and our latent strength. Taking a denominational view of the question, can we not as Congregational Christians, sometimes as churches, and frequently as individuals, employ the pages of the *Spectator* in communicating with each other, in making common property of our best thoughts, prompting each other with spiritual aspirations, and thus diffuse among all our people the knowledge of the wisest, the energy of the strongest, and the piety of the most Christ-like among us? This has not yet been attempted, except in a very general manner, and in relation to the statistics of our organization. We require more knowledge of the Churches than statistics can furnish. We want to know something of the inner life, the spiritual history, attainments, privileges, labours, temptations, afflictions, and general experience which our community of piety have realised. No intrusions upon the privacies of social life are necessary—no publicity for facts which properly belong to the records of individual conscience—no facts, no information, no thought of any kind, even though it may be Christian in its nature, which may properly be held to be the exclusive property either of a Church or an individual. In our aspirations after spiritual communism (if we may borrow a term from Socialists) we may not sacrifice the domain of individuality; but, without touching this tender ground, the ministers and churches of our faith may employ the pages of our monthly periodical in diffusing among our detached community a very large amount of invaluable instruction and sympathy; and while no distinct Church in Australia can complain of its irreparable isolation and obscurity, none can be excused for its exclusive possession of thought or intercourse, which it can, and far as possible ought, to bestow upon others. They cannot communicate and diffuse too much of that thought or feeling which has an intrinsic value for all the Church, nor can they carry out their fraternal principles beyond the legitimate province of Christian love. Perhaps every denomination of Christians may become more communicative among its several Churches, and discover the fact that such fraternal intercourse would do more than almost anything else to increase their aggregate strength and influence. But is there one class of Christians in this hemisphere whose strength and influence admit of so much development and increase as Congregationalists? Or is there any denomination whose social status offers such co-operation, whose history is fraught with associations and incidents so inspiring, or whose destiny, if we are true to our faith and our principles, will be more glorious than that of Congregational Christians who are now invited to loving fraternization? Again, we say that secular society is in the van of the fraternities of our earth ; men of the world know the secrets of association, and wisely do they develop them. They spare no expense, grudge no labour, yield to no difficulty, in order to gain every piece of intelligence, every fact, every symptom, and every discovery which they can turn to practical immediate account. All this, be it remembered, is the offspring of mixed motives, and much of it of selfishness—of a desire which terminates exclusively upon individual minds and interests. But Christians are supposed to cultivate desires, affections and energies, which are intended to benefit the whole family of man ; and, what is more, their Divine Master commands them to aim constantly at fulfilling this their mission. Will Christians ever respond to the entire range of their obligations, will they ever develop the mighty energies of their faith, the latent influence of their renewed nature, without they evince more wisdom, more communicativeness, and more reciprocity? Of course this and every other question on the subject admits of a variety of opinions. But variety in religion should not involve the antagonism of strife. Every reader of this paper may see in it some statements which he might not feel able to endorse ; but let him remember that while we have written some things with all the diffidence of conjecture, and with some of the humility which belongs to a fallible christian mind, we have tried to offer a few thoughts, unpolished perhaps and jagged, which we hope will lead the piety that is among us to develop itself in a freer and more communicative manner. Christians and churches are much too shy, too suspicious of each other, and consequently too unknown to one another, even in the same denomination ; and while we allow this isolation with its train of evils to characterize our standing, we shall leave undeveloped our greatest and best resources, and remain, as we now are, comparative strangers to the immense influence which we might exert upon everything human. The bondage of isolation among Churches as well as individual Christians, is the greatest enemy to the genius of their piety, and to its loveliness, and its power. Let us then love one another—not in words, in protestations of charity, in loud declamations against bigotry and exclusiveness—but by giving to each other, even though at the cost of much self-denial, our most entire esteem, sympathy and co-operation. Let us try, as Congregational followers of Christ, to be practical, exemplary, holy brethren. Let every brother among our churches so demean himself as to command the love of the Church, and the admiration and imitation of mankind.

S.A.   FRATER.

PROGRESS OF THE STATE AID QUESTION IN NEW SOUTH WALES.

It is with no small gratification that we are able to record in our present number that a decided step has been taken by the Parliament of New South Wales in the direction of Voluntaryism. This advance is the more welcome because it is entirely unexpected. The whole question seemed for the moment to be in abeyance, other more inviting political topics having absorbed the public attention. But though unanticipated, the step taken is decisive and irrevocable. In the present political condition of these colonies there can be no retrograde movement in a question of this kind ; there can only be pause, or movement onward. The Schedule of the Constitution Act of New South Wales, like that of Victoria, sets aside a fixed sum for public worship, but the amount has been supplemented in the former colony by an additional vote of nearly half as much again. This has always been protested against by the Voluntaries as a grievance, who thought it bad enough to be compelled to vote the £28,000 fixed by the Schedule, without increasing the evils and injustice of State Aid by adding further to the endowment. The four favored denominations, however, have always been strong enough unitedly to secure the annual vote, until last month, when by a small majority the Assembly rejected the vote. For the year 1859, therefore, nothing more will be voted for religious purposes than is required by the Schedule.

Nor is the mere cancellation of this vote the only sign of advancing Voluntaryism. The government, though proposing the vote for one year longer, admitted its incompatibility with the growing tendencies of the age, and promised next year to introduce into the reformed parliament a Bill to deal with the Schedule itself, and to make provision for the gradual withdrawal of State Aid altogether. At the coming general election, therefore, this will be one of the first questions raised, and the colonists at large will be able to pronounce their opinions on it, by their choice of candidates. There cannot be in New South Wales such a sudden and total cessation of State Aid as there was in South Australia ; for, in the former colony, there are Government Chaplains connected with the old order of the convict system, and others who may be considered to have an equitable claim on the revenue for life, they having been brought out from England on the faith of receiving a permanent salary from Government. But these claims will expire one after another in the course of nature and all sects will then be on a level.

There have been several indications lately in New South Wales, that Voluntaryism, though apparently stationary, was in reality slowly pushing its way. In the conference of Church of England clergy and delegates, there were not a few found who expressed their belief that State Aid would soon cease, and their wish that it should be so ; and who exhorted their brethren to be prepared for self-reliance. The Wesleyans at their last annual gathering passed resolutions condemnatory of the principles of the grant, though with obvious inconsistency they also declared it impolitic to refuse their share as long as it was obtainable. The Presbyterians have been sadly divided amongst themselves relative to the establishment of an affiliated College to the University, the whole cause of the division having its root in the Government Endowment, till many of their best members have come to the conclusion that the State bounty costs more than it is worth. Even among the Roman Catholics, a small party who have joined

the radicals in politics, have agreed to adopt heartily the separation of
Church and State as an inevitable adjunct of democratic principles.   There
is, therefore, no longer a compact unity amongst those denominations that
receive the Government aid.   Each is a house divided against itself, and
the issue is obvious and inevitable.

The step taken in New South Wales cannot fail to have a decided
influence on the progress of the same great question in Victoria and
Tasmania.   We look forward now with confidence to the establishment of
perfect religious equality in all the colonies of Australia.

We may supplement the above remarks of an esteemed correspondent
by saying that the question of the abolition of State Aid to religion is
engaging the attention of Tasmania and Victoria as well as New South
Wales, and in such a way as to give sure presage of its ultimate and speedy
success.   The withdrawment of State support to religious bodies was
moved for in the Tasmanian Legislature not long ago, and only failed in
being carried by a narrow majority.   Argument, zeal and faith were
defeated by self-interest and prejudice ; but only for a time, for the contest
is sure to be renewed again and again until the victory is won.

In the Victorian Legislative the question is not formally, but is considered to be virtually settled.   The abolition was, last Session, carried in
the Assembly by a decided majority, and was thrown out in the Council
by a majority of only one.   Several fresh elections for the Upper House
have since been held, and changes in consequence have taken place of such
a nature as to leave little doubt of the majority being now prepared to
support a measure for abolition.   A Bill for the discontinuance of State
Grants was introduced into the Lower House in the present short session,
but the pressure of other business requiring immediate attention, has caused
its postponement till the Parliament next assembles ; and this is expected
to be at an early period.

Some attempts, however, have been made, if not to tinker up the old
and decaying system, at least to get as much out of it as possible.   A Bill professedly for the better regulation of Ecclesiastical Trusts, but really under that
pretext, which but thinly veiled the true object, to give power to Trustees to sell
church lands granted by the State.   But the device being detected, the
measure was first emasculated and then suffered silently to drop as useless.
Three several private Bills were also brought in to seek, under special
circumstances, power to sell certain church lands ; but meeting with
unexpected opposition and obstruction, they seem at present hanging fire, to
await, perhaps, the fate of a bolder and more comprehensive measure, now
before the Legislature.   This measure proposes to give power to all religious
bodies throughout the colony, holding grants from the Crown for church sites,
to alienate them at pleasure from their proper and designed use, and to traffic
and trade in them as they please, provided, of course, that the proceeds are
devoted to Ecclesiastical purposes.   It is to be hoped that the common
sense of the House and the country will at once quash such a barefaced
proposal, and insist upon the lands, as they *are* granted, being strictly
applied to their original object, viz., sites for churches, schools and par-
sonages.   There is little reason to doubt that the Parliament, soon to be
summoned on the basis of the new Reform Bill, will at once free all the
religious bodies in the colony from all dependence upon the taxes for
support, and free the Legislature also from all pretexts for meddling with
matters ecclesiastical.   It will be a happy day for the peace of the country,

and we believe for the interest of vital religion itself, when that consummation, so devoutly to be wished, shall have arrived throughout the whole of
the Australian colonies.

BRETHREN DWELLING IN UNITY.

A lovely picture, framed and set in Psalm cxxxiii.

In all probability this psalm was written at the gladsome season when
the ark of God was placed in the sacred tent recently erected on mount
Zion. "David," says a learned writer, "brings here to the consciousness
of the people the glory of the fellowship of the saints, which had so long
fallen into abeyance, and the restoration of which had begun with the
setting up of the tabernacle in Zion, after it had been interrupted during
the entire period in which the ark had been buried as in its grave at
Kirjath-jearim." Our psalm was sung with peculiar delight when the
Jews had returned from their captivity in Babylon, for then were re-united
the tribes that had been divided by the folly and rashness of Rehoboam.
In the assemblies of the early Christians they joyfully lauded, in these
inspired words, the grace which had united in one fold pious Jews and the
straying sheep of the Gentile world. Let us take up, perpetuate and
transmit the song which celebrates that divine and comprehensive charity
which would embrace all mankind in the bonds of Christian brotherhood.

What is the object of admiration and delight? It is "brethren dwelling
together in unity." A more beautiful, cheering and heavenly sight earth
does not afford. We are greatly indebted to the Gospel that in this
wretched world many such scenes appear, like green and fertile spots in
the desert. The Gospel effectually breaks down the barriers man's pride
has erected between himself and his fellow-man. This system of love
levels distinctions founded on haughtiness and contempt, selfishness and
ambition, and (which are) supported by deceit and cruel oppression. For
the Bible teaches the common origin of mankind, as the creatures of divine
power; their common degradation and ruin, as being all similarly related to
fallen Adam; their common dependence on the same providence and grace
for bodily and spiritual, temporal and eternal blessings. In a word, we
gather from the Bible the truth that *we are all brethren*—all guilty before
God and needing his mercy. Thus Scripture opposes all unwarrantable
assumptions and domination, while it acknowledges and sanctions every
domestic and public distinction in rank and authority in which the good
of the many is sought by their required subordination to the few.

As "brethren" God would have us "dwell together." For this end he
has endowed us with social and communicative affections and tendencies.
Man is not designed for a solitary life; his mental and physical wants
must be supplied by the ministry of society. While it must be admitted
that, through human depravity, society is productive of much evil, it is
contended, and justly, that more benefits than evils result from man's
association with his kindred race.

But the expression, "brethren dwelling together" implies and requires
—what is indeed stated—that they "dwell together *in unity*"—that is, in
concord and harmony of heart, purpose and act. Here is intended not
merely proximity of dwelling and opportunity for frequent intercourse, but
also nearness and dearness of heart one to another, and an actual interchange of friendly offices.

FIRST CHRISTIAN SERVICE IN NEW ZEALAND.

On Sunday morning, when I was on deck, I saw the English flag flying, which was a pleasing sight in New Zealand: I considered it as the signal and the dawn of civilisation, liberty, and religion in that dark and benighted land. I never viewed the British colours with more gratification; and flattered myself they would never be removed till the natives of that island enjoyed all the happiness of British subjects. About ten o'clock we prepared to go ashore, to publish for the first time the glad tidings of the Gospel. I was under no apprehension for the safety of the vessel, and therefore, ordered all on board to go on shore to attend divine service, except the master and one man. When we landed, we found Koro Koro, Duaterra, and Shungbie dressed in regimentals which Governor Macquarrie had given them, with their men drawn up, ready to be marched into the inclosure, to attend divine service; they had their swords by their sides, and switches in their hands. We entered the inclosure, and were placed on the seats on each side of the pulpit, Koro Koro marched his men, and placed them on the right hand, in the rear of the Europeans, and Duaterra placed his men on the left; the inhabitants of the town, with the women and children, and a number of other chiefs, formed a circle round the whole: a solemn silence prevailed—the sight was truly impressive. I rose up and began the service with singing the Old Hundredth Psalm, and felt my very soul melt within me when I viewed my congregation, and considered the state they were in. After reading the service, during which the natives stood up and sat down at the signals given by Koro Koro's switch, which was regulated by the movements of the Europeans, it being Christmas day, I preached from the second chapter of St. Luke's gospel, and tenth verse,—" Behold, I bring you glad tidings of great joy," etc. The natives told Duaterra that they could not understand what I meant; he replied, that they were not to mind that now, or they would understand by-and-by, and that he would explain my meaning far as he could. When I had done preaching, he informed them what I had been talking about. Duaterra was very much pleased that he had been able to make all the necessary preparations for the performance of divine worship in so short a time, and we felt much obliged to him for his intention. He was extremely anxious to convince us that he would do everything in his power, and that the good of his country was his principal consideration.

" In this manner the Gospel has been introduced into New Zealand; and I fervently pray that the glory of it may never depart from its inhabitants till time shall be no more.—*Life of the Rev. Samuel Marsden.*

DYING WORDS OF A CONVERTED NEW ZEALAND CHIEFTAIN.

Who that has a heart to feel, or any imagination capable of being warmed by strains of exquisite pathos, can read, unmoved, the last words of the dying Karepa? the scene is in the lonely village of Te Hawera, of which he was the chief. Mr. Colenzo, the missionary, arrived just as his people, with loud cries, sitting around his new made tomb, bewailed his departure: at night they gathered around their spiritual father in his tent, and one of the natives thus related the last words of Karepa.

" He summoned us all," said he, " to come close around him, and with much love exhorted us, talking energetically, as was his custom, a long while: he said—' You well know that I have brought you, from time to time, much riches, muskets, powder, hatchets, knives, blankets; I afterwards heard of the new riches, called faith! I sought it—I went to Manawater, in those days a long and perilous journey, for we were surrounded by enemies; no man travelled alone. I saw the few natives who, it was said, had heard of it; but they could not satisfy me. I sought further, but in vain. I heard afterwards of a white man at Otaki, and that with him was the spring where I could fill my empty and dry calabash. I travelled to his place, to Otaki, but in vain; he was gone—gone away ill. I returned to you, my children, dark minded, days passed by, the snows fell, they melted, they disappeared, the buds expanded, and the tangled paths of our low forests were again passable to the foot of the native man. At last we heard of another white man who was going about over mountains, and through forests and swamps, giving drink from his calabash to the secluded native—to the remnants of the tribes of the mighty, of the renowned of former days, now dwelling by twos and threes among the long reeds by the rills in the valley. Yes, my grandchildren, my and your ancestors, once spread over the country, as the koitarcke (quail) and krivi (apteryx) once did, but now their descendants are even as the descendants of these birds, scarce, gone, dead, fast hastening to utter exhaustion. Yes, he heard of that white man; we heard of his going over the high snowy range to Patea, all over the rocks to Turakirae. I sent four of my children to meet him —they saw his face; yes, you, you talked with, you brought me a drop of water from his calabash. You told me he had said he would come to this far-off isle to see me. I rejoiced, I disbelieved his coming; but I said he may. I built the chapel, we waited expecting; you slept at nights, I did not. He came, he emerged from the long forest, he stood upon Te Hawera ground. I saw him, I shook hands with him, we rubbed noses together,—yes, I saw a missionary's face, I sat in his cloth house (tent), I tasted his new food, I heard him talk Maori; my heart bounded within me; I listened, I ate his words; you slept at nights, I did not. Yes, I listened and he told me about God, and his son Jesus Christ, and of peace and of reconciliation, and of a loving father's home beyond the stars. And, now, I too drank from his calabash and was refreshed, he gave me a book as well as words. I laid hold of the new riches for me and for you, and we have it now. My children, I am old, my teeth are gone, my hair is white—the yellow leaf is falling from the T'awai (beech tree) —I am departing—the sun is sinking behind the great western hills, it will soon be night. But, hear me, hold fast the new riches—the great riches—the true riches: we have had plenty of sin, and pain, and death; but now we have the true riches. Hold fast the true riches which Karepa sought out for you.'

"Here he became faint and ceased talking. We all wept like little children around the bed of the dying old man—of our father: he suffered much pain, from which he had scarcely any cessation until death relieved him."—*Life of the Rev. Samuel Marsden.*

———◆———

A CHINESE CONVERT.

The following application for Baptism was received by the Rev. W. Young, written in the Chinese language, and has been translated by him.

Lum-Kheu-Yang, a native of the village of Che-san, in the district of Hook-san in Canton Province, respectfully requests to be baptized. I give seriatim the circumstances connected with my call to a knowledge of the Gospel. From my youth I have studied books, and made myself acquainted with the instructions of Confucius and Mencius. For eleven years I made strenuous efforts in school, but never succeeded in distinguishing myself. This circumstance induced me to give up study and betake myself to trade, in order that I might be able to provide for my family. All of a sudden disturbances occurred in Canton; the Mandarins and people arrayed themselves in battle against the Hak-ka rebels. No place was exempt from trouble; but my native village suffered more from the injuries inflicted by these rebels than any other place. Property was plundered, and houses burned and destroyed. The strong fled to different parts of the country and sought a subsistence, while the weak fell victims to the weapons of the rebels. In their progress of murder and slaughter dead bodies might be seen strewing the roads, and blood might be observed flooding the ground. No one could look on such scenes without feeling his heart saddened; nor could any hear of them without shedding tears. The cruel rebels were permitted to act thus, because our people from ancient times to the present have been ignorant of him who preserved them, and worshipped idols, and have been guilty of a great many wicked practices, and heaped to themselves divine wrath. Hence the infliction of these just temporal punishments. It was a fortunate circumstance, however, that none of my family were personally injured; they have been able, though with the greatest hardship, to maintain themselves to this day. At the time our money and property were plundered, and we had not means of purchasing even a morsel to put into our mouths, and there appeared no way by which we could extricate ourselves from poverty, we happily received intelligence regarding a new gold-field in an English colony. We were told that men from all countries were congregated there, and obtained permission to dig for gold; that money was to be easily made, the people were peaceably disposed, and that the country abounded in everything. The idea of going to such a country was delightful; I told my family of my intention, and they too were delighted and commended my plan.

I then made an effort to get as much money as would pay for my passage to this productive land. I was in this country a whole year without hearing anything about the doctrines of the Gospel. When afterwards I went to Mopoke to dig for gold, I unexpectedly met with my friend Leong-a-t'oe, who was engaged in making known the doctrines of the Gospel. People collected together in large numbers to hear him: I felt glad in my heart, knowing in some measure the tendency of these doctrines, which inculcated on men the practice of virtue, and the reforming of their wicked ways. They taught them also the worship of God, and the grace of the Lord Jesus, who died for man's salvation. At this time I was not successful in gold digging, and I had yet to make great efforts in order to provide for my family left behind in China; so I eventually left Mopoke and removed to the Ovens. There I was about a year, but was not in the slightest degree successful; I then tried Ballaarat, seeking a livelihood east and west. Like a weathercock I was never in one fixed spot, and lived just from hand to mouth. From Ballaarat I wended my way back to Castlemaine, and again met my friend A-t'oe, who consoled me with the words of divine truth, and took me with him to the chapel that I might hear the preaching of God's word. On that occasion he discoursed about a good man of ancient time, who lived in the east, whose name was Job, a person who obeyed God's commandments and practised righteousness. Through God's blessing he became the richest man in the east. But one day Satan devised an artful scheme, destroyed Job's sons and daughters and all that he had, hoping thereby to overturn the piety of Job and make him rebel against God. But notwithstanding these trials Job remained faithful to God, exclaiming "Naked I came into the world, and naked I shall return to the earth. It is God that gives us all things, and it is God that takes them back." As usual, Job praised God without ceasing. When I heard these statements I was much affected. I then began to understand how that all I had enjoyed during my lifetime was the gift of God; and that all the injuries I had endured at the hands of the Hak-ka Chinese, who robbed me of my property, were permitted to befal me by God's appointment. Before I heard the word of God, I considered these trials as great misfortunes. But who would have supposed that God would make use of misfortunes to try the faith of believers and the unbelief of unbelievers? Job, notwithstanding his trials, was patient, and in the end was greatly rewarded. I in like manner, in consequence of disturbances occasioned by the Hak-ka rebels, was forced to flee to these gold-fields; but I have thereby obtained a knowledge of the Saviour, and have become a believer in the truth. At one time I was disposed to consider my reverses a calamity; now I regard them a happiness, inasmuch as by them I have been brought to hear God's holy doctrines. Had I not experienced the cruelties of the Hak-ka rebels, I should never have come to these gold-fields, nor entered the gate of divine truth, nor should I have been favored with the daily instructions and prayers of A-t'oe, who prayed that I might obtain the renewing influence of the Holy Spirit. Having received enlightenment, I perceive the error of my former ways, and also the worthlessness of the worship of spirits, Buddhas and ancestors. I wish to amend my former ways, to place my dependence on the Saviour, to keep his commandments, and to worship God; to make these things the rule of my life all my days.

sins are great and aggravated, and I am afraid I cannot escape. But happy it is for me that the Saviour gave up his life upon the cross in order to restore me, that I believing in him might not perish, but have eternal life; that he can enable me to do his will, to receive his grace, to praise his power, to confide in his name, and to cherish the hope of the life to come. I desire to be baptized, and to shew that I receive the truth in sincerity and joy. To the end of my life I shall not recant. May the triune God have mercy upon me, and grant that I may enjoy the inheritance that fades not away. I hope the ministers of the Gospel will take into their favorable consideration the request I now present.

VARIETIES.

EFFICACY OF THE ATONEMENT.

But if the question be asked, How could one man satisfy for many? how by one man's obedience many may be made righteous? the answer is not far to seek. The transcendant worth of that obedience which Christ rendered, of that oblation which he offered, the power which it possessed of countervailing and counterbalancing a world's sin, lay in this, that he who offered these, while he bore a human nature and wrought human acts, was a divine person; not indeed God alone, for as such he would never have been in the condition to offer; nor man alone, for then the worth of his offering could never have reached so far; but that he was God and man in one person indissolubly united, and in this person performing all those acts, man that he might obey, and suffer, and die; God that he might add to every act of his obedience, his suffering and death, an immeasureable worth, steeping in the glory of his divine personality all of human that he wrought. Christ was able so summarily to pay our debt, because he had another and a higher coin in which to pay it than that in which it was contracted. It was contracted in the currency of earth, he paid it in the currency of heaven.—*Trench*.

PREJUDICE.

Prejudice may be considered as a continual false medium of viewing things, for prejudiced persons not only never speak well, but also never think well of those whom they dislike, and the whole character and conduct is considered with an eye to that particular thing which offends them.—*Butler*.

There is nothing respecting which a man may be so long unconscious, as of the extent and strength of his prejudices.

REVIVALS.

AMERICA.—The Philadelphia *Press* gives a report of the Jayne's Hall prayer-meeting in that city. The attendance continues unabated, and numerous incidents of interest are connected with its daily progress. Monday of last week was set apart to hear statements from gentlemen recently returned from the country, respecting the progress of the revival in the sections they had visited. Rev. John Chambers described the morning prayer-meetings held in the dining-saloon of the hotel at Bedford Springs. The attendance at these meetings had been large, including even drinkers and gamblers; and, indeed so popular was this feature among the guests generally, that an effort to have them discontinued had met with a signal and overwhelming rebuke from nine-tenths of all present. Of all the guests at that delightful resort, none had been more regular in their attendance, or appeared to enter more heartily into the spirit of those meetings, than the President of the United States, who, he believed, had, with but two exceptions, attended every one of them while he was there. Sir William Gore Ouseley, the British Minister and his lady had also been regular in their attendance upon these morning gatherings for worship, and expressed their delight at this progress in the recognition of the claims of religion. Lady Ousely had said to him a day or two previous to his departure, that she had written to the Queen, giving her an account of these meetings at Bedford Springs. He had been interrogated once and again respecting the character and progress of the Jayne's Hall meetings, and none had been more minute and particular in these inquiries than the President. Rev. Dr. Nevins recounted what he had witnessed during the present season at Cape May, Pittsburgh, and other intermediate points, showing that the work was being carried forward by Christians wherever they had gone to spend the summer. A graphic picture was given by another speaker of the extraordinary work now in progress among the Philadelphia firemen, whose former history is anything but creditable to the city.—*New York Chronicle.*

SCOTLAND.—PUBLIC MEETINGS FOR PRAYER.—Meetings are now being organised almost simultaneously in Glasgow, Edinburgh, Dundee, Aberdeen, Inverness, and Liverpool. A feature of similarity in some of these meetings to those which are still taking place on the other side of the Atlantic is this, that they are not only held in the evening, but also in the busiest part of the day, between twelve and one o'clock. In Glasgow, meetings have taken place for a few weeks in Free Anderston Church on Tuesday evenings, and on Wednesdays at noon, which have been well attended. In the Religious Institution Rooms a meeting is held on the Friday evenings, and it is in contemplation to establish another meeting, in the same place, during business hours. The advocate of Protestantism in the eastern end of the city (the Rev. R. Gault), has also initiated the movement in that district, on Tuesday last, at noon, in Suffolk street Chapel, where it is to be continued. On Wednesday evenings a meeting is held in Free St. Mark's Church, in connection with the same movement. At Inverness a meeting takes place every morning at seven o'clock, and every evening at eight. A similar meeting is held in Aberdeen twice a day; and the Dundee Sunday School Teachers' Union have agreed to hold meetings every night, several of which have already taken place. In Liverpool a meeting for business men is held every Monday, Wednesday, and Friday, from half-past twelve till half-past one, p.m., under the auspices of the Young Men's Christian Association of that town.— *Witness.*

ENGLISH CONGREGATIONAL UNION.

Autumnal Session of the Congregational Union of England and Wales, held at Halifax, Yorkshire, in the week commencing on the 18th of October last.

On Monday evening, the 18th, a public devotional meeting was held in Harrison-road Chapel, when an address was delivered by the Rev. J. Kennedy, M.A., of Stepney. The subject was, Those passages of Scripture which describe the Saviour as praying. Similar devotional services were conducted by Dr. Alliott at Warley, Dr. Ferguson at Brighouse, and the Rev. J. C. Harrison at Sowerby Bridge.

On Tuesday morning the delegates assembled in considerable numbers at Harrison-road Chapel. A published list of the names showed that 360 gentlemen were receiving the hospitalities of the friends in Halifax;—Bradford, Huddersfield, Warley, Brighouse, Lightcliffe, and neighbouring villages, contributing their share of accommodation. The arrangements were excellent, the place of meeting most convenient, and the attendance of pastors and delegates was unusually punctual.

At ten o'clock the Rev. Dr. Alliott, the President of the Union, took the chair, and after a devotional exercise he read his address, which was listened to with profound attention. It occupied nearly an hour in delivery.

The subject of the address was the nature of a true revival; the uses and abuses, the dangers and benefits of those religious excitements which are known under that name. We hope to give some extracts from this admirable address in our next number, not having space in the present one.

On the conclusion of the address the Rev. E. Mellor, of Halifax, rose to ??? a resolution by which the assembly expressed its thanks to Dr Alliott, and req??? the document for publication. Mr. Mellor gave a hearty welcome in the ??? his brethren in Halifax to the Union, and said that it had been a ??? of ??? solicitude that a great blessing might result from the meetings, ??? blessing might be left in the town. There was no reason why ??? ???

men meeting together should not draw down from heaven a promised and an abundant blessing. With respect to the paper, he would say that he had never heard Dr. Alliott with more pleasure than while he read this paper, characterised by continuous thought and earnest feeling, rendering it, what all must admit it was—an exquisite production. There was great wisdom in the way in which difficult questions were handled, and he declared himself at a loss to know which most to admire, the judgment displayed in including, or the wisdom shown in omitting. There was no sentence to which he could not add his hearty amen, and he therefore cordially proposed the resolution.

Dr. Halley in a few words seconded it, and made a passing reference to Dr. Alliott's entrance into Homerton, and the promise he then gave of the possession of a metaphysical acumen and logical power of which they had had a display that day. He congratulated his friend upon the position he now occupied, so honourable to himself and so beneficial to the Churches. This motion was carried unanimously, and Dr. Alliott responded to the thanks, and handed his manuscript to the Secretary.

The Rev. George Smith stated that he had received a letter from the Rev. Dr. Legge, of Leicester, regretting that, as chairman elect for the year 1859, he was unable to be present at the meeting at Halifax.

The Rev. T. Rees, of Beaufort, presented to the assembly a most interesting paper on " The State of Congregationalism in Wales," which, in fact, was a history of Dissent in the principality, from the time of John Penry to the present period. This paper will be published in the " Year-book " for 1859.

Thomas Barnes, Esq., of Farnworth, proposed a resolution thanking Mr. Rees in the most emphatic terms for his admirable paper, and took up the question raised in it, of the necessities of the English population.

The Rev. A. Thomson, of Manchester, expressed a genuine interest in the good work going on in the Welsh Churches; and he felt that this clear, honest, and able statement deserved the careful attention of the assembly, and urged that the paper should be pondered well. He saw in it a triumphant answer to Lord Shaftesbury's argument in favour of what was called the " fixed " principle, and he wished that there was more of the freedom and fervour of the Welsh amongst English Churches.

Dr. Massie suggested that the paper should receive a fuller discussion, but it was thought better, on the whole, to adhere to the programme, and proceed at once to the consideration of the paper next on the list.

The subject of this paper was an " Aged Pastor's Fund ;" it was read by the Rev. Dr. Ferguson. This paper was prepared with great care, and was evidently the result of matured thought. It was received by the assembly with attention, and though many failed to concur in all its recommendations, the subject was felt to be of the highest importance. Its main feature was the proposal of a fund of £5000, to be raised for the purpose of granting annuities to aged ministers under certain conditions. It provided that all pastors should be entitled to obtain help, but that priority of claim should be given to such as had themselves subscribed through a period of years. It was thus thought that a way out of the ministry might be provided for such as desired, at an advanced age, to make an honourable retreat.

The Rev. Geo. Smith briefly explained the circumstances under which the movement had originated, and, to give rise to discussion, he moved that the paper be brought up for consideration. The Rev. Thomas James, of London, seconded the motion, and read an interesting letter from the Rev. John Angell James, of Birmingham, his brother, having reference to his offer, two years since, of a sum of money for the fund. Mr. James now amended his offer by adding to the testimonial raised by his people a sum of £500 of his own, and this sum of £1000 he had already put in trust for the purposes of the fund, provided that a further amount of £4000 should be raised within two years, making up the required £5000. If the offer was not met, he should appropriate the sum for the erection of a chapel near Birmingham.

A long discussion then ensued, in which the Revs. John Ashby, Dr. Hewlett, Dr. Massie, Thomas James, J. Kennedy, J. Davis, Dr. Halley, Messrs. Plint, Jupe, Rosely, and others took part, some approving of, and some objecting to Dr. Ferguson's plan. It was ultimately resolved, " That this assembly thankfully expresses its obligation to Dr. Ferguson for the attention he has bestowed on the subject of making suitable provision to aid our aged pastors in retiring from the full work of the ministry,—hereby records its deliberate opinion of the desirableness, alike for pastors and churches, of forming a fund for the accomplishment of this important object; and that it be referred to a sub-committee to nominate and bring up on Thursday morning the names of a special committee to form and mature a plan for such an institution, to be presented for adoption at the next annual meeting of the Congregational Union, and that the following gentlemen form the sub-committee:—Rev. Thomas Scales, Rev. J. Kennedy, T. Barnes, Esq., Rev. T. James, Mr. A. Morley, and the Secretaries."

The dinner took place in the school room of the Harrison-road Chapel, and was provided upon the most liberal scale.

The Rev. Dr. Alliott presided, supported by Mr. Hadfield, M.P.; Mr. Crossley, M.P.; Mr. Barnes, late M.P. for Bolton: J. Crossley, Esq.; S. Morley, Esq., and other gentlemen. More than 300 delegates sat down at the tables. After dinner, the Rev. John Ross made a statement respecting the scheme for a weekly offering.

The Union resumed its sittings on Wednesday, at ten o'clock. After the devotional services, the Rev. J. C. Harrison, of Camden Town, read a paper "On the best means of rightly influencing the religious condition of the people of our country." The paper, which was highly commended, is to be printed. A long discussion ensued, in which the Revs. W. Guest, Dr. Tidman, H. W. Parkinson, G. Richards, Dr. Massie, D. Fraser, D. G. Watt, E. Melor, W. Tyler, S. Clarkson, J. Parsons, J. Davis, Dr. Halley, Mr. Morley, and others took part. The topic most prominent in the discussion was the Sabbath afternoon lectures to the working classes, in public rooms of various kinds, a few of the speakers condemning some of the methods used to attract attention, and others vindicating them.

The following points were also submitted to the meeting for discussion by the Chairman:—Home evangelisation by county and other associations, and by individual churches; can any means be adopted to render our ordinary prayer meetings more attractive and efficient than they are? the propriety of noonday special meetings for prayer; the duties of Church members to each other, and to the members of our congregations; the best method of treating religious inquirers; admission and transference of members; modes of conducting church meetings; the duties of pastors to the baptized children of the congregation; importance of pastoral visitation; the power of the pulpit.

The Rev. Mr. Poore directed attention to the transference of Church members, especially those who were emigrating, so that they could be received into the Colonial Churches on their arrival, and spoke of the necessity of not suffering their young members, especially their young women, to leave the country except under proper care, as they would be subjected during the voyage to various temptations.

The Rev. G. Smith then read an extract from a letter from the Rev. J. S. Clark, of Boston, in which he spoke of the religious revival in America as continuing in many parts unabated. The writer also stated that the number of apostates was comparatively small.

On Wednesday afternoon Messrs. Crossley kindly threw open their works to the inspection of the delegates, and more than 200 of them availed themselves of the courtesy. Mr. Titus Salt also obligingly allowed his extensive works to be seen by many visitors.

The last of the sittings of the Union was held on Thursday, 21st.

A quantity of miscellaneous business was transacted, and the Rev. Dr. Halley read a paper on "Oliver Heywood, or Early Nonconformists in the Border Counties of Lancashire and Yorkshire," a paper full of interesting facts. It will doubtless be published.

On Friday morning a large number took breakfast together, in connexion with the Congregational Board of Education. The attendance at the meetings increased rather than diminished as the week advanced, and the interest was sustained to the last.

An evening meeting was held in Zion Chapel on Tuesday, in favor of denominational evangelistic efforts. Samuel Morley, Esq., in the chair; and addresses were delivered on behalf of the Home Missionary Society, by Dr. Massie; of the Irish Evangelical Society, by the Rev. R. Sewell of Londonderry; and of the Colonial Missionary Society, by the Rev. J. L. Poore, from Australia. The meeting was also addressed by the Rev. A. Thomson, of Manchester, and the Revs. J. W. Richardson and G. Smith, of London.

From those who were present at this eighteenth autumnal Session of the Union we learn, that the spirit of cheerful kindness which existed among the assembled brethren, the unbounded hospitality of the Halifax friends, the absence of all controversy, the serious earnestness with which all parties addressed themselves to the grave and important subjects brought under their notice, the determination to do good, and if possible to do good, manifested in the various speeches, and the rior character of the papers read, all conspired to render the gathering one of the most interesting and useful assemblies which the Union has ever known.

NEW SOUTH WALES.—Congregational Home Missionary Society.—The eighth annual meeting of this society was held on Monday, Nov. 1, in Pitt street Congregational Church, the Rev. Dr. Ross in the chair. Prayer having been offered by the Rev. Mr. Buzacott, the Rev. S. C. Kent, Secretary, read the Report, from which we make the following extracts :—

" When we remember the comparatively short period during which the society has existed, and the number of agents now employed under its direction, and partially sustained by its funds, notwithstanding some drawbacks and discouragements, we cannot but feel that we have much to be grateful for, and that it becomes us to ' thank God and take courage.'

" Through the instrumentality which this society has called into operation, ' the glorious Gospel of the blessed God' is faithfully proclaimed, and the distinctive principles of our church polity, as they are understood, secure approval, and are producing a beneficial influence not only within, but beyond the circle in which the agents are located.

" All who were present at our last annual meeting will remember the gloom which was thrown over the service, and the excitement and sorrow occasioned by the announcement of the shipwreck and death of the Rev. Jacob Jones, late of Melksham, Wilts, who had been designated by the Colonial Missionary Society of London to labor in this colony in connexion with this society.

" On the 29th of August the Rev. Thomas Arnold, late of Smethwick, near Birmingham, arrived in this city, and, after having been introduced to your committee by his old friend and neighbour, the Rev. William Cuthbertson, entered upon his labours at Balmain, with very encouraging prospects of success. Our valued friends, the Rev. Thomas James and Mr. G. A. Lloyd, have laid us under increased obligations for the part they have taken in securing his services.

" Your Committee have also to report the arrival of the Rev. George Wight, late of Portobello, near Edinburgh, by the *Star of Peace*, on the 4th February last. Mr. Wight, after spending some months in this city, during which time he supplied the pulpit at Balmain or the pulpits of those ministers who assisted in conducting the services there, proceeded to Brisbane, in which town he was selected by the Rev. J. L. Poore to commence an interest. Mr. Wight entered upon his labors in Brisbane on the 16th of May, and for a while preached in the National School-room. He has since removed to the School of Arts, a building much better adapted for public worship than the one which he at first occupied. He has succeeded in gathering around him a considerable congregation, and there is every prospect of establishing, by divine aid, a permanent and flourishing cause. Upwards of a hundred sittings have been let in the present place of meeting, and a fund has been commenced to aid in the erection of a Congregational church.

" In reporting the arrivals from England, we have to mention the visit of the Rev. Thomas Binney, one of the fathers and founders of the Colonial Missionary Society—a visit which has already been productive of the most beneficial results, and has afforded pleasure and profit to thousands of our fellow-citizens and colonists. While deeply regretting the illness which rendered rest and change necessary, we cannot but rejoice that we have been favored with his presence, and that our Heavenly Father has been pleased so far to restore his health as to enable him to render signal service to our denomination, and to the cause of Christ generally, in the colonies through which he is now making the tour.

" Mr. Binney arrived in this colony in April, and, although at times suffering much generously devoted himself to the service of your society. Special sermons were preached by him on its behalf in the Pitt street and Redfern churches, after which liberal collections were taken. Services were also held by him at Balmain, Surry-Hills, and Newtown. At the latter place Mr. Binney laid the first stone of an addition to the church recently erected there.

" Mr. Binney, wishing thoroughly to acquaint himself with the state of our missions, did not confine his labors to this city and its suburbs, but visited Newcastle, Maitland, Brisbane, and Ipswich, all of which places enjoyed the advantage of his labors. In addition to the encouragement afforded to the brethren occupying these stations, and the intellectual and spiritual good derived by the people of their charge, the pecuniary benefit resulting must be taken into account. £120 was collected in these four places for purposes connected with their local operations.

" In proceeding to notice the several stations occupied by your agents, it is scarcely necessary to dwell at any length upon those which are in your own immediate neighbourhood.

" The Rev. W. Slayter continues to labor at Surry Hills, and the Rev. G. Charter, reports encouragingly of his success at Wollongong. A large congregation has there been gathered, a flourishing Sunday school is efficiently instructed, and services are regularly conducted in neighboring places The debt upon the church has been nearly if not altogether liquidated ; and those members of your committee, who have visited this station, speak most highly of the praiseworthy exertions of your agent.

" Since your last annual meeting, a new and spacious Gothic church has been opened at West Maitland. The opening services were conducted by the Rev. Messrs. Cuthbertson and Kent. The debt remaining upon the building is comparatively small, and its central position and comfortable accommodation, connected with the zealous efforts of the Rev. E. Griffith, have done much to increase the congregation. Mr. Griffith writes—' The progress at Maitland is, I hope, certain. I cannot tell of rapid advance, but there is real ground of hope, that, though not immediately, by and by there will be a good cause here, and your society will not have to look with regret on what has been done for this locality. In taking up Maitland, the committee were acting under the direction of an all-wise and over-ruling Providence. This the future will reveal.'

"The Rev. J. Gibson has vacated the church at Newcastle, and is about. independently of this society, to establish himself at Campbelltown. The pulpit at Newcastle has been lately occupied by the Rev. A. Buzacott and Mr. J. Halley; and your committee are not without a hope that a permanent arrangement for its regular supply may speedily be made.

"The Rev. J. T. Waraker is laboring at Ipswich with acceptance and success. In addition to the central church there are six stations at present occupied, viz., Little Ipswich, North Ipswich, Bremer Saw Mills, Moggil, Drayton. and Warwick. At all of these Sunday schools have been established, and religious services are regularly held. At the Bremer Saw Mills, a chapel capable of holding 120 persons has been built, on ground presented for this purpose by T. Fleming, Esq.

"Your committee have to report that they have expended some portion of their funds in sustaining Mr. J. Halley as a university student, with a view to his entering upon the Christian ministry, in return for which he has given his services on the Sabbath. He has conducted services at Waterloo, Petersham, Campbelltown, aud in other places; but his chief attention has been given to Woolloomooloo, where two services have been held on the Sabbath and a Sunday school gathered.

"Your Committee feel that they ought not to conclude this report without referring to the place of worship which has recently been built on the Waterloo Estate, through the zealous exertions of the Rev. J. Beazley and his friends. They would also mention that a church is now in course of erection at Paddington, upon land generously granted by the Honorable Sir D. Cooper. Special thanks are due to the Revs. Dr. Ross and J. West, for their exertions in connection with this building. In March last Mr. Rees, the then treasurer of this society, was compelled, through personal and relative affliction, to return to Europe in search of health. It was with deep regret your committee received his resignation.

"We have thus briefly noticed the several events of the year. Something has been done, but much remains to be done. Efficiently to carry on our work it is imperatively necessary that our income should be greatly enlarged, as it is not now sufficient to meet our existing liabilities. We sometimes tremble for the stability of what has already been done, and cannot multiply our agents and stations unless we can first increase the number of our subscribers and the amount of our contributions.

" But we must not forget that even had we all the funds we could desire, and suitable agents to propagate the Gospel, without God's aid we could not hope for success. However complete the machinery, the hand of God is needed to move it. The sacrifice may be provided, but the fire to kindle it must come from heaven. Let us pray, then, as Elijah did (for he was a man of like passions with ourselves), and the sacred element will descend, the sacrifice be accepted, and the people falling down upon their faces will acknowledge—The Lord, he is the God—The Lord he is the God.' "

Mr. FAIRFAX, the treasurer, then submitted the financial statement. The receipts for the year, including balance in hand at the beginning, were £1466 2s. 4d.; and the expenditure £1588 3s., showing the overdrawn account to be £122 0s. 8d. The contributions for the year showed a falling off; and the grants to the ministerial agents had, consequently, been slightly reduced for the coming year. £300 had been remitted to the English Colonial Missionary Society, to assist in paying the passages and outfits of three ministers. Upon the whole, it was expected that the financial account of the year upon which the society is now entering would be augmented by additional subscriptions.

SOUTH SEA MISSION.

Extract of a letter from the Rev. J. Inglis, Aheiteum, to the Rev. Dr. Ross, Sydney, dated 31st July, 1858.

"*Mana,* the Erromanga native who was for several years at Samoa, and who has been with Mr. Gordon since his settlement at Dillon's Bay, was baptised, and sat down at the table of the Lord last sabbath. He is the first native of Erromanga, so far as I know, who has made a public profession of his faith in Jesus. May the little one soon become a thousand!"

Extract of a letter from the Rev. George W. Gordon, a Missionry at Erromanga, to S. Thompson, Esq., of Sydney, dated 14th September, 1858.

"In November we found it would be unsafe for Mrs. G. to remain in the valley at this place, and I built a house for her benefit on a high mountain, and had to pay for, and cut a road to it, which I did at the cost of many a hard day's labor; but the result amply repaid the toil, for under God, I think it was the means of saving her life. We then tried another place, midway between the valley and the mountain, where I built a school-house, but the chief opposed all (from another tribe, to which he did not belong) coming to this place and did not wish the young men of my school to sit in one house with the women, and his wives from attending to the word. We, about this time, found it necessary to make some preparation for building another schoolhouse on the opposite side of the river, where I had previously secured a small piece of land from the murderers of Williams nd Harris; and I subsequently purchased, or got granted from the same party, the land which they had not sold, although others had sold for them. I am now preaching at this side of the river on sabbaths, and Mrs. G. has succeeded here, after 14 months almost fruitless efforts, and has now a small class of women from the tribe attending to daily instruction. I got recently the murderers of Williams and Harris to show me where their bodies were cooked, and can hardly describe my feelings as I followed them to these mournful spots where the stones of the oven on which the bodies of God's slaughtered saints were laid, are still to be found. I took away some bones of the human skeleton. The head of Mr. Williams was buried under a tree, and his watch hidden near the same place; but it is exceedingly difficult to get the guilty parties to search for these things, without whom all search must probably be fruitless; they have a superstitious dread of going to search after the watch, because they regard it as a god; it however, may have been destroyed. I expect now to be able to make another diligent search after these things, meanwhile I am endeavoring to allay their fears. I preached last Lord's Day, what I regard as my first sermon on Erromanga, from these words, "Father forgive them for they know not what they do;" and had my heart filled with solemn thoughts as I looked on two of the murderers and the memorable spot where these horrible deeds were perpetrated by them. One of the murderers would not come to the sermon; two were present, and I think lasting good will be the result.

Now, contrary to our first expectations, God is granting us, I may say, our *first* opening on Erromanga among the murderers of the saints of God who fell there, and seems to be making some use of this sad circumstance for the furtherance of the Gospel—for the heathen say, if we can forgive them, it must be a strange thing—there is truth in the Gospel. Blessed be the holy name of God for this good result of the death of his servants.

P.S. I herewith send you two Erromangan idols, begging that Dr. Ross will accept one from his obliged friend, and send the other to the Mission House, Blomfield-street, London, to the care of the Rev. W. Harbutt, who has written for one. Please to tell the Dr. that these idols are taken from the spot where Williams was killed, or near to it, and the cocoa nuts were left on the trees which spread their branches over them, none daring to touch them. They are the only idols I have found standing erect with one end on the ground."

ISLAND OF AITUTAKI, HERVEY GROUP, SOUTH SEAS.

The following testimony to the efficiency of missionary labors among the South Sea Islanders, from Captain Harvey, of H.B.M. frigate *Havannah*, is extracted from *The Book and its Missions*, and is published in *The Missionary Chronicle* for September. The editor has a personal gratification in introducing it into the *Southern Spectator*, as the excellent missionary and his wife, Mr. and Mrs. Royle, were members of his church in Manchester, and were recommended by himself as suitable laborers for the mission field. Independently of this, the testimony itself is one of the most valuable that has ever been furnished by an impartial witness to Missionary labors.   R. F.

TO THE EDITOR OF "THE BOOK AND ITS MISSION."

"My dear Friend,—The great progress of Christianity in the South Seas has been disputed by many, doubted by some, and scoffed at by others. Perhaps the following statement, forwarded to the British Admiralty by Captain Harvey, of Her Majesty's frigate, the *Havannah*, may be believed by those who have hitherto put no trust in mere "missionary records," because they have not considered them impartial. On my way to Peru, I had recently the pleasure of dining with Captain Harvey, on board his own ship, in the bay of Panama, and from his rough notes I copied the following, which I am able now, with his permission, to present to your readers. I am, &c.   A. J. DUFFIELD,
Agent of the British and Foreign Bible Society for South America."

CAPTAIN HARVEY AT AITUTAKI.

"At 10.30 a.m. on Friday, the 20th February, made the Island of Aitutaki, distant about twenty miles, bearing S.S.E. It first showed as two hummocks. On approaching, it assumed a very pleasing appearance, from the undulating nature of its formation, and the tropical luxuriance of the vegetation. It was well wooded, and apparently with fine trees. The eastern end of the island ran off into a long low spit; near the centre, on the north side, was a round hill of some elevation, having two cocoa-nut trees on its summit; to the westward of this were several smaller rounded hillocks, one showing a bold front of dark stone. From the eastern spit, spreads a broad beach of white sand; and off the western end is a detached island covered with trees: the sea breaks the whole way An American whaling ship was observed standing off east. When we were about five miles off the land, a whaleboat, with a native crew, came alongside, having presents of oranges and pine-apples. Two of them spoke English tolerably well, and informed us that the whaler, the *Alarm*, had communicated with them, but that no one had landed; that there was an English missionary at the place, and that they all much wished us to go on shore. One of the natives, who styled himself

D

"Times" offered to pilot a cutter, and, accompanied by half a dozen men and officers, we put ourselves under the guidance of "Times." The entrance to the lagoon through the coral-reef was marked by a staff with a flag on it. There is a coral-stone jetty built out from the beach, between two and three hundred yards in length; it was covered with natives waiting to receive us. The scene that presented itself on entering the lagoon was beautiful beyond any powers of description; the deep shaded and magnificent foliage—the rich, variegated tints of the deeply-wooded shore—the dazzling white of the sandy beach—the light and beautiful blue of the shallow water of the lagoon in contrast with the darker color of the deeper sea outside, with a clear, bright sky overhead, formed a picture only to be realised in the torrid zones. Add to all this the sincere welcome offered to us by hundreds of the islanders assembled for the purpose, and you may possibly imagine something like the pleasurable excitement experienced on the occasion.

"My first object was to visit the missionary, whose residence we found on the hill side at about an elevation of two hundred feet—so steep, that a rough stone staircase had been constructed to make the approach easy. At the foot of this, on the right hand, in a most picturesque clearance, stood two substantially built, commodious buildings—the church and school-house. On either side, going up, the flowers, shrubs, and trees formed a pleasing approach to the house of the missionary. We found the Rev. Henry Royle prepared to receive our visit, and Mrs. Royle was making her welcome ready in the shape of the various refreshments their establishment could afford.

"I found they had resided in the island between eighteen and nineteen years. They have a family of six daughters, the two eldest at present being in England for education. On first landing, their settlement was opposed by a vast majority of the natives, who twice burnt them out of their houses, as they also did a friendly chief, who protected them to the utmost of his power. After great difficulties, much privation and self-denial, by perseverance they have succeeded, inasmuch as at the present day there is not a man, woman, or child, that would not sacrifice everything for them.

"These islanders do not touch fermented liquor, and but few use tobacco in any shape. The greater portion can both read and write. They are all respectably clothed. Their houses are built of coral stone, with high and well-thatched roofs, having a considerable air of comfort in their interior arrangements. They possess nine whaleboats, some of which were presents to them from American whale ships. Mr. and Mrs. Royle spoke very highly of these people. They provide everything in their power towards making them comfortable, and frequently Mr Royle stated, that tea, sugar, coffee, &c., were found in his verandah, which these kind fellows had obtained from the captains of the ships in exchange for their labor or goods, expressly for the missionary. They also met annually to subscribe towards their domestic and foreign missions, and did so most liberally.

"There are six cows on the island. Cattle are not permitted to increase beyond twelve. On reaching that number they kill them, and divide the flesh among the inhabitants. Pigs, fowls, muscovy ducks, plantains, sweet potatoes, yams, a kind of bran, bread fruit, oranges, pine-apples, and many other fruits and vegetables, are to be had in great quantity. Cocoa-nut oil is made, and, I understand, in tolerable quantity at a reasonable price. I asked Mr. and Mrs. Royle, if seeing the American captains and crews using tobacco and spirits, did not cause some difficulty in persuading the people to abstain from them? They replied they thought not, and spoke very highly of the considerate and kind behaviour of the whaling captains who have visited them. Some seventy ships recruit wood and water annually at this island, and about a hundred vessels call for the same purpose at the larger islands. The value of money is well understood, although much is done by exchange for cloths, linen, stuffs, &c. Captain Whynger, of the Illinois whaler, of New Bedford, who was obtaining his supplies for a passage home, told me it was exceedingly economical to recruit at these islands. There is a schooner belonging to the island, which trades between them, and has been once to Tahiti. The John Williams, a barque belonging to the missions, was daily expected, having left England in July last, on her round, viâ the Cape of Good Hope, in which colony they have an establishment. Beyond that periodical visit, they seldom or never see other than American ships. Let me add, that fourteen hundred of these islanders subscribed 300 dollars towards the Sailor's Home at Honolulu.

"On going down, for the purpose of embarking, I found a large assemblage of the natives, and before a house or shed sat the great men of the island to receive me. The son of the oldest man present, who spoke English better than any other native that I had heard, interpreted. He said they had come together to express their pleasure at seeing 'English man-of-war' captain. That they had never before been so visited; and the fruits, vegetables, tapa, &c., &c., piled in heaps on either side in front, they gave to me. I thanked them very much for their generosity and kindness, and said that I was not prepared for visiting them, that I had no presents to offer in exchange, and that my boats could not carry so great a quantity of these good things. The interpreter replied, 'They make free present—no exchange—no want anything but you, captain, to take all, and ask for anything the island affords, and it is freely at your service—and our own boats shall take everything on board." I then expressed my sorrow that my visit was so necessarily short, and asked if any would now come off to see the ship for the little time I could give them. Ten or eleven said, "Yes;" the old man and his son accompanied me. Four whaleboats, deeply laden with fruits, started, taking the cutter in tow. On board they expressed great delight at everything they saw; refused spirits, wine, or beer, but enjoyed a cup of tea in my cabin; and although the roughest of the rough in costume, they behaved like gentlemen; the men (about eighty) were all over the ship, and not a single thing of any sort was missed. Their common exclamation was, "English, we all English!" As they had shown great wonder at a 56 lb. shot, I told them I would send them one on shore after they had left the ship, but they preferred having it fired off at once. On bidding them good-bye they shook hands with their heads uncovered, several of the older chiefs kissing my hand as they did so.

"I was utterly unprepared for meeting such a civilised, hospitable people, and sincerely regretted not having the means for making them some return for the generous welcome offered to Her Majesty's ship."

———◆———

CHURCH UNION.

Under this head we continued last month the Adelaide correspondence which we commenced inserting the month before. We expressed a hope of being able to give, in the present number, the concluding letter of Mr. Binney, alluded to in the one we then published. Circumstances, however, prevent our doing this. So many things have been demanding our friend's time and attention, in connexion with his visit to us, that he has had no opportunity of preparing what he may deem it necessary to write. As, however, the Bishop of Adelaide has replied to Mr. Binney's Letter, we continue the correspondence by giving insertion to that reply. His Lordship appended to his own letter, in the Adelaide papers, from which we take it, a short private note of Mr. Binney's, which will be found below, and which may require a word of explanation from us. To save himself the trouble of re-writing his letter, Mr. Binney put it into type for the *Spectator* before sending it to the Bishop; but, that his Lordship might receive it before publication, it was sent to him as soon as a copy could be obtained.* Two or three other copies were sent to private friends, with directions to insert it or not in the Adelaide

---

* The printed slip containing the letter was forwarded with the following note, which we are permitted to publish:—

Government House, Toorak,
December 23, 1858.

My Lord.—It would have cost a great deal of trouble to have gone through the form of transcribing the enclosed letter, for the sake of sending it with the intimation that it would be sent to the printer—or before the public—the next day. I should gladly have done this, however, had it been possible, as your lordship was so good as to send the letter to which it is a reply to Mr. Stow's residence, on the evening before its publication.

It was my full intention to have written just one word of *acknowledgment* the next morning before leaving Adelaide, but that was utterly out of my power. As the editor of the *Southern Spectator*, a Magazine connected with the Congregational Churches of Australia, is preserving the more important letters of the Adelaide correspondence in that work, I thought it best to save my hand the labor of transcribing a long letter, and your lordship's eyes (though younger than mine) from having to decipher writing not very clear at the best. I feel sure of your lordship's forgiveness for thus sending you a printed epistle instead of a written one.

I do not see the Adelaide papers now, with any regularity, and know not whether the whole matter may not, by this time, be at an end, so far as they are concerned. I am quite sure that so far as a sincere regard to the interests of truth and love has influenced those who have taken part on either side, it is *not* ended, for good must come, by God's blessing, some time or other, from anything that springs from such a motive, though it may take a shape unexpected by *all* concerned. I shall hope to publish my second (and last) letter, in the Number of the Spectator for February, though I may be disappointed, as I have been very unwell this week. I shall send a copy or two of my present letter to Adelaide, but I am not anxious about its publication in the papers. They may do as they think best.

With earnest prayers for every blessing and all holy influences to be yours, personally and officially.

I am, my lord,
Your lordship's friend and servant,

T. B.

To the Right Reverend the Lord Bishop of Adelaide.

P.S. By "sending a copy or two of the enclosed letter to Adelaide," I do not mean sending to the newspapers; I do not know the state of the question in South Australia now, so as to judge how far it would be wise to recall it to public attention *in that way*. I shall send a copy or two to personal friends, whose action in the matter will be guided by their knowledge of local circumstances.

T. B

papers, as circumstances might determine. It was after these copies were posted that, in finally revising the proof, Mr. B. expunged the sentence referred to,—*which sentence therefore does not appear in his letter as printed in the " Spectator " last month.* He felt it right, on making the alteration, to inform the Bishop of it, and also to try to get it made in the Adelaide edition of his letter, should there be one. In the latter point he was unsuccessful. The Bishop, however, caused Mr. B.'s notification to him of the change to be inserted in the Adelaide papers, by giving the letter in which it was contained, as will be seen below. His Lordship also, in transmitting to Mr. B. a copy of his reply, sent an acknowledgment of the note in question, which we have had the pleasure of perusing, and which we have begged Mr. Binney's permission to print. We feel that if the Bishop thought he took a liberty in publishing Mr. B.'s letter, we are taking a much greater, in assuming the responsibility of publishing his. But we do so on a principle which will fully justify us. Religious controversy is so often disfigured by wrath and rancour, that it is most refreshing to see how it can be conducted after another fashion. It is suggestive and edifying too, to see how two men, though they publicly differ, and have publicly to state and maintain their opposite opinions, and while doing so, firmly and strongly. because as public advocates of their respective views they *must*, they can yet, privately, as Christians and gentlemen, indulge in feelings and expressions of mutual respect and regard. We deem the picture too good to be lost—too beautiful to be hidden,—and trust that our friends (we hope we may use the plural) will not only forgive our putting it forward. but will pardon the words with which we thus accompany it.

No. X.

The Right Reverend the Bishop of Adelaide to the Reverend Thomas Binney.

Dear and Reverend Sir.—When men differ in religion or politics the sooner they get to understand the principle or supposed principle which divides them the sooner are they likely either to agree or differ irreconcilably. So far, therefore, from being " offended by the observations " which you have made on my second letter, I am thankful to learn from so competent an authority " the modes of thought and feeling prevalent in the non-Episcopal denominations ; " and " the way in which they look at certain ecclesiastical subjects."

In England it always seemed to me impossible to disengage those subjects from the surrounding medium ; to separate them from extraneous matter. so as to look at them simply in the light of God's Word interpreted by spiritual understanding. In this colony, on the contrary, where the great offence to your co-religionists of a State Church does not exist, I thought religious questions, and among them that of Church Union, might be approached from *all* sides clear of that " mirage " which deceives the explorer by exaggerating or distorting objects. Nevertheless I have observed from time to time invidious references made to past abuses or present difficulties of the National Established Church of England, as if they were of the essence of Episcopal discipline, and not the accidents of an establishment interwoven with the State for more than one thousand years ; while, on the other hand, the isolation of our clergy from non-Episcopalian ministers, not so much personally as *ministerially*, has not been referred (as you *now* truly do) to its real cause, viz., their *conscientious* holding fast that which they believe to have apostolic and scriptural authority, but to the mere pride of social position, or the domineering spirit of a State-favored Church, or a Baronial Episcopate.

Had it been all along seen, as *you now* clearly see, that we *cannot* recognise your orders (though we do not take upon ourselves to reject as *ineffectuous* your ministerial acts of baptising in the name of the Father, Son, and Holy Ghost), I should not have been asked, as I have frequently been, to admit non-Episcopalian ministers to officiate in our churches, burial-grounds, school-rooms, and to co-operate with them in works essential to the prophetical office of the ministry, such as distribution of religious tracts, missions to the bush, Sunday-school teachers' union, and lately to open *our* pulpits *unconditionally* for their use. The rule, however, on which we act has been plainly laid down for us. We do not *forbid* non-Episcopalian ministers " to cast out devils " by preaching Christ's name and Gospel, *because they follow not us;* but neither on the other hand, do *we* find any warrant for " following " them.

Compelled, then, from time to time to refuse such applications, I was not sorry to seize the opportunity presented by your arrival in South Australia of making it quite *clear* " *why,*" and " *why only,*" we hold ourselves *ministerially* aloof from non-Episcopalian ministers, though as with myself, so with my brethren, our *private* and *personal* " feelings often kick against" our solemn convictions and pledges. I would simply ask you to read the following extracts from the Preface to our Ordination Service, and the twenty-third Article, in order to judge fairly of our position :—

" It is evident unto all men diligently reading the Holy Scripture and ancient authors that from the *Apostles' time* there have been these orders of ministers in Christ's Church—bishops, priests, and deacons; which offices were evermore had in such reverend estimation, that *no man might presume* to execute any of them except he were first called, tried, examined, and known to have such qualities as are requisite for the same; and also by public prayer, with imposition of hands, were approved and admitted thereunto by lawful authority. And, therefore, *to the intent that these* orders *may be continued*, and reverently used and esteemed *in the United Church of England and Ireland*, no man shall be accounted or taken to be a lawful bishop, priest, or deacon in the United Church of England and Ireland, or *suffered to execute* any of the said functions, except he be called, tried, examined, and admitted thereunto according to the form hereafter following, or *hath had* formerly Episcopal consecration or ordination."

Article XXIII.—Of Ministering in the Congregation.

" It is not lawful for any man to take upon him the office of public preaching, or ministering the sacraments in the congregation, before he be lawfully called and sent to execute the same; and those we ought to judge lawfully called and sent which be chosen and called to this work by men who have public authority given unto them in the congregation to call and send ministers into the Lord's vineyard."

As a matter of history, it stands recorded that Whittingham was deprived in 1579 of the deanery of Durham, and Travers of the lectureship of the Temple, because they had received only Presbyterian ordination at the hands of certain ministers on the continent of Europe.

Could I then, as an *honest* man, invite you to preach in our pulpits? But as I *could not do so*, I felt " pressed in spirit " to show you how I, and multitudes of others in the Church of England, valued piety, eloquence, and ability in non-Episcopalian ministers; and how much we wished that *they* would *reconsider* those points of discipline which *they* number with " *things indifferent*," but which *we* are *bound in conscience* to hold fast as being of apostolic origin and possessing scriptural authority. Neither Lutherans, nor Calvinists, nor Wesleyans, nor even " independent " Independents, like yourself, assert Episcopacy or Creeds to be unscriptural or *unlawful*, though they maintain that they are " *not of obligation*." Non-Episcopalians then would violate no rule of conscience by adopting either one or the other; *either* a freely-elected Episcopate in its primitive form, or a form of sound words, whereby " *the sunk fence* " of which you speak, between the Episcopal and more recent Denominational Presbyterian Churches, would so far be filled up and disappear

If it savours of " assumed superiority " on my part in venturing to point out for consideration this condition of union, it is a superiority *forced* upon me, and not of my creating —emanating from former acts of non-Episcopalian bodies. I cannot reverse the history of the Church for eighteen centuries; but I neither " dictated " nor " offered " terms of union; I simply stated what we believe to be our " scriptural and apostolic " rule; and asked non-Episcopalian ministers, in these days of free thought and " independent " Independency, to consider whether future union of " evangelical Churches " on certain principles were possible.

I am not sorry that some few eager spirits, who attempted to clear the " sunk fence " at a bound, should have stumbled and fallen therein; or, to adopt your military metaphor, they have not blown in the counterscarp of the ditch, and planted their banners on the breach of a ruined Episcopacy. That fortress we cannot abandon, because we believe its bulwarks to be of apostolic origin and to have the sanction of Scripture. And if our non-Episcopalian friends cannot join it and form part of the garrison, let them believe and give us credit for acting " conscientiously " in maintaining our ministerial reserve. Let them cease to talk of " dominant Church," " intolerant hierarchy," &c., as the cause of disunion. We have as much right to *remain* Episcopalians as they had to become non-Episcopalians. The foxes in the fable were justified in declining to reform themselves by a " fraternal curtailment."

Nor was it merely with a view to remove " the midwall of partition " between the Church of England and those bodies which have dissented from it that I thought the readoption of the Episcopate an indispensable preliminary to Church Union. If oneness, outward as well as inward, formal as well as spiritual, be the *normal* state of Christ's Church militant as well as triumphant; if we may hope " the Gospel and true Church of God " will finally emerge from Tridentine, Mediæval, or Patristic error, then the " idiosyncrasy " also of the Eastern and Greek mind, as well as of Southern Christian Europe, must be taken into some account; and it certainly would be a greater " miracle " to reform those Churches—Greek, Roman, Syrian, Russian—*down* to the *platform* of John Knox—than that you and other evangelical ministers should be willing to sit side by side with Bishops in some Council like that of Jerusalem, when Paul and Barnabas and Simon Peter, with James presiding, gave forth the decree assented to by the elders and the brethren, condemnatory of a Judaising Christianity. Whether a more extended " fraternization " might not thus result, not only between the clergy of our Church and non-Episcopalian Dissenting ministers, but Lutheran, Swiss, and French divines; whether an *unscriptural* " denominationalism "—" I am of Paul, and I of Apollos, and I of Cephas "—would not thus help to fill up the " sunk fence " between us, and under access to a church catholic *in form* as well as *spirit* easy on *all* sides; whether Heathen ... Antichrists, or those within the Church itself, viz., the unbelief which denies ... bought us—the Father and the Son; or that which exalts the creature—sacra... saint; so as to keep less in view the Saviour himself (a *will-worship* which ...) whether, I say, such enemies of God and Christ will give way *more readily* ... rendered possible by the spirit of love leading us " to walk by the same rule, and in honour to prefer one another," I do not presume to decide. I have simply proposed the question for consideration.

But I am reminded by you that something more than identity of church government, or subscription to the orthodox creed, would be necessary to open your pulpits to the Anglican clergy. I return then to this second preliminary condition, viz., subscription to a creed, which you pronounce to be ineffectual to procure doctrinal purity in pulpit ministrations. You describe some clergymen of our Church as Roman in all but name, and others as Rationalists. neither of whom on any account would you suffer to preach in your pulpit. Neither would I suffer them to preach in mine.

But I proposed nothing of the sort. That preliminary condition of subscription to a creed might remove an existing barrier, but would *compel* no exchange of pulpits. Liberty might have been gained, but no compulsion introduced. Certain conditions being presupposed, it seemed possible that like Peter Martyr and Bucer in the 16th century, so in these days, D'Aubigne or Neander, Chalmers, Cumming, or yourself, might be heard (perhaps to advantage) in St. Paul's or Westminster Abbey—a position for Christian influence which the pastor of the Weigh House might not altogether despise, though he might think it beneath him to covet.

From the fact, however, that in spite of our Articles there are Romanizing and Rationalist clergymen in our Church, you draw the conclusion that formularies of the faith are useless. You also state, as a matter of fact, that the exchange of pulpits between non-Episcopalian ministers, Congregationalists, Wesleyan, Free Kirk, and Baptist is far more carefully guarded than is access to those of our Church. Now is it not owing in great measure to the Thirty-nine Articles themselves that these Romanizing and Rationalizing clergymen are *tested and found out*? Your argument, from the abuse of creeds, *proves too much*; for there *are* Unitarians and papists, despite of the authorised version of the Scriptures and the Latin Vulgate, which led Luther to justification by faith.

If creeds and articles cannot prevent error, neither can the Scriptures! Are the latter, therefore, needless and useless? "The unlearned and unstable wrest St. Paul's Epistles and other Scriptures to their destruction." I do not know that the blame rests with St. Paul for writing his letters to the churches!

Besides, who commanded the Baptismal creed—belief in the name of the Father, Son, and Holy Ghost, as necessary to salvation? "He that *believeth* and is baptized shall be saved!" Who required belief in *himself* as the *Son of God* before the Eunuch could be baptized? *Why* did St. Paul deliver *first* of all to the Corinthians that which he also had received, that "Christ died for our sins according to the Scriptures; that he was buried and rose again according to the Scriptures?" Why did he tell Timothy to "hold fast the form of sound words;" and "to commit the same to faithful men who should be able to teach others?"

Look to the history of Protestanism itself! What Protestant Church did not, at the Reformation, put forth its Confession? Is that of Augsburg a dead letter? Not *until* the Helvetic Confession of Calvin's Church had been *abrogated* by the Rationalistic Government of Geneva as a test for its State Clergy did a new *evangelical* reformation, inaugurated by D'Aubigne and Malan, become seasonable there. Let me further ask what has become of the orthodoxy of the old Presbyterian Churches in England? What is the faith of the Presbyterian Synod of Antrim? Was it not from the absence of a creed that the Lady Hewly Charity came to be dragged into a court of law? Did the absence of articles prevent the "Rivulet" controversy, and preserve the fountain of Gospel truth pure and undefiled? Not long ago I had the pleasure of receiving from you a sermon, entitled "The Apostles' Creed." Now, if the Apostles had a creed, that is, certain truths indispensable to the Gospel of Salvation, and if you have endeavoured to define those truths, surely a *creed* in itself is neither useless nor needless, "yourself being judge." I might refer also to your friends, the Wesleyans, whom you once offended, by plainly telling them "that they must be either Dissenters or Schismatics;" yet *they* have a *creed* and a tolerably long one too—one also of purely uninspired composition, which nevertheless you yourself have morally subscribed before you preached in their chapel! I know not whether you are an Arminian or Calvinist, or neither. But every Wesleyan minister is bound by Wesley's model trust deed to preach no "doctrine or practice contrary to what is contained in certain notes on the New Testament, commonly reputed to be the notes of the said John Wesley, and in the first four volumes of sermons, commonly reputed to be written and published by him." Talk of Popery and the Council of Trent, and of the infallibility of the Pope! those are "motes" not more huge than this Wesleyan beam.

I did not ask you or other non-Episcopalian ministers, to subscribe to the *Thirty-nine Articles and the Book of Homilies* before you could preach in our pulpits, but simply to a creed in accordance with the Nicene Confession. If this will not secure absolute immunity from doctrinal error, it may do something *towards* it. I believe in charts and lighthouses, although in spite of them some master mariners contrive to run their ships on shore.

I believe also as much as you do, that watches, clocks, and even dials must be adjusted to the sun; but the example of adjustment which you have selected, and which you describe as giving "great relief to the clergy and members of the *English Church*," no more affects them than it does you and other non-Episcopalians. You state that the hand of the clock (that is from the context the English Church clock) pointed to this :—"Children having been baptized if they die, are undoubtedly saved; *else not*. The pointer was put back by it.....

not' disappearing, ceased to rule. But what a mighty difference was made by that little change! Instead of *being obliged to* hold the positive destruction of all unbaptized infants, the clergy and members of the English Church are allowed to believe in their *possible* salvation. I am sure it will be a great "relief" to you to learn that this statement, however designed to comfort us, is (so far as the Church of England is concerned) quite unnecessary.

The *first* Liturgy of Edward VI., A.D. 1549, has this rubric in the office for confirmation :—

"And that no man shall think that any detriment shall come to children by deferring of their confirmation, he shall know for truth that it is certain by God's word that children being baptized (if they depart out of this life in their infancy) are undoubtedly saved."

The words "else not" do not appear in our *first reformed Liturgy*, and therefore could not have been omitted.

But to make it quite clear that the doctrine you incorrectly fasten upon the English Church was not held by her leading reformers, take this declaration from the chapter "Concerning Baptism" from the "Reformation of Ecclesiastical Laws," a treatise drawn up by Commissioners appointed in the reigns of Henry VIII. and Edward, of whom Cranmer was the first in rank :—

"Theirs also ought to be considered a scrupulous superstition who so completely tie down the grace of God and the Holy Spirit to the Sacramental elements, as explicitly to affirm that no infant of Christian parents can obtain eternal salvation who dies before it can be brought to baptism—*an opinion far different from ours.* "Quod longe secus habire judicamus."

An expression indeed which had found its way into the baptismal service of the first Liturgy of Edward VI. 1549, from that of *Luther*, through the Latin reformed service of the Archbishop Herman of Cologne (1543), was omitted in the *second* Liturgy of Edward VI. in 1552. It is in the prayer before baptism which ran thus :—"That by this wholesome laver of regeneration, whatsoever sin is in them may be washed clean away : that they, being delivered from Thy wrath, may be received into the ark of Christ's Church, *and so saved from perishing.*"

This prayer is *not* to be found in the *ancient* offices of *the Church of Rome*, but seems to have been originally composed by *Luther*, though it is not in accordance with his sentiments expressed elsewhere.

"Although infants," he remarks, "bring into the world with them the depravity of their origin, yet it is an important consideration that they have never transgressed the Divine commandments ; and since God is merciful, He will not, we may be assured, suffer them to fare the worse because, *without their own fault, they have been deprived of baptism.*"

So that this *chance* expression of Luther's—contrary to his own sentiments, and which escaped notice in the baptismal service of our Liturgy from 1549 to 1552, but was then omitted, and which never existed in the *ancient offices* of the Church—is *small* ground enough on which to express your compassion "for the ministers and clergy of the English Church," in the "great relief" they must have experienced!

In conclusion, let me observe that while minds capacious and independent as yours labor under such misapprehensions in regard to the Church of England and its doctrines, the hope of Church Union will remain "Ideal." But if Episcopalians and non-Episcopalians will honestly, and in the fear of God, try to learn with accuracy *wherein* they do essentially differ, and *why*, then, possibly both may be able eventually, through the grace of God, to adjust their clocks and watches by the sun-dial of His revealed will.

I am rev. sir,
Yours faithfully and respectfully,
AUGUSTUS ADELAIDE.

Rev. T. Binney.

(His Lordship also places at our disposal, for publication, the following letter received from Mr. Binney which he is not specially authorised to publish, but which he thinks will only do justice to Mr. Binney's sentiments and Christian feelings.—*South Australian Register*.)

1.

Rev. T. Binney to the Right Reverend the Bishop of Adelaide.

Glen Urquhart, the Green Hills, Victoria,
December 29, 1858.

MY LORD.—In a last revise of the letter which I had the honor to transmit to your Lordship by last mail, I withdrew the sentence which I have marked in the enclosed piece of proof. There is nothing in the words but what logically follows from the power which a Congregational minister has over his own pulpit—the jealousy with which we guard it against the intrusion of doctrinal error, from the importance we attach to evangelical truth—and the conviction we have of serious departures from that truth, in different directions, by many of the clergy. The words contain nothing but what follows from these things—whether our views of the Gospel (evangelical truth) be scriptural or not, or whether our "conviction" respecting the various forms of clerical opinion be right or wrong. Still, for many reasons, I thought it best to withdraw the words referred to. Your lordship, therefore, will do me the favor to regard them as withdrawn.*

I was very unwell while visiting at Toorak last week; I was obliged to abstain from all public duty last Sunday; I am now between 20 and 30 miles away from Melbourne, at a retired station, in a beautiful locality. A celebrated philosopher and metaphysician used to say that all his great and difficult problems, nice distinctions, and fine theories seemed to vanish into thin air after he had had a good dinner, and was in the company of warm and genial friends. There is something, however, better than this. In the deep solitude of the bush—God's beautiful world spreading and swelling round about us—His glorious blue heaven bending over us all—one's heart feels the blessed softening humanizing influence, and goes forth in tenderness and love towards all God's creatures. How little one heeds the noise of the world of men afar off—the struggle of parties, the clashing of opinion, the controversies, political or religious, which seem so important when we are in the midst of them! I wish your lordship was here, sitting with me in the sunlight; how soon we should be able to put everything right! May we meet in that world where there will be nothing to put right, and where we shall have something better to do than either to mend or mourn over the evils of this! Wishing you, my lord, in the language of the old country, "the compliments of the season"—all the blessings we wish for one another at this happy time, I am, truly and much, yours,

T. BINNEY.

The following is the private note of the Bishop, which accompanied the copy of his printed letter [No. X.], transmitted to Mr. Binney. It is this note, with the one of which it is an acknowledgment, to which we refer in our introductory remarks. Mr. Binney has kindly placed at our disposal his answer to it, which we also give. We have marked this private series 1, 2, 3.

2.

The Right Reverend the Bishop of Adelaide to the Reverend T. Binney.

Bishop's Court, January 10, 1859.

MY DEAR SIR,—Your kind and genial letter from Glen Urquhart, received this morning, quite refreshed me with its inward and outward "sunshine," and the blue heavens, which you so feelingly describe, as teaching us a lesson of holiness and love.

I had written an answer to your *printed* letter, which I duly received, not with a controversial view, but simply to explain more clearly our position as Church of England ministers, that our non-Episcopalian brethren may see that it is not state favour, or social distinction, which keeps us apart from them, but a really conscientious belief that we are bound to hold fast that rule of discipline, which if not instituted by "commandment," and so of absolute obligation, has at least in its favour the "judgment of apostles" according to the testimony of history, and is not in opposition to Scripture.

As your printed letter appeared in both our papers, I propose to print my answer and publish it through the like medium. But you shall also receive copies from the printers.

I thought it well that the passage you desired me to consider "cancelled," should also be noticed by them as *withdrawn*,—not that it hurt *me*, but lest a drop of bitterness should infuse itself in our hitherto amicable correspondence.

The best way, and one I am sure which will place your own feelings of christian kindness towards myself and other members of our Church in the clearest possible light, would be, I thought, to publish, in conjunction with my own, that letter in which you express yourself so kindly and so eloquently. This I feel is to *take a great liberty*, but you will pardon it, if, as I believe, it will help to show how christian men and ministers may differ without forfeiting eac other's esteem and regard. This has been my leading motive in beginning and carrying on this correspondence with you. To diminish if possible the obstacles which hinder the co-operation of Christian ministers and churches, and, if that cannot be done, then to lessen the ill-will which arises from those obstacles. The ice, I think, has been broken; I hope it won't freeze up again. Cordially reciprocating your good wishes, and trusting that the great work may prosper in your hand during the present year,

I am yours sincerely,

Rev. T. Binney.　　　　　　　　　　　　　　　　　　　AUGUSTUS ADELAIDE.

3.

The Rev. T. Binney to the Right Reverend the Bishop of Adelaide.

Collingwood, near Melbourne, Wednesday, Jan. 19, 1859.

To the Right Reverend the Lord Bishop of Adelaide.

MY LORD,—On Monday evening I had the pleasure of receiving your two letters, the written one dated January 10th, and the printed one which is without date, but which appeared in the Adelaide papers on the 11th instant. The latter may call the an explanatory

---

* The words which Mr. Binney wishes to withdraw are the following :—" ...... among the clergy whom I would not suffer to preach to my people—th .... being, for the most part, as I believe, either chaff or poison."

remark or two hereafter. I will only say at present, that my impression is—the impression, however, only of the first perusal—that it misapprehends the true point and bearing of my remarks, and instead of meeting illustrates and confirms them. This, I think, is singularly the case with the latter paragraphs referring to the "old church clock" Whether, however this be the case or no, it is not my purpose, just now, either to inquire or to affirm. My simple object is, to afford myself the pleasure of acknowledging your Lordship's *written* note, and to say how highly I appreciated its tenor and spirit, and how distinctly I recognise the kindness of the act to which it refers I received the newspapers some hours before the letters reached me, and on observing that you had appended my private note to your published letter, I was not only content, but felt that you had done me a great service, and that in a manner honorable alike to your feelings as a man, and your principles as a Christian. I am glad that your lordship read with pleasure what I wrote with sincerity; and I trust that nothing inconsistent with kindly feeling will insinuate itself into anything that may remain to be publicly said by either of us.

In reference to the "cancelled" sentence, I may mention, that in looking over the proof-sheet of the letter for the last time, and on coming to the words referred to, I said to myself—"Don't you think that that is something like a pretty striking illustration of what you say to the Bishop, about people accustomed to certain modes of thought, expressing themselves in a way likely to be offensive to others without their being at the time conscious of it themselves?" I was obliged to confess that I thought it was. "Then," said the judge, "you should withdraw it." So I withdrew it. Perhaps the judge ought to have put his finger on other expressions and blotted them out too. But it is impossible to avoid strong statements altogether, in relation to opinions firmly held, and believed to be of serious moment. Both your lordship and myself may not only fall unconsciously into such, but feel constrained to use them. There will not only be no harm in this, *in the absence of unfriendly personal feelings*, there may be honesty and consistency, as it may be the giving (and only that) of a required and becoming outward form, to some deep, earnest, religious conviction.

When I have given brief utterance to some of the thoughts which your lordship's first letter suggests to me, (and without my doing this, I feel that our correspondence would be imperfect,) I shall, like yourself, leave the matter to "ferment," hoping and believing that, by od's blessing, the amicable discussion initiated by your lordship will not be without results. I had hoped, indeed, to have done this long since; but my time and attention are constantly demanded for some business-matter or other, which cannot be postponed. I came out to these "uttermost parts of the earth" broken down, seeking rest and quiet, and I unexpectedly find myself not only called to pulpit labours and private duties among our own people, but unavoidably drawn, in company with your lordship, into an excursion to the frequently disturbed border lands laid down in our ecclesiastical maps. I hope we shall both get back again safely and soon, without losing ourselves on the road, or parting from each other in the bush; and then, perhaps, one day, in the old land, we may "sit together in the sunshine" after all, and talk over the incidents of what may have proved a not uneventful or bootless journey. I am, my lord, with sentiments of respect and regard,

Your friend and servant,
T. BINNEY.

RELIGIOUS INTELLIGENCE.

THE REV. R. BOWMAN.

(*Late of the Victoria Parade Congregational Church.*)

This talented and excellent clergyman, who so recently as April last came to this city, and who began his labours under hopeful and encouraging auspices, has, we regret to learn, been compelled to relinquish his mission and to return to England, from the serious effect of the climate on his health. He and his family sailed in the *White Star* on Thursday the 13th January. Although the term of Mr. Bowman's residence and services in Melbourne has been short, it has not been without results. He has left behind much by which he will be remembered, not only in the immediate circle of his co-religionists, but in some of the more general departments of duty beyond it. On his departure an address was presented to him by the members of his church, expressive of their high respect, their disappointed hopes, and their deep christian affection. This was accompanied by a pecuniary testimonial to the amount of £150, with a copy of McCombie's Victoria. Mr. Bowman's sudden breaking up of his house and unexpected departure with his family to England, involved, it may be mentioned, not only much expense but great sacrifices. The Young Men's Christian Association connected with the Victoria Parade Church, accompanied their address to Mr. Bowman with a copy of the large well-known work, consisting of views of Victoria. Mrs. Bowman, too, received a small memorial of esteem in the form of a valuable gold brooch, the material and the workmanship being alike colonial. The members of the Evangelical Alliance passed a resolution of sympathy and respect to Mr. Bowman at its usual monthly meeting. It so happened that, from an accidental circumstance, the members of Mr. Bowman's own denomination were absent on that occasion, being unavoidably engaged at the time in a meeting of their own; but, without concert with the Alliance, or knowledge of its intenti⌐

they were in sympathy with it, and passed a resolution of a like nature. At the request of a correspondent we insert these particulars, and append the resolution referred to.

Melbourne, January 5, 1859.

THE CHURCH OF CHRIST ASSEMBLING IN VICTORIA PARADE TO THE REV. R. BOWMAN.

Rev. and Dear Sir,—It is with feelings of deep sorrow that we are made acquainted with the failure of your health, which renders necessary your immediate return to England, and the consequent resignation of your pastorate over us as a Church; which appointment, in the order of Divine providence, you have only been permitted to hold for a very brief period.

It is now little more than eight months ago since your labours amongst us commenced, yet we have reason to believe that within this short space of time good has been effected. The increase both in the church and congregation must have been gratifying to yourself as it was cheering to us; and the manifest tokens of God's blessing filled us with joy and hope for the future.

But the cherished hopes entertained both by yourself and by us are doomed to disappointment; and the desire which was strong in your heart you are not permitted to realise.

May the grace of God enable us as his people, and you as his servant, to submit with a christian resignation to the chastening of his hand.

Our prayer is that you may be sustained under the severe afflictions you have been called to undergo, and that God in his goodness will in his own set time restore you again to health and strength, and fit you for his work and service, and that you may yet be permitted to labour in Christ's vineyard, and be made the honoured instrument in the conversion of many souls.

We beg you to accept of our best wishes for your future welfare, and that of the dear partner of your life and dear children; and may you have a safe and prosperous journey across the mighty deep, and the felicity of being welcomed and received by those near and dear in the fatherland.

And if it be ours to say farewell, and should we not again be permitted to meet on this side of eternity, may we, as one family, meet in the "Heavenly Canaan" where partings and sorrows will be known no more.

We are, Rev. and Dear Sir,

With all christian affection, Yours faith fully,

(*Signed by the Members of the Church.*)

At a meeting of gentlemen, members of the Evangelical Alliance, on Wednesday, January 5th, 1859, it was unanimously resolved:

"That Mr. Hoskins, the Secretary of this Alliance, be requested to convey to the Rev. R. Bowman the expression of our sincere sympathy with him, and our deep regret that his declining health necessitates his return to England. We had hoped long to enjoy the benefit of his presence and counsel in the transactions of this Alliance. But although he may be absent from us in person, we trust he will continue with us in spirit. We earnestly pray for the restoration of his health and the welfare of himself and family in his native land."

The following members of the Alliance were present at the meeting:—His Honour Judge Pohlman, the Right Rev. the Bishop of Melbourne, Rev. James Darling, Rev. M. Goethe, Rev. George Pollard, Rev. James Taylor, Hon. T. T. A'Beckett, Messrs. Hodgson, J. T. Hoskins, Henry Jennings, Dr. Singleton, Messrs. Mars Millar, J. Russell, David Ogilvy.

The following resolution was unanimously agreed to at a meeting of the Fraternal Association of Congregational ministers of Melbourne and its vicinity, held at St. Kilda, January 5th, 1859, there being present Revs. R. Fletcher, W. B. Landells, J. Sunderland, H. Thomas, W. Moss, W. A. Lewis, J. Robinson, and J. Mirams; and as a visitor, the Rev. Thomas Binney of London.

"The brethren having learnt that the Rev. R. Bowman has been compelled, through serious failure of health, to relinquish his charge of the Victoria Parade Congregational Church and arrange to return to England without delay, cordially and affectionately unite in the expression of their sympathy with him and his family in this painful and mysterious dispensation of Providence, and of their sincere regret at this unexpected issue of his self-denying consecration of himself to the service of his Master in a country so much needing ministerial aid; and they assure him that he leaves these shores with their highest esteem for his character, their warmest wishes for his welfare, their fervent prayers for the restoration of his health, and their hopes that a protracted period of usefulness may yet be allotted to him in the land of his birth."

RICHARD FLETCHER,

CHAIRMAN.

REV. J. L. POORE.—Mr. Poore arrived at Melbourne by the *Oneida* January 19, in good health and spirits. He has successfully accomplished the object for which he went to England, the procuring of twelve additional ministers for these colonies. The result of his two journeys home is the sending thence to Australia of 28 ministers, of whom two have died, and one returned from ill-health. The clear accession is therefore 25. That Mr. Poore's efforts on behalf of these colonies have been highly appreciated at home, appears from the following letter, addressed to him on behalf of the Committee of the Colonial Missionary Society at a public meeting held in the Weigh House Chapel (Rev. T. Binney's), London, to bid him farewell.

Colonial Missionary Society, 4, Blomfield-street,
Finsbury, London, Nov. 10th, 1858.

Rev. J. L. Poore,—Dear Sir,—In the name and on the behalf of our Committee we beg to address you on your expected departure to the distant region you have made the land of your adoption. In doing this we avail ourselves of the opportunity thus afforded to express the high estimation in which we hold you personally, and the great value we attach to the indefatigable labors which you have bestowed upon the objects our Society exists to promote. We look back to the period when you, and your excellent friend Mr. Fletcher, nobly responded to our invitation to sacrifice the comforts of your former home, and to go to our antipodes to serve our Divine Master in the Gospel. By the instructions then given you, you were requested not to settle down in any given locality, but to act the part of an evangelist, and to visit all the Colonies for the purpose of inducing the settlers to gather themselves together, to form themselves into congregations, and to make all due preparation for the introduction of suitable ministers. Most effectually, we consider, you have fulfilled the work assigned you. We magnify the grace of God in you that you have been able to accomplish so much in so short a time. We thank God that your life and health have been preserved, and that the "labors more abundant" in which you have been engaged, have not exhausted your energies, or prostrated your strength. When we remember that 27 ministers will have be-n selected, and sent forth to those regions within a period of two years, we cannot but "thank God and take courage" The importance of the work thus accomplished cannot be over-rated. Whatever devotedness the Committee at home might have manifested, they could never have effected so much, had you not prepared the way, by exploring the entire region, and rousing the energies of all in the Colonies who were friendly to the great objects of your mission. We admire the men who, for purposes of science or commerce, will venture into the wilderness, trace the course of rivers, and open up new tracts of country for future occupancy, thereby adding to our stores of knowledge and advancing the material interests of society. But yours is a nobler object, and tends to infinitely more important results, and most thankful do we feel that you have been enabled, in so great a degree, to keep pace with the rapid growth of those truly wonderful communities. We rejoice, too, that by your influence, in a great measure, is to be attributed the munificent liberality of the Australian Churches in meeting the cost incurred by sending so many ministers as have already gone, or are going, to occupy the stations which have been prepared for them, The unexampled progress of the colonies justified, in our esteem, the local committee in Melbourne in urging you to revisit England for the purpose of obtaining an additional number of ministers. Your ready assent to their proposal is a striking evidence of your disinterested zeal, and meets with, as it deserves, our cordial approval. Your efforts have essentially aided us in securing the services of brethren who, we believe, will be found adapted for the work to be assigned to them.

And now, Dear Sir, you are about to return to the field of your labor. We need not assure you of our entire, unabated confidence in you. We shall follow you with our prayers, and shall not cease to implore on your behalf the watchful care of Him who holds the winds in his fist and the waters in the hollow of his hands. We trust you will be preserved in your journeyings by sea and land, and be restored to the society of your beloved partner in life, with whom we sincerely sympathize on account of the lengthened separation to which she has so kindly submitted. That she may be long spared to be your solace in times of trouble and anxiety and your help-meet in all things, is our earnest prayer.

The future we must chiefly leave in your own hands. Your course of action in the past leads us to the confident expectation that you will be able so to arrange your proceedings as to commend them to the approval of your local committees in the Colonies, as well as to ourselves in this country. You will inform us of your safe arrival, which we pray you may in due course realize, and favor us from time to time with information of the settlement of the ministers who have already gone, or will soon take their leave.

We now beg to subscribe ourselves, on behalf of the whole Committee,
Your sincere and faithful friends,

(Signed)   JAMES SPICER, Treasurer.
THOMAS JAMES, Secretary.

At the close of the meeting at which this letter was read, in the vestry of Mr. Binney's Chapel, a few gentlemen of the committee presented Mr. Poore with a

Testimonial of their personal esteem for his character and labors, in the shape of some articles of plate, which might be used in his house and preserved in his family.

MINISTERS FOR AUSTRALIA.—The following is an extract from a letter from the Rev. Thomas James, Secretary of the Colonial Missionary Society :—During the past year fifteen ministers were sent to the Australian colonies, all of whom, with the exception of Mr. Jacob Jones—who, by a mysterious Providence, was lost by shipwreck within sight of his intended home—have found their appropriate spheres of labor.   Mr. J. G. Reed, whose early death you noticed in a recent number of your journal is also an exception.   Of Mr. Arnold's arrival we have not yet heard, though it is hoped he has reached Sydney, and entered on his labors in that city before now.   The remaining thirteen have been cordially received, are faithfully preaching the Gospel of Christ, and will be sustained by the colonists themselves, without any draft on the society's funds.   At the earnest request of the committee in Melbourne, Mr. Poore has been induced again to visit this country, for the purpose of obtaining an additional number of suitable men, for whom important and promising stations are provided.   Since his arrival the committee have been actively engaged in efforts to meet this renewed demand, and are happy in being able to state that they have engaged the services of nine, and are negotiating with two or three others.   One, the Rev. C. E. Palmer of Warrington, has already sailed.   Two others—the Rev. C. Manthorpe, of Newport, Essex, and the Rev. J. W. Shippherd, of Hayes Middlesex,—will embark in a few days.   Four others—the Rev. J. Hill, M.A. of Witham; the Rev. J. C. M'Michael, of Halifax; the Rev. J. W. C. Drane of Hanley; and the Rev. G. Hoatson, of Stoke-upon-Trent—are expected to take their departure in the course of a month.   It is hoped that all at present required will have started for their destination by the end of the year.   Of the twelve now being sent, six are designed for South Australia, four for Victoria, one for Tasmania, and one for Wellington, New Zealand.   The committee would bespeak for these brethren the prayers of their friends, that they may be preserved from the perils of the deep, reach their destination in safety, and find an open door for their entrance on fields " white to the harvest."   It will be gratifying to the friends of the society to know that the funds specially collected last year to meet the charges incident to the voyage and outfit of so many ministers, with their families (the greater proportion of which was contributed by the colonists themselves), will be sufficient to meet the expenses thus incurred, without infringing on the general income of the society.   This would not have been the case had not the committee been favored by some noble-minded ship-owners, who generously consented to convey the ministers either wholly free or at greatly reduced charges. —Nonconformist.

VICTORIA.—REV. THOS. BINNEY AT ST. KILDA.—On the evening of Sunday, Jan. 2, Mr. Binney delivered a discourse to young men, taking for his text the two sentences, " Joseph being seventeen years old was feeding the flock with his brethren," and " Joseph was thirty years old when he stood before Pharoah, king of Egypt." (Gen. xxxvii. 2, and xli. 46.) Nothing could exceed the beauty and effectiveness with which the interval between these two periods, and the influence which the events that happened in that interval had in preparing Joseph for his future destiny, were traced ; and certainly nothing could be more felicitously appropriate to the class of persons specially addressed.   The following suitable remarks upon the service are by a correspondent in the Melbourne Herald :—

" Nearly seven years ago, in the old Weigh House Chapel, we listened to the last sermon we ever listened to in England.   It was from the lips of Thos. Binney.   It was no unusual thing in those days for young men to leave home, and Thomas Binney, essentially the young man's preacher, braced many a heart, and fixed many a principle in those who since have met with few who cared little to take the trouble to do the one or the other.   On Sunday we again, for the first time since leaving home, listened to his preaching ; and again he addressed himself to young men, and with that impressiveness and truth to which so many of the strugglers in Australasian Adventures can so well testify he held up a pattern for their guidance.   And as we watched and waited for his words as they fell, and gazed upon the glorious head and face we have so often looked upon Sabbath after Sabbath in the old time, and followed him in his graphic description of character, sending forcible appeals to conscience, we felt better for his teaching, and hopeful for the people with such a teacher for their guide.   It would be impossible to conceive anything more telling than the succession of pictures pourtrayed by Mr. Binney in illustrating the life and character of Joseph.   Commencing with him at seventeen, and leaving him whilst still a young man at thirty—from the tender, loving, and withal God-fearing boy, to the strong, earnest, honest man—describing, with the facility of a master, the refining influence of his trials, and his eventuating through them to the greatness he achieved—the slavery, the toil, the success, the temptation, the false charge, the abasement and the renewal of good ; the unflinching manliness of endeavour supporting him under all reverses, and the elevation of motive accompanying the whole, were described with a vigour and earnestness only paralleled by the strength of entreaty and exhortation to the hearers to ' do likewise.'   It would be impossible to estimate too highly the influence of such preachings as these, as well upon the spiritual as upon the everyday life of everyday men.   An elevation of sentiment, of feeling, and of character must necessarily and naturally be the result ; and it would be well for us in our new homes to endeavour to retain such a means of good amongst us."

OXFORD STREET INDEPENDENT CHAPEL, COLLINGWOOD.—On Wednesday evening, the 3rd November, the church and congregation connected with Oxford-street Chapel, held their quarterly social meeting. About 350 persons partook of tea, which was prepared by the deacons' wives in the school-house, and then adjourned to the chapel. The pastor (Rev. W. B. Landells) presided. In his address, he reviewed the spiritual state of the church, and the progress of the work of God. Several members then gave brief statements respecting the local agencies with which they were more immediately connected. The subjects thus spoken to, were—spiritual life, individual experience, lay preaching, finance, the Tract Society, the Sunday School, and the Young Men's Christian Association. The choir, at intervals, performed several anthems, which added greatly to the interest and pleasure of the evening. The collection to defray the expense of the tea amounted to £11 7s.

OXFORD STREET CHAPEL, COLLINGWOOD.—The church and congregation connected with the above place of worship, had, on Sunday, 21st November, the long-anticipated pleasure of the sight of the Rev. Thos. Binney in their pulpit. The day was devoted to the Congregational Home Mission, the service in the morning being conducted by the Rev. Thos. Williams, late missionary to the Feejee Islands, and now of the Wesleyan Church, Brunswick-street; and the evening service by the Rev. Thomas Binney, assisted by the former gentleman. The expectations of his admirers were fully realised with regard to the attendance, for not less than a thousand persons were assembled within the chapel, while hundreds were compelled to go away without obtaining admission. His text was chosen from 2 Cor. iv. 8, " We look not at the things which are seen, but at the things which are not seen, for the things which are seen are temporal, but the things which are not seen are eternal." The Australian hot wind had prevailed during the day, and it was manifest the rev. gentleman was suffering from its exhausting influence, but for upwards of an hour his brilliant eluci- dation of the text was eagerly listened to by the congregation. There were many present who have been familiar with the preacher from their boyhood, and to whom his weighty thoughts are as household words. It was an exquisite gratification to such, and perhaps, not less so to those from other communions who then listened to him for the first time. The collection amounted to £20.

RICHMOND CONGREGATIONAL CHAPEL.—On Sabbath morning, Nov. 21, the Rev. T. Binney preached in the above chapel, to a densely crowded audience. After the usual devotional exercises, Mr. Binney announced as the subject of his discourse, Phillippians, 3rd chap. and 10th verse, " The power of his resurrection," which he treated under the following heads:—I. As a fact. To convince the intellect. II. As a doctrine. A great spiritual truth to affect the heart. III. As a type. That we must die to sin and live to holiness. IV. As a motive for Christian progress. V. As a model of what we shall hereafter be. Mr. Binney closed with some practical remarks. On Tuesday evening the half-yearly tea meeting was held, in the same chapel. The Hon. W. Roope, M.L.C., presided. Addresses were delivered by the Revs. Messrs. Binney, I. New, and R. Fletcher. Mr. Russel read the financial state- ment—The floating debt on the chapel was £144 ; towards the liquidation of this amount, the collection and the proceeds of the tea meeting, amounting together to £80, were applied.

ST. KILDA CONGREGATIONAL CHURCH (REV. MR. FLETCHER'S).—This church and congregation held their anniversary social meeting on the evening of the 24th Nov., the Rev. Thos. Binney presided, and interested the assembly much by various short addresses he delivered in the course of the evening. In his introductory remarks he expressed the pleasure he felt in presiding, at the request of his old friend and companion in youth, the pastor of the church. He spoke of social meetings, in connexion with religion, when properly conducted, as in harmony with the customs both of the Ancient Jews and Primitive Christians. The Rev. R. Fletcher gave a report of the proceedings of the church at St. Kilda during the past year, its losses and its gains. He also expressed in feeling terms his joy at meeting his early friend at the antipodes, after an interval of forty years from their youthful days, with their lives spared, and, by the grace of God, their characters untarnished. Robert Smith, Esq., deacon and treasurer, read the cash statement, from which it appeared that the congregation had raised and disbursed through the year, including £133 to the Home Mission Society, about £1000. He also gave an account of the Sunday School, which had increased in number during the year. G. Rolfe, Esq., deacon, read the Home Mission report, which appeared to be prospering. Various resolutions were moved and seconded, and addresses delivered by the Revs. W. B. Landells, A. Scales, J. Sunderland, Mr. Fulton, and others.

PORTLAND: ANNIVERSARY OF THE CONGREGATIONAL CHURCH. — Recently a public social meeting took place at the Congregational Chapel, Tyers-street, which was very numerously attended. An excellent tea was provided, and the interior of the chapel, decorated with flowers, and brilliantly illuminated, had a most cheerful appearance. After tea, the chair being taken by Norman M'Leigh, Esq., Mr. Sleigh, the minister, gave an account of the progress of the cause amongst them from the time of his arrival in January, 1858, and the laying the foundation stone of the present building. Mr. Hearne then made a financial statement. He said that the purchasing the ground and building the chapel had cost above £400, and that efforts would be made to pay that off. The meeting was then addressed by the Rev. Messrs. Richards, Ridley, Boag, and Huntley, and terminated soon after ten o'clock.

CASTLEMAINE.—The Rev. T. Binney preached on Sunday, Dec. 5th, morning and evening, in the Congregational Chapel, to over flowing audiences. A social meeting was held on Monday evening, in the chapel, and was crowded to excess. The Rev. Mr. Day stated the object of the meeting to be to clear the debt of £400 on the chapel. Twenty persons had guaranteed £300, if by collections the sum of £100 could be realised. The collections at the various services, and proceeds of the social meeting, amounted to £117 9s., so that the whole debt is virtually liquidated. The meeting was addressed by the Revs. Messrs. Binney, Fletcher, of St Kilda; Firth, Dr. Preston, and Messrs. Naylor, Fulton, and others.

BRITISH AND FOREIGN BIBLE SOCIETY.—A sermon was preached by the Rev. Thomas Binney on behalf of the Victorian Branch of the above society, on the morning of Sabbath, Dec. 19, in Chalmers' Church, Eastern Hill, Melbourne. The congregation was numerous, the building being crowded in every part. The rev. gentleman chose for his text the last verse of the 17th Psalm—" As for me I will behold thy face in righteousness; I shall be satisfied when I awake, with thy likeness" The collection amounted to £64 18s.

THE REV. THOMAS BINNEY AT BALLAARAT.—A public meeting was held at the Council Chambers on the 10th Dec., to welcome Mr. Binney to Ballaarat. After tea, J. Oddie, Esq., was called to the chair, and the proceedings of the evening opened by prayer by the Rev. W. Henderson. The Rev. J. Beckford moved, and the Rev. Mr. Searle seconded the resolution " that this meeting regards, with satisfaction, the progressive development of the principles of the Evangelical Alliance, and especially does it welcome the Rev. T. Binney among the churches of Ballaarat." Mr. Binney then addressed the meeting at considerable length, and expressed himself as being much interested in the colonies. He prayed God to bless the churches, and establish in this infant nation all the blessings of social and political liberty. The meeting was afterwards briefly addressed by Mr. Fulton, of Melbourne, and the Rev. Mr. Bradney.

BEECHWORTH: CONGREGATIONAL CHURCH.—The opening services in connection with the Independent congregation of this town, were conducted in their new building on Sabbath, Dec. 19, by the Rev. T. H. Jackson, the minister. A social tea meeting took place on the evening of the 22nd, in connection with the above services. The building is substantial, being built of stone, and although not large is still sufficiently capacious for the purpose. The Rev. T. H. Jackson took the chair. He spoke of the pleasure he experienced in meeting his own people, in their own place of worship, for the first time. He adverted to the movement made some two years ago towards procuring a place of worship, and of the expenditure of the money then collected, in the purchase of the suitable site of land on which the present building stood. He stated it to be the intention of the Committee to publish a full account of the moneys received up to the present time, together with the manner in which they had been expended, which he believed would give satisfaction. Mr. Cunningham read the report, which, among other things, stated that in the course of the year an allotment of land had been purchased for a parsonage, and a house erected thereon, at a cost of £420, the money for which had been advanced by friends at interest, a scheme having been put in operation by which the debt will be gradually liquidated, and the property become the freehold of the body. Occupying a hired room, the necessity of possessing a place of worship of their own was strongly felt by the church and congregation. The committee consequently commenced the work. They resolved to proceed according to the means at their disposal, and consequently erected the present substantial, neat, and economical structure; and they were much gratified by expressions of satisfaction which reached them from all quarters. The total income of the year had been £730 16s. 10d., the expenditure, £717 11s. 3d.; while the present liabilities amounted to £80. The meeting was then addressed by the Rev. J. C. Symons, Wesleyan minister, who wished the Congregationalists God speed in their undertaking, and afterwards by Messrs. C. Williams, Dunn, Hazleton, Morris, from the Three-Mile Creek, Darvall, and Young (Solicitor). Subscriptions towards the liquidation of the remaining debt were received, amounting to nearly £30. Thanks being voted to the ladies for the tea, and to the choir for the music, the service closed with the Doxology.

UNION OF PRESBYTERIANS IN VICTORIA.—There have been recently held meetings of the several Synods connected with the Old Kirk, the Free Church, and the United Presbyterians in Victoria, with a view to an amalgamation of the whole into one body of Presbyterians. The terms of union proposed have met with the unanimous approval of all the Synods, and the matter is now referred to the consideration of the congregations separately. So far as they have yet been consulted, we understand they have given their assent. As the ministers and elders constituting the Synods were unanimous in their approval of the union itself, and of the proposed basis on which it should rest, there is every probability that all the congregations also will cordially concur. As the Scottish Presbyterians of every name, all agree in doctrine, church government, and discipline, and in the standards in which these are set forth; and as the points which divided them at home have no significance here, there seems no valid reason why they should not forget their differences and form one great and united Synod. They would thus, instead of presenting the painful spectacle of division and subdivision, the reasons for which persons who are without the pale of Presbyterianism have extreme difficulty in understanding, appear before the public as one compact body, characterised by distinctive principles, and effectively organised for united action. We present one instance, out of many, of the way in which the question is treated before individual congregations:—" PRESBYTERIAN UNION.—According to pulpit on the previous day, a public meeting took place in the Free Church, Lake Learmonth, in the night of Monday, 10th January. Owing to the rainy weather the meeting was well attended only by the male portion of the congregation. Mr. Mackie, minister of the congregation, commenced the proceedings with prayer. Mr. Laidlaw was called to the chair. Mr. Mackie then proceeded to explain the matter which had brought them together. The basis agreed upon in conference at Melbourne last month, recommends itself to all Presbyterians. It is comprehensive, and yet not latitudinarian; it is concise, and yet not exclusive. The adherent of the established Church of Scotland must be satisfied with it, for it does not bring up unnecessary matters of discussion; the Free Churchman must be satisfied it, for it contains all for which he pleads in Scotland—viz., and simply, the carrying out of our common standards in their entirety; and the United Presbyterian must also be satisfied, for it concedes to him all he asks. Who then shall forbid the banns of union among all Presbyterians? No one will do so with a true understanding of the question. The whole country will bid us a right hearty God-speed in this movement, and children's children will bless us for what we are now doing. The more efficiently carrying out the great commission, " to preach the gospel to every creature," demands union; the rearing a native ministry—a ministry purely colonial—demands it; the education of our Presbyterian children cries aloud for it; and the well-being and well-doing of the country, morally, socially, and politically will be bettered by this union. Various gentlemen expressed their concurrence and hearty approval of the contemplated union. After which, the following motions were very cordially carried, viz.—" That this meeting of members and adherents of the Free Church of Lake Learmonth, is of opinion that the basis agreed upon at the Melbourne Conference of 15th ult., is sufficient to secure a true and lasting union among all Presbyterians. 2nd,—That in the contemplated Presbyterian Church of Victoria, no State aid be received." The meeting was then closed with prayer.

NEW SOUTH WALES.—MAITLAND.—ANNIVERSARY.—During the week, the anniversary of the Congregational Church, West Maitland, was celebrated—commencing, on Sunday, with two services by the Rev. W. Cuthbertson, B.A., and ending with a public meeting on Tuesday evening, in the church. On that occasion the Rev. E. Griffith, pastor of the congregation, presided, and about 200 persons were present. The proceedings having been opened with devotional exercises, Mr. Griffith made a statement as to the financial position of the church, from which it appeared that the building had cost £4,700; that when the accounts were last audited, at the end of March, there was a balance of debt remaining, inclusive of interest, amounting to £671; that the interest from that time was £45; that during the year, the sum of £119 had been raised and paid; and that the debt had thus been reduced to £611, which he hoped, ere long, to see entirely wiped off. The Rev. Joseph Beazley enforced the duty and privilege of contributing not merely towards the support of the Gospel, but to the removal of the debt in question, pointing out how this could be most easily accomplished. He had been present at the first meeting of the denomination in Maitland—at the opening of the little weatherboard structure six or seven years ago—and it was with peculiar emotions of delight that he witnessed such altered circumstances, and stood in so noble and spacious an edifice erected for the worship of God The Rev. W. Cuthbertson followed with a powerful address. A collection was then made, which, added to what had been raised at the previous meeting, amounted to £22 19s.

TASMANIA.—TAMAR STREET INDEPENDENT CHAPEL, LAUNCESTON.—The anniversary of the Sunday schools connected with this church took place on Sunday, November 28th, and the following day. The Rev. Mr. Lindsay, of the Free Church, preached in the morning, and the Rev. W. Law, of St. John's Square Church, in the evening. A social tea meeting was held in the school-room on Monday evening. After tea, the meeting adjourned, to the chapel, and under the presidency of the pastor of the church, the Rev. C. Price, topics connected with Sunday schools were spoken to by the Rev. Mr. Law and Messrs. Aikenhead, Stephens, Cowl, Gurr, and C. Price, jun. From a statement read it appeared that there were 9 male and 5 female teachers, 83 boys and 61 girls at Tamar-street school, making 144 scholars, which shows an increase of 1. During the year 69 have been admitted, 66 have left, and two have been expelled. At New Town School there were 3 male and 2 female teachers, 18 boys and 17 girls. The total last year was 143, this year it is 179, showing an increase of 36 children. During the year a building has been erected at New Town, which, with the land, cost £225. A debt of £55 remains. The cost of flooring the second school-room under the chapel will exceed £50, and has not yet been paid for.

WESTERN AUSTRALIA.—A public tea meeting, in aid of the building fund of the Congregational Chapel, was held at Fremantle, on Tuesday evening, the 5th October, and was numerously attended. After tea the meeting was addressed by the Revs. Z. Berry, J. Johnstone, S. Hardey, R. Alderson, and Mr. Trigg. and the proceedings of the evening were varied by the performance of sacred music, executed by the Freeman. Choir, aided by their Perth friends who had kindly volunteered their services for the occasion.—*Perth Independent.*

SOUTH AUSTRALIA.—CONGREGATIONAL CHAPEL, FREEMAN STREET.—On Sunday morning a sermon was delivered by the Rev. Thomas Binney, at the above chapel, on the occasion of its eighteenth anniversary; and a collection was made in aid of the fund for bringing out ministers from England. The chapel was filled with a most attentive congregation. The Rev. preacher took his text from Romans, xiv. 17—"For the kingdom of God is not meat and drink, but righteousness, and peace, and joy in the Holy Ghost." He glanced at the state of the early Christian Church in Rome, and the heartburnings which had arisen there, as in most other places, between Jewish and Gentile converts. He pointed out the way in which St. Paul, who always insisted strongly upon essential points, reprehended any intolerance upon those which were non-essential, and upon which good men might conscientiously differ. This he applied to the question of church union, which had recently been so much discussed; and placed in the strongest light the duty of Christians of all denominations to carry out as far as possible, the spirit of the apostle's injunctions. In the afternoon the Holy Sacrament was administered by Mr. Binney to the members of several Congregational churches, and there were present nearly the whole of the members belonging to the denomination in Adelaide and its vicinity. In the evening the Rev. T. Q. Stow, preached from 1st Corinthians, vi. 20—"For ye are bought with a price; therefore glorify God in your body, and in your spirit, which are God's." After the sermon the Rev. gentleman took occasion to remark that it was a double anniversary, inasmuch as he had preached his first sermon in South Australia on that day 21 years ago, three years before the opening of the Freeman-street Chapel. A collection was made for the same object as that in the morning.

KAPUNDA.—On Sunday, November 14, the Independent Chapel, newly erected in this town, was opened for public worship by the performances of three services, at each of which the chapel was crowded with highly respectable congregations. The morning service was taken by the Rev. Mr. Stow, who chose for his text the first portion of the fifth chapter of St. Paul's Epistle to the Romans, in which he so ably and explicitly sets forth the doctrine of justification through faith in Jesus Christ. In the afternoon the Rev. Mr. Brown, the Wesleyan minister resident at Kapunda, delivered a very appropriate and truly Christian address on the 8th and 9th verses of the 132nd Psalm; and in the evening the pulpit was occupied by the Rev. Mr. Cox, of Ebenezer Chapel, Adelaide, who gave an admirable sermon on a portion of the 19th verse of the 1st chapter of the 1st General Epistle of Peter.

CONGREGATIONAL CHAPEL, GLENELG.—We understand that the Rev. Mr. Palmer, late of Warrington, Lancashire, has engaged to occupy the pulpit of the Congregational Chapel Glenelg, for the next three months, with a view to permanent settlement.

TESTIMONIAL.—On Thursday evening, the 25th ult., the second anniversary of the Bible Class in connection with the Baptist Chapel, Lefevre terrace, North Adelaide, was held in the school room, when a silver cup, of colonial workmanship, with a suitable inscription, and bearing the appropriate devices of an open Bible and a spreading vine richly laden with fruit, as an emblem of "the true vine," was presented by the members of the class to Mr. E. S. Wigg, as an acknowledgment of the benefits they have received from his instructions.

PROPOSED RESTORATION OF PALESTINE TO THE JEWS.—Recently, the Rev. Ridley H. Herschell delivered a lecture at Edinburgh, on "The present state of the Jews in the East, and on the Continent of Europe, with some account of the openings for their return to the Holy Land." He gave interesting details regarding the present condition of the Jews, both in Europe and Palestine. It was a curious fact, but he was prepared to prove it, that in proportion to their respective numbers there was a far greater amount of Jewish Christians in the world than there was of Gentile. During the last twenty years too, Jewish converts had been more numerous than they had ever been at any previous period since the time of the Apostles. This was especially true of the educated and influential classes, and in proof of this he might simply mention that there were at the present moment no fewer than twenty-six professors in the University of Berlin, who were either converted Jews or of Jewish origin. Among them was Professor Kirsch, the famous ecclesiastical historian. In regard to the openings for the return of the Jews to the Holy Land, he (the lecturer) might mention that he lately had an interview with the Turkish Minister in London, and that, referring to the recent disturbances in Jaffa (the ancient Joppa), His Excellency had asked him what ought to be done. He (Mr. Herschell) then stated to him, that the best plan to adopt in the circumstances, and the only plan which would tend to effectually secure peace and prosperity to Palestine, would be for the Sultan to allow the Jews once more to take possession of it. Being an active, enterprising and industrious people, they would soon rid the land of the marauding Arab tribes, and promote its welfare in every respect. The Turkish Minister highly approved of this proposal, and promised to lay it before the Sublime Porte, who would, he doubted not, at once accede to it. (Applause.) Mr. Herschell concluded by a reference to the glorious results which might be expected to flow from the restoration of the Jews to their own land in the mannner alluded to, and strongly pressed upon the benevolent sympathies of his audience the claims of a "model farm" which had been established at Jaffa.

W. FAIRFAX AND CO., STEAM PRINTERS, COLLINS STREET, EAST, MELBOURNE.

The Southern Spectator.

MARCH, 1859.

NOTES ON THE RELIGIOUS CONDITION OF SCOTLAND.

Scotland is the most religious country in the world. Not only is the Sabbath-day better kept there ; not only are the places of worship, in proportion to the gross number of the population, better attended there : but also, and best of all, there you will find a greater amount of those spiritual and moral elements that constitute religion, in the highest sense, existing and operating among the people, than among the people of any other country. You will, indeed, find Sabbath desecration, and that not a little ; you will find men at church on the Lord's day, and the same men will over-reach you (if they can) in the market-place and the exchange on the week day ; you will find men who put on religion as a cloak, as in every other country ; but there, in dear old Scotland, we are bound to say, you will find by the fair rule of proportion, a greater amount of the genuine article than in any other country under the sun. In this statement, the Scotch reader who has a competent knowledge of the subject, and who is true to his fatherland, will readily acquiesce ; and from it even the English reader is not likely to dissent, for two reasons :—1st. he (the Englishman), has been accustomed from his earliest days, to hear that in the matter of religion and education *only*, can Scotland hold up her old head in the presence of more highly favoured England. But in these respects she *does* hold her head erect, proud and unbending, like the free and bold peaks of her own granite mountains. 2nd. Strangers know so little of the religious condition of Scotland, that, in virtue of the aforesaid " tradition," they find it the safest course at once to admit the claim. No one will call in question the wisdom of this course in present circumstances, at least we shall not. Nor are those who live beyond the bounds of a country to be blamed, if they should be found but partially or even ill-informed on such a subject as its religious condition. And, in the case of Scotland, there are obstacles, peculiar to herself, which those who are interested in such inquiries as these have to encounter. Although the mass of her population be Presbyterian, yet these are broken up into so many sects—there are so many divisions, subdivisions, and sub-sub-divisions —that a stranger must have a special qualification for gathering the splintered fragments of the mirror into a whole again, who makes himself thoroughly master of this complicated subject. Now, smart reader, don't imagine that we are, in these instances, covertly putting forth our own qualifications for this work. Honestly, we are not, nor do we need ; for, *first*, we are no strangers to that land, but in the exercise of our calling have been brought into close contact with her religious communities ; *secondly*, we are not so ambitious as to attempt

a full discussion of this question, so vast and so many-sided, but only
such a hasty and fragmentary sketch as a person might pen in the unrest
and bustle that obtain on board ship, and under the feelings that
crowd upon him as he looks back on the country and the friends from
which he has parted for ever, and thinks of the land of his adoption,
and of what, under a benign Providence, may be his possible future.*
    We have said that the great mass of the population is Presbyterian.
All the large sects are of this persuasion, and one or two of the
smaller ones.   The Established Church, the Free Church, the United
Presbyterian Church, the three great religious communities that share
among them about two millions of the population, occupy the same
ecclesiastical platform, and their processes and practices are substantially identical.   The only thing that breaks up the harmony is the
principle of endowments.   We make no remark on this theory of
church government; Presbyterianism is the same all the world over,
and doubtless it is known sufficiently to the reader to preclude the
possibility of serious regret at the course we have chosen to pursue.
Not only are their church polity and modes of procedure substantially
the same, but we venture to go further, and assert that in doctrine
also, there is a wide-spread and gratifying similarity.   We are, of
course, speaking now in general terms ; doubtless a keen eye might
detect exceptions.   Orthodox all of them in their creeds, the evangelical
doctrines, as a rule, are every week promulgated from their numerous
pulpits.   Narrow-minded men, in connection with each sect, may be
found, who may demur to this statement in its bearings on the sects to
which they themselves do not happen to belong; but this demur to the
contrary notwithstanding, the reader may be well assured that we
express the belief of liberal-minded men—a belief which greatly
rejoices the hearts of all those who would rather see the development
of Christian character than the growth of party peculiarities.   The
remainder of the population is portioned out to the Congregationalists,
the Episcopalians, the Baptists, the Methodists, the Roman Catholics,
and various other sects, too small in numbers, and too crotchety in
their notions, to be of any possible importance, excepting always in
their own eyes.
    We must be somewhat more particular, and shall endeavour to be
so without wearying the reader ; for, although the theme forbids us to
seek his amusement, it prompts us to minister to his gratification, by
discoursing in such a manner as shall, if possible, interest and please him,
as well as, mayhap, contribute a little to his information.
    The country is divided into small districts or parishes, in each of
which there is a church and schoolroom, in connection with the
church established by law ; generally speaking there is one clergyman
only to each church, in which he performs service twice each Lord's
day.   In country districts the two services are frequently merged into
one, which arrangement, it is alleged, suits both the people and the
pastor.   Some few churches are collegiate, and in the more populous
parishes additional accommodation is provided in the shape of chapels
of ease, &c.   As there are many more churches and chapels, so there
are also many more schoolrooms spread over the length and breadth
of the land than those that stand connected with the Established

---

* Written on board the Star of Peace.

Church. These owe their existence to private enterprise and energy, or they have been founded by the liberality of the other sects, or by the charitable bequests of deceased donors.

From time to time sections, more or less numerous and influential, have come out from the communion of the Established Church, and formed themselves into separate and independent communities. These branches of the old tree flourished for a time, and several of them still flourish, side by side with the parent stem. Witness the Free Church and the United Presbyterian Church, under whose umbrageous shades many of the best of the land find shelter and repose. Upwards of a century ago, the *Secession* Church took its rise in the manner above alluded to, under the leadership of the Erskines and Fishers, of fragrant memory; some years later, another section sought relief from the evils of patronage, and formed themselves into what was called the *Relief Presbytery*. On these two occasions the Established Church suffered much more in the loss of moral and spiritual influence than in numbers. A goodly number, however, followed the " Seceding " brethren, and the new communities throve and spread apace. The greatest shock which the Establishment has ever received was the loss, in one day, of so many of her ablest, most learned, and most active ministers, together with thousands of her most devoted and god-fearing people, at the recent Disruption. It will be long before she recovers from that shock, and, in some respects, it may be fairly questioned whether she will ever again recover from it, during the term of her present ecclesiastical existence. The General Assembly of the Church of Scotland had met in St. Andrew's Church, Edinburgh, and when the conflict between the Civil and Ecclesiastical powers reached its crisis, almost all her best men—her men of mark— deliberately left the Court, presided over though it was, by the representative of Royalty, and walked in long and solemn procession, in the presence of many thousands of spectators, to the Hall at Canon-mills. By this act they at once ceased to be her clergy, and secured their freedom. It was a grand moral spectacle, and few among the vast multitude that witnessed it, whatever were their ideas on ecclesiastical matters, were unmoved by the sight. Many hastened to give in their adhesion to the new party; and some, when they saw how matters were going, trimmed off, and hurried home to their manses and glebes, and—empty churches. Some four hundred pulpits had been vacated in one day, and it was no easy matter for the Old Church to supply the demand thus created, from her ministerial resources. She did what she could, but the natural consequence was, that many men were suddenly clothed with the ministerial functions whom neither nature nor art had intended for other than tolerable school-masters and passable tutors. From this cause she will suffer for many a day. The " dominie's " desk was emptied to fill the pulpit, and the change was not destined to raise the intellectual status of the Church. But it was a terrible necessity; and, if there is not an over-abundance of *power* in the Scotch Established Church, it is no small consolation to reflect that, generally speaking, what power there is, is exerted in behalf of Evangelical Truth. This sketch is intended to be both faithful and true, imbued with as little bias as may be, and it therefore affords us sincere pleasure to add, that for pattern pastors the Church of Scotland still has Drs. Smith and Muir; for scholars, Principal Tulloch and Dr. R. Lee; and for men of eloquence she has a MacLeod and a Caird.

The Free Church next demands our attention, as being the largest sect after the Established Church. The rise of this influential community is so recent, and must be so familiar to most readers, even at the antipodes, that the facts already noticed regarding its origin and immediate popularity, may be deemed sufficient. During the few years in which this Church has been in existence, upwards of seven hundred congregations have been gathered and consolidated by its unexampled efforts and liberality. To these congregations regular ministerial service is supplied, and in connection with almost all of them, a well-appointed school will be found. But, it must not be concluded that the Free Church alone cares and provides for the education of the children of Scotland. Its members certainly do their part, but they are fellow-workers with others in this field, the importance of which it is impossible to over-estimate. In addition to these efforts, the new community has, in the free exercise of its young energies, erected a handsome college, at large expense, and instituted an efficient system for the thorough training of her candidates for the sacred office.* At the Disruption we have seen that the Old Church was exposed to a peculiar evil, arising from the sudden evacuation of so many of her pulpits in one day. The Free Church suffered after a similar manner. There were many congregations that separated themselves from the old, and attached themselves to the new community, in parishes where the incumbent did *not* " leave the manse." How to supply these congregations with ministerial service, with the least possible delay, was the question. Much depended upon its prompt and wise solution. The leaders of the movement, men of penetration and experience, were fully alive to this, and gave it their immediate attention. Many young men engaged in preparatory studies joined the ranks of the Free Church, as might have been expected of ingenuous youth, such as those who generally compose the candidates for the Scottish ministry. Still, a sufficient number of thoroughly educated, and otherwise qualified persons to supply the *immediate* demand, was not forthcoming. And, notwithstanding every effort, numbers got permanently settled in churches who brought little intellectual weight to the ministerial order, and scarcely sustained the credit and character of their sect, even though backed by the momentum of recent victory and continued popular applause. This was a cause of weakness to the Free Church, but the consequences have not been all on the wrong side. There can be no doubt that this consideration had its own weight in urging the leaders of the party to do so much for ministerial education, as well as for ministerial support. There was great wisdom in this course, for if you put into the pulpit men of education, possessing at the same time other requisite qualifications, and give them a fair remuneration for their labour, in ninety-nine cases in the hundred, the work performed, by the blessing of Heaven, will be satisfactory. The adherents of the Free Church are very numerous, comprising multitudes from all ranks, and in all social positions—from the noble, proud of his long line of ancestry, to the maid-of-all-work that obeys the behests of his lordship's head-groom. And among them

---

* Much more has been done since this paper was written.

you will find many of the most generous, liberal, and active Christians, whose schemes of Christian effort are intended to better the home population, as well as to send the means of education and christianization to lands less favoured than their own. Time has worked a great change in regard to the evil above referred to, and now we may safely affirm that in few churches will there be found a body of men more worthy of their sacred calling. Still, there are but few names among them that command attention beyond the boundaries of their own community. It is not difficult to account for this state of matters. The period immediately preceding, and the period immediately succeeding the Disruption, must of necessity have been periods of *practical* work, not of profound study. It need not surprise us, then, if when we have named Candlish, Cunningham, Bruce, Buchanan, Tweedie, Fairbairn, and Guthrie, we have about exhausted the list of distinguished men whose names are familiarly known beyond the bounds of their own church. Public expectation is directed towards the younger portion of the ministers of the Free Church, and we predict, although prophecy is not our vocation, that that expectation will not be disappointed.

(*To be continued.*)

BRETHREN DWELLING IN UNITY.
(*Continued from Page* 39.)

In the utter absence of this bond and cement of active charity, and in its place, enmity and contest, it would be better for men to dwell far asunder, lest they " bite and devour, and be consumed one of another." Explosive tempers " easily provoked," are frequently like coals, which burn hotly when collected together, and become extinguished when scattered. We have an illustration of the evil of too close contiguity of men with unhappy tempers, in the strife of the herdsmen of Abraham and Lot ; and such unseemly quarrels and discords on a large scale, and in many hideous forms, have disfigured the records of history in every subsequent age.

However, our business at present is not with war, but with peace : not with hatred, but with love. Let us picture to ourselves a state of things which God requires and approves, and which the Gospel is designed and adapted to bring about, rather than what may really now exist. The standard and pattern being thus high, our desires, efforts, and prayers for universal harmony may be elevated and quickened. " Behold, how good and how pleasant it is for brethren to dwell together in unity ! "

How good and pleasant is *family love and unity*. The family is the first school in which man is instructed to deny himself for others, and so curb his selfishness. It is the garden where the social and kindly sympathies of our nature are intended to be cherished, and made to flourish in beauty and fragrance. With this intent God has implanted strong natural affection between parents and children, brethren and their sisters. It is only in comparatively few cases, and after the heart has been hardened by long continuance in vicious and abandoned courses, that these natural affections can be destroyed. In after life, we are greatly indebted for kindly feelings and benevolent actions in ourselves and others, to family connexions and influences in our early days.

Hence the importance of parents promoting natural kindness, self-denial, generosity and benevolence to all around, among their children. In this way, parents may open up and replenish in their offspring little bubbling fountains of benevolence and love, which may swell into rivers of the most comprehensive charity, fertilizing the waste places of the earth, refreshing many thirsty and saving many dying souls. How delightful is the picture of a whole family living in love and harmony! What can surpass the beauty of such a scene, especially when domestic love is refined and strengthened by true religion? We spontaneously exclaim with our Watts—

> "Blessed are the sons of peace
>   Whose hearts and hopes are one;
> Whose kind designs to serve and please,
>   Through all their actions run.
> Blessed is the pious house
>   Where zeal and friendship meet;
> Their songs of praise, their mingled vows,
>   Make their communion sweet."

How good and how pleasant is *neighbourly love and unity*. Next to the members of our respective families come those who live nearest to us in our several vicinities. As family happiness cannot be secured without the exercise of love, and a faithful discharge of family duties, no more can the social happiness of the same street, hamlet, village, or town, be realized apart from a manifestation of neighbourly love, and a discharge of neighbourly obligations. It is a painful sight, yet one too frequently seen, to behold neighbours picking quarrels one with another, living at variance, "hateful and hating one another," raising and propagating slander, deceiving and defrauding, and constantly engaged in schemes of mutual annoyance. On the other hand, how good and pleasant it is to witness those, whom God has in his providence placed near each other, bound together in love; studying to do good to one another instead of evil, observing a strict regard to truth between neighbour and neighbour, and displaying in their intercourse, justice, respectful esteem, and every social excellence. This can occur only through the operation of the golden law,—"Thou shalt love thy neighbour as thyself," and "Whatsoever ye would that men should do unto you, do ye even so to them." Those are truly loyal people who fulfil the "royal law of love," the love which not only "worketh no ill to his neighbour," but seeks his welfare, and "overcomes evil with good." Thanks to God for the softening and humanizing influence of the Gospel, through which we are permitted to behold many of these fruits of love among neighbours,—a readiness to relieve the distressed, in imitation of the Good Samaritan, and a sympathizing spirit in bereavement, like that of the friends of Martha and Mary when they had lost their beloved brother Lazarus.

How good and pleasant is *patriotic love and unity*. Patriotism, the love of our country, is a sentiment which every one more or less feels and recognizes. For it seems to be inwrought into our nature by Him who formed us, and doubtless it has its great and various uses, although frequently perverted. Love to the place which gave us birth leads the way to love for our best friends, from whose kind regards we derived our earliest and most valuable blessings. Indeed, the affection we have for our country appears to be inseparably connected with a like love for its inhabitants at large. Of this sentiment poets have sung, historians have written: philosophers have explained it, and

and warriors appealed to it when a political change was to be brought about, an invading foe expelled, or civil discord subdued. But a far better way to prove the excellence and utility of patriotism, and to exalt its praises, would be to cultivate love and unity among our countrymen by spreading among them the Gospel of peace. If its heavenly principles were universally embraced and acted upon, they would assuredly correct abuses in government, and vices and errors in society; they would bind in one the shattered community which faction had severed, uproot the bitter weeds of enmity, and plant the olive-branch of peace. It is pre-eminently desirable that we thus advance the welfare of these Australian colonies. We who have migrated to these regions, call many different countries our father-land, and our infant lips were taught various vernacular languages or provincial dialects, and around our young hearts not a few narrow old-world prejudices may have twined and fastened themselves. Do we heartily desire the prosperity of this our adopted land? Then, without ignoring natural predilections in favour of the lands that gave us birth, these preferences *must be subordinated* to mutual love and esteem as men, as Christians, as Australians and the founders of a new nation; and while shaking off the coil of undue national prepossessions, let us in this sunny land, emerge from the chrysalis tomb of dead formalism and stereotyped religious error, and soar aloft on the wings of intelligent faith and fervent love. In this way alone can we make Australia " great, glorious, and free," happy in herself, and a light and a blessing to heathen lands.

How good and pleasant is the prospect of *universal love and unity*. All mankind are in reality brethren; all are citizens of the same great world. The Gospel aims at nothing less than the union of earth's millions in one great family of love. The time when this shall be has not yet arrived. For " wars and rumours of wars" are still abroad, and men's angry, covetous, and, ambitious passions are still effecting more misery than the most desolating famines and pestilences that have ever scourged the nations. But universal peace *shall* arrive. The word of truth has declared it. " Wars shall cease unto the ends of the earth." The bow and the arrow shall be broken, the spear shall be snapped asunder, and the sword be commanded to return and rest in its scabbard. Nay, these weapons shall be melted and remoulded in the fire of love. The spear shall be converted into a pruning-hook, and the sword into a ploughshare. What lately drew blood from men and ministered death, shall draw food from the earth and minister sustenance and life. The metal which ere-while glittered in the battle-field, and created the clatter of arms, and gave impetus to the din of infuriated and bloodthirsty men, shall adorn the humble cottage of the peasant, and make music under the mower's whetstone, with the accompaniment of the ploughboy's cheerful notes. Happy period! when the " Prince of Peace " shall rule victoriously and universally; when He, the most mighty, shall gird his bloodless sword of truth upon his thigh, with his glory and his majesty, and in his majesty shall ride prosperously, because of truth, and meekness, and righteousness; and his right hand, clearing the way to dispense the blessings of redemption, shall teach him terrible things. Jesus shall gather together in himself all the families of the world, and shall unite heaven with a sanctified earth.

Finally, how good is it to behold the Church dwelling in love and unity. The Church of God is the medium and instrument by which those still wandering are to be reclaimed. Love is the very essence of true religion ; the element in which it " lives and moves and has its being." Love to God and our neighbour comprehends all the duties of the Moral Law. In the character of Jesus, as foreshadowed in prophecy and as developed in his life, the purest love, the warmest philanthropy, are conspicuous. In the commands he has given, his " new commandment," to love one another, outshines and outweighs the rest. In the lives and labours of his apostles and of the first Christians, love is the most conspicuous of the graces : selfishness was condemned to death, and the most expansive charity was the vital spirit that filled their breasts. Justly, therefore, might we expect to find love triumphant in the Church, whose very foundation was laid in bleeding love, and whose perfection in holiness is but " love made perfect." But do we see there *only* love and peace ? It must be allowed that a higher standard of morality and a purer pacific feeling actually exist within the pale of the Christian Church than can elsewhere be found ; yet it must also be sorrowfully admitted that many professed followers of Jesus fall far short of full compliance, in this respect, with the religion of their Lord. There needs much faithful self-scrutiny, more earnest prayer, and more constant watchfulness, and an abundant outpouring of the Holy Spirit, ere the Church of Christ will exhibit that oneness of affection for which our Lord so earnestly prayed. The Word of God also must be more generally elevated to its rightful and supreme position, and appealed to as an authority decisive and final. The sacred pages must receive, on a wider scale, a study more devout, candid, and diligent. Thus alone may Christians, entertaining different sentiments, hope to approximate towards each other, and to accelerate the time when their faith in great truths shall be less disfigured by diversity of views on numerous less important topics. \. ho does not feel it incumbent to plead with God for the advent of that happy period ? Because, when the Church is more fully in spirit, and more visibly in acts, and perhaps in form, ONE, the world will become one with her, for the world will then believe in Christ. " Pray for the peace of Jerusalem, they shall prosper that love thee. Peace be within thy walls, and prosperity within thy palaces. For my brethren and companion's sakes, I will now say, Peace be within thee. Because of the house of the LORD our God, I will seek thy good."

Surely no renewed and enlightened mind can fail to acknowledge that the loving union of brethren merits the commendation bestowed upon it in this gem-like psalm.

Christian unity is of *unspeakable value.* " It is precious." " The ornament of a meek and quiet spirit is in the sight of God of great price." Christian love is exceedingly " good," and therefore precious. It is comparatively rare in its higher forms, and its rarity should increase our estimation of it as is usual in other valuables. Love *shines by its own light*, carries with it its own evidence, and commends itself even to the most depraved, as music delights those uninstructed in that science, and unskilled in that art. Love is fragrant as the costly compounded perfume, poured on Aaron's head: it is useful and refreshing as the dew. It is *of heavenly origin*, poured from above as the dew and the consecrating ointment. Such love is no longer natural to earth since the fall of man. It flows from Christ the Head of the Church, who was himself anointed above measure by the Father. Love is *wide-reaching* in its influence. How penetrating and fast-spreading are perfumed oil and the heavenly dew! the former came down on Aaron's person, and filled with delicious odour the whole sanctuary ; the dew cheers the humblest plant and flower. So, evangelical love benefits both the political and the religious in society: it sanctifies the intellect, softens and subdues the heart, teaches the bowels compassion, incites the hands to minister to the needy, and the feet to run on errands of mercy, and to walk in the way of obedience. Love is the life of Zion's regenerated children, and the vital principle of all their truly pious acts. It is a grace blessed and blessing, that carries in its bosom all else that is good and benignant. Love shall live and flourish in the heavenly Jerusalem as an essential element of " spiritual life for evermore." " Charity never faileth."

THE SOLEMN OBLIGATIONS OF THE CHURCH TO SPREAD THE GOSPEL.

No man actuated by Christian principles, and admitting the value of immortal souls, can look upon those around him in a state of profound ignorance, and sunk in vice, with indifference. To do so would give a powerful reason to call in question the sincerity of his profession. In time past when the extent of such an evil was known but to few—seldom heard of—and but little understood, there might have been some color of excuse for apathy ; but now that information has been circulated, and the awful reality is fully before us, no man can remain inactive and be innocent. If an individual possesses talents, whether they are talents of intellect, of property, or influence, as they were entrusted to him by God to be put to a good use, it is his duty to lay them on the altar, and consecrate them to the glory of God, and the welfare of his fellow man. In the present state of society in this colony, this duty might be urged upon every good man simply on the ground of *expediency*, apart from all religious considerations, with a view to insure the peace and good order of society. But we take the higher and holier ground of *religious obligation*, which devolves upon the Christian Church at large. Great solemnity has been attached to this obligation by an authoritive Act of the great Lawgiver of the Church. He has charged his people with the duty of conveying spiritual instruction to their fellow-men. His language is, " Go out *quickly* into the *streets* and *lanes* of the city, and bring in hither THE POOR." And when taking leave of his little church on Mount Olivet, he solemnly devolved upon them the charge to go among all nations, and preach the Gospel to *every creature*, beginning at Jerusalem. Here then is our *duty*, and here follows our *encouragement*, " Lo, I am with you always even to the end of the world."

God, if he had pleased, could have wrought the work by other means, or employed other agents, so as to have superseded all human intervention ; but he has seen fit to appoint man to be his instrument in the instruction and salvation of his fellow-man. Those who are themselves the partakers of divine grace, are to carry the glad tidings of the Gospel to those who are not. On this principle rests every missionary effort, whether at home or abroad. A principle which was most acknowledged—felt—and acted upon, when the Church was in a state of the greatest purity and spiritual prosperity. The *mode* of discharging the obligation has been different according to the light enjoyed or the circumstances of providence at the time, but the *duty* itself is fixed and unchangeable. It derives its authority and character from the law, "Thou shalt love thy neighbor as thyself." This law we are required to *honor ;* but such honor is not rendered by faith *only,* or a simple recognition of the obligation which the law imposes upon us. Something more is necessary. That recognition of duty should lead to deeds of benevolence—kind sympathy—and holy enterprise, under the full influence of a melting compassion for souls. On those who are actuated by these principles, has God put the honor of extending his kingdom among men. And unquestionably it is an honor of no ordinary kind to be chosen for such a purpose. In what a position does this view place the Christian Church in relation to the world ? In what a solemn point of light she has to look at the moral state of mankind ! And yet what a great and glorious enterprise is placed before her ! She is designed to be the salt of the earth, the light of the world. She has to contemplate millions of unenlightened, unconverted, yet immortal beings in the aggregate, who must sit in darkness until she diffuses her light ; and in a state of impurity, until sanctified by the purifying influence of the Gospel. May we not well cry in the language of inspiration, "Arise—shine—for thy light is come, and the glory of the Lord is risen upon thee."

Each church should be the centre of a circle over which its light should radiate, the circle extending as far as its resources will allow. This was one of the great designs of God, in constituting Christians into one body— THE CHURCH. Bishop Butler says, "it being an indispensable law of the Gospel that Christians should unite in religious communities, and these being intended for repositories of the written oracles of God, for standing memorials of religion to unthinking men, and for the propagation of it in the world ; Christianity is very particularly to be considered as a trust deposited with us *on behalf of mankind,* as well as for our own instruction. No one has a right to be called a Christian who does not do something in, his station towards the discharge of his trust, and who does not assist in keeping up and spreading the profession of Christianity where he lives." The Church is called upon to fulfil her Lord's behests, and therefore should arise, "put on her strength" and address herself to her assigned work. In connection with a spirit of glowing piety, she should be richly imbued with a *missionary spirit.* These are identified the one with the other. The object she has before her is a glorious one, if the removal of ignorance—the rooting out of error—the propagation of truth—the communication of moral principle—the renovation of the heart—and the preparing a people for the Lord, constitute such an object. How far this will be realized in our time depends much upon the faithfulness of God's people in the discharge of their solemn trust, and the zeal with which they prosecute their labors. We possess the knowledge of principles which are calculated to effect it. If we earnestly desire to prove their efficacy, let them be zealously brought into operation. They differ from principles which are only of human origin. *They,* may fail—*have* failed a thousand times ; but the principles of the Gospel will not, cannot fail. Wherever they obtain a lodgement in the judgment and conscience they *must* prevail. "My word shall not return unto me void, but it shall accomplish that which I please, and prosper in the thing whereto I sent it." With such an assurance we may "go forward."

An encouragement to do so may be derived from the consideration that we are not called upon to exert an influence which we do not possess. In the church there are to be found the constituent parts of a moral and spiritual machinery of mighty power, which may be fitly compacted together, and brought to bear upon those gigantic evils that are to be grappled with—and an extent of piety which has only to be placed in a proper position, to exert a holy and extensive influence. Some of the churches have already sent forth into the field of the world their pioneer laborers, quite sufficient in number to show what might be done, if the fact of personal obligation to work for God were more generally realized and acted upon. We daily pray, "Thy kingdom come, thy will be done in earth as it is in heaven;" let us follow our prayers by making greater effort to send "more laborers into the harvest." Each church must become much more productive and active before the world will be converted to the faith of the Cross, or before the inhabitants of these colonies will be brought fully under the influence of the Gospel.

If obedience to the commands of Christ had uniformly characterized the conduct of his people in reference to an ungodly world, we have reason to believe that its inhabitants would long ago have been not only nominal but real Christians. With a greater extent of piety, additional means would have been provided, and the Gospel would have been diffused over a much larger portion of the globe than at present. Had Christians followed the example of Christ, this would have been done. "He went about doing good." He sought every occasion to enlighten the understandings of the people—to counteract their prejudices—to interest them in the great and spiritual truths of religion—to direct them in the way of life eternal—and when they would not come to him that they might have life, he *wept* over their impenitence. What might not have been accomplished, had all his followers imbibed his spirit and followed in his steps!

Is it not the duty of every Christian to do this? Are we not required to be followers of him, as dear children? Is not the same mind to be in us, as was also in him? He delighted to do the will of his heavenly Father — it was his meat and drink. When will the members of his Church reach to that state of glowing piety, which will thus make the *habit* of their spiritual being as natural and energetic in the pursuit of spiritual objects, as their bodily appetites are in supplying stimulous for procuring daily food! The early Christians were largely imbued with this spirit. Until the general persecutions they were actively engaged at Jerusalem, for, "daily in the temple, and in *every house*, they ceased not to teach, and preach Jesus Christ." Subsequently, while smarting under the severity of their sufferings, "they went *everywhere*, preaching the word," "the Lord working with them, and confirming the word with signs following." They had too much love for souls, and too much regard to the honor of their Master, to be deterred from prosecuting their object. If men blasphemed, and endeavored to do them dishonor, they bound the scorn to their brow, as their glory, and rejoiced that they were counted worthy to suffer shame for their Master's sake. Instead of being severed from their object they adhered to it with more tenacity. They concentrated all their powers of body and mind on one point—the honor of God in the salvation of a perishing world. Noble purpose! Well was it rewarded with success. The word of the Lord mightily prevailed. Tertullian, who flourished in the early part of the third century, tells us to what an extent it had prevailed as the result of their labors, and the labors of those Christians who succeeded them, and who were baptized with their spirit. He says; "We witness the accomplishment of the words of the Psalmist : their sound is gone out into all the earth, and their words unto the end of the world ! For not only the various countries from which worshippers were collected at Jerusalem on the day of pentecost, but the most distant regions have received the faith of Christ. He reigns among the people whom the Roman arms never yet subdued ; among the different tribes of Getulia and Mauritania ; in the farthest extremities of Spain, and Gaul, and Britain; among the Samaritans, Dacians, Germans, and Scythians; in countries and islands scarcely known to us by name."

To what can we attribute all this success ? Directly, to the blessing of the great Head of the Church, there can be no doubt, for all increase is of God. But *instrumentally* we trace it to the principle of individual and collective obligation, which was fully felt, and acted out by all the primitive Christians. As *churches* they were active—as *individuals* they were active. Let the same principle become as generally operative in all our modern churches, and it would not be difficult to foretell the results which would follow. There are *thousands* of Christians in the Australias who have recognized the principle of personal obligation, from the time of taking upon themselves a christian profession, but in too many cases it has been a principle dormant and inoperative. Could they but perceive this solemn obligation in a clearer light—were it to present itself to their view with a sacredness commensurate with its importance—were they to recognize more closely its connection with the kingdom of Christ among men and the immortal destiny of souls, what would be the result ? We should see the great body of the servants of Christ baptized with the spirit of the primitive believers—feeling and laboring as they did. But alas ! this spectacle is not fully realized; here we fall short. This is what Christians and the Church ought to be, but what they *are* not. The Church in general has been too much under the power of selfishness, to allow of such an unreserved consecration of herself to the service of her Lord and Master.

(To be continued in our next.)

EXTRACTS.

SOPHISTRY.

To reason justly from a false principle is the perfection of sophistry, which it is much more difficult to expose, than to refute false reasoning. It is easy to discover any error in false reasoning, and by just reasoning to refute it. But if men reason justly from any principle, whether true or false, their reasoning is conclusive, and the more it is examined the more conclusive it will appear. We find as strong and conclusive reasoning in favor of error as in favor of truth. The only proper way, therefore, to expose the errors of profound sophisters, is to make it appear that they have built all their just and conclusive reasonings upon some false or absurd principle.— *Emmons.*

THE SATISFACTION OF CHRIST.

Christ satisfied herein—not the divine anger—but the divine craving and yearning after a perfect holiness, righteousness, and obedience in man, God's chosen creature, the first fruits of his creatures; which craving no man had satisfied, but all had disappointed, before. There had been a flaw in every other man's escutcheon : every other, instead of repairing the breach which Adam had made, had himself left that breach wider than he found it. But here at length was one, a son of man, yet fairer than all the children of men, one on whom the Father's love could rest with a perfect complacency, in regard of whom he could declare, " This is my beloved Son in whom I am well pleased," in whom he had pleasure without stint and without drawback. And that life of his, the long self-offering of that life of love, was crowned, consummated, and perfected by the sacrifice of his death, wherein he satisfied to the uttermost every demand which God had made upon all the other children of men, and which they had not satisfied for themselves.— *Trench.*

CORRESPONDENCE.

To the Rev. the Editor of the Southern Spectator, per favor of Church of England Record.

Bishopscourt, January 26, 1859.

MY DEAR SIR,—I have just read, with much pain, your editorial comment upon the correspondence published in your number for December, between the Bishop of Adelaide and the Rev. T. Binney. I confess that I am at a loss to understand how a person really desirous, as I believe you to be, to promote brotherly union among all those who love the Lord Jesus Christ in sincerity, could have penned and published such observations upon an ecclesiastical rule of what, although you have separated from it, you appear to regard in the main as a sound branch of the Church of Christ.

Surely any particular church must, according to your own principles, be at liberty to make its own rules respecting those whom it will admit to minister in the congregation; and it would, I think, be difficult for any church to adopt a rule more wise and judicious in itself, or expressed in language less likely to offend the members of other churches than that of the Church of England. That rule is as follows :—" It is not lawful for any man to take upon him the office of public preaching, or ministering the sacrament in the congregation, before he be lawfully called, and sent to execute the same. And those we ought to judge lawfully called and sent, which be chosen and called to this work by men who have public authority given unto them in the congregation, to call and send ministers into the Lord's vineyard."—Art. xxiii.

The Church of England does not, either in this Article or in any other authoritative document pronounce that " no man is a proper and authorised minister of the Gospel," in the particular church to which he belongs, " whose ordination is not derived immediately from a bishop;" but it very properly claims to itself the right of determining in what manner its own ministers shall be " chosen and called,"—viz., according to the practice of the Primitive Church, by Episcopal Ordination. It is not, however, as I believe, absolutely bound to the observance of this mode out of the United Kingdom ; for it is a law of the State, and not of the Church, which requires of necessity Episcopal Ordination ; and I doubt whether that law applies to the colonies. At the same time, I do not hesitate to express my own opinion that it would be exceedingly *inexpedient*, except in cases of necessity, to deviate from it. If it were deviated from, the license from the bishop could alone authorise any person, according to the 23rd article, to minister in a Church of England congregation.

You affirm that this rule of the Church of England is the *real barrier* to an effective and thoroughly cordial union of Christians and churches of different denominations. I cannot agree with you in this. I can understand how it may be the chief barrier to a cordial union between the Episcopal Church of England and the Presbyterian Church of another land, which are in agreement with one another upon all doctrinal matters ; have articles of religion and a confession of faith, which constitute respectively an acknowledged standard of doctrines ; and recognise each a regularly ordained ministry. But how can it be the real barrier to an union between the Church of England and those congregations or Churches (for I am quite willing to give them the name) which have, upon conscientious objections to its doctrine or constitution, separated itself from its communion ? If these objections are well-founded, then the matters to which they relate are the " real barrier " to an union. If they are groundless, then the mistaken views of the separatists are the barrier. But, in either case, I cannot see how those who have conscientiously separated, or who conscientiously continue in a state of separation, can desire an union. I can assent to the doctrine that a dissenter is not necessarily guilty of schism ; but I cannot assent to the doctrine that a dissenter on any ground, so unimportant in his own opinion as not to constitute a " barrier to an effective and thoroughly cordial union " with the church from which he has separated, *is not guilty of schism.* To represent the exclusion of ministers of other denominations from the pulpit of the Church of England, as "the real barrier" to an union of the churches, appears to me therefore to be casting a most unjust stigma upon all conscientious nonconformists.

Moreover, a person must be very little acquainted with the relative positions of the Church of England and the various non-conformist churches in this colony, if he suppose that the admission of their ministers to its pulpits would avail to effect a "free, cordial, and compact union of Protestants." I will not enter into particulars on this, to me very painful part of the subject; I will only say, that I think each particular church will most effectually "make head against a papistical and infidel world," by endeavoring to promote true religion and piety among its own members, and avoiding, as much as possible, any offensive remarks upon the principles and practices of others.

Such remarks upon the Church of England are sometimes heard on public occasions, as recently at Bendigo, from the lips of ministers of other denominations; and I regret to say that the tone of your own comment partakes of the same character. It seems to me calculated rather to prevent the union of individual Christians than to promote the union of churches. I am sure, however, that you did not intend this.

There is one sentence in your observations which I am unwilling to pass unnoticed. You say,—"To fit such as these (a Calvin or Melancthon, &c.) for admission (to the humblest pulpit of the Anglican Church), they must ignore their previous orders, acknowledge the invalidity of all their past ministerial acts, and begin de novo by receiving from a duly consecrated bishop, deacon's orders, the lowest in the clerical scale, and rising to higher grades in due time." Now, undoubtedly, any such person, if he desire to become a minister in the Church of England, must begin in the lowest grade. But this is, from the very nature of the case, necessary, and does not appear to me to imply any degradation. He may, if the bishop see fit, remain in that lowest grade a few days, or only a few hours; and, having been admitted to priest's orders, becomes at once eligible to the highest grade—of bishop. Nor is it necessary, as you state, that he should "ignore his previous orders," and "acknowledge the invalidity of all his past ministerial acts." He may retain his own opinion upon these points, while he consents, as Archbishop Leighton did, to receive ordination again in another form.

It would be well if our nonconformist brethren would remember, that Episcopal ordination is an essential characteristic of the Church of England; and that, while they may, if they think right to do so, make that or any other characteristic, a ground for separating from the Church, they are not justified in complaining, after such separation, of its operating as a barrier against the maintenance of an ecclesiastical union with them.

I am, my dear sir,
With sincere personal esteem,
Your faithful brother in Christ,
C. MELBOURNE.

To the Rt. Rev. the Bishop of Melbourne.

St. Kilda, February 18, 1859.

MY LORD,—I freely express to you my deep regret that anything I have written should have inflicted a moment's pain upon one for whom I have so high a personal respect as your lordship. I carefully read over the Adelaide correspondence, and merely put down the first thoughts that rose to my mind on a review of the whole. I admit that I did this rather hastily, for I was on the eve of a journey to the interior, and had to leave everything ready for the press before I went away. This prevented me from revising the proof of the article in question, which will also account for some typographical *errata*. Upon reviewing what I wrote I clearly perceive that the tone of it is faulty; it might have been more mildly expressed; and I sincerely lament that I have given any ground of complaint in this respect. Having readily and frankly made this concession, permit me to say that I am persuaded the chief cause of the pain, which you and others may have felt, has arisen, to a large extent, from a misapprehension of my meaning.

1. I never meant by "union of Christians and churches of different denominations" the fusion of different bodies into one. True, the Bishop of Adelaide's notion was something of that kind,—he projected a grand ideal scheme of the visible Protestant Church under a modified episcopacy,—but the proposition really applied to him to open occasionally the pulpits of episcopal ministers

ministers of other bodies, and to Mr. Binney in particular, repudiated any such scheme as at present visionary and impracticable. All they urged was friendly interchange of pulpits when circumstances seemed to render it desirable.

2. The question being thus changed, from amalgamation or organic union to a mere interchange of pulpit-services, when mutually convenient and wished for, such as now obtains among all other non-episcopal evangelical denominations, and to such an amount of public recognition as that interchange involves, I had no idea, when speaking of " a free, cordial, compact, and effective union of Protestants to make head against a papistical and infidel world," of a close, organic union, the blending of many churches into one visible community. I agree with the Governor of South Australia, and the gentleman with whom he united in a memorial to the Bishop of that diocese, that such an organization, if it be ever realised, is, at present, in the far distance. With such an understanding and impression on the subject under discussion, the most of what I said about episcopal ordination, as usually viewed, being the real barrier to union among Protestants, referred to the sort of union actually proposed, and to its influence on other than strictly church efforts to propagate the Gospel. With this explanation it will at once appear obvious that the greater part of your lordships letter has little or no bearing upon what I wrote.

3. That agreement among Christians in matters of church government as well as doctrine is abstractedly desirable no one can doubt. It would be a goodly spectacle to see reproduced that approach to uniformity in organization and practice which marked the primitive assemblies during the life-time of the apostles. But whether that state of things will ever occur again appears to me questionable. There are manifestly some things comparatively non-essential, and respecting which no positive and clearly defined law is laid down in our Divine Statute Book. About these, as the human mind is constituted, liberty being allowed to all, there possible always will be difference of judgment. Nor does it appear to me that outward uniformity is the sort of union so much insisted on in Scripture, or that it is, in itself, so important as some imagine. That differences existed even among the primitive believers is well-known ; nor did the apostles put them down with a high hand and insist on rigid uniformity. " Whereto they had attained " they had to " walk by the same rule and mind the same thing," but no further. Everyone was to be " fully persuaded in his own mind," but to allow to others the same liberty he assumed for himself, even in some matters which he might deem points of conscience. We find many inculcations to union and oneness, but it was to unity of the spirit and oneness of heart. It was a union of love, which involved forbearance and forgiveness, something to put up with, which tried the temper and put charity and candour to the test. And so it, very likely, ever will be. The notion of one visible Church seems to me to have no place in the New Testament. Wherever visible Christianity is spoken of in its organized and social form, it is as churches, assemblies, societies. But where the grand idea of one universal Church is the theme, it always refers to the aggregate of true Christians, the spiritual body of Christ. The notion of a Catholic Visible Church, uniform in observance and strictly subordinated under one form of government, was clearly a post-apostolic idea, the gradual growth of time, and the product of pre-existing notions of both Jews and Gentiles,—the former having been used to a single visible church under a High Priest in connexion with the Mosaic Theocracy, and the latter to a Pontifex Maximus and other hierarchs who exercised authority over the superstitions of the people.

Our blessed Lord in his high-priestly intercession with his Father says,—" I pray that they all may be one, as thou Father art in me and I in thee; that they also may be one in us; that the world may believe that thou hast sent me." This is often referred to as an argument for uniformity, and the idea in many minds is, that the prayer will be fulfilled only when there shall be one form of church-government, one set of articles, and complete uniformity of worship. But what is the reason why our Intercessor prays for oneness? Is it not for its moral effect?— the effect it would have upon the world in inducing faith in Christ's mission ? But may not external uniformity exist with serious inward discrepancies, as in the churches of Rome and England? And is there any particular tendency in uniformity as such, and developed as it has heretofore been, to produce moral conviction? Supposing that the state of things among Christians were such that, while different views on church-government prevailed, distinct organizations existed, and differences also on minor points of doctrine characterized the various creeds, there yet was universally displayed a spirit of genuine brotherly love,—showing itself in frank recognition, mutual good-will, ready co-operation in all wherein agreement existed, and manifest delight in each other's success,—would not this be a grander, more imposing moral spectacle and more influential in producing conviction, in the carnal mind, of the truth and value of Christianity than any form of outward Christianity however compactly organized?

4. In the remarks I made on the Church of England notion of the exclusive validity of episcopal ordination being the real barrier to an *effective union* among Protestant Christians, I had in view, not, as I have said, strictly church union, but union for such objects as are compatible with ecclesiastical diversity. I heartily rejoice that there are many practical objects of great moment where this barrier does not to much extent interfere, such as the circulation of the Bible and religious tracts, and even the working of city missions; and in such objects it has been my delight for many years to take a very active part, having been for a long time secretary to a Bible society of which the present Archbishop of Canterbury, when Bishop of Chester, was the patron, and on the platform of which it was often our lot to meet. But there were *other* objects and departments of work where the idea of a specific virtue attaching to episcopal ordination and episcopal consecration operated as a real and indeed insurmountable barrier to cordial co-operation. What troubles and heart-burnings have arisen in the matter of interments, not only from other than episcopally ordained ministers not being permitted to officiate at the burial of their dead in the parish churchyard, but in the refusal or inability of episcopalian clergymen to inter in public cemeteries that were not consecrated. In such cemeteries the barrier of separation has been carried to the grave itself, one portion of the ground and one chapel being consecrated and the other not, and sometimes a wall or hedge being insisted on to divide off the consecrated from the unconsecrated parts. Ministers of various denominations advocate missionary societies together on the platform; an Episcopalian proposes, and a Presbyterian seconds, a motion recommending prayer—united prayer—for the out-pouring of the Spirit: but when it comes to the *practical* part, they cannot carry it out: an Episcopalian cannot go to the Presbyterian chapel and take part in the public services at a united prayer-meeting, and the Presbyterian is not allowed to enter the Episcopalian church pulpit to join in such a service there. Social services are constantly being held for promoting the erection of places of worship, and ministers of all evangelical denominations freely meet together to sympathise with and encourage each other, except, generally speaking, the Episcopalians: even your lordship recommends your clergy not to attend such meetings; and what can the barrier be that separates the Episcopalian from others, but some such notion as the one under consideration? The *Evangelical Alliance* in Britain was a noble movement, in which many of the devoutest minds among the clergy of the Church of England took a sincere and earnest part. But its influence was confined to a *select few*, to ministers and leading laymen in the several churches, who could meet in committee-rooms and school-houses, and there exhort one another and pray together. And there it stopped: the masses of Christians were never touched, and took scarcely any interest in the Alliance. For when any movement was made to hold Alliance meetings in places of worship, where alone the people could be reached, and where they might be addressed by ministers of different communions, and devotional exercises carried on, it was always frowned upon. The Episcopalian could not enter the chapel, the Dissenter would not be permitted to enter the church: all the other ministers could freely interchange, but the single one, the episcopally ordained, could not. And this, in my opinion, is the real reason why the Alliance never has been popular with the bulk of Christians. Your lordships therefore, will perceive that I had in view some practical modes and manifestations of union—which I deem of as great or greater importance than the fusion of many churches into one—when I spoke of the real barrier to united action.

5. The right of each church to frame such regulations as it deems scriptural and proper for the admission of ministers to serve in its congregations cannot be questioned. All communions do it, and to have any organization and government at all they must do it. There must be some mode, more or less formal, by which recognition of ministerial status is given. But, if I mistake not, it is not the general custom, when a minister duly ordained in one communion transfers himself to another, to require him to be *re*-ordained, to go through precisely the same process as one who is newly entering on the ministry. Among Congregationalists, Presbyterians, and Wesleyans, the validity of the previous ordination is admitted, and a service of recognition,—in which the change of sentiment and adhesion to the principles and regulations of the adopted church are avowed—suffices. A similar course, I understand, is adopted in your lordship's church in the event of Roman Catholic priests joining it. Their status as clergymen is admitted, and

they are received into your communion, I know not by what process, but by something which differs from a first ordination. Now, what Protestants of other communions complain of, is, that the courtesy which they all show to one another, and which is extended by the English Church to Roman Catholics, is not extended by the English Church to *them*; and they cannot account for this but on the principle that there is some mystic virtue supposed to inhere in *epi-copal* ordination as such, and perhaps in apostolical succession, which distinguishes it *per se* from all other ordinations, and renders it necessary to any one's being recognised as really invested with the ministerial office. I know that this is not your lordship's own opinion, as you have distinctly stated the contrary, but it is clearly the doctrine of the English Church, if we may judge from what it invariably requires from all who go over to its ranks from other bodies.

Your lordship considers that the requirement of re-ordination does not imply a denial of the validity of the previous ministry. If there be any force in the above remarks, it does involve that implication. The question is not what the individual who submits to re-ordination thinks about his previous ministry, but how the church he has joined treats it, and, in this case, it obviously treats it as a nullity. That this is no fanciful and unimportant point is obvious from the manner in which it affected some of the most eminent and moderate of the ejected ministers. One of the chief stumbling-blocks in their way was the inexorable requirement of re-ordination from all who, however eminent for gifts, usefulness, or position, could show nothing more than ordination by a Presbytery. So it was with Philip Henry and John Howe.[*]

6. To recur, however, to the original question which raised the present controversy, the admission of ministers not episcopally ordained to officiate in episcopal pulpits, not as incumbents, but occasionally, when specially invited. Why might not this be allowed without the stranger being required to submit to re-ordination, or without his acceptance of the invitation being supposed to imply his approval of all and every thing in the church, which asks from him passing ministrations? When I admit Presbyterians or Wesleyans to my pulpit, which I have often done, I never supposed their preaching for me implied their conversion to Independency: nor when I have preached in their pulpits did I mean to convey an approval of their systems wherein they differed from my own. Such friendly interchanges are well understood as expressions of kindly and brotherly feeling, as personal proofs, on the part of the inviters, that they regard the parties invited to be true and faithful ministers of Jesus Christ, whose services are likely to edify their flocks; and those who comply, by their very act, reciprocate the compliment; nor does there result from such interchange the least relaxation of discipline or loosening of the arrangements of the most compactly organized communities. And if conforming and nonconforming ministers were occasionally to preach for each other when expediency dictated such a step, each, of course, conducting the worship of the respective churches according to their custom, I see no surrender of principle in this, or interference with the strictest discipline any church may please to exercise over its *own* ministers. The rule your lordship quotes from the 23rd article, defining who are to be regarded as ministers of the Church, is, I think, a very proper one and inoffensively expressed, but I apprehend it refers only to the *regular* and *stated* ministers of your own communion, to those who alone are to be recognised as *its* clergymen; and, if so, is not applicable to the case in hand. But if it *do* refer to others as well, and *so* refer to them as to compel the inference that they have taken upon themselves the office of the ministry without being lawfully called

---

[*] Matthew Henry says of his father, Philip Henry: "His reasons for his nonconformity were very considerable. It was no rash act, but deliberate and well-weighed in the balances of the sanctuary. He could by no means submit to be re-ordained, so well satisfied was he in his call to the ministry and his solemn ordination to it, by the laying on of the hands of the Presbytery, which God had graciously owned him in, that he durst not do that which looked like a renunciation of it, as null and sinful, and would be at least a tacit invalidating and condemning of all his administrations. This, of re-ordination, was the first and great bar to his conformity, and which he mostly insisted on. He would sometimes say, 'that for a Presbyter to be ordained a Deacon, is at best *suscipere gradum Simeonis*.'"—*Sir J. B. William's Life of Philip Henry*, p. 97.

The celebrated John Howe after his ejectment had a friendly interview with Dr. Seth Ward, Bishop of Exeter. The bishop asked him his reasons for refusing to conform. Howe replied, "that without taxing his lordship's patience beyond all decency, he could not give such an account of his objections as justice to himself required." The bishop then requested him to mention any one of the points at which he scrupled. On this Howe specified, *re-ordination*. "Pray sir," said th bishop, "what *hurt* is there in being twice ordained." "*Hurt*, my lord, it *hurts* my understanding; the thought is shocking; it is an absurdity, since nothing can have two beginnings. I am sure I am a minister of Christ, and am ready to debate that matter with your lordship, but I cannot begin again to be a minister.["]—*Roger's Life of Howe*, p. 151.

and sent to execute the same, and if those who have public authority in the episcopal congregation (or church) exclude them even from occasional ministration *on that account*, I say the more's the pity: it would seem to me on such interpretation to establish the point, which your lordship does not hold, that ministers of other communities are unauthorised intruders into the sacred office.

Trusting that this passage-at-arms into which I have unexpectedly and unintentionally been drawn may not interfere with the kindly and christian feeling which has all along subsisted between your lordship and myself, I am, your lordship's true and

Faithful friend and servant,
THE EDITOR.

SELF-DENIAL.

Lines written by the late Mrs. Beazley, wife of the Rev. Joseph Beazley, Redfern, Sydney, addressed to a young Friend. *

Not mine each splendid deed to sing,
Which may from self-denial spring;
For these but rarely are afforded,
And then by nobler bards recorded.
But there are times of self-denial
When few appreciate the trial,
(Though much we need the potent spell
Of that most Christian principle),
When no kind words the deed applaud,
And no fond glances give reward;
Nought to subdue the swelling heart
And bid it act a gentle part,
Save Duty's stern, unyielding voice,
And her's alone, to aid our choice.

'Tis hard to check retaliation,
To spare a giddy friend's vexation,
While she, unconscious, (we suppress
All answer to her bitterness
From such kind motive,) carries on
The taunting jest and critic tone,
While other listeners standing by,
Who hear *her* words—not read *your* eye,
May call you spiritless and tame;
'Tis hard indeed to bear such blame.
Why should we?   We have our reward—
Ah! known to few - the smile of God.
The praise of men fails in this light,
The calm sweet sense of acting right.

Again, when o'er the couch we bend
Of some lov'd convalescent friend
Who all our care, our love, has known;
How sad to hear the peevish tone
Remaining weakness may create.
Our eyes are filled,—we scarce can wait
For the heart's reas'ning—but we burn
To upbraid this harsh unkind return;
But the example of our Lord,
The utterance of his holy word—
" Bless'd are the meek," descends like balm;
The bosom's storm subsides to calm.

Again, when we delight to rove
Through scenes which youth and fancy love,
Each high and cherished thought set free
To weave a web of poesy,—

---

* The above was found among her papers, and is a juvenile production. It is inserted, less for the sake of the poetry than for the excellency and maturity of the sentiments at so early an age, and for the gratification of a large circle of friends, who revere the memory of the authoress.

How difficult to check these dreams
And turn to common home-spun scenes;
To leave our fancied elevation,
And take with joy our real station.
Nay, smile not thus, ye sober band,
Who never tread this fairy land,
These are real trials—harder far
To bear than deeper sufferings are:
For then we heavenly influence seek,
Nor meet our foes unarm'd and weak.

Unnumber'd seasons might we mention,
But these suffice for our intention,
To show how magnanimity
E'en in a girlish heart may lie.
When real religion is the root
It thus will yield the sweetest fruit;
Bliss will from self-denial flow,
The purest kind we taste below.
Then, Clara, may it be our aim
To 'stablish and make good our claim
To this great virtue; it will prove
Parent of meekness, patience, love;
When we secure this blessed train,
Life will be peace and death be gain.

Tottenham, April 6, 1880.   S. T. J

REV. THOMAS BINNEY.—Mr. Binney after nearly three months' stay in Victoria, during which he preached in nearly all the Congregational places of worship and in several others, and once or twice gave lectures, large crowds of people of all denominations always being present, left per steamer for Launceston, on Wednesday, February 16th. He purposes serving the cause of religion in Tasmania as he has done in the other colonies, so far as the state of his health, which is now much improved, will permit. When his visit to Tasmania is completed he will return to Melbourne, and thence proceed to Sydney.

THOMAS FULTON, ESQ.—*Death and Funeral.*—The cause of religion, of Congregationalism, of temperance, of honest government municipal and general, and of almost every good cause, has suffered a severe loss by the sudden death of Mr. Fulton. The manner of his death has added to the painfulness of the bereavement. Engaged in erecting some machinery at a quartz-mine at Sandhurst, on descending a deep shaft to inspect the work, when about half-way down some derangement of the apparatus at the top by which he was being lowered, caused him to be suddenly precipitated to the bottom. He was completely crushed by the fall, both legs being broken, one completely shattered. Amputation became necessary, and the operation was performed some three or four hours after he was conveyed to the house of Mr. Bannerman, of the Bank of New South Wales. He expired about half an hour afterwards. Between the accident and the departure of the breath from the body he was for the most part conscious, but scarcely able to speak, certainly not to converse. Mrs. Fulton was happily there to soothe his last moments. His remains were brought down from Sandhurst to his own residence at St. Kilda, from whence they were removed to the place of interment. The funeral took place on Tuesday, February 22nd, at the Melbourne cemetery. The procession left St. Kilda at one o'clock and reached the Cemetery at three. The corpse was followed by a long string of mourning coaches, containing the numerous relatives of the deceased, and by a procession on foot of his workmen from the foundry, by whom he was much respected. Private carriages and vehicles were numerous; upwards of fifty passed through the St. Kilda toll-bar, and the number swelled to a full hundred before the procession had cleared the streets of Melbourne. Nearly all the shops, inns, offices, and banks on the entire line of road were closed, and the blinds of private houses drawn down. The flag on the Town Hall was hoisted half-mast high, and so were those of the steamers, ships, and lighters in the river. Large crowds on both sides of roads and streets watched the procession, many a hat was reverentially taken off as it passed along, and a general grief seemed to pervade all classes. Among the persons who followed the hearse in vehicles were the pastor and deacons of the church of which Mr. Fulton was a member and a deacon, the ministers of the Congregational body, and various ministers of other denominations; a vast number of old colonists, of whom Mr. Fulton was one of the oldest, the mayor and several of the aldermen and council of the corporation, Mr. F. having till very lately been one of their number; together with a miscellaneous assembly of members of the Legislature, lawyers, merchants, and others, who came to show their respect for the deceased. Seldom has such a funeral been seen in Melbourne. Sympathy for the melancholy fate of the deceased, and for the bereaved condition of the widow and family; respect for ability energy and industry, honesty straightforwardness and frankness, for public spirit benevolence and charity, and, as the basis and crowning ornament of all, sincere earnest and consistent piety, thoroughly wrought into all his character and actions, combined to call forth this unusual measure of public sorrow and esteem. The funeral service at the grave was conducted jointly by the Rev. R. Fletcher, the present, and the Rev. T. Odell, the former, pastors of the deceased. "Blessed are the dead that die in the Lord, from henceforth: yea, saith the spirit, that they may rest from their labors, and their works do follow them."

MISSIONS.
CHINESE MISSION, VICTORIA.

We are pained to have to state that this society, after existing upwards of three years, has come to a close for want of funds. The particulars will be found in the subjoined report, which was read at a special meeting, held in the Mechanics' Institution, Melbourne, and convened for the purpose of winding up the affairs of the Society. The meeting was held on Tuesday afternoon, November 30, the Dean of Melbourne presiding. The statement of the committee, read by the Rev. J. Darling, of St. John's Church, we submit, somewhat abridged.

The Committee of the Chinese Mission have deemed it desirable to convene a general meeting of its friends and supporters to lay before them a statement of their proceedings and prospects in order to determine on the course to be taken under present circumstances.

The presence of a large body of Chinese heathen, numbering between 25,000 and 30,000 souls, created a painful anxiety in the hearts of Christians in Victoria, and they felt desirous of doing something for the spiritual welfare of these heathen strangers. Two native Christians unexpectedly arrived from China. Their services were immediately engaged, and subsequently the services of the Rev. W. Young, formerly a missionary in China, who arrived in Sydney, was secured, to superintend the mission. Three agents were thus at once obtained, and that without any cost whatever of passage or outfit to the society. Thus the finger of providence seemed to indicate the way to the establishment of the Society.

The first and second public meetings held in this city, on behalf of the Chinese mission, were numerously attended, and a deep and lively interest in its object was manifested on both occasions. It was thus inaugurated under auspices, which seemed to foretel future prosperity to the new Christian cause. But it is to be regretted these anticipations have not been realised.

The limited supplies, furnished by subscriptions to the treasurer, time after time, made it a matter of extreme difficulty for him to meet the current expenses during the first year, and were it not that advances were made, the affairs of the mission must have come to a stand after the first six months. The same financial difficulty was felt during the second year, though not to the same extent. During the third year matters were still more discouraging. The committee being in arrears to the agents for their salaries, jeopardised the very existence of the mission, so that on the 15th of September last, the following resolution was passed by the committee:—

"That it is incumbent on the Church in the colony, either to carry on the mission without debt, or to abandon it altogether, and that the alternative be made a matter of special consideration at the next meeting of committee, October 13th proximo.

" That in the mean time a circular embodying the above resolution, with a copy of the last report, be forwarded to the ministers of the several religious denominations in the colony, requesting contributions to be guaranteed either by way of annual subscriptions or congregational collections." The above resolution having been carried out, your committee regret to say the result proved unfavorable. The Rev. Mr. Young therefore announced his intention of resigning his connection with the mission on the 31st October. On his tendering his resignation, the committee, at a meeting held on the 20th October, passed the following resolution :—

" The Rev. William Young having tendered his resignation, the committee, whilst accepting the same, desire to record their regret that Mr. Young has not been cheered in his labors by the more hearty co-operation of the christian churches in this country, and they would express their confidence that his past faithful exertions have not been in vain, together with a fervent hope that the Lord of the harvest may still employ him as an instrument for carrying on his work of mercy on behalf of the Chinese."

The committee have had to contend with the following, among other difficulties :—

1. The low state of the funds, which may be attributed, in a great measure to the local claims on the various churches in this colony. These claims have been of a pressing and immediate nature and have precluded the churches from giving substantial aid to this cause, though we must ever remember it is a first duty to give to him that needs as well as to provide for our own wants. 2. The strong feeling of prejudice in the minds of a great many Europeans against the Chinese, has made the mission very unpopular. It is moreover frequently asserted, in reply to applications for aid in behalf of this mission, that there is much to be done among our European population in the colony, and that while such want exists it is imprudent to expend our means in relieving the spiritual wants of the Chinese. With this feeling, however, your committee cannot sympathise. 3. The catholic basis on which the mission has been conducted, appears, in the view of some, to have operated against its success. It is to be feared that there are some grounds for this opinion ; for the Church seems to require much more of the love of Christ, and the unity of the Spirit pervading all its branches, before there could be displayed that sympathy and liveliness of interest in the mission which would be a certain pledge of its perpetuity and success. But if there have been obstacles and discouragements, there are also encouraging circumstances which, perhaps, more than counterbalance them :

1. The accessibility of the Chinese. There is nothing like caste among them, as among the Hindoos. The missionary who knows their language can gain ready admittance into their habitations everywhere, and will find them willing to listen to his message. 2. There is always to be found a goodly number among them who are disposed to assist the missionary, to a certain extent, in the attainment of some of his objects, such as erecting schools and places of worship. It is true they may do this from a friendly regard to his character, and not to the cause he seeks to promote ; still it is a disposition of which he can avail himself with advantage. 3. The insulated position of these people in this colony is a circumstance greatly in favor of the mission. It is a great advantage to have them removed far away from the atmosphere of heathenism. The absence of priests, fortune tellers, pompous paradings of idols, stated idolatrous festivals, tombs, ancestral tablets, halls, and a variety of other objects and observances, which foster superstition and nourish idolatry, is no small advantage. Their long continued absence from home has, to a great extent, loosened the hold of idolatry on the hearts of several of the Chinese, and the removal of this obstacle has assisted the missionary to recommend to them the Gospel of Christ. 4. The reception given to the agents by the people, has, on the whole, been cordial and encouraging. The journals and reports that have been published, it is hoped, afford satisfactory proof of this. 5. The results of the mission, although it has been carried on under the most depressing influence at times, are of an encouraging character. Two chapels

have been built, with money collected almost entirely amongst the Chinese.
A third one would have been completed before this, had the agents met with
more encouragement. More than £300 has been raised *entirely* among the
Chinese in three years for the erection or repairs of places of worship. They
have thus contributed towards christian objects at the rate of £100 annually,
and in addition to this there are some in Melbourne who are contributors to the
funds of the mission. 6. The applications for baptism, received recently from
three Chinese, show that the preaching of the word of God to the heathen has
not been in vain, and ought to encourage the churches to strive still more in
efforts of love on behalf of these heathen.

While the committee regret that the mission has not been supported by the
more hearty co-operation of the christian churches collectively, yet they
indulge a hope that the encouraging prospects, above referred to, may be taken
advantage of by the several churches taking up separate spheres of labor in the
various gold-fields where the Chinese are located. H. Jennings, Esq. read a
financial statement, showing a deficiency of about £150. A series of resolutions were moved and seconded by the Revs. Messrs. Sunderland, Draper, and
Taylor, expressing regret at the necessity of dissolving the society, and hope
for its speedy resuscitation in another form by the various denominations in
the colony. A letter was read from the Bishop of Melbourne, promising on
behalf of the Episcopal church, a quarter of the debt, and Robert Kerr, Esq.,
made a similar promise on behalf of the Baptist denomination. It is some
consolation to know that with the close of this Institution, efforts for the
evangelization of the Chinese in Victoria will not cease. There is still a
society, based upon general principles, sustained by friends at Geelong and
Ballaarat, of which Lo Sam Yuen is the able and useful agent. And at Castlemaine, it is understood, the Wesleyans are prepared to take up the work and to
engage Leong-a-toe as their agent ; and perhaps other branches of the church
may take separate action on other gold-fields. That past labors have not been
altogether in vain, may be seen from the following narrative in addition to the
two others of a similar kind referred to above and which have been published
in this magazine.

———————◆———————

OUR ENGLISH CORRESPONDENT'S TALK ABOUT BOOKS.

December 16, 1858.

When I drop a letter into the post for Australia, it seems like casting the precious product of one's brains into the mouth of a bottomless abyss, which silently
swallows everything, and gives no sign. I may, indeed, exercise my imagination in
following the mail-bag, which has the honor of bearing my valuable communication,
as it travels, according to circumstances, over the ocean, or through the wonders
of "foreign parts." Projecting my personality into my literary offspring, I may
indulge in virtuous indignation as we pass through the part of our journey indicated by "*via* Marseilles," at the monstrous flunkey-despotism which is astonishing
our self-satisfied nineteenth century with its bloated foulness in the land of France.
I may farther nurse my sentimentalism with historic reminiscences and high-flown
soliloquies on the "blue" Mediterranean. I may turn aside with the learned
Gladstone on his hopeful mission to the Ionian Isles, and hear him discuss in
wonderful Italian the advantages of our protection to a people who don't want to
be protected, or express to him my unlearned astonishment at the webs he has
wrought out of split moonbeams on "Homer and the Homeric age." But by that
time I confess the wing of my fancy begins to tire, till, to parody Hood's celebrated
song, over Egypt it falls asleep, and travels through in a dream, haunted by strange
images of eld, Sphinxes, and Memnons, and Winged Spheres, grinning in misty
derision of the poor bamboozled creature, who soon loses all consciousness in the
Cimerian darkness beyond, and wakes up to the tune of "Cheer boys, cheer," on
the one hand, and "Poor dog Tray" on the other, ground out on either side of
the window by rival barrel-organs, amid the cold reality of an English December.
I suppose there *is* a region beyond Egypt, and by a strong exercise of faith I can
believe that the present missive will pass that limit ; but all results and consequences thereof are so utterly remote and enveloped in cloudland, that really one
would feel as much personal interest in planting a centenial aloe, that the great-
grand children of some unknown stranger might gaze upon its bloom, as in writing

for the benefit of you dim, shadowy spectres, walking so uncomfortably with your heads downwards, like flies on a ceiling, at the other side of the world. It was needful to say something of this kind, because I have an uneasy consciousness of having neglected you.

However, though we may forget each other for a time, I suppose we are both busily going our own ways all the while—you, for instance, originating new histories, and we writing old ones; a thought suggested to me by the prominence of Carlyle's new book in my mind at present ("History of Frederick the Great, 4 vols. 8vo. London: Chapman and Hall, 1858"); only two vols. at present out; a capital book, worthy the author of the "French Revolution." Style as usual— *monstrum horrendum informe* (excuse reminiscences of the Eton grammar)—horrible when imitated, but singularly tolerable, nay striking, dramatic, exciting, as the own proper body of that soul of fire. Don't be afraid, most excellent and judicious friend, I am no Carlyle worshipper; but any one who can't see the stamp of genius in that book, because he dislikes the author's influence, must indeed be in a state of distractedly blind terror for the cause of orthodoxy. I speak feelingly, for I read at the same time a one-volume history of Gustavus Adolphus, by some Rev. Mr. Chapman, which has come out recently. O, dear! well, no more of that, only this: Carlyle occupied half his first volume with a preliminary sketch of Brandenburg history to the end of the first king's reign, and in the midst of this, of course he sketches the part that great king played in European politics. What I mean to affirm is this, that you know almost as much about Gustavus Adolphus after reading those few pages of Carlyle, as you would after reading the whole volume of Chapman; not but that the latter gentleman says a greater number of things in his book, but the difference is here: however well you may cover a man up with sand while he is lying down, it will certainly all run off when he gets up, except what, to his discomfort, sticks in his eyes, ears, and mouth; whereas a properly constructed garment will remain on him whatever be his position. I have been too lazy to take notes; I have read in a very self-indulgent manner, seated in an armchair, feet frizzling on the fender, and other circumstances tending rather to sleepiness than particular distinctness of mental vision, and I don't mean to say I could stand creditably a stiff three-hour examination on the history of Prussia; but this I do say, that I am astonished at the amount which our apparently chaotic author has managed to stamp and burn into my memory by his pyrotechnic illuminations of the dim gulf of past ages. As to his estimation of character, I don't doubt that a mind of such powers has considerable insight, but it does seem to a poor individual, perhaps eaten up by the rotting conventionalisms of an age of course inferior to times when murder and burglary were more respectable occupations than at present, that to be rough and ready, especially if there be plenty of self-confidence, is, in the opinion of our author, not only the mother of all the virtues, but really and truly all the virtues rolled into one. Carlyle's love of physical force, and the brute element most nearly allied to it in mental power, as though these were necessarily and under all circumstances the opposite of unreality and eternal foes to humbug, betrays him at times into strange and inconsistent eulogies of most imperfect characters. This burly Frederick William, for instance, father of Frederick the Great, is set up as an uncompromising enemy to shams in an age of lies, and is also much lauded for his spirit of economy. This economy, it seems, led him, when expecting a visit from Czar Peter, to issue orders to his officials that this visit was not to cost him a penny above a certain very modest, if not shabby, sum mentioned, but at the same time they were strenuously to give out that four or five times that sum had been expended. Talk about shams! can anything more paltry be imagined? Perhaps I have now characterised the book as well as I can, in a limited space: it is a magnificent illumination of the salient points of the past, and, on the whole, of a decidedly healthful tendency for well-balanced minds, but the lights are certainly colored by the author's subjectivity. Most who read it will be anxious for the remaining two volumes.

While ruminating on Germany, one thinks with a cold shudder, or a glow of enthusiasm, as the case may be, of its theology; and here is a specimen thereof, which I imagine will do you no harm, and may throw a great deal of light on a difficult subject. I mean "The Sinlessness of Jesus, an Evidence for Christianity, by Dr. C. Ullmann. Translated from the sixth German edition. Edinburgh: T. and T. Clark, 1858." The most interesting feature of this book is its investigation of the possibility of temptation in the case of a sinless creature. But it is also valuable for the mode in which it displays the inter-penetration of the immaculate purity of its founder with the whole life of Christianity. I do not know of any more suitable book to put into the hands of those who may be laboring under difficulties about this important matter: for all objections, both *a priori* and *a posteriori*, meet with a fair examination.

Here is another theological book, of a different stamp.—" Studies of Christianity, by James Martineau. London : Longman and Co., 1858." These are a series of papers mostly contributed to reviews, but containing some sermons, and also some things entirely new : all together make up a small 8vo. volume. As a specimen of what the English language can be made to do in the way of prose, some of these papers could perhaps hardly be surpassed—elegance and perspicuity, elaboration and power being set to the melody of a most wonderful word-music, enchanting at once to . e intellect and ear. But indeed this is not all that can be said for the book. Many of Mr. Martineau's ideas are as profoundly true as they are splendid, and are often penetrated by an evangelical spirit, which would perhaps be surprising to some, coming from such a quarter.* I am very sorry that Mr. Martineau should have incorporated with this series a sermon on vicarious redemption, apparently preached in the heat of the Liverpool controversy. It is quite unworthy of the catholic spirit which marks a paper first in the series,—" Distinctive Type· of Christianity." In the former article this writer treats a rude distortion of the doctrine of the atonement as though it were its only possible form in the evangelical idea of redemption, and then denounces it with a violence of indignation which is indeed quite deserved by the hideousness of the effigy set up, but which makes one wretchedly uncomfortable, with the feeling that it is directed against something ineffably holy, something interwoven with the foundations of the universe, something so grand, loving, and pure, that one shudders at the pretended resemblance, more than at the violence so painfully exhibited. For those who are strong, and have had considerable experience in religious thought and reading, this book may be a valuable indication of the prevailing tendencies of opinion in some important quarters. Far from being a hopeless sign in my opinion, none of your high and dry Unitarianism will do in these days. There must be more or less of a certain evangelism in it, if it is to lay hold of the mind of the age at all,—a fact which is far from uncomfortable to reflect upon.

Here is a Christmas book with a queer name,—" The Scouring of the White Horse, or the Vacation Rambles of a London Clerk. By the author of Tom Brown's School Days. Illustrated by Richard Doyle. Cambridge : MacMillan and Co., 1858." This writer of " Tom Brown," a very excellent fellow in his way, is quite one of the " physical force Christians," of whom Kingsley is the head, or major-general, I suppose we ought to call him, if he were not a clergyman. And along with this worship of physical force (a man being incompetent to enter this muscular church under clear six feet in his stockings), these gentlemen are likewise most intensely, nay, spasmodically, English in their feelings, so much so that I am inclined to think one of the essential articles of their creed is that all Frenchmen eat frogs, and wear wooden shoes, from the Emperor down to the "gamin." However, this spasmodic Englishism takes a very innocent form in the present book. It appears that somewhere in Berkshire there is, on one of the hill sides, a sprawling figure of a colossal horse, scratched through the turf into the chalky ground. The origination of this horse is associated by country-side tradition with the great battle of Ashdown, fought in this neighborhood by the Danes against Alfred the Great, or by the latter against the former, whichever is the proper way to put it. However, the Danes were beaten, and in memory thereof it is said this rude figure was scratched in the hill side, and has been kept clear ever since by patriotic and periodic scrapings on the part of the rustics around, greatly to the delight of muscular English Christians, such as the author of " Tom Brown." It seems that last year one of these scrapings or scourings took place, celebrated, as is the wont, by greased-pig hunts, greased-pole climbing, sack-races, and all the other edifying spectacles

* This change of tone in Unitarianism is one for the better in two respects. It may be considered as a virtual abandonment of the ground taken by Priestly, Belsham, and the authors of the "Improved Version of the New Testament," that Unitarianism was the genuine doctrine taught in Scripture, and orthodoxy a false interpretation. Hence all the appliances of an overstrained criticism were brought to bear upon the text to make it speak something else than its obvious meaning. Now, this application of the screw seems to be quietly given up, and the orthodoxy of the apostles, on some leading points at least, conceded. True, they are regarded as having been prejudiced, biassed by Jewish ideas, and to have misunderstood the simple nature of Christianity. But it is something to have it allowed that they did teach evangelical doctrine. The other favorable change is the infusion, above referred to, of a certain evangelical element in productions of modern writers of that class, and even the adoption of a semi-evangelical phraseology. This would seem to admit that human nature requires something more than a mere system of ethics to satisfy its inward cravings and moral necessities. But the concession is not without its danger, for all that is good in it is made to rest, less on the solid testimony of revealed truth, than upon a man's own subjectivity ; *i.e.*, upon the varying and uncertain frames, yearning and instincts which each man has, or fancies he has, in himself.—ED.

which from time immemorial have proved the superiority of Englishmen over Frenchmen. However, a pretty thing enough is made of it in this book. A London clerk comes down to visit his friend, sees the scouring, describes the traditions, falls in love with his friend's sister, and is altogether very entertaining,—indeed, I should say, very welcome to some of you down there, who may not have completely forgotten the land of your birth, with its Alfred the Great and sublime self-satisfaction.

Have you got Longfellow's " Miles Standish, and Other Poems," yet ? I hav'n't patience to look at "Miles Standish," for it is in one of those wretched galvanised hexameters than which I would far rather meet a "skeleton in armour" taking a turn some night in a dark lane to stretch his legs after his long sleep in the adjoining heath. But the " Other Poems " contain some very pretty things, in fact, as beautiful as Longfellow has ever yet produced, or more so. One on Florence Nightingale is very fine, and with the opening verses of this I make my obeisance till next month, or the month after.

> " Whene'er a noble deed is wrought,
> Whene'er is spoken a noble thought,
> Our hearts in glad surprise
> To higher levels rise.
> The tidal wave of deeper souls
> Into our inward being rolls
> And lifts us unawares
> Out of our meaner cares."

CONGREGATIONAL MINISTERS FOR AUSTRALIA.

Since our last notice of the Rev. Mr. Poore's proceedings in England in procuring ministers for these colonies, we have the pleasure to announce that seven have safely arrived ; four of these being intended for South Australia, and three for Victoria. Those bound for South Australia were the Rev. C. E. Palmer, late of Warrington, Lancashire ; Rev. S. W. Shipperd, Hayes, Middlesex ; Rev. G. Hoatson, Stoke upon Trent, and Rev. J. W. C. Drane, of Hanley, Staffordshire. All these brethren landed at Melbourne, preached in a few of the Congregational churches, and then sailed for Adelaide. We hope shortly to receive detailed information of their settlement in that colony. The most recent arrivals are the Rev. J. Hill, M.A., late of Witham, Essex ; the Rev J. Beer, of Kirkheaton, Yorkshire ; and the Rev. J. C. McMichael, of Halifax, in the same county. Mr. Hill and Mr. Beer are at present fulfilling temporary engagements in the neighbourhood of Melbourne, and Mr. McMichael has proceeded to Geelong, having been sent out with a special view to occupying an important vacancy in that city.

As we happen to have fallen in with a Halifax paper containing particulars of the farewell services connected with Mr. McMichael's departure from his former sphere of labour, and as they are highly creditable to himself and adapted to excite hope that he will prove a valuable accession to the " working clergy " of this country, we are persuaded we shall gratify many of our readers if we present these particulars, abridged indeed, but still pretty much at length.

Farewell Tea Party to the Rev. J. C. McMichael, Halifax, Yorkshire, on his departure for Geelong, Austr..lia.

On Wednesday evening, October 13, 1858, the members of the congregation assembling in Harrison Road Chapel, Halifax, held a tea party in the school-room, to take leave of their esteemed pastor. His departure from them was as unexpected as it was generally regretted. Mr. Poore had but a few weeks before proposed to Mr. McMichael to go out to Australia, and the latter, after seriously considering the matter and advising with friends, had seen it his duty to comply with the call. On the previous Sunday evening he had preached his farewell sermon to a crowded congregation, in which he acknowledged the uniform kindness he had received from all parties. About five or six hundred attended the tea meeting. The chair was taken by the Rev James Pridie, the oldest minister of the town who knew Mr. McMichael in his boyhood when Mr. Pridie was pastor of the church in Salford, of which Dr. Clunie, Mr. M's uncle, was a deacon and chief supporter. He spoke of the great difficulty he had in giving advice to Mr. McMichael when consulted by him about going to Australia, as, his brother ministers did not want to part with him, and yet they saw the importance of efficient ministers being sent to Australia.

An address from the church and congregation to Mr. McMichael was then read by Mr. M. Oates, one of the deacons, in feeling terms. The following is a copy of the document :—

To the Rev. John Clunie McMichael, Minister and Pastor of the Church and Congregation assembing at Harrison-Road Chapel, Halifax.

Dear Rev. Sir,—There is something painful in the parting of friends, when the separation is likely to be for any lengthened period of time. It is so when the connection which has subsisted between the parties has only related to this world. But when the relationship has had more immediately to do with spiritual things, and the intercourse has had an influence that may be expected to affect future happiness and eternal interests, the separation becomes one of very great solemnity. The church and congregation of this place of worship has had (if measured by years or months) but a very brief connection with yourself, but in that brief period great and momentous changes have taken place, which will affect yourself, the church, the congregation, and an unknown, though doubtless large, number of individuals who belong to both, and also others who belong to neither.

Without referring to the circumstances which led to your settlement as the pastor of this church and congregation, we need only call to remembrance the 1st of January, 1856, when, in this room, you first took your place as the pastor of our choice. Those of us who were happily present on that occasion believe that no minister ever experienced a more cordial, sincere, and warm-hearted reception than that which greeted you then. With the prudence which has marked all your proceedings, you doubtless took your seat that evening, with the determination to be chary of your promises, lest by raising expectations which you might not be able to carry out in your ministry, disappointment might result. But the hearty welcome you received, and the smiling countenances which surrounded you, broke down the barriers of restraint, and called forth such expressions of intended labor, as raised expectation and hope to a very high degree. The most sanguine expectations and the most fondly cherished hopes have all been fully realized; and it must be most gratifying to yourself, as it is to us this night, to behold and to contemplate the results. In our sanctuary how many seats then empty, are now occupied; at our monthly communion the portions of the chapel then appropriated to spectators is now filled on the right hand and on the left with members of the church, and a very much larger number than usual occupy the galleries, as interested and hopeful witnesses of the commemoration of our Saviour's love. Not only is the congregation greatly increased, but the number of church members also; whilst a spirit of harmony, zeal, and christian union seems to pervade every portion of your pastoral charge. No wonder that the younger portion of your people cherish towards you feelings of the warmest attachment and deepest gratitude. What have you not done to promote their improvement and happiness, both temporal and eternal? Have you not cheerfully responded to every request, when your presence, your instructions, or your counsels could benefit or gratify them? How much thought and toil have you endured to promote every plan attempted for their good? Sir, they may well love you, and they do; but this is not the time or place for further reference to them on our part,—they both can and will speak for themselves.

We would not omit special reference to High-road Well. Although so many of our friends there are united with us here, and are one with us as part of ourselves, yet it must be recorded that your efforts at High-road Well, for the spiritual good of the people there have been great, unwearied, and eminently successful Your labours in connection with that place will cause your name to be a household word in many a family in that neighbourhood, and will occasion many a tear of grateful remembrance, to be followed by thanksgiving to God, who brought you to that place, and prayers for your happiness and usefulness in the far distant land to which you go.

There is another department in which you have been eminently blessed, and in which we believe your soul has delighted. The "inquirers' classes" have not only been a source of unspeakable pleasure to all who have attended them, but we feel assured have, under God, been exceedingly blessed to many souls now present ; and the remembrance of them will be attended with increasing gratitude in this life, and happiness in the life that is to come. To estimate the amount of your ministerial and pastoral labour, both mental and physical, it must be recollected that every one of these departments, to be of use, requires previous study and preparation, and that not occasionally and fitfully, but continuously ; for the various duties are constantly recurring, and to neglect any of them would involve failure and grief. We thank God that you were induced to give them your attention, that you have been enabled to bear up under them so well, and that by the Holy Spirit they have been so largely blessed.

We trust we are not forgetful of our deep obligation to God for every blessing we have, through your instrumentality, received ; and whilst we appreciate your talents, your untiring zeal, your great energy, and your unceasing labours for our collective prosperity, and for our individual happiness and good, we know you would think little of our esteem were it not at the same time accompanied by an evidence that we are aware of the source of all that is good and great. We honour you the most when we recognise you as God's servant seeking to glorify your divine Master, by seeking to promote our everlasting welfare.

But this is not a perfect world, and all our enjoyments and privileges here are liable to changes and removals. Your labours here have been abundant ; your preaching has been acceptable ; your pastoral visitations have been sought after ; and highly esteemed ; your prayers have been mingled with ours, your friendship has been coveted and enjoyed ; and all your ministrations have been owned of God and blessed ; but now how changed our positions! As pastor and people we are to meet no more ; we are to hear you preach no more ; in sickness and sorrow, in joy and gladness, you will have present sympathy with us no more. As our minister and pastor we shall see your face no more. This is a painful thought, which for your sake and our own, we will pursue no further. We believe "it is the will of God," whose you are, and whom you serve, who orders our footsteps and yours, and to him we will say, "Thy will be done." Death might have called you away and not duty; even then we should not have sorrowed as others who have no hope; and shall we now give way to undue grief when your removal from us to a far-off land, is only to labour in another field? Souls are there as valuable as ours, as dear to Christ as ours, as much in need of the faithful preaching of the gospel, and perhaps as ready as we, yea possibly more ready than we, to receive it as the word of God, and to receive it into their hearts. We trust your ministry has not been without fruit in each of us; but if we had been more attentive, more diligent, and more prayerful, many of us would have derived more profit. May you, in yonder clime, find a more earnest, zealous, prayerful people to listen to your ministry, and to welcome you to their homes, their sanctuaries, and their hearts, than you have found here! May you and your dear wife and children, with all who sail in your company, ride safely over the billows that shall bear you to your future home. May your lives be preserved, your health be established, your strength invigorated, and may your souls prosper and be in health; and should there be on board with you, any who call not upon their God, may you be instrumental in awakening them to a sense of their sin and danger; so that, however varied their spiritual condition when you set sail, every soul that lands may be a Christian indeed in whom there is no guile! May your reception there be as happy as it was here when first you were welcomed by us; and may the Lord of the harvest, who sends forth laborers into his harvest, make your spiritual children a thousand fold more than they are this day. The Lord bless and keep you! The Lord lift up his countenance upon you; and when you move up higher, even into the city whose streets are gold, may you meet all there whom you now meet here, to part no more for ever.

> " This is the hope, the blissful hope,
> Which Jesus' grace has given ;
> The hope, when days and years are past,
> We all shall meet in heaven."

Signed on behalf of the church and congregation,

MATTHEW OATES.

The address was beautifully engrossed on vellum, and as beautifully bound in morocco covers. The silk lining inside bore an inscription detailing the circumstances under which the address was presented. On the fourth leaf was a photograph of the members taken in one group.

Mr. J. C. Hoatson then presented to Mr. McMichael an address from the Sunday School, observing that he could not do so with pleasure, because of the regret he felt at being called upon to part with him. He was glad, however, that he was going to engage in a work not second to the one he had performed here, and cordially concurred in the address he had just read. The following is a copy of the address, which has been beautifully engrossed, and mounted in the form of a scroll, and with gilt rollers, covering of blue velvet lined with satin and hung with orange tassels.

To the Rev. John Clunie McMichael, pastor of the Church and Congregation assembling in Harrison-Road Chapel, Halifax.

Dearly beloved Pastor,—We cannot allow you to depart for another land without an expression of our feelings of attachment and respect created and fostered by an intimate connection with you for nearly three years in works of faith and labors of love. When entering upon your pastoral duties in Halifax, of those by whom you were welcomed, we believe, none received you more cordially than we; and now, none have greater cause to regret your removal from us. Aware of your previous exertions in similar spheres of Christian effort, we expected that you would devote yourself especially to the adoption of means by which our young men and our young women should be led to embrace Christ as their Saviour, and give their hearts unreservedly to Him and to His people. In this expectation we have experienced no disappointment. By the blessing of God, and the out-pourings of His Holy Spirit, many such additions have been made to the Church to which you are now discharging your last duty as overseer. Should we and they see your face no more, this token of our regard will testify that you have kept back nothing that was profitable unto us, but have continually taught repentance toward God, and faith toward our Lord Jesus Christ.

To our branch school at Highroad Well you have devoted especial attention. In that village some of your friends united in Sabbath-school efforts 30 years ago, but until a short time prior to your settlement in Halifax, the Sabbath-school there was not connected with any particular place of worship. The services commenced and carried on by you upon the Sabbath afternoons and weekday evenings, coupled with the faithful and affectionate instructions of the teachers, have been rendered a greater good to Highroad Well than pen can describe or time develop. Not a few of those who join in the presentation of this testimonial have been brought to the feet of Jesus through your instrumentality, and deeply feel your approaching separation from them. Regarding our Sabbath-schools as the nursery of the church, you have constantly sought to render them promotive of the spiritual interests of our charge, and during your pastorate a larger proportion than formerly of our elder scholars have become the disciples of Jesus. We had hoped that your efforts, attended with like results, would have continued to be put forth amongst us; but God, in His over-ruling providence, has otherwise appointed. Believing that by Him you have been directed to the new sphere of labour opened up to you in our colonial possessions, we would bow to His all-wise arrangements, and rejoice in the hope of successes amongst the young there far greater than any yet realized in our Sabbath schools. We would fervently pray for the presence of God to attend you in all the relations you may sustain, and in all the duties you may be called upon to discharge. We desire that as a minister you may be happy and prosperous in your life and labors, and, as the head of a family, have grace to command your children and household after you to keep the way of the Lord. And when, faithful unto death, you stand in your lot at the end of the days, may it be your happiness to receive the crown of righteousness, and the welcome plaudit, " Enter thou into the joy of the Lord."

Signed on behalf of the teachers of Harrison-road and High-road Well Sabbath schools,

JOHN CROSSLEY, Sen, } Presidents.
JOHN TULEY,
JOSEPH C. HOATSON, Secretary.

This address was followed by a third from the young men of High-road Well Sunday school, a branch belonging to Harrison-road church.

Mr. John Tuley, secretary to the Young Men's Society in connection with the chapel, rose to present the address. He said he was anxious to refer to what had already been touched upon, the active interest Mr. McMichael had taken in the Sunday school at High-road Well. He (Mr. Tuley) had spent some of the happiest years of his life at High-road Well, and he wished to say that that happiness had been increased by the encouragement and help which he and his fellow teachers had received at the hands of their minister. On behalf of himself, and on behalf of his friends at High-road Well—many of whom had that night deserted their homes to be present at that meeting—he begged to tender him their best thanks, and their heartfelt wishes that God's blessing might still rest upon him, and attend him to the end of his journey. He (Mr. Tuley) stood there that night as the representative of the Young Men's Society, a society which had been the means of doing much good, and an institution similar to which if established in connection with other places of worship, might, he was sure, be an instrument of effecting incalculable good. There were many connected with that place of worship and with the school attached, who had been drawn into this relationship entirely through the means of their Young Men's Society. Mr. Tuley then read and presented the address, which ran as follows :—

To the Rev. J. C. McMichael.

Dear Sir,—The members of the Harrison road chapel Young Men's Society cannot suffer your connection with them to be severed, without tendering to you some expression of their gratitude for the uniform interest you have taken in their proceedings, and the valuable services you have from time to time rendered the society.

During the period you have had the oversight of the church at Harrison road, the Young Men's Society has materially profitted at your hands. Though in active discharge of all the onerous duties inseparable from an important religious interest, you have often presided at our meetings, and have always readily assisted us with your information and advice.

In the essays which you have read before us, we have had an earnest of your desire to contribute to our instruction and improvement; in the arrangement of the series of Biblical questions which now form a portion of the subjects brought under our notice, your thorough acquaintance with the contents of the inspired volume has proved of great value; while the unvarying regard you have manifested for the general success of our association warrants us in believing, not only that you have been solicitous for our well-being, but that were you to remain with us, your solicitude would suffer no abatement.

We trust, dear sir, we appreciate the efforts you have made to promote our true welfare; and, while we indulge the assurance that our society will long have a place in your memory and in your prayers, we doubt not your influence and acquirements will be enlisted on behalf of the young men who may form a portion of the people of whom you are about to take the pastoral charge, and in whom we hope you will find valuable coadjutors, both in the Sabbath school and in the church.

In conclusion, dear sir, our heartfelt wish is that eminent usefulness, and an unsullied name may continue to characterise you, and that on both yourself and your family the blessing of that Divine Being whose " goodness and mercy" it is your privilege to make known, may ever abide.

Signed on behalf of the members,

JOHN TULEY, Hon. Sec.

The Rev. E. Mellor, minister of the splendid new church which has superseded the old Square Chapel in Halifax, made a feeling speech expressing his regret at losing such a neighbour as Mr. McMichael. He was followed by the Rev. W. Thomas, the Rev. D. Jones, and others, who spoke in a similar strain.

Mr. McMichael, in coming forward to acknowledge these addresses was welcomed with demonstrations of affection. After a feeling allusion to Mr. Pridie, the chairman, as an old friend, and to the Rev. Messrs. Hoatson, Moffett, and Thomas as fellow students, and to the sacrifice he was making in parting with them, Mr. M. said—" With regard to the step I have taken, I met a gentleman in Halifax the other day, who reminded me that years ago I had said to him that if my uncle, Dr. Clunie, were not living, I should undoubtedly go to Australia. I don't remember saying so, but very likely I did. I will, however, briefly give you the reasons which have induced me to leave you. In the spring of this year a severe and fatal affiction laid hold of Dr. Clunie. As his only relative I felt it my duty to pay every attention to him during his illness, and I shall not tell you how many journeys I made to Manchester, and yet never failed to appear in this pulpit. My uncle died, but the labour that was thrown upon me by his illness, and subsequently in arranging his affairs, proved a serious tax upon my strength and time. Soon after I removed to another house, and never felt more settled in my life, and yet five days after, while in Manchester, I met Mr. Poore. When he proposed that I should go to Australia, I positively refused. I told him I was comfortable. He said he knew that, and did not want a man who was not. I said I was doing good. He said he knew that, and did not want a man who was not. I told him my age—which I am not going to tell you—(laughter), but even that was no objection. You can know nothing of the confusion which seized on my mind when this proposal was made to me. I came home, and believing that God guided those who trust in him, consulted my best friends and the best friends of Harrison road. It is only fair to say that when I had laid the matter fully before them, there was not one of them who could say it was not my duty to go. Then came the question, " Are you not doing good here ?" Yes, I was. But is a minister never to leave his people until he has done doing good ?—until he has lost the affection of his people ? That is a doctrine which I do not think any one of you will endorse. It may perhaps be said I was thinking of moving. Never was I more settled in this world than when this application came to me through Mr. Poore. Nor was I biased by pecuniary considerations. If I were to stay here, I should at the end of the next twelve months be a richer man than I shall be now that I am going. I think it right to state these things, because the motives of a minister in changing his place should be thoroughly understood—(hear, hear.) As to my adaptability to the work I am about to enter upon; it has been my fortune to take charge of several churches that were in a low condition, and thanks to God I have been able to raise them. When I went to Farnworth the church numbered 120 members; when I left, after a stay of six years, it numbered 240 members. The same was the case at Staleybridge I left both these places at the call of other churches. My friend Mr. Thomas wished me to give him permission to mention my name at Harrison-road while I was at Staleybridge; but I refused. You all know the rest. I came among you, and I have no reason to believe that it was other than by the providence of God. When I came among you I found a great deal of seed sown by your late pastor, and God made me a means of causing it to bring forth fruit. I have, sir, though I say it before you, had the best set of deacons in the town—[the CHAIRMAN: " That you don't know, sir")—(laughter.) —and a valuable body of young men. I had, however, no little difficulty in coming to the decision at which I arrived. But I am as satisfied that the cloud has moved off Harrison-road and guides me elsewhere, as I am that it moved off Staleybridge and settled here. I have not the least doubt upon this point. The course upon which I have entered is, I am aware, no trifle. But in weighing this matter various things had to be considered. I have never been seriously ill in my life. I have never, until last year, been two Sundays together from the pulpit since I entered the ministry. I have not had a holiday for the last eleven years; and next Sunday will be the first holiday in my ministerial life. But the fact is, I have done too much. I feel that three services a day must be given up, but I cannot give up the services at High-road Well. In addition to this, the death of my uncle removed the last family tie that bound me to England. To these things I had to add the fact that Mr. Poore had thought of me, that the health of my family was concerned, and there was a prospect of doing good when I got there. This, therefore, is the history of the process of thought through which my mind has passed. You have not driven me away. You have not made me unhappy. I have not received a remark or a look which was unkind. I shall carry with me remembrances of all my pastorates, but the most pleasing will be the last. You have, however, but a faint idea of the emotion I have to suppress in making this statement, and if I were to speak further on this matter, neither you nor myself would be able to endure it. I assure you, however, that next to my mother, the first pleasing news from me shall be received by you. As to the state of this church now that I am leaving it, few are aware of the hope it holds out. There are many on the point of declaring for Christ, and I trust nothing will be done to stifle their intentions. That God may send you a man to reap the abundant harvest which is promised by the state of this church is my heartfelt wish. I almost envy him the work; but thus it ever is—one sows and another reaps. I see many mothers here, and I would impress upon them the fact that they have an influence over their children far greater than they suppose, an influence which I trust they will exert to the spiritual good of those children. If I change my pastorate again, may I do so with feelings as painful and yet as pleasing as those which I experience to-night. I thank God we have been so happy together as pastor and people, and that we part under circumstances so gratifying to ourselves, and forming so good an example for the world. You have my earnest wish that inquirers among you may be directed to Christ, and that the undecided may decide to-night. And let me say to those who are hearers of the gospel only, " I charge you to meet me at the last day, and to meet me not again to be separated." I pray God that I may meet you all where separation is for ever unknown. '

Similar scenes to the above have occurred in connection with the departure of most of the ministers who have come out from England to Australia, and had we been favored with the particulars, we should have been glad to give publicity to a selection of them. We present the above as a specimen. Those who derive the benefit of the ministers' services who are sent for may see at how great a cost to the churches there really efficient men are obtained and sacrifice not to be estimated by money.

RELIGIOUS INTELLIGENCE.

VICTORIA.—EVANGELICAL ALLIANCE OF VICTORIA.—On Monday morning, a special meeting of this association was held in the large hall of the Criterion Hotel, Collins-street. Upwards of thirty members sat down to breakfast. After partaking of a well arranged and neatly served repast, the company adjourned to another apartment, considerately placed at their disposal by Mr. Wedel. His Honor Judge Pohlman, as president of the Alliance, took the chair. After a hymn had been sung, the Rev. Dr. Perry, Bishop of Melbourne, offered prayer; and the Rev. James Taylor read the Scriptures. Dr. Cairns then addressed the company, and in a few appropriate and emphatic sentences introduced the Rev. Thomas Binney. Before Mr. Binney rose, Dr. Perry offered a few remarks, expressing his great satisfaction at meeting with the honoured guest of the morning, and his anxiety for the promotion of Christian union among the followers of the one Lord Jesus. The Rev. Thomas Binney delivered a long and most interesting address, full of wise counsel, genial humour, and manly eloquence. The Rev. R. Fletcher, of St. Kilda, was the last speaker. He referred to his long friendship with Mr. Binney, and to the great delight he had experienced in being permitted to renew intercourse with him in Australia. Mr. Fletcher closed the proceedings of the morning with prayer. The various sections of the Christian Church in this land were well represented at the meeting, and it was felt that brethren holding different views of Church order and discipline, can meet for prayer and pleasant social intercourse without any compromise of principle.

VICTORIA AUXILIARY TO THE BRITISH AND FOREIGN BIBLE SOCIETY.—The annual meeting of the above society was held on Monday evening, February 1, in the hall of the Mechanics' Institution, Melbourne. There was a very large meeting, the hall being densely crowded in every part. His Excellency Sir Henry Barkly, patron of the society, presided, and was surrounded by a large body of influential citizens, among whom were Dr. Perry, Bishop of Melbourne; Revs. Thomas Binney, Dr. Cairns, R. Fletcher, Seddon, Odell, Thomas, Jarrett, Hetherington, J. L. Poore, Taylor, His Honor Judge Pohlman, John Hodgson, Esq., M.L.C., Charles Vaughan, Esq., M.L.C., Robert Kerr, Esq.; and in the body of the hall were among other well-known citizens, Sir J. Palmer, A. Frazer, Esq., M.L.C., J. H. Patterson, Esq., M.L.C. There was also a large attendance of ladies.

The proceedings commenced shortly after seven o'clock, by the Rev. James Taylor reading the 19th Psalm, after which, the Rev. D. Seddon, of St. Kilda, offered prayer. His Excellency then rose, amid loud applause, to address the meeting. In a short, but very excellent speech, he referred to the importance of circulating the word of God. He believed it was their duty to put the Scriptures into the hands of every living creature, for by that book they would one day all be judged at the judgment seat of God. In most approximate and impressive terms His Excellency alluded to the openings made, through the providential interposition of God, for the circulation of the word of God in India, China, and Japan, and closed by calling upon the secretary to read the annual report. Mr. Hoskins then read the following report:—

"Your Committee, in compliance with their duty, now report their proceedings since the last general meeting. Amongst the objects which have particularly engaged their attention, there was none which appeared to them of greater moment than to make the institution of this society generally known. With this object in view, the secretary has maintained an extensive correspondence with the supporters and friends of the institution in every part of the colony. The sixteen Branch Associations in connection with this society, still continue their operations, subject to those fluctuations which seriously affect the permanency of all institutions on the gold-fields. Free grants have been made to the amount of £18 1s. The number of Bibles received from the parent society has been 4307. The entire issue from the depository has amounted to 5178, besides a large number of the Chinese Scriptures. The Rev. Kerr Johnstone continues to promote the sale of Bibles among the seamen in the port. The Committee desire to express their thanks to the clergymen who have preached for the society, and to the ladies who, by means of cards, have added a considerable sum to the funds. It is hoped that in the course of this year the secretary will visit the Branch Associations. The receipts amount to £1430 12s. 8d.; the payments to £1437 3s. 6d. Balance due the Treasurer, £6 10s. 9d.

The meeting was then addressed with great effect by the Bishop of Melbourne and Dr. Cairns.

The second resolution was moved by the Rev. Thomas Binney, of London—"That this meeting expresses its sympathy with all kindred associations, and rejoices in the success which, by the blessing of God, attends their operations in various parts of the world." Mr. Binney, after referring to his bodily indisposition, and to his unwillingness to take any prominent part in public meetings, delivered an address, full of profound thought, and which evidently made a deep impression on the assembly. He alluded, in impressive terms, to the fact that he had been a reader of the Bible for half a century—acknowledged that he had felt difficulty in understanding parts of it—that, like others, he had passed through his seasons of doubt and perplexity, but the result of all his reading and study was, a profound conviction that the Bible is from God. In a manner that will not be forgotten by many of his hearers, Mr. Binney next described the effects produced by the study of the "Book" on the minds of some sceptics, alluding specially to the conversion of the celebrated William Hone, and the admission of that well-known writer and a portion of his family to the fellowship of the Weighhouse Church. The resolution was seconded by the Rev. J. L. Poore, in a thoroughly earnest and practical speech, and, like the preceding motion, was unanimously adopted.

The meeting was subsequently addressed by the Revs. W. Jarrett and J. S. Waugh. H Jennings, Esq.; Mr. Justice Pohlman, and Robert Kerr, Esq. proposed a vote of thanks to His Excellency who returned thanks, when the meeting closed with the doxology and benediction.

AUXILIARY TO THE LONDON MISSIONARY, COLLINS STREET INDEPENDENT CHURCH. —The anniversary services of the Auxiliary to the London Missionary Society, connected with the Independent Church, Collins-street, under the pastoral care of the Rev. A. Morison, were held on Sabbath, 30th Jan. The Rev. W. Waugh, of Richmond, preached in the morning, and the Rev. Henry Thomas, B.A., in the evening. On the Tuesday evening following, the annual public meeting of the society was held, at which the Rev. A. Morison presided, who opened the engagements of the evening by the hymn, "Come let us join our cheerful songs," &c., and afterwards reading the 135th Psalm. The Rev. H. Kidgel offered prayer. The chairman made some remarks on the prevalent deficiency of a missionary spirit among the people, and the manifest dislike to contribute for the sustenance of missionary operations; and that while the money spent on matters of religion among ourselves in this colony might be reckoned by hundreds of thousands, he would venture to assert that £500 would cover the actual amount contributed for the purposes of missions, foreign to ourselves, amongst all the denominations. Letters from the Revs. Messrs. New, Fletcher, W. Miller, and Sunderland, were read, excusing their absence from the meeting. Mr. E. M. Gibbs, in the unavoidable absence of the secretary, read the report. It stated that letters had been received from Rev. A. Busacott, informing us of the wants of Danger and Savage Islands, and recommending that our Auxiliary should provide for the native teachers left there. Also, that letters from the Rev. James Russell, of the mission at Nagercoil, South India; and from the Revs. Messrs. Barff, of Tahaa; and Jones, of Mare, had been received, in relation to their several spheres of labour. That the Rev. A. Morison had delivered five lectures on the missions in Madagascar, in the Fiji Islands, among North American Indians, in Ceylon and in the Tonga Islands. That the ladies' committee had continued their working parties, and that articles to the value of £14 had been made. The letter of Rev. Mr. Jones to the Secretary, Mrs. Drew, had excited the sympathies especially of the children of the Sabbath school, in behalf of the children on the island of Mare, whom one pound a year would suffice to feed and educate, and who, without this help, could not, from the pressure of hunger, be so kept and taught as to prove ultimately useful in the work of God. The acknowledgments of the Committee were made to Messrs. G. Horne and Meares, and the ladies who had helped, by contributing gratuitously materials to be made into dresses for the natives and missionaries' families.

The report of the Branch Auxiliary of the Victoria Grammar school, was then read. The list of subscribers, among whom we observed His Excellency the Governor's name, with a liberal sum attached, was read by the President, in the absence of the treasurer, and the balance sheet showed an income of £140 6s. 9½d., with an expenditure of £10 9s. 6d., leaving £129 17s. 3½d, to be remitted to the Parent Society.

The meeting was afterwards addressed by the Revs. J. Mirams, H. Thomas, J. L. Poore, and W. Jarrett. The pastor of the Church added a few remarks, intimating that the Church was pledged to maintain eight native teachers in the South Seas; and the meeting closed with a doxology and the apostolic benediction.

JANEFIELD CHAPEL, UPPER PLENTY ROAD.—On Sunday, January 30th, this place of worship was opened by the Rev. W. B. Landells, of Oxford street chapel. On the following Tuesday, February 1st, a public meeting was held to celebrate the event. One of Mr. Landells' deacons, who has preached to the congregation regularly since February last year, gave a progress report of the cause; from which it appeared, that in November last a church was formed consisting of three Independents, two Baptists, two Presbyterians, one Wesleyan, and one convert. (The basis of the church expressing Congregational church polity, but otherwise excluding all denominational peculiarities.) Through the kindness of John Bakewell, Esq., who has presented and conveyed to the church free of all cost, half an acre of land near the twelve mile post, and also of Mr. White, who has given up his right to the lease of the said land, the congregation were induced to build the chapel at a cost of about £180. It is of strong weatherboards, and slate roof; 30 feet long, 20 feet wide, the walls 14 feet high; seats about 120 persons; it has a porch 9 feet wide, and projecting 8 feet at entrance. Addresses were delivered by the Revds. Messrs. Landells, Poore and Hoatson. There were about 200 persons present, many of whom had come miles; and including the collection on the Sabbath £127 was collected and promised, which has since been made up to £160. The tea, which was tastefully and gratuitously furnished by the ladies of the congregation, and the public meeting appeared to be heartily enjoyed.

CAULFIELD UNION CHAPEL, NEAR ST. KILDA.—This very neat and commodious chapel, erected by the Independents and Baptists in the beautiful district of Caulfield, was opened for Divine worship on Sabbath, 16th January. Sermons were preached by the Revds. W. B. Landells, of Collingwood, and I. New, of Melbourne. On the following Sabbath, 23rd January, the preachers were the Revds. R. Fletcher, and J. L. Poore. On both Sabbaths the congregations were large. On Tuesday evening 25th inst., there was a social meeting; the chapel was quite crowded by a delighted assembly. Among the ministers present we observed—

The Revds. J. L. Poore, W. B. Landells, Lewis, Moss, and J. Taylor. Upwards of £100 was collected. We rejoice to see the Independents and Baptists, whose sentiments on almost every point, so nearly accord, uniting in the good work of supplying new districts with the Gospel of the grace of God.

SUNDAY SCHOOL UNION.—On Tuesday evening 18th January, the monthly meeting of the Sunday School Union was held at the Independent Chapel, Tyers street, when Mr. Bonwick gave an address on the subject of Education. The meeting, which was well attended, was presided over by the Rev. J. Sleigh, the minister of the chapel.—*Portland Guardian.*

OXFORD STREET CHAPEL, COLLINGWOOD.—The Sixth Anniversary of the Independent Church, meeting in the above place of worship, was celebrated on Sunday, the 20th February. The Rev. W. B. Landells, pastor, preached in the morning, from Psalm cxxii. 7, " Peace be within thy walls, and prosperity within thy palaces." The evening service was conducted by the Rev. J. Hill, M.A., one of the ministers recently from England. His text was from Psalm xcii. 12, "The righteous shall flourish like the palm tree ; he shall grow like a cedar in Lebanon." A tea meeting was held in the school-room, on the Wednesday following, at which about 300 persons were present. The tables were handsomely decorated and well supplied, under the gratuitous management of the ladies of the congregation. After tea, a large public meeting was held in the chapel above. Dr. Embling, M.L.A. who was called to the chair, alluded to the melancholy event that had caused the postponement of the meeting from the previous day, and paid a graceful tribute to the memory of the late Thomas Fulton, Esq. The Secretary then read a report upon the progress of the Church and congregation, which stated that the church which began with 12 members has had 304 on its books, and that its present number was 153. The treasurer stated that in the course of six years £12,000 had been raised by the church and friends ; and that during the last year, a special effort had resulted in £250 being contributed towards the £1,000 mortgage remaining on the property. Interesting speeches were given by the Revds. W. Robinson, J. Townend, James Ballantyne, Thomas Odell, Isaac New, J. Hill, and J. Beer. The two latter gentlemen have only recently arrived from England. A letter was received from the Rev. R. Fletcher, apologizing for his absence, on account of engagements connected with his own church. Several other ministers and influential gentlemen were present, and the engagements of the evening were very interesting, and rendered exceedingly pleasing by the services of the choir, who sung three select anthems in a most effective manner.

NEW SOUTH WALES.—The annual public meeting of the N. S. W. Auxiliary Bible Society was held last Monday evening, the 17th inst., in the Infant School Room, Castlereagh street, His Excellency Sir W. Denison, in the chair. The Rev. S. C. Kent, the secretary, read the report. The treasurer's account showed that the receipts for the year had been £2417 12s. 11d. ; and that the expenditure was £1711 6s. 11d. ; leaving a balance in hand of £706 6s. The meeting was addressed by the Revds. G. King, T. Arnold, —Steele, A. Buscott, R. Amos, and J. Malvern, in highly interesting speeches. His Excellency in accepting thanks made some very pertinent and cordial remarks.

CONGREGATIONAL CHAPEL, PADDINGTON, SYDNEY.—On Tuesday, 13th Jan., the new Congregational Chapel, Point Piper road, Paddington, was opened. The Rev. W. Cuthbertson, B.A., preached a morning sermon, and in the evening there was a tea meeting, after which speeches were made by several ministers who were present. On Sunday the 16th, sermons were preached, that in the morning by the Rev. Mr. Arnold, of Balmain ; and that in the evening by the Rev. J. Beasley, of Redfern.

EDUCATION IN ENGLAND.—The Rev. J. A. James, of Birmingham, is desirous that the views expressed in the following communication, should be made known to parties in these colonies who may be interested in them. We therefore beg to call attention to them. Mr. James writes, with reference to Spring Hill College, near Birmingham—

"At our last annual meeting, it was suggested that as we admit *lay* students to the college, it is probable there may be some of the wealthier inhabitants of our colonies, who may wish for their sons a thoroughly good classical and philosophical education, and who would be glad to avail themselves of such an institution as ours, where they would have all the advantages of moral and religious, as well as of intellectual culture. It is not necessary that the youths entrusted to our care should be members of a church, or even truly converted to God ; but they must bring credentials of good morals and behaviour, and be recommended by some minister. They would have opportunity to attend all the classical, philosophical, mathematical, logical, and belles lettres classes ; and, if they choose, the theological and ecclesiastical history classes. They could also study French and German. As we are incorporated with the London University, they can, of course, graduate there.

The college is very beautifully situated in an enclosure of twenty acres of land in a very healthy locality. The expense for board, lodging and education is eighty pounds per annum. The students in addition would have to pay for washing, books, and the modern languages, and board and lodging during the vacation. Their accommodations consist of a study and dormitory.

There may possibly be found some who may be glad to have their sons under such supervision as this institution affords. While I live, and that cannot be very many years, I feel it my duty to cultivate intercourse with the students, and exercise an un-professional paternal care of them. They are often at my house, dining with me, and receiving such counsels as a long life and much experience and observation enable me to impart."

W. FAIRFAX AND CO., STEAM PRINTERS, COLLINS STREET EAST, MELBOURNE.

The Southern Spectator.

APRIL, 1859.

THE LATE THOMAS FULTON, ESQ., OF MELBOURNE.

THE accident recorded in our last, which so suddenly terminated the life of Mr. Fulton, has awakened so unwonted a sympathy in the public at large, that we feel justified in publishing the substance of the sermon delivered on the Sabbath morning after his interment to the church and congregation which he served as deacon in the presence of the bereaved family, and of many old friends of the deceased.

FUNERAL SERMON.

My aim in this discourse shall be not to eulogise the dead, but to benefit the living, not by attempting to work upon the feelings of the audience, but by directing attention to matters of a practical and useful character. With this object in view, the following text has occurred to me as adapted to the occasion; as a motto not unsuitable to be engraven on the tomb-stone of our friend, and as a stimulus to us who survive so to frame our lives that it might, without incongruity, be inscribed upon our own.

Acts xiii. 36. "David, after he had served his own generation by the will of God, fell on sleep, and was laid unto his fathers."

These words occur in a speech delivered by Paul in the synagogue at Antioch in Pisidia. His object was to prove to his hearers that Jesus, who had been crucified at Jerusalem, had risen again from the dead, and was therefore the true Messiah promised in their own Scriptures. In support of this, he quotes from the 16th Psalm a verse which declares that God would "not suffer his Holy One to see corruption," and affirms that that assertion could not apply to David himself, because he *did* see corruption, but only to him who was David's son, Lord, and antitype; "For David, after he had served his own generation by the will of God, fell on sleep, and was laid unto his fathers, and saw corruption; but he whom God raised again saw no corruption." Leaving the main argument in proof of the resurrection, we shall confine ourselves to the striking epitome of David's life and death, which is thus incidentally introduced; his serving his generation according to God's will, and then his being gathered to the congregation of the pious dead.

I. Here is a striking description of the living career of a good and useful man : "He served his own generation according to the will of God." In putting into brief phrase what was characteristic of David's life as a whole, the Apostle does not say he was a fortunate and successful man, a glorious and mighty king, a man famous in his day who won for himself a great name, nor even simply a good and pious man : but, "*he served his generation*," and he did this, not after a fashion of his own, as became a great genius, but "*according to the will of God*." Herein he is a model to us all.

G

1. The Scripture idea of our position in this world, in relation to God, is that he is our Proprietor and Lord, and the Supreme Disposer of our lot. He made us, and not we ourselves, and he endowed us with whatever faculties of mind or body we possess. We owe every thing to his sole will and pleasure; and as he created so he sustains us: "In him we live and move, and have our being." Our dependence on him is therefore absolute, and his right to control and govern us, and to use us for such purposes as he thinks fit, is indisputable.

2. Now he has thought fit to make us, not strictly his instruments but his servants. He has not constituted man as he has constituted the sun, the moon, minerals and plants,—unconscious instruments, guided by fixed material laws to do his sovereign will,—but responsible agents, with intelligence, thought, and affection, susceptibility of motive, and choice of action. These faculties are to be used in a way suitable to their nature. From the Scriptures we learn that God made man "for himself," to shew forth his glory, and that to this end he has conferred endowments and talents upon him in the manner of a trust, and placed him in circumstances to bring them into active and useful employment. We are in the condition of stewards set over a charge with certain discretionary powers confided to us, but accountable to the Lord of All for the use we make of that discretion.

3. Leaving out of consideration at present, other aspects of our condition as responsible agents, I observe, it is the will of our Divine Master that we should address ourselves to serve *our generation*. " David served *his* generation according to the will of God," and in so doing did his duty.

The race of man, unlike that of angels, is successive. As a whole, it is continuous for ages, and has a long history. The individuals composing it have but a brief period allotted to them, and a limited part to play. A generation is the aggregate of the individuals living on the world at any one time; and "one generation goeth, and another cometh."

We are not to regard ourselves as units, independent atoms, having no relation to those around us, but as parts of the race. Not that we are forbidden to love ourselves, or to seek our own interest, and especially our own salvation. This, by the law of our own nature, is our first duty; but we are not to stop there. We must consider ourselves as associated with others, bound to love our neighbour as ourselves, and to seek and labour for his good; not to be selfish, but generous, not useless but serviceable. In a sense each man is his " brother's keeper," and accountable for the influence he exerts upon him, or has it in his power to exert.

With respect to the generations gone by, we cannot affect them; their course is run and their state is fixed. With regard to the future, the influence of any one generation, or any one individual in it, may be perpetuated for good or for evil, to the end of time. Nor are we forbidden, in our plans of usefulness, to think of the future, and to aim at the welfare of coming generations; to sow now that others may reap. All this is lawful and proper, and is the special vocation of intellects of the highest order, and of some men in influential positions. But even they must do this chiefly by operations upon their own generation, and by discharging the special duty of the hour. David has indeed served *all* generations by the psalms which he wrote, but he composed them under the influences of the times passing over him, and with reference primarily to his own circumstances and experience. The community at large however have mainly, if not wholly, to do with their contemporaries and with their own times. Their first and chief duty is to serve their *own* generation, and through *it*, if at all, generations to come.

4. The *manner* in which we may serve our generation is to be decided partly by general, and partly by special considerations. The general considerations apply to us and to David alike, the special ones are such as affect each individual in particular.

I will not now, in our present circumstances, refer to the service a man may do to his generation by science, by literature, by legislation, by industrial developments or social reforms. These, important as they are, must give place on this occasion, to a higher kind of service, that which influences the spiritual, the religious, the eternal condition of man. It was this kind of influence the Apostle had in view in speaking of David. He was a great warrior, a great king, a great poet, a great musician, but above all, he was an eminent believer, a distinguished servant of God, a profoundly devout and religious man, and he served his generation chiefly by infusing into it a large amount of the religious element. He was pious while a youth ; when rising into manhood, and becoming suddenly exposed to the dangers of popularity, he was not carried away with it so as to forget his God ; when harassed with malicious persecutions he still made God his refuge ; when occupied and pressed with the cares of empire he found time to commune with his Father in heaven ; when crowned with success, and at the height of his glory, he laid all his honors down at the footstool of him to whom he devoutly acknowledged he owed them all ; and when sinking under the weight of years, and worn out with hard service, God was still "the strength of his heart, and his portion for ever." And so, to serve our generation effectively, we must serve it religiously. If the religious element be left out, the main thing God regards is left out.

Now this cannot be done without *being* religious ourselves. Personal piety is indispensable to the propagation of piety. A man is disqualified by the very nature of the case for spreading religion, making others religious, if he has not religion himself ; and to be of any real use, such religion should be decided in its stamp, undoubted as to its genuineness. It loses all influence if it be equivocal and suspicious. It ought to begin, too, in early life, like David's. Life is short enough to serve our generation without our wantonly making it shorter by putting off securing the main qualifications for usefulness till it is nearly wasted away. And this piety must be evangelical, the piety which Christ and his Gospel require : embracing, repentance towards God, faith in the Lord Jesus Christ, the renewal of the Holy Ghost, communion with God, and a life of holy obedience.

Nor is the bare possession of this piety enough. It should be strong and *earnest* to do good service. The salt must not be savourless, the light must not be dim, the life must not be feeble and sickly, or no perceptible effect will be exerted on the world around. Force of character is required to lead others in secular matters, and it requires force of piety to impress and draw others to religion. The secret of David's power in serving his generation was the fervour, the elevation, the intensity of his personal piety.

This, however, must be backed by consistent *conduct* in all the walks of morality.   David did grievous harm by his sad fall, but his deep repentance and his consciencious conduct in the main, must have had a mighty influence for good on the men of his age.   He was diligent as a shepherd youth, faithful as a commander under Saul, attached as a friend to Jonathan, wise and just and beneficent as a monarch of the realm ; in short, a good man in all the relations of life.   Every man who has a conscience void of offence, who is blameless and harmless and without rebuke, who attends to " whatsoever things are true, honest, just, pure, lovely, and of good report," is serving his generation, and is a benefactor to the age in which he lives.

Direct, designed, active, self-denying *efforts* to render service to our generation, are required.   The silent influence of example is not enough ; the positive outgoings of the mind and labours of the hand in works of benevolence and in the propagation of religion, are imperatively demanded.   David wrote psalms, taught lessons, set up the ark, provided for the building of the temple.   He served his generation by developing and bringing to perfection the religious worship of the economy under which he lived ; by applying the vast resources which his high station placed at his disposal, to the great work required in that generation, the establishment on Mount Zion of the typical worship of that preparatory period, in all its glory and fulness.   Paul served *his* generation by labouring more abundantly to preach the Gospel to Jew and Gentile, and to plant Christian churches all over the Roman Empire.   And in like manner it is binding on all Christians to propagate the faith to the extent of their ability.   In this respect " no man liveth to himself, no man dieth to himself."   As we have opportunity it behoves us to do good to all men ; to preach the Gospel, or assist others in preaching it; to teach the young, to arouse the careless, to call in the wanderers, to circulate the Bible and religious books, to be instant in season and out of season, in devising means and carrying them into execution, to save the souls of men.

5. The " will of God" intimates the *special* way in which we may serve our generation.   Each generation has its peculiar wants and its peculiar duties, and invites to a peculiar line of action.   The state of the age and its wants indicate the direction which efforts to serve it should take.   I have just intimated the way in which David and Paul served their generations ; in like manner the will of God pointed out the work of reformation, as the service required of Luther, Calvin, and Knox ; of testimony for the rights of conscience, as the special work of Baxter, Howe, and Henry; of evangelization of the masses, as the call of Whitfield and Wesley ; of sending the [Gospel to the heathen, as the service demanded of Carey, Morrison, and Martin.   The Providence of God is indicating the organization of resources for the circulation of the word of God, and the maintenance of numerous agencies for working upon society at every point, as the duty of Christians in Britain at the present time ; and it is pointing out with equal plainness, the founding of new churches and the planting of religious institutions as the special duty of Christians in this land if they would serve their generation effectually.

6. When a man by the grace of God has done this, has thus served his generation, he has done his duty ; he has " finished his course," as Paul ; performed his assigned task, taken his share in the

events which constitute the history of Providence. What he does may be a trifle compared with the whole of the work done for the good of the entire race, or even of one generation, but it is enough for one man. Much work may remain yet to be done, but other agents will be raised up to do it. David only developed Judaism ; it was left to the Apostles to introduce Christianity. The Apostles only laid the foundations of the Christian Church ; their successors had to carry on the super-structure. A higher encomium cannot be passed upon a man than that he served his generation according to the will of God, in such a way, as God by his Providence pointed out to him, before he fell on sleep and was laid to his fathers.

II. The Apostle gives an equally striking description of the *close* of such an active and useful course. David, after he had served his generation, "fell on sleep, and was laid unto his fathers."

It is appointed unto all men once to die. The sentence of death has been passed by the Giver of Life, and there is no escape from it. It is impartially executed upon kings and subjects, ministers and people, masters and men, upon the sublimest geniuses and untutored savages. The keys of the invisible world are held by him whose servants we are. He assigns us our specific task and fixes the time we are to do it in. " We are immortal till our work is done," and when it is done, he summons us into his presence to give an account of our stewardship. Death is God's mode of severing man's connection with his generation and with all the interests of time. " There is no work, nor device, nor knowledge, nor wisdom in the grave," so far as relates to the life that now is. All our personal and active service for our gen-eration has then come to an end, and can never be renewed.

The time and mode of calling us away from our work, till the event occurs, are to us unknown. This only we know, that the time allowed is brief at longest, and the period of its close uncertain at all times. "Death's thousand doors stand open." This night our souls may be re-quired of us. Disease, storm, fire, flood; our neighbour's violence or our own carelessness : the fright of an animal, or the derangement of a ma-chine, may precipitate us at once into the abyss of eternity. And these sudden deaths not only may, but do occur, and that frequently, and in the most unlikely cases, no doubt to remind survivors of the uncertain tenure on which they hold their life. The lesson is thus impressed upon all, " Be ye therefore ready, for in such an hour as ye think not, the Son of Man cometh."

And what a blessed change death is to those who die in the Lord. A new scene of wonder is unfolded to view. And to the "faithful servant," who like David, has served his generation according to the will of God, the translation to the world of spirits is abundant gain. Blessed is he who is found watching and ready when his Lord comes. He will be greeted with the approving welcome, "Well done, good and faithful servant, enter thou into the joy of thy Lord." The fatiguing toil ceases, work does not ; the sphere of the soul's activity is only changed. There, in the immediate presence of the Master, service shall still be rendered in some nobler and higher form of em-ployment. The reward of the faithful service on earth shall be promo-tion to a more honourable and extended field of action in heaven.

Such we are assured is the change that comes upon the soul when the body dies. But the body itself, what is *its* fate? It falls into a *sleep*, a deep sleep; all consciousness is gone; the animal life is extinct; the material structure falls to pieces; it sees corruption; it must be buried out of sight of the living, that it may not offend or injure them; it is gathered to the vast and ever-increasing congregation of the dead; laid to and joined with fathers and predecessors, where, in the dark chambers of the tomb, it gradually returns to the dust whence it was taken.   The funeral procession may be imposing, the tears of affection may be copiously shed upon the grave, the praises of the dead may be sounded by many a voice, yet nothing can ward off this humiliating decay of the mortal frame.   But why should we mourn? It is but a sleep after all; a sleep in Jesus, in his arms and under his eye.   He who said "I am the resurrection and the life," will, at the appointed time, awake the slumberers from their long repose, re-fashion their bodies like unto his own most glorious body, and crown them with glory, honor, and immortality.   Then death itself shall die, and the redeemed shall enter upon a career of pure enjoyment and intelligent service unmarred by the presence of suffering or the apprehension of another dissolution.

The active and useful life, and sudden death of our late friend, Mr. Fulton, has suggested these reflections.   He possessed aptitudes for effective service, and had an ample sphere for their exercise.   We believe he was faithful to the task committed to him, and served his generation zealously according to the will of God. We fondly hoped that many more years of useful labour would have been allowed to him. But his sun has gone down while it was yet day.   In the prime of bodily health, and in the full vigour of his mental capacities he has been called to his account.   It now appears that his work was done, and we submit without a murmur to the all-wise will of God.   While we gratify our affection by indulging our grief, though without repining at Providence, let us try to learn a useful lesson from the event.   That lesson is, to be ready in case our removal should be as unexpected as his.   Youth, manly strength, important relations, are no guarantees for continued life.   Be therefore upon your watch-tower, looking for the coming of the Son of Man.   Have your loins girt and your lamps burning, that "whether he come in the second watch or come in the third watch" he may find you prepared to welcome his approach. Nor let your preparation interfere with active service for your generation. Rather let that service form part of the preparation. Combine diligence in business with fervency in spirit.   Your master will be best pleased if, when he comes, he finds not only your hearts yearning after his presence, but your hands actively employed in the work he gave you to do.

MEMOIR.

I have stated that I deemed the text on which the above remarks are founded—" He served his own generation according to the will of God, and then fell on sleep, and was laid unto his fathers."—as not inappropriate to the life and death of our late friend, Mr. Fulton. He appeared to me to serve his generation faithfully, to do the work that was required of him in this rising colony, and to employ the talents committed to him in the very way best fitted to serve his generation.

I have not particulars for more than a mere outline.

He was born in Scotland, in the neighbourhood of Dundee, in the year 1813. His parents belonged to the working classes. He himself when a lad first wrought with his father, and afterwards was apprenticed to a machine-maker in Dundee. He made rapid progress in learning his trade, and his energy, talent, and aptitude, even at that early period, displayed themselves so strongly, that two years before he was out of his time he was entrusted by his master to put up machinery in various towns in that part of Scotland.

He was brought up in connexion with the Established Church of Scotland, and joined in its communion before, according to his subsequent views, he was really converted to God. Dr. Russell was at that time the Independent minister at Dundee, and drew great crowds of people by his eloquence and fervour as a preacher. To this ministry Mr. Fulton in his youth was attracted ; and instructions and impressions received under the parental roof, deeply serious feeling awakened by the death at that time of a beloved brother, and other previously planted good seeds of truth, were all quickened into fresh life and vigor under the powerful preaching of Dr. Russell. I have heard him speak with rapture of the deep impressions that preaching made upon his mind, and of the delight and profit it so abundantly yielded him. He seemed to regard Dr. Russell without an equal as a minister, and especially as an expositor of the word of God. It was there, too, in connexion with Dr. Russell's congregation, that he got, or at least began to cultivate, a taste for psalmody, which he retained to the last.

He married and had a small family while yet he resided in Dundee. One main inducement to him to emigrate was the oppression which children in factories were at that time subject to, and which it was a constant pain to him to be compelled to witness, while following his occupation in putting up machinery. He and his family sailed from Scotland in the year 1841. The voyage lasted six months, and was not without risks and adventures, one of which was the shipping of a heavy sea, which so completely submerged the vessel, that the captain was lifted from the deck, and found himself clinging to the rigging when the wave passed off and the ship righted herself. In February, 1842, they landed safely in Melbourne.

Mr. Fulton formed a partnership and commenced business as a founder, in a small way, shortly after his arrival. I am told that the difficulties to be encountered, in introducing such a busiuess into a new country, can hardly be conceived by those who follow that trade at home; for the sort of work to be done being strange and novel, and the materials doing it—iron, fuel, loam, and other things—being all to be sought for and experimented upon. But his skill, enterprise, and patient perseverance, tried as they were to the utmost, finally overcame all difficulties. The little concern grew, and was ultimately able to bear transplanting from its original site to the place where it now stands. The first partnership being dissolved, another was formed with the late Mr. Annand, and then, after that, with Mr. Robert Smith ; and latterly the business was carried on by Mr. Fulton alone. The last change and development was that commencement of operations at Sandhurst, which has mysteriously led to Mr. Fulton's sudden death.

It was by faithfully doing his duty and employing diligently his great natural abilities, as an apprentice and as a journeyman, that he rose to be a master ; and it was by the strenuous and continued application of the same qualities that, from a small master struggling with early difficulties, he became a large employer of labour. By his frankness and fairness, his consideration for his men and sympathy with their condition, he won and retained their confidence and esteem: unfortunately too rare a sight between masters and men where many hands are employed. It was only five months ago that a handsome piece of plate, value sixty guineas, together with an Address,* was presented to Mr. Fulton by his men, as a token of their esteem, at a dinner to which they invited him. The matter was kept profoundly secret till all was ready, and I had it from Mr. Fulton's own lips that hardly anything more deeply affected him than this unexpected testimony from such a quarter; and the striking appearance his workmen made in the funeral procession, when upwards of a hundred walked after the hearse, is an evidence that that feeling of gratitude and confidence continued unabated till their master was no more.

Mr. Fulton beheld the city of Melbourne develop from a mere village to what it now is; and in the various public institutions which sprung up in it he took a fair share of interest and trouble. His public spirit, his benevolence, and his ready powers of effective speech, brought him not a little before the eyes of his fellow-citizens as one of the most energetic and useful of their number. I need only advert to his advocacy of the temperance cause, and latterly to his labours in the City Council, to bring to your recollection some of the ways in which he laid himself out to serve his generation.

But, after all, Religion was the ruling element in our friend's character. He did not leave his youthful piety behind him when he left Scotland, nor lose it on the voyage, as too many do; nor suffer it to be choked when the cares of a growing family and a growing business, and calls into public life multiplied upon him. Nor was he ashamed of it when

---

*   Address to Thomas Fulton, Esq., J.P., C.C.

SIR,—We feel proud of this demonstration and of this desire to establish and perpetuate a good feeling between the employer and the employed.

We are fully sensible of your sterling character as an employer, as a friend, as a citizen, and as a gentleman. Your name stands high in the list of those who have done and suffered much for the happiness of mankind. We have frequently witnessed with feelings of gratitude and pleasure your disinterested acts of benevolence; the stranger and all in distress find instantaneous access to your sympathy and support; Nor do your labours stop here; it is well known that you have both by precept and example done much to benefit your fellow-men; you have devoted your time and your talents to stimulate the great principle of self-culture among the operative classes of society, and to promote their moral and intellectual improvement; and above all, you have laboured almost incessantly to advance the sacred cause of religion; thereby exemplifying that man has nobler duties and higher pleasures than can be found in merely supplying his physical necessities, or in adding house to house. We therefore feel that you are justly entitled to the most devoted thanks to which all well-wishers of their country can bestow upon the exercise of a sound and vigorous philanthropy.

The kindness and courtesy which you have on all occasions manifested have won for you the golden opinion of those in your employment; and, sir, we rejoice to see the employer and the employed assembled together; for we think with Dr. Cairns "it would tend greatly to sweeten the blood of society could all classes unbend a little now and then, and pass a few hours together in innocent recreation;" and we further agree with him that lawful labour should be confined to a period consistent with the workman's highest interests, so that the youth might improve his mind, and the father attend to his household.

With best wishes for your prosperity and happiness, we now have the honour to present to you this small token of our regard.

That God may long spare your life, to enjoy the reward of virtue and industry, is the sincere desire of, sir,

Your faithful servants,
THE MEN IN YOUR EMPLOYMENT.

Signed by the committee—David Black, chairman; William R. Douglas, Richard Bowen, John Gilmour; James Ingham, hon. sec.
Melbourne, September 24th, 1858.

he rose from the condition of a workman to that of a master, a merchant, a city councillor, and a magistrate. While he did not offensively obtrude his religion on others, he never took any pains to conceal it from them. He was *known* to be a man professing godliness, and was respected for his honest avowal of it.

Mr. Fulton's ecclesiastical connexions in this colony began with the church in Collins-street, under the Rev. W. Waterfield, its first pastor, and continued subsequently under the Rev. A. Morison, his successor. He and his friend, Mr. R. Smith, were the first deacons that were chosen in any Independent church in Victoria, and he was an office-bearer in one or other of the churches until his death. He was among those who began a Sunday-school at the west end of Melbourne, which ultimately ripened into the church in Lonsdale street, of which the Rev. Thomas Odell is now pastor. In the first list of members of that church he was included, and he served it faithfully as a member of the diaconate till he removed from town. The foundation of the church at St. Kilda is mainly owing to the princely liberality of Mr. Fulton, Mr. Smith, and Mr. Sargood, who defrayed out of their own pockets the greater part of the costs ; and he, in conjunction with the gentlemen named and others, acted for that church as deacon till he was called away to his heavenly rest.

The body of Christians to which we belong is largely indebted to the zeal and liberality of our late friend. He served his generation by encouraging the building of places of worship, the formation of Christian churches, and the bringing out of ministers from home. Thousands of pounds he freely consecrated to these objects. He was one of the £1,000 donors to the £5,000 subscription raised when Mr. Poore, Mr. Day, and myself landed in Victoria ; and it was a sore trial to him, as the wants and calls of the denomination increased, that losses in trade disabled him from doing as he had formerly done, and as his heart still inclined him to do.

There was scarce an anniversary social meeting of any of our chapels or churches near Melbourne at which our friend was not asked to officiate as chairman or take part as a speaker; his open heart, his good humour, his fluent tongue, and his homely and racy eloquence universally fitting him for such a service ; and we shall sadly miss the sight of his cheerful face, the sound of his pleasant voice, and the aid of his liberal purse on these festive occasions.

He did not forget to entertain strangers and discharge the duties of hospitality. His house was ever open to ministers ; and many of those who have come out lately from England have found solace and encouragement in a strange land from the kindness shown to them by himself and family. One case I may specify, that of the late Rev. J. G. Reed, who left England to become minister of McKillop street Chapel, Geelong. When increasing debility incapacitated him for work, he, together with Mrs. Reed, was invited by Mr. Fulton to come to his house and remain there till the issue of the illness should be known ; and, there, all was done for the sufferer that sympathy and kindness and assiduous attention could do, till death closed the scene.

Mr. Fulton was not much of a traveller; the urgent claims of a business which, for the most part, required personal superintendence, confining him to Melbourne and its immediate locality. He managed, however, to pay a visit to Tasmania in February of last year, as a del gate to the Congregational Conference held at that time in Hobart Town. While his journey yielded him a gratification he was fond of referring to, it left, among the friends he there associated with, impressions of respect and affection which are not likely to wear out; and the news of his death produced, we know, a deep and sorrowful feeling in that quarter.

Mr. Fulton was deeply interested in the visit of the Rev. T. Binney, and his first connexion with Sandhurst arose from his engaging to accompany that gentleman in his journey to that part of the country. He was with Mr. Binney at all the services he conducted, and the meetings in which he took part at Sandhurst, Castlemaine, and Ballaarat, and he returned home much delighted and refreshed with his trip.

This visit, which was the first Mr. Fulton had ever paid to any of the diggings, led to fresh openings in business. A new field of enterprise presented itself in connexion with quartz-mining, and Mr. Fulton entered into one or more contracts for the erection of machinery. He considered his personal superintendence of the works desirable, and therefore made arrangements for a temporary residence at Sandhurst, and Mrs. Fulton and one of his daughters followed him up for the sake of company.

The last Sabbath he spent on earth was a happy one, for on the evening of that day he expressed himself as having been highly edified and refreshed by the services. On the Monday evening he attended a social meeting at the new Baptist Chapel, where he made a characteristic speech,—a speech which excited hopes in the Sandhurst people that on many a similar occasion they would have the benefit of his acceptable help. This was the last public service in which he engaged.

On the morning of the fatal day Mr. Fulton was in good spirits, and remarked to Mrs. Fulton that he never was in better health in his life. At family worship she took notice that he was particularly fervent and earnest in praying for his family, distant as they were from him at the time, entreating God to give them grace that they might serve him in youth, and that they all might meet together in the mansions of bliss above,—a prayer which I trust will be answered to the letter. He was busy throughout the day; and in the afternoon, being anxious to inspect the works at the bottom of the shaft, he descended in company with his foreman. By some accident, when they were about half-way down, the windlass by which they were lowered got out of gear, and the rope on which they were suspended running rapidly off the cylinder, Mr. Fulton was instantly jerked off the plank on which he stood and precipitated to the bottom. Assistance was soon brought, when he was found to be alive and sensible, but dangerously injured. On being raised to the top he was conveyed to his friend, Mr. Bannerman's house, at the Bank of New South Wales. Medical aid was soon at hand, and on examination it was ascertained that both legs were broken, one of them shattered so severely that immediate amputation was necessary. The accident occurred at four o'clock in the afternoon, and death took place about nine. Though he was conscious to a certain extent almost to the last, he was too much stunned to be able to converse. There is therefore no dying experience to relate; we fall back upon the safer evidence of a life of service for God and his generation; and doubt not but that sudden death was to him sudden glory.

Through that grace that made him what he was, he has entered into the joy of his Lord and met his reward.

The public has not been wanting in tokens of respect. The funeral was the most remarkable one ever seen in Melbourne. The body had been removed down from Sandhurst, and the interment took place at the Melbourne Cemetery, on Tuesday, February 22. The hearse was followed by a numerous body of relatives, by the pastor and deacons of the St. Kilda Congregational Church and most of the Congregational ministers in the neighbourhood, in mourning coaches; by the Mayor and members of the City Council; by old colonists and gentlemen of the city, some in carriages and some on horseback; and by a long procession of his workmen and numerous other friends on foot. The procession, as it passed through Melbourne to the cemetery, exceeded a mile in length. Nearly all the shops, inns, offices, and banks, on the entire line of road were closed, and the blinds of private houses drawn down. The flag on the Town Hall was hoisted half-mast high all day, and so were those of the steamers, ships, and lighters in the river. Large crowds of people lined the roads and streets on both sides, and many a hat was reverentially touched as the procession moved along. The funeral service at the grave was conducted by the Rev. R. Fletcher, the deceased's pastor, and by the Rev. T. Odell, his former pastor. Grief for the loss of so valuable a citizen, and sympathy for the bereaved family, seemed to pervade all classes.

In politics Mr. Fulton was an ardent and sincere advocate of all measures tending to do away with class legislation, and to promote the establishment of free institutions, and was a staunch and persevering opponent of all State-aid to religion in any form whatever. As he was unsuccessful in the single attempt he made to obtain a seat in the Legislature, the only way in which his interest in political affairs could be shown was by delivering speeches and acting as president at public meetings, which he not unfrequently did.

But it was, after all, Religion,—the religion I have already spoken of,—which was the basis of all those excellencies of our friend's character that have won for him so much respect. That religion was genuine, simple, earnest, hearty, evangelical. He dearly loved the glorious Gospel of the blessed God with all its rich peculiarities. The Sabbath was his joy and refreshment. The offering at the family altar was never neglected. The word of God was his spiritual meat and drink day by day. Private devotion was habitually kept up. And in this way it was that, by nourishing the religion of his heart by unremitting attention to the means of grace and spiritual improvement both secret and public, he acquired that strength of piety and energy of benevolence which enabled him to serve his generation so effectually as he has done. While admiring what was good in his character, let us seek to imitate it. "Be not slothful, but followers of them who through faith and patience are now inheriting the promises."

R. F.

STRENGTH AND WEAKNESS.

There is many a man who is not ashamed to loose his temper or his patience, because his servant has been negligent, who, upon being visited with some serious calamity, would probably display the resignation of a Christian.—*Henry Rogers*.

NOTES OF THE RELIGIOUS CONDITION OF SCOTLAND.
(Concluded from page 69).

THE United Presbyterian Church has an honorable history, which it is no part of our present purpose fully to rehearse. We shall refer to the past only so far as may be deemed necessary to enable the reader to have a tolerable understanding of its present position and influence in the country. It has been stated already that upwards of a century ago the Secession Church took its rise, under the Erskines and others. Those who left the Church of Scotland under the auspices of these men went on increasing both in numbers and in influence ; but in course of time there sprung up causes of dispute, and reasons (as they thought) for separation. The quarrel ran high, and " the strife of tongues " filled the land. In the controversies that followed, the qualities of acute reasoning and keen sarcasm, which are apparently inseparable from the Scotch mind when warm in theological or ecclesiastical debate, were called into active and frequent operation. They separated after the Burgess oath. Time passes, the fire of controversy burns itself out, wiser counsels prevail, men wonder at past estrangements, and those who never should have parted company, meet and mingle again as friends, under the name of the " United Secession Church." But although the great body of both " old " and " new lights," as the Burghers and anti-Burghers were derisively called, entered into the union with right good will, yet there were many who did so with reluctance, and a " remnant " on each side was left behind. These, and one or two other small sects of Presbyterians, managed to maintain a separate existence, without producing any marked effect, either on the social or religious character of the country. One of these " remnants," a small but sturdy sect, has had the good sense to strike a match with the Free Church, and, it is alleged, on very favourable terms. The others choose to stand alone in their glory ; and under an inexorable law of nature, must " become small by degrees, and beautifully less," till that which they refuse to do as bodies corporate, will be effectually accomplished by the exercise of the individual will, an entire absorption in the larger and more popular Presbyterian communities. The lion's share will fall to the Free Church. To return from this digression :— Upwards of twenty years ago, the question began to be agitated in two bodies who had hitherto stood apart, the " United Secession " and the " Relief," whether a union might not be effected between the followers of the Erskines and the followers of Gillespie, the founder of the Relief Presbytery. This union did take place a few years ago, under the auspices of Dr. McKelvie, who still lives, in a green old age, to rejoice in the many good fruits which that union, under the favour of heaven, has produced. These united sects constitute the numerous and influential community whose position and power we are now endeavouring to fix. The United Presbyterian Church is, perhaps, the most compact religious community in Scotland. It has a maturity and ripeness about it which are not observable in the others. Its adherents are numerous, but not so numerous as those attached to the Free Church. They have been trained to exercise a large and steady liberality in all matters pertaining to the support and extension of the Gospel, and they have done and are still doing great things in the wide field of practical Christian duty. Scotland owes a deep debt of gratitude to the United Presbyterian—(we hate the common abbreviation used even by themselves, " U. P.")—Church ; for the moral and spiritual influence of this Church is very great indeed. There are upwards of 500 congregations, ministered to by men who are thoroughly trained in all the branches of a liberal and theological education. The fame of the United Presbyterian " Hall " is the growth of many years ; it needs no help from our pen ; and no theological seminary in Scotland sends forth an annual supply of young men better fitted to discharge the onerous and responsible duties of the Christian ministry. The present incumbents of this church take a high place among the clergy of Scotland ; and were one who belonged to neither of the three great sections of the Presbyterian Church candidly to state his opinion, he would, in all probability, say, that, upon the whole, the standard of ministerial excellence is higher in the United Presbyterian than it is either in the Established or in the Free Churches. From the general body, in which so much excellence exists, such men as Cairns and Eadie and Brown* stand forth as types of clerical character that would shed lustre on any church. We should not omit to mention that recently an imposing show, on the part of the laity of both churches, was made in favour of union between the Free Church and the United Presbyterians ; but it was " pooh poohed !" by the clerical leaders, especially on the side of the Frees. United, they would out-balance the Established Church in many important respects ; but the time for union is not yet. Great men, and good men, too ; men who can make great sacrifices for Christ's crown and kingdom; men who can redeem the ministerial character from sordidness, and make the mere worldling stand silent in amazement at the moral grandeur of their actions ;— such men, with pain we say, can find reasons why the body of Christ should continue bruised and torn, even when the lacerated and bleeding parts make common cause to come together.—The disruption is too recent.

The remaining sects must be classed in one paragraph, otherwise this sketch would expand far beyond its intended proportions. These consist of Episcopalians, Independents, Baptists, Methodists, and Roman Catholics. There are other sects still ; but they are so small and so unimportant, comparatively, that we may, without serious detriment to the subject, leave them in their obscurity. Although the sects abovementioned are none of them large, yet their influence on the religious condition of Scotland has been, and still is, considerable. Presbyterian though the country be, no one acquainted with the subject will deny that Presbyterian preaching and polity have alike been quickened and liberalized by the presence and practice of Independents. The English Independents, as everyone knows, are a numerous and influential body of Christians ; and as they have for generations been a recognised power in the land, so they have, from time to time, since the days of the " Pilgrim Fathers " till now, sent forth men holding their principles to all parts of the world. Nay, more.—In many places those principles specially embodied in Independency have sprung up immediately when religion has begun to shake itself free of the iron

* The home newspapers report the death of this able minister of the Gospel, and ablest of Scotch Biblical critics. He was the last of the old ministers of that name, all so distinguished, who sprung from John Brown, of Haddington, of revered memory. The only remaining representative of this name is the Rev. John Crombie Brown, Aberdeen, grandson to old John Brown, and a much younger man than the deceased professor.

fetters of a cold and dead formalism. Upwards of three score years ago, it sprung up a promising sapling in Presbyterian Scotland. Under the fostering care of the Haldanes and the Ewings, now no more, it struck its roots and extended its branches over the whole land, and many who longed for the privileges of a pure and spiritual religion sate gratefully under its shade. Time passed, and the goodly tree of goodlier promise was blighted. Concord was broken, unity was destroyed, and usefulness retarded. Differences crept in among the leading ministers and congregations, and the disputations became sharp and portentous. Amid the throes that so terribly convulsed the community, the Baptist body rose into separate ecclesiastic existence. And now, instead of one, we have two religious communities, composed chiefly of those who had adopted the principles and polity of Independency. That was a terrible shock, a shock from which neither party has perfectly recovered. The congregations or " churches " are, indeed, more numerous; but they are not so strong. Unity and brotherly love are the human elements that constitute the strength, as they constitute the beauty and glory of Christian communities; divisions are fatal to them both. Years of peace and usefulness have healed up many wounds, and removed many of the anticipated consequences; and now you will see those who were formerly estranged, engaged, with the utmost cordiality, in every good work. Many of the Baptist churches have no salaried minister, some brother being appointed to discharge the duties of the pastorate, with the usual results. On the other hand, the Independents, both those included in the " Congregational Union of Scotland " and those who remain without, have a body of ministers thoroughly trained for the work, and who hold a most respectable position among the clergy of Scotland. Their preaching powers are more frequently called into exercise, their influence as men and as ministers is more seriously tested, and certain virtues in them are more largely taxed than those of the ministers in any other denomination. It is more difficult, humanly speaking, to succeed as a minister in this communion than in any other; and whilst those who minister at her altars bear, in one respect at least, a close resemblance to the early preachers of the Gospel, like them, too, they need " to possess their souls in patience," and " to endure as seeing Him who is invisible !" The sect that had, till recently, a Wardlaw and a Russell, and that still has an Alexander, a Raleigh, and a Pulsford, must have had its own share in producing and sustaining, under God, that spiritual life and moral greatness that characterize in such a marked manner the land of Melville and Knox.

The Scotch Episcopalians are not a numerous, but they are, in a worldly sense, a highly respectable community. In truth, it is composed chiefly of the upper classes, and since the disruption it has been considerably augmented. Many who were well to do in the world, and who loved repose more than controversy, during that stormy period went quietly off from both parties, and attached themselves to this community. Here they find repose, but not so absolute and unbroken as may have been anticipated; for even here the waves of controversy ruffle the surface, if they do not move the waters in their depths. The Scotch Episcopalians are generally reputed Tractarians, and it would not be surprising though they were: but in justice it must be said that there are many among them as thoroughly evangelical in their faith, and as much given to Christian well-doing in their life, as are those in connexion with the Presbyterian sects. It is further alleged that from this community the ranks of the Roman Catholic Church have been considerably recruited. It is true that some members of the aristocracy have openly acknowledged their adhesion to the Papacy ; but, in the first place, the number is very small ; and secondly, it is much more a change of position or connexion than a change of principle ; and it is not followed by a corresponding number of the people. The Roman Catholic Church is not strong in Scotland ; and though it has increased of late years, yet everyone knows that it is not owing to Protestants having departed from their principles, but chiefly to the influx of Irish as "navvies" and farm labourers. The Roman Catholic Church in Scotland can scarcely be called a power,—certainly it is not a great power ; and the cry of the spread of Popery is less founded in fact than it is helpful to the dreaded innovation. The Methodists, too, are but a small sect, and exercise but a feeble influence on the religious character and condition of that country. They are, indeed, there, as everywhere else, a zealous people ; but what can even zeal do when there is no field for its operation ? In this last sentence we must be understood as at once speaking to their honor and accounting for their non-success.

Notwithstanding the divisions that break up the unity and mar the beauty of the Church of Christ in Scotland, the religious principle has a powerful hold on the minds and hearts of the community. Divisions and sectional strife have not been unmitigated evils ; they have created a commendable rivalry, sustained a spirit of theological inquiry, stimulated zeal, and greatly multiplied Christian exertion. Paradoxical as it may seem, they have provoked to "love" and to "good works." You will, indeed, meet with persons who, with marvellous presumption and impertinence, set the whole matter down as fanaticism, cant, and humbug. Believe them not. They know not the price that Scotchmen of past generations have paid for their religion ; they know not the depth and strength of the religious principle in the souls of her ablest sons ; they have not the capacity to grasp the strong points in Scotch theology, nor the candour to admit that religious feeling is not of necessity spurious because it is strong. Fools ! What is religion if it is not sincere ? What is principle if it is not embodied in practice ? What is a name to live if one is dead ? Shall a man mock God ? There is a deep and steady flow of healthy religious feeling all over the land, which the surface-currents of controversy rarely touch ; and this is the life-principle of the nation. Her strength, her conserving principle, the hope of her future, are all bound up in her religion. And it is not, as many suppose, a metaphysical abstract principle ; it is thoroughly practical, and hence some of the finest illustrations of disinterestedness, devotedness, liberality, and self-sacrifice, are to be met with in dear old Scotland.   W.

THE HARMONY OF TRUTH.

A diamond when set in the midst of diamonds seems to acquire a new brilliancy foreign to its natural state. This, however, is but a seeming change, arising from the harmony of effect produced by skilful arrangement. Its angles remain the same, its properties are unaltered, the amount of reflected and refracted light is just as it was when we looked at the jewel as it lay in the palm of our hand previous to its being wrought in with the rest of the cluster. Truths are often called diamonds, but the setting of any of them produces a marked difference in their effect. An isolated truth is in reality a distorted truth. It has no doubt a brilliancy peculiar to itself, but its light may be broken, fitful, and apparently impure. A truth set among other truths actually undergoes an important change, not in appearance merely, but in fact : it is more resplendent ; it develops new properties, reflects new light, increases both the quantity and the quality of its illumination. Truths, like the radii of a circle, are, when removed from their position, but fragments of straight lines ; by their relation to the unseen centre they are more than lines, they are full of the mysterious beauty of the geometric harmony of the sphere.

Short-sighted men, both philosophers and theologians, have failed to grasp the harmony of the many truths presented at once to the mind. The result of this is, each has chosen out his favorite dogmas, *taken them out of the circle,* and thus isolated, they have almost ceased to be truths. Many gifted intellects in both walks of speculation have seen this error and tried to remedy it. Assuming that in every doctrine and opinion which has swayed men's hearts there is some truth, however small, they have tried to collect these fragments and recombine them into a harmonious whole. In philosophy these attempts have failed, as, in modern times we have an example of, in the brilliant but useless eclecticism of Cousin. In theology, which comes from God, such attempts have been eminently successful. Not uniformly has this been the case, as we know, alas, from the mistakes, and discords, and persecutions which disfigure the history of the Church of Christ ; but the life of many a noble hero of the Cross proclaims to us the harmony of the truth of God with the truth of man ; the truth in theory, with the truth in practice.

The ancient chronicles, narrating the wars of a semi-barbarous period, tell us of a certain heroic king whose career was an unbroken succession of victories ; and of him it is recorded, that he owed all his success to one manœuvre or plan of action. He divided the main body of his forces into three parts, over each of these appointing a commander, and arranging the whole in the form of a *triangle* or *wedge.* In attack, the whole force of a side of the wedge was opposed to the enemy ; in defence, the sharp angle only was presented for them to send their missiles against. To be taken in flank was impossible, to be broken almost equally so, and if it was not always practicable to gain the victory, the commander might count upon never being defeated while he adhered to these formidable tactics. Each host was more than itself. It had the strength of a mere line of forces and the strength of its close relationship to the other lines added to this ; and in thus giving to the others accessions of power it was not weakened by parting with any of its own. Honest fighting could never overcome this great hero. He was at last defeated, 'tis true, but only by deceit ; a feigned flight on the part of the enemy caused the component parts of the wedge, flushed with the pride of their imaginary success, to break from their order and to join in the pursuit of the flying foe. They were taken in the rear and defeated.

In similar manner may the great Christian doctrines be marshalled. They may be arranged in three great divisions, and these divisions united as an impenetrable triangle. By so doing these cardinal doctrines augment more than they were before, in shedding light on minor truths and on each other.

And *first* come the great doctrines of *Immortality:* The Christian Scriptures alone tell us of the unknown future world. That such a region is, is essentially a truth of revelation, for philosophy can but vaguely surmise and dream of what lies beyond mortal life on earth. We say first come the *doctrines* of immortality, for here we have a whole phalanx of truths,—*heaven*, its character, its duration, its employments, its sympathy with earth and its inhabitants, the pre-requisites for attaining its bliss, and the perpetuation of individual existence in the super-mortal state ;—*hell*, too, its nature, its terrors, its justice, and the consignment of the unworthy to a continuance of their sin and misery ; all these are among the verities of the Christian faith. It is a grand band of truths. The whole host is ever looking upward, ever cheerful ; their leader is named *Hope*, and they are ranged under a wide spread white banner on which is embroidered a rising sun.

And next come the doctrines which gather around and are included in the *Atonement*. These again are peculiarly a Christian host. In any other army they are scouted as poor soldiers unfit for ordinary warfare, but not so here : they are mighty in themselves, and, allied with the rest of the forces, are full of indomitable courage. In their ranks we may recognize,—the *law*, its precepts, its rightness, its sanctions ; *sacrifice*, its seat in human nature, its universality, its prophetic character ; the *incarnation*, with its glance into the past and the future of the mercy of Jehovah's purposes, the God-man, the suffering Saviour, the appointed lamb ; *pardon*, free pardon for all sins through his precious blood. Here, too, is a vast array of truths, not buoyant like those under the command of Hope, but of soberer aspect, bespeaking concealed power. Silent are they but resolute ; not mercenary, attracted by promised rewards, but marshalled by conviction in the defence of the right. They have one common leader, well known for his victories, *Faith*, and over them floats a dark colored standard, on which is wrought a crimson cross.

But even with these two mighty forces the army is incomplete ; the third side of the triangle is wanting. What power would a distant immortality possess even when joined with the Atonement, unless there were revealed to us, likewise, the privilege of communion.

Then lastly come the doctrines of *Prayer*. Earth and heaven are to the Christian one. " Dead to sin," he is already " risen with Christ." *Now* he dwells among the blessed, and his heart and God's are open to the most intimate fellowship. This it is which makes the splendour of immortality to our eyes so great. It is ours now. And this it is which makes the slain Lamb so precious ; he now " walks among the seven golden candlesticks," and is visibly present to the eye of faith. This part of the great army, no less than the others, is composed of many ranks. The doctrines involved in prayer are important,—communion with God, intercession for others. Providence, mighty as are its workings, is yet influenced by prayer. The Spirit of God himself dwells in the praying heart. The Bible and life and death are all interpreted by prayer. The example and name of Christ are incentives to devotion. This is the most practical part of religion, for it is here that the ambassadors and emissaries of the army are placed and negotiations are carried on. It is here that the messengers from the enemy are received, and it is to the commandant of this division that the great King of all makes known his will by direct personal intercourse. The other generals come here for advice and encouragement, for there is wisdom in prayer which all will do well to learn. In these ranks are no downcast looks, no hatred or jealousy marring the concert of their action, no hesitancy and no fear.   It is at this point that the enemy is most anxious to make a break in the invincible triangle, for this side once burst through, Faith and Hope may call in vain to their forces to stand ; whereas, if the other lines be thrown into disorder and this be unmoved, there is even yet but small chance for the foe.   And he who has the command here is *Love*, the chosen servant of the Most High, who, both here below and in heaven itself, ranks among the highest.   And over his head waves the great consecrated banner of the whole host, having a ground of pure white, wrought with a circle of rainbow colours around two clasped hands, the hand of God and the hand of man.

In this way we may present to our minds the power of the united body of Christian truth, and perceive plainly the cause of the weakness of even a truthful idea when held alone.   Orthodox faith is often seen powerless, because prayer has been neglected.   Bright dreams of poetry and fancy have been but dreams, because the hope of immortality has not been founded on the atonement and upheld by communion.   And prayer itself has passed into fanaticism because not supported by reasonable faith in revelation.   Truth united must advance.   The individual, the church, the nation which is allied with this three-sided phalanx of Christian doctrine must be victorious in the great battle, which we all must wage with sin, temptation and death.

EXTRACTS.

THE OUTLAWRY OF VICE.

If he that, amidst the hazards of a dubious war, betrays the interest and honor of his country, be justly infamous, and thought worthy severest punishments, I see not why a debauched sensualist, that lives as if he were created only to indulge his appetite ; that so vilifies the notion of man, as if he were made but to eat and drink and sport, to please only his sense and fancy ; that in this time and state of conflict between the powers of this present world, and those of the world to come, quits his party, bids open defiance to humanity, abjures the noble principles and ends, forsakes the laws and society of all that are worthy to be esteemed men, abandons the common and rational hope of mankind concerning a future immortality, and herds himself among brute creatures : I say, I see not why such a one should not be scorned and abhorred as a traitor to the whole race and nation of reasonable creatures, as a fugitive from the tents, and deserter of the common interest of men ; and that both for the vileness of his practice and the danger of his example.—*Howe.*

GROWTH OF TOLERATION.

The three centuries which have passed over the world since the Reformation have soothed the theological animosities which they have failed to obliterate. An enlarged experience of one another has taught believers of all sorts that these differences need not be pressed into mortal hatred ; and we have been led forward unconsciously into a recognition of a broader Christianity than as yet we are able to profess in the respectful acknowledgment of excellence wherever excellence is found.   Where we see piety, continence, courage, self-forgetfulness, there, or not far off, we know is the spirit of the Almighty ; and as we look around us among our living contemporaries, or look back with open eyes into the history of the past, we see—we dare not in voluntary blindness say we do not see—that God is no respecter of " denominations " any more than he is a respecter of persons.   His highest gifts are shed abroad with an even hand among the sects of Christendom, and petty distinctions melt away and become invisible in the palaces of a grander truth.   Thus, even among those whose theories allow least room for latitude, liberty of conscience has become a law of modern thought. It is as if the ancient Catholic unity which was divided in the sixteenth century into separate streams of doctrine, as light is divided by the prism, was again imperceptibly returning; as if the colored rays were once more blending themselves together in a purer and more rich transparency.—*Froude's History of England.*

GOD'S DESIGN IN AFFLICTION.

We may err in thinking some particular offence must be fastened upon as the cause. If it clearly can, it ought; if not, it is better to forbear judging than to misjudge. Possibly, chastening for a particular sin may not be God's design; it is not always. We may be sure it never is his principal design, in taking away one relative from another. He made all things (principally) for himself; he made us but secondarily for one another. If his principal design in making such a creature was not to please me, his principal design in taking it away was not to displease or afflict me. He hath his own greater and higher end concerning his own creature, to glorify himself upon it, and by it, in a greater world than this.—*Howe.*

WHY SOME RELIGIOUS MEN DON'T "GET ON" IN THE WORLD.

In like manner, I think that religion should not be charged with the blundering, and failure, and want of success of those good men whom our friend referred to. He has known, it seems, many of the "excellent of the earth" that never got on; never succeeded as masters, and never rose very high as servants. So have I. But the *religion* of the men did not hinder them. I have known such in positions where, other things being equal, it would have weighed in their favor, and done them service. The fact is, the sort of men referred to are generally such as, whether they have religion or not, will never succeed in anything. They are slow, dull, well-meaning men. Heavy, rather, at both ends—head and feet alike acting as if weighed down by something that impeded them. They want tact, perspicacity, vigor, ambition. They look at things as if their eyes were made of glass;—they lay hold of them as if they had no fingers on their hands. They can't be looked to, when a thing presses, to get through it with cleverness and dexterity. They will lose the post because they cannot write without mending their pen;—and they will go leisurely, too, about the operation,—though the very sight of the thing will vex and irritate those who are longing to see the boy off with the letter. Men of this sort may be very good, very pious. I quite believe it. I don't doubt that. But it's all nonsense attributing their want of advance and success in life to their *religion.* They are true, worthy, conscientious; they are spiritual, holy, excellent men; but they are not fitted for getting on, in the highest form of the thing, or the largest meaning of the phrase. They do best as servants; with their duties defined, their powers directed, and their salary secure. They cannot be trusted to be employers and principals,—having plans to form, and speculations to enter into, and modes of action to choose or to originate. They are sure to fail in all that. But they would have done so, had they been as destitute of religion as they are of ability. The fact is, that religion, as regenerating, sanctifying, and making a man into "a new creature," does not make him into a different natural man from what he was before—though it makes him into a *spiritual* one by the infusion of a Divine principle of life. As a man, he will be morally improved and elevated, but he will not be different—in talent, genius, or original aptitude—from what he previously was. He will be a better but not a cleverer man. It is to be observed, therefore, that the excellent unsuccessful men of our friend here, are, for the most part, such because of their natural destitution of some one or more of those attributes of mind and character on which success depends; and that they are indebted to their religion, not for having done so badly, but for not having done a great deal worse. It is not the source of what is defective in them, but of what is good. Without religion, they might have been dishonest and immoral as well stupid. So that, you see, balancing natural defect by spiritual principle, religion, after all, that helps them to get on as well as they do. They pass through the world worthy, reputable people, filling with honor subordinate positions in the great household of humanity,—whereas had they not had religion to quicken and enoble them as men of God, they might have been so dragged downwards by the sluggishness of nature, as to deserve turning into the streets as dishonest and unfaithful, to wander and starve like ejected vagabonds.— *Binney's "Both Worlds,"* page 128.

GRATITUDE FOR CHRISTIAN PRIVILEGES.

A Hymn for British Colonists.

To Thee, oh! Lord of all the earth!
  Our cheerful songs arise,
Tho' left the land that gave us birth,
  And distant far its skies.

No silent harps on willows hung
  Upon a foreign strand,
Behold us weeping, anguish-wrung,
  As aliens in the land.

Our fathers' God we still approach,
  Our fathers' songs we sing ;
Thro' Jesus, still, without reproach,
  Our wonted off'rings bring.

His pleading blood and righteousness
  We mention, as of old,
Still coming to a throne of grace,
  Thy mercy making bold.

And here, as we renew our vows,
  We ask for help anew,
To press towards our Father's House
  With earnest step, and true.

Nor shall the land forgotten be,
  The land that gave us birth ;
God bless the land of liberty,
  The glory of the earth.

Hymns for the Colonies by E. S.

POSTURES IN PUBLIC WORSHIP.

At a recent meeting of the Victoria Bible Society, the Rev. Mr. Binney, in the course of his speech, related some instances of the conversion of Roman Catholics of the poorer classes in Italy to simple and Evangelical Christianity ; and, in describing their meetings for devotion, he said they all *stood* during prayer, and then remarked, as a singular co-incidence, that such was the custom of Christians of the primitive ages. This remark brought forth the following letter, which appeared in the Melbourne Christian Times of February 12 :—

"PRIMITIVE USAGE IN WORSHIP.—*To the Editor of the Christian Times.*

"Sir,—At the last meeting of the Bible Society in the Mechanics' Institute, the Rev. Mr. Binney, in the course of his speech, and turning round to the Bishop of Melbourne, said that his lordship would bear him out in saying that it was the custom of the Church in the early ages to *stand* while praying on Sundays, and to *kneel* on other days. I find, on referring to Mosheim's Ecclesiastical History, he says, that during the third century, "at those festivals which recalled the memory of some joyful event, and were to be celebrated with expressions of thanksgiving and praise, they prayed standing, as they thought that posture the fittest to express their joy and confidence. On days of contrition and fasting, they prostrated themselves upon their knees before the throne of the Most High to express their profound humiliation and self-abasement.''

" Now, sir, this very idea is carried out by the Church of England, for part of the prayers (that is, the Psalms for the day of the month, and which generally consist mostly of thanksgiving and praise) is repeated while standing; and the other part (that is, confession, supplication, intercession, &c.) is repeated while kneeling.

I am, Sir, yours respectfully,
ONE WHO HAS JOINED THE CHURCH OF ENGLAND FROM CONVICTION."

WHAT the real usage of the early ages was may be learnt from the extract given below from Bingham, a higher authority than Mosheim. Though lengthy, it is curious and interesting :—

" The next considerable circumstance in their worship was the *posture* observed in their addresses and adorations of God ; and of this we find four kinds generally practised and allowed, namely,—standing, kneeling, bowing, and prostration ; for sitting, which some add as a fifth sort, was never allowed by the ancients as an ordinary posture of devotion. Standing, was the general observation of the whole church on the Lord's day, and the fifty days between Easter and Pentecost, in memory of our Saviour's resurrection. This custom may be traced as high as Irenæus, who derives it from apostolical authority. For the author, under the name of Justin Martyr, gives this account of the use of both postures in prayer :—' Forasmuch as we ought to remember both our fall by sin, and the grace of Christ by which we rise again from our fall, therefore we pray kneeling six days, as a symbol of our fall by sin ; but our not kneeling on the Lord's day is a symbol of the resurrection, whereby through the grace of Christ we are delivered from our sins, and from death, that is mortified thereby.' And this custom took its original from the times of the Apostles, as St. Irenæus says in his book concerning Easter, wherein he also makes mention of Pentecost, during which time we kneel not, because it is of the same nature with the Lord's day, according to the reason that has been given. Not long after, Tertullian speaks of it as an observation, among many others, handed down from ancient tradition. And Cyprian may be supposed to hint it when he speaks of their standing in prayer.

" It is mentioned also by Clemens, of Alexandria, and Peter, bishop of Alexandria, who died some years before the Council of Nice. He says :—' We keep the Lord's day as a day of joy, because then our Lord rose from the dead, and our tradition is not to kneel on that day.' In the time of the Council of Nice there was some disagreement about this practice, and therefore that council made a canon to bring all churches to a uniformity in this matter ; ' Because there are some who kneel on the Lord's day and in the days of Pentecost ; that all things may be uniformly performed in every parish or diocese, it seems good to the holy synod, that prayers be made to God standing.' After this, St. Hilary speaks of it again as an apostolical practice, neither to fast nor worship kneeling on the Lord's day, or the fifty days between Easter and Pentecost. Epiphanius says, that on the appointed days they prayed kneeling, but during the whole fifty days of Pentecost they neither fasted nor kneeled.

" St. Jerome reckons it among the traditions of the universal Church, neither to fast nor kneel on the Lord's day or Pentecost. St. Austin is a little doubtful as to the practice of the Church universal, but he assures us that as far as he knew, all churches in Africa forbore fasting and prayed standing, and sung hallelujah at the altar every Lord's day and all the days of Pentecost, in token of our Saviour's resurrection. We find the same in St. Basil, who derives it from apostolical practice. And Cassian testifies of the Egyptian churches, that from Saturday night to Sunday night, and all the days of Pentecost, they neither kneeled nor fasted. And in another place he gives the reason of this, because kneeling was a sign of deep repentance and mourning, which they omitted on those days out of respect and reverence to our Saviour's resurrection. Hence it was, that the author of the "Constitutions" makes it one of his apostolical orders, that all men should pray three times, or three prayers, on the Lord's day standing, in memory of him who rose the third day from the dead. And from hence came that usual form so often mentioned by St. Chrysostom and others, of the deacon's calling upon the people in prayer, "Ὀρθῶς στῶμεν καλῶς," 'Let us stand upright with reverence and decency,' alluding to the posture then commonly used in prayer on the Lord's day.

"How long this custom continued in the Church is not easy to determine ; but we may observe it to be mentioned by Martin Bracarensis in the sixth century, and the Council of Trullo in the seventh century, and third Council of Tours in the time of Charles the Great. Nor do we meet with any exception to this rule all this time, save only one relating to the penitents, or those that were under the discipline of the Church ; who being, by their falling into scandalous sins, reduced to a state of penance, were not allowed this privilege of standing at prayers on the Lord's day, but were obliged in token of their humiliation to kneel at all times, not excepting the days of relaxation, as the fourth Council of Carthage words it in a canon made in this behalf. And so we have seen the concurrent testimony of all writers for the antiquity and universality of this practice."—*Bingham's Christian Antiquities*, book xiii. chap. 8, sect. 3.

It would appear from this that the primitive Christians did not regulate their devotional postures according to the *tenor* of the devotions themselves, but according to the *day* on which they were offered, standing, during all their devotions, whether confessions or thanksgivings, on the Sundays, and kneeling throughout the whole of them on other days; and during the fifty days of Pentecost, standing on all days alike. If our friend, the writer of the letter, above, changes from one denomination to another from a love of antiquarian usages (though, in his taste for antiquities, stopping short of the *apostolic* period) he should look out for some Church that really does copy the ancients. One would have thought he would have been attracted rather to the Presbyterians, who stand *all the time* during prayer, whereas the Episcopalians stand and kneel *alternately*. Nor is the standing of the latter regulated by the eucharistic tone of the service, as many of the Psalms are deeply penitential, while many of the Collects and other parts of the service are full of joy and thanksgiving. Yet *all* the Psalms are repeated standing and *all* the collects and other prayers kneeling.

COLONIAL MISSIONARY SOCIETY.

The Society in England for furnishing Congregational ministers for the Colonies has commenced the publication of a small quarterly periodical, entitled the "Colonial Chronicle," intended to contain a brief record of the transactions of the Society, both at home, and in the various colonies whither its ministers are sent. The following is an extract from their prospectus:—

"The operations of the Colonial Missionary Society having of late been greatly extended, the committee have felt the importance, indeed the absolute necessity, of some medium of communication with their subscribers and friends throughout the country. Heretofore they have published an "occasional paper," containing information which might have been recently received from one or more of the stations occupied by the agents of the society. They have also had access to the pages of the magazines. But they consider that many advantages will result from a more direct intercourse with their friends, especially by the means of Auxiliary Societies and Congregational Associations, the multiplication of which is greatly to be desired. They have therefore resolved, after mature consideration, to publish a quarterly record of their proceedings, which, they trust, will sustain the interest felt in the operations of the society, and awaken it where hitherto it does not exist.

"It is intended the 'Chronicle' should contain extracts from the correspondence, which, though it may not possess the novelty, not to say romance, which sometimes characterises communications from heathen or foreign countries, will convey intelligence of the work of God amongst our 'kinsmen according to the flesh,' resident in the various colonies of the British empire, which, it is presumed, will be cordially received by the churches of the mother country.

"The quarterly paper will also be a chronicle of the most important transactions of the committee, so far as it may be deemed expedient to publish them. This will show to their constituents how far they have discharged the important duties devolved upon them; and will awaken on their behalf the sympathies they so much value, and call forth the prayers they so earnestly desire.

"The establishment of auxiliary societies or associations will here find a suitable record. As the committee are anxious to multiply these institutions, as a means of diffusing information and raising funds, they indulge the hope that no number of their little serial will be issued without the announcement of some such organisations. They have proved of essential service wherever they have been established, and as they are not found to interfere with public or other means of raising funds, their proceeds have been clear gain to the general income of the society. The contributions received from all sources during the quarter will be acknowledged in the Chronicle."

The two numbers for October and January, which have come to hand, contain all details of the Rev. J. L. Poore's successful proceedings in England, and of the farewell services at his departure, but these have already been printed in our pages. We make the following extract relating to ministers whose arrival is daily expected :—

"Since the publication of the last number of the ' Chronicle,' the committee have engaged the services of two young brethren, who they believe to be eminently fitted for great usefulness, the Rev. James Jefferis, LL.B., and the Rev. John E. Vetch, B.A., who was one of the Alumni of New College, and who has been induced by domestic circumstances to devote himself to the ministry of the Gospel in Australia. Both these young brethren are warmly recommended by the College authorities, so that the committee felt no hesitation in sending them under the auspices of the Society.

"They were ordained to the work of the ministry at Westminster Chapel on the 16th of December, which solemn service was conducted by the Revs. Dr. Halley, S. Martin, J. C. Harrison, J. S. Pearsall, F. S. Turner, B.A., and T. James, with other ministers. It was an occasion long to be remembered, and produced a great interest in the beloved young brethren, and, it is hoped, in the Society in connexion with which they go forth to the land of their adoption. They sailed with their wives from Liverpool in the Beechworth, on the 21st of December. May God protect and speed them on their voyage, and give them an abundant entrance on the scene of their anticipated labors."

An account is given of the various fields of the society's operations in British America, Nova Scotia and New Brunswick, Port Natal, and British Columbia, Vancouver's Island. We extract the last-named :—

"BRITISH COLUMBIA.
" VANCOUVER'S ISLAND.

"The chief attraction of British America at the present time is the new gold region recently discovered in the territory occupied by the Hudson's Bay Company. A considerable population has already arrived, and still multitudes are hastening to this new El Dorado. A correspondent, writing from Victoria, Vancouver's Island, under date of June 9th, states :—' Immigration has commenced from Washington and Oregon territories, and from California alone about 2,000 arrive weekly. Nearly 100,000 it is expected will arrive by November next.' Though this is probably an over estimate, it cannot be doubted that a very large population will soon be gathered. In Victoria already there are probably 10,000 English-speaking people. Under these circumstances the committee have resolved to send, with the least possible delay, two or three well-qualified individuals to direct the attention of the congregated multitudes to the ' things pertaining to the kingdom of God,' the importance of which cannot be exaggerated. Apart from the discovery of gold on the main land, Vancouver's Island cannot fail to prove eminently attractive to Britain's hardy sons, who, finding a difficulty to provide for themselves and their families, are prepared to seek a new home in more auspicious regions. A gentleman who has resided there for eight years says, that for the beauty of its scenery, the salubrity of its climate, and its general adaptation to commerce, the territory on the shores of the Pacific cannot be surpassed by any country in the world. The soil, too, is fertile in the highest degree, and possesses great agricultural capabilities. The mineral wealth of the island is enormous. Besides iron, copper, and gold, there is abundance of excellent coal, ' very like the West Riding of Yorkshire coal.' 'There is coal enough,' the Right Hon. E. Ellice testified, in his evidence before the House of Commons, ' to supply the whole British navy. Vessels of 500 tons burden may reach within forty yards of the pit's mouth to take in their cargo.' Besides these internal riches, the surrounding waters teem with fish in such enormous quantities, that ' no one who has not seen them can possibly credit the value and extent of the fisheries.' Many thousand barrels of salted salmon are now annually sent from her shores by the Hudson's Bay Company to their depot in the Sandwich Islands. The trade in salmon and herrings might be indefinitely extended.

" The committee, notwithstanding the importance of this new field of missionary enterprise, feel they cannot enter upon it unless the friends of the Society aid them with special contributions for the purpose. As it is obvious that, for some little time, no pecuniary returns could be expected, they consider they ought to possess from £1,500 to £2,000, to enable them to enter on this work free from anxiety, and on the scale requisite to justify a hope of success. The committee would very earnestly appeal to the friends of the society to aid them in this enterprise, than which few of greater importance have ever been undertaken."

RELIGIOUS INTELLIGENCE.

GENERAL SOCIETIES.—N. S. W. BIBLE SOCIETY, SYDNEY.—We add to the brief notice of the annual meeting of the above Society, held on 17th January, which appeared in our last, the following extract from the report which we were compelled to omit for want room :—" Your committee have to report that during the past year the sales to the public from the depot have been slightly in excess of the previous year, viz.,—Bibles, 975, and testaments 565. The sales to the branches have been—bibles, 741, and testaments, 834. The branches have been further supplied with bibles 222, and testaments 171, but for these payment has not yet been received. Free grants have been made to Sunday schools and other institutions of 463 bibles, and 889 testaments. £210 17s. 7d. has been paid to the parent society in the course of the year on purchase account, and £1,000 has been remitted as a free contribution. The branches and associations connected with this auxiliary have largely contributed to its funds, and your committee hereby desire to acknowledge their obligation to those gentlemen who have from time to time, as their services have been needed, travelled to distant places to advocate the claims of this society. Mr. Rees, early in the year, kindly placed at our disposal a case of Chinese Testaments. In the distribution of these among the Chinamen who have visited our shores great assistance has been received from Leau Appa, a Christian Chinaman. It has long been a subject of complaint that the free contributions of subscribers should be taxed to enable your committee to sell at the London invoice prices to non-subscribers, the larger and better class of Bibles. To remedy this, a special general meeting of this society was held in the School of Arts, on July 20th, 1858, when on the motion of Dr. Charles, seconded by the Rev. F. Ashwin, the 5th rule, which prevented a higher price being charged, was rescinded."

MAITLAND BIBLE SOCIETY.—The third annual meeting of the Maitland Branch of the New South Wales Auxiliary to the British and Foreign Bible Society was held in the Congregational Church, West Maitland, on Tuesday evening, January 18, 1859. The attendance, though good, was much affected by a severe storm of wind and rain, which arose just at the time fixed for the meeting to commence. The chair was occupied by the president, J. Douglas, Esq., and after the reading of the report by the secretary, John Whytlaw, Esq., the various resolutions were moved and seconded by the Revs. W. Slatyer and Hugh Darling, of Sydney, Rev. E. Griffith, and Messrs. C. Long, A. Dickson, T. W. Robinson, and J. Whytlaw. The report stated that there had been a falling off in the receipts during the past year —that £60 had been forwarded to the Sydney society, and that the branch committee recommended the severance of the connection between it and the Sydney auxiliary, and the establishment of a separate auxiliary which should embrace the whole of the Hunter River district, and be styled the " Hunter River Auxiliary to the British and Foreign Bible Society." A resolution expressive of this latter part of the report was warmly and unanimously adopted, and the society was constituted as the auxiliary for the district. It is hoped that during the coming year various towns will be visited for the purpose of holding public meetings and forming branch associations, and thus the wish of the friends of the parent society be realised by more efficacious effort than could be made whilst associated as a branch with an auxiliary. The collection amounted to £13 18s.

THE N. S. W. WELSH CHRISTIAN SOCIETY. SYDNEY.—According to the emigration returns, about 14,000 Welsh-speaking people have left Wales for the different colonies of Australia and New Zealand, during the last thirty years. Of the thousands now located among us, a considerable number can but imperfectly understand the service in an English place of worship. To meet the wants of this class, divine services are conducted in the Welsh language in South Australia, Victoria, Tasmania, and New Zealand; but in our own colony, from the absence of this provision, many neglect the ordinances of religion altogether. The more serious among them thought it desirable to form a society to supply this deficiency, and a meeting was recently held for that purpose in the lecture-room, Jamison-street, where divine service has been performed for some weeks by the Rev. John Roberts, a Welsh clergyman from Caernarvon, when the following resolution was adopted:—That a society be formed, to be called "The New South Wales Welsh Christian Society," the objects of which will be—the propagation of the Gospel, and the promotion of Christian knowledge among the Welsh-speaking people of Sydney, in their native language, by means of preaching, conducting adult Sunday schools, &c. The following persons were named as the committee— Rev. John Roberts, Messrs. John Morgan, William Jones, John Thomas Roberts, Joseph Parry, William Humphrey, William Evans, Richard Owen, William Davis, William Williams, and Robert Roberts, with power to add to their number; the Rev. John Roberts, president; Mr. John Thomas Roberts, treasurer; and Mr. Wm. Davis, secretary. Mr. J. T. Roberts was elected precentor; and it was also agreed that Messrs. W. Davis and W. Evans be requested to conduct the singing. In accordance with the above arrangements, divine service is conducted in Welsh every Sunday morning and evening.

SYDNEY JUVENILE CITY MISSIONARY SOCIETY, for the City and Neighbourhood.— This is a society for employing young people to act as city missionaries in visiting neglected neighbourhoods, to canvass for Sabbath school children, to induce the inhabitants to attend public worship, and otherwise to promote vital religion among the masses. It holds quarterly meetings to hear reports of proceedings and to stir up the zeal of the members. One of these meetings was held on Jan. 18, at the school, Bathurst-street. Invitations had been sent to about 110 members and friends, amongst whom were the Rev. Messrs. Threlkeld and Voller. Although a sudden storm came on just at tea-time, about eighty friends sat down to tea, after which a meeting was held. The Rev. J. Voller being moved into the chair, a hymn was sung, after which Mr. Walker engaged in prayer. The chairman called on the hon. secretary to read the report, which was an abstract of the past year's transactions. The principal items were the relinquishing the projected school at Five Dock; the establishment of Sabbath schools at Riley-street, Surrey Hills, and at Kent-street; the sending out itinerant suburban missions during the Christmas holidays to Coogee, Balmain Estate, Lane Cove, Middle Harbour and Manly, Kirkham and suburbs of Camden. The treasurer also gave an account of finance matters. The meeting was afterwards addressed by Messrs. Glassop, Clarke, and Addison. Several of the members then related their experience in the itinerant mission, which has well succeeded and given great encouragement for others at future periods. The benediction being pronounced, the meeting separated.

LAUNCESTON TOWN MISSION.—The annual meeting of the Town Mission was held on the 27th of January. His Worship the Mayor, treasurer of the society, presided. The report read by the secretary, was, on the whole encouraging. The receipts amounted to £175 14s. 10d.; a balance of £2 16s. 8d. remained. The following is a summary of the missionary's labours and results:—visit to familes, 4,577; to sick, 474; to hospital, 95; to vessels, 447; total number of visits, 5,593. Meetings held for prayers, 94; tracts distributed, 13,271; induced to attend public worship, 12; couple induced to marry, 1; induced to take temperance pledge, 9; children sent to Sunday school, 5. The meeting was addressed by several ministers and other gentlemen, and the various resolutions proposed, were unanimously adopted.

EVANGELICAL ALLIANCE, BALLAARAT.—A meeting was held in the Wesleyan Church, Lydiard-street, on Thursday, February 10, for the purpose of forming an Evangelical Alliance for Ballaarat and district. There were from 150 to 200 persons present, including clergymen and laymen of all the Protestant Churches in Ballaarat. The Rev. Mr. Bickford opened the meeting by giving out a hymn, which was followed by reading the Scriptures and prayer. In the absence of Mr. Lynn, Mr. James Oddie was voted to the chair. The meeting was afterwards addressed by the Revs. Messrs. Searle (E.), Henderson (B.), Bradney (U. M.) Lind (C.), Mackie (P.), Sutton (B.), and Lane (W.), and by Messrs. J. Gray and Bonwick.

SAILORS' MISSION, MELBOURNE.—The second annual meeting of the Victorian Bethel Union and Seamens' Mission in Hobson's Bay, was held on March 4th, 1859, in the Mechanics' Institution, Melbourne. The room was comfortably filled, and there was a large proportion of ladies present. After prayer had been offered by the Rev. J. P. Sunderland, His Worship the Mayor, H. S. Walsh, Esq., was called to the chair, and in opening the proceedings, he expressed his gratification at being called upon to fill the honorable position of chairman, and said he yielded to no one in his sincere desire to ameliorate the position of the British sailor, and he was glad to know that, in his official position, he might further the objects of the Mission. He had been informed by the honorary secretary that his Excellency the Governor would have taken the chair that evening but for the fact of His Excellency having been occupied recently on a tedious journey, and in the preparation of his despatches for England. In perusing the annual report, he was pleased to recognise the warmth and excellent feelings which His Excellency the Governor had invariably shown to the society, and on this account he regretted that His Excellency was not present. But as he (the chairman) said before, he yielded to no one in his warm sympathy with the efforts of the society, and in his wish that the labors of the officers and committee might be crowned with success. He was glad to hear that the ladies had exerted themselves in the cause, and he was of opinion that when the ladies did interest themselves in institutions of this nature success was certain. He was also delighted to find that the institution was of such a catholic nature, as was represented that evening on the platform by representatives of all denominations.

Apologies were given by the honorary secretary for the absence of the Bishop, the Dean, Dr. Cairns, the Revs. W. Byrnes, S. L. Chase, H. H. P. Handfield, Isaac New, James Taylor, D. J. Draper, W. L. Binks, T. Williams, W. P. Wells, J. Hutchinson, R. Fletcher, A. Morison, J. L. Poore, and Messrs Mackay (of Mackay, Baines and Co.) and T. Dickson. Mr. W. Fairfax then read the report for the past year. While thanking the great Head of the Church for the progress made during the past year, much surprise was expressed that an institution for the moral and spiritual benefit of our sailors had not been in operation before. It was also regretted that many of the first subscriptions had not been continued, but, it was added, some others had been forthcoming. In October, 1858, a number of ladies had formed themselves into a committe to collect subscriptions for the institution, and their efforts had been attended with marked success. Though their labors had only just commenced, they had collected £93. Melbourne and suburbs were divided into districts for canvassing. The report spoke favorably of the labors of the mission in Hobson's Bay, in the ministrations of the chaplain, distribution of tracts, bibles, and other books, visiting sick sailors, &c. Since its establishment upwards of 30,000 had attended the religious services on the Bethel or various other ships. After some consideration it had been deemed advisable to moor the Bethel opposite Williamstown. The report in conclusion adverted to the desirability of establishing a Sailors' Home for the port of Melbourne, and that steps had been taken to accomplish this very desirable object.

Captain B. R. Matthews read the treasurer's statement for the past year. £561 16s. 9d. had been received; the expenses had been £618 11s. 6d. There was a balance of £56 14s. 8d. in the bank, but there were liabilities over £150, leaving a deficiency of about £100. The treasurer stated that since he entered the room a lady had given him £10, which sum she would contribute annually.

The Rev. Kerr Johnston, the chaplain gave an account of his labors among the shipping in Hobson's Bay.

Resolutions were then submitted to the meeting expressive of the spiritual necessities of seamen, thanking God for his blessing upon the labors of the society, shewing the desirableness of increased exertions, and thanking the ladies for their timely help in raising funds, were proposed and seconded by the Rev. J. P. Sunderland, Lieut. Amsinck, R.N., Captain Perry, M.L.A., Dr. Embling, M.L.A., Hon. A. Fraser, M.L.C., C. Vaughan, M.L.C., and Messrs. Freeman, White, Haller, Newell, and H. Langlands, M.L.A. The following are the ladies and gentlemen's committees for the ensuing year:—

Ladies' Committee—President, Mrs. MacLachlan; Vice-President, Mrs. H. Langlands; Hon. Treasurer, Mrs. Ridley; Hon. Secretary, Mrs. Embling; Mrs. Cutts, Mrs. Dinwoodie, Mrs. A. Dove, Mrs. C. Ferguson, Mrs. E. M. Gibbs, Mrs. Goethe, Mrs. Haller, Mrs. Hetherington, Mrs. R. Kerr, Mrs. Lewis, Mrs. Russell, Mrs. M'Callum, Mrs. Mathews, Mrs. R. Thompson, Mrs. Thorp, Miss Thorp, Mrs. Webb.

Gentlemen's Committee—Patron, His Excellency Sir Henry Barkly; President, the Hon. C. Vaughan, M.L.C.; Vice-President, Captain C. Ferguson; Hon. Treasurer, Captain B. R. Mathews; Hon. Secretary, Mr. W. Fairfax; the Hon. J. Hodgson, M.L.C.; H. Langlands, Esq., M.L.A.; Captain Perry, M.L.A.; Captain A. Dove, Captain W. H. Hawken, Captain J. Dalgarno, Captain D. M'Callum, Captain G. Burrell, Captain Probert, J. M'Culloch, Esq., M.L.A.; J. Henty, jun., Esq.; J. Lorimer, Esq.; F. Haller, Esq.; A. H. Newell, Esq.; T. Dickson, Esq.; B. Cully, Esq.; E. M. Gibbs, Esq. Both committees with power to add to their number.

YOUNG MEN'S MUTUAL IMPROVEMENT ASSOCIATION, LONSDALE STREET, MELBOURNE.— Among the social meetings which have been held during the past month, we have to notice the first half yearly tea meeting of the above very interesting and useful association which was held in Wesley Church schoolroom on the 7th of March. The room was elegantly hung with flags, evergreens, and flowers. About 150 ladies and gentlemen sat down to tea. After which, the president—Rev. W. L. Binks—took the chair and opened the meeting by calling upon the secretary to read the report. The following gentlemen addressed the meeting during the evening upon various resolutions:—Revs. W. P. Wells, James Hutchinson, Dr. Philips, Messrs. J. D. Fetch, A. J. Smith, R. Hodgson, T. J. Trowell, Amos Fenton, Francis Brown, William McComas, and William Chellew. A vote of thanks having been accorded to the chairman, the meeting dispersed, having spent a very agreeable evening.

SUNDAY SCHOOLS.—LAUNCESTON SUNDAY SCHOOL ASSOCIATION MOVEMENT.— On Tuesday evening, January 18, a very important and interesting meeting took place in the Temperance Hall, Launceston. Its object was to inaugurate a movement for the canvass of the whole town for Sabbath-school scholars by means of congregational agency. Tea was provided, and the hall was quite full, half the company consisting of ladies. Amongst those present we noticed the Mayor, the Hon. W. S. Button, M.L.C.; the Revs. Messrs. Price, Ewing and Law; a large number of influential gentlemen and most of the teachers connected with the Sunday schools. After tea, Mr. Gleadow took the chair and said he could not refuse the invitation to preside, although there were others no doubt more competent. He had been long connected with Sabbath schools, almost longer than any one in the community—one individual who was present excepted; and therefore he was desirous the work should progress. The design of the meeting was to devise some plan by which the work might be extended, and the advantages of the Sabbath school made more general. The plan by which it was proposed to do this was one which all must approve; namely, that all the schools of various denominations might join in the work. It was considered that whilst good would no doubt result from the efforts of each separate organization, still greater good would be the result of the combination—a combination of Christian men and women to extend the work of Sabbath schools. The speakers were Messrs. Aikenhead, Sinclair, Caseley, Barrett, Button, Turner, Dowling, and Price. Among the subjects we name the following—"The necessity and success of canvassing for Sabbath school scholars;" "The benefit of Sabbath school instruction;" "The punctuality of teachers;" "The importance of visiting houses;" and "Quarterly Tea Meetings of teachers and friends."

BALLAARAT SUNDAY SCHOOL UNION.—The second half-yearly meeting of this association was held in January. In the absence of Mr. Price, the president, Mr. Francis was called to the chair. Mr. C. Martin, honorary secretary, read the report, and the treasurer his financial statement, which were adopted. During the six months that had elapsed, lectures had been delivered on "The reciprocal influences of Churches and Sabbath schools," by the Rev. W. Henderson; on "Paul in Athens," by the Rev. M. W. Bradney; and on "the Women of the Bible," by the Rev. W. Sutton. The Rev. W. A. Lind had undertaken to deliver a lecture, but illness had prevented. He delivered it on Tuesday evening February 1, in the Wesleyan school-room, it being the usual monthly one in connection with the Sabbath school Union. The subject was "The History of the Jews, from the destruction of Jerusalem to the present time." At the conclusion, the rev. lecturer was loudly applauded for his exceedingly interesting, able, and masterly discourse to a crowded and attentive audience.

PORTLAND SUNDAY SCHOOL UNION.—The annual treat given to the children belonging to the Sunday schools, took place on Wednesday, March 2. The children assembled at one o'clock on the grounds adjoining the Wesleyan Chapel, whence after a short address from the Rev. Mr. Sleigh, they walked in procession to the Survey Paddock. Before them was carried a large banner, on which was worked the words, "Peace on earth, and good will toward man." At the paddock they enjoyed themselves right heartily, being amply provided with tea, cake, &c. About 250 children were present, making in all, with the teachers and friends, fully 300 persons. The whole of the proceedings were under the management of Mr. Hearne, to whom much praise is due for the efficient manner in which they were carried out.

CONGREGATIONALISTS.—SANDHURST CONGREGATIONAL CHURCH.—The Congregational church at this place, commenced a few months previously, for the use of the Rev. W. Roby Fletcher, M.A., was opened for Divine worship on Sunday, November 28th last, by the Rev. Thomas Binney, who preached two sermons on the occasion. Notwithstanding the rain poured in torrents, the congregations were good. On the Tuesday evening following, a soirée was held to commemorate the event, when a large number of people assembled. The chair was taken by the Rev. R. Fletcher, of St. Kilda, father of the pastor, who expressed his joy at the success which had so far attended his son's labors in this new enterprise. The report, read by Mr. Miller, stated, that when Mr. Fletcher, jun., came up, a few friends gathered around him and took a store for preaching in. A removal soon took place to a larger store; this becoming dilapidated, the Episcopal school-room was kindly lent; and at length a movement was made towards obtaining a permanent place of worship. The present eligible site, with a good dwelling-house upon it, was purchased, and a mortgage obtained to provide for the purchase-money. The church was then erected, which cost £800. About half the money (except the mortgage) had been obtained by subscriptions in Sandhurst and Melbourne, and the balance had remained on as a floating debt, which it was proposed to clear off as soon as possible. The meeting was addressed by the Revs. Messrs. Nish, Butler, W. R. Ffetcher, and others. Mr. Binney deeply interested the meeting by his address. He expressed great interest in the labors of his young friend Mr. Fletcher, whom he had known in England, and in whose successful university career he had warmly sympathised.

COLONIAL MISSIONARY SOCIETY, TASMANIA.—The annual meeting of the local branch of this society was held in St. John's square Congregational chapel, Launceston, on Monday evening, 21st ult. The Hon. W. S. Button, presided. The chapel was filled. After the usual devotional services and an excellent address from the chairman, the Rev. W. Law read the report, from which we select the following sentences:—The society whose interests we are here met to promote was first established in Hobart Town under the name of the Van Diemen's Land Colonial Missionary and Christian Instruction Society. The immediate object of the society was to supply the destitute districts of this colony with the glorious Gospel of the blessed God, and chiefly in connection with the Congregational churches of the colony

An auxiliary was formed at Launceston on the 29th December, 1845, at a meeting held in St. John's Square Congregational church, presided over by J. G. Jennings, Esq., and addressed by the Revs. Messrs. West, Dowling, Hastie, Butters, Jarrett, and other gentlemen and friends. One of the earliest stations of the society was at the River Forth, N.W. coast, which station the society still retains, and one of its earliest agents was the Rev. W. Waterfield, now of Green Ponds. On the commencement of the effort of the Rev. J. L. Poore to secure a number of ministers for Australasia, the committee of this auxiliary was one of the first to co-operate with him. A meeting of committee was held in the Tamar-street school-room on the 25th July, 1856, when Mr. Poore, having stated the purpose for which he was about to proceed to England, it was resolved, "That a subscription be entered into by the Northern Branch of the Tasmanian Colonial Missionary Society, to assist Mr. Poore in introducing ministers into the Australian colonies." After the reading of the report, Mr. Button read a statement of the society's expenditure, from which it appeared that the latter had been £241 19s. 4d., leaving a balance due to the treasurer of £3 7s. 1d. The collections made on the previous day amounted to about £45. The meeting was afterwards addressed by the Rev. J. Lindsay, his Worship the Mayor, Revs. C. Price, Mr. Crookes, Rev. Thomas Binney, who spoke at great length, Rev. T. B. Hains, and other friends of the society.

UNION CHAPEL, SCHNAPPER POINT, PORT PHILLIP.—On March 2nd a number of ladies and gentlemen connected with the Independent and Baptist denominations formed a party, and proceeded from Melbourne, in the "Prince Albert" steamer, to Schnapper Point, to inaugurate the new chapel erected for the use of Christian friends residing in that pleasant watering place. Amongst the party were the Revs. Sunderland, Hill, and Lemmon, the Hon. George Harker, Messrs. Richardson, Goodhugh, Barlow, Kerr, Haigh, &c, with their families, and Mr. Bakewell, of Adelaide. On landing at Schnapper Point, the party (who were received by Rev. J. L. Poore and several residents) proceeded to the Mornington Hotel, and partook of a substantial Luncheon, after which they adjourned to the chapel, and according to previous arrangement, Mr. Robert Kerr took the chair. The chairman congratulated the meeting on the neat and commodious character of the building, and on the fact that for once, the Independents and Baptists were before the Wesleyans, who were generally the pioneers in carrying the Gospel and religious ordinances into newly-formed settlements. He further stated that the ground, which was spacious and beautifully situated, overlooking the bay, had been generously given by Mr. Sykes, who lived close by, and who would convey the property in trust, for the joint use of the Independents and Baptists: that Mr. James Robinson had guaranteed the cost of the erection, and thus had enabled the work to be proceeded with. The Oxford street church, Collingwood, had presented the pulpit as a gift, and Mr. Huckson of Melbourne, had given the doors. Mr. Robinson then read the financial report, from which it appeared that the building had cost £190; that about £100 had been collected and promised, which left about £90 due to the worthy treasurer, Mr. Barrett. The Rev. J. L. Poore (who had opened the chapel on the previous Sabbath) then addressed the meeting in a lively speech, after which a collection was made toward the building fund, and the very handsome sum of £43 3s. was received. The meeting was further addressed by the Hon. George Harker, and the Revs. Sunderland, Lemmon, and Hill. An excellent tea was provided on the lawn in front of Mr. Sykes's residence, and after the party had regaled themselves with this refreshing beverage, they proceeded on board, and reached town at eight o'clock. The Rev. J. L. Poore has engaged to find pulpit supplies for Schnapper Point for the present.

REV. JAMES MIRAMS.—On Thursday evening a meeting of the friends and supporters of this esteemed minister was held in the Victoria Parade chapel. After tea the Rev. W. Jarrett was called on to preside. An address was read expressive of the sympathy felt by the friends of Mr. Mirams, on account of his trials in connection with his retirement from the North Collingwood Independent church. To this address Mr. Mirams returned a suitable reply, and then entered on a long explanation and defence of his conduct. A resolution expressing unabated confidence in the Rev. James Mirams, and earnest wishes for his future comfort and success, was moved by the Rev. R. Fletcher, seconded by Dr. Cairns, and supported by the Rev. W. B. Landells.

ADELAIDE.—The Rev. J. W. C. Drane, one of the ministers selected by Mr. Poore for South Australia, has arrived, and is settling at Kensington over the church raised by the exertions of the Rev. J. H. Barrow. The other ministers sent out, are for the most part comfortably and usefully settled.—South Australian Paper.

BAPTISTS.—BAPTIST CHAPEL, MORETON BAY.—A new chapel for the use of Baptists has recently been built in Brisbane. Its size is 67 feet by 37 feet, and the style is Pisan, or early Italian. The cost is £2,000. It is described as an ornament to the town. It was opened in January by the pastor, and the Rev. Mr. Voller, of Sydney: who preached an effective sermon to a crowded congregation.

BAPTIST CHAPEL, SANDHURST.—On Sabbath, February 15, a small wooden chapel was opened for the use of the Baptists of Sandhurst. The Rev. James Taylor, of Melbourne, conducted the services. At the close of the morning service Mr. Taylor read the resolutions agreed upon by the parties to be associated together as a church, and the names of twenty-one persons formerly connected with Baptist churches in England and then and there constituted the church. In the afternoon, after a discourse, on the ordinances of the gospel, individuals were baptised, on a profession of faith in the Lord Jesus Christ. At the close of the evening service, the ordinance of the Lord's Supper was observed, the Rev. W. R. Fletcher, of Sandhurst, taking part in the service. The chapel was crowded at all the services, and the collections in aid of the building-fund amounted to £20. On the following evening a public tea-meeting was held. The chapel was again crowded. The Rev. James Taylor presided; and, after the reading of the report by the secretary, Mr. R. Bentley, interesting and instructive addresses were delivered on the following subjects:—" Denominational distinctions no barrier to Christian Love," by the Rev. James Nish, of the Free Church; " Christianity, a nation's greatness," Rev. W. R. Fletcher, Congregational Church; " The difference between nominal and real religion," Rev. J. Watts, Primitive Methodist; " The value of Christian unity," Rev. Mr. Butler, Congregational minister; " The past, present and future," Rev. C. Dubourg, Wesleyan minister; " The advantages of earnest piety," Rev. J. J. Buckhardt, German Lutheran; " The connection between the small and the great—its religious aspect," Mr. J. Bentley. In the course of the evening, the late Mr. Fulton, J.P., of Melbourne, then on a visit to Sandhurst, delivered an earnest and characteristic address. The evening was most pleasantly and profitably spent; the collection and the proceeds of tea, which was provided gratuitously by kind Christian ladies, amounted to about £20.

BAPTIST CHURCH, ALBERT-STREET, MELBOURNE.—The opening of the above church, for the ministry of the Rev. Isaac New, was celebrated on Sunday, February, 27th. A prayer-meeting was held in the morning at a quarter past seven o'clock. Three sermons were preached; that in the forenoon, by the Rev. W. B Landells, Independent; in the afternoon, by the Rev. James Hutchinson, Wesleyan; in the evening, by the Rev. James Taylor. At this service the place was crowded in every part to excess, by nearly 1,000 people. The collections amounted to £101 16s. The above place of worship was designed by Thomas Watts, Esq., architect, who has given untiring attention to it throughout. The interior arrangements and aspect have drawn forth universal admiration. The dimensions are 75 feet by 52 feet 6 inches clear of the walls The seats are arranged in the form of an amphitheatre, having three entrances; one on the floor, with a lobby under the seats, and two upper entrances, approached by flights of steps from the outside. The interior is decorated with pilasters of the Corinthian order, carrying an entablature, having a dentiled cornice. A trellised cone interposes between the cornice and the ceiling, which is divided into fifteen coffres, deeply inlaid and enriched with centre flowers. The angles are circular, and are occupied by the upper entrances and niches. The pulpit is of cedar, decorated with Corinthian pilasters and columns, and is placed in front of a pediment, also of the Corinthian order. The baptistry is on a platform before the pulpit. The cost is nearly £4,000. The front is not yet completed, but in due time it is proposed to erect a Corinthian portico, flanked by two towers of 120 feet. On Tuesday evening, March 1, a tea-meeting was held, when between 600 and 700 sat down to tea, filling the old chapel, and nearly filling the new. At half-past seven a public meting was held, when the Rev. Isaac New took the chair, supported by Henry Langlands, Esq., M.L.A. and the Hon. Charles Vaughan the two deacons, and by a number of ministers of various denominations. The Rev. W. Moss, Independent, engaged in prayer. After which effective addresses were delivered by the Revs. A. M. Ramsay, United Presbyterian, A. Morrison and R. Fletcher, Independents. D. J. Draper, President of the Australian Wesleyan Conference, J. P. Sutherland, Independent, and James Taylor, Baptist. Resolutions of thanks were then passed—To Thomas Watts, Esq., for his generous donation in the form of gratuitous services as architect of the new church; to the ministers, for their eloquent sermons on the Lord's day; and to the ladies, for their devoted efforts in originating and carrying out the bazaar, by which more than £600 was cleared. The collection at the tea-meeting, including promises, amounted to £335 10s. But other sums are expected to be added to this, reducing the debt on the new building to little more than £1,400.

PRESBYTERIANS. — UNITED PRESBYTERIAN CHURCH, COLLINS-STREET, MELBOURNE.—Soirée to the Rev. A. M. Ramsay.—On Tuesday evening, 15th of February, a public soirée was held in the United Presbyterian Church, Collins-street (Mr. Ramsay's), on the occasion of his return from Britain per Emeu. There was a very large attendance, the commodious church being filled with a respectable and attentive assemblage. On the platform we observed the Rev. Dr. Cairns, Chalmers' Church; Rev. Mr. Goethe, Lutheran Church; Rev. Richard Fletcher, St. Kilda Congregational Church; Rev. William Moss, Prahran; Rev. R. Hamilton, Collingwood; H. Langlands, Esq., M.L.A.; Wm. Robertson, Esq., J.P. Wooling; John Macgregor, Esq.; Alexander Cairns, Esq.; and other friends. Apologies were received expressive of kindest wishes from the Rev. Messrs. New, Taylor, Sunderland, Williams, Meek, Hetherington, Landells, and Walker of Ballaarat, who had made prior engagements, as the invitations were only issued on Saturday, in consequence of the hasty manner in which the meeting had been got up. The Rev. Robert Hamilton, Napier-street United Presbyterian Church, occupied the chair. The Rev. Mr. Moss opened the meeting with prayer. The Rev. Dr. Cairns addressed the meeting, expressing his heartfelt satisfaction at Mr. Ramsay's return, and the hope that he would have a long career of usefulness before him still in this land. The rev. gentleman, in conclusion, strongly urged upon the meeting the great desirability of a general union of the Presbyterians in this colony. A congratulatory address from the congregation, beautifully engrossed on parchment, was then presented to Mr. Ramsay by John Macgregor, Esq., solicitor, prefaced by a few remarks. Mr. Ramsay then rose and was received with great applause. He gave a short but most interesting narrative of the voyage home, alluding to the various points of interest in the overland route, King George's Sound, Ceylon, Aden, Suez, and Malta, and to his impressions of the old country, after an absence of thirteen years, and the great improvement observable in society there. He then referred particularly to the object of his mission to the mother country, which was to induce several ministers to emigrate to this colony. He alluded to the fact that the Rev. James Henderson, of Duntocher, near Glasgow, Scotland, had been induced by him to give up his charge in that district, where he was much esteemed and beloved, to cast in his lot with the brethren here. Mr. Henderson, together with his wife and family, had sailed per Lightning, from Liverpool, on the 5th of January, and two more ministers might be expected soon to follow. He referred to the great want experienced here of ministerial assistance, and the numerous vacancies at present existing, such as Warnambool, Geelong, and North Melbourne, in all which places ministers could be planted with every prospect of success. In concluding, he thanked those ministers most heartily who had fulfilled their engagements in the supply of the pulpit, and congratulated the congregation on not having been left a single day without supply. The Rev. Richard Fletcher, of St. Kilda, then addressed the meeting, and spoke in high terms of Mr. Ramsay as an energetic and laborious servant of Christ. Mr. Fletcher's speech was highly interesting. In concluding, he referred to the struggle which was again proposed to be made to effect the abolition of State-aid to religion in the colony, and to Mr. Ramsay's former exertions in that cause. The Rev. Mr. Goethe also addressed the meeting at some length. He referred to Mr. Ramsay as being the father of the German Lutheran cause in this colony, on account of his exertions to obtain his (Mr. Goethe's) settlement, and as it were to induct him into the sphere which he had since filled in that body. The following resolution was then proposed by John Macgregor, Esq., and seconded by Alexander Cairns, Esq., and carried unanimously:—"This congregation tenders its grateful acknowledgments to the ministers of the various denominations and the lay preachers of the Wesleyan and Independent Churches who so generously lent their aid in supplying the pulpit of this church during the absence of our pastor." After the usual votes of thanks, the meeting dispersed about half-past ten o'clock.

ADELAIDE.—The very beautiful edifice erected in Wakefield-street for the Rev. Robert Haining, minister of the Church of Scotland, was opened for divine worship on Sunday, February 13, when eloquent sermons were preached by the pastor, the Rev. T. Q. Stow, Independent, and the Rev. W. Ross, Scotch Church, Inverbrackie, to large and deeply interested congregations. At the close of each service a collection was made in aid of the building-fund, the proceeds of which amounted to £35. The church is 60 feet by 40 feet, in the Gothic style, with a spire 138 feet high. It is deemed an ornament to the city.

FREE PRESBYTERIAN CHURCH, MANNING RIVER, N.S.W.—The congregation at Manning River, in connection with the Presbyterian Church of Eastern Australia, have lately completed another neat and substantial church at Redbank, which was opened for public worship on Sabbath, the 30th of January, by the Rev. Allan M'Intyre, pastor of the congregation. Mr. M'Intyre preached from Acts xvii. 30, the subject being "Repentance." A Gaelic sermon was also preached, from the same text, in the afternoon; and in the evening another English service was held, followed by a devotional service. A liberal collection was made. The church is built of sawed wood, and on the same plan as the other Free Churches in the district. The site, which is a very valuable one, was presented by Mr. Archibald Cameron. The present is the third church that has been built in this district by the Free Church within the last three years, the aggregate cost of which has been about £600. In addition to this, they have within the last few months subscribed about £500 towards the erection of a manse for their pastor. It may be also worthy of remark, by way of showing the progress that has been made by the congregation, since organised by the synod some five years ago, that its first contribution to the Sustentation Fund of the Church amounted only to £30, whereas the last annual contribution exceeded £200, and this by a congregation but newly settled in the locality, and, consequently, having many private demands on their resources, and without State or other extraneous aid.—*Sydney Morning Herald.*

FREE CHURCH, SYDNEY.—SYNOD OF EASTERN AUSTRALIA.—The ordinary quarterly meeting of the Presbytery of Sydney was held in Macquarie-street church, on Wednesday, 2nd February, the Rev. Dr. Mackay, Moderator, *pro tempore.* A call was laid on the table from the congregation of Chalmer's Church, in favor of Mr. John L. M'Skimming, a probationer of the Free Church of Scotland, recently arrived in this colony, and who since his arrival has ministered to the congregation who now invite him to be their pastor. The call having been placed by the Moderator in Mr. M'Skimming's hands, he declared his acceptance of the same. The Presbytery thereupon prescribed to him subjects for trials, with a view to ordination; and agreed to meet on Wednesday, the 23rd Feb., for the purpose of examining him upon the subjects now appointed. The resignation of the Rev. W. Lumsdaine was then considered and accepted by the Presbytery.

TASMANIAN PRESBYTERY.—The Presbytery of Tasmania met at Oatlands on the 9th of February. The *Launceston Examiner* contains a report, extending to about twelve columns, of the proceedings. Various matters of considerable interest engaged the attention of the reverend court. The case of Mr. Farons, formerly an elder of Mr. Ewing's church, occupied a long time, but ended without any division being reached.

PORTLAND FREE PRESBYTERIAN CHURCH.—The induction of the Rev. S. Kelso to the pastorship of the Presbyterian church in Tyers-street, took place March 6th. The church was crowded. Dr. Cairns, who officiated on the occasion, proceeded after the sermon to put the usual questions to Mr. Kelso, after which he addressed a few words to him relative to his duties as a minister, and gave some counsel to the congregation generally, touching their new pastor. Mr. Kelso then proceeded to the door of the church, according to the usual custom, so that each of the congregation on retiring might have an opportunity of giving him the hand of fellowship and welcome. A social meeting of the congregation and friends took place in the Free Church building in Hurd-street. The chair was taken by W. Learmonth, Esq., and the meeting was addressed at some length by Dr. Cairns, who gave an account of the origin of the present movement towards a general union of the Presbyterian bodies, described the obstacles and difficulties they had to contend with, and which even still threatened to impede their progress and prevent the attainment of their object, and enumerated some of the benefits which would probably result from their union. The Rev. J. Sleigh and the Rev. S. Kelso also addressed the meeting.

ARARAT FREE PRESBYTERIAN CHURCH.—The Rev. Dr. Cairns and the Rev. Mr. Moir visited this place, and officiated in the Wesleyan church, lent for the occasion. Subsequently the Rev. W. Mackintosh, recently arrived from Scotland, received and accepted a call to be the minister. In the meantime a new church was built. The opening of the church and the ordination of the pastor took place on Thursday, February 10. The Revs. W. Anderson, A. Adams, and G. Mackie conducted the various services. In the evening a soiree was held, at which Mr. Mackintosh presided. A report, containing a history of the rise and progress of the church, was read by Mr. Allan, the secretary, and the meeting was then addressed by the above-named ministers and others. The services were well attended, and the interest excited was great.

UNITED PRESBYTERIAN CHURCH, GEELONG.—A numerously-attended meeting of the members of this Church was held on the evening of the 18th March, John Brebner, Esq., in the chair. The Rev. R. Hamilton, of Melbourne, was present. It was unanimously resolved, "That it is inexpedient for this congregation to enter into the present proposed General Presbyterian Union while the question of State aid to religion remains unsettled, inasmuch as by so doing the protest which the United Presbyterian Synod of Victoria (with which the congregation is connected) has hitherto maintained against the continuance of that system, would be compromised by its forming part of a State aid receiving body."

FREE PRESBYTERIAN CHURCH, PUNT-ROAD, NEAR MELBOURNE.—A tea meeting was held on the evening of March 22nd, in the Free Presbyterian Church, Punt-road. South Yarra; the minister of the congregation, the Rev. George Divorty, presiding. After tea had been partaken of by those who were present, the Rev. Mr. Divorty addressed the assemblage, and introduced to them Mr. Thomas Dickson, the treasurer, who entered into particulars respecting the financial affairs of the church. It appeared that the church, manse, &c., which were erected in the year 1854, had originally cost about £6,500, which amount had all been paid off, with the exception of about £750. In addition to the £5,750 thus paid off by the congregation, and other friends, a further sum had been raised by them during the past five years of £2,625, which had been expended in paying the interest of the original debt and other church purposes. After the treasurer had made his financial statement, the meeting was addressed by the Rev. Charles Moir, of St. Kilda, the Rev. Mr. Morse, the Rev. Mr. Clarke of Williamstown, and other clergymen of various denominations. Most of the clergymen particularly alluded to the great advantage that would be derived from the approaching union of the various branches of the Presbyterian body in this colony, which is expected to take place during the ensuing month, under the provisions of the Victorian Synod Act, passed during the late Parliamentary session. The usual and appropriate devotional services took place at various periods during the evening.

WESLEYANS.—THE AUSTRALASIAN WESLEYAN CONFERENCE.—This Conference commenced its sittings in the York-street Wesleyan Chapel, Sydney, on the 20th of January. The following particulars are taken from the Sydney Christian Pleader of February 5th:— "The Conference was opened by the Rev. W. Butters, of Adelaide, who introduced the new President, the Rev. D. J. Draper, of Melbourne, who had been appointed by the British Conference, at the request of the Australasian Conference of last year. The Rev. S. Rabone was elected secretary, and the Revs. H. M. Gaud and T. Buddle sub-secretaries. The Revs. Charles Colwell and William D. Lelean were unanimously received into full connexion, and the chairmen of the districts in which they are stationed were directed to publicly ordain them. The following candidates for the ministry were received as preachers on trial:—Thos. Barker, John Clifton, E. J. Watkin, Jesse Carey, E. B. Burns, R. O. Cook, Thomas Skewa, Henry Bath, H. T. Burgess, C. H. Goldsmith, and R. S. Casely. Three native assistant missionaries were admitted into full connexion. Three ministers have exchanged mortality for life in the past year—the Rev. W. Woon, New Zealand; the Rev. Theophilus Taylor, Victoria; and the Rev. John Crawford, Fiji. A resolution was adopted, giving permission to the New South Wales Finance District Committee to establish a Wesleyan Church Sustentation and Extension Society, its object, as described in the rules of the society, being 'to stimulate and combine, in a larger and more systematic scale, the efforts of the Wesleyan Methodist Church in New South Wales, to establish and extend the ordinances of God for the spread of Scriptural holiness throughout the land.' A special service was held in York-street Church on Monday evening, the 24th Jan., for the ordination of the Revs. J. K. Piddington, T. Angwin

W. Clarke, W. Kelynack, H. Mack, J. G. Turner, and R. W. Vanderkiste, several of whom had some time previously been received into the full ministry, but their public ordination had been deferred for want of a suitable opportunity.

NUMBER OF CHURCH MEMBERS.

	Members.	Increase.	On trial.		Members.	Increase.	On trial
N. S. W. District	3,158	144	336	Wellington District	814	...	22
Victoria „	3,937	743	439	Friendly Is. „	6,846	31	258
S. Australia „	2,477	274	269	Fiji Islands „	8,345	1,296	3,452
W. Austral. „	74	...	9				
Tasmania „	843	10	39	Total ...	28,138	2,685	5,000
Auckland „	1,844	107	176				

On Thursday morning, the 27th, the General Missionary Committee met for the despatch of business. The committee being informed that power of attorney to transfer the ship John Wesley had been received from England, it was resolved, 'That the ship John Wesley be vested in the following gentlemen upon trust for the Australasian Wesleyan Methodist Missionary Society, namely, Stephen Rabone, John Egglestone, George Wigram Allen, Alexander M'Arthur, and John Caldwell.' The income of the Society was stated to be £9,500, and the expenditure about £13,450, leaving a balance of nearly £4,000 to be paid by the parent society at home. It having been stated that many Chinese in Victoria wished to attend the Wesleyan ministry, and had subscribed £200 for the erection of a Chinese Wesleyan Chapel, and also that there was a fair prospect for the opening of a Chinese mission in this colony, the committee recommended the establishment of Wesleyan missions to the Chinese in the colonies of New South Wales and Victoria, to be under the same management as the other missions of the society."

KILMORE NEW WESLEYAN CHURCH.—This commodious church was opened for public worship on Sunday, February 13th, by the Rev. J. Dare, of Sandhurst, who preached three sermons to good congregations. On the following evening a tea-meeting was held, presided over by Mr. S. King, of Melbourne. A report was read by the Rev. J. Mewton, and addresses delivered by the Revs. S. Catterall, R. Hart, and J. Dare, Mr. Wilkinson, &c. The whole cost of the building was £972. From the Church Extension Fund £300 was received, about £230 from subscriptions, and £135 was obtained or promised at the opening services, leaving a debt of some £617.

CRESWICK.—The new Wesleyan Chapel at Mount Bolton was opened for public worship on Sunday, March 6, when two sermons were preached, in the morning by the Rev. C. Lane, and in the evening by the Rev. J. W. Crisp. The tea-meeting on Monday was well attended by the farmers and other residents, with their families. The building is quite an ornament to the neighborhood; it is a substantial brick structure, and the style of architecture is Gothic. It is capable of holding 150 persons. The total cost was £400, towards which £270 have been made paid or promised, leaving £130 on the building. There is to be a day school opened immediately in connexion with the chapel.

EPISCOPALIANS. — TRINITY CHURCH, GEELONG. — The foundation stone of this Church, intended for the use of the Rev. G. M. Brough, L.L.D. and the congregation attached to him, was laid September 29, 1858. From its position and appearance it is one of the chief ornaments of Geelong. It is in the style of early English architecture, with steep roof, lancet windows, and spire over the entrance porch. The dimensions are 70 feet by 35 feet, and height to the ridge of open roof 45 feet. It was opened for worship on Sunday February 20, when Dr. Brough preached in the morning, and the Rev. Mr. Hill, Wesleyan, in the evening; the attendance at both services was numerous and the collections amounted to £53.

NEW CHURCH, ESSENDON.—On 6th March the new Church of England at Essendon was opened for Divine service. It is a very neat and commodious building, capable of accommodating 250 persons. The architecture is of the early English order. The morning and evening sermons were preached respectively by the Revs. R. B. Barlow, of St. Mark's, and D. Seddon, of St. Kilda. The incumbent is the Rev. E. Puckle, formerly of St. Anthony's, near Falmouth, in the diocese of Exeter. The singing was very good, and the congregation numbered many of different Christian denominations. The collection in the morning amounted to over £53, and in the evening exceeded £17.

MELBOURNE "CHRISTIAN TIMES."—This Religious Weekly Newspaper, conducted on Evangelical Alliance principles, has now completed its experimental stage of six months, to which period the guarantees extended their liability. The expenses connected with the commencement of such an undertaking have absorbed the sums guaranteed, but it is now in a paying condition or nearly so. A meeting of the original promoters of the Paper was recently held, when it was resolved to carry it on, and a further sum has been subscribed. A little effort at this crisis on the part of friends, to extend its circulation, would place it altogether in a satisfactory position. The Rev. James Taylor continues his gratuitous services as Editor. The work is excellently conducted. We are largely indebted to it for articles in our Religious Intelligence Department. It is henceforth to be printed and published by Mr. Goodhugh, Flinders-lane.

W. FAIRFAX AND CO., STEAM PRINTERS, COLLINS STREET EAST, MELBOURNE.

The Southern Spectator.

MAY, 1859.

A REVIEW OF THE STATE OF RELIGION IN OUR CHURCHES

AT THE COMMENCEMENT OF THE YEAR 1859.

BY THE REV. JOHN ANGELL JAMES.

The solemn march of time continues with silent and measured tread towards eternity. Another year has opened upon us with its coming, but unknown, unanticipated events. All minds and hearts are turning to the future with new plans and purposes, new hopes or fears. The commencement and close of each year call for reflection, examination, and determination. As individual Christians, the question ought to arise at such a season, "What is my state? In what condition am I setting out afresh on the journey and business of life? What old defects have I to supply what new duties to discharge?" So it should be with churches and whole denominations. I propose, in the following papers, to take up this question with reference to our body as Congregationalists, and to point out what appear to me to be our excellences, our faults, and our defects. What I say of ourselves will, perhaps, apply, to a considerable extent, to other bodies; and, therefore, what I shall advance may be considered as my opinion of the condition of the Christian world at large; and, as my individual opinion, it must, of course, be taken only for what it is worth.

It is not my intention to dwell at any length on what may be called the historical details of our denomination. Public confidence in statistics does not strengthen, and I shall not attempt anything in reference to numbers, beyond the assertion of the fact, that we, like other bodies of Christians, are sadly behind the increase of population It is a deplorable consideration for us all, that the domain of Satan is far more rapidly filling up than that of Christ As regards the general features of our churches, it is but too apparent that while they are multiplying and strengthening in the metropolis and large towns, they are, at least in many places, getting smaller and poorer in the lesser towns, and require the serious consideration of our body. It is equally evident, that the churches are characterised too much by fastidiousness and fickleness, in regard to the choice and retention of their pastors, while the pastors are no less characterised by restlessness and mobility in regard to the churches. I am aware that fixedness may, and does, too strongly prevail in some cases; but in the present day, it seems as if all ministers might be regarded as movable, and as if mobility were a virtue and a means of usefulness,—and so it would be in some cases. But much mischief will result to us if the bond which unites the pastor and the church be considered so slight a thing as to be soon and easily broken.

I

Our col'eges, on which so much depends, are, I hope, as regards their theological teaching, in a sound and healthful state ; but some of them are only half full of students, and, perhaps, needing to be reminded that, with all their concern to train up learned men, they should unite the greatest solicitude and care to send forth earnest preachers and judicious pastors.   How few me i of great promise come from any of them !   How is this ?

It is not, however, on these matters, or any cognate subject, that I mea. now to dwell, but upon the internal and spiritual condition of our churches.   Lik ᵢ the Lord Jesus in the survey which he took of the seven Asiatic churches, I would mention—

First of all. their EXCELLENCES ; and some very distinguished ones present themselves.   The most superficial observers cannot fail to be impressed with the Christian *activity* and *liberality* which prevail everywhere nd which thus conform them to our Lord's metaphorical description. that they are as " the salt of the earth, and the light of the world."   This is a high commendation ; and it is, happily, a true one. This has come on ᵗy such gradual advances, that they who have grown up within the last thirty years can have no conception of the different state of things in this age to what it was half a century ago.   Those of us who were on the public stage at the commencement of 1809, and can remember what the aspect of things was then, can scarcely believe we are in the same church in the b ginning of 1859, any more than we can realize the fact that we are inhabitants of the same p anet, when we see night turned into day in our streets by gaslight, distance annihilated by railways, and intelligence conveyed by lightning.   When I became pastor of my church more than fifty-three years ago, the only object of Congregational benevolence and action was the Sunday school, which was then conducted in a private house, hired for the purpose. There was nothing else ; literally, nothing we set our hands to.   We h d not then taken up even the Missionary Society.   And our state was but a specimen of the inactivity of the great bulk of our churches, at least in the provinces, throughout the whole country.   You may well wonder what the Christians of those days coul have been thinking of.   Now, look at the state of things at the opening of the year 1859.   If I allude to my own church, it is not for the sake of ostentation or self-commendation ; for we are not one whit better than some others.   Ours is but a specimen and average of the rest.   We have now an organization for the London Missionary Society, which raises, as its regular contribution, nearly £500 per annum, besides occasional donations to meet special appeals, which, upon an average, may make up another £100 a year.   For the Colonial Missionary Society we raise, annually, £70.   For our Sunday and day schools, which comprehend nearly two thousand children, we raise £200.   We support two Town Missionaries, at a cost of £200.   Our ladies conduct a working society for Orphan Mission Schools in the East Indies, the proceeds of which reach, on an average, £50 a year ; they sustain also a Dorcas Society for the poor of our own town ; a Maternal Society, of many branches, in various localities of the town ; and a Female Benevolent Society, for visiting the sick poor.   We have a Religious Tract Society, which employs ninety distributors, and spends £50, nearly, a year in the purchase of tracts.   Our Village Preachers' Society, which employs twelve or fourteen lay agents, costs us scarcely anything.   We raise

£40 annually for the County Association. We have a Young Men's Brotherly Society, for general and religious improvement, with a library of 2,000 volumes. Besides all this, we have night-schools for young men and women, at small costs, and Bible classes for other young men and women.

I again say that this is but an average of Congregational exertion and liberality in this day of general activity. Yea, many churches of our own and other denominations, perhaps, greatly excel us. And after all, we none of us come up to our resources, our opportunities, or our obligations. We all could do more, ought to do more, must do more. Still, compare this with what my congregation did with its single object, the Sunday-school, fifty-three years ago. We have since then laid out £22,000 in improving the old chapel, and building the new one; in the erection of school-rooms, the college, and in building seven country and town small chapels. We have also formed two separate Independent churches, and have, jointly with another congregation, formed a third, and all but set up a fourth, and are at this time in treaty for a piece of freehold land, which will cost £600, to build another chapel in one of the suburbs of the town. I am afraid that this will savour of boasting and self-glorification. I can only say, this is not its design, but simply to exhibit the features of the age and the spirit of our churches, in the way of activity and liberality; and also to show what a concentration of power is contained in one church, and what an amount of good it might do. Oh, that the churches of Christ did but consider what a power, both for kind and degree, they possess. What *ought* to be the influence upon the population of the place in which it is situated, and upon the world at large, of a church consisting of 500, 700, or 1,000 members; and what *would* it be if each member did what he or she could do? The churches of Christ have even yet to learn the full extent of both their power and their obligations.

In addition to this, there are, in all our congregations, many and liberal subscribers to our public societies, such as the Bible Society, the Society for the Conversion of the Jews, and all other objects of Christian zeal and benevolence. What, I ask, does this manifest and prove? Why, that activity and liberality have been at length pretty generally recognised as no less obligatory upon the individual conscience, than the sanctity of the Sabbath, the duty of private worship, and the observance of the Lord's Supper. The man who now stands back from these things, who lends no helping hand to the evangelization of his country and the world, is looked at with much the same suspicion as he who is never at the house of God. Zeal, activity, liberality are now no longer considered matters of religious taste, but of solemn duty, as essentials of true piety, evidences of genuine faith, and concomitants of a Christian profession. It was not so, at least generally and conspicuously, when I commenced my ministry. The thing was not understood and felt as it is now. The founders of the Missionary societies had to preach and print apologies for attempting the conversion of the heathen. Witness Dr. Bogue's elaborate sermon at the first Missionary meeting, entitled, "Objections against Missions to the heathen answered." Christians went to the house of God, sat still in their pews, heard sermons, attended sacraments, and doled out an occasional guinea to a charity sermon or the building of a chapel, and there their liberality ended. It is not so now. People have begun to ask, in serious earnestness, "Lord, what wilt thou have *me* to DO?" and are laying money, time, labour, influence, upon the altars of God. It is really surprising and delightful to see what sacrifices, not only of their leisure, which they would ladly devote to the soft enjoyments of their own hearths, firesides, and family circles, but also of the time they would give to their business, many noble-minded men are constantly making to promote the cause of God and the good of their fellow-creatures.

Now, what do we see in all this? What? Why the very dawn of millennial glory. It is not merely in the various organizations of Christian zeal that I delight, but in the principle that raised and that supports them. Were they all to be dissolved to-morrow, that principle, if it survived them, would raise for itself other and nobler institutions. The church of God, being wakened up to this knowledge of its mission, and this sense of its duty, will, I believe, never let the work of God stand still. It has started in a career of zeal for Christ, in which it will never stop till it has brought the world to Him. As a ground of this hope, I ask, how does the year 1859 open as regards this matter? Do we see any symptoms of decline in the zeal, activity, and liberality of our churches? Do we see a spirit of lukewarmness creeping over them? Do we see the men of wealth closing their hands, locking their coffers, and saying, "I have done giving?" Do we see our middle-class men retiring from committees, and saying, "I am weary of this work"? Do we see our tract distributors and Sunday-school teachers throwing up their offices and saying, "We will labour no more"? If so, it would be a sad beginning of the New Year, a dark omen for the future. But the most timid and suspicious eye can detect nothing of the kind. Never was there more activity or liberality, or a stronger disposition for both than now. Let any new object be presented to the Christian public, it is sure to find supporters, even in cases of a doubtful nature. The spirit is up, and no signs of decadence are yet visible, but many signs of increasing vigour.

Here, then, I say, is a glorious feature of our times. Nothing like it has been known in the Christian church since the days of the apostles. Still, I do not mean to assert either that this, as a whole, proceeds from pure Christian principle, or has reached the point to which it ought to extend. Vanity, regard to reputation, the compulsion of entreaty, motiveless liberality, the fashion of the times, mere love of activity, and a dread of being behind others, have all much to do in swelling the stream of public benevolence, and prevent us from regarding it as a true and exact estimate of the amount of spiritual religion in existence. It is a good thing, as regards the world, for liberality to be in fashion, even where it is in a great part only fashion. I believe, however that a large portion of what is now devoted to the cause of Christ and humanity is given from conscientious motives, and as a matter both of duty and privilege.

We must also guard against the mistake of supposing that the wealth now devoted to the cause of Christ and humanity comes up to the full measure of our obligation, or the necessities of the case. It is our felicity, could we but think so, to live in an age and a country in which Christianity is beginning—and only beginning—in modern times to manifest its expansive powers both in the hearts of its professors and in the world. Instead of thinking that all the ways of spending it, either in this country or abroad, are yet found out, we may be perfectly sure that the ingenuity which has opened so many channels of spiritual influence has not exhausted its inventive skill, but will find out many more.

We are ready to suppose that in the organizations for Jew and Gentile,—for heathen abroad, and heathen at home—for male and female—adult and infant—soldier and sailor—Bible and tract—preventive and reformatory schemes—vice and misery—the city and the village—the school and the college—and for others too numerous to mention,—we have found out every dark corner of our world into which the light of Christianity can be introduced, every part of Satan's domain where immortal souls may be rescued from his grasp, and every scheme for diffusing the knowledge of Christ. Let us not deceive ourselves in this matter, and imagine that we have reached all the objects that can be found, or the opportunities that can be embraced, or that we have arrived at the maximum of our liberality for supporting them. No such thing. The circle of Christian activity will certainly go on continually widening, and the obligations of Christian liberality will go on continually increasing. There is a spirit up, that will show us yet in how many more ways we can spread abroad the principles of our holy religion. Be it so, that some of the divisions of sacred labour might be—as perhaps they should be—amalgamated; yet others will present themselves. If, therefore, that excellence of the churches to which this paper alludes be maintained, their resources must be called out still more profusely than they have ever yet been. If God's providence open to us new fields of labour, new channels of influence, as it undoubtedly will, both abroad and at home, we must be prepared to embrace them. At the present moment, God is throwing open to our evangelizing operations the whole Eastern world—India, China, Japan; and also Africa. His dispensations at this juncture are wonderful. Nothing like it has occured in the history of our planet. At such a time, it will not do for us to content ourselves with ordinary contributions, and that measure of liberality we had twenty, nay even ten years ago. It will not do for us to be ever advancing in our luxurious habits of life, which is now really the case, and be satisfied with the same amount of Christian beneficence. The parsimonious cry, when a new object is presented to us, or a new demand for an old one is made upon us, "What, something new! Really, there is no end of it: I am tired out with applications. It will not do." A new object! Yes, and another and another yet; and as long as a new one can be found, and we have the means of supporting it, we must not be weary in well doing. We must abridge our luxuries, if need be, to raise the means of supporting it. Have any of us done this yet? Yea, we must curtail what we have been accustomed to consider our comforts, and even our very necessaries, till we are reduced to the widow's two mites, if we cannot by any other means embrace the opportunities which God is opening before us for carrying on His cause in the earth. For my own part, it seems to me as if our wealthy men must take a few more steps yet, towards the beneficence recorded in Acts ii. iv. They have yet given of their abundance; the abundance itself must be given next.

How much depends upon us as to what the church and the world are to be in future ages; Our individual existence has derived additional importance from the circumstances in which we are placed. We each of us help to mould the age, and are moulded by it. We never could have lived in a more momentous era, and should, every one of us, be aware of this. Never before had men such work to do. We have awful responsibilities lying upon us, in consequence of all this ; may we have grace to know our position, and the day of our merciful visitation !

J. A. J.

A WORD TO THE FATHERLESS.

" WE are orphans and fatherless; our mothers are as widows."* This is language that expresses a simple truth with respect to some who may read this paper. It was true some thousands of years ago, when used by the desolate ones in Judea, and in similar circumstances, t as lost none of its deep and touching import by the lapse of time. The great features of human history, as of human nature itself, remain the same in all ages and countries. In this as in many other respects there is nothing new under the sun. Like the people of olden time we pass through the same general routine of birth, sorrow, labour, joy, sickness and death. Thus too will it be with our descen ants. There exist slight national, local and individual distinctions, but the leading facts and incidents of human life are perpetually repeating themselve . The orphans who first uttered this particular wail of sorrow had many of them become so b the rude hand of war ; the enemy entered the land, trampled down their vineyards, raz d their ha itations to the ground, and slew their fathers with the edge of the sword—hence group after group might be seen passing along the desolate streets of Jerusalem clad in the like garments of sorrow, uttering one sad and touching retrain. " We are orphans and fatherless, our mothers are as widows." Your fathers have not thus perished, but have died perhaps in their o n peaceful homes in varied circumsta ces of age, wealth, and general comfort ; but your lot now is a common one—a brotherhood of woe— a sisterhood of sorr w. You can painfully understand in its full and mystic force the dirge of grief bewailing a father's loss. .We premise that while our remarks and counsels will be chiefly addressed to the fatherless, yet where any have lost both parents they will in the main ap ly to t eir circumstances with double force. Next, that we shall very much fail in the object of this brief pap r, if those who may read it, and are still blessed with both living parents, do not attach a higher value to them. They will see the sorrows and other incidents of even a partial orphanage, and will doubtless bless God that their cup of enjoyment still runneth over.

W would fain give a word of sympathy and counsel to the fatherless. Your condition is one calculated to awaken the deepest emotions of pitying human love—to arrest the attention of angels as they pass to and fro in this our world on their varied ministries of benevolence and help, a condition which God has been pleased to take under His especial protection; for a judge of the widow and a father of the fatherless is God in his holy habitation. In your sorrow we deeply sympathise, and would fain comfort those that mourn. The father once loved and honored is no more—your heart is very desolate—earth seems gloomy, and the skies as if they wore a sadder hue. You sorrow over the graves of the

---

* Lamentations, 5th chap. 3rd verse.

loved and lost; they live, however, in grateful remembrance, and memory busies itself in recalling scenes of enjoyment never more to return. The kind fatherly greeting is past, the quiet talk by the winter's fireside is a tale that is told; the chair emphatically *his* is vacant; the grave-yard, 'God's acre,' has received one more seed waiting the trumpet call, and the resurrection body; heaven another spiri and an added charm. In that far-off land they forget not this; amidst the spirits of just men made perfect they think of you, and beckon you home. Deep-toned is the fine old hymn for Christian mourners from the 'Land of Luther.'

> " Our beloved have departed,
> While we tarry broken-hearted,
>   In the dreary empty house;
> They have ended life's brief story,
> They have reached the home of glory,
>   Over death victorious.
> .   .   .   .   .   .
> On we haste, to home invited,
> There with friends to be united,
>   In a surer bond than here;
> Meeting soon, and met for ever!
> Glorious hope! forsake us never,
>   For thy glimmering light is dear."

Alas! that the position of some of you is one of severe *privation*. You are tasting the sorrows of cheerless poverty. Whilst your father lived you had bread enough and to spare for others' need. You had many friends then, and could occasionally partake of innocent pleasures; but now with a diminished income you can too well realize the privations and sorrows of the fatherless. The poor make few new friends to replace those who have forgotten to call. Well might the dying child ask if all her father's friends died when he died. The memories of the past, said often to visit the dying in their last moments, were suddenly called from their sleeping places and led to the question with its un esigned b t bitter satire upon the friends who live in sunshine and wealth—the question was almost the last, for an angel entered the room and two left it—the bright rays of the rising sun shone upon a darkened house, and the little mourner was at rest. You will beware of *danger*. We speak not of the danger of injustice, though truth compels us to say that as in the time of Christ there were some who devoured widows' houses, and for a pretence made ong prayers, so in these days their successors and imitators can be found. A defenceless state instead of awakening pity and help, is a temptation to the mean and the vile, and thousands have received an added sorrow in the loss of all their substance through misplaced confidence. There is extreme *moral* danger. It is too often seen, that orph ns have become the prey of wicked and designing men. Many a sad history of sorrow and shame has been enacted, because of the lack of controlling parental authority. It is well for you to survey your position,—a man sailing over a dangerous sea frequently consults his chart—better for him to know of the sandbanks around him, in order to avoid them, than to sail on in blind security, only to awake to a knowledge of his danger when it is too late.

Yet, amidst all your sorrows, privations, and dangers, you have a powerful protector, and a loving, gentle friend in the Father of all flesh. Good to all, he will be especially so to you. If you seek him you shall find that his eye never sleeps; that his ear can attend the softest call; that he is ready to show himself strong on behalf of those who trust him. He asks for your love and reverence. " My son or my daughter give me thine heart." He is ready to adopt y u, to make you a partaker of the divine nature; to give you a new name; to instruct you in the holy and honorable duties of your sacred position; to give you in the noblest sense all things in time and in eternity, as the heir of God and joint heir with our Lord Jesus Christ. If recognising sin as the fruitful cause of all human misery—its too powerful prevalence in y ur own heart—you seek, by repentance towards God and faith in our Lord Jesus, to escape the consequences of all past sins, and in humble dependance upon the renewing and sanctifying grace of the Holy Spirit, to walk worthy of the Lord to all well-pleasing, the Holy One will say, " I will be a Father unto you, and ye shall be my sons and daughters, saith the Lord God Almighty." Like a father, the Almighty One will te ch you to profit, and guide you by his eye and his voice in the pleasant paths of wisdom and virtue. He will seek to promote your welfare, by making all things work together for your good. He will watch over you in sickness and minister to your wants—you can cast all your care upon Him, for he careth for you. You may consult Him in all life's perplexities, and always with satisfaction. "Wilt thou not from this time say—My Father, thou art the guide of my youth ? " " Thou shalt guide me by thy counsel, and afterwards receive me to glory." The love of God is like that which a tender father feels. His words are those of gentleness—his deeds are mercies. He will never leave you nor forsake you. Y u will find him always at your side, and ever the same. Of his days there is no end, and he changeth not. Even now you may say, " Our Father who art in heaven," and rejoice in hope of the time when He shall bring you to His own glorious and heavenly home to meet the good of all times. " In all thy days acknowledge him, and he shall direct thy paths," making all life's varying ways terminate at his own right hand, where there is fulness of joy and pleasures for evermore—freedom from sin, and no more sorrow, sighing, or death, for the former things have passed away.　　　　　　　W. L.

COMMUNION THOUGHTS.

" This is my beloved, and this is my friend, O daughter of Jerusalem."* Such is the reply of the Church to a pointed and pressing question. There are two aspects in which the language may be viewed,—one, as it illustrates the position of the Church; and next, as it illustrates the character sustained by Christ to his people. The Church appears before us as an ardent and outspoken admirer of the Lord Jesus,

* The Song of Solomon, 5th chap. 16th verse. The songs of Solomon were a thousand and five, and yet among them all this is *the song of songs*. What Homer's Iliad is to other songs, real or supposed of the same author, Paradise Lost to other poems of Milton, so is this song to all other poetical productions of Solomon. At what period of his life it was written is still a moot point among Biblical critics. If in early life it is a striking instance of youthful love and devotion—if in the mature period of his days, a cheering instance of restoring mercy and light at eventide—evidencing, too, most impressively the adoring and satisfied gratitude of a reclaimed prodigal. We at once and without controversy assume the book to be divine, and believe it to be a Christian's book, a manual for the Church member *only*, and only for him when, above the usual wont, his heart is purified from all earthly leaven, and the spirit upborne on the wings of a sanctified imagination, seeketh for closer fellowship with him whom it loveth.

having contemplated all the glorious attributes of his nature—the perfect sinlessness of his character, with all its positive, active virtues, the saving love and power manifest d in his life, death, and resurrection, and prevailing intercession—she exultingly says, " This is my beloved and this is my friend." *Great is the honor possessed by those who can truly use this language.* Men feel honored when they can number among their intimate friends, those who are distinguished by real worth, tried wisdom, extensive usefulness, great moral and social influence. As the rays of the sun fall upon the moon, and gild her with their rich lustre, so the rays of our friend's greatness and goodness fall upon us, and as we point to them we exultingly say, " This is my beloved and this is my friend." Jesus is the most glorious of all beings. He is the King of kings, and the Lord of lords ; ruling over all times, all places, all persons and all events. He is almighty, all wise, supremely good, possessed of vast moral influence ever increasing as his people multiply, and the same yesterday, to-day, and for ever. This honor have all the saints, to look up to him as their beloved and friend.

Intimate is the relation here indicated. Friendship implies acquaintance, appreciation, familiarity, confidence, frequent intercourse personally or by communications. All this a Christian believer claims. He is acquainted with Christ. He has searched the Scriptures which testify concerning Immanuel. The wondrous revelation, from its first utterances in the forfeited garden of Eden to the fulness of time, is a theme well known. The New Testament records of his Saviour's twofold life, with its deeds of mercy and lessons of love, are familiar as household words. Each Sabbath he sees afresh the place where the Lord lay, and guided by unerring wisdom he has seen the gates of the everlasting city thrown open, that the King of glory might enter in, leading captivity captive, and richly laden with the spoils of moral victories. He has seen heaven opened, and Jesus sitting as the only Mediator at the right hand of God. He appreciates his love, and is sacredly familiar, not in the use of endearing appellatives, which an intelligent and chastened friendship ever eschews, but in devout meditation, prayer and acquaintance with His purposes. " Henceforth, I call you not servants, for the servant knoweth not what his Lord doeth : but I have called you friends ; for all things that I have heard of my father I have made known unto you." A more sacred relation than even friendship is intimated. This is my beloved. A union closer than that between a parent and child : for this cause shall a man leave his father and mother, and be joined to his wife, and they twain shall be one flesh ; but he that is joined to the Lord is one spirit. Christ is the bridegroom and the Church is his bride. He loved the Church, and gave himself for it. He adorns his bride with the garments of salvation and the robes of praise—gently sustains her in the pathway through the wilderness, and brings her to a glorious home. He requires her to forget her own people and her father's house, and to delight herself in his infinite and faithful love. The Church, conscious evermore that he is the chief among ten thousand, and the altogether lovely, says with a full glad heart, " This is my beloved this is my friend."

This shows the designed constancy of the relation. It is the God himself that " the woman which hath an husband is the law to her husband, so long as he liveth ; but if the husband be dead, she is loosed from the law of her husband," Rom. vii. 2. " Wherefore, my brethren, ye also are become dead to the law (the law of sin) by the body of Christ ; that ye should be married to another, even to him who is raised from the dead, that we should bring forth fruit unto God." Christ abideth for ever after the power of an endless life, and we are bound to him by sacred bonds for perpetuity. The surrender we made was once for all. Our vows are ratified and sealed to him, who merits all our love and service. Nor would we willingly violate them—our joyful experience exceeds our fondest hopes and expectations, and with an ever deepening satisfaction we say, " This is my beloved and this is my friend."

This illustrates the joy of the Church. God is love, and God is the blessed, the happy God. To love is to be happy. There is the pleasure of realized wealth and fame ; the higher pleasure of the student, as with a true spirit he pursues his anxious and successful researches ; but of all pleasures sage experience has declared that reciprocated love is the sweetest and most satisfying. It is the quickener of the mental powers—of all high hopes and noble purposes a sure ally—and a welcome pillow for a weary heart. Christians have not seen Christ, but they love him, though unseen by mortal vision. Faith gives us a realizing power, and we joy in God through our Lord Jesus Christ, by whom we have now received the atonement. Accepted in the beloved, we drink of that river of joy which maketh glad the city of our God. We rejoice with a joy unspeakable and full of glory ; while we feel nothing shall be able to separate us from the love of God, in Christ Jesus our Lord—our beloved and our friend.

Having seen the position of the Church, we may now meditate upon the passage, as it illustrates or suggests the special character of the Saviour's friendship. We cannot find a friend in every man : some we love for God's sake more than their own—there may be much that is good and valuable about them, but they lack to us individually that mysterious magnetic power that makes two hearts one. Christ, because of the expansiveness of his nature, is a friend to every man, and especially to his people. He can meet and satisfy the wants of every longing soul.

His friendship is full of tender sympathy. The human heart is often the seat of sorrow and anguish. Poverty, sickness, desolation, death may enter my dwelling, and open wide the flood gates of trouble. Deep may call unto deep, as the waterspouts burst with all their collected sorrows, and the winds and the waves roll over my spirit, tempest tossed and half a wreck. It is then we need and wish for a sympathising friend, whose heart is full of tenderness and pity— in whose eye love lights up a glory all its own—on whose lips grace is poured—whose hands are ready helpers of another's need— who by an instinct of prized sacredness can see my hidden grief, and will not vex me with vain words, but by the eloquence of silence and the appropriate deed, will help me to bear my heavy burden, and so fulfil the law of Christ. Jesus is full of tender sympathy. The bruised reed he will not break. He takes up the lambs in his bosom, and tempers the wind to the shorn one. He enters in at the opened door, and binds up the broken-hearted, giving the oil of joy for that of mourning, and the garment of praise for the spirit of heaviness.

His friendship is eminently practical. We require friends who will help us according to our need and their ability. He is my friend who, when I am in poverty and sorrow, comes to help and bless—who will seek to deliver me from danger at his own personal risk and sacrifice. It is thus with Christ. He visited men forlorn and wretched with words of hope and love, ready offers of help, and all with a grace and goodness rendering doubly sweet his manifold blessings. He made our cause his own by a complete identification with us—made like unto his brethren—and gave at last the noblest proof; for greater love hath no man than this, that a man lay down his life for his friend. It embraces and consummates all other gifts and sacrifices; even when we were enemies he died the just for the unjust, that he might bring us to God; and now he is in heaven ordering all things after the counsel of his own will, and making them work together for good to them that love God, and for whom he is also preparing a glorious mansion, that where he is there they may be also.

His friendship is ever the same. Sometimes it is seen in our observation of human life, that friendship is a stronger tie than mere family relationship—a friend sticketh closer than a brother. Yet all human friendships are liable to decay, and some to entire extinction. We give all the earnest fondness of a young and unsophisticated heart to an object afterwards found to be unworthy—we have been " entangled with a poisonous bosom snake," then our revulsion and distaste are proportionate to our former love. Christ always saw the worst of us, and became our friend to make us holy—meet for the inheritance of the saints in light. Human friendships decay from change of abode, wide separation, and difficulty of intercommunication. There is regret felt at this; but other friends are found — even solemn and pressing duties co-operate—our friendship dies by slow decay—and in our widely varying pathway of life, perhaps never more to be renewed, till all the chosen seed meet in their heavenly home. But Christ is ever present with his people. " Lo! I am with you in all ages, world without end; " with us in sorrow and in joy—in the land that gave us birth, and in this of our adoption and love. Sometimes human friendships are severed by the exaltation of one who speedily forgets the other. The chief butler did not remember Joseph, but forgat him, and many have played the same ignoble part in the shifting scenes of their life's history. Jesus was ever exalted—he stoops to raise us up—he seeks to make us like himself—and he will not leave us nor forsake us; the work of His grace on earth shall be crowned with glory in heaven, and so shall we be for ever with the Lord. " This is my beloved and this is my friend, O daughter of Jerusalem! " Wherefore, Christian brethren, let us comfort one another with these words, and while from time to time we come to the banqueting house, let us remember that in this divine, as in all human friendships, " He that hath friends must show himself friendly." W. L.

CHRISTIANITY IMPARTIAL.

The genius of Christianity, be it recollected, pays no deference to mere greatness; it prescribes exactly the same rules of conduct to all; no power can terrify, no splendour can dazzle it; with sublime indifference to all that bewilders and perverts the judgment of this world's too compliant moralists, it considers guilt on a throne precisely in the same light with guilt on the scaffold —*Henry Rogers.*

PIOUS MOTHERS—PROFITABLE REMEMBRANCE OF THEM.*

" Save the son of thine handmaid."—Psalm lxxxvi. 16.

Scripture history supplies a very limited account of David's parentage, and especially of his mother. We first read of David himself when Samuel anointed him as the future king of Israel. His father, Jesse the Bethlemite, called him before the prophet, but his mother is not mentioned. David was then a youth, probably about fifteen years of age, ruddy and well-favored,—usually occupied in keeping his father's's sheep. A few years later, he was sent by Jesse to the field of strife, where his elder brothers were serving, and where David himself shortly encountered the giant of Gath. The narrative indicates that David's father was, at that time, advanced in years. (See 1 Sam. xvii. 12—14.) About a year after, when David fled from Saul's persecuting malice to the cave of Adullam, he committed his parents to the care of the king of Moab, saying, " Let my father and my mother, I pray thee, come forth, and be with you, till I know what God will do for me." They continued there, while David was in the hold ; but no further reference is made to them in the sacred narrative. It is probable, that being well stricken in years they were soon removed by death.

It may be proper, however, to notice a passage, which has conveyed the impression that David's parents eventually abandoned him, through fear of Saul's displeasure,—" When my father and my mother forsake me, then the Lord will take me up." But this language is simply hypothetical. David expresses his assurance, that should he be abandoned by his nearest kindred, God's paternal care would be available and all sufficient. Perhaps his parents died about this time, or he was deprived of the solace of their company ; and thus he was led to feel that God's favour and succour would more than compensate for the loss of earthly friends. We do not conceive then that David intended to reflect upon his parents for their unkindness, and especially upon his mother. Of his father he makes no further mention ; but of his mother he cherished a sweet and hallowed remembrance, as one who was devoted to God. Hence in the trials of after-years, this was his prayer—" Save the son of thine handmaid."

I. A peculiar relation is here recognised. David was the son of a pious mother. Such a mother will supply sacred *training*. We have no record of David's childhood ; but we know that he received early instruction, for in old age he thus acknowleges God's goodness in placing this instruction within his reach,—" O God, thou hast taught me from my youth." Now as God works by means and instrumentalities of his own appointment, what more probable than that David's mother, the handmaid of the Lord, was the teacher that God employed, to train that bright-faced boy for his service ? We read of another mother, who thus instructed a royal son ; for we have recorded in Prov. xxxi., " The words of King Lemuel, the prophecy that his mother taught him." Timothy too, knew the Scriptures from his youth, doubtless instructed by his grandmother Lois and his mother Eunice.

The son of a pious mother, like David, will also be instructed by her *example.* Happy the mother, whose spirit is so habitually holy —enduring, that her children arise and call her blessed.

* Thoughts embodied in a discourse delivered by the Rev. ? receiving intelligence of the death of his mother.

mother, whose demeanour in domestic trials and in all the changing scenes of life, leaves the mind of her son, after the lapse of many years, full of fragrant and precious memories!

The son of a pious mother will have a mother's *prayers;* and this may render precious to the heart the name of a mother, who perhaps is imperfectly remembered, or who may have been removed before her children could know her value. But, whatever the period of separation, it is certain that a son of a pious mother (whether he can recall her teaching and example or not), is a child of many prayers; and shall not this persuasion be cherished with a thoughtful melting heart? Shall it not suggest and sustain the personal appeal—"Let my mother's prayers be answered!—Save the son of thine handmaid."

II. The prayer, appropriate to this relation is here recorded. "Save the son of thine handmaid," that distinguished privileges may not issue in deeper condemnation.—The child of a pious mother may well remember that solemn responsibility as well as high privilege is involved in that relation. If after all the pleadings of a Christian parent, the way of evil be chosen, how terrible must be the condemnation of that guilty soul? There is sometimes a frightful abuse of the privilege this relation involves, and sinful ways are pursued with the impression that, sooner or later, God will interpose in answer to a mother's prayers, and save the soul from ultimate ruin. But this is a vain and perilous delusion: and of those who thus pervert a mother's piety into an argument for continued impenitence and sin, it may surely be said—"Their damnation is just." Let then the remembrance of a pious mother prompt the prayer—"Save the son of thine handmaid from trampling under foot the blessings which a mother most highly prized. Let not my soul be stung throughout eternity by the hissing reproach of many a taunting demon—'Thou art the son of a pious mother, but thou hast rejected her God: and now the hottest hell is thy appropriate place!'"

"Save the son of thine handmaid," that maternal consecration may be ratified and sustained by personal dedication to God. This may well be the prayer of those who have been devoted to the Lord from their earliest years by pious mothers. In all such cases, this is the cry which maternal solicitude suggests—"Let my child live, live to God! Let him be the subject of renewing and sanctifying grace. Let him grow up to serve his generation according to the will of God."—This cry is answered, when the "child of many prayers" says—"Lord, I am thine, save me. Save me from a worldly mind—a procrastinating spirit—a divided heart. Save me from all my sins, and uphold me in thy ways. Give thy strength to thy servant, and save the son of thine handmaid."—Let this self-consecration be often renewed; and especially let it be prompted by the call which comes, with tender and solemn accents, from a mother's grave.

"Save the son of thine handmaid," that in prosecuting the Christian path, the incentives to devotedness and perseverance which this relation supplies may be prayerfully and practically improved. We speak now of a son who is "looking unto Jesus," and concerned to follow in the course, which his mother pursued. Often may he be animated in this course, by the recollections which she supplies. Is there the temptation to moral weariness—to sloth and inaction? Do toils and trials seem to be almost profitless? The remembrance of a mother's patient continuance in well-doing may revive the fainting spirit and rouse the sluggish heart. Is the mind fretted and chafed by the perverse ways of men—by the disquieting agencies which are so often found in this world of sin and strife? The remembrance of a mother's "patience in tribulation" may well sooth the agitated spirit, and bid the unruly heart be still. And so—is the fainting Christian himself a parent—longing for the conversion of his children, and yet failing to realize the full blessing? Perhaps he may remember his own early waywardness; and yet, as a mother's prayers were answered in him, he may well "continue in prayer" that God's mercy may be unto children's children.

The final prayer must be—that a happy reunion may be realized in a higher state of being. "Save the son of thine handmaid" that I may meet again with a sainted mother.

The reflections we have recorded, although specially applicable to one relation, are susceptible of a wider range. They may be suitably pondered by all who may have been favored with pious relatives or friends. Moreover, Sabbath School Teachers often supplement domestic training, and sometimes, alas! work alone. There are few young persons in the present day who do not realize in the family, or in the "nursery of the Church," lessons for the soul's good. Let the removal of faithful counsellors, whether parent—teacher—or friend—excite solicitude to profit yet more fully by early privileges, and, with love and holy zeal, to obey

"The counsels of the dead."

CONGREGATIONAL UNION, GREEN PONDS, TASMANIA.

This small but rising town, situated about 27 miles from Hobart, has lately been the scene of unusual excitement. The Congregational Union had decided to hold its annual gathering there on March the 16th and 17th, to which a special interest was attached from the anticipation that the Rev. Mr. Binney would take part in the proceedings. The anxiety to see and hear a man whose name has been so prominently brought before the public in these colonies, and who is known to be "a pillar in the Church" of Christ, drew together many persons from Hobart, as well as from the immediate neighbourhood.

There is a Congregational Church and Chapel at Green Ponds, established through the labours of the Rev. J. Beazley (now of Sydney), of which the Rev. W. Waterfield (the first pastor of the Independent Church, Collins-street, Melbourne) is the minister. A public service was held in the chapel on Wednesday evening, March 16. The Rev. F Miller conducted the devotional exercises, and the Rev. Thos. Binney preached to a large congregation from 1 Cor. i., 21—24. A collection, which realised upwards of £16, was then made on behalf of the Colonial Missionary Society.

The congregation having separated, a *pro formâ* meeting was held, of which the Rev. W. Law, president of the last annual meeting, was chairman. The names of ministers, delegates, &c., were announced. The ministers present were:—Revs. Messrs. Miller, Clarke, Price, Waterfield, Law, Day and Nisbet. The delegates:—Messrs. Woolley, Perkins, Lumsden, W. Giblin, R. Morgan, E. Rout, Hopkins, Facey, Walch, Searle, Aikenhead, Powell, Gorringe, Speak. Colonial Missionary Society agents:—Messrs. Blackwood and Giles; and officers of Colonial Missionary Society, Messrs. Dear and B. Rout. It was resolved, on the motion of Rev. C. Price, seconded by Rev. W. Waterfield, that the Rev. Mr. Binney be requested to preside at the present meeting of the Union, which he kindly consented to do. The Rev. Mr. Shippherd's application to become a member of the Union, terminated the business of the meeting.

On Thursday morning the ministers and delegates re-assembled in the chapel at 9½ o'clock. The Rev. Mr. Binney, chairman, opened the proceedings by singing, reading and prayer, and then read a lengthened but deeply interesting address, listened to with marked attention by a numerous auditory. It was devoted to an explanation of the peculiar relation of the speaker to the correspondence which took place in Adelaide on Christian Union among Evangelical Protestants, and to a review of certain propositions of the Bishop of Adelaide out of which the correspondence arose. The Bishop's letter, with replies thereto, have already appeared in the *Spectator*, and as Mr. Binney's address is to be published *in extenso*, it is needless to do more than simply to indicate the main points of the review. They were,—

1st. That the Bishop's proposals are inconsistent and contradictory. There are two opposing tones running through the letter which tended to defeat its object. The one displayed the man ; the other the ecclesiastic.

2nd. The concessions to be made to secure " the Church of the Future " were not mutual but one-sided. The other denominations are to give up their principles, episcopacy is to remain intact.

3rd. The Bishop overlooks the possible existence of conscientious convictions of spiritual minds in other communions than the Church of England. He seems to infer that members of non-conforming bodies can change their principles as readily as their garments.

In commenting on the Bishop's views, the Chairman referred to his own predilections in favor of Episcopacy, and stated the grounds on which he was compelled to be a non-conformist—" a schismatical layman "—rather than a perjured ecclesiastic In support of his views, and in defence of his conduct, Mr. Binney quoted a paragraph from a charge by Bishop Nixon, whom, by the way, he proved, in consequence of his rejection of the decision of the Privy Council on the Gorham question, to be a dissenter from the Church of England, while he remains a member of the Church of the Prayer-book,—theologically consistent but ecclesiastically wrong.

We have not attempted to give the precise language the Chairman employed, and only a faint idea of the line of reasoning he adopted. When the address was concluded the Rev. F. Miller moved, and the Rev. W. Law seconded a resolution,—

" That the best thanks of this meeting be given to the Rev. Thos. Binney for his very valuable address, and that he be requested to allow of its publication."

The meeting having concurred, the Chairman said he had not come to the colonies for controversy, nor to print books, but that if arrangements could be made to relieve him from the expense, he would prepare the address for printing, accompanied by the documents to which he had occasion to refer. Mr. Hopkins engaged to secure Mr. Binney against all loss, believing that the circulation of the address would effect much good.

The Secretary then moved the suspension of the 3rd Rule, in order that the Rev. J. W. Shippherd be admitted by declaration of hands, instead of by ballot. Agreed to, and Mr. Shippherd was admitted a member of the Union.

The annual report was read by the Secretary. It referred to matters of local interest, but contained nothing to call for special notice here. Its adoption was moved by the Rev. W. Day, and seconded by the Rev. W. Waterfield. The Chairman, on putting the resolution before the meeting, remarked that 40 years ago he was sitting at Mr. Day's feet as a student, Mr. Day being at that time Classical Tutor at the college in which he (Mr. B.) had just entered, and that his first essay as a student was read to Mr. Day.

The general business of the Union occupied the remainder of the day. The subjects brought before the meeting were, Missions in the Colony, Miss Watkins's Legacy, Statistical Returns, *Southern Spectator*, Law of Marriage and Divorce, Cemetery Bill, Correspondence with the Congregational Union of England and Wales, the election of a Delegate to the Australian Congregational Conference, to be held at Adelaide, and the appointment of Officers and Executive Committee for the ensuing year. The appointments made are, the Rev. G. Clarke, to be the Delegate to Adelaide : the Rev. W. Law, to preside at the next Annual Meeting to be held in Launceston ; H. Hopkins, Esq., to be Treasurer ; and the Rev. J. Nisbet, Secretary. The proceedings were closed at 4 o'clock by a brief address, and the benediction by the Chairman.

This report would not be complete if it omitted to notice the very liberal scale on which supplies were provided by the friends at Green Ponds, to meet the physical requirements of members of the Union and their friends. Tables were neatly arranged and largely furnished in the schoolroom attached to the chapel, around which the ministers and delegates gathered at 1 o'clock; and in the evening a tea meeting was held, which was numerously attended by the friends more immediately resident at Green Ponds and its vicinity. At this meeting the esteemed pastor of the church, the Rev. W. Waterfield, presided; and addresses were delivered by Messrs. Aikenhead and Dear, and by the Rev. Messrs. Price, Day, Miller, Law and Binney.

The meetings were instructive and refreshing, and will not readily be forgotten by those who had the privilege of attending them.

EXTRACTS AND VARIETIES.

TENDENCY TO FORMALISM.

As the soul is clothed in flesh, and only thus is able to perform its functions on the earth, where it is sent to live; as the thought must find a word before it can pass from mind to mind, so every great truth seeks some body, some outward form in which to exhibit its powers. It appears in the world, and men lay hold upon it, and represent it to themselves in histories, in forms of words, in sacramental symbols; and these things which, in their proper nature, are but illustrations, stiffen into essential fact, and become part of the reality. So arises, in era after era, an outward and mortal expression of the inward and immortal life; and at once the old struggle begins to repeat itself between the flesh and the spirit, the form and the reality. For awhile the lower tendencies are held in check. The meaning of the symbolism is living and fresh. It is a living language vivid and suggestive. By-and-by, as the mind passes into other phases, the meaning is forgotten. The language becomes a dead language, and the living robe of life becomes a winding sheet of corruption. The form is represented as everything; the spirit as nothing—obedience is dispensed with. Sin and religion arrange a compromise, and outward observances and technical inward emotions are converted into jugglers' tricks, by which men are enabled to enjoy their pleasures and escape the penalties of wrong. Then such religion becomes no religion, but a falsehood; and honorable men turn away from it, and fall back in haste upon the naked elemental life."—*Froude* (History of England).

(Perhaps the most remarkable illustration of this is the history of Quakerism. Commencing as a special protest against forms in religion, abjuring them all, relying wholly upon the Spirit and inward life, and confining itself in its outward manifestation to the extremest possible simplicity, it has, in the course of a century and a half, become petrified and stiffened into the most rigid and punctilious of formalisms.)

CONVERSION OF WILBERFORCE.

In the summer of 1785 Wilberforce was travelling on the Continent, and had taken for his carriage companion Isaac Milner, afterwards Dean of Carlisle. Dr. Milner, a man of extensive learning and great ability, was a firm holder of Evangelical opinions, though at that time he was not much influenced by them. Wilberforce afterwards declared that had he been aware of his peculiar sentiments he should have taken special care not to choose him for his travelling companion. One day as they journeyed along, a clergyman's name was mentioned in conversation, with respect to whom Mr. Wilberforce said he thought *he went too far* in his religion. Dr. Milner controverted this, showing, from the nature of religion, that such a thing was impossible. Various interesting discussions ensued, day by day, as they travelled amidst the sublime scenery of Switzerland. The result was a thorough awakening of Mr. Wilberforce's mind to the subject of religion. No sudden and violent emotions were felt, but he became interested, determined like the Bereans to search the Scriptures for himself, and see if these things were so. And feeling his need of Divine guidance, in so momentous an inquiry, he bent his knees in prayer to the Father of lights, to supplicate the tuition of the Holy Spirit. His prejudicies, previously very inveterate, gradually melted; his difficulties gave way; he saw clearly that those views of religion usually denominated Evangelical were truly and veritably the doctrines of Holy Scripture; and when this conviction was once formed, with his characteristic honesty and sincerity, he openly avowed the change. For awhile the alteration in him was rather in the head than the heart; more in his opinions than his feelings. But so frank a nature as his could not long hold such sentiments as he now embraced without perceiving their importance and feeling their influence. Gradually the new leaven penetrated the recesses of his heart and pervaded his whole character. He became a deeply experimental Christian, a man of prayer, a devout reader of the Bible. He came out in the face of the world a *new man*. There was little indeed to change externally for he had few or no vices to lop off, but what was before mere worldly *virtue*, now assumed the warm tints and lovely hues of Gospel *holiness*. His conversion produced quite a sensation in the fashionable world. Strange reports and caricatured accounts of his altered habits were circulated, and it required no small amount of courage and resolution to breast this tide of ridicule. But he held on his way, and was faithful unto death.

THE BIBLE NOT THE SAME TO ALL.

Look at the way in which the Bible seems to speak to this wretched man here; and do you, young men, take a warning from it. Never forget that the Bible will be to you what you are to it. You will find in it what you bring to it. "To the merciful, thou wilt show thyself merciful; to the upright, thou wilt show thyself upright; to the pure, thou wilt show thyself pure; and to the froward, thou wilt show thyself froward." "Thus saith the Lord God: Every man that setteth up his idols in his heart, and cometh to the prophet, I the Lord will answer him that cometh, according to the multitude of his idols." A good man, in reading the Scriptures, never notices the passages that terrify others. In relation to these, he reads the book as a little child reads it in relation to such as the corrupt and impure ridicule or pervert,—he does not see them, does not understand them,—they have no message or meaning for him. To his eye every page is covered with a mild radiance, with Divine light, laughter, and sunshine. If he casually opens it, he is sure to be addressed by some great promise, some pregnant word of consolation and strength; or to see some picture of the blessedness of the righteous, or some bright gleam of the glory of heaven! He cannot help it. An instinct in himself detects the words, —a secret life in the words themselves, makes them stand out prominent and lustrous. In the same way the agitated and terrified, the sinner alarmed by the recollection of his sins, with his soul disturbed by foul passions and his conscience blackened by fearful guilt, to him the Book seems to be nothing but a message of wrath; every column is covered with characters of fire, every syllable seems sharp as the point of an arrow, pungent as if tipped with poison, constructed only to pierce and wound! He cannot find the texts which he thinks he remembers. They are not there. When he looks for them it is the alarming only that start into view, and become terribly alive and vocal! Now, all this is perfectly natural. The Bible will reveal itself to you, according to your state of mind. As I have just said, you will find, when you go to it, what you take. In ordinary cases, how different the same Book would be to one opening it reeking from a debauch, and to another returning from some act of mercy or self-sacrifice!—*Binney.*

HE WILL GIVE YOU REST.

Are you travailing with sorrow? Are you heavy-laden with the burden of oppression or woe? Christ will give you rest. Doubtless the heavy-laden with the burden of sin are first invited; but they exclude no other sufferers. There is no exception of age, or rank, or clime, the extent of the travail, or weight of the burden; the childish sorrows of the weeping schoolboy are as much the subject of the Saviour's sympathy as the matured wretchedness of the aged man; all come within the Saviour's invitation.—*H. Blunt.*

K

CHRIST THE FOUNTAIN OF LIFE.

Oh! what a melting consideration is this, that out of his agony comes our victory; out of his condemnation, our justification; out of his pain, our ease; out of his stripes, our healing; out of his gall and vinegar, our honey; out of his curse, our blessing; out of his crown of thorns, our crown of glory; out of his death, our life! If *he* could not be released, it was that *you* might. If Pilate gave sentence against him, it was that the great God might not give sentence against you. If he yielded, that it should be with Christ as they required, it was that it might be with our souls as well as we can desire — *Flavel.*

THE COURSE OF SIN.

Sin is first easy, then pleasant, then agreeable, then delightful, then the man is far from God, then he is obstinate, then he resolves never to repent, and then he is damned. – *Jeremy Taylor.*

TEMPERANCE AND INDUSTRY.

"No one's enemy but his own." – How often are these words used to excuse, if not to justify, the conduct of the unhappy drunkard! But is it true that he *alone* suffers? In thousands of cases is he not the enemy of every person with whom he has to do? He mostly squanders his own property, then incurs debts, and calls on his friends for loans; reduces his wife to beggary; leaves his orphan children to the public; and, after having indulged himself to the last shilling, entails a life of misery on his family, and too often leaves behind him that ill-understood reputation of harmless folly, which is more injurious to society than some positive crimes. The utter waste of life, the neglect of all relative and social duties, an evil example, and a worthless character, are more or less the fruits of the conduct of him who is " *no one's enemy but his own.*"

HOW TO SECURE PEACE AT HOME.

It is just as possible to keep a calm house as a clean one: a cheerful house, an orderly house, as a furnished house, if the heads set themselves to do so. Where is the difficulty of consulting each other's weakness, as well as each other's wants; each other's tempers, as well as each other's health; each other's comfort, as well as each other's character? Oh! it is by leaving the peace at home to chance, instead of pursuing it by system, that so many homes are unhappy. It deserves notice, also, that almost any one can be courteous and forbearing and patient in a neighbour's house. If anything go wrong, or be out of time, or disagreeable there, it is made the best of, not the worst; even efforts made to excuse it, and to show that it is not felt; or, if felt, it is attributed to accident, not design; and this is not only easy, but natural, in the house of a friend. I will not, therefore, believe that what is so natural in the house of another is impossible at home; but maintain, without fear, that all the courtesies of social life may be upheld in domestic societies. A husband as willing to be pleased at home and as anxious to please as in his neighbour's house, and a wife as intent on making things comfortable every day to her family as on set days to her guests, could not fail to make their own home happy. Let us not evade the point of these remarks by recurring to the maxim about allowances for temper. It is worse than folly to refer to our temper, unless we could prove that we ever gained anything good by giving way to it. Fits of ill-humour punish us quite as much, if not more, than those they are vented upon; and it actually requires more effort, and inflicts mor pain to give them up, than would be required to avoid them.—*Philip.*

PURPOSES AND PROSPECTS.

The King of kings adore!
  The Lord of Glory praise!
Whose sceptre evermore
  In sov'reign wisdom sways,
And even from the stormy deep,
Oft brings to his beloved sleep!

Oh! bless the Guiding hand,
  That bade us hither come!
May peace be on the land
  The Lord hath made our home.
Here he hath made the cloud to rest,
Here blessings may we be, and blest!

We purpose to be thine,
    To serve thee, with our house ;
Our all to thee resign,
    Oh ! Lord accept our vows.
Yea ! thou hast promis'd, and wilt do,
Our faith beholds the promise true.

Leap, leap, ye rocks and hills !
    Oh ! clap your hands ye trees !
The Lord Jehovah wills
    The borders shall be his !
O'er hill and dale the shout shall ring
Jehovah, Jesus is our king !

And we, sweet harps above !
    We soon shall harp with them,
And chant redeeming love
    In yon Jerusalem !
Its sea of glass, its streets of gold,
Ev'n now our raptur'd eyes behold.

The joy shall ever last
    Within those pearly gates ;
Earth's trials overpast,
    No second trial waits.
Hail ! stormless sea ! and city bright !
Hail ! everlasting life and light !

Hymns for the Colonies.

HOUSES IN SAMOA, OR NAVIGATORS' ISLANDS.

The Samoans have a tradition that of old their forefathers had no houses
They say that in those days the people were " housed by the heavens ; " and
describe the ingenuity of a chief who first contrived to build houses. He had
two sons, and, out of love to them, built for each of them a house. The places
where the houses stood are also pointed out, and form the names of two
divisions of a district at the east end of Upolu. The one is called the "upper
house," and the other the " lower house."

But leaving tradition, imagine a gigantic bee-hive, thirty feet in diameter, a
hundred in circumference, and raised from the ground about four feet, by a
number of short posts, at intervals of four feet from each other all round, and
you have a good idea of the appearance of a Samoan house. The spaces
between these posts, which may be called open doors or windows, all round the
house, are shut in at night by roughly-plaited cocoanut-leaf blinds. During the
day, the blinds are pulled up, and all the interior exposed to a free current of
air. The floor is raised six or eight inches with rough stones, then an upper
layer of smooth pebbles, then some cocoanut-leaf mats, and then a layer of fine
matting. Houses of important chiefs are erected on a raised platform of stones
three feet high. In the centre of the house there are three posts or pillars,
twenty feet long, sunk three feet into the ground, and extending to, and supporting the ridge pole. These are the main props of the building. Any *Samson*
pulling them away would bring down the whole house. The space between the
rafters is filled up with what they call *ribs*, viz., the wood of the bread-fruit
tree, split up into small pieces, and joined together so as to form a long rod the
thickness of your finger, running from the ridge pole down to the eaves. All
are kept in their places—an inch and a half apart—by cross pieces, made fast
with cinet. The whole of this upper cage-like work looks compact and tidy,
and, at the first glance, is admired by strangers as being alike novel, ingenious,
and neat. The wood of the bread-fruit tree, of which the greater part of the
best houses are built, is durable, and, if preserved from wet, will last fifty
years.

The thatch also is laid on with great care and taste. The long dry leaves of
the sugar-cane are strung on to pieces of reed five feet long. They are made
fast to the reed by overlapping the one end of the leaf and pinning it with the

κ 2

rib of the cocoanut-leaflet, run through from leaf to leaf horizontally. These reeds, thus fringed with the sugar-cane leaves hanging down three or four feet, are laid on, beginning at the eaves and running up to the ridge pole, each one overlapping its fellow about an inch or so, and made fast one by one with cinet to the inside rods or rafters. Upwards of a hundred of these reeds of thatch will be required for a single row running from the eaves to the ridge pole. Then they do another row, and so on all round the house. Two, three, or four thousand of these fringed reeds may be required for a good-sized house. This thatching, if well done, will last for seven years. To collect the sugar cane leaves, and "sew," as it is called, the ends on to the reeds, is the work of the women. An active woman will sew fifty reeds in a day ; and three men will put up and fasten on to the roof of the house some five hundred in a day. Zinc, felt, and other contrivances are being tried by European residents ; but, for coolness and ventilation, nothing beats the thatch. The great drawback is, that in gales it stands up like a field of corn : and then the rain pours into the house. That, however, may be remedied by a network of cinet to keep down the thatch, or by the native plan of covering all in with a layer of heavy cocoa-nut leaves on the approach of a gale.

These great circular roofs are so constructed that they can be lifted bodily off the posts, and removed anywhere, either by land or by a raft of canoes. But in removing a house, they generally divide the roof into four parts, viz., the two sides, and the two ends, where there are particular joints left by the carpenters, which can easily be untied, and again fastened. There is not a single nail in the whole building: all is made fast with cinet. As Samoan houses often form presents, fines, doweries, as well as articles of barter, they are frequently removed from place to place. The arrangement of the houses in a village has no regard whatever to order. You rarely see three houses in a line. Every one puts his house on his little plot of ground, just as the shade of the trees, the direction of the wind, the height of the ground, &c., may suit his fancy.

A house, after the usual Samoan fashion, has but *one* apartment. It is the common parlour, dining-room, &c., &c., by day, and the bed-room of the whole family by night. They do not, however, herd indiscriminately. If you peep into a Samoan house at midnight, you will see five or six low oblong *tents* pitched (or rather strung up) here and there throughout the house. They are made of native-cloth, five feet high, and close all round down to the mat. They shut out the musquitoes, and enclose a place some eight feet by five ; and these said tent-looking places may be called the *bed-rooms* of the family. Four or five mats laid loosely, the one on the top of the other, form the *bed*. The *pillow* is a piece of thick bamboo, three inches in diameter, three to five feet long, and raised three inches from the mat by short wooden feet. The sick are indulged with something softer, but the hard bamboo is the invariable pillow of health. The *bedding* is complete with a single sheet of calico or native-cloth. After private prayer in the morning, the tent is unstrung, mats, pillow, and sheet rolled together, and laid up over head on a shelf between the posts in the middle of the house. Hence, to "make the bed" in Samoa, is no doubt much the same thing which Peter meant when he said to Æneas (Acts ix. 34), "Arise, and make thy bed."

These rolls of mats and bedding, a bundle or two done up in native cloth, on the same shelf in the centre of the house, a basket, a fan or two, and a butcher's knife stuck into the thatch within reach, a fishing net, a gun strung up along the rafters, a few paddles, a wooden chest in one corner, and a few cocoanut-shell water-bottles in another, are about all the things in the shape of furniture or property you can see in looking into a Samoan house. The fire-place is about the middle of the house. It is merely a circular hollow, two or three feet in diameter, a few inches deep, and lined with hardened clay. It is not used for cooking, but for the purpose of lighting up the house at night. A *flaming fire* was the regular evening offering to the gods, as the family bowed the head, and the fathers prayed for prosperity from the "gods great and small." The women collect during the day, a supply of dried cocoanut leaves, &c., which, with a little management, keep up a continued blaze in the evening, while the assembled family group have their supper and prayer, and sit together chatting for an hour or two afterwards. Many now-a-days burn an oil lamp instead ; and you see in their houses a table it may be, a sofa, a form, a chair or two, a few earthenware dishes, and some other conveniences of civilized life.

Oblong houses, divided into two or three apartments, more suited to the devotional and other wants of a well-regulated Christian family, are now seen here and there ; and a bedstead, instead of the mats laid on the floor.

CHILDREN OF MISSIONARIES.

To the Editor of the Southern Spectator.

Sir,—At the recent Conference held in Hobart Town, and ably presided over by yourself, among other resolutions it was agreed, on the motion of Mr. Hopkins, seconded by Mr. Thompson,—" That a committee be formed, consisting of the Revds. Messrs. West, Cuthbertson, and Kent, and Messrs. Fairfax, Thompson, and Mills, to raise and provide a fund to assist in the education of the children of those missionaries of the London Missionary Society in the South Seas, who may be disposed to avail themselves of such aid : that such committee apply the funds as occasion may require, and report their proceedings at the next Conference." Can you or the committee furnish any information as to the steps they have taken in the matter? An attempt is being made to open a school in Tasmania, where the junior children of such missionaries as may be disposed to avail themselves of the provision may be sent as to a home. Till the plan is fully matured it would not be wise to say more ; but should not the central committee immediately move and enlarge the proposed plan by furnishing funds, so that the elder children who may arrive from the islands may be at once distributed among the higher schools in New South Wales, or other colonies; and that the younger children in the home, as they reach the age of ten or twelve years, may be likewise sent to other schools, as their parents may direct or circumstances render desirable? It being a general conviction, I presume, among all who have thought upon the matter, that a careful distribution of the elder children among existing schools would be the most satisfactory method. Surely the day is not far distant when the Australian churches will be able to take up the South Sea Missions altogether, the Society at home assisting as needed for a few years. Begging your insertion of this in your next issue, and with much gratitude for your labors in connection with our Magazine,

I am, sir, your obedient servant,

Tasmania. A.

MISSIONS.

Rev. Wm. Henry.—-The *Sydney Morning Herald* announces the death, at the advanced age of eighty-nine years, of the Rev. William Henry, formerly one of the London Missionary Society's agents in the South Sea Islands. Mr. Henry was one of the first band of missionaries (thirty in number) sent out by the Society in 1796. The *Herald*, in a very able and interesting article, refers to the labors, discouragements, and successes of the missionaries. We can only quote a few sentences :—" In whatever light the labors of Mr. Henry, the Nestor of missionaries, are surveyed, the world will unanimously pronounce him worthy of honor. As a pioneer of civilisation and commerce, and as a teacher of the Christian faith, he maintained an unblemished reputation through all the trials of his long public life. As few men have lived so long, so few men have been permitted to contribute so largely to the elevation of the human race. At this present moment there are hundreds of Christian teachers of various denominations scattered over the islands of Polynesia. Often, by the mere agency of the natives themselves, their countrymen are turned from idols, and initiated into the doctrines of Christianity. Wherever a missionary residence is found, there is not only a welcome, but refreshment to every visitor of whatever nation. We have seen numerous testimonies to the value of their services, in their own proper sphere, and especially in relation to commerce. Sometimes, indeed, unreasoning men, who expect the highest style of human virtue in a people lately savages ; or bad men, who, throwing off themselves all the restraints of morality and civilisation, go with the hope of indulging the lowest passions at the native expense—rise up and tell the world that the efforts to Christianize the natives are all a delusion. We prefer to rely on her Majesty's Service, who, with one voice, assure us that the exertions of these gentlemen not only benefit the islanders, but spread the fame and protect the interests of their own country. Looking forward, as we must, to the increased connection of these colonies with those sunny regions, we have no doubt that curiosity with respect to the first pioneers of civilization will enlarge with the advance of time. And when the innumerable islands shall be brought under the various flags of European civilization, and in every place Christianity shall be established—when all the grosser forms of idolatrous customs and worship shall disappear, the name of Mr. Henry will rise high in the calendar of the regenerated nations. The spot to which we have confided his remains will be visited with something of the veneration which consecrates the sepulchre of the wise, the powerful, and the just ; and the children of the southern islands, in their growing enlightment, will pay their homage to the memory of one who devoted his life to their welfare."—*Melbourne Christian Times.*

MISSIONARY SERVICES IN VICTORIA.

The arrival in Hobson's Bay of some Missionaries on their way from England to the South Seas, and the visit from Sydney of the Rev. A. Buzzacott, for many years a devoted and successful Missionary at Raratonga, have given occasion for holding a series of meetings for promoting the cause of Missions to the heathen. Among the brethren from England were the aged Mr. Platt, who has spent the prime of his days in labour on the Society Islands, and now, superannuated, goes to end his days where he spent his strength, and where some of his family are resident. He is accompanied by an aged maiden sister, who has left her birth-place, for the first time, to be the companion of her brother during the remainder of his pilgrimage. The active Missionaries consist of the Rev. E. R. W. Krause, the Rev. G. Macfarlane, and the Rev. W. Baker. Mr. Krause, a German Lutheran, has spent twenty years in Missionary service in the South Seas, and is now returning with Mrs. Krause to resume his labours. Mr. Macfarlane and Mr. Baker are both young men, newly devoted to the work, and they, with their wives, are designated to Lifu, in one of the Westward Groups.

Sermons have been preached by these brethren, and Mr. Buzzacott, in Independent and Presbyterian Churches in Geelong, Williamstown, Richmond, Brighton, Collingwood, St. Kilda, Melbourne, &c. In addition to sermons on the Sabbath, there have, in several instances, been meetings held on week evenings, in different places of worship, when addresses were delivered, and interesting details of Missionary operations given by Mr. Buzzacott, Mr. Krause, and Mr. Sunderland, of Richmond. Several meetings have also been held in connexion with Sunday Schools, to interest the young people in the work of missions.

A large Public United Meeting was held in Chalmers' Church, Rev. Dr. Cairns's, Eastern Hill, Melbourne, on Wednesday Evening, April 24. The Hon. G. Harker, M.L.A., Colonial Treasurer, presided. Dr. Cairns and a few of the town ministers spoke briefly, but all made way for the veteran missionaries, Messrs. Buzzacott and Krause, who gave vivid descriptions of the wretched islands still in a state of heathenism and cannibalism ; of others now in a transition state, casting off their idolatries and their savage customs, and, embracing the glorious Gospel ; and of the numerous Christian islands where |

not a vestige of idolatory is now to be found; where all the people are under instruction and attend Christian worship; where industry, morality and humanity have superseded idleness, war, and cruelty; and where nurseries of Native Teachers exist, and are abundantly supplied with students for carrying the Gospel as pioneers into the heathen portions of Polynesia. The meeting was also addressed by Taevae, a Native Raratongan Teacher, in his own language, his speech being interpreted by Mr. Buzzacott. He is a modest, sensible, and intelligent man, and gives a favorable idea of the native agency now so extensively employed by the Missionaries.

Considerable interest has been awakened by these various services, and collections to aid the funds of the London Missionary Society have been made in the several places of worship. A detailed list has not yet been furnished, but the aggregate amount will not, it is hoped, fall short of £250 or £300. Besides the money contributions much has been done in furnishing clothing for the Mission families, the Native Teachers and their wives, and the Christian islanders generally. One lady has collected and sent packages to the extent of three tons (by measurement), and others have despatched large boxes. These articles are extremely useful to the natives, and are much prized.

The missionary party (except Mr. Buzzacott and Taevae) sailed in the steamer on the 21st April for Sydney, where the missionary barque " John Williams " waits to convey them to their destination.

Mr. Buzzacott remains behind in Victoria a little longer, in order to visit the interior towns with a view to stir up zeal on behalf of Missions.

WANT OF MISSIONARIES IN THE SOUTH SEAS.

The following extract from a letter written by the Rev. William Gill, missionary at the Island of Mangaia, to his brother Mr. Edwin Gill, of Malmsbury, Victoria, and communicated by the latter to the Rev. A. Morison, is worthy of serious attention :—

"We are expecting to go to Raratonga next year to occupy Mr. George Gill's place, that is, if nobody comes out. I am very sorry for our people. I love Mangaia. Alas! for my people, to be left simply in charge of native teachers! God have pity upon *his* people! For it does not seem as if our society could, or they would have re-inforced our mission long ago. I would that a board of Congregational and Presbyterian ministers could be constituted in the colonies, with the sanction and under the auspices of that in London, for the ordination of suitable young men and their dedication to the work in the Islands. Something *must* be done, or the South Sea Missions, eastward, westward, and northward, are all lost. *This* Mission, and the westward (*i. e.* New Hebrides) Missions, are all alike,—no European Missionaries to direct and sustain our native evangelists, who will not, *cannot* do *alone.*"

The gentleman to whom this earnest and pathetic letter was written suggests that it should appear in our pages, that the attention of the churches may be called to the subject. It is obvious that the directors in England have their hands full, and more than full, with South Africa, India, and China. The openings all at once and so suddenly made into those vast regions, the millions upon millions of people that inhabit them, and the loud calls to reinforce the Missionary staffs who are making preparations to go in and possess them for Christ, altogether constitute an exigency extremely embarrassing to a directory with limited means both of money and men. The danger therefore is imminent of the first and favorite field of the London Missionary Society's operations, the scene of its earliest and greatest triumphs, and now in a more hopeful state of religious improvement and progress than ever, being forgotten and neglected from the pressure of what appear to be more urgent demands. Is not this a call in Providence upon the friends and supporters of the London Missionary Society, and all Christains who approve of and are willing to work upon its fundamental principles, to take charge of these missions themselves, and thus relieve the Society at home of the burden? The Wesleyans have done so with their South Sea Missions; might not we do the same with ours? EDITOR.

SAMOAN MISSION SEMINARY FOR NATIVE TEACHERS.

In a Mission such as ours, which employs in Samoa alone a native agency of about two hundred, the annual demand for fresh teachers is necessarily considerable. Our limited number of missionaries, failure of health, and other causes, have, during the past year, made an unusual demand on the Institution. We have not been able, in all cases, to respond to applications as efficiently as we could have wished ; still we are glad to report that we have sent out in the course of the year *twenty-three* young men, in whose piety we have confidence, and whose usefulness, we trust, will, under God's blessing, prove that our confidence in them has net been misplaced. Two have been dismissed. Two have retired, the one on account of sickness, and the other unqualified. The places of all have been filled up, and with the addition of nine young men from the youths' class, who have been admitted to the church, and are preparing for the work of the ministry, the number of young men now in the Institution is *sixty-eight*. Natives from Nengone, Fate, Tokelau, and Savage Island, to the number of eight, who were with us last year, have been taken home in the "John Williams" to their respective lands. Of this class of strangers, we have now five natives of Savage Island, and one from Fate, of the New Hebrides.

The wives of the teachers number *forty-eight*, and, with hardly a single exception, show as much anxiety as their husbands to acquire all the knowledge they can while they are on the premises, to prepare them for conducting classes with the women and girls, and also special classes for mothers wherever they may be located.

The youths' class, including natives from the westward islands, and the elder sons of the teachers in the Institution numbers *forty-three*.

During the year, the attention of the young men has been, as usual, principally directed to Scripture history, Scripture exposition, and pastoral duties, as the great essentials, under God's blessing, of making them useful ministers of the Gospel of Christ. In Scripture exposition, we have finished the Gospel of Matthew since last Report, and are now lecturing through the book of Psalms. In the course of the year the young men have received and copied, in connection with their class duties, Scripture comments and lectures, amounting to four hundred and forty-five pages. Being, for the present, without a fellow-tutor, we cannot do as much as we could wish to Arithmetic, Geography, Natural Philosophy, Natural History, and the English language. Still, we have endeavoured to keep up regularly four classes a week, for the special purpose of attending to these minor, yet not to-be neglected, departments in the training of native pastors and teachers.

The industrial day—every Wednesday, has been devoted during the year, to sawing, fencing, weather-boarding, and other necessary employments to keep the premises in repair; and, as usual, all devote, on an average an hour every morning at sunrise to their plantations.

We have still the pleasure of reporting favourably of the uniform good conduct of the members of the Institution. There are some exceptions, but remarkably few, considering the number assembled from all parts of the group. The marked respect and gratitude which they shew to Mrs. Turner and myself are very grateful to our feelings, and tend much to lighten our burden, and cheer us in our work. It is the same with those who have been with us in past years. We have often letters from them full of affectionate remembrance and expressions of gratitude, which we consider ample returns for all the pains we took in instructing them.

It is worthy of special remark in our present report, that among other friends who are interested in our Institution, the Sabbath-schools in connection with the Rev. F. Miller's church and congregation, Hobart Town, have come forward, and promised to supply us annually with whatever articles we please to order to the amount of £40 or £50. We feel grateful to these dear children, and also to the missionary-spirited men who are their teachers. This efficient aid, with the occasional help which we receive from other quarters, will amply meet our current expenses, and save our drawing further on the funds of the London Missionary Society for the support of the Institution.

Our expenditure during the year for tools, stationery, and a suit of clothes for *two hundred and forty-eight* men, women, and children, amounts to *fifty pounds ;* and the entire number now in the Institution is *two hundred and fifty-three.*

Malua, Sept. 1858. GEORGE TURNER.

CHINA.
PROPOSED MISSIONARY CONFERENCE.

We have received from the Rev. Dr. Wentworth, a well-known missionary of the Methodist Episcopal Church, the following letter on the subject of the meeting of a great Missionary Conference. It will be observed that his scheme is a large one, involving the attendance of representative men from all the churches of Europe and America. We do not feel ourselves in a position to express a decided opinion. We willingly, however, publish the letter, as the time may come, if not already present, when the carrying out of such a plan may be highly beneficial :—

FUH-CHAU, CHINA, Sept. 28, 1858.

I have a proposition to submit, through your valuable paper, to the Christian public of Great Britain, and, indeed, to the evangelical promoters of Christian missions throughout the world. It is that a convention of the friends of missions, and the directors of missionary societies, both in Europe and America, assemble, by delegation or otherwise, to devise ways and means for the further-of the Gospel in India and China at this present juncture. The moment is favourable. The four great powers of the globe are awaiting the signatures of treaties with China,* alike favourable to commerce and religion. Each of them contains an article expressly guaranteeing the toleration of the Christian religion, and provision is made for the safe progress of the teachers of that religion, under a system of passports, through any and every province in the empire. Five new ports immediately, and nine more ultimately, in addition to thsee already open, are to be made accessible to commerce and foreign residenoc. The French treaty not only contains an article guaranteeing free toleration of religion, but also one abrogating all former acts and edicts of the Government against Christianity and its advocates, in all the provinces of the empire ; by which it is understood that all acts of confiscation under former reigns may be rendered null and void ; and that thus the Roman Catholics will not only come into the enjoyment of the right to travel and preach in common with Protestants, but also of the possession of numerous churches, lots of land and other property, owned and lost by them in the persecutions of former days. Protestants may well conceive what an immense advantage will instantly accrue to Rome on the adoption of this treaty, and may rest assured that she will not fail to profit by it to the full extent of her consummate policy and ability. Under these circumstances, what is the duty of the Protestant world ? Clearly, *to call a delegated convention of all the missionary societies in Europe and America, and map out the eighteen provinces of China and the adjacent islands for immediate occupancy.* I say *map out,* because I believe it will better secure the occupancy of the *entire territory.* Let the London Missionary Society choose, or have assigned to it, its province or field of labour, the Church Missionary Society have another, the American Board another, the Wesleyans another, the Methodist Episcopal Church one, the M. E. Church South another, the Presbyterians another, and so on till *all* are allotted, *all* manned, and *all* under Christian culture.

India demands similar treatment. The terrible storm that has swept flourishing mission establishments from the face of several of the provinces is allayed. India will be a safe and successful field to work in for a century to come. It should be *all* occupied, and how can this be done better than by convention and

---

* These treaties have since been ratified.

mutual agreement? This is an age of wonderful achievements. Protestant Christianity should not be behind the age in grand conceptions, and fearless execution of undertakings as stupendous as the building of Great Easterns, and the submerging of Atlantic Telegraphs.

                       Very truly yours, ERASTUS WENTWORTH.

—*News of the Churches.*

RELIGIOUS INTELLIGENCE.

THE REV. THOMAS BINNEY IN SYDNEY.—After an absence of about nine months Mr. Binney has returned to Sydney to fulfil engagements which, on his previous visit, he was obliged to postpone in consequence of having to leave for Melbourne sooner than he anticipated. During his absence he has visited South Australia, Victoria, and Tasmania. To each of the two former he devoted three months; travelling and preaching in all directions, visiting the churches of his own denomination, but officiating also for other bodies, and aiding by his advocacy religious societies and general benevolent institutions. In Tasmania he was only able to stay three weeks, being obliged to leave unexpectedly, but with the promise and purpose to return, if possible. When he first arrived in Sydney he was in a very enfeebled state of health—he appeared to have derived little or no advantage from the voyage, but during his stay here his strength was so materially restored, that he was enabled to undertake many important public services. His sojourn in the other colonies completed what this began, and as health improved labours multiplied. His visit to South Australia gave rise to what has been called the "Adelaide Correspondence," which originated with the Bishop and has been read with interest not only in all the Australian colonies, but in the Old Land. When in Tasmania, Mr. Binney was invited to preside at the meeting of its Congregational Union, and availed himself of the opportunity of delivering an address, in which he examined and discussed the Bishop of Adelaide's scheme for an union of all Protestant Evangelical Denominations, as enunciated in the Bishop's letter to himself. This address (or "charge," as the local newspapers called it, making the speaker a bishop for the occasion!) is to be published, with the more important portions of the "Adelaide Correspondence." The circumstances, however, which obliged Mr. B. to leave Tasmania when about to prepare it for the press, will unfortunately occasion some delay in its appearance. During the reverend gentleman's present residence in Sydney it is hoped that he will be able not only to serve his own but kindred denominations, and to visit other important towns in the colony. The members of the Congregational body, to which Mr. B. belongs, have derived so much advantage from his visit (in various ways), and still feel that so much remains to be done which he may be instrumental in accomplishing, that they are willing to believe his friends in England will not grudge their wish to detain him a month or two longer in lands in which they have always felt a great interest, and in which, when he has once left, it is too certain, he will never be seen again. It has been, we understand, the wish of many that he could have been prevailed upon to spend a year or two more amongst us—three or four months at a time in each of our colonies; but any such plan is, we are told, utterly hopeless. After fulfilling such engagements as may appear to himself important or desirable, he will return to England, taking his departure by the overland route some time in the course of the winter.

    THE REV. T. JOHNSON, late of Hinckley, Leicestershire, one of the ministers sent out by the Colonial Missionary Society, through Rev. J. L. Poore's agency, has just arrived at Melbourne by the *Prince of the Seas*. The following account of the farewell services, on his leaving Hinckley, is taken from the *Patriot*:—The Corn Exchange of this town was, on Tuesday week, the scene of a gathering to which a painful interest attached. The Rev. Thomas Johnson, who has for the past five years presided over the Independent Church at Stockwell-Head, and whose ministry there has been very successful, has bidden adieu to the people of his charge. The Colonial Missionary Society solicited him to occupy one of the important spheres of labour in Australia, with which request, after consultation with ministerial brethren, he has considered it his duty to comply. The Rev. T. Mays, of Ashby-de-la-Zouch, was unanimously voted to the chair, and the Rev. Robert Massie, of Atherstone, offered a short prayer. Mr. Mays said that he had known Mr. Johnson for upwards of twenty-three years; and that, having been his pastor at Wigston Magna, and counsellor upon his entering the ministry of the Gospel, he felt a peculiar interest in his movements. Although it might be painful to many of the present assembly, he must say that he thought that his friend, Mr. Johnson, had acted right in deciding to resign his present charge for a sphere of labour in Australia. Some one hundred and twenty-eight years ago a party walked down the streets of Wigston, having been cast out on the ground of Nonconformist principles. One of the company was carrying a pulpit—and that man was a Johnson—there were at this present moment three Johnsons in the assembly, descendants of the same man, and their pastor, as one of them, was not unworthy of being upon the honoured roll. The Rev. R. W. McAll, of Leicester, expressed himself as opposed to Mr. Johnson's saving; but seeing that it must be, he trusted that all usefulness would be granted to him in his new sphere of labour. T. Nunneley, Esq., of Leicester, delivered a serious address to the people upon the separation now taking place between pastor and flock. The Rev. W. Woods, of Harney-lane, Leicester, and the Rev. T. Burgess, of Tamworth, both gave expression to much kind feeling on the occasion, the latter of whom will be Mr. Johnson's successor. Mr. Simpson, one of the Hinckley congregation, then in an affectionate address presented to his pastor, on behalf of the friends at Hinckley and Tamworth, as well as in other parts of the country, 54 volumes of "Clark's Foreign Theological Library," as a small and feeble expression of their affection and regret upon the separation now taking place betwixt them as pastor and people. A handsome china tea service was then presented to Mrs. Johnson with the best wishes of the contributors. Mr. Kiddle, as one of the choir, presented Mr. Johnson with a handsomely bound volume of music, as an expression of gratitude for the warm interest he had ever shown in their peculiar department. The Rev. T. Johnson feelingly replied. He assured them of his affection, though about to be separated from them, and that he would never forget his friends in Hinckley, who had from the first to the last of his intercourse amongst them shown him nothing but kindness. Other ministers of the town, the Revs. E. Toyne and Burgess of the Wesleyan, Shaw of the Primitive Methodist, and Parkinson of the Baptist denominations, also expressed their fraternal regard towards Mr. Johnson: and the Rev. Robert Massie, of Atherstone, added his emphatic testimony to Mr. Johnson's worth, and to the usefulness of his friend in his sphere at home, which was the best proof of his suitableness for the work assigned him abroad. The usual votes of thanks having been given, the benediction was pronounced, and the meeting dispersed.

CONGREGATIONALISTS.—MOUNT CLEAR, NEAR BALLAARAT.—On Wednesday, March 16, Mr. Potter was ordained pastor of the Union Church of Baptists and Independents, Mount Clear. The following ministers were present :—Revs. K. Johnston, Melbourne; Strongman, Lind, Sutton, Bradney, and Niquet, of Ballaarat; and E. Day, Castlemaine. Mr. Johnson preached the introductory discourse. The Rev. W. A. Lind read the invitation of the church, and the reply of Mr. Potter accepting the invitation; he also asked the questions usual upon these occasions. After suitable replies were given to these questions, the ordination prayer was offered by Mr. Johnston, and the services concluded with an address to the pastor and people on their mutual duties. The building in which Mr. Potter is to officiate has been lately erected, and is capable of accommodating about 120 or 130 people. It is a very neat unpretending structure, and is situated about midway between Ballaarat and Buninyong, the cost of which has, within a few pounds, been defrayed.

PORTLAND CONGREGATIONAL CHURCH.—On Lord's day, March 20th, the Rev. J. L Poore preached two excellent sermons in the above place of worship. The morning discourse was founded on St. Luke x. 24.; the evening, on Eccl. xi. 1. The attendance was numerous and the collections liberal. On the 22nd, a tea and public meeting was held in the Free Church building, kindly lent for the occasion. A few friends generously gave the tea and all incidental expenses, in aid of the building fund. J. N. McLeod, Esq., presided at the meeting. The Rev. M. McInnes offered prayer. After the secretary's brief statement, the Rev. J. Sleigh in few words reviewed his labors since his arrival at Portland in January, 1858. The Rev. S. Kelso, Presbyterian, then gave an appropriate address. The Rev. J. L. Poore characterised Congregationalism, stated the efforts made to supply the spiritual wants of these colonies by the Colonial Missionary Society, London, in conjunction with zealous Christians at Melbourne and throughout Australia. He congratulated Mr. Sleigh and his flock on what had been accomplished, and urged the meeting to wipe off the remaining debt on the building. Thanks to the chairman, and for the use of the room, with prayer, concluded the meeting. The following are the financial particulars, exclusive of the debt on the land :— The cost of the building for the Congregational Church was £393 2s., and after defraying the incidental expenses of the year, which amounted to £95, the balance was £148 13s. 2d., the collections on Sunday, together with the profits of the tea and subscriptions promised at the meeting, amount to £123 17s. 9d., leaving a balance of little more than £25. On the 23rd, the children of the Congregational Sabbath-school took tea in the chapel with their teachers and friends. A meeting was afterwards held and addressed by the Revds. J. Sleigh, J. L. Poore, and several of the teachers.

LONSDALE-STREET, MELBOURNE.—The ninth anniversary services connected with this Church, were held on the 10th instant, when suitable and instructive discourses were delivered by the Rev. J. C. M'Michael, of Geelong. On Tuesday, the 12th instant, the annual meeting of the congregation was held in the school-room. After tea, prayer was offered by the Rev. A. Morison. The Hon George Harker was called to the chair, and in the course of his opening address stated that, although not partial to tea-meetings, he felt himself called upon (if desired) to be present, and preside at meetings of the kind connected with the congregation with which he had so long worshipped. The report, which was encouraging, was read by

R. C. Dunn. Esq., the Secretary. From the Treasurer's Report, it appeared that there had been raised by the congregation during the past year—

For the Building Fund £295 1 8	Foreign missions...	14 16 10
By weekly collections 486 18 10	For Hospital	44 6 0
By donation from one member of	City Mission	40 4 0
the congregation 35 0 0	Sunday school	28 12 11
Tickets, &c. 15 19 5		
Ordinance collections 21 5 2		£982 4 10

In addition to this, it was stated sums had been subscribed to other objects, besides £60 for purposes of private benevolence; and as a balance of about £200 was due to the Treasurer, chiefly expended in building purposes, upwards of £130 had been subscribed, or promised, for its liquidation, the balance being hoped for as the result of sale of tickets and collections connected with the anniversary services. The meeting was then suitably addressed by the Revs. H. Thomas, B.A., R. Fletcher, W. R. Lewis, A. Scales, W. Jarrett, T. O'dell (the pastor) and H. Langlands, Esq., M.L.A., and closed by devotional services The attendance was good.

PRAHRAN INDEPENDENT CHURCH.—The opening services of the new Independent Church, Commercial Road, Prahran, were commenced on Lord's Day, April 10th. A prayer-meeting was held in the morning, which was well attended. During the day, three sermons were preached by the Revs. J. L. Poore, D. J. Draper, and James Ballantyne. The church' morning and evening, was crowded, every available space being occupied. The services were resumed on Lord's Day, 17th. The Rev. W. B. Landells preached in the morning, and the Rev. James Taylor in the afternoon. The Rev. Thomas Odell was expected to preach in the evening, but was prevented by sudden illness, and the Rev. W. Jarrett kindly took his place. On Tuesday evening, 19th, a Public Tea Meeting was held in the old chapel and school-rooms,— between four and five hundred persons were in attendance. After tea the meeting adjourned to the new church, which was soon crowded. The devotional exercises were conducted by the Rev. W. Moss, pastor, and the Rev James Mirams. F. Haller, Esq., occupied the chair. The meeting was addressed by the Revs. I. New, H. Thomas, J. P. Sunderland, R. Fletcher, and W. R. Lewis and Mr. Vetch, late of New College, London; and by R. Smith, J. Browning, T. Dickson, G. Rolf, and J. Craven, Esqs. The Revs. T. James, Wesleyan minister, W. Jarrett, W. B. Landells, James Ballantyne, and G. Divorty were also present. The following ministers, who were expected to take part in the proceedings, were unavoidably absent:—Revs. J. L. Poore, T. Odell, James M'Gaw, James Taylor, W. R. Robinson, and John Ballantyne. The Report of the Building Committee was read by Mr. W. Green, sen., from which we make the following extracts:—The memorial stone was laid on November 2nd, last, by His Excellency Sir H. Barkly. The Rev. Thomas Binney was also present, and delivered an address. In the evening a Tea Meeting was held, at which the late Thomas Fulton, Esq., presided. To the ladies of the congregation the Committee tendered their warmest thanks for their exertions in collecting subscriptions, and (on the occasion alluded to) supplying the tea free of cost; also to Messrs. Craven and Joseph, who stained and varnished the whole of the pews. The following is the balance sheet :—

Total cost of land, building, fittings, &c. £3,140	Obtained by subscriptions and collections	1,270
	Mortgage	1,500
	Balance	£370
£3,140		£3140

An effort to remove the floating debt, £370, was then made, and the collections, together with promises to collect in three months, amounted to £249, leaving a balance of £121. The meeting closed with the doxology, and prayer by Rev. B. Lemmon. The following is a brief description of the building:—Style, Gothic; dimensions in the clear—length, 70 feet; width, 40 feet; height from floor to ridge of open roof, 47 feet. The floor has a slight inclination towards the pulpit, and the side-seats are placed at an acute angle with the walls. The roof is in part supported by ornamental timber columns, finished with rich composition capitals, from which spring carved ribs longitudinally and across the nave, forming at once a very strongly-framed roof, and adding very greatly to the effect of the interior. The church will comfortably accommodate 500 persons. The external appearance of the edifice, though unfinished, is exceedingly neat. On the principal elevation there is a large geometrical three-light window, and two octagonal turrets rising to the height of 60 feet. On the east side there is an ornamental porch. When completed, there will be at the north-west angle a chaste tower and broach spire rising to the height of 105 feet, and finished with an ornamental vane. It is a very handsome structure, and reflects great credit on Messrs. Crouch and Wilson, its architects.

MARYBOROUGH.—A public tea meeting, in connection with the Congregational Church, was held in the Freemasons' Hall, Maryborough, on Thursday evening, 14th April. Its object was to give a welcome to the Rev. John Hill. There was a numerous attendance. On the removal of the tables, the room was filled by a large and attentive audience. Mr. Peter Virtue was unanimously called to the chair, and opened the proceedings by a few appropriate remarks, tendering to the Rev. Mr. Hill, on behalf of the meeting, a warm and cordial welcome to Maryborough. The Rev. Mr. Hill, who was greeted with acclamation, stated, he regretted that all the reverend gentlemen who had been expected to address the meeting, had been from various causes prevented from being present, and proceeded to read letters of apology. One from the Rev. Mr. Fletcher, of St. Kilda, informing him that the Rev. J. L. Poore had met with an accident, by which his collar-bone had been broken, so that, although he was progressing favorably, it was impossible for him to be present. Also letters from the Revs. Messrs. Day and Beer. Mr. Hill continued, that of course the whole work, by their absence, being thrown upon his shoulders, he would endeavour to do his best. The rev. gentleman then spoke at considerable length, giving a narrative of the feelings entertained at home in regard to all that concerned this rising colony, and his own motive for coming out. He described his overland journey with such useful reflections as it suggested. He then entered into the distinguishing features of Congregationalism, and concluded a long address, which was listened to throughout with marked attenton by all present. Mr. M'Landress proposed a vote of thanks to the ladies who had presided at the tea tables, which being seconded by Mr. Kerr, was carried by acclamation. After a vote of thanks to the chair, the meeting separated, all apparently well satisfied with the pleasant manner in which the evening had been spent.

McKILLOP-STREET CONGREGATIONAL CHURCH, GEELONG.—*Recognition Service.*—A meeting was held on Wednesday evening, April 27th, to recognise the Rev. J. C. McMichael as pastor of this Church, and to welcome him to his sphere of labour. Tea was provided. The meeting was presided over by Mr. Allen, one of the deacons. Prayer was offered by the Rev. B. Cuzens. The chairman gave a brief account of the history of the church and of the measures taken to procure a pastor, which had resulted in Mr. McMichael's settlement among them. Mr. McMichael related the manner in which he had been asked to come out to Australia, and the circumstances which had induced him to accede to the request. After preaching two months at McKillop-street, the church had given him a unanimous invitation to assume the pastorship, which invitation he had accepted. He gave a simple, earnest, and interesting statement of his feelings, views, and purposes, in relation to his new and important sphere of labor. The Rev. J. L. Poore, through whose agency Mr. M. was sent out, was to have been present at the meeting and taken a prominent part in its proceedings, but an accident, which confined him to the house, compelled him, much to his regret and to the disappointment of the meeting, to be absent. The Rev. R. Fletcher of St. Kilda cordially welcomed Mr. M. to Australia. He stated that he had known him from his childhood and was well acquainted with every step in his career. He expressed his belief in Mr. M.'s peculiar adaptedness to the position assigned to him, and his hope that he would prove eminently useful to Geelong and to the colony at large. Mr. F. also adverted to the past history of the church at McKillop-street, its difficulties and perplexities, and his hope that the things which had happened to it would turn out rather to the furtherance of the Gospel. There were present at the meeting :— the Revds. Messrs. Henderson, Presbyterian ; Symonds and Hill, Wesleyans ; Dr. Brough, Episcopalian ; and B. Cuzens, J. Apperley, and Mr. Pausey, Independents, most of whom briefly addressed the meeting. Apologies for the unavoidable absence of the Revds. Messrs. Tait and Love were given. The meeting was largely attended and deeply interested. Nearly £200 is about to be expended in completing and improving the capacious chapel, which is one of the best Congregational places of worship in Victoria.

IPSWICH, NEW SOUTH WALES.—The fourth anniversary of the Congregational Church was celebrated on Sabbath, March 13, when two sermons were preached by the Rev. J. T. Waraker, pastor. A social meeting was held on Tuesday, 15th March, and largely attended. The report, read by Mr. Whitehead, one of the deacons, contained several interesting items. The state of the schools is encouraging. In the central schools the number of scholars is 120, teachers 14. Three branch schools are also well attended. In aid of the various schools, £25 9s. 11d. had been contributed ; of this sum upwards of £20 had been expended on books. The church and congregation were in a prosperous state. The financial statement, read by Dr. Chullinor, showed that upwards of £400 had been collected for religious and educational purposes during the year. Addresses were delivered by Revs. T. Deacon and G. Wight. On the following evening, the Rev. G. Wight delivered a lecture to a numerous and attentive audience, on " Religion a life, not a profession." The anniversary services realised about £30.

BALMAIN.—The recognition service in connexion with the settlement of the Rev. Thomas Arnold, as the pastor of the above church, was held on Thursday evening, the 7th April. The devotional parts of the service were conducted by the Rev. Messrs. Slayter, Cuthbertson, Beazley, and Kent. The reasons for leaving England and coming to this colony for the purpose of becoming the minister of that place of worship, and his intentions as to the future, were clearly stated by Mr. Arnold. The Rev. Thomas Binney then delivered an address, dividing it into two parts,—the first portion being advice and counsel to the minister, founded upon the words of St. Peter, 1st epistle, 5th chapter, the first four verses ; and the latter to the church and congregation, from Philippians, 2nd chapter, 14—16 verses, defining their duties and obligations. The entire discourse was a truly masculine and apostolical one, and was listened to with intense interest by a large and respectable audience. After this service a tea meeting was held in a large marquee tastefully decorated for the occasion, which was followed by a public meeting, presided over by the Rev. Thomas Binney. Speeches were delivered by the chairman, and by the above-named gentlemen. Mr. Mullens laid a statement of the financial condition of the church before the meeting and propounded a plan, suggested by Mr. Fairfax, by which it was hoped the whole might be paid off. The debt upon the church, amounting to £3000, was the chief topic of consideration, and, after several gentlemen had spoken specially to the desirableness of its entire liquidation, subscriptions were entered into—the collection for the most part extending over three years—to the amount of nearly £2,400. The residue it was hoped would be supplied by friends who were unable to be present.

CAMPBELLTOWN, NEW SOUTH WALES.—A public tea meeting was held at Campbelltown, by the Congregationalists and their friends, on Tuesday, 15th April, in connexion with the settlement of the Rev. John Gibson as pastor. About 300 people were present. The Hon. David Jones, M.L.C., occupied the chair. Addresses were delivered by the Revs. J. Robinson, T. Arnold, and T. Gibson, and by Messrs. John Row, Kendall, and Booking. On the following afternoon, the children of the Sabbath School were entertained by their teachers. About 120 were present.

COLONIAL MISSIONARY SOCIETY, HOBART TOWN.—The annual public meeting of the Congregational Colonial Missionary Society, was held in the Congregational Church, Davey-street, on Monday evening. Henry Hopkins, Esq., in the chair. The report showed that the Rev. W. Shippherd, who has recently arrived from England, has been appointed as minister at Pontville, where a chapel has been erected. The receipts of the society during the year were £526 7s. 7d.; and there was a balance due to the treasurer of £33 11s. 9d. The meeting was addressed by the Revs. T. Binney of London, J. Nisbett, Shippherd, and G. Clarke.

BRISBANE-STREET CONGREGATIONAL CHAPEL, HOBART TOWN.—The anniversary services in connexion with the Sunday-schools were held on Sunday, April 10, when sermons were preached by the Revs. J. Cope and J. G. M'Intosh, and the Rev. F. Miller addressed the children. The usual tea meeting took place in the chapel on Monday. From the report read we extract the following:—It noticed the necessity of Sabbath-school teachers endeavoring to prepare themselves to give a higher order of instruction than that previously given in such schools. Teachers were wanted who could convey to their pupils the living truths of Christ in their most attractive form—men who, with their own hearts filled with the love of Christ, burnt with a holy desire that His love should be felt and shared by others. It was also recommended that the teachers should meet and study together the lessons which they intended to give to the scholars. During the past year the sum of £25 had been contributed by the Brisbane-street schools to the Missionary Native School at Samoa. In the three schools there were 472 children and 45 teachers. During the past year the committee and teachers agreed to contribute annually the amount required for the support of the Native Missionary Training Institution at Samoa, at an annual cost of £50; and the second contribution, consisting of stationery, clothing, tools, &c., had been forwarded by the Tasmania on her last trip to Sydney, with a view to being shipped on board the John Williams, missionary ship, for Samoa. The total sum contributed during the year by the three schools for the support of the Samoan Institution amounted to £57 16s. 4d. A very interesting letter had been received from the young men training for native missionaries, and a large case, containing specimens of native manufacture, canoes, and various native implements, had been forwarded to the Sabbath-schools from Samoa. These articles had been manufactured by the young people in the Samoan school, and had been forwarded as a token of gratitude to the three schools. It was proposed by the committee that these interesting articles should form the nucleus of a Sabbath-school Museum.

GAWLER CONGREGATIONAL CHAPEL, SOUTH AUSTRALIA.—The anniversary services of this place of worship were held on Sunday and Monday, the 14th and 15th November last, as follows:—On Sunday two excellent discourses were delivered in the Free Presbyterian Church, by the Rev. W. Wilson, of Hindmarsh; and on Monday a public tea meeting took place in St. George's Schoolroom, and a public meeting afterwards in the Free Church, on which accasion Mr. T. Reynolds, M.P., presided, and the Revs. G. D. Mudie, T. Ayling, T. Hannay, T. W. Charlesworth. S. Keen, T. Howie, T. Counter, W. Wilson, and T. Leonard, and Messrs. W. Peacock and W. Duffield severally spoke. Votes of thanks were cordially passed to the ladies who had so liberally provided the tea; to Mr. L. S. Burton for the use of the schoolroom for the tea; to the trustees and friends of the Free Church, for the use of their place of worship for both the services of Sunday and for the public meeting; and to the chairman for his kind and efficient presidence on that occasion. The above services were well attended, and it is hoped proved both interesting and edifying to many. The object of these services this year (which object was first introduced to the public by the Rev. T. Binney, on the occasion of his visit to Gawler) being more especially the enlargement of the Congregational Chapel in this town, the resolutions and addresses at the public meeting were framed with reference thereto, and were cordially received and responded to by the meeting. The proceeds of these services amounted to upwards of £40, which, added to the donations and promises already received towards the proposed enlargement, make a total of upwards of £200.

KENSINGTON, SOUTH AUSTRALIA.—On Sunday, March 13, the worship of the congregation assembled in Clayton Chapel, Kensington, was suspended for a few minutes by a circumstance pleasing, it is believed, to all present. Mr. Bruce, one of the deacons, read to the people the invitation which had been given to the Rev. Mr. Drane. He then read the answer, accepting that invitation. Both the call and the response were frank and cordial.

GLENELG, SOUTH AUSTRALIA.—A new Independent Chapel is about to be erected at Glenelg, the old building having been found, since the arrival of the Rev. C. E. Palmer, entirely inadequate to its intended purpose. Mr. Palmer, who was formerly settled at Warrington, in Lancashire, has been stationed at Glenelg during the last three months, and, as may be inferred from the above statement, the congregation has increased under his ministry to a very great extent. The site chosen for the new building is on the south side of the Jetty road, immediately opposite to the end of Nile-street. The chapel, for which tenders have been invited, will be built in the Gothic style of architecture, from a very beautiful design by Mr. James Macgeorge, of Adelaide, and, when completed, will form a great ornament to the neighbourhood.

PRESBYTERIANS.—The great event among the Presbyterians of Victoria, during the past month, has been the consummation of the UNION of the Old Kirk, the Free Church, and the United Presbyterians into one body, with the exception of a portion of each of the two latter Synods, who have not yet seen their way clear to join the new organization. Preparations for this Union have been for some time going on. Resolutions favorable to it were passed in each of the Synods, and the matter was then referred to the congregations separately. The next step was to procure the introduction of a bill into the Victorian Legislature to give permission to any congregation, desirous of joining the Union, to alter the Trusts of their church property so as to be in harmony with their new position. This bill became law. All this being done, the Synods of the Church of Scotland and of the Free Church, and the two Synods into which the United Presbyterians had formed themselves, severally passed definite resolutions to join the Union. On Wednesday, April 6th, a conference of these Synods was held in Rev. J. Hotherington's church Melbourne, the Rev. James Ballantyne in the chair. The Rev. Mr. Tait, of Geelong, read the minutes of what had been transacted at the separate meetings of the committees of each of the Synods, previous to the present Conference. From these it appeared that each of the four bodies, viz., the Church of Scotland, the Free Church, the United Presbyterian Church of Australia, and the United Presbyterian Church of Victoria, had pronounced in favor of the proposed Union. The Rev. Mr. Hetherington, as convener of the conference, then read the report of the Union committee, and congratulated the meeting upon the Union that was about to be accomplished. The moderators of the four Synods reported that the latter bodies had determined to enter the Union, three of them unanimously, and the fourth—the United Presbyterian Church of Victoria—by a majority. The report of the Committee on the proposed arrangements for consummating the Union was adopted, and the formula to be signed by all the members of the various Synods on entering the Union, was agreed upon. On Thursday afternoon, April 7th, the ministers, elders, and a large congregation assembled in Collins-street church, to ratify the terms of the Union agreed upon by the conference on Wednesday evening. After devotional services, the different Synod clerks read the minutes of their respective Synods concurring in the Union. On the motion of the Rev. Mr. Story, seconded by the Rev. Mr. Nish, the Rev. Mr. Clow was elected moderator of the new Synod. After devoutly invoking the blessing of God upon the united Synod of Victoria, the moderator addressed the Assembly, and afterwards read the basis of Union, to which sixty ministers and elders appended their signatures. The Lord's supper was then administered, Dr. Cairns presiding. In the evening a very large congregation met in the Exhibition building. After devotional services, conducted by the Rev. I. Hetherington, the moderator addressed the large assembly in a very impressive manner. He had witnessed many changes in the colony during his residence of twenty years, and many great events had taken place, but the Union now consummated, he considered the most important of all. The Rev. Dr. Cairns spoke at great length, and was followed by D. Ogilvie, Esq., and by the Revds. W. Jarrett, James Ballantyne, and A. McNichol. The 122nd Psalm was then sung, after which the moderator pronounced the benediction, and the meeting separated. And thus terminated this movement, replete with important issues to the future of Evangelical religion in these colonies. The reasons assigned by that portion of the United Presbyterians who have declined at present to join the new Synod are twofold; first, its complicity in the question of State Aid to religion, as many of its members are recipients of such aid; and secondly, its reception of certain parties into its body on whom they allege acts of suspension and excision are now resting. It is to be hoped, however, that circumstances, in the providence of God, will soon occur, which, without any sacrifice of principle, may lead to a re-union of those now severed, and the blending of all the scattered fragments of the great Presbyterian denomination into a compact whole. The State Aid objection is fully and clearly set forth in the following resolutions, unanimously passed at a meeting of the church in Collins-street, of which the Rev. A. M. Ramsay is the respected pastor, held on the evening of Wednesday, March 22rd, Alexander Cairns, Esq., in the chair :—1. "That this congregation, at its commencement in 1845, and when regularly organised as a Presbyterian church in 1847, under the ministry of the present pastor (the Rev. A. M. Ramsay), was founded on the principle that all State connection and support was unscriptural, derogatory to the honor of the Christian ministry, calculated to affect the independence of the Church of Christ, and detrimental to the interests of true religion ; and that, by the good hand of God upon pastor and people, the congregation has been enabled to preserve that fundamental principle, intact and inviolate." 2. "That this congregation has ever been ready to sympathise and co-operate with other evangelical churches in all general movements for the extension of the Gospel and the moral advancement of the people; that, in common with many sincere Christians, the congregation has lamented the divided state of the Presbyterian Churches in this colony, and that a general Presbyterian union, based on common and scriptural grounds, pursued in a Christian spirit, and regularly and constitutionally effected, would be hailed as an event of the happiest kind, and fraught with incalculable benefit to the interests, not only of Presbyterianism, but of our common Christianity." 3.

"That this congregation regards State-aid as the great, if not the sole, barrier to Presbyterian union in this colony, and that while it continues to be received by any of the Presbyterian Churches, no satisfactory Presbyterian union can be maintained." 4. That this congregation, having had before it the Act recently passed by the Legislature, intituled 'An Act,' &c., and also the basis of union thereto annexed, and having duly considered the same, finds that it leaves the question of State-aid undisposed of, and that this congregation could not enter into the projected Union without forming part of a State-aid receiving denomination, and thus violating a fundamental principle of the Church. While, therefore the enormous evil of State-aid continues, this congregation feels that it must occupy a position in which it can testify clearly, conscientiously, and effectively against it."

UNITED PRESBYTERIAN CHURCH, NAPIER-STREET, COLLINGWOOD. — The seventh anniversary of the United Presbyterian Congregation, Napier-street, was celebrated on the evening of Tuesday, March 22nd, by a soirée. The chair was occupied by the Rev. R. Hamilton, the pastor. The meeting was addressed by the Revs. A. M. Ramsay, New, Williams, and Mr. Mollis, Jewish missionary, in able, instructive, and impressive speeches. The chairman gave a brief sketch of the past history of the congregation. The same topic was ably followed up by Mr. Ramsay, who was present at the laying of the foundation stone, more than two years before the present minister entered upon his labours in the place. He gave a prominent place in his address to the *voluntary principle* on which this church was founded and had ever consistently acted, accepting neither money nor land from Government. Mr. New spoke on Divine influence, Mr. Williams on missionary labours in the Figi Islands, and Mr. Mollis on the state of Palestine.

CURZON STREET, NORTH MELBOURNE.—PRESBYTERIAN CHURCH.—On April 8th, the day after the General Union was completed, the foundation stone of this building was laid by His Excellency Sir Henry Barkly in the presence of a large number of the ministers and elders of the newly constituted Synod. In the evening a soirée was held and was largely attended. The church when completed will seat from 700 to 800 worshippers.

ERSKINE CHURCH, LONSDALE-STREET, MELBOURNE.—On Sabbath, April 10th, three sermons were preached at this place of worship, on the occasion of its reopening and anniversary; that in the morning, by the Rev. James Ballantyne; in the afternoon, by the Rev. James Taylor; and in the evening, by the Rev. Dr. Cairns. On Monday evening a public soirée was held, at which were present the Revs. James Ballantyne (who presided), D. MacDonald, John Ballantyne, Seaborn, Moss, Nish, Jarrett, and Taylor. The chairman reviewed the progress of the church since its establishment. After the building was finished, it was found that the roof was in an unsafe condition, and it had to be replaced, which entailed a considerable extra expenditure. The requisite funds were, however, at once readily and cheerfully contributed. Through the liberality of a few Christian friends, a vestry has also been erected. The Rev. chairman alluded to the recent "Union" expressed his gratification thereat, and his opinion that it would be productive of the most glorious results. Several short addresses were delivered. Not the least interesting part of the proceedings was the presentation of a purse of sovereigns and a silver salver to the pastor, by the ladies of his congregation accompanied by an address, expressive of their esteem and respect for him; to which he replied in suitable terms. The meeting was well attended. The collections at the various services amounted to £53.

WESLEYANS.—Three small chapels, adapted to rural neighborhoods, have recently been opened for worship in Tasmania: viz. at Bothwell, on Monday, March 21st., by the Revs. J. Tuckfield, and J. B. Smith; at Hagley, on Sunday, March 27, by the Rev. J. A. Manton; and at Newtown, Tuesday, March 29, by a tea meeting, when S. Crisp, Esq., presided, and the meeting was addressed by the Revs. Messrs. Cope and Lelean, and other gentlemen. At Colac, Victoria, also a neat brick chapel was opened on March 20, by the Revs. D. J. Draper and W. Hill. On the following evening a social meeting was held, when J. Lowe, Esq., presided, and Messrs. Draper, Blair, and others spoke.

UNITED FREE METHODIST CHURCH, ST. KILDA EAST.—On Tuesday, March 29, the foundation stone of a new chapel was laid in Packington-street, St. Kilda east, by Mr. Orr. For some time the United Free Methodists have been holding preaching services in a house lent by a friend. The congregation increasing it was necessary to erect a chapel; and Henry Jennings, Esq., kindly gave the land for the purpose. The chapel is to be built of brick, 30 feet by 26 feet.

EPISCOPALIANS.—PADDINGTON, SYDNEY.—The ceremony of laying the foundation stone of a new church at Paddington was performed by the Bishop of Sydney on Thursday afternoon, March 24. A very large company assembled to witness the proceedings. After devotional services, the Bishop laid the stone in the usual form. After further devotional services, the Bishop addressed the large company, and Mr. Cape one of the trustees, gave a statement in relation to the size and cost of the new church. When finished the building will afford accommodation to 1,040 persons, and is expected to cost £4,200. In the evening a social meeting was held in a large tent, tea being provided by the ladies connected with the church. The Bishop presided, and various gentlemen delivered addresses.

AT DELORAINE, TASMANIA, a new church was opened on March 31st. The attendance was large. Archdeacon Reiley preached, and the Communion was administered.

W. FAIRFAX AND CO., STEAM PRINTERS, COLLINS STREET EAST, MELBOURNE.

The Southern Spectator.

JUNE, 1859.

THE PRESENT STATE OF OUR CHURCHES.

BY THE REV. JOHN ANGELL JAMES.

In my last paper I gave an encouraging and, I believe, a true representation of the excellences of our churches, as manifested by their zeal, activity, and liberality: and a glorious feature of the age it is. But there are dark shadows as well as bright lights on the picture, and I now, therefore, proceed to give a less favorable view of the case, and present for consideration their faults. It is somewhat difficult to form, at any time, a correct estimate of the existing state of religion as compared with some previous periods. And it is well for us all, and always, to remember Solomon's exhortation, "Say not, What is the cause that the former days were better than these? for thou dost not wisely inquire concerning this." (Eccles. vii. 10.) The more eminently pious of every age have been prone to complain of the faults of their own times, and to think them greater than those of bygone periods of the Church's history. We *see* the evils of our own times: we only *read* of those of the men which have gone before us. Dropping, then, for the most part, a comparison of our present state with past times, I shall appeal to the true standard of all spiritual religion, and endeavour by *that* to ascertain our real state.

1. As the first, most prominent, and most prevailing fault of our churches now, I mention worldliness, or, as it is frequently designated, earthly-mindedness. The least acquaintance with the Christian records and the Christian system must convince us, one should think, that it is the intention of these to form a character which, in reference to things both temporal and eternal, shall, in its spirit and manifestation, be different from, and contrary to, that of an unconverted man. In this, Christianity has a vast advantage over Judaism. The latter was, to a considerable extent, a worldly system ;—its revelation of a future state was dim; its promises were of earthly things; its ecclesiastical polity, though administered by God himself, was in part worldly. There seemed little to foster an unearthly, spiritual, and heavenly mind, even as regards the more pious Israelites. It is altogether different with us. We are under a covenant "established upon better promises." All in the way of motive is spiritual and heavenly. Life and immortality are brought to light by the Gospel. Eternal life in heaven is the grand theme of the New Testament. Fruitful seasons, temporal comforts, augmented wealth, worldly prosperity, are no longer the incentives to obedience, or the promised rewards of good conduct. God, by his almost entire silence about these things, and his constant exhibition of " all *spiritual blessings in heavenly places,*" has somewhat disparaged the objects of human ambition, and taught *us* to disparage

them too, at least in comparison with *heavenly* things.   By the very revelation, to our faith and hope, of the glories of the celestial world, he intends, not indeed to annihilate nor entirely to hide earthly things, but certainly to throw them in some measure into the shade, to lessen their importance, and to draw off, in some degree, our attention from them.   Just see what is said about these two classes of objects in the New Testament: " If ye then be risen with Christ, seek those things which are above, where Christ sitteth on the right hand of God.   Set your affection on things above, not on things on the earth.   For ye are dead, and your life is hid with Christ in God." (Col. iii. 1—3.) " We look not at the things which are seen, but at the things which are not seen : for the things which are seen are temporal; but the things which are not seen are eternal."   " Let those that buy be as though they possessed not, and they that use the world as not abusing it." "Love not the world, neither the things that are in the world.   If any man love the world, the love of the Father is not in him.   For all that is in the world, the lust of the flesh, and the lust of the eyes, and the pride of life, is not of the Father, but is of the world." (1 John ii. 15, 16.) "Dearly beloved, I beseech you as strangers and pilgrims, abstain from fleshly lusts, which war against the soul." " Having food and raiment, let us be therewith content." " Lay not up for yourselves treasures on earth, but lay up for yourselves treasures in heaven."

Now, in the view of these passages, and very many others, how forcibly does the question of the Apostle come to us: " Seeing all these things shall be dissolved, what manner of persons ought ye to be, in all holy conversation and godliness?" (2 Pet. iii. 11.) What an unearthly spirit—what an impress of eternity—what a temper of heaven should there be in us!   Professing to believe all this, to hope for all this, to love all this, to yield up ourselves to all this, ought we not to be a people really, practically different from the people of the world?—*seen* to be different, *known* and *acknowledged* to be different: different in our prevailing spirit, in our pleasures, in our tastes, in our mode of doing business, in our feelings and conduct in regard to wealth, in our behaviour under losses, and in the maxims which govern us?   Ought we not to appear to be the conquerors and not the captives of the world?   But *is it so?*   Is not the very opposite to all this the present characteristic of many professors?   Has not an inundation of worldliness flowed in upon the church?   Do we not see a heap of *débris*, accumulations of mud, around the walls and in the streets of Zion?   Do we not see it in the intense worldly spirit of professors?

It is, of course, admitted that a Christian may and must engage in secular business, if he has not a competent fortune to do without it; that he may become a skilful, clever man of business; ought to be diligent, and may, by honest industry, acquire wealth.   An incompetent or idle tradesman does no honour to religion.   And it is also admitted that it was never more difficult than in this age to get on in business and maintain a conscience void of offence.   The temptations to depart from the strict line of integrity were never so many and so powerful as they are now.   It is hard work to live and follow whatsoever things are true and honest.   But, then, if we are Christians, it must be done.   Now, then, look at the conduct of many professors of religion.   Are they not almost as completely swallowed up in the eagerness to be rich,—in the ever-widening circle of their trading speculations,—in their hard, grinding, grubbing way of doing business,—in their adopting the same tricks, artifices, half-falsehoods, half-dishonourables, half-dishonesties of unprofessing worldlings? Read the advertisements in our journals and magazines, and the placards upon our walls; what puffings and praises—what assertions of transcendent excellence, and declarations of superiority above all others—what mendacious attractives—what little, mean, ridiculous arts to catch attention—do we meet with in some who ought to know better! We do not, as may be supposed, object to advertising,—trade cannot be carried on without it; nor do we condemn such modest ingenuity in attracting notice as is consistent with truth and with things of good report; but when this degenerates, as it often does, into half-falsehoods, it is what no professing Christian ought to resort to.

Do we not see many practically rejecting the apostolic rules of trade and commerce, disregarding whatsoever things are true, honest, just, pure, lovely, and of good report, and who smile at the simplicity of the man who would tie them down to such rules? I am aware of the rage of competition, of the rivalries of trade, of the absolute necessity of skill, diligence, and even shrewdness, to cope with jealousy, envy, and trickery; but still, I say, the apostolic rule holds good, and the man who cannot get on without trampling it under foot, must not get on at all. If a Christian cannot get rich without losing his religion, he must be content to be poor. In a commercial country like this, and in times so *intensely* commercial as ours, this is the great snare—for Christians to act like worldly men in many of the looser maxims and questionable practices of the age.

Is not this worldly spirit manifested in many instances by a *rash and reckless speculation?* Surely there must be meaning in the Apostle's words, and meaning applicable to all ages and states of society: "Having food and raiment, let us be therewith content." (1 Tim. vi. 8.) Not that this is to be interpreted rigidly and literally. Yet certainly its *spirit* must be supposed to condemn an excessive eagerness after wealth. This is plain from what follows: "They that will be rich fall into temptation and a snare, and into many foolish and hurtful lusts, which drown men in destruction and perdition. For the love of money is the root of all evil: which while some coveted after, they have erred from the faith, and pierced themselves through with many sorrows." What is it but this *determination, at almost all hazards, and almost by any means, to be rich,* that makes so many go on ever enlarging their already wide circle of trade, launching out beyond their capital, speculating largely and imprudently, having recourse to fictitious capital in accommodation paper, following the bubbles which others have blown, and then resorting, by a kind of compulsion, as they suppose and feel, to means for meeting an exigency which commercial honour, to say nothing of Christian principle, forbids? What is it, I say, but a worldly spirit that leads to all this? Not content with plodding on at a slow pace in the humbler and more obscure path of patient and honest industry, many must gallop towards wealth on the high road of speculation. They have seen some fortunate adventurers in this way leap to affluence, and they too must try their luck. Ah! but how few are the *great* prizes in this lottery, how numerous the small ones, and how multiplied the blanks. How many scandals occur in this way to the ruin of the individuals themselves,
and to the discredit of religion. Have we not all b.. .

kind: of men who were not dishonest, who would have shuddered at the very idea of a deliberate and intentional fraud, and never perpetrated one; but who, in consequence of some unexpected failure of a rash and unwise and unwarranted speculation, have resorted to means for averting a crash, which, in other circumstances, they would have avoided with detestation? They never designed to rob any one, but fully purposed to pay every one their own when the speculation brought them the fortune they confidently expected. The cloud, which they hoped would pour down a shower of gold upon their cherished object, sent forth a thunderbolt which shivered it to pieces. Promises made with other anticipations all failed; injured and exasperated creditors heaped reproach upon the author of their loss: and the people, who wait for the halting of professors, tauntingly exclaimed, "This is your *religious* man!"

Such cases, I regret to say, are not uncommon. Not that they are more frequent with professors than with persons who make *no* profession. I will venture to affirm that for one such among the former, there are ten among the latter; but then, as one execution of a criminal makes more noise than the lives of ten exemplary honest men, so one disgraceful failure of a professing Christian occasions more reproachful talk than the still *more* disgraceful failure of ten men of the world does. Some malignantly pretend, they would sooner do business with a man who does *not* profess religion, than with one who does. This, I believe, is falsehood—mere calumnious hatred of religion, and enmity against God.

Still, what a lesson and a warning does this hold out to professing Christians, to be most circumspect and cautious in all their secular transactions, and most resolute in their determination to be willing to suffer, like the Apostle—though in different matters—the loss of all things, for the excellency of the knowledge of Christ Jesus the Lord.

I am sure I do but express the feelings of all my brethren in the ministry, when I say I am sick and weary of the reports which are floating about the world—though not, perhaps, affecting our own members—of the misconduct of professing Christians in reference to money matters. Of the three prevailing sins to which Christians in every age are exposed and tempted—*intemperance, licentiousness,* and *worldliness*—the most prevailing is of course the last; and, as regards its turpitude, it is the most difficult to fasten upon the individual conscience and to bring under the discipline of the church. How many are there who would feel exquisite pangs of remorse for one act of intoxication or licentiousness, who would go on through a whole series of inconsistencies in money matters, and yet their conscience scarcely ever trouble them: and who, while the church would take cognisance of the former, would, with regard to the latter, be suffered to go on uncited and unreproved.

It is utterly inconceivable, the mischief which is done to the credit of religion, and the souls of men, by the want of honourable and, in some cases, honest principle among the professors of religion. Infidels are confirmed in their infidelity, the profane in their profanity, and the worldly in their worldliness, by these occurrences. A single inconsistency of this kind in the conduct even of a professor who never did such a thing before, and will never do it again, may produce, on more minds than one, an ineffaceable impression and an inextinguishable prejudice against religion. Therefore, let us watch and be circumspect always, in everything, and before everybody. There are words of our Lord which ought to be ever sounding in our ears—" Woe to the world because of offences : it must needs be that offences will come, but woe to that man by whom they come." Let it only be imagined, what an impression would be produced on the unconverted part of mankind, if all who profess to be converted carried out the apostolic rule of trade : if in all cases it were an established and well-known fact, that every professor of religion were an honest and honourable man—one whose word was his bond, who would rather suffer wrong than do it, and was neither a rogue nor a screw. I am aware that the advantage which would redound to religious people, to whom honesty would be found the best policy, would, in that case, be so great, that many would hypocritically simulate religion for the sake of its benefits ; for, as all would be led to deal with people they could thoroughly trust, it would be palpable to every one that "godliness is profitable for all things, having the promise of the life that now is, as well as of that which is to come." But even by them an undesigned compliment would be paid to religion, when it was intentionally counterfeited for the sake of its temporal advantages. And is it not, then, the solemn duty of every professing Christian to be thus known as an honest, generous, and honourable man? *Ought* not his religion to be carried from the sanctuary, and the church, and the family altar, into the shop, to the exchange, to the market? *Ought* it not to preside over buying and selling, and enter into bargains and covenants? Why, half the prophetic writings of the Old Testament, and no small part of those of the New, are about these very matters. " Holiness to the Lord " should be written on all our merchandise. Are we not commanded by Christ to let our light shine before men? Now, this intimates not only that our religion must be *visible,* but *resplendent.* A rushlight is visible, but is it resplendent? And to shine *before men,* it must be conspicuous in those matters that fall more immediately under their notice. They do not see us in our closets, or at our family altars ; and though they see us in the sanctuary, yet there is nothing in that which they do not engage in themselves. But they *do* see us in matters of trade and in all money transactions. It is there we are a city set on a hill, which cannot be hidden. Nothing can shine which is not radiant as compared with what is around it; and we cannot shine before men unless we are honest, honourable, and true. A Christian is not only to be *as* moral as a moral worldling, but *more so,* else he cannot shine before that man. And yet, are there not some men, making no profession of religion, and possessing none, who outshine many who are church members, in the sterling integrity, the truthfulness, and the honour of their money transactions? Just before I penned this sentence, I was conversing with one of the richest and most fortunate men in this town, who told me he was started in life by a most upright, generous, and noble-minded man, who was an infidel, and endeavoured to make him one, and had almost succeeded, by the force of his beautiful moral conduct, especially as contrasted with the gross inconsistencies of many who called themselves Christians. Oh, what is a profession of religion worth, which in the moralities of trade is outshone by the conduct of an infidel?

What an opportunity, were they but eager to embrace it, have professing Christians to shine, in this age of corrupt trading principles ! How infected, to its very core, with unsound principles, is the great commercial body! Some have gone so far as to say all trade is a lie. Truth, justice, honesty, honour, seem weakening in trade. In such an age, in such a country, and in such circumstances, the *Christian* now carries on *his* business. Trying, severely trying, I know it is, and much do I pity him. So I should have done the believer in primitive times, when, under the Roman Empire, he was required to burn incense to the statues of the emperors, or suffer martyrdom. What must he now do, seeing what he was then required to do? To refuse to do evil, and determine to do good, at all risks and all sacrifices. If religion would not bend to the feelings of humanity when *life* itself depended upon such seemingly slight a circumstance as burning a few grains of incense before a statue, rest assured it will not be more flexible when it is only *property* and *worldly comfort* that are at stake. The test of religion then was idolatry; now it is property. Ours is far the less severe of the two. " Skin for skin, all that a man hath he will give for his life." If we cannot now refrain from getting money by untruthfulness, dishonesty, dishonour, trickery, how could we have refrained, in times of persecution, from forbidden means of saving life? What, at most, is it that men fear now, by following the things that are true, honest, just, and by sacrificing gains dishonourably obtained? Absolute poverty? No. There is little danger of that, at least in most cases. It is only a little lower grade in society. If they do not get so much profit, they cannot live quite so genteelly, so luxuriously. They cannot inhabit so large a house, cannot have such elegant furniture, cannot keep a carriage, cannot have such entertainments. It is to support these things that the laws of honesty and honour in trade must by some be sacrificed. They are not satisfied with competency, but they must have abundance. And even some professors of religion are carried away by this ambitious and aspiring disposition.

This, then, I aver, is a prevailing *fault* of the churches in this day. And how is it to be amended? The Apostle has told us : " God forbid that I should glory, save in the cross of our Lord Jesus Christ, by whom the world is crucified unto me, and I unto the world." How dim, how worthless, does everything earthly appear when seen in the sunlight of the cross! It is by losing sight of that, by living so far from that, by forgetting that, we let the world get so much the upper hand of us. You must meditate more upon the cross, you must dwell more upon Calvary, you must be more familiar with the crucified One. So again, in another place, it is said : Whatsoever is born of God overcometh the world : this is the victory that overcometh the world, even our faith." (1 John v. 4.)

What is wanted is a stronger belief of the reality of an eternal existence beyond the grave,—a firmer grasp by the hand of faith upon the glory, honour, and immortality which are promised to those who continue patient in well-doing,—a more frequent and serious consideration of the shortness of time, and the brevity and uncertainty of life. Oh Christians, what is time to eternity? what is earth to heaven? Do think more about laying up treasures in heaven, and less about laying up treasures on earth. Even supposing you get safe to heaven at last, notwithstanding a too-prevailing worldliness of disposition, and some inconsistencies, what a diminution of the heavenly inheritance will all this occasion! The Christian, who increases his worldly portion by means unworthy of his profession, is perpetually lessening his ortion in paradise.   There are degrees of glory in heaven; and the greatest will be obtained by them, who by divine grace obtain the most signal victory over the world : and take it as a most certain truth, that, even upon earth, there is more real and sublime felicity to be obtained from a crucified world than from an idolised one.   **J. A. J.**

PLAIN THOUGHTS ON PUBLIC WORSHIP.

Does the reader attend public worship ?   If not, why not ?

Is it not a *duty ?*   The great God who created, sustains and governs you, to whom you must give account, and by whose grace redemption is provided for you, claims your homage and praise.   And he claims it in public, in company with your fellow creatures.   For you have received mercies in common and should acknowledge them in common. He has made your nature social, capable of being acted upon by others, and of acting upon them in return, for good or for evil.   And if men associate so much for secular purposes, surely they should do so to honour God and to cultivate the religious principle.

The Scriptures, given for your guidance in religious matters, require it.   The patriarch, his family and tribe, offered sacrifice together around a common altar.   The Israelites had their appointed tabernacle and temple, where, as a " congregation," they assembled at stated times for worship.   In addition to these temple services, the institution of the synagogue, combining instruction and worship, sprang up, being introduced by Ezra and sanctioned by Christ and his Apostles.   The Christian services began in little meetings held by Christ with his apostles ; were continued by the disciples after their master's ascension, and were extended and organised into a regular system as the converts multiplied.   We are commanded " not to forsake the assembling of ourselves together, as the manner of some is," but to " come together " for prayer, praise, instruction, and edification.   He who has " all power in heaven and on earth," has bidden his servants " preach the gospel to every creature," and it is therefore the duty of every creature to " hear " it.

Is not this duty of public worship one which the common instincts of our nature suggest, and which all religions sanction ?   Where is the nation without its temples, sacred places, or public ceremonies ? Shall Mahommedans, idolaters and pagans of every degree be attentive to *their* worship in common, and shall men called Christians be alone distinguished for neglect of this obvious duty ?

Is not public worship a *benefit ?*   Those who condemn it, or speak lightly of it, as of no utility, are those who neglect it altogether, or who take no pains to profit by it.   Ask the most regular and con-scientious attendants upon the worship of the congregation whether they do not find it a comfort and a benefit ; look forward to it with pleasure, and reflect on it with satisfaction ?   It eases them of their cares, soothes their sorrows, instructs their minds, and warns them of their dangers ; it brings their sins to remembrance and directs them to the means of pardon and of peace, probing and at the same time curing their wounds.   It improves character, teaches the true use of life, and prepares for a safe and happy death.   What multitudes have sincerely exclaimed from their own exeperience—

" I have been there and still would go,
'Tis like a little heaven below ! '

Is it not a *family* benefit? promoting early rising, cleanliness and order, agreeable diversity of occupation, and, above all, moral and spiritual improvement? Look at the households that habitually neglect public worship, and see how late they are in getting up, what disorder marks their proceedings, what listlessness prevails, how heavy time hangs on their hands, what trashy books they read to help them through the day ; or if they look out of doors for some recreation, what shifts they are put to to find something fresh and entertaining. No wonder that such families often lack want of proper subordination, and enjoy little of real domestic happiness, when they have no fear of God before their eyes.

Is not public worship a benefit to *society* at large? What would a people be without it? What security for good morals and common decency ; for safety of property or even of life ; for social order or respect to law? Look at a new rush, where thousands suddenly congregate before there has been time to erect places of worship, to procure religious teachers, and to make arrangements for Divine service. What drunkenness and vice, what rudeness and fighting, what noise and tumult, what robbery and violence, and even maiming and killing each other! Little do those who neglect public worship know how much they are indebted for their own peace and security, and the good order that prevails around them, to the holy, elevating influences which, emanating from the sanctuary, tend to the good of the whole community. Every one who would be a patriotic citizen, should be a firm supporter of public worship, and constant attendant upon its services.

Have you any *excuses* for neglect? Of course you have. And some of these excuses may be valid. If you are confined to bed through illness, you cannot go; neither can you if the distance from your house to a place of worship be too great to reach it and return the same day. But if you were very anxious about the matter, perhaps you might do something to *originate* services in your own neighbourhood ; or you might remove nearer the sanctuary. Why not take into account, in fixing on a residence, its convenience for cultivating your religious and higher interests, as well as the secular and lower?—You want the day for rest, recreation, visiting friends and receiving visits from them. These are all very good in their place. But should they push aside other and higher duties? Will they be allowed as sufficient excuses by the God who has to judge you, and who, knowing what man needs, has instituted public worship for his benefit? Do they even satisfy yourselves? Is it not obvious that those who make a conscience of paying regard to the Sabbath and attending public worship, enjoy as much relief from the fatigue of work, and as much of social intercourse with their friends as those do who make these a pretext for neglecting their duty to their Maker and their own souls?

Timothy J. was a workman in a factory at home. He and his family made a point of regularly attending the worship of Almighty God. One Saturday afternoon two of his fellow-workmen came up to him and said, " Timothy, will you go with us to-morrow to Longton?" " What are you going for?" asked Timothy. " Oh, for health and pleasure." " No, I can't go, I must go to chapel." " Chapel!" rejoined one of them, " are you going to be prisoned up in a chapel! We are prisoned up enough here all the week, without being prisoned on Sundays too." "I don't call it prisoning," said Timothy, "I like it : it always does me good." "Well, you may do as you please," replied they both together; "but we'll be off to the country and enjoy ourselves." On Monday morning Timothy was at the factory door punctual to his time a few minutes before six o'clock. Fresh, vigorous and in good spirits he set to work. His companions were not there. He thought they were perhaps tired with their Sunday's walk and had overslept themselves, but that they would turn up at breakfast time. Nine o'clock came, but the men did not make their appearance. " I hope nothing's happened to them," said Timothy to himself. After dinner, however, one of them came; he looked, as Timothy expressed it, rather *seedy* and woe-begone. "What's the matter with you, John?" asked he. "Rather done up with yesterday's out." "Done up," rejoined Timothy with a tone of surprise, "I thought you went out for your health." "So we did," said John, "but you see we couldn't but go into the public house to get a snack, and of course we had some drink, and to tell you the truth, we got a drop too much, and got home late ; and this morning I couldn't get up, what with head-ache and being tired." Timothy, who was a very quiet man and did not usually say much, felt that the opportunity was now given him of turning round upon his fellow-workmen who had tried to induce him to absent himself from public worship and to break the Sabbath, under the plea of seeking health. He therefore said, " Well, this is a pretty story; you went to seek rest and health, and you have got head-ache and weariness, and made yourselves unfit for work. And if I had gone with you it might have been the same with me. But I and my family were at chapel twice yesterday. My mind was instructed and refreshed ; it was a happy day for me ; and I slept sound last night, and rose like a lark this morning at five o'clock, and was ready to begin my week's work at six as brisk as a bee." Then looking significantly at John, lowering his tone and at the same time jingling some change in his breeches pocket, he said, " Where's your *money? mine* is *here !* "

Perhaps the reader makes the excuse of being *unsettled.* At home you went to the House of God regularly, but there you lived always in one neighbourhood, went constantly to one place of worship, knew all the people, were at home among them and felt comfortable. But you have been tossed about in the colony and you are not sure of remaining long where you are, and those that attend the churches or chapels in your neighbourhood are strangers to you and distant and cold, and you don't like going among them. Now we all know there are many discomforts in Colonial life ; but are we to give way to them, or to make the best of them? They are trials meant to test and try us and see whether we can serve God under difficulties or not. Many, alas! have shown that the religion they seemed to have at home was of a very poor and weak kind, by their laying it aside as soon as they got away from the eye of their friends and had a few inconveniences to cope with. But surely these are flimsy excuses, that won't bear examining. Your duty to God and your own soul is paramount, and must not be set aside by trifling interests. If you are only *one* Sunday in a place, go to the House of God ; and if you are more, attach yourself to some Christian people while you stay in the locality, and this will make that stay profitable.

Reader, whether married or single, whether old or young, whether rich or poor, whether learned or ignorant, regularly attend upon the public worship of God. Your duty to your never-dying *soul* requires it. *That* demands appropriate food as well as the body, and the food provided is the word of God. Salvation is only to be expected in the way of God's appointment, through the preaching of Christ crucified, which is the power of God and the wisdom of God to all that believe. And "faith cometh by hearing and hearing by the word of God."

TEMPTATION.

There are no dangers so fatal as hidden and unsuspected dangers. When a mariner sees before him a rocky island, with its steep cliffs rising perpendicularly out of the waters, and the surf breaking at its base, he takes good care to keep clear of all danger. He puts his ship about or bears away, so as to get a good offing. In fact the danger may be partially said not to exist at all, when it is so clearly seen and so easily avoided. But if there are sunken rocks about, which he does not know of, then there is danger, especially if a sharp look out is not being kept. Just so is it with the Christian's career; overt dangers to his soul, great temptations, proclaim themselves—there is hardly need to warn him about *them*. There is no mistaking them, and no doubt about how he ought to act. It is hidden dangers that call most for watchfulness, that are most likely to entrap him unawares, to involve him in difficulties when he thinks all is safe and going on well, and perhaps to cause shipwreck of character.

It is not uncommon for us to talk of the need of *clinging* to Christ as a resource against the devil and his arts, as though the thing we most wanted were *force* enough to withstand very powerful efforts to tear us away, as it were, from the embrace of the cross. Yet this phrase hardly gives an accurate idea of the general nature of the Christian conflict. It is true there are times in almost every man's life when temptation is *violent*—great crises when there is some tremendous inducement to do what is wrong, when there is a frightful inward struggle, when great issues depend upon the result. But these are only occasional, and some experience but very few of them even in the course of a long career. The greater portion of temptations are small ones, such as in their initial stages are apt to be overlooked or almost despised as not of much importance. It is against these that we most need to be upon our guard. The devil always tries to take us at a disadvantage. It is not when we are in our highest moods that he assails us most powerfully, but when we are off our guard, and even then the temptation comes sometimes in a form almost imperceptible at first, till we find ourselves committed. Hence our Saviour, who knew what was in man, and knew also what spiritual dangers surrounded man, enjoined his disciples to watch and pray *lest they entered* into temptation. He did not so much enjoin them to cultivate great force wherewith to be able to resist, as great vigilance, and prudence to see that they did not allow themselves to get into a position in which such force should be necessary. There may be some temptations which spring up entirely outside of a man, and for the existence and power of which he is in no way responsible. But mostly they originate within him, and prayerful watchfulness would have nipped them in the bud. It is prudence more than power that we need, to keep us safe. Our instructions from the Divine Master are to do our utmost to keep clear of danger ; to be always on the look out for the first signs of it, to be tremblingly anxious that we do not get involved even by a few steps taken in a wrong direction.

We all know the force of habit. How many men groan under the tyranny of passions, appetites, and infirmities ! Yet all these troublesome foes to the mind's peace began in little unresisted temptations. Prayerful watchfulness would have been an effectual preventative against them, but it was intermitted at the right time ; they " entered into temptation," and did not retreat precipitately, as they should have done, and guard against similar transgressions in future. And so the temptation has wound its cords around them, and they are in perpetual and painful entanglement.

"Surely in vain the net is spread in the sight of any bird." The "great fowler " never sets his snares with ostentation. Light and airy as gossamer is the web he weaves around the gay thoughtless youth, who feels it not and sees it not. Year by year the fatal cords thicken and strengthen. But even when conscious at last of their existence, they seem to the young man, proud of his strength of will, to be as packthread, which he can easily break through when he likes. He recognises no restraint in such bonds. Confident that he can escape from them, he too often does not make the attempt, and does not learn the amount of resistance that is necessary, till he finds that it is more or almost more than he possesses. The cords grow into ropes—the ropes harden into cable chains, and the once self-confident soul is taken captive by the devil at his will.

Generally speaking, the Christian does not fall under *great* temptations, unless his spiritual-mindedness has been sapped and undermined by a course of yielding to minor ones. But mostly in such cases the issues are so clearly seen, and the whole powers of the soul are called into such violent action, that principle gains the mastery over impulse. But the very same man who has come triumphantly out of a fierce conflict, may succumb almost immediately to a smaller temptation of a different character, which takes him unawares. " Watch and pray therefore lest ye *enter* into temptation."

EARLY SOWING, LATE REAPING.

A sailor lad, 15 years of age, belonging to the port of Dartmouth, in Devonshire, went one Sunday to hear the pithy and pathetic Flavel, the celebrated nonconformist minister of that town, preach. The text of the sermon happened to be, " If any man love not the Lord Jesus Christ let him be anathema maranatha." The discourse was more than usually solemn and affecting. The preacher described in pointed terms the characters of those who were destitute of the love of Christ, and depicted in glowing colours the fearfulness of the curse the text denounced upon such as continued in that state. When the service was just concluding Mr. Flavel rose, as usual, to pronounce the benediction. But when his hands were lifted up and the words were about to drop from his lips, he suddenly paused, and in a tone of deep feeling said, " How shall I bless those whom the Lord curses ? " A scene of indescribable emotion ensued ; the whole congregation burst into tears, and an impression of unwonted seriousness was made upon many minds.

Among the rest the young sailor was deeply affected. But he had to go to sea almost immediately, and the society of godless companions, and absence from all religious ordinances soon obliterated the sacred impressions made upon his mind. He roamed over the ocean for forty years, visiting most parts of the world, and at length settled in New England, North America. Here he became a proprietor of a farm, upon which he supported himself in moderate competency for fifty-five years, till he reached the patriarchal age of 100. During all this time he was living without God in the world. His early impressions had worn completely off, and he had spent a thoughtless, carnal life, blotted, during the seafaring period particularly, with many vices.

A century of years having thus passed over him, and being still in vigorous health, he was walking one day across a part of his land, when he sat down to rest upon a stone. Falling into a musing mood his thoughts rapidly ran over his long life, with its varied and eventful scenes; and among the rest the scene in Mr. Flavel's meeting house, 85 years before, rose up from the store-house of memory where it had lain undisturbed all this long time. It presented itself before him as fresh as if it had been yesterday. He seemed to see the preacher's look, and to hear his voice and the sobbings of the weeping crowd; and above all, the impression of the theme itself, the neglected Saviour, the want of love to him, the fearful anathema pronounced by inspired authority upon all Christless souls, was revived with increased force. And then the thought of a life drawn out to so unusual a length being *all* spent without God and without Christ, added aggravation to his sense of ingratitude and guilt. The dangers, too, he had passed through, the narrow escapes he had had of being plunged into eternity utterly unprepared, came into recollection and made him tremble with terror. The arrows of conviction penetrated deep into his conscience; he saw himself a sinner of crimson dye, and despaired of mercy.

The old man, however, lived in the neighbourhood of means of grace, which had been provided by the piety of the puritan founders of the colony. He had never troubled this sanctuary, being known as a godless man, and regarded in his extreme age as in an incorrigible and hopeless state of impenitency. But *now* he thought of this neglected house of God, and repaired thither on the next Sabbath. We will not speak of the wonder and surprise produced upon the congregation by the sight of the centenarian scoffer crossing the threshold and taking his seat among the worshippers. Suffice it to say there he heard the *Gospel*, as pure as it flowed from the lips of the venerated Flavel of his youthful days; and there he learnt there was mercy even for *him*, the chief of sinners. The Saviour whom he so long had refused to love, still pitied him and invited him to partake of his free salvation even at the eleventh hour. A heart was given to him to comply: the old man, with brokenness and contrition of spirit, cried out, "God be merciful to me a sinner," and with a believing, trusting heart he embraced the promise of pardon. He obtained peace, and gave all the love of which he was capable to the long-slighted Saviour.

Nor was this conversion produced by the mere fear of death, and the genuineness of which there was no means of proving. Old as the convert was, his life was protracted for 16 years longer; during which time, having joined the communion of the church, he adorned his profession by a consistent course of life. He acquired the confidence of his fellow-members, was chosen a deacon, and served the church faithfully till his death, which took place at the unwonted age of 116 years. While we aim at the conversion of the young, let us not limit the Holy One of Israel, by despairing of the conversion of the old.

———————————◆———————————

THE HARD WAY.

"Frank, I have got one more errand for you; then you may go and play all the rest of the afternoon."

"Yes, father, thank you, what is it?"

Frank's father went around behind the counter and drew out a little ____ from under it. In the meantime Frank had come up to the opposite ____ counter. His father handed him a silver dollar, saying:

"You may carry this to widow Boardman. Be careful not to ____

"Yes, sir, I will," said Frank, and then went out of doors. I___ of vacation. Frank felt very happy as he trudged along the road. He was thinking of the fine times ahead—two weeks and no school! Perhaps the pleasant day, the fresh air, and the sunlight, had something to do with making him happy. Sunshine generally makes us feel more pleasant than clouds. But something else helped to make Frank happy, although he was not thinking about it. He had been a good boy. He had done right and was doing right. It makes a wonderful difference with a boy's feelings whether he knows that he is doing right, or whether there is the uneasy feeling of sin in his heart. He can have no quiet satisfaction with this feeling.

Mrs. Boardman lived at some distance up the road. Frank had already got by the school-house, and the little pond, and was just passing the willow grove, when, all of sudden, it came into his head to make himself a whistle to blow along the way. So, putting the dollar in his jacket-pocket, he climbed over the fence and cut several of such willow twigs as he thought would be suitable for his purpose. He did not make the whistle there, but went along with the twigs in his hand, till he reached a log lying on a grass plat by the road-side. Here he sat down and made two whistles. They sounded admirably.

As he shut the widow's gate, he put his hand in his pocket to take out the dollar, so that he might have it ready for her when she should come to the door. It was not there. Thinking he had felt it in the wrong pocket, he put his hand in the other, fully expecting to feel the dollar between his fingers immediately. *It was not there.* Frank felt a little alarmed. Could he have lost it? He searched carefully every pocket, but it was not to be found. He turned around and went slowly back, looking carefully along the road for the lost dollar. He searched around the log, in the willow grove, by the roadside, every step of the way, but no dollar was to be seen. He went over the road again with no better success. At length he sat down upon the log, feeling very badly, to consider what he should do.

The dollar was lost, there was no doubt of that. His father had told him to be careful, and he had not been. Now what should he do? His first thought was to go back to the store, and tell his father all about it. This he felt would be the right way ; but he disliked to go, for he knew that his father would blame him and perhaps would punish him. Boys dislike to be punished, whether they deserve it or not. In fact, Frank had a feeling very common, that of drawing back from a disagreeable duty. Was there no other way? He stayed to think. Ah! here was a great fault! Frank knew that he had found the right path, but, instead of pursuing it immediately, he waited and cast about to find another, easier way of getting out of the difficulty. An *easier* way. O, what a mistake! There was no road easier than the right road. There never is. Frank thought he would not go to his father then. He would go and play with the boys awhile. Perhaps his father might never know it. At any rate he would not tell him then. So he got up from the log and walked slowly toward the school-house green. How differently everything seemed to him. The warm summer day, the blue sky, the grass, the trees, the very air—all were changed. A few minutes ago they all looked bright and pleasant, but now not so. The change was in his own heart. An uneasy feeling of wrong-doing made him unhappy. He was not fit to enjoy the summer day.

Pretty soon he reached the school-house and engaged with the other boys in play. But still the unhappy feeling remained in his heart. Once in a while, to be sure, he would forget his sin and laugh as loudly as the merriest. But the remembrance soon came back to trouble him. There was no peace. At night he went home and sat down at the supper table with the rest. Soon after the blessing had been asked, while his brothers and sisters were talking with each other about what they had been doing through the day, his father turned to him and said :

" O, Frank, did you carry the dollar?"

" Yes, sir," said Frank.

The question was asked so suddenly that he had no time to make up his mind what to answer. He felt then less like telling the truth than he had at first. It seemed too hard. He thought to take the easier way by answering "yes." The easier way! Poor boy, he had not learned yet that it was the hard way. He had already, during the afternoon, suffered more than if he had gone to his father at the first and frankly told him all. And now he had made the matter far worse by telling a lie about it. Pretty soon after supper he went up stairs to bed. But when he repeated his evening prayer, he could not help feeling that God did not listen to him, and that he had no right to pray while he kept on in this wrong course. He passed a restless, dreamy night.

In the morning he woke up to find the sun shining broadly into his room. He leaped out of bed in high spirits and began dressing, thinking over at the same time some schemes for the day. But very soon the remembrance of the lost dollar came into his mind and blotted out at once all his happy feelings. It brought back the old wretchedness.

The day went by slowly and wearily. Frank was continually troubled by the fear of his father's finding out about the dollar, and still more by the consciousness of his own guilt; and yet he found it harder and harder every hour to make up his mind that he would tell all about the matter and bear such punishment as his father might inflict upon him. In the evening he could endure it no longer. The easy way had indeed become the hard way. While sitting by the parlor window he had made up his mind to go and confess the whole thing. He started toward the study, where his father was. Once on the way thither his courage almost failed him; but he kept steadily on. Every new step toward the right gave him new strength. He opened the study door and came up to the table where his father sat writing.

"Well, Frank," said he kindly, "what is it?"

"O father," said Frank, but he could not go on. He bowed his head upon the table, and bursting into tears sobbed and wept as though his heart would break. His father with tears in his own eyes gently tried to soothe him. In a few minutes Frank raised his head and began again:

"I want to tell you, father,"—but it was too much. A fresh burst of crying interrupted his words, as the thought of his father's kindness and his own wretchedness and wickedness came over his mind.

"Wait a minute, Frank. Let me tell you first," said his father. "You want to tell me that you did not carry the dollar to Mrs. Boardman, that you lost it on the way, that last night you told a lie about it, that you felt very wretched all the time and wanted to tell me but did not dare to. Is it not so?"

"Yes, sir," sobbed Frank.

"And now, my poor, dear boy, you have been suffering all this time, and I have been longing to have you come and tell me about your fault and be forgiven —and all this because you wanted to take a way easier than the right way; and yet you have found it a great deal harder."

Frank saw now that he had. He saw that he might have spared himself a great deal of uneasiness and sorrow and sin, and his father considerable pain and anxiety, by only choosing the right way at first. He told his father so, and decided in his own mind never to choose the foolish course again. His father freely forgave him, and then they knelt together and asked forgiveness of God.

Frank's punishment was that he should earn a dollar as soon as he could and carry it to Mrs. Boardman in the place of the dollar lost. Accordingly Frank set about earning his dollar, and before vacation was over, he carried it with a light heart and gave it to Mrs. Boardman. But the strangest part of the whole matter was this. While Frank was returning from Mrs. Boardman's his shoe struck something hard; he looked down and saw—the very dollar he had lost. Frank's father had found out about the loss in the following way:—After sending Frank he started on some business for a place beyond Mrs. Boardman's but went by another road. On his way back he saw his son walking slowly along and looking down as if searching for something on the road. Thinking it might be the dollar, he stepped into Mrs. Boardman's and asked her if Frank had been there. He had not. He waited all the afternoon hoping that Frank would come and tell him about it. At night he asked him, still hoping that, when asked, he would confess the loss. The result has been seen. The punishment was not for the loss but for the falsehood. It only remains to say that Frank did not after this choose the hard way again.　　　*New York Independent.*

BOOKS.—ENGLISH CORRESPONDENT'S LETTER.

February 22nd, 1859.

Since I last wrote to you I have read the first volume (which is all that is yet published) of Masson's "Life of Milton, related in connection with the history of his times." The work will consist of two more large octavo volumes, as bulky, I suppose, as the present one, and will form the first biography of our great poet that has been conceived in a spirit worthy of the dignity of the subject, or extended to a length commensurate with its magnitude. Milton's life almost involves the history of his country through one of its most thrillingly interesting periods, and you will observe by the title that Mr. Masson has fully appreciated the importance of this fact. It is surprising what fresh interest the almost threadbare narrative of those times acquires when looked at in this aspect. For in these days of democracy, when the Puritans are no longer "crop-eared roundheads," but our "heroic forefathers," when every young demagogue goes off into sublime enthusiasm about the Petition of Right, and every bore in a debating society sharpens his tusks against Cromwell's Ironsides, one is really troubled in spirit at the thought of another book on the history of those times. But it is a very different matter when we examine them, as the soil which developes so mighty a tree, flashing the splendour of its gorgeous foliage through the rolling storms and war-clouds of the day,—when we view them as the tumultuous deluges and piercing frosts and grinding glaciers that shaped the sublime front of so lofty a mountain peak, which at one time awes us by its solemn grandeur, and at another, catching the sunbeams as they fly, flings them down upon us in golden showers of gladdening light. Nor has Mr. Masson neglected to present us, as the Professor of English Literature in University College, London, is so well able to do, with a very interesting sketch of the progress of our literature previous to Milton's time, and a very full account of its position at that critical period, together with notices more or less extended, of all contemporary authors. This, from such a hand, forms a very valuable feature in the book. I think, also, that his treatment of the various religious parties of the day is fair, and shows noble sympathies. The present volume may be said to contain the period of Milton's education; extending from his birth to the period of his return from Italy, just before the civil war. A very interesting account is given of his earlier works, produced towards the close of this period,—as Comus, L'Allegro and Il Penseroso ; and we have also very full notices of his career at Cambridge, with, what is quite new to the general public, copious extracts from compositions which were produced as college exercises. Perhaps Mr. Masson runs some risk of being considered tedious here. Altogether, this is a great book on a great subject.

The Dean of Westminster (Trench) published, a few months since, five sermons preached before the University of Cambridge, on " The Person and Work of Christ." Perhaps you will be pleased with them ; I confess I am not. I cannot think them quite worthy of their author. They seem to me to be somewhat wordy, and to make up what they lack in cogency of proof by force of dogmatism. It is very unfortunate when this is the case in connection with a subject so overwhelmingly important as this, for I cannot help thinking that while people are squabbling and snarling about some indefinite and undefinable notions of inspiration, which they fondly look upon as a mighty bulwark, there is some danger of forgetting the real citadel of Christianity, in the " Person and Work of Christ." I would not have you suppose there is anything in the book which is likely to offend evangelical feelings, but I cannot think it is satisfactory, as against the Unitarians. I only give, however, what is my impression, on somewhat hastily looking into the book. It is very small, clearly printed, and is quite worth reading.

I wonder whether the same precocity is to be marked in the rising generation amongst you as is said to be painfully prevalent in the United States, where, I suppose, young gentlemen at fifteen or sixteen quite despise the authority of " the governor," and even plunge into the vortex of matrimony. I should hope it is not so, and with a view of doing something to keep the young mind amongst you fresh and tender, yet ever aspiring towards noble ends, let me suggest for their perusal a book I am reading myself, and which, in fact, I have just laid down to write this letter to you,—" Agnes Hopetown's Schools and Holydays ; the experiences of a little girl, by Mrs. Oliphant, author of Katie Stewart." There is a freshness of nature about the book and, in general, an absence of misrepresentation or exaggeration of possibilities in regard to children's thoughts, which is even yet unusual, notwithstanding the great strides which this branch of literature has made. I do not say that this

book is altogether free from such defects; still, compared with t
Petticoats," and "Madame Guyons in Short Frocks," which v
to regard as prodigies, the children of this story are very refresh
of the foolishness which people in old-fashioned times fondly i
"bound up in the heart of a child," and to require somethir
striking in its application to drive it out than is to be found in
narratives of a milk and water sentimentality. The religious tor
is healthful and natural on the whole, and the homeliness of the
conversations is likely to suggest the applicability of its lessons
consciences of our young friends, to whom I commend it.

De Quincey has published another volume on "The Cæsars
read it, so that I can say nothing about it, only that if the sa
issued a book on "The White of an Egg," I should look forward
with anticipations of the greatest delight.

The correspondence of Mr. Binney with the Bishop of South
of course, been looked upon with great interest here. Such a c
would, you know, be impossible in this country, but the very fac
place amongst you proves that the deep-rooted prejudices of the
are not after all so tenacious in their hold as that they can b
their vitality to the other side of the world. The bishop is cert
menon of liberality; but I admire the outspoken candour wi
Binney reminded him that any treaty which might be effected
as between equals; and also the keenness and force with which t
obstacle to any such arrangement is pointed out in the assumpti
of the Episcopalian clergy that their "orders" have a peculia
sanctity. It is greatly to be feared that this childish relic of
superstitions which saw sanctity not in truths and principles,
and incantations, in cups and platters, in peculiar forms of mai
genuflexion, will for an age to come keep this great and gl
fountain of so much splendour in scholarship and art, mothe
bright angelic spirit, centre of so many dear and cherished, so i
holy associations, from taking her proper place in the shining ph;
church militant, which at the present time seems to have felt
its common life thrilling throughout with a sense of deep
stronger than sectarian differences. How sad, how painful, h
how shameful, that the men raised highest by their splendid cult
ing by their exalted position the widest, most ennobling prospe
vastness of which, names, orders, manipulations, mummeries of
to nothingness, while truths and principles shine with etern
growing glory, should be of all reformed ecclesiastics, the mc
bent upon clinging to a bauble which grows more ridiculous i
which by the wretchedly narrow idolatry which it engenders, s
souls against the more manly and generous feelings which we
are struggling for entrance.

THE ESSENCE OF RELIGION.

As I often think of that saying of an ancient, Clement of Alex;
courted not that philosophy, which was peculiar to this or that sect,
of truth was to be found in any of them; so I say of Christiani
which is appropriate to this or that party, but whatsoever of sincere
be found common to them all.—*Howe.*

THE DECEITFULNESS OF SIN.

We never do wrong, but we attempt in some way to palliate
and the sophistry is repeated so often and so earnestly, that at lengt
be regarded as sound argument. The crime, still repeated, dem
excuse, till at length we think we can not only excuse, but justify
thus justly punished for having done wrong, by being permitted to
done right.—*Henry Rogers.*

MIDNIGHT, 1858—1859. *

I STAND upon a point sublime;
 The parting and the coming year
Meet in this narrow speck of time,
 And press upon my spirit here.—
The past with all its blessings gone,
 Its gifts renewed from day to day :
The future, with its scenes unknown,
 Its mingled cup, and chequered way.

Then, on the past let memory dwell,
 Jehovah's goodness to recount.
But who the wondrous tale can tell,
 Or reckon up the vast amount ?
The mercies, every evening new,
 With every opening morn renewed,
More numerous than the drops of dew,
 Or stars, in countless multitude !

In helpless infancy, His hand
 My tottering footsteps well sustained,
And angel guards, a constant band,
 Their ministry of love maintained ;
Mid childhood's wayward course, and youth,
 Where perils lurked on every side,
He, with unfailing light and truth,
 Has been my guardian and my guide.

When heavy on this troubled breast, [share,
 O'erwhelmed with burdens none could
A thousand anxious cares have pressed,
 And sought to make their dwelling there ;
I've borne the burden to His throne,
 I've told Him all my tale of grief ;
Nor did He e'er my claim disown,
 Or fail to yield me prompt relief.

Such is the past. And to His praise
 I thus His constant care record ;
My EBENEZER here I raise,
 And still I lean upon His word.
Strong in his strength, I still endure,
 Still happy in His power to bless ;
Nor shall the future less ensure
 His never-failing faithfulness.

And soon these scenes of time shall fade,
 And all of life be past to me ;
The present—death's funeral shade ;
 The future—all Eternity ;
Eternity !—that boundless sea,
 That dark, unfathomed, dread abyss—
By faith in Christ, shall prove to me
 One vast Eternity of b.iss !

LIVERPOOL, January 1, 1859.

             T. RAFFLES.

MISSIONS.
CONGREGATIONAL HOME MISSION OF VICTORIA.

 The annual meeting of this Institution, was held on Thursday evening, May 12, in the Victoria Parade chapel, Melbourne. Dr. Embling, M.L.A. presided. Rev. Mr. Vetch offered prayer. The Rev. R. Fletcher read the annual report, and G. Rolfe, Esq., treasurer, presented the cash statement, from which it appeared that the receipts of the year amounted to £603 16s. 8d., and the expenditure to £588 2s. 1d., leaving a balance in hand of £15 14s. 7d. The several resolutions were moved and seconded by the Hon. G. Harker, Colonial Treasurer, the Revs. J. P. Sunderland, J. L. Poore, T. Johnson, J. Mirams, W. Moss, J. Vetch, R. Fletcher, &c. Mr. Poore in his speech entered into many interesting details of his proceedings in England, his journeys in the colonies, and plans of proceeding for the future. Mr. Harker generously offered to give a tenth of whatever sum the Society might raise in the course of the year, provided the income did not exceed £1,000. The report, from the fulness of its information respecting the results of Mr. Poore's visits to England, and the distribution of the ministers who have been sent out by his instrumentality, we present entire.

SECOND ANNUAL REPORT OF THE COMMITTEE OF THE CONGREGA-
TIONAL HOME MISSION FOR VICTORIA.

 Since the annual meeting held on the 12th April, 1858, the operations of the Society have progressed steadily and satisfactorily. Its great object is to raise up new congregations where wanted, to strengthen weak ones, and to settle ministers. At the date of last report there had arrived from England, sent out by the Rev. J. L. Poore, the Revs. W. C. Robinson, W. R. Lewis, J. Sleigh, J. H. Jackson, J. Summers, R. Bowman, and J. G. Reed, and these had entered on their labors respectively, at Williamstown, Brighton, Portland, Beechworth, Sandhurst, Victoria Parade Melbourne, and Geelong.

---

* The Editor has received the above in a private letter from Dr. Raffles. It was read and sung at the early prayer meeting, on January 1st of the present year, being the 48th production of this kind the author has furnished for those occasions in the same place of worship. His numerous friends will be happy to see that age has not chilled his poetic fire, much less the ardour of his piety

M

Mr. Robinson's settlement at Williamstown has been one of grati
success.   A church is formed, a respectable and steady congregation of h
is gathered, and a Sunday school is in operation.   The iron store which
temporarily used, has been purchased, with the ground on which it st
and has, by additional outlay, been made convenient and suitable for wo
This place will answer every purpose until the congregation is strong e
to build a more tasteful and enduring structure.   The expenses connected
this movement have been provided or procured by the congregation thems
The pastor has also been sustained by the people throughout the year, wit
exception of a grant from this Society of £15, and it is expected that f
aid will not be necessary.

Not less pleasing is the account the committee have to give of Mr. L
settlement at Brighton.   On his entrance on that sphere, in January
year, there was a church of 10 or 12 members, a congregation varying fr
to 50, and a small, frail, and inconvenient chapel.   An eligible piece of
however, had been purchased for a place of worship.   Mr. Lewis's labors
blessed, and it was soon necessary to proceed with a new erection.   A
church has consequently been reared.   It was opened Sabbath day, Octob
and a social meeting was held on the Tuesday evening following.   The
cost of land and church was £1,175.   A mortgage of £500 was obtained
the remaining £675, has been raised either in cash or promises.   The
has been supported by the people themselves, with the exception of a gr
£50 from this Society for the first half-year.   The church will hold
persons and is well attended.

The Rev. Mr. Sleigh's labors at Portland have also been successful.
last report mentioned the purchase of a piece of ground and the erectio
small church as having just then occurred, a debt remaining of about
which was rather oppressive to a people not very wealthy or very num
The anniversary services were held on March 20th and 22nd, when Mr.
officiated, and the whole debt, exclusive of the cost of the land, was clea
with the exception of some £25.   A grant towards Mr. Sleigh's salar
made by this Society, for the first year, of £50, and another by the C
Missionary Society of England of £50), but henceforth it is expected the
will be self-sustaining, or nearly so.

We have the pleasure of presenting an equally favorable report of the
Mr. Jackson's proceedings at Beechworth.   At our last anniversary he ha
just entered upon his labors there.   A small church had been previously fo
and a site of land purchased, but there was no chapel, and services were s
time suspended.   Mr. Jackson was welcomed by the people ; a room for pre
in was procured, and an encouraging congregation obtained ; the c
has been reorganized ; a house built for the pastor at a cost of £50(
measures are in progress for the erection of a commodious place of wo
No grant from your Society has been necessary this year.   Mr Jackson's
are very acceptable and useful in Beechworth, and he extends them as op
nity serves to the population of the surrounding diggings.

The Rev. J. Mirams was sent up, at the expense of the Society, t
Jackson's request, to the Indigo diggings, and he preached there a few Sabt
but there being no minister at liberty to occupy the sphere, nothing perm
resulted from the visit beyond the erection of a large tent for preaching.

At Sandhurst a prosperous cause has been established.   After Mr. Sun
removal to Daylesford, service, which had been conducted in the G
Church, was discontinued.   At the request of the Committee, the Rev.
Fletcher, who had temporarily assisted his father at St. Kilda and Brighto
ceeded to Sandhurst, and he having collected a few friends together, comm
preaching in an empty store ; this being soon filled was vacated for a larg
as it was frail and incommodious, the Episcopal school room was kind
until measures were taken to purchase land and erect a church.
site with a good dwelling house upon it, was procured for about £1,
brick church, which is ultimately designed to be the school
built at a cost of £800, making £1,000 in all.   A mortgage of

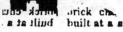

procured, and the greater part of the remaining £900 has been subscribed by the congregation itself and by friends in Melbourne and elsewhere. The new church was opened by services held on November 28th and 30th, when the Rev. T. Binney preached, and the Rev. R. Fletcher, father of the pastor, occupied the pulpit for the two following Sabbaths. A church has now been formed, a promising Sunday school commenced, and other operations for acting on the population are carried on. With the exception of £15 given by this Committee to Mr. Fletcher to meet preliminary expenses, all the costs have been defrayed by the people themselves.

The *Rev. J. Summers*, after leaving Sandhurst, was sent by your Committee to *Daylesford*, where it was understood there was great need of Evangelical ministrations. He has labored hard, preaching and itinerating among the people, and has gained general esteem and affection. His success has been considerably checked by rushes to other diggings, and consequent fluctuations in the population. A church has not yet been organized, nor a permanent place of worship erected. The committee of the congregation have striven hard to raise a maintenance for their minister, but this Society has been obliged to assist them to the extent of £52 8s. 6d. This place, from the nature and necessities of the neighbourhood, will still require the fostering care of the Society.

The *Rev. R. Bowman* having, immediately on his arrival, acceded to the wishes of the church at *Victoria Parade* to undertake that cause, commenced his ministry with every prospect of success. But ere long his health began to fail, and it soon became manifest that the climate of Australia was not suited to his constitution; and the unanimous testimony of four medical men of eminence was, that immediate return to England was necessary to his safety. He and his family consequently left, much to the regret of a numerous circle of friends. The funds of your Society were not drawn upon to meet any of the expenses.

The *Rev. J. G. Reed*, who came out in feeble health, went to *Geelong*, for which place he was designed, but his strength rapidly failed and death soon closed his career. He was carried to the grave beloved and lamented by all who knew him. Of course the funds of this Mission had no portion of the charges to bear.

The Ministers who have arrived since the last anniversary are Messrs. Firth, Hill, Beer, Vetch, Johnson, and McMichael.

The Rev. *J. C. McMichael*, who was sent out by Mr. Poore with a view to taking Mr. Reed's place at McIllop street Geelong, after preaching two months there received and accepted a unanimous call from the church, and has every prospect of doing well.

The committee being informed that there was an opening at *Maldon* for a new cause, sent the *Rev. J. Firth* thither, after he had preached for a few weeks in the neighbourhood of Melbourne. At that time there was no Presbyterian minister in the township, and many of the Scotch attended Mr. Firth's preaching, but shortly afterwards one of their own ministers arriving, they consequently withdrew, and as there were scarcely any Independents in the place, Mr Firth was left with very few adherents. He carried on the experiment for six months altogether, but not succeeding, he abandoned it with the approval of the committee. He has since gone to New South Wales, for which colony he was originally selected, and he is now making trial of Newcastle, at the mouth of the Hunter.

The *Rev. J. Hill, M.A.*, and the *Rev. J. Beer*, recently arrived, have both commenced very hopeful causes, the one at Maryborough, the other at Dunolly. Information having reached the committee that there was an opening at these places, Mr. Poore, in a tour among the gold-fields in that vicinity, had an interview with the friends in both those towns, which resulted in his promising to send ministers up on their arrival. *Mr. Hill*, after preaching at Victoria Parade a few Sabbaths, went to Maryborough, and met with a most cordial reception. A public hall has been engaged, an enthusiastic tea meeting held, and a large congregation collected; and it is hoped that this auspicious beginning will issue in the organization of a church, and the erection of a chapel ere long.

Mr. Hill, however, went to Maryborough with a distinct understandi
would not permanently remain there, and Mr. Johnson is likely to s
At *Dunolly*, a minister, unconnected with any specific denomination, ha
congregation, and was accomplishing much good, when he was arrested
by failure of health, which occasioned him to return to England.
gation, thus left destitute, applied, through their managing co
various bodies for information respecting their principles, with a vi
them in their choice of a denomination to which they should attach
and among others they wrote to the Independents. The result of
conference with them was a resolution to ask for the probationary
an Independent minister, and thither the Rev. Mr. Beer has gor
already received and accepted an unanimous call to become
measures are being taken to build a new chapel, and all appearance
hope that a self-sustaining and efficient cause will be establishe
grant of £20 for the first six months has been made to this enterpr
however, expected that neither of these places will entail any
burden upon the Society's funds.

Mr. *Vetch* is at present preaching for the Church at Victoria
Mr. *Johnson*, whose health suffered severely during the voyage
awhile for the purpose of recruiting his strength. The committe
but these brethren will soon find appropriate spheres of labor.

On the settlement of the *Rev. J. M. Strongman*, at *Ballaarat*, a
as mentioned in last report, was made by this Society, of which £77 1
duly paid during this year. Mr. Strongman resigned in the course
and the Rev. W. Lind, formerly a South Sea missionary, has suc
An application was made to continue the grant towards his maint
the committee did not feel warranted, from the state of their fu
prior claims of the ministers who were on their way, in complyi
request.

From this rapid review it appears that during the two years
has been in existence, *eight* new congregations have been formed, a
with ministers, four of these during the year just closed, all i
centres of population, and all, except one, now strong enough, o
to do without further subsidy. This is obviously a great success a
devout thankfulness to Almighty God.

It may not be out of place to give a summary of the labors of th
Poore in procuring ministers for these colonies. Home Mission opera
a stand still for want of ministers. Inviting spheres were not lacki
to occupy them were. Ministerial brethren occasionally came out
accord, but these were far too few and uncertain to meet the deman
circumstances Mr. Poore visited all the Australian colonies, and
friends to subscribe towards procuring a supply of ministers, offerir
to England at his own expense, to raise additional funds ther
ministers, and send them hither. This he accomplished, obtaining f
friends by much persevering journeying, and no little toil, the nee
mentary funds, and despatching fifteen ministers. He returned to
scarcely had landed, before he perceived that the colonies requii
number of men, and that the shortest way would be to return at on
them. He offered to do this again at his own expense, with the
£50 the committee of this Society promised to contribute. This
was undertaken, and the whole was accomplished in the short s
months. As many as thirteen ministers have been sent, as the
second visit. The total number of ministers selected and sent to th
by Mr. Poore is 28. Of these twelve have come to Victoria,
Australia, four to New South Wales, one to Tasmania, and
Zealand. Two have died, Mr. Jones designed for Sydney, and
Geelong, and Mr. Bowman has broken down through ill health.
men left are twenty-five. The total cost in subscriptions, and fre
passages, has been £4,696 2s. of which sum Great Britain
cash £1,500, in free and reduced passages £896,

raised the remainder, viz., New South Wales £310; Tasmania £250; South Australia £600; Victoria, Melbourne £810 2s., Geelong £240, Kyneton £20, Castlemaine £50, Sandhurst £20, in all £1,140. Total for the Colonies, £2,300 2s. Grand Total, £4,696 2s.

All these moneys have been disbursed under the direction of the committee of the Colonial Missionary Society in England, a statement of which will be published in their accounts. It thus appears that the average expense of bringing hither twenty-eight ministers with their wives and families, including outfit, passage money, travelling and other expenses in ·England, has been £167 each.

Much as has been done, the work seems only opening up. The occupation of central positions reveals the necessities of outlying districts. Schnapper Point, where there is a chapel built on Union principles, is in want of a minister, so also is Queenscliff, and probably Kyneton will require one ere long. And ample spheres exist for the operations of Congregationalists in such places as Ararat, Pleasant Creek, Indigo, Back Creek, Amherst, Creswick's Creek, McIvor, Avoca, Ballan, Kilmore, &c., to say nothing of some of the suburbs of Melbourne. In a few years *twenty* more places might be occupied. But how is this to be done? Men and money are indispensable. Ministers must be sent out from England, as candidates for the ministry, in sufficient numbers, are not likely to spring out of our own churches for many years to come

And larger funds will be required, in proportion, in time to come than in time past. The places most ripe for ministers have already procured them, because they were prepared to take them off the Society's hands and sustain them at once. Other places, where little or nothing has yet been done, will require more working and more extraneous aid. The Society may fairly reckon upon having to make larger grants, and for a longer period, to such places than heretofore. But there is little doubt of their rewarding such outlay, by sooner or later becoming self-sustaining.

The funds of the Society have been very scanty, many of our churches not being in a condition to do much. The committee have been, during the past year, seasonably assisted by special collections made in various chapels by Mr. Binney, who kindly placed himself at the disposal of the committee for that purpose, and by a special subscription which was entered into. Now that our churches are increased in number, and several of them are surmounting their pecuniary difficulties arising from purchasing land and building chapels, the time is come for combined movement and consentaneous action. Every church should have an association among its own members to obtain monthly or weekly subscriptions, and should, besides, make a yearly collection. Then, a considerable sum would be raised without the burden falling with special weight upon any particular churches or individuals. The committee would then be in a condition to maintain always one or two spare ministers to be employed in opening up new spheres either for themselves or others. Arrangements also might be made with the Colonial Missionary Society at home, to send out at frequent intervals, a minister or two to take charge of the congregations prepared for them, or themselves to enter upon itinerating and preparatory work. Are the churches willing to combine and exert themselves for this purpose?

The committee have referred to the Rev. Mr. Binney, and they cannot suffer this occasion to pass without expressing their deep sense of the obligations that gentlemen has conferred upon this Society in particular, and the Congregational body in general, by his visit to these colonies. Coming hither in search of health, after a season of unwonted prostration, it is matter of thankfulness and joy, that he has not only, to a considerable extent, recruited his strength, but has also had the satisfaction, by his abundant labors, of doing an incalculable amount of good. Not only has the Congregational body been benefited by his services, in a pecuniary point of view and otherwise, but still more, numbers of persons, little used to attend upon Christian ordinances, have been attracted to hear discourses as distinguished for their fidelity, plainness, and adaptedness to arouse the conscience, as by universal testimony they are for the high qualities of oratory and genius. Surely not a little spiritual fruit will result from these labors.

CONGREGATIONAL UNION, SOUTH AUSTRALIA.—The annual asser
Congregational Union of South Australia was held at Adelaide, on V
April 20th, and by adjournment on Thursday, the 21st. On Tuesd
the annual sermon was preached in Rundle-street Congregational
the Rev. James Howie. The preacher chose for his text 1 Cor
showed, in an eloquent and lucid discourse that the wisdom of the gr
of antiquity, so far from making the knowledge of God clearer
minds, only obscured it; and when this had been fully proved, t
God brought salvation by Christ Jesus, and published it by what
esteem the foolishness of preaching. On Wednesday morning a
united prayer was held in Freeman-street Chapel, conducted by
W. Evan; and at half-past 11 the ministers and delegates met in R
Chapel for despatch of business. Prayer was offered by the Re
Drane, and the Rev. James Howie was appointed Secretary for
The new ministers were then admitted members of the Union by
Assembly, the names being called by the chairman as follows:—
Palmer, Charles Manthorpe, J. W. C. Drane, George Hoatson,
Morrison Howie. The chairman for the year—the Rev. W.
delivered the address, in which he referred to the events of the
affecting the interests of religion in the colony, and especially as i
interests of their own denomination—such as the arrival of the ne
their difficulties and prospects, the visit of the Rev. Thomas Binne
chapels opened, or in prospect. Then the chairman passed on to th
in the way of the spread of religion in the colony, contrasting the n
difficulties here and in England, and pointing out some cases of ir
between their professed principles and their practice. The followir
among others, were laid before the meeting:—Congregational min
whom 5 are at this moment unattached. Chapels 39, and preach
11, total 40; 31 of these are reported to seat 5,090 persons, averag
The other nine are estimated to seat 720 persons. Total chapel
tion, 5,810. Only 5 chapels have debts, which together amoun
average £88 12s. each. Number of hearers reported in 39 ph
average 86 to each. Church members in 23 churches, 655; av
each. Sunday-scholars in 30 schools, 1561; average 52 to eac
school teachers, 203. Lay preachers, 15. Three churches prov
manse for their minister, namely, Hindmarsh, Middleton, and En
On the evening of Wednesday, the annual tea and public me
Home Missionary Society were held. The latter was, perhaps, one
interesting ever held on such an occasion, the company being ver
the interest warmly excited by the presence of so many new minis
singing, prayer, and an opening address by the chairman, Mr. Ale
M.P., the report was read by Mr. Shawyer, the secretary. The r
was of considerable length, was in many respects very satisfactor
resolutions were unanimously adopted. The proceeds of the tea-1
collections at the various services, amounted to £50.

FOREIGN MISSIONS.

LONDON MISSIONARY SOCIETY.

The annual meeting of the New South Wales Auxiliary to
Missionary Society was held on Monday evening, May 23rd, in tl
tional Church, Pitt-street. This anniversary, usually held at an e
of the year, has been delayed for the arrival of some missionaries v
returned from a visit to England. There were several other
religion on the platform. The chair was taken by the Rev. Thoma
The proceedings were commenced by the singing of a hymn;
the Rev. S. C. Kent offered up prayer.
The Rev. chairman, in opening the proceedings, expressed
the Rev. Dr. Ross, who usually presided, was not able

recommended the missionaries in their speeches to confine themselves to facts, and to leave the arguments and application to home ministers who had not seen mis-ionary service. He dwelt with strong emphasis upon the three most wonderful things in the world—the Bible, Christianity, and the Church—and stated that the object of missionary societies was to circulate the first, teach the second, and to extend the last, until all mankind was embraced in this social institution. He also touched upon the benefits which the world generally had derived from the labors of eminent missionaries. The Rev. Joseph Beazley read the report, which contained a summary of the parent society's proceedings in various parts of the world, and a more detailed account of the operations carried on in the Western Islands of Polynesia, Aneiteum, Erromanga, Nengone, Lifu, and others, in the midst of which Mr. Creagh and Mr. Jones, to whose support the Sydney contributions chiefly go, are laboring. Joseph Thomson, Esq., read the treasurer's account, calling special attention to the fact that there had been a falling off in the contributions during the year, from £408 to £266 2s.

The Rev. George Platt, an aged missionary, who had seen upwards of forty years' service, moved the adoption of the report, together with the appointment of the following gentlemen as officers and committee for the ensuing year:—President, Rev. Dr. Ross; treasurer, Joseph Thomson, Esq.; joint secretaries, Rev. J. Beazley, Mr. A. H. Eagar; committee, all Ministers of contributing congregations, Messrs. John Fairfax, A. Foss, A. Fairfax, R. Garrett, A. Garran, T. Holt, R. N. Jenkins, D. Jones, R. Nott, J. Thompson, S. Thomson, Rev. J. West. He detailed some interesting reminiscences of the olden time of the missions in the South Seas. The Rev. Mr. Krause, of the Lutheran Church, but for many years a missionary of the non-sectarian London Missionary Society, also gave numerous and interesting particulars of his experience as a missionary in Tahiti and other parts, and of the improved condition of the natives who had embraced Christianity, especially their simplicity of manners, liberality, and prayerfulness. The Rev. W. Cuthbertson then followed with an earnest and eloquent speech, in which he reviewed the general field of missions, pressed the special claims of China and India, expressed his hope that young men would come forward to emulate the noble heroes who had distinguished themselves in the missionary enterprise, and that means and measures would be adopted to enable them to be sent out when they offered. The Rev. Mr. Darling, who had spent forty-two years as a missionary in Polynesia and is now superannuated, related something of his experience in the work. Simeoni, a native of Aitutaki, was then introduced to the meeting, and made an address (interpreted by the Rev. Mr. Platt), setting forth the advantages, social and moral, which his countrymen had received through the instrumentality of missionaries, and of his and their gratitude to Almighty God and the Missionary Society for their ameliorated circumstances.

Two young missionaries, who with their wives had just been sent out from England to proceed in the *John Williams* to the island of Lifu, then delivered addresses, after which the doxology was sung, and the benediction pronounced by the reverend chairman, and the meeting broke up.

THE REV. A. BUZACOTT.—This esteemed missionary, whose various services in and around Melbourne were recorded in our last number, accompanied by Teavae, the native teacher, has proceeded to the interior of Victoria to preach on behalf of the London Missionary Society, to diffuse missionary information and excite a missionary spirit. He has visited Kyneton, Castlemaine, Sandhurst, Maryborough, Amherst, Back Creek, Ballaarat, and other places, but the particulars and results have not yet reached us. It is his intention shortly to go on to Adelaide to carry out the same objects.

TRUE PRAYER

Prayer is not eloquence, but earnestness; not the definition of helplessness, but the feeling of it; not figures of speech, but compunction of soul.—*Hannah More.*

RELIGIOUS INTELLIGENCE.

CONGREGATIONALISTS.—CONGREGATIONAL CHURCH, CARLTON,]
—On Monday evening, April 27, the anniversary social meeting of this chur
The Rev. H. Thomas, in his address, stated that during the year 15 members ha
church. The number at its formation was 11, and 2 having left, the present nun
The children in the Sabbath-school amounted to 177 on the books, and 12
attendance. The disposition to attend public worship by the population of the ne
was stated to be small; and measures were resolved upon to circulate the
among the people, and take other measures to stir them up to the discharge of th
duties.

OXFORD-STREET INDEPENDENT CHURCH, COLLINGWOOD.—On Wednes
May 18th, the church and congregation connected with the above place of worshi
quarterly social meeting. About 200 persons took tea in the school-room, after
adjourned to the chapel. The pastor, the Rev. W. B. Landells, presided. In
remarks he alluded to the present apparently prosperous condition of the
pointed out some of the indications of the Divine presence and blessing. He the
all the absolute necessity of continually seeking the aid of the Holy Spirit, in ord
the high results which are contemplated by the Church of Christ. Several membe
gregation afterwards spoke upon topics of interest connected with the Ch
Treasurer's statement was regarded with satisfaction, as showing that it only
help of all, according to their means, in order to attain complete success in a pec
of view. A proposal was made shortly to erect a vestry and meeting room at th
present building, in order to secure the comfort of the minister, and to provide fo
night services. It was stated that Mr. R. T. Hills, one of the deacons, had rece
tation from the church at Janefield, River Plenty, to become its pastor, which
accepted. In the remarks which Mr. Hills afterwards made, he alluded to the r
the practicability of making Young Men's Christian Associations so many tra
for the colonial ministry. The choir contributed its share to the enjoyment of
by the performance of several anthems in a most efficient manner.

REV. THOMAS BINNEY.—This gentleman is still in Sydney, where he b
ducting various services with his usual attractiveness and power. It is understo
also engaged in seeing through the press the address he delivered as Chairman
gregational Union Meeting, recently held at Green Ponds, Tasmania: an ac
contains a minute examination of the Bishop of Adelaide's scheme of Church
movement has been commenced to induce Mr. Binney to remain and exercise
in Melbourne. A memorial expressing this desire and extensively signed has be
to him in Sydney, and a subscription has been entered into, amounting to £1,
meeting the first year's expenses, should he comply. The subscriptions
given and obtained in a very short time.

NORTH COLLINGWOOD INDEPENDENT CHURCH.—The Rev. E. Henders
for some time laboured usefully in connexion with the City Mission. Colli
accepted an invitation to become the pastor of this church, and is expected to en
stated duties on the first Sabbath in June. We understand that in addition to h
duties he will still devote the greater portion of his time to the work of an Evan
locality.

CLAYTON CHAPEL, KENSINGTON, SOUTH AUSTRALIA.—A tea meeting
with the anniversary services of this chapel was held on Monday evening, 11th
Institute, Kensington; after which a public meeting took place in the chapel fo
nition of the Rev. J. W. C. Drane as minister of the place. The chair was taken
Bakewell, M.P., and on the platform were also Mr. Glyde, M.P., the Revs. T.
W. Evan, F. W. Cox, M. H. Hodge, H. Cheetham, G. Hoatson, and J. W. C.
chairman stated that the meeting had two objects in view—that of recognizin
minister, whom, on behalf of the congregation, he heartily welcomed, and also
senting a testimonial to the Rev. T. Q. Stow, who had gratuitously officiated at
that chapel since the resignation of Mr. J. H. Barrow. He called upon Mr. I
read a letter containing 140 signatures, thanking Mr. Stow for his services,
M.P., then came forward, and stated that the Committee which had been form
subscriptions for the purpose of presenting Mr. Stow with some testimonial in r
his services had purchased a gold watch and chain, which, with some appropriate
presented to that gentleman. Mr. Stow rose amidst continued acclamations a
thanks. He said he had felt it his duty to do as he had done, and his conscienc
have allowed him to have refused. But he had his reward, not only in the test
had been presented to him, but also in seeing them met that evening in order
Mr. Drane as their minister. The Rev. Mr. Drane was then called upon. He
brief but most interesting sketch of the manner in which he had become connect
Congregationalists, and his reason for coming to South Australia. The meeti
addressed by Revs. Messrs. Hoatson, Evan, Cox, Drane and others.

PRESBYTERIANS.—PRESBYTERIAN UNION.—To complete our summ
proceedings which led to this event, it is necessary to state that several of tho
are connected with the Union are opposed to State Aid, and that they joir
brethren who keep aloof in the expression of their opinion on the subject.

utions, passed April 26, 1855, in the United Presbyterian Church, Collins-street. The resolutions are as follow :—" 1. That inasmuch as the three Presbyterian denominations are one in doctrine, discipline, and government, and inasmuch as the Confession of Faith is the received and acknowledged compendium of their doctrinal belief and worship, that said Confession be the basis of proposed union, except in so far, &c., &c. 2. That in the exercise of charity, and of a prudent regard to interests and arrangements entered into prior to the union; those ministers and churches at present in the receipt of Government aid shall not be required to forego the same without their own consent. 3. That in the matter of churches originated AFTER the union shall have been consummated, should any propose to apply for Government assistance, it shall be competent for the united Synod to decide as to whether or not they shall receive it. 4. That the right to expound and discuss, on all suitable occasions, the principle of Government interference and aid in the cause of religion, be reserved to all parties, but that the members of the united body shall agree to avoid all unnecessary severity in such discussions, and shall conduct them in the spirit of liberality, forbearance, and Christian love."

WESLEYANS.—As this is the season when the ministers of this body of Christians change their circuits, various interesting valedictory meetings have been recently held. The Rev. J. S. Waugh bid farewell to his congregation, at Richmond, at a social meeting, on March 29th ; the Rev. W. L. Binks at the Wesley Church, Melbourne, when a presentation of a silver service took place ; and the Rev. G. Daniel, at Yarra-street, Geelong, on April 6th, when also a presentation was made ; the Rev. J. A. Manton, at Hobart Town and Campbell Town, on April 12, when Baxter's Comprehensive Bible was presented ; and various others in other places. A delightful spirit of harmony prevailed at these meetings, indicating the high appreciation of the services and estimation of the characters of these brethren.

VARIOUS SOCIETIES.—MISSION TO THE ABORIGINES.—On Thursday evening, April 28, the annual meeting of the Church of England Mission to the Aborigines was held in St. Paul's school-room, Swanston-street, Melbourne. His Excellency Sir Henry Barkly presided. The proceedings were opened with prayer, by the Dean of Melbourne. Sir Henry then addressed the meeting. After which the secretary read the annual report, from which a few items are extracted. " The committee present their report of the past year with humble acknowledgments of the Divine goodness, but with mingled feelings of pleasure and pain. With grateful feelings they record the continued support of the mission by its friends, and the patient labours of its missionaries; but experience proves that the work of winning souls to Christ from amongst the Aborigines is a most arduous work, and calls for the increase of faith and patience. The claims of this society have been urged amongst a very limited circle of friends, owing to the want of advocates, both clerical and lay, yet, notwithstanding this circumstance, sufficient means have been provided to pay all the expenses of the year, and to leave a small balance in hand. The Missionaries are now three in number, instead of two, as reported last year. During his stay in Melbourne, in January, 1858, Mr. Bulmer was married to one who appeared suited to forward the great work, to which her husband has devoted his own life. Having received training as a school teacher, Mrs. Bulmer may be considered as peculiarly fitted to impart instruction to the children on the station ; and the native women also, it is expected, will find in her such a friend as they most urgently need." After the reading of the report, resolutions were moved and seconded—by the Rev. the Dean of Melbourne, Mr. Lock, His Honor Justice Molesworth, and the Revs. Messrs. Seddon and Chase, and H. Jennings, Esq. After a vote of thanks to His Excellency for presiding, the Rev. Mr. Chase engaged in prayer, and the meeting separated.

WESLEYAN CHURCH, GOLDEN-SQUARE, SANDHURST.— The foundation stone of a new church was laid on Tuesday, April 19, by the Rev. D. J. Draper, President of the Conference. A silver trowel was presented to him by the Rev. J. Dare, on behalf of the congregation, in a suitable speech, which was responded to by a feeling reply from Mr. Draper. The concourse of people was large and the proceedings excited great interest.

TARADALE NEW WESLEYAN CHURCH.—The ceremony of laying the foundation stone of a new Wesleyan church at Taradale was performed by the Rev. T. Williams, on Monday, 18th April. The rev. gentleman delivered an eloquent and appropriate address to the large company assembled. To celebrate the event a tea-meeting was afterwards held in a large tent erected for the purpose, in which Mr. Williams had preached the previous day. Addresses were delivered by the Revs. T. Williams, J. Mewton, J. Catterall, Messrs. Hutcheson and Orwin; Mr. Ward occupying the chair. The building is to be of brick with stone dressings, in the Gothic style, and capable of seating 150 persons. The estimated cost is £450, towards which £185 has been received, the principal part of which was raised on the occasion.

WESLEYAN MISSIONS.—Sermon by the Rev. T. Binney.—A sermon on behalf of the Wesleyan Missionary Society was, on May 2nd, preached by the Rev. T. Binney, in the Centenary Chapel in York-street, Sydney. The rev. gentleman delivered a powerful and impressive discourse, taking for his text, Acts xvii. 2, 3, 22, 23.

RICHMOND YOUNG MEN'S CHRISTIAN ASSOCIATION.—A public soirée in connexion with the first anniversary of this Association, was held in the National School-room, Lennox-street, on Monday evening, May 16, which was attended by about 100 of the members and friends of this and other kindred societies. After the duties of the tea table were completed, the chair was taken by the President, who opened the meeting by demonstrating the importance of such associations in respect to those who have been some time in the colony, and especially to those who may arrive, as a means more particularly of bringing connexion with that department of the Church of Christ to which they migh belong, and also, that it was distinctly wished to be understood, that this society unsectarian in character and design.   Mr. Wilmot, the Secretary, read the repor the proceedings and success which had attended the efforts of the members anc make the Institution worthy the attention of those who feel the value and im Christian intercourse and edification.   Mr. Inglis, one of the members, read an e: "Age we live in," and its demands on young men,—expatiating on the duties wl urge every member to action—and also on the advancement of science and literatt conclusion of this admirable essay, Mr. Petch, one of the delegates, Mr Ha Mirams, Messrs. John Russell, Britton, sen., Geo. Bell, and Biggs, severally ad meeting, interspersed by the performances of the choir, under the direction of M Votes of thanks were then awarded to the ladies for providing the tea ; to the ch the efficient manner he displayed in conducting the meeting ; to the choir in admi: the enjoyments of the evening ; and after singing the Doxology, and the Bene plored, the meeting separated.

REV. G. W. CONDER.—*To the Editor of the Christian Times, M* Dear Sir,—Extracts from English papers having appeared in the *Christ* announcing that the Rev. G. W. Conder, of Leeds, was coming to Melbourne, I tl interest many of your readers, if you will insert the following portion of a letter 1 received from that gentleman.   It will show that he was not coming out on spec: that certain arrangements had been entered into between himself and me, but w h be of no advantage for me to specify :—

Leeds, Feb. :

"My Dear Friend,—At the close of last year my throat became so much worse obliged to resign my charge, and fully intended to set out for Australia as soon as cir should allow me to do so.   My resignation was received in a way wholly unexpected 1 immediately evoked in the breasts of my people an amount of sympathy and love of wh not have any idea.   They proposed to me to withdraw my resignation and offered me i with to travel until my health should be restored.   I had memorials from all the soci place and so many private representations of the desire felt for my remaining with then two months of deliberation I have come to the conclusion that there is no course open t accept their offer, and dismiss at all events for the present, the idea of making my home We leave England for Italy in a few days.   I hope this will be in time to stay any pro your part with respect to me.   I much regret any trouble I have put you to, as it seen vain ; but perhaps the result will show that it has not been in vain.   It may be that in t Great Head of the Church has been preparing me for a step in the future, when the w made clear.   At all events you will believe that I have been simply anxious to know anc of God in the matter."

Yours very sincerely, G. W. CO

Thus, Sir, my hope, if not broken off, is deferred, and I greatly fear that Riding of Yorkshire will not allow the man who can gather thousands to hear h them on their duties and follies, to leave England for the Antipodes—strong as hi to help in doing something to make this young nation good and worthy.

May 17, 1859.   Yours faithfully, J. L. I

EDITORIAL ANNOUNCEMENT.

It is with pain the Editor has to announce, that this will be the last n the Southern Spectator, at least for the present.   The sole cause of the si pecuniary difficulties, and these arising, not from the series now termina: which began last August, but from the previous bi-monthly one, upc considerable losses have been incurred, from copies returned, tardy rei and various expenses incurred.   The whole subject of the Magazine will b considered by the Conference, which is expected to meet sometime th Adelaide.   The Editor, having had many testimonies of the usefulness of as supplying a want extensively felt, hopes that that body will see it de: resume it, and that, guided by the experience already gained, they will l make such arrangements as will secure its permanency in such form : most acceptable, and suitable.

The Editor tenders his warmest thanks to those few brethren who hav: sympathised with him in his labors, and have rendered him gratuitious assistance by the articles they have so cheerfully contributed, and to thos: also who have exerted themselves to promote the circulation of the wor equal interest in it had been shewn by others, from whom the Editor, as : a public capacity, and by the request of the representatives of the bodi: right to expect it, he has no doubt the result would have been very :

INDEX.

AUGUST TO DECEMBER, 1858.

INDEX.

JANUARY TO JUNE, 1859.

W. FAIRFAX AND CO., STEAM PRINTERS, COLLINS-STREET EAST,

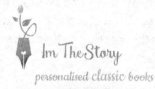

CPSIA information can be obtained
at www.ICGtesting.com
Printed in the USA
BVHW071442140819
555860BV00025B/2061/P